ADVANCED ACCOUNTING

THIRD EDITION

ADVANCED ACCOUNTING

DANIEL L. JENSEN
The Ohio State University

EDWARD N. COFFMAN
Virginia Commonwealth University

RAY G. STEPHENS
Kent State University

THOMAS J. BURNS
The Ohio State University

McGRAW-HILL, INC.
New York   St. Louis   San Francisco   Auckland   Bogotá   Caracas
Lisbon   London   Madrid   Mexico City   Milan   Montreal   New Delhi
San Juan   Singapore   Sydney   Tokyo   Toronto

ADVANCED ACCOUNTING

This book is printed on acid-free paper.

1 2 3 4 5 6 7 8 9 0   DOH   DOH   9 0 9 8 7 6 5 4 3

ISBN 0-07-032667-3

This book was set in Times Roman by York Graphic Services, Inc.
The editors were Alan Sachs and Bernadette Boylan;
the designer was Leon Bolognese;
the production supervisor was Paula Keller.
R. R. Donnelley & Sons Company was printer and binder.

Material from the Uniform CPA Examination Questions and Unofficial Answers, copyright © 1948, 1950, 1951, 1953, 1955, 1957, 1960, 1961, 1962, 1963, 1964, 1965, 1966, 1967, 1969, 1970, 1971, 1972, 1973, 1974, 1975, 1976, 1977, 1978, 1979, 1980, 1981, 1982, 1983, 1984, 1985, 1986, 1989, 1990, 1991, 1992 by the American Institute of Certified Public Accountants, Inc., is reprinted (or adapted) with permission.

Material from the Certified Management Accountant Examinations, copyright © 1975, 1977, 1991 by the Institute of Certified Management Accountants is reprinted (or adapted) with permission.

Material from the Certificate in Internal Auditing Examinations, copyright © 1983 by The Institute of Internal Auditors, Inc., is reprinted (or adapted) with permission.

Library of Congress Cataloging-in-Publication Data is available:
LC Card #93-21688

INTERNATIONAL EDITION

Copyright 1994. Exclusive rights by McGraw-Hill, Inc., for manufacture and export. This book cannot be re-exported from the country to which it is consigned by McGraw-Hill. The International Edition is not available in North America.

When ordering this title, use ISBN 0-07-113400-X.

ABOUT THE AUTHORS

DANIEL L. JENSEN is Professor of Accounting at The Ohio State University. He is coauthor of *Financial Accounting* (1992, in its fourth edition) and *Accounting for Changing Prices* (1984). In addition to service on many editorial boards, Professor Jensen served as editor of *Issues in Accounting Education* and was recently elected director of publications for the American Accounting Association. His research has been published in various journals, including *The Accounting Review,* the *Journal of Accounting Research,* the *Quarterly Review of Economics and Business,* the *Journal of Business Finance and Accounting,* and *Financial Management.* In addition, he has edited monographs on educational issues including *Information Systems in Accounting Education* (1985) and *The Impact of Rule-Making on Intermediate Accounting Textbooks* (1982). His national committee work includes service on the AICPA's Education Executive Committee and the Executive Committee, Council, Nominating Committee, and Education Advisory Committee of the American Accounting Association. In 1991, Professor Jensen received the Outstanding Ohio Accounting Educator Award. Professor Jensen served on the faculties at the University of Illinois at Urbana-Champaign and Purdue University and was a visiting professor at Indiana University. A certified public accountant, he received a Ph.D. from The Ohio State University and master's and bachelor's degrees from the University of Minnesota.

EDWARD N. COFFMAN is Professor of Accounting at Virginia Commonwealth University. He is coeditor of *Historical Perspectives of Selected Financial Accounting Topics* (1992) and coauthor of *Accounting for Changing Prices* (1984). His research has been published in the *Journal of Accounting Research, Abacus,* the *International Journal of Accounting, Issues in Accounting Education,* and the *Journal of Accountancy.* Professor Coffman has served as president of the Academy of Accounting Historians, chairman of its Board of Trustees, and editor of *The Accounting Historians Journal.* He has also served on various committees of professional organizations including the Education Advisory Committee and the Model Library Committee of the American Accounting Association. Professor Coffman has been a visiting professor at The Ohio State University, Southern Methodist University, and Swinburne University of Technology (Australia). His honors and awards include Beta Alpha Psi's Accountant of the Year in Education Award (1990) and designation as the 1991 Virginia Outstanding Accounting Educator by the Institute of Management Accountants (IMA) Student Chapter of James Madison University. He received his bachelor's and master's degrees from Virginia Commonwealth University and his doctorate from George Washington University.

RAY G. STEPHENS is KPMG Peat Marwick Professor and accounting department chair at Kent State University. He is coauthor of *Financial Reporting by Privately Held Business Enterprises: Diagnosis and Analysis* (1983) and author of *Uses of Financial Information in Bank Lending Decision* (1980). His research has been published in *The Accounting Review, Auditing: A Journal of Practice and Theory,* the *Quarterly Review of Economics and Business, Instructional Science,* and *The Ohio CPA,* among other journals. In addition to serving on many editorial boards, Professor Stephens was editor of the *Case Research Journal* and associate editor for *Issues in Accounting Education.* He has served as president of the North American Case Research Association, chair of the American Accounting Association Section on Accounting, Behavior and Organizations, and vice-president and Executive Committee member for the Ohio Society of CPAs. Professor Stephens earned a doctorate at Harvard University and holds M.B.A. and bachelor's degrees from East Carolina University and the University of Georgia, respectively. He was a member of the faculty at The Ohio State University and served as Academic Accounting Fellow at the Securities and Exchange Commission.

THOMAS J. BURNS is Deloitte & Touche Professor of Accounting at The Ohio State University. He is coeditor of *The Accounting Sampler* (1986, in its fourth edition) and coauthor of *The Accounting Primer: An Introduction to Accounting* (1972). He has edited many monographs including *Doctoral Programs in Accounting Education* (1984) and the annual *Accounting Trends: Innovative Accounting and Information Systems Course Outlines,* now in its twenty-fourth year. He has served as national president of Beta Alpha Psi, director of education for the American Accounting Association, and president of the Academy of Accounting Historians. His papers have been published in various journals including *The Accounting Review,* the *Journal of Accounting Research,* and the *Journal of Accountancy.* His many honors and awards include the Outstanding Accounting Educator Award from both the American Accounting Association (1992) and the American Institute of CPAs (1989); he was also the first recipient of the Ohio Outstanding Educator Award. Professor Burns has been a member of the accounting faculty at The Ohio State University since 1963 and has held visiting professorships at the University of California at Berkeley, Harvard University, and Stanford University. A certified public accountant, he earned a Ph.D. from the University of Minnesota and bachelor's and master's degrees from the University of Wisconsin and the University of Michigan, respectively.

CONTENTS

PREFACE   xix

PART ONE | **MULTIPLE-CORPORATION ENTITIES**

CHAPTER 1
BUSINESS COMBINATIONS
PAGE 2

BUSINESS COMBINATIONS FROM VARIOUS VIEWPOINTS   3

The Acquiring Company *4* / **ISSUES: Evaluation of Proposed Expansion by Combination** *4* / The Acquired Company *5* / **ISSUES: A Tender Offer** *6* / Regulatory Agencies *7* / Accounting Rule-Making Agencies *7*

COMBINATION TRANSACTIONS   8

Four Basic Forms of Business Combination *8* / Acquisitions of Assets Subject to Liabilities *10* / Corporate Structure of Business Combinations *11*

AN OVERVIEW OF ACCOUNTING FOR BUSINESS COMBINATIONS   11

Criteria That Distinguish Purchases and Poolings *11* / Valuation of Acquired Net Assets *12* / Taxes and Business Combinations *12*

ACCOUNTING FOR PURCHASE COMBINATIONS   13

Measuring Acquisition Cost *13* / Allocating the Acquisition Cost *15* / Recording Purchase Combinations *17*

ACCOUNTING FOR POOLING-OF-INTERESTS COMBINATIONS   21

ISSUES: A Critique of Pooling-of-Interests Accounting *21* / Recording Pooling of Interests *22* / Par Value Issued and the Reclassification of Stockholders' Equity *24*

COMBINED NET INCOME IN YEAR OF COMBINATION   26

SUMMARY   *28*
APPENDIX A: CRITERIA FOR POOLINGS OF INTERESTS   *28*
APPENDIX B: CONTINGENT CONSIDERATION AND PREACQUISITION CONTINGENCIES   *33*
SELECTED READINGS   *36*
QUESTIONS   *37*
EXERCISES   *38*
PROBLEMS   *49*
ISSUES IN ACCOUNTING JUDGMENT   *59*

CHAPTER 2
ACQUISITIONS OF STOCK AND DATE-OF ACQUISITION CONSOLIDATION
PAGE 64

BUSINESS COMBINATIONS AND CONSOLIDATIONS   65

MINORITY INTEREST AND CONSOLIDATION CRITERIA   68

Controlling Interest *68* / **ISSUES: Judgment on Control of Investee** *69* / Unconsolidated Subsidiaries *72* / Disclosure of Consolidation Policy *73*

PURPOSES AND LIMITATIONS OF CONSOLIDATED FINANCIAL STATEMENTS   74

ISSUES: Consolidated versus Separate Financial Statements *75*

DATE-OF-ACQUISITION CONSOLIDATION PROCEDURES FOR PURCHASE COMBINATIONS WITH MINORITY INTEREST   77

Analysis of the Valuation Differential *77* / Consolidation Worksheet Procedures *79* / Consolidated Financial Statements *82* / Comprehensive Illustration *88*

CONCEPTUAL BASIS FOR CONSOLIDATION   91

SUMMARY   *94*
APPENDIX A: THE CONSOLIDATED BALANCE SHEET UNDER ALTERNATIVE CONCEPTS OF CONSOLIDATION   *94*
APPENDIX B: DATE-OF-ACQUISITION CONSOLIDATION PROCEDURES FOR POOLINGS OF INTERESTS WITH MINORITY INTEREST   *102*
SELECTED READINGS   *104*
QUESTIONS   *105*
EXERCISES   *107*
PROBLEMS   *119*
ISSUES IN ACCOUNTING JUDGMENT   *131*

CHAPTER 3
THE EQUITY METHOD AND POSTACQUISITION CONSOLIDATION
PAGE 134

ACCOUNTING FOR LONG-TERM INVESTMENTS IN COMMON STOCK   135

The Cost Method *136* / The Equity Method *138* / **ISSUES: Cost Method versus Equity Method** *138*

POSTACQUISITION CONSOLIDATION FINANCIAL STATEMENTS   146

Consolidation of Balance Sheets at Date of Acquisition *147* / Consolidated Financial Statements One Year after Acquisition *148* / Consolidation of Financial Statements Two Years after Acquisition *161* / Interim Acquisition *164*

SUMMARY   *170*
APPENDIX A: POSTACQUISITION CONSOLIDATION FOR POOLINGS OF INTERESTS   *171*
APPENDIX B: CONSOLIDATION PROCEDURES FOR THE COST METHOD   *173*
APPENDIX C: THE TRIAL BALANCE FORMAT FOR CONSOLIDATION WORKSHEETS   *176*
SELECTED READINGS   *178*
QUESTIONS   *179*

EXERCISES *180*
PROBLEMS *191*
ISSUES IN ACCOUNTING JUDGMENT *212*

CHAPTER 4
INTERCOMPANY MERCHANDISE TRANSFERS
PAGE 214

REVENUE RECOGNITION AND MERCHANDISE TRANSFERS 215

ISSUES: Non-Arm's Length Transactions and Revenue Recognition *215* / Gross Margin on Intercompany Merchandise Transfers *217*

THE EQUITY METHOD FOR MERCHANDISE TRANSFERS 218

Merchandise Transfers (Upstream) from Subsidiary to Parent *218* / Merchandise Transfers (Downstream) from Parent to Subsidiary *220* / Comprehensive Illustration of Equity Method for Merchandise Transfers *222*

CONSOLIDATION AND MERCHANDISE TRANSFERS 223

Total versus Fractional Deferral for Upstream Transfers *223* / **ISSUES: Consequences of Deferral Methods** *224* / Consolidation Adjustments for Upstream Merchandise Transfers *224* / Comprehensive Illustration of Consolidation Procedures for Merchandise Transfers *228*

SUMMARY *235*
APPENDIX: FRACTIONAL DEFERRAL METHOD OF CONSOLIDATION *236*
SELECTED READINGS *237*
QUESTIONS *237*
EXERCISES *238*
PROBLEMS *243*
ISSUES IN ACCOUNTING JUDGMENT *255*

CHAPTER 5
INTERCOMPANY PLANT ASSET TRANSFERS
PAGE 256

TRANSFERS OF LAND 257

Upstream Land Transfers *257* / Downstream Land Transfers *261* / **ISSUES: Income Effects of Omitted Deferrals** *263*

TRANSFERS OF DEPRECIABLE ASSETS 263

Upstream Transfers of Depreciable Assets *264* / Downstream Transfers of Depreciable Assets *268* / **ISSUES: Variations in Intercompany Asset Transfers** *269*

COMPREHENSIVE ILLUSTRATION 269

SUMMARY *275*
QUESTIONS *275*
EXERCISES *276*
PROBLEMS *282*
ISSUES IN ACCOUNTING JUDGMENT *298*

CHAPTER 6
INTERCOMPANY DEBT TRANSACTIONS
PAGE 300

CREATION OF NEW INTERCOMPANY DEBT   301

ISSUES: Motivation for Creation of New Intercompany Debt *301* / A Parent Lends to Its Subsidiary *301* / Equity Method for New Intercompany Debt *302* / Consolidation Procedures for New Intercompany Debt *304*

ACQUISITION OF OUTSTANDING DEBT   307

Gains and Losses *307* / **ISSUES: Motivation for Acquisition of Affiliate Debts** *307* / Attribution of Gain or Loss *308* / Acquisition of Parent's Debt by Subsidiary *309* / Acquisition of Subsidiary's Debt by Parent *314*

SUMMARY   *321*
APPENDIX A: THE FACE-VALUE METHOD FOR GAINS AND LOSSES ON INTERCOMPANY DEBT   *323*
APPENDIX B: DISCOUNTING AND INTERCOMPANY NOTES   *328*
SELECTED READINGS   *329*
QUESTIONS   *329*
EXERCISES   *330*
PROBLEMS   *335*
ISSUES IN ACCOUNTING JUDGMENT   *354*

CHAPTER 7
TRANSACTIONS IN SUBSIDIARY COMMON STOCK
PAGE 356

PARENT'S TRANSACTIONS IN SUBSIDIARY COMMON STOCK   357

Multiple-Step Stock Acquisitions of Subsidiaries *357* / Sale of Subsidiary Shares by Parent *361*

NEW ISSUES OF SUBSIDIARY COMMON STOCK   369

ISSUES: Minority Stockholders and Subsidiary Stock Issues *370* / Subsidiary Sells Stock to Parent *371* / Subsidiary Sells Stock to Minority Stockholders *373* / Subsidiary Sells Stock to Parent and Minority Stockholders *376*

SUBSIDIARY TRANSACTIONS IN COMMON TREASURY SHARES   376

Transactions with the Parent *376* / Transactions with Minority Stockholders *377*

APPENDIX: OWNERSHIP CHANGES AND INTERCOMPANY GROSS MARGIN   *378*
SELECTED READINGS   *382*
QUESTIONS   *383*
EXERCISES   *384*
PROBLEMS   *390*
ISSUES IN ACCOUNTING JUDGMENT   *401*

CHAPTER 8
CONSOLIDATION IN COMPLEX ENVIRONMENTS
PAGE 402

MULTIPLE SUBSIDIARIES AND INDIRECT OWNERSHIP   403

Multiple Subsidiaries *403* / Indirect Ownership *404* / Consolidation Procedures *406*

MUTUAL HOLDINGS   409

Mutual Holdings between Subsidiaries *409* / Mutual Holdings between Parent and Subsidiary *413* / The Treasury-Stock Method for Mutual Holdings between Parent and Subsidiary *414* / The Allocation Method for Mutual Holdings between Parent and Subsidiary *418*

PARENT'S INVESTMENT IN SUBSIDIARY PREFERRED STOCK   422

Book Value of Preferred Stockholders' Equity *423* / Intercompany Preferred Stock Investment and Consolidated Entities *424* / A Parent Invests in Subsidiary Preferred Stock *424* / Consolidation at Date of Acquisition *424* / The Equity Method *426* / Consolidation Worksheet Adjustments *427* / Consolidation Worksheet One Year after Acquisition *427* / Consolidation Worksheet Two Years after Acquisition *429*

JOINT VENTURES   430

Accounting for Joint Venture Investments *431* / Proportionate Consolidation *431*

DEFERRED INCOME TAXES   435

Consolidated and Separate Tax Returns *435* / Undistributed Investee Income *435* / Intercompany Merchandise Transactions *436* / Comprehensive Example with Separate Tax Returns *439* / Business Combinations *443*

SELECTED READINGS   *449*
QUESTIONS   *449*
EXERCISES   *450*
PROBLEMS   *456*
ISSUES IN ACCOUNTING JUDGMENT   *465*

CHAPTER 9
REPORTING DISAGGREGATED FINANCIAL INFORMATION
PAGE 468

HISTORICAL PERSPECTIVE ON THE NEED FOR DISAGGREGATED FINANCIAL INFORMATION   469

REPORTING NONHOMOGENEOUS SUBSIDIARIES   469

SEGMENT REPORTING   470

Segment Information by Industry *473* / Segment Information by Geographic Area and Export Sales *478* / Sales to Major Customers *480* / Disposal of a Segment of a Business *484*

SIGNIFICANT INVESTEES AND JOINT VENTURES   484

PARENT-COMPANY-ONLY FINANCIAL INFORMATION   485

SEPARATELY ISSUED FINANCIAL STATEMENTS FOR SUBSIDIARIES AND PUSH-DOWN ACCOUNTING   486

APPENDIX: INTERIM FINANCIAL REPORTING   *491*
Financial Accounting Standards for Interim Reporting *491*
SELECTED READINGS   *498*
QUESTIONS   *500*
EXERCISES   *501*
PROBLEMS   *507*
ISSUES IN ACCOUNTING JUDGMENT   *516*

CHAPTER 10
REPORTING UNDER NEW BASIS ACCOUNTING
PAGE 518

FOUR RATIONALES FOR NEW BASIS ACCOUNTING   519

PURCHASE BUSINESS COMBINATIONS AND PUSH-DOWN ACCOUNTING   520

LEVERAGED BUYOUTS   520

Recording LBOs without New Basis Accounting *520* / Recording LBOs Using New Basis Accounting *521* / Guidance from Emerging Issues Task Force *523* / Stockholders' Equity in the LBO *525* / LBO Financial Statements *525* / Analyzing LBOs *525*

REORGANIZATION ACCOUNTING   526

Restructuring-Recapitalization *526* / Quasi-Reorganization *526* / Bankruptcy *527*

REORGANIZATION UNDER THE BANKRUPTCY CODE   528

Accounting When the Petition Is Filed *529* / Accounting during the Bankruptcy *532* / Accounting When Emerging from Bankruptcy *533* / New Basis Accounting for the Emerging Entity *534* / Accounting for Enterprises Emerging from Bankruptcy When New Basis Is Not Allowed *535*

SUMMARY   *536*
SELECTED READINGS   *537*
QUESTIONS   *537*
EXERCISES   *538*
PROBLEMS   *542*
ISSUES IN ACCOUNTING JUDGMENT   *550*

CHAPTER 11
RESEARCHING ACCOUNTING PRINCIPLES
PAGE 552

RESEARCHING FINANCIAL ACCOUNTING PRONOUNCEMENTS   553

Accounting Measurements *553* / Accounting Presentation and Disclosures *554*

THE HIERARCHY OF GAAP   554

Framework of the Hierarchy *554* / Parallel Hierarchies for Private and Public Sectors *555*

IMPACT OF REGULATORY AGENCIES   556

Banking Regulators and the Call Report *556* / Securities and Exchange Commission *558* / Insurance and Utility Regulators *561*

THE RESEARCH PROCESS   561

Terminology and Research *561* / Standards and Interpretative Guidance *562* / Iteration and Consultation *562*

A RESEARCH EXAMPLE   562

SUMMARY   *565*
SELECTED READINGS   *565*
QUESTIONS   *566*

EXERCISES   *566*
PROBLEMS   *568*
ISSUES IN ACCOUNTING JUDGMENT   *573*

PART TWO   **MULTINATIONAL COMPANIES**

CHAPTER 12
**RESTATEMENT OF
FOREIGN FINANCIAL
STATEMENTS**
PAGE 576

FOREIGN CURRENCY RESTATEMENT   577

Restatement and Conversion *577* / Currency Exchange Rates *578*

MEASUREMENT ISSUES IN FOREIGN STATEMENT RESTATEMENT   578

Conformity with U.S. Generally Accepted Accounting Principles *578* / Historical
Rate and Current Rate Restatement *579* / Treatment of Restatement
Adjustments *581* / **ISSUES: Restatement Adjustments as Income Elements or
Direct Equity Adjustments** *581*

THE FUNCTIONAL CURRENCY CONCEPT   582

TRANSLATION   584

Translation at Date of Acquisition *584* / Translation One Year after
Acquisition *585* / Translation Two Years after Acquisition *587*

REMEASUREMENT   590

Remeasurement Procedures *593* / Remeasured Financial Statements *598* /
Translation of Remeasured Trial Balances *599* / Inventory Remeasurement and the
Lower-of-Cost-or-Market Adjustment *601*

SUBSIDIARIES IN HIGHLY INFLATIONARY ECONOMIES   602

SUMMARY   *603*
APPENDIX A: EQUITY-METHOD AND CONSOLIDATION PROCEDURES FOR
FOREIGN SUBSIDIARIES   *603*
APPENDIX B: COMPOSITION OF TRANSLATION ADJUSTMENT   *616*
SELECTED READINGS   *616*
QUESTIONS   *618*
EXERCISES   *619*
PROBLEMS   *627*
ISSUES IN ACCOUNTING JUDGMENT   *639*

CHAPTER 13
**FOREIGN CURRENCY
TRANSACTIONS**
PAGE 642

FOREIGN CURRENCY RESTATEMENT   644

Currency Exchange Rates *644*

RECORDING FOREIGN SALES AND PURCHASES   645

Transaction and Settlement Dates *645* / Restatements and Exchange Rate
Movements *646* / **ISSUES: Historical Perspective on Foreign Currency
Standards** *646* / Recording Foreign Sales *647* / Recording Foreign Purchases *649*

HEDGES AND FOREIGN CURRENCY   652

Forward Contracts *653* / **ISSUES: Interest Differentials and Forward Rates** *654* /
Hedging Exposure to Foreign Currency Assets and Liabilities *655* / Hedges of
Identifiable Foreign Currency Commitments *658* / Hedges of Net Investment
Positions *664* / Disclosures Rules for Transaction Gains and Losses *665*

SPECULATIVE FORWARD EXCHANGE CONTRACTS   665

Recording the Speculative Forward Contract *666* / Transaction Gain on Forward
Contract *666* / Recognition of Transaction Gain at Year-End *667* / Recording
Exercise of the Speculative Forward Contract *667*

SUMMARY   *667*
SELECTED READINGS   *668*
QUESTIONS   *669*
EXERCISES   *670*
PROBLEMS   *676*
ISSUES IN ACCOUNTING JUDGMENT   *681*

PART THREE

PARTNERSHIPS AND BRANCHES

CHAPTER 14
**PARTNERSHIPS:
FORMATION, OPERATION,
AND OWNERSHIP
CHANGES**
PAGE 684

PARTNERSHIPS AS ORGANIZATIONS   685

Partnership Agreements *685* / Distinctive Characteristics *686*

OWNERSHIP EQUITY ACCOUNTS FOR PARTNERSHIPS   686

ISSUES: Partnership versus Corporate Ownership Equity *686* / Initial Capital
Balances *687* / Partners' Drawing Accounts *688* / Other Payments to Partners *690*

ALLOCATION OF PARTNERSHIP INCOME OR LOSS   690

Bases for the Allocation of Income and Loss *690* / Specified Numerical Ratio *691* /
Capital Investment Bases *691* / Service Contributions Bases *694* / Deficiencies of
Income Relative to Salaries and Interest *695* / Partners' Salaries and Interest in the
Income Statement *697* / Correction of Prior Years' Net Income *698*

FINANCIAL REPORTING AND TAXATION   698

Financial Statements of Partnerships *698* / Federal Income Tax Law and
Partnerships *699*

CHANGES IN OWNERSHIP   701

Admission of a New Partner *702* / **ISSUES: Reevaluation and Ownership
Changes—Corporations and Partnerships** *704* / Admission by Investment *705* /
Admission by a Purchased Interest *711* / Withdrawal or Death of a Partner *717* /
ISSUES: Total versus Fractional Revaluation *719*

SUMMARY   *719*
SELECTED READINGS   *720*
QUESTIONS   *720*

EXERCISES   *721*
PROBLEMS   *731*
ISSUES IN ACCOUNTING JUDGMENT   *745*

CHAPTER 15
PARTNERSHIPS: LIQUIDATION
PAGE 748

STATEMENT OF PARTNERSHIP LIQUIDATION   749

Liquidation Transactions *749* / **ISSUES: Personal Liability of a Liquidation Officer** *751* / Single-Step and Installment Distributions *751*

SINGLE-STEP DISTRIBUTIONS   752

ISSUES: Limited and Unlimited Liability *752* / Debit Balances in Capital Accounts *752* / Insolvency and Distribution Priorities *754* / Liquidation of Insolvent Partnerships *755*

INSTALLMENT DISTRIBUTIONS   756

A Two-Installment Distribution to Partners *756* / The Safe-Payment Calculation *756* / Installment Distribution Schedules *759*

SUMMARY   *763*
QUESTIONS   *763*
EXERCISES   *764*
PROBLEMS   *769*
ISSUES IN ACCOUNTING JUDGMENT   *777*

CHAPTER 16
ACCOUNTING FOR BRANCHES
PAGE 780

BRANCH ACCOUNTING SYSTEMS   781

ISSUES: Variations in Branch Accounting Systems *781*

ACCOUNTING FOR BRANCH TRANSACTIONS   782

Branch Investment and Home Office Accounts *782* / Transfers from Home Office to Branch *783* / Branch Operating Transactions and Transfers to Home Office *787* / End-of-Period Reporting by Branch and Closing Procedures *787*

PREPARATION OF COMBINED FINANCIAL STATEMENTS   790

Worksheet for Combined Financial Statements *790* / Combined Financial Statements *794*

MERCHANDISE TRANSFERS BILLED IN EXCESS OF COST   794

ISSUES: Branch versus Home Office Margin *794* / Recording Merchandise Transfers from Home Office to Branch Billed in Excess of Cost *796* / Combination Worksheet when Merchandise Transfers are Billed in Excess of Cost *798*

MULTIPLE BRANCHES   804

INTERBRANCH TRANSFERS   804

SUMMARY   *805*

QUESTIONS   *805*
EXERCISES   *806*
PROBLEMS   *813*
ISSUES IN ACCOUNTING JUDGMENT   *823*

PART FOUR   **GOVERNMENTAL AND NONPROFIT ENTITIES**

CHAPTER 17
**ACCOUNTING FOR
GOVERNMENTS:
FUNDAMENTALS AND
THE GENERAL FUND**
PAGE 826

ACCOUNTING FOR GOVERNMENTS   827

ISSUES: Financial Reporting Objectives *828* / Accounting Standards for State and Local Governments *828* / Fund Accounting Systems *831* / Measurement and Recognition *833* / Budgets and Expenditures Control *839* /   / **ISSUES: Appropriations and Expenditures** *839* / Encumbrance Accounting *842*

ACCOUNTING FOR THE GENERAL FUND   845

Recording General Fund Budget *848* / Recording General Fund Revenues and Other Financial Sources *848* / Recording General Fund Encumbrances and Expenditures *853* / General Ledger Accounts and Closing Entries *856* / Financial Reporting for the General Fund *857*

INTERFUND TRANSACTIONS   858

Quasi-External Transactions and Reimbursements *858* / Transfers *860* / Interfund Loans *861*

ACCOUNTING FOR GRANTS, ENTITLEMENTS, AND SHARED REVENUES   863

SUMMARY   *864*
SELECTED READINGS   *864*
QUESTIONS   *865*
EXERCISES   *866*
PROBLEMS   *877*
ISSUES IN ACCOUNTING JUDGMENT   *887*

CHAPTER 18
**ACCOUNTING FOR
GOVERNMENTS SPECIFIC
PURPOSE FUNDS,
ACCOUNT GROUPS, AND
ANNUAL FINANCIAL
REPORTING**
PAGE 890

ACCOUNTING FOR SPECIAL REVENUE FUNDS   891

ACCOUNTING FOR CAPITAL PROJECTS FUNDS   891

Bond Premium and Discount *892* / Budgets and Encumbrances *892* / Recording Capital Projects Fund Transactions *892* / Financial Reporting for the Capital Projects Fund *897*

ACCOUNTING FOR DEBT SERVICE FUNDS   898

Recording Debt Service Fund Transactions *899* / Financial Reporting for Debt Service Fund *903* / Accounting for Serial Bonds and Interest in Debt Service Fund *904*

GENERAL FIXED ASSETS ACCOUNT GROUP   905

Classification of Fixed Assets *907* / Recording General Fixed Assets *907* / Financial Reporting for General Fixed Assets Account Group *907*

GENERAL LONG-TERM DEBT ACCOUNT GROUP   907

Recording Transactions in the Long-Term Debt Account Group *910* / Financial Reporting for General Long-Term Debt Account Group *911*

ACCOUNTING FOR PROPRIETARY FUNDS   911

Distinctive Aspects of Enterprise Funds *913* / Distinctive Aspects of Internal Service Funds *916*

ACCOUNTING FOR SPECIAL ASSESSMENTS   917

Services Financed by Special Assessments *918* / Capital Improvements Financed by Special Assessments *918*

ACCOUNTING FOR FIDUCIARY FUNDS   919

Recording Agency Fund Transactions *920* / Recording Trust Fund Transactions *921* / Financial Reporting for Nonexpendable and Expendable Trust Funds *924*

ANNUAL FINANCIAL REPORTING   924

Level 1: General Purpose Financial Statements *926* / Level 2: Combining Statements by Fund Type *930* / Level 3: Individual Fund and Account Group Statements *931* / Level 4: Schedules *933* / **ISSUES: Classification of Revenues and Expenditures** *933*

SUMMARY   *934*
SELECTED READINGS   *935*
QUESTIONS   *938*
EXERCISES   *939*
PROBLEMS   *951*
ISSUES IN ACCOUNTING JUDGMENT   *963*

CHAPTER 19
ACCOUNTING FOR NONPROFIT ORGANIZATIONS
PAGE 966

ISSUES: Objectives, Revenues, and Governance of Nonprofit Organizations *967*

ACCOUNTING STANDARDS FOR NONPROFIT ORGANIZATIONS   968

Historical Development *968* / The GAAP Hierarchy *968*

NONPROFIT ACCOUNTING PRACTICES   969

ISSUES: Revenue from Contributions *969*

COLLEGES AND UNIVERSITIES   971

Fund Structure *971* / Accounting Methods of Colleges and Universities *972* / Accounting for College and University Current Funds *974* / Accounting for College and University Loan Funds *978* / Accounting for College and University Endowment and Similar Funds *978* / Accounting for College and University

Annuity and Life Income Funds *980* / Accounting for College and University Plant Funds *982* / Accounting for College and University Agency Funds *985* / Closing Entries for Funds Other Than Current Funds *985* / Annual Financial Statements of Colleges and Universities *990*

HOSPITALS   990

Fund Structure *993* / Classification and Recognition of Hospital Revenues *993* / Classification of Operating Expenses *998* / Accounting for Hospital Unrestricted and Restricted Funds *998* / No Closing Entries for Restricted Funds *1007* / Annual Financial Statements of Hospitals *1007*

VOLUNTARY HEALTH AND WELFARE ORGANIZATIONS   1010

Accounting Methods of Voluntary Health and Welfare Organizations *1010* / Fund Structure *1011* / Accounting for VHWO Funds *1013* / Annual Financial Statements *1013*

OTHER NONPROFIT ORGANIZATIONS   1013

Accounting Methods of Other Nonprofit Organizations *1022* / Fund Structure *1023* / Annual Financial Statements *1024*

SUMMARY   *1025*
SELECTED READINGS   *1026*
QUESTIONS   *1028*
EXERCISES   *1029*
PROBLEMS   *1039*
ISSUES IN ACCOUNTING JUDGMENT   *1051*

INDEX   1053

PREFACE

Our purpose in writing this book is to present the topics of advanced accounting—multiple corporation entities, multinational entities, partnerships and branches, and governmental and nonprofit entities—in an up-to-date and thorough fashion. We give attention to both conceptual and procedural aspects of each topic and to the institutional setting in which they arise. Particular attention is given to producing a readable text that applies consistent pedagogical techniques throughout, giving students every possible assistance in mastering the challenging topics of the advanced accounting course.

THIRD EDITION ADDITIONS AND REVISIONS

New Features

The third edition of *Advanced Accounting* adds several new features to those of the preceding two editions:

1. *New Chapter on Disaggregated Financial Reporting.* Chapter 9 describes situations requiring disaggregation of consolidated financial information. This new chapter discusses nonhomogeneous subsidiaries, segment reporting, significant investees and joint ventures, parent-company-only financial information, separately issued subsidiary financial statement and push-down accounting, and interim financial reporting. Although these topics are frequently treated in different chapters, we believe that the disaggregation idea helps students understand and master these forms of accounting.

2. *New Chapter on Reporting under New Basis Accounting.* A new Chapter 10 describes several situations requiring a new basis of accounting including leveraged buyouts, quasireorganizations, and reorganizations under the bankruptcy code. This chapter emphasizes the relationship among this group of topics and helps students recognize the diversity of situations calling for new basis accounting.

3. *New Chapter on Researching Accounting Principles.* The literature of accounting standards, regulations, and scholarship is expanding at an unprecedented rate. Recognizing the impossibility of treating this literature exhaustively in a single book, we have created a new chapter to encourage students to explore the complexities of accounting research. This new Chapter 11 describes research by professional accountants, presents the hierarchy of generally accepted accounting principles, discusses aspects of accounting in governmental regulation emphasizing the role of the Securities and Exchange Commission, and illustrates the research process. The assignment materials for this chapter include challenging opportunities for students to research the professional literature.

4. *Issues in Accounting Judgment.* A new form of assignment material is added at the end of each chapter. "Issues in Accounting Judgment" are brief cases that challenge students to think through various aspects of accounting. These "judgment cases" are a logical pedagogical extension of the "issues sections" presented in the text. Some of

these cases require students to visit their school's library and to extend their understanding beyond the discussion presented in the text.

Revisions and Updates

In addition, we have incorporated many editorial updates and improvements including the following:

1. *Recent Financial Accounting Pronouncements and Literature.* The entire text has been updated to reflect important changes in the professional literature. Of course, the three new chapters introduce a significant amount of new material. Here are some examples of other additions: The discussion of consolidation concepts has been revised to reflect thinking presented in the 1991 FASB discussion memorandum written by Professor Paul Pacter. As in previous editions, a discussion of conceptual consolidation issues is placed in Chapter 2 and is supported by a presentation of alternative consolidation concepts in an appendix to the chapter. We have added a brief discussion of foreign consolidation standards to Chapter 2. Discussions of accounting for income taxes, which appear in the text and footnotes of various chapters, have been updated to reflect FASB Statement No. 109, although we have not endeavored to treat these topics exhaustively. Finally, the end-of-chapter lists of selected readings have also been revised to incorporate scholarly writing on new and emerging issues.

2. *Recent Developments in Governmental and Nonprofit Accounting.* Governmental and nonprofit accounting are undergoing significant change. Although implementation of all the proposed changes is likely to occur gradually, our revision includes discussion of the general direction of proposed changes. For example, our presentation of accounting for state and local governments includes general discussion of the wide-ranging *GASB Statement No. 11.* Similarly, our presentation of accounting for nonprofit organizations includes discussion of the implications of *SAS No. 69* for change and improvement in this tangled and contested area of accounting standards. In addition, of course, our revision updates the presentation to reflect significant changes in specific standards including *FASB statements Nos. 116 and 117.*

3. *New and Revised End-of-Chapter Assignment Materials.* On the basis of a review of recent accounting literature and professional examinations, we have added new exercises and problems and revised a significant number of assignment materials appearing in prior editions.

4. *Combination of Partnership Chapters.* The three partnership chapters of the second edition have been combined into two chapters, with the result that partnership formation, operations, and ownership changes are now discussed in a single chapter. Partnership liquidation continues to be treated in a separate chapter.

The chapters of the text are divided into four parts, as in earlier editions; however, some of the parts have been renamed and the location of one chapter has been changed. The addition of the three new chapters led us to change the title of the "Business Combinations and Consolidations" section to "Multiple Corporation Entities." We have also moved the branches chapter to share a section with the partnership chapters.

HELPING STUDENTS LEARN COMPLEX MATERIAL

Chapter Structure

Advanced accounting topics exhibit logical complexities that place heavy demands on the learning abilities of students. Most students do not master advanced accounting topics in a single reading; instead, they learn advanced accounting in an iterative process that involves repeated exposure to segments of the text and related problem material. In such a process, it is important that the text assist the student in partitioning each topic into segments and in establishing a structure that shows the relationship among the various segments. The extensive use of headings and subheadings to organize discussions and illustrations throughout this book is designed to provide such assistance. In addition, the detailed outline that precedes each chapter repeats the headings and subheadings that partition the chapter and provides page references. Students will find these outlines to be useful in organizing their study.

The book is written in a way that students will appreciate. Recurring entries, schedules, and computations are presented in standardized formats throughout the text. These standard forms become familiar to students and aid them in developing an understanding of complex problems unfolded through several chapters. Another aspect of the book that students will appreciate is the extensive use of verbal explanations of entries, schedules, and computations. Rather than relying on the numbers to speak for themselves, we put important relationships into words.

Study Guide

The text is accompanied by a study guide prepared by the authors and Eric E. Spires. Carefully coordinated with the text, each chapter of the study guide contains review material in the form of learning objectives, a review outline, a summary of critical points, a key term review accompanied by statement-completion items, a true-false self-test, and practice problems with solutions.

Working Papers

This supplement provides students with typeset working papers for all the problems in the text.

Spreadsheet Templates

Eugene R. Rozzinski (Illinois State University) has prepared a set of 40 Lotus 1-2-3 templates for selected problems in the text. Problems included are identified in the text by a computer icon. The templates are free to the instructor upon request.

TEACHING FLEXIBILITY AND FEATURES

Flexibility

Recognizing that most advanced accounting courses do not have enough time to cover all chapters exhaustively, we have designed most of our chapters to permit instructors to vary the extent of coverage. Chapters present basic issues first. Extensions are placed in appendixes, some of which are described earlier in this preface, or in separate sections appearing late in the chapter. An important example of this type of flexibility appears in Chapter 12, which discusses the restatement for foreign financial statement with a brief discussion of the related consolidation procedures; detailed consolidation procedures for foreign statements are described and illustrated in an appendix to the chapter. This permits instructors considerable latitude in the time devoted to this topic. In addition, Chapter 13 on foreign currency transactions is written so that instructors may assign it prior to Chapter 12, if they wish to do so. We have also made extensive use of explanatory footnotes, which removes many complexities and fine points from the main flow of the text.

Issues Sections

The issues sections, an innovation of the second edition, establish the nature and importance of theoretical and professional issues without needlessly disrupting the presentation of the basic concepts and procedures. Each issues section is a brief discussion of a professional or theoretical issue related to the accounting topic under discussion. Although each issue is related to the surrounding text, it is set off from the text to highlight its distinctive character and to permit students to read around it in developing a basic understanding of the text. Most chapters contain one or more issues sections, and related essay questions are presented in the test bank.

End-of-Chapter Assignment Materials

Each exercise, problem, and judgment case bears a carefully constructed descriptive label to assist instructors in selecting an appropriately balanced set of items for assignment to students. An abundance of assignment materials is presented at the end of every chapter to permit the instructor wide latitude in selection and to allow the assignment of different items in different terms.

Solutions Manual

Fully worked out solutions to all questions, exercises, and problems in the text are provided. The solutions include extensive supporting schedules and computations that are consistent with those presented in the text.

Check Figures

Check figures are provided for end-of-chapter problems and are available to instructors from the publisher, upon request, in quantity for distribution to students.

Test Bank

Prepared by Edward N. Coffman, the test bank contains over 850 multiple-choice questions in addition to computational problems and essay questions. The test bank is also available in a computerized version.

Instructor's Resource Manual

An instructor's resource manual has been prepared for this edition by Edward N. Coffman. This manual offers recommendations on teaching the text supported by chapter outlines, teaching suggestions for every chapter, and other teaching aids.

Overhead Transparencies

These transparencies are available for solutions to many end-of-chapter problems.

ACKNOWLEDGMENTS

It is impossible to list all the persons whose assistance and cooperation have aided the preparation of this book. We are grateful to our students who have made innumerable contributions and worthy suggestions that improved both the text and the supporting materials. In addition, the text and its supplements have been enriched by the comments and reactions of the many reviewers of all three editions. We are indebted to each of them and particularly to the following persons who assisted us with the third edition: Steven Cahan, University of Wyoming; Jim Chan, University of Illinois at Chicago; Roger Chope, University of Oregon; Steve Courtenay, The University of North Carolina at Wilmington; Janie Flynt, Louisiana State University, Shreveport; Abo Habib, Mankato State University; John Hamer, University of Massachusetts at Lowell; Kendrall C. Hardy, Catonsville Community College; Ernest Hicks, Ohio State University (retired); Jesse Hughes, Old Dominion University; Steven Kachelmeier, University of Texas at Austin; Joanne Rockness, North Carolina State University; and Forrest Thompson, Florida A&M University.

We wish to express our appreciation to the American Institute of Certified Public Accountants, the Institute of Management Accountants, and the Institute of Internal Auditors for permission to reprint their published materials.

Finally, we wish to thank Martha Anderson, who assisted with the manuscript and solutions manual, and Alan Sachs and the editorial staff at McGraw-Hill, including Bernadette Boylan, whose skill and patience helped us refine the effectiveness of our text.

Daniel L. Jensen
Edward N. Coffman
Ray G. Stephens
Thomas J. Burns

ADVANCED ACCOUNTING

ONE

Multiple- Corporation Entities

1

Business Combinations

BUSINESS COMBINATIONS FROM VARIOUS VIEWPOINTS 3

THE ACQUIRING COMPANY 4

THE ACQUIRED COMPANY 5

REGULATORY AGENCIES 7

ACCOUNTING RULE-MAKING AGENCIES 7

COMBINATION TRANSACTIONS 8

FOUR BASIC FORMS OF BUSINESS COMBINATION 8

Acquisitions of Net Assets for Cash 8 Acquisitions of Net Assets for Stock 9 Acquisitions of Stock for Cash 9 Acquisitions of Stock for Stock 10

ACQUISITIONS OF ASSETS SUBJECT TO LIABILITIES 10

CORPORATE STRUCTURE OF BUSINESS COMBINATIONS 11

AN OVERVIEW OF ACCOUNTING FOR BUSINESS COMBINATIONS 11

CRITERIA THAT DISTINGUISH PURCHASES AND POOLINGS 11

VALUATION OF ACQUIRED NET ASSETS 12

TAXES AND BUSINESS COMBINATIONS 12

ACCOUNTING FOR PURCHASE COMBINATIONS 13

MEASURING ACQUISITION COST 13

Security Registration and Issue Costs 14 Direct and Indirect Costs of Acquisition 14

ALLOCATING THE ACQUISITION COST 15

Unrecorded Assets Received 15 Analysis of the Valuation Differential for Net Assets 15

RECORDING PURCHASE COMBINATIONS 17

ACCOUNTING FOR POOLING-OF-INTERESTS COMBINATIONS 21

RECORDING POOLINGS OF INTERESTS 22

PAR VALUE ISSUED AND THE RECLASSIFICATION OF STOCKHOLDERS' EQUITY 24

COMBINED NET INCOME IN YEAR OF COMBINATION 26

SUMMARY 28

APPENDIX A: CRITERIA FOR POOLINGS OF INTERESTS 28

APPENDIX B: CONTINGENT CONSIDERATION AND PREACQUISITION CONTINGENCIES 33

Business combinations bring together the net assets of two or more business enterprises in a single accounting entity. Historically, the popularity of business combinations has been strongly influenced by the economic and political climate. Consequently, the extent of combination activity and the business purposes served by combination are subject to change. For example, the two decades preceding the turn of the century saw extensive combination activity stimulated by improvements in transportation and communication systems and directed at building *horizontally integrated* business entities (combining companies engaged in the same type of production or the sale of the same general product) with broad control over certain industries. Combinations in this period were particularly effective in high-volume, continuous-process, and capital-intensive industries such as food processing, steel, and petroleum where significant cost reductions and distributional advantages were to be obtained. Examples are United States Steel, Standard Oil Company, American Sugar Refining Company, and American Tobacco Company. Following World War I, a second wave of the combination activity emphasized the building of *vertically integrated* business entities (combining companies engaged in different stages of production and distribution of a common product). Combinations in this period were particularly effective in distribution and marketing-oriented industries where combinations secured the benefits of effective administrative functions. Examples are Continental Can, General Electric, and Union Carbide. A third wave of combination followed World War II and continues to this day. Combination activity was particularly widespread in the late 1960s and has shown an upturn in recent years. Many recent combinations have been directed at diversifying business risk by forming large multi-industry organizations known as *conglomerates* (combining companies that are neither horizontally nor vertically integrated).[1]

This chapter begins by describing business combinations from the viewpoint of the combining companies and the various regulatory and accounting agencies concerned with business combinations. The chapter continues with a description of four basic forms of business combinations and a discussion of several important aspects of combination transactions. The chapter then turns to a discussion of two methods of accounting for business combinations—purchase accounting and pooling-of-interests accounting. The chapter concludes by demonstrating differences in the calculation of net income under the purchase and pooling-of-interests methods. Two appendixes follow the chapter. Appendix A describes the 12 criteria that characterize poolings of interests. Appendix B discusses the accounting for contingent consideration used in business combinations under purchase accounting.

BUSINESS COMBINATIONS FROM VARIOUS VIEWPOINTS

In most business combinations, one company acquires control over the net assets of another company. The transfer of control from one group of owners to another affects the economic interests of many people, including the owners, managers, creditors, and customers of both the acquired and acquiring companies. Each group is interested in its impact on their prospects and welfare. Owners of the acquiring company are interested in the impact of the acquired net assets on the value and income-producing capability of their investment and in the amount and form of the price paid. Owners of the acquired company are interested in the adequacy of the price received and the form of the payment. Creditors of both acquired and acquiring companies are interested in the impact of the combination on the security of their debt holdings, including any instruments issued as part of the combination. Managers of both acquired and acquiring companies are interested in the combination's effect on their managerial positions. Customers are interested in its effect on the level of price and quality of goods and services produced. In addition, regulatory agencies and accounting rule-making groups hold distinctive viewpoints regarding business combinations. The paragraphs that follow illustrate these different viewpoints on combinations.

---

[1] See Chandler (1977) for additional discussion of business combination in the history of American business; also see Chandler (1990), particularly for historical developments in Great Britain and in Germany.

The Acquiring Company

The acquiring company must carefully consider the economic consequences of any proposed business combination. In the issues section that follows, we examine a proposed business combination from the perspective of the acquiring company's management.

Evaluation of Proposed Expansion by Combination

General Electronics, Inc. is a large manufacturer of electronic production equipment. The company currently enjoys a significant market share, but management recognizes that market share is very sensitive to technological change. A new technology could sweep the market and significantly reduce the market share in a matter of two or three years. In fact, recent advances in technology have made possible the creation of highly versatile robots that are applicable to a variety of manufacturing operations. General Electronics' management has decided to undertake production of these robots and to secure a share in this rapidly developing market. Two alternative strategies are currently under consideration:

Strategy 1: Expansion by Internal Development. Assemble the research and engineering staff to build and equip the required manufacturing facility.

Strategy 2: Expansion by Combination. Negotiate a business combination with Robotec, Inc., a smaller company that pioneered in the field of robot technology. (Since the proposed combination brings together two businesses that sell the same general product, electronic production equipment, the combination qualifies as a horizontal combination.)

Let us consider some of the strategic questions faced by General Electronics' management.

1. *What impact will the two strategies have on the capital structure of General Electronics?*

General Electronics intends to finance the expansion by issuing new common stock regardless of the plan undertaken. If expansion by internal development is undertaken, stock will be sold to the general public and the proceeds used to develop the new product line. If expansion by combination is undertaken, over half of the stock will be used to acquire the outstanding voting stock of Robotec and the remainder will be sold to the general public with the proceeds used to develop the new product line. An analysis prepared by the controller of General Electronics shows that expansion by combination will require a significantly smaller stock issue than expansion by internal development. Moreover, the controller notes that expansion by combination draws a much smaller amount of capital from financial markets and, in her view, leaves the company in a stronger position to secure equity capital for other purposes.

2. *What impact will the two strategies have on marketing the new product?*

General Electronics' marketing vice-president predicts that both strategies will produce about the same market share; however, expansion by combination will enable the company to reach the market about 18 months earlier than expansion by internal development. Consequently, the combination offers a decided advantage in terms of anticipated future revenues.

3. *What impact will the two strategies have on the production of the new product?*

General Electronics' operating vice-president predicts that the cost of new facilities under Strategy 1 would be about the same as the cost of acquiring Robotec's existing facilities. Moreover, the existing facilities will have about the same useful life and annual operating costs as newly constructed facilities. However, Strategy 1 would require significant outlays for assembling the required research and production staff and for establishing a program of product research and development. Under Strategy 2, the outlays for assembling new staff can be avoided by a carefully considered program to integrate Robotec's personnel into the organization. On the other hand, it is recognized that integrating personnel—particularly research and development personnel—into a new organization is very difficult.

4. *What impact will the two strategies have on the administrative structure of the company?*

The management of General Electronics believes that it could not undertake the internal development of the new product without significant increases in its ranks. The company recognizes that building a new management team—particularly one to handle a new, high-technology product—is time-consuming and costly. However, the company also recognizes the difficulty in transferring management from a small company to a larger one.

5. *How should the company choose between the two strategies?*

The choice between the two strategies should be made on the basis of a careful analysis of the economic consequences of each strategy and an assessment of those consequences in terms of the objectives for the company. Although the information presented here is not sufficient for such an analysis, it would appear that expansion by combination has better economic consequences than expansion by internal development. The decision must also consider the way in which the combination would be viewed under applicable antitrust laws and the impact of the combination on taxation and financial statements. Consideration of such technical issues frequently requires the company to seek the counsel of outside legal and accounting experts.

Thus, the decision to expand by business combination rather than internal development raises complex questions about the effects on capital structure, marketing, production, and administration. We turn now from the acquiring company's viewpoint to the viewpoint of the company acquired in a business combination.

The Acquired Company

Various conditions motivate companies to be acquired in business combinations. For example, an acquired company may have exhausted its sources of capital with the result that a business combination is the only way it can grow. In other cases, an acquired company with a regional orientation or a limited product line may gain access to larger markets through combination with a firm with a national distribution system or a more complete product line. In some cases, a small company may combine with a larger company rather than risk being swamped by impending changes in technology or markets. Acquired companies may also be motivated to enter a business combination by personal financial circumstances of the owners.[2] Ultimately, of course, the price and other arrange-

---

[2] The retirement of major stockholders from key management positions of closely held companies, particularly when no suitable replacements have been developed, may bring a combination with another company. In some cases, owners of a closely held corporation may wish to liquidate their stockholdings or to diversify their personal stock portfolios. Since holdings in closely held companies are not readily marketed to the general public, a business combination is an attractive alternative. Sometimes business combinations offer tax advantages to owners or to their future estates.

ments offered by the acquiring company must be more attractive than the acquired company's prospects for future profit.

Many business combinations are negotiated by the managements and boards of directors of the acquired and acquiring companies without direct involvement of the acquired company's stockholders. In such cases, the managers and directors of the acquired company who favor combination must either own or hold proxies for enough shares to effect the combination. In some cases, the acquiring company may bypass management and go directly to the stockholders of the acquired company with a "tender offer." A *tender offer* is an offer to purchase the target company's shares at a specified price from any stockholder who "tenders" his or her shares. The issues section that follows examines a tender offer from the viewpoint of the company targeted for acquisition.

ISSUES

A Tender Offer

Bonworth Products is a profitable, medium-sized company that produces software for personal computers. Although the price of its stock has advanced little in recent years, it is generally believed that the company has excellent prospects for future growth and development given the right financing and management. A recent issue of the *Wall Street Journal* carried a full-page letter addressed to the stockholders of Bonworth Products from the management of ZBN Corporation, a large producer of personal computer software. The tender-offer letter agreed to buy for cash any outstanding shares of Bonworth at a 20% premium over the current market price, provided that those shares are tendered to ZBN within 30 business days. Let us consider some of the questions faced by the stockholders and management of Bonworth Products.

1. *What concerns does the tender offer raise for the management of Bonworth Products?*

The management of Bonworth has serious misgivings about the impact of the combination on their managerial positions and on the performances of production and development personnel. If the takeover occurs, it is quite likely that many managers will either resign or be replaced. Indeed, senior managers have very generous severance pay provisions, known as "golden parachutes," in their employment contracts that are effective in the event of a takeover and provide a strong incentive for them to resign if the takeover is successful.

In order to combat the takeover effort, the management of Bonworth has written a letter to all stockholders arguing that the 20% premium of the tender offer is well under the current value of the company if its long-run prospects are considered. The letter advises all stockholders to refuse to sell their shares. In order to discourage ZBN Corporation, senior managers have issued a public statement indicating their intention to resign and exercise their golden parachutes if the takeover is successful; such action will virtually strip the company of its working capital.

2. *What concerns does the tender offer raise for the stockholders of Bonworth Products?*

The stockholders of Bonworth must decide whether the 20% premium over the current market price is sufficient to reflect the future prospects for growth and development offered by Bonworth. Perhaps the current market price reflects a temporary depression of stock prices that makes the premium too low. Perhaps the stockholders will be unable to invest the amount offered in equally attractive securities. On the other hand, if the stockholders decide not to sell and the takeover is successful, then the stockholders must live with the decisions of ZBN Corporation's controlling interest. Although the information given here is not sufficient to evaluate the offer, each stockholder has only 30 days in which to gather and analyze information as a basis for his or her decision.

Tender offers, like the one described above, are called "hostile takeovers" (rather than "friendly takeovers") when they generate stiff resistance from the management or owners of the target company; the would-be acquirer in such cases may be called a "shark" or "raider." Defenses against hostile takeovers, which are sometimes called "shark repellents," include "golden parachutes" (generous severance benefits for management that deplete the target company resources), "poison pills" (securities issued by a target company to its stockholders to give them, in the event that the raider manages to acquire a specified level of ownership, a disproportionately large number of voting shares or an expensively redeemable security), or "scorched earth" policies (whereby the company sells valuable assets, pays large dividends, or takes other action to reduce the value of the target company to the raider). In some cases, the target company may seek the protection of a "white knight," an alternative acquirer who is more acceptable to the target company. We turn now to a third perspective on business combinations—the perspective of the regulatory agency.

Regulatory Agencies

Although business combinations are motivated by a desire on the part of both acquired and acquiring companies to enhance their profitability, when carried to an extreme, business combinations can impair the functioning of competitive market structures by concentrating market power in the hands of one or a small number of entities. Various federal statutes—including the Sherman Act of 1890, the Clayton Act of 1914, the Federal Trade Commission Act of 1914, and the 1950 Celler-Kefauver amendment to the Clayton Act—have been enacted to prevent excessive concentrations of market power. These statutes are administered by the Federal Trade Commission (FTC) and enforced by the Antitrust Division of the Justice Department. Either the Antitrust Division or the FTC may block a business combination by bringing suit under the Clayton Act and proving that the combination would result in a substantial lessening of competition. Both the FTC and the Antitrust Division of the Justice Department are open to precombination consultation with the combining parties. In such consultations, the combining parties secure advice concerning the proposed combination and an indication of whether or not the combination is likely to provoke legal action.[3] Identification and consideration of the applicable regulations are important aspects of any business combination for which combining parties usually seek the assistance of expert legal and accounting consultants.

Accounting Rule-Making Agencies

A fourth perspective on business combinations is that of the accounting rule-making agencies. Business combinations raise many difficult accounting issues concerning financial statements issued by the constituent enterprises and the combined entity. Much of this

---

[3] Business combinations in certain industries are subject to regulation by other specialized agencies. For example, combinations in the banking industry are subject to regulations of the Federal Reserve, the Treasury Department, and the Federal Deposit Insurance Corporation. Combinations in the interstate trucking industry are subject to regulations of the Interstate Commerce Commission. In addition, business combinations must also be reported to the Securities and Exchange Commission.

book is devoted to the discussion of these issues and the arguments and rules that resolve them. Accounting rule-making agencies—most notably, the Financial Accounting Standards Board and its predecessor, the Accounting Principles Board—have issued standards that resolve many important issues raised by business combinations. These accounting standards establish uniform ways of handling various types of business combinations. Such uniformity makes it easier for readers of financial statements to discern both the impact of a combination and the effects of subsequent events on the newly created business entity.

COMBINATION TRANSACTIONS

Most business combinations consist of not one, but several transactions involving stockholders and creditors as well as the constituent companies themselves. Some combinations are brought about by transactions between the constituent companies, as when two companies combine by an exchange of newly issued shares in one company for the assets of another. Other combinations do not involve transactions between the constituent companies, as when one company acquires all the outstanding stock of another directly from its stockholders. In general, business combinations are composed of transactions between constituent companies and transactions between a constituent company and an equity-holding group.

Four Basic Forms of Business Combination

Although business combinations can take an unlimited variety of forms, the essential character of most combinations is either an acquisition of net assets or an acquisition of stock taking one of four basic forms:

1. An acquisition of net assets for cash
2. An acquisition of net assets for stock
3. An acquisition of stock for cash
4. An acquisition of stock for stock

The first two forms are frequently referred to collectively as acquisitions of net assets and the last two forms, as acquisitions of stock. Let us consider each of the four basic forms of business combination.

Acquisitions of Net Assets for Cash

When one company acquires the net assets of another in exchange for cash, the acquiring company records the detailed assets and liabilities acquired. To illustrate, suppose that Gilmore Corporation acquires the assets and liabilities of Hall, Inc. for $90,000 cash; the various assets of Hall are valued at a total of $130,000 and the liabilities at $40,000. Accordingly, Gilmore makes the following entry:

Acquiring company's entry to record the acquisition of net assets in exchange for cash:

Various assets (listed individually)	130,000	
Various liabilities (listed individually)		40,000
Cash		90,000

The recipient of the net assets is identified as the acquiring company and the recipient of the cash is identified as the acquired company. Unlike certain other forms of combination, an acquisition of net assets for cash completely dissolves the acquired company's equity interest in the net assets. The acquired company receives cash, which it may reinvest or distribute to its stockholders, but has no further interest in its former net assets. Of course, if the acquired company reinvests the cash, then the purpose of the continuing company differs from that of the precombination company.

Acquisitions of Net Assets for Stock

Following the second form of business combination, one corporation can acquire the net assets of another in exchange for stock of the acquiring corporation. For example, if Gilmore had issued common stock valued at $90,000 rather than paying cash of $90,000, Gilmore would have made the following entry:

> *Acquiring company's entry to record the acquisition of net assets in exchange for stock:*

Various assets (listed individually) 130,000		
Various liabilities (listed individually)		40,000
Common stock accounts		90,000

Although the stock given up is usually newly issued shares of the acquiring company, it may include treasury shares as well. The amount of the stock given up must be negotiated by the constituent companies, but it generally does not exceed the number of shares held by the acquiring company's stockholders prior to the combination.[4]

Acquisitions of Stock for Cash

A third form of business combination is an acquisition of stock for cash in which the recipient of the stock is identified as the acquiring company. To illustrate, suppose that Roberts Corporation acquires all the outstanding common stock of Simpson, Inc. for $70,000 cash; Roberts makes the following entry:

> *Acquiring company's entry to record the acquisition of stock in exchange for cash:*

Investment in Simpson, Inc. 70,000		
Cash		70,000

The acquiring company establishes an investment account rather than recording the detailed assets and liabilities of the acquired company. When the stockholders of the acquired company surrender their shares in exchange for cash, they also surrender their equity interest in the assets of the acquired company. The acquired company may continue to exist, but to the extent that its stock is held by the acquiring company, it has no substance apart from the acquiring company.

---

[4] If the amount of stock given up exceeds the number of shares held by the acquiring company's stockholders prior to the combination, then the combination is no longer an acquisition of assets for stock. If so many shares are issued that the company receiving the shares ends up controlling the issuing company, then the combination is an acquisition of stock (in exchange for assets) rather than an acquisition of assets (in exchange for stock) and, further, the identities of the acquired and acquiring companies are reversed.

Acquisitions of Stock for Stock

A fourth form of business combination is accomplished by exchanging shares of stock. Usually, the acquiring corporation issues new shares of its stock in exchange for the outstanding stock of the acquired corporation. In most cases, the acquiring corporation will secure the outstanding shares directly from the stockholders of the acquired corporation in a tender-offer procedure. To illustrate, suppose that Roberts had acquired Simpson's outstanding shares by issuing common stock valued at $70,000 rather than by paying $70,000 in cash; Roberts would make the following entry:

Acquiring company's entry to record the acquisition of stock in exchange for stock:

Investment in Simpson, Inc. 70,000
　　Common stock accounts .... 　　70,000

Again, the acquiring company establishes an investment account rather than recording the detailed assets and liabilities of the acquired company. However, acquisitions of stock for stock do not reduce the liquid assets available to the combined entity as do acquisitions of stock or assets for cash. However, acquisitions of stock (or net assets) for stock do divide control over the combined assets between the stockholders of the acquired and acquiring companies.

Acquisitions of Assets Subject to Liabilities

In some acquisitions of assets, the liabilities of the acquired company are liquidated as part of the combination. Alternatively, the assets may be acquired subject to the liabilities, which means that the acquiring company agrees to pay the liabilities of the acquired corporation as they come due. The assumption of liabilities of one company by another usually requires approval of the creditors. For example, suppose that Johnson Corporation acquires the assets of Kelley, Inc., which have a fair value of $160,000, in exchange for $100,000 cash and the assumption of Kelley's liabilities, which have a fair value[5] of $60,000. This intercompany transaction may be viewed in two ways. First, the transaction may be viewed as an acquisition of assets valued at $160,000 in exchange for consideration with the same total value ($160,000 = $100,000 + $60,000); in this case, the assets are valued separately, and the liability assumption is treated as an element or component of the consideration. Second, the transaction may be viewed as an acquisition of *net* assets valued at $100,000 ($160,000 − $60,000) in exchange for consideration with the same value; in this case, the assets are valued net of related liabilities, and therefore consideration given does not include the liability assumption. The two views of the transaction are equivalent, but the second or "net asset" view simplifies explanations and calculations. Consequently, it is adopted throughout this text unless otherwise indicated.[6]

---

[5] The fair value of liabilities assumed equals the present value of the amounts to be paid thereunder computed at appropriate *current* interest rates. For example, the present value of a debt security assumed by an acquiring company should be computed at the effective rate or current yield rate for a comparable security *(APB Opinion No. 16,* par. 72). If the current yield on comparable securities is above the rate at which debt securities were issued by the acquired company, then the fair value of the debt securities will be less than their book value on the records of the acquired company.

[6] Some preferred stock issues offer very strong assurances on the payment of future dividends and par amounts. Such preferred stock issues may be sufficiently similar to debt securities to call for their treatment as assumed liabilities in business combinations. Although valuation of preferred stock is certain to be a subjective task, financial accounting standards suggest that "the fair value of nonvoting, nonconvertible preferred stock which lacks characteristics of common stock may be determined by comparing the specific dividend and redemption terms with comparable securities and by assessing market factors" *(APB Opinion No. 16,* par. 73).

Corporate Structure of Business Combinations

Some business combinations create a new corporate structure, whereas others use only existing corporate structures. If the combined entity takes the form of a newly created corporation, then the combination is called a *consolidation*. For example, Corporation X and Corporation Y combine by consolidation if the combined entity takes the form of a newly created Corporation Z. On the other hand, if the combined entity takes the form of one of the original corporate parties to the combination, then the combination is called a *merger*. For example, Corporation A and Corporation B are said to combine by merger if the combined entity takes the form of Corporation A. For the sake of simplicity, all business combinations described in this book are assumed to be mergers unless a consolidation is specifically indicated.

Some business combinations result in the liquidation of one or more of the corporate parties to the combination. *Corporate liquidation* is the process of converting all corporate assets into cash or another distributable form, paying all creditors and expenses, and distributing any remainder to stockholders. For example, if Corporation A and Corporation B combine by merger in Corporation A, then Corporation B may or may not liquidate.[7]

Thus, the corporate structure of a business combination depends on whether the combination is a merger or a consolidation, and whether the acquired company liquidates or continues. The structure of a particular combination depends on the needs and wishes of the combining companies as reflected in the combination agreement. Income tax laws frequently have an important influence on the structure of business combinations. Of course, the structure is also influenced by the objectives of the constituent companies' managements.

Business combinations are subject to the provisions of state statute, which vary from one state to another, and in some cases to the rules of regulatory agencies including the Securities and Exchange Commission. When a business combination leads to the liquidation of all but one of the constituent corporations, whether by merger or consolidation, the combination is subject to state laws and is called a *statutory merger* or a *statutory consolidation*. Most state laws require that the terms of such statutory combinations be approved by the boards of directors of the combining corporations. Frequently, the stockholders of acquired companies must ratify the combination agreement, and sometimes the stockholders of the acquiring company must do so as well.

AN OVERVIEW OF ACCOUNTING FOR BUSINESS COMBINATIONS

From an accounting point of view, there are two types of business combinations—*purchases* and *poolings of interests*. The terms of a purchase combination differ from the terms of a pooling-of-interests combination. Further, different accounting methods are applicable to purchases and poolings of interests. Let us begin by briefly considering the criteria that distinguish purchases from poolings and then turn to a discussion of the valuation methods that are applicable to the two types of business combination.

Criteria That Distinguish Purchases and Poolings

A business combination is identified as a purchase or a pooling on the basis of the terms of its transactions and by reference to criteria established by financial accounting standards. The theoretical difference between purchases and poolings is that the stockholders of the acquired company relinquish their ownership in the acquired company's net assets in a

---

[7] Similarly, if Corporation X and Corporation Y consolidate in the newly created Corporation Z, Corporations X and Y may be liquidated; on the other hand, Corporations X and Y may survive the combination and not liquidate. Accounting for corporate liquidations is discussed in Chapter 11.

purchase but not in a pooling. For example, if a significant number of former stockholders of the acquired company accept cash for their stock, those stockholders relinquish their interests in the acquired company and the related combination is a purchase. In contrast, a pooling of interests merely joins two stockholder groups and their related net assets. For example, if the former stockholders of the acquired company merely exchange their shares for shares in the acquiring company, they do not relinquish their ownership interest. Rather, the former stockholders of the acquired company become stockholders of the combined entity.[8] Although poolings are possible, most business combinations result in the relinquishment of significant ownership interests in the acquired company and are treated as purchases.

Although the differences between purchases and poolings are fairly easy to state in theoretical terms, purchases and poolings are quite difficult to distinguish in practice. In an effort to clarify the distinction between the two types of business combination, financial accounting standards establish 12 conditions—all of which must be met—for a combination to qualify as a pooling of interests. For example, one of the conditions requires that the acquiring company issue voting common stock for at least 90% of the voting common stock of the acquired company. This important condition implies that most poolings of interests are substantially acquisitions of stock in exchange for stock; in contrast, purchase combinations may be organized around any of the four basic forms of business combination mentioned earlier. The 12 conditions, which are summarized in Appendix A to this chapter, were promulgated by the Accounting Principles Board (APB) in 1970 following a wave of combination activity.

Valuation of Acquired Net Assets

Although other differences between accounting for purchases and poolings are described later in this chapter, the most striking difference concerns the valuation of acquired net assets. If a business combination constitutes a purchase, then the acquiring company is viewed as the purchaser of the acquired company. Accordingly, net assets from the acquired company are revalued and recorded by the acquiring company at amounts that total the *acquisition cost*. On the other hand, if a combination constitutes a pooling, then the net assets from the acquired company are not revalued but are recorded by the acquiring company at their *book value* to the acquired company. In both purchases and poolings, the valuation of net assets held by the *acquiring* company prior to the combination is unaffected by the combination.

Taxes and Business Combinations

Under the federal income tax law, business combinations may be either taxable or nontaxable to the acquired company or its stockholders. In a *nontaxable combination,* the acquired company's tax basis is transferred to the acquiring company, and no tax is paid by either company on any implied gain or loss from the combination. Further, the acquiring company may be able to receive the tax benefits of net operating loss carryforwards of the acquired company. In a *taxable combination,* the tax basis of the acquired company is adjusted (usually raised) to equal the consideration given by the acquirer, and a taxable gain or loss is recognized by the acquired company. In most taxable combinations, the tax

---

[8] Theoretically, a pooling of interests does not constitute an acquisition; consequently, it is more appropriate to refer to the combining parties as *issuing company* and *combinee* rather than as *acquiring company* and *acquired company.* However, for the sake of simplicity, we use the latter designations for the parties to both poolings and purchases.

benefits of the acquired company's net operating loss carryforwards are not transferable to the acquiring company. Thus, the tax accounting for taxable combinations usually results in equality between the tax basis and book value of the acquired company.

Chapter 8 extends this discussion of differences between tax basis and book value in business combinations and describes the accounting for deferred taxes related to such differences. For the sake of simplicity, we assume throughout this book, unless the contrary is specifically indicated, that all combinations are structured such that no deferred taxes are recognized in recording the combination.

Rather complicated tax rules restrict the availability of nontaxable combination to statutory mergers or consolidations and to combinations resulting in control by the acquiring company of at least 80% of the acquired company's stock. In these and other respects, the tax treatment of business combinations can be influenced by the transaction details of a combination; thus, provisions of the tax law frequently provide strong incentives for the various parties to a business combination to prefer one set of transactions over others in negotiating the final terms of the combination.[9]

We now turn to a more detailed description of accounting for purchase combinations and poolings of interests, beginning with purchase combinations.

ACCOUNTING FOR PURCHASE COMBINATIONS

The essence of accounting for purchase combinations is that the net assets of the acquired company are reported by the acquiring company at acquisition cost. Measurement of the acquisition cost—both total cost and the cost assignable to individual assets and liabilities acquired—is a formidable task when an entire corporation is acquired. Let us consider the measurement of acquisition cost and then illustrate the recording of a business combination using the purchase accounting method.

Measuring Acquisition Cost

The principles of historical cost accounting dictate that the net assets acquired by an entity be recorded at cost on the date of their acquisition. Cost, in this context, "may be determined by the fair value of the consideration given or by the fair value of the property acquired, whichever is the more clearly evident" (*ARB No. 43*, as quoted by *APB Opinion No. 16*, par. 67); however, the standards indicate a preference for setting acquisition cost at the fair value of the consideration given.

An acquiring corporation may give up cash, noncash assets, equity securities (common or preferred stock), debt securities (bonds and notes payable), or some combination of these items. If the consideration given is entirely cash, then the cost of the acquired assets is the amount of cash given. If the consideration given is entirely *noncash assets,* then the cost of the acquired assets is the fair value of the noncash assets given. If the consideration given is entirely *securities* issued by the acquiring corporation and if the securities have an established market value, then the acquisition cost is the market value of the securities given up (*APB Opinion No. 16*, par. 74). However, if the fair value of net assets acquired is more clearly evident than the fair value of the securities given up, then

---

[9] For an excellent discussion of the tax consequences of the differing characteristics of business combinations and related research on the impact of taxes on the incidence and form of business combinations, see Scholes and Wolfson (1992), especially Chapters 23 through 26; also see Knight and Knight (1989).

the acquisition cost is the fair value of the net assets received.[10] In general, the fair value of noncash consideration—whether it be securities or noncash assets—is the cash that would have been given had the consideration been entirely cash.

The measurement of acquisition cost is complicated by various outlays made in connection with business combinations. We begin by considering outlays for the registration and issuance of securities and then turn to other costs of consummating an acquisition. Appendix B at the end of this chapter discusses the measurement of acquisition cost that involves contingent consideration—payments by the acquiring company that depend on the occurrence of a future event.

Security Registration and Issue Costs

The costs of registering and issuing securities in a purchase combination are not included in the acquisition cost but ''are a reduction of the otherwise determinable fair value of the securities'' (*APB Opinion No. 16,* par. 76). For example, suppose that Warran Corporation acquires the assets of Zimmerman, Inc., which have a fair value of $900, subject to liabilities of $100; Warran Corporation issues 80 shares of common stock, which have a par value of $7 and a current market value of $10 per share. In addition, Warran incurs registration costs (the cost of registering the securities with the Securities and Exchange Commission) and issue costs of $60 on the 80 shares. The fair value of the newly issued shares is $740 ($800 − $60), and Warran records the acquisition with the following entry:

> *Acquiring company's entry to record the acquisition of net assets in exchange for stock:*

Various assets (listed individually) 900		
Various liabilities (listed individually)	100	
Common stock ($7 × 80)	560	
Excess over par ($800 − $60 − $560)	180	
Cash	60	

If *unregistered securities* are issued in an acquisition with the promise of subsequent registration, then the credit to cash in the foregoing entry is replaced by a credit to a liability for the anticipated registration costs (*AICPA Accounting Interpretations of APB Opinion No. 16,* Interpretation No. 35).

Direct and Indirect Costs of Acquisition

Direct costs of acquisition are to be included in acquisition cost. Direct cost, in this context, is interpreted to mean '' 'out-of-pocket' or incremental costs rather than the recurring internal costs which may be directly related to an acquisition'' and to exclude all recurring internal costs (*AICPA Accounting Interpretations of APB Opinion No. 16,* Interpretation No. 33). Thus, fees paid to outside accountants, lawyers, engineers, and apprais-

---

[10] If ''the number of shares issued is relatively large, the market for shares issued is relatively thin, the stock price is volatile or other uncertainties influence the quoted price,'' then the fair value of securities issued should be calculated in terms of the fair value of the net assets received (*APB Opinion No. 16,* par. 23).

ers for services in connection with acquisitions are direct costs and are capitalized, but the cost of an internal acquisition department is indirect and charged to expense as incurred.

The reader should note that both security registration and issue costs and direct costs of acquisition are handled differently in poolings, as explained later in this chapter.

Allocating the Acquisition Cost

Immediately after an acquisition, a combined balance sheet shows the cost of the individual assets and liabilities acquired. The cost of the individual assets and liabilities acquired is determined by allocating the acquisition cost. As mentioned earlier, the procedure assigns a portion of the acquisition cost to each asset and liability—a portion that is normally equal to its fair value at the date of acquisition.

Unrecorded Assets Received

An excess of acquisition cost over the fair value of recorded net assets received is evidence of unrecorded assets. An effort should be made to identify specific additional assets received and to measure their fair value. For example, unrecorded, fully depreciated equipment or unrecorded, fully amortized patents may possess fair value that should be recorded by the acquiring company. If an excess of acquisition cost remains after every effort has been made to attribute it to *identifiable assets,* then that excess is attributed to unidentifiable assets (*APB Opinion No. 16,* par. 68). Such an unidentifiable remainder frequently represents expectations of future earnings in excess of those normally expected, and thus is usually called *goodwill.*

Analysis of the Valuation Differential for Net Assets

The net assets of an acquired company are characterized in three measurements: (1) the *acquisition cost* to the acquiring company, (2) the *fair value of identifiable net assets acquired,* and (3) the *book value* of the net assets acquired, as recorded by the acquired company. The *valuation differential* is the name we shall use for the difference between the first and the last of these measurements—that is, the difference between acquisition cost and book value.

To illustrate, consider Corporation X, which acquires all the net assets of Corporation Y in exchange of $1,000 cash. On the date of acquisition, Corporation Y has the following balance sheet:

Date-of-Acquisition Balance Sheet of Acquired Company

Current assets	$100	Liabilities	$120
Plant and equipment (net)	750	Common stock	400
		Retained earnings	330
		Total liabilities and	
Total assets	$850	stockholders' equities	$850

In this illustration, the acquisition cost of $1,000 exceeds the $730 book value of net assets acquired ($730 = $850 − $120); therefore, the valuation differential is $270 calculated as follows:

Calculation of the Valuation Differential

Acquisition cost	$1,000
Less: Book value of net assets required ($850 − $120)	730
Valuation differential	$ 270

In the foregoing analysis, the book value of net assets acquired ($730) is calculated by subtracting the book value of liabilities assumed from the book value of assets acquired ($730 = $850 − $120). Alternatively, the book value of net assets acquired can be calculated by reference to the stockholders' equity accounts of the acquired company ($730 = $400 + $330).

The analysis of the valuation differential into its two principal parts requires a third measure of the acquired net assets—the fair value of identifiable net assets acquired. The following schedule gives the fair values[11] of the individual identifiable net assets of the acquired company, which total $900:

Fair Values and Book Values of Identifiable Assets and Liabilities

	Fair Value	Book Value	Difference
Current assets	$ 125	$100	$ 25
Plant and equipment (net)	835	750	85
Patent	60	0	60
Total assets	$1,020	$850	$170
Liabilities	(120)	(120)	
Net assets	$ 900	$730	$170

The schedule shows that the fair values of current assets and plant and equipment (net) exceed their corresponding book values by $25 and $85, respectively. In addition, Corporation Y holds a patent with a fair value of $60 and a book value of zero (the cost of the

---

[11] The measurement of fair value for noncash assets calls for the use of various sources of information. For some assets, like marketable securities, current market values are readily available. For other assets, like inventories and fixed assets, fair value must frequently be derived from special purpose price indexes and appraisals. *APB Opinion No. 16* (par. 88, as amended) provides guidelines for the determination of the fair value of identifiable assets and liabilities of the acquired company. Receivables and liabilities are assigned an amount equal to their present values. Marketable securities, finished goods, and work-in-process inventories are assigned an amount equal to their net realizable values. Nonmarketable securities, land, natural resources, and intangible assets are assigned an amount equal to their appraised values. Material inventories and plant assets held for long-term use are assigned an amount equal to their replacement cost. Plant assets to be used temporarily should be assigned their net realizable values, and depreciation should be provided for the period of their expected use.

FASB Interpretation No. 4 (par. 4) requires that identifiable assets resulting from research and development activities of the acquired company—including patents, blueprints, formulas, designs for new products or processes, and equipment and supplies to be used in research and development activities of the combined entity—should be allocated a portion of the acquisition cost in proportion to their fair value and without regard to their book value on the records of the acquired company.

The treatment of pension plans and other post-retirement benefits is discussed in *FASB Statement No. 87* (pars. 74–75 and 251–253) and *FASB Statement No. 106* (pars. 86–89 and 383–387). Preacquisition contingencies of the acquired company are discussed in Appendix B at the end of this chapter.

patent has been completely amortized). The fair value of the liabilities is correctly measured by the reported present value of $120.

The valuation differential is divided into two segments called the revaluation increment and goodwill. The *revaluation increment* is the sum of all differences between book value and fair value for the identifiable assets and liabilities. The revaluation increment is $170 in our example. *Goodwill* is the remainder of the valuation differential after subtracting the revaluation increment as shown in the following schedule:

Calculation of Valuation Differential and Goodwill

Acquisition cost		$1,000
Less: Book value of net assets acquired ($850 − $120)		730
Valuation differential		$ 270
Less: Revaluation increment:		
Current assets	$25	
Plant and equipment	85	
Patent	60	170
Goodwill		$ 100

Throughout this chapter, we assume that both the valuation differential and goodwill are positive. The next chapter discusses cases in which the valuation differential and goodwill are negative.

The following diagram depicts the structure of the valuation differential in terms of its two components—goodwill and the revaluation increment—and shows their relationship to the three measures of acquired net assets:

Analysis of the Valuation Differential for Net Assets

Acquisition cost ($1,000)	Fair value of identifiable net assets acquired ($900)	Book value of net assets acquired ($730)
Goodwill = $100	Revaluation increment = $170	
Valuation differential = $270		

The valuation differential is divided into two segments by the fair value of identifiable net assets acquired ($900). Reading from right to left, the first segment of the valuation differential is the revaluation increment ($170) attributed to identifiable assets and liabilities to raise them from book value to fair value ($170 = $900 − $730, or $170 = $25 + $85 + $60). The second segment is goodwill ($100), which represents that portion of the acquisition cost not attributable to identifiable assets or liabilities. The analysis of the valuation differential is the basis for recording purchase combinations on the records of the acquiring company as illustrated in the next section.

Recording Purchase Combinations

Purchase combinations—whether accomplished by acquisitions of assets or acquisitions of stock—are recorded at acquisition cost on the records of the acquiring company. To illustrate, consider an acquisition of stock for stock that does not qualify as a pooling of interests. On January 1, 19X4, Graham Corporation acquired all the outstanding common stock of Katz, Inc. in exchange for newly issued shares of Graham's stock, and Katz, Inc. was liquidated. In return, Graham issued one share of its $10 par, common stock for every two shares of Katz $6 par, common stock. The fair value of Graham's newly issued stock was estimated to be $35 per share. Immediately before the combination, the two corporations had the balance sheets shown in Exhibit 1-1, where the statement for Katz, Inc. shows fair values as well as book values.

The information in the balance sheet can be used to infer several important characteristics about the combination of Graham and Katz. Since Katz, Inc. has 16,000 common shares outstanding (16,000 = $96,000 ÷ $6), Graham must have issued 8,000 new common shares on January 1, 19X4 (8,000 = 16,000 ÷ 2), to acquire Katz. Accordingly, the acquisition cost to Graham of acquiring the net assets of Katz is $280,000 ($35 × 8,000), which is the fair market value of the stock issued by Graham. Since the fair value of the net assets acquired is $218,000 ($292,000 − $4,000 − $70,000), goodwill equals $62,000 ($280,000 − $218,000), calculated as follows:

Calculation of Valuation Differential and Goodwill

Acquisition cost ($35 × 8,000 shares)		$280,000
Less: Book value of net assets acquired		
($226,000 − $4,000 − $75,000)		147,000
Valuation differential		$133,000
Less: Revaluation increment:		
Inventories ($82,000 − $75,000)	$ 7,000	
Land ($78,000 − $55,000)	23,000	
Buildings and equipment [($200,000 −		
$80,000) − ($140,000 − $56,000)]	36,000	
Bonds payable ($70,000 − $75,000)	5,000	71,000
Goodwill		$ 62,000

To record the business combination as a purchase and to record the liquidation of Katz, Graham Corporation makes the following journal entries on the date of the exchange of shares:

Acquiring company's entry to record acquisition of stock in exchange for stock as a purchase:

Investment in Katz, Inc. 280,000		
Common stock (8,000 shares at $10 par)		80,000
Excess over par		200,000

Acquiring company's entry to record liquidation of acquired company:

Cash...	12,000	
Inventories....................................	82,000	
Land	78,000	
Buildings and equipment ($200,000 − $80,000)	120,000	
Discount on bonds payable	5,000	
Goodwill	62,000	
Accounts payable		4,000
Bonds payable		75,000
Investment in Katz, Inc.		280,000

	EXHIBIT 1-1	**BALANCE SHEETS BEFORE COMBINATION**

Graham Corporation and Katz, Inc.

BALANCE SHEETS
IMMEDIATELY BEFORE COMBINATION
ON JANUARY 1, 19X4

	Graham	Katz	
	Book Value	Book Value	Fair Value
Assets			
Cash	$ 90,000	$ 12,000	$ 12,000
Inventories	160,000	75,000	82,000
Land	285,000	55,000	78,000
Buildings and equipment	810,000	140,000	200,000
Accumulated depreciation	(370,000)	(56,000)	(80,000)
Total assets	$975,000	$226,000	$292,000
Liabilities and Stockholders' Equity			
Accounts payable	$ 40,000	$ 4,000	$ 4,000
Bonds payable	250,000	75,000	70,000
Common stock	400,000	96,000	
Excess over par	35,000		
Retained earnings	250,000	51,000	
Total liabilities and stockholders' equity	$975,000	$226,000	

The newly issued stock is recorded at its fair value of $280,000, which is divided between the par value of $80,000 ($10 × 8,000 shares) and the excess over par of $200,000 ($280,000 − $80,000). The acquisition of Katz's stock is recorded by a debit to an investment account in the first entry, and the debit is reversed by the second entry, which records the liquidation. Notice that buildings and equipment are recorded at the net fair value ($120,000), without separating accumulated depreciation on the current cost of comparable new assets. The same procedure would be followed in recording the purchase of any used asset, whether or not associated with a business combination. When a single used asset is acquired for cash, the cash outlay is recorded as the acquisition cost rather than recording the fair value of a comparable new asset reduced by an allowance for accumulated depreciation. Observe that the assumed bonds payable are recorded at par value ($75,000) less a discount of $5,000; it is necessary to record the discount to reduce the bonds to their fair value on the date of acquisition ($70,000).

The foregoing journal entries by Graham record two events—the acquisition of Katz's common stock and the liquidation of Katz. The Graham-Katz combination, which involves both events, also could be recorded in a single entry as shown here:

Acquiring company's entry to record acquisition of stock in exchange for stock as a purchase and to record liquidation of acquired company:

Cash..	12,000	
Inventories.....................................	82,000	
Land	78,000	
Buildings and equipment ($200,000 − $80,000)	120,000	
Discount on bonds payable	5,000	
Goodwill	62,000	
Accounts payable		4,000
Bonds payable		75,000
Common stock (8,000 shares at $10)..............		80,000
Excess over par		200,000

Of course, if Katz had continued as a separate corporation (rather than liquidated), then only the first of the two entries would be appropriate and the foregoing combined entry would not be available as an option.

The comparative statements in Exhibit 1-2 illustrate the impact of the purchase combination on the balance sheet of the acquiring corporation. The first column gives Graham's balance sheet immediately before the purchase combination, and the last column

---

EXHIBIT 1-2 **BALANCE SHEETS BEFORE AND AFTER PURCHASE COMBINATION**

Graham Corporation

BALANCE SHEETS

	Before Combination	Difference	After Combination
Assets			
Cash	$ 90,000	$ 12,000	$ 102,000
Inventories	160,000	82,000	242,000
Land	285,000	78,000	363,000
Buildings and equipment	810,000	120,000	930,000
Accumulated depreciation	(370,000)		(370,000)
Goodwill		62,000	62,000
Total assets	$975,000	$354,000	$1,329,000
Liabilities and Stockholders' Equity			
Accounts payable	$ 40,000	$ 4,000	$ 44,000
Bonds payable	250,000	75,000	325,000
Discount on bonds payable	–0–	(5,000)	(5,000)
Common stock	400,000	80,000	480,000
Excess over par	35,000	200,000	235,000
Retained earnings	250,000		250,000
Total liabilities and stockholders' equity	$975,000	$354,000	$1,329,000

gives Graham's balance sheet immediately after the combination. The middle column gives the difference between the two, namely, the effect of the journal entry required to record the purchase combination.

The difference column in Exhibit 1-2 shows the fair value of all net assets (including goodwill) acquired by Graham. Since Graham purchased these net assets with stock, Graham's common stock accounts are increased in an equal amount. Notice, however, that the combination has no effect on retained earnings.

We turn now to poolings of interests.

ACCOUNTING FOR POOLING-OF-INTERESTS COMBINATIONS

A combination may be constructed so that the stockholders of *both* corporations come through the combination holding common stock in the combined net assets, where the holdings represent essentially the same ownership interests as represented by the precombination stock holdings. Such combinations are called *poolings of interests*. Combinations that qualify as poolings of interests are characterized by a fusion of equity interests, continuity of both ownership and operations, and very limited disbursals of assets. The objective of pooling-of-interests accounting under financial accounting standards is "to present as a single interest two or more common stockholder interests which were previously independent and the combined rights and risks represented by those interests" (*APB Opinion No. 16,* par. 45).

Although accounting standards restrict the use of pooling-of-interests accounting to a small subset of business combinations, the standards are still open to criticism, as the following issues section explains.

ISSUES

A Critique of Pooling-of-Interests Accounting

"Pooling of interests" was originally used by accountants to indicate a combination of two or more interests of comparable size and complementary, if not similar, operations. Subsequent development of criteria for poolings, however, has emphasized the continuity of ownership interests and operations and has given little consideration to relative size or compatibility of operations. Further, the criteria for poolings permit significant exceptions as noted in Appendix A. Can we really argue that a purchase has not occurred when one of the combining companies is several times, perhaps many times, the size of the other; when as much as a 10% minority interest does not participate in the exchange of shares; when one party to the combination converts its nonmarketable shares into readily marketable shares; or when the combining companies are in different and unrelated lines of business? Some accountants have argued that a purchase occurs whenever one company gains control over the net assets of another, as is clearly the case in many combinations treated as poolings of interests under current standards. "No basis exists in principle for . . . 'pooling-of-interests' accounting *if* the business combination involves an exchange of assets and/or equities between independent parties" (Wyatt, 1963, p. 105; essentially the same conclusion is reached by Catlett and Olson, 1968, pp. 106, 109). Professor Wyatt argued that pooling-of-interests accounting should be reserved for combinations "in which no substantive changes occur, as in a combination between two legally separate but formerly related entities" (pp. 105–106).

From a purchase perspective, pooling-of-interests accounting is deficient in that it provides no accountability for acquired goodwill (which is effectively written off upon acquisition), results in misstated asset and income amounts, and fails to disclose the current fair value of the acquiring company's stock given in exchange. Further, combining parties may have incentives to use pooling-of-interests accounting whether or not it misrepresents the economic substance of the combination; for example, in times of rising prices, it is often easier to maintain earnings per share under pooling-of-interests accounting than under purchase accounting.[12]

Although most business combinations are accounted for as purchases, pooling remains an option. It should be noted that the United States is not the only country that allows pooling-of-interests accounting, although it is rarely used outside the United States (Arthur Andersen & Co., 1991; Peller and Schwitter, 1991, p. 4.18).

Recording Poolings of Interests

The essence of the pooling-of-interests method is that the assets and liabilities of the combining companies are merged or combined without revaluation. Subject to conformity with generally accepted accounting principles, the combined balance sheet reports assets and liabilities at their *book values* from the records of the combining companies. In a parallel way, the stockholders' equity sections of the two companies are merged, subject to par value restrictions, to produce combined stockholders' equity. This procedure, of course, is in sharp contrast to the method of accounting for purchase combinations that revalues net assets acquired and treats the acquiring company's retained earnings as combined retained earnings. The section that follows demonstrates the accounting procedures for poolings of interests.

Let us reconsider the combination of Graham and Katz wherein Graham issued new common stock to acquire all the outstanding common stock of Katz and wherein Katz was liquidated. Since the combination involves an exchange of shares, it could be structured to have little impact on ownership interests.[13] To illustrate the recording of poolings of interests, let us assume that the unstated terms of the Graham-Katz combination satisfy all 12 conditions for a pooling of interests.

Since the book value is the basis for recording poolings of interests, all market values and fair values can be ignored. Graham Corporation records the acquisition and liquidation of Katz using Katz's book values as shown in Exhibit 1-1 by the following entries:

Acquiring company's entry to record acquisition of stock in exchange for stock as a pooling of interests:

Investment in Katz, Inc. 147,000
    Common stock (8,000 shares at $10)   80,000
    Excess over par ($96,000 − $80,000)   16,000
    Retained earnings   51,000

---

[12] But see Nurnberg and Sweeney (1989) for illustrations of cases in which purchase accounting results in higher postcombination income.

[13] The typical pooling involves an acquisition of stock for stock. Although acquisitions of assets usually alter ownership interests and do not qualify as poolings of interests, it is possible to structure a pooling around an acquisition of assets. When all the assets of a corporation are acquired in exchange for stock *and* the acquired corporation liquidates by distributing the stock received to the stockholders of the acquired corporation, then the combination *may* qualify as a pooling of interests. In such cases, the acquired corporation acts as an intermediary between the acquiring corporation and the stockholders of the acquired corporation, and the combination may have the same effect on ownership interests as a direct exchange of shares between the acquiring corporation and the stockholders of the acquired corporation.

Acquiring company's entry to record liquidation of acquired company:

Cash...	12,000	
Inventories.....................................	75,000	
Land	55,000	
Buildings and equipment	140,000	
Accumulated depreciation		56,000
Accounts payable		4,000
Bonds payable		75,000
Investment in Katz, Inc.		147,000

The first entry records the acquisition of Katz's stock in an investment account, which is reversed by the second entry to record the liquidation. Notice that the net assets of Katz are recorded at their respective book values and that buildings and equipment are entered at their original cost with an offsetting amount entered for accumulated depreciation. Making due allowance for par value restrictions, Katz's stockholders' equity balances (including retained earnings) are entered in the corresponding accounts of Graham Corporation. The newly issued shares of Graham create par value of only $80,000, which is $16,000 less than the par value in Katz's common stock account. Accordingly, in merging the two stockholders' equity sections, $16,000 of Katz's par value is reclassified as excess over par.

The foregoing journal entries by Graham record two events—the acquisition of Katz's common stock and the liquidation of Katz. Alternatively, the pooling could have been recorded in a single entry as shown here:

Acquiring company's entry to record acquisition of stock in exchange for stock as a pooling of interests and liquidation of acquired company:

Cash...	12,000	
Inventories.....................................	75,000	
Land	55,000	
Buildings and equipment	140,000	
Accumulated depreciation		56,000
Accounts payable		4,000
Bonds payable		75,000
Common stock (8,000 shares at $10)		80,000
Excess over par ($96,000 − $80,000)..............		16,000
Retained earnings		51,000

Of course, if Katz had continued as a separate corporation (rather than liquidating), then only the first of the two entries would be appropriate, and the foregoing combined entry would not be available as an option.

The comparative statements in Exhibit 1-3 on the following page show the impact of the pooling of interests on the balance sheet of Graham Corporation. The first column gives Graham's balance sheet immediately before the pooling, and the last column gives Graham's balance sheet immediately after. The middle column gives the difference between the two, namely, the book value of all assets and liabilities of Katz, Inc., which have been pooled with the corresponding assets and liabilities of Graham Corporation. Graham's stockholders' equity accounts are increased in an amount equal to the total book value of Katz's assets and liabilities—in other words, in an amount equal to Katz's stockholders' equity.

EXHIBIT 1-3	BALANCE SHEETS BEFORE AND AFTER POOLING-OF-INTERESTS COMBINATION

Graham Corporation

BALANCE SHEETS

	Before Combination	Difference	After Combination
Assets			
Cash	$ 90,000	$ 12,000	$ 102,000
Inventories	160,000	75,000	235,000
Land	285,000	55,000	340,000
Buildings and equipment	810,000	140,000	950,000
Accumulated depreciation	(370,000)	(56,000)	(426,000)
Total assets	$975,000	$226,000	$1,201,000
Liabilities and Stockholders' Equity			
Accounts payable	$ 40,000	$ 4,000	$ 44,000
Bonds payable	250,000	75,000	325,000
Common stock	400,000	80,000	480,000
Excess over par	35,000	16,000	51,000
Retained earnings	250,000	51,000	301,000
Total liabilities and stockholders' equity	$975,000	$226,000	$1,201,000

Par Value Issued and the Reclassification of Stockholders' Equity

In a pooling of interests, as illustrated in Exhibit 1-3, the stock-issuing corporation credits its equity accounts, in total, with the book value of the stockholders' equity that the newly issued stock replaces. The issuer's individual equity accounts must be credited, however, so that par value is correctly reflected and a proper distinction is maintained between contributed capital (which includes capital stock and excess-over-par amounts) and retained earnings. Let us consider several complications that arise in this reclassification of stockholders' equity.

Consider a pooling of interests in which Corporation V acquires all the outstanding stock of Corporation W in exchange for 80 newly issued shares of V. Corporation W has the following stockholders' equity section on the date of combination:

Stockholders' Equity of Corporation W

Common stock—par value	$175
Excess over par	125
Retained earnings	200
Total	$500

On the date of combination, Corporation V increases its stockholders' equity by $500, the book value of stockholders' equity in Corporation W. The form of the investment entry that records the $500 increase in V's stockholders' equity depends on the par value of the newly issued stock in V and on the structure of W's stockholders' equity.

Let us consider three different par values for the newly issued shares of V—$2 per share, $3 per share, and $4 per share. The calculation in Exhibit 1-4 shows the relationship between the newly created par value and the structure of the acquired stockholders' equity.

The calculation in Exhibit 1-4 serves as the basis for the following entry by Corporation V under each of the three different par value assumptions:

Entry by V to record acquisition of W's stock in exchange for 80 newly issued shares of V's stock:

	Par = $2	Par = $3	Par = $4
Investment in W	500	500	500
Excess over par of V	0	0	20
Common stock	160	240	320
Excess over par	140	60	0
Retained earnings	200	200	200

If V's par value is $2 per share, then the new par value created by V ($160 = $2 × 80 shares) is $340 less than the acquired stockholders' equity of W ($340 = $500 − $160), which is the amount available for addition to retained earnings and excess-over-par accounts of Corporation V. Since pooling calls for the transfer of W's retained earnings balance ($200) to V's retained earnings account, the $140 remainder ($340 − $200) is credited to V's excess-over-par account. Observe that the entry to V's excess-over-par account exceeds the balance of W's excess-over-par account by $15 ($140 − $125) and that the newly created par value of V is less than the common stock balance of W by $15 ($175 − $160). In other words, the pooling of the two stockholders' equity sections reclassifies $15 of W's par value as "excess over par."

If V's par value is $3 per share, then only $60 is entered in V's excess-over-par account, which implies that pooling reclassifies $65 of W's excess-over-par balance as V's par value ($65 = $240 − $175).

If V's par value is $4 per share, then the new par value created by V ($320 = $4 × 80 shares) is only $180 less than the total stockholders' equity of W. Consequently, the

EXHIBIT 1-4	**RELATIONSHIP BETWEEN NEW PAR VALUE AND BOOK VALUE OF ACQUIRED STOCKHOLDERS' EQUITY**		
	Par = $2	**Par = $3**	**Par = $4**
Book value of acquired stockholders' equity	$500	$500	$500
New par values (80 shares)	160	240	320
Book value available for retained earnings and excess over par	$340	$260	$180
Book value of acquired retained earnings	200	200	200
Remainder (deficiency)	$140	$ 60	$ (20)

amount available for addition to retained earnings and excess-over-par accounts is $20 short of the required $200 credit to retained earnings of V. Instead of reducing the entry to retained earnings of V to $180, financial accounting standards require that retained earnings be credited with the full book value of $200 and that the $20 deficiency be debited to "excess over par" of the issuing corporation. If the issuing corporation's excess-over-par account is not sufficient to absorb the deficiency, then—and only then—the combined retained earnings will absorb the deficiency. These procedures, which are required by *APB Opinion No. 16* (par. 53), may result in an amount of combined retained earnings that is less than the total of the amounts shown by the separate pooling corporations, but combined retained earnings will never be more than that total.

COMBINED NET INCOME IN YEAR OF COMBINATION

Purchase combinations and poolings of interests exhibit different combined net income calculations. Purchase combinations usually give rise to valuation differentials that are subject to amortization and depreciation (which is discussed in Chapter 3). Poolings of interests do not create such differentials; consequently, one source of difference between the two combined income calculations is that purchase calculations include a deduction for amortization of the valuation differential, whereas pooling calculations do not. A second difference between the combined net income calculations arises only in the year of combination. The difference concerns the treatment of the acquired company's income in the precombination segment of the year; purchase calculations exclude it from combined net income, whereas pooling calculations include it. A third difference concerns the treatment of incidental acquisition costs—costs of registering and issuing securities and direct acquisition costs. Such costs of acquisition are charged to combined expense in a pooling of interests. In a purchase, security registration and issue costs reduce the fair value of the related securities, and direct acquisition costs are capitalized, as noted earlier.

Consider an example of a pooling of interests. Suppose that Corporation K acquires Corporation L on September 30, 19X1, that both corporations survive the merger, and that their separate records reveal the information given in Exhibit 1-5. Corporation K incurred direct acquisition costs for the services of a business combinations consultant in the

EXHIBIT 1-5	NET INCOME FOR ACQUIRING AND ACQUIRED CORPORATION FOR ACQUISITION YEAR		
	First 9 Months of 19X1	**Last 3 Months of 19X1**	**Total**
Corporation K (Acquiring Company)			
Revenue	$900	$300	$1,200
Expense	(700)	(220)	(920)
Income before income from L	$200	$ 80	$ 280
Corporation L (Acquired Company)			
Revenue	$400	$200	$ 600
Expense	(280)	(140)	(420)
Net income	$120	$ 60	$ 180

EXHIBIT 1-6	COMBINED NET INCOME FOR ACQUISITION YEAR

Combination of K and L

INCOME STATEMENTS
FOR YEAR ENDED DECEMBER 31, 19X1

	Purchase Combination		Pooling-of-Interests Combination	
Revenue		$1,400		$1,800
Amortization of valuation differential	$ 15		$ 0	
Acquisition expense	0		33	
Other expenses	1,060*	1,075	1,340†	1,373
Net income		$ 325		$ 427

* $1,060 = $920 + $140

† $1,340 = $920 + $420

amount of $33, which are not included in the expenses shown in Exhibit 1-5. Assume that the valuation differential leads to a total annual amortization of $60, of which $15 is applicable to the postacquisition portion of 19X1 ($15 = $60 × 3/12).

Both the purchase combination income statement and the pooling-of-interests income statement for the K-L combination are shown in Exhibit 1-6.[14] The purchase-accounting revenue ($1,400) consists of K's revenue for the entire year ($1,200) and L's revenue for the postcombination period ($200). Pooling-accounting revenue ($1,800) consists of the

[14] For purposes of comparison, financial information from earlier periods is frequently reported alongside current financial information. When that information comes from periods prior to a combination, financial accounting standards may require that it be retroactively restated for the combination—adjusted as if the combination had occurred at the beginning of the earliest period for which information is presented. This represents an exception to the general requirement that the cumulative effect of a change in accounting principle be recognized in the year of the change and that prior-period information not be retroactively restated. In the case of poolings, prior-year information presented in comparative statements or footnotes must be restated as if the pooling had occurred at the beginning of the earliest period for which information is presented and must be identified as restated information obtained by combining information from previously separate entities (APB Opinion No. 16, pars. 56–57). In the case of purchases, the acquiring company's prior-year information is presented in comparative statements without adjustment. However, footnotes to the acquiring company's financial statements must disclose restated, pro forma results in the year of the purchase. Specifically, the purchaser must disclose (1) the results of operations for the current (purchase) year as if the purchase had occurred at the beginning of the year (unless the purchase was at or near the beginning of the year) and (2) the results of operations for the immediately preceding year as if the purchase had occurred at the beginning of that year (unless comparative financial statements are not presented). Such disclosures of prepurchase pro forma results are limited to results for the period immediately preceding the period of the purchase (APB Opinion No. 16, par. 96). Although required of all public enterprises, these pro forma disclosures are not required of nonpublic enterprises—enterprises whose securities are not traded in a public market and whose financial statements are not filed with a regulatory agency in preparation for the sale of securities (FASB Statement No. 79, pars. 4–5).

entire year's revenue for both corporations ($1,800 = $1,200 + $600). A parallel analysis can be made of other expenses. The amortization of the valuation differential is subtracted only on the purchase-combination statement; acquisition expense is subtracted only on the pooling-of-interests statement.

The differences between pooling-of-interests accounting and purchase accounting—particularly the differences in the accounting for income—may motivate managers who seek to manipulate income to press for one accounting method when the other is more appropriate. Further, some have argued that some companies have entered business combinations for the express purpose of manipulating income. In an effort to reduce, if not remove, the incentive for such behavior, accounting standards require a number of disclosures in notes to the financial statements that reveal to the careful reader attempts to use business combinations to manipulate income.[15]

SUMMARY

Business combinations are complex and varied transactions that bring together the net assets of two or more business enterprises in a single accounting entity. Most business combinations can be characterized as the acquisition of one firm by another via the acquisition of stock or acquisition of assets. If a business combination satisfies certain conditions, which are detailed in Appendix A, it must be accounted for as a pooling of interests. Otherwise, it must be accounted for as a purchase. Under purchase accounting, the net assets of the acquired firm are revalued and recorded by the acquiring firm at their acquisition cost. Under pooling accounting, the net assets of the acquired firm are recorded by the acquiring firm at their book value to the acquired firm and are not revalued. In neither case are the net assets of the acquiring firm revalued. Purchases and poolings also require different calculations of combined net income in the year of the combination. These differences are attributable to three main sources—the valuation differential amortization (which is recognized in purchases but not poolings), the precombination income of the acquired corporation for the year of the combination, and the incidental acquisition costs. The measurement of acquisition cost in purchases presents a variety of complications, including the presence of security registration and issue costs and direct and indirect acquisition costs (which are discussed in the foregoing chapter) and contingent consideration (which is discussed in Appendix B). The adjustment to the stockholders' equity of the acquiring firm in poolings also presents a variety of complications that are illustrated in the chapter.

APPENDIX A: CRITERIA FOR POOLINGS OF INTERESTS

The existence of so many different vehicles for a business combination makes the identification of poolings a complex task. Specifically, the use of convertible stocks, convertible bonds, stock warrants, treasury stock, and contingent consideration (see Appendix B) makes it difficult to discern whether a purchase or a pooling has occurred. In fact, the financial accounting standards lay down 12 conditions, all of which must be satisfied, for

---

[15] In addition to the pro forma disclosures described in footnote 14, accounting standards also require footnote disclosure of (1) the name and a brief description of the acquired company, (2) the number of shares and a description of stock issued, and (3) the method of accounting used to record the combination. Further, footnotes for poolings must disclose the revenue, extraordinary items, and net income of the separate companies from the beginning of the period to the combination date (or the end of the interim period nearest the combination date); footnotes for purchases must disclose the period for which the results of operations of the acquired company are included in the combined income. For details and additional disclosure requirements, see *APB Opinion No. 16,* especially pars. 63–65, and 95.

a combination to be recorded as a pooling of interests. The 12 conditions are described in the paragraphs that follow.

Combining Company Attributes

In order to qualify as a pooling of interests, the combining companies must satisfy two conditions concerning attributes of the combining companies.[16]

Condition 1: Autonomy

A two-year autonomy condition requires that each of the combining companies be *autonomous from each other* and must not have been a subsidiary or division of another corporation for a period of at least two years before the plan of combination is initiated; a combination plan is initiated when its major terms have been negotiated and are announced to the public or communicated to stockholders (*APB Opinion No. 16,* par. 46a, and *AICPA Interpretations of APB Opinion No. 16,* Interpretations Nos. 1 and 2). For example, suppose that a combination of A and B has just been initiated but that B was owned by A until one year ago when A sold its stock in B. The present combination of A and B does not meet the two-year autonomy condition and must be recorded as a purchase. When the present combination of A and B and the recent sale of B are interpreted together, it is difficult to argue that a purchase has not occurred. But a new company incorporated within the last two years (provided it is not a successor to a nonautonomous company) meets the autonomy condition.

Condition 2: Independence

The independence condition requires that no combining company may have an investment in another combining company of more than 10% of the latter's voting common stock[17] (*APB Opinion No. 16,* par. 46b, and *AICPA Interpretations of APB Opinion No. 16,* Interpretations Nos. 3 and 4). Thus a corporation that acquires another corporation's outstanding common stock in multiple steps over a period of time (in a "step acquisition") is precluded from pooling-of-interests accounting if more than 10% and less than 90% (see Condition 4) of the stock is acquired in any step.

Conditions on the Combination

The combination itself, as distinguished from combining company attributes and postcombination events, must satisfy seven conditions to qualify as a pooling of interests. The general objective of the conditions is to designate as purchases all "exchanges of common stock that alter relative voting rights, that result in preferential claims to distributions of profits or assets for some common stockholder groups, or that leave significant minority interests in combining companies." In addition, the conditions direct purchase accounting

---

[16] Although *APB Opinion No. 16* does not require the combining companies to have significant operations, as evidenced by significant sales and operating activity, the Securities and Exchange Commission (SEC) has denied pooling-of-interests accounting in at least one combination in which the acquired company held significant assets but had only nominal sales and operations ("An Unpublished . . . ," 1974).

[17] The percentage limit does not apply to stock acquired after the initiation of the combination plan *provided* it is acquired in exchange for voting common stock issued to effect the combination.

for "acquisitions of common stock for assets or debt, reacquisition of outstanding stock for the purpose of exchanging it in a business combination, and other transactions that reduce the common stock interests" (*APB Opinion No. 16,* par. 47). Combination transactions that possess any of these characteristics alter ownership interests and cannot be recorded as poolings of interests. As we review these conditions in more detail, notice that a combination transaction can qualify as a pooling of interests even if more than one corporation survives the combination.

Condition 3: Time Limit

The combination must be effected in a single transaction or completed in accordance with a specific plan on which a time limit is imposed. If more than one year expires between the initiation of the combination plan and its consummation, then the combination cannot qualify as a pooling of interests. If the duration of a combination is extended beyond one year by proceedings of a government authority (excluding security registrations), by litigation (including antitrust suits and suits by dissenting minority stockholders), or by other factors beyond the control of the combining parties, then the condition is not violated (see *APB Opinion No. 16,* par. 47a, and *AICPA Accounting Interpretations of APB Opinion No. 16,* Interpretations Nos. 4 and 5).

Condition 4: Substantially All Stock Exchanged

A condition is imposed on the stock exchanged to effect a pooling of interests:

> A corporation offers and issues only common stock with rights identical to those of the majority of its outstanding voting common stock in exchange for substantially all of the voting common stock interest of another company at the date the plan of combination is consummated.

"Substantially all of the voting common stock" means at least 90% of the acquired company's shares outstanding at the date the combination is consummated, excluding any shares acquired before initiation of the combination, excluding any shares acquired during the combination in exchange for consideration other than common voting shares, and of course excluding any shares held by parties other than the parties to the combination (see *APB Opinion No. 16,* par. 47b). Further, an adjustment must be made for any investment in the acquiring company by the acquired company. To illustrate, suppose that York Corporation wishes to know whether its recent acquisition of Small Manufacturing, Inc. through an exchange of shares (two shares of York for each share of Small) qualifies for pooling-of-interests accounting. Small has 20,000 voting common shares issued of which 1,000 are treasury shares and 500 have been held by York since before the initiation of the combination. An additional 17,400 Small shares were acquired by York as part of the combination—200 for cash and the remainder in exchange for York shares—and 1,100 Small shares remain in the hands of parties other than York and Small. In addition, Small has a long-standing investment in 600 shares of York. If the combination is to qualify as a pooling, at least 17,100 York shares [(20,000 − 1,000) × 90%] must have been exchanged. The calculation of the equivalent Small shares exchanged is as follows:

Calculation of Equivalent Shares Exchanged		
Total Small shares issued		20,000
Less: Shares in Small's treasury		1,000
Total Small shares outstanding		19,000
Less: Small shares held by York prior to initiation of combination	500	
Small shares acquired by York for cash as part of combination	200	
Small shares held by stockholders other than York or Small	1,100	1,800
Total Small shares acquired in exchange for York shares		17,200
Less: Equivalent number of Small shares represented by Small's investment in York's common stock (600 × 2)		1,200
Equivalent shares exchanged		16,000

The 17,200 Small shares exchanged on the date of combination are restated to an equivalent of 16,000 shares, which is less than the required minimum of 17,100 shares (90% of York's outstanding common shares). Thus, the treatment of the combination as a pooling of interests is precluded.[18]

Condition 5: Equity Changes

The fifth condition prohibits equity changes in contemplation of combination, specifically:

> None of the combining companies changes the equity interest of voting common stock in contemplation of effecting the combination either within two years before the plan of combination is initiated or between the dates the combination is initiated and consummated.

Although poolings may be accompanied by normal dividends, this condition requires that combinations preceded or accompanied by unusual distributions to owners ("distributions to stockholders and additional issuances, exchanges, and retirements of securities") be treated as purchases and not as poolings of interests (see *APB Opinion No. 16,* par. 47c).

Condition 6: Treasury Stock

The sixth condition precludes abnormal acquisitions of treasury stock:

> Each of the combining companies reacquires shares of voting common stock only for purposes other than business combinations, and no company reacquires more than a

---

[18] Accounting standards deal with a number of complications in the application of this important "substantially all" criterion, including a limited exception available to certain companies (see *APB Opinion No. 16,* par. 99, as amended by *FASB Statement No. 10*). The Emerging Issues Task Force has considered a variety of complications (see *FASB Technical Bulletin No. 85-5,* pars. 16–20, which overturned *EITF Issue No. 84-38;* and *EITF Issue Nos. 85-14, 86-10, 87-15, 87-16,* and *87-27*).

normal number of shares between the dates the plan of combination is initiated and consummated.

Treasury shares may be acquired in poolings of interests to satisfy stock option and compensation plans and other recurring distributions (''provided a systematic pattern of reacquisition is established at least two years before the plan of combination is initiated''), but reacquisitions of shares as part of the business combination mandates purchase accounting. Under the second clause of this condition, the purchase of one combining company's voting common shares by another combining company, after the combination plan is initiated, is equivalent to reacquisition of the shares by the issuing company (see *APB Opinion No. 16*, par. 47d).

Treasury shares that fail to meet this condition are called *tainted treasury shares.* Difficulties in implementing this condition have brought forth interpretations from both the AICPA and the SEC (*AICPA Interpretation of Opinion No. 16*, Interpretation No. 20, and *SEC Accounting Series Release Nos. 146 and 146A;* see also ''Implementing . . . ,'' 1974).

Condition 7: Proportionate Treatment

A seventh condition requires that each stockholder receive the same exchange terms; ''each individual common stockholder who exchanges his stock receives a voting common stock interest exactly in proportion to his relative voting common stock interest before the combination is effected.'' For example, if A and B pool by an exchange of shares, then if one of B's stockholders receives one share of A's stock for every four shares of B's stock, then all of B's stockholders should receive one share of A for every four shares of B. Otherwise, ownership interests are altered and a purchase is indicated (see *APB Opinion No. 16*, par. 47e).

Condition 8: Voting Rights

The eighth requirement concerns the exercise of voting rights:

> The voting rights to which the common stock ownership interests in the resulting combined corporation are entitled are exercisable by the stockholders.

In other words, the stockholders in a pooling ''are neither deprived of nor restricted in exercising'' voting rights as, for example, when voting shares are transferred to a voting trust (see *APB Opinion No. 16*, par. 47f).

Condition 9: Contingent Consideration

A ninth condition on pooling-of-interests transactions precludes contingent consideration. A pooling combination must be ''resolved at the date the plan is consummated and no provisions of the plan relating to the issue of securities or other consideration are pending.'' This requirement is not intended to preclude pooling treatment for a combination in which the number of shares issued is ''revised for the later settlement of a contingency [such as a settlement of a lawsuit] at a different amount than that recorded by a combining company'' (see *APB Opinion No. 16*, par. 47g, *AICPA Interpretation of APB Opinion No. 16*, Interpretation No. 30, and Appendix B).

Conditions on Postcombination Transactions

The last group of conditions concerns transactions that follow the combination and counteract its effect. Pooling-of-interests accounting is available only if the combined corporation satisfies the following prohibitions.

Condition 10: Reacquisition of Stock

The combined corporation does not agree directly or indirectly to retire or reacquire all or part of the common stock issued to effect the combination.

Condition 11: Other Financial Arrangements

The combined corporation does not enter into other financial arrangements for the benefit of the former stockholders of a combining company, such as a guaranty of loans secured by stock issued in the combination, which in effect negates the exchange of equity securities.

Condition 12: Asset Dispositions

The combined corporation does not intend or plan to dispose of a significant part of the assets of the combining companies within two years after the combination other than disposals in the ordinary course of business of the formerly separate companies and to eliminate duplicate facilities or excess capacity.

Failure to satisfy one or more of these prohibitions signals a change in ownership interests that calls for purchase accounting (see *APB Opinion No. 16,* par. 48).

APPENDIX B: CONTINGENT CONSIDERATION AND PREACQUISITION CONTINGENCIES

Contingent consideration is the issuance of additional shares or the payment of additional cash or assets that a party to a purchase combination (usually the acquiring company) agrees to make contingent on a specified future event. If the specified event occurs, then the additional consideration (securities, cash, or other assets) is given. If the specified event does not occur, then the additional consideration is not given. In some cases, the contingency is based on future earnings, as when the acquiring company agrees to give additional consideration if the earnings of the new subsidiary reach a specified level during the year following acquisition. In other cases, the contingency is based on future securities prices, as when the acquiring company agrees to give additional consideration if the price of the acquiring company's common stock falls below a specified level. Whatever its form, the presence of contingent consideration in a business combination precludes treatment of the combination as a pooling of interests (*APB Opinion No. 16,* par. 47g).[19]

---

[19] *AICPA Accounting Interpretation of APB Opinion No. 16,* Interpretation Nos. 30, 31, and 32 sanction strictly limited exceptions for (1) ''general management representations'' that promise small adjustments in the number of shares exchanged during a reasonable period (usually a few months) following combination, during which the acquiring company has an opportunity to determine whether the representations of the acquired company respecting such things as inventories and receivables are correct; (2) reasonable employment contracts or deferred compensation agreements granted by the acquired company to continuing employees; and (3) stock options granted by the acquired company as compensation for employment of persons who are also its former stockholders.

Financial accounting standards provide that the liability or stockholders' equity items associated with contingent consideration should not be recorded at the date of acquisition. Rather, "contingent consideration should usually be recorded when the contingency is resolved and consideration is issued or becomes issuable." If the contingent consideration is based on future earnings, then an additional element of acquisition cost is recorded upon resolution of the contingency. But if the contingent consideration is based on future securities prices, then resolution of the contingency does not change the amount of recorded acquisition cost. Let us illustrate these provisions of *APB Opinion No. 16* (pars. 78–79) by reference to two examples.

Contingency Based on Earnings

Let us begin by considering a purchase combination involving a contingency based on earnings. To illustrate, suppose that Anderson acquires all the assets and liabilities of Baxter in exchange for 100 shares of newly issued common stock ($5 par) with a total fair value of $650 and a promise to pay an additional $90 cash if combined earnings during the two years following the acquisition exceed the specified amount. On the date of acquisition, Baxter has assets totaling $700 and liabilities totaling $100, all carried at fair value. Accordingly, the entire valuation differential of $50 [$650 − ($700 − $100)] is allocated to goodwill, and Anderson records the acquisition with the following entry:

Identifiable assets (listed individually)	700	
Goodwill	50	
Liabilities (listed individually)		100
Common stock ($5 × 100)		500
Excess over par		150

If the combined earnings exceed the specified amount, then Anderson pays the $90 to Baxter and records an addition to the acquisition cost by the following entry:

Goodwill	90	
Cash		90

In cases in which the contingency payment is made in securities rather than in cash, the adjustment to acquisition cost (usually recorded by a debit to goodwill) equals the then current fair value of the securities and this amount is credited to the appropriate securities accounts. Of course, if combined earnings equal or fall short of the specified amount, then no additional amount is paid and no adjustment to the acquisition cost is appropriate.

Contingency Based on Security Prices

The standards direct a different treatment if the contingency is tied to security prices rather than to earnings. To illustrate, suppose that Calder acquires all of Donner's assets and liabilities (which have fair values of $5,000 and $1,100, respectively) by issuing 330 shares of common stock ($8 par) with a total fair value of $3,960 ($12 per share). In addition, Calder promises to issue additional shares in two years if the then current price of Calder's stock falls below its date-of-acquisition level. The total value of the additional shares will equal the decline in the market price times the number of shares originally issued. Calder records the acquisition with the following entry:

Identifiable assets (listed individually)	5,000	
Goodwill [$3,960 − ($5,000 − $1,100)]	60	
Liabilities (listed individually)		1,100
Common stock ($8 × 330 shares)		2,640
Excess over par ($3,960 − $2,640)		1,320

If Calder's stock price is not below its date-of-acquisition level two years after the acquisition, then no additional shares are issued under the contingency clause and the contingency clause has no effect on the records.

On the other hand, if the price of the stock two years after acquisition is $11, which is $1 less than the date-of-acquisition price, then Calder must issue 30 additional shares to Donner [30 shares = ($1 × 330 shares) ÷ $11]. Calder records the additional issue, which has a market value of $330 ($11 × 30 shares), by the following entry:

Excess over par	240	
Common stock ($8 × 30)		240

No adjustment of acquisition cost occurs; the entry merely transfers an amount from excess over par to provide for the par value of the newly issued shares ($240 = $8 × 30).

In some cases, the contingency based on future security prices may be payable in cash rather than in securities. Suppose, for example, that Calder's contingency is payable in cash rather than in common stock and that the price of Calder's stock is $11 two years after acquisition. Then Calder would make the following entry:

Excess over par	330	
Cash		330

Again, no adjustment of acquisition cost occurs; it merely changes the means by which the cost is paid. On the acquisition date, the cost was paid by issuing common stock with a fair value of $3,960. After recording the $330 payment, the total is still $3,960, but it consists of $330 for cash paid and $3,630 for stock issued (*APB Opinion No. 16*, pars. 81–82).

In some cases, the contingent consideration may be tied to both future earnings and future stock prices. Financial accounting standards require that "additional cost of the acquired company should be recorded for the additional consideration contingent on earnings, and previously recorded consideration should be reduced to current value of the consideration contingent on security prices" (*APB Opinion No. 16*, par. 83).

Preacquisition Contingencies of Acquired Companies

Contingent consideration in business combinations must be distinguished from *preacquisition contingencies* of acquired companies. Contingent consideration is an aspect of the consideration given by the acquiring company in a business combination. Preacquisition contingencies, in contrast, represent contingent assets, liabilities, and asset impairments of acquired companies existing prior to the date of combination. As these contingencies resolve, after the combination date, the related assets and liabilities of the acquired company may require adjustment. The question is whether such adjustments should alter the original allocation of acquisition cost to those assets and liabilities or should be included in the net income of the combined entity. *FASB Statement No. 38* requires the determination of an "allocation period" beginning at the date of combination and usually extending one year or less from that date. Information about preacquisition contingencies received during the allocation period may be used to adjust the allocation of the acquisition cost among the identifiable net assets and goodwill. Information received after the allocation period, however, should not be used to adjust the allocation of acquisition cost. Rather, the adjustments should be included in the net income of the combined entity.

SELECTED READINGS

"An Unpublished Requirement," *The CPA Journal* (June 1974), p. 16.

Andrews, Wesley T. "The Evolution of *APB Opinion No. 17—Accounting for Intangible Assets:* A Study of the U.S. Position on Accounting for Goodwill," *Accounting Historians Journal* (Spring 1981), pp. 37–49.

Arthur Andersen & Co. *International Research Project on Accounting for Business Combination, Goodwill and Other Intangibles. . . .* Chicago: Arthur Andersen & Co., 1991.

Beresford, Dennis R., and Bruce J. Rosen. "Accounting for Preacquisition Contingencies," *The CPA Journal* (March 1982), pp. 39–42.

Catlett, George R., and Norman O. Olson. *Accounting for Goodwill,* Accounting Research Study No. 10. New York: American Institute of Certified Public Accountants, 1968.

Chandler, Alfred D., Jr. *The Visible Hand: The Managerial Revolution in American Business.* Cambridge, MA: Harvard University Press, 1977.

Chandler, Alfred D., Jr. *Scale and Scope: The Dynamics of Industrial Capitalism.* Cambridge, MA: Harvard University Press, 1990.

Choi, F. D. S., and G. G. Mueller. *International Accounting.* Englewood Cliffs, NJ: Prentice-Hall, 1984.

Davis, Michael. "APB 16: Time to Reconsider—Acquisitions Disguised as Poolings Can Lead to Misleading Improvements in Earnings," *Journal of Accountancy* (October 1991), pp. 99–107.

Dunne, Kathleen M. "An Empirical Analysis of Management's Choice of Accounting Treatment for Business Combinations," *Journal of Accounting and Public Policy* (Summer 1990), pp. 111–133.

Eiteman, Dean S. *Pooling and Purchase Accounting: The Effect of Alternative Practices on Financial Statements.* Ann Arbor, MI: The University of Michigan, 1967.

FASB Discussion Memorandum. *Accounting for Business Combinations and Purchased Intangible.* Stamford, CT: Financial Accounting Standards Board, August 19, 1976.

Getz, Lowell V. *Mergers, Acquisitions, and Sales,* Technical Consulting Practice Aid No. 8. New York: American Institute of Certified Public Accountants, 1986.

Gunther, Samuel P. "The CPA's Role in Mergers and Acquisitions," *Journal of Accountancy* (February 1979), pp. 47–56.

Hermanson, Roger H., and Hugh P. Hughes. "Pooling vs. Purchase and Goodwill: A Long-Standing Controversy Abates," *Mergers & Acquisitions* (Fall 1980), pp. 15–22.

Hughes, Hugh P. *Goodwill in Accounting: A History of the Issues and Problems.* Atlanta: College of Business Administration, Georgia State University, 1982.

"Implementing SEC Rules on ASR Nos. 146 and 146A," *Journal of Accountancy* (November 1974), pp. 76–82.

Kimmel, Dennis L. "Consolidation Models at Acquisition: Purchase and Pooling of Interest Methods," *The Accounting Review* (July 1976), pp. 629–632.

Knechel, W. Robert, and Charles L. McDonald. "Accounting for Income Taxes Related to Assets Acquired in a Purchase Business Combination," *Accounting Horizons* (September 1989), pp. 44–52.

Knight, Ray A., and Lee G. Knight. "Have Recent Tax Acts Provided a Level Playing Field for Corporate Mergers and Acquisitions?" *Accounting Horizons* (September 1989), pp. 28–37.

Nurnberg, Hugo, and Corwin Grube. "Alternative Methods of Accounting for Business Combinations," *The Accounting Review* (October 1970), pp. 783–789.

Nurnberg, Hugo, Clyde P. Stickney, and Roman L. Weil. "Combining Stockholders' Equity Accounts under Pooling of Interest Method," *The Accounting Review* (January 1975), pp. 179–183.

Nurnberg, Hugo, and Jan Sweeney. "The Effect of Fair Values and Historical Costs on Accounting for Business Combinations," *Issues in Accounting Education* (Fall 1989), pp. 375–395.

Peller, Philip R., and Frank J. Schwitter. "A Summary of Accounting Principal Differences around the World," Chap. 4 in *Handbook of International Accounting,* F.D.S. Choi (ed.). New York: John Wiley, 1991.

Rayburn, Frank R., and Ollie S. Powers. "A History of Pooling of Interests Accounting for Business Combinations in the United States," *The Accounting Historians Journal* (December 1991), pp. 155–192.

Scholes, Myron S., and Mark A. Wolfson. *Taxes and Business Strategy: A Planning Approach.* Englewood Cliffs, NJ: Prentice-Hall, 1992.

Willens Robert. "Taxes and Takeovers," *Journal of Accountancy* (July 1986), pp. 86–95.

Wyatt, Arthur R. *A Critical Study of Accounting for Business Combinations.* Accounting Research Study No. 5. New York: American Institute of Certified Public Accountants, 1963.

QUESTIONS

Q1-1 Define the following terms:

a) Business combination

c) Goodwill

b) Corporate liquidation

d) Valuation differential

Q1-2 The stockholders of Ivy Computers received a tender offer from the management of Hardware, Inc. to buy, for cash, all the outstanding shares of Ivy at a 25% premium over the current market price. Define the term *tender offer,* and identify some of the questions faced by the management and the stockholders of Ivy concerning the tender offer.

Q1-3 Distinguish among horizontal, vertical, and conglomerate combinations.

Q1-4 Describe the following defenses used by a target company against a hostile takeover:

a) Golden parachutes

c) Scorched earth

b) Poison pills

d) White knight

Q1-5 On January 10, 1990, the *Richmond Times-Dispatch* reported that the Justice Department will file an antitrust suit aimed at blocking Gillette Company's plan to acquire most of Wilkinson Sword's worldwide razor-blade business. Gillette is the nation's largest manufacturer of razor blades for shaving. Why might the Justice Department want to block this acquisition?

Q1-6 How would the acquiring company's recording of a business combination differ if the business combination were accomplished by an acquisition of net assets versus an acquisition of stock? Assume the acquired company does not liquidate.

Q1-7 What is the difference between the purchase method and the pooling-of-interests method of accounting for business combinations in relation to:

a) The impact of each method on the ownership interest of precombination stock holdings?

b) The accounting for net assets of the acquired company under each method of business combination?

Q1-8 Company X acquired the net assets of Company Y by paying $200 cash and issuing 80 shares of common stock with a market value of $5 per share. Assuming X incurred registration and issue costs of $75 on the 80 shares, determine the acquisition cost of the net assets of Y.

Q1-9 Distinguish between business combinations that are considered *consolidations* and those that are considered *mergers.*

Q1-10   What is the objective of pooling-of-interests accounting under financial accounting standards?

Q1-11   Under what conditions would the consolidated retained earnings under a pooling of interests be less than the total of the separate retained earnings of the combining companies?

Q1-12   Discuss three differences between combined net income in the year of combination under purchase combinations and poolings of interests.

Q1-13   Company M acquired all outstanding voting shares of Corporation N in exchange for newly issued stock of M. Indicate the proper accounting treatment for each of the following costs associated with the purchase combination:

a) Cost of registering securities issued in the combination

b) Professional fees paid to outside accountants and lawyers for general advice concerning the combination

c) Indirect costs associated with maintaining an internal acquisition department

Q1-14   Explain why you agree or disagree with the following statement: Purchase accounting and pooling-of-interests accounting are alternative methods of accounting for business combination.

Q1-15   Briefly comment on the difference between a nontaxable business combination and a taxable business combination.

QUESTIONS FOR APPENDIX A

Q1-16   Briefly describe the 12 conditions that must be met in order for a business combination to be accounted for by the pooling-of-interests method.

Q1-17   One of the conditions for a pooling of interests is that ''a corporation offers and issues only common stock with rights identical to those of the majority of its outstanding voting common stock in exchange for substantially all of the voting common stock interest of another company at the date the plan of combination is consummated.'' Explain what is meant by ''substantially all of the voting common stock.''

QUESTIONS FOR APPENDIX B

Q1-18   Define the term *contingent consideration* as related to business combinations.

Q1-19   Is a contingent consideration for a purchase combination recorded as part of the acquisition cost on the date of acquisition of the business combination, or is it recorded at the time the contingency is resolved and consideration is issued or becomes issuable?

Q1-20   Describe the accounting treatment in a purchase combination of:

a) A contingent consideration tied to earnings

b) A contingent consideration tied to stock prices

EXERCISES

E1-1   **Business Combination from Viewpoint of Regulatory Agency**   The following information is paraphrased from an article that appeared in the *Richmond Times-Dispatch* on January 10, 1990: In April of 1989, American Safety Razor Co. acquired the outstanding shares of Ardell Industries Inc. for $12.7 million. American Safety Razor and Ardell were the nation's largest and second-largest sellers of industrial single-edge blades for cutting, trimming, and scraping. However, you read in the local newspaper that the Justice Department filed suit to block the merger of the two industrial razor-blade companies.

REQUIRED

Discuss why the Justice Department would want to block the merger of the two companies.

E1-2 **Identification of Type of Expansion and Type of Accounting Entity** The following discussion is paraphrased from an article that appeared in the *Richmond Times-Dispatch* on December 28, 1989: In 1989, the executives of Pearle Inc. considered their company to be the fastest growing retail chain in the country.

In late 1989, Pearle Inc., an optical company based in Dallas, Texas, announced the purchase of Richard Bartley Optical Inc., a Virginia Beach–based chain of 24 retail eye care stores across the state of Virginia. Plans are to convert the Richard Bartley stores to Pearle Vision Express stores with larger inventories and a larger on-site laboratory than the conventional, original Pearle Vision Centers.

Earlier in 1989, Pearle announced plans to acquire Eyelab Inc., an eye care chain with 72 stores on the East Coast and in the Midwest. In 1988, Pearle also bought two smaller chains.

Pearle is a wholly owned subsidiary of Grand Metropolitan of London. Grand Metropolitan also owns Pillsbury, Burger King, Haagen-Dazs Heublein, and Alpo in the United States.

REQUIRED

a) What is a primary factor contributing to the fast growth of Pearle Inc.?

b) What type of organization would you describe Grand Metropolitan as being? What would be a motivation for forming this type of organization?

E1-3 **Defining Terms Associated with a Takeover** The following discussion is paraphrased from an article that appeared in the *Richmond Times-Dispatch* on December 24, 1989: Your company's president never calls meetings on short notice, but today she did. And now, every manager in the corporation, including you, is crammed into a tiny room, worrying about what might be wrong. The news, you know deep inside, must be bad. And you're right.

"Well, I want you to know that our company is the target of a hostile takeover attempt," the president says. "There's not a lot we can do. We don't have any shark repellent. The tender offer is above market value, but it still isn't what we're worth. The corporate raiders want us for the breakup value. Without a poison pill, we need to find a white knight."

REQUIRED

a) What does the president mean by her statement that "our company is the target of a hostile takeover attempt"? How would this differ if the takeover attempt had been friendly?

b) What are shark repellents, and how might they be beneficial to the target company?

c) What is a tender offer?

d) What are corporate raiders, and what did the president mean by her statement that "the corporate raiders want us for the breakup value"?

e) What are poison pills, and how might they be used by the target company?

f) What does the president mean by her statement that "we need to find a white knight"?

E1-4 **Combination Considerations: Tender Offer and Golden Parachutes** Rimco, a large manufacturer of wheel rims, is contemplating expanding into the fast-growing computer software field by combining with Software, Inc., a medium-sized developer of software packages. Software, Inc. is considered to be financially sound with adequate working capital. Software's senior management is considered one of the best in the industry.

Rimco's strategy includes making a tender offer to the stockholders of Software, Inc. However, Rimco is concerned about a recent rumor that senior management would resign and exercise their "golden parachutes" if a takeover of Software was successful.

REQUIRED

1. The combination under consideration by Rimco would be identified as what form of expansion?

2. Define what is meant by a tender offer.

3. What are golden parachutes, and why might senior management exercise them and resign from the company?

4. Why might Rimco be concerned if senior management exercised their golden parachutes and resigned?

E1-5 **Acquisition Cost: Fair Value of Securities Issued or Assets Acquired**   Hagueman Company acquired all of the 200,000 shares of the common stock of Forest Company, a manufacturer of forest products, in exchange for 100,000 newly issued common shares of Hagueman. The combination is to be accounted for as a purchase. Hagueman's common stock is traded on a regional stock exchange. The controller of Hagueman Company is not clear as to whether the acquisition cost of Forest Company should be based on the market price of Hagueman's stock or based on the fair value of the net assets acquired.

REQUIRED

Discuss conditions under which it would be appropriate for the controller to record the acquisition cost of Forest Company using:

1. The market price of the stock issued

2. The fair value of the net assets acquired

E1-6 **Analysis of Valuation Differential**   Corporation A and Corporation B agree to a business combination. Just prior to combination, the balance sheets of the two firms appeared as follows:

	Corporation A	Corporation B
Assets		
Current assets	$ 300	$400
Plant and equipment (net)	500	200
Land	200	100
Total assets	$1,000	$700
Liabilities and Stockholders' Equity		
Liabilities	$ 200	$100
Common stock	700	300
Retained earnings	100	300
Total liabilities and stockholders' equity	$1,000	$700

REQUIRED

a) Following the diagram presented in the chapter, prepare an *analysis of the valuation differential for net assets* associated with each of the following independent purchase combinations:

1. Corporation A acquired all the outstanding stock of Corporation B in exchange for 200 newly issued shares in A, which have an established market price of $4 per share. Both firms' balance sheets reflect fair values.

2. Corporation A acquired all the outstanding stock of Corporation B for $750 cash. Both firms' balance sheets reflect fair values except for B's plant and equipment, which have a fair value of $300.

3. Corporation A acquired the net assets of Corporation B, paying $700. Corporation A incurred $25 out-of-pocket costs concerning the acquisition. Both firms' balance sheets reflect fair values except for B's balance sheet, which does not reflect an unrecorded, fully depreciated patent with a fair value of $50.

b) The accountant for Corporation A contends that the computed valuation differential for the business combination in part (a)(1) would be the same amount had the combination been accounted for as a pooling of interests and not as a purchase combination. Discuss.

E1-7 **Arguments for Purchase and Pooling**   When a business combination is effected by an exchange of common stock, the transaction is accounted for as a purchase or as a pooling of interests, depending on the circumstances. The methods are not optional, and each yields significantly different results as to financial position and results of operations.

REQUIRED

Discuss the *supportive* arguments for each of the following:

1. Purchase method

2. Pooling-of-interests method

Do *not* discuss in your answer the rules for distinguishing between a purchase and a pooling of interests.

(AICPA adapted)

E1-8 **Allocation of Investment Cost: Purchase and Pooling**   On January 2, 19X5, Asch Corporation paid $1,000,000 cash for all of Bacher Company's outstanding stock. The recorded amount (book value) of Bacher's net assets on January 2 was $880,000. Both Asch and Bacher had operated profitably for many years, both have December 31 accounting year-ends, and each has only one class of stock outstanding. This business combination should be accounted for by the purchase method, in which Asch should follow certain principles in allocating its investment cost to the assets acquired and liabilities assumed.

REQUIRED

a) Describe the principles that Asch should follow in allocating its investment cost to the assets purchased and liabilities assumed for a January 2, 19X5, combined balance sheet. Explain.

b) Independent of your answer to part (a), assume that on January 2, 19X5, Asch acquired all of Bacher's outstanding stock in a stock-for-stock exchange and that all other conditions prerequisite to a pooling of interests were met. Describe the principles that Asch should follow in applying the pooling-of-interests method to this business combination when combining the balance sheet accounts of both companies in the preparation of a combined balance sheet on January 2, 19X5.

(AICPA adapted)

E1-9 **Journal Entries: Purchase and Pooling**   On January 1, 19X7, Middle issued its common stock to the stockholders of End in exchange for all the outstanding stock of End. End plans to liquidate after paying creditors. The combination is to be treated as statutory merger. The balance sheets for the two companies immediately before the combination appear here:

	Middle Company	End Company
Assets		
Cash	$ 2,000	$1,000
Other assets	8,000	2,000
Total assets	$10,000	$3,000
Liabilities and Stockholders' Equity		
Liabilities	$ 2,000	$ 500
Common stock ($5 par)	5,000	
Common stock ($10 par)		1,000
Excess over par	2,000	500
Retained earnings	1,000	1,000
Total liabilities and stockholders' equity	$10,000	$3,000

Middle exchanges two of its shares for each of the outstanding shares of End. Middle's common stock is currently selling in the market at $20 per share. Both companies agree that the balance sheets represent fair values except for End's other assets, which have a fair value of $3,000.

REQUIRED

a) Prepare the entries on the books of Middle to record the merger as

    1. A purchase

    2. A pooling of interests

b) Prepare the entries on the books of Middle to record the merger as a pooling of interests, assuming Middle exchanges one of its shares for each of the outstanding shares of End.

E1-10   Multiple Choice Questions on Pooling

1. Ethel Corporation issued voting common stock with a stated value of $90,000 in exchange for all the outstanding common stock of Lum Company. The combination was properly accounted for as a pooling of interests. The stockholders' equity section of Lum Company at the date of the combination was as follows:

Common stock	$ 70,000
Excess over stated value	7,000
Retained earnings	50,000
	$127,000

What should be the increase in the stockholders' equity of Ethel Corporation at the date of acquisition as a result of this business combination?

    a) $ –0–   **c)** $ 90,000

    b) $37,000   **d)** $127,000

Items 2 and 3 are based on the following information: On June 30, 19X5, Axel, Inc., acquired Belle, Inc., in a business combination properly accounted for as a pooling of interests. Axel exchanged six of its shares of common stock for each share of Belle's outstanding common stock. June 30 was the fiscal year-end for both companies. The balance sheets immediately before the combination follow:

	Axel	Belle	
	Book Value	Book Value	Fair Value
Current assets	$ 40,000	$ 30,000	$ 45,000
Equipment (net)	150,000	120,000	140,000
Land	30,000		
	$220,000	$150,000	$185,000
Current liabilities	$ 35,000	$ 15,000	$ 15,000
Notes payable	40,000		
Bonds payable		100,000	100,000
Common stock ($1 par)	75,000 *60,000 sh*		
Common stock ($5 par)		50,000 *10,000 sh*	
Retained earnings	70,000	(15,000)	
	$220,000	$150,000	

2. What was the retained earnings balance on the combined balance sheet at June 30, 19X5?

a) $45,000

b) $55,000

c) $70,000

d) $80,000

3. How should the combined net income for the year be computed?

a) Use only Axel's income because the combination occurred on the last day of the fiscal year.

b) Use only Belle's income because the combination occurred on the last day of the fiscal year.

c) Add together both companies' incomes even though the combination occurred on the last day of the fiscal year.

d) Add together both companies' incomes and subtract the annual amortization of goodwill.

4. Which of the following is a potential abuse that can arise when a business combination is accounted for as a pooling of interests?

a) Assets of the investee may be overvalued when the price paid by the investor is allocated among specific assets.

b) Earnings of the pooled entity may be increased because of the combination only and not as a result of efficient operations.

c) Liabilities may be undervalued when the price paid by the investor is allocated to the specific liabilities.

d) An undue amount of cost may be assigned to goodwill, thus potentially allowing for an overstatement of pooled earnings.

5. The Troy Corporation was organized to consolidate the resources of Able Company and Baker, Inc., in a business combination appropriately accounted for by the pooling-of-interests method. On January 1, 19X0, Troy issued 65,000 shares of its $10 par-value voting stock in exchange for all the outstanding capital stock of Able and Baker. The stockholders' equity account balances of Able and Baker on this date were:

	Able	Baker	Total
Par value of common stock	$150,000	$450,000	$600,000
Additional paid-in capital	20,000	55,000	75,000
Retained earnings	110,000	210,000	320,000
	$280,000	$715,000	$995,000

What is the balance in Troy's "Additional Paid-in Capital" account immediately after the business combination?

   a) $–0–

   b) $ 25,000

   c) $ 75,000

   d) $395,000

E1-11   **Journal Entries: Purchase and Pooling**   The board of directors of Reynolds and Redford have agreed upon a business combination by merger in which Reynolds will issue 2,000 shares of its common stock to the stockholders of Redford for all the stock of Redford. The market value per share of Reynolds' stock is $20. The balance sheets of the two companies just prior to the merger are as follows:

	Reynolds	Redford
Assets		
Cash	$10,000	$ 2,000
Receivables	5,000	7,000
Inventory	25,000	12,000
Machinery and equipment (net)	50,000	9,000
Total assets	$90,000	$30,000
Stockholders' Equity		
Common stock ($5 par)	$60,000	$10,000
Excess over par	20,000	15,000
Retained earnings	10,000	5,000
Total stockholders' equity	$90,000	$30,000

Fair values of the assets and liabilities of Redford are equal to their book value except for machinery and equipment, which have a fair value of $15,000. Redford is to liquidate.

REQUIRED

a) Record entries on the books of Reynolds to record the merger as

   1. A purchase

   2. A pooling of interests

b) Prepare the entries on the books of Reynolds to record the merger as a pooling of interests, assuming Reynolds issues 5,500 shares of its stock for all the stock of Redford.

E1-12   **Acquisitions, Results of Operations: Purchase and Pooling**   Midway through their respective fiscal year, Schwartz, Inc. and McEwen Company entered into a business combination in which Schwartz agreed to exchange its common shares for all the common shares of McEwen. The costs to Schwartz to register and issue the common shares totaled $6,000. In addition, Schwartz paid outside accountants, lawyers, and appraisers $10,000 for services in connection with the acquisition.

REQUIRED

a) How should the costs of registration and issuing securities and the direct acquisition costs be handled if the business combination were recorded as

   1. A purchase

   2. A pooling of interests

b) How should the results of operations for the year in which the business combination took place be reported if the business combination were recorded as

1. A purchase

2. A pooling of interests

E1-13 **Stockholders' Equity: Pooling**   On December 31, 19X6, Company W issues 100 new shares of its common stock in exchange for all the outstanding common stock of Company Z. The newly issued shares of Company W have a total market value of $2,000. The combination is to be recorded as a pooling of interests. Just before the combination, the stockholders' equity sections of the companies' balance sheets were as follows:

	Company W	Company Z
Common stock of W (par)	$1,000	
Common stock of Z (par)		$ 500
Excess over par	250	400
Retained earnings	1,750	600
Total stockholders' equity	$3,000	$1,500

REQUIRED

a) Prepare the entries on the books of Company W under each of the following independent exchanges of stock between Company W and Company Z:

1. The par value of Company W's common stock is $4 per share.

2. The par value of Company W's common stock is $6 per share.

3. The par value of Company W's common stock is $10 per share.

4. The par value of Company W's common stock is $12 per share.

b) Present the combined stockholders' equity section of the combined balance sheet after each of the independent exchanges of stock in part (a).

E1-14 **Combined Net Income in Year of Combination: Purchase and Pooling**   Corporation P acquired all of the common stock of Corporation S on March 31, 19X3; both corporations survive the combination. Both P and S issue financial statements on a calendar-year basis. Their separate records reveal the following information concerning their own operations for the year ended December 31, 19X3.

	First 3 Months of 19X3	Last 9 Months of 19X3	Total
Corporation P			
Revenue	$4,000	$14,000	$18,000
Expense	(2,000)	(8,000)	(10,000)
Income before income from S	$2,000	$ 6,000	$ 8,000
Corporation S			
Revenue	$3,000	$10,000	$13,000
Expense	(1,000)	(6,000)	(7,000)
Net income	$2,000	$ 4,000	$ 6,000

This information has not been included in the data presented above:

1. The cost of P's investment in S exceeded S's book value; the valuation differential amortization applicable to the postacquisition portion of 19X3 is $500.

2. Direct acquisition costs totaled $100.

REQUIRED

Prepare the combined income statement of P and S as of December 31, 19X3, assuming the combination was accounted for as

1. A purchase combination

2. A pooling-of-interests combination

E1-15 **Combinations: Purchase and Pooling** Corporation X and Corporation Y agree to a business combination. The following are balance sheets for both companies just before the combination:

	Corporation X	Corporation Y
Assets		
Cash	$1,200	$300
Other assets	800	400
Total assets	$2,000	$700
Liabilities and Stockholders' Equity		
Liabilities	$ 300	$ 40
Common stock (par)	1,200	400
Excess over par	150	–0–
Retained earnings	350	260
Total liabilities and stockholders' equity	$2,000	$700

The fair value of other assets held by Y is $520. The fair value of Y's liabilities is $40, which equals their book value.

REQUIRED

Using the preceding information, answer the questions associated with the independent requirements (a) and (b) that follow:

a) Corporation X acquires all the assets and liabilities of Corporation Y in exchange for $850 cash. The combination is recorded as a purchase combination. Assume that Corporation Y does not liquidate.

   1. Determine the valuation differential and the portion that is applicable to revaluation increment and goodwill.

   2. Prepare the entry on the books of X to record the acquisition of Y's net assets.

   3. Prepare a balance sheet for Corporation X immediately after the business combination.

b) Corporation X acquires all the outstanding common stock of Corporation Y directly from Y's stockholders in exchange for newly issued shares of X's common stock, which have a total par value of $430 and a fair value of $900. The combination is recorded as a pooling of interests. Assume that Corporation Y does not liquidate.

   1. Prepare the entry on the books of X to record the acquisition of Y's stock.

   2. Prepare a separate balance sheet of Corporation X immediately after the business combination.

E1-16 **Multiple Choice Questions on Conditions for Pooling**

APPENDIX A   **1.** Which of the following transactions relating to a business combination would require that the combination be accounted for as a purchase?

a) The combination is to be completed within 12 months from the date the plan was initiated.

b) Ninety-two percent of one company's common stock is exchanged for only common stock in the other company.

c) The combined company is to retire a portion of the common stock exchanged to effect the combination within 12 months of the combination.

d) The combined company will dispose of numerous fixed assets representing duplicate facilities subsequent to the combination.

(AICPA adapted)

2. In order to report a business combination as a pooling of interests, the minimum amount of an investee's common stock that must be acquired during the combination period in exchange for the investor's common stock is

a) 100%	**c)** 80%
b) 90%	**d)** 51%

3. Which of the following types of transactions or situations would preclude a company from accounting for a business combination as a pooling of interests?

a) The combined company sells assets that were acquired in the combination representing duplicate facilities.

b) The acquiring corporation acquires only 90% of the voting common stock of the other corporation in exchange for its voting common stock.

c) The combination is effected within nine months of the initiation of the plan of combination.

d) The combined company enters into a financial arrangement for the benefit of the former stockholders of a combining company, whereby it guarantees the loans of the former stockholders that are secured by the stock issued in the combination.

(AICPA adapted)

4. Which of the following cannot exist if a business combination is to be accounted for as a pooling of interests?

a) The combined corporation does not agree to retire or reacquire part of the common stock issued to effect the combination.

b) The combined corporation does not enter into other financial arrangements for the benefit of the former stockholders of a combining company.

c) Up until 12 months before the plan of combination was initiated, each of the combining corporations was a division of another corporation.

d) One corporation's common stock is exchanged for 95% of the common stock in the other corporation.

5. In order to report a business combination as a pooling of interests, the maximum amount of outstanding voting common stock that any combining company can hold in the other combining company at the dates the plan of combination is initiated and consummated is

a) 15%	**c)** 20%
b) 10%	**d)** 90%

6. Which of the following would negate the use of pooling of interests for a business combination?

a) It is expected that two years will expire between the date the combination plan is initiated and the date it is consummated.

b) The acquiring company will issue more common shares to certain common stockholders of the acquired company than it will to other common stockholders of the acquired company.

c) The combination plan provides for additional common stock to be issued by the acquiring company if the market price of the common shares does not reach a certain price within the next two years.

d) All of the above.

E1-17   On July 1, 19X8, Anderson Company and Edwards, Inc. initiated a business combination in which Anderson would exchange two shares of its common stock for each outstanding share of Edwards' common stock. Currently, Edwards has 25,000 common shares issued and 24,500 shares outstanding (500 are held by Edwards in treasury shares). Edwards has owned 800 shares of Anderson's common stock since 19X2. Anderson has 2,000,000 shares issued and outstanding.

Prior to July 1, 19X8, Anderson had acquired 400 common shares of Edwards for cash. On July 17, 19X8, Anderson acquired 300 common shares of Edwards for cash; and on July 25, 19X8, Anderson exchanged 45,600 shares of its common stock for 22,800 outstanding shares of Edwards. One thousand common shares of Edwards, Inc. remain in the possession of parties other than Anderson or Edwards.

REQUIRED
Determine if Anderson's acquisition of Edwards' common shares satisfies the condition for pooling that Anderson issue common stock in exchange for at least 90% of the outstanding shares of Edwards at the date the combination was consummated, July 25, 19X8.

E1-18   **Multiple Choice Questions on Contingent Consideration**   Kitt Corporation agreed to the follow-
APPENDIX B   ing terms in order to acquire the net assets of Lee, Inc. on January 1, 19X1:

1. To issue 200 shares of common stock ($10 par) with a fair value of $50 per share.

2. To assume Lee's liabilities, which have a fair value of $500.

The book value of Lee's net assets on January 1, 19X1, was $9,000, which reflected fair value.

The following Part A and Part B are independent of each other.

Part A. In addition to the preceding terms, assume Kitt agreed to pay an additional $1,000 cash for the net assets of Lee if the combined earnings for 19X1 exceeded $6,000.

1. On the date of acquisition, January 1, 19X1, Kitt's acquisition cost of the net assets of Lee would be

a) $10,000   c) $11,500

b) $10,500   d) $11,000

2. The amount of goodwill on January 1, 19X1, associated with the acquisition of net assets would be

a) $1,000   c) $2,500

b) $1,500   d) $ –0–

3. Assuming Kitt reported combined earnings of $8,000 for 19X1, Kitt's entry to record the contingent consideration would be

a) Equipment 1,000
    Cash   1,000

b) Goodwill 1,000
    Cash   1,000

c) Common stock 1,000
    Cash   1,000

d) No entry is necessary

4. After taking into account the contingent consideration in item 3, the total cost and goodwill associated with Kitt's acquisition of the net assets of Lee would be

a) $11,000 and $1,000, respectively

b) $11,000 and $2,000, respectively

c) $10,000 and $1,000, respectively

d) $10,000 and $2,000, respectively

Part B. In addition to the terms preceding Part A, assume Kitt agreed to pay additional cash in one year for the net assets of Lee if the then current price of Kitt's stock falls below its date-of-acquisition price; the amount of cash to be paid will equal the decline in market price times the number of shares originally issued.

5. On the date of acquisition, January 1, 19X1, Kitt's acquisition cost of the net assets of Lee would be

a) $10,000 c) $11,500
b) $10,500 d) $ 9,000

6. The amount of goodwill on January 1, 19X1, associated with the acquisition of net assets would be

a) $1,000 c) $2,500
b) $1,500 d) $ –0–

7. If the current market price for Kitt's stock one year after the date of acquisition is $45 per share, Kitt's entry to record the contingent consideration would be

a) Equipment 1,000
    Cash 1,000
b) Goodwill 1,000
    Cash 1,000
c) Excess over par 1,000
    Cash 1,000
d) No entry is necessary

8. After taking into account the contingent consideration in item 7, the total cost and goodwill associated with Kitt's acquisition of the net assets of Lee would be

a) $11,000 and $1,000, respectively c) $10,000 and $1,000, respectively
b) $11,000 and $2,000, respectively d) $10,000 and $2,000, respectively

E1-19 Preacquisition Contingencies On January 1, 19X4, Bookbinder acquired all the voting stock of Saddlestitch for $5,000. Fair values of Saddlestitch's net assets exceeded book values by $1,000, which was allocated to goodwill. At the time of combination, Saddlestitch had an unrecorded contingent liability as a result of its being named as a defendant in a lawsuit. On April 1, 19X4, the legal department of the combined company notified the accounting department that it was probable that the company would have to pay $400 as a result of the lawsuit. The lawsuit was settled on March 14, 19X5, with the company having to pay $570.

REQUIRED

a) Define preacquisition contingencies.

b) Describe how Bookbinder would account for the lawsuit in years 19X4 and 19X5.

PROBLEMS

P1-1 Journal Entries and Balance Sheet for a Purchase On January 1, 19X2, the stockholders of Corporation B and Corporation C approved a statutory merger of the two firms. The merger provides for B to issue one share of its stock in exchange for every two shares of C, and for B to assume C's liabilities upon the liquidation of C. The common stock of B has an established market value of $10 per share. Just prior to the combination, the book values and fair values of B and C were as follows:

	Corporation B		Corporation C	
	Book Value	**Fair Value**	**Book Value**	**Fair Value**
Assets				
Cash	$ 400	$ 400	$ 200	$ 200
Other assets	1,600	2,100	800	950
Total assets	$2,000	$2,500	$1,000	$1,150
Liabilities and Stockholders' Equity				
Liabilities	$ 700	700	$ 200	200
Common stock, B ($3 par)	900			
Common stock, C ($2 par)			400	
Excess over par	300		100	
Retained earnings	100		300	
Total liabilities and stockholders' equity	$2,000		$1,000	

REQUIRED

a) Assuming the business combination is to be accounted for as a purchase, prepare the entries on the books of B to record the investment in C and the liquidation of C.

b) Prepare a balance sheet for B after the merger.

P1-2   Journal Entries and Balance Sheet for a Pooling   Using the same information in Problem 1-1, complete the following requirements.

REQUIRED

a) Assuming the business combination is to be accounted for as a pooling, prepare the entries on the books of B to record the investment in C and the liquidation of C.

b) Prepare a balance sheet for B after the merger.

P1-3   Journal Entries: Purchase and Pooling   Effective December 31, 19X9, Wesco Corporation proposes to acquire, in a one-for-one exchange of common stock, all the assets and liabilities of Southco Corporation and Eastco Corporation, after which the latter two corporations will distribute the Wesco stock to their shareholders in complete liquidation and dissolution. Wesco proposes to increase its outstanding stock for purposes of these acquisitions. Balance sheets of each of the corporations immediately prior to merger on December 31, 19X9, are given here. The assets are deemed to be worth their book values:

	Wesco	Southco	Eastco
Current assets	$ 2,000,000	$ 500,000	$ 25,000
Fixed assets (net)	10,000,000	4,000,000	200,000
Total assets	$12,000,000	$4,500,000	$225,000
Current liabilities	$ 1,000,000	$ 300,000	$ 20,000
Long-term debt	3,000,000	1,000,000	105,000
Common stock ($10 par)	3,000,000	1,000,000	50,000
Retained earnings	5,000,000	2,200,000	50,000
Total liabilities and stockholders' equity	$12,000,000	$4,500,000	$225,000

Other data relative to acquisition:

Shares outstanding	300,000	100,000	5,000
Fair market value per share	$40	$40	$30
Number shares of Wesco stock to be exchanged for Southco assets		100,000	
Number shares of Wesco stock to be exchanged for Eastco assets			5,000

The fair market value of the common shares of Wesco reflects the impact of the increased number of shares to be issued.

REQUIRED

a) Prepare the entries on the books of Wesco to record the combination as a purchase.

b) Prepare the entries on the books of Wesco to record the combination as a pooling of interests.

(AICPA adapted)

P1-4 **Journal Entries and Financial Statements for a Pooling**   On the last day of its fiscal year, December 31, 19X2, Company P acquired Company S through an exchange of common stock. P is to issue three shares of its common stock for each common share of S. Condensed financial statements of both companies as of December 31, 19X2, just prior to combination, are as follows:

	Company P	Company S
Income Statements		
Sales	$20,000	$ 6,000
Cost of goods sold	8,000	1,000
Gross margin	$12,000	$ 5,000
Expenses	4,000	3,000
Net income	$ 8,000	$ 2,000
Balance Sheets		
Assets		
Cash	$ 2,000	$ 1,500
Inventories	8,000	500
Plant and equipment (net)	50,000	12,000
Other assets	20,000	6,000
Total assets	$80,000	$20,000
Liabilities and Stockholders' Equity		
Accounts payable	$10,000	$ 2,000
Common stock ($5 par)	30,000	
Common stock ($10 par)		10,000
Excess over par	10,000	2,000
Retained earnings	30,000	6,000
Total liabilities and stockholders' equity	$80,000	$20,000

Additional information:

1. Direct costs associated with the combination totaled $1,000. These costs have been paid by P but not yet recorded.

2. The combination is to be treated as a statutory merger with S liquidating and P assuming all liabilities of S.

3. All the assets and liabilities of S were fairly valued except for plant and equipment, which had a fair value of $20,000.

4. The fair value of P's newly issued stock was determined to be $12 per share.

REQUIRED

a) Assuming the business combination is to be accounted for as a pooling, prepare the entries on the books of P to record its investment in S and the liquidation of S.

b) Prepare a December 31, 19X2, income statement and balance sheet for Company P after the merger.

P1-5   Journal Entries and Financial Statements for a Purchase   Using the same information presented in Problem 1-4, complete the following requirements.

REQUIRED

a) Assuming the business combination is to be accounted for as a purchase (and not a pooling as required in Problem 1-4), prepare the entries on the books of P to record its investment in S and the liquidation of S.

b) Prepare a December 31, 19X2, income statement and balance sheet for Company P after the merger.

P1-6   Multiple Choice Questions on Purchase and Pooling

1. In a business combination, how should plant and equipment of the acquired corporation generally be reported under each of the following methods?

Pooling of Interests	Purchase
a) Fair value	Recorded value
b) Fair value	Fair value
c) Recorded value	Recorded value
d) Recorded value	Fair value

2. How should long-term debt assumed in a business combination be shown under each of the following methods?

Purchase	Pooling of interests
a) Recorded value	Recorded value
b) Recorded value	Fair value
c) Fair value	Fair value
d) Fair value	Recorded value

Items 3 and 4 are based on the following data: On March 1, 19X2, Agront Corporation issued 10,000 shares of its $1 par-value common stock for all the outstanding stock of Barcelo Corporation, when the fair market value of Agront's stock was $50 per share. In addition, Agront made the following payments in connection with this business combination:

Finder's and consultants' fees	$20,000
SEC registration costs	7,000

3. If this business combination is treated as a pooling of interests, how much should be recorded as business combination expenses in 19X2?

a) $ –0–   **c)** $20,000

b) $ 7,000   **d)** $27,000

4. If this business combination is treated as a purchase, Agront's acquisition cost would be capitalized at

a) $ –0–   c) $520,000

b) $500,000   d) $527,000

Items 5 and 6 are based on the following data: On January 1, 19X1, Rolan Corporation issued 10,000 shares of common stock in exchange for all of Sandin Corporation's outstanding stock. Condensed balance sheets of Rolan and Sandin immediately prior to the combination are as follows:

	Rolan	Sandin
Total assets	$1,000,000	$500,000
Liabilities	$ 300,000	$150,000
Common stock ($10 par)	200,000	100,000
Retained earnings	500,000	250,000
Total liabilities and stockholders' equity	$1,000,000	$500,000

Rolan's common stock had a market price of $60 per share on January 1, 19X1. The market price of Sandin's stock was not readily ascertainable.

5. Assuming that the combination of Rolan and Sandin qualifies as a purchase, Rolan's investment in Sandin's stock will be stated in Rolan's balance sheet immediately after the combination in the amount of

a) $100,000   c) $500,000

b) $350,000   d) $600,000

6. Assuming that the combination of Rolan and Sandin qualifies as a pooling of interests rather than as a purchase, what should be reported as retained earnings in the combined balance sheet immediately after the combination?

a) $500,000

b) $600,000

c) $750,000

d) $850,000

7. What is the most appropriate basis for recording the acquisition of 100% of the stock in another company if the acquisition was a noncash transaction involving the use of preferred stock?

a) At the book value of the consideration given

b) At the par value of the stock acquired

c) At the book value of the stock acquired

d) At the fair value of the consideration given

Items 8 and 9 are based on the following information: On December 1, 19X6, Company B was merged into Company A, with Company B going out of existence. Both companies report on a calendar-year basis. This business combination should have been accounted for as a pooling of interests, but it was mistakenly accounted for as a purchase.

8. As a result of this error, what was the effect upon Company A's net earnings for the year ended December 31, 19X6?

a) Overstated, if B had a net loss from December 1, 19X6, to December 31, 19X6

b) Understated, if B had a net loss from January 1, 19X6, to November 30, 19X6

c) Overstated, if B had net earnings from December 1, 19X6, to December 31, 19X6

d) Understated, if B had net earnings from January 1, 19X6, to November 30, 19X6

9. What was the effect of this error upon Company A's asset valuations at December 1, 19X6?

    a) Overstated, under any circumstances

    b) Understated, under any circumstances

    c) Overstated, if the fair value of B's assets exceeded their book value

    d) Understated, if the fair value of B's assets exceeded their book value

10. Expenses related to effecting a business combination accounted for by the pooling-of-interests method should be

    a) Deducted in determining the net income of the resulting combined corporation for the period in which the expenses are incurred

    b) Capitalized and amortized over a discretionary period elected by management

    c) Charged to retained earnings when incurred

    d) Treated as a prior period adjustment   *(AICPA adapted)*

P1-7 **Journal Entries and Financial Statements for a Pooling** On December 31, 19X5, Ritz Company acquired all the net assets of Welch Company through an exchange of common stock. Ritz is to issue two shares of its common stock for each of the common shares of Welch. The common stock of Ritz has an established market value of $35 per share. The financial statements of each of the companies immediately prior to the business combination on December 31, 19X5, the last day of their fiscal year, are presented below; the balance sheet for Welch shows fair values as well as book values.

	Ritz Company	Welch Company
Income Statements		
Sales	$40,000	$15,000
Cost of goods sold	12,000	4,000
Gross margin	$28,000	$11,000
Expenses	8,000	5,000
Net income	$20,000	$ 6,000

	Ritz Company	Welch Company Book Value	Welch Company Fair Value
Balance Sheets			
Assets			
Cash	$ 3,500	$ 500	$ 500
Inventories	7,500	2,500	3,100
Plant and equipment	70,000	22,000	30,000
Accumulated depreciation	(14,000)	(7,000)	(12,000)
Patents	20,000	8,000	11,000
Total assets	$87,000	$26,000	$32,600
Liabilities and Stockholders' Equity			
Accounts payable	$ 5,000	$ 4,000	$ 4,000
Common stock ($13 par)	50,000		
Common stock ($20 par)		9,000	
Excess over par	1,200	1,000	
Retained earnings	30,800	12,000	
Total liabilities and stockholders' equity	$87,000	$26,000	

Additional information:

1. Ritz incurred the following costs associated with the combination; these costs have been paid by Ritz but not yet recorded.

Finder's and consultants' fees	$1,900
Cost to register securities with the SEC	1,100

2. The combination is to be treated as a statutory merger with Welch liquidating and Ritz assuming all liabilities of Welch.

REQUIRED

a) Assuming the business combination is to be accounted for as a pooling, prepare the entries on the books of Ritz to record its investment in Welch and the liquidation of Welch.

b) Prepare a December 31, 19X5, income statement and balance sheet for Ritz after the merger.

P1-8 **Journal Entries and Financial Statements for a Purchase** Using the same information presented in Problem 1-7, complete the following requirements.

REQUIRED

a) Assuming the business combination is to be accounted for as a purchase (and not a pooling, as required in Problem 1-7), prepare the entries on the books of Ritz to record its investment in Welch and the liquidation of Welch.

b) Prepare a December 31, 19X5, income statement and balance sheet for Ritz after the merger.

P1-9 **Concepts Underlying Purchase and Pooling** The boards of directors of Kessler Corporation, Bar Company, Cohen, Inc., and Mason Corporation are meeting jointly to discuss plans for a business combination. Each of the corporations has one class of common stock outstanding; Bar also has one class of preferred stock outstanding. Although terms have not as yet been settled, Kessler will be the acquiring, or issuing, corporation. Because the directors want to conform to generally accepted accounting principles, they have asked you to attend the meeting as an adviser.

REQUIRED

Consider each of the following questions independently of the others, and answer each in accordance with generally accepted accounting principles. Explain your answers.

a) Assume that the combination will be consummated August 31, 19X3. Explain the philosophy underlying the accounting and how the balance sheet accounts of each of the four corporations will appear on Kessler's combined balance sheet, on September 1, 19X3, if the combination is accounted for as a

    1. Pooling of interests

    2. Purchase

b) Assume that the combination will be consummated August 31, 19X3. Explain how the income statement accounts of each of the four corporations will be accounted for in preparing Kessler's combined income statement for the year ended December 31, 19X3, if the combination is accounted for as a

    1. Pooling of interests

    2. Purchase

(AICPA adapted)

P1-10 **Journal Entries for a Pooling** Holton Company and Miller Company agreed to a business combination in which Holton is to issue 900 shares of its stock to the stockholders of Miller for all the outstanding shares of Miller and Miller is liquidated. The common stock of Holton has an established market value of $320 per share. Just before the combination, January 1, 19X1, Holton and Miller had the balance sheets presented here, where the balance sheet for Miller shows fair values as well as book values:

| | Holton Company | Miller Company | |
	Book Value	Book Value	Fair Value
Assets			
Cash	$ 25,000	$ 20,000	$ 20,000
Inventory	175,000	60,000	65,000
Plant and equipment	850,000	225,000	275,000
Accumulated depreciation	(200,000)	(75,000)	(92,000)
Patents	100,000	50,000	82,000
Total assets	$950,000	$280,000	$350,000
Liabilities and Stockholders' Equity			
Accounts payable	$ 50,000	$ 30,000	$ 30,000
Bonds payable	160,000	50,000	45,000
Common stock ($100 par)	450,000	100,000	
Excess over par	150,000	75,000	
Retained earnings	140,000	25,000	
Total liabilities and stockholders' equity	$950,000	$280,000	

REQUIRED

a) Assuming the business combination is to be accounted for as a pooling, prepare the entries on the books of Holton to record the investment in Miller and the liquidation of Miller.

b) Assuming Holton issued 2,000 shares of its stock (and not 900 shares as previously indicated) to the stockholders of Miller for all the outstanding shares of Miller, prepare the entry on the books of Holton to record the investment in Miller and the liquidation of Miller.

P1-11 **Journal Entries for a Purchase** Using the same information in Problem 1-10, complete the following requirements.

REQUIRED

Assuming the business combination is to be accounted for as a purchase for the issuance of 900 shares of stock (and not a pooling as required in Problem 1-10), prepare the entries on the books of Holton to record the investment in Miller and the liquidation of Miller.

P1-12 **Journal Entries, Stock Exchange Ratio: Pooling** The balance sheets of the Georgia Corporation and Duke Corporation as of June 30, 19X2, follow:

	Georgia Corporation	Duke Corporation
Assets		
Cash	$ 25,500	$ 1,500
Receivables	32,100	7,500
Inventories	42,000	8,800
Fixed assets (net)	59,500	35,780
Other assets	4,500	200
Total assets	$163,600	$53,780
Liabilities		
Accounts and notes payable	$ 22,600	$43,000
Accrued expenses payable	11,000	2,200
Total liabilities	$ 33,600	$45,200
Stockholders' Equity		
Capital stock, $10 par	$ 50,000	$ –0–
Capital stock, $100 par		25,000
Paid-in capital in excess of par	30,000	32,000
Retained earnings	50,000	(48,420)
Total stockholders' equity	$130,000	$ 8,580
Total liabilities and stockholders' equity	$163,600	$53,780

On July 1, 19X2, Duke Corporation transferred to Georgia Corporation all its assets, subject to all liabilities, in exchange for unissued Georgia Corporation capital stock. The terms of the merger provided that the fair value of the stock in each case is to be its book value.

REQUIRED

a) Compute

1. The number of shares of Georgia Corporation to be distributed to shareholders of Duke Corporation

2. The number of shares of Georgia Corporation stock to be exchanged for each share of Duke stock

b) Prepare the entry on the books of Georgia Corporation recording the merger with Duke Corporation as a pooling of interests.

(AICPA adapted)

P1-13
APPENDIX A
Conditions for Pooling versus Purchase The boards of directors of Kessler Corporation, Bar Company, Cohen, Inc., and Mason Corporation are meeting jointly to discuss plans for a business combination. Each of the corporations has one class of common stock outstanding; Bar also has one class of preferred stock outstanding. Although terms have not as yet been settled, Kessler will be the acquiring, or issuing, corporation. Because the directors want to conform to generally accepted accounting principles, they have asked you to attend the meeting as an adviser.

REQUIRED

Consider each of the following questions independently of the others, and answer each in accordance with generally accepted accounting principles. Explain your answers.

a) Some of the directors believe that the terms of the combination should be agreed upon immediately and that the method of accounting to be used (whether pooling of interests, purchase, or a mixture) may be chosen at some later date. Others believe that the terms of the combination and the method to be used are very closely related. Which position is correct?

b) Kessler and Mason are comparable in size; Cohen and Bar are much smaller. How do these facts affect the choice of accounting method?

c) Bar was formerly a subsidiary of Tucker Corporation, which has no other relationship to any of the four companies discussing combination. Eighteen months ago Tucker voluntarily spun off Bar. What effect, if any, do these facts have on the choice of accounting method?

d) Kessler holds 2,000 of Bar's 10,000 outstanding shares of preferred stock and 15,000 of Cohen's 100,000 outstanding shares of common stock. All of Kessler's holdings were acquired during the first three months of the current year. What effect, if any, do these facts have on the choice of accounting method?

e) It is almost certain that Mrs. Victor Mason, Sr., who holds 5% of Mason's common stock, will object to the combination. Assume that Kessler is able to acquire only 95% (rather than 100%) of Mason's stock, issuing Kessler common stock in exchange. Which accounting method is applicable?

f) Since the directors feel that one of Mason's major divisions will not be compatible with operations of the combined company, they anticipate that it will be sold as soon as possible after the combination is consummated. They expect to have no trouble in finding a buyer. What effect, if any, do these facts have on the choice of accounting method?

(AICPA adapted)

P1-14
APPENDIX B

Journal Entries for Contingent Considerations   On January 1, 19X2, Humphreys Company acquired all the net assets of Walker Company in exchange for 9,000 newly issued common shares of Humphreys with a par value of $10 and a market value of $25. Immediately prior to the combination, on January 1, 19X2, the book values and fair values of Walker were presented in the following balance sheet:

	Walker Company	
	Book Value	**Fair Value**
Assets		
Cash	$ 10,000	$ 10,000
Inventory	30,000	30,000
Plant and equipment (net)	165,000	200,000
Total assets	$205,000	$240,000
Liabilities and Stockholders' Equity		
Notes payable	$ 20,000	$ 20,000
Common stock	100,000	
Excess over par	25,000	
Retained earnings	60,000	
Total liabilities and stockholders' equity	$205,000	

As part of the combination plan, Humphreys agreed to give additional consideration to Walker if certain future events or transactions occur.

REQUIRED

a) Prepare the entry on the books of Humphreys to record the purchase of the net assets of Walker.

b) Using the information computed in part (a), prepare the entry for each of the following independent contingent considerations.

1. Humphreys agreed to issue 1,000 additional shares of common stock to the former stockholders of Walker if Humphreys' total net income for the next two years exceeds a specified amount. Assume the contingency is met and that the market price of Humphreys' common shares at the end of the contingency period is $30 per share.

2. Humphreys agreed to pay $25,000 cash to the former stockholders of Walker if Humphreys' total net income for the next three years exceeds a specified amount. Assume the contingency is met.

3. Humphreys agreed to pay cash to the former stockholders of Walker for any difference between the $25 assigned the securities at the combination date and the market price of the securities at the end of one year. The market price of Humphreys' stock at the end of the contingency period was $20.

4. Humphreys agreed to issue additional shares of common stock for any difference between the $25 assigned the securities at the combination date and the market price of the securities at the end of one year. The market price of Humphreys' stock at the end of the contingency period was $20.

c) How are contingent considerations that are tied to both future earnings and future stock prices accounted for?

ISSUES IN ACCOUNTING JUDGMENT

I1-1 **Instant Earnings through Late-in-the-Year Pooling** Some have argued that an unscrupulous manager, whose stockholders expect a high earnings per share, can go out after his or her own operations have failed and find a profitable pooling partner that will result in combined net income for the year that is in line with their stockholders' expectations.

REQUIRED

a) Explain how this might occur. Would purchase accounting prevent this abuse?

b) What does your explanation assume about the attitude toward earnings of the profitable pooling partner?

c) Do required disclosures for poolings present information that would reveal this manipulation?

I1-2 **Business Combinations in the Financial Press and Financial Statements** Business combinations are usually reported in the financial press in addition to being described in the published financial statements of the acquiring company.

REQUIRED

a) Visit your library, and locate the *Wall Street Journal General Index* or another index that includes the financial press. Use the index to identify a particular business combination (see "mergers and acquisitions") that occurred two or three years ago, and make a list of all articles (title, periodical, and date) that discuss the combination.

b) Locate and read the articles pertaining to the combination. Make a list describing the reported information about the combination; list both accounting and nonaccounting information. If an item of information is reported in more than one article, you need not list it more than once.

c) Write a short essay comparing the information obtained from the financial press (as described in your list) with the information that would be reported in the financial statements (as described in Chapter 1). Note any differences, and comment on their significance.

I1-3 **Taxable versus Nontaxable Combinations** Standard Manufacturing, Inc. is discussing a business combination with a larger more profitable company, Mega Products Corporation. Standard has experienced sizable net operating losses (NOL) in recent years and has no prospect of generating future operating income large enough to realize the tax benefits of those losses. The current market value of Standard's net assets exceeds the corresponding book value by a substantial amount.

REQUIRED
Review the discussion of taxes and business combinations in Chapter 1, and write a brief analysis of the way in which tax considerations might enter the negotiation of a combination between Standard Manufacturing and Mega Products.

I1-4 **Footnote Disclosures for Purchases and Poolings** In the year of a business combination, a footnote to the financial statements of the acquiring company describes the combination. Two such footnotes and related information are described below. One describes a pooling of interests involving Rubbermaid Incorporated and Eldon Industries; the other, a purchase of Meredith/Burda by R. R. Donnelley & Sons Company.

Excerpts from the Financial Statements of Rubbermaid Incorporated

The "acquisitions" footnote gives the following information about the pooling: "In October 1990, 6,236,758 common shares were issued in exchange for all the outstanding common shares of Eldon Industries, Inc. (Eldon), primarily a manufacturer and marketer of office products.

"The acquisition has been accounted for as a pooling of interests, and accordingly, the accompanying financial information has been restated to include the accounts of Eldon for all periods presented.

"Net sales and net earnings of the separate companies for the period preceding the acquisition were (in thousands of dollars):

	January 1, 1990 through October 29, 1990	Years Ended December 31,	
		1989	1988
Net sales:			
Rubbermaid	$1,184,249	$1,343,873	$1,193,539
Eldon	88,732	108,492	98,045
Combined	$1,272,981	$1,452,365	$1,291,584
Net earnings:			
Rubbermaid	$ 117,366	$ 116,410	$ 99,290
Eldon	6,440	8,574	7,568
Combined	$ 123,806	$ 124,984	$ 106,858

The Rubbermaid comparative financial statements report net income, net assets, and stockholders' equity accounts for the years 1990 and 1989 as follows (in thousands of dollars):

	1990	1989
Net income	$ 143,520	$ 124,984
Net assets	1,114,250	985,005
Common shares (par)	79,993	79,557
Paid-in capital	37,857	24,715
Retained earnings	638,551	541,042
Foreign currency translation adjustment	11,803	7,162
Total stockholders' equity	$1,114,250	$ 985,005

The consolidated statement of stockholders' equity shows that the change in common shares is entirely attributable to employee stock plans.''

Excerpt from the Financial Statements of R. R. Donnelley & Sons Company

The ''acquisitions'' footnote gives the following information about the purchase: ''On September 4, 1990, the company acquired the Meredith/Burda companies for $180 million in cash, two interest-free installments of $157.3 million and $149.3 million, payable in May and October 1991, respectively, and related expenses of approximately $10 million. The acquisition was accounted for using the purchase method; accordingly, the assets and liabilities (including debt of $49.9 million) of the acquired entities have been recorded at their estimated fair values at the date of acquisition. The excess of purchase price over the estimated fair value of the net assets acquired ('goodwill' of $227 million) is being amortized on a straight-line basis over 40 years. The Meredith/Burda companies' results of operations have been included in the Consolidated Statement of Income since acquisition.

''The following table presents unaudited pro forma results of operations as if the acquisition had occurred on January 1, 1989. These pro forma results have been prepared for comparative purposes only and do not purport to be indicative of what would have occurred had the acquisition been made at the beginning of 1989 or of results which may occur in the future. Furthermore, no effect has been given in the pro forma information for operating and synergistic benefits that are expected to be realized through the combination of the entities because precise estimates of such benefits cannot be quantified.

	1990	1989
Thousands of dollars, except per share data (unaudited)		
Net sales	$3,800,304	$3,590,395
Earnings from operations	373,816	358,712
Earnings before income taxes	347,935	332,274
Net income	214,567	205,855
Net income per share	$ 2.76	$ 2.64

''In July 1990, the Federal Trade Commission (FTC) initiated an action to enjoin the Meredith/Burda acquisition on grounds that it would create an illegal concentration in an alleged 'high volume gravure printing market.' Despite a Federal District Court ruling that the action was legally proper, the FTC has begun an administrative proceeding again challenging the acquisition. Although the outcome of this proceeding cannot be determined with certainty, this new action raises issues similar to those heard before the Federal District Court. Company management continues to believe this acquisition is legally proper.''

The R. R. Donnelley comparative financial statements report net income, net assets, and stockholders' equity accounts for the years 1990 and 1989 as follows (in thousands of dollars):

	1990	1989
Net income	$ 225,846	$ 221,857
Net assets	1,595,616	1,445,787
Common stock	231,481	231,481
Retained earnings	1,435,872	1,265,953
Treasury stock	(71,737)	(51,647)
Total stockholders' equity	$1,595,616	$1,445,787

The ''Debt Financing and Interest Expense'' footnote states that the noninterest-bearing notes issued in connection with the combination are carried at a discounted value of $282 million and that interest at approximately 9.3% has been imputed on these notes. The comparative balance sheets report goodwill as follows:

	1990	1989
Goodwill	$489,040	$259,448
Amortization	26,664	16,919
	$462,376	$242,529

REQUIRED

a) Consider the summary journal entry to record each business combination. Are the disclosures in the annual reports sufficient to enable you to prepare the entry for each combination? What information are you lacking? Would you be able to secure the missing information from other public sources? (Hint: See footnote 15 in Chapter 1.)

b) How much of the 1990 combined net income is attributable to the acquired company in each combination?

c) Write a paragraph evaluating the adequacy of the disclosure rules for business combinations.

Acquisitions of Stock and Date-of-Acquisition Consolidation

BUSINESS COMBINATIONS AND CONSOLIDATIONS 65

MINORITY INTEREST AND CONSOLIDATION CRITERIA 68

CONTROLLING INTEREST 68

Policy-Making and Control 69   Majority Ownership and
Control 70   Control without Majority Ownership 71
Foreign Consolidation Standards 71

UNCONSOLIDATED SUBSIDIARIES 72

DISCLOSURE OF CONSOLIDATION POLICY 73

PURPOSES AND LIMITATIONS OF CONSOLIDATED
FINANCIAL STATEMENTS 74

DATE-OF-ACQUISITION CONSOLIDATION PROCEDURES FOR
PURCHASE COMBINATIONS WITH MINORITY
INTEREST 77

ANALYSIS OF THE VALUATION DIFFERENTIAL 77

CONSOLIDATION WORKSHEET PROCEDURES 79

Consolidation Worksheet Adjustments 79   The Minority
Interest Column 80   Completing the Consolidation
Worksheet 81

CONSOLIDATED FINANCIAL STATEMENTS 82

Reporting Minority Interest 82   Intercompany Loans 83
Unpaid Subsidiary Cash Dividends 83   Allocation of
Excess of Initial Fair Value over Cost 84   Treasury Stock
of Subsidiaries 86   Goodwill on Subsidiary's Records 88
Differing Fiscal Years of Parent and Subsidiary 88

COMPREHENSIVE ILLUSTRATION 88

CONCEPTUAL BASIS FOR CONSOLIDATION 91

SUMMARY 94

APPENDIX A: THE CONSOLIDATED BALANCE SHEET UNDER
ALTERNATIVE CONCEPTS OF CONSOLIDATION 94

APPENDIX B: DATE-OF-ACQUISITION CONSOLIDATION
PROCEDURES FOR POOLINGS OF INTERESTS WITH
MINORITY INTEREST 102

A business combination—whether accomplished by acquisition of net assets or by acquisition of stock—brings together the net assets of two or more business enterprises in a single accounting entity. In other words, a business combination creates a new accounting entity called the combined or consolidated entity that is distinct from the constituent enterprises. In combinations accomplished by an acquisition of net assets, the financial statements of the combined entity are the same as the financial statements of the acquiring company. However, in combinations accomplished by an acquisition of stock, the financial statements of the combined entity may differ from the financial statement of the acquiring company. In such cases, preparation of the combined entity's financial statements requires the application of a special accounting procedure to the separate financial statements of the acquiring and acquired companies. This special accounting procedure is called a *consolidation of financial statements*. The resultant financial statements for the combined entity are called *consolidated financial statements*, and they are distinct from the separate financial statements of the acquired and acquiring companies. The purpose of this chapter is to explain the consolidation procedures required to produce a consolidated balance sheet for the combined entity immediately after an acquisition of stock that results in a business combination. Appendixes to this chapter illustrate the effect of alternative conceptual structures on the date-of-acquisition consolidated balance sheet (Appendix A) and explain the application of date-of-acquisition consolidation procedures for poolings of interests (Appendix B). Later chapters explain consolidation procedures required subsequent to the acquisition date (see Chapters 3 through 8) and also consider more complex acquisitions, including acquisitions that occur in several steps (see Chapter 7).

BUSINESS COMBINATIONS AND CONSOLIDATIONS

A business combination requires a consolidation procedure whenever it results in an *investment in stock account* on the records of the acquiring company. For example, a combination by acquisition of stock produces an investment account whenever the acquired company is not liquidated but, rather, survives the combination. If the acquired company is liquidated, the entry by the acquiring company to record the liquidation on its records replaces the investment account with the detailed net assets it represents. Thereafter, no consolidation procedure is required, as illustrated by the Graham-Katz combination in Chapter 1. But if the acquired company survives (does not liquidate), then so does the investment account, and a consolidation procedure is required to produce the combined statements. As illustrated in the preceding chapter, not all business combinations create an investment account on the books of the acquiring company. For example, a combination by acquisition of net assets never produces such an investment account. The net assets acquired in an acquisition of net assets are listed in appropriate detail on the postcombination balance sheet of the acquiring company, which also represents the postcombination balance sheet of the combined entity. Consequently, a combination by acquisition of net assets never requires a consolidation procedure.[1]

The balance of the investment in stock account is a single number representing the net assets of the acquired company that are owned by the acquiring company. The consolidation procedure, which is aided by a worksheet, replaces this single number, investment in stock, with the detailed net assets of the acquired company. The result of the consolidation procedure is a consolidated balance sheet, which presents the assets and equities of the acquired and acquiring companies as if they were a single accounting entity.

Let us illustrate the consolidation procedure by reference to an acquisition of stock for cash. Pacific Corporation acquired 100% of the outstanding voting stock of South Sea, Inc. in exchange for $500 cash. The separate and consolidated balance sheets, immediately after the acquisition, are shown in Exhibit 2-1 on the following page. The acquisition cost of $500 is recorded by Pacific in its investment in the South Sea account by the following entry:

---

[1] An apparent exception may arise when assets are acquired for a sufficiently large stock issue that the company receiving the stock is designated the acquiring company, but such a transaction, by definition, must be an acquisition of *stock* and not an acquisition of assets.

EXHIBIT 2-1	SEPARATE AND CONSOLIDATED BALANCE SHEETS IMMEDIATELY AFTER ACQUISITION

BALANCE SHEETS
AT DATE OF ACQUISITION

	Separate Balance Sheets		Consolidated Balance Sheet
	Pacific Corporation	South Sea, Inc.	
Assets			
Current assets	$ 250	$ 60	$ 310
Investment in South Sea	500		
Plant and equipment (net)	1,000	500	1,530
Goodwill			10
Total assets	$1,750	$560	$1,850
Liabilities and Stockholders' Equity			
Liabilities	$ 350	$100	$ 450
Common stock	1,000	300	1,000
Retained earnings	400	160	400
Total liabilities and stockholders' equity	$1,750	$560	$1,850

Acquiring company's entry to record acquisition of stock in exchange for cash:

Investment in South Sea 500
     Cash   500

Pacific paid $40 more than the book value of South Sea's stockholders' equity because the fair value of South Sea's plant and equipment exceeds its book value by $30. All other assets and liabilities on South Sea's balance sheet are carried at their fair value.

    The following schedule shows the calculation of the valuation differential and goodwill:

Calculation of Valuation Differential and Goodwill

Acquisition cost	$500
Less: Book value of net assets acquired ($60 + $500 − $100)	460
Valuation differential	$ 40
Less: Revaluation increment:	
Plant and equipment	30
Goodwill	$ 10

The following diagram shows the valuation differential in terms of its two components— goodwill and the revaluation increment:

Analysis of the Valuation Differential for Net Assets Acquired

Acquisition cost ($500)	Fair value of identifiable net assets acquired ($490)*	Book value of net assets acquired ($460)†
Goodwill = $10		Revaluation increment = $30
Valuation differential = $40		

* $490 = $60 + $500 + $30 − $100

† $460 = $60 + $500 − $100

Thus, the valuation differential is attributed to the undervalued plant and equipment in the amount of $30 and to goodwill in the amount of $10.

The consolidated balance sheet can be viewed as a modification of Pacific Corporation's balance sheet that is achieved with the aid of a worksheet and a worksheet adjustment. The worksheet is shown in Exhibit 2-2. The first two columns of the worksheet contain the separate date-of-acquisition balance sheets of the two companies. The worksheet adjustment—which is strictly a worksheet adjustment and is not recorded on the records of either company—has the journal entry form shown on the top of page 68.

EXHIBIT 2-2	**CONSOLIDATION OF ACQUIRED AND ACQUIRING COMPANY BALANCE SHEETS AT DATE OF ACQUISITION: AN ACQUISITION OF 100% OF STOCK**

	Separate Financial Statements		Consolidation Adjustments		Consolidated Financial Statement
	Pacific	South Sea	Dr.	Cr.	
Assets					
Current assets	250	60			310
Investment in South Sea	500			(1) 500	–0–
Plant and equipment (net)	1,000	500	(1) 30		1,530
Goodwill			(1) 10		10
Total assets	1,750	560			1,850
Liabilities and Stockholders' Equity					
Liabilities	350	100			450
Common stock:					
Pacific	1,000				1,000
South Sea		300	(1) 300		–0–
Retained earnings:					
Pacific	400				400
South Sea		160	(1) 160		–0–
Total liabilities and stockholders' equity	1,750	560	500	500	1,850

(1) *Worksheet adjustment to eliminate and reclassify investment account:*

Common stock of South Sea................................. 300
Retained earnings of South Sea 160
Plant and equipment (net) *30*
Goodwill *10*
      Investment in South Sea   500

The worksheet adjustment performs two functions. First, it *eliminates* the investee's stockholders' equity accounts (representing the book value of the investor's equity) by offsetting them against the investor's investment balance. The first function of the adjustment is accomplished by the first two lines of the adjustment in conjunction with the bottom line of the adjustment. This part of the adjustment eliminates the entire stockholders' equity of the investee, but only part of the investment balance of the investor; a remainder equal to the valuation differential is not eliminated. Second, the adjustment *reclassifies* the remainder of the investor's investment balance as a revaluation increment (here an adjustment to plant and equipment) and goodwill. The second function of the adjustment is accomplished by the third and fourth lines (in italics) in conjunction with the bottom line. Thus, the last line of the adjustment includes the effect of both the elimination and the reclassification.

    The amounts in the consolidated balance sheet column are obtained by simply adding across each row taking due account of the debit and credit adjustments. Once the consolidation worksheet is complete, the consolidated balance sheet, which is presented in the third column of Exhibit 2-1, may be prepared from the information in the worksheet's consolidated balance sheet column.

    Our prior discussion of combinations by acquisition of stock has been restricted to combinations that transfer all the voting stock of the acquired firm to the acquiring firm. In the following discussion, we relax this restriction and consider combinations in which a portion of the acquired firm's stock does not change hands.[2] The introduction of this possibility complicates accounting and reporting for the combination.

MINORITY INTEREST AND CONSOLIDATION CRITERIA

Any voting shares of the acquired company that the acquiring company does not purchase are called the *minority interest in the acquired company*, and the holders of those shares are called the *minority stockholders*. The presence of a continuing minority interest ensures the survival of the acquired company, which implies that production of the combined financial statements will require a consolidation procedure.

Controlling Interest

When the investing company acquires less than 100% of the investee company, what determines whether or not consolidation is appropriate? The answer depends on whether or not the acquisition of stock gives a controlling interest to the acquiring company. If the acquiring company secures a controlling interest in the investee, then a consolidation procedure is in order. Further, the acquiring company in such cases is called the *parent*

---

[2] Some state laws require corporate directors to hold a nominal number of shares that cannot be held by the acquiring company. In addition, the acquiring company may be unable to locate all stockholders, or some stockholders may refuse to sell their shares—even when a special settlement is offered. Consequently, a 100% acquisition may be impossible to accomplish.

company and the acquired company is called the *subsidiary company.* On the other hand, if the acquiring company does not secure such an interest, then a consolidation procedure is not appropriate.[3]

Policy-Making and Control

In general, a controlling interest gives the parent company the ability to establish the subsidiary's operating and financing policies and to direct the subsidiary's economic activities as if they were the economic activities of its branches or divisions. Thus, the parent is able to elect or remove a majority of the subsidiary's board of directors. This enables the parent to determine the composition of the board and control a majority of votes cast at any meeting of the board. Further, the parent is usually able to obtain stockholder approval of any decision requiring such approval. Thus, control is the final or ultimate ability to establish the operating and financing policies of an investee. It goes well beyond the ability to influence those policies—as major customers may be able to do—or to veto certain acts specified in laws, bylaws, or contracts, as the following issues section shows.

ISSUES

Judgment on Control of Investee

Manhattan Corporation owns 55% of the outstanding voting stock of Condor Industries, Inc. Condor is incorporated in a state that has enacted a law intended to discourage hostile takeovers. The law requires all corporations chartered by the state to secure a two-thirds vote of its stockholders before a statutory merger or combination can occur.

1. *Could Manhattan effect the statutory merger or combination of Condor?*

Since the will of the 45% minority interest is unknown, it is possible that Manhattan would be unable to secure sufficient support within the minority interest to effect a statutory merger or combination. However, if the prospect of merger or combination has a sufficiently positive effect on Condor's stock price, it is likely that enough minority stockholders will support Manhattan.

2. *Does Manhattan control Condor?*

Although control is usually interpreted to require the ability to obtain stockholder approval of any decision requiring such approval, limited restrictions like those imposed by anti-takeover statutes or bylaw provisions do not negate the ability of the investor to establish the operating and financing policies of the investee; therefore, they should not stand in the way of consolidation. Further, neither the presence of a large and influential customer nor the delegation by an investor of some of its power to establish operating and financing policies of the investee—whether through a direct delegation of routine operating decisions or a decision not to elect a majority of directors—necessarily denies the existence of control by the investor. See Pacter (1991, p. 43) for additional discussion of control.

---

[3] Although a parent may control many subsidiaries, a subsidiary can have only one parent; if several investors exercise *joint or common control* over an investee, the investee is a *joint venture* (see Chapter 9), not a subsidiary.

Of course, the judgment on control requires an evaluation of the complete package of restrictions on control of the investee within the framework of current financial accounting standards.

Majority Ownership and Control

Under current standards, a controlling interest is indicated whenever one company owns, directly or indirectly, over 50% of the outstanding voting shares of another company. An investor has direct ownership to the extent that it holds title to shares of the investee; this is the usual meaning of ownership. An investor has indirect ownership of an investee to the extent that it owns shares in a third company that, in turn, owns shares of the investee.

To illustrate the way in which indirect ownership leads to a requirement for consolidation, consider the example depicted in Exhibit 2-3. Company X owns 45% of Z directly and 12% indirectly by holding 30% of Company Y, which holds, in turn, 40% of Z (12% = 30% × 40%); thus, Company X owns 57% of Company Z in total (57% = 45% + 12%), which constitutes a controlling interest. Therefore, the financial statements of Company X and Company Z should be consolidated. The other 43% of Company Z is held by two stockholder groups that together constitute the minority (noncontrolling) interest: (1) the stockholders of Company Z, other than Company X and Company Y, who have a 15% direct ownership of Company Z; and (2) the stockholders of Company Y, other than Company X, who have a 70% direct ownership of Company Y and thus a 28% indirect ownership (28% = 70% × 40%) in Company Z. Thus, the minority (noncontrolling) interest (43% = 15% + 28%) includes both stockholders of Company Z and stockholders of Company Y.

EXHIBIT 2-3	DIRECT AND INDIRECT OWNERSHIP

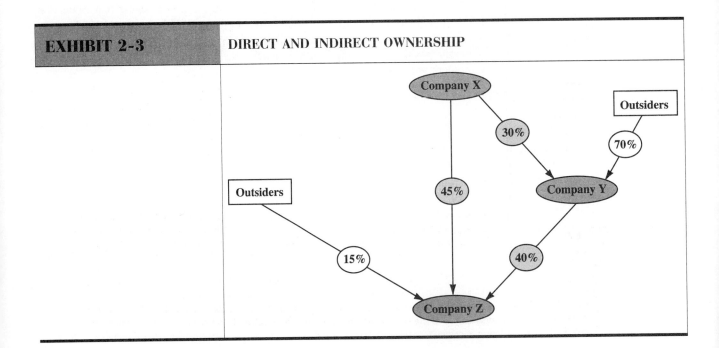

Control without Majority Ownership

The requirement that all majority-owned subsidiaries be consolidated should not be read to preclude consolidation of investor and investee when the investor owns less than 50% of the investee voting stock. Although current standards do not require it, consolidation may be appropriate in cases of less than 50% ownership provided that one company controls another. An investor holding a large minority of voting shares may be able to control an investee if the remaining stockholders are widely dispersed, disorganized, or apathetic. Further, once such a minority interest elects a majority of directors and installs its management team, proxy machinery may encourage perpetuation of control by the minority. Proxy rules permit management to propose a slate of directors and to ask stockholders for their proxies to vote for that slate. Control by minority ownership interests of 30% to 40% is frequently observed, and control by interests of 10% or even less is not uncommon. Of course, the possibility always exists that other stockholders will unite in a ''proxy fight'' and unseat the controlling minority. Thus, control in the absence of majority ownership is never assured indefinitely. In practice, consolidation in the absence of majority ownership occurs infrequently and is usually restricted to cases of large minorities (in the 40% to 50% range) for which control is not open to dispute (Pacter, 1991, pp. 45–47).[4]

To simplify our presentation, we shall assume throughout this book that all majority-owned investees are consolidated with their parent and that all other investees are not consolidated unless the contrary is specifically indicated.

Foreign Consolidation Standards

Although most industrialized countries require consolidated financial statements to be prepared by publicly held companies listed on stock exchanges, the consolidated statements may not be the primary financial statements (Price Waterhouse, 1990). For example, Japan requires listed companies to prepare consolidated statements as supplementary information; however, the separate company statements, which account for all investees on a cost basis, are the primary statements, and consolidated statements may not be widely distributed. Although the membership in Europe's Economic Community (EC) requires large companies to prepare consolidated financial statements, most member countries continue to view the separate company statements, in which investments in other companies are carried at cost, as the primary financial statements.

---

[4] In rare cases, control in the absence of majority ownership may be effected through contract or lease or through securities that are convertible into a majority ownership. For example, control may be effected through very long-term restrictive purchase agreements or leases whereby a purchaser or lessee—who lacks a majority interest in the common stock of the seller or lessor—controls sales or assets. In other cases, control may be effected by holding bonds that are convertible into a sufficiently large number of common shares—even if the bonds have not been converted and the bondholder owns very little common stock. Although Regulation S-X [Rule 4-2(a)(1)] of the Securities and Exchange Commission (SEC) supports this treatment when an analysis of the particular facts and circumstances indicates that one company controls another, accountants are very reluctant to consolidate on the basis of contracts, leases, or unexercised conversion rights; see Pacter (1991, pp. 47–49) for additional discussion of this topic.

Further, consolidation methods exhibit many differences from country to country. To illustrate, consider just a few of them. Most countries define control in terms of majority ownership, but most also permit exceptions for various nonhomogeneous subsidiaries. The United States and Australia permit the fewest exceptions to the requirement for consolidation. The reporting of minority interest also varies from country to country. For example, Australian and German companies present minority interest as part of ownership equity, whereas U.S. companies report it between long-term liabilities and ownership equities. Efforts to secure greater uniformity in international standards—sometimes referred to as "international harmonization" of accounting standards—continue but proceed slowly and face difficult obstacles. For additional discussion of international issues in consolidation, see Neuhausen (1991).

Unconsolidated Subsidiaries

Although the general rule calls for consolidation of all majority-owned subsidiaries, *FASB Statement No. 94* sanctions two exceptions. First, majority-owned subsidiaries should not be consolidated if control is likely to be temporary, as when a parent anticipates selling enough of its subsidiary's stock to reduce its ownership percentage below 50%. Second, majority-owned subsidiaries should not be consolidated if control does not rest with the majority owners, as when a subsidiary involved in a bankruptcy is controlled by a court-appointed trustee or when the subsidiary is located outside the United States and the availability of its assets and net income is restricted by circumstances or actions of foreign governments. In all these cases, consolidated financial statements would not be as meaningful to shareholders and creditors as the separate statements of the constituent companies.[5]

The choice between consolidation and nonconsolidation affects the parent's accounting for the subsidiary. The detailed assets and liabilities of an unconsolidated subsidiary are not included with the corresponding assets and liabilities of its parent company. Rather, unconsolidated subsidiaries are reported among the long-term investments of the parent company. An unconsolidated subsidiary may be accounted for using either the equity method or the cost method depending on the nature of the exception leading to

---

[5] Additional exceptions occur when the parent and subsidiary have different fiscal periods. *SEC Regulation S-X* [Rule 4-2 (a)(2)] precludes consolidation by registrants when the difference between company year-ends exceeds 93 days [17 CFR 210.4-2(a)(2)]. However, financial accounting standards also state that a "difference in fiscal periods of a parent and a subsidiary does not of itself justify the exclusion of the subsidiary from consolidation" (*ARB No. 51*, par. 5). If, for example, the parent's fiscal year ends on December 31 and the subsidiary's fiscal year ends on November 30, that fact does not preclude consolidation of the two companies. The subsidiary's data might be adjusted to a calendar-year basis in each year for purposes of consolidation, or the fiscal year of one company might be changed to coincide with the other. Frequently, however, such adjustments or changes are infeasible, and consolidation proceeds despite the fact that the underlying accounting periods do not coincide. If this occurred in our example, consolidated statements would be dated December 31 (the parent's year-end) incorporating the subsidiary's unadjusted (November 30) information. In addition, any December events that materially affect the subsidiary must be disclosed.

nonconsolidation. For example, if control is temporary because a parent plans to reduce its ownership in a subsidiary from 60% to 40%, then the equity method is appropriate. On the other hand, if the parent plans to reduce its ownership to 15%, then the cost method is appropriate.[6] The cost and equity methods of accounting for long-term investments in stock are discussed in Chapters 3 and 7.

Disclosure of Consolidation Policy

APB Opinion No. 22 (par. 8) states that "a description of all significant accounting policies of the reporting entity should be included as an integral part of the financial statements." Further, *ARB 51* (par. 5) states that "consolidated statements should disclose the consolidation policy which is being followed." Accordingly, most consolidated financial statements are accompanied by a statement of consolidation policy setting forth the general rules applied and describing any exceptions to the general rules.

The following statement of consolidation policy is taken from the "summary of accounting policies" included in the 1990 annual report of Unocal Corporation:

> The consolidated financial statements of the company include the accounts of subsidiaries more than 50 percent owned, except for certain Brazilian subsidiaries which are accounted for by the cost method due to current restrictions imposed by the Brazilian government.

The Brazilian government tightly controls the rate at which its highly inflationary currency may be used in international transactions, making it difficult to interpret the detailed Brazilian financial statements restated in U.S. dollars; consequently, Unocal does not consolidate the financial statements with those of the parent and its other subsidiaries. Rather, the Brazilian operations are included in Unocal's consolidated financial statements as an investment accounted for by the equity method.

Prior to 1989, an exception to the required consolidation of all majority-owned subsidiaries was provided for financial subsidiaries—including financial service, banking, insurance, and real estate subsidiaries—of a parent engaged primarily in manufacturing or other nonfinancial businesses. *FASB Statement No. 94* removed this "nonhomogeneity exception" but also imposed a requirement to disclose summarized information about subsidiaries that were not consolidated prior to the effective date of the statement. The note shown at the top of page 74 is from the 1990 annual report of Honeywell, Inc. and illustrates the form of this required disclosure.

---

[6] The other exceptions to the majority-owned consolidation rule offer additional examples. If control over a subsidiary has been transferred from the parent to a trustee as a result of a bankruptcy proceeding, then the cost method is appropriate for the subsidiary. On the other hand, control over a recently acquired subsidiary may rest with a government agency that is required to approve the acquisition, yet the parent may be able to influence the subsidiary significantly. In such cases, the equity method is appropriate. If a foreign subsidiary is not consolidated because of restrictions on the availability of its assets, then the parent should account for the investment using the cost method.

Note 13—Finance and Real Estate Subsidiaries
Following is summarized financial information pertaining to finance and real estate sub-sidiaries:

	1990	1989	1988
Condensed Income Statement			
Revenues and other income	$ 19.5	$ 19.6	$ 51.2
Costs and expenses	14.4	14.6	19.7
Income taxes	1.7	1.5	1.7
Net income	$ 3.4	$ 3.5	$ 29.8
Condensed Statement of Financial Position			
Receivables	$191.2	$189.5	$186.5
Receivables from Honeywell	24.1	23.9	25.1
Property	42.8	47.1	48.3
Other	2.4	2.5	2.2
	$260.5	$263.0	$262.1
Payables and accruals	$ 4.6	$ 8.3	$ 9.7
Short-term debt	0.5	2.0	0.5
Long-term debt	56.4	58.6	60.5
Payable to Honeywell	42.2	40.7	41.4
Stockholders' equity	156.8	153.4	150.0
	$260.5	$263.0	$262.1

Receivables include customer obligations purchased from Honeywell by Honeywell Finance Inc. Collection of these receivables is performed by Honeywell and the cost of this service is paid by Honeywell Finance, Inc.

Revenues and other income consist primarily of financing fees paid by Honeywell to Honeywell Finance Inc. and rental income from buildings owned by the real estate subsidiaries. The financing fees are based upon expenses and interest income. Fees are paid to Honeywell Finance Inc. under a formula providing fixed-charges coverage of 150 percent. In 1988 revenues included $29.8 from gains on sales of real estate.

An alternative form of disclosure for nonhomogeneous subsidiaries is followed by Ford Motor Company, which reports the assets and liabilities of its financial services operations in separate sections of its 1990 consolidated balance sheet. Disclosures such as these allow creditors, investors, and others to understand the varied activities of the consolidated entity and to assess the effects of their differing risks and rewards.

PURPOSES AND LIMITATIONS OF CONSOLIDATED FINANCIAL STATEMENTS

Consolidated financial statements are prepared primarily for use by stockholders and creditors—both present and potential—whose interest focuses on the parent company and its subsidiaries as a single, aggregated entity. The standards that bear on consolidation policies are based on the view that consolidated financial information is useful when the parent has a controlling interest in a subsidiary, and that separate-company financial information is *not* useful when the parent has such an interest in a subsidiary. The grounds for this view and the character of the standards based on it represent a continuing source of research and debate, but it is clear that consolidated information is subject to a variety of limitations as demonstrated by the following issues section:

Two accounting students, Mr. Hosmer and Ms. Sanders, at Midwestern University have prepared an informal debate for presentation in their advanced accounting class. The question to be debated is: "Are consolidated financial statements superior to separate financial statements as a basis for financial reporting to stockholders?" Mr. Hosmer has prepared the case for the affirmative side, arguing that the consolidated statements are superior, and Ms. Sanders has prepared the case for the negative, arguing that they are not superior to separate statements. After introductory remarks by the instructor, the following discussion takes place:

MR. HOSMER: "The purpose of my remarks is to establish the superiority of consolidated financial statements over separate financial statements as a basis for financial reporting about an entity. When one company controls the operations and finances of another, the two companies function as if they were a single entity. Sometimes companies establish many corporations simply to secure legal or tax benefits, and the corporate structure bears no other relationship to the structure of operations or finances. In such cases, consolidated financial statements are necessary to give a meaningful picture of the entity. Even when the related companies are few in number and partition the entity along natural lines, consolidated statements are an important element of financial reporting. If each company simply issues its separate financial statements without consolidation, then the stockholders of the parent company will be denied information about the amount and makeup of the subsidiary's net assets and the extent to which the subsidiary's assets are derived from liabilities. Unless the parent's stockholders are able to secure the separate balance sheet of the subsidiary—and this may be difficult unless the parent's stockholders are also stockholders of the subsidiary—only the net investment will be known to the stockholders. Even if the parent's stockholders secure the subsidiary's balance sheet, the stockholders' information and technical understanding may not be sufficient to permit them to consolidate it with the parent's balance sheet. Consequently, consolidated financial statements are of considerable importance to the parent's stockholders."

MS. SANDERS: "I do not dispute the importance of consolidated financial statements to stockholders of the parent company. But I do not believe that Mr. Hosmer has established the superiority of consolidated statements over separate statements for all users of financial information or even for the parent's stockholders. Consolidated financial statements are limited in a number of important ways. Let's consider some of the important limitations.

"First, consolidated statements are not designed to serve the needs of minority stockholders. Consolidated statements contain very little information about assets, equities, and income of the subsidiary; such information must be obtained from the subsidiary's separate financial statements. Furthermore, neither consolidated nor separate financial statements reveal the extent and character of transactions of a subsidiary with its parent; yet such information may be of great interest to minority stockholders in view of the dominance of the parent over the subsidiary.

"Second, consolidated statements do not satisfy the information needs of creditors. Consolidated assets may be an indication of the overall security of debt, but consolidated assets are not generally available to satisfy the claims of creditors; consequently, creditors are also interested in the separate financial statements of borrowers. Furthermore, liens on assets, pledges of stock to secure debt, and similar arrangements are frequently complicated and difficult to disclose in footnotes; consequently, such disclosures are often omitted or severely abbreviated. Yet these arrangements constrain the availability of assets and alter the priority of interests in combined assets. For example, the pledging of subsidiary stock to secure the debt of a parent means that the holders of the parent's secured debt, as well as the creditors of the subsidiary, have an interest in subsidiary assets.

"Third, consolidated statements do not completely satisfy the information needs of the parent's stockholders in several important respects. First, the aggregation of data in consolidated financial statements does not convey much information about the mixture of strong and weak results among the constituent entities. This fact complicates the interpretation of consolidated income and financial position as well as its use in ratio analysis. Second, the income of subsidiaries is not available for the payment of dividends by the parent until it is transferred as dividends to the parent; consequently, consolidated net income is not a reliable indicator of dividend policy since it depends on the ability and willingness of two or more companies to pay dividends."

MR. HOSMER: "Ms. Sanders misconstrues my arguments and the fundamental question that is at issue here. I did not argue that consolidated financial statements remove the need for separate financial statements. Ms. Sanders argues that separate financial statements contain additional information. I accept her arguments, but I also contend that Ms. Sanders has not established the superiority of separate statements over consolidated statements; she merely establishes that consolidated financial statements are not sufficient to satisfy the needs of all users of financial statements. The limitations she identifies are mitigated or eliminated by the reporting of the separate financial statements of affiliated companies along with the consolidated statements. Indeed, financial accounting standards encourage the reporting of separate financial statements when it is necessary to indicate adequately the position of bondholders and other creditors or preferred stockholders of the parent (*ARB No. 51*, par. 24). Despite their limitations, however, I would argue that consolidated financial statements are superior to separate statements as representations of the accounting entity. Consolidated financial statements represent an aggregation of company data into financial information about the larger accounting entity that would be extremely difficult to obtain from separate statements of affiliated companies, owing to the complexity and subtlety of the measurement problem."

For additional discussion of the usefulness of consolidated financial statements, see the exchange between Hylton (1988) and Sharp and Thompson (1989). Chapter 9 contains further discussion of the separate financial statements of affiliated companies. We turn now to a discussion of date-of-acquisition consolidation procedures for cases involving minority interest and a variety of additional complications. We begin with a discussion of the underlying consolidation concept and then illustrate the related consolidation procedures.

DATE-OF-ACQUISITION CONSOLIDATION PROCEDURES FOR PURCHASE COMBINATIONS WITH MINORITY INTEREST

Consolidation of a partially owned subsidiary—like consolidation of a wholly owned subsidiary—replaces the parent's investment account with the subsidiary's detailed assets and liabilities. The replacement is accomplished by a worksheet adjustment that eliminates the book value of the parent's investment from the subsidiary's stockholders' equity accounts and from the parent's investment accounts. This adjustment leaves a remainder in both the parent's investment account and the subsidiary's stockholders' equity accounts. As in the case of the wholly owned subsidiary, the remainder in the parent's investment account equals the valuation differential, representing the revaluation increment and goodwill, which is properly reclassified by the same adjustment. The remainder in the subsidiary's stockholders' equity accounts, which does not arise in cases of wholly owned subsidiaries, equals the interest of the minority stockholders in the net assets of the subsidiary. This minority interest must be reclassified as a separate balance sheet item which is usually presented between long-term liabilities and stockholders' equity on the consolidated balance sheet.

Current accounting practice generally follows the parent-company concept in determining the interrelated amounts on consolidated balance sheets for minority interest and subsidiary net assets. The *parent-company concept* requires subsidiary assets and liabilities to be included in the consolidated balance sheet at their book value plus revaluation increments and goodwill arising in the analysis of the parent's valuation differential. As we shall see, this implies that minority interest is reported at its book value.

The preparation of the consolidated balance sheet at the date of acquisition immediately following the acquisition of stock is based on an analysis of the related valuation differential. The paragraphs that follow demonstrate this analysis and the related consolidation worksheet procedures by reference to the acquisition of Sherman, Inc. by Parker Corporation. On January 1, 19X1, Parker Corporation pays $800 cash for an 80% interest in the voting stock of Sherman, Inc. and makes the following entry:

Acquiring company's entry to record acquisition of stock in exchange for cash:

Investment in Sherman 800
    Cash 800

The supporting financial information, immediately after the acquisition, is given in Exhibit 2-4 shown on the following page.

Analysis of the Valuation Differential

The parent's valuation differential, the difference between the acquisition cost incurred by the parent and the book value of the net assets acquired, is summarized in Exhibit 2-5 on page 78. Since the parent acquired only 80% of the subsidiary, the book value of the net assets acquired equals 80% of the total book value of the subsidiary [$584 = ($850 − $120) × .80]. Similarly, the fair value of the identifiable assets acquired equals 80% of the total fair value of the subsidiary's net assets [$720 = ($1,020 − $120) × .80]. As shown earlier, goodwill is the excess of the acquisition cost over the identifiable fair value acquired ($80 = $800 − $720), and the revaluation increment is the excess of the identifiable fair value acquired over the book value acquired ($136 = $720 − $584).

The diagrammatic analysis of the valuation differential in Exhibit 2-5 emphasizes the impact of partial ownership on the analysis. A more complete analysis is shown in Exhibit 2-6 on page 79, which shows, in addition, the composition of the revaluation increment. Notice that the revaluation increment includes, for each asset and liability of the

EXHIBIT 2-4	SEPARATE BALANCE SHEETS IMMEDIATELY AFTER ACQUISITION

BALANCE SHEETS
AT JANUARY 1, 19X1

	Parker Corporation	Sherman, Inc.	
	Book Value	Book Value	Fair Value
Assets			
Current assets	$ 500	$100	$ 125
Investment in Sherman	800		
Plant and equipment (net)	1,700	750	835
Patent			60
Total assets	$3,000	$850	$1,020
Liabilities and Stockholders' Equity			
Liabilities	$1,100	$120	$ 120
Common stock	1,000	400	
Excess over par		100	
Retained earnings	900	230	
Total liabilities and stockholders' equity	$3,000	$850	

subsidiary, 80% of that item's excess of fair value over book value. Thus, the revaluation increment for plant and equipment is 80% of the excess of fair value over book value for plant and equipment [$68 = ($835 − $750) × .80]. This means that the purchased subsidiary net assets will be included in the consolidated balance sheet, not at their fair values, but at 100% of their book values plus 80% of the excess of fair value over book value.

EXHIBIT 2-5	ANALYSIS OF VALUATION DIFFERENTIAL FOR NET ASSETS ACQUIRED WITH MINORITY INTEREST

Acquisition cost ($800)	Fair value of identifiable net assets acquired ($720)*	Book value of net assets acquired ($584)†
Goodwill = $80	Revaluation increment = $136	
Valuation differential = $216		

* $720 = ($1,020 − $120) × .80

† $584 = ($850 − $120) × .80

EXHIBIT 2-6	CALCULATION OF VALUATION DIFFERENTIAL AND GOODWILL WITH MINORITY INTEREST

Acquisition cost		$800
Less: Book value of net assets acquired*		584
Valuation differential		$216
Less: Revaluation increment:		
Current assets [($125 − $100) × .80]	$20	
Plant and equipment (net) [($835 − $750) × .80]	68	
Patent [($60 − $0) × .80]	48	136
Goodwill		$ 80

* $584 = ($850 − $120) × .80
 = ($400 + $100 + $230) × .80

This practice is consistent with the parent-company concept of consolidation. Thus, for example, plant and equipment is reported in the consolidated balance sheet at its book value of $750 plus 80% of the excess of its fair value over its book value [$818 = $750 + ($835 − $750)(.80)].

The analysis presented in Exhibit 2-6 is used as a basis for the worksheet adjustments required to consolidate the date-of-acquisition balance sheets of the parent and subsidiary.

Consolidation Worksheet Procedures

We begin our discussion of consolidation worksheet procedures by considering the form of the consolidation worksheet adjustments. We then turn to the handling of minority interest in a special column of the worksheet.

Consolidation Worksheet Adjustments

Consolidation worksheet adjustments are of two fundamentally different types: (1) reclassification adjustments and (2) elimination adjustments. *Reclassification adjustments* merely change the label or account title associated with an element of assets or equities. *Elimination adjustments*, on the other hand, offset an asset recorded by one company against an equity (creditors' or owners') recorded by another company and thereby avoid double-counting assets and equities. In other words, elimination adjustments offset reciprocal balances against one another.

The date-of-acquisition worksheet adjustment required for the consolidation of Parker and Sherman performs both an elimination and a reclassification. The elimination offsets the parent's equity in the subsidiary's stockholders' equity accounts against the reciprocal amount in the parent's investment account. Without this elimination, the consolidated entity would report its own stock as an asset, which is clearly inappropriate. The reclassification removes the valuation differential from the parent's investment account and distributes it among appropriate assets and liabilities. Both functions are accomplished by the following worksheet adjustment:

(1) *Worksheet adjustment to eliminate and reclassify parent's investment account:*

Common stock of Sherman 320
Excess over par of Sherman 80
Retained earnings of Sherman 184
Current assets (inventory) 20
Plant and equipment (net) 68
Patent 48
Goodwill 80
    Investment in Sherman   800

The information for this adjustment is obtained from the analysis of the parent's valuation differential prepared in the previous section. The first three lines of the adjustment eliminate the book value of the parent's interest ($584 in total) from the stockholders' equity accounts of the subsidiary; the last line of the adjustment includes a $584 elimination from the parent's investment account. The fourth through seventh lines of the adjustment (all in italics) reclassify the valuation differential ($216 in total) among the appropriate assets, and the last line of the adjustment includes a $216 elimination from the parent's investment account. As a result of this worksheet adjustment, the entire balance of the investment account ($800) is either eliminated or reclassified. The combined elimination and reclassification is entered as adjustment (1) on the worksheet in Exhibit 2-7.

The Minority Interest Column

The presence of minority interest adds an additional step to the worksheet procedure. The equity interest of minority stockholders in subsidiary net assets is represented by portions of common stock, excess over par, and retained earnings balances on the subsidiary's records. An additional worksheet column is introduced to separate the minority interest in these balances and to summarize that interest in a single-equity account on the consolidated balance sheet. In other words, the minority interest column performs a reclassification adjustment.[7] Use of such a column is shown in Exhibit 2-7. The minority interest column receives the remainder of subsidiary stockholders' equity accounts after elimination of the parent's equity therein. The preparer of the worksheet must then sum the three elements of minority interest ($80 + $20 + $46 = $146) and transfer the sum to the consolidated financial statement column. Notice that the minority interest in each stockholders' equity account can be calculated in two ways—as the minority ownership percentage (20%) times the account balance or as the remainder in the account after the elimination of the parent's interest.

---

[7] Use of the minority interest column is equivalent to the following worksheet adjustment:

Common stock of Sherman 80
Excess over par of Sherman 20
Retained earnings of Sherman 46
    Minority interest   146

The use of the minority interest column may seem an awkward way to accomplish a simple reclassification adjustment, but it simplifies worksheet procedures in the more complex situations considered in later chapters.

EXHIBIT 2-7	CONSOLIDATION OF PARENT AND SUBSIDIARY BALANCE SHEETS AT DATE OF ACQUISITION: MINORITY INTEREST RECLASSIFIED BY A WORKSHEET COLUMN

	Separate Financial Statements		Consolidation Adjustments		Minority Interest	Consolidated Financial Statement
	Parker	Sherman	Dr.	Cr.		
Assets						
Current assets	500	100	(1) 20			620
Investment in Sherman	800			(1) 800		–0–
Plant and equipment (net)	1,700	750	(1) 68			2,518
Patent			(1) 48			48
Goodwill			(1) 80			80
Total assets	3,000	850				3,266
Liabilities and Stockholders' Equity						
Liabilities	1,100	120				1,220
Common stock:						
Parker	1,000					1,000
Sherman		400	(1) 320		80	
Excess over par:						
Parker	–0–					–0–
Sherman		100	(1) 80		20	
Retained earnings:						
Parker	900					900
Sherman		230	(1) 184		46	
Minority interest					(146)	146
Total liabilities and stockholders' equity	3,000	850	800	800	–0–	3,266

Completing the Consolidation Worksheet

When the consolidation worksheet adjustments are entered on the worksheet, as shown in Exhibit 2-7, the consolidated balance sheet is obtained in the far right-hand column by simply summing the entries in each row, taking due account of the worksheet adjustments. *Remember, the adjustments are strictly worksheet adjustments and are not entered on the company records of either the parent or the subsidiary.* Observe that the parent's investment account does not appear on the consolidated balance sheet; the entire investment balance is either eliminated against the related stockholders' equity or reclassified as goodwill and revaluation increments. Also note that consolidated stockholders' equity (excluding minority interest) is identical with stockholders' equity of the parent company; subsidiary stockholders' equity accounts are either eliminated against the related investment account of the parent or reclassified as minority interest, which represents the equity of minority stockholders in the net assets of the subsidiary.

Consolidated Financial Statements

The consolidated balance sheet is prepared using the information in the far right-hand column of the consolidation worksheet in Exhibit 2-7 and is shown in Exhibit 2-8. The following paragraphs discuss the reporting of minority interest in consolidated financial statements and several complications that arise in consolidation, including intercompany loans, unpaid subsidiary dividends, negative goodwill, and subsidiary treasury stock.

Reporting Minority Interest

The reporting of minority interest in a subsidiary's net assets has three aspects—its title, the degree to which it is disaggregated, and its location among the equities. Minority interest is identified by various titles, including *minority interest, minority shareholders' interest, equity of minority shareholders in consolidated subsidiaries,* and *minority interest in subsidiaries*. Minority interest is usually presented as a single item. However, in addition, the amount of minority interest associated with the various subsidiaries or with various elements of subsidiary stockholders' equity—common stock, excess over par, and retained earnings—may be disclosed in a footnote. If more than one subsidiary exists, the minority interest in all subsidiaries is usually presented as a single item.

The FASB has indicated that minority interests ''do not represent present obligations of the enterprise to pay cash or distribute other assets to minority stockholders. Rather, those stockholders have ownership or residual interests in components of the consolidated enterprise'' (*FASB Concepts Statement No. 6*, par. 254). This suggests that minority interest should be reported as part of stockholders' equity on the consolidated balance sheet. However, minority interest is frequently reported as the last long-term liability or in a

EXHIBIT 2-8	CONSOLIDATED BALANCE SHEET IMMEDIATELY AFTER ACQUISITION

Parker Corporation

CONSOLIDATED BALANCE SHEET
AT JANUARY 1, 19X1

Assets	
Current assets	$ 620
Plant and equipment (net)	2,518
Patent	48
Goodwill	80
Total assets	$3,266
Liabilities and Stockholders' Equity	
Liabilities	$1,220
Minority interest	146
Common stock	1,000
Retained earnings	900
Total liabilities and stockholders' equity	$3,266

separate category between liabilities and stockholders' equity. The FASB indicates some tolerance for different practices by saying that it did not intend to ''preclude showing minority interests separately from majority interests or preclude emphasizing the interests of majority stockholders for whom consolidated statements are primarily provided'' (*Ibid.*). Throughout this text, we shall follow the common practice of reporting minority interest in a separate category between long-term liabilities and stockholders' equity.

Intercompany Loans

Parents and subsidiaries frequently transact business with one another. Although such intercompany transactions are considered at length in subsequent chapters, a simple intercompany loan will illustrate the nature of such transactions and their impact on consolidation procedures. Consider Corporation A, which acquires 90% of the outstanding stock of Corporation B. On the date of acquisition, Corporation B owes Corporation A $20,000 cash as a result of a loan prior to the acquisition. The loan is reported on Corporation A's balance sheet as a note receivable of $20,000 and on Corporation B's balance sheet as a note payable of $20,000. Consolidation of A and B at the acquisition date requires that the intercompany loan be eliminated by the following worksheet adjustment:

Worksheet adjustment to eliminate intercompany loan:

Notes payable 20,000
    Notes receivable   20,000

The generally accepted practice is to eliminate 100% of the loan despite the 90% ownership percentage. The elimination is necessary because the consolidated entity cannot create assets and liabilities by lending money to itself. Consolidated financial statements reflect only those transactions between the reporting consolidated entity (parent and subsidiary) and unaffiliated parties (outsiders).

Unpaid Subsidiary Cash Dividends

If a purchase combination occurs after the subsidiary declares a cash dividend, but before the dividend's date of record, then the dividend associated with the acquired shares is payable to the parent company. A portion of the consideration given by the parent was given to acquire the dividend payment. Accordingly, that amount should be charged to dividends receivable by the parent rather than to the investment account. Suppose that a parent pays $100,000 cash for a 90% interest in a subsidiary, after the subsidiary declared a $10,000 dividend but before the date of record. The parent records the investment by the following entry:

Parent's entry to record investment in subsidiary with acquired subsidiary dividend:

Dividends receivable (.90 × $10,000) 9,000
Investment in subsidiary (90%). 91,000
    Cash.   100,000

Preparation of the date-of-acquisition consolidated balance sheet will require the following worksheet adjustment:

Worksheet adjustment to eliminate acquired subsidiary dividend:

Dividend payable 9,000

          Dividend receivable   9,000

This adjustment eliminates the dividend receivable, which appears on the parent's balance sheet, by offsetting it against the dividend payable, which appears on the subsidiary's balance sheet.

On the other hand, if the purchase combination occurs between the date of record and the payment date, then subsidiary dividends are payable to the former holders of the parent's shares in the subsidiary and no intercompany dividend accounts arise. Suppose that a parent pays $100,000 cash for a 90% interest in a subsidiary, after the date of record for a $10,000 subsidiary dividend but before payment of the dividend. The parent records the investment by the following entry:

Parent's entry to record investment in subsidiary without acquired subsidiary dividend:

Investment in subsidiary (90%). 100,000

          Cash.   100,000

Allocation of Excess of Initial Fair Value over Cost

In some purchase combinations, the initial determination of the fair value of identifiable net assets exceeds the acquisition cost. One might conclude, in such cases, that the acquired company could have liquidated its assets and liabilities individually and be left with a larger sum than received for selling them intact to the acquiring company. However, it seems much more likely that the initial estimates of fair value are too high and should be revised downward. Further, the usual presumption in historical cost accounting is that net assets acquired should not be recorded at an amount in excess of cost. Accordingly, financial accounting standards (*APB Opinion No. 16*, pars. 87 and 91) provide that any excess of initial fair value over cost should be allocated to reduce proportionately the fair values initially assigned to *noncurrent assets* (other than long-term investments in marketable securities). In the unlikely event that this procedure reduces the noncurrent assets to zero value, the remainder should be classified as a deferred credit and amortized over a period not to exceed 40 years. The deferred credit is frequently called *negative goodwill*.[8]

To illustrate, consider a parent company that acquires for $6,900 cash, a 90% interest in a subsidiary whose net assets have a book value of $5,500 and an initial fair value estimate of $9,000 composed as follows:

---

[8] DeMoville and Petrie (1989) suggest that bargain purchases are not uncommon in business combinations and that recording bargain purchases in the required manner misrepresents such transactions. These authors argue that all assets and liabilities acquired in a bargain purchase should be recorded at their fair values (without an arbitrary reduction) and that the excess of total fair value over cost should be reported as an unrealized gain in the stockholders' equity section.

Book Values and Initial Estimates of Fair Value for Subsidiary Net Assets

	Book Value	Initial Fair Value
Current assets	$1,400	$ 1,700
Long-term investments in marketable securities	1,000	1,800
Buildings and equipment (net)	3,500	4,800
Land	2,100	3,200
Total assets	$8,000	$11,500
Liabilities	2,500	2,500
Net assets	$5,500	$ 9,000

On the basis of this information, we can prepare the following analysis of the valuation differential:

Calculation of Valuation Differential with Excess of Initial Fair Value over Cost

Acquisition cost		$ 6,900
Less: Book value of net assets acquired		4,950
Valuation differential		$ 1,950
Less: Initial revaluation increment:		
Current assets [($1,700 − $1,400) × .90]	$ 270	
Long-term investments in marketable securities [($1,800 − $1,000) × .90]	720	
Buildings and equipment (net) [($4,800 − $3,500) × .90]	1,170	
Land [($3,200 − $2,100) × .90]	990	3,150
Excess of initial fair value over cost		$(1,200)

The standards require that the $1,200 excess of initial fair value over cost be allocated among noncurrent assets in proportion to their respective fair values as shown in the following schedule:

Allocation of Excess of Initial Fair Value over Cost among Noncurrent Assets

	Initial Fair Value Estimate			Allocation
	Amount	Percent		
Buildings and equipment (net)	$4,800	60%	$1,200 × .60 =	$ 720
Land	3,200	40	$1,200 × .40 =	480
Total	$8,000	100%		$1,200

The $1,200 excess of initial fair value over cost is not allocated to current assets, long-term investments in marketable securities, or liabilities. Accordingly, the entire excess is allocated among buildings and equipment and land. The allocations reduce the initial revaluation increments associated with these noncurrent assets as shown in Exhibit 2-9 on the following page.

| | EXHIBIT 2-9 | ALLOCATION OF EXCESS OF INITIAL FAIR VALUE OVER COST AMONG CERTAIN NONCURRENT ASSETS OF SUBSIDIARY |

	Initial Fair Value (100%) (1)	Book Value (100%) (2)	Excess of Initial Fair Value over Book Value (100%) (3)	Initial Revaluation Increment* (90%) (4)	Allocation of Excess of Fair Value over Cost (5)	Adjusted Revaluation Increment (6)
Current assets	$ 1,700	$1,400	$ 300	$ 270	$	$ 270
Long-term investments in marketable securities	1,800	1,000	800	720		720
Buildings and equipment (net)	4,800	3,500	1,300	1,170	(720)	450
Land	3,200	2,100	1,100	990	(480)	510
Total assets	$11,500	$8,000	$3,500	$3,150	$(1,200)	$1,950
Liabilities	2,500	2,500				
Net assets	$ 9,000	$5,500	$3,500	$3,150	$(1,200)	$1,950

*Following the parent-company concept of consolidation, the revaluation increment represents 90% of the excess of fair value over book value because the parent acquired 90% of the subsidiary.

Treasury Stock of Subsidiaries

When a subsidiary has treasury stock at the date of acquisition, the treasury shares should be treated as if they had been retired for purposes of consolidation calculations. The treasury shares must be excluded from total shares outstanding in calculating the parent's ownership percentage. In addition, a special worksheet adjustment accomplishes the retirement of the treasury stock for purposes of consolidation. To illustrate, let us consider the case of Fisher, Inc., which pays $30,000 cash for 900 common shares of Ziebur Corporation. On the date of acquisition, Ziebur's net assets have a fair value equal to their book value and its stockholders' equity has the following composition:

Stockholders' Equity of Subsidiary

Common stock (1,200 shares × $10)	$12,000
Excess over par	6,000
Retained earnings	16,000
Subtotal	$34,000
Less: Treasury stock (200 shares at cost)	3,800
Total stockholders' equity	$30,200

The following worksheet adjustment retires the subsidiary's treasury stock for purposes of consolidation:

Worksheet adjustment to retire subsidiary's treasury stock for consolidation purposes:

Common stock (200 shares × $10). 2,000
Excess over par ($6,000 × 200/1,200) 1,000
Retained earnings ($3,800 − $2,000 − $1,000)   800
    Treasury stock.   3,800

The 900 shares acquired by Fisher represent a 90% interest in Ziebur [.90 = 900 ÷ (1,200 − 200)]. Accordingly, the following worksheet adjustment is required to eliminate and reclassify the parent's investment account:

Worksheet adjustment to eliminate and reclassify parent's investment account:

Common stock [.90 × ($12,000 − $2,000)] 9,000
Excess over par [.90 × ($6,000 − $1,000)] 4,500
Retained earnings [.90 × ($16,000 − $800)] 13,680
Goodwill 2,820
    Investment in Ziebur   30,000

The acquired equity in each stockholders' equity account equals the ownership percentage (90%) times the balance of each account *after* adjustment for the retirement of treasury stock. Observe that acquired stockholders' equity ($27,180 = $9,000 + $4,500 + $13,680) equals 90% of total stockholders' equity at the date of acquisition (.90 × $30,200 = $27,180). In a parallel way, minority interest at the date of acquisition equals 10% of total stockholders' equity at the date of acquisition (.10 × $30,200 = $3,020).

The preceding illustration assumed that the subsidiary (Ziebur Corporation) used the *cost method* in recording the initial acquisition of its treasury shares. Had the subsidiary recorded the purchase of treasury shares using the *par value* method, its stockholders' equity would have the following composition on the date of acquisition:

Stockholders' Equity of Subsidiary		
Common stock (1,200 shares × $10)	$12,000	
Less: Treasury stock (200 shares × $10)	2,000	$10,000
Excess over par ($6,000 − $1,000)		5,000
Retained earnings ($16,000 − $800)		15,200
Total stockholders' equity		$30,200

The following worksheet adjustment retires the subsidiary's treasury stock for purposes of consolidation when the par value method was used to record the acquisition of treasury shares:

Worksheet adjustment to retire subsidiary's treasury stock for consolidation purposes:

Common stock 2,000
    Treasury stock.   2,000

The worksheet adjustment required to eliminate and reclassify the parent's investment account would be as follows:

Worksheet adjustment to eliminate and reclassify parent's investment account:

Common stock (.90 × $10,000) 9,000
Excess over par (.90 × $5,000) 4,500
Retained earnings (.90 × $15,200) 13,680
Goodwill *2,820*
        Investment in Ziebur 30,000

This adjustment is identical to the one required when treasury shares were recorded using the cost method.

Goodwill on Subsidiary's Records

At the date of its acquisition, a subsidiary's separate financial statements may show goodwill resulting from earlier transactions of the subsidiary. For purposes of calculating the valuation differential and assigning revaluation increments, such goodwill is assigned a fair value of zero. Thus only one goodwill item for a purchase acquisition is placed on the consolidated balance sheet, and it is calculated by reference to the parent's cost of acquiring the subsidiary (*APB Opinion No. 16*, par. 88). In a pooling of interests, however, goodwill on the subsidiary's records is reported at book value on the consolidated balance sheet.

Differing Fiscal Years of Parent and Subsidiary

Subsidiaries may use an accounting period different from that of their parent to conform with industry practice or to reduce year-end accounting work of the parent. When this occurs, consolidation should use the best available data from the subsidiary giving preference to timely data. In the interests of timeliness, it is usually best to use interim data of the subsidiary to match the parent's fiscal year as closely as possible; however, unreliable interim data may force consolidation of the subsidiary's year-end data just as if the two fiscal year-ends were the same. The difference between year-ends and any material events should be disclosed (*Accounting Research Bulletin No. 51*, par. 4). The SEC will not accept consolidated statements for parents and subsidiaries whose year-ends differ by more than 93 days [17 CFR 210.4.2(a)(2)]; consequently, parent and subsidiary year-ends rarely differ by more than three months.

Comprehensive Illustration

Let us review and summarize consolidation procedures by reference to Platt Corporation's acquisition of an 80% interest in Stern, Inc. On January 1, 19X1, Platt pays $664 in cash for the stock of Stern, which includes both $64 for a dividend declared by Stern (with a date of record following acquisition) and $50 for brokerage fees. Exhibit 2-10 presents the separate balance sheets prepared immediately after the acquisition and the fair values of Stern's assets and liabilities. The intercompany loan of $160 was made prior to the acquisition. Notice that Platt has recorded $600 ($664 − $64) as the acquisition cost of the investment in Stern, which includes the brokerage fees, and has recorded the dividend receivable from Stern ($64) in a separate account. Using this information and the data in Exhibit 2-10, we can prepare the calculation of the valuation differential shown in Exhibit 2-11 and the related diagram shown in Exhibit 2-12 (on page 90).

EXHIBIT 2-10	SEPARATE BALANCE SHEETS IMMEDIATELY AFTER ACQUISITION

BALANCE SHEETS
AT JANUARY 1, 19X1

	Platt Corporation	Stern, Inc.	
	Book Value	**Book Value**	**Fair Value**
Assets			
Cash	$ 86	$ 10	$ 10
Inventory	200	80	75
Dividend receivable from Stern	64		
Note receivable from Stern	160		
Investment in Stern	600		
Plant and equipment (net)	2,200	810	850
Patent			75
Total assets	$3,310	$900	$1,010
Liabilities and Stockholders' Equity			
Accounts payable	$ 180	$ 60	$ 70
Dividends payable		80	80
Notes payable	900	160	160
Common stock	1,100	300	
Treasury stock*		(70)	
Excess over par	400	55	
Retained earnings	730	315	
Total liabilities and stockholders' equity	$3,310	$900	

* Stern uses the par value method for treasury stock.

EXHIBIT 2-11	CALCULATION OF VALUATION DIFFERENTIAL AND GOODWILL

Acquisition cost ($664 − $64)		$600
Less: Book value of net assets acquired		
[($900 − $60 − $80 − $160) × .80]		480
Valuation differential		$120
Less: Revaluation increment:		
Inventories [($75 − $80) × .80]	$ (4)	
Plant and equipment (net) [($850 − $810) × .80]	32	
Patent [($75 × $0) × .80]	60	
Accounts payable [($60 − $70) × .80]	(8)	80
Goodwill		$ 40

EXHIBIT 2-12	ANALYSIS OF VALUATION DIFFERENTIAL FOR NET ASSETS ACQUIRED WITH MINORITY INTEREST

Acquisition cost ($600)	Fair value of identifiable net assets acquired ($560)*	Book value of net assets acquired ($480)†

Goodwill = $40	Revaluation increment = $80

Valuation differential = $120

* $560 = [($10 + $75 + $850 + $75) − ($70 + $80 + $160)] × .80
      = $700 × .80

† $480 = [($10 + $80 + $810) − ($60 + $80 + $160)] × .80
      = $600 × .80

Following the procedures described in the foregoing chapter, four worksheet adjustments are required; the adjustments are shown in Exhibit 2-13. Adjustment (1) eliminates and reclassifies the parent's investment account and is based on information displayed in the analysis of the valuation differential (Exhibit 2-12). Adjustment (2) retires Stern's treasury stock assuming that Stern has employed the par-value method of accounting for

EXHIBIT 2-13	CONSOLIDATION WORKSHEET ADJUSTMENTS

(1) *Worksheet adjustment to eliminate and reclassify parent's investment account:*
Common stock of Stern [($300 − $70*) × .80] 184
Excess over par of Stern ($55 × .80) 44
Retained earnings of Stern ($315 × .80). 252
Plant and equipment (net) *32*
Patent *60*
Goodwill *40*
    Inventory *4*
    Accounts payable *8*
    Investment in Stern 600

(2) *Worksheet adjustment to retire subsidiary's treasury stock for consolidation purposes:*
Common stock 70
    Treasury stock 70

(3) *Worksheet adjustment to eliminate intercompany dividend:*
Dividends payable 64
    Dividend receivable from Stern 64

(4) *Worksheet adjustment to eliminate intercompany loan:*
Notes payable 160
    Notes receivable from Stern 160

* Treasury stock.

treasury stock. Adjustment (3) eliminates the $64 subsidiary dividend payable to the parent; notice that the $16 remainder is included among the consolidated liabilities. Finally, adjustment (4) eliminates the intercompany loan. The consolidation worksheet is shown in Exhibit 2-14. The consolidated balance sheet, which is prepared from the far right-hand column of the worksheet, is shown in Exhibit 2-15 on the following page.

CONCEPTUAL BASIS FOR CONSOLIDATION

Consolidated financial statements bring together the separate financial statements of two companies when one company controls the other. The fundamental conceptual question is whether the form of the consolidated statements should emphasize the controlling company's ownership of the economic entity or the assets and liabilities of the economic entity as a whole. Two theories of financial reporting—the proprietary theory and the entity

EXHIBIT 2-14	CONSOLIDATION OF PARENT AND SUBSIDIARY BALANCE SHEETS AT DATE OF ACQUISITION: COMPREHENSIVE ILLUSTRATION

	Separate Financial Statements		Consolidation Adjustments			Minority Interest	Consolidated Financial Statement
	Platt	Stern	Dr.		Cr.		
Assets							
Cash	86	10					96
Inventory	200	80		(1)	4		276
Dividend receivable from Stern	64			(3)	64		–0–
Note receivable from Stern	160			(4)	160		–0–
Investment in Stern	600			(1)	600		–0–
Plant and equipment (net)	2,200	810	(1)	32			3,042
Patent			(1)	60			60
Goodwill			(1)	40			40
Total assets	3,310	900					3,514
Liabilities and Stockholders' Equity							
Accounts payable	180	60		(1)	8		248
Dividends payable		80	(3)	64			16
Notes payable	900	160	(4)	160			900
Common Stock:							
Platt	1,100						1,100
Stern		300	(1)	184		46	
			(2)	70			
Treasury stock		(70)			(2) 70		–0–
Excess over par:							
Platt	400						400
Stern		55	(1)	44		11	
Retained earnings:							
Platt	730						730
Stern		315	(1)	252		63	
Minority interest						(120)	120
Total liabilities and stockholders' equity	3,310	900		906	906	–0–	3,514

EXHIBIT 2-15	CONSOLIDATED BALANCE SHEET

Platt Corporation

CONSOLIDATED BALANCE SHEET
AT DECEMBER 31, 19X1

Assets

Cash	$ 96
Inventory	276
Plant and equipment (net)	3,042
Patent	60
Goodwill	40
Total assets	$3,514

Liabilities and Stockholders' Equity

Accounts payable	$ 248
Dividends payable	16
Notes payable	900
Minority interest	120
Common stock	1,100
Excess over par	400
Retained earnings	730
Total liabilities and stockholders' equity	$3,514

theory—lead to different answers. The *proprietary theory* emphasizes the ownership of the economic entity by the proprietor. In the context of a multicorporation entity, "proprietor" is translated to mean "controlling stockholder group," usually the stockholders of the parent company. Thus, the proprietary theory separates or excludes the equity interests of minority stockholders and leads to consolidated financial statements that are of primary interest to the parent company's stockholders. The *entity theory* emphasizes the assets and liabilities of the economic entity represented by the totality of the interrelated corporate entities, and the equity interests of minority stockholders are viewed as a component of owners' equity. The entity theory leads to consolidated financial statements that are intended for all parties interested in the economic entity.

The proprietary and entity theories of financial reporting are the basis for several alternative conceptual structures for consolidated financial statements. The conceptual structure that most closely resembles current accounting practice is a hybrid of proprietary and entity concepts called the *parent-company concept of consolidation*. The parent-company concept views the consolidated financial statements as an extension of the parent's financial statements intended to convey better information about the parent's total ownership holdings. Following the parent-company concept, consolidated plant and equipment is determined by adding together the amounts for plant and equipment of the parent and of its subsidiary without any adjustment for the ownership interests of minority (noncontrolling) stockholders in the subsidiary's portion. This practice, which is followed in consolidating all identifiable subsidiary assets and liabilities, is consistent with the entity theory but not with the proprietary theory. The proprietary theory, strictly interpreted, would exclude the portion of assets and liabilities associated with the ownership interests of minority stockholders—a practice followed for goodwill. In contrast to the consolidation of identifiable assets, the consolidation of equity under the parent-company concept takes a step in the direction of proprietary theory. Minority interest in the assets and liabilities of a subsidiary is reported separately and usually removed from the stockholders' equity section of the consolidated balance sheet. Further, it is accounted for on a somewhat different basis than the equity of majority stockholders. Entity theory would view minority interest as an element of consolidated stockholders' equity to be accounted for on the same basis as the equity of majority stockholders.

Of course, a strict interpretation of proprietary theory would exclude minority interest from the consolidated balance sheet just as it would exclude the minority interest's share of assets and liabilities from the consolidated balance sheet. This strict interpretation of proprietary theory is called the *proportionate-consolidation concept*; it is applied to special multiple-company stock arrangements called joint ventures, as described and illustrated in Chapter 8.

A strict interpretation of the entity theory leads to the *economic-unit concept* of consolidation, which is described in detail in Appendix A along with other consolidation concepts. Thus, the consolidation concepts can be traced to the two theories of financial reporting as shown diagrammatically in Exhibit 2-16.

EXHIBIT 2-16	FINANCIAL REPORTING THEORIES, CONSOLIDATION CONCEPTS, AND CONSOLIDATION PRACTICE

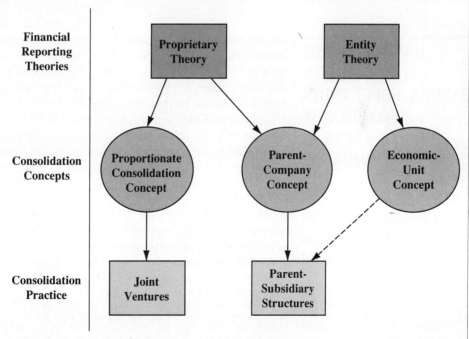

The consolidation of parent and subsidiary financial statements in practice most closely resembles the parent-company concept but also reflects aspects of the economic-unit concept. An understanding of the various concepts of consolidation enhances our appreciation of the conceptual choices made in the design of consolidation standards and practices; however, the parent-company concept is followed throughout this book unless an alternative concept is specifically noted.

SUMMARY

When the acquired company continues to exist and is not liquidated following a business combination, preparation of the date-of-acquisition balance sheet for the combined entity requires a consolidation procedure. Such a consolidation procedure is required whether the combination is a purchase or a pooling of interests. The body of this chapter describes the procedure for purchases, and Appendix B describes the slightly modified procedure for poolings. The consolidation procedure substitutes the detailed assets and liabilities of the subsidiary for the parent's investment account. In addition, the procedure recognizes an item called minority interest when the parent acquires less than 100% of the subsidiary outstanding voting stock. In practice, consolidation usually observes the parent-company concept, which views the consolidated entity as an extension of the parent company. Under this concept, the net assets of the subsidiary are revalued on the date-of-acquisition balance sheet but only to the extent that the valuation differential is reflected in the parent's acquisition cost. This means that minority interest is reported at its book value to the subsidiary. Minority interest is usually reported between long-term liabilities and stockholders' equity. The chapter also considers the impact of intercompany loans, unpaid subsidiary dividends, negative goodwill, and subsidiary treasury stock on date-of-acquisition consolidation procedures.

APPENDIX A: THE CONSOLIDATED BALANCE SHEET UNDER ALTERNATIVE CONCEPTS OF CONSOLIDATION

As noted in the foregoing chapter, alternative conceptions of consolidation are different interpretations of two theories of financial reporting—the proprietary theory and the entity theory. The parent-company concept of consolidation, which most closely resembles accounting practice, is a hybrid of the proprietary and entity theories. The proprietary theory is the basis for the proportionate-consolidation concept, which is sometimes applied to the consolidation of joint ventures as explained in Chapter 8. The entity theory is the basis for the economic-unit concept of consolidation. In the presence of minority interest, the three consolidation concepts produce different consolidated financial statements. The purpose of this appendix is to explain and illustrate these differences based on an expanded analysis of the valuation differential.[9]

An Expanded Analysis of the Valuation Differential

Each consolidation concept leads to a different way of valuing the net assets of the subsidiary on the consolidated balance sheet. In addition, each concept leads to a different way of valuing and reporting minority interest in the subsidiary. In order to understand these different treatments of subsidiary net assets and minority interest, we must compute

[9] Moonitz (1942; 1944, pp. 1–21) and Vatter (1947, pp. 2–10) present classic statements of the proprietary and entity theories and also discussions of other theories of financial reporting (see also Hendriksen and van Breda, 1992, pp. 765–778). Pacter (1991, pp. 23–35) presents a thorough discussion of consolidation concepts (see also Baxter and Spinney, 1975).

a fair value for the entire subsidiary and consider an expanded form of the valuation differential. To illustrate, let us consider Burns Corporation's acquisition for $70,000 cash of a 70% interest in the common stock of Hendrickson, Inc. Exhibit 2-17 presents the relevant financial information.

Fair Value of Entire Subsidiary

The acquisition cost gives the fair value of the parent's interest in its subsidiary and serves as the basis for estimating the fair value of the entire subsidiary. Thus Burns's acquisition cost of $70,000 gives the fair value of 70% of the Hendrickson, Inc., but not the fair value of the remaining 30% held by investors other than Burns, that is, by minority stockholders. If the fractional valuation of $70,000 is appropriately extended in linear fashion, then the total fair value is $100,000 ($70,000 ÷ .70), of which $70,000 is the fair value of Burns Corporation's equity interest and $30,000 is the *implied* fair value of the minority stockholders' interest.

Analysis of the Total Valuation Differential

We can use this extrapolated value to construct the expanded analysis of the valuation differential, called the *total valuation differential*, shown in Exhibit 2-18 on the following page. The exhibit presents three related analyses of the total valuation differential. The middle analysis has the same general form as that presented in the foregoing chapter and represents the portion of the valuation differential related to the parent's 70% interest in the subsidiary. This analysis of the parent's valuation differential is sufficient for consolidation under the parent-company concept. Consolidation under the entity concept, how-

EXHIBIT 2-17	**SEPARATE BALANCE SHEETS IMMEDIATELY AFTER ACQUISITION**		
	Burns Corporation	Hendrickson, Inc.	
	Book Value	Book Value	Fair Value
Assets			
Cash	$ 2,000	$ 1,000	$ 1,000
Accounts receivable	15,000	7,000	7,000
Inventories	24,000	11,000	11,000
Investment in Hendrickson	70,000		
Plant and equipment (net)	89,000	65,000	82,000
Total assets	$200,000	$84,000	$101,000
Liabilities and Stockholders' Equity			
Liabilities	20,000	$ 4,000	$ 4,000
Common stock	100,000	50,000	
Retained earnings	80,000	30,000	
Total liabilities and stockholders' equity	$200,000	$84,000	

EXHIBIT 2-18	ANALYSIS OF THE TOTAL VALUATION DIFFERENTIAL

Analysis of Valuation Differential for Total Net Assets of Subsidiary

Implied fair value of subsidiary ($100,000)*		Fair value of identifiable net assets ($97,000)†		Book value of net assets ($80,000)
	Goodwill = $3,000		Revaluation increment = $17,000	
		Total-subsidiary valuation differential = $20,000		

$$* \ \$100,000 = \$70,000 \div .70$$
$$† \ \$97,000 = \$101,000 - \$4,000$$

Analysis of Valuation Differential for Net Assets Acquired (Parent's Interest)

Acquisition cost ($70,000)		Fair value of identifiable net assets acquired ($67,900)‡		Book value of net assets acquired ($56,000)§
	Goodwill = $2,100		Revaluation increment = $11,900	
		Parent's valuation differential = $14,000		

$$‡ \ \$67,900 = (\$101,000 - \$4,000) \times .70$$
$$= \$97,000 \times .70$$
$$§ \ \$56,000 = (\$80,000 \times .70)$$

Analysis of Valuation Differential for Minority Interest

Minority interest in implied fair value of subsidiary ($30,000)‖		Minority interest in fair value of identifiable net assets ($29,100)#		Minority interest in book value of net assets ($24,000)**
	Goodwill = $900		Revaluation increment = $5,100	
		Minority interest valuation differential = $6,000		

$$‖ \ \$30,0000 = \$100,000 - \$70,000$$
$$= \$100,000 \times .30$$
$$\# \ \$29,100 = \$ \ 97,000 - \$67,900$$
$$= \$ \ 97,000 \times .30$$
$$** \ \$24,000 = \$ \ 80,000 - \$56,000$$
$$= \$ \ 80,000 \times .30$$

ever, requires an analysis of the valuation differential for the entire subsidiary—including both the parent's 70% interest and the 30% minority interest. This analysis of the total-subsidiary valuation differential is presented at the top of Exhibit 2-18. The total-subsidiary valuation differential based on the implied fair value of the entire subsidiary ($100,000) is extrapolated from the cost to the parent of a 70% interest ($100,000 = $70,000 ÷ .70). The fair value of the subsidiary's identifiable net assets ($97,000) is obtained from the fair values in Exhibit 2-17 ($97,000 = $101,000 − $4,000), and the book value of the subsidiary ($80,000) is obtained from its date-of-acquisition balance sheet. The third analysis presented at the bottom of Exhibit 2-18, which pertains to the minority interest, is calculated by simply subtracting each number in the analysis of the parent's valuation differential from the corresponding number in the analysis of the total-subsidiary valuation differential.

We turn now to a demonstration of the concepts of consolidation using the expanded analysis of the valuation differential.

Proportionate-Consolidation Concept

The proportionate-consolidation concept, which derives from the proprietary theory of financial reporting, defines the consolidated entity narrowly in terms of the parent company's ownership equity. The consolidated balance sheet for Burns Corporation prepared using proportionate consolidation is shown in the first column of Exhibit 2-19. Proportion-

EXHIBIT 2-19	CONSOLIDATED BALANCE SHEETS UNDER THREE CONCEPTS OF CONSOLIDATION

Burns Corporation
CONSOLIDATED BALANCE SHEETS
AT DATE OF ACQUISITION

	Proportionate-Consolidation Concept	Parent-Company Concept	Economic-Unit Concept
Assets			
Cash	$ 2,700	$ 3,000	$ 3,000
Accounts receivable	19,900	22,000	22,000
Inventories	31,700	35,000	35,000
Plant and equipment (net)	146,400	165,900	171,000
Goodwill	2,100	2,100	3,000
Total assets	$202,800	$228,000	$234,000
Liabilities and Stockholders' Equity			
Liabilities	$ 22,800	$ 24,000	$ 24,000
Minority interest		24,000	
Common stock	100,000	100,000	100,000
Retained earnings	80,000	80,000	80,000
Minority interest			30,000
Total liabilities and stockholders' equity	$202,800	$228,000	$234,000

ate consolidation substitutes for the investment account 70% of the fair value of each of Hendrickson's assets and liabilities. Since the total of the substituted fair values equals the investment account, no provision is made for minority interest in the consolidated balance sheet.

The principal characteristics of the proportionate-consolidation balance sheet are listed in Exhibit 2-20. The most striking characteristic is that proportionate consolidation leads to reporting fractional assets and fractional liabilities on the consolidated balance sheet (see item 1 in Exhibit 2-20). For example, as illustrated in Exhibit 2-19, consolidated cash would include only 70% of the subsidiary's cash [$2,700 = $2,000 + (.70 × $1,000)] and consolidated plant and equipment includes only 70% of the fair value of every element of the subsidiary's plant and equipment [$146,400 = $89,000 + (.70 ×

EXHIBIT 2-20	DIFFERENCES AMONG DATE-OF-ACQUISITION BALANCE SHEETS PREPARED UNDER DIFFERENT CONSOLIDATION CONCEPTS		
Balance Sheet Characteristic	**Concepts of Consolidation**		
	Proportionate-Consolidation	**Parent-Company**	**Economic-Unit**
1. Description of consolidated assets and liabilities	The parent's assets and liabilities aggregated with the parent's share only of the subsidiary assets and liabilities	The parent's assets and liabilities aggregated with the subsidiary assets and liabilities	The parent's assets and liabilities aggregated with the subsidiary assets and liabilities
2. Classification of minority interest	Minority interest excluded	Between liabilities and owners' equity	An element of owners' equity
3. Valuation of parent's assets and liabilities	Book value to parent	Book value to parent	Book value to parent
4. Valuation of subsidiary's *identifiable* assets and liabilities	Fair value of parent share only (acquisition cost to parent)	Fair value of parent share plus book value of minority-interest share[*]	Implied fair value of both parent and minority-interest shares[**]
5. Valuation of goodwill	Recognize only purchased goodwill	Recognize only purchased goodwill	Recognize total implied goodwill
6. Valuation of minority interest	Minority interest excluded	Book value to subsidiary[*]	Implied fair value

[*] A departure from the parent-company concept is allowed in practice wherein both parent and minority-interest shares of the subsidiary's net assets are valued at fair value, which is the same amount assigned to the subsidiary's net assets under the economic-unit concept. If this procedure is followed, of course, minority interest is based on the fair value of identifiable net assets rather than the book value of the subsidiary's identifiable net assets. Although this procedure is allowed in practice, the parent-company concept as described in the table above (which reports minority interest at its book value to the subsidiary) is followed throughout this book, unless specifically noted otherwise.

[**] A variation of the economic-unit concept reports the implied fair value for identifiable assets and liabilities but reports only the purchased portion of goodwill; this variation reports the same date-of-acquisition consolidated net asset amounts as reported under the practice-sanctioned departure from the parent-company concept described in the preceding footnote.

$82,000)]. Some accountants argue that it does not make sense to report 70% of an asset—particularly an asset like a building that is not divisible into small parts. Equity interests are divisible because they are divided into shares that can be held or traded in varying numbers. However, assets like buildings cannot be subdivided but must be sold or used in their entirety.

The proportionate-consolidation balance sheet is also striking because it excludes minority interest; only the parent's ownership interests are represented in consolidated owners' equity.

Economic-Unit Concept

Emphasizing control rather than ownership, the economic-unit concept defines the consolidated entity broadly to include all assets and liabilities. The principal characteristics of the economic-unit concept balance sheet are listed in Exhibit 2-20. Minority stockholders are viewed as owners of the consolidated entity, and minority interest is reported as an element of consolidated owners' equity (see item 2 in Exhibit 2-20).[10] The consolidated balance sheet for Burns Corporation prepared using the economic-unit concept is shown in the right-most column of Exhibit 2-19. The economic-unit concept of consolidation replaces the investment account with the implied fair value of the entire subsidiary, consolidating the full amount of the subsidiary's assets and liabilities (recall that proportionate consolidation recognized just the parent's share). For example, consolidated plant and equipment ($171,000) is the sum of the parent's book value and 100% of the subsidiary's fair value ($171,000 = $89,000 + $82,000). Thus, the economic-unit concept is a "full consolidation concept" requiring minority interest in the subsidiary's net assets to be reported. Since Hendrickson's fair value exceeds the investment account by $30,000 (representing the fair value of the minority interest), the consolidated balance sheet reports minority interest of $30,000 as an element of stockholders' equity.

Although the economic-unit concept of consolidation avoids the problem of reporting fractional assets and liabilities, it forces reliance on an implied fair value for the subsidiary calculated by extrapolation from the parent's acquisition cost. Accountants are reluctant to recognize such implied values because implied values are inconsistent with cost-based accounting and may be unreliable indicators of market value.

Parent-Company Concept

Among the three alternative concepts, the parent-company concept most closely resembles consolidation practice. Like the economic-unit concept, the parent-company concept is a "full consolidation concept" that avoids the problem of fractional assets; but unlike the economic-unit concept, it stops short of reporting the full fair value of such net assets.

---

[10] Moonitz (1944, pp. 88–89) presents the following argument against the treatment of minority interest as a liability: "The tendency to view minority interest as a liability is clearly undesirable and the practice is logically indefensible. No obligation, as that term is used in connection with debts, exists to pay off the outside shareholders beyond the general right to demand that their vested interest in the *subsidiary* be respected. A claim of this nature is undoubtedly important; but it is not a debt or liability in the accounting sense." Accepting the economic-unit viewpoint, *FASB Statement of Financial Accounting Concepts No. 6* (par. 254) argues against treating minority interest as a liability; instead, both the economic-unit concept and the concepts statement favor treating minority interest as an element of owners' equity, provided that it is separately identified as indicating the portion of consolidated net assets that is not assignable to the majority stockholders. As explained in the next section, most consolidation practice follows the parent-company concept by presenting minority interest between the long-term liability and stockholders' equity sections of the consolidated balance sheet.

The consolidated statements are viewed as an extension of the parent's financial statements. Thus, the parent's perspective dominates the classification and measurement of minority interest in the subsidiary. The minority (noncontrolling) shareholders are viewed as outsiders whose interest in the consolidated entity is not an ownership interest but is akin to a liability and appropriately stated at its book value to the subsidiary.

Exhibit 2-21 shows diagrammatically the differing net asset values reported under the range of consolidation concepts considered in this text. This range of valuation alterna-

EXHIBIT 2-21	VALUATION OF SUBSIDIARY NET ASSETS UNDER THREE CONSOLIDATION CONCEPTS

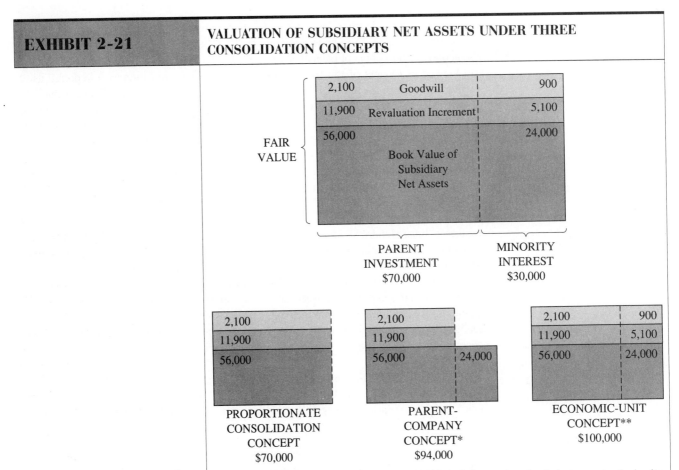

* A departure from the parent-company concept is allowed in practice wherein both parent and minority-interest shares of the subsidiary's net assets are valued at fair value, which is the same amount assigned to the subsidiary's net assets under the economic-unit concept. If this procedure is followed, of course, minority interest is based on the fair value of identifiable net assets rather than the book value of the subsidiary's identifiable net assets. In the Burns-Hendrickson example, this variation adds $5,100 to both consolidated net assets and minority interest. Although this procedure is allowed in practice, the parent-company concept as portrayed in the diagram above (wherein minority-interest is reported at its book value to the subsidiary) is followed throughout this book, unless specifically noted otherwise.

** A variation of the economic-unit concept reports the implied fair value for identifiable assets and liabilities but reports only the purchased portion of goodwill; this variation reports the same date-of-acquisition consolidated net asset amounts as reported under the practice-sanctioned departure from the parent-company concept described in the preceding footnote.

tives is a useful backdrop against which to explain net asset valuation under the parent-company concept and under the variations of that concept found in practice. In addition, the diagram shows the relationship between differing net asset valuations and the valuation of minority interest. Let us begin with the proportionate-consolidation concept under which the $70,000 investment account is replaced with net assets valued at $70,000 and no minority interest is reported. Accordingly, the proportionate-consolidation diagram in Exhibit 2-21 omits all three components of the minority interest in the subsidiary's net assets. The economic-unit concept procedure replaces the $70,000 investment account with net assets valued at $100,000, the implied fair value of the entire subsidiary, and $30,000 ($100,000 − $70,000) is reported for minority interest. Thus the economic-unit concept diagram in Exhibit 2-21 includes all three components of minority interest in the subsidiary's net assets, showing that the parent interest and the minority interest in the subsidiary are accounted for on the same basis. The parent-company concept replaces the $70,000 investment account with net assets valued at $94,000. Consequently, $24,000 ($94,000 − $70,000) must be reported for minority interest. Thus the parent-company diagram in Exhibit 2-21 omits the two components of minority interest associated with goodwill and the revaluation of identifiable net assets but includes the component associated with the book value of subsidiary net assets.

The principal features of the parent-company concept are summarized in the middle column of Exhibit 2-20. Under all three concepts, the parent's net assets are consolidated at their book values (row 3 of Exhibit 2-20). The three concepts differ, however, in the way they consolidate the subsidiary's net assets. Under the parent-company concept, the identifiable net assets of the subsidiary are reported in the date-of-acquisition consolidated balance sheet at the fair value of the parent's share (which includes the parent's share of the revaluation increment) plus the book value of the minority-interest share (row 4 of Exhibit 2-20). As in proportionate consolidation, only purchased goodwill (the parent's share of goodwill) is recognized (row 5 of Exhibit 2-20). To illustrate, consider the $165,900 for plant and equipment reported by the parent-company consolidated balance sheet in Exhibit 2-19. This amount is the sum of the book value of the parent's plant and equipment ($89,000), the fair value of the parent's share of subsidiary plant and equipment ($57,400 = .70 × $82,000), and the book value of the minority interest's share of subsidiary plant and equipment ($19,500 = .30 × $65,000). Goodwill is $2,100, the amount of purchased goodwill. Notice that minority interest ($24,000) is reported between liabilities and stockholders' equity on the parent-company balance sheet in Exhibit 2-19.

Current Practice   Although the parent-company concept closely resembles current accounting practice, current practice departs from the parent-company concept in several ways. First, the parent-company concept is frequently interpreted to require consolidation of all majority-owned investees and use of the equity or cost method for all other investees. In contrast, as noted in the foregoing chapter, current practice sanctions consolidation for less-than-majority-owned investees when control is present and also supports use of the equity or cost method for majority-owned investees when control is temporary or does not reside with the majority owners.

A second departure of current practice from the parent-company concept concerns the valuation of the subsidiary's identifiable assets and liabilities and the related valuation of minority interest. Under the parent-company concept, the subsidiary's identifiable assets and liabilities are valued at a mixture of fair value and book value on the date-of-acquisition consolidated balance sheet, as explained in row 4 of Exhibit 2-20; thus minority interest is reported at its book value (see row 6 of Exhibit 2-20). Current standards, which are ambiguous on this point, permit an alternative procedure that values the subsidiary's identifiable assets and liabilities at their total fair value, which then becomes the basis for valuing minority interest. Although this alternative procedure sees some use in practice (see *FASB Discussion Memorandum*, 1976, p. 107), we account for minority interest at book value throughout this text unless specifically stated otherwise.

Additional differences between current practice and the parent-company concept, including differences related to consolidated income and multiple-step acquisitions, are discussed in later chapters.

APPENDIX B: DATE-OF-ACQUISITION CONSOLIDATION PROCEDURES FOR POOLINGS OF INTERESTS WITH MINORITY INTEREST

The consolidation procedures required for poolings of interests are somewhat simpler than those required for purchases owing to the absence of the valuation differential. Let us illustrate these procedures by reference to a pooling of interests that leaves a minority interest in the subsidiary. Exhibit 2-22 contains the separate balance sheets of Corporation PY and Corporation SY prepared on January 1, 19X1. Corporation PY issues 200 shares of common stock ($3 par value) in exchange for 95% of the outstanding common shares of SY. The transaction is a business combination that qualifies as a pooling of interests. Consequently, Corporation PY records the pooling of interests with the following entry:

Entry by PY to record acquisition of SY's stock with newly issued shares of PY's stock:

Investment in SY	950	
Common stock (200 × $3)		600
Excess over par ($665 − $600)		65
Retained earnings (.95 × $300)		285

EXHIBIT 2-22	SEPARATE BALANCE SHEETS IMMEDIATELY AFTER ACQUISITION

BALANCE SHEETS
AT JANUARY 1, 19X1

	Corporation PY	Corporation SY
Assets		
Current assets	$ 600	$ 400
Investment in SY	950	
Plant and equipment (net)	2,450	1,200
Total assets	$4,000	$1,600
Liabilities and Stockholders' Equity		
Liabilities	$ 750	$ 600
Common stock	1,500	500
Excess over par	465	200
Retained earnings	1,285	300
Total liabilities and stockholders' equity	$4,000	$1,600

Observe that the investment in SY is recorded by PY at its book value [$950 = .95 × ($500 + $200 + $300)]. Following pooling-of-interests accounting, the stockholders' equity accounts of PY are increased by PY's share of the corresponding accounts of SY. PY's share of SY's retained earnings is $285 (.95 × $300). PY's share of SY's contributed capital accounts is $665 [.95 × ($500 + $200)]. Since the newly issued shares of PY create a par value of $600 (200 × $3), $600 of PY's share in SY's contributed capital is classified as common stock and the $65 remainder ($65 = $665 − $600) is classified as excess over par.

Consolidation Adjustments and Worksheet

The consolidation worksheet adjustment, which follows, eliminates the investment account and the related stockholders' equity:

(1) *Worksheet adjustment to eliminate parent's investment account:*

Common stock of SY (.95 × $500) 475
Excess over par of SY (.95 × $200) 190
Retained earnings (.95 × $300)................................ 285
    Investment in SY   950

Note that the foregoing elimination adjustment is *not* a simple reversal of PY's entry to record the investment. The consolidation worksheet is given in Exhibit 2-23.

EXHIBIT 2-23	POOLING OF INTERESTS CONSOLIDATION OF BALANCE SHEETS AT DATE OF ACQUISITION					

	Separate Financial Statements		Consolidation Adjustments		Minority Interest	Consolidated Financial Statement
	PY	SY	Dr.	Cr.		
Assets						
Current assets	600	400				1,000
Investment in SY	950			(1) 950		–0–
Plant and equipment (net)	2,450	1,200				3,650
Total assets	4,000	1,600				4,650
Liabilities and Stockholders' Equity						
Liabilities	750	600				1,350
Common stock:						
Corporation PY	1,500					1,500
Corporation SY		500	(1) 475		25	
Excess over par:						
Corporation PY	465					465
Corporation SY		200	(1) 190		10	
Retained earnings:						
Corporation PY	1,285					1,285
Corporation SY		300	(1) 285		15	
Minority interest					(50)	50
Total liabilities and stockholders' equity	4,000	1,600	950	950	–0–	4,650

Transactions between Companies under Common Control

Business combinations bring together, in a single entity, two or more formerly separate companies. Pooling-of-interests accounting should be used for business combinations that meet all the conditions described in Appendix A of Chapter 1. Pooling-of-interests accounting is also appropriate for a number of transactions between companies under a common control that do not qualify as business combinations. Consider the following examples: (1) a parent transfers the net assets of a wholly owned subsidiary into the parent company and liquidates the subsidiary; (2) a parent transfers some of its net assets to a newly formed subsidiary; and (3) a parent exchanges some of its net assets or some of its shares in a wholly owned subsidiary for shares issued by a partially owned subsidiary, thereby increasing its ownership in the latter but leaving minority interests unaffected.[11] No outsiders are involved in any of these transactions; consequently, they do not bring together previously separate entities and do not qualify as poolings of interests. In such cases, accounting standards provide that the assets and liabilities so transferred "be accounted for at historical cost in a manner similar to that in pooling of interests accounting" (*AICPA Accounting Interpretations of APB Opinion No. 16*, Interpretation No. 39).

SELECTED READINGS

AAA Committee on Concepts and Standards. "Consolidated Financial Statements," *Supplementary Statement No. 7*. American Accounting Association, 1954.

Accountants' International Study Group. *Consolidated Financial Statements: Current Recommended Practices in Canada, the United Kingdom, and the United States*. Plaistow, England: Curwen Press, 1973.

AICPA Accounting Standards Division, Task Force on Consolidation Problems. "Certain Issues That Affect Accounting for Minority Interest in Consolidated Financial Statements," *Issues Paper*. New York: American Institute of Certified Public Accountants, March 17, 1981.

Baxter, George C., and James C. Spinney. "A Closer Look at Consolidated Financial Statement Theory," *CA Magazine* (Canada) (January 1975), pp. 31–36; and (February 1975), pp. 31–35.

Bierman, Harold, Jr. "Proportionate Consolidation and Financial Analysis," *Accounting Horizons* (December 1992), pp. 5–17.

Byrd, Clarence. *Business Combinations and Long-Term Investments: The Canadian View*, 2nd ed. The Society of Management Accountants of Canada, 1979.

Campbell, J. D. "Consolidation vs. Combination," *The Accounting Review* (January 1969), pp. 99–102.

Colley, J. Ron, and Ara G. Volkan. "Accounting for Goodwill," *Accounting Horizons* (March 1988), pp. 35–41.

DeMoville, Wig, and A. George Petrie. "Accounting for a Bargain Purchase in a Business Combination," *Accounting Horizons* (September 1989), pp. 38–43.

Grinyer, J. R., A. Russell, and M. Walker. "The Rationale for Accounting for Goodwill," *British Accounting Review* (September 1990), pp. 223–235.

[11] If the effect of a transfer or exchange is to acquire all or part of the minority interest in a subsidiary, then the transaction is between entities under a common control (because outsiders are involved) and purchase accounting is appropriate. This conclusion holds whether the minority shares are acquired by the parent, the subsidiary itself, or another affiliate (*APB Opinion No. 16*, par. 34; see *AICPA Accounting Interpretations of APB Opinion No. 16*, Interpretation No. 26, for discussion of a rare exception in which pooling-of-interests treatment would be allowed).

Heian, James B., and James B. Thies. "Consolidation of Finance Subsidiaries: $230 Billion in Off-Balance-Sheet Financing Comes Home to Roost," *Accounting Horizons* (March 1989), pp. 1–9.

Hendriksen, Eldon S., and Michael F. van Breda. *Accounting Theory*, 5th ed. Homewood, IL: Richard D. Irwin, 1992.

Husband, George R. "The Corporate-Entity Fiction and Accounting Theory," *The Accounting Review* (September 1938), pp. 241–253.

Hylton, Delmer P. "On the Usefulness of Consolidated Financial Statements," *The CPA Journal* (October 1988), pp. 74–77.

Mohr, Rosanne M. "Unconsolidated Finance Subsidiaries: Characteristics and Debt/Equity Effects," *Accounting Horizons* (March 1988), pp. 27–34.

Moonitz, Maurice. "The Entity Approach to Consolidated Statements," *The Accounting Review* (July 1942), pp. 236–242.

Moonitz, Maurice. *The Entity Theory of Consolidated Statements*. American Accounting Association, 1944. Reprinted Brooklyn: The Foundation Press, 1951; New York: Arno Press, 1978.

Neuhausen, Benjamin S. "Consolidated Financial Statements and Joint Venture Accounting," Chap. 15 in *Handbook of International Accounting*, Frederick D. S. Choi (ed.). New York: John Wiley, 1991.

Ordway, Nicholas, and Jacqualyn A. Fouse. "New Rules for Allocating the Purchase Price of a Business," *Management Accounting* (May 1988), pp. 50–53.

Pacter, Paul. *An Analysis of Issues Related to Consolidation Policies and Procedures*, Financial Accounting Standards Board Discussion Memorandum. Norwalk, CT: Financial Accounting Standards Board, September 10, 1991.

Price Waterhouse. *A Survey and Analysis of Consolidations/Equity Accounting Practices in Australia, Canada, France, Germany, Italy, Japan, The Netherlands, United Kingdom*. New York: Price Waterhouse, November 1990.

Rezaee, Azbihollah. "The Impact of New Accounting Rules on the Consolidation of Financial Statements of Multinational Companies," *The International Journal of Accounting*, 26:3 (1991), pp. 206–219.

Rosenfield, Paul, and Steven Rubin. "Minority Interest: Opposing Views," *Journal of Accountancy* (March 1986), pp. 78–89.

Sharp, Andrew D., and James H. Thompson. "SFAS 94: The Prodigal Son Becomes Part of the Family Picture," *The CPA Journal* (February 1989), pp. 40–44.

Vatter, William J. *The Fund Theory of Accounting and Its Implications for Financial Reports*. Chicago: The University of Chicago Press, 1947.

QUESTIONS

Q2-1 Define the following terms:

a) Parent company

b) Subsidiary company

c) Controlling interest

d) Direct ownership in a company

e) Indirect ownership in a company

f) Minority interest

Q2-2   Explain why you agree or disagree with the following statement: When the acquiring company acquires a controlling interest in the acquired company, the preparation of combined statements requires a consolidation procedure regardless of whether the acquired company liquidates or continues in existence after the acquisition.

Q2-3   When the investing company acquires less than 100% of the investee company, what determines whether or not consolidation is appropriate?

Q2-4   If P owns 40% of S and 30% of R, which owns in turn 50% of S, what percentage of ownership does P have in S?

Q2-5   Explain why you agree or disagree with the following statement: In general, a controlling interest of the parent company in the subsidiary company gives the parent the ability to influence, but not to control, the subsidiary's operating and financing policies.

Q2-6   Discuss the circumstances under which an investor and investee might consolidate even though the investor owns less than 50% of the investee voting stock.

Q2-7   Describe two exceptions to the requirement of *FASB Statement No. 94* that all majority-owned subsidiaries be consolidated.

Q2-8   Under what circumstances will a minority interest exist in the net assets of the subsidiary? What are some of the titles used to describe minority interest, and where on the consolidated balance sheet might minority interest be classified?

Q2-9   Under the parent-company concept of consolidation, does minority interest appearing on the consolidated balance sheet represent minority interest in the fair value of the subsidiary net assets or the book value of the subsidiary net assets?

Q2-10   Consolidation worksheet adjustments are classified into two fundamentally different types. Identify and briefly describe these two types.

Q2-11   Are consolidation worksheet adjustments entered on the company records of the parent or subsidiary? Explain.

Q2-12   What is the purpose of preparing consolidated financial statements?

Q2-13   Explain why you agree or disagree with the following statement: Consolidated net income is a reliable indicator of the income available for payment of dividends by the parent.

Q2-14   When consolidated financial statements are being prepared, what accounting treatment is accorded intercompany transactions such as intercompany loans?

Q2-15   If there is treasury stock on the books of the subsidiary at the date the parent acquires an interest in the subsidiary, what accounting treatment is accorded the treasury shares in the preparation of consolidated statements?

Q2-16   If the subsidiary declared cash dividends prior to the parent's acquisition, what impact, if any, would the declared dividends have on the parent's recording of the investment?

Q2-17   If the parent paid less than book value for all the outstanding common stock of the subsidiary and the subsidiary's book values reflected fair values, how would the excess fair value over cost be handled in the preparation of the consolidated balance sheet?

Q2-18   Discuss the basic difference between the proprietary theory and the entity theory of financial reporting, and explain how the adoption of each would affect the form of the consolidated financial statements.

Q2-19 Briefly describe the parent-company concept of consolidation, and discuss why it is considered a hybrid of the proprietary and entity concepts of financial reporting.

QUESTIONS FOR APPENDIX A

Q2-20 In the consolidation of a partially owned subsidiary, the parent's investment account is replaced with the subsidiary net assets. Briefly describe the difference in the valuation of subsidiary net assets under each of the following concepts of consolidation:

a) Proportionate-consolidation concept

b) Economic-unit concept of consolidation

c) Parent-company concept of consolidation.

Q2-21 Describe how minority interest is measured and classified on the consolidated balance sheet under the proportionate-consolidation concept, parent-company concept, and economic-unit concept of consolidation.

QUESTION FOR APPENDIX B

Q2-22 Explain why you agree or disagree with the following statement: The consolidation procedures for poolings of interests are very simple because the consolidation worksheet adjustment to eliminate the parent's investment account is always a reversal of the parent's entry to record the investment.

EXERCISES

E2-1 **Record Investment, Consolidation Adjustment** Pointer Company acquired for cash 2,200 shares of the common stock of Setter Company on December 31, 19X9, for $115 per share. On the acquisition date, the stockholders' equity section of Setter's balance sheet consisted of the following:

Common stock ($35 par)	$ 77,000
Retained earnings	156,600

It was agreed by both Pointer and Setter that Setter's building and land were undervalued by $8,000 and $7,000, respectively.

REQUIRED

a) Prepare the entry to record Pointer's investment in Setter.

b) What percentage of Setter's common shares was acquired by Pointer?

c) Prepare in journal entry form the consolidation worksheet adjustment at the date of acquisition to eliminate the investment of Pointer in Setter.

d) Assuming Pointer acquired 1,980 shares of the voting stock of Setter and not 2,200 shares:

1. Prepare the entry to record Pointer's investment in Setter.

2. What percentage of Setter's common shares was acquired by Pointer?

3. Prepare in journal entry form the consolidation worksheet adjustment at the date of acquisition to eliminate Pointer's investment in Setter.

E2-2 **Direct and Indirect Ownership** The following diagram presents the various ownership interests in Perch Company and Croaker Company.

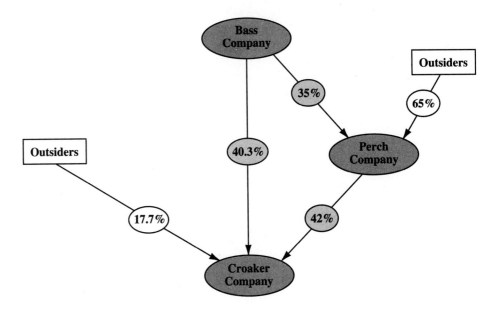

REQUIRED

a) Determine the percentage of ownership that Bass Company has in Croaker Company. Should the financial statements of Bass and Croaker be consolidated?

b) For purposes of your answer to this requirement only, assume Bass and Croaker consolidate. Determine the total minority interest percentage that would appear on consolidated statements, and identify the percentages represented by the stockholders of Perch and the stockholders of Croaker.

E2-3   Unconsolidated Subsidiaries   Generally accepted accounting principles require that all majority-owned subsidiaries be consolidated.

REQUIRED
Discuss two exceptions to the above requirement sanctioned by *FASB Statement No. 94*.

E2-4   Limitations of Consolidated Statements   Consolidated financial statements are prepared primarily for use by stockholders and creditors of the parent company. The assumption is that consolidated statements are more useful than separate financial statements. Consolidated statements, however, do not serve all the purposes for which separate financial statements may be used.

REQUIRED
Discuss several limitations of consolidated financial statements.

√ **E2-5** **Consolidation Adjustments, Minority Interest, Consolidated Assets** Company A purchased 90% of the common stock of Company B. The book values of B's assets and liabilities are equal to their fair values. The balance sheets of both companies immediately after the acquisition are presented as follows:

	Company A	Company B
Assets		
Cash	$ 25,000	$20,000
Accounts receivable	45,000	15,000
Inventory	30,000	25,000
Investment in Company B	57,000	
Total assets	$157,000	$60,000
Liabilities and Stockholders' Equity		
Accounts payable	$ 40,000	$10,000
Common stock ($30 par)	60,000	30,000
Excess over par	20,000	10,000
Retained earnings	37,000	10,000
Total liabilities and stockholders' equity	$157,000	$60,000

REQUIRED

Using the preceding information, answer the following questions based on Company A and its subsidiary consolidating at the date of acquisition. Each question is to be answered in light of the answer to the previous question(s):

1. Determine the amount of minority interest.

2. Assuming $5,000 of the accounts payable of A are obligations to B, what adjustment would you make on the consolidation worksheet?

3. Record in journal entry form the consolidation worksheet adjustment to eliminate A's investment in B.

4. Determine the total consolidated assets.

E2-6 **Multiple Choice Questions on Consolidations**

1. Which of the following is the best theoretical justification for consolidated financial statements?

  a) In form the companies are one entity; in substance they are separate.

  b) In form the companies are separate; in substance they are one entity.

  c) In form and substance the companies are one entity.

  d) In form and substance the companies are separate.

2. On April 1, 19X8, Dart Co. paid $620,000 for all the issued and outstanding common stock of Wall Corp. in a transaction properly accounted for as a purchase. The recorded assets and liabilities of Wall Corp. on April 1, 19X8, follow:

Cash	$ 60,000
Inventory	180,000
Property and equipment (net of accumulated depreciation of $220,000)	320,000
Goodwill (net of accumulated amortization of $50,000)	100,000
Liabilities	(120,000)
Net assets	$540,000

On April 1, 19X8, Wall's inventory had a fair value of $150,000, and the property and equipment (net) had a fair value of $380,000. What is the amount of goodwill resulting from the business combination?

   a) $150,000

   b) $120,000

   c) $ 50,000

   d) $ 20,000

3. P's cost of investment in M exceeded its equity in the book value of M's net assets at the acquisition date. The excess is not attributable to specific assets. In the consolidated statements, this excess should be

   a) Eliminated

   b) Allocated proportionately to the subsidiary's noncurrent assets

   c) Shown on the balance sheet as a liability from consolidation

   d) Shown on the balance sheet as an excess of cost of stock of the subsidiary over book value (goodwill)

4. P's cost of investment in J was less than its equity in the book value of J's net assets at the acquisition date. The difference is related to the decline in value of J's machinery. In the consolidated statements, this difference should be shown on the balance sheet as

   a) A reduction in machinery

   b) Goodwill

   c) An addition to machinery

   d) An excess of book value over purchase price

5. Meredith Company and Kyle Company were combined in a purchase transaction. Meredith was able to acquire Kyle at a bargain price. The sum of the market or appraised values of identifiable assets acquired less the fair value of liabilities assumed exceeded the cost to Meredith. After noncurrent assets were revalued to zero, there was still some "negative goodwill." Proper accounting treatment by Meredith is to report the amount as

   a) An extraordinary item

   b) Part of current income in the year of combination

   c) A deferred credit

   d) Paid-in capital

6. Fast Corporation paid $50,000 cash for the net assets of Agge Company, which consisted of the following:

	Book Value	Fair Value
Current assets	$10,000	$14,000
Plant and equipment	40,000	55,000
Liabilities assumed	(10,000)	(9,000)
	$40,000	$60,000

The plant and equipment acquired in this business combination should be recorded at

   a) $55,000

   b) $50,000

   c) $45,833

   d) $45,000

7. Consolidated statements are proper for Neely, Inc., Randle, Inc., and Walker, Inc., if

   a) Neely owns 80% of the outstanding common stock of Randle and 40% of Walker; Randle owns 30% of Walker

b) Neely owns 100% of the outstanding common stock of Randle and 90% of Walker; Neely bought the stock of Walker one month before the balance sheet date and sold it seven weeks later

c) Neely owns 100% of the outstanding common stock of Randle and Walker; Walker is in legal reorganization

d) Neely owns 80% of the outstanding common stock of Randle and 40% of Walker; Reeves, Inc., owns 55% of Walker

(AICPA adapted)

E2-7   **Record Investment, Consolidation Adjustment, Minority Interest**   On November 1, 19X9, AB purchased, in the open market, 765 shares (85%) of the common stock of CD at $210 per share. The balances in CD's common stock ($50 par) and retained earnings were $45,000 and $125,000, respectively. The book values of CD's assets and liabilities reflected fair values except for land, which had a book value of $10,000 and a fair value of $16,000.

REQUIRED

a) Prepare the entry to record AB's investment in CD.

b) Prepare in journal entry form the consolidation worksheet adjustment to eliminate AB's investment in CD at the date of acquisition.

c) Determine minority interest at the date of acquisition.

E2-8   **Record Investment, Consolidation Adjustment, Minority Interest**   Eagle, Inc., acquired 75% of the common stock of Robin Company on September 1, 19X9, for $204,750. On the date of acquisition, the book values and fair values of the assets and liabilities of Robin were as follows:

	Book Value	Fair Value
Assets		
Cash	$ 35,000	$ 35,000
Accounts receivable	30,000	28,000
Inventory	110,000	140,000
Plant and equipment (net)	100,000	80,000
Total assets	$275,000	$283,000
Liabilities and Stockholders' Equity		
Accounts payable	$ 20,000	$ 14,000
Common stock ($25 par)	200,000	
Excess over par	40,000	
Retained earnings	15,000	
Total liabilities and stockholders' equity	$275,000	

REQUIRED

a) Prepare the entry to record Eagle's investment in Robin.

b) Prepare in journal entry form the consolidation worksheet adjustment to eliminate Eagle's investment in Robin at the date of acquisition.

c) Determine minority interest at the date of acquisition.

E2-9   **Consolidation Adjustment, Consolidated Balance Sheet**   The CPA Company acquired 90% of the outstanding common stock of CMA Company on August 1, 19X7. The balance sheets for both companies immediately after acquisition are shown below. The entire valuation differential is attributable to goodwill.

	CPA Company	CMA Company
Assets		
Cash	$ 118,749	$ 53,758
Accounts receivable	306,115	126,718
Inventory	217,843	96,810
Investment in CMA	300,000	
Plant and equipment (net)	457,293	232,152
Total assets	$1,400,000	$509,438
Liabilities and Stockholders' Equity		
Accounts payable	$ 172,953	$ 83,308
Notes payable	190,000	106,130
Common stock ($10 par)	800,000	200,000
Retained earnings	237,047	120,000
Total liabilities and stockholders' equity	$1,400,000	$509,438

REQUIRED

a) Prepare in journal entry form the consolidation worksheet adjustment to eliminate CPA's investment in CMA.

b) Prepare a consolidated balance sheet as of August 1, 19X7.

E2-10 **Consolidation Adjustment** Ace Corporation acquired all the common stock of Deuce Company in the open market on January 1, 19X7. At the time of acquisition, it was agreed by both companies that Deuce's book values were equal to their fair values except for accounts receivable and inventory, which were overvalued by $5,000 and $10,000, respectively. The balance sheets of the two firms immediately after acquisition are as follows:

	Ace Corporation	Deuce Corporation
Assets		
Cash	$157,000	$ 97,000
Accounts receivable	214,000	152,000
Inventory	169,000	106,000
Land	85,000	50,000
Investment in long-term marketable securities	219,000	78,000
Investment in Deuce	123,000	
Total assets	$967,000	$483,000
Liabilities and Stockholders' Equity		
Accounts payable	$208,000	$154,000
Notes payable	163,000	136,000
Bonds payable	200,000	
Common stock	300,000	100,000
Retained earnings	96,000	93,000
Total liabilities and stockholders' equity	$967,000	$483,000

REQUIRED

Prepare in journal entry form the consolidation worksheet adjustment at the date of acquisition to eliminate Ace's investment in Deuce.

E2-11 **Multiple Choice Questions on Consolidation**

1. Consolidated statements are intended, primarily, for the benefit of
   a) Stockholders and creditors of the parent company
   b) Taxing authorities
   c) Management of the parent company
   d) Minority stockholders of the subsidiary company

2. A consolidated statement for X, Y, and Z is proper if
   a) X owns 100% of the outstanding common stock of Y and 49% of Z; Q owns 51% of Z
   b) X owns 100% of the outstanding common stock of Y; Y owns 75% of Z
   c) There is no interrelation of financial control among X, Y, and Z; however, they are contemplating the joint purchase of 100% of the outstanding common stock of W
   d) X owns 100% of the outstanding common stock of Y and Z. Z is in bankruptcy

3. H is the parent company and would probably treat K as an investment, and not a consolidated subsidiary, in the proposed consolidated statement of H, J, and K if
   a) H and J manufacture electronic equipment; K manufactures ball bearings
   b) H and J manufacture ball-point pens; K is in bankruptcy
   c) K has assets of $1,000,000 and an outstanding bond issue of $750,000; H holds the bonds
   d) H and J manufacture cars, and K provides financial services

4. Parent company P has a fiscal year ending June 30, 19X1. Subsidiary S's fiscal year ends May 31, 19X1. Therefore
   a) A consolidated statement cannot properly be prepared for P and S
   b) S's May 31, 19X1, statement can be used for consolidation with P's June 30, 19X1, statement, provided disclosure is made of any June event that materially affected S and the consolidated statement is dated June 30, 19X1
   c) If the consolidated statement is permissible, it will be dated May 31, 19X1
   d) None of the above

5. P owns 90% of the stock S. W owns 10% of S's stock. In relation to P, W is considered as
   a) An affiliate
   b) A subsidiary not to be consolidated
   c) A minority interest
   d) A holding company

6. If goodwill arising from the consolidation appears among the assets on the consolidated balance sheet of a parent company and its only subsidiary, then this indicates that the subsidiary
   a) Was acquired at a price that was less than the underlying book value of its tangible assets
   b) Was accounted for as a pooling of interests
   c) Already had goodwill on its books
   d) Was acquired at a price in excess of the underlying book value of its net assets

(AICPA adapted)

E2-12 **Unpaid Subsidiary Cash Dividend** Gotcha Company acquired 85% of the outstanding common stock of Never Company for $420,000 cash. On June 15, 19X2, Never declared a cash dividend of $30,000 payable on July 15, 19X2, to common stockholders of record on July 5, 19X2.

REQUIRED

a) Prepare the entry to record Gotcha's investment in Never under each of the following:
   1. Gotcha's investment in Never took place on July 1, 19X2.
   2. Gotcha's investment in Never took place on July 10, 19X2.

b) Assuming a consolidated balance sheet is prepared at the date of acquisition, July 1, 19X2, prepare in journal entry form the consolidation worksheet adjustment (if any) to eliminate intercompany dividends under each of the conditions described in (a) above.

E2-13   **Treasury Stock of Subsidiary**   On June 1, 19X2, Pastry, Inc., acquired 3,150 shares of the voting stock of Dough Company for $87,750. Dough's stockholders' equity on the date of acquisition was as follows:

Common stock ($15 par)	$60,000	
Excess over par	20,000	
Retained earnings	30,000	$110,000
Less: Treasury stock (500 shares at cost)		12,500
Total stockholders' equity		$ 97,500

REQUIRED

a) Prepare in journal entry form consolidation worksheet adjustments to (1) retire the subsidiary treasury stock and (2) eliminate Pastry's investment in Dough.

b) Determine the minority interest in Dough.

c) Assuming the preceding investment cost and ownership percentage, prepare in journal entry form consolidation worksheet adjustments to (1) retire the subsidiary treasury stock and (2) eliminate Pastry's investment in Dough. Assume Dough's stockholders' equity on the date of acquisition was as follows:

Common stock ($15 par)	$60,000	
Less: Treasury stock (at par)	(7,500)	$52,500
Excess over par		17,500
Retained earnings		27,500
Total stockholders' equity		$97,500

E2-14   **Relationships between Consolidated and Separate Firms' Accounts**   On January 1, 19X9, Company P acquired, for cash, 90% of the voting stock of Company S from the latter's stockholders. The balance sheet for Company P just prior to acquisition and the consolidated balance sheet of Company P and its subsidiary, Company S, are as follows:

	Company P	Consolidated
Assets		
Cash	$170,500	$110,000
Plant and equipment	108,500	148,500
Land	85,000	114,500
Goodwill		10,000
Total assets	$364,000	$383,000
Liabilities and Stockholders' Equity		
Liabilities	$ 34,000	$ 44,000
Common stock	210,000	210,000
Paid-in capital	20,000	20,000
Retained earnings	100,000	100,000
Minority interest		9,000
Total liabilities and stockholders' equity	$364,000	$383,000

Immediately before consolidation, the assets and liabilities of Company S were fairly valued at book value except for land, which had a fair value in excess of book value of $5,000. Company S's common stock and paid-in capital balances were $80,000 and $40,000, respectively.

REQUIRED

Using the preceding information, answer the following questions:

1. What was the balance in the retained earnings account of S at the date of acquisition?

2. What was the book value of the land of S at the date of acquisition?

3. What was the valuation of the liabilities of S at the date of acquisition?

4. What was the acquisition cost of P's investment in S?

5. What individual stockholders' equity amounts constitute the $9,000 of minority interest?

E2-15   **Multiple Choice Questions on Goodwill and Negative Goodwill**

1. On June 30, 19X9, Needle Corporation purchased for cash at $10 per share all 100,000 shares of the outstanding common stock of Thread Company. The total appraised value of identifiable assets less liabilities of Thread was $1,400,000 at June 30, 19X9, including the appraised value of Thread's property, plant and equipment (its only noncurrent asset) of $250,000. The consolidated balance sheet of Needle Corporation and its wholly owned subsidiary at June 30, 19X9, should reflect

   a) A deferred credit (negative goodwill) of $150,000

   b) Goodwill of $150,000

   c) A deferred credit (negative goodwill) of $400,000

   d) Goodwill of $400,000

2. During 19X8 the Henderson Company purchased the net assets of John Corporation for $800,000. On the date of the transaction, John had no long-term investments in marketable securities and had $100,000 of liabilities. The fair value of John's assets when acquired were as follows:

Current assets	$ 400,000
Noncurrent assets	600,000
	$1,000,000

How should the $100,000 difference between the fair value of the net assets acquired ($900,000) and the cost ($800,000) be accounted for by Henderson?

   a) The $100,000 difference should be credited to retained earnings.

   b) The noncurrent assets should be recorded at $500,000.

   c) The current assets should be recorded at $360,000, and the noncurrent assets should be recorded at $540,000.

   d) A deferred credit of $100,000 should be set up.

3. On April 1, 19X3, Union Company paid $1,600,000 for all the issued and outstanding common stock of Cable Corporation in a transaction properly accounted for as a purchase. The recorded assets and liabilities of Cable on April 1, 19X3, were as follows:

Cash	$160,000
Inventory	480,000
Property, plant and equipment (net)	960,000
Liabilities	(360,000)

On April 1, 19X3, it was determined that Cable's inventory had a fair value of $460,000, and the property, plant and equipment (net) had a fair value of $1,040,000. What is the amount of goodwill resulting from the business combination?

a) $ –0–   c) $300,000

b) $ 20,000   d) $360,000

4. On November 30, 19X8, Eagle, Incorporated, purchased for cash at $25 per share all 300,000 shares of the outstanding common stock of Perch Company. Perch's balance sheet at November 30, 19X8, showed a book value of $6,000,000. Additionally, the fair value of Perch's property, plant and equipment on November 30, 19X8, was $800,000 in excess of its book value. What amount, if any, will be shown in the balance sheet caption "Goodwill" in the November 30, 19X8, consolidated balance sheet of Eagle, Incorporated, and its wholly owned subsidiary, Perch Company?

a) $ –0–   c) $ 800,000

b) $ 700,000   d) $1,500,000

5. On July 31, 19X9, Light Company purchased, for cash of $8,000,000, all the outstanding common stock of Shirk Company when Shirk's balance sheet showed net assets of $6,400,000. Shirk's assets and liabilities had fair values that were different from the book values as follows:

	Book Value	Fair Value
Property, plant and equipment (net)	$10,000,000	$11,500,000
Other assets	1,000,000	700,000
Long-term debt	6,000,000	5,600,000

As a result of the preceding transaction, what amount, if any, will be shown as goodwill in the July 31, 19X9, consolidated balance sheet of Light Company and its wholly owned subsidiary, Shirk Company?

a) $ –0–   c) $1,200,000

b) $ 100,000   d) $1,600,000

6. On April 1, 19X9, the Jack Company paid $800,000 for all the issued and outstanding common stock of Ann Corporation in a transaction properly accounted for as a purchase. The recorded assets and liabilities of Ann Corporation on April 1, 19X9, follow:

Cash	$ 80,000
Inventory	240,000
Property and equipment (net)	480,000
Liabilities	(180,000)

On April 1, 19X9, it was determined that the inventory of Ann had a fair value of $190,000, and the property and equipment (net) had a fair value of $560,000. What is the amount of goodwill resulting from the business combination?

a) $ –0–   c) $150,000

b) $ 50,000   d) $180,000

(AICPA adapted)

E2-16
APPENDIX A

Alternative Concepts of Consolidation   On January 1, 19X1, P acquired 80% of the common stock of S for $400,000. The fair values of the net assets of S were equal to their book values except for patents, which were undervalued by $20,000.

REQUIRED
Determine the amount of minority interest that would appear in the consolidated balance sheet under each of the following alternative concepts of consolidation:

1. Proportionate-consolidation concept

2. Economic-unit concept

3. Parent-company concept

E2-17 **Alternative Concepts of Consolidation** Lightfoot, Inc. acquired 85% of the outstanding voting shares of Toano Company for $361,250 cash on August 1, 19X3. On the date of acquisition, the book values of the net assets of Lightfoot and Toano were $800,000 and $300,000, respectively. The net assets of Toano had a fair value of $410,000.

REQUIRED

Determine the amount of net assets, goodwill, and minority interest that would appear in the consolidated balance sheet under each of the following alternative concepts of consolidation:

1. Proportionate-consolidation concept

2. Parent-company concept

3. Economic-unit concept

E2-18 **Multiple Choice Questions on Pooling of Interests**

APPENDIX B 1. If all other conditions for consolidation are met, how should subsidiaries acquired in a business combination be shown under each of the following methods?

Purchase	Pooling of Interests
a) Consolidated	Not consolidated
b) Consolidated	Consolidated
c) Not consolidated	Consolidated
d) Not consolidated	Not consolidated

2. How would the retained earnings of a subsidiary acquired in a business combination usually be treated in a consolidated balance sheet prepared immediately after the acquisition?

   a) Excluded for both a purchase and a pooling of interests

   b) Excluded for a pooling of interests but included for a purchase

   c) Included for both a purchase and a pooling of interests

   d) Included for a pooling of interests but excluded for a purchase

3. On December 31, 19X7, Kim, Inc., had 2,000,000 shares of authorized $10 par-value voting common stock of which 1,600,000 were issued and outstanding. On December 1, 19X8, Kim issued 250,000 additional shares of its $10 par-value voting common stock in exchange for all 100,000 shares of Terry Company's outstanding $20 par-value voting common stock in a business combination appropriately accounted for by the pooling-of-interests method. The market value of Kim's voting common stock was $30 per share on the date of the business combination. What is the total consolidated common stock issued and outstanding for Kim and its subsidiary, Terry, at December 31, 19X8?

   a) $17,000,000

   b) $18,500,000

   c) $22,500,000

   d) $55,500,000

(AICPA adapted)

E2-19 **Acquisition Cost, Consolidation Adjustment, Minority Interest, Retained Earnings** Lexus issued 1,000 shares ($23 par) common stock with a market value of $28 per share in exchange for 90% of the outstanding common stock of Infiniti. The combination is to be accounted for as a pooling of interests. Just prior to the date of combination, the stockholders' equity sections of Lexus and Infiniti were as follows:

	Lexus	Infiniti
Common stock	$ 80,000	$20,000
Excess over par	10,000	15,000
Retained earnings	30,000	(7,000)
	$120,000	$28,000

REQUIRED

a) Prepare the entry to record Lexus' investment in Infiniti.

b) Prepare in journal entry form the consolidation worksheet adjustment to eliminate Lexus' investment in Infiniti at the date of acquisition.

c) Determine minority interest at the date of acquisition.

d) Determine the amount of consolidated retained earnings at the date of acquisition.

E2-20 **Acquisition Cost, Consolidation Adjustment, Balance Sheet** On November 15, 19X7, Bowman Company and Millner, Inc. agreed to a business combination in which Bowman will issue 1,500 shares of its $10 par common stock to the stockholders of Millner for 95% of the stock of Millner. The market value per share of Bowman's stock is $30. The business combination is to be accounted for as a pooling of interests. The balance sheets of the two companies just prior to the business combination are as follows:

	Bowman	Millner
Assets		
Cash	$ 5,000	$ 2,000
Accounts receivables	10,000	7,000
Inventory	25,000	8,000
Machinery and equipment (net)	70,000	13,000
Total assets	$110,000	$30,000
Stockholders' Equity		
Common stock	$ 65,000	$12,000
Excess over par	30,000	14,000
Retained earnings	15,000	4,000
Total stockholders' equity	$110,000	$30,000

Fair values of the assets and liabilities of Millner are equal to their book value except for inventory and machinery and equipment (net), which have fair values of $8,500 and $20,000, respectively.

REQUIRED

a) Prepare the entry to record Bowman's investment in Millner.

b) Prepare in journal entry form the consolidation worksheet adjustment to eliminate Bowman's investment in Millner at the date of combination.

c) Prepare a consolidated balance sheet as of November 15, 19X7.

PROBLEMS

P2-1 **Consolidation Worksheet: Wholly Owned Subsidiary, Valuation Differential** Bengels, Inc. acquired all of the outstanding common stock of Cavalier Company for $36,700 cash on January 1, 19X3. On this date, all the assets and liabilities of Cavalier were properly valued except for a fully depreciated piece of equipment with a fair value of $500.

The balance sheets of the two companies immediately after the combination on January 1, 19X3, were as follows:

	Bengels, Inc.	Cavalier Company
Assets		
Cash	$ 25,000	$ 5,000
Inventories	30,000	7,500
Investment in Cavalier Company	36,700	
Plant and equipment (net)	153,300	28,500
Total assets	$245,000	$41,000
Liabilities and Stockholders' Equity		
Accounts payable	$ 52,500	$ 5,500
Common stock	140,000	20,000
Excess over par	30,000	12,500
Retained earnings	22,500	3,000
Total liabilities and stockholders' equity	$245,000	$41,000

REQUIRED

Prepare a consolidation worksheet for Bengels, Inc. and its subsidiary as of January 1, 19X3.

P2-2 **Consolidation Worksheet: Partially Owned Subsidiary, Valuation Differential** On January 1, 19X4, Company X acquired, for cash, 90% of the common stock of Company Y in the open market. Company Y's net assets were properly valued except for equipment and buildings, which were undervalued by $7,200 and $4,500, respectively. The balance sheets of both companies immediately after the combination on January 1, 19X4, were as follows:

	Company X	Company Y
Assets		
Cash	$ 28,000	$20,000
Accounts receivable	24,000	10,000
Inventory	26,000	30,000
Investment in Company Y	80,000	
Equipment (net)	4,000	5,000
Buildings (net)	22,000	20,000
Total assets	$184,000	$85,000
Liabilities and Stockholders' Equity		
Accounts payable	$ 34,000	$10,000
Common stock	100,000	60,000
Retained earnings	50,000	15,000
Total liabilities and stockholders' equity	$184,000	$85,000

REQUIRED

Prepare a consolidation worksheet as of January 1, 19X4, for Company X and its subsidiary.

P2-3　**Consolidation Worksheet: Wholly Owned Subsidiary, Valuation Differential**　The balance sheets of Companies P and S on January 1, 19X1, just after P had acquired all the voting stock of S in the open market, appear here:

	Company P	Company S
Assets		
Cash	$ 50,000	$10,000
Inventories	60,000	15,000
Investment in Company S	80,000	
Plant and equipment (net)	300,000	57,000
Total assets	$490,000	$82,000
Liabilities and Stockholders' Equity		
Accounts payable	$ 30,000	$ 6,000
Bonds payable	75,000	15,000
Common stock ($5 par)	280,000	45,000
Paid-in capital	60,000	10,000
Retained earnings	45,000	6,000
Total liabilities and stockholders' equity	$490,000	$82,000

The net assets of Company S were properly valued except for inventories and accounts payable, which had fair values of $30,000 and $4,000, respectively.

REQUIRED

Prepare a consolidation worksheet for Company P and its subsidiary as of January 1, 19X1.

P2-4　**Multiple Choice Questions on Consolidation**

1. Corporation A purchases the net assets of Corporation B for $110,000. On the date of A's purchase, Corporation B had no long-term investments in marketable securities and $15,000 (representing both book and fair value) of liabilities. The fair values of Corporation B's assets, when acquired, were:

Current assets	$ 55,000
Noncurrent assets	75,000
Total	$130,000

How should the $5,000 difference between the fair value of the net assets acquired ($115,000) and the cost ($110,000) be accounted for by Corporation A?

    a) Credit retained earnings for $5,000.

    b) Record current assets at $50,000.

    c) Record current assets of $52,885 and noncurrent at $72,115.

    d) Record noncurrent assets of $70,000.

2. On April 1, 19X6, Ash Company paid $400,000 for all the issued and outstanding common stock of Tray Corporation in a transaction that was properly accounted for as a purchase. The assets and liabilities of Tray Corporation on April 1, 19X6, follow:

Cash	$ 40,000
Inventory	120,000
Property and equipment (net)	240,000
Liabilities	(90,000)

On April 1, 19X6, it was determined that the inventory of Tray had a fair value of $95,000 and the property and equipment (net) had a fair value of $280,000. What should be the amount recorded as goodwill by Ash as a result of the business combination?

a) $ –0–   **c)** $75,000

b) $25,000   **d)** $90,000

Items 3 and 4 are based on the following information: Apex Company acquired 70% of the outstanding stock of Nadir Corporation. The separate balance sheet of Apex immediately after the acquisition and the consolidated balance sheet are as follows:

	Apex	**Consolidated**
Current assets	$106,000	$146,000
Investment in Nadir	100,000	
Goodwill		8,100
Fixed assets (net)	270,000	370,000
	$476,000	$524,100
Current liabilities	$ 15,000	$ 28,000
Capital stock	350,000	350,000
Minority interest		35,100
Retained earnings	111,000	111,000
	$476,000	$524,100

Ten thousand dollars of the excess payment for the investment in Nadir was ascribed to undervaluation of its fixed assets; the balance of the excess payment was ascribed to goodwill. Current assets of Nadir included a $2,000 receivable from Apex, due to a cash loan on the date of acquisition. The following two items relate to Nadir's separate balance sheet prepared at the time Apex acquired its 70% interest in Nadir:

3. What was the total of the current assets on Nadir's separate balance sheet at the time Apex acquired its 70% interest?

a) $ 38,000   **c)** $ 42,000

b) $ 40,000   **d)** $104,000

4. What was the total stockholders' equity on Nadir's separate balance sheet at the time Apex acquired its 70% interest?

a) $ 64,900   **c)** $100,000

b) $ 70,000   **d)** $117,000

Items (5) and (6) are based on the following information: The Nugget Company's balance sheet on December 31, 19X6, is as follows:

Assets

Cash	$ 100,000
Accounts receivable	200,000
Inventories	500,000
Property, plant and equipment (net)	900,000
	$1,700,000

Liabilities and Stockholders' Equity

Current liabilities	$ 300,000
Long-term debt	500,000
Common stock ($1 par)	100,000
Additional paid-in capital	200,000
Retained earnings	600,000
	$1,700,000

On December 31, 19X6, the Bronc Company purchased all the outstanding common stock of Nugget for $1,500,000 cash. On that date, the fair (market) value of Nugget's inventories was $450,000; and the fair value of Nugget's property, plant and equipment was $1,000,000. The fair values of all other assets and liabilities of Nugget were equal to their book values.

5. As a result of the acquisition of Nugget by Bronc, the consolidated balance sheet of Bronc and Nugget should reflect goodwill in the amount of

    a) $500,000   **c)** $600,000

    b) $550,000   **d)** $650,000

6. Assuming the balance sheet of Bronc (unconsolidated) at December 31, 19X6, reflected retained earnings of $2,000,000, what amount of retained earnings would you show in the December 31, 19X6, consolidated balance sheet of Bronc and its new subsidiary, Nugget?

    a) $2,000,000   **c)** $2,800,000

    b) $2,600,000   **d)** $3,150,000

(AICPA adapted)

P2-5   **Acquisition Cost, Consolidation Worksheet: Partially Owned Subsidiary, Valuation Differential**   On January 1, 19X6, Kitty Company acquired 90% of the outstanding common shares of Hawk Company in exchange for 4,000 shares of Kitty's common stock, which have a par value of $25 and a current market value of $42. Kitty's costs to register the securities with the Securities and Exchange Commission and issue the securities totaled $2,000. Balance sheets of both companies just prior to the business combination are as follows:

	Kitty Company	Hawk Company
Assets		
Cash	$300,000	$ 50,000
Inventory	150,000	25,000
Accounts receivable	60,000	10,000
Machinery and equipment (net)	400,000	60,000
Land	40,000	15,000
Total assets	$950,000	$160,000
Liabilities and Stockholders' Equity		
Accounts payable	$ 50,000	$ 5,000
Common stock ($25 par)	500,000	100,000
Excess over pay	100,000	35,000
Retained earnings	300,000	20,000
Total liabilities and stockholders' equity	$950,000	$160,000

The fair values of the net assets of Hawk were the same as their book values except for machinery and equipment, which had a fair value of $75,000, and land, which was appraised at $20,000.

REQUIRED

a) Prepare the entry on the books of Kitty to record its investment in Hawk as a purchase combination.

b) Prepare a consolidation worksheet for Kitty and its subsidiary at the date of acquisition, January 1, 19X6, assuming the business combination was recorded as a purchase combination.

P2-6 **Consolidation Worksheet: Partially Owned Subsidiary, Valuation Differential** On July 1, 19X6, the Stone Corporation acquired 90% of the 2,000 outstanding shares of the common stock of Tonic, Inc., from shareholders for cash of $400,000. The balance sheets for both companies immediately after acquisition are presented here. Also shown are the agreed-upon fair values of the assets of Tonic; liabilities are fairly valued as shown:

	Stone Corporation	Tonic, Inc.	
	Book Value	Book Value	Fair Value
Assets			
Cash	$ 300,000	$100,000	$100,000
Accounts receivable (net)	30,000	20,000	15,000
Notes receivable	10,000*		
Inventories	100,000	50,000	60,000
Investment in Tonic	400,000		
Property, plant and equipment (net)	500,000	400,000	450,000
Patent	5,000	5,000	5,000
Total assets	$1,345,000	$575,000	$630,000
Liabilities and Stockholders' Equity			
Accounts payable	$ 20,000	$ 90,000	
Notes payable		10,000*	
Long-term liabilities	40,000	90,000	
Common stock ($100 par)	600,000	200,000	
Excess over par	85,000	45,000	
Retained earnings	600,000	140,000	
Total liabilities and stockholders' equity	$1,345,000	$575,000	

* Tonic owed Stone $10,000 (notes payable) due to a cash loan on the date of acquisition.

REQUIRED

a) Prepare a consolidation worksheet at the date of acquisition for Stone Corporation and its subsidiary.

b) Prepare a consolidated balance sheet for Stone Corporation at July 1, 19X6.

P2-7   **Consolidation Worksheet: Wholly Owned Subsidiary, Negative Goodwill**   The Buckwheat

Company acquired, on April 30, 19X6, all the common stock of Alfalfa Company for $84,500 cash.
At the date of stock purchase, it was determined that all Alfalfa's assets and liabilities were recorded
at their fair value except land, which was overvalued by $5,000. Balance sheets for both companies
immediately after acquisition are as follows:

	Buckwheat Company	Alfalfa Company
Assets		
Cash	$ 93,000	$ 76,000
Accounts receivable	107,000	92,000
Inventory	80,000	40,000
Investment in Alfalfa	84,500	
Investment in marketable securities (long-term)	103,500	59,000
Land	95,000	60,000
Buildings (net)	70,000	45,000
Total assets	$633,000	$372,000
Liabilities and Stockholders' Equity		
Accounts payable	$ 89,000	$ 62,000
Notes payable	71,000	130,000
Bonds payable	100,000	80,000
Common stock	250,000	90,000
Retained earnings	123,000	10,000
Total liabilities and stockholders' equity	$633,000	$372,000

REQUIRED

Prepare a consolidation worksheet at the date of acquisition, April 30, 19X6, for Buckwheat Company and its subsidiary.

P2-8   Consolidation Worksheet: Partially Owned Subsidiary, Valuation Differential   Corporation PX acquired 2,000 shares of the voting stock of Corporation SX in the open market at $48 per share. Direct costs associated with the acquisition total $4,000. Balance sheets of both companies on January 1, 19X6, immediately after the acquisition of shares by PX, are as follows:

	Corporation PX	Corporation SX
Assets		
Cash	$ 50,000	$ 10,000
Temporary investments	80,000	40,000
Receivables (net)	95,000	10,000
Investment in Corporation SX	100,000	
Machinery and equipment (net)	100,000	45,000
Land	50,000	20,000
Total assets	$475,000	$125,000
Liabilities and Stockholders' Equity		
Accounts payable	$ 75,000	$ 25,000
Common stock ($20 par)	250,000	50,000
Excess over par	90,000	30,000
Retained earnings	60,000	20,000
Total liabilities and stockholders' equity	$475,000	$125,000

The fair values of PX and SX assets on January 1, 19X6, are presented below. Liabilities of both companies are properly valued at their respective book value:

	PX	SX
Cash	$ 50,000	$ 10,000
Temporary investments	100,000	50,000
Receivables (net)	95,000	8,000
Investment in Corporation SX	100,000	
Machinery and equipment (net)	110,000	40,000
Land	100,000	30,000
	$555,000	$138,000

REQUIRED

a) Prepare a consolidation worksheet for Corporation PX and its subsidiary as of January 1, 19X6.

b) Prepare a consolidated balance sheet for Corporation PX at January 1, 19X6.

P2-9 **Consolidation Worksheet: Two Partially Owned Subsidiaries** On January 1, 19X1, Carl Company acquired, for cash, an 80% interest in Flip Company and a 90% interest in Flop Company. Balance sheets of all three companies immediately after acquisition are as follows:

	Carl Company	Flip Company	Flop Company
Assets			
Cash	$ 47,000	$ 7,500	$ 8,600
Accounts receivable	39,250	2,900	4,125
Inventory	36,710	8,850	8,600
Investment in:			
Flip	16,740		
Flop	25,000		
Notes receivable	27,800		
Plant and equipment (net)	20,000	8,000	9,325
Total assets	$212,500	$27,250	$30,650
Liabilities and Stockholders' Equity			
Accounts payable	$ 7,500	$ 3,200	$ 5,025
Notes payable			1,425
Common stock:			
Carl	100,000		
Flip		20,000	
Flop			29,000
Retained earnings	105,000	4,050	(4,800)
Total liabilities and stockholders' equity	$212,500	$27,250	$30,650

Additional information:

1. Any differences in the investment cost and book value of the net assets acquired in Flip and Flop are considered to be an overvaluation or undervaluation of the subsidiary's plant and equipment.

2. On the date of acquisition, Carl loaned $500 to Flop to provide working capital. Flop signed a note for the loan.

REQUIRED

Prepare a consolidation worksheet at the date of acquisition, January 1, 19X1, for Carl Company and its subsidiaries.

P2-10   **Acquisition Cost, Consolidation Worksheet: Partially Owned Subsidiary, Valuation Differential**   On January 1, 19X6, Richmond Company acquired 90% of the outstanding common shares of Hanover Company in exchange for 10,000 shares of its $50 par-value common stock. On this date, Richmond's common stock had a market value of $60 per share. Balance sheets of both companies just prior to the business combination are as follows:

	Richmond Company	Hanover Company
Assets		
Cash	$ 600,000	$200,000
Inventory	300,000	100,000
Accounts receivable	120,000	40,000
Machinery and equipment (net)	800,000	200,000
Patents	80,000	60,000
Total assets	$1,900,000	$600,000
Liabilities and Stockholders' Equity		
Accounts payable	$ 100,000	$ 25,000
Common stock:		
Richmond ($50 par)	1,000,000	
Hanover ($40 par)		400,000
Excess over par	200,000	100,000
Retained earnings	600,000	75,000
Total liabilities and stockholders' equity	$1,900,000	$600,000

The fair values of the net assets of Hanover were the same as their book values except for machinery and equipment, which had a fair value of $250,000, and patents, which were appraised at $70,000.

REQUIRED

a) Prepare the entry on the books of Richmond to record its investment in Hanover as a purchase combination.

b) Prepare a consolidation worksheet for Richmond and its subsidiary at the date of acquisition, January 1, 19X6, assuming the business combination was recorded as a purchase combination.

P2-11 **Consolidation Worksheet: Partially Owned Subsidiary, Treasury Stock, Cash Dividends, Valuation Differential**   Mann Company acquired 810 shares of the outstanding common stock of Rayburn Company for $100 per share on December 31, 19X4. Immediately after the acquisition, the balance sheets of both companies appeared as follows:

	Mann Company	Rayburn Company
Assets		
Cash	$ 27,000	$10,100
Temporary investments	15,000	5,000
Accounts receivable	12,000	8,000
Dividends receivable	1,215	
Inventory	25,000	15,000
Investment in Rayburn	79,785	
Machinery and equipment (net)	25,000	10,000
Buildings (net)	38,200	25,250
Land	16,000	18,000
Total assets	$239,200	$91,350
Liabilities and Stockholders' Equity		
Accounts payable	$ 35,200	$10,000
Dividends payable	4,000	1,350
Common stock ($50 par)	100,000	50,000
Treasury stock (at par)	(10,000)	(5,000)
Retained earnings	110,000	35,000
Total liabilities and stockholders' equity	$239,200	$91,350

Additional information:

1. On November 1, 19X4, Rayburn acquired shares of its own common stock in the open market at $60 per share. The treasury stock was recorded using the par-value method.

2. Rayburn declared, on December 20, 19X4, a cash dividend of $1.50 per share on its outstanding common shares of record on January 20, 19X5.

3. The accounts receivable of Rayburn include $2,000 due from Mann as a result of a cash loan on the date of acquisition.

4. All the assets and liabilities of Rayburn are recorded at their fair values except for the following:

	Book Value	Fair Value
Temporary investments	$ 5,000	$ 4,000
Machinery and equipment (net)	10,000	15,000
Accounts payable (portion for which book and fair values differ)	5,700	5,000

REQUIRED

a) Prepare a consolidation worksheet at the date of acquisition, December 31, 19X4, for Mann Company and its subsidiary.

b) Prepare a consolidated balance sheet for Mann Company at December 31, 19X4.

P2-12   **Alternative Concepts of Consolidation**   On January 1, 19X1, P acquired an 80% interest in S,
APPENDIX A   paying $140,000 in cash. Immediately after the acquisition, the balance sheets of both companies
appeared as follows. Also shown is the fair value of the net assets of S:

	P	S	
	Book Value	Book Value	Fair Value
Assets			
Cash	$ 10,000	$ 20,000	$ 20,000
Investment in S	140,000		
Other assets	75,000	140,000	150,000
Total assets	$225,000	$160,000	$170,000
Liabilities and Stockholders' Equity			
Accounts payable	$ 5,000	$ 10,000	$ 10,000
Common stock	200,000	100,000	
Retained earnings	20,000	50,000	
Total liabilities and stockholders' equity	$225,000	$160,000	

REQUIRED

a) Prepare consolidated balance sheets as of January 1, 19X1, applying each of the following
alternative concepts of consolidation:

1. Proportionate-consolidation concept

2. Parent-company concept

3. Economic-unit concept

b) Which of the preceding concepts of consolidation is applied in this text?

P2-13   **Acquisition Cost, Consolidation Worksheet: Partially Owned Subsidiary**   On July 1, 19X6,
APPENDIX B   Crosby acquired 90% of the outstanding common shares of Sanborn in exchange for newly issued
shares of Crosby. The combination is to be accounted for as a pooling of interests. Prior to the
acquisition, the following balances appeared in the balance sheets of Crosby and Sanborn. Also
shown are the agreed-upon fair values of the assets of Sanborn:

	Crosby	Sanborn	
	Book Value	Book Value	Fair Value
Cash	$ 70,000	$10,000	$ 10,000
Accounts receivable	30,000	5,000	15,000
Inventory	40,000	20,000	30,000
Plant and equipment (net)	100,000	60,000	75,000
	$240,000	$95,000	$130,000
Accounts payable	$ 20,000	$20,000	
Common stock ($10 par)	150,000	40,000	
Excess over par	20,000	10,000	
Retained earnings	50,000	25,000	
	$240,000	$95,000	

REQUIRED

a) Prepare the entry on the books of Crosby to record its investment in Sanborn. Crosby is to exchange one share of its stock for each share of Sanborn's stock.

b) Prepare a consolidation worksheet for Crosby and its subsidiary at the date of acquisition.

P2-14
APPENDIX B

Acquisition Cost, Consolidation Worksheet: Partially Owned Subsidiary   The following information is the same as that presented in Problem 2-10. It is reproduced here to assist the student in referring to information needed to solve the new requirement. On January 1, 19X6, Richmond Company acquired 90% of the outstanding common shares of Hanover Company in exchange for 10,000 shares of its $50 par-value common stock. On this date, Richmond's common stock had a market value of $60 per share. Balance sheets of both companies just prior to the business combination are as follows:

	Richmond Company	Hanover Company
Assets		
Cash	$ 600,000	$200,000
Inventory	300,000	100,000
Accounts receivable	120,000	40,000
Machinery and equipment (net)	800,000	200,000
Patents	80,000	60,000
Total assets	$1,900,000	$600,000
Liabilities and Stockholders' Equity		
Accounts payable	$ 100,000	$ 25,000
Common stock:		
Richmond ($50 par)	1,000,000	
Hanover ($40 par)		400,000
Excess over par	200,000	100,000
Retained earnings	600,000	75,000
Total liabilities and stockholders' equity	$1,900,000	$600,000

The fair values of the net assets of Hanover were the same as their book values except for machinery and equipment, which had a fair value of $250,000, and patents, which were appraised at $70,000.

REQUIRED

a) Prepare the entry on the books of Richmond to record its investment in Hanover as a pooling of interests.

b) Prepare a consolidation worksheet for Richmond and its subsidiary at the date of acquisition, January 1, 19X6, assuming the business combination was recorded as a pooling of interests.

ISSUES IN ACCOUNTING JUDGMENT

I2-1   **Minority Interest as a Liability**   Some accountants argue that minority interest is a liability and should be classified as such on the consolidated balance sheet. The principal basis for this argument is a strict interpretation of the parent-company concept of consolidation which views the consolidated financial statements as an extension of the parent's separate financial statements intended primarily for the parent's stockholders and others interested in the parent company. *FASB Statement* *of Financial Accounting Concepts No. 6* (par. 35) states, ''Liabilities are probable future sacrifices of economic benefits arising from present obligations of a particular entity to transfer assets or provide services to other entities in the future as a result of past transactions or events.''

REQUIRED

a) Using the FASB's definition of a liability, construct an argument *against* the classification of minority interest as a liability in consolidated balance sheets.

b) Consider the case of a parent company that has acquired many subsidiaries over the year and has followed the policy of pushing toward 100% ownership as soon as possible. Would your argument hold as well in this special case as it does in general? Explain.

I2-2   Control and Ownership   Deciding whether or not to consolidate an investee involves an analysis of control and ownership of a majority of voting rights in the investee by the parent company. Some accountants have argued that control is the principal basis for consolidation decisions and that ownership is merely an indicator of control. Others have argued that ownership is the principal basis because presence of control cannot be detected directly.

REQUIRED

a) Write a paragraph supporting the argument that control, not ownership, is the principal basis for consolidation decisions. Support your argument by reference to general and conceptual considerations as well as current accounting standards.

b) Write a paragraph supporting the position that ownership, not control, is the principal basis for consolidation decisions. Support your argument by reference to general and conceptual considerations as well as current accounting standards.

I2-3   Valuing Acquired Research and Development Projects   Harvey Enterprises, Inc. has recently purchased an 80% interest in Randall Development Corporation. Randall is engaged in a number of ongoing research and development projects. One of these projects, known as the Widler Project, is potentially important to the future of the combined entity but is in its early stages and has not produced any patents or designs. Further, it is a rather specialized project requiring materials, equipment, and facilities that are not likely to be useful in other projects. Harvey's controller, Mr. Stanley V. Jones, has asked you, an accountant on his staff, to determine the appropriate treatment of the Widler Project for purposes of recording the purchase of Randall and for purposes of preparing Harvey's consolidated financial statements.

REQUIRED

a) Prepare a list of the relevant professional pronouncements. Read the pronouncements.

b) Why doesn't any amount for the Widler Project appear on the books of Randall Development? Quote and cite appropriate pronouncements to support your answer.

c) How should the Widler Project be treated in recording the purchase combination?

The Equity Method and Postacquisition Consolidation

ACCOUNTING FOR LONG-TERM INVESTMENTS IN COMMON STOCK 135

THE COST METHOD 136
Journal Entries for the Cost Method 136   Cumulative Dividends in Excess of Earnings Share 136   Use of Cost Method for Subsidiaries as a Record-Keeping Convenience 137

THE EQUITY METHOD 138
Journal Entries for the Equity Method 139   Presentation in Investor's Financial Statements 141   Special Problems under the Equity Method 142

POSTACQUISITION CONSOLIDATED FINANCIAL STATEMENTS 146

CONSOLIDATION OF BALANCE SHEETS AT DATE OF ACQUISITION 147
Analysis of the Valuation Differential 147   Consolidation Adjustment at Date of Acquisition 148   Minority Interest Column 148

CONSOLIDATED FINANCIAL STATEMENTS ONE YEAR AFTER ACQUISITION 148
Analysis of Subsidiary Stockholders' Equity 150   Analysis of Investment Account 150   Consolidated Net Income 152   Consolidated Income Statement 154   The Consolidated Statement of Cash Flows 156   Consolidation Worksheet Procedure 156   Entry of Parent and Subsidiary Separate Financial Statements 156   Consolidation Adjustments One Year after Acquisition 158   Minority Interest Column 159   Consolidated Financial Statements Column 160

CONSOLIDATION OF FINANCIAL STATEMENTS TWO YEARS AFTER ACQUISITION 161
Analysis of Investment Account 162   Consolidation Adjustments Two Years after Acquisition 162

INTERIM ACQUISITIONS 164
The Equity Method 167   Two Forms of Consolidated Income Statements for Acquisition Year 168   Form I Consolidation Procedures 168   Form II Consolidation Procedures 169   Calculation and Amortization of Valuation Differential 170

SUMMARY 170

APPENDIX A: POSTACQUISITION CONSOLIDATION FOR POOLINGS OF INTERESTS 171

APPENDIX B: CONSOLIDATION PROCEDURES FOR THE COST METHOD 173

APPENDIX C: THE TRIAL BALANCE FORMAT FOR CONSOLIDATION WORKSHEETS 176

After the date of acquisition, the preparation of both separate and consolidated financial statements must take account of a subsidiary's activities in the interval since acquisition. The separate financial statements of the parent reflect these postacquisition activities in an investment account, a related income account, and other accounts of the parent used under the equity method. The postacquisition consolidated financial statements include an income statement, a statement of retained earnings, and a statement of cash flows in addition to a balance sheet. Like the date-of-acquisition consolidated balance sheet, the postacquisition consolidated financial statements are prepared from a worksheet based on the separate financial statements of the parent and its subsidiary. The preparation of such a worksheet requires an extension of the worksheet adjustments described in the previous chapter to accommodate the activities of the subsidiary since the date of acquisition.

This chapter begins by discussing two methods of accounting for investments—the cost method and the equity method—before turning to a discussion of the extended procedures required to consolidate parent and subsidiary financial statements subsequent to the acquisition date. The chapter includes a comprehensive illustration that demonstrates three consolidations—consolidation at the date of acquisition, consolidation one year after acquisition, and consolidation two years after acquisition. The chapter concludes with a discussion of consolidation procedures for interim acquisitions. Three appendixes follow the chapter: The first describes postacquisition consolidation procedures for poolings of interests, the second describes consolidation procedures for the cost method, and the third illustrates the trial balance form of the consolidation worksheet.

ACCOUNTING FOR LONG-TERM INVESTMENTS IN COMMON STOCK

In keeping with the principles of historical cost accounting, long-term investments in common stock are recorded at acquisition cost on the date of acquisition. The only exception to this general rule is for investments recorded as poolings of interests, which are recorded at book value. Two methods are used to account for the investments subsequent to acquisition—the cost method and the equity method. The cost method is usually applied to small stock holdings, whereby the investor cannot significantly influence the company whose stock is held; ''an investment of less than 20% of the voting stock of an investee should lead to a presumption that an investor does not have the ability to exercise significant influence unless such ability can be demonstrated'' (*APB Opinion No. 18,* par. 17). Whenever an investor can exercise significant influence over an investee (usually whenever an investor owns 20% or more of the investee's stock), then the equity method is used in the investor's separate financial statements.[1] (Since poolings always result in

---

[1] If the evidence indicates that an investor owning 20% or more of the voting stock of an investee cannot exercise significant influence over the investee's operating and financial policies, then the cost method should be used instead of the equity method. For example, an investor may be unable to exercise significant influence over an investee when investee opposition challenges the investor's ability to such exercise; when an investor surrenders the right to exercise significant influence by signing an agreement with the investee; when the majority ownership of the investee is concentrated in a small group that operates the investee without regard to the investor; when the investor is unsuccessful in efforts to obtain information (such as quarterly financial information) required to apply the equity method; or when the investor is unsuccessful in efforts to obtain representation on the investee's board of directors. [See *FASB Interpretation No. 35,* ''Criteria for Applying the Equity Method of Accounting for Investments in Common Stock'' (May 1981).] Although the 20% rule can be overridden by such evidence, the 20% rule is applicable in the typical case and is applied throughout this book.

investments representing more than 20% ownership, only the equity method is applicable to such investments.) The paragraphs that follow explain and illustrate both the cost and equity methods of accounting for long-term investments in common stock.

The Cost Method

A simple illustration will demonstrate the application of the cost method. Bryant Corporation acquires 15% of the outstanding voting stock of Nelson Corporation for $25,000 cash on January 1, 19X1. On December 31, 19X1, Nelson declares and pays a cash dividend of $4,000 (paying $600 to Bryant) and reports a net income of $7,800. The ownership percentage (15%) indicates that Bryant must use the cost method in reporting its investment in Nelson.

Journal Entries for the Cost Method

The cost-method journal entries made by Bryant for its investment in Nelson are shown on the left-hand side of Exhibit 3-1. The first entry records the acquisition of the investment at its cost of $25,000. The reporting of net income by the investee occasions no entry by the investor under the cost method, but declaration of the dividend occasions the recording of income by the investor in the amount of the dividend. Bryant records this income for 19X1 by making the second cost-method entry shown in Exhibit 3-1. Since Nelson pays the dividend in cash during the year under consideration, a debit is made to cash; if the dividend had been declared but not paid at year-end, the debit would be made to dividend receivable.

EXHIBIT 3-1	COST AND EQUITY METHOD OF ACCOUNTING FOR LONG-TERM INVESTMENTS IN COMMON STOCK

Cost Method	Equity Method
Entry by Bryant to record acquisition of 15% of Nelson's shares on January 1, 19X1:	Entry by Thompson to record acquisition of 60% of Winslow's shares on January 1, 19X1:

Investment in Nelson 25,000
    Cash   25,000
	Investment in Winslow 60,000
	    Cash 60,000

No entry by Bryant to record share of Nelson's 19X1 net income or to amortize valuation differential:	Entry by Thompson to record share of Winslow's 19X1 net income and to amortize valuation differential:
No entry	Investment in Winslow . . . . 13,860 Income from subsidiary 13,860
Entry by Bryant to record declaration and receipt of cash dividend from Nelson:	Entry by Thompson to record declaration and receipt of cash dividend from Winslow:

Cash. 600
    Dividend income   600
	Cash. 6,000
	    Investment in Winslow 6,000

Cumulative Dividends in Excess of Earnings Share

Under the cost method, the balance of the investment account remains at the acquisition cost unless the accumulated dividends paid to an investor since acquisition of an investment exceed the investor's share of investee earnings accumulated over the same period.[2] When this occurs, the excess is a return of the investment (a liquidating dividend) and should be credited to the investment account rather than to income. Consider an extension of our Bryant-Nelson illustration into a second year following acquisition. Suppose that Nelson reports a $2,000 loss in 19X2, the second year following the acquisition of Nelson, and that Nelson declares and pays a cash dividend of $3,800 (paying $570 to Bryant) on December 31, 19X2. The cost method requires the investor, Bryant, to make the following entry at the end of 19X2:

> *Bryant's entry to record dividend income and return of investment:*
>
> Cash. 570
>   Dividend income ($570 − $300).   270
>   Investment in Nelson   300

The reduction in the investment account of $300 ($1,170 − $870) is the excess of total dividends received since acquisition ($1,170 = $600 + $570) over the investor's share of total income and loss since acquisition [$870 = (.15 × $7,800) − (.15 × $2,000)].

Use of Cost Method for Subsidiaries as a Record-Keeping Convenience

A parent-subsidiary relationship exists when one company owns more than 50% of the outstanding voting shares of another. Of course, the equity method must be used by all parent companies in their separate financial statements since control of the subsidiary investee implies an ability to significantly influence the investee. Although the equity method must be used for all subsidiaries on the parent's separate financial statements, some parents do not prepare separate financial statements; rather, they prepare only consolidated financial statements. In such cases, either the cost method or the equity method can be used to account for subsidiaries that are to be consolidated. If the parent's separate financial statements are not prepared, then it does not matter how consolidated subsidiaries are accounted for in the parent's separate records, provided that consolidation worksheet adjustments properly accommodate the parent's records and produce the correct consolidated amounts. Since the cost method is somewhat simpler to use than the equity method, companies that do not prepare separate financial statements may find it expedient

---

[2] The balance of the investment account under the cost method may also be reduced when the value of the investment declines below cost when the decline is other than temporary. When a long-term investment exhibits an *other than temporary* decline in value, the cost method requires that the investor reduce the investment. For example, a series of operating losses reported by an investee may indicate a nontemporary decline in the value of the investment that should be recognized by a credit to the investment account and a charge to the investor's net income. Once the cost of an investment has been reduced for a nontemporary decline in value, the adjusted cost should be treated as the cost basis of the investment and the original cost basis should not be restored if the investment value recovers.

to use the cost method. Notwithstanding this possibility, we shall assume throughout this text that parent companies use the equity method for all subsidiaries.[3]

The Equity Method

The fundamental difference between the cost method and the equity method of accounting for long-term investments is the manner in which the investor recognizes income from the investee. Under the cost method, income generated by the investee enters the investor's income upon distribution to the investor in the form of dividends. Under the equity method, the investor's share of investee income or loss enters the investor's income when it is reported by the investee. Further, the investor's share of the income must be adjusted for amortization of the valuation differential associated with the investment.

An equity-method investor follows the same general income recognition principles (augmented by valuation differential adjustments) as are followed by the investee. To this extent, equity-method financial statements reflect the entity theory, which emphasizes a single-entity approach to investor and investee; whereas cost-method financial statements reflect the proprietary theory, which emphasizes the legal form of the investor-investee relationship. The following issues section explains and examines the difference between cost and equity methods in the context of an erroneous use of the cost method.

ISSUES

Cost Method versus Equity Method

For the sake of comparing the cost and equity methods of accounting for long-term investments in common stock, consider an investor company that erroneously uses the cost method for an investment in 30% of another company's stock.

1. *At the end of the first year following acquisition of the investment, the investee reports a sizable net income and pays a relatively small cash dividend. Describe the impact of erroneously using the cost method on income and net assets.*

The investor's net income for the first year following acquisition will be *understated* by the investor's share of the investee's *undistributed* net income reduced by any valuation differential amortization for the year. In addition, the investor's assets at the end of that year will be understated by the same amount.

2. *At the end of the second year following acquisition of the investment, the investee company reports a net loss but pays the same dividend as in the preceding year. Describe the impact of erroneously using the cost method on income and net assets.*

The investor's net income for the second year will be *overstated* by the investor's share of the investee's loss plus the dividend and plus any valuation differential amortization. Further, readers of the investor's separate financial statements will be given the impression that the investment generated the same income in both years. Yet maintenance of the dividend in the face of losses may actually imperil future earnings by distributing cash needed for operations. Use of the equity method would avoid giving this misleading impression to readers of the investor's financial statements.

---

[3] Although the cost method may be applied to *consolidated* subsidiaries as an expedient (when separate financial statements are not prepared), the cost method should *not* be applied to *unconsolidated* subsidiaries that require use of the equity method. Consolidation procedures do not alter accounts reflecting unconsolidated subsidiaries. Consequently, unconsolidated subsidiaries are reported on consolidated statements (and on separate financial statements of the parent, if separate statements are prepared) just as they are represented on the parent's records.

The following paragraphs describe and illustrate the use of the equity method by a parent for its subsidiary. The same procedures are used for nonsubsidiary (20% to 50% owned) investees. The term "valuation differential," applied to subsidiary investees, is the same as "excess of cost over underlying book value," which is the term frequently used for nonsubsidiary investees.

Journal Entries for the Equity Method

To illustrate the equity method, let us consider the acquisition by Thompson, Inc. of 60% of the outstanding voting stock of Winslow Corporation in exchange for $60,000 cash on January 1, 19X1. Since Thompson acquires 60% of Winslow, Thompson and Winslow have a parent-subsidiary relationship. On the date of acquisition, the fair value of Winslow's identifiable net assets ($85,000) exceeded the corresponding book value ($80,000) by $5,000 as the following schedule shows:

Date-of-Acquisition Book and Fair Values of Subsidiary Net Assets

	Book Value	Fair Value	Excess of Fair Value
Assets:			
Cash	$ 1,500	$ 1,500	$ –0–
Inventory	5,000	5,600	600
Equipment (net)	49,500	49,500	–0–
Building (net)	31,000	35,400	4,400
Total assets	$87,000	$92,000	$5,000
Less: Liabilities	7,000	7,000	–0–
Net assets	$80,000	$85,000	$5,000

On the basis of this information, the following diagrammatic analysis of the valuation differential can be prepared:

Analysis of the Valuation Differential for Net Assets Acquired

Acquisition cost ($60,000)	Fair value of identifiable net assets acquired ($51,000)*	Book value of net assets acquired ($48,000)†

Goodwill = $9,000	Revaluation increment = $3,000

Valuation differential = $12,000

* $51,000 = $85,000 × .60

† $48,000 = $80,000 × .60

A more complete analysis of the valuation differential is given in the following schedule:

Calculation of Valuation Differential and Goodwill

Acquisition cost		$60,000
Less: Book value of net assets acquired		
[($87,000 − $7,000) × .60]		48,000
Valuation differential		$12,000
Less: Revaluation increment:		
Inventories [($5,600 − $5,000) × .60]	$ 360	
Building [($35,400 − $31,000) × .60]	2,640	3,000
Goodwill		$ 9,000

The equity method requires investors to amortize valuation differentials [*APB Opinion No. 18,* par. 19(b)]. The revaluation increment is amortized (unless allocated to land) over the remaining life of the related assets or liabilities as determined by the parent. Goodwill is amortized over a period not to exceed 40 years. Let us assume that Thompson amortizes the valuation differential as shown in the following schedule:

Amortization of Valuation Differential

	19X1		19X2–X8		19X9–X20	
Goodwill ($9,000 ÷ 20)		$ 450		$450		$450
Revaluation increment:						
Inventory ($360 ÷ 1)	$360		$–0–		$–0–	
Building ($2,640 ÷ 8)	330	690	330	330	–0–	–0–
Amortization of valuation differential		$1,140		$780		$450

The foregoing schedule shows that Thompson amortizes goodwill at a straight-line rate of $450 per year over 20 years. Thompson follows the usual treatment of inventory write-ups included in the revaluation increment. The entire inventory write-up ($360) is included in the first-year amortization, which is appropriate if the inventory is sold (or used in production that is sold) during the first year. Finally, the schedule shows that Thompson amortizes the revaluation increment that is associated with the building at a straight-line rate of $330 per year over 8 years.

The equity-method journal entries made by Thompson are shown on the right-hand side of Exhibit 3-1 on page 136. The first entry records Thompson's acquisition of a 60% interest in its subsidiary, Winslow. Observe that the acquisition of a long-term investment in stock is recorded at acquisition cost whether the cost method or the equity method is employed. The second equity-method entry records the investor's share of the investee's reported net income of $25,000, which has been adjusted for the investor's amortization of the valuation differential:[4]

---

[4] As explained in Chapter 9, the application of push-down accounting for subsidiary financial statements alters the parent's calculation of income from subsidiary. A push-down subsidiary's income will already include amortization of the valuation differential, making unnecessary all or part of the amortization adjustment in the parent's calculation of income from subsidiary.

Parent's Calculation of 19X1 Income from Subsidiary

Subsidiary's reported net income	$25,000
Parent's ownership percentage	×.60
Parent's share of subsidiary net income	$15,000
Amortization of valuation differential	(1,140)
Income from subsidiary	$13,860

Observe that the credit to income from subsidiary[5] is accompanied by an equal debit to the investment account. In this way, the parent's share of net assets generated by the subsidiary enters the investment account in the same period that it enters the accounts of the subsidiary. Of course, the amount recognized in this way is adjusted for the parent's amortization of the valuation differential.[6]

The third entry on the right-hand side of Exhibit 3-1 records the declaration and receipt of the $6,000 dividend from the subsidiary ($6,000 = .60 × $10,000). The dividend is recorded as a reduction of the investment account because it represents a distribution of a portion of the earnings recorded in the investment account by the preceding entry. In other words, the balance of the investment account includes the parent's share of the undistributed subsidiary net income. Notice that the amount of income from subsidiary is unaffected by the amount of the subsidiary's dividend. Rather, the dividend represents a reduction of the investment.[7]

The following T-account summarizes the application of the equity method to the investment in Winslow:

Investment in Winslow

Acquisition cost	60,000	Valuation differential amortization	1,140
Net income share	15,000	Dividend	6,000
Balance, 12-31-X1	67,860		

The acquisition cost ($60,000) is recorded by the first entry in Exhibit 3-1, the parent's net income share ($15,000 = .60 × $25,000) and the offsetting valuation differential amortization ($1,140) are recorded as a single amount ($13,860 = $15,000 − $1,140) by the second entry in Exhibit 3-1, and the dividend ($6,000 = .60 × $10,000) is recorded by the third entry in Exhibit 3-1.

Presentation in Investor's Financial Statements

The equity method, when applied to subsidiaries, is sometimes characterized as a "one-line consolidation." This characterization reflects the equity-method practice of reporting the parent's share of subsidiary net assets as a single balance sheet item (investment in

---

[5] When the equity method is applied to nonsubsidiary (less than 50% owned) investees, then the income items should be called *income from investments* or *equity in earnings of investees* rather than *income from subsidiary*. Of course, the exact words used in practice vary considerably.

[6] Although amortization of the valuation differential is deducted under the equity method, it is not deductible in the calculation of taxable income unless it arises from a taxable combination. However, the financial press has reported recent court decisions that may expand the deductibility of intangibles.

[7] In addition, investments, like other long-term assets, should be reduced for *other than temporary* declines in their value. Accordingly, an investment balance may include such adjustments.

subsidiary) and the parent's share of subsidiary income as a single income statement item (income from subsidiary). The characterization of the equity method as "one-line consolidation" also reflects the fact that the parent's net income under the equity method usually equals consolidated net income. From a conceptual point of view, the equity method is a highly aggregated application of the proportionate-consolidation concept.

The equity-method items, "investment in subsidiary" and "income from subsidiary," appear in the parent's separate financial statements but not in the parent's consolidated financial statements, where they are replaced in the consolidation process. On the other hand, equity-method items for nonsubsidiary investees (less than majority-owned investees) appear in both the parent's separate financial statements and the consolidated financial statements.

The investor's share of income from equity-method investments is reported in the investor's income statement in a variety of ways. When the investee is an integral part of operations, the investee's income may be reported as part of income from operations—frequently as a separate revenue item. "Income from subsidiaries" is shown in this way throughout this book in the separate income statements of parent companies. Sometimes income from subsidiaries (or investees) is offset against a closely related expense item. In a classified income statement, income from equity-method investees may be reported following income from operations and before income tax expense; this presentation is particularly appropriate if investees produce significant income yet are not an integral part of operations. In all of these cases, income tax expense should include any taxes borne by the investor as a consequence of the investment and income from the investee should include the investor's share of taxes borne by the investee.[8]

Special Problems under the Equity Method

Let us consider several special problems that arise in accounting for long-term investments in stock and demonstrate their treatment under the equity method. The paragraphs that follow consider equity-method accounting for (1) identifiable fair value in excess of acquisition cost, (2) investee losses, (3) investee stock dividends, (4) preferred dividends of investee, (5) investor's share of investee's extraordinary items, and (6) disclosure of separate financial information about investee.

Identifiable fair value acquired in excess of acquisition cost

When acquisition cost exceeds the fair value of identifiable net assets acquired, the excess represents an asset called goodwill that is amortized over time as shown in the Thompson-Winslow illustration. On the other hand, when the fair value of identifiable net assets acquired exceeds acquisition cost, the excess represents a credit that must be allocated to reduce proportionately the fair values initially assigned to noncurrent assets (except long-term investments in marketable securities). The allocation of such a credit was illustrated in Chapter 2 in the context of a date-of-acquisition consolidation. A similar allocation is required under the equity method. To illustrate, consider Arthur Enterprises' investment in

---

[8] When the investor and investee qualify for filing a combined tax return (see Chapter 8 for an introductory discussion), it may be necessary to allocate the tax expense between investor (parent) and investee (subsidiary) in order to meet requirements for the disclosure of separate-company financial information. See *FASB Statement No. 109,* pars. 49 and 159, for additional details. Some companies report income from equity-method investees following income tax expense, in which case the reported amount should be adjusted for any tax consequences of the income for the investor.

Young, Inc. Arthur acquired the investment, which represents 75% of the outstanding voting shares of Young, for $45,000 cash on January 1, 19X1. On that date, the estimated fair value of Young's identifiable net assets ($75,000) exceeded the corresponding book value ($64,000) by $11,000 as shown in column (3) of Exhibit 3-2. On the basis of this information, we can prepare the following analysis of the valuation differential:

Calculation of Valuation Differential with Excess of Initial Fair Value over Cost

Acquisition cost		$45,000
Less: Book value of net assets acquired		48,000
Valuation differential (negative)		$ (3,000)
Less: Initial revaluation increment:		
Inventory [($19,500 − $17,000) × .75]	$1,875	
Building and equipment		
[($52,900 − $46,400) × .75]	4,875	
Land [($12,000 − $10,000) × .75]	1,500	8,250
Excess of initial fair value over cost		$(11,250)

Financial accounting standards require that the excess of fair value over cost be allocated among noncurrent assets in proportion to their respective fair values as shown in the following schedule:

Allocation of Excess of Fair Value over Cost among Noncurrent Assets

	Initial Fair Value Estimate		
	Amount	Percent	Allocation
Building and equipment (net)	$52,900	81.5%	$11,250 × .815 = $ 9,169
Land	12,000	18.5	$11,250 × .185 = 2,081
Total	$64,900	100.0%	$11,250

EXHIBIT 3-2	ALLOCATION OF EXCESS OF INITIAL FAIR VALUE OVER COST AMONG CERTAIN NONCURRENT ASSETS OF SUBSIDIARY

	Initial Fair Value (100%) (1)	Book Value (100%) (2)	Excess of Initial Fair Value over Book Value (100%) (3)	Initial Revaluation Increment (75%) (4)	Allocation of Excess of Fair Value over Cost (5)	Adjusted Revaluation Increment (6)
Cash	$ 2,600	$ 2,600	$	$	$	$
Inventory	19,500	17,000	2,500	1,875		1,875
Building and equipment (net)	52,900	46,400	6,500	4,875	(9,169)	(4,294)
Land	12,000	10,000	2,000	1,500	(2,081)	(581)
Total assets	$87,000	$76,000	$11,000	$8,250	$(11,250)	$(3,000)
Liabilities	12,000	12,000				
Net assets	$75,000	$64,000	$11,000	$8,250	$(11,250)	$(3,000)

The $11,250 excess of fair value over cost is not allocated to current assets, long-term investments in marketable securities, or liabilities. Accordingly, the entire excess is allocated among building and equipment (net) and land. The allocation alters the initial revaluation increment that is associated with these noncurrent assets as shown in Exhibit 3-2. The amortization of the $11,250 excess of fair value over cost completely eliminates the revaluation increment that is associated with noncurrent assets and results in a $4,294 write-down of building and equipment and a $581 write-down of land. The calculation of the valuation differential is summarized in the following schedule:

Calculation of Valuation Differential and Goodwill

Acquisition cost		$45,000
Less: Book value of net assets acquired		
[($76,000 − $12,000) × .75]		48,000
Negative valuation differential		$ (3,000)
Less: Revaluation increment:		
Inventory [($19,500 − $17,000) × .75]	$1,875	
Building and equipment (net)		
[(($52,900 − $46,400) × .75) − $9,169]	(4,294)	
Land [(($12,000 − $10,000) × .75) − $2,081]	(581)	(3,000)
Goodwill		$ −0−

As long as the book value of the investee's noncurrent assets is sufficient to absorb the excess of fair value over cost, goodwill remains zero. If, however, the excess of fair value over cost is sufficiently large, the entire book value may be offset and negative goodwill results. Negative goodwill results when the allocated excess of fair value over cost (the total of column 6 in Exhibit 3-2) exceeds the book value of noncurrent assets (except long-term investments in marketable securities). Under the equity method, negative goodwill must be amortized over a period that is not to exceed 40 years. In consolidation, unamortized negative goodwill must be removed from the investment balance and reclassified as a deferred credit. In the Arthur-Young illustration, let us assume amortization of the adjusted revaluation increment proceeds according to the following schedule:

Amortization of Adjusted Valuation Differential

	19X1	19X2–X9
Revaluation increment:		
Inventory ($1,875 ÷ 1)	$1,875	$−0−
Building and equipment (net) ($4,294 ÷ 9)	(477)	(477)
Land ($581)	−0−	−0−
Amortization of valuation differential	$1,398	$(477)

The foregoing schedule shows that the entire inventory write-up is included in the first-year amortization. The schedule also shows that Arthur amortizes the negative revaluation increment that is associated with building and equipment on a straight-line basis over nine years. Note that the negative revaluation increment that is associated with land is not subject to amortization. Thus, $1,398 would be *subtracted* in the 19X1 calculation of income from subsidiary and $477 would be *added* in the 19X2 through 19X9 calculations.

Investee losses

Under the equity method, the investor's share of investee net income *increases* both the investor's net income and the investor's investment balance. Correspondingly, the investor's share of investee losses *decreases* both the investor's net income and the investor's investment balance. When the investee incurs such heavy losses that the investment balance is reduced to zero, further losses are not recognized by the investor. When an investment balance is reduced to zero by investee losses and the investee subsequently reports a net income, the investor should not recognize its share of such income until that share of income equals the investor's share of investee losses incurred after the investment balance reached zero. In other words, the application of the equity method is suspended when the investment balance reaches zero and is not resumed until losses recognized during the period of suspension are recovered through a subsequent net income [*APB Opinion No. 18,* par. 19 (i)].[9]

Subsidiary stock dividends and ownership percentage

A subsidiary stock dividend, unlike a subsidiary cash dividend, does not transfer assets to the parent. Accordingly, a stock dividend occasions only a memorandum entry by the parent as to the number and identity of the new shares received; neither the assets nor the ownership percentage of the parent is altered by a stock dividend. The subsidiary, of course, must transfer an amount of retained earnings (usually the par value or the fair value of the new shares) to its common stock and excess-over-par accounts. This treatment is also accorded stock dividends under the cost method of accounting for long-term investments in common stock.

Preferred dividends and parent's income share

If a subsidiary has outstanding preferred stock, then preferred dividends should be subtracted from the subsidiary's net income before multiplication by the parent's ownership percentage to obtain the parent's income share. Of course, the amount subtracted for dividends depends on the characteristics of the preferred stock. If preferred stock is cumulative, then the entire dividend should be subtracted whether or not it has been paid. Preferred stock is also discussed in Chapter 7.

Parent's share of extraordinary items

Financial accounting standards require that the extraordinary items and prior-period adjustments reported by an investee be shown separately (and net of applicable income tax effects) in the investor's income statement and statement of retained earnings, respectively [see *APB Opinion No. 18,* par. 19(d), as amended, and *APB Opinion No. 30* for additional details].

Consider an 80%-owned subsidiary acquired at book value that reports a net income of $20,000, including an extraordinary loss (net of tax) of $6,000. The parent records its share of the income and extraordinary loss by the following entry:

---

[9] If the investor has guaranteed obligations of the investee or is otherwise committed to supporting the investee, then losses in excess of the investment balance should be recognized to the extent of such commitments and the corresponding liabilities should be recorded. In other words, the equity method is suspended when losses reduce the investment balance to zero and, in addition, result in the recording of all guaranteed amounts among the investor's liabilities.

Parent's entry to record extraordinary loss and income from subsidiary:

Investment in subsidiary (.80 × $20,000).................	16,000	
Extraordinary loss (.80 × $6,000).......................	4,800	
Income from subsidiary [.80 × ($20,000 + $6,000)].....		20,800

The parent's share of the extraordinary loss, $4,800, should be reported in the parent's income statement in the same manner as an extraordinary item from the parent's separate operations. Similarly, the parent's share of a subsidiary's prior-period adjustment should be reported in the parent's statement of retained earnings (see *APB Opinion No. 30*).

Separate financial information

Under certain conditions, the SEC's Regulation S-X requires that public companies present separate financial information and, in some cases, separate financial statements for significant investees for which the equity method has been used. Separate financial statements are required in Form 10-K for any investee that individually constitutes more than 20% of consolidated assets or income for the latest year. Further, summarized financial information is required as a minimum for any investees that aggregate more than 10% of consolidated assets or income. Chapter 9 contains additional discussion of the rules governing the separate financial statements of affiliated companies.

Deferred income taxes

Another important complication is that investors must recognize income tax expense and the related deferred tax liability for undistributed income of investees. This complication is discussed in Chapter 8. Throughout this book, unless stated otherwise, we assume that consolidated returns are filed making such deferred tax recognition unnecessary, or, if consolidated returns cannot be filed, that deferred tax amounts are immaterial and not recorded.

POSTACQUISITION CONSOLIDATED FINANCIAL STATEMENTS

We turn now from the parent's accounting for investments in subsidiaries to the preparation of consolidated financial statements. The essence of balance sheet consolidation is the replacement of the parent's investment account with the detailed assets and liabilities of the subsidiary and the creation of minority interest equity, if one exists. The previous chapter demonstrated consolidations at the date of acquisition. The present chapter considers consolidations of financial statements one or more years after acquisition. Although postacquisition consolidations follow the same basic procedure outlined in Chapter 2, the procedures must be extended. Date-of-acquisition consolidations entail neither postacquisition income and dividends nor amortizations of goodwill and revaluation increments. But postacquisition consolidations must account for all these events, which complicate the substitution of subsidiary assets and liabilities for the parent's investment account and the calculation of minority interest.

    The consolidation worksheet is the controlling document for both date-of-acquisition and postacquisition consolidations. But the form of the worksheet—in particular, the form of worksheet adjustments—depends on the parent's accounting for postacquisition income, dividends, and amortization related to investments in subsidiaries (i.e., on whether the cost method or equity method has been used). Throughout the remainder of this text, we assume that all parent companies use the equity method for investments in subsidiaries unless use of the cost method is specifically indicated.

Consolidation of Balance Sheets at Date of Acquisition

Consolidation of the balance sheets at the date of acquisition is reviewed here to establish a point of departure for the additional procedures required subsequent to acquisition. We shall illustrate consolidation procedures both at the date of acquisition and subsequent to acquisition by reference to Broad Corporation's 80% acquisition of High, Inc. Data concerning the acquisition will be presented as they are required in the discussion that follows.

Analysis of the Valuation Differential

Let us begin by analyzing the valuation differential associated with the acquisition. On January 1, 19X1, Broad Corporation acquired 80% of the outstanding voting stock of High, Inc., for $80,000 cash. On January 1, 19X1, High's total stockholders' equity is $90,000, consisting of common stock of $60,000 and retained earnings of $30,000. Book values equal fair values for all assets and liabilities of High on January 1, 19X1, except for the building, which has a fair value that is $6,250 more than book value.

The analysis of the valuation differential is the first computational step in consolidating at the date of acquisition. The $8,000 excess of acquisition cost over the book value of net assets acquired (the excess of cost over acquired equity) is analyzed as follows for the Broad and High illustration:

Analysis of the Valuation Differential for Net Assets Acquired

Acquisition cost ($80,000)	Fair value of identifiable net assets acquired ($77,000)*	Book value of net assets acquired ($72,000)†
Goodwill = $3,000	Revaluation increment = $5,000	
Valuation differential = $8,000		

* $77,000 = ($90,000 + $6,250) × .80
    = $72,000 + $5,000

† $72,000 = $90,000 × .80

The calculation of the valuation differential and goodwill is presented in the following schedule:

Calculation of Valuation Differential and Goodwill

Acquisition cost	$80,000
Less: Book value of net assets acquired ($90,000 × .80)	72,000
Valuation differential	$ 8,000
Less: Revaluation increment:	
Building ($6,250 × .80)	5,000
Goodwill	$ 3,000

Consolidation Adjustment at Date of Acquisition

Recall that a consolidation worksheet adjustment is required at the date of acquisition to perform two functions: (1) to eliminate the acquired stockholders' equity and the related investment and (2) to reclassify the valuation differential. The book value of the parent's equity in the subsidiary is a component of both the parent's investment account and the subsidiary's stockholders' equity accounts. Before parent and subsidiary balance sheets can be consolidated, this component must be eliminated from both the parent's assets and the subsidiary's equities. Although the component is appropriately included among the parent's separately reported assets, the consolidated entity cannot report its own equity securities as an asset. In addition, the adjustment must reclassify the remainder of the investment account as goodwill and revaluation increment. Recall that the entire revaluation increment is associated with the subsidiary's building account. The following worksheet adjustment accomplishes the required elimination and reclassification at the date of acquisition:

Worksheet adjustment to eliminate and reclassify beginning-of-the-year balance of parent's investment account:

Common stock of High ($60,000 × .80) 48,000
Retained earnings of High ($30,000 × .80) 24,000
Building (net) *5,000*
Goodwill *3,000*
    Investment in High   80,000

Once again, the reclassification of the valuation differential is shown in italic type. The adjustment is entered in the worksheet shown in Exhibit 3-3.

Minority Interest Column

The foregoing adjustment reduces the investment account balance to zero, but it leaves remainders in the subsidiary's common stock and retained earnings accounts of $12,000 ($60,000 − $48,000) and $6,000 ($30,000 − $24,000), respectively. These remainders constitute the interest of minority stockholders in common stock and retained earnings of the subsidiary and are carried to a minority interest column in Exhibit 3-3, where they are summed and transferred to the consolidated balance sheet column as a single item. Notice that the parent's common stock and retained earnings balances are carried to the consolidated balance sheet without adjustment.

Consolidated Financial Statements One Year after Acquisition

Postacquisition consolidation procedures must reflect the parent's application of the equity method. In particular, consolidation procedures must accommodate the recognition of subsidiary income and dividends and the amortization of the valuation differential by the parent company. The demonstration of postacquisition consolidation procedures that follows is based on additional information about the Broad and High example pertaining to the year following acquisition. Recall that at the date of acquisition, the valuation differential that is associated with Broad Corporation's 80% interest in High, Inc., is $8,000, consisting of goodwill of $3,000 and a revaluation increment of $5,000. The following schedule describes the amortization of this valuation differential:

Amortization of Valuation Differential

	19X1–X5	19X6–X15
Goodwill ($3,000 ÷ 15)	$ 200	$200
Revaluation increment: Building ($5,000 ÷ 5)	1,000	–0–
Amortization of valuation differential	$1,200	$200

The schedule shows that goodwill is amortized on a straight-line basis for 15 years and that the revaluation increment, all of which is associated with a building, is amortized on a straight-line basis over five years. Thus, the rate of amortization is $1,200 per year for the first five years and $200 per year for the next ten years.

During 19X1 High, Inc., reports a net income of $9,000 and declares and pays a dividend of $4,000, as shown in the following analysis of the stockholders' equity accounts of High presented at the top of the next page.

EXHIBIT 3-3	CONSOLIDATION OF BALANCE SHEETS AT DATE OF ACQUISITION

	Separate Financial Statements		Consolidation Adjustments		Minority Interest	Consolidated Financial Statement
	Broad	High	Dr.	Cr.		
Assets						
Current assets	120,000	10,000				130,000
Investment in High	80,000			(1) 80,000		–0–
Equipment (net)	400,000	70,000				470,000
Building (net)	300,000	30,000	(1) 5,000			335,000
Land	100,000	10,000				110,000
Goodwill			(1) 3,000			3,000
Total assets	1,000,000	120,000				1,048,000
Liabilities and Stockholders' Equity						
Current liabilities	40,000	5,000				45,000
Long-term liabilities	340,000	25,000				365,000
Common stock:						
Broad	500,000					500,000
High		60,000	(1) 48,000		12,000	
Retained earnings:						
Broad	120,000					120,000
High		30,000	(1) 24,000		6,000	
Minority interest					(18,000)*	18,000
Total liabilities and stockholders' equity	1,000,000	120,000	80,000	80,000	–0–	1,048,000

* Parentheses indicate decreases.

Stockholders' Equity Accounts of Subsidiary for 19X1			
	Subsidiary Common Stock	Subsidiary Retained Earnings	Total Subsidiary Stockholders' Equity
Balance, Jan. 1, 19X1	$60,000	$30,000	$90,000
Add: 19X1 net income of High		9,000	9,000
Less: 19X1 dividend of High		(4,000)	(4,000)
Balance, Dec. 31, 19X1	$60,000	$35,000	$95,000

The paragraphs that follow present analyses of subsidiary stockholders' equity and the parent's investment account, which are designed to enhance understanding of postacquisition consolidation procedures. Then we turn to discussions of consolidated net income and minority interest in subsidiary net income before illustrating the consolidation worksheet and related adjustments for the year following acquisition.

Analysis of Subsidiary Stockholders' Equity

Stockholders' equity of the subsidiary can be allocated between the parent company and minority stockholders. In the Broad–High illustration, the parent company's 80% share of subsidiary stockholders' equity is $72,000 (.80 × $90,000) on January 1, 19X1, and $76,000 (.80 × $95,000) on December 31, 19X1. The remainder of subsidiary stockholders' equity is attributable to minority stockholders—$18,000 (.20 × $90,000) on January 1, 19X1, and $19,000 (.20 × $95,000) on December 31, 19X1.

The parent's share of subsidiary equity can be further subdivided into *acquired equity* and *earned equity,* as shown in Exhibit 3-4. On December 31, 19X1, the parent's equity interest of $76,000 consists of acquired equity of $72,000 and earned equity of $4,000. *Earned equity is the parent's share of subsidiary earnings in excess of dividends since acquisition.* The parent's shares of 19X1 earnings and dividends are $7,200 (.80 × $9,000) and $3,200 (.80 × $4,000), respectively. The difference between the two shares equals the increase in the parent's earned equity during 19X1 ($4,000 = $7,200 − $3,200). The dividend transfers assets in the amount of $3,200 from High to Broad. Consequently, the equity in the transferred assets is no longer reflected in the equity accounts of the subsidiary and must be subtracted in calculating the parent's share of subsidiary equity.

Analysis of Investment Account

Before we analyze the parent's investment account, let us consider in general terms the components of the investment account. Under the equity method, the investment account has two primary components, each of which is divisible into two additional secondary components. The two primary components of the investment account are (1) the book value of the parent's equity in the subsidiary and (2) the valuation differential, that is, the excess of acquisition cost over the book value of *acquired* equity in the subsidiary. The first component, the book value of the parent's equity in the subsidiary, is divisible into *acquired equity* and *earned equity,* which parallels the division of the parent's share of subsidiary stockholders' equity into acquired and earned equity. The second component,

EXHIBIT 3-4	ANALYSIS OF SUBSIDIARY STOCKHOLDERS' EQUITY ONE YEAR AFTER ACQUISITION

Broad Corporation
ANALYSIS OF STOCKHOLDERS' EQUITY FOR SUBSIDIARY, HIGH, INC.
FOR THE YEAR ENDED DECEMBER 31, 19X1

	Subsidiary Stockholders' Equity	Parent's Equity in Subsidiary		Minority Interest
		Acquired	Earned	
Common stock of High, Inc.	$60,000	$48,000		$12,000
Retained earnings of High, Inc.:				
Balance on Jan. 1, 19X1	$30,000	$24,000		$ 6,000
Add: 19X1 net income	9,000		$7,200	1,800
Less: 19X1 dividend	(4,000)*		(3,200)	(800)
Balance on Dec. 31, 19X1	$35,000	$24,000	$4,000	$ 7,000
Subsidiary stockholders' equity on Dec. 31, 19X1	$95,000	$72,000	$4,000	$19,000

* Parentheses indicate decreases.

the valuation differential, is divisible into *goodwill* and the *revaluation increment*. This two-level classification, which is the basis for the analysis of the parent's investment account, is shown in the headings of Exhibit 3-5 on the following page. Acquired equity arises from all the subsidiary's transactions in ownership equity (earnings, dividends, and capital transactions) that occur *before* the date of acquisition. The book value of such equity is said to be *acquired* by the parent on the date of acquisition. On the other hand, earned equity arises from the subsidiary's earnings and dividends that occur *after* the date of acquisition. The book value of such equity is said to be *earned* by the parent.

Analysis of the investment account must track these four components of the investment over time from the date of acquisition onward. The analysis of the investment account one year after acquisition reflects the parent's entries for subsidiary income, dividends, and amortization. The analysis for Broad Corporation's investment in High, Inc., is presented in Exhibit 3-5. A separate column of Exhibit 3-5 depicts the 19X1 changes in each of the four components of the investment account. Let us consider each of the two primary components in turn.

Book value of parent's equity in subsidiary

The book value of *acquired* equity (which equals the book value of net assets acquired) is unaltered by changes in the investment account during 19X1; it remains $72,000. But the book value of *earned* equity is increased by $4,000, the difference between the parent's income share and the dividend ($4,000 = $7,200 − $3,200). At year-end, the total book value of the parent's equity in High, Inc., is $76,000 ($72,000 + $4,000), which agrees with the analysis of subsidiary ownership equity shown in Exhibit 3-4.

EXHIBIT 3-5	ANALYSIS OF PARENT'S INVESTMENT ACCOUNT ONE YEAR AFTER ACQUISITION

Broad Corporation

ANALYSIS OF INVESTMENT IN HIGH, INC.
FOR THE YEAR ENDED DECEMBER 31, 19X1

	Total Investment	Book Value of Parent's Equity in Subsidiary		Unamortized Valuation Differential	
		Acquired	Earned	Goodwill	Revaluation Increment
Balance, January 1, 19X1	$80,000[2]†	$72,000*	$ –0–	$3,000	$5,000
Add: Income from subsidiary [(.80 × $9,000) − $1,200]	6,000[1]		7,200	(200)	(1,000)
Less: Parent's share of subsidiary dividend (.80 × $4,000)	(3,200)[1]		(3,200)		
Balance, December 31, 19X1	$82,800	$72,000	$4,000	$2,800	$4,000

* The book value of *acquired* equity is $72,000, including equity in common stock of $48,000 ($60,000 × .80) and acquired equity in retained earnings of $24,000 ($30,000 × .80). Notice that the book value of acquired equity equals the book value of net assets acquired [$72,000 = .80 ($120,000 − $5,000 − $25,000)] which is used in the calculation of the valuation differential at the date of acquisition.

† The numerical superscripts in the investment analysis above identify the various components of the investment balance with the consolidation worksheet adjustments (see Exhibit 3-7 on page 157) that eliminate or reclassify the component.

Unamortized valuation differential

The valuation differential is composed of goodwill and the revaluation increment. The amortization during 19X1 reduces goodwill by $200 and the revaluation increment by $1,000. The result at year-end is an unamortized valuation differential of $6,800 ($2,800 + $4,000). Unlike the book value of the parent's equity in the subsidiary, which is reflected in both the investment account and the ownership equity accounts of the subsidiary, the unamortized valuation differential is not recorded on the books of the subsidiary but is strictly a manifestation of the parent's records.

Before we turn to the consolidation worksheet procedure required one year after acquisition, it is useful to consider the general nature of consolidated net income and minority interest, which play important roles in the consolidation procedure.

Consolidated Net Income

The balance sheet is the only consolidated financial statement at the date of acquisition for purchase combinations. Subsequent to acquisition, however, the income statement must also be presented on a consolidated basis. *Consolidated net income* is the difference

EXHIBIT 3-6	SEPARATE AND CONSOLIDATED INCOME STATEMENTS

Broad Corporation and High, Inc.

SEPARATE AND CONSOLIDATED INCOME STATEMENTS*
FOR THE YEAR ENDED DECEMBER 31, 19X1

	Separate Income Statements		Consolidated Income Statement
	Broad	**High†**	
Revenue	$2,800,000	$150,000	$2,950,000
Income from subsidiary	6,000		
Cost of goods sold	(1,800,000)	(90,000)	(1,890,000)
Depreciation expense—equipment	(80,000)	(14,000)	(94,000)
Depreciation expense—building	(30,000)	(6,000)	(36,000)
Other expense	(800,000)	(31,000)	(831,000)
Amortization of goodwill			(200)
Depreciation of valuation increment			(1,000)
Minority interest in subsidiary income (.20 × $9,000)			(1,800)
Net income	$ 96,000	$ 9,000	$ 96,000

* The unconventional format of the income statement shown here is consistent with the form of the consolidation worksheet. Although the statements do not display gross margin or income from operations, problems and exercises may require the computations of such amounts. Observe that the *parent's income from its own operations* is $90,000 (the parent's net income of $96,000 less the income from its subsidiary of $6,000). The subsidiary's income from operations is $9,000, which equals the subsidiary's net income.

† High, Inc., is an 80%-owned subsidiary of Broad Corporation.

between consolidated revenues and expenses (after the elimination of the parent's income from the subsidiary account) reduced by the amortization of the valuation differential and the minority interest in the subsidiary's net income. The 19X1 consolidated income statement for the Broad and High illustration is shown in the third column of Exhibit 3-6. (For the sake of comparison, the separate income statements of Broad and High are shown in the first two columns of Exhibit 3-6. Of course, only the third column is reported on the consolidated income statement.) Consolidated net income can also be calculated as the *parent's income from its own operations* plus the parent's share of *income from the subsidiary* (including the amortization of goodwill and revaluation increments). Thus, *consolidated net income equals the parent's separate net income* when the parent uses the equity method of accounting for investments in subsidiaries.[10] In other words, we consider three income figures—the parent's net income, the subsidiary's net income, and the consolidated net income—and two of them are equal (consolidated net income equals the parent's net income), as shown in Exhibit 3-6.

---

[10] Several exceptions to this general rule are discussed in later chapters.

Broad Corporation's net income of $96,000 includes $6,000 for income from High, Inc., which is Broad's share of High's net income ($7,200 = .80 × $9,000) reduced by the amortization of goodwill and revaluation increments ($6,000 = $7,200 − $200 − $1,000). Observe that both the parent's net income and consolidated net income equal $96,000. Yet the computation of consolidated net income differs from the computation of the parent's net income. In the parent's net income statement, income from the subsidiary is shown as a single item of $6,000. In contrast, the consolidated income statement shows a net income from the subsidiary distributed among the appropriate revenue and expense items with a deduction for minority interest. As shown in Exhibit 3-6, 100% of subsidiary revenue is included in a consolidated revenue of $2,950,000 ($2,800,000 + $150,000). The consolidated net income statement includes 100% of every element of the subsidiary net income. Yet only 80% of the subsidiary's net income is assignable to the parent—the remainder being assignable to minority interest. The minority interest in all elements of the subsidiary net income is removed from the calculation by a single deduction of $1,800 (.20 × $9,000).

Observe that consolidated net income includes amortization of goodwill and revaluation increment ($200 and $1,000, respectively) as separate items. On the parent's income statement these additional expenses are adjustments to the income from the subsidiary ($6,000 = $7,200 − $1,200).

In short, the consolidated income statement is obtained from the parent's income statement by a process of *substitution*—"income from subsidiary," a single item on the parent's income statement, is replaced by (1) the detailed revenues and expenses of the subsidiary, (2) the amortization of the valuation differential, and (3) an adjustment for the minority interest in subsidiary net income.

This view of consolidated net income characterizes current accounting practice. It is also consistent with the parent-company concept of consolidation because it results in a consolidated net income equal to the parent's net income.[11]

Consolidated Income Statement

The structure and captions used in practice for consolidated income statements vary considerably. Even the placement of minority interest varies. In some consolidated income statements, minority interest—particularly if it is not material—is reported (after-tax) among the consolidated expenses. In other statements—particularly if it is material—it is reported just after the deduction of income taxes expense, as shown in the following consolidated income statement issued by Corning:

---

[11] Following the proprietary theory, some authors interpret the parent-company concept to mean that minority interest in subsidiary net income is an *expense* and that minority interest in subsidiary stockholders' equity is a *liability* (Accountants International Study Group, 1973, par. 24). Thus, the expense of minority interest increases the parent company's liability to pay dividends to minority stockholders. However, other interpreters of the parent-company concept would not support this view (Pacter, 1991, p. 25). Instead, they view minority interest in subsidiary net income as an aggregate adjustment to consolidated net income items. Further, they view minority interest in subsidiary stockholders' equity as having characteristics of both a liability and an equity. This view has elements of both proprietary and entity theory.

Consolidated Statements of Income
Corning Incorporated and Subsidiary Companies

YEARS ENDED DECEMBER 29, 1991, DECEMBER 30, 1990, AND DECEMBER 31, 1989
(IN MILLIONS, EXCEPT PER-SHARE AMOUNTS)

	1991	1990	1989
Revenues			
Net sales	**$3,259.2**	$2,940.5	$2,439.2
Royalty, interest and dividend income	**27.6**	39.9	29.6
Non-operating gains	**8.1**	69.2	107.1
	3,294.9	3,049.6	2,575.9
Deductions			
Cost of sales	**2,121.6**	1,925.7	1,600.9
Selling, general and administrative expenses	**622.5**	581.8	491.8
Research and development expenses	**130.7**	124.5	109.6
Interest expense	**58.1**	54.0	44.5
Provision for restructuring costs			54.4
Other, net	**34.6**	35.5	20.9
Income before taxes on income	**327.4**	328.1	253.8
Taxes on income	**110.6**	136.1	116.9
Income before minority interest and equity earnings	**216.8**	192.0	136.9
Minority interest in earnings of subsidiaries	**(17.3)**	(10.4)	(4.2)
Equity in earnings of associated companies	**111.7**	107.5	126.7
Income before Extraordinary Credit (per common share, $1.66/1991; $1.53/1990; $1.39/1989)	**311.2**	289.1	259.4
Tax benefit of loss carryforwards	**5.6**	2.9	1.6
Net Income (per common share, $1.69/1991; $1.55/1990; $1.40/1989)	**$ 316.8**	$ 292.0	$ 261.0

Notice that the Corning consolidated income statement includes "equity in earnings of associated companies"; this item represents the parent's share of equity-method income from nonsubsidiary (20% to 50% owned) investees.

When the subsidiary reports net income, the minority interest in subsidiary net income is a negative number on the consolidated income statement, as shown above. When the subsidiary reports a net loss, the minority interest is a positive number. Minority interest in income usually appears after the caption for income tax expense and before consolidated net income.[12] To simplify our presentation, most of our illustrations and problems in this book do not consider income taxes.

---

[12] The economic-unit concept of consolidation leads to an alternative form of the consolidated income statement in which consolidated net income *includes* minority interest in the subsidiary's net income or loss. This consolidated net income, which would be $97,800 for our Broad and High example, must be allocated between parent-company and minority interests, either on the bottom of the income statement or in a separate schedule. In the example, $96,000 would be allocated to the parent and $1,800 to the minority interests.

The Consolidated Statement of Cash Flows

Consolidated financial statements also include a consolidated statement of cash flows as required by *FASB Statement No. 95.* Such statements are prepared from *consolidated* income statements and balance sheets rather than from the *separate* financial statements of parents and subsidiaries. The preparation of such statements follows the procedures described in intermediate accounting textbooks.

Consolidation Worksheet Procedure

One year after acquisition, the consolidation procedure yields a consolidated income statement, statement of retained earnings, and balance sheet. The worksheet procedure demonstrated for date-of-acquisition consolidated balance sheets can be extended to yield all three consolidated financial statements. The extension requires that two new sections be added to the top of the consolidation worksheet—one for the consolidated income statement and another for the consolidated statement of retained earnings. Exhibit 3-7 shows such a worksheet for the consolidation of Broad and High's separate financial statements for 19X1. The worksheet is comprised of one section for each of the three financial statements. The worksheet procedure consists of the following sequence of procedures, which correspond to the column headings in Exhibit 3-7:

1. Enter the separate financial statements of the *parent company* in the first column.
2. Enter the separate financial statements of the *subsidiary company* in the second column.
3. Enter the *consolidation adjustments.*
4. Calculate and enter the elements of *minority interest* in the subsidiary company in the minority interest column.
5. Calculate and enter the *consolidated financial statements* in the far right-hand column.

The paragraphs that follow describe and demonstrate the performance of these procedures leading to the consolidation worksheet shown in Exhibit 3-7.

Entry of Parent and Subsidiary Separate Financial Statements

Entry of the separate financial statements of the parent and its subsidiary (the first of the five procedures described previously) entails the following five steps:

1. Enter income statement items, and calculate net income.
2. *Carry forward* net income to the statement of retained earnings.
3. Enter all other elements of retained earnings, and calculate the year-end balance of retained earnings.
4. *Carry forward* the year-end balance of retained earnings to the balance sheet.
5. Enter all other assets and equities, and calculate total assets and total liabilities.

EXHIBIT 3-7	CONSOLIDATION OF FINANCIAL STATEMENTS ONE YEAR AFTER ACQUISITION

	Separate Financial Statements		Consolidation Adjustments		Minority Interest	Consolidated Financial Statements
	Broad	High	Dr.	Cr.		
Income Statement						
Revenue	2,800,000	150,000				2,950,000
Income from subsidiary	6,000		(1) 6,000			–0–
Cost of goods sold	(1,800,000)*	(90,000)				(1,890,000)
Depreciation and amortization	(110,000)	(20,000)	(3) 1,200			(131,200)
Other expense	(800,000)	(31,000)				(831,000)
Minority interest					1,800	(1,800)
Net income	96,000	9,000	7,200		1,800	96,000
Retained Earnings Statement						
Retained earnings, 1-1-X1:						
Broad	120,000					120,000
High		30,000	(2) 24,000		6,000	
Net income	96,000	9,000	7,200		1,800	96,000
Dividends	(40,000)	(4,000)		(1) 3,200	(800)	(40,000)
Retained earnings, 12-31-X1	176,000	35,000	31,200	3,200	7,000	176,000
Balance Sheet						
Current assets	153,200	32,000				185,200
Investment in High	82,800			(1) 2,800		–0–
				(2) 80,000		
Equipment (net)	420,000	56,000				476,000
Building (net)	270,000	24,000	(2) 5,000	(3) 1,000		298,000
Land	100,000	10,000				110,000
Goodwill			(2) 3,000	(3) 200		2,800
Total assets	1,026,000	122,000				1,072,000
Current liabilities	60,000	8,000				68,000
Long-term liabilities	290,000	19,000				309,000
Common stock:						
Broad	500,000					500,000
High		60,000	(2) 48,000		12,000	–0–
Retained earnings	176,000	35,000	31,200	3,200	7,000	176,000
Minority interest					(19,000)	19,000
Total liabilities and stockholders' equity	1,026,000	122,000	87,200	87,200	–0–	1,072,000

* Parentheses indicate decreases.

It is especially important to notice two points at which amounts carried forward are entered in a lower section of the worksheet. First, net income is calculated in the income section and carried forward to the retained earnings section. Second, year-end retained earnings are calculated and carried forward to the balance sheet. This sequence of carry-forwards parallels the fundamental articulation of the three financial statements.

Consolidation Adjustments One Year after Acquisition

Three worksheet adjustments, which follow, are required to consolidate the financial statements one year after acquisition and may be prepared by reference to Exhibit 3-5:

(1) *Worksheet adjustment to reverse parent's recording of subsidiary income and eliminate subsidiary dividend to parent for current year:*

Income from subsidiary	6,000	
Dividends		3,200
Investment in High.		2,800

(2) *Worksheet adjustment to eliminate and reclassify beginning-of-the-year balance of parent's investment account:*

Common stock of High ($60,000 × .80)	48,000	
Retained earnings of High ($30,000 × .80)	24,000	
Building (net)	*5,000*	
Goodwill	*3,000*	
Investment in High.		80,000

(3) *Worksheet adjustment to record amortization of valuation differential for current year:*

Depreciation and amortization.	1,200	
Building (net)		1,000
Goodwill		200

The foregoing adjustments have been entered in the consolidation worksheet shown in Exhibit 3-7. Let us consider each of the three worksheet adjustments in turn.

Reversal of parent's recording of subsidiary income and elimination of subsidiary dividend to parent.

The first adjustment reverses Broad's recording of subsidiary income [$6,000 = ($9,000 × .80) − $1,200] and eliminates the subsidiary's dividend to Broad ($3,200). The $6,000 debit to income from the subsidiary prevents the double-counting of subsidiary net income, which is already provided for when the subsidiary's income statement is added, item by item, to the parent's income statement. Notice that the $6,000 debit to income from the subsidiary is carried forward through the total of income-statement adjustments and also reduces the retained earnings balance in both the retained earnings and balance sheet segments of the worksheet. The first adjustment also eliminates the subsidiary's $3,200 dividend to Broad. From the viewpoint of the consolidated entity, dividend payments by the subsidiary to the parent are merely transfers of cash from one cash account to another. Consequently, the parent's credit to the investment account and the subsidiary's debit to the dividend account must be offset against one another. Notice that the adjustment to the subsidiary's dividend account is carried forward to adjust the subsidiary's retained earnings account on the balance sheet.[13] The first adjustment reduces the end-of-the-period balance of the parent's investment account ($82,800) to its beginning-of-the-period balance ($80,000).

Elimination and reclassification of beginning-of-the-year investment balance

The second adjustment eliminates or reclassifies the beginning-of-the-year investment balance. It eliminates the portion of the beginning-of-the-period investment balance associated with acquired equity in the subsidiary ($72,000), which equals 80% of the subsidiary's common stock and retained earnings balances on the date of acquisition. It reclassifies the beginning-of-the-period unamortized valuation differential consisting of an unamortized goodwill of $3,000 and an unamortized revaluation increment of $5,000 associated with a building. The amounts for the second adjustment are displayed in the first row of the investment account analysis in Exhibit 3-5.

Recording parent's amortization of valuation differential for current year

The third adjustment simply records the amortization of the valuation differential for the current period—$200 for goodwill and $1,000 for the building revaluation increment—by reducing the balances established in the preceding adjustment and by recording the appropriate amounts of expense.

Additional adjustments

The three adjustments demonstrated here are not the only consolidation adjustments encountered. Later sections of the text will demonstrate adjustments for intercompany debt, intercompany transfers of merchandise and other assets, and a variety of other complications.

Minority Interest Column

At the date of acquisition, minority interest in the subsidiary equals the minority interest percentage times subsidiary stockholders' equity. Subsequent to the date of acquisition, minority interest in the subsidiary is increased for the minority interest share in subsidiary net income and decreased for the minority interest share in subsidiary losses and dividends. The minority interest column of the consolidation worksheet summarizes the effects of subsidiary income, losses, and dividends on minority interest. The following worksheet procedures are required to complete the minority interest column in Exhibit 3-7:

1. Calculate the minority interest in subsidiary net income ($1,800 = .20 × $9,000), and enter it in the minority interest column and in the consolidated income statement column. When the *subsidiary reports net income,* the minority interest in the subsidiary net income should be entered as a *positive* number in the minority interest column and a *negative* number in the consolidated income column. When the *subsidiary reports a net loss,* the minority interest in the subsidiary net loss should be entered as a *negative*

[13] The reversal of the dividend restores equity in the amount of $3,200 to subsidiary retained earnings. Since the restored equity is related to a $3,200 cash transfer from High to Broad, the parent's (Broad's) assets include $3,200 that is supported by retained earnings of the subsidiary.

number in the minority interest column and a *positive* number in the consolidated income column.

2. Carry forward the minority interest in the subsidiary net income to the statement of retained earnings.

3. Calculate minority interest in the beginning balance of subsidiary retained earnings ($6,000 = .20 × $30,000) and minority interest in subsidiary dividends ($800 = .20 × $4,000), and enter the amounts in the minority interest column.

4. Total to find the minority interest in year-end subsidiary retained earnings ($7,000 = $6,000 + $1,800 − $800), and carry forward to balance sheet section.

5. Calculate the minority interest in the common stock of the subsidiary, and enter it in the minority interest column ($12,000 = .20 × $60,000).

6. Total to find the minority interest in the subsidiary equity ($19,000 = $12,000 + $7,000), and transfer it from the minority interest column to the consolidated balance sheet column.

The minority interest is represented at two points in the consolidated financial statements of Broad Corporation. First, the *minority interest in subsidiary net income,* $1,800, is subtracted in the income calculation to yield a consolidation net income of $96,000.[14] Second, *minority interest in the subsidiary ownership equity,* $19,000, is displayed as a single item on the equity side of the consolidated balance sheet.

Consolidated Financial Statements Column

The final step in the preparation of the consolidation worksheet is the completion of the consolidated financial statements column. Let us consider the completion of each of the three segments of this column in turn.

Worksheet segment for income

The income statement segment of the consolidation worksheet is completed by summing across the row for each statement item and calculating consolidated net income. For example, consolidated depreciation and amortization expense, $131,200, is the sum of the separate companies' depreciation expense deductions adjusted for the additional amortization of goodwill and the revaluation increment ($131,200 = $110,000 + $20,000 + $1,200). Since the parent uses the equity method to account for its investment in the subsidiary, consolidated net income *equals the net income of the parent company.* The net income segment of the worksheet is completed by summing the adjustment columns and carrying forward the entire net income row to the retained earnings segment of the worksheet.

---

[14] Minority interest in subsidiary net income is subtracted to yield consolidated net income provided that minority interest has a positive equity balance. In the unusual case that minority interest in subsidiary equity falls to zero, all further losses are charged against the parent's equity (see *Accounting Research Bulletin No. 51,* par. 15).

Worksheet segment for retained earnings

The retained earnings segment of the worksheet is completed by summing across the row for each statement item and computing the ending balance of consolidated retained earnings. For example, consolidated dividends, $40,000, equal the sum of the separate company dividends adjusted for the subsidiary's dividend to the parent of $3,200 and for the subsidiary's dividend to minority stockholders of $800 ($40,000 = $40,000 + $4,000 − $3,200 − $800). The result, of course, is that the consolidated dividend equals the parent's dividend. Notice that retained earnings of the parent *equal consolidated retained earnings.* This equality characterizes both beginning and ending balances as long as the parent uses the equity method of accounting for its investment in the subsidiary. The retained earnings segment of the worksheet is completed by summing the adjustment columns and carrying forward the entire year-end retained earnings row to the balance sheet segment of the worksheet.

Worksheet segment for balance sheet

The balance sheet segment of the worksheet is also completed by summing across the row for each statement item and computing the totals of consolidated assets and consolidated equities. Observe that the entire balance of the investment account is eliminated or reclassified. Of course, investment accounts for *unconsolidated* subsidiaries accounted for by the equity method would be reported in the asset section of the consolidated balance sheet under the caption ''Investments.'' Also observe that the entire balance of the subsidiary's common stock account is either eliminated or reclassified as minority interest. The remainder of minority interest consists of the minority stockholders' share of the subsidiary's ending retained earnings. The balance sheet segment of the worksheet is completed by summing the adjustment columns, which include the adjustments carried forward from the retained earnings segment, to determine that they exhibit equal totals.

Consolidation of Financial Statements Two Years after Acquisition

In the second and subsequent years following acquisition, the parent's earned equity in the beginning balance of subsidiary retained earnings is the basis for an additional consolidation adjustment. Let us illustrate the required procedures for a consolidation two years after acquisition by extending the information for the Broad and High combination into the second year following acquisition. The following data pertain to Broad Corporation's 80% interest in High, Inc., during 19X2, the second year following acquisition:

1. The valuation differential is amortized on the same basis as in the preceding year: $200 for goodwill and $1,000 for the building revaluation increment.

2. During 19X2 High, Inc., reported a net income of $18,000 and paid a cash dividend of $3,000 ($2,400 to Broad).

The foregoing data are reflected in the analysis of subsidiary stockholders' equity at December 31, 19X2, which is presented in Exhibit 3-8 on the following page. Observe that the parent's share of subsidiary retained earnings at December 31, 19X1, includes earned equity in the amount of $4,000, which represents the parent's share of subsidiary income in excess of dividends during the first year after acquisition [$4,000 = (.80 × $9,000) − (.80 × $4,000) = $7,200 − $3,200].

EXHIBIT 3-8	ANALYSIS OF SUBSIDIARY STOCKHOLDERS' EQUITY TWO YEARS AFTER ACQUISITION

Broad Corporation

ANALYSIS OF STOCKHOLDERS' EQUITY FOR SUBSIDIARY, HIGH, INC.
FOR THE YEAR ENDED DECEMBER 31, 19X2

	Subsidiary Stockholders' Equity	Parent's Equity		Minority Interest
		Acquired	Earned	
Common stock of subsidiary	$ 60,000	$48,000		$12,000
Retained earnings of subsidiary:				
Balance on Dec. 31, 19X1	35,000	24,000	4,000	7,000
Add: 19X2 net income	18,000		14,400	3,600
Less: 19X2 dividend	(3,000)		(2,400)	(600)
Balance on Dec. 31, 19X2	$ 50,000	$24,000	$16,000	$10,000
Subsidiary stockholders' equity on Dec. 31, 19X2	$110,000	$72,000	$16,000	$22,000

Analysis of Investment Account

The analysis of the investment account two years after acquisition takes essentially the same form as the analysis one year after acquisition. The investment account is partitioned into the book value of the parent's equity (acquired and earned) and the unamortized valuation differential. The primary difference between the second-year and first-year analyses is that the beginning investment balance for the second-year analysis reflects the first year's earned equity and differential amortization, whereas the beginning investment balance for the first-year analysis equals the acquisition cost, which, by definition, includes neither earned equity nor differential amortization.

Both first-year and second-year analyses for Broad Corporation's investment account are shown in Exhibit 3-9. During 19X2 High, Inc., reported a net income of $18,000 and paid a cash dividend of $3,000 ($2,400 to Broad). In addition, Broad amortized the valuation differential in the total amount of $1,200. Observe that the beginning investment balance for 19X2 reflects earned equity in High of $4,000, which is Broad Corporation's *undistributed* share of the subsidiary's 19X1 net income. Also observe that the January 1, 19X2, balance includes an *unamortized* valuation differential in the total amount of $6,800 ($6,800 = $2,800 + $4,000). The *year-end* investment balance ($93,600) includes the parent's share of undistributed subsidiary income ($16,000) for *both* 19X1 and 19X2 and, in addition, the unamortized valuation differential to be amortized in years after 19X2 ($5,600 = $2,600 + $3,000).

Consolidation Adjustments Two Years after Acquisition

The consolidation worksheet adjustments, based on the analysis in Exhibit 3-9 of Broad Corporation's investment in High, Inc., are presented in Exhibit 3-10. For purposes of

EXHIBIT 3-9

Broad Corporation

ANALYSIS OF INVESTMENT IN HIGH, INC.
FOR THE YEARS ENDED DECEMBER 31, 19X1, AND DECEMBER 31, 19X2

	Total Investment	Book Value of Parent's Equity in Subsidiary		Unamortized Valuation Differential	
		Acquired	Earned	Goodwill	Revaluation Increment
Balance, January 1, 19X1	$80,000^2†	$72,000*	$ –0–	$3,000	$5,000
Add: Income from subsidiary [(.80 × $9,000) − $1,200]	6,000^1		7,200	(200)	(1,000)
Less: Parent's share of subsidiary dividend (.80 × $4,000)	(3,200)^1		(3,200)		
Balance, January 1, 19X2	$82,800^2	$72,000	$ 4,000	$2,800	$4,000
Add: Income from subsidiary [($18,000 × .80) − $1,200]	13,200^1		14,400	(200)	(1,000)
Less: Parent's share of subsidiary dividend ($3,000 × .80)	(2,400)^1		(2,400)		
Balance, December 31, 19X2	$93,600	$72,000	$16,000	$2,600	$3,000

* Acquired stockholders' equity on the date of acquisition is $72,000 including acquired equity in common stock of $48,000 ($60,000 × .80) and acquired equity in retained earnings of $24,000 ($30,000 × .80).
† The numerical superscripts in the investment analysis above identify the various components of the investment balance with the consolidated worksheet adjustments (see Exhibits 3-10 below and 3-11 on page 165) that eliminate or reclassify the component.

EXHIBIT 3-10

	Date of Acquisition		One Year after Acquisition		Two Years after Acquisition	
(1) Reverse parent's recording of subsidiary income and eliminate subsidiary dividend to parent for current year:						
Income from subsidiary			6,000		13,200	
Dividends	No entry			3,200		2,400
Investment in High				2,800		10,800
(2) Eliminate and reclassify beginning-of-the-year balance of parent's investment account:						
Common stock of High	48,000		48,000		48,000	
Retained earnings of High	24,000		24,000		28,000	
Building (net)	5,000		5,000		4,000	
Goodwill	3,000		3,000		2,800	
Investment in High		80,000		80,000		82,800
(3) Amortize valuation differential for current year:						
Depreciation and amortization expense			1,200		1,200	
Building (net)				1,000		1,000
Goodwill	No entry			200		200

comparison, Exhibit 3-10 presents the date-of-acquisition and first-year consolidation adjustments as well as second-year adjustments. Second-year adjustments are posted to the consolidation worksheet shown in Exhibit 3-11. It is important to remember that consolidation worksheet adjustments are posted to the consolidation worksheet only and not to the books of the parent or its subsidiary.

Reversal of parent's recording of subsidiary income and elimination of subsidiary dividend to parent

At the end of the second year following acquisition, adjustment (1) reverses the equity-method entry made by the parent to record its adjusted share of subsidiary income for the second year [$13,200 = (.80 × $18,000) − $1,200] and eliminates the parent's share of the second-year subsidiary dividend ($2,400 = .80 × $3,000). Although the amounts differ from those in the corresponding worksheet adjustment made at the end of the first year following acquisition, the two adjustments alter the same accounts. Notice, as shown in Exhibit 3-10, that adjustment (1) is not required at the date of acquisition. Adjustment (1), whether made at the end of the first or second year following acquisition, adjusts the investment account to its beginning-of-the-year balance; at the end of the second year, this adjustment reduces the parent's investment account to $82,800 ($93,600 − $10,800), which, as shown in Exhibit 3-9, is the balance of the parent's investment account on January 1, 19X2.

Elimination and reclassification of beginning-of-year investment balance

At the end of the second year following acquisition, adjustment (2) eliminates the book value of the parent's investment as of the beginning of the second year and reclassifies the valuation differential that remains unamortized at the beginning of the year. The book value of the parent's investment increased by $4,000 during the first year following acquisition, which represents the parent's share of subsidiary earnings in excess of dividends and valuation differential amortization. The $4,000 increase is shown in the fourth row of Exhibit 3-9 as a component of the investment account balance at the beginning of the second year. As a consequence of this increase in the book value of the parent's investment, an additional $4,000 must be eliminated from subsidiary retained earnings. Accordingly, as shown in Exhibit 3-10, $28,000 is eliminated from subsidiary retained earnings at the end of the second year, whereas only $24,000 is eliminated from subsidiary retained earnings at the end of the first year. Notice that adjustment (2) is exactly the same at the end of the first year as at the date of acquisition.

Recording parent's amortization of valuation differential for current year

Adjustment (3) records the parent's $1,200 amortization of the valuation differential for the second year. Observe that this adjustment is exactly the same at the end of the second year following acquisition as at the end of the first. Also note that adjustment (3) is not required at the date of acquisition.

Interim Acquisitions

All prior examples demonstrate acquisitions that occur at the very end or the very beginning of a year. In other words, demonstrations have been restricted to acquisitions that occur at the beginning or end of income determination periods. The purpose of this section

| EXHIBIT 3-11 | CONSOLIDATION OF FINANCIAL STATEMENTS TWO YEARS AFTER ACQUISITION | | | | | |

	Separate Financial Statements		Consolidation Adjustments		Minority Interest	Consolidated Financial Statements
	Broad	High	Dr.	Cr.		
Income Statement						
Revenue	3,000,000	170,000				3,170,000
Income from subsidiary	13,200		(1) 13,200			–0–
Cost of goods sold	(1,900,000)*	(94,000)				(1,994,000)
Depreciation and amortization	(120,000)	(24,000)	(3) 1,200			(145,200)
Other expense	(900,000)	(34,000)				(934,000)
Minority interest					3,600	(3,600)
Net income	93,200	18,000	14,400		3,600	93,200
Statement of Retained Earnings						
Retained earnings, 1-1-X2:						
Broad	176,000					176,000
High		35,000	(2) 28,000		7,000	–0–
Net income	93,200	18,000	14,400		3,600	93,200
Dividends	(45,000)	(3,000)		(1) 2,400	(600)	(45,000)
Retained earnings, 12-31-X2	224,200	50,000	42,400	2,400	10,000	224,200
Balance Sheet						
Current assets	155,600	29,000				184,600
Investment in High	93,600			(1) 10,800		–0–
				(2) 82,800		
Equipment (net)	440,000	73,000				513,000
Building (net)	240,000	18,000	(2) 4,000	(3) 1,000		261,000
Land	100,000	10,000				110,000
Goodwill			(2) 2,800	(3) 200		2,600
Total assets	1,029,200	130,000				1,071,200
Current liabilities	65,000	9,000				74,000
Long-term liabilities	240,000	11,000				251,000
Common stock:						
Broad	500,000					500,000
High		60,000	(2) 48,000		12,000	–0–
Retained earnings	224,200	50,000	42,400	2,400	10,000	224,200
Minority interest					(22,000)	22,000
Total liabilities and stockholders' equity	1,029,200	130,000	97,200	97,200	–0–	1,071,200

* Parentheses indicate decreases.

is to demonstrate the effect of *interim acquisitions,* which occur within an income determination period, on the application of the equity-method and consolidation procedures. The following paragraphs demonstrate consolidation procedures for an interim acquisition. As a basis for the demonstration, consider the acquisition by Dublin, Inc., of 90% of Granville Corporation's outstanding stock on March 31, 19X1, for $128,250 in cash. Both companies issue financial statements on a calendar-year basis. Granville Corporation, the subsidiary, has outstanding common stock of $100,000 and retained earnings of $40,000

EXHIBIT 3-12	CONSOLIDATION OF FINANCIAL STATEMENTS FOR AN INTERIM ACQUISITION: FORM I						

	Separate Financial Statements		Consolidation Adjustments			Minority Interest	Consolidated Financial Statements
	Dublin	Granville	Dr.		Cr.		
Income Statement							
Revenue	250,000	60,000					310,000
Income from subsidiary	6,750		(1)	6,750			
Expenses	(180,000)*	(50,000)					(230,000)
Purchased preacquisition subsidiary income			(2)	2,250			(2,250)
Minority interest						1,000	(1,000)
Net income	76,750	10,000		9,000		1,000	76,750
Retained Earnings Statement							
Retained earnings, 1-1:							
Dublin	150,000						150,000
Granville		40,000	(2)	36,000		4,000	
Net income	76,750	10,000		9,000		1,000	76,750
Dividends	–0–	(4,000)			(1) 3,600	(400)	–0–
Retained earnings, 12-31	226,750	46,000		45,000	3,600	4,600	226,750
Balance Sheet							
Investment in Granville	131,400				(1) 3,150		–0–
					(2) 128,250		
Other assets	495,350	146,000					641,350
Total assets	626,750	146,000					641,350
Common stock:							
Dublin	400,000						400,000
Granville		100,000	(2)	90,000		10,000	–0–
Retained earnings	226,750	46,000		45,000	3,600	4,600	226,750
Minority interest						(14,600)	14,600
Total liabilities and stockholders' equity	626,750	146,000		135,000	135,000	–0–	641,350

* Parentheses indicate decreases.

on January 1, 19X1. Granville reports a net income of $10,000 for 19X1 ($2,500 for the first quarter) and pays a $4,000 dividend to stockholders of record on April 15, 19X1. The separate financial statements for 19X1 are entered in the first two columns of Exhibit 3-12.

The book value of the equity acquired on March 31, 19X1, is $128,250, which represents 90% of subsidiary stockholders' equity on that date and is calculated as follows:

Calculation of Book Value of Subsidiary Equity Acquired

Common stock of Granville ($100,000 × .90)		$ 90,000
Retained earnings of Granville:		
Balance, Jan. 1, 19X1:	$40,000 × .90 = $36,000	
Income from first quarter:	2,500 × .90 = 2,250	
Balance, March 31, 19X1:	$42,500 × .90 =	38,250
Book value of equity acquired by Dublin		$128,250

Since Dublin paid $128,250 for its 90% interest—an amount equal to the book value acquired—the valuation differential is zero.

The following schedule summarizes the 19X1 income statements of the two companies and allocates a subsidiary net income between preacquisition and postacquisition periods:

19X1 Income Statements and Allocation of Subsidiary Income

	Parent (Dublin)	Subsidiary (Granville) Total	First 3 Months	Last 9 Months
Revenue	$250,000	$60,000	$15,000	$45,000
Expense	180,000	50,000	12,500	37,500
Operating income	$ 70,000	$10,000	$ 2,500	$ 7,500
Income from subsidiary	6,750			
Net income	$ 76,750	$10,000	$ 2,500	$ 7,500

The straight-line allocation of subsidiary income shown here is appropriate if income arises at a uniform rate throughout the year; if seasonalities or other nonuniformities are present, they should be taken into account.

The Equity Method

Subsidiary net income earned prior to acquisition is not properly recognized by the parent as income from the subsidiary, as shown in the following calculation for our illustration:

Parent's Calculation of Income from Subsidiary

Subsidiary net income for 19X1	$10,000
Less: Preacquisition portion of subsidiary net income for 19X1	2,500
Adjusted subsidiary net income	$ 7,500
Parent's ownership percentage	×.90
Income from subsidiary	$ 6,750

The calculation reduces the subsidiary net income for the portion earned in the first three months of 19X1—the preacquisition portion of $2,500—before applying the parent's ownership percentage.

Two Forms of Consolidated Income Statements for Acquisition Year

The portion of the subsidiary net income earned in the first three months of 19X1 is not part of consolidated net income because it was earned prior to acquisition. Consequently, it is excluded from consolidated net income. The consolidated income statement for the acquisition year may accomplish the exclusion in one of two ways, as follows:

Two Forms of Consolidated Income Statements

	Form I	Form II
Revenue	$310,000	$295,000
Expense	230,000	217,500
	$ 80,000	$ 77,500
Less: Purchased preacquisition subsidiary income (.90 × $2,500)	2,250	
Combined income	$ 77,750	$ 77,500
Less: Minority interest	1,000	750
Consolidated net income	$ 76,750	$ 76,750

Observe that both forms of the consolidated income statement exhibit the same net income. Although both forms are allowed, financial accounting standards evidence a preference for Form I because it "presents results which are more indicative of the current status of the [consolidated] group, and facilitates future comparison with subsequent years" (*ARB No. 51,* par. 11).

Form I of the acquisition-year consolidated income statement includes subsidiary revenues and expenses for the entire year in consolidated net income. Thus, a preacquisition subsidiary income of $2,500 enters the consolidated income statement. But Form I also provides for the exclusion of the preacquisition income by two deductions. First, a deduction of $2,250 excludes the parent's share of the preacquisition subsidiary income from the consolidated net income ($2,250 = $2,500 × .90). Second, the deduction of minority interest includes $250 for the minority stockholders' share of the preacquisition income ($250 = $2,500 × .10). Of course, the minority interest deduction also includes $750 for the minority stockholders' share of *postacquisition* subsidiary income.

Form II of the acquisition-year consolidated income statement includes only the postacquisition portion of subsidiary revenues and expenses. Consequently, a deduction for preacquisition income is unnecessary. Observe that minority interest is only $750 on Form II, which represents the minority stockholders' share of the postacquisition subsidiary income. Their share of preacquisition income ($250) is already excluded from consolidated revenues and expenses.

Form I Consolidation Procedures

The following worksheet adjustments are required to produce a Form I consolidated income statement for the acquisition year in our illustration:

(1) *Worksheet adjustment to reverse parent's recording of subsidiary income and eliminate subsidiary dividend to parent for current year:*

Income from subsidiary 6,750
    Dividend   3,600
    Investment in Granville   3,150

(2) *Worksheet adjustment to eliminate and reclassify beginning-of-the-period balance
of parent's investment account (Form I):*

Common stock of Granville 90,000
Retained earnings of Granville (1-1-X1) 36,000
Purchased preacquisition subsidiary income *2,250*
    Investment in Granville   128,250

Let us begin by considering the second worksheet adjustment. Since the valuation differential is zero, adjustment (2) involves no reclassification of valuation differential. Instead,
the sole purpose of the second adjustment is to eliminate the beginning-of-the-period book
value of the parent's investment that (since this is the first period following acquisition
and the valuation differential is zero) equals the acquisition cost. For purposes of consolidation, the beginning of this first period is the date of acquisition, March 31, 19X1. The
book value of equity acquired by the parent on that date resides in three places on the
subsidiary's records: (1) $90,000 (.90 × $100,000) resides in the subsidiary's common
stock account; (2) $36,000 (.90 × $40,000) resides in the January 1, 19X1, balance of
subsidiary retained earnings; and (3) $2,250 (.90 × $2,500) resides in the income accounts of the subsidiary. The third element of book value acquired ($2,250) is the parent's
90% share of the subsidiary's first quarter income of $2,500. Since the acquired equity
resides in three places, the elimination adjustment makes three corresponding eliminations.

    The first adjustment is a familiar form but deserves a word of explanation. It is
important to notice that the adjustment eliminates the parent's share of subsidiary dividends paid to stockholders of record after the date of acquisition. Subsidiary dividends
paid to stockholders of record *before* the date of acquistion do not require elimination as
part of the first adjustment. However, they must be provided for in the second adjustment.
Dividends paid to stockholders of record in the preacquisition segment of the acquisition
year reduce the book value of acquired equity. Accordingly, the elimination of acquired
equity and related investment will require a credit against subsidiary dividends for the
parent's share of such preacquisition dividends. Such credits are not required in adjustment to Form II worksheets. Exhibit 3-12 shows the consolidation worksheet prepared at
the end of 19X1 for our illustration following Form I.

Form II Consolidation Procedures

The consolidation procedures for a Form II consolidated income statement differ from
Form I procedures in just three respects. First, only the postacquisition portion of subsidiary revenues and expenses is entered on the worksheet. In our illustration, the subsidiary
column of the Form II worksheet would display revenues of $45,000, expenses of
$37,500, and a net income of $7,500. Second, the date-of-acquisition balance of subsidiary retained earnings is entered as the beginning balance in the retained earnings segment
of the worksheet. In our illustration, the subsidiary retained earnings balance at March 31,

19X1, would be entered in place of the balance at January 1, 19X1. And third, the second worksheet adjustment would eliminate the entire acquired interest in subsidiary retained earnings against the beginning (March 31) balance of subsidiary retained earnings, as shown for our illustration in the following adjustment:

(2) *Worksheet adjustment to eliminate and reclassify beginning-of-the-period balance of parent's investment account (Form II):*

Common stock of Granville (.90 × $100,000). 90,000
Retained earnings of Granville, 3-31-X1 (.90 × $42,500) . . . 38,250
    Investment in Granville   128,250

Adjustment (1) is the same as for the Form I income statement. Unless specifically directed to do otherwise, Form I should be used in solving problems and exercises.

Calculation and Amortization of Valuation Differential

Recall that the valuation differential is the excess of acquisition cost over the book value of acquired stockholders' equity *on the date of acquisition.* If acquisition occurs at an interim date, then subsidiary stockholders' equity must be determined at that date. Beginning-of-the-year stockholders' equity balances must be updated for earnings, dividends, and other transactions that occur during the preacquisition segment of the year as a basis for calculating the valuation differential. In addition, the valuation differential must be prorated over the first year.

SUMMARY

This chapter describes the basic accounting procedures that underlie a parent's postacquisition financial statements. A parent company may prepare two sets of financial statements—the separate financial statements of the parent and the consolidated financial statements of the parent and its subsidiaries. The separate financial statements are prepared directly from the records of the parent company. A subsidiary is reflected in the separate financial statements by an investment account and an income from the subsidiary account maintained under the equity method. The consolidated financial statements are prepared by applying a worksheet procedure to the separate financial statements of both the parent and its subsidiary. The consolidation procedure substitutes the detailed assets and liabilities of the subsidiary for the investment in the subsidiary account, and substitutes the detailed revenues and expenses of the subsidiary for the income from the subsidiary account. In this process, minority interest in subsidiary net income and minority interest in subsidiary net assets are placed on the consolidation income statement and consolidated balance sheet, respectively, if a minority interest exists. The foregoing chapter explores the complexities of postacquisition consolidation procedures including the three basic worksheet adjustments and the treatment of interim acquisitions.

Although a subsidiary is accounted for by the equity method in the parent's separate financial statements and is consolidated with the parent in the consolidated financial statements, both sets of financial statements exhibit the same net income and the same retained earnings. Consolidated net income equals the net income of the parent company, and consolidated retained earnings equals the retained earnings of the parent company. Although several exceptions to these equalities are considered in later chapters, the equalities hold in most cases considered in this book.

The parent's accounting for its subsidiary's income in both separate and consolidated financial statements differs from the subsidiary's accounting for that income. The principal difference discussed in this chapter is the additional expense charged against the subsidiary income by the parent—expense arising from the amortization of the valuation differential. Both income from the subsidiary (under the equity method) and consolidated net income are reduced for this additional expense. Later chapters discuss other sources of difference between parent and subsidiary accounting for the subsidiary income including different treatments of operating transactions between the parent and its subsidiary.

APPENDIX A: POSTACQUISITION CONSOLIDATION FOR POOLINGS OF INTERESTS

As noted in Appendix B to Chapter 2, consolidation procedures for poolings of interests are simpler than those required for purchases owing to the absence of the valuation differential. Let us illustrate these procedures by extending the PY–SY pooling described in Appendix B to Chapter 2. Recall that Corporation PY acquired 95% of the outstanding common stock of Corporation SY on January 1, 19X1, in exchange for 200 newly issued shares of PY's $3-par common stock. The separate financial statements of the two companies issued shortly after December 31, 19X1, are summarized in the first two columns of Exhibit 3-13 on the following page. Observe that Corporation PY recognizes income from its subsidiary in the amount of $171, which is 95% of SY's net income of $180, following the equity method of accounting for the investment. Since the combination of PY and SY qualifies as a pooling of interests, no valuation differential is recognized, and therefore, no additional amortizations of goodwill or the valuation increment are recorded by the parent.

The following two worksheet adjustments are required:

(1) *Worksheet adjustment to reverse parent's recording of subsidiary income and eliminate subsidiary dividend to parent for current year:*

Income from subsidiary	171	
Dividends		95
Investment in SY		76

(2) *Worksheet adjustment to eliminate beginning-of-the-year balance of parent's investment account:*

Common stock of SY ($500 × .95)	475	
Excess over par of SY ($200 × .95)	190	
Retained earnings of SY ($300 × .95)	285	
Investment in SY		950

The first simply reverses the parent's recognition of the subsidiary income in the amount of $171 and eliminates the subsidiary's dividend to the parent in the amount of $95 (.95 × $100). The minority interest in the subsidiary net income is simply the minority ownership percentage (5%) times the subsidiary net income ($9 = 0.5 × $180). Since the parent uses the equity method (adapted for a pooling of interests), parent-company net income equals consolidated net income under pooling-of-interests accounting (as shown in Exhibit 3-13) just as it does under purchase accounting. The second adjustment eliminates the beginning-of-the-year balance of the parent's investment account. Since the beginning of 19X1 is the date of acquisition, the elimination from retained earnings ($285) equals the date-of-acquisition elimination from retained earnings. Next year (two years

EXHIBIT 3-13	POOLING-OF-INTERESTS CONSOLIDATION ONE YEAR AFTER ACQUISITION

	Separate Financial Statements		Consolidation Adjustments		Minority Interest	Consolidated Financial Statements
	PY	SY	Dr.	Cr.		
Income Statement						
Revenue	2,200	1,000				3,200
Income from subsidiary	171		(1) 171			
Cost of goods sold	(1,441)*	(635)				(2,076)
Depreciation and amortization	(200)	(110)				(310)
Other expense	(164)	(75)				(239)
Minority interest					9	(9)
Net income	566	180	171		9	566
Statement of Retained Earnings						
Retained earnings, 1-1-X1:						
PY Corporation	1,285					1,285
SY Corporation		300	(2) 285		15	
Net income	566	180	171		9	566
Dividends	(220)	(100)		(1) 95	(5)	(220)
Retained earnings, 12-31-X1	1,631	380	456	95	19	1,631
Balance Sheet						
Current assets	1,120	580				1,700
Investment in SY	1,026			(1) 76		
				(2) 950		
Plant and equipment (net)	2,250	1,090				3,340
Total assets	4,396	1,670				5,040
Current liabilities	800	590				1,390
Common stock:						
PY Corporation	1,500					1,500
SY Corporation		500	(2) 475		25	
Excess over par:						
PY Corporation	465					465
SY Corporation		200	(2) 190		10	
Retained earnings	1,631	380	456	95	19	1,631
Minority interest					(54)	54
Total liabilities and stockholders' equity	4,396	1,670	1,121	1,121	–0–	5,040

* Parentheses indicate decreases.

after acquisition), the elimination from retained earnings will be $361 ($380 × .95), which is larger by the amount of the parent's share of undistributed 19X1 subsidiary net income [$76 = $361 − $285, or $76 = ($180 − $100) × .95]. Of course, the corresponding elimination from the investment account also will be larger by $76. The computation of minority interest is the same under the pooling-of-interests method and the purchase method.

APPENDIX B: CONSOLIDATION PROCEDURES FOR THE COST METHOD

As noted in the foregoing chapter, a parent company may use the cost method for consolidated subsidiaries. This appendix demonstrates consolidation procedures for the cost method by reference to the consolidation of Byrd Corporation and its 60%-owned subsidiary, Taylor, Inc. Byrd Corporation acquired a 60% interest in Taylor, Inc. on January 1, 19X1, for $10,000 cash. Accordingly, an investment in the subsidiary account is established in the amount of $10,000 on January 1, 19X1. On the date of acquisition, Taylor's stockholders' equity consists of common stock of $10,000 and retained earnings of $4,000. Assume that the fair value of Taylor's identifiable net assets is $15,833 and that all assets and liabilities are carried at fair values except for its undervalued building, which has a book value of $10,000 and a fair value of $11,833. On the basis of this information, the following analysis of the valuation differential can be prepared on January 1, 19X1:

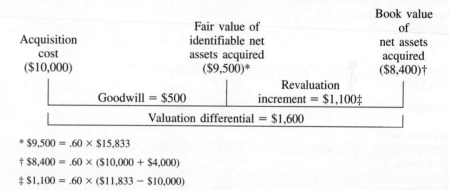

* $9,500 = .60 × $15,833

† $8,400 = .60 × ($10,000 + $4,000)

‡ $1,100 = .60 × ($11,833 − $10,000)

Let us assume that goodwill is amortized at a rate of $50 per year and that the revaluation increment is amortized at a rate of $200 per year over its remaining life of 5 1/2 years. Although the foregoing analysis of the valuation differential is not required for application of the cost method, it is required for purposes of consolidating a subsidiary that has been accounted for using the cost method.

The separate financial statements prepared by the two companies at the end of 19X2 (two years after the date of acquisition) are presented in the first two columns of Exhibit 3-14 on the following page. Recall that net income and retained earnings of Byrd Corporation under the cost method reflect the dividends from the subsidiary rather than the parent's share of subsidiary net income adjusted for amortization of the valuation differential, as under the equity method. Taylor, Inc., declared dividends of $2,200 in 19X2, of which $1,320 was paid to Byrd.

Worksheet Adjustments for Cost Method

When the parent uses the cost method to account for its investment in a consolidated subsidiary, consolidation worksheet adjustments must be tailored to the use of the cost method. Consolidation of Byrd and Taylor at the end of 19X2 requires three worksheet adjustments when Byrd uses the cost method, just as it does when Byrd uses the equity method. However, the form of the adjustments is somewhat different.

EXHIBIT 3-14	CONSOLIDATION OF FINANCIAL STATEMENTS TWO YEARS AFTER ACQUISITION: COST METHOD					

	Separate Financial Statements		Consolidation Adjustments		Minority Interest	Consolidated Financial Statements
	Byrd	Taylor	Dr.	Cr.		
Income Statement						
Revenue	100,000	17,000				117,000
Dividend income	1,320		(1) 1,320			–0–
Cost of goods sold	(57,000)*	(8,600)				(65,600)
Depreciation and amortization	(17,500)	(2,500)	(3) 250			(20,250)
Other expenses	(16,200)	(2,900)				(19,100)
Minority interest					1,200	(1,200)
Net income	10,620	3,000	1,570		1,200	10,850
Statement of Retained Earnings						
Retained earnings, 1-1-X2						
Byrd	37,880					37,880
Taylor		5,400	(2) 2,400		2,160	590
			(3) 250			
Net income	10,620	3,000	1,570		1,200	10,850
Dividends	(5,000)	(2,200)		(1) 1,320	(880)	(5,000)
Retained earnings, 12-31-X2	43,500	6,200	4,220	1,320	2,480	44,320
Balance Sheet						
Current assets	5,400	300				5,700
Investment in Taylor	10,000			(2) 10,000		–0–
Equipment (net)	71,200	8,700				79,900
Building (net)	34,700	9,000	(2) 1,110	(3) 400		44,400
Land	28,700	2,000				30,700
Goodwill			(2) 500	(3) 100		400
Total assets	150,000	20,000				161,100
Current liabilities	2,500	200				2,700
Long-term liabilities	34,000	3,600				37,600
Common stock:						
Byrd	70,000					70,000
Taylor		10,000	(2) 6,000		4,000	
Retained earnings	43,500	6,200	4,220	1,320	2,480	44,320
Minority interest					(6,480)	6,480
Total liabilities and stockholders' equity	150,000	20,000	11,820	11,820	–0–	161,100

* Parentheses indicate decreases.

Adjustment (1) eliminates the subsidiary's $1,320 dividend to the parent during the current year:

(1) *Worksheet adjustment to eliminate subsidiary dividend to parent for current year:*

Dividend income 1,320		
Dividends (retained earnings of subsidiary)	1,320	

Recall that under the equity method, the current year's dividend is eliminated on the consolidation worksheet by a debit to *income from subsidiary* and a credit to dividends, whereas under the cost method, it is eliminated by a charge to the *dividend income* and a credit to *dividends.*

Adjustment (2) reduces the parent's investment account balance to zero by eliminating the subsidiary stockholders' equity acquired by the parent on the date of acquisition ($8,400 = $6,000 + $2,400) and reclassifying the related valuation differential as goodwill ($500) and a revaluation of building ($1,100):

(2) *Worksheet adjustment to eliminate and reclassify beginning-of-the-year balance of parent's investment account:*

Common stock of Taylor ($10,000 × .60) 6,000
Retained earnings of Taylor ($4,000 × .60)................ 2,400
Building (net) *1,100*
Goodwill *500*
    Investment in Taylor 10,000

Adjustment (3) records the amortization of the valuation differential—both the portion that is applicable to the current year ($250 for 19X2) and the portion that is applicable to all prior years ($250 for 19X1):

(3) *Worksheet adjustment to amortize valuation differential for current and prior years:*

Depreciation and amortization expense 250
Retained earnings of Taylor 250
    Building (net) 400
    Goodwill 100

Under the equity method, the amortization is recognized on the records of the parent (in the calculation and recording of the parent's income from its subsidiary), and consolidation adjustments merely reclassify that amortization. In contrast, the amortization is not recognized by the parent under the cost method and must be recorded as part of consolidation procedures. Observe that the amortization for the current year ($250) is charged to depreciation and amortization expense, whereas the amortization for prior years ($250) is charged to retained earnings of the subsidiary.

Consolidation Worksheet for Cost Method

Under the equity method, consolidated net income equals the net income of the parent company, and consolidated retained earnings equals retained earnings of the parent company. Under the cost method, these equalities do not hold as shown in Exhibit 3-14. Consolidated net income ($10,850) exceeds the parent's separate net income ($10,620) by $230 ($10,850 − $10,620), representing the excess of the parent's income from its subsidiary under the equity method [$1,550 = ($3,000 × .60) − $250] over the parent's income from its subsidiary under the cost method ($1,320 = .60 × $2,200). Consolidated retained earnings at year-end ($44,320) exceed the parent's separate retained earnings at year-end

($43,500) by $820 ($44,320 − $43,500), representing the excess of the parent's equity-method income from its subsidiary over its cost-method income from its subsidiary during the two years since acquisition.

The calculation of beginning-of-the-year minority interest in subsidiary retained earnings is somewhat more difficult as a result of the inequality between consolidated and parent retained earnings. As evidenced by the change in subsidiary retained earnings during 19X1 (from $4,000 to $5,400), the subsidiary had an undistributed net income of $1,400 in 19X1, of which $840 (.60 × $1,400) is earned equity of the parent at January 1, 19X2. The minority interest in subsidiary retained earnings at January 1, 19X2 ($2,160), is simply the subsidiary retained earnings balance ($5,400) adjusted for the portion acquired by the parent on January 1, 19X1, and the portion subsequently earned by the parent ($2,160 = $5,400 − $2,400 − $840). Alternatively, of course, minority interest in retained earnings can be calculated directly as 40% of subsidiary retained earnings on January 1, 19X2 ($2,160 = .40 × $5,400). Notice, however, that minority interest in subsidiary retained earnings does not equal the balance of subsidiary retained earnings after all consolidation adjustments have been applied; $2,160 does not equal the $2,750 remainder of subsidiary retained earnings after the application of the consolidation adjustments required by the cost method ($2,750 = $5,400 − $2,400 − $250). Consequently, it is necessary to prepare a separate calculation of the minority interest in beginning-of-the-year retained earnings when the cost method is applied to consolidated subsidiaries, as shown in the following schedule:

**Calculation of Minority Interest in Subsidiary Retained Earnings
at the Beginning of the Year**

Retained earnings of subsidiary, 1-1-X2		$5,400
Less: Parent's equity in subsidiary retained earnings at 1-1-X2:		
Portion acquired (.60 × $4,000)	$2,400	
Portion earned since acquisition [.60 × ($5,400 − $4,000)]	840	3,240
Minority interest in subsidiary retained earnings at 1-1-X2		$2,160

The $2,750 remainder of subsidiary retained earnings after the application of cost-method consolidation adjustments has two components: (1) the minority interest in subsidiary retained earnings ($2,160) and (2) the parent's equity in subsidiary retained earnings earned in prior years and adjusted for amortization of the valuation differential ($590 = $840 − $250). The second component ($590) is carried to the consolidated financial statements column of the worksheet in Exhibit 3-14 but does not represent a separate financial statement item. Instead, it represents a component of beginning-of-the-year consolidated retained earnings ($38,470 = $37,880 + $590), which is reported as a single amount ($38,470) in the consolidated statement of retained earnings.

APPENDIX C: THE TRIAL BALANCE FORMAT FOR CONSOLIDATION WORKSHEETS

The *three-section statement format* is used to construct consolidation worksheets throughout this text. However, another worksheet format, call the *trial balance format,* may be encountered in practice. The principal difference between the trial balance and three-section statement formats is that the adjusted (preclosing) trial balance is entered in the first two (left-hand) columns of the trial balance format, whereas the financial statements are entered in the first two columns of the three-section statement format. In constructing the trial balance consolidation worksheet, we usually enter the owners' equity accounts of the parent and subsidiary on separate lines in order to facilitate the consolidation process

EXHIBIT 3-15	TRIAL BALANCE FORMAT FOR CONSOLIDATION TWO YEARS AFTER ACQUISITION

	Trial Balance		Consolidation Adjustments		Consolidated Income Statement	Minority Interest	Consolidated Retained Earnings	Consolidated Balance Sheet
	Broad	High	Dr.	Cr.				
Debits								
Current assets	155,600	29,000						184,600
Investment in High	93,600		(1) 10,800					–0–
			(2) 82,800					
Equipment (net)	440,000	73,000						513,000
Building (net)	240,000	18,000	(2) 4,000	(3) 1,000				261,000
Land	100,000	10,000						110,000
Cost of goods sold	1,900,000	94,000			(1,994,000)*			
Depreciation and amortization	120,000	24,000	(3) 1,200		(145,200)			
Other expense	900,000	34,000			(934,000)			
Dividends of Broad	45,000						(45,000)	
Dividends of High		3,000		(1) 2,400		(600)		
Goodwill			(2) 2,800	(3) 200				2,600
	3,994,200	285,000						1,071,200
Credits								
Current liabilities	65,000	9,000						74,000
Long-term liabilities	240,000	11,000						251,000
Common stock of Broad	500,000							500,000
Common stock of High		60,000	(2) 48,000			12,000		
Retained earnings of Broad	176,000						176,000	
Retained earnings of High		35,000	(2) 28,000			7,000		
High revenue	3,000,000	170,000			3,170,000			
Income from subsidiary	13,200		(1) 13,200		–0–			
	3,994,200	285,000	97,200	97,200				
Minority interest in subsidiary income					(3,600)	3,600		
Consolidated net income					93,200		93,200	
Minority interest						22,000		22,000
Consolidated retained earnings							224,200	224,200
								1,071,200

* Parentheses indicate decreases.

since the subsidiary owners' equity accounts are eliminated. Another important difference is that the trial balance format usually has a separate column for each consolidated financial statement. A trial balance consolidation worksheet is shown in Exhibit 3-15 for the consolidation two years after the acquisition of High, Inc., by Broad Corporation, an illustration presented earlier in this chapter. The comparable three-section statement format worksheet for this combination is shown in Exhibit 3-11. Note the treatment of *minority interest in subsidiary income, consolidated net income,* and *minority interest* in the trial balance format. The consolidation worksheet adjustments, which are shown in Exhibit 3-10, have the same form for both worksheet formats. Consequently, the difference between the two worksheet formats is substantially one of format. Although the three-section statement format is used throughout this text, exercises and problems are readily solved by the application of either the three-section statement format or the trial balance format.

SELECTED READINGS

Accountants' International Study Group. *Consolidated Financial Statements: Current Recommended Practices in Canada, the United Kingdom, and the United States.* Plaistow, England: Curwen Press, 1973.

Arthur Andersen & Co. *International Research Project on Accounting for Business Combinations, Goodwill and Other Intangibles.* . . . Chicago: Arthur Andersen & Co., 1991.

Burton, John C. *Accounting for Business Combinations.* New York: Financial Executives Research Foundation, 1970.

Catlett, George R., and Norman O. Olson. *Accounting for Goodwill,* Accounting Research Study No. 10. New York: American Institute of Certified Public Accountants, 1968.

Colley, J. Ron, and Ara G. Volkan. "Accounting for Goodwill," *Accounting Horizons* (March 1988), pp. 35–41.

Davis, Michael. "Goodwill Accounting: Time for an Overhaul," *Journal of Accountancy* (June, 1992), pp. 75–83.

Falk, Haim, and L. A. Gordon. "Imperfect Markets and the Nature of Goodwill," *Journal of Business Finance and Accounting* (April 1977), pp. 443–463.

Grinyer, J. R., A. Russell, and M. Walker. "The Rationale for Accounting for Goodwill," *British Accounting Review* (September 1990), pp. 223–235.

King, Thomas E., and Valdean C. Lembke. "Reporting Investor Income under the Equity Method," *Journal of Accountancy* (September 1976), pp. 65–71.

Neuhausen, Benjamin S. "Consolidation and the Equity Method—Time for an Overhaul," *Journal of Accountancy* (February 1982), pp. 54–66.

Nurnberg, Hugo. "Combining Stockholders' Equity Accounts under the Pooling of Interests Method," *The Accounting Review* (January 1975), pp. 179–183.

Pacter, Paul. *An Analysis of Issues Related to Consolidation Policies and Procedures,* Financial Accounting Standards Board Discussion Memorandum. Norwalk, CT: Financial Accounting Standards Board, September 10, 1991.

Pacter, Paul. "Consolidations: An Overview of the FASB DM," *Journal of Accountancy* (April 1992), pp. 56–61.

Tearney, Michael G. "Accounting for Goodwill: A Realistic Approach," *Journal of Accountancy* (July 1973), pp. 41–45.

QUESTIONS

Q3-1 Discuss when it is appropriate to use the cost method and when it is appropriate to use the equity method in accounting for long-term investments in common stock.

Q3-2 Discuss the differences in accounting for an investment in the common stock of an investee under the cost method and the equity method. Which method is more consistent with accrual accounting principles and why?

Q3-3 Assuming the investor uses the cost method for its investment and the cumulative dividends received by the investor since acquisition exceed the investor's share of investee earnings accumulated since acquisition, how should the excess dividends be treated?

Q3-4 Company A paid $6,000 on January 1, 19X3, for an 80% interest in Company B. The investment cost is $1,000 less than the book value of the identifiable net assets acquired. The excess book value is attributable to overvalued equipment owned by Company B, which has a remaining life of ten years. Company B reported a net income of $2,000 for 19X3. How would the excess book value over investment cost be accounted for by Company A when recording its share of Company B's income?

Q3-5 Describe the financial accounting guidelines for the amortization of goodwill. Is the amortization of goodwill deductible in computing taxable income?

Q3-6 Define *consolidated net income*. Does consolidated net income equal the parent's separate net income when the parent uses the equity method of accounting for investments in subsidiaries?

Q3-7 How is the minority interest in the subsidiary net income determined, and how is it reported on the consolidated income statement?

Q3-8 How is minority interest in the net loss of a subsidiary reported on the consolidated income statement?

Q3-9 Briefly state the five procedures leading to the completion of a consolidation worksheet in periods subsequent to the date of acquisition.

Q3-10 Why is it necessary to make the following consolidation worksheet adjustment?

Income from subsidiary X		
Dividends		X
Investment in subsidiary		X

Q3-11 Where on consolidated financial statements are the parent's investments in *unconsolidated* subsidiaries reported? Should the cost method or equity method be used in reporting the parent's investments in *unconsolidated* subsidiaries?

Q3-12 Explain why you agree or disagree with the following statement: Consolidated statements will be the same whether the cost method or the equity method is used in accounting for investments in consolidated subsidiaries.

Q3-13 Discuss how the parent's share of extraordinary items and prior period adjustments of a subsidiary should be reported in the parent's financial statements.

Q3-14 If P uses the equity method of accounting for its investment in subsidiary S, would the retained earnings of P equal consolidated retained earnings?

Q3-15 Companies P and S issue financial statements on a calendar-year basis. If P acquired a 90% interest in S on April 1, 19X1 (purchase method), would the subsidiary net income earned prior to acquisition be properly recognized by the parent as income from its subsidiary?

Q3-16   When a subsidiary is acquired during the fiscal year of the affiliated firms (purchase method), two alternative forms of reporting the subsidiary revenues and expenses in the consolidated income statement are allowed. Describe these two forms. Does the form adopted affect consolidated net income?

Q3-17   Explain why you agree or disagree with the following statement: The equity method, when applied to subsidiaries, is sometimes referred to as a "one-line consolidation."

Q3-18   Assume the balance in the parent's investment in subsidiary account has been reduced to zero as a result of the parent recognizing its share of subsidiary losses under the equity method. Describe how the parent should account for its share of subsequent subsidiary losses and net income.

QUESTIONS FOR APPENDIX A

Q3-19   On January 1, 19X6, P acquired a 90% interest in S for $3,000 in excess of book value of the equity acquired. The excess cost is attributable to the fact that patents owned by S are undervalued. The combination is to be accounted for as a pooling of interests. Following the equity method of accounting for the investment in S, prepare the entry on P's books to record income from the subsidiary assuming S reported a net income of $10,000.

Q3-20   If the equity method is used by the parent company in accounting for its investment in a subsidiary, would the net income of the parent equal the consolidated net income whether the combination was a pooling of interests or a purchase?

QUESTIONS FOR APPENDIX B

Q3-21   If McCools accounts for its investment in subsidiary Bon Air using the cost method, would the net income and retained earnings of McCools equal the consolidated net income and retained earnings?

Q3-22   When the parent uses the cost method to account for its investment in a consolidated subsidiary, the consolidation worksheet adjustments would be in the same form as those used had the investment in the subsidiary been accounted for by the equity method. Discuss.

QUESTIONS FOR APPENDIX C

Q3-23   Discuss the principal differences between the trial balance format and the three-section statement format of the consolidation worksheet.

Q3-24   Explain why you agree or disagree with the following statement: The consolidation worksheet adjustments are the same whether the trial balance format or the three-section statement format of the consolidation worksheet is used.

EXERCISES

E3-1   Each of the two parts of this exercise is independent of the other. Prepare proper solutions to each of the following requirements.

Part I. Cost and Equity Method Identification   The cost method or the equity method is generally used to account for long-term investments in common stock. However, firms may not choose freely between these two methods; rather, the method must be chosen that is appropriate for the particular investment at hand.

REQUIRED

Indicate whether the cost method or the equity method would be used in accounting for the following long-term investments in common stock:

1. Investment totaling 15% of the voting stock of an investee

2. Investment in common stock of a subsidiary reported in the parent company's separate financial statements prepared for issuance to stockholders of the parent

3. Investment totaling 35% of the voting stock of an investee

4. Investment in common stock of an unconsolidated subsidiary reported on consolidated financial statements

5. Investment totaling 17% of the voting stock of an investee. Investor purchases 30% of the investee's output and has representation on the investee's board of directors.

Part II. Cost and Equity Method Fundamentals   Rebound Company acquired a 60% interest in Sandbridge Company on January 1, 19X1, at book value. At that time Sandbridge's common stock and retained earnings balances were $150,000 and $50,000, respectively. During the fiscal year ended December 31, 19X1, Sandbridge earned a net income of $30,000 and paid dividends of $4,000.

REQUIRED

Determine the balance in Rebound's investment account as of December 31, 19X1, under each of the following methods of accounting for its investment in Sandbridge:

1. Cost method

2. Equity method

Cost and Equity Method Entries   Ram Corporation acquired 80% of the outstanding voting stock of Colonial, Inc., for $88,000 cash on January 1, 19X2. The stockholders' equity of Colonial was $100,000 at that date. The excess acquisition cost over the book value of the acquired equity is attributable to expected future earnings of Colonial (goodwill) and is to be amortized over 40 years. On December 31, 19X2, Colonial declared and paid a cash dividend of $15,000 and reported net income of $35,000.

REQUIRED

On the books of Ram Corporation, record the entries for its investment in Colonial, Inc., during 19X2 under

1. The cost method

2. The equity method

Also, indicate the balance that would appear in Ram's investment account at the end of 19X2 under each of these methods.

E3-3   **Discussion of the Fundamentals of Equity Method**   The most common method of accounting for unconsolidated subsidiaries is the equity method.

REQUIRED

Answer the questions shown here with respect to the equity method:

a) Under what circumstances should the equity method be applied?

b) At what amount should the initial investment be recorded, and what events subsequent to the initial investment (if any) would change this amount?

c) How are investment earnings recognized under the equity method, and how is the amount determined?

(AICPA adapted)

E3-4   **Discussion of Proper Accounting Method for Investor**   On July 1, 19X1, Dynamic Company purchased, for cash, 40% of the outstanding common stock of Cart Company. Both Dynamic Company and Cart Company have a December 31 year-end. Cart Company, whose common stock is actively traded in the over-the-counter market, reported its total net income for the year to Dynamic Company and also paid cash dividends on November 15, 19X1, to Dynamic Company and its other stockholders.

REQUIRED

How should Dynamic Company report the preceding facts in its December 31, 19X1, balance sheet and its income statement for the year then ended? Discuss the rationale for your answer.

(AICPA adapted)

E3-5 **Calculation and Amortization of Goodwill** On September 1, 19X7, the Horn Company purchased 200,000 shares representing 45% of the outstanding common stock of Mat Company for cash. As a result of the purchase, Horn has the ability to exercise significant influence over the operating and financial policies of Mat. Goodwill of $500,000 was appropriately recognized by Horn at the date of the purchase.

On December 1, 19X8, Horn purchased 300,000 shares representing 30% of the outstanding common stock of Simon Company for cash of $2,500,000. The stockholders' equity section of Simon's balance sheet at the date of the acquisition was as follows:

Common stock, par value $2.00 a share	$2,000,000
Additional paid-in capital	1,000,000
Retained earnings	4,000,000
	$7,000,000

Furthermore, at the date of acquisition, the fair value of Simon's property, plant and equipment, net, was $3,800,000, whereas the book value was $3,500,000. For all the other assets and liabilities of Simon the fair value and book value were equal. As a result of the transaction, Horn has the ability to exercise significant influence over the operating and financial policies of Simon.

Assume that Horn amortizes goodwill over the maximum period allowed and takes a full year's amortization in the year of purchase.

REQUIRED

Compute the amount of goodwill and accumulated amortization at December 31, 19X8, and the goodwill amortization for the year ended December 31, 19X8.

(AICPA adapted)

E3-6 **Equity Method Entries, Consolidation Adjustments** Bold purchased, on January 1, 19X1, 80% of the outstanding common stock of Tide, paying $70,000 cash. At that time, Tide's stockholders' equity consisted of common stock, $30,000; excess over par, $20,000; and retained earnings, $10,000. Any difference in acquisition cost and book value of the acquired equity is to be identified as goodwill and amortized over ten years. During the next two years, Tide reported net incomes and paid dividends as follows:

	December 31	
	19X1	**19X2**
Net income	$12,000	$5,000
Dividends	8,000	4,000

REQUIRED

a) Prepare the entries on the books of Bold for the years 19X1 and 19X2 concerning its investment in Tide.

b) Prepare in journal entry form the consolidation adjustments that would appear on the December 31, 19X1, and 19X2 consolidation worksheets of Bold and its subsidiary.

E3-7 **Cost and Equity Method Entries** On January 1, 19X5, Bates Company acquired 60% of the previously issued voting shares of Pride Company for $50,000 cash. The stockholders' equity of Pride at the date of acquisition was $80,000. Any difference in acquisition cost and book value of the acquired equity is due to a difference in the fair value and book value of equipment, which has a remaining life of five years. On December 31, 19X5, Pride declared and paid a cash dividend of $8,000 and reported a net loss of $10,000.

REQUIRED

Prepare entries during 19X5 for Bates Company concerning its investment in Pride Company under

1. The cost method

2. The equity method

Also, indicate the investment account balance at the end of the year 19X5 under each of these methods.

E3-8 **Investment Account Analysis, Consolidation Adjustments, and Computations** Flick acquired, on January 1, 19X4, a 70% interest in Bic, paying $63,500. Bic's stockholders' equity consisted of common stock, $60,000, and retained earnings, $20,000. The difference in the cost of the investment and the book value of the subsidiary's net assets cannot be identified with any specific assets or liabilities. During the year ended December 31, 19X4, Flick and Bic each reported income from its own operations and paid dividends as indicated here. Intangible assets are amortized over 25 years:

	Net Income	Dividends
Flick	$25,000	$5,000
Bic	8,000	1,500

REQUIRED

a) Prepare an analysis of the parent's investment account of 19X4 using the format shown in the chapter.

b) Prepare in journal entry form the consolidation adjustments that would appear on the December 31, 19X4, consolidation worksheet of Flick and its subsidiary.

c) Determine total minority interest to be reported on the December 31, 19X4, consolidated balance sheet of Flick and its subsidiary.

d) Determine the consolidated net income for the year ended December 31, 19X4.

 E3-9 **Equity Method Entries, Consolidation Adjustments and Computations** Shad acquired, on January 1, 19X9, 55% of the outstanding voting stock of Spot for $51,000 cash, when the stockholders' equity of Spot consisted of common stock of $70,000 and retained earnings of $30,000. The excess book value of acquired equity over investment cost is attributable to the fact that the fair value of a building owned by Spot is different from its book value. The building has a remaining life of eight years. On December 31, 19X9, Spot reported a net loss of $10,000 and declared a cash dividend of $4,000 payable to shareholders of record on January 15 of next year. From its own operations, Shad reported an income of $25,000 for 19X9.

REQUIRED

a) Prepare the entries on the books of Shad for the year 19X9 concerning its investment in Spot.

b) Prepare in journal entry form the consolidation adjustments that would appear on the December 31, 19X9, consolidation worksheet of Shad and its subsidiary.

c) Determine consolidated net income for 19X9.

E3-10   **Investment Account Analysis Consolidation Adjustments**   On January 1, 19X7, AJ Company acquired 80% of Good Times, Inc. for $100,000 cash. Good Times' stockholders' equity consisted of common stock, $80,000, and retained earnings, $40,000. Book values equal fair values of all assets and liabilities of Good Times except for equipment, which has a fair value that is $4,000 more than book value. The equipment has a remaining life of eight years, and any intangibles are to be amortized over ten years. During the years 19X7 and 19X8, Good Times earned a net income and paid dividends as follows:

	19X7	19X8
Net income	$8,000	$13,000
Dividends	3,000	6,000

REQUIRED

a) Prepare the entries on the books of AJ for the years 19X7 and 19X8 concerning its investment in Good Times.

b) Prepare an analysis of the parent's investment account for 19X7 and 19X8, using the format shown in the chapter.

c) Prepare in journal entry form the consolidation adjustments that would appear on the December 31, 19X7, and 19X8 consolidation worksheets of AJ and its subsidiary.

E3-11   **Multiple Choice Questions on Cost and Equity Methods**

1. On January 2, 19X3, Ben Company purchased 40% of the outstanding common stock of Clarke Company for $1,000. On that date, Clarke's net assets were $2,000, and Ben cannot attribute the excess of the cost of its investment in Clarke over its equity in Clarke's net assets to any particular factor. Clarke's 19X3 net income is $250. Ben plans to retain its investment in Clarke indefinitely. Ben accounts for its investment in Clarke by the equity method. The maximum amount that could be included in Ben's 19X3 income before taxes to reflect Ben's ''equity in net income of Clarke'' is

a) $ 95	**c)** $200
b) $100	**d)** $245

2. Investor, Inc., owns 40% of Alimand Corporation. During the calendar year 19X5, Alimand had net earnings of $100,000 and paid dividends of $10,000. Investor, Inc., mistakenly recorded these transactions using the cost method rather than the equity method of accounting. What effect would this have on the investment account, net earnings, and retained earnings, respectively?

a) Understate, overstate, overstate	**c)** Overstate, overstate, overstate
b) Overstate, understate, understate	**d)** Understate, understate, understate

3. On January 1, 19X5, the Swing Company purchased at book value 100,000 shares (20%) of the voting common stock of Harpo Instruments, Inc., for $1,200,000. Direct costs associated with the purchase were $50,000. On December 1, 19X5, the board of directors of Harpo declared a dividend of $2 per share payable to holders of record on December 28, 19X5. The net income of Harpo for the year ended December 31, 19X5, was $1,600,000. What should be the balance in Swing's ''Investment in Harpo Instruments, Inc.'' account at December 31, 19X5?

a) $1,200,000	**c)** $1,370,000
b) $1,250,000	**d)** $1,520,000

4. How should goodwill be written off?

a) As soon as possible to retained earnings

b) By systematic charges to retained earnings over the period benefited, but not in excess of 40 years

c) As soon as possible as a one-time charge to expense and reported as an extraordinary item

d) By systematic charges to an operating expense over the period benefited, but not in excess of 40 years

5. Ray Company has invested in several domestic manufacturing corporations. Ray would be most likely to use the equity method to determine the amount to be reported as an investment in its consolidated balance sheet for its holding of

a) 2,000 of the 50,000 outstanding common shares of Locke Company

b) 3,000 of the 10,000 outstanding preferred shares of Dawes Company

c) 15,000 of the 60,000 outstanding common shares of Bates Company

d) 20,000 of the 25,000 outstanding common shares of Welch Company

6. Polk Corporation purchased a controlling interest in Irwin Corporation for an amount that reflects the fact that Irwin's depreciable assets have a market value in excess of their book value. In the separate statements of Polk, this difference should be

a) Charged against investment revenue over the remaining useful life of the assets

b) Included in the carrying value of the investment until disposition of the stock

c) Charged against investment revenue in the year of acquisition

d) Charged to depreciation expense over the remaining useful life of the assets

7. On January 1, 19X2, Investor Corporation purchased, for $20,000, a 15% common stock interest in Investee Corporation, whose total common stock equity had a fair and book value of $100,000. The investment is accounted for by the cost method. If Investee's net income during 19X2 is $30,000 and Investor receives dividends of $5,000 from Investee, for 19X2 Investor Corporation should report income from this investment of

a) $5,000   **c)** $4,500

b) $4,875   **d)** $4,375

8. Assume the same facts as in item (7) except that Investor Corporation pays $50,000 for a 40% common stock interest in Investee Corporation, accounts for the investment by the equity method, and receives $13,333 in dividends from Investee during 19X2. For 19X2, Investor Corporation should report, as income from this investment, the single amount of (any excess cost over the book value is amortized over 40 years using the straight-line method)

a) $13,333   **c)** $12,000

b) $13,083   **d)** $11,750

9. The investment described in item (8) should be reported as a long-term investment in Investor Corporation's balance sheet at December 31, 19X2, as a single amount of

a) $63,083   **c)** $48,667

b) $50,000   **d)** $48,417

10. Drab, Inc., owns 40% of the outstanding stock of Gloom Company. During 19X5, Drab received a $4,000 cash dividend from Gloom. What effect did this dividend have on Drab's 19X5 financial statements?

a) Increased total assets   **c)** Increased income

b) Decreased total assets   **d)** Decreased investment account

(AICPA adapted)

E3-12   **Equity Method Treatment of Investee Extraordinary Items and Prior-Period Adjustments**
Cedar Company acquired 75% of the voting stock of Deck, Inc., for $75,000 cash when the stockholders' equity of Deck was $100,000. Cedar accounts for its investment in the subsidiary under the equity method.

REQUIRED

Record the entries on Cedar's books to recognize its share of the following independent operating performances of Deck:

1. Deck reported a net income of $40,000 including an extraordinary gain (net of tax) of $12,000.

2. Deck reported a net income of $20,000 including an extraordinary loss (net of tax) of $8,000.

3. Deck incurred a net loss of $10,000 including an extraordinary gain (net of tax) of $16,000.

4. Included in Deck's net income of $34,000 is an extraordinary gain (net of tax) of $4,000 and an extraordinary loss (net of tax) of $6,000.

5. Deck reported a net loss of $5,000 including an extraordinary loss (net of tax) of $2,000, In addition, Deck reported a prior-period adjustment (net of tax) of $4,000 (previous year's depreciation expense understated due to a calculation error).

E3-13   Investment Account Analysis, Consolidation Adjustments   Newton acquired, for $50,000, 75% of the voting stock of Jackson on January 1, 19X6, at which time Jackson's stockholders' equity consisted of common stock, $50,000, and retained earnings, $10,000. The difference in cost and book value of acquired equity is due to the fair value of the machinery (remaining life, ten years) of Jackson being different from its book value. During the next two years, Jackson reported net incomes and dividend payments as follows:

	December 31	
	19X6	**19X7**
Net income	$6,000	$8,000
Dividends	4,000	3,000

REQUIRED

a) Prepare an analysis of the parent's investment account for 19X6 and 19X7, using the format shown in the chapter.

b) Prepare in journal entry form consolidation adjustments that would appear on the December 31, 19X6, and 19X7 consolidation worksheets of Newton and its subsidiary.

E3-14   Multiple Choice Question on Cost and Equity Methods

1. The equity method of accounting for an investment in the common stock of another company should be used when the investment

    a) Is composed of common stock and it is the investor's intent to vote the common stock

    b) Ensures a source of supply such as raw materials

    c) Enables the investor to exercise significant influence over the investee

    d) Is obtained by an exchange of stock for stock

2. When an investor uses the equity method to account for investments in common stock, the equity in the earnings of the investee reported in the investor's income statement will be affected by which of the following?

	Cash Dividends from Investee	Goodwill Amortization Related to Purchase
a)	No	Yes
b)	No	No
c)	Yes	No
d)	Yes	Yes

3. When an investor uses the equity method to account for investments in common stock, cash dividends received by the investor from the investee should be recorded as

a) Dividend income

b) A deduction from the investor's share of the investee's profits

c) A deduction from the investment account

d) A deduction from the stockholders' equity account, dividends to stockholders

4. When an investor uses the equity method to account for investments in common stock, the investment account will be increased when the investor recognizes

a) A proportionate interest in the net income of the investee

b) A cash dividend received from the investee

c) Periodic amortization of the goodwill related to the purchase

d) Depreciation related to the excess of market value over the book value of the investee's depreciable assets at the date of purchase by the investor

Items (5) and (6) are based on the following information:

5. On January 1, 19X8, Avow, Inc., purchased 30% of the outstanding common stock of Depot Corporation for $129,000 cash. Avow is accounting for this investment on the equity method. On the date of acquisition, the fair value of Depot's net assets was $310,000. Avow has determined that the excess of the cost of the investment over its share of Depot's net assets has an indeterminate life. Depot's net income for the year ended December 31, 19X8, was $90,000. During 19X8 Depot declared and paid cash dividends of $10,000. There were no other transactions between the two companies. On January 1, 19X8, the investment in Depot should have been recorded as

a) $ 93,000   **c)** $129,000

b) $120,000   **d)** $165,000

6. Ignoring income taxes, Avow's statement of income for the year ended December 31, 19X8, should include "equity in the net income of Depot Corporation" in the amount of

a) $17,000   **c)** $27,000

b) $26,100   **d)** $27,900

7. On January 1, 19X9, Star Company paid $1,200,000 for 40,000 shares of Comet Corporation's common stock, which represents a 25% investment in the net assets of Comet. Star has the ability to exercise significant influence over Comet. Star received a dividend of $3 per share from Comet in 19X9. Comet reported a net income of $640,000 for the year ended December 31, 19X9. The balance in Star's balance sheet account "Investment in Comet Corporation" at December 31, 19X9, should be

a) $1,200,000   **c)** $1,360,000

b) $1,240,000   **d)** $1,480,000

8. On January 2, 19X0, Troquel Corporation bought 15% of Zafacon Corporation's capital stock for $30,000. Troquel accounts for this investment by the cost method. Zafacon's net incomes for the years ended December 31, 19X0, and December 31, 19X1, were $10,000 and $50,000, respectively. During 19X1, Zafacon declared a dividend of $70,000. No dividends were declared in 19X0. How much should Troquel show on its 19X1 income statement as income from this investment?

a) $1,575   **c)** $ 9,000

b) $7,500   **d)** $10,500

9. On January 1, 19X8, Grade Company paid $300,000 for 20,000 shares of Medium Company's common stock, which represents a 15% investment in Medium. Grade does not have the ability to exercise significant influence over Medium. Medium declared and paid a dividend of $1 per share to its stockholders during 19X8. Medium reported a net income of $260,000 for the year ended December 31, 19X8. The balance in Grade's balance sheet account ''Investment in Medium Company'' at December 31, 19X8, should be

    a) $280,000   **c)** $319,000

    b) $300,000   **d)** $339,000

10. When an investor uses the cost method to account for investments in common stock, cash dividends received by the investor from the investee should normally be recorded as

    a) Dividend income

    b) An addition to the investor's share of the investee's profit

    c) A deduction from the investor's share of the investee's profit

    d) A deduction from the investment account

(AICPA adapted)

E3-15   **Interim Acquisition: Investor and Consolidation Computations** On April 1, 19X7, Tuna acquired 80% of the common stock of Sandfiddler for $248,000. The common stock and retained earnings balances of Sandfiddler on January 1, 19X7, were $200,000 and $100,000, respectively. Any excess cost over the book value of acquired equity is goodwill and is to be amortized over the maximum period allowed under generally acceptable accounting principles. At the end of their fiscal year, December 31, 19X7, the following information was presented summarizing operating activities of the two firms:

	Tuna	Sandfiddler		
	Total	Total	First 3 Months	Last 9 Months
Revenue	$500,000	$120,000	$30,000	$90,000
Expense	360,000	100,000	25,000	75,000
Operating income	$140,000	$ 20,000	$ 5,000	$15,000
Income from subsidiary	11,925			
Net income	$151,925	$ 20,000	$ 5,000	$15,000

Sandfiddler declared and paid $8,000 of dividends on May 1, 19X7.

REQUIRED

a) Show the calculation producing the income from the subsidiary reported by the parent.

b) Determine the balance in Tuna's ''Investment in Sandfiddler'' account as of December 31, 19X7.

c) Present consolidated income statements for 19X7, showing two alternative forms of reporting the subsidiary revenues and expenses.

E3-16   **Interim Acquisition: Investor Computations and Entries, Consolidation Adjustments** P Company acquired a 90% interest in S Company on April 1, 19X3, for $64,125. On January 1, 19X3, the subsidiary's outstanding common stock and retained earnings balances were $50,000 and $20,000, respectively. The subsidiary reported a net income of $5,000 for 19X3 and declared and paid a cash dividend of $2,000 on April 15, 19X3. The income of the subsidiary is earned at a constant rate throughout the year. Both P and S issue financial statements on a calendar-year basis.

REQUIRED

a) Determine the book value of equity acquired by P in S.

b) Prepare entries on the books of P for 19X3 concerning its investment in S.

c) Prepare in journal entry form the consolidation worksheet adjustments for 19X3, assuming the consolidated income statement is to include subsidiary revenues and expenses for the entire year.

d) Prepare in journal entry form the consolidation worksheet adjustments for 19X3, assuming the consolidated income statement is to include only the postacquisition portion of subsidiary revenues and expenses.

E3-17 **Consolidated Stockholders' Equity for a Pooling** On January 1, 19X6, Peters, Inc., issued
APPENDIX A 200,000 additional shares of its voting common stock in exchange for 100,000 shares of Clarkin Company's outstanding voting common stock in a business combination appropriately accounted for by the pooling-of-interests method. The market value of Peters' voting common stock was $40 per share on the date of the business combination. The balance sheets of Peters and Clarkin immediately before the business combination contained the following information:

PETERS, INC.

Common stock, par value $5 per share; authorized, 1,000,000	
shares; issued and outstanding, 600,000 shares	$ 3,000,000
Additional paid-in capital	6,000,000
Retained earnings	11,000,000
Total liabilities and stockholders' equity	$20,000,000

CLARKIN COMPANY

Common stock, par value $10 per share; authorized, 250,000	
shares; issued and outstanding, 100,000 shares	$1,000,000
Additional paid-in captial	2,000,000
Retained earnings	4,000,000
Total liabilities and stockholders' equity	$7,000,000

The net income for the year ended December 31, 19X6, was $1,150,000 for Peters and $350,000 for Clarkin. During 19X6 Peters paid $900,000 in dividends to its stockholders, and Clarkin paid no dividends.

REQUIRED

Prepare the consolidated stockholders' equity section of the balance sheet for the combined companies as of December 31, 19X6. Provide a supporting schedule for retained earnings.

(AICPA adapted)

E3-18 **Multiple Choice Questions on Pooling** *Items (1) through (5) are based on the following informa-*
APPENDIX A *tion:* On June 30, 19X7, Post, Inc. issued 630,000 shares of its $5 par common stock, for which it received 180,000 shares (90%) of Shaw Corp.'s $10 par common stock, in a business combination appropriately accounted for as a pooling of interests. The stockholders' equities immediately before the combination were:

	Post	Shaw
Common stock	$ 6,500,000	$2,000,000
Additional paid-in capital	4,400,000	1,600,000
Retained earnings	6,100,000	5,400,000
	$17,000,000	$9,000,000

Both corporations continued to operate as separate businesses, maintaining accounting records with years ending December 31. For 19X7, net income and dividends paid from separate company operations were:

	Post	Shaw
Net Income		
Six months ended 6/30/X7	$1,000,000	$300,000
Six months ended 12/31/X7	1,100,000	500,000
Dividends Paid		
April 1, 19X7	1,300,000	—
October 1, 19X7	—	350,000

1. In the June 30, 19X7, consolidated balance sheet, common stock should be reported at

a) $9,650,000   c) $8,500,000

b) $9,450,000   d) $8,300,000

2. In the June 30, 19X7, consolidated balance sheet, additional paid-in capital should be reported at

a) $4,400,000   c) $5,840,000

b) $4,490,000   d) $6,000,000

3. In the June 30, 19X7, consolidated balance sheet, retained earnings should be reported at

a) $6,100,000   c) $10,960,000

b) $9,660,000   d) $11,500,000

4. In the 19X7 consolidated income statement, net income should be reported at

a) $2,550,000   c) $2,820,000

b) $2,600,000   d) $2,900,000

5. In the December 31, 19X7, consolidated balance sheet, total minority interest should be reported at

a) $950,000   c) $915,000

b) $945,000   d) $900,000

(AICPA adapted)

E3-19
APPENDIX B

Cost Method Entries, Consolidation Adjustments, and Computations Shuler Company acquired 60% of Stroh Company on January 1, 19X6, for $70,000 when Stroh's common stock was $70,000 and its retained earnings was $20,000. Book values equal fair values of all assets and liabilities of Stroh except for buildings (ten-year remaining life), which have a fair value that is $10,000 more than book value. All intangibles are amortized over five years. During 19X6 and 19X7, Stroh earned a net income and paid dividends as follows:

	19X6	19X7
Net income	$15,000	$20,000
Dividends	5,000	10,000

REQUIRED

a) Prepare the entries on the books of Shuler for 19X6 and 19X7 concerning its investment in Stroh assuming Shuler uses the cost method.

b) Prepare in journal entry form the consolidation adjustments that would appear on the December 31, 19X6, and 19X7 consolidation worksheet of Shuler and its subsidiary assuming the cost method was used in accounting for the investment in Stroh.

c) Determine minority interest in the subsidiary retained earnings on January 1, 19X7.

PROBLEMS

P3-1 Valuation Differential and Amortization Schedule Calculations, Cost and Equity Method Entries On January 1, 19X1, Dunn Company purchased, in the open market, 75% of the outstanding common stock of Hunt Company for $105,000 cash. At that time, Hunt's common stock and retained earnings were $100,000 and $30,000, respectively. On the date of acquisition, the net assets of Hunt were fairly valued except for the following assets:

	Book Value	Fair Value
Equipment (net)	$ 60,000	$ 62,000
Buildings (net)	100,000	103,000
Land	25,000	28,000

The equipment and buildings have a remaining life of five years, and any intangible assets are amortized over a ten-year period. On December 31, 19X1, Hunt reported a net income of $20,000 and paid dividends of $10,000. At the end of the calendar year 19X2, Hunt reported a net loss of $8,000 and paid dividends of $6,000.

REQUIRED

a) Determine the valuation differential associated with the purchase of Hunt by Dunn.

b) Prepare a composition of the revaluation increment.

c) Prepare an amortization schedule for goodwill and the revaluation increment.

d) Prepare entries for 19X1 and 19X2 for Dunn concerning its investment in Hunt under (1) the cost method and (2) the equity method.

P3-2 Equity Method Entries, Consolidation Worksheet: Wholly Owned Subsidiary, Valuation Differential On January 1, 19X2, Prime Company issued 240 shares of its stock and paid cash of $1,000 for all the shares of Rib Company. Prime's stock was selling on the market at $50 per share at this time. At the date of acquisition, the book value of the assets and liabilities of Rib represented fair values. Any excess cost over the book value of acquired equity is considered goodwill and amortized over 30 years. The following information was made available on the two companies as of December 31, 19X2:

	Prime Company	Rib Company
Cash	$ 7,000	$ 4,000
Inventory	24,000	11,000
Investment in Rib	13,900	
Accounts payable	5,000	4,000
Common stock ($50 par)	25,000	6,000
Retained earnings, Jan. 1, 19X2	12,000	4,000
Dividends	4,000	1,000
Sales	20,000	20,000
Cost of goods sold	10,000	15,000
Operating expenses	5,000	3,000
Income from subsidiary	1,900	

REQUIRED

a) Prepare the entries that Prime Company would have recorded on its books to produce the balances of $13,900 in the investment in Rib Company account and $1,900 in the income from subsidiary account.

b) Prepare a consolidation worksheet as of December 31, 19X2, for Prime and its subsidiary.

P3-3 **Equity Method Entries, Consolidation Computations** On January 1, 19X6, Todd Corporation made the following investments:

1. Todd acquired, for cash, 80% of the outstanding common stock of Meadow Corporation at $70 per share. The stockholders' equity of Meadow on January 1, 19X6, consisted of the following:

Common stock, par value $50	$50,000
Retained earnings	20,000

2. Todd acquired, for cash, 70% of the outstanding common stock of Van Corporation at $40 per share. The stockholders' equity of Van on January 1, 19X6, consisted of the following:

Common stock, par value $20	$60,000
Capital in excess of par value	20,000
Retained earnings	40,000

After these investments were made, Todd was able to exercise significant influence over the operations of both companies. An analysis of the retained earnings of each company for 19X6 is as follows:

	Todd	Meadow	Van
Balance, 1-1-X6	$240,000	$20,000	$40,000
Net income (loss) from own operations	104,600	36,000	(12,000)
Cash dividends paid	(40,000)	(16,000)	(9,000)

REQUIRED

a) What entries should have been made on the books of Todd during 19X6 to record the following?

  1. Investments in subsidiaries

  2. Parent's share of subsidiary income or loss

  3. Subsidiary dividends received

b) Compute the amount of minority interest in each subsidiary's stockholders' equity at December 31, 19X6.

c) What amount should be reported as consolidated retained earnings of Todd Corporation and subsidiaries as of December 31, 19X6?

(AICPA adapted)

P3-4 **Multiple Choice Questions on Equity Method and Consolidation**

1. On January 1, 19X6, Tom Kat, Inc., purchased 25% of the outstanding shares of stock of Carmel for $115,000 cash. The investment will be accounted for by the equity method. On that date, Carmel's net assets (book and fair values) were $300,000. Tom Kat has determined that the excess of the cost of its investment in Carmel over its share of Carmel's net assets has an indeterminate life and is to be amortized over the maximum allowed period of time. Carmel's net income for the year ended December 31, 19X6, was $50,000. During 19X6, Tom Kat received $5,000 cash dividends from Carmel. There were no other transactions between the two companies. Tom Kat's income statement for the year ended December 31, 19X6, should include "equity in 19X6 net income of Carmel" in the amount of

  a) $ 7,500   **c)** $12,500

  b) $11,500   **d)** $13,500

2. A parent company that uses the equity method of accounting for its investment in a 40%-owned subsidiary, which earned $20,000 and paid $5,000 in dividends, made the following entries:

Investment in subsidiary	8,000	
Income from subsidiary		8,000
Cash	2,000	
Dividend income		2,000

What effect will these entries have on the parent's balance sheet?

a) Financial position will be fairly stated.

b) Investment in the subsidiary will be overstated, retained earnings understated.

c) Investment in the subsidiary will be understated, retained earnings understated.

d) Investment in the subsidiary will be overstated, retained earnings overstated.

3. On January 1, 19X7, the Pint Corporation paid $400,000 for 10,000 shares of Quart Company's common stock which represents a 10% investment in Quart. Pint received dividends of $1 per share from Quart in 19X7. Quart reported a net income of $150,000 for the year ended December 31, 19X7. The market value of Quart's common stock on December 31, 19X7, was $42 per share. The amount reported in Pint's 19X7 income statement as a result of Pint's investment in Quart was

a) $10,000   **c)** $30,000

b) $15,000   **d)** $35,000

4. Which of the following describes the amount at which a parent company should carry its unconsolidated domestic subsidiary on its separate financial statements in periods subsequent to acquisition?

a) Original cost of the investment to the parent company

b) Original cost of the investment adjusted for the parent's share of the subsidiary's earnings, losses, and dividends

c) Current market value of the investment adjusted for dividends received

d) Current market value of the investment

5. In a parent's unconsolidated financial statements, which accounts, other than cash, are affected when reflecting a subsidiary's earnings and dividends?

a) Dividend revenue, income from subsidiary, and retained earnings

b) Dividend revenue and retained earnings

c) Investment in subsidiary, income from subsidiary, dividend revenue, and retained earnings

d) Investment in subsidiary, income from subsidiary, and retained earnings

6. On January 1, 19X7, the Robohn Company purchased, for cash, 40% of the 300,000 shares of voting common stock of the Lowell Company for $1,800,000 when 40% of the underlying equity in the net assets of Lowell was $1,400,000. Robohn amortizes goodwill over a 40-year period with a full year's amortization taken in the year of the purchase. As a result of this transaction, Robohn has the ability to exercise significant influence over the operating and financial policies of Lowell. Lowell's net income for the year ended December 31, 19X7, was $600,000. During 19X7, Lowell paid $325,000 in dividends to its stockholders. The income reported by Robohn for its investment in Lowell should be

a) $120,000   **c)** $230,000

b) $130,000   **d)** $240,000

7. How is the portion of consolidated earnings to be assigned to minority interest in consolidated financial statements determined?

a) The net income of the parent is subtracted from the subsidiary's net income to determine the minority interest.

b) The subsidiary's net income is extended to the minority interest.

c) The amount of the subsidiary's earnings recognized for consolidation purposes is multiplied by the minority's percentage ownership.

d) The amount of consolidated earnings determined on the consolidated working papers is multiplied by the minority interest percentage at the balance sheet date.

8. What would be the effect on the financial statements if an unconsolidated subsidiary is accounted for by the equity method but consolidated statements are being prepared with other subsidiaries?

a) All the unconsolidated subsidiary's accounts would be included individually in the consolidated statements.

b) The consolidated retained earnings would not reflect the earnings of the unconsolidated subsidiary.

c) The consolidated retained earnings would be the same as if the subsidiary had been included in the consolidation.

d) Dividend income from the unconsolidated subsidiary would be reflected in consolidated net income.

9. The Mon Corporation acquired a 30% interest in the Soon Company on January 1, 19X4, for $600,000. At that time, Soon had 2,000,000 shares of its $1 par value common stock issued and outstanding. During 19X4, Soon paid cash dividends of $20,000 and thereafter declared and issued a 5% common stock dividend when the market value was $2 per share. Soon's net income for 19X4 was $120,000. What should be the balance in Mon's "Investment in Soon Company" account at the end of 19X4?

a) $570,000

b) $600,000

c) $630,000

d) $636,000

(AICPA adapted)

P3-5 **Consolidation Worksheet: Partially Owned Subsidiary, Valuation Differential** Bach Company acquired 75% of the voting stock of Mason Company on January 1, 19X3, for $18,000 cash. At the date of acquisition, the book values of Mason's net assets were equal to their fair values except for equipment, which had a fair value exceeding the book value by $6,000 and a remaining life of nine years. The financial statements of both companies as of December 31, 19X3, are as follows:

	Bach Company	Mason Company
Income Statement		
Sales	$44,000	$22,000
Income from subsidiary	4,000	
Cost of goods sold	(15,000)	(11,000)
Operating expenses	(10,000)	(5,000)
Net income	$23,000	$ 6,000
Statement of Retained Earnings		
Retained earnings, 1-1-X3	$16,000	$ 8,000
Net income	23,000	6,000
Dividends		(2,000)
Retained earnings, 12-31-X3	$39,000	$12,000
Balance Sheet		
Assets		
Cash	$11,000	$ 3,000
Accounts receivable	6,000	2,000
Inventory	12,000	2,000
Investment in Mason	20,500	
Equipment (net)	22,000	14,000
Other assets	20,000	3,000
Total assets	$91,500	$24,000
Liabilities and Stockholders' Equity		
Accounts payable	$ 3,000	$ 2,000
Common stock	49,500	10,000
Retained earnings	39,000	12,000
Total liabilities and stockholders' equity	$91,500	$24,000

REQUIRED

Prepare a consolidation worksheet as of December 31, 19X3, for Bach Company and its subsidiary.

P3-6 **Consolidation Worksheet: Partially Owned Subsidiary, Valuation Differential** Muse Company acquired, in the open market, 80% of the common stock of Dodge Company for $35,000 on January 1, 19X3. The stockholders' equity of Dodge Company at the date of acquisition consisted of common stock of $25,000 and retained earnings of $10,000. On the date of acquisition, the book values of the net assets of Dodge were equal to their fair values except for a piece of equipment, which had a fair value of $14,250, a book value of $8,000, and a remaining estimated life of ten years. All intangibles are amortized over 20 years. As of December 31, 19X3, the trial balances of Muse and Dodge appeared as follows:

	Muse Company	Dodge Company
Debits		
Cash	$ 17,000	$ 4,000
Inventory	25,000	14,000
Investment in Dodge	38,400	
Equipment (net)	12,000	22,000
Dividends	10,000	5,000
Cost of goods sold	30,000	25,000
Depreciation and other expenses	20,000	5,000
	$152,400	$75,000
Credits		
Common stock ($50 par)	$ 45,000	$25,000
Retained earnings	20,000	10,000
Sales	80,000	40,000
Income from subsidiary	7,400	
	$152,400	$75,000

REQUIRED

For Muse Company and its subsidiary, prepare a consolidation worksheet for the year ended December 31, 19X3.

P3-7 **Consolidation Worksheet: Partially Owned Subsidiary, Valuation Differential** Van Company acquired 80% of the voting stock of Halen Company on January 1, 19X3, for $22,200 cash. On this date, the book values of Halen's net assets were equal to their fair values except for machinery, which had a fair value exceeding book value by $3,000 (remaining life of six years). All intangible assets are amortized over ten years. The financial statements of both companies as of December 31, 19X3, are as follows:

	Van Company	Halen Company
Income Statement		
Sales	$ 40,000	$24,000
Income from subsidiary	7,540	
Cost of goods sold	(13,000)	(9,000)
Operating expenses	(12,540)	(5,000)
Net income	$ 22,000	$10,000
Statement of Retained Earnings		
Retained earnings, 1-1-X3	$ 30,000	$14,000
Net income	22,000	10,000
Dividends	(8,000)	(2,000)
Retained earnings, 12-31-X3	$ 44,000	$22,000
Balance Sheet		
Assets		
Cash	$ 9,000	$ 2,000
Accounts receivable	12,000	4,000
Inventory	15,000	6,000
Investment in Halen	28,140	
Machinery (net)	12,860	18,000
Building (net)	40,000	7,000
Total assets	$117,000	$37,000
Liabilities and Stockholders' Equity		
Accounts payable	$ 13,000	$ 5,000
Common stock	60,000	10,000
Retained earnings	44,000	22,000
Total liabilities and stockholders' equity	$117,000	$37,000

REQUIRED

a) Prepare an analysis of the parent's investment account for 19X3 using the format shown in the chapter.

b) Prepare a consolidation worksheet as of December 31, 19X3, for Van Company and its subsidiary.

P3-8   **Consolidation Worksheet (End of Second Year): Wholly Owned Subsidiary, Valuation Differential** The Redskins Company acquired, on January 1, 19X1, all the outstanding common stock of the Cowboys Company for $51,000; net asset book values equal fair values on this date for both companies. At the date of acquisition, the common stock and retained earnings balances of Cowboys were $30,000 and $15,000, respectively. During the year 19X1, Cowboys earned a net income of $7,000 and paid dividends of $2,000. Both companies amortize intangible assets over a six-year period. Financial statements for the two companies as of December 31, 19X2, are as follows:

	Redskins Company	Cowboys Company
Income Statement		
Sales	$100,000	$100,000
Income from subsidiary	9,000	
Cost of goods sold	(50,000)	(75,000)
Other expenses	(25,000)	(15,000)
Net income	$ 34,000	$ 10,000
Statement of Retained Earnings		
Retained earnings, 1-1-X2	$ 60,000	$ 20,000
Net income	34,000	10,000
Dividends	(20,000)	(5,000)
Retained earnings, 12-31-X2	$ 74,000	$ 25,000
Balance Sheet		
Assets		
Cash	$ 45,000	$ 20,000
Notes receivable	100,000	30,000
Inventory	20,000	25,000
Investment in Cowboys	59,000	
Total assets	$224,000	$ 75,000
Liabilities and Stockholders' Equity		
Accounts payable	$ 25,000	$ 20,000
Common stock	125,000	30,000
Retained earnings	74,000	25,000
Total liabilities and stockholders' equity	$224,000	$ 75,000

REQUIRED

Prepare a consolidation worksheet for the Redskins Company and its subsidiary for the year ended December 31, 19X2.

P3-9 **Consolidation Worksheet (End of Second Year): Partially Owned Subsidiary, Valuation Differential** The Miller Company acquired 90% of the common stock of Rhoads Company for $102,350 on January 1, 19X2. At the date of acquisition, the book values of the assets and liabilities of Rhoads represented fair values except for a piece of equipment which had a book value of $2,000, a fair value of $3,500, and a remaining estimated life of five years. All intangible assets are amortized over twenty years.

	Miller Company	Rhoads Company
Income Statement		
Sales	$110,000	$ 90,000
Income from subsidiary	8,630	
Cost of goods sold	(60,000)	(55,000)
Other expenses	(20,630)	(25,000)
Net income	$ 38,000	$ 10,000
Statement of Retained Earnings		
Retained earnings, 1-1-X3	$ 57,000	$ 44,000
Net income	38,000	10,000
Dividends	(20,000)	(5,000)
Retained earnings, 12-31-X3	$ 75,000	$ 49,000
Balance Sheet		
Assets		
Cash	$ 10,000	$ 16,000
Notes receivable	22,000	26,000
Inventory	20,000	29,000
Investment in Rhoads	109,710	
Plant & equipment (net)	80,000	65,000
Total assets	$241,710	$136,000
Liabilities and Stockholders' Equity		
Accounts payable	$ 26,710	$ 17,000
Common stock	140,000	70,000
Retained earnings	75,000	49,000
Total liabilities and stockholders' equity	$241,710	$136,000

Additional information:

1. Rhoads reported a net income of $6,000 in 19X2 and paid dividends of $2,000 during the same year.

2. Rhoads' stock and retained earnings balances were $70,000 and $40,000, respectively, at the date of acquisition, January 1, 19X2.

REQUIRED

a) Prepare an analysis of the parent's investment account for 19X2 and 19X3 using the format shown in the chapter.

b) Prepare a consolidation worksheet for Miller Company and its subsidiary as of December 31, 19X3.

P3-10   **Investment Account Analysis, Consolidation Worksheet (End of Second Year): Partially Owned Subsidiary, Valuation Differential**   Ping Company acquired an 80% interest in Pong Company on January 1, 19X2, for $110,000. The cost of the acquisition included $10,000 in excess of the book value, which is attributable to the fact that Pong's building is undervalued. The building had a ten-year remaining estimated life at the time of the acquisition. The following information is made available about the two companies as of December 31, 19X3:

	Ping Company	Pong Company
Cash	$142,000	$ 80,000
Inventory	100,000	75,000
Investment in Pong	136,000	
Building (net)	35,000	25,000
Accounts payable	41,000	20,000
Common stock	200,000	100,000
Retained earnings, Jan. 1, 19X3	150,000	50,000
Dividends	50,000	25,000
Sales	225,000	150,000
Cost of goods sold	150,000	100,000
Depreciation expense	20,000	10,000
Other expenses	10,000	5,000
Income from subsidiary	27,000	

Additional information:

1. Pong Company reported a net income of $35,000 in 19X2 and paid dividends of $10,000 during the same year.

2. Pong's common stock and retained earnings balances were $100,000 and $25,000, respectively, at the date of acquisition.

REQUIRED

a) Prepare an analysis of the parent's investment account for 19X2 and 19X3 using the format shown in the chapter.

b) Prepare a consolidation worksheet for Ping Company and its subsidiary as of December 31, 19X3.

P3-11 **Consolidation Worksheet (End of Second Year): Partially Owned Subsidiary, Valuation Differential** On January 1, 19X1, Martin Company acquired 80% of the outstanding common stock of Daniels Company for $119,000. Trial balances of the two companies for the year ended December 31, 19X2, are as follows:

	Martin Company	Daniels Company
Debits		
Cash	$ 28,000	$ 20,000
Accounts receivable	20,000	46,000
Inventory	70,000	30,000
Investments in Daniels	132,600	
Building (net)	25,000	20,000
Equipment (net)	75,000	60,000
Dividends	30,600	20,000
Cost of goods sold	125,000	105,000
Depreciation and amortization expense	20,000	15,000
Other expenses	57,000	58,000
	$583,200	$374,000
Credits		
Accounts payable	$ 40,000	$ 24,000
Common stock	212,600	115,000
Retained earnings	15,000	35,000
Sales	300,000	200,000
Income from subsidiary	15,600	
	$583,200	$374,000

Additional information:

1. The common stock and retained earnings balances of Daniels at the date of acquisition, January 1, 19X1, were $115,000 and $15,000, respectively.

2. At the date of acquisition, Martin paid $15,000 in excess of the book value of the net assets of Daniels. Of the $15,000 excess, $6,000 was allocated to building (estimated remaining life, six years), $4,000 to equipment (estimated remaining life, five years), and $5,000 to goodwill (estimated life, 25 years).

3. During the fiscal year ended December 31, 19X1, Daniels reported a net income of $30,000 and dividend payments of $10,000.

REQUIRED
Prepare a consolidation worksheet for the year ended December 31, 19X2, for Martin Company and its subsidiary.

P3-12   **Interim Acquisition—Consolidation Worksheet (Form I): Partially Owned Subsidiary, Valuation Differential**   On May 1, 19X2, Company P acquired a 75% interest in Company S for $35,250. Any excess cost over the book value of equity acquired is goodwill and is amortized over four years. Financial statements of both companies for the 12-month period ending December 31, 19X2, are as follows:

	Company P	Company S
Income Statement		
Sales	$ 88,000	$44,000
Income from subsidiary	5,000	
Cost of goods sold	(30,000)	(22,000)
Operating expenses	(20,000)	(10,000)
Net income	$ 43,000	$12,000
Statement of Retained Earnings		
Retained earnings, 1-1-X2	$ 32,000	$16,000
Net income	43,000	12,000
Dividends	(8,000)	(4,000)
Retained earnings, 12-31-X2	$ 67,000	$24,000
Balance Sheet		
Assets		
Cash	$ 19,000	$ 7,000
Accounts receivable	12,000	4,000
Inventory	24,000	4,000
Investment in Company S	38,000	
Plant and equipment (net)	84,000	34,000
Total assets	$177,000	$49,000
Liabilities and Stockholders' Equity		
Accounts payable	$ 11,000	$ 5,000
Common stock	99,000	20,000
Retained earnings	67,000	24,000
Total liabilities and stockholders' equity	$177,000	$49,000

Additional information:

1. Both companies paid their respective dividends in equal amounts each quarter.

2. Income of the subsidiary is earned at a constant rate throughout the year.

REQUIRED

a) Prepare a consolidation worksheet as of December 31, 19X2, for Company P and its subsidiary. The consolidated income statement is to include subsidiary revenues and expenses for the entire year.

b) Prepare a consolidated income statement for Company P and its subsidiary for the year ended December 31, 19X2.

P3-13 **Interim Acquisition—Journal Entries and Consolidation Worksheet (Form 1): Partially Owned Subsidiary, Valuation Differential** Hugo Company acquired 85% of the outstanding common stock of Perry on April 1, 19X5, in exchange for 3,000 common shares ($20 par) of Hugo with a fair value of $50 per share. In addition, Hugo paid $6,000 to have the securities registered and $4,000 to a local firm as a ''finder's fee'' for arranging the combination. At the date of acquisition, the book values of the assets and liabilities of Perry are equal to their respective fair values. All intangible assets are amortized over five years.

Financial statements of both companies for the 12-month period ending December 31, 19X5, are presented below. However, the financial statements of Hugo are *incomplete* as to the amounts for ''Income from subsidiary'' and ''Investment in Perry.''

	Hugo	Perry
Income Statement		
Sales	$150,000	$ 78,000
Income from subsidiary		
Cost of goods sold	(45,000)	(30,000)
Operating expenses	(29,000)	(26,000)
Net income	$	$ 22,000
Statement of Retained Earnings		
Retained earnings, 1-1-X5	$ 70,000	$ 50,000
Net income		22,000
Dividends	(12,000)	(8,000)
Retained earnings, 12-31-X5	$	$ 64,000
Balance Sheet		
Assets		
Cash	$ 19,000	$ 12,000
Accounts receivable	41,000	10,000
Inventory	68,000	27,000
Investment in Perry		
Plant and equipment (net)	213,800	125,000
Total assets	$	$174,000
Liabilities and Stockholders' Equity		
Accounts payable	$ 15,000	$ 20,000
Common stock	250,000	80,000
Excess over par	90,000	10,000
Retained earnings		64,000
Total liabilities and stockholders' equity	$	$174,000

Additional information:

1. The subsidiary declared a $2,000 cash dividend on March 15, payable on April 25 to stockholders of record on April 12.

2. The income of the subsidiary is earned at a uniform rate throughout the year.

REQUIRED

a) Determine the amounts that would appear in the December 31, 19X5, financial statements of Hugo for ''Income from subsidiary'' and ''Investment in Perry'' accounts.

b) For purposes of preparing your answer to this item only, assume that the amounts in the December 31, 19X5, financial statements of Hugo for "Income from subsidiary" and "Investment in Perry" were $9,476 and $156,676, respectively. Prepare a consolidation worksheet as of December 31, 19X5, for Hugo and its subsidiary. The consolidated income statement is to include subsidiary revenue and expenses for the entire year.

P3-14　**Consolidation Worksheet (End of Fifth Year): Partially Owned Subsidiary, Valuation Differential**　Venus Company acquired a 90% interest in Pluto Company on January 1, 19X1, for $125,000. On that date, the common stock and retained earnings of Pluto Company totaled $75,000 and $25,000, respectively. Of the $35,000 excess cost over the book value, equipment, building, and land, each was allocated $9,000; the remaining $8,000 was allocated to goodwill. Financial statements of Venus and Pluto for the year ending December 31, 19X5, are as follows:

	Venus Company	Pluto Company
Income Statement		
Sales	$ 75,000	$ 50,000
Income from subsidiary	11,300	
Cost of goods sold	(30,000)	(25,000)
Operating expenses	(15,000)	(10,000)
Net income	$ 41,300	$ 15,000
Statement of Retained Earnings		
Retained earnings, 1-1-X5	$ 71,000	$ 50,000
Net income	41,300	15,000
Dividends	(10,000)	(5,000)
Retained earnings, 12-31-X5	$102,300	$ 60,000
Balance Sheet		
Assets		
Cash	$ 25,500	$ 15,000
Accounts receivable	25,000	20,000
Inventory	40,000	35,000
Investment in Pluto	145,500	
Equipment (net)	45,000	35,000
Building (net)	30,000	20,000
Land	30,000	30,000
Total assets	$341,000	$155,000
Liabilities and Stockholders' Equity		
Accounts payable	$ 38,700	$ 20,000
Common stock	200,000	75,000
Retained earnings	102,300	60,000
Total liabilities and stockholders' equity	$341,000	$155,000

Additional information:

1. On the date of acquisition, Pluto's equipment and building had a remaining life of nine years.

2. All intangible assets are amortized over a 40-year period.

REQUIRED

Prepare a consolidation worksheet for Venus and its subsidiary as of December 31, 19X5.

P3-15 **Consolidation Worksheet (End of Third Year): Two Partially Owned Subsidiaries, One Acquired in Excess of Book Value and One at Less Than Book Value** On January 1, 19X1, Thunderbird acquired an 80% interest in Hawk and a 90% interest in Lark. Thunderbird paid $10,000 in excess of the book value for the investment in Hawk; the book value and fair value of the assets and liabilities of Hawk were the same. Thunderbird paid $8,000 less than the book value for its equity in Lark. The difference in the cost of Thunderbird's investment and Lark's book value is equally divided between the land and the building owned by the subsidiary. Both subsidiaries had estimated a 20-year remaining life on all long-term tangible and intangible assets. Trial balances for the three companies as of December 31, 19X3, are as follows:

	Thunderbird	Hawk	Lark
Debits			
Cash	$ 59,500	$ 25,000	$ 25,000
Accounts receivable	20,000	18,000	23,000
Inventory	50,000	35,000	30,000
Investment in Hawk	98,100		
Investment in Lark	120,400		
Land	26,000	10,000	20,000
Buildings (net)	40,000	25,000	35,000
Other assets	22,000	14,000	19,000
Cost of goods sold	60,000	40,000	42,000
Depreciation and other expenses	21,000	20,000	18,000
Dividends	25,000	10,000	8,000
	$542,000	$197,000	$220,000
Credits			
Accounts payable	$ 25,300	$ 15,000	$ 10,000
Common stock ($25 par)	200,000	60,000	80,000
Paid-in capital	75,000	12,000	20,000
Retained earnings	80,000	20,000	30,000
Sales	120,000	90,000	80,000
Income from subsidiary, Hawk	23,500		
Income from subsidiary, Lark	18,200		
	$542,000	$197,000	$220,000

REQUIRED
Prepare a consolidation worksheet for Thunderbird and its subsidiaries as of December 31, 19X3.

P3-16

APPENDIX A

Consolidation Worksheet: Partially Owned Subsidiary   On January 1, 19X5, Mitchem Company acquired 90% of the outstanding common shares of Carpenter, Inc., in exchange for newly issued shares of Mitchem. The combination is to be accounted for as a pooling of interests. Immediately before the combination, the assets and liabilities of Carpenter were fairly valued at book value except for equipment, which had a fair value in excess of book value of $5,000 (remaining life, ten years).

Financial statements for Mitchem and Carpenter for the year ended December 31, 19X5, are as follows:

	Mitchem Company	Carpenter, Inc.
Income Statement		
Sales	$ 70,000	$ 50,000
Income from subsidiary	13,500	
Cost of goods sold	(30,000)	(25,000)
Operating expenses	(15,000)	(10,000)
Net income	$ 38,500	$ 15,000
Statement of Retained Earnings		
Retained earnings, 1-1-X5	$ 73,800	$ 50,000
Net income	38,500	15,000
Dividends	(10,000)	(5,000)
Retained earnings, 12-31-X5	$102,300	$ 60,000
Balance Sheet		
Assets		
Cash	$ 25,500	$ 15,000
Accounts receivable	25,000	20,000
Inventory	40,000	35,000
Investment in Carpenter	121,500	
Equipment (net)	45,000	35,000
Building (net)	54,000	20,000
Land	30,000	30,000
Total assets	$341,000	$155,000
Liabilities and Stockholders' Equity		
Accounts payable	$ 38,700	$ 20,000
Common stock	200,000	75,000
Retained earnings	102,300	60,000
Total liabilities and stockholders' equity	$341,000	$155,000

REQUIRED

Prepare a consolidation worksheet for Mitchem and its subsidiary as of December 31, 19X5.

P3-17

APPENDIX A

Consolidation Worksheet: Partially Owned Subsidiary   On January 1, 19X8, Normal, Inc. acquired 90% of the outstanding common stock of Eccentric Company in exchange for 4,000 shares of Normal's $5 par common stock. The combination is to be accounted for as a pooling of interests. At the date of acquisition, the book values of the assets and liabilities of Eccentric represented fair values. Following are the financial statements of both companies as of December 31, 19X8.

	Normal Inc.	Eccentric Company
Income Statement		
Sales	$160,000	$ 75,000
Income from subsidiary	22,500	
Cost of goods sold	(60,000)	(25,000)
Operating expenses	(50,000)	(25,000)
Net income	$ 72,500	$ 25,000
Statement of Retained Earnings		
Retained earnings, 1-1-X8	$200,000	$ 75,000
Net income	72,500	25,000
Dividends	(50,000)	(15,000)
Retained earnings, 12-31-X8	$222,500	$ 85,000
Balance Sheet		
Assets		
Cash	$ 90,000	$ 50,000
Accounts receivable	97,500	40,000
Inventory	100,000	60,000
Investment in Eccentric	135,000	
Total assets	$422,500	$150,000
Stockholders' Equity		
Common stock	$200,000	$ 65,000
Retained earnings	222,500	85,000
Total stockholders' equity	$422,500	$150,000

REQUIRED

Prepare a consolidation worksheet for Normal, Inc., and its subsidiary for the year ended December 31, 19X8.

P3-18 **Consolidation Worksheet: Partially Owned Subsidiary** Angelfish acquired 95% of the out-
APPENDIX A   standing common stock of Bluefish on January 1, 19X5, in exchange for newly issued common
shares of Angelfish. The combination was accounted for as a pooling of interests. At the date of
acquisition, the book values of the assets and liabilities of Bluefish were equal to their respective fair
values, except for a fully amortized patent which had a fair value of $12,000 (estimated life, six
years). All intangible assets are amortized over ten years.

Financial statements of both companies ending December 31, 19X6, are presented below.

	Angelfish	Bluefish
Income Statement		
Sales	$300,000	$156,000
Income from subsidiary	43,700	
Cost of goods sold	(90,000)	(80,000)
Operating expenses	(129,700)	(30,000)
Net income	$124,000	$ 46,000
Statement of Retained Earnings		
Retained earnings, 1-1-X6	$140,000	$ 50,000
Net income	124,000	46,000
Dividends	(24,000)	(16,000)
Retained earnings, 12-31-X6	$240,000	$ 80,000
Balance Sheet		
Assets		
Cash	$ 20,000	$ 12,000
Accounts receivable	44,000	10,000
Inventory	75,000	25,000
Investment in Bluefish	152,000	
Plant and equipment (net)	249,000	123,000
Total assets	$540,000	$170,000
Liabilities and Stockholders' Equity		
Accounts payable	$ 30,000	$ 10,000
Common stock	200,000	70,000
Excess over par	70,000	10,000
Retained earnings	240,000	80,000
Total liabilities and stockholders' equity	$540,000	$170,000

REQUIRED
Prepare a consolidation worksheet for Angelfish and its subsidiary as of December 31, 19X6.

P3-19 **Consolidation Worksheet (Cost Method): Partially Owned Subsidiary, Valuation Differential**
APPENDIX B On January 1, 19X2, Blue Ridge, Inc., acquired 75% of the common stock of Afton Company for
$21,000. The book values of Afton's assets and liabilities were equal to their fair values except for
equipment, which had a book value of $10,000, a fair value of $20,000, and a 15-year remaining life.
The separate financial statements of Blue Ridge and its subsidiary as of December 31, 19X2, are
presented here. Blue Ridge uses the cost method to account for its investment in Afton:

	Blue Ridge, Inc.	Afton Company
Income Statement		
Sales	$ 42,000	$20,000
Dividend income	1,500	
Cost of goods sold	(13,000)	(9,000)
Operating expenses	(10,000)	(5,000)
Net income	$ 20,500	$ 6,000
Statement of Retained Earnings		
Retained earnings, 1-1-X2	$ 49,000	$ 8,000
Net income	20,500	6,000
Dividends		(2,000)
Retained earnings, 12-31-X2	$ 69,500	$12,000
Balance Sheet		
Assets		
Cash	$ 12,500	$ 4,000
Inventory	20,000	7,000
Investment in Afton	21,000	
Equipment (net)	39,000	9,000
Other assets	20,000	4,000
Total assets	$112,500	$24,000
Liabilities and Stockholders' Equity		
Accounts payable	$ 3,000	$ 2,000
Common stock	40,000	10,000
Retained earnings	69,500	12,000
Total liabilities and stockholders' equity	$112,500	$24,000

REQUIRED

a) Prepare a consolidation worksheet as of December 31, 19X2, for Blue Ridge and its subsidiary.

b) Explain what caused the consolidated net income to be different from the net income reported on
the parent's (Blue Ridge, Inc.) separate financial statements. Supporting computations should be
provided.

c) Assuming Blue Ridge had accounted for its investment in Afton using the equity method and not
the cost method, would the consolidated amounts be different?

P3-20 **Consolidation Worksheet (Cost Method, End of Second Year): Partially Owned Subsidiary,**
APPENDIX B **Valuation Differential**   Michener Company acquired an 80% interest in Homer, Inc., on January 1,
19X2, for $110,000 when Homer's common stock was $100,000 and its retained earnings $25,000.
Of the excess investment cost over the book value of equity acquired, $6,000 was allocated to
buildings (ten-year life) and the remainder to goodwill (eight-year life). The financial statements of
Michener and its subsidiary as of December 31, 19X3, are presented here. Michener accounts for its
investment in Homer using the cost method.

	Michener Company	Homer, Inc.
Income Statement		
Sales	$220,000	$150,000
Dividend income	12,000	
Cost of goods sold	(140,000)	(100,000)
Depreciation and amortization expense	(25,000)	(15,000)
Other expenses	(10,000)	(5,000)
Net income	$ 57,000	$ 30,000
Statement of Retained Earnings		
Retained earnings, 1-1-X3	$150,000	$ 65,000
Net income	57,000	30,000
Dividends	(30,000)	(15,000)
Retained earnings, 12-31-X3	$177,000	$ 80,000
Balance Sheet		
Assets		
Cash	$140,000	$ 80,000
Accounts receivable	20,000	15,000
Inventory	90,000	70,000
Investment in Homer	110,000	
Building (net)	57,000	25,000
Total assets	$417,000	$190,000
Liabilities and Stockholders' Equity		
Accounts payable	$ 40,000	$ 10,000
Common stock	200,000	100,000
Retained earnings	177,000	80,000
Total liabilities and stockholders' equity	$417,000	$190,000

Additional information:
Homer reported net income of $50,000 in 19X2 and paid dividends of $10,000 during the same year.

REQUIRED
Prepare a consolidation worksheet for Michener and its subsidiary as of December 31, 19X3.

P3-21
Consolidation Worksheet (Trial Balance Format): Partially Owned Subsidiary, Valuation Differential Ramm Company purchased 80% of the common stock of Cavalier Company on January 1, 19X2, for $60,000 when Cavalier had common stock of $50,000 and retained earnings of $20,000. Any difference between the acquisition cost and the book value of Cavalier is identified as goodwill and amortized over ten years. Trial balances for Ramm and Cavalier as of December 31, 19X2, are as follows:

	Ramm Company	Cavalier Company
Debits		
Cash	$ 40,000	$ 15,000
Inventory	20,000	30,000
Investment in Cavalier	71,600	
Machinery (net)	50,000	55,000
Dividends	10,000	5,000
Cost of goods sold	45,000	20,000
Operating expenses	15,000	10,000
	$251,600	$135,000
Credits		
Current liabilities	$ 16,000	$ 6,000
Long-term liabilities	20,000	9,000
Common stock	75,000	50,000
Retained earnings	25,000	20,000
Sales	100,000	50,000
Income from subsidiary	15,600	
	$251,600	$135,000

REQUIRED

Prepare a consolidation worksheet as of December 31, 19X2, for Ramm Company and its subsidiary using the trial balance format.

P3-22   **Consolidation Worksheet (End of Second Year, Trial Balance Format): Partially Owned Sub-**

APPENDIX C   **sidiary, Valuation Differential**   Wallace, Inc., paid $131,500 for a 90% interest in Accent Company on January 1, 19X3, when Accent's common stock was $100,000 and its retained earnings $30,000. On the date of acquisition, the book values of the net assets of Accent were equal to their fair value except for machinery, which had a fair value of $5,000 more than book value and a remaining life of 15 years. All intangibles are amortized over 20 years. Trial balances for the two companies as of December 31, 19X4, appear here:

	Wallace, Inc.	Accent Company
Debits		
Cash	$ 60,000	$ 45,000
Accounts receivable	10,000	35,000
Investment in Accent	170,400	
Machinery (net)	120,000	110,000
Dividends	20,000	10,000
Cost of goods sold	100,000	40,000
Operating expenses	50,000	20,000
	$530,400	$260,000
Credits		
Accounts payable	$ 20,000	$ 5,000
Notes payable	29,700	10,000
Common stock	150,000	100,000
Retained earnings	100,000	50,000
Sales	200,000	95,000
Income from subsidiary	30,700	
	$530,400	$260,000

REQUIRED

Prepare a consolidation worksheet as of December 31, 19X4, for Wallace, Inc., and its subsidiary using the trial balance format.

P3-23   **Consolidation Worksheet (End of Second Year, Trial Balance Format): Partially Owned Sub-**

APPENDIX C   **sidiary, Valuation Differential**   Using the same information in Problem 3-11, complete the following requirement.

REQUIRED

Prepare a consolidation worksheet as of December 31, 19X2, for Martin Company and its subsidiary using the trial balance format.

ISSUES IN ACCOUNTING JUDGMENT

I3-1   **Disclosures for the Equity Method**   Visit your library and locate the annual report of a company that has one or more investments in stock that are accounted for by the equity method. Disregard joint ventures.

REQUIRED

a) Read paragraph 19 of Accounting Principles Board Opinion No. 18, "The Equity Method of Accounting for Investments in Common Stock," and make a list summarizing the disclosures under the equity method for long-term investments in common stock (disregarding joint ventures) required in notes to the financial statements. Leave space under each subparagraph on your list for the next requirement of this exercise.

b) Under each item on your list of disclosure requirements, quote the words and/or numbers from the footnotes in your chosen annual report that satisfy the requirement. Is any information disclosed that is not specifically required?

c) Write a paragraph that discusses the usefulness of the required disclosures to stockholders of the disclosing company and to other readers of the financial statements.

I3-2 **International Issues in Accounting for Goodwill** In the United States, purchased goodwill is recognized as an asset on the consolidated balance sheet and is subject to straight-line amortization over a maximum of 40 years. In contrast, Germany, Italy, The Netherlands, and the United Kingdom permit purchased goodwill to be charged to consolidated equity at acquisition; thus, it is not amortized over future years.

REQUIRED

a) Read Accounting Principles Board Opinion No. 17, ''Intangible Assets,'' and briefly describe the conceptual basis for the treatment of purchased goodwill in the United States.

b) What are the consequences of international differences in goodwill accounting for the United States and foreign companies competing in capital markets? What are the consequences for efforts to secure international uniformity in goodwill accounting?

I3-3 **Income Effects of Mid-Year Purchases** John C. Burton (1970, p. 47) notes the following problem with purchase accounting: ''It has been noted that net income growth can be made to appear very substantial as a result of purchasing a company even though internal operating growth is not taking place. When a company purchases another midway through a year, it includes the purchased earnings from the date of acquisition. If the acquired company is substantial, the combined net earnings in the year of acquisition will show an increase over the prior year due to its inclusion for part of the year. Then the earnings in the year following the acquisition will show considerable growth over the acquisition year due to the inclusion of the full year results of the acquired company compared to the partial year's results included in the former year.''

REQUIRED

a) Prepare a numerical example to illustrate Professor Burton's point.

b) Why is this effect of mid-year purchases a potential problem?

c) Do current financial accounting standards include any provisions that mitigate this problem?

Intercompany Merchandise Transfers

REVENUE RECOGNITION AND MERCHANDISE TRANSFERS 215

GROSS MARGIN ON INTERCOMPANY MERCHANDISE TRANSFERS 217

THE EQUITY METHOD FOR MERCHANDISE TRANSFERS 218

MERCHANDISE TRANSFERS (UPSTREAM) FROM SUBSIDIARY TO PARENT 218

MERCHANDISE TRANSFERS (DOWNSTREAM) FROM PARENT TO SUBSIDIARY 220

COMPREHENSIVE ILLUSTRATION OF EQUITY METHOD FOR MERCHANDISE TRANSFERS 222

CONSOLIDATION AND MERCHANDISE TRANSFERS 223

TOTAL VERSUS FRACTIONAL DEFERRAL FOR UPSTREAM TRANSFERS 223

CONSOLIDATION ADJUSTMENTS FOR UPSTREAM MERCHANDISE TRANSFERS 224

Elimination of Transfer Prices 226   Deferral of Gross Margin to Future Period 226   Recognition of Gross Margin Deferred from Prior Period 227

COMPREHENSIVE ILLUSTRATION OF CONSOLIDATION PROCEDURES FOR MERCHANDISE TRANSFERS 228

Analysis of Parent's Investment Account 228   Consolidation Worksheet Adjustments 229   First-Year Consolidation Worksheet and Composition of Minority Interest 233   Second-Year Consolidation Worksheet and Composition of Minority Interest 233   Minority Interest in Beginning Subsidiary Retained Earnings 235   Intercompany Gross Margin Deferral for Poolings 235

SUMMARY 235

APPENDIX: FRACTIONAL DEFERRAL METHOD OF CONSOLIDATION 236

Intercompany transactions are transactions between affiliated companies—transactions between a parent and its subsidiary or between two subsidiaries of the same parent.[1] Transactions between affiliates lack an arm's-length character when one transacting affiliate controls the actions of the other or when the actions of both transacting affiliates are controlled by a third affiliate. Such transactions are easier to execute than transactions between unaffiliated companies because there is little opportunity for the transacting parties to disagree over transaction terms. Indeed, the relative ease of transactions between

---

[1] Transfers between subsidiaries of the same parent are called *lateral transfers* and are considered in Chapter 8.

affiliated companies is an inducement to the establishment of parent-subsidiary relationships. However, the lack of an arm's-length character denies recognition in consolidated financial statements for such transactions.

Intercompany transactions in previous chapters were restricted to income distributions—dividends paid to the parent and recognition of subsidiary income by the parent—and simple examples of short-term loans. However, intercompany transactions also include long-term borrowings and transfers of merchandise, partially completed products, depreciable assets, and land. The present chapter considers accounting procedures that are applicable to intercompany transactions involving merchandise. The word *merchandise* is used throughout this chapter to mean the product held in inventories of the parent or its subsidiary and to include intermediate or partially completed products as well as finished merchandise. Intercompany merchandise transfers refer to transfers between affiliated companies, both of which inventory the transferred merchandise. This chapter demonstrates the effect of such transfers on the equity method of accounting for the investment in the subsidiary and on consolidation procedures. The next chapter considers procedures that are applicable to transfers of land and depreciable assets.

Merchandise may move between a parent and its subsidiary in two directions. Transfers of merchandise from a parent to its subsidiary are called *downstream transfers*; transfers of merchandise from a subsidiary to its parent are called *upstream transfers*.[2]

REVENUE RECOGNITION AND MERCHANDISE TRANSFERS

It is customary to recognize revenue on the basis of sales. When a sales transaction occurs (usually when merchandise is transferred to a customer), the selling price is taken into revenue and the related merchandise costs are taken into cost of goods sold. The propriety of the sales transaction as a basis for revenue recognition requires, among other things, that the transaction be arm's-length; that is, the transaction must be consummated with an unrelated party. But the transactions between parent and subsidiary companies cannot be arm's-length because the parent controls the subsidiary. Consequently, sale transactions between parent and subsidiary companies cannot serve as a basis for the recognition of revenue. Recognition of revenue on such transactions requires a subsequent sale to an unaffiliated party, as the following issues section illustrates.

ISSUES

Non-Arm's-Length Transactions and Revenue Recognition

Sherritt Inc., of Harrisburg, Pennsylvania, is a 100%-owned subsidiary of Field Corporation, which is located in Wilmington, Delaware. Sherritt produces steel castings required for heavy industrial equipment manufactured by Field. Since state taxes on corporate income are significantly lower in Delaware than in Pennsylvania, Field transfers castings at the lowest possible price from its Pennsylvania subsidiary. Pennsylvania tax laws and regulations permit transfers at any price in excess of the full cost of transferred merchandise. Consequently, castings are transferred from Sherritt at a price equal to cost plus a small profit margin.

---

[2] *Accounting Interpretation of APB Opinion No. 18, No. 1*, issued in November of 1971, uses *upstream and downstream* in this way. Although the designation of transfers as upstream and downstream is especially apt when parent and subsidiary are vertically integrated and the subsidiary represents a later stage of production than the parent, the designations are also consistent with the flow of control in the parent-subsidiary relationship.

1. *How does this transfer price differ from an arm's-length transaction?*

In an arm's-length transaction, the seller is not compelled to sell and the buyer is not compelled to buy. The seller is free to choose another buyer who offers a higher price, and the buyer is free to choose another seller who offers a lower price. Such freedom of choice means that we can interpret the related selling price as an indicator of the traded asset's market value. More precisely, the price is no more than the seller was willing to accept and no more than the buyer was willing to pay. The transfer price in the Field-Sherritt illustration differs from an arm's-length transaction because one party is under the control of the other. Sherritt is the 100%-owned subsidiary of Field. Consequently, Sherritt is not free to choose to whom it will sell its castings and it is not free to seek the highest possible price for those castings. Sherritt's sales and prices are under the control of its parent, Field, and Field sets the transfer price to minimize the amount of state taxes paid by the consolidated entity. Consequently, the transfer price is not a reliable indicator of the market value of the transferred castings. Further, Field could repudiate the transaction and order the castings returned to its inventory.

2. *What is the impact of these non-arm's-length transactions on the separate financial statements of the two corporations?*

The transfer price understates the market value of the castings. Consequently, the net income of Sherritt is understated (because its revenue is understated) and the net income of Field is overstated (because its cost of goods sold is understated). In other words, net income that might have been reported by Sherritt is reported by Field, which means that it is taxed at Delaware's lower rates.

3. *What is the impact of these non-arm's-length transactions on the consolidated financial statements?*

From the viewpoint of the consolidated entity, the transfer of castings is merely a movement of a material input from one location within the accounting entity to another. Accordingly, it should not affect consolidated net income (apart from a possible effect on tax expense). Income related to a casting should not be recognized until the equipment, of which the casting is a component, is sold to a party outside the consolidated entity in an arm's-length transaction.

In other words, revenue and gross margin on both downstream and upstream transfers should be recognized when the transferred merchandise is sold to parties outside the parent-subsidiary affiliation, even though the transaction is recorded on the date of transfer in the sales and cost of goods sold accounts of the affiliated seller and buyer. Under this line of reasoning, a parent's gross margin on merchandise transferred (downstream) to a subsidiary should be excluded from both the *parent's separate net income* and *consolidated net income* until the subsidiary sells the merchandise to an unaffiliated party. If the merchandise is sold to an unaffiliated party in the year following the year of the intercompany transfer, then the related gross margin must be deferred to the year of the sale. Similarly, the subsidiary's gross margin on merchandise transferred (upstream) to the parent should be excluded from both the *parent's share of subsidiary net income* and *consolidated net income* until the parent sells the merchandise to an unaffiliated party. If the merchandise is sold to an unaffiliated party in the year following the year of the intercompany sale, then the related gross margin must be deferred to the year of the unaffiliated sale.[3]

Gross Margin on Intercompany Merchandise Transfers

Gross margin is the excess of the transfer price over the cost of the related goods to the seller. Accordingly, the gross margin associated with any transfer price can be calculated by subtracting the cost from the related transfer price. For example, if the inventory of a subsidiary contains merchandise transferred from a parent at a transfer price of $10,000 and the cost of the merchandise to the parent was $8,000, then the related gross margin is $2,000 ($10,000 − $8,000). Usually, however, the transfer price is known but the related cost is unknown. Consequently, the gross margin must be calculated using information about the general relationship between the gross margin and either cost or transfer prices. Let us illustrate two approaches to the calculation of gross margin when the cost is unknown by reference to merchandise with a transfer price of $10,000 transferred from a parent to its subsidiary.

First, suppose that the parent sells to all customers at 25% above cost (i.e., the parent's *markup percentage on cost* is 25%). Then the parent's cost must be $8,000 ($10,000 ÷ 1.25), and the related gross margin must be $2,000 [$10,000 − ($10,000 ÷ 1.25)]. In general, gross margin is calculated using the markup percentage on cost by the following formula:

$$\begin{bmatrix} \text{Gross} \\ \text{margin} \end{bmatrix} = \begin{bmatrix} \text{Transfer} \\ \text{price} \end{bmatrix} - \begin{bmatrix} \dfrac{\text{Transfer price}}{1 + \text{markup percentage on cost}} \end{bmatrix}$$

An alternative and equivalent calculation depends on the relationship between gross margin and transfer prices rather than on the relationship between gross margin and cost. Suppose that the parent's gross margin in our example is known to average 20% of the transfer prices (i.e., the parent's *gross margin rate on sales* is 20%). Then the parent's gross margin ($2,000) is simply the product of the transfer price and the gross margin rate ($2,000 = $10,000 × .20). In general, gross margin is calculated using the gross margin rate on transfer prices by the following formula:

$$\begin{bmatrix} \text{Gross} \\ \text{margin} \end{bmatrix} = \begin{bmatrix} \text{Transfer} \\ \text{price} \end{bmatrix} \times [\text{Gross margin rate on transfer price}]$$

Of course, the markup percentage on cost can be converted into the corresponding gross margin rate on sales by dividing the markup percentage by 1 plus the markup percentage. In our example, the gross margin rate on sales of 20% can be obtained by dividing the markup percentage of 25% by 125% (.20 = .25 ÷ 1.25).

---

[3] The deferral of gross margin on transfers of merchandise between the parent and subsidiary may be complicated by the effect of income taxes and related interperiod tax deferrals. Parents and subsidiaries may file either separate or consolidated tax returns. If a selling affiliate files a separate return, gross margin is taxed in the period of the intercompany transfer but included in parent-company and consolidated net incomes in a later period when the merchandise is sold to outsiders. This temporary difference occasions the deferral of a portion of the subsidiary's taxes from the period of the transfer to the period of the outside sale. On the other hand, if parent and subsidiary file a consolidated return, the gross margin related to intercompany transfers will be taxed in the period in which the merchandise is sold to outsiders. Hence, no temporary difference arises and no interperiod tax deferral is appropriate. Additional discussion of these income tax issues is presented in Chapter 8. Throughout this book we assume that parent and subsidiaries file consolidated tax returns unless the contrary is specifically indicated.

The deferral of gross margin[4] on intercompany transfers affects both the application of the equity method by the parent and the preparation of consolidated financial statements. Let us begin by considering the impact of upstream and downstream transfers on the equity method of accounting for investments in subsidiaries and then consider the impact of such transfers on consolidation procedures.

THE EQUITY METHOD FOR MERCHANDISE TRANSFERS

The typical accounting system records all sales—including sales to affiliated companies—in exactly the same way.[5] Consequently, a parent's gross margin (before consolidation adjustments) incorrectly includes the gross margin on all transfers to subsidiaries; therefore, an adjusting entry is required at year-end to defer the gross margin on downstream transfers that remain in subsidiary inventories and to recognize the income deferred at the end of the preceding year. In addition, a subsidiary's net income includes gross margin on all transfers to its parent company. Although a subsidiary does not adjust its records for deferred gross margin on upstream transfers, the parent must adjust its share of subsidiary net income for such amounts. The paragraphs that follow demonstrate the parent's adjustments under the equity method for deferred gross margin arising in both upstream and downstream transfers.

Merchandise Transfers (Upstream) from Subsidiary to Parent

Recall that an upstream transfer of merchandise is a sale by a subsidiary to its parent. To illustrate, consider an upstream transfer from Michigan Corporation, a 90%-owned subsidiary, to its parent, Ohio Corporation. During 19X1 Michigan transfers merchandise to Ohio in exchange for $175,000. The cost to Michigan of the upstream transfer was $100,000. Hence, Michigan (the subsidiary) recognizes a gross margin of $75,000 on the transaction. The two corporations make the following entries to record the upstream transfer:[6]

Subsidiary's (Michigan's) journal entries to record sale to parent (Ohio):

Accounts receivable	175,000	
Sales		175,000
Cost of goods sold	100,000	
Inventory		100,000

Parent's (Ohio's) journal entry to record purchase from subsidiary (Michigan):

Inventory	175,000	
Accounts payable		175,000

At the end of 19X1, the parent's inventory includes 20% of the merchandise transferred from the subsidiary, the remainder having been sold to unaffiliated parties.

---

[4] Gross margin deferrals for intercompany transfers in inventory should be reduced by the amount of any related lower-of-cost-or-market write-downs of inventory recorded by the buying affiliate. Such write-downs imply that the buying affiliate expects to realize a lesser gross margin from the sale of such goods and, further, that the difference between the transfer price and the cost to the selling affiliate overstates gross margin by the amount of the write-down.

[5] Some accounting systems may record transactions with affiliated parties in separate accounts; this facilitates the identification of such transactions. Even if transactions with affiliated corporations are recorded in separate accounts, the adjustments described in this paragraph are still necessary.

[6] Here and throughout this chapter, we shall assume that all companies use a perpetual inventory system.

The equity method requires that the parent company adjust its income from subsidiary for the deferred gross margin on upstream transfers. The subsidiary, Michigan Corporation, reports a 19X1 net income of $220,000, including the intercompany gross margin of $75,000, 20% of which is not yet confirmed by sales to unaffiliated parties. Exhibit 4-1 shows the calculation of the income from the subsidiary to be reported by the parent; assume that the parent's valuation differential is completely amortized and, therefore, does not affect the calculation. Observe that the subsidiary's reported net income ($220,000) is reduced by the amount of deferred subsidiary gross margin ($15,000 = .20 × $75,000) *before* application of the parent's ownership percentage.

The foregoing calculation by the parent leads to the following entry on the records of the parent corporation:

Parent's entry to record income from subsidiary:

Investment in Michigan 184,500
        Income from subsidiary   184,500

The $184,500 credit to income is the parent's share of the subsidiary net income adjusted for deferred gross margin on upstream transfers.[7]

The year-end deferral of subsidiary gross margin transfers subsidiary income from the current year into the next year. Hence, the amount of the deferral is *subtracted* from the subsidiary net income for the current year in the calculation of income from subsidi-

---

[7] As noted earlier, a parent's year-end inventory includes any unsold goods transferred from its subsidiary. Moreover, such goods are carried on the parent's separate records at their transfer price (the purchase price paid to the subsidiary), which includes the gross margin of the subsidiary that must be deferred. One might argue that this gross margin should be removed from the inventory and recorded in a separate account to indicate that it represents unconfirmed valuation based on transfers from an affiliated corporation. However, in the interests of maintaining a simple presentation, the remainder of the text assumes that such adjustments are not made on parent company records.

EXHIBIT 4-1	PARENT'S CALCULATION OF INCOME FROM SUBSIDIARY WITH ADJUSTMENTS FOR DEFERRED GROSS MARGIN ON UPSTREAM TRANSFERS

Ohio Corporation

CALCULATION OF INCOME FROM MICHIGAN CORPORATION
FOR THE YEAR ENDED DECEMBER 31, 19X1

Subsidiary net income	$220,000
Add: Deferred gross margin on *upstream* transfers at 1-1-X1	–0–
Less: Deferred gross margin on *upstream* transfers at 12-31-X1 ($75,000 × .20)	(15,000)
Adjusted subsidiary net income	$205,000
Parent's ownership percentage	×.90
Income from subsidiary	$184,500

ary. The beginning-of-the-year deferral of subsidiary gross margin (the year-end deferral of the previous year) transfers subsidiary income from the previous year into the current year. Hence, the amount of the deferral is *added* to the subsidiary net income in the calculation of income from subsidiary. For example, the 19X2 calculation of Ohio's income from its subsidiary, Michigan, will *add* $15,000 to the 19X2 subsidiary net income, whereas the 19X1 calculation subtracted it. This procedure is appropriate if all intercompany transfers that are unsold at the end of one year are sold during the next year. The procedure is appropriate even if some of last year's transfers are not sold in the current year, provided that the related gross margin is included in the deferral at both the beginning and the end of the year. This deferral procedure is illustrated later in this chapter.

Merchandise Transfers (Downstream) from Parent to Subsidiary

A downstream transfer of merchandise is a sale by a parent to its subsidiary. To illustrate, consider a downstream transfer from McKinsey Corporation to its 80%-owned subsidiary, Sinclair Corporation. During 19X1 McKinsey transferred merchandise to Sinclair in exchange for $22,000. The cost to McKinsey of the downstream transfer is $12,000. Hence, McKinsey recognizes a gross margin of $10,000 on the transaction. At December 31, 19X1, the subsidiary's inventory includes 30% of the merchandise transfers from its parent, the remainder having been sold to unaffiliated parties. The subsidiary reports a 19X1 net income of $14,000, which is the starting point for the parent's calculation of income from its subsidiary shown in Exhibit 4-2; assume that the parent's valuation differential is completely amortized and, therefore, does not affect the calculation. Observe that the calculation format begins with adjustments to the subsidiary net income for *upstream* transfers, although no such adjustments are appropriate in this illustration. The calculation ends with the adjustment for *downstream* transfers, which follow application of the parent's ownership percentage.

EXHIBIT 4-2	PARENT'S CALCULATION OF INCOME FROM SUBSIDIARY WITH ADJUSTMENTS FOR DEFERRED GROSS MARGIN ON DOWNSTREAM TRANSFER

McKinsey Corporation

CALCULATION OF INCOME FROM SINCLAIR CORPORATION
FOR THE YEAR ENDED DECEMBER 31, 19X1

Subsidiary net income	$14,000
Add: Deferred gross margin on *upstream* transfers at 1-1-X1	–0–
Less: Deferred gross margin on *upstream* transfers at 12-31-X1	(–0–)
Adjusted subsidiary net income	$14,000
Parent's ownership percentage	×.80
Parent's share of subsidiary net income adjusted for upstream transfers	$11,200
Add: Deferred gross margin on *downstream* transfers at 1-1-X1	–0–
Less: Deferred gross margin on *downstream* transfers at 12-31-X1	(3,000)
Income from subsidiary	$ 8,200

The equity method requires that the parent defer from *its* net income any gross margin on downstream transfers that are not yet confirmed by sales to unaffiliated parties. Rather than deferring such amounts directly by reducing the parent's revenue and cost of goods sold, the amounts are deferred indirectly by reducing the parent's income from its subsidiary. In our illustration, the parent (McKinsey) must defer $3,000 from its 19X1 net income, representing 30% of the gross margin on the downstream transfers during 19X1 [$3,000 = .30 × ($22,000 − $12,000)]. The $3,000 deferred gross margin is the difference between $6,600 (.30 × $22,000) included in the parent's sale and $3,600 (.30 × $12,000) included in the parent's cost of goods sold. Exhibit 4-2 illustrates the indirect procedure whereby the parent's gross margin on downstream transfers in inventory ($3,000) is deferred by adjusting income from its subsidiary. This permits adjustments for both downstream and upstream deferrals to be handled as adjustments to the parent's calculation of income from subsidiary.

Based on the calculation in Exhibit 4-2, the parent's entry to record income from the subsidiary takes the following form:

Parent's entry to record income from subsidiary:

Investment in Sinclair	8,200	
Income from subsidiary		8,200

The foregoing entry includes a $3,000 *debit* to the income account and an equal *credit* to the investment account, which operate to reduce the parent's income in 19X1 and to establish a deferred margin credit as part of the investment account.[8] As illustrated in the following section, the deferral will be reversed and recognition of the related gross margin will be triggered in 19X2 by the addition of $3,000 to the 19X2 subsidiary income recorded by the parent.

It is important to note that gross margin deferrals associated with *upstream* transfers represent deferrals of subsidiary gross margin. Therefore, the related adjustments are made *before* application of the parent's ownership percentage (as shown in Exhibit 4-1). On the other hand, gross margin deferrals associated with *downstream* transfers represent

---

[8] This method of adjusting for deferrals of downstream gross margin is indirect in that the income from the *subsidiary* is adjusted for a deferral of the *parent's* gross margin. The direct way to defer the $3,000 gross margin would be to reduce sales by $6,600 and cost of goods sold by $3,600, crediting the investment account for the $3,000 difference, as shown in the following entry:

Sales	6,600	
Investment in Sinclair	8,200	
Cost of goods sold		3,600
Income from subsidiary		11,200

Following this direct procedure, income from the subsidiary ($11,200) is calculated without adjustment for downstream deferrals [$11,200 = ($14,000 × .80)]. The adjustment to the investment account ($8,200) is the income from subsidiary adjusted for the downstream deferral ($8,200 = $11,200 − $3,000). In the next year, when the transferred merchandise is sold to unaffiliated parties, the parent must credit sales for $6,600, debit the cost of goods sold for $3,600, and debit the investment account for $3,000, thereby removing the deferred credit. Although this direct adjustment procedure is appropriate for non-arm's-length transfers between parent and subsidiary, it results in the same parent-company and consolidated net incomes as the indirect method. In the interests of maintaining a simple presentation, we shall follow the indirect method shown in Exhibit 4-2 throughout this book.

deferrals of the parent's gross margin. Thus, the related adjustments are made *after* application of the parent's ownership percentage (as shown in Exhibit 4-2).[9]

Comprehensive Illustration of Equity Method for Merchandise Transfers

Consider a parent and subsidiary that engage in both upstream and downstream merchandise transfers. The parent, York Corporation, acquired 90% of the outstanding stock of Rippon, Inc., the subsidiary on January 1, 19X1, by paying $154,000 in cash. The valuation differential is amortized at a rate of $750 per year.

The parent's calculation of income from the subsidiary for 19X1 and 19X2 is presented in Exhibit 4-3. The subsidiary reported a net income of $12,000 for 19X1 and $15,000 for 19X2. Upstream and downstream transfers of merchandise and the related amounts of gross margin subject to deferral during the years 19X1 and 19X2 are given in the following schedule:

Computation of Deferred Gross Margin on 19X1 and 19X2 Transfers

	19X1		19X2	
	Upstream	Downstream	Upstream	Downstream
Transfer price	$4,000	$22,000	$5,625	$21,000
Cost to seller	2,400	16,500	3,375	15,750
Gross margin	$1,600	$ 5,500	$2,250	$ 5,250
Percentage in year-end inventory of purchaser	×.20	×.20	×.20	×.20
Deferred gross margin	$ 320	$ 1,100	$ 450	$ 1,050

Both the upstream and downstream end-of-19X1 deferrals are *subtracted* in the parent's calculation of 19X1 income from the subsidiary, as shown in Exhibit 4-3. Observe that both these deferrals are *added* in the parent's calculation of 19X2 income from the subsidiary, also as shown in Exhibit 4-3. Similarly, both the upstream and downstream end-of-19X2 deferrals are subtracted in the parent's calculation of income from the subsidiary as shown in Exhibit 4-3. These end-of-year deferrals, in turn, are added in the parent's calculation of 19X3 income from subsidiary, a calculation that is not shown.

---

[9] This treatment of downstream gross margin in the calculation of income from subsidiary is appropriate whenever the downstream transaction is not arm's-length. Thus, all downstream transfers from parent to subsidiary must use this calculation. However, when the investor owns less than a controlling interest in the investee, financial accounting standards permit deferral of only the fraction of downstream gross margin associated with the investee's equity interest (see *AICPA Interpretations of APB Opinion No. 18*, Interpretation No. 1); thus, the downstream transfer is viewed as arm's-length to the extent that the transacting parties are not affiliated. Although this procedure is acceptable in practice, it is difficult to conceive of a partially arm's-length transaction. The arm's-length characteristic is not a matter of degree; a transaction is either arm's-length or not arm's-length. In keeping with this view, and to simplify our presentation, we defer the entire gross margin on all downstream transfers throughout this book unless an exception is specifically noted. (See the appendix at the end of this chapter for additional discussion of this issue; also see the discussion of joint ventures in Chapter 9.)

EXHIBIT 4-3	PARENT'S CALCULATION OF INCOME FROM SUBSIDIARY WITH ADJUSTMENTS FOR DEFERRED GROSS MARGIN

York Corporation

CALCULATION OF INCOME FROM RIPPON, INC.
FOR THE YEARS ENDED DECEMBER 31, 19X1, AND DECEMBER 31, 19X2

	19X1	19X2
Subsidiary net income	$12,000	$15,000
Add: Deferred gross margin on *upstream* transfers at January 1	–0–	320
Less: Deferred gross margin on *upstream* transfers at December 31	(320)	(450)
Adjusted subsidiary net income	$11,680	$14,870
Parent's ownership percentage	×.90	×.90
Parent's share of subsidiary net income adjusted for upstream transfers	$10,512	$13,383
Add: Deferred gross margin on *downstream* transfers at January 1	–0–	1,100
Less: Deferred gross margin on *downstream* transfers at December 31	(1,100)	(1,050)
Parent's share of subsidiary net income (adjusted for both upstream and downstream transfers)	$ 9,412	$13,433
Amortization of valuation differential	(750)	(750)
Income from subsidiary	$ 8,662	$12,683

CONSOLIDATION AND MERCHANDISE TRANSFERS

Intercompany gross margin is deferred under the equity method to achieve a proper matching with sales activity. Similar deferrals of gross margin are made in the preparation of consolidated financial statements. The paragraphs that follow describe these consolidation adjustments and the related worksheet procedures. We begin with a discussion of two deferral methods[10] and then turn to the consolidation adjustments and a comprehensive illustration.

Total versus Fractional Deferral for Upstream Transfers

As explained earlier, the intercompany gross margin associated with unsold intercompany transfers of merchandise is deferred into the period in which the merchandise is sold to unaffiliated parties. In the case of upstream transfers, the deferred gross margin represents the gross margin of the subsidiary. If the subsidiary is 100% owned by the parent, it is clearly appropriate to defer 100% of the subsidiary's gross margin on transfers in inventory. But if the subsidiary is partially owned, some accountants have argued that only the majority interest's share of the gross margin should be deferred; these accountants view the intercompany transaction as arm's-length to the extent of the minority interest in the subsidiary—a view that derives some support from the proprietary theory of financial reporting. Consider a 90%-owned subsidiary whose current net income includes a gross

---

[10] These deferral methods are frequently referred to as *elimination* methods. Since gross margin is not really eliminated by the adjustments considered here—but is merely deferred from one period to a later period—we prefer *deferral methods* and use these words throughout this book.

margin of $320 that is associated with transferred merchandise in the parent's year-end inventory. Following the *total deferral method*, $320 is deferred for purposes of consolidation. Following the *fractional deferral method*, only $288 (.90 × $320) is deferred for purposes of consolidation; the remaining $32 (.10 × $320) is viewed as arising from an arm's-length transaction.

Financial accounting standards are usually interpreted to require the total deferral method.[11] Accordingly, the total deferral method is used throughout this book unless the fractional method is specifically indicated. The following issues section discusses the consequences of using fractional and total deferral methods.

ISSUES

Consequences of Deferral Methods

Pfeifer Outlet Stores sells a number of products manufactured by its newly acquired (60%-owned) subsidiary, Sanderson Manufacturing. Pfeifer's controller has asked Jane Taylor, a new member of the controller's staff, to prepare a report on the differing consequences of using total and fractional deferral methods for upstream transfers. After reviewing her advanced accounting textbook and preparing a numerical demonstration using Pfeifer's data for the current year, Jane reports that consolidated net income will be the same whether the total deferral method or the fractional deferral method is used. She finds that if the fractional deferral method is used, consolidated cost of goods includes a provision for the minority interest's share of the net deferred gross margin adjustment that it does not include if the total deferral method is used; however, this difference is exactly offset by an equal difference in the amount of minority interest in subsidiary net income. (Under the total elimination method, minority interest in subsidiary net income includes adjustments for deferred upstream gross margin; as explained in the appendix to this chapter, no such adjustments are included if the fractional deferral method is used.) Although consolidated net income is unaffected, Jane reports that consolidated inventory and minority interest will be reported at higher amounts under the fractional deferral method to the extent of the minority interest in upstream gross margins that are deferred at year-end. She also notes that downstream transfers produce exactly the same results under both methods.

The sections that follow develop your understanding of the basis for the conclusions summarized in the foregoing issues section.

Consolidation Adjustments for Upstream Merchandise Transfers

Let us use an example to illustrate the impact of intercompany merchandise transfers on the consolidation adjustments. Five years ago, Campbell Corporation acquired 90% of Stanley Corporation at book value. During 19X5 the subsidiary (Stanley) transferred merchandise to its parent (Campbell) in exchange for $2,000 cash. At December 31, 19X5, the parent's inventory contains $500 representing the unsold remainder of these transfers. The parent's beginning inventory included $300 representing merchandise

---

[11] *Accounting Research Bulletin No. 51*, (par. 14) indicates a preference for total deferral, and *AICPA Interpretations of APB Opinion No. 18*, Interpretation No. 1, supports that preference. However, *ARB No. 51* also suggests that minority interest may or may not adjust for upstream gross margin deferrals, which may be interpreted to sanction fractional elimination after all. For additional discussion of this point, see King and Lembke (1976).

transferred from the subsidiary during prior years, all of which was sold during 19X5. Assume that a gross margin rate on sales of 45% is applicable to all transfers. The first two columns in Exhibit 4-4 show the separate income statements for Campbell and Stanley. Following the equity method, Campbell records 19X5 income from its subsidiary calculated as follows:

Parent's Calculation of Income from Subsidiary

Subsidiary net income	$1,550
Add: Deferred gross margin on *upstream* transfers at 1-1-X5 ($300 × .45)	135
Less: Deferred gross margin on *upstream* transfers at 12-31-X5 ($500 × .45)	(225)
Adjusted subsidiary net income	$1,460
Parent's ownership percentage	×.90
Income from subsidiary	$1,314

Exhibit 4-4 also shows the consolidated income statement and the effect of the consolidation worksheet adjustments used to create that statement. Four worksheet adjustments

---

EXHIBIT 4-4	SEPARATE COMPANY AND CONSOLIDATED INCOME STATEMENTS

	Campbell Corporation (Parent)		Stanley Corporation (Subsidiary)		Consolidation Adjustment Effect			Consolidated Income Statement
Sales	$10,000	+	$7,000	−	(2)	$2,000	=	$15,000
Cost of Goods Sold								
Beginning inventory	$ 1,800	+	$ 600	−	(4)	135	=	$ 2,265
Add: Purchases	7,000	+	3,600	−	(2)	2,000	=	8,600
Goods available for sale	$ 8,800		$4,200					$10,865
Less: Ending inventory	2,000	+	350	−	(3)	225	=	2,125
Cost of goods sold[1]	$ 6,800		$3,850					$ 8,740
Gross margin	$ 3,200		$3,150					$ 6,260
Other expenses	1,200	+	1,600				=	2,800
Operating income	$ 2,000		$1,550					$ 3,460
Add: Income from subsidiary	1,314	+	–0–	−	(1)	1,314	=	—
Less: Minority interest[2]	—		—					146
Net income	$ 3,314		$1,550					$ 3,314

[1] Hereafter, we shall assume that all separate income statements present a single cost of goods sold figure (as is consistent with a perpetual inventory system) rather than a detailed calculation of cost of goods sold. Accordingly, the consolidation adjustments used to defer intercompany gross margin will be made to cost of goods sold rather than to beginning inventory, purchases, and ending inventory.

[2] Notice that the minority interest is 10% of subsidiary net income *after adjustment for deferral of upstream gross margin* [$146 = .10 × ($1,550 + $135 − $225)].

affect the consolidated income statement. The first, which is identified by the number (1), is the familiar adjustment to reverse the parent's recording of the subsidiary income by debiting the income from subsidiary account for $1,460 and by crediting the investment in Stanley account. The remaining are new adjustments associated with intercompany merchandise transfers. Each is discussed in the paragraphs that follow.

Elimination of Transfer Prices

When merchandise is transferred between the parent and its subsidiary, the transfer price is recorded as a sale by the selling affiliate and as a purchase by the buying affiliate. However, from the viewpoint of the consolidated entity, no sale or purchase has occurred. Merchandise has merely been transferred from one location to another within the same consolidated entity. Accordingly, the recorded effects of the sale and purchase must be removed from the consolidated statements. In the case of the upstream transfer from Stanley to Campbell, $2,000 must be removed from the subsidiary's sales and $2,000 must be removed from the parent's cost of goods sold. This removal is done by adjustment (2) in Exhibit 4-4 and has the following form:

(2)   *Worksheet adjustment to eliminate transfer prices from sales and cost of goods sold for current year:*

Sales 2,000
     Cost of goods sold[12]   2,000

Notice that the same adjustment would be appropriate in the case of a *downstream* transfer from the parent to the subsidiary. In that case, however, the transfer price would be removed from the parent's sales and from the subsidiary's cost of goods sold. Since the adjustment eliminates the same amount from sales and cost of goods sold, consolidated gross margin (and consolidated income) is unaltered by the adjustment. Accordingly, two additional adjustments are needed to accomplish the deferral of gross margin—one related to the ending inventory and the other related to the beginning inventory.

Deferral of Gross Margin to Future Period

Recall that Campbell's ending inventory includes $500 representing goods transferred from its subsidiary that have not yet been sold to unaffiliated parties. Yet the subsidiary has recognized a gross margin of $225 ($500 × .45) on these inventoried goods. From the viewpoint of the consolidated entity, this amount of gross margin should be deferred to the future period in which the related goods are sold to unaffiliated parties. Further, the related goods should be included in consolidated inventory at their cost ($275 = $500 − $225) rather than at their transfer price ($500). This deferral of gross margin and adjustment of the inventory are accomplished by the following worksheet adjustment:

---

[12] If the income statements presented by the parent and subsidiary report cost of goods sold with supporting detail relating to inventories and purchases, then this worksheet adjustment must credit purchases instead of cost of goods sold.

(3)   *Worksheet adjustment to defer gross margin at the end of current year:*

Cost of goods sold[13] 225

   Inventory   225

The $225 increase in cost of goods sold reduces the consolidated gross margin and thereby postpones recognition by the consolidated entity of the subsidiary gross margin associated with the parent's ending inventory. The decrease in the parent's inventory provides for the inclusion of the transferred goods in consolidated inventory at their cost rather than at their transfer price.

   The same adjustment would be appropriate in the case of unsold *downstream* transfers in a subsidiary's ending inventory. In that case, however, the increase in cost of goods sold would defer gross margin recognized by the parent and the decrease in inventory would be related to inventory held by the subsidiary.

Recognition of Gross Margin Deferred from Prior Period

Just as the intercompany gross margin in the ending inventory must be deferred from the current period to be recognized in a future period, so intercompany gross margin in the beginning inventory must be deferred from a prior period to be recognized in the current period. Returning to the upstream transfer from Stanley to Campbell, subsidiary gross margin in the amount of $135 ($300 × .45) is associated with the parent's beginning inventory. This amount was recognized by the subsidiary as part of last year's gross margin. For purposes of consolidation, however, this amount should be recognized as part of the current year's gross margin. Accordingly, the following worksheet adjustment is made to recognize the deferral of the subsidiary gross margin from last year:

(4)   *Worksheet adjustment to recognize upstream gross margin deferred from prior year:*

Retained earnings of subsidiary 135

   Cost of goods sold[14]   135

The $135 decrease in the beginning balance of subsidiary retained earnings removes from the retained earnings balance the gross margin recognized by the subsidiary in the previous year. The decrease in the cost of goods sold increases the consolidated gross margin and thereby provides for recognition by the consolidated entity of the subsidiary's gross margin associated with the parent's beginning inventory.

---

[13] If the income statements presented by the parent and subsidiary report cost of goods sold with supporting detail relating to inventories and purchases, then this worksheet adjustment must debit the ending inventory account that appears on the income statement instead of cost of goods sold. The debit to the ending inventory account, like the debit to cost of goods sold, increases cost of goods sold and thereby postpones recognition of gross margin.

[14] If the income statements presented by the parent and subsidiary report cost of goods sold with supporting detail relating to inventories and purchases, then this worksheet adjustment must credit the beginning inventory that appears on the income statement instead of cost of goods sold. The credit to the beginning inventory account, like the credit to cost of goods sold, reduces cost of goods sold and thereby recognizes the gross margin deferred from the last period.

A somewhat different adjustment is required to recognize gross margin deferred from prior periods into the current period when the related transfers are downstream rather than upstream. The worksheet adjustment for unsold *downstream* transfers in a subsidiary's beginning inventory takes the following form:

Worksheet adjustment to recognize downstream gross margin deferred from prior year:

Investment in subsidiary XXX
    Cost of goods sold XXX

The adjustment debits the parent's investment in subsidiary account rather than the subsidiary's retained earnings account, as in the upstream case. Recall that the parent, following the equity method, reduces its income from its subsidiary (and its investment account) by the amount of deferred gross margin on downstream transfers in the subsidiary's ending inventory. Hence, the investment account includes a credit (see analysis of York-Rippon investment account in Exhibit 4-5 and note the $1,100 credit included in the balance at December 31, 19X1) that represents deferred gross margin on downstream transfers that remain unsold at the end of the prior year (and the beginning of the current year). This credit to the investment account is reversed by the downstream adjustment previously shown.

Comprehensive Illustration of Consolidation Procedures for Merchandise Transfers

As the basis for a comprehensive illustration of consolidation procedures for merchandise transfers, let us use the information presented earlier in this chapter for York Corporation and its 90%-owned subsidiary Rippon, Inc. Exhibit 4-3 on page 223 shows the parent's calculation of income from the subsidiary in each of the two years covered by the illustration. The separate financial statements for the parent (York) and subsidiary (Rippon) are entered in the consolidation worksheets prepared at the end of each year, 19X1 and 19X2, as shown in Exhibits 4-7 (on page 232) and 4-9 (on page 234). York Corporation acquired its 90%-owned subsidiary on January 1, 19X1, for $154,000 cash when the book value of Rippon's stockholders' equity was $160,000 (common stock of $100,000 and retained earnings of $60,000). Analysis of the $10,000 valuation differential [$154,000 − (.90)($100,000 + $60,000)] on the acquisition date reveals goodwill of $7,500 and a revaluation increment associated with equipment of $2,500. Goodwill is amortized on a straight-line basis over 30 years ($250 per year), and the revaluation increment is amortized on a straight-line basis over five years ($500 per year).

Analysis of Parent's Investment Account

The analysis of the parent's investment account is presented in Exhibit 4-5, which is prepared using the information about York and Rippon given in Exhibit 4-3 and the additional information given earlier. Observe that the analysis incorporates an *additional column* to reflect adjustments to the parent's net income that are instead incorporated in the parent's income from its subsidiary. Specifically, the *adjustments to parent's net income* column in Exhibit 4-5 shows the annual adjustment for the deferral of gross margin on downstream transfers. In 19X1, $1,100 is deferred to 19X2; in 19X2, $1,050 is deferred to 19X3 and the $1,100 deferral from 19X1 is recognized, making a net debit to

EXHIBIT 4-5	ANALYSIS OF PARENT'S INVESTMENT ACCOUNT

York Corporation

ANALYSIS OF INVESTMENT IN RIPPON, INC.
FOR THE YEARS ENDED DECEMBER 31, 19X1, AND DECEMBER 31, 19X2

		Book Value of Parent's Equity in Subsidiary		Unamortized Valuation Differential		
	Total Investment	Acquired*	Earned	Goodwill	Revaluation Increment	Adjustments to Parent's Net Income
Balance, 1-1-X1	$154,000	$144,000^{2†}		$7,500^2	$2,500^2	
Add: Income from subsidiary for 19X1 (see Exhibit 4-3)	8,662^1		10,512	(250)	(500)	(1,100)
Less: Parent's share of subsidiary dividend for 19X1 (.90 × $6,000)	(5,400)^1		(5,400)			
Balance, 12-31-X1	$157,262	$144,000^2	$ 5,112^2	$7,250^2	$2,000^2	$(1,100)^7
Add: Income from subsidiary for 19X2 (see Exhibit 4-3)	12,683^1		13,383	(250)	(500)	50
Less: Parent's share of subsidiary dividend for 19X2 (.90 × $5,000)	(4,500)^1		(4,500)			
Balance, 12-31-X2	$165,445	$144,000	$13,995	$7,000	$1,500	$(1,050)

* The parent acquired 90% of the outstanding stock of the subsidiary on January 1, 19X1, for cash of $154,000. Acquired equity on the date of acquisition is $144,000 including acquired equity in common stock of $90,000 (.90 × $100,000) and acquired equity in retained earnings of $54,000 (.90 × $60,000).

† The numerical superscripts in the investment analysis above identify the various components of the investment balance with the consolidation worksheet adjustments (see Exhibit 4-6) that eliminate or reclassify the component.

the investment account of $50 ($1,100 − $1,050). The entries in the *book value of earned entity* column represent the parent's share of subsidiary net income adjusted for *upstream* transfers ($10,512 for 19X1 and $13,383 for 19X2, as calculated in Exhibit 4-3) and the parent's share of subsidiary dividends ($5,400 for 19X1 and $4,500 for 19X2).

Consolidation Worksheet Adjustments

Consolidation worksheet adjustments take exactly the same form as those in the previous chapter except that two groups of additional worksheet adjustments are used—one for upstream merchandise transfers and another for downstream merchandise transfers. As described earlier, each added group contains three adjustments—one defers gross margin from a prior period into the current period, a second defers gross margin from the current period into a subsequent period, and a third eliminates the aggregate transfer price from sales and cost of goods sold of the current period.[15] Exhibit 4-6 displays all nine consolidation worksheet adjustments for the York-Rippon illustration. The first three adjustments have exactly the same form as the adjustments considered in the preceding chapter. The remaining adjustments are new and relate to intercompany transfers of merchandise. Adjustments (4), (5), and (6) relate to upstream transfers; and adjustments (7), (8), and (9) relate to downstream transfers.[16] A review of the computation of deferred gross margin on 19X1 and 19X2 transfers, which is shown on page 222, will assist the reader in interpreting these adjustments.

Since the upstream and downstream adjustments to eliminate transfer prices from the current period sales and cost of goods sold [adjustments (6) and (9)] have the same form, they can be combined in a single adjustment as follows:

Worksheet adjustment to eliminate combined upstream and downstream transfer prices from sales and cost of goods sold for current year:

	19X1	19X2
Sales	26,000	26,625
Cost of goods sold	26,000	26,625

The upstream and downstream adjustments to defer gross margin at year-end [adjustments (5) and (8)] also have the same form. Consequently, they too can be combined into a single adjustment as follows:

Worksheet adjustment to defer combined upstream and downstream gross margin at end of current year:

	19X1	19X2
Cost of goods sold	1,420	1,500
Inventory, 12-31 (balance sheet)	1,420	1,500

In contrast, the upstream and downstream adjustments that recognize the gross margin deferred at the end of the previous year [adjustments (4) and (7)] do not have the same form. Consequently, they are not as readily combined into a single adjustment. Observe that the first year following acquisition does not require such adjustment,[17] but that both upstream and downstream transfers during 19X1 give rise to deferrals at December 31, 19X1, which are recognized in 19X2.

---

[15] In earlier chapters, all consolidation adjustments either eliminated reciprocal balances or reclassified balances. The adjustments that defer gross margin represent a third class of worksheet adjustments, which should be distinguished from elimination and reclassification adjustments.

[16] An additional adjustment related to intercompany merchandise transfers will be required when affiliates transfer goods on account. When this occurs, reciprocal balances of accounts receivable and accounts payable must also be eliminated by a consolidation worksheet adjustment.

[17] We have assumed that no transfers are included in the inventory on January 1, 19X1. Even if the January 1, 19X1 inventory includes transfers, the authors believe that no adjustment is appropriate since the transfers preceded acquisition and are correctly treated as sales between unaffiliated parties. Of course, if such transfers lack an arm's-length character, then related gross margin is appropriately deferred.

EXHIBIT 4-6   CONSOLIDATION WORKSHEET ADJUSTMENTS

York Corporation

WORKSHEET ADJUSTMENTS FOR THE CONSOLIDATION OF RIPPON, INC.

	For the Year Ended December 31,			
	19X1 (One Year after Acquisition)		19X2 (Two Years after Acquisition)	

(1) *Reverse parent's recording of subsidiary income and eliminate subsidiary dividend to parent for current year:*

Income from subsidiary	8,662		12,683	
Dividends		5,400		4,500
Investment in Rippon		3,262		8,183

(2) *Eliminate and reclassify beginning-of-the-year balance of parent's investment account:*

Common stock of Rippon	90,000		90,000	
Retained earnings of Rippon	54,000		59,112	
Goodwill	7,500		7,250	
Plant and equipment (net)	2,500		2,000	
Investment in Rippon		154,000		158,362*

(3) *Amortize valuation differential for current year:*

Depreciation and amortization expense	750		750	
Goodwill		250		250
Plant and equipment (net)		500		500

(4) *Recognize upstream gross margin deferred from prior year:*

Retained earnings, 1-1	–0–		320	
Cost of goods sold		–0–		320

(5) *Defer upstream gross margin at end of current year:*

Cost of goods sold	320		450	
Inventory, 12-31		320		450

(6) *Eliminate upstream transfer prices from sales and cost of goods sold for current year:*

Sales	4,000		5,625	
Cost of goods sold		4,000		5,625

(7) *Recognize downstream gross margin deferred from prior year:*

Investment in Rippon	–0–		1,100	
Cost of goods sold		–0–		1,100

(8) *Defer downstream gross margin at end of current year:*

Cost of goods sold	1,100		1,050	
Inventory, 12-31		1,100		1,050

(9) *Eliminate downstream transfer prices from sales and cost of goods sold for current year:*

Sales	22,000		21,000	
Cost of goods sold		22,000		21,000

---

*As shown in Exhibit 4-5, the beginning-of-the-year balance of the parent's investment account (a $157,262 *debit*) includes a $1,100 *credit* representing gross margin on downstream transfers deferred from the preceding period. This $1,100 deferred credit is recognized and eliminated from the investment account by adjustment (7); adjustment (2) eliminates or reclassifies the $158,362 remainder [$158,362 = $157,262 − (−$1,100)]. In general, adjustment (2) eliminates the beginning-of-the-year investment balance *except for* components of that balance representing deferred gross margin or profit on *downstream* transfers, which is eliminated by other adjustments.

EXHIBIT 4-7	CONSOLIDATION OF FINANCIAL STATEMENTS ONE YEAR AFTER ACQUISITION

	Separate Financial Statements		Consolidation[†] Adjustments		Minority Interest	Consolidated Financial Statements
	York	Rippon	Dr.	Cr.		
Income Statement						
Sales	400,000	60,000	(6) 4,000 (9) 22,000			434,000
Income from subsidiary	8,662		(1) 8,662			–0–
Cost of goods sold	(231,000)*	(37,600)	(5) 320 (8) 1,100	(6) 4,000 (9) 22,000		(244,020)
Depreciation and amortization expense	(17,000)	(1,000)	(3) 750			(18,750)
Other expenses	(69,000)	(9,400)				(78,400)
Minority interest					1,168	(1,168)
Net income	91,662	12,000	36,832	26,000	1,168	91,662
Statement of Retained Earnings						
Retained earnings, 1-1-X1:						
York	320,000					320,000
Rippon		60,000	(2) 54,000		6,000	–0–
Net income	91,662	12,000	36,832	26,000	1,168	91,662
Dividends	–0–	(6,000)		(1) 5,400	(600)	–0–
Retained earnings, 12-31-X1	411,662	66,000	90,832	31,400	6,568	411,662
Balance Sheet						
Cash	70,000	4,800				74,800
Accounts receivable	131,400	20,000				151,400
Inventory, 12-31-X1	23,000	6,200		(5) 320 (8) 1,100		27,780
Investment in Rippon	157,262	—		(1) 3,262 (2) 154,000		–0–
Plant and equipment (net)	930,000	157,000	(2) 2,500	(3) 500		1,089,000
Goodwill	—	—	(2) 7,500	(3) 250		7,250
Total assets	1,311,662	188,000				1,350,230
Liabilities	300,000	22,000				322,000
Common stock:						
York	600,000					600,000
Rippon		100,000	(2) 90,000		10,000	
Retained earnings	411,662	66,000	90,832	31,400	6,568	411,662
Minority interest					(16,568)	16,568
Total liabilities and stockholders' equity	1,311,662	188,000	190,832	190,832	–0–	1,350,230

* Parentheses indicate decreases.

[†] Adjustments (4) and (7) do not appear on the 19X1 consolidation worksheet because neither York nor Rippon had inventory on January 1, 19X1.

First-Year Consolidation Worksheet and Composition of Minority Interest

The first-year consolidation worksheet for the York-Rippon illustration is presented in Exhibit 4-7. The far left-hand columns reproduce the separate financial statements of the parent and its subsidiary. The worksheet adjustments shown in Exhibit 4-6 are entered in the usual way. Further, the worksheet is completed in exactly the same way as in the previous chapter except that the calculation of minority interest in subsidiary income involves several additional steps. In the previous chapter, minority interest in subsidiary income was simply the minority interest percentage (10%) times subsidiary income ($12,000), but the result of that computation ($1,200) exceeds the minority interest shown on the worksheet ($1,168). The reason for the difference is that the worksheet's minority interest was computed using an adjusted subsidiary net income. Subsidiary net income must be adjusted for deferred gross margin on *upstream* transfers before application of the minority interest percentage. Exhibit 4-8 shows the calculation of minority interest in subsidiary net income. In effect, the calculation *allocates* the gross margin adjustment for upstream transfers between minority and majority interests in proportion to their ownership interests. Observe that the minority interest in subsidiary net income is not influenced by gross margin adjustments related to downstream transfers; such gross margins accrue to the parent and not to the minority stockholders of the subsidiary.

Second-Year Consolidation Worksheet and Composition of Minority Interest

The second year consolidation worksheet for the York-Rippon illustration is presented in Exhibit 4-9 on the following page. The worksheet adjustments shown in Exhibit 4-6 are entered in the usual way. The calculation of minority interest in 19X2 subsidiary income is given in Exhibit 4-8.

EXHIBIT 4-8	CALCULATION OF MINORITY INTEREST IN SUBSIDIARY INCOME

York Corporation

CALCULATION OF MINORITY INTEREST IN RIPPON'S NET INCOME

	Year Ended December 31,	
	19X1	**19X2**
Subsidiary net income	$12,000	$15,000
Add: Deferred gross margin on *upstream* transfers at Jan. 1	–0–	320
Less: Deferred gross margin on *upstream* transfers at Dec. 31	(320)	(450)
Adjusted subsidiary net income	$11,680	$14,870
Minority ownership percentage	×.10	×.10
Minority interest in subsidiary income	$ 1,168	$ 1,487

EXHIBIT 4-9	CONSOLIDATION OF FINANCIAL STATEMENTS TWO YEARS AFTER ACQUISITION					

	Separate Financial Statements		Consolidation Adjustments		Minority Interest	Consolidated Financial Statements
	York	Rippon	Dr.	Cr.		
Income Statement						
Sales	440,000	70,000	(6) 5,625 (9) 21,000			483,375
Income from subsidiary	12,683		(1) 12,683			–0–
Cost of goods sold	(261,000)*	(44,000)	(5) 450 (8) 1,050	(4) 320 (7) 1,100 (6) 5,625 (9) 21,000		(278,455)
Depreciation and amortization expense	(19,000)	(2,000)	(3) 750			(21,750)
Other expenses	(70,000)	(9,000)				(79,000)
Minority interest					1,487	(1,487)
Net income	102,683	15,000	41,558	28,045	1,487	102,683
Retained Earnings Statement						
Retained earnings, 1-1-X2:						
York	411,662					411,662
Rippon		66,000	(2) 59,112 (4) 320		6,568	
Net income	102,683	15,000	41,558	28,045	1,487	102,683
Dividends	–0–	(5,000)		(1) 4,500	(500)	–0–
Retained earnings, 12-31-X2	514,345	76,000	100,900	32,545	7,555	514,345
Balance Sheet						
Cash	80,000	5,000				85,000
Accounts receivable	143,900	25,500				169,400
Inventory, 12-31-X2	25,000	7,500		(5) 450 (8) 1,050		31,000
Investment in Rippon	165,445		(7) 1,100	(1) 8,183 (2) 158,362		–0–
Plant and equipment (net)	950,000	168,000	(2) 2,000	(3) 500		1,119,500
Goodwill			(2) 7,250	(3) 250		7,000
Total assets	1,364,345	206,000				1,411,900
Liabilities	250,000	30,000				280,000
Common stock:						
York	600,000					600,000
Rippon		100,000	(2) 90,000		10,000	
Retained earnings	514,345	76,000	100,990	32,545	7,555	514,345
Minority interest					(17,555)	17,555
Total liabilities and stockholders' equity	1,364,345	206,000	201,340	201,340	–0–	1,411,900

* Parentheses indicate decreases.

Minority Interest in Beginning Subsidiary Retained Earnings

Completion of the minority interest column of the consolidation worksheet requires beginning-of-the-year minority interest in subsidiary retained earnings, which is calculated as follows for the York-Rippon illustration:

Calculation of Minority Interest in Subsidiary Retained Earnings		
	January 1, 19X1	January 1, 19X2
Subsidiary retained earnings at 1-1	$60,000	$66,000
Less: Gross margin on *upstream* transfers deferred from prior year [adjustment (4)]	(–0–)	(320)
Adjusted retained earnings at 1-1	$60,000	$65,680
Minority ownership percentage	×.10	×.10
Minority interest in subsidiary retained earnings at 1-1	$ 6,000	$ 6,568

Observe that the minority interest in subsidiary retained earnings is unaffected by deferred gross margin on *downstream* transfers. As noted earlier, deferred gross margin on downstream transfers is the gross margin of the parent company in which the minority stockholders have no equity interest.

Intercompany Gross Margin Deferral for Poolings

All the illustrations presented in this chapter have involved purchase accounting rather than pooling-of-interests accounting. However, precisely the same equity method and consolidation adjustments are used to defer intercompany gross margin in poolings as are used in purchases.

SUMMARY

Merchandise may be sold upstream by a subsidiary to its parent or downstream by a parent to its subsidiary. Parents and subsidiaries record such intercompany transfers on their separate records like sales to unaffiliated parties, but intercompany transfers should not enter parent company net income or consolidated net income until the merchandise is transferred to an unaffiliated party. Both the equity method and consolidation procedures provide for the deferral of gross margins on such transactions until the period in which the related merchandise is sold to an unaffiliated party. In addition, consolidation procedures eliminate all effects of intercompany merchandise transfers from the consolidated financial statements. Following the preferred total deferral method, deferrals are made for 100% of the related gross margin without regard to the existence of minority interest. This means that the income and equity interests of minority stockholders reported in consolidated financial statements are subject to deferral of their pro rata share of such gross margins.

APPENDIX: FRACTIONAL DEFERRAL METHOD OF CONSOLIDATION

Let us illustrate the fractional deferral method by reference to the York-Rippon example. The *fractional deferral method* alters only two of the nine worksheet adjustments shown in Exhibit 4-6—the two adjustments that deal with the deferral of subsidiary gross profit related to upstream transfers, namely, adjustments (4) and (5).[18] Under the fractional deferral method, the fifth adjustment, which defers upstream gross margin at year-end, has the following altered form for 19X1 and 19X2:

(5) *Defer upstream gross margin at end of current year:*

	19X1		19X2	
Cost of goods sold	288		405	
Inventory, 12-31		288		405

The year-end deferrals represent 90% of the subsidiary gross margin associated with the parent's *ending* inventories ($288 = .90 \times $320, and $405 = .90 \times $450). The fractional deferral method leads to the following replacement for the fourth adjustment in Exhibit 4-6, which recognizes upstream gross margin deferred from a prior year:

(4) *Recognize upstream gross margin deferred from prior year:*

	19X1		19X2	
Retained earnings, 1-1	0		288	
Cost of goods sold		0		288

The $288 represents 90% of the subsidiary gross profit associated with the parent's *beginning* inventory for 19X2.

The fractional deferral method simplifies the calculation of minority interest in subsidiary net income. Instead of the calculation shown in Exhibit 4-8, minority interest in subsidiary net income is simply the minority ownership percentage times the net income reported by the subsidiary:

Calculation of Minority Interest in Subsidiary Net Income under Fractional Deferral method

	19X1	19X2
Net income reported by subsidiary	$12,000	$15,000
Minority ownership percentage	×.10	×.10
Minority interest in subsidiary income	$ 1,200	$ 1,500

It is important to notice that the choice between fractional and total deferral methods *does not affect consolidated net income.* The fractional deferral method results in a larger minority interest in income that is exactly offset by a smaller consolidated cost of goods sold. The result is that both methods produce the same consolidated net income. On the balance sheet, the fractional deferral method produces higher carrying amounts for both inventory and minority interest—higher by the amount of the minority interest's share of the subsidiary's deferred gross margin—than produced by the total deferral method.

---

[18] This follows the usual interpretation of the fractional deferral method which recognizes the minority interest share of gross margin on upstream transfers but defers the entire gross margin on downstream transfers. Pacter (1991, par. 79) states that some accountants interpret the fractional deferral method to require recognition of the minority interest share of both upstream and downstream gross margin.

The equity method is unaffected by the use of the fractional deferral method. The fractional deferral method does not alter the deferral of the parent's gross margins associated with downstream transfers because minority stockholders have no interest in such margins. Although the minority stockholders have an interest in the subsidiary's gross margins associated with upstream transfers, the equity method defers only the parent's share, and it does so whether fractional or total deferral is used for consolidation purposes.

SELECTED READINGS

King, Thomas E., and Valdean C. Lembke. "Reporting Investor Income under the Equity Method," *Journal of Accountancy* (September 1976), pp. 65–71.

Pacter, Paul. *An Analysis of Issues Related to Consolidation Policies and Procedures.* Financial Accounting Standards Board Discussion Memorandum. Norwalk, CT: Financial Accounting Standards Board, September 10, 1991.

Spiller, Earl A., Jr. "Teaching Consolidated Financial Statements—A Realistic Approach," *The Accounting Review* (April 1962), pp. 336–342.

Thomas, Arthur L. "Consolidated Adjustments: Three Simple Rules," *Cost and Management* (Canada) (November–December 1973), pp. 17–24.

QUESTIONS

Q4-1 Intercompany transfers of merchandise are described as either downstream transfers or upstream transfers. Define the terms *downstream transfer* and *upstream transfer.*

Q4-2 Why is it necessary to eliminate intercompany profits and losses in the preparation of a consolidated income statement?

Q4-3 When intercompany inventory profit is deferred at the end of one year, what assumption is made concerning this deferred profit during the next year?

Q4-4 Explain why you agree or disagree with the following statement: The net income reported by the subsidiary need not be adjusted for deferred gross margins on downstream and upstream transfers of merchandise when calculating minority interest in subsidiary net income.

Q4-5 Partially owned subsidiary B sells merchandise to the parent company A. In preparing consolidated statements for A and B, would 100% of the subsidiary's gross margin on transfers in the parent's inventory be deferred (total deferral) or would only the parent's share of the gross margin (fractional deferral) be deferred?

Q4-6 Describe the three types of consolidation worksheet adjustments relating to intercompany upstream and downstream transfers of merchandise.

Q4-7 Explain why you agree or disagree with the following statement: It is customary to accept sale transactions between parent and subsidiary companies as an appropriate basis for the recognition of revenue and related expense.

Q4-8 When is the gross margin on intercompany transfers of inventory recognized for consolidation purposes?

Q4-9 Explain why you agree or disagree with the following statement: In the parent's calculation of income from a partially owned subsidiary, gross margin deferrals on both upstream and downstream inventory transfers are adjustments to the subsidiary net income before application of the parent's ownership percentage.

Q4-10   What rationale is used to support the deferral of only the parent's share (fractional deferral) of the subsidiary's gross margin on transfers in inventory?

QUESTION FOR APPENDIX
Q4-11   What are the effects on the consolidated income statement and balance sheet if the fractional deferral method rather than the total deferral method is used in the preparation of consolidated statements?

EXERCISES

E4-1   **Upstream Transfers of Inventory (Beginning and Ending): Consolidation Adjustments**   The parent acquired all the common stock of the subsidiary on January 1, 19X1. The parent acquires all its inventory from the subsidiary at a markup of 25% above the cost to the subsidiary. The 19X1 ending inventory of the parent consisted of unconfirmed gross margin of $2,000.

During 19X2, the subsidiary sold merchandise to the parent for $30,000, recognizing a gross profit of $6,000. Thirty percent of the intercompany transfers of merchandise was in the 19X2 ending inventory of the parent.

REQUIRED
Prepare in journal entry form consolidation worksheet adjustments for 19X2 relating to intercompany upstream transfers of merchandise. Also, explain the reasons for having to make each of such worksheet adjustments.

E4-2   **Downstream Transfers of Inventory (Ending): Consolidation Adjustments, Compute Parent and Minority Interest in Subsidiary Income**   During 19X4 Blues Alley sold merchandise costing $24,000 to its 70%-owned subsidiary, Jazz, for $44,000. At the end of 19X4, the inventory of Jazz included 40% of the transferred merchandise. For the year 19X4, Jazz reported a net income of $28,000.

REQUIRED
a) On the books of Blues Alley, record the entry to recognize its income from the subsidiary.

b) Prepare in journal entry form consolidation worksheet adjustments for 19X4 relating to intercompany transfers of merchandise.

c) Determine minority interest in the net income of the subsidiary.

E4-3   **Downstream Transfers of Inventory (Beginning and Ending): Consolidation Adjustments, Compute Parent and Minority Interest in Subsidiary Income**   During the preparation of consolidated statements on December 31, 19X5, for Ajax Printing Company and its 80%-owned subsidiary, Northern Press, the following intercompany transactions were noted. During the year Ajax sold Northern merchandise totaling $32,000, which included the usual 30% markup over cost. Northern's beginning inventory contained $6,500 of merchandise purchased from Ajax in the previous year, and its ending inventory contained $5,200 of the current year purchases. The 19X5 net income of Northern was $12,000.

REQUIRED
a) On the books of Ajax, record the entry to recognize its income from the subsidiary.

b) Prepare in journal entry form consolidation worksheet adjustments for 19X5 relating to intercompany transfers of merchandise.

c) Determine minority interest in the net income of the subsidiary.

E4-4   **Upstream Transfers of Inventory (Ending): Consolidation Adjustments, Compute Parent and Minority Interest in Subsidiary Income**   Pattie, an 80%-owned subsidiary of Peppermint, sold merchandise during 19X2 to Peppermint for $80,000. The merchandise cost Pattie $50,000. Twenty percent of the transferred merchandise was included in Peppermint's 19X2 ending inventory. For the year 19X2, Pattie reported a net income of $30,000.

REQUIRED

a) Prepare the entry on the parent's books to record its income from the subsidiary.

b) Prepare in journal entry form consolidation worksheet adjustments for 19X2 relating to intercompany transfers of merchandise.

c) Determine minority interest in the net income of the subsidiary.

E4-5   **Analysis of Comments on Upstream and Downstream Transfers of Merchandise**   Indicate whether you agree or disagree with each of the following statements. If you disagree with a statement, provide an explanation as to why.

1. Transfers of merchandise from a subsidiary to its parents are called *downstream transfers;* whereas transfers of merchandise from a parent to its subsidiary are called *upstream transfers.*

2. The sale of merchandise between parent and subsidiary companies constitutes arm's-length transactions and thus provides the basis for the recognition of revenue and gross margin on such transfers.

3. Under the equity method, gross margins on upstream merchandise transfers associated with the parent's ending inventory are subtracted from subsidiary net income for the current year in the calculation of parent's income from subsidiary. These year-end deferrals are then added to the next year's subsidiary net income in the calculation of parent's income from the subsidiary. This procedure is inappropriate because all the intercompany transfers unsold at the end of one year may not be sold in the next year.

4. For consolidation purposes, 100% (total deferral method) of the subsidiary's gross margin on merchandise transfers in the parent's inventory is deferred even though the subsidiary is partially owned.

5. The consolidation worksheet adjustment below, to eliminate merchandise transfer prices from sales and cost of goods sold for the current year, would be the same for both upstream and downstream transfers of merchandise.

    Sales XXX
        Cost of goods sold   XXX

6. Merchandise transfers from a parent to its subsidiary that have not yet been sold to unaffiliated parties should be included in consolidated inventory at their cost rather than at their transfer price.

7. Minority interest in subsidiary net income is not influenced by deferred gross margins on upstream and downstream transfers of merchandise. In essence, minority interest in subsidiary income is determined by simply applying the minority interest percentage times the reported subsidiary income.

8. The consolidation worksheet adjustment below, to recognize gross margin deferred on upstream merchandise transfers from prior year, would be the same for such situations involving downstream transfers of merchandise.

    Retained earnings of subsidiary XXX
        Cost of goods sold   XXX

E4-6   **Upstream Transfers of Inventory (Beginning and Ending): Consolidation Adjustments, Compute Parent and Minority Interest in Subsidiary Income**   During 19X9, Tomac (a 75%-owned subsidiary of Teal) sold merchandise costing $35,000 to its parent Teal for $45,500. Teal's 19X9 ending inventory contained 20% of the transferred merchandise. The beginning inventory of Teal consisted of $13,000 of merchandise acquired from Tomac in 19X8. Tomac has always sold merchandise to all customers at the 30% markup above cost. For the year 19X9, Tomac reported a net income of $50,000.

REQUIRED

a) Prepare the entry on the parent's books to record its income from the subsidiary.

b) Prepare in journal entry form consolidation worksheet adjustments for 19X9 relating to intercompany transfers of merchandise.

c) Determine minority interest in the net income of the subsidiary.

E4-7 **Downstream Transfers of Inventory (Beginning and Ending): Consolidation Adjustments, Compute Parent and Minority Interest in Subsidiary Income**   PH has a 90% ownership interest in SH. During 19X5 PH sold merchandise to SH for $20,000. The merchandise cost PH $16,000. Thirty percent of the transferred merchandise remains in SH's ending inventory. The beginning inventory of SH consisted of $5,000 of merchandise purchased from PH in 19X4. PH sells merchandise to all customers at 25% above its cost. At the end of 19X5, SH reported a net income of $50,000.

REQUIRED

a) Prepare the entry for 19X5 on the books of PH to record its income from the subsidiary.

b) Prepare in journal entry form consolidation worksheet adjustments for 19X5 relating to intercompany transfers of merchandise.

c) Determine minority interest in the net income of the subsidiary.

E4-8 **Upstream/Downstream Transfers of Inventory (Beginning and Ending): Minority Interest Computations**   Walnut acquired an 80% interest in Sycamore on January 1, 19X1. Each company sells merchandise to the other at its normal markup. Following is the amount of intercompany gross margin in the ending inventory of each company for a three-year period of time:

| | Intercompany Gross Margin Ending Inventory | | |
	19X1	19X2	19X3
Walnut	$1,000	$3,000	$2,000
Sycamore	5,000	4,000	6,000

REQUIRED

Assuming Sycamore reported net income of $20,000 in each of the years 19X1, 19X2, and 19X3, calculate the minority interest in the subsidiary's net income.

E4-9 **Upstream/Downstream Transfers of Inventory (Beginning and Ending): Consolidation Adjustments, Compute Parent and Minority Interest in Subsidiary Income**   During 19X6 Hunter, an 85%-owned subsidiary of Flippen, sold merchandise costing $40,000 to Flippen for $70,000, reflecting a gross margin of $30,000 over Hunter's cost. Hunter purchased merchandise from Flippen during the same period for $50,000, which included a gross margin for Flippen of $10,000. The 19X6 ending inventory of Hunter and Flippen consisted of 30% and 40%, respectively, of the intercompany sales of merchandise.

The 19X6 beginning inventory of Hunter and Flippen consisted of unconfirmed gross margins on intercompany merchandise sales of $6,000 and $8,000, respectively. For the year 19X6, Hunter reported a net loss of $4,000.

REQUIRED

a) Record on the books of Flippen the entry to record its income (loss) from Hunter.

b) Prepare in journal entry form consolidation worksheet adjustments for 19X6 relating to intercompany transfers of merchandise.

c) Determine minority interest in the net income (loss) of Hunter.

E4-10 **Upstream/Downstream Transfers of Inventory (Beginning and Ending): Consolidation Adjustments, Compute Parent and Minority Interest in Subsidiary Income** Company X owns 80% of the voting stock of Company Y. Starting in the year 19X4, X and Y began selling merchandise to each other with each recording intercompany sales at a 20% markup above cost. At the end of 19X4, X had $4,200 and Y had $6,000 of intercompany transfers in their respective inventories.

During 19X5, X sold merchandise to Y for $24,000 and purchased from Y $12,000 of merchandise. The 19X5 ending inventory of X and Y consisted of intercompany sales of $12,000 and $8,400, respectively. At the end of 19X5, Y reported a net income of $25,000.

REQUIRED

a) Prepare the 19X5 entry on the books of Company X to record its income from the subsidiary.

b) Prepare in journal entry form consolidation worksheet adjustments for 19X5 relating to intercompany transfers of merchandise.

c) Determine minority interest in Y's 19X5 net income.

E4-11 **Multiple Choice Questions on Intercompany Inventory Transfers**

1. Hecht's, a 90% owner of Robious, sold merchandise at a sales price of $60,000 to Robious during the 19X5 fiscal year. This represented a markup of 10% on the selling price. Robious' ending inventory contained 30% of the merchandise purchased during the year from Hecht's. When preparing the 19X5 consolidated statements the accountant failed to adjust for the intercompany profit in ending inventory. The impact of this omission on consolidated statements was to

a) Overstate net income, $1,800, and understate ending inventory, $1,800

b) Understate net income, $6,000, and overstate retained earnings, $6,000

c) Overstate net income, $1,800, and overstate ending inventory, $1,800

d) Understate net income, $1,800, and overstate ending inventory, $1,800

2. Lipstock, a wholly owned subsidiary as of January 1, 19X6, purchases all its merchandise from the parent company. At the date of acquisition, Lipstock's inventory was $36,000. During the fiscal year the parent recorded $45,000 of merchandise sales to Lipstock; this represented a selling price of 40% above cost. On December 31, 19X6, the parent's ending inventory was $52,000 and the consolidated ending inventory was $69,000. The consolidated working paper elimination that was made in respect to intercompany profit was

a) Cost of goods sold 6,800
  Inventory, Dec. 31, 19X6.   6,800

b) Inventory, Jan. 1, 19X6 6,800
  Cost of goods sold   6,800

c) Cost of goods sold 3,600
  Inventory, Dec. 31, 19X6.   3,600

d) Inventory, Jan. 1, 19X6 3,600
  Cost of goods sold   3,600

3. Eltro Company acquired a 70% interest in the Samson Company in 19X2. For the years ended December 31, 19X3, and 19X4, Samson reported a net income of $80,000 and $90,000, respectively. During 19X3 Samson sold merchandise to Eltro for $10,000 at a profit of $2,000. The merchandise was later resold by Eltro to outsiders for $15,000 during 19X4. For consolidation purposes, what is the minority interest's share of Samson's net income for 19X3 and 19X4, respectively?

a) $23,400 and $27,600   c). $24,600 and $26,400

b) $24,000 and $27,000   d) $26,000 and $25,000

4. In the preparation of consolidated financial statements, the intercompany profits on inventory acquired by a parent from its subsidiary should

a) Not be eliminated

b) Be eliminated in full

c) Be eliminated to the extent of the parent's controlling interest in the subsidiary

d) Be eliminated to the extent of the minority interest of the subsidiary

5. King Corp. owns 80% of Lee Corp.'s common stock. During October 19X7, Lee sold merchandise to King for $100,000. At December 31, 19X7, one-half of the merchandise remained in King's inventory. For 19X7, gross profit percentages were 30% for King and 40% for Lee. The amount of unrealized intercompany profit in ending inventory at December 31, 19X7, that should be eliminated in consolidation is

a) $40,000   c) $16,000

b) $20,000   d) $15,000

6. Parker Corp. owns 70% of Smith Inc.'s common stock. During 19X1, Parker sold Smith $250,000 of inventory on the same terms as sales made to third parties. Smith sold all of the inventory purchased from Parker in 19X1. The following information pertains to Smith and Parker's sales for 19X1:

	Parker	Smith
Sales	$1,000,000	$700,000
Cost of sales	400,000	350,000
	$ 600,000	$350,000

What amount should Parker report as cost of sales in its 19X1 consolidated income statement?

a) $750,000   c) $500,000

b) $680,000   d) $430,000

(AICPA adapted)

E4-12　**Upstream Transfers of Inventory (Beginning and Ending): Consolidation Adjustments, Com-**
APPENDIX　**pute Parent and Minority Interest in Subsidiary Income**　Knight, a 90%-owned subsidiary of Rider, sold merchandise during 19X5 to Rider for $30,000. The merchandise cost Knight $25,000. Ten percent of the transferred merchandise was included in Rider's 19X5 ending inventory.

The 19X5 beginning inventory of Rider consisted of $1,000 of intercompany gross margin deferred from the previous year. Knight reported a net income of $15,000 for the year 19X5.

For purposes of consolidation, the fractional deferral method is used to account for deferrals of upstream gross margin on transfers in inventory.

REQUIRED

a) Prepare the entry on the books of Rider to record its income from the subsidiary.

b) Discuss the effect, if any, on the equity method of using the fractional deferral method rather than the total deferral method to account for deferrals relating to upstream transfers.

c) Prepare in journal entry form consolidation worksheet adjustments for 19X5 relating to intercompany transfers of merchandise.

d) Determine minority interest in the net income of the subsidiary.

e) Discuss the effect, if any, on the consolidated net income of using the fractional deferral method rather than the total deferral method to account for deferrals relating to upstream transfers.

E4-13
APPENDIX

Upstream/Downstream Transfers of Inventory (Beginning and Ending): Consolidation Adjustments, Compute Parent and Minority Interest in Subsidiary Income Using the same information in Exercise 4-10, complete the following requirements assuming, for purposes of consolidation, that the fractional method is used to account for deferrals of upstream gross margin on transfers in inventory.

REQUIRED

a) Prepare the 19X5 entry on the books of Company X to record its income from the subsidiary.

b) Prepare in journal entry form consolidation worksheet adjustments for 19X5 relating to intercompany transfers of merchandise.

c) Determine minority interest in Y's 19X5 net income.

PROBLEMS

P4-1

Consolidation Worksheet: Downstream Transfer of Inventory (Ending) Dallas Inc. acquired 80% of the outstanding common stock of Dynasty Company for the book value on January 1, 19X3. At the date of acquisition, the stockholders' equity of Dynasty consisted of $75,000 common stock and $50,000 retained earnings.

During 19X3 Dallas sold merchandise costing $10,000 to Dynasty for $14,000. The 19X3 ending inventory of Dynasty consisted of 40% of the intercompany profit on transfers of merchandise.

The financial statements of both companies as of December 31, 19X3, are presented here:

	Dallas Inc.	Dynasty Company
Income Statement		
Sales	$130,000	$ 60,000
Income from subsidiary	12,800	
Cost of goods sold	(70,000)	(30,000)
Operating expenses	(20,800)	(12,000)
Net income	$ 52,000	$ 18,000
Statement of Retained Earnings		
Retained earnings, 1-1-X3	$ 80,000	$ 50,000
Net income	52,000	18,000
Dividends	(10,000)	(5,000)
Retained earnings, 12-31-X3	$122,000	$ 63,000
Balance Sheet		
Assets		
Cash	$ 12,000	$ 15,000
Inventory	40,000	33,000
Investment in Dynasty	108,800	
Buildings (net)	82,000	100,000
Total assets	$242,800	$148,000
Liabilities and Stockholders' Equity		
Accounts payable	$ 20,800	$ 10,000
Common stock ($25 par)	100,000	75,000
Retained earnings	122,000	63,000
Total liabilities and stockholders' equity	$242,800	$148,000

REQUIRED
Prepare a consolidation worksheet for Dallas Inc. and its subsidiary as of December 31, 19X3.

P4-2 Consolidation Worksheet: Upstream Transfers of Inventory (Ending), Valuation Differential

Stuart Company acquired 80% of the previously issued voting stock of Peaco Company for $32,000 on January 1, 19X7. At that time, Peaco's common stock and retained earnings were $25,000 and $10,000, respectively. Any excess cost over the book value of acquired equity is to be considered goodwill and amortized over 20 years. During 19X7 Peaco sold merchandise costing $20,000 to Stuart for $30,000. Ten percent of the transferred merchandise was included in Stuart's ending inventory. As of December 31, 19X7, the financial statements of Stuart and Peaco were as follows:

	Stuart Company	Peaco Company
Income Statement		
Sales	$ 80,000	$40,000
Income from subsidiary	7,000	
Cost of goods sold	(55,000)	(25,000)
Amortization expense	(5,000)	(3,000)
Other expenses	(3,000)	(2,000)
Net income	$ 24,000	$10,000
Statement of Retained Earnings		
Retained earnings, 1-1-X7	$ 30,000	$10,000
Net income	24,000	10,000
Dividends	(25,000)	(5,000)
Retained earnings, 12-31-X7	$ 29,000	$15,000
Balance Sheet		
Assets		
Cash	$ 15,800	$15,000
Accounts receivable	30,000	25,000
Inventory	20,000	10,000
Investment in Peaco	35,000	
Total assets	$100,800	$50,000
Liabilities and Stockholders' Equity		
Accounts payable	$ 21,800	$10,000
Common stock ($25 par)	50,000	25,000
Retained earnings	29,000	15,000
Total liabilities and stockholders' equity	$100,800	$50,000

REQUIRED
Prepare a consolidation worksheet as of December 31, 19X7, for Stuart Company and its subsidiary.

P4-3 Multiple Choice Questions on Downstream and Upstream Transfers of Inventory Bradley Company acquired 75% of Marshal, Inc., on January 1, 19X8, paying $10,000 over book value; $400 amortized annually.

Intercompany transfers of merchandise between the two affiliated firms were $90,000 during 19X8 and $60,000 during 19X9. Intercompany gross margin included in the ending inventories as a result of these intercompany transfers amounted to $15,000 at December 31, 19X8, and $10,000 at December 31, 19X9.

Income statements for the two firms for 19X8 and 19X9 are presented here. The amounts presented for Bradley are a result of its own operations and exclude income from the subsidiary:

	Bradley Company		Marshal, Inc.	
	19X8	**19X9**	**19X8**	**19X9**
Sales	$200,000	$300,000	$100,000	$150,000
Cost of goods sold	(110,000)	(150,000)	(50,000)	(80,000)
Operating expenses	(50,000)	(80,000)	(30,000)	(40,000)
Net income	$ 40,000	$ 70,000	$ 20,000	$ 30,000

REQUIRED

Part A. Assume that all intercompany transfers of merchandise for 19X8 are upstream from Marshal to Bradley.

1. The amount of sales that would appear in the 19X8 consolidated income statement of Bradley and its subsidiary would be

a) $300,000   c) $240,000

b) $210,000   d) $450,000

2. The consolidated cost of goods sold for 19X8 would be

a) $ 70,000   c) $ 85,000

b) $160,000   d) $175,000

3. The parent's income from subsidiary for 19X8 would be

a) $15,000   c) $19,600

b) $ 5,000   d) $ 3,350

4. Minority interest in subsidiary income for 19X8 would be

a) $5,000   c) $1,250

b) $4,600   d) $2,000

5. Consolidated income for 19X8 would be (*Reminder:* Bradley's income statement amounts are a result of its own operations and exclude income from subsidiary)

a) $43,350   c) $55,000

b) $45,000   d) $59,600

Part B. Assume that all intercompany transfers of merchandise for 19X8 and 19X9 are downstream from Bradley to Marshal.

6. The parent's income from subsidiary for 19X9 would be

a) $22,500   c) $27,500

b) $27,100   d) $25,850

7. Minority interest in subsidiary income for 19X9 would be

a) $12,500   c) $7,500

b) $12,100   d) $8,750

8. The consolidated cost of goods sold for 19X9 would be

a) $230,000   c) $180,000

b) $170,000   d) $165,000

9. Consolidated income for 19X9 would be (*Reminder:* Bradley's income statement amounts are a result of its own operations and exclude income from the subsidiary)

a) $100,000   c) $90,000

b) $115,000   d) $97,100

10. The amount of sales that would appear in the 19X9 consolidated income statement of Bradley and its subsidiary would be

a) $390,000   c) $360,000

b) $450,000   d) $425,000

P4-4   Consolidation Worksheet: Downstream Transfers of Inventory (Beginning and Ending)   On January 1, 19X1, Macbride Company acquired 90% of the outstanding common shares of Ryan Company at book value. The stockholders' equity of Ryan at the date of acquisition consisted of common stock of $50,000 and retained earnings of $30,000. At the end of 19X1, Ryan reported a net income of $15,000 and paid dividends of $2,000. During 19X2 Macbride sold merchandise costing $22,000 to Ryan for $30,000. Thirty percent of the transferred merchandise was in Ryan's ending inventory. The 19X2 beginning inventory of Ryan included the intercompany gross margin of $3,000. December 31, 19X2, trial balances for Macbride and Ryan are as follows:

	Macbride Company	Ryan Company
Debits		
Cash	$129,500	$103,000
Inventory	40,000	20,000
Investment in Ryan	99,300	
Cost of goods sold	70,000	35,000
Operating expenses	20,000	10,000
Dividends	10,000	5,000
	$368,800	$173,000
Credits		
Accounts payable	$ 19,700	$ 10,000
Common stock	100,000	50,000
Retained earnings	86,000	43,000
Sales	140,000	70,000
Income from subsidiary	23,100	
	$368,800	$173,000

REQUIRED

Prepare a consolidation worksheet for Macbride and its subsidiary for the year ended December 31, 19X2.

P4-5 **Consolidation Worksheet: Upstream Transfers of Inventory (Beginning and Ending)**   Alpha Company purchased 90% of the outstanding common stock of Beta Company at book value on January 1, 19X2. At the date of acquisition, the balances in Beta's common stock and retained earnings were $125,000 and $25,000, respectively. Beta reported a net income of $10,000 in 19X2 and paid no dividends. As of the end of the fiscal year December 31, 19X3, the following financial statements were made available concerning the two companies:

	Alpha Company	Beta Company
Income Statement		
Sales	$350,000	$125,000
Income from subsidiary	27,900	
Cost of goods sold	(180,000)	(70,000)
Operating expenses	(60,000)	(20,000)
Net income	$137,900	$ 35,000
Statement of Retained Earnings		
Retained earnings, 1-1-X3	$107,200	$ 35,000
Net income	137,900	35,000
Dividends	(40,000)	(10,000)
Retained earnings, 12-31-X3	$205,100	$ 60,000
Balance Sheet		
Assets		
Cash	$ 99,000	$ 80,000
Accounts receivable	75,000	85,000
Inventory	120,000	35,000
Investment in Beta	161,100	
Total assets	$455,100	$200,000
Liabilities and Stockholders' Equity		
Accounts payable	$ 50,000	$ 15,000
Common stock	200,000	125,000
Retained earnings	205,100	60,000
Total liabilities and stockholders' equity	$455,100	$200,000

While Alpha buys its merchandise from several suppliers, Beta is its main supplier. During the fiscal year 19X3 Alpha purchased $120,000 of its merchandise from Beta. Beta sells merchandise to all customers at 20% above cost. Although Alpha's beginning inventory for 19X3 contained only $12,000 of merchandise purchased from Beta, its ending inventory consisted of $36,000 of merchandise purchased from Beta.

REQUIRED
Prepare a consolidation worksheet for Alpha and its subsidiary as of December 31, 19X3.

P4-6   **Consolidation Worksheet: Downstream Transfers of Inventory (Beginning and Ending)** On January 1, 19X1, Everett Company acquired 90% of the outstanding common shares of Waddey Company for $51,000. The stockholders' equity of Waddey at the date of acquisition consisted of common stock of $40,000 and retained earnings of $15,000. At the date of acquisition, the book values of the assets and liabilities of Waddey represented fair values. Any excess cost over book value is considered goodwill and amortized over five years. At the end of 19X1, Waddey reported a net income of $15,000 and paid dividends of $5,000. During 19X2 Everett sold merchandise costing $18,000 to Waddey for $24,000. Twenty percent of the transferred merchandise was in Waddey's ending inventory. The 19X2 beginning inventory of Waddey included the intercompany gross margin of $400. December 31, 19X2, financial statements for Everett and Waddey are as follows:

	Everett Company	Waddey Company
Income Statement		
Sales	$175,300	$105,000
Income from subsidiary	16,900	
Cost of goods sold	(90,000)	(55,000)
Operating expenses	(40,200)	(30,000)
Net income	$ 62,000	$ 20,000
Statement of Retained Earnings		
Retained earnings, 1-1-X2	$ 58,000	$ 25,000
Net income	62,000	20,000
Dividends	(29,000)	(7,000)
Retained earnings, 12-31-X2	$ 91,000	$ 38,000
Balance Sheet		
Assets		
Cash	$ 14,000	$ 12,000
Accounts receivable	35,000	9,000
Inventory	64,000	23,000
Investment in Waddey	69,900	
Equipment (net)	90,000	43,000
Total assets	$273,500	$ 87,000
Liabilities and Stockholders' Equity		
Accounts payable	$ 32,500	$ 9,000
Common stock	150,000	40,000
Retained earnings	91,000	38,000
Total liabilities and stockholders' equity	$273,500	$ 87,000

REQUIRED

Prepare a consolidation worksheet for Everett and its subsidiary for the year ended December 31, 19X2.

P4-7 **Consolidation Worksheet: Upstream Transfers of Inventory (Beginning and Ending), Valuation Differential**   On January 1, 19X1, Delta Corporation acquired 80% of the outstanding common stock of Midas Company for $89,600. At the date of acquisition, the common stock and retained earnings balances of Midas were $87,000 and $15,000, respectively. At the date of acquisition, the book values of the assets and liabilities of Midas represent fair values except for a building that has a book value of $20,000 and a fair value of $27,000 (estimated remaining life of eight years). All intangible assets are amortized over four years. During the fiscal year ended December 31, 19X1, Midas reported a net income of $19,000 and dividend payments of $10,000. Financial statements for the two companies as of December 31, 19X2, are presented here:

	Delta	Midas
Income Statement		
Sales	$225,000	$150,000
Income from subsidiary	12,300	
Cost of goods sold	(105,000)	(78,000)
Depreciation and amortization expenses	(30,000)	(24,000)
Other expenses	(60,300)	(32,000)
Net income	$ 42,000	$ 16,000
Statement of Retained Earnings		
Retained earnings, 1-1-X2	$ 78,000	$ 24,000
Net income	42,000	16,000
Dividends	(12,000)	(3,000)
Retained earnings, 12-31-X2	$108,000	$ 37,000
Balance Sheet		
Assets		
Cash	$ 9,600	$ 10,000
Accounts receivable	26,000	20,000
Inventory	54,000	32,000
Investment in Midas	103,400	
Buildings (net)	90,000	70,000
Total assets	$283,000	$132,000
Liabilities and Stockholders' Equity		
Accounts payable	$ 23,000	$ 8,000
Common stock	152,000	87,000
Retained earnings	108,000	37,000
Total liabilities and stockholders' equity	$283,000	$132,000

During 19X2 Midas sold merchandise costing $20,000 to Delta for $25,000. Thirty percent of the transferred merchandise was included in Delta's ending inventory. The 19X2 beginning inventory of Delta consisted of $12,500 of intercompany merchandise transfers. Midas has always sold merchandise to Delta at 25% above cost.

REQUIRED

a) Prepare an analysis of the parent's investment account for 19X1 and 19X2, using the format shown in the chapter.

b) Prepare a consolidation worksheet as of December 31, 19X2, for Delta and its subsidiary.

P4-8   **Consolidation Worksheet: Downstream and Upstream Transfers of Inventory (Beginning and Ending)**   O'Brienstein, Inc., acquired a 75% interest in Swiss Company on January 1, 19X7, for a book value of $75,000. Swiss stockholders' equity consisted of common stock of $75,000 and retained earnings of $25,000. The two companies sell their merchandise to each other at a price 20% above cost. During 19X7 Swiss reported a net income of $20,000 and paid dividends of $6,000. On December 31, 19X8, the following information is made available concerning the two companies:

	O'Brienstein, Inc.	Swiss Company
Cash	$ 79,300	$ 50,000
Accounts receivable	100,000	61,000
Investment in Swiss	94,550	
Inventory, Dec. 31, 19X8	80,000	40,000
Accounts payable	40,000	20,000
Common stock	150,000	75,000
Retained earnings, Jan. 1, 19X8	70,000	39,000
Dividends	25,000	8,000
Sales	300,000	200,000
Cost of goods sold	95,000	90,000
Operating expenses	105,000	85,000
Income from subsidiary	18,850	

During the current 19X8 fiscal year O'Brienstein sold $20,000 of merchandise to Swiss and purchased $35,000 of merchandise from Swiss. The amount of intercompany merchandise transfers in the 19X8 beginning and ending inventory of each firm is as follows:

	Beginning Inventory	Ending Inventory
O'Brienstein, Inc.	$14,400	$16,800
Swiss Company	12,000	9,600

REQUIRED

Prepare a consolidation worksheet for O'Brienstein, Inc., and its subsidiary for December 31, 19X8.

P4-9 **Consolidation Worksheet: Downstream and Upstream Transfers of Inventory (Beginning and Ending), Valuation Differential** January 1, 19X3, Johnston Company paid $12,000 cash for 90% of the outstanding shares of Miller Company. At the date of acquisition, Miller's common stock and retained earnings balances were $6,000 and $4,000, respectively. At the date of acquisition, the book value of the assets and liabilities of Miller represented fair values. Any excess cost over book value is considered goodwill and amortized over 20 years. The financial statements for both companies as of December 31, 19X4, are presented as follows:

	Johnston Company	Miller Company
Income Statement		
Sales	$30,000	$20,000
Income from subsidiary	2,240	
Cost of goods sold	(20,000)	(15,000)
Depreciation and amortization expense	(3,000)	(2,000)
Other expenses	(2,000)	(1,000)
Net income	$ 7,240	$ 2,000
Statement of Retained Earnings		
Retained earnings, 1-1-X4	$15,000	$ 7,000
Net income	7,240	2,000
Dividends	(5,000)	(1,000)
Retained earnings, 12-31-X4	$17,240	$ 8,000
Balance Sheet		
Assets		
Cash	$ 4,220	$ 5,000
Inventory	10,000	5,000
Investment in Miller	15,020	
Equipment (net)	18,000	9,000
Total assets	$47,240	$19,000
Liabilities and Stockholders' Equity		
Accounts payable	$10,000	$ 5,000
Common stock	20,000	6,000
Retained earnings	17,240	8,000
Total liabilities and stockholders' equity	$47,240	$19,000

During 19X4, Johnston Company sold merchandise costing $2,000 to Miller Company for $3,000. Johnston purchased merchandise from Miller during the same period for $4,000, which included a gross profit for Miller of $2,000. The 19X4 ending inventory of Johnston and Miller consisted of 10% of the intercompany profit on transfers of merchandise. The 19X4 beginning inventory of Johnston and Miller consisted of unconfirmed gross margins of $300 and $600, respectively, on intercompany transfers of merchandise. Miller reported, for 19X3, a net income of $4,000 and dividend payments of $1,000.

REQUIRED

a) Prepare an analysis of the parent's investment account for 19X3 and 19X4, using the format shown in the chapter.

b) Prepare a consolidation worksheet as of December 31, 19X4, for Johnston and its subsidiary.

P4-10 **Consolidation Worksheet: Downstream Transfers of Inventory (Beginning and Ending), Valuation Differential** Bee Company acquired, on January 1, 19X2, 2,000 shares (80%) of the common stock of Cee Company in the open market paying $35 per share. At the date of acquisition, all the assets and liabilities of Cee were recorded at their fair value, and Cee's stockholders' equity consisted of $62,500 common stock ($25 par) and $20,000 retained earnings. It was estimated that all long-lived tangible and intangible assets of Cee had an estimated remaining life of 20 years. The financial statements of both companies as of December 31, 19X3, are presented here:

	Bee Company	Cee Company
Income Statement		
Sales	$150,000	$ 80,000
Income from subsidiary	11,200	
Cost of goods sold	(70,000)	(42,000)
Operating expenses	(35,000)	(25,000)
Net income	$ 56,200	$ 13,000
Statement of Retained Earnings		
Retained earnings, 1-1-X3	$ 95,000	$ 35,000
Net income	56,200	13,000
Dividends	(15,000)	(6,000)
Retained earnings, 12-31-X3	$136,200	$ 42,000
Balance Sheet		
Assets		
Cash	$ 52,000	$ 24,500
Accounts receivable	40,000	32,000
Inventory	50,000	18,000
Investment in Cee	84,200	
Buildings (net)	110,000	50,000
Total assets	$336,200	$124,500
Liabilities and Stockholders' Equity		
Accounts payable	$ 50,000	$ 20,000
Common stock ($25 par)	150,000	62,500
Retained earnings	136,200	42,000
Total liabilities and stockholders' equity	$336,200	$124,500

Additional information:

1. Cee acquires all its merchandise from Bee at 20% above Bee's cost.

2. Intercompany inventory transfers to Cee from Bee during 19X3 totaled $36,000.

3. The 19X3 beginning inventory of Cee included intercompany gross margin of $4,000.

4. Cee reported net income of $20,000 and dividend payments of $5,000 for 19X2.

REQUIRED

a) Prepare an analysis of the parent's investment account for 19X2 and 19X3, using the format shown in the chapter.

b) Prepare a consolidation worksheet for Bee Company and its subsidiary as of December 31, 19X3.

P4-11   **Consolidation Worksheet: Downstream and Upstream Transfers of Inventory (Beginning and Ending), Valuation Differential**   On January 1, 19X1, Company P acquired 80% of the outstanding common stock of Company S. At the date of acquisition, the common stock and retained earnings balances were $115,000 and $15,000, respectively. Company P paid $15,000 in excess of book value of the net assets of S. The excess is allocated as follows: $6,000 to building (estimated remaining life—six years) and $9,000 to equipment (estimated remaining life—nine years). During the fiscal year ended December 31, 19X1, Company S reported a net income of $30,000 and dividend payments of $10,000. Financial statements for the two companies as of December 31, 19X2, are presented here:

	Company P	Company S
Income Statement		
Sales	$300,000	$200,000
Income from subsidiary	12,720	
Cost of goods sold	(111,120)	(105,000)
Depreciation expense	(20,000)	(33,000)
Other expenses	(60,000)	(40,000)
Net income	$121,600	$ 22,000
Statement of Retained Earnings		
Retained earnings, 1-1-X2	$ 15,000	$ 35,000
Net income	121,600	22,000
Dividends	(30,000)	(2,000)
Retained earnings, 12-31-X2	$106,600	$ 55,000
Balance Sheet		
Assets		
Cash	$ 27,600	$ 38,000
Accounts receivable	20,000	46,000
Inventory	50,000	20,000
Investment in Company S	141,000	
Building (net)	25,000	20,000
Equipment (net)	75,000	60,000
Total assets	$338,600	$184,000
Liabilities and Stockholders' Equity		
Accounts payable	$ 20,000	$ 14,000
Common stock	212,000	115,000
Retained earnings	106,600	55,000
Total liabilities and stockholders' equity	$338,600	$184,000

Since the date of acquisition, both companies have been selling merchandise to the other at 20% above cost. At the end of 19X1, Company P had $8,400 and Company S had $12,000 of intercompany merchandise transfers in their inventory. During 19X2, P sold merchandise to S for $48,000 and purchased from S $24,000 of merchandise. The 19X2 ending inventory of P and S consisted of intercompany transfers of $24,000 and $16,800, respectively.

REQUIRED

Prepare a consolidation worksheet as of December 31, 19X2, for Company P and its subsidiary.

P4-12 **Consolidation Worksheet: Upstream Transfers of Inventory (Beginning and Ending); Frac-**
APPENDIX **tional Deferral Method**   On January 1, 19X2, Bentley Company purchased 90% of the common
stock of Bishop Company at book value. At the date of acquisition, the balances in Bishop's
common stock and retained earnings were $110,000 and $40,000, respectively. Bishop reported a
net income of $11,000 in 19X2 and paid no dividends.

During the year 19X3 Bentley purchased $125,000 of merchandise from Bishop. Bishop sells
merchandise to all customers at 25% above cost. Bentley's beginning and ending inventories for
19X3 contained $15,000 and $36,000, respectively, of merchandise purchased from Bishop. Following are the financial statements of Bentley and Bishop for the year ended December 31, 19X3.

	Bentley Company	Bishop Company
Income Statement		
Sales	$320,000	$120,000
Income from subsidiary	23,220	
Cost of goods sold	(200,000)	(70,000)
Operating expenses	(60,000)	(20,000)
Net income	$ 83,220	$ 30,000
Statement of Retained Earnings		
Retained earnings, 1-1-X3	$161,880	$ 51,000
Net income	83,220	30,000
Dividends	(40,000)	(10,000)
Retained earnings, 12-31-X3	$205,100	$ 71,000
Balance Sheet		
Assets		
Cash	$ 90,000	$ 60,000
Accounts receivable	78,680	85,000
Inventory	120,000	46,000
Investment in Bishop	156,420	
Total assets	$445,100	$191,000
Liabilities and Stockholders' Equity		
Accounts payable	$ 40,000	$ 10,000
Common stock	200,000	110,000
Retained earnings	205,100	71,000
Total liabilities and stockholders' equity	$445,100	$191,000

REQUIRED
Prepare a consolidation worksheet for Bentley and its subsidiary as of December 31, 19X3. The
fractional deferral method is to be used to account for deferrals of upstream gross margin on
transfers in inventory.

P4-13 **Consolidation Worksheet: Downstream and Upstream Transfers of Inventory (Beginning and**
APPENDIX **Ending), Valuation Differential; Fractional Deferral Method**   Using the same information in
Problem 4-11, complete the following requirement.

REQUIRED
Prepare a consolidation worksheet for Company P and its subsidiary as of December 31, 19X2. The
fractional method is to be used to account for deferrals of upstream gross margin on transfers in
inventory.

ISSUES IN ACCOUNTING JUDGMENT

I4-1 **Fractional versus Total Deferral** James Manufacturing is the 70%-owned subsidiary (and the only subsidiary) of Floor-Mart, Inc., a retailer of floor-covering products through a network of stores. During 19X7, James transferred merchandise to Floor-Mart at a transfer price of $1,200,000. Transferred merchandise in Floor-Mart's ending inventory had a total transfer price of $240,000, and the beginning inventory contained no transferred merchandise. The gross margin rate on these upstream transfers is 35%; thus gross margin of $84,000 (.35 × $240,000) is associated with the ending inventory of Floor-Mart. The cost to James of all transfers to Floor-Mart during 19X7 was $780,000 [$1,200,000 − (.35 × $1,200,000)].

REQUIRED

a) If Floor-Mart's objective was to maximize consolidated net income, would it use fractional deferral or total deferral? Explain, using the numbers.

b) What would be the effect on Floor-Mart's consolidated balance sheet of using the fractional deferral rather than the total deferral method.

I4-2 **Failure to Defer and Effect on Consolidated and Separate Statements** Magnum Corporation manufactures and sells personal computers. Most of the disk drives for its computers are manufactured by its 55%-owned subsidiary, Tandem Sales, Inc. Magnum uses the total deferral method in constructing its consolidated financial statements; however, through an error, Magnum's accountants and auditors failed to defer gross margin of $400,000 (revenue of $900,000 less cost of $500,000) associated with *upstream* transfers from Tandem that remained in Magnum's inventory at year-end.

REQUIRED

a) Describe the effect of this error on Magnum's consolidated financial statements for the current year. If you studied the appendix on fractional elimination, answer the following question: Would the effect have differed if the fractional deferral method had been used?

b) Describe the effect of this error on Tandem's separate financial statements for the current year.

c) Describe the long-term effect of this error on both Magnum's consolidated financial statements and Tandem's separate financial statements.

d) How might auditors detect omitted transfers?

CHAPTER

5

Intercompany Plant Asset Transfers

TRANSFERS OF LAND   257

UPSTREAM LAND TRANSFERS   257

Application of the Equity Method 257   Consolidation Worksheet Adjustments 258   Effect of Deferral on Minority Interest 259

DOWNSTREAM LAND TRANSFERS   261

Application of the Equity Method 261   Consolidation Worksheet Adjustments 262

TRANSFERS OF DEPRECIABLE ASSETS   263

UPSTREAM TRANSFERS OF DEPRECIABLE ASSETS   264

Application of the Equity Method 264   Consolidation Worksheet Adjustments 265   Minority Interest in Subsidiary Net Income 267   Minority Interest in Subsidiary Retained Earnings 267

DOWNSTREAM TRANSFERS OF DEPRECIABLE ASSETS   268

COMPREHENSIVE ILLUSTRATION   269

SUMMARY   275

As discussed in the preceding chapter, gross margin on merchandise transfers between parents and subsidiaries must be deferred and excluded from both the parent's separate net income and consolidated net income until the merchandise is sold to an unaffiliated party. The present chapter develops similar total-deferral procedures to defer gains and losses on transfers of plant assets between parents and subsidiaries. Gains and losses related on intercompany transfers of plant assets should be deferred and excluded from both the parent's net income and consolidated net income until the asset is either sold to an unaffiliated party or used to generate revenue from unaffiliated parties.[1] This chapter describes the impact of such deferred gains and losses on both the equity method and consolidation

---

[1] The deferral of gains and losses on transfers of plant assets between the parent and subsidiary—like the deferral of gross margin on transfers of merchandise between the parent and subsidiary—may be complicated by the effect of income taxes and related interperiod tax deferrals. If a selling affiliate files a separate tax return, gains and losses are taxed in the period of the intercompany transfer but included in parent-company and consolidated net incomes in later periods as the asset is used by the buying affiliate. This temporary difference gives rise to an interperiod tax deferral. On the other hand, if parent and subsidiary file a consolidated return, the gain or loss related to intercompany plant asset transfers will be taxed as the asset is used. Hence, no temporary difference arises and no interperiod tax deferral is appropriate. Throughout this book, we assume that the parent and subsidiary file consolidated tax returns unless the contrary is specifically indicated.

procedures. We begin by considering intercompany transfers of land and then turn to intercompany transfers of depreciable assets. The chapter concludes with a comprehensive example.

TRANSFERS OF LAND

When land is transferred from one affiliate to another, the selling affiliate recognizes a gain or loss equal to the difference between the amount received from the buying affiliate and the selling affiliate's book value for the transferred asset. For example, when land is transferred *upstream,* a gain or loss may be recorded by the subsidiary. The parent must exclude such gains and losses from its income-from-subsidiary account until the land is sold to an unaffiliated party. Similarly, when land is transferred *downstream,* the parent may record a gain or loss that should not be included in the parent's net income until the land is sold to an unaffiliated party. In addition, consolidated net income should defer gains and losses on both upstream and downstream land transfers until the land is sold to a party outside the consolidated entity. Let us begin with an illustration of an upstream land transfer.

Upstream Land Transfers

During 19X4 Cable, Inc., a 90%-owned subsidiary of Barnes Corporation, sells land with a cost of $12,000 to its parent for $20,000 cash, and the subsidiary records a gain of $8,000. This is the only intercompany asset transfer that bears on 19X4, and the subsidiary reports 19X4 net income of $43,000 (including the $8,000 gain). The subsidiary's retained earnings is $92,000 on January 1, 19X4, and the subsidiary pays no dividends; the parent's valuation differential is completely amortized by 19X4. The land is held by the parent until 19X7, when it is sold to an unaffiliated party for $31,000. The subsidiary reports net income of $35,000 for 19X5, $40,000 for 19X6, and $50,000 for 19X7. In 19X7, the parent records a gain of $11,000 ($31,000 − $20,000) on the land sale, the excess of the selling price over the price paid to the subsidiary. Observe that the total gain on the land to the consolidated entity is $19,000 ($31,000 − $12,000), of which $8,000 is recorded by the subsidiary in 19X4 and $11,000 is recorded by the parent in 19X7.

Application of the Equity Method

The parent's (Barnes's) calculations of income from its subsidiary (Cable) for 19X4 and 19X7 following the upstream transfer of land are shown in Exhibit 5-1 on the following page. The subsidiary's net income for 19X4 includes an $8,000 gain that must be deferred and recognized in 19X7 for purposes of applying the equity method. Accordingly, the $8,000 gain is subtracted in the parent's calculation of income from subsidiary for 19X4 and added in the calculation for 19X7. Of course, if the subsidiary had transferred the land at a *loss,* then the loss would be *added* to the subsidiary net income in 19X4 and *subtracted* in 19X7. Whether the land transfer produces a gain or a loss, the income-from-subsidiary calculations for the intervening years (19X5 and 19X6) are unaffected by the transaction.

On the basis of the calculations in Exhibit 5-1, the parent would make the following entries in the years 19X4 and 19X7 to record income from its subsidiary:

Parent's entry to record income from subsidiary:

	19X4		19X7	
Investment in Cable	31,500		52,200	
Income from subsidiary		31,500		52,200

EXHIBIT 5-1	PARENT'S CALCULATIONS OF INCOME FROM SUBSIDIARY FOLLOWING UPSTREAM LAND TRANSFER

Barnes Corporation

CALCULATION OF INCOME FROM SUBSIDIARY, CABLE, INC.

	Years Ended December 31,	
	19X4	19X7
Subsidiary net income	$43,000	$50,000
Less: Deferral of gain on upstream land transfer	(8,000)	
Add: Recognition of deferred gain on upstream land transfer		8,000
Adjusted subsidiary net income	$35,000	$58,000
Parent's ownership percentage	×.90	×.90
Income from subsidiary	$31,500	$52,200

Thus, under the equity method, the parent recognizes its share of the subsidiary's $8,000 gain but not until the transferred land is sold to an unaffiliated party, at which time, the entire gain (including both the parent's share of the $8,000 gain recorded by the subsidiary and the $11,000 gain recorded by the parent) is included in the parent's net income.[2]

Consolidation Worksheet Adjustments

The consolidated net income for 19X4 must also defer the $8,000 gain recorded by the subsidiary (Cable, Inc.). Further, consolidated assets must present the land at its original cost to the subsidiary and not at its transfer price to the parent. Accordingly, the following consolidation worksheet adjustment is made for 19X4, the year of the transfer:

Worksheet adjustment to defer gain on land transferred from subsidiary during current year:

Gain on land sale 8,000
    Land   8,000

The foregoing adjustment offsets the subsidiary's gain against the parent's land account, and thereby defers recognition of the gain and reduces the carrying amount of land to its original cost to the subsidiary. Since recognition of the gain must be deferred until the land

---

[2] While held by the parent, the land is carried on the parent's separate records at its transfer price (the purchase price paid to the subsidiary), which includes the $8,000 gain that must be deferred. One might argue that this gain should be removed from the parent's land account and recorded in a separate account to indicate that it represents unconfirmed valuation based on a transfer price established by an affiliated company. However, in the interests of maintaining a simple presentation, the remainder of this book assumes that such adjustments are not made by parents on their separate records.

is sold by the parent to an unaffiliated party, the following consolidation worksheet adjustment is required for 19X5 and 19X6 consolidated financial statements:

Worksheet adjustment to defer gain on land transferred from subsidiary in prior year:

Retained earnings, 1-1 (subsidiary) 8,000
     Land 8,000

This adjustment is required in every year (subsequent to the year of the transfer and until the land is sold) to remove from the subsidiary's retained earnings account the gain recognized in 19X4 and to reduce the carrying amount of land to its original cost.

    In 19X7, the land is sold to an unaffiliated party and the following consolidation worksheet adjustment is appropriate:

Worksheet adjustment to recognize subsidiary's gain on transferred land sold by parent during current year:

Retained earnings, 1-1 (subsidiary) 8,000
     Gain on land sale 8,000

The foregoing adjustment adds $8,000 to the $11,000 gain recorded by the parent on its separate records. As a consequence, the consolidated income statement reflects a gain of $19,000, which represents the gain to both the parent ($11,000) and the subsidiary ($8,000) on the sale of the transferred land.

Effect of Deferral on Minority Interest

The consolidation adjustments described for upstream land transfers follow the total deferral method and, therefore, defer both the parent's share and minority interest share of the $8,000 gain to the subsidiary. Accordingly, minority interest in subsidiary net income for the years 19X4 and 19X7 is computed as follows:

Calculation of Minority Interest in Subsidiary Net Income

	Year Ended December 31,	
	19X4	19X7
Subsidiary net income	$43,000	$50,000
Less: Deferral of gain on upstream land transfer	(8,000)	
Add: Recognition of deferred gain on upstream land transfer		8,000
Adjusted subsidiary net income	$35,000	$58,000
Minority interest ownership percentage	×.10	×.10
Minority interest in subsidiary net income	$ 3,500	$ 5,800

Minority interest in subsidiary retained earnings can be calculated in two ways, as shown in Exhibit 5-2 on the following page for the Barnes-Cable illustration. Recall that the balance of subsidiary retained earnings was $92,000 on January 1, 19X4, and that the balances at subsequent year-ends are larger by the amount of subsequent subsidiary net income (the subsidiary pays no dividends). Calculation I in Exhibit 5-2 adjusts minority

EXHIBIT 5-2	TWO CALCULATIONS OF MINORITY INTEREST IN RETAINED EARNINGS FOLLOWING UPSTREAM TRANSFER OF LAND

Barnes Corporation

CALCULATION OF MINORITY INTEREST IN RETAINED EARNINGS OF CABLE, INC.

	For the Years Ended December 31,			
	19X4	19X5	19X6	19X7
Calculation I				
Minority interest in subsidiary retained earnings, 1-1	$ 9,200	$ 12,700	$ 16,200	$ 20,200
Add: Minority interest in subsidiary net income (including adjustments for deferral of gain on land transfer)	3,500	3,500*	4,000†	5,800
	$ 12,700	$ 16,200	$ 20,200	$ 26,000
Less: Dividend to minority stockholders	–0–	–0–	–0–	–0–
Minority interest in subsidiary retained earnings, 12-31	$ 12,700	$ 16,200	$ 20,200	$ 26,000
Calculation II				
Subsidiary retained earnings, 1-1	$ 92,000	$135,000	$170,000	$210,000
Add: Subsidiary net income	43,000	35,000	40,000	50,000
	$135,000	$170,000	$210,000	$260,000
Less: Subsidiary dividend	–0–	–0–	–0–	–0–
Subsidiary retained earnings, 12-31	$135,000	$170,000	$210,000	$260,000
Less: Deferral of gain on upstream land transfer	(8,000)	(8,000)	(8,000)	
Adjusted subsidiary retained earnings, 12-31	$127,000	$162,000	$202,000	$260,000
Minority ownership percentage	×.10	×.10	×.10	×.10
Minority interest in subsidiary retained earnings, 12-31	$ 12,700	$ 16,200	$ 20,200	$ 26,000

* $3,500 = .10 × $35,000

† $4,000 = .10 × $40,000

interest in *beginning-of-the-year* retained earnings for minority interest in subsidiary income (as calculated previously) and dividends (if any). Calculation II adjusts *end-of-the-year* retained earnings for the amount of the deferred gain related to upstream transfers. Total-deferred consolidation procedures defer the entire $8,000 gain from the year of the land's transfer (19X4) to the year of the land's sale to unaffiliated parties (19X7). Thus, the entire gain is deferred to 19X7, and minority interest does not receive its $800 share of the gain (.10 × $8,000) until 19X7.

Although the calculation of minority interest in subsidiary net income is adjusted for subsidiary gains and losses on upstream asset transfers, no adjustment is made for downstream asset transfers. The deferred gains and losses related to downstream transfers are gains and losses of the parent in which the minority stockholders have no equity interest.

Downstream Land Transfers

When land is transferred downstream, the *parent* may record a gain or loss (equal to the difference between the amount received from the buying affiliate and the parent's book value for the transferred asset) in the year of the transfer. Such gains or losses are excluded from the parent's net income and from consolidated net income until the land is sold by the subsidiary to an unaffiliated party. Consider a parent, Jennings Corporation, that sells land during 19X3 with a cost of $36,500 to its 80%-owned subsidiary, Kendall, Inc. The subsidiary pays $39,000 cash for the land and holds the land until 19X6, when it is sold to an outsider for $40,600. This is the only intercompany asset transfer that bears on either 19X3 or 19X6, and the subsidiary reports 19X3 net income of $18,000 and 19X6 net income of $19,000. The parent's valuation differential is completely amortized. The total gain on the land to the consolidated entity is $4,100 ($40,600 − $36,500), of which $2,500 is recorded by the parent in 19X3 and $1,600 is recorded by the subsidiary in 19X6.

Application of the Equity Method

The parent's (Jennings's) calculations of income from subsidiary (Kendall) for 19X3 and 19X6 following the downstream transfer of land are shown in Exhibit 5-3. These calculations are the basis for the following entries by the parent:

Parent's entry to record income from subsidiary:

	19X3		19X6	
Investment in Kendall 11,900		17,700		
Income from subsidiary	11,900		17,700	

EXHIBIT 5-3	PARENT'S CALCULATIONS OF INCOME FROM SUBSIDIARY FOLLOWING DOWNSTREAM LAND TRANSFER

Jennings Corporation

CALCULATION OF INCOME FROM SUBSIDIARY, KENDALL, INC.

	Years Ended December 31,	
	19X3	**19X6**
Subsidiary net income	$18,000	$19,000
Parent's ownership percentage	×.80	×.80
Parent's share of subsidiary net income	$14,400	$15,200
Less: Deferral of gain on downstream land transfer	(2,500)	
Add: Recognition of deferred gain on downstream land transfer		2,500
Income from subsidiary	$11,900	$17,700

Observe that the equity method adjusts the parent's share of *subsidiary* net income for the deferred gain to the *parent*. As a result, the parent's 19X3 income statement will exhibit a $2,500 gain that is reversed by a component of income from subsidiary. The $2,500 gain is deferred until 19X6, when it is added to the parent's share of subsidiary net income for 19X6.[3]

Consolidation Worksheet Adjustments

The consolidated net income must not reflect the $2,500 gain on the land transfer until 19X6. Further, consolidated assets must present the land at its original cost to the parent, Jennings Corporation (and not at its transfer price to the subsidiary). Accordingly, the following worksheet adjustment is required in 19X3, the year of the transfer:

> *Worksheet adjustment to defer gain on land transferred from parent during current year:*
>
> Gain on land sale 2,500
>   Land 2,500

The foregoing adjustment defers the gain and reduces the carrying amount of the land to its original cost. The consolidation worksheets prepared for 19X4 and 19X5 will each require the following adjustment:

> *Worksheet adjustment to defer gain on land transferred from parent in prior year:*
>
> Investment in subsidiary 2,500
>   Land 2,500

This consolidation adjustment, made in 19X4 and again in 19X5, offsets the overvaluation of land against the investment account, which contains, as a *credit,* the deferred gain recognized by the parent on the downstream transfer. Recall that the 19X3 income from

---

[3] The method of adjusting for deferrals of downstream gains and losses is indirect in that income from the *subsidiary* is adjusted for a deferral of the *parent's* gain or loss. The direct way to defer the $2,500 gain would be to debit the gain account and credit the investment account as shown in the following entry by the parent for 19X3:

> Gain on land sale 2,500
> Investment in subsidiary 11,900
>   Income from subsidiary 14,400

Following this direct procedure, income from subsidiary ($14,400) is calculated without adjustment for downstream deferrals ($14,400 = $18,000 × .80). The debit to the investment account ($11,900) is income from subsidiary adjusted for the downstream deferral ($11,900 = $14,400 − $2,500). In 19X6, when the transferred land is sold to an unaffiliated party, the parent would credit the gain account and debit the investment account as shown in the following entry:

> Investment in subsidiary 17,700
>   Gain on land sale 2,500
>   Income from subsidiary 15,200

Although this direct adjustment procedure is appropriate for non-arm's-length transfers (like those between the parent and subsidiary), it results in the same parent-company and consolidated net incomes as the indirect method. In the interests of maintaining a simple presentation, we shall follow the indirect method throughout this book.

subsidiary (see Exhibit 5-3), which was debited to the investment account, was reduced by the $2,500 deferred gain on the downstream transfer.

In 19X6, Kendall, Inc., the subsidiary, sells the land to an unaffiliated party for $40,600, resulting in a gain to the subsidiary of $1,600. The following consolidation worksheet adjustment is required in 19X6:

Worksheet adjustment to recognize parent's gain on transferred land sold by subsidiary during current year:

Investment in subsidiary 2,500
　　Gain on land sale . . . . 　　　2,500

The foregoing adjustment adds $2,500 to the $1,600 gain recorded in 19X6 by the subsidiary on its separate records, with the result that the consolidated income statement for 19X6 exhibits a total gain of $4,100 ($2,500 + $1,600).

In summary, both net income under the equity method and consolidated net income are adjusted so that any gain or loss on the sale of land to an affiliated entity is deferred to the date on which the land is sold to an outside third party. In the intervening periods, the land is carried on the consolidated balance sheet at its original cost to the selling affiliate. The following issues section considers the effects of failing to make such deferrals.

ISSUES

Income Effects of Omitted Deferrals

Failure to defer gain or loss on parent-subsidiary transactions results in a misstatement of income in two or more periods. Failure to defer gross margin on intercompany merchandise transfers overstates income in the period of the transfer and understates income in the period of the sale to unaffiliated parties. Failure to defer gain (loss) on intercompany land transfers overstates (understates for losses) income in the period of the transfer and understates (overstates for losses) income in the period of the sale to unaffiliated parties. In both cases, the error is self-correcting in the sense that the overstatement in one period is exactly offset by the understatement in another period. In the case of merchandise, the self-correcting process is likely to be complete in two years. However, in the case of land, the self-correcting process may last the life of the enterprise.

Let us turn now to transfers of depreciable assets between affiliated companies.

TRANSFERS OF DEPRECIABLE ASSETS

The depreciation expense associated with depreciable asset transfers has a different relationship to net income than the cost of goods sold expense associated with merchandise transfers. The cost of merchandise transfers is a *product cost* that enters cost of goods sold expense when the related merchandise is sold to an unaffiliated party. Any unsold transfers from affiliates that remain in inventories of recipients form the basis for postponement of the seller's gross margin under both the equity method and consolidation procedures. In other words, all gross margin on merchandise transfers is realized for consolidation and equity-method purposes when the transferred merchandise is sold to an unaffiliated third party. In contrast, depreciation expense is a *period cost*[4] that enters the expense of the

---

[4] We assume throughout this chapter that all depreciable assets transferred between affiliates are associated with selling and administration rather than with production.

periods in which the services of the depreciable asset are consumed without regard to the specific period in which their consumption produces sales. Period costs cannot be identified with particular sales. Consequently, the *use* of inputs related to such costs, rather than the *sale* of such inputs (in the form of merchandise), must serve as the basis for recognition of the transferring affiliate's gross margin, gain or loss. Thus, when transfers create period costs, the recipient's *recording* of the expense replaces the recipient's *sale* as the event that signals the entry of the related gross margin, gain, or loss into consolidated and parent-company net income.

When depreciable assets are transferred from one affiliate to another, the selling affiliate recognizes a gain or loss equal to the difference between the amount received from the buying affiliate and the selling affiliate's book value for the transferred asset. Such gains and losses are not appropriately included in consolidated net income because the transfer does not constitute an arm's-length transaction. Similarly, the consolidated depreciation expense related to transferred assets should be based on the selling affiliate's book value and not on the transfer price paid by the buying affiliate, which differs from the book value by the amount of any gain or loss.[5] Let us illustrate by considering the treatment of an upstream transfer of a depreciable asset.

Upstream Transfers of Depreciable Assets

On January 1, 19X1, Riley Corporation, a 90%-owned subsidiary of Heath, Inc., transfers a machine with a six-year life (four of which remain) to its parent in exchange for $40,000 cash. Just prior to transfer, the subsidiary's (Riley's) records carry the machine at a cost of $54,000 less accumulated depreciation of $18,000. Upon transfer, the subsidiary recognized a gain of $4,000 [$40,000 − ($54,000 − $18,000)]. The machine has no salvage value, and straight-line depreciation is applied. Thus, the parent (Heath) will depreciate the machine at a rate of $10,000 per year ($10,000 = $40,000 ÷ 4), whereas the subsidiary had depreciated the machine at a rate of $9,000 per year ($9,000 = $54,000 ÷ 6). In this sense, the transfer creates additional depreciation of $1,000 per year ($1,000 = $10,000 − $9,000).

The subsidiary reports net income of $26,000 for 19X1, $23,000 for 19X2, $24,000 for 19X3, and $25,000 for 19X4. Assume that the machinery transfer on January 1, 19X1, is the only intercompany transaction and that the valuation differential has been completely amortized. The subsidiary's retained earnings balance on January 1, 19X1, is $140,000, and the subsidiary pays no dividends.

Application of the Equity Method

The parent's (Heath's) calculation of income from subsidiary for our illustration is shown in Exhibit 5-4, which results in the following entries for the years 19X1 through 19X4 to record income from subsidiary:

---

[5] To the extent that a loss on intercompany transfers represents book value in excess of fair value, the loss should be recognized by the selling affiliate as an impairment prior to the sale rather than being deferred and recognized over the remaining life of the asset through depreciation charges. If, after the write-down of the asset, its book value still exceeds the proceeds from its transfer, then its fair value also exceeds the proceeds and the recipient of the asset has made a "bargain purchase." In the case of downstream transfers, such a loss may benefit minority stockholders at the expense of majority stockholders; in the upstream case, such a loss may benefit majority stockholders at the expense of minority stockholders.

Parent's entries to record income from subsidiary:

	19X1	19X2	19X3	19X4
Investment in Riley	20,700	21,600	22,500	23,400
Income from subsidiary . .	20,700	21,600	22,500	23,400

The subsidiary's 19X1 net income of $26,000 includes a $4,000 gain on the transferred machine. The subsidiary's gain is deferred by a $4,000 subtraction in the calculation of income from subsidiary. The subsidiary's gain is appropriately recognized only as the parent uses the transferred machine. In essence, gains (or losses) on intercompany transfers of depreciable assets are deferred (for equity-method purposes) until the relevant asset is depreciated by the purchasing affiliate firm. As long as straight-line depreciation procedures are appropriate for the machine, it is reasonable to recognize an equal portion of the gain in each period of the remaining life of the transferred asset. Accordingly, $1,000 ($4,000 ÷ 4) is added annually in the calculation of income from subsidiary. The adjustment for the portion of the gain recognized in each year may also be calculated as the excess of depreciation based on the transfer price ($10,000 = $40,000 ÷ 4) over depreciation based on the subsidiary's book value [$9,000 = ($54,000 − $18,000) ÷ 4]. From the viewpoint of this alternative calculation, the adjustments in Exhibit 5-4 restore subsidiary income for 19X1 through 19X4 to the amounts that would have been reported if the machine had not been transferred.

Consolidation Worksheet Adjustments

Exhibit 5-5 on the following page shows three consolidation worksheet adjustments for the Heath-Riley illustration identified by the numbers (1), (2), and (3). The first adjustment is the familiar elimination of the parent's share of subsidiary net income. Under the

EXHIBIT 5-4	**PARENT'S CALCULATION OF INCOME FROM SUBSIDIARY FOLLOWING UPSTREAM TRANSFER OF DEPRECIABLE ASSET**

Heath, Inc.

CALCULATION OF INCOME FROM RILEY CORPORATION

	For the Years Ended December 31,			
	19X1	**19X2**	**19X3**	**19X4**
Subsidiary net income	$26,000	$23,000	$24,000	$25,000
Less: Deferral of gain on upstream machine transfer	(4,000)			
Add: Recognition of deferred gain on upstream machine transfer	1,000	1,000	1,000	1,000
Adjusted subsidiary net income	$23,000	$24,000	$25,000	$26,000
Parent's ownership percentage	×.90	×.90	×.90	×.90
Income from subsidiary	$20,700	$21,600	$22,500	$23,400

| EXHIBIT 5-5 | CONSOLIDATION WORKSHEET ADJUSTMENTS REQUIRED BY UPSTREAM TRANSFER OF DEPRECIABLE ASSET |

Heath, Inc.

WORKSHEET ADJUSTMENTS FOR CONSOLIDATION OF RILEY, INC.

	For the Years Ended December 31,							
	19X1		19X2		19X3		19X4	
(1) *Worksheet adjustment to reverse parent's recording of subsidiary income:*								
Income from subsidiary	20,700		21,600		22,500		23,400	
Investment in Riley		20,700		21,600		22,500		23,400
(2) *Worksheet adjustment to eliminate gain on upstream equipment transfer and to restore date-of-transfer cost and depreciation:*								
Gain on sale of machine	4,000							
Retained earnings, 1-1 (subsidiary)			4,000		4,000		4,000	
Machinery	14,000		14,000		14,000		14,000	
Accumulated depreciation		18,000		18,000		18,000		18,000
(3) *Worksheet adjustment to eliminate additional depreciation created by transfer:*								
Accumulated depreciation	1,000		2,000		3,000		4,000	
Depreciation expense		1,000		1,000		1,000		1,000
Retained earnings, 1-1 (subsidiary)				1,000		2,000		3,000

equity method, the subsidiary's gain on the transferred machine is deferred as a result of adjustments included in the calculation of income from subsidiary. By reversing the parent's equity-method recording of subsidiary income, adjustment (1) in Exhibit 5-5 removes the current year's deferral adjustments from the parent's "income from subsidiary" and "investment in subsidiary" financial statement balances. Adjustment (2) in Exhibit 5-5 removes the subsidiary's gain from the subsidiary's income or equity balances and from the parent's "machinery" and "accumulated depreciation" balances. As a result of the second adjustment, the machine is adjusted to its original cost to the subsidiary and subsidiary's date-of-transfer accumulated depreciation is restored to the accumulated depreciation. Note that the gain is removed from "gain on sale of machine," in 19X1 and from the beginning balance of retained earnings in subsequent years. Adjustment (3) in Exhibit 5-5 eliminates the additional depreciation created by the transfer and thereby recognizes a portion of the subsidiary's gain in each of the years 19X1 through 19X4.[6] The $1,000 annual reduction of the parent's depreciation expense recognizes a $1,000 gain in each year. In addition, retained earnings are increased to reflect the portion of the gain recognized in prior years, and the parent's accumulated depreciation is reduced to reflect depreciation on the basis of the subsidiary's book values.

---

[6] The second and third adjustments reinstate the very same deferral of the subsidiary's gain that was accomplished by the equity method (and reversed by the first adjustment) in a form that is consistent with the less aggregated account structure of the consolidated financial statements.

Minority Interest in Subsidiary Net Income

The consolidation adjustments described for the upstream machinery transfer follow the total deferral method, which is used throughout this book for all upstream transfers unless specified otherwise. Consequently, the adjustments defer both the parent's share and the minority interest's share of the $4,000 gain to the subsidiary. The calculation of the minority interest in subsidiary net income for our upstream machinery transfer, which is required to prepare the consolidation worksheet, is shown in Exhibit 5-6. Minority interest in subsidiary net income is based on subsidiary net income adjusted for deferrals related to upstream transfers but not downstream transfers. Adjustments for downstream transfers do not affect minority interest calculations because such adjustments are related to gains and losses of the parent in which the minority stockholders of the subsidiary have no equity interest.

Minority Interest in Subsidiary Retained Earnings

Minority interest in subsidiary retained earnings can be calculated in two ways, as demonstrated in Exhibit 5-7 for the Heath-Riley illustration. Recall that the balance of subsidiary retained earnings was $140,000 on January 1, 19X1, and that the balances at subsequent year-ends are larger by the amount of subsequent subsidiary net income (the subsidiary pays no dividends). Calculation I in Exhibit 5-7 adjusts minority interest in *beginning-of-the-year* retained earnings for the minority interest in subsidiary income (as calculated in Exhibit 5-6) and dividends (if any). Calculation II adjusts *end-of-the-year* retained earnings for the amount of deferred gain related to upstream transfers. Total-deferral consolidation procedures eliminate the entire $4,000 gain at the date of transfer and subsequently recognize the gain only as the machine is used and depreciated. Thus, the gain is recognized at a rate of $1,000 per year; and minority interest on the consolidated balance sheet includes a $100 (.10 × $1,000) interest in the gain at December 31, 19X1, a $200 (.10 × $2,000) interest at December 31, 19X2, a $300 (.10 × $3,000) interest at December 31, 19X3, and the full $400 (.10 × $4,000) interest at December 31, 19X4.

EXHIBIT 5-6	**MINORITY INTEREST IN SUBSIDIARY NET INCOME FOLLOWING UPSTREAM TRANSFER OF DEPRECIABLE ASSET**

Heath, Inc.

CALCULATION OF MINORITY INTEREST IN NET INCOME OF RILEY CORPORATION

	For the Years Ended December 31,			
	19X1	**19X2**	**19X3**	**19X4**
Subsidiary net income	$26,000	$23,000	$24,000	$25,000
Less: Deferral of gain on upstream machine transfer	(4,000)			
Add: Recognition of deferred gain on upstream machine transfer	1,000	1,000	1,000	1,000
Adjusted subsidiary net income	$23,000	$24,000	$25,000	$26,000
Minority ownership percentage	×.10	×.10	×.10	×.10
Minority interest in subsidiary income	$ 2,300	$ 2,400	$ 2,500	$ 2,600

Downstream Transfers of Depreciable Assets

When depreciable assets are transferred downstream at a gain, the parent's calculation of income from subsidiary must include adjustments that defer the *parent's* gain on the transferred asset to the periods in which the *subsidiary* uses the transferred asset. Such adjustments take the same form as the upstream adjustments in Exhibit 5-4 except that the downstream adjustments *follow* the application of the parent's ownership percentage in the calculation of income from subsidiary rather than precede it.

Downstream consolidation adjustments for depreciable asset transfers have the same general form as upstream consolidation adjustments for depreciable asset transfers except that in years subsequent to the year of sale, gains or losses are treated as adjustments to the investment in subsidiary account rather than to retained earnings. Since minority stockholders have no interest in gains on downstream transfers, no adjustments to subsidiary

EXHIBIT 5-7	TWO CALCULATIONS OF MINORITY INTEREST IN RETAINED EARNINGS FOLLOWING UPSTREAM TRANSFER OF DEPRECIABLE ASSET

Heath, Inc.

CALCULATION OF MINORITY INTEREST IN RETAINED EARNINGS OF RILEY CORPORATION

	For the Years Ended December 31,			
	19X1	**19X2**	**19X3**	**19X4**
Calculation I				
Minority interest in subsidiary retained earnings, 1-1	$ 14,000	$ 16,300	$ 18,700	$ 21,200
Add: Minority interest in subsidiary net income*	2,300	2,400	2,500	2,600
	$ 16,300	$ 18,700	$ 21,200	$ 23,800
Less: Dividend to minority stockholders	–0–	–0–	–0–	–0–
Minority interest in subsidiary retained earnings, 12-31	$ 16,300	$ 18,700	$ 21,200	$ 23,800
Calculation II				
Subsidiary retained earnings, 1-1	$140,000	$166,000	$189,000	$213,000
Add: Subsidiary net income	26,000	23,000	24,000	25,000
	$166,000	$189,000	$213,000	$238,000
Less: Subsidiary dividend	–0–	–0–	–0–	–0–
Subsidiary retained earnings, 12-31	$166,000	$189,000	$213,000	$238,000
Less: Deferral of gain on upstream machine transfer	(4,000)	(4,000)	(4,000)	(4,000)
Add: Accumulated recognition of deferred gain on upstream machine transfer	1,000	2,000	3,000	4,000
Adjusted subsidiary retained earnings, 12-31	$163,000	$187,000	$212,000	$238,000
Minority ownership percentage	×.10	×.10	×.10	×.10
Minority interest in subsidiary retained earnings, 12-31	$ 16,300	$ 18,700	$ 21,200	$ 23,800

* Includes adjustments for deferral of gain on upstream machinery transfer; see Exhibit 5-6.

income are required for such gains in the calculation of minority interest. The comprehensive illustration that follows demonstrates the equity method and consolidation procedures for both upstream and downstream transfers of depreciable assets.

Since all transfers of plant assets illustrated in this chapter are associated with selling and administration rather than with production, the cost of the assets does not enter the inventories of either party to the transfer. Further, we assume that transferred depreciable assets are subject to depreciation on the separate records of both the parent and its subsidiary and do not represent merchandise to either affiliate. The following issues section relaxes these rather restrictive assumptions.

ISSUES

Variations in Intercompany Asset Transfers

Let us consider two cases of asset transfers that are not restricted to plant assets used in selling and administrative functions.

Seller's Merchandise Subject to Depreciation by Buyer Suppose that a subsidiary manufactures loading equipment that is purchased by its parent for use in its distribution activities. The subsidiary's gross margin on the transfer must be deferred and recognized over the life of the equipment. Consolidation worksheet adjustments must combine aspects of the merchandise transfer adjustments considered in Chapter 4 and the depreciable asset adjustments described in the present chapter.

Plant Asset Transfers Used in Production Suppose that a subsidiary transfers used factory equipment to its parent. The subsidiary's gain or loss on the transaction must be deferred and applied to production cost over the life of the equipment. Thus, adjustments to depreciation will alter the parent's cost of production rather than the parent's period expense. As a result, the subsidiary's gain or loss is deferred into the periods in which the production associated with the equipment is sold. The impact of this deferral on each year's income, which is required for the parent's calculation of income from subsidiary under the equity method, must take account of changes in the buying affiliate's inventory. Of course, if such changes are small, it may be appropriate to use the adjustment to production cost as an approximation of the income effect.

COMPREHENSIVE ILLUSTRATION

Ridge, Inc. acquired a 90% interest in West Corporation on January 1, 19X3, for $200,000. At the date of acquisition, the stockholders' equity of West consisted of common stock of $150,000 and retained earnings of $50,000. Consequently, a valuation differential of $20,000 [$200,000 − (.90)($150,000 + $50,000)] is associated with the acquisition. The entire valuation differential is attributed to goodwill and is amortized over ten years at a rate of $2,000 per year ($20,000 ÷ 10).

West reported a net income in 19X3 of $25,000 and paid dividends of $4,000. Thus, the balance of West's retained earnings on December 31, 19X3, is $71,000 ($50,000 + $25,000 − $4,000). Financial statements for both companies for the fiscal year ended December 31, 19X4, the second year following acquisition, are shown in Exhibit 5-8 on the following page.

The following information describes the intercompany transactions, both upstream and downstream, that are related to 19X4:

1. West sold merchandise to its parent during 19X3 at a gross margin of $15,000. Twenty percent of the transferred merchandise was in the parent's 19X3 ending inventory. Consequently, Ridge's (the parent's) inventory at *January 1, 19X4,* contains uncon-

EXHIBIT 5-8	FINANCIAL STATEMENTS FOR COMPREHENSIVE ILLUSTRATION	

	Ridge, Inc.	West Corporation
Income Statements		
for Fiscal Year Ended December 31, 19X4		
Sales	$110,000	$ 40,000
Income from subsidiary	13,080	
Gain on land sale	1,000	
Cost of goods sold	(60,000)	(20,000)
Depreciation and amortization expense	(10,000)	(5,000)
Other expenses	(17,000)	(2,000)
Net income	$ 37,080	$ 13,000
Statements of Retained Earnings		
for Fiscal Year Ended December 31, 19X4		
Retained earnings, 1-1-X4	$119,300	$ 71,000
Net income	37,080	13,000
Dividends	(14,000)	(3,000)
Retained earnings, 12-31-X4	$142,380	$ 81,000
Balance Sheets		
at December 31, 19X4		
Assets		
Cash	$ 55,000	$ 32,000
Accounts receivable	45,000	70,000
Inventory	80,000	50,000
Investment in West	211,320	
Plant and equipment	620,000	107,000
Accumulated depreciation	(330,000)	(27,000)
Land	11,000	19,000
Total assets	$692,320	$251,000
Liabilities and Stockholders' Equity		
Accounts payable	$ 60,940	$ 20,000
Common stock	489,000	150,000
Retained earnings	142,380	81,000
Total liabilities and stockholders' equity	$692,320	$251,000

firmed *upstream* gross margin of $3,000 (.20 × $15,000). The corresponding merchandise was sold during 19X4. No intercompany merchandise transfers occurred during 19X4.

2. On January 1, 19X3, West sold equipment to Ridge (upstream) for $21,600; its estimated remaining life is eight years. On the sale date, the records of West indicated equipment cost of $40,000 and accumulated depreciation of $28,000 or a net book value of $12,000. Consequently, West recognized a gain of $9,600 ($21,600 − $12,000) in 19X3, and the upstream equipment transfer created additional depreciation of $1,200 per year ($9,600 ÷ 8).

3. In 19X4, Ridge sold land to West (downstream) at a gain of $1,000.

4. On June 30, 19X3, Ridge sold a building to its subsidiary (downstream) for $86,000. The estimated remaining life of the building was ten years. On the date of sale, the records of the parent (Ridge) indicated an original cost for the building of $300,000 and accumulated depreciation of $220,000, or a net book value of $80,000. Consequently, Ridge recognized a gain of $6,000 ($86,000 − $80,000) in 19X3, and the downstream building transfer created additional depreciation of $600 per year ($6,000 ÷ 10), or $300 (1/2 × $600) for 19X3 since the intercompany transfer took place on June 30.

5. At December 31, 19X4, Ridge owes West $16,000 on noninterest-bearing account. The amount is included in Ridge's accounts payable and West's accounts receivable.

Using this information, we can perform the calculations required for the equity method and the consolidation worksheet. The parent's calculation of income from its subsidiary for 19X4 is presented in Exhibit 5-9 and an analysis of the parent's investment account for 19X4 is presented in Exhibit 5-10. Notice that Exhibit 5-10 incorporates an additional column to reflect adjustments to provide for the deferral of the *parent's* gain on downstream asset transfers; these adjustments are also incorporated in the calculation of the parent's share of subsidiary income (see Exhibit 5-9).

Exhibit 5-11 shows the calculation of minority interest in the subsidiary at December 31, 19X4, and Exhibit 5-12 shows the consolidation worksheet adjustments required at December 31, 19X4. The completed consolidation worksheet is given in Exhibit 5-13.

EXHIBIT 5-9	PARENT'S CALCULATION OF INCOME FROM SUBSIDIARY

Ridge, Inc.

CALCULATION OF INCOME FROM WEST CORPORATION

	For the Year Ended December 31,	
	19X3	19X4
Subsidiary net income	$25,000	$13,000
Add: Deferred gross margin on upstream merchandise transfers at 1-1-X4		3,000
Less: Deferred gross margin on upstream merchandise transfers at 12-31-X3	(3,000)	
Less: Deferred gain on upstream equipment transfer	(9,600)	
Add: Recognition of deferred gain on upstream equipment transfer	1,200	1,200
Adjusted subsidiary net income	$13,600	$17,200
Parent's ownership percentage	×.90	×.90
Parent's share of adjusted subsidiary net income	$12,240	$15,480
Less: Deferred gain on downstream building transfer	(6,000)	
Add: Recognition of deferred gain on downstream building transfer	300	600
Less: Deferred gain on downstream land transfer		(1,000)
Parent's share of subsidiary net income (adjusted for both upstream and downstream transfers)	$ 6,540	$15,080
Amortization of valuation differential	(2,000)	(2,000)
Income from subsidiary	$ 4,540	$13,080

EXHIBIT 5-10

ANALYSIS OF PARENT'S INVESTMENT ACCOUNT

Ridge, Inc.

ANALYSIS OF INVESTMENT IN WEST CORPORATION
FOR THE YEARS ENDED DECEMBER 31, 19X3, AND DECEMBER 31, 19X4

		Book Value of Parent's Equity in Subsidiary		Unamortized Valuation Differential		
	Total Investment	Acquired*	Earned	Goodwill	Revaluation Increment	Adjustments to Parent's Net Income
Balance, January 1, 19X3	$200,000	$180,000	$ –0–	$20,000	$ –0–	$ –0–
Add: Income from subsidiary for 19X3 (see Exhibit 5-9)	4,540		12,240‡	(2,000)		(5,700)§
Less: Parent's share of subsidiary dividends for 19X3 (.90 × $4,000)	(3,600)		(3,600)			
Balance, December 31, 19X3	$200,940	$180,000^2†	$ 8,640^2	$18,000^2	$ –0–	$(5,700)^{9,10}
Add: Income from subsidiary for 19X4 (see Exhibit 5-9)	13,080^1		15,480	(2,000)		(400)$^\parallel$
Less: Parent's share of subsidiary dividends for 19X4 (.90 × $3,000)	(2,700)^1		(2,700)			
Balance, December 31, 19X4	$211,320	$180,000	$21,420	$16,000	$ –0–	$(6,100)

* The parent acquired 90% of the outstanding stock of the subsidiary on January 1, 19X3, for cash of $200,000; acquired equity on the date of acquisition is $180,000 including acquired equity in common stock of $135,000 (.90 × $150,000) and acquired equity in retained earnings of $45,000 (.90 − $50,000).

† The numerical superscripts in the investment analysis above identify the various components of the investment balance with the consolidation worksheet adjustments (Exhibit 5-12) that eliminate or reclassify the component.

‡ $12,240 = .90 × ($25,000 − $3,000 − $9,600 + $1,200)

§ $5,700 = (.50 × $600) − $6,000

$\parallel$ ($400) = $600 − $1,000

EXHIBIT 5-11

CALCULATION OF MINORITY INTEREST IN SUBSIDIARY

Minority interest in 19X4 subsidiary net income [.10 × $17,200 adjusted subsidiary net income (see computation in Exhibit 5-10)]	$ 1,720
Minority interest in beginning retained earnings, 1-1-X4 [.10 × ($71,000 − $3,000 − $9,600 + $1,200)]	5,960
Minority interest in common stock (.10 × $150,000)	15,000
Subtotal	$22,680
Less: Dividends from subsidiary during 19X4	(300)
Total minority interest, 12-31-X4	$22,380

EXHIBIT 5-12	CONSOLIDATION WORKSHEET ADJUSTMENTS

(1) *Reverse parent's recording of subsidiary income, and eliminate subsidiary dividend to parent for current year:*

Income from subsidiary	13,080	
Dividends.....................................		2,700
Investment in West		10,380

(2) *Eliminate and reclassify beginning-of-the-year balance of parent's investment account:*

Common stock of West	135,000	
Retained earnings of West	53,640*	
Goodwill	*18,000*	
Investment in West		206,640

(3) *Amortize valuation differential for current year:*

Depreciation and amortization expense	2,000	
Goodwill		2,000

(4) *Recognize upstream gross margin deferred from prior year:*

Retained earnings, 1-1-X4	3,000	
Cost of goods sold		3,000

(5) *Eliminate gain on upstream equipment transfer, and restore date-of-transfer cost and depreciation:*

Retained earnings, 1-1-X4	9,600	
Plant and equipment	18,400	
Accumulated depreciation.......................		28,000

(6) *Eliminate additional depreciation created by upstream equipment transfer:*

Accumulated depreciation..........................	2,400	
Depreciation and amortization expense		1,200
Retained earnings, 1-1-X4		1,200

(7) *Eliminate intercompany accounts receivable and accounts payable:*

Accounts payable	16,000	
Accounts receivable		16,000

(8) *Defer gain on downstream land transfer during current year:*

Gain on land sale	1,000	
Land..		1,000

(9) *Eliminate gain on downstream building transfer, and restore date-of-transfer cost and depreciation:*

Investment in West	6,000	
Plant and equipment	214,000	
Accumulated depreciation.......................		220,000

(10) *Eliminate additional depreciation created by downstream building transfer:*

Accumulated depreciation..........................	900	
Depreciation and amortization expense		600
Investment in West		300†

* $53,640 = .90 ($71,000 - $3,000 - $9,600 + $1,200)$
$\qquad = ($180,000 - $135,000) + $8,640$

† $300 = .50 \times 600 for one-half year.

EXHIBIT 5-13	CONSOLIDATION OF FINANCIAL STATEMENTS TWO YEARS AFTER ACQUISITION

	Separate Financial Statements		Consolidation Adjustments		Minority Interest	Consolidated Financial Statement
	Ridge	West	Dr.	Cr.		
Income Statement						
Sales	110,000	40,000				150,000
Income from subsidiary	13,080		(1) 13,080			
Gain on land sale	1,000		(8) 1,000			
Cost of goods sold	(60,000)*	(20,000)		(4) 3,000		(77,000)
Depreciation and amortization expense	(10,000)	(5,000)	(3) 2,000	(6) 1,200 (10) 600		(15,200)
Other expenses	(17,000)	(2,000)				(19,000)
Minority interest					1,720	(1,720)
Net income	37,080	13,000	16,080	4,800	1,720	37,080
Statement of Retained Earnings						
Retained earnings, 1-1-X4						
Ridge	119,300					119,300
West		71,000	(2) 53,640 (4) 3,000 (5) 9,600	(6) 1,200	5,960	
Net income	37,080	13,000	16,080	4,800	1,720	37,080
Dividends	(14,000)	(3,000)		(1) 2,700	(300)	(14,000)
Retained earnings, 12-31-X4	142,380	81,000	82,320	8,700	7,380	142,380
Balance Sheet						
Cash	55,000	32,000				87,000
Accounts receivable	45,000	70,000		(7) 16,000		99,000
Inventory	80,000	50,000				130,000
Investment in West	211,320		(9) 6,000	(1) 10,380 (2) 206,640 (10) 300		
Plant and equipment	620,000	107,000	(5) 18,400 (9) 214,000			959,400
Accumulated depreciation	(330,000)	(27,000)	(6) 2,400 (10) 900	(5) 28,000 (9) 220,000		(601,700)
Land	11,000	19,000		(8) 1,000		29,000
Goodwill			(2) 18,000	(3) 2,000		16,000
Total assets	692,320	251,000				718,700
Accounts payable	60,940	20,000	(7) 16,000			64,940
Common stock	489,000	150,000	(2) 135,000		15,000	489,000
Retained earnings	142,380	81,000	82,320	8,700	7,380	142,380
Minority interest					(22,380)	22,380
Total liabilities and stockholders' equity	692,320	251,000	493,020	493,020	–0–	718,700

* Parentheses indicate decreases.

SUMMARY   Gains and losses on plant asset transfers between parents and subsidiaries must be deferred to the subsequent period or periods in which the transferred asset is sold to an unaffiliated party or used in the generation of sales. The deferral accounting illustrated for land is applicable to other assets where cost is maintained (or is part of the accounting) by the receiving affiliate until sold. The deferral accounting illustrated for depreciable assets is applicable to other assets that are amortized or depleted. These deferrals affect both separate parent-company net income and consolidated net income over the life (or holding period) of the transferred asset. Separate parent-company income is adjusted through the parent's calculation of income from its subsidiary. Consolidated net income is adjusted through consolidation worksheet adjustments.

QUESTIONS

Q5-1   A parent company sells land to its subsidiary in 19X0 at a profit of $5,000. In 19X5, the subsidiary sells the land to an unaffiliated party at a price equal to what it paid for the land when acquired from the parent in 19X0. Should the profit on the land sale be included in the 19X0 or 19X5 consolidated income? Explain.

Q5-2   When are gains on intercompany transfers of depreciable assets realized for consolidation purposes?

Q5-3   Describe three distinct operations performed by the consolidation worksheet adjustments relating to intercompany transfers of depreciable assets.

Q5-4   As a result of the parent selling land to its subsidiary during 19X1, the following consolidation worksheet adjustment was made at the end of 19X1:

Gain on sale of land	2,000	
Land		2,000

Explain what the foregoing adjustment accomplishes. Would the consolidation worksheet adjustment be different had the subsidiary sold land to the parent?

Q5-5   How do downstream sales of land and depreciable assets affect the computation of minority interest in the subsidiary net income?

Q5-6   Explain why you agree or disagree with the following statement: Consolidated depreciation expense on intercompany transfers of depreciable assets should be based on the transfer price paid by the buying affiliate.

Q5-7   Describe the effects on the consolidated net income of failing to defer gain (loss) on intercompany land transfers.

Q5-8   Discuss what is meant by the following statement: The depreciation expense associated with depreciable asset transfers has a different relationship to net income from the cost of goods sold expense associated with merchandise transfers.

Q5-9   Discuss why you agree or disagree with the following statement: Subsidiary gains or losses on transfers of depreciable assets are treated the same way under the equity method whether the transferred assets are associated with the parent's selling and administration activities or production activities.

Q5-10   Discuss why you agree or disagree with the following statement: Downstream and upstream consolidation worksheet adjustments for depreciable asset transfers have the same general form.

EXERCISES   **E5-1**   **Multiple Choice Questions on Upstream and Downstream Transfers of Land**   Pinehurst, Inc.
acquired an 80% interest in Smallwood Company on January 1, 19X7, for an amount equal to book
value.

An intercompany transfer of land took place between the two affiliated firms in 19X7 at a profit
of $5,000. The land is held by the buying affiliate firm until 19X9, when it is sold to an unaffiliated
party for a profit of $6,000.

Smallwood reported net income for 19X7, 19X8, and 19X9 of $30,000, $40,000, and $50,000,
respectively.

REQUIRED
Part A. Assume that the 19X7 intercompany transfer of land was upstream from Smallwood to
Pinehurst.

1. The parent's income from the subsidiary for 19X7 would be
   a) $30,000   c) $20,000
   b) $24,000   d) $28,000

2. The parent's income from the subsidiary for 19X8 would be
   a) $32,000   c) $36,000
   b) $28,000   d) $40,000

3. The parent's income from the subsidiary for 19X9 would be
   a) $40,000   c) $44,800
   b) $44,000   d) $35,200

4. The consolidation worksheet adjustment required on December 31, 19X7, concerning the intercompany sale of land would be

   a) Gain on sale of land 5,000
      Land   5,000
   b) Land 5,000
      Gain on sale of land   5,000
   c) Retained earnings, 1-1-X7 5,000
      Land   5,000
   d) Investment in Smallwood 5,000
      Land   5,000

5. The consolidation worksheet adjustment on December 31, 19X8, concerning the intercompany
sale of land would include
   a) A debit to gain on sale of land for $5,000
   b) A credit to gain on sale of land for $6,000
   c) A debit to retained earnings (1-1-X8) for $5,000
   d) A debit to investment in Smallwood for $5,000

6. The 19X9 consolidated income statement would reflect a gain on sale of land in the amount of
   a) $ 6,000   c) $11,000
   b) $ 5,000   d) $ 1,000

7. Minority interest in subsidiary income for 19X7, 19X8, and 19X9 would be
   a) $6,000, $8,000, and $10,000, respectively
   b) $7,000, $9,000, and $11,200, respectively
   c) $5,000, $5,000, and $10,000, respectively
   d) $5,000, $8,000, and $11,000, respectively

Part B. Assume that the 19X7 intercompany transfer of land was downstream from Pinehurst to Smallwood.

8. The parent's income from the subsidiary for 19X7, 19X8, and 19X9 would be

    a) $19,000, $32,000, and $45,000, respectively

    b) $20,000, $32,000, and $44,000, respectively

    c) $24,000, $32,000, and $40,000, respectively

    d) $24,000, $28,000, and $44,000, respectively

9. The consolidation worksheet adjustment required on December 31, 19X8, concerning the intercompany sale of land would be

    a) Gain on sale of land 5,000

           Land 5,000

    b) Investment in Smallwood 5,000

           Land 5,000

    c) Retained earnings, 1-1-X8 5,000

           Land 5,000

    d) Land 5,000

           Gain on sale of land 5,000

10. The consolidation worksheet adjustment required on December 31, 19X9, concerning the intercompany sale of land would be

    a) Gain on sale of land 6,000

           Land 6,000

    b) Retained earnings, 1-1-X9 5,000

           Gain on sale of land 5,000

    c) Land 5,000

           Gain on sale of land 5,000

    d) Investment in Smallwood 5,000

           Gain on sale of land 5,000

11. Minority interest in subsidiary income for 19X7, 19X8, and 19X9 would be

    a) $5,000, $8,000, and $11,000, respectively

    b) $3,800, $6,400, and $9,000, respectively

    c) $4,000, $6,000, and $10,500, respectively

    d) $6,000, $8,000, and $10,000, respectively

E5-2 **Upstream Transfer of Land** On January 1, 19X6, Dugout, Inc., a 90%-owned subsidiary of Triple Play Company, sold land costing $20,000 to Triple Play for $30,000. At the end of 19X6, Dugout reported a net income of $25,000. Triple Play sold the land to an unaffiliated party on July 1, 19X8, for $35,000. During the same year Dugout reported net income of $20,000.

REQUIRED

a) Prepare the entry on Triple Play's books to record its 19X6 income from its subsidiary.

b) Prepare in journal entry form the 19X6 consolidation worksheet adjustment relating to intercompany transfer of land.

c) Prepare in journal entry form the 19X7 consolidation worksheet adjustment relating to intercompany transfer of land.

d) Prepare the entry on Triple Play's books to record its 19X8 income from its subsidiary.

e) Prepare in journal entry form the 19X8 consolidation worksheet adjustment relating to the sale of land.

E5-3 **Downstream Transfer of Land** Bixby Company sold a parcel of land on August 1, 19X1, to its 80%-owned subsidiary, Wilby Company, at a $8,000 profit. At the end of 19X1, Wilby reported a net income of $40,000. The subsidiary sold the land at a profit of $6,000 in 19X3. At the end of 19X3, Wilby reported a net income of $15,000.

REQUIRED

a) Prepare the 19X1 entry for Bixby to record its income from its subsidiary.

b) Prepare in journal entry form the 19X1 consolidation worksheet adjustment relating to the inter-company transfer of land.

c) Prepare in journal entry form the 19X2 consolidation worksheet adjustment relating to the inter-company transfer of land.

d) Prepare the 19X3 entry for Bixby to record its income from its subsidiary.

e) Prepare in journal entry form the 19X3 consolidation worksheet adjustment relating to the sale of land.

E5-4 **Downstream Transfer of Depreciable Asset** On January 1, 19X2, Dwyer Company transferred a machine with a six-year life (three of which remain) to its 75%-owned subsidiary in exchange for $51,000 cash. Just prior to the transfer, Dwyer's records carried the machine at a cost of $84,000 less accumulated depreciation of $42,000. The machine has no salvage value, and straight-line deprecia-tion is applied. The subsidiary reported net income of $32,000 for 19X2 and $28,000 for 19X3.

REQUIRED

a) Calculate Dwyer's income from subsidiary for 19X2 and 19X3.

b) Prepare in journal entry form the 19X2 and 19X3 consolidation worksheet adjustments relating to the intercompany transfer of machine.

c) Determine minority interest in the net income of subsidiary for 19X2 and 19X3.

E5-5 **Multiple Choice Questions on Upstream Transfers of Depreciable Asset** Poodle purchased equipment from its 85%-owned subsidiary, Rent-a-Pet, for $15,000 on January 1, 19X2. The equip-ment and its accumulated depreciation were carried on the books of Rent-a-Pet at $20,000 and $10,000, respectively. Poodle estimates the remaining life of the equipment to be five years, at which time no salvage value is expected to exist. Straight-line depreciation is used. Rent-a-Pet reported a net income for 19X2 of $15,000.

1. The amount of gain on the sale of equipment reported by Rent-a-Pet on its separate financial statements would be

a) $10,000	**c)** $15,000
b) $ 5,000	**d)** $20,000

2. The parent's share of the 19X2 net income of the subsidiary would be

a) $12,750	**c)** $ 9,350
b) $ 8,500	**d)** $13,600

3. Minority stockholders' interest in the 19X2 net income of the subsidiary would be

a) $2,250	**c)** $2,400
b) $1,500	**d)** $1,650

4. On the 19X2 consolidated balance sheet, the equipment cost and accumulated depreciation, respectively, would be

a) $20,000 and $12,000	**c)** $20,000 and $13,000
b) $15,000 and $ 3,000	**d)** $15,000 and $ 2,000

5. The amount of depreciation expense on the 19X2 consolidated income statement relating to this particular equipment would be

a) $2,000   c) $4,000

b) $3,000   d) $1,000

E5-6   **Upstream and Downstream Transfers of Depreciable Assets**   On January 1, 19X0, an 80%-owned subsidiary transferred equipment with a ten-year life (six of which remain) and no salvage value to its parent in exchange for $42,000 cash. At the date of transfer, the subsidiary's records carried the equipment at a cost of $60,000 less accumulated depreciation of $24,000. Straight-line depreciation is used. Upon transfer, the subsidiary recognized a gain of $6,000. The subsidiary reported for 19X0 and 19X1 net incomes of $14,000 and $16,000, respectively.

REQUIRED

a) Calculate the parent's income from the subsidiary for 19X0 and 19X1.

b) Prepare in journal entry form the 19X0 and 19X1 consolidation worksheet adjustments relating to the intercompany transfer of assets.

c) Assuming all the preceding information to be the same except that the parent sold the equipment to the subsidiary on January 1, 19X0 (and not the subsidiary to the parent), calculate the parent's income from the subsidiary for 19X0 and 19X1.

E5-7   **Upstream Transfer of Depreciable Asset**   On January 1, 19X1, Medical Leasing, a 90%-owned subsidiary of Medway, Inc., sold machinery to the parent for $20,000. At the date of the asset transfer, the records of the subsidiary showed the cost of the machinery as $27,000 and the accumulated depreciation as $9,000. The machinery is estimated to have a remaining life of four years, and straight-line depreciation is applied. Medical Leasing reported a net income of $15,000 for 19X1 and $20,000 for 19X2.

REQUIRED

a) Prepare the entries on the books of Medway to record its income from subsidiary for 19X1 and 19X2.

b) Prepare in journal entry form consolidation worksheet adjustments for 19X1 and 19X2 relating to the intercompany sale of machinery.

c) Calculate minority interest in the 19X1 and 19X2 net incomes of the subsidiary.

E5-8   **Upstream Transfer of Depreciable Asset**   True Company acquired 85% controlling interest in Temper, Inc., on January 1, 19X1, when the retained earnings of Temper was $40,000. On December 31, 19X1, Temper sold to True equipment having an estimated remaining life of ten years for $45,000. The equipment cost Temper $60,000, and accumulated depreciation was $21,000 at the date of transfer. Straight-line depreciation is used. During the years 19X1 and 19X2, Temper earned net incomes of $28,000 and $21,000, respectively, and paid dividends each year equal to 20% of net income.

REQUIRED

a) Prepare the entries on the books of True to record its income from subsidiary for 19X1 and 19X2.

b) Prepare in journal entry form consolidation worksheet adjustments for 19X1 and 19X2 relating to the intercompany sale of equipment.

c) Determine minority interest in the 19X1 and 19X2 net incomes of the subsidiary.

d) Determine the minority interest in the 19X2 and 19X3 beginning retained earnings of the subsidiary.

E5-9 **Multiple Choice Questions on Downstream Transfer of Depreciable Assets** Ginnie sold machinery to a 90%-owned subsidiary, Mae, for $25,000 on December 31, 19X1 (after adjusting entry for the current year's depreciation). At the time of the transfer, the machinery and its accumulated depreciation were carried on Ginnie's books at $45,000 and $30,000, respectively. The machinery has no salvage value and is to be depreciated using the straight-line method over a ten-year period. Mae reported net income of $28,000 for 19X1 and $22,000 for 19X2.

  1. Ginnie would report a gain on the sale of machinery on its 19X1 separate financial statements of
   a) $25,000   c) $10,000
   b) $15,000   d) $ 5,000

  2. The parent's share of the 19X1 net income of the subsidiary would be
   a) $25,200   c) $28,000
   b) $16,200   d) $15,200

  3. Minority interest in the 19X1 subsidiary net income would be
   a) $2,800   c) $1,900
   b) $1,800   d) $1,520

  4. On the consolidated balance sheet at December 31, 19X1, the machinery cost and accumulated depreciation should be
   a) $45,000 and $32,500, respectively
   b) $25,000 and $ 2,500, respectively
   c) $45,000 and $30,000, respectively
   d) $25,000 and $ 1,000, respectively

  5. The amount of depreciation expense on the 19X1 consolidated income statement related to this particular machinery would be
   a) $2,500   c) $1,000
   b) $1,500   d) $4,500

  6. The consolidation worksheet adjustment required at December 31, 19X1, concerning the intercompany sale of machinery would be
   a) Retained earnings, 1-1-X1 10,000
      Machinery 20,000
         Accumulated depreciation............................   30,000
   b) Gain on sale of machinery 10,000
      Machinery 20,000
         Accumulated depreciation............................   30,000
   c) Investment in Mae 10,000
      Machinery 25,000
         Accumulated depreciation............................   35,000
   d) Retained earnings, 1-1-X0 10,000
      Accumulated depreciation.............................. 6,000
         Machinery   16,000

  7. The parent's share of the 19X2 net income of the subsidiary would be
   a) $19,800   c) $10,800
   b) $11,800   d) $20,800

  8. Minority interest in the 19X2 subsidiary net income would be
   a) $2,300   c) $1,300
   b) $1,880   d) $2,200

9. On the consolidated balance sheet at December 31, 19X2, the machinery cost and accumulated depreciation should be

   a) $45,000 and $35,000, respectively

   b) $25,000 and $ 2,000, respectively

   c) $25,000 and $ 5,000, respectively

   d) $45,000 and $31,500, respectively

10. The amount of depreciation expense on the 19X2 consolidated income statement related to this particular machinery would be

a) $2,500	**c)** $1,000
b) $1,500	**d)** $4,500

E5-10   **Downstream Transfers of Land and Depreciable Asset**   Perry Company acquired 90% of Stempf, Inc. on January 1, 19X2, for $64,800. At the date of acquisition, Stempf's common stock and retained earnings balances were $50,000 and $20,000, respectively. Any excess cost over equity acquired is allocated to equipment, which has a remaining life of six years.

Perry sold a parcel of land to Stempf on March 1, 19X2, at a profit of $1,100. On January 1, 19X3, Perry sold equipment with a remaining life of seven years to Stempf for $18,000. At the date of sale, Perry's records indicated the equipment had a book value of $14,500 (cost—$32,000, accumulated depreciation—$17,500). Straight-line depreciation is applied.

Stempf reported net income of $23,000 for 19X2 and $28,000 for 19X3. In each of the years 19X2 and 19X3, Stempf declared and paid dividends equal to 20% of net income.

REQUIRED

a) Prepare an analysis of the parent's investment account for 19X2 and 19X3, using the format shown in the chapter.

b) Prepare in journal entry form the 19X2 and 19X3 consolidation worksheet adjustments relating to the above.

c) Determine minority interest in the net income of subsidiary for 19X2 and 19X3.

PROBLEMS   **P5-1**   **Consolidation Worksheet: Upstream Land and Equipment Transfers**   On January 1, 19X9, Second Lap, Inc., a dealer in racing car equipment, acquired a 90% interest in Hub Company for a book value of $78,300. Financial statements for the two firms as of December 31, 19X9, are as follows:

	Second Lap, Inc.	Hub Company
Income Statement		
Sales	$ 90,000	$ 60,000
Income from subsidiary	9,450	
Gain on sale of equipment		3,000
Gain on sale of land		2,000
Cost of goods sold	(55,720)	(45,000)
Depreciation and other expenses	(10,000)	(5,000)
Net income	$ 33,730	$ 15,000
Statement of Retained Earnings		
Retained earnings, 1-1-X9	$ 77,800	$ 37,000
Net income	33,730	15,000
Retained earnings, 12-31-X9	$111,530	$ 52,000
Balance Sheet		
Assets		
Cash	$ 22,000	$ 25,000
Accounts receivable	31,000	15,000
Inventory	60,000	40,000
Investment in Hub	87,750	
Equipment	80,000	40,000
Accumulated depreciation	(20,000)	(5,000)
Land	25,000	7,000
Total assets	$285,750	$122,000
Liabilities and Stockholders' Equity		
Accounts payable	$ 9,500	$ 20,000
Common stock	164,720	50,000
Retained earnings	111,530	52,000
Total liabilities and stockholders' equity	$285,750	$122,000

Additional information:

1. During 19X9 Hub sold land to Second Lap at a profit of $2,000.

2. Second Lap purchased unused equipment from Hub on January 1, 19X9, for $8,000. The equipment cost Hub $5,000 and has an estimated life of six years. Straight-line depreciation is used.

REQUIRED

Prepare a consolidation worksheet for Second Lap, Inc., and its subsidiary as of December 31, 19X9.

P5-2 **Consolidation Worksheet: Downstream Land and Equipment Transfers** Scott, Inc., acquired an 80% interest in Bolt Company on January 1, 19X7, for a book value of $48,000.

On the date of acquisition, January 1, 19X7, Scott sold equipment to Bolt for $10,000; its estimated remaining life is five years. On that date, the records of Scott indicated equipment cost of $11,000 and accumulated depreciation of $3,500. Straight-line depreciation is applied.

In 19X7, Scott sold land to the subsidiary at a profit of $1,000.

Financial statements for both companies as of December 31, 19X7, are as follows:

	Scott, Inc.	Bolt Company
Income Statement		
Sales	$ 96,830	$30,000
Income from subsidiary	3,400	
Gain on sale of equipment	2,500	
Gain on sale of land	1,000	
Cost of goods sold	(60,000)	(20,000)
Depreciation and other expenses	(10,000)	(2,000)
Net income	$ 33,730	$ 8,000
Statement of Retained Earnings		
Retained earnings, 1-1-X7	$ 77,800	$35,000
Net income	33,730	8,000
Retained earnings, 12-31-X7	$111,530	$43,000
Balance Sheet		
Assets		
Cash	$ 22,000	$ 8,000
Accounts receivable	31,000	12,000
Inventory	60,000	20,000
Investment in Bolt	51,400	
Equipment	80,000	30,000
Accumulated depreciation	(20,000)	(4,000)
Land	25,000	9,000
Total assets	$249,400	$75,000
Liabilities and Stockholders' Equity		
Accounts payable	$ 9,500	$ 7,000
Common stock	128,370	25,000
Retained earnings	111,530	43,000
Total liabilities and stockholders' equity	$249,400	$75,000

REQUIRED

Prepare a consolidation worksheet for Scott, Inc., and its subsidiary as of December 31, 19X7.

P5-3 **Consolidation Worksheet: Upstream Inventory and Land Transfers; Downstream Machinery Transfer**   Pitt Company acquired all the common stock of Hugh Company on December 31, 19X1, paying book value per share. On January 1, 19X2, Pitt sold machinery to Hugh at a $3,000 profit; an estimated three-year life was established, and straight-line depreciation is applied. Pitt's records indicate machinery cost of $7,000 and accumulated depreciation of $5,000. Hugh sells merchandise to Pitt at a markup of 5% above cost. Twenty-five percent of Pitt's 19X2 ending inventory was intercompany purchases. This represented one-half of the purchases from Hugh during the year. In 19X2, Hugh sold land to Pitt at a $2,000 profit. Financial statements for the two companies as of December 31, 19X2, are as follows:

	Pitt Company	Hugh Company
Income Statement		
Sales	$ 75,000	$25,000
Income from subsidiary	3,500	
Gain on sale of land		2,000
Gain on sale of machinery	3,000	
Cost of goods sold	(35,000)	(12,000)
Depreciation expense, machinery	(5,000)	(2,000)
Other expenses	(15,000)	(5,000)
Net income	$ 26,500	$ 8,000
Statement of Retained Earnings		
Retained earnings, 1-1-X2	$ 60,000	$20,000
Net income	26,500	8,000
Retained earnings, 12-31-X2	$ 86,500	$28,000
Balance Sheet		
Assets		
Cash	$ 22,500	$15,000
Accounts receivable	31,000	10,000
Inventory	42,000	25,000
Investment in Hugh	68,500	
Machinery	55,000	40,000
Accumulated depreciation	(15,000)	(7,000)
Land	8,000	5,000
Total assets	$212,000	$88,000
Liabilities and Stockholders' Equity		
Accounts payable	$ 35,500	$15,000
Common stock	90,000	45,000
Retained earnings	86,500	28,000
Total liabilities and stockholders' equity	$212,000	$88,000

REQUIRED

Prepare a consolidation worksheet for Pitt Company and its subsidiary as of December 31, 19X2.

P5-4   **Consolidation Worksheet: Upstream Land and Equipment Transfers**   Pledger Company purchased 90% of the outstanding common stock of Spectra Company at book value on January 1,
19X2. At the date of acquisition, the balances in Spectra's common stock and retained earnings were
$125,000 and $25,000, respectively. Spectra reported a net income of $10,000 in 19X2 and paid no
dividends. As of the end of the fiscal year December 31, 19X3, the following financial statements
are made available concerning the two companies:

	Pledger Company	Spectra Company
Income Statement		
Sales	$349,100	$121,000
Income from subsidiary	28,800	
Gain on sale of equipment		4,000
Cost of goods sold	(180,000)	(70,000)
Operating expenses	(60,000)	(20,000)
Net income	$137,900	$ 35,000
Statement of Retained Earnings		
Retained earnings, 1-1-X3	$107,200	$ 35,000
Net income	137,900	35,000
Dividends	(40,000)	(10,000)
Retained earnings, 12-31-X3	$205,100	$ 60,000
Balance Sheet		
Assets		
Cash	$100,800	$ 80,000
Inventory	120,000	35,000
Investment in Spectra	159,300	
Equipment	80,000	100,000
Accumulated depreciation	(20,000)	(25,000)
Land	15,000	10,000
Total assets	$455,100	$200,000
Liabilities and Stockholders' Equity		
Accounts payable	$ 50,000	$ 15,000
Common stock	200,000	125,000
Retained earnings	205,100	60,000
Total liabilities and stockholders' equity	$455,100	$200,000

Additional information:

1. During the year 19X2, Spectra sold a parcel of land costing $10,000 to Pledger for $15,000.

2. On January 1, 19X3, Spectra sold equipment to Pledger for $40,000. At the date of the asset
transfer, the records of the subsidiary showed the cost of the equipment as $54,000 and the accumu-
lated depreciation as $18,000. The equipment is estimated to have a remaining life of four years, and
straight-line depreciation is used.

REQUIRED
Prepare a consolidation worksheet for Pledger Company and its subsidiary as of December 31,
19X3.

P5-5   **Consolidation Worksheet: Upstream Land Transfer; Downstream Machinery Transfer; Valuation Differential**   Martin Company purchased a 90% interest in Knapp Company for $85,000 on January 1, 19X6. At the date of acquisition, Knapp's stockholders' equity consisted of $60,000 common stock and $30,000 retained earnings. The excess cost over equity acquired is allocated to an undervalued building, which has an estimated remaining life of ten years.

Martin sold machinery with a remaining life of five years to Knapp on December 31, 19X6, for $11,000. Straight-line depreciation is used. At the date of sale, Martin's records indicated the machinery had a book value of $8,000 (cost—$13,000, accumulated depreciation—$5,000). Knapp paid no dividends during 19X6 but reported $15,000 of net income.

Knapp sold Martin land in 19X7 at a profit of $2,600. The financial statements of Martin and Knapp as of December 31, 19X7, are as follows:

	Martin Company	Knapp Company
Income Statement		
Sales	$119,640	$ 62,800
Income from subsidiary	15,860	
Gain on land sale		2,600
Cost of goods sold	(43,700)	(35,400)
Depreciation expense	(13,000)	(7,000)
Other expenses	(38,800)	(3,000)
Net income	$ 40,000	$ 20,000
Statement of Retained Earnings		
Retained earnings, 1-1-X7	$ 95,000	$ 45,000
Net income	40,000	20,000
Dividends	(20,000)	(5,000)
Retained earnings, 12-31-X7	$115,000	$ 60,000
Balance Sheet		
Assets		
Cash	$ 33,540	$ 20,000
Inventory	15,000	30,000
Investment in Knapp	106,460	
Machinery	25,000	37,000
Accumulated depreciation	(5,000)	(2,000)
Buildings (net)	30,000	25,000
Land	20,000	15,000
Total assets	$225,000	$125,000
Liabilities and Stockholders' Equity		
Accounts payable	$ 10,000	$ 5,000
Common stock	100,000	60,000
Retained earnings	115,000	60,000
Total liabilities and stockholders' equity	$225,000	$125,000

REQUIRED

a) Prepare an analysis of the parent's investment account for 19X6 and 19X7, using the format shown in the chapter.

b) Prepare a consolidation worksheet for Martin and its subsidiary as of December 31, 19X7.

P5-6 **Consolidation Worksheet: Upstream Inventory, Land and Equipment Transfers; Valuation Differential** Atlantic Sound acquired a 90% interest in Pioneer on January 1, 19X1, for $147,000. At the date of acquisition, the stockholders' equity of Pioneer consisted of common stock of $100,000 and retained earnings of $50,000. Any excess cost over book value of acquired equity is due to anticipated future superior earnings of Pioneer for the next five years. Pioneer reported a net income in 19X1 of $24,000 and paid no dividends. Financial statements for both companies as of December 31, 19X2, are presented below.

	Atlantic Sound	Pioneer
Income Statement		
Sales	$180,000	$120,000
Income from subsidiary	19,740	
Gain on sale of equipment		6,000
Cost of goods sold	(120,000)	(86,000)
Depreciation and other expenses	(20,000)	(10,000)
Net income	$ 59,740	$ 30,000
Statement of Retained Earnings		
Retained earnings, 1-1-X2	$155,600	$ 74,000
Net income	59,740	30,000
Dividends	(10,000)	(5,000)
Retained earnings, 12-31-X2	$205,340	$ 99,000
Balance Sheet		
Assets		
Cash	$ 67,500	$ 45,000
Accounts receivable	88,900	30,000
Inventory	120,000	80,000
Investment in Pioneer	176,040	
Equipment	160,000	80,000
Accumulated depreciation	(40,000)	(10,000)
Land	50,000	14,000
Total assets	$622,440	$239,000
Liabilities and Stockholders' Equity		
Accounts payable	$ 17,100	$ 40,000
Common stock	400,000	100,000
Retained earnings	205,340	99,000
Total liabilities and stockholders' equity	$622,440	$239,000

Additional information:

1. During the year 19X1, Pioneer sold merchandise to the parent at a profit of $10,000. Twenty percent of the transferred merchandise was in the 19X1 ending inventory of the parent. Pioneer acquires all its merchandise from outside vendors.

2. The subsidiary sold, during 19X2, merchandise to the parent for $21,000, recognizing a profit on the transfer of $6,000. Forty percent of the merchandise remained a part of the parent's 19X2 ending inventory.

3. In 19X1, the subsidiary sold land carried at $6,000 to the parent for $10,000.

4. On January 1, 19X2, the parent acquired equipment from the subsidiary for $16,000; its estimated remaining life is six years. On the sale date, the subsidiary records indicated equipment cost of $20,000 and accumulated depreciation of $10,000. Straight-line depreciation is used.

REQUIRED

Prepare a consolidation worksheet for Atlantic Sound and its subsidiary as of December 31, 19X2.

P5-7 **Consolidation Worksheet: Downstream Inventory Transfers; Upstream Land and Equipment Transfers; Valuation Differential** The following financial statements are made available as of December 31, 19X6, for the Jennings Company and its 85%-owned subsidiary, Emroch, Inc.:

	Jennings Company	Emroch, Inc.
Income Statement		
Sales	$100,000	$80,000
Income from subsidiary	10,630	
Gain on sale of equipment		8,000
Gain on sale of land	2,000	
Cost of goods sold	(70,000)	(60,000)
Depreciation expense	(7,000)	(5,000)
Other expenses	(3,000)	(8,000)
Net income	$ 32,630	$15,000
Statement of Retained Earnings		
Retained earnings, 1-1-X6	$ 90,000	$30,000
Net income	32,630	15,000
Dividends	(30,000)	(10,000)
Retained earnings, 12-31-X6	$ 92,630	$35,000
Balance Sheet		
Assets		
Cash	$ 28,750	$10,000
Accounts receivable	25,000	15,000
Inventory	50,000	25,000
Investment in Emroch	68,880	
Equipment	100,000	35,000
Accumulated depreciation	(25,000)	(10,000)
Land	15,000	20,000
Total assets	$262,630	$95,000
Liabilities and Stockholders' Equity		
Accounts payable	$ 25,000	$10,000
Common stock	145,000	50,000
Retained earnings	92,630	35,000
Total liabilities and stockholders' equity	$262,630	$95,000

Additional information:

1. Jennings acquired 85% control of Emroch for $64,500 on January 1, 19X5. All Emroch's identifiable net assets were fairly valued at their carrying values on January 1, 19X5. Any excess cost over acquired equity paid by Jennings for its investment is attributable to goodwill and is to be amortized over ten years. At the date of acquisition, Emroch's common stock and retained earnings balances were $50,000 and $20,000, respectively.

2. In 19X5, the subsidiary sold land costing $10,000 to the parent for $15,000. In 19X6, the parent sold the land for $17,000 to an unaffiliated firm.

3. Equipment of the subsidiary, having a book value of $10,000 (cost $15,000, accumulated depreciation $5,000), was sold to the parent on January 1, 19X6, for $18,000. The estimated remaining life of the equipment is ten years, and straight-line depreciation is applied.

4. During the year 19X5 Jennings sold merchandise costing $20,000 to Emroch for $25,000. Thirty percent of the merchandise remained in Emroch's 19X5 ending inventory. Emroch discovered it could buy merchandise at a lower price from outside suppliers. Therefore, only $6,250 of merchandise was acquired from Jennings in 19X6, which included the usual 25% markup above cost. All the 19X6 intercompany purchases were in Emroch's 19X6 ending inventory.

REQUIRED

Prepare a consolidation worksheet for Jennings Company and its subsidiary as of December 31, 19X6.

P5-8 **Consolidation Worksheet: Upstream Inventory and Land Transfers; Downstream Machinery Transfer; Valuation Differential**   Beta acquired 90% of the outstanding common stock of Gamma on January 1, 19X3, for cash of $60,000. On this date, Gamma's common stock and retained earnings balances were $40,000 and $15,000, respectively. The fair values of Gamma's net assets were equal to book values except for a fully depreciated patent, which had a fair value of $4,000 and a remaining life of 9 years. Any goodwill recognized is to be amortized over 15 years.

Gamma reported a net income in 19X3 of $20,000 and paid dividends of $4,000. Financial statements for both companies as of December 31, 19X4, are presented below.

	Beta	Gamma
Income Statement		
Sales	$100,000	$ 80,000
Income from subsidiary	13,510	
Gain on sale of land		850
Cost of goods sold	(55,000)	(45,300)
Depreciation and other expenses	(30,510)	(20,550)
Net income	$ 28,000	$ 15,000
Statement of Retained Earnings		
Retained earnings, 1-1-X4	$ 75,000	$ 31,000
Net income	28,000	15,000
Dividends	(10,000)	(4,000)
Retained earnings, 12-31-X4	$ 93,000	$ 42,000
Balance Sheet		
Assets		
Cash	$ 18,937	$ 17,000
Accounts receivable	25,000	15,000
Inventory	45,000	25,000
Investment in Gamma	80,063	
Machinery	85,000	60,000
Accumulated depreciation	(40,000)	(10,000)
Land	16,000	12,000
Total assets	$230,000	$119,000
Liabilities and Stockholders' Equity		
Accounts payable	$ 17,000	$ 37,000
Common stock	120,000	40,000
Retained earnings	93,000	42,000
Total liabilities and stockholders' equity	$230,000	$119,000

Additional information:

1. On September 15, 19X4, Gamma sold land costing $750 to Beta for $1,600.

2. On January 1, 19X3, Beta sold Gamma machinery that had cost Beta $25,000. At the time of the machinery sale, accumulated depreciation was $17,000. Gamma paid $12,500 for the machinery; its estimated remaining life is three years, and straight-line depreciation is applied.

3. During 19X4, Gamma sold merchandise costing $4,000 to Beta for $5,400. The 19X4 ending inventory of Beta consisted of 20% of the 19X4 intercompany transfers of merchandise. The 19X4 beginning inventory of Beta consisted of unconfirmed gross margins of $430 in intercompany transfers of merchandise.

REQUIRED

Prepare a consolidation worksheet for Beta and its subsidiary as of December 31, 19X4.

P5-9 **Consolidation Worksheet: Upstream Inventory Transfers; Downstream Warehouse Transfer; Valuation Differential** Airco Corporation acquired all the outstanding $10 par-voting common stock of Timbers, Inc., on January 1, 19X2, in exchange for 50,000 shares of its $10 par-voting common stock. On December 31, 19X1, Airco's common stock had a closing market price of $15 per share on a national stock exchange. The acquisition was appropriately accounted for as a purchase. Both companies continued to operate as separate business entities maintaining separate accounting records with years ending December 31.

The financial statements for both companies as of December 31, 19X2, are as follows:

	Airco Corporation	Timbers, Inc.
Income Statement		
Sales	$1,900,000	$1,500,000
Income from subsidiary	132,000	
Gain on sale of warehouse	30,000	
Cost of goods sold	(1,180,000)	(870,000)
Operating expenses	(550,000)	(440,000)
Net income	$ 332,000	$ 190,000
Statement of Retained Earnings		
Retained earnings, 1-1-X2	$ 110,000	$ 156,000
Net income	332,000	190,000
Dividends		(40,000)
Retained earnings, 12-31-X2	$ 442,000	$ 306,000
Balance Sheet		
Assets		
Cash	$ 285,000	$ 150,000
Accounts receivable	430,000	350,000
Inventory	530,000	410,000
Investment in Timbers	842,000	
Land, plant, and equipment	660,000	680,000
Accumulated depreciation	(185,000)	(210,000)
Total assets	$2,562,000	$1,380,000
Liabilities and Stockholders' Equity		
Accounts payable	$ 670,000	$ 594,000
Common stock ($10 par)	1,200,000	400,000
Excess over par	250,000	80,000
Retained earnings	442,000	306,000
Total liabilities and stockholders' equity	$2,562,000	$1,380,000

Additional information:

1. At the acquisition date, the current value of Timbers' machinery exceeded its book value by $54,000. The excess will be amortized over the estimated average remaining life of six years. The fair values of all Timbers' other assets and liabilities were equal to their book values. Any goodwill resulting from the acquisition will be amortized over a 20-year period.

2. On July 1, 19X2, Airco sold a warehouse facility to Timbers for $129,000 cash. At the date of sale, Airco's book values were $33,000 for the land and $66,000 for the undepreciated cost of the building. Timbers allocated the $129,000 purchase price to the land for $43,000 and to the building for $86,000. Timbers is depreciating the building over its estimated five-year remaining useful life by the straight-line method with no salvage value.

3. During 19X2 Airco purchased merchandise from Timbers at an aggregate invoice price of $180,000, which included a 100% markup on Timbers' cost. At December 31, 19X2, Airco owed Timbers $75,000 on these purchases, and $36,000 of the merchandise purchased remained in Airco inventory.

REQUIRED
Prepare a consolidation worksheet for Airco Corporation and its subsidiary as of December 31, 19X2.

(AICPA adapted)

P5-10   **Consolidation Worksheet: Downstream Land and Equipment Transfers; Valuation Differential**   Wallace, Inc., acquired a 90% interest in Weston Company on January 1, 19X3, for $160,000. At the date of acquisition, the stockholders' equity of Weston consisted of common stock of $100,000 and retained earnings of $50,000. Any difference in investment cost and acquired equity is attributed to goodwill and is amortized over five years.

Weston reported net income in 19X3 of $23,000 and paid dividends of $2,000. Financial statements for both companies for the fiscal year ended December 31, 19X4, are as follows:

	Wallace, Inc.	Weston Company
Income Statement		
Sales	$115,000	$ 60,000
Income from subsidiary	17,200	
Gain on sale of land	4,000	
Cost of goods sold	(60,000)	(20,000)
Depreciation and amortization expense	(15,000)	(7,000)
Other expenses	(19,000)	(5,000)
Net income	$ 42,200	$ 28,000
Statement of Retained Earnings		
Retained earnings, 1-1-X4	$120,000	$ 71,000
Net income	42,200	28,000
Dividends	(10,000)	(5,000)
Retained earnings, 12-31-X4	$152,200	$ 94,000
Balance Sheet		
Assets		
Cash	$ 50,000	$ 30,000
Accounts receivable	40,000	60,000
Inventory	80,000	40,000
Investment in Weston	179,600	
Plant and equipment	100,000	97,000
Accumulated depreciation	(30,000)	(7,000)
Land	10,000	14,000
Total assets	$429,600	$234,000
Liabilities and Stockholders' Equity		
Accounts payable	$ 45,000	$ 40,000
Common stock	232,400	100,000
Retained earnings	152,200	94,000
Total liabilities and stockholders' equity	$429,600	$234,000

Additional information:

1. In 19X4, Wallace sold land to its subsidiary at a gain of $4,000.

2. On January 1, 19X3, Wallace sold equipment to its subsidiary for $20,000; its estimated remaining life is eight years. Straight-line depreciation is used. On the sale date, the records of Wallace indicated equipment cost of $30,000 and accumulated depreciation of $18,000.

REQUIRED

Prepare a consolidation worksheet for Wallace, Inc., and its subsidiary as of December 31, 19X4.

P5-11   Consolidation Worksheet: Upstream Inventory and Equipment Transfers; Downstream Inventory and Land Transfers; Valuation Differential   On January 1, 19X1, Colling acquired 95% of the outstanding common stock of Wood for cash of $120,000. In addition, out-of-pocket costs paid by Colling for accounting and legal fees relating to the business combination totaled $2,500. At the time of the purchase, Wood's common stock and retained earnings balances were $80,000 and $30,000, respectively. The fair value of Wood's assets was equal to book value except for the following:

	Book Value	Fair Value	Estimated Remaining Life (years)
Equipment	$20,000	$28,000	10
Land	8,000	10,000	

Any goodwill is to be amortized over 25 years. Wood reported a net income in 19X1 of $28,000 and paid dividends of $3,000. Financial statements for both companies as of December 31, 19X2, are presented below.

	Colling	Wood
Income Statement		
Sales	$200,000	$150,000
Income from subsidiary	17,210	
Gain on sale of equipment		5,000
Cost of goods sold	(110,000)	(90,000)
Depreciation and other expenses	(60,000)	(40,000)
Net income	$ 47,210	$25,000
Statement of Retained Earnings		
Retained earnings, 1-1-X2	$150,790	$ 55,000
Net income	47,210	25,000
Dividends	(12,000)	(7,000)
Retained earnings, 12-31-X2	$186,000	$ 73,000
Balance Sheet		
Assets		
Cash	$ 63,650	$ 34,000
Accounts receivable	80,000	30,000
Inventory	136,080	50,000
Investment in Wood	152,270	
Equipment	120,000	80,000
Accumulated depreciation	(50,000)	(20,000)
Land	40,000	24,000
Total assets	$542,000	$198,000
Liabilities and Stockholders' Equity		
Accounts payable	$ 31,000	$ 45,000
Common stock	325,000	80,000
Retained earnings	186,000	73,000
Total liabilities and stockholders' equity	$542,000	$198,000

Additional information:

1. On August 1, 19X1, Colling sold land costing $1,700 to Wood for $3,200.

2. On January 1, 19X2, Wood sold Colling equipment that had cost Wood $50,000. At the time of the equipment sale, accumulated depreciation was $30,000. Colling paid $25,000 for the equipment; its estimated remaining life is five years (straight-line depreciation used).

3. The two companies sell their merchandise to each other at a price 25% above cost. During the current 19X2 fiscal year, Colling sold Wood merchandise at a selling price of $40,000 and Wood sold Colling merchandise at a price of $60,000. At year-end, 10% of the intercompany purchases made by Colling are unpaid and 15% of the intercompany purchases made by Wood are unpaid. The amount of intercompany profit in the 1-1-X2 and 12-31-X2 inventory of each firm is as follows:

Date	Intercompany Profit in Colling's Inventory	Intercompany Profit in Wood's Inventory
1-1-X2	$1,200	$ 800
12-31-X2	2,400	1,300

REQUIRED

Prepare a consolidation worksheet for Colling and its subsidiary as of December 31, 19X2.

P5-12 **Consolidation Worksheet: Upstream and Downstream Land and Equipment Transfers; Valuation Differential** Webster Company acquired a 90% interest in Arnold Company on January 1, 19X3, for $15,000. At the date of acquisition, the stockholders' equity of Arnold consisted of common stock of $8,000 and retained earnings of $4,000. Any valuation differential is attributed to goodwill and is amortized over seven years.

Arnold reported net income in 19X3 of $7,000 and paid dividends of $1,000. Financial statements for both companies for the fiscal year ended December 31, 19X4, are as follows:

	Webster Company	Arnold Company
Income Statement		
Sales	$40,000	$25,000
Income from subsidiary	3,890	
Gain on sale of equipment		500
Gain on sale of land	700	
Cost of goods sold	(22,000)	(15,000)
Depreciation and amortization expense	(4,000)	(2,000)
Other expenses	(3,590)	(3,500)
Net income	$15,000	$ 5,000
Statement of Retained Earnings		
Retained earnings, 1-1-X4	$20,000	$10,000
Net income	15,000	5,000
Dividends	(7,000)	(2,000)
Retained earnings, 12-31-X4	$28,000	$13,000
Balance Sheet		
Assets		
Cash	$ 3,500	$ 6,000
Accounts receivable	9,000	4,000
Inventory	12,000	8,000
Investment in Arnold	19,950	
Equipment	25,000	11,000
Accumulated depreciation	(5,000)	(3,000)
Land	6,000	2,000
Total assets	$70,450	$28,000
Liabilities and Stockholders' Equity		
Accounts payable	$10,450	$ 7,000
Common stock	32,000	8,000
Retained earnings	28,000	13,000
Total liabilities and stockholders' equity	$70,450	$28,000

Additional information:

1. In 19X3, Arnold sold land costing $2,000 to its parent for $2,600. The parent sold the land to an unaffiliated party in 19X4 for $3,000.

2. On January 1, 19X3, Webster sold equipment to its subsidiary for $6,000; its estimated remaining life is eight years. On the sale date, the records of Webster indicated equipment cost of $5,400 and accumulated depreciation of $1,000. Straight-line depreciation is used.

3. Webster sold land to its subsidiary in 19X4 at a gain of $300.

4. On December 31, 19X4, Arnold sold equipment to its parent for $3,500. On this date, Arnold's records indicated equipment cost of $9,000 and accumulated depreciation of $6,000. The equipment is estimated to have a remaining life of five years, and straight-line depreciation is applied.

REQUIRED

Prepare a consolidation worksheet for Webster Company and its subsidiary as of December 31, 19X4.

P5-13 **Consolidation Worksheet: Upstream and Downstream Transfers of Inventory, Land, and Equipment; Valuation Differential** Prizm acquired 85% of the outstanding common stock of Saturn on January 1, 19X1, for cash of $135,715. On this date, Saturn's common stock and retained earnings balances were $100,000 and $30,000, respectively. The fair values of Saturn's net assets were equal to book values except for a patent, which had a book value of $6,300, a fair value of $4,200, and a remaining life of 7 years. Any goodwill recognized is to be amortized over 12 years. Financial statements for both companies as of December 31, 19X4, are presented below.

	Prizm	Saturn
Income Statement		
Sales	$218,470	$160,000
Income from subsidiary	18,220	
Gain on sale of land	700	
Loss on sale of equipment		(2,500)
Cost of goods sold	(105,000)	(92,000)
Depreciation and other expenses	(65,000)	(44,500)
Net income	$ 67,390	$ 21,000
Statement of Retained Earnings		
Retained earnings, 1-1-X4	$140,610	$ 70,000
Net income	67,390	21,000
Dividends	(15,000)	(9,000)
Retained earnings, 12-31-X4	$193,000	$ 82,000
Balance Sheet		
Assets		
Cash	$ 25,575	$ 22,400
Accounts receivable	71,800	25,000
Inventory	104,000	80,000
Investment in Saturn	159,625	
Equipment	190,000	115,000
Accumulated depreciation	(50,000)	(30,000)
Land	49,000	34,000
Patent		3,600
Total assets	$550,000	$250,000
Liabilities and Stockholders' Equity		
Accounts payable	$ 35,000	$ 68,000
Common stock	322,000	100,000
Retained earnings	193,000	82,000
Total liabilities and stockholders' equity	$550,000	$250,000

Additional information:

1. During 19X4, Saturn sold merchandise costing $28,000 to Prizm for $34,000. The 19X4 ending inventory of Prizm consisted of 30% of the 19X4 intercompany transfers of merchandise. The 19X4 beginning inventory of Prizm consisted of unconfirmed gross margins of $2,700 in intercompany transfers of merchandise.

2. During the year 19X4 Saturn purchased $60,000 of merchandise from Prizm. Prizm sells merchandise to all customers at 25% above cost. Saturn's beginning and ending inventories for 19X4 contained $12,000 and $19,000, respectively, of merchandise purchased from Prizm.

3. On June 1, 19X2, Saturn sold land costing $4,200 to Prizm for $3,000.

4. On November 20, 19X4, Prizm sold land costing $1,700 to Saturn for $2,400.

5. On July 1, 19X2, Prizm sold Saturn equipment that had cost Prizm $30,000. At the time of the equipment sale, accumulated depreciation was $17,000. Saturn paid $27,000 for the equipment; its estimated remaining life is seven years. Straight-line depreciation is used.

6. On January 1, 19X4, Saturn sold Prizm equipment that had cost Saturn $70,000. At the time of the equipment sale, accumulated depreciation was $35,000. Prizm paid $32,500 for the equipment; its estimated remaining life is five years. Straight-line depreciation is used.

REQUIRED
Prepare a consolidation worksheet for Prizm and its subsidiary as of December 31, 19X4.

ISSUES IN ACCOUNTING JUDGMENT

I5-1 **Failure to Defer Gain on Intercompany Asset Transfer** FlyBy Aviation manufactures and sells custom-made propeller-type airplanes. Most of the components are made by independent suppliers; however, seats and other internal furnishings are made by Plush Fittings, Inc., a 70%-owned subsidiary. On January 1, 19X4, FlyBy sells a piece of specialized equipment to Plush Fittings for $45,000. The equipment has a book value to FlyBy of $30,000 and a remaining life of six years, at which time it will have no salvage value. Through an error, FlyBy's accountants and auditors failed to make equity-method and consolidation adjustments for the transfer, which was recorded as a sale to outside parties with recognition of a $15,000 gain.

REQUIRED
a) Describe the effect of this error on FlyBy's consolidated financial statements for 19X4.

b) Describe the long-term effect of this error on FlyBy's consolidated financial statements.

c) How might auditors detect improperly recorded transfers?

I5-2 **Losses on Intercompany Asset Transfers** On January 1, 19X2, Emerson Corporation sells production equipment to Johnson Manufacturing, an 80%-owned subsidiary of Emerson, for cash in the amount of its fair value, $500,000. The equipment has a book value to Emerson of $640,000 and a remaining life of 5 years, at which time it will have no salvage value.

REQUIRED
a) What effect will the loss have on consolidated net income?

b) What effect will the loss have on the subsidiary's separate net income?

c) How might majority stockholders view the transfer if the fair value of the equipment had exceeded $500,000, the amount paid by the subsidiary?

Intercompany Debt Transactions

CREATION OF NEW INTERCOMPANY DEBT **301**

A PARENT LENDS TO ITS SUBSIDIARY **301**

EQUITY METHOD FOR NEW INTERCOMPANY DEBT **302**

Income from Subsidiary 302 Parent's Separate-Company Income Statement 303

CONSOLIDATION PROCEDURES FOR NEW INTERCOMPANY DEBT **304**

Elimination of Intercompany Debt and Interest 306 Consolidated Net Income 306 Minority Interest 307

ACQUISITION OF OUTSTANDING DEBT **307**

GAINS AND LOSSES **307**

ATTRIBUTION OF GAIN OR LOSS **308**

ACQUISITION OF PARENT'S DEBT BY SUBSIDIARY **309**

Equity Method for Acquisition of Parent's Debt by Subsidiary 311 Consolidation Procedures for Acquisition of Parent's Debt by Subsidiary 312 Effect of Consolidation Adjustments on Separate-Company Balances 313

ACQUISITION OF SUBSIDIARY'S DEBT BY PARENT **314**

Equity Method for Acquisition of Subsidiary's Debt by Parent 317 Consolidation Procedures for Acquisition of Subsidiary's Debt by Parent 318 Effect of Consolidation Adjustments on Separate-Company Balances 320

SUMMARY **321**

APPENDIX A: THE FACE-VALUE METHOD FOR GAINS AND LOSSES ON INTERCOMPANY DEBT **323**

APPENDIX B: DISCOUNTING AND INTERCOMPANY NOTES **328**

Intercompany *asset* transfers, the subject of the preceding two chapters, are transacted by two affiliated companies; unaffiliated parties are not involved in intercompany asset transfers. In contrast, transactions in intercompany *debt* may or may not involve unaffiliated parties. When a parent acquires its subsidiary's outstanding bonds on the open market or when a subsidiary acquires its parent's outstanding bonds on the open market, the investing affiliate (the parent or subsidiary) acquires the bonds from an outside (unaffiliated) party. Of course, a parent or subsidiary may acquire newly issued bonds from an affiliate, in which case the transacting parties *are* affiliated.

This chapter describes the equity-method and consolidation procedures for acquisition of an affiliated company's debt whether that debt is newly issued or outstanding. The chapter begins by discussing the purchase of new debt from an affiliated company. Accounting for such transactions is relatively straightforward and lays the groundwork for the somewhat more complex accounting required by purchases of an affiliate's outstanding debt on the open market from unaffiliated parties, which is discussed later in the chapter.

CREATION OF NEW INTERCOMPANY DEBT

When a parent transfers funds to a subsidiary in exchange for a note, the parent establishes an asset (note receivable from subsidiary) and the subsidiary establishes an equal liability (note payable to parent). As interest accrues, the parent records interest revenue and the subsidiary records an equal amount of interest expense. Similarly, when a subsidiary transfers funds to a parent in exchange for a note, the subsidiary establishes the note receivable and interest revenue accounts and the parent establishes the note payable and interest expense accounts, but corresponding balances are still equal in amount. Although the creation of new intercompany debt is merely an internal cash transfer whose effects must be eliminated from the consolidated financial statements, such intercompany debt may benefit the consolidated entity as the following issues section illustrates.

ISSUES

Motivation for Creation of New Intercompany Debt

Home Burger Corporation is a recently acquired subsidiary of Fast Franchise, Inc., which holds a controlling interest in several fast-food companies. Home Burger plans to introduce a "salad bar" into its establishments; the addition to the menu will require an outlay for development and advertising activities, which Home Burger expects to recover through additional revenues within a year or so. Banks, tending to view Home Burger as somewhat risky, charge the corporation 18% on short-term loans. Banks view Fast Franchise, a larger and more diversified corporation, as somewhat less risky and charge the corporation only 15% on such loans. Consequently, Home Burger prevails upon Fast Franchise to increase its short-term debt by borrowing the required amount from the bank and lending that amount to Home Burger at 15.5%. By assuming the risk of its subsidiary's short-term debt, the parent makes the consolidated entity better off.

Let us illustrate the accounting for such intercompany debt by reference to an example.

A Parent Lends to Its Subsidiary

Consider a case in which a parent lends cash to its newly acquired subsidiary. On January 1, 19X1, Jordan Corporation acquires 90% of the outstanding voting stock of Harris, Inc., by paying $450,000 cash, which equals the book value of stock acquired. The subsidiary's balances of common stock and retained earnings on January 1, 19X1, were $400,000 and $100,000, respectively. On the date of acquisition, the parent lends $100,000 to its newly acquired subsidiary in exchange for a three-year note (payable on December 31, 19X3) that requires annual interest payments at a rate of 7% due on December 31. Assume that the parent's loan to its subsidiary represents the only intercompany transaction during the three years considered. The following T-accounts show the related note payable and note receivable accounts for the three-year term of the note.[1]

---

[1] Ordinarily, interest and principal are recorded in separate accounts. However, for purposes of emphasizing the total impact of the intercompany debt and its reciprocal character, we have recorded interest and principal in a single account.

Note Payable (Subsidiary's Account)

		Balance 1-1-X1	100,000
Payment 12-31-X1	7,000	19X1 interest	7,000
		Balance 12-31-X1	100,000
Payment 12-31-X2	7,000	19X2 interest	7,000
		Balance 12-31-X2	100,000
Payment 12-31-X3	107,000	19X3 interest	7,000
		Balance 12-31-X3	–0–

Note Receivable (Parent's Account)

Balance 1-1-X1	100,000		
19X1 interest	7,000	Receipt 12-31-X1	7,000
Balance 12-31-X1	100,000		
19X2 interest	7,000	Receipt 12-31-X2	7,000
Balance 12-31-X2	100,000		
19X3 interest	7,000	Receipt 12-31-X3	107,000
Balance 12-31-X3	–0–		

Observe that the two accounts record equal amounts but on different sides of the account. For example, the first year's interest is recorded as a credit to notes payable (with an equal debit to interest expense) on the subsidiary's records and as a debit to notes receivable (with an equal credit to interest revenue) on the parent's records. Consequently, both accounts exhibit the same numerical balance at each year-end but on opposite sides of their respective accounts. All corresponding borrower and lender accounts exhibit a similar reciprocity when debt arises from fund transfers between the parent and its subsidiary.

Loans by a subsidiary to its parent also exhibit this reciprocal relationship except that the related note payable account is part of the parent's records and the related note receivable account is part of the subsidiary's records.

Additional information from the separate-company income statements of Jordan and Harris is presented in Exhibit 6-1. Observe that intercompany interest revenue is included in the revenues of the parent and intercompany interest expense is included in the expenses of the subsidiary in each of the three years.

Equity Method for New Intercompany Debt

The parent's calculations under the equity method are unaffected by intercompany debt arising from transfers of funds *between* the parent and its subsidiary, because the parent's share of subsidiary income offsets the loan interest recorded separately by the parent, leaving only the portion related to minority interest. Let us illustrate by reference to the Jordan and Harris example.

Income from Subsidiary

Jordan Corporation (the parent) calculates income from the subsidiary as follows:

Parent's Calculation of Income from Subsidiary

	For the Years Ended December 31,		
	19X1	19X2	19X3
Subsidiary net income	$38,000	$44,000	$48,000
Parent's ownership percentage	×.90	×.90	×.90
Income from subsidiary	$34,200	$39,600	$43,200

Observe that the parent's calculation does not adjust subsidiary net income for the effects of the intercompany debt. In each year, subsidiary net income includes $7,000 for intercompany interest expense. Accordingly, the parent's income from the subsidiary includes an intercompany interest expense of $6,300 in each year ($7,000 × .90).

In the case of loans by a subsidiary to its parent, the parent's income from the subsidiary includes intercompany interest revenue, but still no adjustment is required.

Parent's Separate-Company Income Statement

The parent's separate-company income statement, which is shown in Exhibit 6-1, includes income from the subsidiary, as calculated in the preceding paragraph. Interest on the intercompany debt is represented in two places on the parent's income statement—as interest revenue of $7,000 and as interest expense of $6,300 ($7,000 × .90) included in the parent's income from the subsidiary. The net effect of the intercompany debt on the parent's net income is the $700 excess of interest revenue over interest expense. In other words, the net effect on the parent's net income is the $700 portion of the parent's interest *revenue* attributed to minority interest in the subsidiary. Of course, when the parent is the borrower rather than the lender of intercompany funds, the net effect on the parent's net

---

EXHIBIT 6-1	**SEPARATE-COMPANY INCOME STATEMENTS FOLLOWING LOAN BY PARENT TO ITS SUBSIDIARY**

	For the Years Ended December 31,		
	19X1	19X2	19X3
Income Statements of Parent (Jordan)			
Sales	$290,000	$310,000	$360,000
Income from subsidiary	34,200	39,600	43,200
Interest revenue (received from subsidiary)	7,000	7,000	7,000
Operating expenses	(115,000)	(135,000)	(150,000)
Net income	$216,200	$221,600	$260,200
Income Statements of Subsidiary (Harris)			
Sales	$ 80,000	$100,000	$120,000
Operating expenses	(35,000)	(49,000)	(65,000)
Interest expense (paid to parent)	(7,000)	(7,000)	(7,000)
Net income	$ 38,000	$ 44,000	$ 48,000

income is the portion of the parent's interest *expense* that is attributable to minority interest in the subsidiary.

In summary, when the parent is the lender, the equity method automatically eliminates (without any adjustments to subsidiary net income) all the parent's intercompany interest *revenue* except the portion associated with minority interest in the borrowing subsidiary. Similarly, when the subsidiary is the lender, the equity method automatically eliminates all the parent's intercompany interest *expense* except the portion associated with minority interest in the lending subsidiary. No special adjustments to the parent's calculation of income from its subsidiary are required to effect the appropriate elimination.

Consolidation Procedures for New Intercompany Debt

Although equity-method calculations can ignore new intercompany debt, consolidation procedures *cannot* ignore it. In every year, consolidation worksheet adjustments must eliminate reciprocal asset and liability balances as well as reciprocal interest revenue and interest expense balances. Consider our illustration in which the parent, Jordan Corporation, lent $100,000 to Harris, Inc., its 90%-owned subsidiary. The consolidation adjustments for each of the three years are shown in Exhibit 6-2. In addition, the consolidation worksheet for 19X2 is given in Exhibit 6-3. Since the consolidation worksheets for 19X1 and 19X3 are similar to the one for 19X2, they are not shown.

The first worksheet adjustment in Exhibit 6-2 reverses the parent's recording of subsidiary income in each year. The second adjustment in Exhibit 6-2 eliminates and reclassifies the beginning-of-the-year balance of the parent's investment account for each

EXHIBIT 6-2	CONSOLIDATION WORKSHEET ADJUSTMENTS FOLLOWING LOAN BY PARENT TO ITS SUBSIDIARY

Jordan Corporation

WORKSHEET ADJUSTMENTS FOR CONSOLIDATION OF HARRIS, INC.
FOR THE YEARS ENDED DECEMBER 31, 19X1, DECEMBER 31, 19X2, AND DECEMBER 31, 19X3

	19X1		19X2		19X3	
(1) *Reverse parent's recording of subsidiary income for current year:*						
Income from subsidiary	34,200		39,600		43,200	
Investment in Harris		34,200		39,600		43,200
(2) *Eliminate and reclassify beginning-of-the-year balance of parent's investment account:*						
Common stock of Harris	360,000		360,000		360,000	
Retained earnings of Harris, 1-1	90,000		124,200		163,800	
Investment in Harris		450,000		484,200		523,800
(3) *Eliminate intercompany debt and interest:*						
Notes payable	100,000		100,000		–0–	
Interest revenue	7,000		7,000		7,000	
Notes receivable		100,000		100,000		–0–
Interest expense		7,000		7,000		7,000

EXHIBIT 6-3	19X2 CONSOLIDATION WORKSHEET FOR JORDAN-HARRIS ILLUSTRATION: 19X1 LOAN BY PARENT TO ITS SUBSIDIARY

	Separate Financial Statements		Consolidation Adjustments		Minority Interest	Consolidated Financial Statements
	Jordan	Harris	Dr.	Cr.		
Income Statement						
Revenue	310,000	100,000				410,000
Interest revenue	7,000		(3) 7,000			
Income from subsidiary	39,600		(1) 39,600			
Expense	(135,000)*	(49,000)				(184,000)
Interest expense		(7,000)		(3) 7,000		
Minority interest ($44,000 × .10)					4,400	(4,400)
Net income	221,600	44,000	46,600	7,000	4,400	221,600
Retained Earnings Statement						
Retained earnings, 1-1-X2:						
Jordan	416,200					416,200
Harris		138,000	(2) 124,200		13,800	
Net income	221,600	44,000	46,600	7,000	4,400	221,600
Retained earnings, 12-31-X2	637,800	182,000	170,800	7,000	18,200	637,800
Balance Sheet						
Current assets	106,000	86,500				192,500
Investment in Harris	523,800			(1) 39,600		–0–
				(2) 484,200		
Notes receivable	100,000			(3) 100,000		–0–
Plant and equipment (net)	700,000	619,000				1,319,000
Total assets	1,429,800	705,500				1,511,500
Current liabilities	27,000	4,500				31,500
Notes payable		100,000	(3) 100,000			–0–
Long-term liabilities	290,000	19,000				309,000
Common stock						
Jordan	475,000					475,000
Harris		400,000	(2) 360,000		40,000	–0–
Retained earnings	637,800	182,000	170,800	7,000	18,200	637,800
Minority interest					(58,200)	58,200
Total liabilities and stockholders' equity	1,429,800	705,500	630,800	630,800	–0–	1,511,500

* Parentheses indicate decreases.

year. Since no dividends are paid by the subsidiary, the annual increase in the amount eliminated from retained earnings equals the subsidiary income recognized by the parent in the previous year. These adjustments have essentially the same form as the corresponding adjustments in earlier chapters. The third adjustment, which represents a new form, is explained in the following section.

Elimination of Intercompany Debt and Interest

The third adjustment in Exhibit 6-2 eliminates all balances related to intercompany debt and interest from the consolidated financial statements. The 19X2 worksheet (see Exhibit 6-3) shows that this adjustment removes all traces of the intercompany debt from consolidated assets and liabilities[2] and from consolidated income. In the last year, 19X3, no adjustment to notes payable and notes receivable accounts is required because the entire loan is repaid on December 31, 19X3.

Consolidated Net Income

The worksheet adjustments presented in Exhibit 6-2 lead to the following summary statements of consolidated net income:

Statements of Consolidated Net Income

	For the Years Ended December 31,		
	19X1	19X2	19X3
Revenue	$370,000	$410,000	$480,000
Expenses	150,000	184,000	215,000
	$220,000	$226,000	$265,000
Minority interest	(3,800)	(4,400)	(4,800)
Consolidated net income	$216,200	$221,600	$260,200

Observe that consolidated net income equals the parent's separate-company net income in every year as shown in Exhibit 6-1. After the worksheet adjustments have been made, consolidated revenues and expenses consist of the revenues and expenses exclusive of intercompany elements. For example, consolidated revenue for 19X2 is the sum of the parent's sales revenue and the subsidiary's sales revenue, which excludes the intercompany interest revenue.

---

[2] Since the initial loan balance equals the loan balance at the end of every year except the last, the third adjustment also eliminates *year-end* note balances for every year except the last. Since intercompany interest is paid at each year-end, no interest is accrued on year-end statements. If interest were accrued on year-end statements, then the following additional worksheet adjustment is required to eliminate the reciprocal accrued balances:

Worksheet Adjustment to Eliminate Accrued Intercompany Interest for Current Year
Interest payable..XX
    Interest receivable...   XX

When the debt arises from an intercompany fund transfer, the parent and its subsidiary accrue equal amounts of interest. When interest is accrued in the loan accounts rather than in separate accrued interest accounts, then accrued interest must be eliminated from the loan accounts. Accrued interest on intercompany debt is assumed to be recorded in separate accrued interest accounts unless otherwise indicated.

Minority Interest

Minority interest in each year's subsidiary net income is simply the minority ownership percentage multiplied by the subsidiary net income for the year. Accordingly, minority interest includes the minority's share of intercompany interest in each year. In our example, the minority interest includes the intercompany interest expense of $700 (.10 × $7,000) in each of the three years.

Although the foregoing discussion of newly created intercompany debt is illustrated by reference to notes, the same basic principles can be applied to newly created intercompany debt arising from the issuance of bonds. We turn now to intercompany debt created through the acquisition of already outstanding debt, which we illustrate by reference to bonds.

ACQUISITION OF OUTSTANDING DEBT

Intercompany debt also arises when a parent or subsidiary acquires from an unaffiliated party the previously issued and outstanding debt of an affiliate. The acquisition by a parent or subsidiary of previously issued and outstanding debt of an affiliated company is tantamount to retirement of the debt from the viewpoint of the consolidated entity. Accordingly, the acquisition of an affiliate's outstanding debt is often called *constructive retirement* of the debt, and the associated gain or loss is reported as an extraordinary item on the consolidated income statement (*FASB Statement No. 4,* par. 8).

Gains and Losses

When a company acquires the bonds of an affiliated company directly from the affiliate, then no gain or loss arises on the transaction because corresponding investment and liability balances are equal. However, when a company acquires the *outstanding* bonds of an affiliate, the difference between the corresponding investment and liability balances gives rise to a gain or loss. If the investment exceeds the related portion of the liability, there is a loss to the consolidated entity because the transfer of funds to unaffiliated parties exceeds the book value of the related debt. On the other hand, if the investment is less than the related liability, then the consolidated entity gains because the transfer of funds to unaffiliated parties is less than the book value of the related debt.

To illustrate, suppose that a parent acquired for $96,000 bonds previously issued by its subsidiary and carried on its subsidiary's books at $101,000. The transaction gives rise to a gain of $5,000 ($101,000 − $96,000) to the consolidated entity. In general, the gain or loss on the acquisition of intercompany debt is the difference between (1) the *carrying amount* or book value of the acquired debt on the records of the issuing company and (2) the *cost* of the debt to the affiliate acquiring the debt.

The following issues section considers some of the factors that affect the decision to acquire the outstanding debt of an affiliated company.

ISSUES

Motivation for Acquisition of Affiliate Debt

Several years ago, Janis Construction, Inc. was acquired as a subsidiary of Morgan Enterprises. Just prior to the acquisition, when interest rates were high, Janis issued, at par value, $1,000,000 of long-term bonds that bear interest at an effective interest rate of 14%. The bonds were not revalued in the business combination. Interest rates have declined, and the current market price of the issue is $1,200,000. Morgan is considering borrowing money to acquire its subsidiary's outstanding bonds.

1. *Will Morgan pay $1,200,000 to repurchase the issue?*

As explained in textbooks on corporate finance, a definitive answer to this question is not possible without additional information about tax effects, costs of repurchase, effects on existing debt covenants, costs and commitments associated with new borrowing, and future market conditions. However, the present value of the improvement in future interest payments (the excess of bond interest formerly paid to outsiders over the interest on new borrowings) is exactly offset by the $200,000 loss on the constructive retirement. Consequently, in terms of the facts given, repurchase would seem to offer no advantage to the consolidated entity.

2. *Assume that the bonds are callable at 105. Will Morgan repurchase the issue?*

Again, additional information is required to give a definitive answer. However, the call price is $150,000 below the current market price, which favors repurchase. However, the effect of calling the bonds is the recognition of an immediate extraordinary loss of $50,000, which is offset by the avoided future interest expense. An extraordinary loss affects consolidated net income; reporting such a loss may have negative consequences.

3. *How would you answer the second question if interest rates had increased since issuance?*

As before, repurchase at market price would not offer an economic advantage in terms of the limited facts given. Further, an increase in interest rates would result in a current market price below the issue price (par in this case) and therefore below the call price; hence, the call price would not be attractive. On the other hand, repurchasing the bonds at market would result in the recording of an extraordinary gain, which would be offset by additional future interest expense. An extraordinary gain affects consolidated net income; reporting such a gain may have positive consequences.

Attribution of Gain or Loss

Gains and losses on the acquisition of intercompany debt present an attribution problem. What share, if any, of the gain or loss should be allocated to the minority interest in the subsidiary? Some accountants argue that the entire gain or loss should be attributed to the bond-issuing affiliate following what is called the *issuing-company method.* They view the investor as an agent of the issuing affiliate and argue that the gain should be handled as if the issuing affiliate had redeemed its own bonds. Under this interpretation, which is consistent with the entity theory of financial reporting, the minority interest shares in the gain or loss only when the subsidiary is the issuing affiliate. A second group of accountants argue that the gain or loss should be allocated between the debt issuer and the debt purchaser by reference to the face value following what is called the *face-value method.* They prefer this method, which is consistent with the proprietary theory of financial reporting, because it allocates a portion of the gain or loss to the subsidiary. Thus, the interest of minority stockholders in the gain or loss is recognized. A third group of accountants argue that the entire gain or loss should be attributed to the parent company, whether the parent is the issuing affiliate or the purchasing affiliate, following what is called the *parent-company method.* The justification for this method is that the parent dominates the decision to acquire the debt, whether the parent or the subsidiary makes the acquisition. Hence, the entire gain or loss should be attributed to the parent. Under this interpretation, no gain or loss is attributed to the minority stockholders.

To illustrate these methods, suppose that a subsidiary acquired for $98,500 bonds with a face value of $100,000 previously issued by its parent and carried on the parent's books at $102,000. Following the issuing-company method, the entire $3,500 gain ($102,000 − $98,500) is attributed to the parent company, which issued the bonds, and the minority interest does not share in the gain. On the other hand, the issuing-company method would attribute entirely to the subsidiary any gain or loss on outstanding subsidiary bonds acquired by a parent. In this case, minority stockholders would share in the gain or loss. Following the face-value method, a $1,500 gain ($100,000 − $98,500) would be attributed to the parent corporation and a $2,000 gain ($102,000 − $100,000) would be attributed to the subsidiary. Accordingly, minority stockholders would share in the $2,000 gain attributed to the subsidiary but not in the $1,500 gain attributed to the parent company. Finally, following the parent-company method, the entire $3,500 would be attributed to the parent company. Under this method, no gain or loss is attributed to a subsidiary and minority stockholders do not share in the gain or loss.

Since financial accounting standards do not direct the use of a particular method, various methods are used in practice. For pedagogical reasons, we prefer the issuing-company method. It involves somewhat less difficult computations than the face-value method, yet it illustrates the attribution of gain or loss to both the majority and minority stockholders, depending on the identity of the debt issuer. The issuing-company method is discussed in the paragraphs that follow, and the face-value method is explained in Appendix A to this chapter.

Acquisition of Parent's Debt by Subsidiary

The acquisition by one company of the outstanding debt of an affiliated company may occur in two ways: a parent may acquire its subsidiary's outstanding debt, or a subsidiary may acquire its parent's outstanding debt. Let us begin by considering the acquisition by a subsidiary of debt previously issued by its parent. Following the issuing-company method, the entire gain or loss on the acquisition is attributed to the parent company. Let us demonstrate the required equity-method and consolidation procedures by reference to an example. Nicholson, Inc., acquires an 80% ownership interest in Small Corporation on January 1, 19X1, by paying $400,000 cash. Since Small reports common stock of $400,000 and retained earnings of $100,000 on this date, the cash paid by Nicholson equals the book value of the outstanding stock acquired [$400,000 = .80 × ($400,000 + $100,000)]. Several years ago, Nicholson issued 9% bonds with a face value of $100,000 at a premium; the bonds mature in three years. Nicholson uses the straight-line amortization method for bonds, and the unamortized premium is $2,400 on January 1, 19X1.[3] The straight-line method produces an annual premium amortization of $800 and an annual interest expense of $8,200 ($9,000 − $800) in each of the three years remaining until the

---

[3] Throughout the remainder of this chapter, unless otherwise stated, the straight-line method is used to amortize bond discounts and bond premiums. Although the effective interest method is conceptually superior to the straight-line method and is generally required (*APB Opinion No. 21*, pars. 2 and 14), the straight-line method is simpler and makes it easier to understand the distinctive aspects of accounting for intercompany debt. Further, an exception to the effective interest method requirement is provided for intercompany transactions (*APB Opinion No. 21*, par. 3f). Of course, the standards permit the straight-line method when it yields approximately the same results. Here and throughout this chapter, amounts are rounded to the nearer dollar.

bonds' maturity.[4] The following T-account summarizes the balances and changes in Nicholson's bond liability during the three years following its acquisition of Small:

Bonds Payable (Parent's Account)

		Balance 1-1-X1	102,400
Payment 12-31-X1	9,000	19X1 interest expense	8,200
		Balance 12-31-X1	101,600
Payment 12-31-X2	9,000	19X2 interest expense	8,200
		Balance 12-31-X2	100,800
Payment 12-31-X3	9,000	19X3 interest expense	8,200
Payment 12-31-X3	100,000		
		Balance 12-31-X3	–0–

Since the bonds were issued at a premium, the annual interest expense of $8,200 is less than the annual coupon payment of $9,000 by $800, the amount of the annual amortization of the premium ($2,400 ÷ 3).

On January 1, 19X1, the date Nicholson acquired Small, Small (the subsidiary) acquires from unaffiliated parties all the previously issued and outstanding bonds of Nicholson, which have a face value of $100,000. Small acquires the bonds at a $3,300 discount and pays $96,700 ($100,000 − $3,300). Since the subsidiary pays $5,700 less than the carrying amount of the debt on the parent's records ($5,700 = $102,400 − $96,700), a gain of $5,700 is attributed to the parent by the issuing-company method. Small's acquisition and holding of Nicholson's bonds is the only intercompany transaction that affects the three-year holding period. The investment in bonds account, which appears on Small's records, is summarized for the three-year holding period in the following T-account:

Investment in Bonds (Subsidiary's Account)

Balance 1-1-X1	96,700		
19X1 interest revenue	10,100	Receipt 12-31-X1	9,000
Balance 12-31-X1	97,800		
19X2 interest revenue	10,100	Receipt 12-31-X2	9,000
Balance 12-31-X2	98,900	Receipt 12-31-X3	9,000
19X3 interest revenue	10,100	Receipt 12-31-X3	100,000
Balance 12-31-X3	–0–		

Since the bonds were acquired at a $3,300 discount, the annual interest revenue of $10,100 exceeds the annual coupon payment of $9,000 by $1,100, the amount of the annual amortization of discount ($3,300 ÷ 3).

---

[4] The straight-line method amortizes the premium or discount in direct proportion to the passage of time. As a result, equal time periods are assigned equal amortizations. Further, the interest expense for a given interest period equals the coupon payment, made at the end of the period, adjusted for the premium or discount amortization assigned to the interest period. For example, Nicholson's annual interest expense of $8,200 equals the $9,000 annual coupon reduced for the $800 annual amortization of premium. Notice that amortizations of premium are subtracted from the coupon payment to reach the interest expense or revenue, whereas amortizations of discount are added.

The separate-company income statements of Nicholson and Small for 19X1, 19X2, and 19X3 are shown in Exhibit 6-4. Neither company declares any dividends during this three-year period. Observe that the subsidiary's interest revenue from the parent's bonds exceeds the parent's interest expense for those bonds by $1,900 in each of the three years and that the sum of these differences equals the gain on intercompany debt ($5,700 = $1,900 + $1,900 + $1,900). In other words, the subsidiary's acquisition of the parent's debt saves the consolidated entity $1,900 per year for three years or a total of $5,700.

Equity Method for Acquisition of Parent's Debt by Subsidiary

When a subsidiary purchases previously issued and outstanding debt of its parent, the parent (as the issuing company) must recognize the entire gain or loss on the constructive retirement of the debt. Rather than reporting the gain or loss as a separate item on its income statement, however, the parent adjusts its income from subsidiary for the amount of the gain or loss. For example, when Small acquires the outstanding debt of its parent, Nicholson, the $5,700 gain is added to Nicholson's calculation of income from subsidiary, as shown in Exhibit 6-5 on the following page.

Under the issuing-company method, any gain or loss on the constructive retirement of debt is viewed as an adjustment to the future interest expense of the issuer. Accordingly, recognition of the gain or loss in the first period must be accompanied by appropriate adjustments to the interest expense of the issuer over the remaining life of the bonds. For example, Nicholson's $5,700 gain occasions an annual increase of $1,900 in Nicholson's interest expense. Rather than adjusting the parent's interest expense directly, the parent's calculation of income from subsidiary is simply increased by $1,900 in each year, as shown in Exhibit 6-5.

EXHIBIT 6-4	SEPARATE-COMPANY INCOME STATEMENTS FOR NICHOLSON-SMALL ILLUSTRATION		
	For the Years Ended December 31,		
	19X1	**19X2**	**19X3**
Income Statements of Nicholson (Parent)			
Sales	$ 500,000	$ 600,000	$ 700,000
Operating expenses	(230,000)	(275,000)	(340,000)
Interest expense on debt held by subsidiary	*(8,200)*	*(8,200)*	*(8,200)*
Income from subsidiary (Exhibit 6-5)	59,880	64,580	66,180
Net income	$ 321,680	$ 381,380	$ 417,980
Income Statements of Small (Subsidiary)			
Sales	$ 110,000	$ 145,000	$ 170,000
Interest revenue from debt issued by parent	*10,100*	*10,100*	*10,100*
Operating expenses	(50,000)	(72,000)	(95,000)
Net income	$ 70,100	$ 83,100	$ 85,100

EXHIBIT 6-5	PARENT'S CALCULATION OF INCOME FROM SUBSIDIARY FOR NICHOLSON-SMALL ILLUSTRATION

	For the Years Ended December 31,		
	19X1	19X2	19X3
Subsidiary net income (including interest revenue from parent)	$70,100	$83,100	$85,100
Parent's ownership percentage	×.80	×.80	×.80
Parent's share of subsidiary net income	$56,080	$66,480	$68,080
Gain on subsidiary's acquisition of parent's debt	5,700		
Adjustment of parent's interest expense	(1,900)	(1,900)	(1,900)
Income from subsidiary	$59,880	$64,580	$66,180

Consolidation Procedures for Acquisition of Parent's Debt by Subsidiary

The consolidation worksheet adjustments for the Nicholson-Small illustration are given in Exhibit 6-6 for the three years following the acquisition of Nicholson's debt by its subsidiary, Small. The first two adjustments are the familiar forms that (1) reverse the parent's

EXHIBIT 6-6	CONSOLIDATION WORKSHEET ADJUSTMENTS FOR NICHOLSON-SMALL ILLUSTRATION

Nicholson, Inc.
WORKSHEET ADJUSTMENTS FOR THE CONSOLIDATION OF SMALL CORPORATION

	For the Years Ended December 31,					
	19X1		19X2		19X3	
(1) *Reverse parent's recording of subsidiary income for current year:*						
Income from subsidiary	59,880		64,580		66,180	
Investment in Small stock		59,880		64,580		66,180
(2) *Eliminate and reclassify beginning-of-the-year balance of parent's investment account:*						
Common stock of Small..............	320,000		320,000		320,000	
Retained earnings of Small, 1-1	80,000		136,080		202,560	
Investment in Small stock		400,000		456,080		522,560
(3) *Eliminate intercompany debt and interest:*						
Bonds payable (net)	101,600		100,800		–0–	
Interest revenue	10,100		10,100		10,100	
Investment in Nicholson bonds (net)...................		97,800		98,900		–0–
Interest expense.................		8,200		8,200		8,200
Gain on intercompany debt		5,700		–0–		–0–
Investment in Small stock		–0–		3,800		1,900

recording of subsidiary income for the current year and (2) eliminate and reclassify the beginning-of-the-year balance of the parent's investment account. Notice that the elimination from retained earnings increases each year by 80% of the increase in subsidiary retained earnings during the preceding year. For example, an additional $56,080 ($136,080 − $80,000) is eliminated from retained earnings in 19X2, which represents 80% of the 19X1 increase in the subsidiary's retained earnings ($56,080 = .80 × $70,100).

The third adjustment eliminates all *end-of-the-period* intercompany debt balances from the consolidated balance sheet. The entries made at the date of maturity by the separate companies remove the related bonds payable and investment in bonds accounts from the separate-company records. Consequently, the adjustment for 19X3 does not involve those accounts.

In addition, the third adjustment records the gain or loss on intercompany debt in the first year and provides for the related adjustment of the issuer's interest expense in subsequent years. The gain or loss is reported as a separate element of consolidated income in the year of the constructive retirement. In subsequent years, the portion of the gain or loss associated with the parent's interest expense in the current and future years is adjusted to the parent's investment-in-subsidiary-stock account. For example, Nicholson's investment-in-subsidiary-stock account receives a credit adjustment of $3,800 at the end of 19X2 representing the portion of the $5,700 gain associated with Nicholson's interest expense for 19X2 and 19X3 ($1,900 per year). The $3,800 credit adjustment eliminates the portion of the beginning investment balance related to the recognition of the gain on intercompany debt. Later in this chapter, we illustrate an acquisition of subsidiary debt by a parent in which retained earnings, rather than investment in subsidiary stock, receives the adjustments for the portion of the gain or loss associated with current and future periods.

Effect of Consolidation Adjustments on Separate-Company Balances

Exhibit 6-7 on the following page shows the effect of the consolidation adjustments displayed in Exhibit 6-6 on the separate-company balances for the Nicholson-Small illustration. Each column of Exhibit 6-7 represents a row of the consolidation worksheet that is affected by one or more of the consolidation adjustments. The rows of Exhibit 6-7 are divided into three sections, one section for each of the three consolidation worksheets for the years 19X1, 19X2, and 19X3. The exhibit demonstrates that the consolidation adjustments accomplish the elimination of the investment-in-subsidiary-stock balance in each year as well as the elimination of the intercompany debt accounts. The remaining balances in subsidiary common stock and retained earnings represent the interest of minority stockholders in those accounts. In other words, the sum of the remaining balances in subsidiary common stock and retained earnings equals the *beginning-of-the-year* balance of minority interest. For example, the minority interest on January 1, 19X2, is $114,020, which is the sum of the two adjusted balances ($114,020 = $80,000 + $34,020). Of course, the minority interest on January 1, 19X2, can also be calculated as 20% of the unadjusted stockholders' equity of the subsidiary [$114,020 = .20 × ($400,000 + $170,100)]. Notice that part of the investment-in-subsidiary-stock elimination is accomplished by the third adjustment ($3,800 in 19X2 and $1,900 in 19X3). Exhibit 6-8 on page 315 shows the effect of these adjustments and minority interest calculations on the consolidation worksheet for 19X2.

EXHIBIT 6-7	CONSOLIDATION ADJUSTMENTS AND RELATED BALANCES FOR NICHOLSON-SMALL ILLUSTRATION

| | Parent's Accounts | | | | Subsidiary's Accounts | | | | Gain on Intercompany Debt |
	Bonds Payable	Interest Expense	Investment in Stock of Subsidiary	Income from Subsidiary	Investment in Bonds of Parent	Interest Revenue	Common Stock	Retained Earnings on Jan. 1	
Balances and Adjustments from 19X1 Consolidation Worksheet									
Balances per separate statements	$(101,600)	$8,200	$459,800	$(59,880)	$97,800	$(10,100)	$(400,000)	$(100,000)	$ –0–
(1) Reverse income from subsidiary			(59,880)	59,880					
(2) Eliminate acquired and earned equity			(400,000)				320,000	80,000	
(3) Eliminate intercompany debt and interest	101,600	(8,200)			(97,800)	10,100			(5,700)
Balances per consolidated statements	$ –0–	$ –0–	$ –0–	$ –0–	$ –0–	$ –0–	$ (80,000)*	$ (20,000)*	$(5,700)
Balances and Adjustments from 19X2 Consolidation Worksheet									
Balances per separate statements	$(100,800)	$8,200	$524,460	$(64,580)	$98,900	$(10,100)	$(400,000)	$(170,100)	$ –0–
(1) Reverse income from subsidiary			(64,580)	64,580					
(2) Eliminate acquired and earned equity			(456,080)				320,000	136,080	
(3) Eliminate intercompany debt and interest	100,800	(8,200)	(3,800)		(98,900)	10,100			
Balances per consolidated statements	$ –0–	$ –0–	$ –0–	$ –0–	$ –0–	$ –0–	$ (80,000)*	$ (34,020)*	$ –0–
Balances and Adjustments from 19X3 Consolidation Worksheet									
Balances per separate statements	$ –0–	$8,200	$590,640	$(66,180)	$ –0–	$(10,100)	$(400,000)	$(253,200)	$ –0–
(1) Reverse income from subsidiary			(66,180)	66,180					
(2) Eliminate acquired and earned equity			(522,560)				320,000	202,560	
(3) Eliminate intercompany debt and interest		(8,200)	(1,900)			10,100			
Balances per consolidated statements	$ –0–	$ –0–	$ –0–	$ –0–	$ –0–	$ –0–	$ (80,000)*	$ (50,640)*	$ –0–

* Component of beginning-of-the-year minority interest.

Acquisition of Subsidiary's Debt by Parent

We turn now to the acquisition by a parent company of previously issued and outstanding debt of its subsidiary. Following the issuing-company method, the entire gain or loss on the acquisition is attributed to the subsidiary company. Let us demonstrate the required equity-method and consolidation procedures by reference to an example. Dohr, Inc., acquires a 90% ownership interest in Inghram Corporation on January 1, 19X1, by paying $450,000 cash, which equals the book value of the stock acquired. Several years ago,

EXHIBIT 6-8	19X2 CONSOLIDATION WORKSHEET FOR NICHOLSON-SMALL ILLUSTRATION: ISSUING-COMPANY METHOD FOR 19X1 ACQUISITION OF PARENT'S OUTSTANDING DEBT BY SUBSIDIARY

| | Separate Financial Statements | | Consolidation Adjustments | | Minority Interest | Consolidated Financial Statements |
	Nicholson	Small	Dr.	Cr.		
Income Statement						
Revenue	600,000	145,000				745,000
Interest revenue		10,100	(3) 10,100			
Income from subsidiary	64,580		(1) 64,580			
Operating expense	(275,000)	(72,000)				(347,000)
Interest expense	(8,200)			(3) 8,200		
Minority interest ($83,100 × .20)					16,620	(16,620)
Net income	381,380	83,100	74,680	8,200	16,620	381,380
Retained Earnings Statement						
Retained earnings, 1-1-X2:						
Nicholson	112,000					112,000
Small		170,100	(2) 136,080		34,020	
Net income	381,380	83,100	74,680	8,200	16,620	381,380
Retained earnings, 12-31-X2	493,380	253,200	210,760	8,200	50,640	493,380
Balance Sheet						
Current assets	151,540	81,100				192,500
Investment in Small stock	524,460			(1) 64,580		–0–
				(2) 456,080		
				(3) 3,800		
Investment in Nicholson bonds		98,900		(3) 98,900		–0–
Plant and equipment (net)	544,000	530,000				1,074,000
Total assets	1,220,000	710,000				1,306,640
Current liabilities	25,820	16,800				42,620
Bonds payable	100,800		(3) 100,800			–0–
Other long-term liabilities	100,000	40,000				140,000
Common stock:						
Nicholson	500,000					500,000
Small		400,000	(2) 320,000		80,000	–0–
Retained earnings	493,380	253,200	210,760	8,200	50,640	493,380
Minority interest					(130,640)	130,640
Total liabilities and stockholders' equity	1,220,000	710,000	631,560	631,560	–0–	1,306,640

Inghram issued 8% bonds, with a face value of $80,000, at a premium to mature on December 31, 19X3. The unamortized premium is $2,100 on January 1, 19X1. The following T-account displays Inghram's liability related to the bonds for the three-year holding period:

Bonds Payable (Subsidiary's Account)

		Balance 1-1-X1	82,100
Payment 12-31-X1	6,400	19X1 interest expense	5,700
		Balance 12-31-X1	81,400
Payment 12-31-X2	6,400	19X2 interest expense	5,700
		Balance 12-31-X2	80,700
Payment 12-31-X3	6,400	19X3 interest expense	5,700
Payment 12-31-X3	80,000		
		Balance 12-31-X3	–0–

Since the bonds were issued at a premium, the annual interest expense of $5,700 is less than the annual coupon payment of $6,400 by $700, the amount of the annual amortization of premium using the straight-line amortization method ($2,100 ÷ 3).

On January 1, 19X1, Dohr (the parent) acquires from unaffiliated parties all the previously issued and outstanding bonds of Inghram, which have a face value of $80,000 and a carrying amount of $82,100. Dohr acquires the bonds at a $3,979 discount and pays $76,021 ($80,000 − $3,979). Since the parent pays $6,079 less than the carrying amount (book value) of the debt on the subsidiary's records ($6,079 = $82,100 − $76,021), a gain of $6,079 is attributed to the subsidiary (the issuing company).[5] Dohr's acquisition and holding of Inghram's bonds is the only intercompany transaction that affects the three-year holding period. The investment in bonds account, which appears on Dohr's records, contains the following information for the three-year holding period:

Investment in Bonds (Parent's Account)

Balance 1-1-X1	76,021		
19X1 interest revenue	7,726	Receipt 12-31-X1	6,400
Balance 12-31-X1	77,347		
19X2 interest revenue	7,726	Receipt 12-31-X2	6,400
Balance 12-31-X2	78,673		
19X3 interest revenue	7,727	Receipt 12-31-X3	6,400
		Receipt 12-31-X3	80,000
Balance 12-31-X3	–0–		

Since the bonds are purchased at a discount, the annual interest revenue of $7,726 from the bonds exceeds the annual coupon payments of $6,400 by the $1,326 discount amortization ($1,326.33 = $3,979 ÷ 3); the rounding error is corrected in the 19X3 amortization of $1,327.

---

[5] In the Dohr-Inghram illustration, the gain on acquisition of debt is $6,079—the balance of Inghram's bonds payable account on January 1, 19X1 ($82,100), less the balance of Dohr's "Investment in Bonds" account on the same date ($76,021). A gain arises because Dohr transfers $6,079 less to unaffiliated parties than the carrying amount of the debt satisfied by the transfer. When a company acquires just a portion of the outstanding debt of an affiliate, the calculation of the gain or loss requires the segregation of the related portion of the affiliate's carrying amount of the debt.

EXHIBIT 6-9 — SEPARATE-COMPANY INCOME STATEMENTS FOR DOHR-INGHRAM ILLUSTRATION

	For the Years Ended December 31,		
	19X1	19X2	19X3
Income Statements of Dohr (Parent)			
Sales	$300,000	$350,000	$400,000
Interest revenue from debt issued by subsidiary	7,726	7,726	7,727
Operating expenses	(120,000)	(150,000)	(180,000)
Income from subsidiary (Exhibit 6-10)	52,518	56,047	65,046
Net income	$240,244	$263,773	$292,773
Income Statements of Inghram (Subsidiary)			
Sales	$100,000	$120,000	$150,000
Operating expenses	(40,000)	(50,000)	(70,000)
Interest expense on debt held by parent	(5,700)	(5,700)	(5,700)
Net income	$ 54,300	$ 64,300	$ 74,300

The separate-company income statements of Dohr and Inghram for 19X1, 19X2, and 19X3 are shown in Exhibit 6-9. Neither company declares any dividends during this three-year period.

Equity Method for Acquisition of Subsidiary's Debt by Parent

When a parent purchases previously issued and outstanding debt of its subsidiary, the subsidiary (as the issuing company) recognizes the entire gain or loss on the constructive retirement of the debt. For example, when Dohr acquires the outstanding debt of its subsidiary, Inghram, the $6,079 gain is added to the subsidiary's reported net income before the multiplication by the parent's ownership percentage in the calculation of income from subsidiary, as shown in Exhibit 6-10.

EXHIBIT 6-10 — PARENT'S CALCULATION OF INCOME FROM SUBSIDIARY FOR DOHR-INGHRAM ILLUSTRATION

	For the Years Ended December 31,		
	19X1	19X2	19X3
Subsidiary net income (including interest expense to parent)	$54,300	$64,300	$74,300
Gain on parent's acquisition of subsidiary's debt	6,079		
Adjustment of subsidiary's interest expense	(2,026)	(2,026)	(2,027)
Adjusted subsidiary net income	$58,353	$62,274	$72,273
Parent's ownership percentage	×.90	×.90	×.90
Income from subsidiary	$52,518	$56,047	$65,046

Under the issuing-company method, the gain or loss on the constructive retirement of debt represents an adjustment to the issuer's future interest expense. Accordingly, recognition of the gain or loss in the first period must be accompanied by appropriate adjustments to the issuer's interest expense. For example, Inghram's $6,079 gain occasions an annual increase of $2,026 ($6,079 ÷ 3) in Inghram's interest expense, as shown in Exhibit 6-10.

Consolidation Procedures for Acquisition of Subsidiary's Debt by Parent

The consolidation worksheet adjustments for the Dohr-Inghram illustration are given in Exhibit 6-11 for the three years following the acquisition of Inghram's outstanding bonds by its parent, Dohr. The first two adjustments are the familiar forms that (1) reverse the parent's recording of income from subsidiary for the current year and (2) eliminate and reclassify the beginning-of-the-year balance of the parent's investment account. In order to calculate the adjustment to retained earnings, however, one must make provision for the portion of the subsidiary's gain or loss on the intercompany debt related to the current and future years. This portion of the gain or loss is attributed to the subsidiary by the issuing-

EXHIBIT 6-11	CONSOLIDATION WORKSHEET ADJUSTMENTS FOR DOHR-INGHRAM ILLUSTRATION

Dohr, Inc.

WORKSHEET ADJUSTMENTS FOR THE CONSOLIDATION OF INGHRAM CORPORATION

	For the Years Ended December 31,					
	19X1		19X2		19X3	
(1) *Reverse parent's recording of subsidiary income for current year:*						
Income from subsidiary	52,518		56,047		65,046	
Investment in Inghram stock		52,518		56,047		65,046
(2) *Eliminate and reclassify beginning-of-the-year balance of parent's investment account:*						
Common stock of subsidiary	360,000		360,000		360,000	
Retained earnings of subsidiary	90,000		142,518		198,565	
Investment in Inghram stock		450,000		502,518		558,565
(3) *Eliminate intercompany debt and interest:*						
Bonds payable (net)	81,400		80,700		–0–	
Interest revenue	7,726		7,726		7,727	
Investment in Inghram's bonds (net)..................		77,347		78,673		–0–
Interest expense..................		5,700		5,700		5,700
Gain on intercompany debt		6,079		–0–		–0–
Retained earnings of subsidiary, 1-1................		–0–		4,053		2,027

company method but has not been recorded by the subsidiary. Prior to this provision, retained earnings of the subsidiary is summarized by the T-account that follows.

Retained Earnings (Subsidiary's Account)

	Balance 1-1-X1	100,000
	19X1 net income	54,300
	Balance 12-31-X1	154,300
	19X2 net income	64,300
	Balance 12-31-X2	218,600
	19X3 net income	74,300
	Balance 12-31-X3	292,900

Since the gain is recognized at the beginning of 19X1 (and is included in the 19X1 minority interest in net income on the consolidation worksheet), the retained earnings balance on January 1, 19X1, requires no adjustment and the elimination from retained earnings at the end of 19X1 is simply 90% of the beginning-of-the-year balance reported by the subsidiary ($90,000 = .90 × $100,000). The elimination from retained earnings at the end of 19X2, however, is based on an *adjusted* beginning-of-the-year balance of $158,353 ($154,300 + $4,053), where the adjustment of $4,053 equals the portion of the gain related to 19X2 and 19X3 ($4,053 = $2,026 + $2,027), which is not recorded in the subsidiary's accounts. Accordingly, the elimination from retained earnings at the end of 19X2 is $142,518 (.90 × $158,353). Similarly, the elimination at the end of 19X3 is based on a retained earnings balance adjusted for the portion of the gain related to 19X3 ($2,027). Accordingly, the elimination from retained earnings at the end of 19X3 is $198,565 = [.90 × ($218,600 + $2,027)].

The third adjustment eliminates all end-of-the-period balances that are related to the intercompany debt balances from the consolidated financial statements. The entries by the separate companies made at maturity of the intercompany debt remove the related bonds payable and investment in bonds accounts from the separate-company records. Consequently, the adjustment for 19X3 does not involve those accounts.

In addition, the third adjustment records the gain or loss on the intercompany debt in the first year and provides for the related adjustment of the issuer's interest expense in subsequent years. Whether the subsidiary or the parent is the issuer of the intercompany debt, the gain or loss is reported as part of the element of consolidated income in the year of the constructive retirement. When the parent is the issuer, subsequent adjustments for gains and losses on the intercompany debt are made to the parent's investment in subsidiary stock account. However, when the subsidiary is the issuer, such adjustments are made to the subsidiary's beginning retained earnings account. In the Dohr-Inghram illustration, the subsidiary is the issuer and the portion of the gain associated with the subsidiary's interest expense in the current and future years is adjusted in 19X2 and 19X3 to the subsidiary's retained earnings account. Accordingly, Inghram's retained earnings account receives a credit of $4,053 in 19X2 representing the portion of the $6,079 gain associated with Inghram's interest expense in 19X2 and 19X3 ($2,026 in 19X2 and $2,027 in 19X3). The $4,053 credit records the portion of the interest savings related to current and future years that have not yet been realized by the subsidiary.

Effect of Consolidation Adjustments on Separate-Company Balances

Exhibit 6-12 shows the effect of the consolidation adjustments displayed in Exhibit 6-11 on the separate-company balances for the Dohr-Inghram illustration. Each column of Exhibit 6-12 represents a row of the consolidation worksheet that is affected by one or more of the consolidation adjustments. The rows of Exhibit 6-12 are divided into three

EXHIBIT 6-12	**CONSOLIDATION ADJUSTMENTS AND RELATED BALANCES FOR DOHR-INGHRAM ILLUSTRATION: ISSUING COMPANY METHOD**								
	Parent's Accounts				**Subsidiary's Accounts**				**Gain on Inter-company Debt**
	Investment in Bonds of Subsidiary	Interest Revenue	Investment in Stock of Subsidiary	Income from Subsidiary	Bonds Payable	Interest Expense	Common Stock	Retained Earnings on Jan. 1	
Balances and Adjustments from 19X1 Consolidation Worksheet									
Balances per separate statements	$77,347	$(7,726)	$502,518	$(52,518)	$(81,400)	$5,700	$(400,000)	$(100,000)	$ –0–
(1) Reverse income from subsidiary			(52,518)	52,518					
(2) Eliminate acquired and earned equity			(450,000)				360,000	90,000	
(3) Eliminate intercompany debt and interest	(77,347)	7,726			81,400	(5,700)			(6,079)
Balances per consolidated statements	$ –0–	$ –0–	$ –0–	$ –0–	$ –0–	$ –0–	$ (40,000)*	$ (10,000)*	$(6,079)
Balances and Adjustments from 19X2 Consolidation Worksheet									
Balances per separate statements	$78,673	$(7,726)	$558,565	$(56,047)	$(80,700)	$5,700	$(400,000)	$(154,300)	$ –0–
(1) Reverse income from subsidiary			(56,047)	56,047					
(2) Eliminate acquired and earned equity			(502,518)				360,000	142,518	
(3) Eliminate intercompany debt and interest	(78,673)	7,726			80,700	(5,700)		(4,053)	
Balances per consolidated statements	$ –0–	$ –0–	$ –0–	$ –0–	$ –0–	$ –0–	$ (40,000)*	$ (15,835)*	$ –0–
Balances and Adjustments from 19X3 Consolidation Worksheet									
Balances per separate statements	$ –0–	$(7,727)	$623,611	$(65,046)	$ –0–	$5,700	$(400,000)	$(218,600)	$ –0–
(1) Reverse income from subsidiary			(65,046)	65,046					
(2) Eliminate acquired and earned equity			(558,565)				360,000	198,565	
(3) Eliminate intercompany debt and interest		7,727				(5,700)		(2,027)	
Balances per consolidated statements	$ –0–	$ –0–	$ –0–	$ –0–	$ –0–	$ –0–	$ (40,000)*	$ (22,062)*	$ –0–

* Component of beginning-of-the-year minority interest.

sections, one section for each of the three consolidation worksheets for the years 19X1, 19X2, and 19X3. The exhibit proves that the consolidation adjustments accomplish the elimination of the investment-in-subsidiary-stock balance in each year as well as the elimination of the intercompany debt accounts. The remaining balances in subsidiary common stock and retained earnings represent the interest of minority stockholders in those accounts, and the sum of the remainders in these two accounts equals the beginning-of-the-year balance of minority interest.

Recall that the elimination of the parent's interest in subsidiary retained earnings by the second adjustment is based on an adjusted balance of subsidiary retained earnings. Exhibit 6-12 suggests a short-cut method of calculating the elimination from retained earnings. Since the second adjustment must also eliminate the remaining balance of the investment-in-subsidiary-stock account, the required elimination from retained earnings can be calculated by reference to the remaining balance of the investment account rather than by reference to the adjusted balance of retained earnings. For example, the elimination from retained earnings by the second adjustment in 19X2 ($142,518) can be calculated as the difference between the remainder of the investment-in-subsidiary-stock account ($502,518 = $558,565 − $56,047) and the elimination from common stock ($142,518 = $502,518 − $360,000).

Notice that the third adjustment increases subsidiary retained earnings for the portion of the gain on the intercompany debt associated with current and future years. This increase is offset by the elimination of the parent portion of that gain, which is included in the adjustment to retained earnings by the second adjustment, leaving only the minority interest share of the gain associated with current and future years. Exhibit 6-13 on the following page shows the effect of these adjustments and calculations on the consolidation worksheet for 19X2.

SUMMARY

Intercompany debt may occur when a parent or subsidiary purchases the newly issued debt of an affiliate, when a parent acquires its subsidiary's outstanding debt, or when a subsidiary acquires its parent's outstanding debt. From the viewpoint of the consolidated entity, intercompany debt does not represent debt at all and must be eliminated from the assets of the lender and from the liabilities of the borrower. Intercompany debt arising from fund transfers between affiliated companies, as described in the preceding paragraphs in relation to notes receivable and notes payable, merely signifies a transfer of funds from one segment of the consolidated entity to another. Since an entity cannot owe money to itself, the intercompany debt and interest accounts (which will have equal balances) must be eliminated as part of the consolidation procedure. If intercompany debt arises from the acquisition of already outstanding debt, as in the case with bonds illustrated in this chapter, the intercompany debt and interest accounts may not be equal, owing to changes in the market rate of interest since issuance of the debt. Such changes in the market rate of interest are reflected in the acquisition price of the debt but not in its book value on the records of the issuing affiliate. In such cases, elimination of the intercompany debt and interest balances gives rise to a gain or loss to the consolidated entity, and proper recognition of that gain or loss requires modifications of both the equity-method and consolidation procedures.

EXHIBIT 6-13	19X2 CONSOLIDATION WORKSHEET FOR DOHR-INGHRAM ILLUSTRATION: ISSUING-COMPANY METHOD FOR 19X1 ACQUISITION OF SUBSIDIARY'S OUTSTANDING DEBT BY PARENT

	Separate Financial Statements		Consolidation Adjustments		Minority Interest	Consolidated Financial Statements
	Dohr	Inghram	Dr.	Cr.		
Income Statement						
Revenue	350,000	120,000				470,000
Interest revenue	7,726		(3) 7,726			
Income from subsidiary	56,047		(1) 56,047			
Other operating expenses	(150,000)*	(50,000)				(200,000)
Interest expense		(5,700)		(3) 5,700		
Minority interest [($64,300 − $2,026) × .10]					6,227	(6,227)
Net income	263,773	64,300	63,773	5,700	6,227	263,773
Retained Earnings Statement						
Retained earnings, 1-1-X2:						
Dohr	147,927					147,927
Inghram		154,300	(2) 142,518	(3) 4,053	15,835	
Net income	263,773	64,300	63,773	5,700	6,227	263,773
Retained earnings, 12-31-X2	411,700	218,600	206,291	9,753	22,062	411,700
Balance Sheet						
Current assets	62,762	93,000				155,762
Investment in Inghram stock	558,565			(1) 56,047		–0–
				(2) 502,518		
Investment in Inghram bonds	78,673			(3) 78,673		–0–
Plant and equipment (net)	850,000	650,000				1,500,000
Total assets	1,550,000	743,000				1,655,762
Current liabilities	38,300	8,700				47,000
Bonds payable		80,700	(3) 80,700			–0–
Other long-term liabilities	300,000	35,000				335,000
Common stock						
Dohr	800,000					800,000
Inghram		400,000	(2) 360,000		40,000	–0–
Retained earnings	411,700	218,600	206,291	9,753	22,062	411,700
Minority interest					(62,062)	62,062
Total liabilities and stockholders' equity	1,550,000	743,000	646,991	646,991	–0–	1,655,762

* Parentheses indicate decreases.

APPENDIX A: THE FACE-VALUE METHOD FOR GAINS AND LOSSES ON INTERCOMPANY DEBT

The preceding pages demonstrate the issuing-company method for gains and losses on intercompany debt. Under the issuing-company method, the entire gain or loss is attributed to the issuer of the intercompany debt. This appendix demonstrates an alternative method, called the face-value method, that allocates the gain or loss between the parent and its subsidiary by reference to the face value or par value of the intercompany debt. Let us illustrate the application of the face-value method by reference to the Dohr-Inghram example presented earlier. Recall that the parent, Dohr, acquired for $76,021 previously issued and outstanding bonds carried on the books of its 90%-owned subsidiary, Inghram, at $82,100. The constructive retirement results in a gain of $6,079 ($82,100 − $76,021).

Allocation of Gain or Loss by Reference to Face Value

The face-value method divides the gain or loss between the debt issuer and the investor by reference to the face or par value of the intercompany debt. The allocation for the Dohr-Inghram illustration is shown in the following diagram:

Allocation of Gain on Acquisition of Intercompany Debt

Book value to issuer ($82,100)	Face value ($80,000)	Acquisition price to investor (76,021)
Gain to issuer = $2,100	Gain to investor = $3,979	
Gain on acquisition = $6,079		

The issuer's gain equals the issuer's unamortized premium at the date of acquisition, and the investor's gain equals the investor's discount at the date of acquisition. Of course, in other examples, this allocation procedure may result in a gain to one affiliate and a loss to another, as when one affiliate purchases debt at a premium that was issued by another affiliate at a premium.

Equity Method for Acquisition of Subsidiary's Debt by Parent

The recognition of gains and losses on intercompany debt acquisitions and the attribution of such gains and losses influence adjustments to the parent's calculation of income from its subsidiary. Income from the subsidiary for the acquisition year must include the gain or loss on the acquisition of intercompany debt in accordance with its attribution to the parent and its subsidiary. In addition, income from the subsidiary for each year of the holding period must include the adjustments to interest revenues and expenses implied by the allocation of the gain or loss.

Reported net income of the subsidiary must be increased for the subsidiary's share of the gain (or reduced for the subsidiary's share of the loss), as shown in Exhibit 6-14 on the following page for the Dohr-Inghram illustration for the three-year remaining life of the bonds. In addition, the parent's share of the gain or loss is also included in the income from subsidiary. Observe that only 90% of the subsidiary's $2,100 gain enters the income from subsidiary. As we shall see later, the remaining 10% of the subsidiary's gain enters the minority interest.

EXHIBIT 6-14	PARENT'S CALCULATION OF INCOME FROM SUBSIDIARY FOR DOHR-INGHRAM ILLUSTRATION

Dohr, Inc.
CALCULATION OF INCOME FROM INGHRAM CORPORATION

	For the Years Ended December 31,		
	19X1	**19X2**	**19X3**
Subsidiary net income (including intercompany interest expense)	$54,300	$64,300	$74,300
Subsidiary's gain on intercompany debt purchase	2,100		
Adjustment of subsidiary's interest *expense*	(700)	(700)	(700)
Adjusted subsidiary net income	$55,700	$63,600	$73,600
Parent's ownership percentage	×.90	×.90	×.90
Parent's share of adjusted subsidiary net income	$50,130	$57,240	$66,240
Parent's gain on intercompany debt purchase	3,979		
Adjustment of parent's interest *revenue*	(1,326)	(1,326)	(1,327)
Income from subsidiary	$52,783	$55,914	$64,913

Consolidation Procedures for Acquisition of Subsidiary's Debt by Parent

Consolidation worksheet adjustments are given in Exhibit 6-15 for the three postacquisition years. Recall that Dohr acquired a 90% interest in Inghram for book value on January 1, 19X1, when Inghram's common stock and retained earnings balances were $400,000 and $100,000, respectively. The first and second adjustments are familiar forms that (1) reverse the parent's recording of subsidiary income for the current year and (2) eliminate and reclassify the beginning-of-the-year balance of the parent's investment account. The $140,130 adjustment to retained earnings by the second adjustment for 19X2 is the parent's share of beginning-of-the-year subsidiary retained earnings adjusted for the subsidiary's gain on the intercompany debt purchase associated with current and future years [$140,130 = .90 × ($154,300 + $2,100 − $700)].

The third adjustment eliminates all end-of-the-period balances related to intercompany debt from the consolidated financial statements. The third adjustment also records the gain or loss on intercompany debt in the first year and provides for the related adjustment of interest in subsequent years. The $1,400 credit to subsidiary retained earnings by the third adjustment for 19X2 is the portion of the *subsidiary's* gain on the intercompany debt purchase associated with the current and future years ($1,400 = $2,100 − $700). The $2,653 credit to the parent's investment in subsidiary stock account is the portion of the *parent's* gain on the intercompany debt purchase associated with interest adjustments in the current and future years ($2,653 = $3,979 − $1,326).

Although we do not illustrate the face-value method for the acquisition of a parent's debt by its subsidiary, the procedures are the same as those illustrated above. In both cases, the third adjustment debits or credits retained earnings of the subsidiary.

EXHIBIT 6-15	CONSOLIDATION WORKSHEET ADJUSTMENTS FOR DOHR-INGHRAM ILLUSTRATION: FACE-VALUE METHOD

Dohr, Inc.
WORKSHEET ADJUSTMENTS FOR THE CONSOLIDATION OF INGHRAM CORPORATION

	For the Years Ended December 31,					
	19X1		**19X2**		**19X3**	

(1) *Reverse parent's recording of subsidiary income for current year:*

Income from subsidiary	52,783		55,914		64,913	
Investment in Inghram stock		52,783		55,914		64,913

(2) *Eliminate and reclassify beginning-of-the-year balance of parent's investment account:*

Common stock of subsidiary	360,000		360,000		360,000	
Retained earnings of subsidiary	90,000		140,130*		197,370**	
Investment in Inghram stock		450,000		500,130		557,370

(3) *Eliminate intercompany debt and interest:*

Bonds payable (net)	81,400		80,700		–0–	
Interest revenue	7,726		7,726		7,727	
Investment in Dohr's bonds (net) ...		77,347		78,673		–0–
Interest expense		5,700		5,700		5,700
Gain on intercompany debt		6,079		–0–		–0–
Retained earnings of subsidiary		–0–		1,400		700
Investment in Inghram stock		–0–		2,653		1,327

$$* \ 140{,}130 = .90 \times (\$154{,}300 + \$2{,}100 - \$700)$$
$$** \ \$197{,}370 = .90 \times (\$154{,}300 + \$64{,}300 + \$1{,}400 - \$700)$$

Effect of Consolidation Adjustments on Separate-Company Balances

Exhibit 6-16 on the following page shows the effect of the consolidation adjustments displayed in Exhibit 6-15 on the separate-company balances for the Dohr-Inghram illustration. Each column of Exhibit 6-16 represents a row of the consolidation worksheet that is affected by one or more of the consolidation adjustments. The rows of Exhibit 6-16 are divided into three sections, one section for each of the three consolidation worksheets for the years 19X1, 19X2, and 19X3. The exhibit demonstrates that the consolidation adjustments accomplish the elimination of the investment-in-subsidiary-stock balance in each year as well as the elimination of the intercompany debt accounts. The remaining balances in subsidiary common stock and retained earnings represent the interest of minority stockholders in those accounts, and the sum of the two remainders equals the beginning-of-the-year balance of minority interest. Exhibit 6-17 shows the effect of these adjustments on the consolidation worksheet for 19X2.

EXHIBIT 6-16	CONSOLIDATION ADJUSTMENTS AND RELATED BALANCES FOR DOHR-INGHRAM ILLUSTRATION: FACE-VALUE METHOD

	Parent's Accounts				Subsidiary's Accounts				Gain on Inter-company Debt
	Investment in Bonds of Subsidiary	Interest Revenue	Investment in Stock of Subsidiary	Income from Subsidiary	Bonds Payable	Interest Expense	Common Stock	Retained Earnings on Jan. 1	
Balances and Adjustments from 19X1 Consolidation Worksheet									
Balances per separate statements	$77,347	$(7,726)	$502,783	$(52,783)	$(81,400)	$5,700	$(400,000)	$(100,000)	$ –0–
(1) Reverse income from subsidiary			(52,783)	52,783					
(2) Eliminate acquired and earned equity			(450,000)				360,000	90,000	
(3) Eliminate intercompany debt and interest	(77,347)	7,726			81,400	(5,700)			(6,079)
Balances per consolidated statements	$ –0–	$ –0–	$ –0–	$ –0–	$ –0–	$ –0–	$ (40,000)*	$ (10,000)*	$(6,079)
Balances and Adjustments from 19X2 Consolidation Worksheet									
Balances per separate statements	$78,673	$(7,726)	$558,697	$(55,914)	$(80,700)	$5,700	$(400,000)	$(154,300)	$ –0–
(1) Reverse income from subsidiary			(55,914)	55,914					
(2) Eliminate acquired and earned equity			(500,130)				360,000	140,130	
(3) Eliminate intercompany debt and interest	(78,673)	7,726	(2,653)		80,700	(5,700)		(1,400)	
Balances per consolidated statements	$ –0–	$ –0–	$ –0–	$ –0–	$ –0–	$ –0–	$ (40,000)*	$ (15,570)*	$ –0–
Balances and Adjustments from 19X3 Consolidation Worksheet									
Balances per separate statements	$ –0–	$(7,727)	$623,610	$(64,913)	$ –0–	$5,700	$(400,000)	$(218,600)	$ –0–
(1) Reverse income from subsidiary			(64,913)	64,913					
(2) Eliminate acquired and earned equity			(557,370)				360,000	197,370	
(3) Eliminate intercompany debt and interest		7,727	(1,327)			(5,700)		(700)	
Balances per consolidated statements	$ –0–	$ –0–	$ –0–	$ –0–	$ –0–	$ –0–	$ (40,000)*	$ (21,930)*	$ –0–

* Component of beginning-of-the-year minority interest: $40,000 = .10 \times $400,000; $10,000 = .10 \times $100,000; $15,570 = .10 \times ($154,300 + $2,100 − $700); and $21,930 = .10 \times ($218,600 + $2,100 − $700 − $700).

EXHIBIT 6-17	19X2 CONSOLIDATION WORKSHEET FOR DOHR-INGHRAM ILLUSTRATION: FACE-VALUE METHOD FOR 19X1 ACQUISITION OF SUBSIDIARY'S OUTSTANDING DEBT BY PARENT

	Separate Financial Statements		Consolidation Adjustments		Minority Interest	Consolidated Financial Statements
	Dohr	Inghram	Dr.	Cr.		
Income Statement						
Revenue	350,000	120,000				470,000
Interest revenue	7,726		(3) 7,726			
Income from subsidiary	55,914		(1) 55,914			
Other operating expenses	(150,000)*	(50,000)				(200,000)
Interest expense		(5,700)		(3) 5,700		
Minority interest						
[($64,300 − $700) × .10]					6,360	(6,360)
Net income	263,640	64,300	63,640	5,700	6,360	263,640
Retained Earnings Statement						
Retained earnings, 1-1-X2:						
Dohr	148,192					148,192
Inghram		154,300	(2) 140,130	(3) 1,400	15,570**	
Net income	263,640	64,300	63,640	5,700	6,360	263,640
Retained earnings, 12-31-X2	411,832	218,600	203,770	7,100	21,930	411,832
Balance Sheet						
Current assets	62,762	93,000				155,762
Investment in Inghram stock	558,697			(1) 55,914		–0–
				(2) 500,130		
				(3) 2,653		
Investment in Inghram bonds	78,673			(3) 78,673		–0–
Plant and equipment (net)	850,000	650,000				1,500,000
Total assets	1,550,132	743,000				1,655,762
Current liabilities	38,300	8,700				47,000
Bonds payable		80,700	(3) 80,700			–0–
Other long-term liabilities	300,000	35,000				335,000
Common stock						
Dohr	800,000					800,000
Inghram		400,000	(2) 360,000		40,000	–0–
Retained earnings	411,832	218,600	203,770	7,100	21,930	411,832
Minority interest					(61,930)	61,930
Total liabilities and stockholders' equity	1,550,132	743,000	644,470	644,470	–0–	1,655,762

* Parentheses indicate decreases.
** $15,570 = .10 × ($154,300 + $2,100 − $700)

Impact of Choice Between Face-Value and Alternative Methods

As noted earlier, the attribution of the gain or loss on acquisition of intercompany debt on the basis of face value is but one of several possible methods of attributing the gain or loss between majority and minority interests. Inspection of the parent's calculation of income from the subsidiary, as given in Exhibit 6-14 or 6-10, reveals that any change in the attribution will also change the parent's separate net income. A change in the attribution alters the portion of the gain that is shared with the minority stockholders, which in turn alters both the parent's income pickup and the parent's separate-company net income. Whereas annual results are altered, the *total* parent's income for the postacquisition term of the intercompany debt will be the same regardless of the attribution of the gain or loss. In a similar way, a change in the attribution of the gain or loss will shift amounts of consolidated net income and minority interest in subsidiary net income from one year to another during the postacquisition life of the debt but does not alter the total amount of consolidated net income or minority interest in subsidiary net income recognized over that period. In short, changes in the attribution of the gain alter the rate of income recognition but not the total amount of income recognized.

APPENDIX B: DISCOUNTING AND INTERCOMPANY NOTES

A lender discounts a note by selling the note to another party in exchange for cash. Frequently, the initial lender is contingently liable for the payment of the discounted note. The discounting of notes by affiliated companies takes two forms: (1) a parent or subsidiary may discount an *intercompany note* with an *unaffiliated party,* and (2) a parent or subsidiary may discount an *unaffiliated note* with an *affiliate.* Both forms of discounting influence consolidation procedures. The first form of discounting transforms an intercompany debt into a liability due to an unaffiliated party (frequently a financial institution) that must be reflected in consolidated financial statements. The second form of discounting transfers an unaffiliated note receivable from one affiliated company to another but does not alter the amount of consolidated assets or liabilities.

Discounting Intercompany Notes with Unaffiliated Parties

When a parent or subsidiary discounts an intercompany note with an unaffiliated party and credits notes receivable, the intercompany note receivable is removed from its records. The intercompany note payable, however, remains on the records of the original borrowing affiliate and now represents a liability of the consolidated entity, which is ultimately payable to an unaffiliated party. Accordingly, the intercompany note payable should not be eliminated in consolidation. Similarly, interest expense accrued subsequent to the date of discount should be included in consolidated net income. Of course, interest expense accrued prior to the date of discount should be offset against related interest revenue in consolidation.

If the discounting affiliate credits the notes receivable discounted account, rather than the notes receivable account, for the discounted intercompany note, then a consolidation adjustment should offset notes receivable discounted against notes receivable. As before, the intercompany note payable and postdiscounting interest expense on the records of the original borrowing affiliate should be reflected as notes payable and interest expense on consolidated financial statements.

Discounting Unaffiliated Notes with an Affiliated Company

When a note receivable from an unaffiliated party is discounted with an affiliated company, the asset (note receivable) is merely transferred from one affiliate to another, and consolidated financial statements should be unaffected. The note receivable should be included in consolidated assets, and the interest revenue should be included in consolidated net income. Of course, if the discounting affiliate credits notes receivable discounted rather than notes receivable, then a consolidation worksheet adjustment must eliminate the balance of notes receivable discounted against the balance of notes receivable.

SELECTED READINGS

Goodman, Hortense, and Leonard Lorensen. *Updated Illustrations of the Disclosure of Related Party Transactions,* Financial Report Survey No. 30. New York: American Institute of Certified Public Accountants, 1985.

Keister, Orville R. "Consolidation and Intercompany Bond Holdings," *The Accounting Review* (April 1967), pp. 375–376.

QUESTIONS

Q6-1 The parent lends funds to a 90%-owned subsidiary in exchange for a note receivable from the subsidiary. In the calculation of the parent's income from subsidiary, is the subsidiary net income adjusted for the effects of interest on intercompany notes? Discuss.

Q6-2 Explain why you agree or disagree with the following statement: Consolidation procedures can ignore intercompany notes receivable/payable when they arise from intercompany transfers of funds.

Q6-3 Cash transfers from a parent to a subsidiary in exchange for a note create new intercompany debt. Although the creation of the new intercompany debt is merely an internal cash transfer, such debt may benefit the consolidated entity. Discuss conditions under which the consolidated entity would be better off.

Q6-4 Define the term *constructive retirement.*

Q6-5 From the viewpoint of the consolidated entity, how does the acquisition of outstanding bonds of one affiliate by another affiliate parallel early extinguishment of debt by payments to unaffiliated parties?

Q6-6 How is the gain or loss on the acquisition of intercompany bonds determined?

Q6-7 Discuss three alternative methods of assigning the gain or loss on the acquisition of intercompany bonds to the affiliated firms. Comment on how the minority interest in the gain or loss is influenced by the method adopted. Which method is followed in this text?

Q6-8 Subsidiary outstanding bonds with a par value of $100,000 and a book value of $110,000 were acquired by the parent in the open market for $115,000. Using the procedure followed in this text, determine the amount of the gain or loss on the acquisition of intercompany bonds that would be assigned to the parent and the subsidiary.

Q6-9 Explain why you agree or disagree with the following statement: When a company acquires the bonds of an affiliate directly from the affiliate, no intercompany gain or loss would result.

Q6-10 Explain why you agree or disagree with the following statement: The acquisition by one company of the outstanding debt of an affiliate, at a price different from the book value of the related debt, gives rise to a gain or loss that is reported as a separate item on the income statement of the purchasing affiliate.

Q6-11   The parent acquired in the open market for $95,000 subsidiary bonds with a par value of $80,000 and a book value of $90,000. Determine the amount of the gain or loss on the intercompany bond purchases that would be allocated to the parent and the subsidiary using the face-value method, and describe the guidelines followed in determining the gain or loss identified with each affiliate firm.

Q6-12   Explain why you agree or disagree with the following statement: The method used to assign the gain or loss on the acquisition of intercompany bonds to affiliated firms will alter the total amount of consolidated net income reported during the postacquisition life of the bonds.

Q6-13   Discuss how each of the following discounting of notes by affiliated companies would alter, if at all, the amount of consolidated assets or liabilities:

a) A parent or subsidiary discounted an intercompany note with an unaffiliated party.

b) A parent or subsidiary discounted an unaffiliated note with an affiliate.

EXERCISES

E6-1   **Intercompany Note: Compute Parent Interest in Subsidiary Income, Consolidation Adjustments**   Howe Company, a 90%-owned subsidiary of Edmonton, Inc., borrowed $50,000 from Edmonton on January 1, 19X5, signing a 6% note in return. The note is due on January 1, 19X7, with the first year's interest payment due on December 31, 19X5, and the second year's interest due at the time the note matures. For the years 19X5 and 19X6, Howe reported net incomes of $45,000 and $65,000, respectively. The subsidiary was acquired at book value.

REQUIRED

a) Prepare the entry to record Edmonton's income from the subsidiary for 19X5 and 19X6.

b) Prepare in journal entry form the consolidation worksheet adjustments relating to the intercompany debt for the years 19X5 and 19X6.

c) How would the consolidation worksheet adjustments be different, if at all, had Edmonton (the parent) been the borrower rather than Howe Company?

E6-2   **Intercompany Note: Compute Parent and Minority Interest in Subsidiary Income, Consolidation Adjustments**   On January 1, 19X1, Pepperhill acquired 80% of the outstanding common stock of Salter at a book value of $240,000. At the date of acquisition, Salter's common stock and retained earnings balances were $200,000 and $100,000, respectively. On the date of acquisition, Salter borrowed $10,000 from Pepperhill under a three-year note requiring annual year-end interest payments of 8%, with the principal of the note due on December 31, 19X3. The net incomes reported by Salter for a three-year period are as follows: 19X1, $9,200; 19X2, $6,200; 19X3, $7,200.

REQUIRED
For the years 19X1, 19X2, and 19X3:

a) Prepare the entry to record Pepperhill's income from the subsidiary.

b) Prepare in journal entry form all necessary consolidation worksheet adjustments.

c) Determine the minority interest in the subsidiary net income.

E6-3   **Parent Acquires Subsidiary Debt: Determine Gain or Loss on Intercompany Debt, Consolidation Adjustments**   Several years ago, Pastore Company acquired 80% of the outstanding common stock of Sabatini Company. At the beginning of the current year, January 1, 19X7, Pastore acquired, in the open market, all the outstanding $50,000 par value, 6% bonds of Sabatini. Pastore paid $50,929 for the bonds. The book value of the bonds on the date of purchase by Pastore was $49,096. The bonds pay interest on December 31 and mature on January 1, 19X9.

REQUIRED

a) Determine the 19X7 consolidated gain or loss on the purchase of intercompany bonds.

b) Prepare in journal entry form the consolidation worksheet adjustments for 19X7 and 19X8 relating to intercompany bonds.

E6-4 **Multiple Choice Questions on Parent's Acquisition of Subsidiary Debt**   On January 1, 19X2, Vertical, a 70%-owned subsidiary of Horizontal, issued $100,000 of 7%, four-year bonds for $96,688. Interest is paid annually each December 31. On January 1, 19X4, Horizontal acquired all the outstanding bonds of Vertical for $96,482. There was no accrued interest on the bonds purchased. Vertical reported a net income of $60,000 for the year ended December 31, 19X4.

REQUIRED

Using the preceding information, select the best answer for each of the following multiple choice questions:

1. The 19X4 consolidated gain or loss on the purchase of intercompany bonds would be

   a) $1,862 gain

   b) $3,518 loss

   c) $ 206 gain

   d) $1,735 loss

2. The gain or loss on the purchase of intercompany bonds attributed to the subsidiary would be

   a) $1,862 gain

   b) $3,518 gain

   c) $1,683 gain

   d) $–0–

3. The gain or loss on the purchase of intercompany bonds attributed to the parent would be

   a) $1,783 loss

   b) $3,518 gain

   c) $1,683 gain

   d) $–0–

4. The parent's 19X4 income from subsidiary would be

   a) $44,463

   b) $42,652

   c) $42,000

   d) $40,752

5. The minority interest in the 19X4 income of the subsidiary would be

   a) $18,000

   b) $18,521

   c) $18,279

   d) $17,465

E6-5 **Subsidiary Acquires Parent Debt: Determine Gain or Loss on Intercompany Debt, Consolidation Adjustments**   Hogge Company owns all the common stock of Lambert, Inc. The December 31, 19X1, balance sheet of Hogge contained the following concerning its bonds payable:

- Bonds payable ($500,000 par, 7%, due 1-1-X5), $512,638; interest is paid each December 31.
- On January 1, 19X2, Lambert acquired, in the open market, all the bonds of Hogge at par value.

REQUIRED

a) Determine the 19X2 consolidated gain or loss on the purchase of intercompany bonds.

b) Prepare in journal entry form the consolidation worksheet adjustments for 19X2, 19X3, and 19X4 relating to intercompany bonds.

E6-6 **Subsidiary Acquires Parent Debt: Determine Gain or Loss on Intercompany Debt, Consolidation Adjustments**   Jones, Inc., owns 100% of the voting shares of Smith Company. Jones presented the following bond information in its December 31, 19X5, balance sheet:

- Bonds payable ($200,000 par, 5%, due 1-1-X9), $189,838; interest is paid each December 31.
- Smith acquired one-half the par value bonds of Jones on January 1, 19X6, for $92,269.

REQUIRED

a) Determine the 19X6 consolidated gain or loss on the purchase of intercompany bonds.

b) Prepare in journal entry form the consolidation worksheet adjustments for 19X6, 19X7, and 19X8 relating to intercompany bonds.

E6-7   Subsidiary Acquires Parent Debt: Determine Gain or Loss on Intercompany Debt, Compute Parent and Minority Interest in Subsidiary Income, Consolidation Adjustments   Rose Company issued 10%, six-year bonds at face value of $100,000 on January 1, 19X2. Interest is paid on December 31, and the bonds mature on January 1, 19X8. On January 1, 19X5, Tulip, Inc., an 80%-owned subsidiary of Rose, acquired all the parent's bonds in the open market for $105,151. For the years 19X5, 19X6, and 19X7 the subsidiary reported income of $20,000, $25,000, and $35,000, respectively.

REQUIRED

a) Determine the 19X5 consolidated gain or loss on the purchase of intercompany bonds.

b) Prepare the entry to record the parent's income from subsidiary for 19X5, 19X6, and 19X7.

c) Prepare in journal entry form the consolidated worksheet adjustments for 19X5, 19X6, and 19X7 relating to intercompany bonds.

d) Calculate minority interest in the net income of the subsidiary for the years 19X5, 19X6, and 19X7.

E6-8   Parent Acquires Subsidiary Debt: Determine Gain or Loss on Intercompany Debt, Consolidation Adjustments   Recycling Company, a wholly owned subsidiary of Aluminum Company, issued at face value, on January 1, 19X1, $100,000 of 6%, four-year bonds maturing on January 1, 19X5. Interest is paid on December 31. On January 1, 19X3, Aluminum Company acquired, in the open market, $20,000 (face value) of the bonds of Recycling Company for $19,286.

REQUIRED

a) Determine the 19X3 consolidated gain or loss on the purchase of intercompany bonds.

b) Prepare in journal entry form the consolidation worksheet adjustments for 19X3 and 19X4 relating to intercompany bonds.

E6-9   Parent Acquires Subsidiary Debt: Determine Gain or Loss on Intercompany Debt; Compute Parent and Minority Interest in Subsidiary Income; Consolidation Adjustments   Company A acquired 90% of the outstanding common stock of Company B on January 1, 19X3, at book value. The balance sheets for both companies immediately after acquisition are shown as follows:

	Company A	Company B
Assets		
Cash	$150,000	$ 58,107
Accounts receivable	81,000	10,000
Inventory	100,000	50,000
Investment in Company B	103,500	
Long-lived assets (net)	75,000	125,000
	$509,500	$243,107
Liabilities and Stockholders' Equity		
Accounts payable	$ 35,000	$ 21,158
Bonds payable (net)		106,949*
Common stock ($10 par)	400,000	100,000
Retained earnings	74,500	15,000
	$509,500	$243,107

* $100,000, 6%, ten-year bonds, issued January 1, 19X2; interest is paid each December 31.

Additional information:

1. On January 1, 19X4, Company A purchased, in the open market, $40,000 (par value) of the bonds of Company B for $37,611.

2. For the years 19X4 and 19X5, the subsidiary reported income of $25,000 and $35,000, respectively.

REQUIRED

a) Determine the 19X4 consolidated gain or loss on purchase of intercompany bonds.

b) Prepare the entry to record the parent's income from subsidiary for 19X4 and 19X5.

c) Prepare in journal entry form the consolidation worksheet adjustments for 19X4 and 19X5 relating to intercompany bonds.

d) Calculate the minority interest in the net income of the subsidiary for the years 19X4 and 19X5.

E6-10 **Subsidiary Acquires Parent Debt: Determine Gain or Loss on Intercompany Debt, Consolidation Adjustments** Kidd, Inc., owns 90% of the voting shares of Sibley Company. The January 1, 19X7, financial records of Kidd contained bonds payable ($100,000 par, 5% due 1-1-X9) of $96,612. Bond interest is paid each December 31.

Sibley acquired one-half the $100,000 par value bonds of the parent company, Kidd, for $47,423 on January 1, 19X7. For the years 19X7 and 19X8, Sibley reported a net income of $60,000 and $70,000, respectively.

REQUIRED

a) Determine the 19X7 consolidated gain or loss on the purchase of intercompany bonds.

b) Prepare the entry to record Kidd's income from subsidiary for 19X7 and 19X8.

c) Prepare in journal entry form the consolidation worksheet adjustments for 19X7 and 19X8 relating to intercompany bonds.

d) Calculate minority interest in the net income of the subsidiary for 19X7 and 19X8.

E6-11 **Parent Acquires Subsidiary Debt: Determine Gain or Loss on Intercompany Debt, Consolidation Adjustments** Several years ago, Mills Company acquired 90% of the outstanding voting stock of Duncan, Inc. On January 1, 19X7, Mills acquired, in the open market, all the outstanding $50,000 par value 6% bonds of Duncan for $51,000. Interest on the bonds is paid each December 31, and the bonds mature January 1, 19X9. The book value of the bonds on the date of purchase by Mills was $49,096. For 19X7 and 19X8, Duncan reported a net income of $45,000 and $30,000, respectively.

REQUIRED

a) Determine the 19X7 consolidated gain or loss on the purchase of intercompany bonds.

b) Prepare the entry to record Mills' income from subsidiary for 19X7 and 19X8.

c) Prepare in journal entry form the consolidation worksheet adjustment for 19X7 and 19X8 relating to intercompany bonds.

d) Calculate minority interest in the net income of the subsidiary for 19X7 and 19X8.

E6-12 **Two-Part Exercise: Parent Acquires Subsidiary Debt and Subsidiary Acquires Parent Debt** PX acquired 80% of the outstanding voting stock of SX on January 1, 19X1, at book value. On January 1, 19X2, the affiliate companies issued bonds as follows:

● PX issued $50,000 of 9%, ten-year bonds at a price of $53,356. Interest is paid annually on December 31.

• SX issued $25,000 of 7%, five-year bonds at a price of $24,002. Interest is paid annually on December 31.

As of December 31, 19X3, the balances in the bonds payable accounts of the two companies were as follows:

Bonds Payable (Net)

PX	$52,684
SX	24,402

For the years ended December 31, 19X3, and 19X4, SX reported a net income of $40,000 and $50,000, respectively. *Prepare independent solutions to PART A and PART B that follow.*

PART A

REQUIRED

Assuming PX acquired in the open market all the outstanding bonds of SX on December 31, 19X3, for $23,135, prepare solutions to the following:

a) Determine the 19X3 consolidated gain or loss on purchase of intercompany bonds.

b) Prepare the entry to record PX's income from subsidiary for 19X3 and 19X4.

c) Prepare in journal entry form the consolidation worksheet adjustments relating to intercompany bonds for the years 19X3 and 19X4.

d) Calculate minority interest in the net income of the subsidiary for 19X3 and 19X4.

PART B

REQUIRED

Assuming SX acquired $25,000 (face value) of PX's bonds on December 31, 19X3, from an unaffiliated firm for $27,985, prepare solutions to the following:

a) Determine the 19X3 consolidated gain or loss on purchase of intercompany bonds.

b) Prepare the entry to record PX's income from subsidiary for 19X3 and 19X4.

c) Prepare in journal entry form the consolidation worksheet adjustments relating to intercompany bonds for the years 19X3 and 19X4.

d) Calculate minority interest in the net income of the subsidiary for 19X3 and 19X4.

E6-13
APPENDIX A

Determine Gain or Loss on Intercompany Debt, Allocation Using Face-Value Method   Home Corporation, a builder of residential homes nationwide, purchased in the open market, over a period of years, the following bond issues of its various subsidiaries. In each of the following independent cases, Home Corporation acquired all the bonds outstanding.

1. Home paid a $1,000 premium for Mortgage Company's bonds, which had an unamortized issuance discount of $300.

2. Home purchased Insulators Corporation's bonds for $1,500 below face value. The bonds had a $1,000 unamortized issuance premium.

3. Home paid $2,000 below face value for the bonds of Jayhawk Safety Lock Corporation. The bonds had an unamortized issuance discount of $2,000.

4. Home purchased Lamplighter Company's bonds for $2,500 below face value. The bonds had an unamortized issuance discount of $2,000.

5. Home purchased the bonds of Plywood Corporation for $500 above face value. The bonds had an unamortized issuance premium of $750.

REQUIRED

a) Describe how the consolidated gain or loss on the acquisition of intercompany bonds is determined, and describe the face-value method of allocating the consolidated gain or loss to the bond-issuer and the bond-investor.

b) Calculate the amount of consolidated gain or loss, if any, for each purchase of intercompany bonds, and allocate the consolidated gain or loss to the bond-issuer and the bond-investor using the face-value method.

E6-14

APPENDIX A

Subsidiary Acquires Parent Debt: Determine Gain or Loss on Intercompany Debt, Consolidation Adjustments   Using the same information in E6-10, complete the requirements of E6-10 assuming the face-value method of allocating gains and losses on intercompany debt is followed.

E6-15

APPENDIX A

Parent Acquires Subsidiary Debt: Determine Gain or Loss on Intercompany Debt, Consolidation Adjustments   Using the same information in E6-11, complete the requirements of E6-11 assuming the face-value method of allocating gains and losses on intercompany debt is followed.

E6-16

APPENDIX A

Two-Part Exercise: Parent Acquires Subsidiary Debt and Subsidiary Acquires Parent Debt   Using the same information in E6-12, complete the requirements of E6-12 assuming the face-value method of allocating gains and losses on intercompany debt is followed.

E6-17

APPENDIX B

Discounting Intercompany Notes   Indicate whether you agree or disagree with each of the following statements. If you disagree with a statement, provide an explanation as to why.

1. When a parent or subsidiary discounts an intercompany note with an unaffiliated party and credits notes receivable, the intercompany note receivable is removed from its records. However, the intercompany note payable remains on the original borrowing affiliate's records and now represents a liability to the consolidated entity.

2. When a parent or subsidiary discounts an intercompany note with an unaffiliated party and credits notes receivable discounted rather than notes receivable for the discounted note, a consolidation adjustment is necessary to offset notes receivable discounted against notes receivable.

3. If a note receivable from an unaffiliated party is discounted with an affiliated party (parent or subsidiary), the asset (note receivable) is transferred from one affiliate to another and thus must be excluded from consolidated assets.

4. If a subsidiary discounts an intercompany note with an unaffiliated party and removes the intercompany note receivable from its records by crediting notes receivable, the intercompany note payable remains on the records of the original borrowing affiliate. Therefore, the interest expense accrued on the note payable subsequent to the date of discount should be excluded from consolidated income.

5. An unaffiliated party note discounted by an affiliate party (parent or subsidiary) transfers an unaffiliated note receivable from one affiliated party to another but does not alter the amount of consolidated assets or liabilities.

PROBLEMS

P6-1

Consolidation Worksheet: Intercompany Loan and Bond Purchase by Subsidiary   On January 1, 19X8, 90% of the outstanding common stock of Warren Corporation was acquired at a book value of $126,000 by Haskins Corporation. The following are the financial statements of both companies as of December 31, 19X8:

	Haskins Corporation	Warren Corporation
Income Statement		
Sales	$160,000	$ 75,000
Income from subsidiary	21,433	
Interest revenue	300	1,600
Cost of goods sold	(60,000)	(15,000)
Interest expense	(1,733)	(300)
Other expenses	(50,000)	(36,300)
Net income	$ 70,000	$ 25,000
Retained Earnings Statement		
Retained earnings, 1-1-X8	$192,800	$ 75,000
Net income	70,000	25,000
Dividends	(50,000)	(15,000)
Retained earnings, 12-31-X8	$212,800	$ 85,000
Balance Sheet		
Cash	$ 90,000	$ 40,300
Accounts receivable	97,500	40,000
Interest receivable	300	
Notes receivable	10,000	
Inventory	100,000	60,000
Investment in Warren stock	133,933	
Investment in Haskins bonds (net)		20,000
Total assets	$431,733	$160,300
Interest payable	$	$ 300
Notes payable		10,000
Bonds payable (net)	18,933	
Common stock	200,000	65,000
Retained earnings	212,800	85,000
Total liabilities and stockholders' equity	$431,733	$160,300

Additional information:

1. On July 1, 19X8, Haskins transferred $10,000 cash to Warren. In exchange, Warren signed a 6%, one-year note. Interest is payable on the date the note is due.

2. Warren acquired in the open market all the outstanding $20,000 par value bonds of Haskins on January 1, 19X8. Warren paid par value for the bonds. The book value of the bonds on the date of purchase by Warren was $18,800. The 8%, ten-year bonds were initially issued by Haskins on January 1, 19X7; interest is paid on December 31.

REQUIRED

Prepare a consolidation worksheet for Haskins Corporation and its subsidiary for the year ended December 31, 19X8.

P6-2 **Consolidation Worksheet: Intercompany Bond Purchase by Parent** On January 1, 19X5, Cash Company acquired 90% of the outstanding common stock and all the outstanding $25,000 par value bonds of Williams Company for $63,750 and $24,389, respectively. Any excess cost over book value of common shares is identified as goodwill and amortized over 15 years. The book value of the bonds on January 1, 19X5, was $25,584. The 10%, five-year bonds were initially issued by Williams on January 1, 19X3, with interest payments on December 31. Financial statements of both companies for the fiscal year ending December 31, 19X5, are as follows:

	Cash Company	Williams Company
Income Statement		
Sales	$ 80,000	$ 37,500
Interest revenue	2,704	
Income from subsidiary	9,517	
Cost of goods sold	(30,000)	(12,500)
Interest expense		(2,306)
Other expenses	(34,914)	(12,694)
Net income	$ 27,307	$ 10,000
Retained Earnings Statement		
Retained earnings, 1-1-X5	$100,000	$ 37,500
Net income	27,307	10,000
Dividends	(25,000)	(5,000)
Retained earnings, 12-31-X5	$102,307	$ 42,500
Balance Sheet		
Cash	$ 23,837	$ 40,000
Accounts receivable	24,178	30,000
Inventory	50,000	30,000
Investment in Williams stock	68,767	
Investment in Williams bonds (net)	24,593	
Total assets	$191,375	$100,000
Accounts payable	$ 14,068	$ 2,110
Bonds payable (net)		25,390
Common stock	75,000	30,000
Retained earnings	102,307	42,500
Total liabilities and stockholders' equity	$191,375	$100,000

REQUIRED
Prepare a consolidation worksheet as of December 31, 19X5, for Cash Company and its subsidiary.

P6-3 **Consolidation Worksheet: Intercompany Bond Purchase by Parent** Pardon Company acquired an 80% interest in Lee Company on January 1, 19X2, for $220,000. Any excess cost over book value of acquired equity is allocated to an undervalued building of Lee. The building has a ten-year remaining estimated life at the time of the acquisition, and straight-line depreciation is applied. The following financial statements are made available for the two companies as of December 31, 19X3:

	Pardon Company	Lee Company
Income Statement		
Sales	$448,763	$300,000
Interest revenue	838	
Income from subsidiary	54,399	
Cost of goods sold	(300,000)	(200,000)
Depreciation expense	(40,000)	(20,000)
Interest expense		(1,534)
Other expenses	(20,000)	(8,466)
Net income	$144,000	$ 70,000
Retained Earnings Statement		
Retained earnings, 1-1-X3	$300,000	$100,000
Net income	144,000	70,000
Dividends	(100,000)	(50,000)
Retained earnings, 12-31-X3	$344,000	$120,000
Balance Sheet		
Cash	$274,570	$160,000
Inventory	200,000	150,000
Investment in Lee stock	272,399	
Investment in Lee bonds (net)	9,031	
Buildings (net)	70,000	50,000
Total assets	$826,000	$360,000
Accounts payable	$ 82,000	$ 20,940
Bonds payable (net)		19,060
Common stock	400,000	200,000
Retained earnings	344,000	120,000
Total liabilities and stockholders' equity	$826,000	$360,000

Additional information:

1. Lee Company reported a net income of $70,000 in 19X2 and paid dividends of $20,000 during the same year.

2. Lee's common stock and retained earnings balances were $200,000 and $50,000, respectively, at the date of acquisition.

3. On January 1, 19X1, Lee issued at a discount, $20,000 par value, 7%, ten-year bonds with interest payments on December 31. Pardon purchased one-half the outstanding bonds of Lee in the open market on January 1, 19X3, for $8,893. The book value of these bonds on the date of purchase by Pardon was $9,463.

REQUIRED

Prepare a consolidation worksheet for Pardon Company and its subsidiary as of December 31, 19X3.

P6-4 **Consolidation Worksheet: Intercompany Bond Purchase by Subsidiary, Inventory Transfers**
On January 1, 19X2, Plotkin Company paid cash of $13,000 for all the voting shares of Spivey Company. At the date of acquisition, the book value of the assets and liabilities of Spivey represented fair values. Any excess cost over book value of acquired equity is considered goodwill and is amortized over 30 years. Financial statements for the two companies as of December 31, 19X2, are as follows:

	Plotkin Company	Spivey Company
Income Statement		
Sales	$20,000	$20,000
Interest revenue		231
Income from subsidiary	1,577	
Cost of goods sold	(10,000)	(15,000)
Interest expense	(500)	
Other expenses	(4,177)	(3,231)
Net income	$ 6,900	$ 2,000
Retained Earnings Statement		
Retained earnings, 1-1-X2	$12,000	$ 4,000
Net income	6,900	2,000
Dividends	(4,000)	(1,000)
Retained earnings, 12-31-X2	$14,900	$ 5,000
Balance Sheet		
Cash	$ 7,573	$ 2,862
Accounts receivable	5,000	6,000
Interest receivable		250
Inventory	24,000	11,000
Investment in Spivey stock	13,577	
Investment in Plotkin bonds (net)		5,323
Total assets	$50,150	$25,435
Accounts payable	$ 5,000	$14,435
Interest payable	250	
Bonds payable	5,000	
Common stock	25,000	6,000
Retained earnings	14,900	5,000
Total liabilities and stockholders' equity	$50,150	$25,435

During the year 19X2, Plotkin acquired merchandise from the subsidiary for $10,000. As of December 31, 19X2, all the transferred merchandise had been sold by the parent. However, the parent still owes Spivey for one-half the purchase price of the merchandise. The open account obligation to Spivey is noninterest-bearing.

On July 1, 19X2, Spivey purchased all the outstanding bonds of the parent, paying $5,342. The $5,000 par value, 10%, ten-year bonds were issued by the parent on July 1, 19X1, at par value with interest paid on June 30 and January 1.

REQUIRED
Prepare a consolidation worksheet as of December 31, 19X2, for Plotkin and its subsidiary.

P6-5 **Consolidation Worksheet: Intercompany Loan and Bond Purchase by Parent**   On January 1, 19X2, Jeans, Inc., acquired a 75% controlling interest in Lee Company, paying cash of $42,000. During 19X2, Lee reported a net income of $8,000 and dividend payments of $2,000. Trial balances for both companies as of December 31, 19X3, are as follows:

	Jeans, Inc.	Lee Company
Debits		
Cash	$ 70,956	$ 29,226
Notes receivable	72,367	13,000
Inventory	49,000	7,915
Investment in Lee stock	47,395	
Investment in Lee bonds (net)	9,838	
Land	15,000	2,000
Plant and equipment (net)	20,000	15,000
Cost of goods sold	78,000	24,127
Interest expense	500	718
Depreciation and other expenses	25,738	6,282
Dividends	12,500	
	$401,294	$ 98,268
Credits		
Notes payable	$ 53,987	$ 10,377
Bonds payable		10,164
Capital stock	120,000	24,000
Paid-in capital	30,000	7,000
Retained earnings	75,000	10,000
Sales	119,123	36,227
Interest revenue	881	500
Income from subsidiary	2,303	
	$401,294	$ 98,268

Additional information:

1. Lee had a balance in retained earnings of $4,000 on January 1, 19X2.

2. The $15,750 excess cost over book value paid by Jeans for its investment in Lee is allocated to plant and equipment ($7,750; ten-year remaining life; straight-line depreciation used) and goodwill ($8,000; eight-year remaining life).

3. On January 1, 19X3, Lee forwarded $5,000 cash to Jeans in exchange for a three-year note signed by Jeans to Lee. The note bears interest of 10%, payable each December 31, with the third year's interest due with the payment of the note.

4. On January 1, 19X1, Lee issued at a premium $10,000 par value, 8%, five-year bonds with interest payments on December 31. Jeans purchased all the outstanding bonds of Lee in the open market on January 1, 19X2, for $9,676. The book value of the bonds on the date of purchase by Jeans was $10,328.

REQUIRED

Prepare a consolidation worksheet as of December 31, 19X3, for Jeans, Inc., and its subsidiary.

P6-6 **Consolidation Worksheet: Intercompany Bond Purchase by Parent** On January 1, 19X5, Crum, Inc., acquired a 90% interest in Knight Company for $66,000. On the date of acquisition the common stock and retained earnings balances of Knight were $30,000 and $40,000, respectively. Any excess cost over book value of acquired equity is attributable to the equipment being undervalued (15-year remaining life, straight-line depreciation used).

    Crum also acquired all the outstanding $25,000 par value, 10%, five-year bonds of Knight on January 1, 19X5, for $24,000. The bonds were initially issued by Knight on January 1, 19X2; interest is paid on December 31, and the bonds mature on January 1, 19X7. The book value of the bond on the date they were purchased by Crum was $25,390.

    Financial statements of both companies for the fiscal year ending December 31, 19X6, are as follows:

	Crum, Inc.	Knight Company
Income Statement		
Sales	$ 80,000	$ 37,000
Interest revenue	3,000	
Income from subsidiary	7,900	
Cost of goods sold	(30,000)	(12,200)
Interest expense		(2,305)
Other expenses	(35,000)	(12,800)
Net income	$ 25,900	$ 9,695
Retained Earnings Statement		
Retained earnings, 1-1-X6	$100,000	$ 50,000
Net income	25,900	9,695
Dividends	(15,000)	(5,000)
Retained earnings, 12-31-X6	$110,900	$ 54,695
Balance Sheet		
Cash	$ 18,174	$ 40,000
Accounts receivable	24,000	32,000
Inventory	50,000	30,000
Investment in Knight stock	78,826	
Investment in Knight bonds (net)	25,000	
Property, plant and equipment (net)	30,000	20,000
Total assets	$226,000	$122,000
Accounts payable	$ 15,100	$ 12,305
Bonds payable (net)		25,000
Common stock	100,000	30,000
Retained earnings	110,900	54,695
Total liabilities and stockholders' equity	$226,000	$122,000

REQUIRED

Prepare a consolidation worksheet for Crum, Inc., and its subsidiary for the year ended December 31, 19X6.

P6-7   Consolidation Worksheet: Intercompany Bond Purchase by Parent, Inventory Transfers
Perez Company acquired, in the open market, 90% of the common stock of Sims Company on January 1, 19X9, for $175,000. Any valuation differential is goodwill and amortized over 20 years. The financial statements as of December 31, 19X9, for both companies are presented as follows:

	Perez Company	Sims Company
Income Statement		
Sales	$627,750	$342,500
Interest revenue	3,800	
Cost of goods sold	(510,000)	(306,000)
Loss from subsidiary	(49,475)	
Operating expenses	(92,000)	(70,000)
Other expenses	(22,180)	(15,500)
Net income (loss)	$ (42,105)	$ (49,000)
Retained Earnings Statement		
Retained earnings, 1-1-X9	$107,000	$ 84,000
Net income (loss)	(42,105)	(49,000)
Dividends	(20,000)	(10,000)
Retained earnings, 12-31-X9	$ 44,895	$ 25,000
Balance Sheet		
Cash	$ 20,570	$ 32,500
Accounts receivable	94,000	60,000
Inventory	80,000	45,000
Investment in Sims stock	116,525	
Investment in Sims bonds (net)	51,800	
Plant and equipment (net)	445,000	210,000
Total assets	$807,895	$347,500
Accounts payable	$163,000	$ 17,100
Bonds payable, 5% (net)		205,400
Common stock	600,000	100,000
Retained earnings	44,895	25,000
Total liabilities and stockholders' equity	$807,895	$347,500

Additional information:

1. In the open market, Perez acquired, on January 1, 19X9, one-fourth ($50,000 face amount) of the bonds of Sims for $52,000. On the date of the bond purchase, the bonds had a remaining life of ten years until maturity and an unamortized premium of $6,000.

2. During 19X9, Sims purchased inventory from Perez for $180,000, which included a 20% markup on cost to Perez. Fifteen percent of this inventory remains in the ending inventory of Sims.

REQUIRED
Prepare a consolidation worksheet for Perez Company and its subsidiary for the year ended December 31, 19X9.

P6-8 **Consolidation Worksheet: Intercompany Bond Purchase by Subsidiary, Inventory Transfers, Management Service Transfers** On June 30, 19X2, Linskey, Inc., purchased 100% of the outstanding common stock of Cresswell Corporation for $3,605,000 cash and Linskey's common stock valued at $4,100,000. At the date of purchase, the book and fair value of Cresswell's assets and liabilities were as follows:

	Book Value	Fair Value
Cash	$ 160,000	$ 160,000
Accounts receivable (net)	910,000	910,000
Inventory	860,000	1,025,186
Property, plant and equipment (net)	6,550,000	9,800,000
Intangible assets (net)	150,000	220,000
	$8,630,000	
Accounts payable	$ 580,000	$ 580,000
Note payable	500,000	500,000
5% mortgage note payable	4,000,000	3,710,186
Common stock	2,900,000	
Retained earnings	650,000	
	$8,630,000	

By the year-end, December 31, 19X2, the net balance of Cresswell's accounts receivable at June 30, 19X2, had been collected; the inventory on hand at June 30, 19X2, had been charged to cost of goods sold; the accounts payable at June 30, 19X2, had been paid; and the $500,000 note had been paid.

As of June 30, 19X2, Cresswell's property, plant, and equipment had an estimated remaining life of 10 years. All intangible assets had an estimated remaining life of 20 years. All depreciation and amortization are to be computed using the straight-line method.

As of June 30, 19X2, the 5% mortgage note payable had eight equal annual payments remaining with the next payment due June 30, 19X3. The fair value of the note was based on a 7% rate.

Prior to June 30, 19X2, there were no intercompany transactions between Linskey and Cresswell. However, during the last six months of 19X2 the following intercompany transactions occurred:

1. Linskey sold $400,000 of merchandise to Cresswell. The cost of the merchandise to Linskey was $360,000. Of this merchandise, $75,000 remained on hand at December 31, 19X2.

2. On December 31, 19X2, Cresswell purchased, in the market, $300,000 of Linskey's 7 1/2% bonds payable for $312,500, including $22,500 interest receivable. Linskey had issued $1,000,000 of these 20-year, 7 1/2% bonds payable 8 years ago for $960,000. Interest is payable January 1.

3. Many of the management functions of the two companies have been consolidated since the merger. Linskey charges Cresswell as $30,000 per month management fee. Management fees are treated as period expenses.

4. At December 31, 19X2, Cresswell owes Linskey two months' management fees and $18,000 for merchandise purchases.

The trial balances for both companies as of December 31, 19X2, follow. Linskey's profit and loss figures are for the 12-month period, whereas Cresswell's are for the last 6 months. Both companies made all the adjustment entries required for separate financial statements.

	Linskey, Inc. Dr. (Cr.)	Cresswell Corporation Dr. (Cr.)
Cash	$ 507,000	$ 200,750
Accounts receivable (net)	1,890,000	817,125
Inventory	2,031,000	1,009,500
Property, plant and equipment (net)	13,200,000	5,950,000
Intangible assets (net)		146,250
Investment in Cresswell stock	7,541,757	
Investment in Linskey 7 1/2% bonds (net)		290,000
Interest receivable		22,500
Accounts payable	(1,843,000)	(575,875)
Interest payable	(200,500)	(100,000)
Mortgage notes payable, 5%	(6,786,500)	(4,000,000)
7 1/2% bonds payable	(976,000)	
8 1/4% bonds payable	(3,900,000)	
Common stock	(8,772,500)	(2,900,000)
Retained earnings	(2,167,500)	(650,000)
Sales	(26,000,000)	(6,000,000)
Cost of goods sold	18,000,000	3,950,000
Selling, general, and administrative expenses	3,130,000	956,000
Management service income	(180,000)	
Management service expense		180,000
Interest expense	662,000	100,000
Depreciation expense	3,701,000	600,000
Amortization expense		3,750
Loss from subsidiary	163,243	
	$ –0–	$ –0–

REQUIRED

Prepare a consolidation worksheet for Linskey, Inc., and its subsidiary for the year ended December 31, 19X2.

(AICPA adapted)

P6-9 **Consolidation Worksheet: Intercompany Upstream Inventory Transfers, Downstream Equipment Transfer, Bond Purchase by Parent; Valuation Differential** On January 1, 19X5, Atlantic purchased, for $255,000, 90% of Pacific's common shares. On this date, the fair value of Pacific's assets and liabilities equaled their carrying value. Atlantic amortizes intangibles over a ten-year period.

The financial statements for both companies as of December 31, 19X5, are presented as follows:

	Atlantic	Pacific
Income Statement		
Sales	$300,000	$116,000
Interest revenue	5,600	
Income from subsidiary	25,100	
Cost of goods sold	(100,000)	(49,000)
Depreciation and amortization expense	(27,000)	(10,000)
Interest expense	(6,500)	(12,000)
Other expenses	(70,200)	(15,000)
Loss on sale of equipment	(7,000)	
Net income	$120,000	$ 30,000
Retained Earnings Statement		
Retained earnings, 1-1-X5	$ 92,000	$ 75,000
Net income	120,000	30,000
Dividends	(22,000)	(14,000)
Retained earnings, 12-31-X5	$190,000	$ 91,000
Balance Sheet		
Cash	$ 57,100	$ 19,000
Accounts receivable	30,000	25,000
Interest receivable	1,400	
Inventory	62,000	57,000
Investment in Pacific stock	267,500	
Investment in Pacific bonds (net)	70,000	
Land	130,000	82,000
Plant and equipment (net)	225,000	195,000
Total assets	$843,000	$378,000
Accounts payable	$ 53,000	$ 10,000
Interest payable		2,000
Bonds payable (net)		100,000
Common stock	600,000	175,000
Retained earnings	190,000	91,000
Total liabilities and stockholders' equity	$843,000	$378,000

Additional information:

1. During the current fiscal year 19X5, Atlantic purchased $60,000 of merchandise from Pacific. At December 31, 19X5, one-fourth of the merchandise remained in Atlantic's inventory. For 19X5, gross profit percentages based on selling price were 50% for Atlantic and 40% for Pacific.

2. On July 1, 19X5, Atlantic sold to Pacific for $19,000 equipment with a book value of $26,000; the estimated life of the equipment is seven years, and straight depreciation is applied.

3. On May 1, 19X1, Pacific issued at face value $100,000, 12% ten-year bonds with interest payable semiannually on April 30 and October 31. Atlantic purchased $70,000 of Pacific's bonds for face value on May 1, 19X5.

REQUIRED
Prepare a consolidation worksheet for Atlantic and its subsidiary for the year ended December 31, 19X5.

P6-10 **Consolidation Worksheet: Intercompany Downstream Inventory Transfers, Upstream Machinery Transfer, Bond Purchase by Parent; Valuation Differential** George Company acquired a 75% interest in Washington Company on January 1, 19X2, for $64,500. The common stock and retained earnings balances of Washington on January 1, 19X2, were $62,000 and $8,000, respectively. Any excess cost over book value of acquired equity is considered goodwill and amortized over ten years.

The financial statements for both companies as of December 31, 19X3, are presented as follows:

	George Company	Washington Company
Income Statement		
Sales	$120,000	$ 63,300
Interest revenue	2,500	700
Income from subsidiary	7,001	
Gain on sale of machinery		3,000
Cost of goods sold	(58,000)	(38,000)
Depreciation and amortization expense	(7,500)	(5,300)
Interest expense	(4,500)	(2,000)
Other expenses	(20,501)	(5,700)
Net income	$ 39,000	$ 16,000
Retained Earnings Statement		
Retained earnings, 1-1-X3	$ 80,000	$ 15,000
Net income	39,000	16,000
Dividends	(12,000)	(4,000)
Retained earnings, 12-31-X3	$107,000	$ 27,000
Balance Sheet		
Cash	$ 34,359	$ 7,000
Accounts receivable	20,000	15,000
Inventory	55,000	22,000
Investment in Washington stock	72,965	
Investment in Washington bonds (net)	19,676	
Land	30,000	28,000
Plant and machinery	125,000	71,000
Accumulated depreciation	(50,000)	(23,000)
Total assets	$307,000	$120,000
Notes payable	$ 50,000	$ 10,672
Bonds payable		20,328
Common stock	150,000	62,000
Retained earnings	107,000	27,000
Total liabilities and stockholders' equity	$307,000	$120,000

Additional information:

1. During 19X2, George sold merchandise costing $8,000 to Washington for $11,200; 10% of these transfers of merchandise remained in the 19X2 ending inventory of Washington.

2. During the current fiscal year 19X3, Washington purchased $28,000 of merchandise from George. George sells merchandise to all customers at 40% above cost. The 19X3 ending inventory of Washington consisted of one-fourth of the 19X3 merchandise transfers.

3. Washington sold machinery with a remaining life of six years to George on January 1, 19X3, for $17,000. At the date of sale, Washington's records indicated the machinery had a book value of $14,000 (cost, $27,000; accumulated depreciation, $13,000). Straight-line depreciation is applied.

4. On January 1, 19X2, George acquired, in the open market, all the $20,000 par value, 8%, five-year bonds of Washington for $19,352. The book value of the bonds on the date of purchase by George was $20,656. The bonds were issued on January 1, 19X1, with interest payments on December 31.

5. During 19X2, Washington reported net income of $9,000 and dividend payments of $2,000.

REQUIRED
Prepare a consolidation worksheet for George Company and its subsidiary for the year ended December 31, 19X3 (round all amounts to the nearest dollar).

P6-11 **Consolidation Worksheet: Intercompany Upstream Inventory and Land Transfers, Downstream Machinery Transfer, Bond Purchase by Subsidiary; Valuation Differential** Mandy Company acquired an 85% interest in Sparky Company on January 1, 19X3, for $77,000. The common stock and retained earnings balances of Sparky on January 1, 19X3, were $70,000 and $10,000, respectively. On the date of acquisition, the book values of the net assets of Sparky were equal to their fair values except for land, which had a fair value exceeding book value by $9,000. All intangibles are amortized over ten years.

The financial statements for both companies as of December 31, 19X8, are presented as follows:

	Mandy Company	Sparky Company
Income Statement		
Sales	$160,000	$ 70,000
Interest revenue	1,500	3,700
Income from subsidiary	14,595	
Cost of goods sold	(69,000)	(32,000)
Loss on sale of land		(3,000)
Depreciation and amortization expense	(8,500)	(6,300)
Interest expense	(5,600)	(2,000)
Other expenses	(39,995)	(10,400)
Net income	$ 53,000	$ 20,000
Retained Earnings Statement		
Retained earnings, 1-1-X8	$ 90,000	$ 45,000
Net income	53,000	20,000
Dividends	(15,000)	(4,500)
Retained earnings, 12-31-X8	$128,000	$ 60,500
Balance Sheet		
Cash	$ 32,965	$ 7,000
Accounts receivable	25,000	11,000
Inventory	56,000	22,400
Investment in Sparky stock	112,835	
Investment in Mandy bonds (net)		33,600
Land	50,000	21,000
Plant and equipment	145,000	80,000
Accumulated depreciation	(50,000)	(24,000)
Total assets	$371,800	$151,000
Accounts payable	$ 40,000	$ 20,500
Bonds payable (net)	28,800	
Common stock	175,000	70,000
Retained earnings	128,000	60,500
Total liabilities and stockholders' equity	$371,800	$151,000

Additional information:

1. During 19X8, Sparky sold merchandise costing $18,000 to Mandy for $22,500; 40% of these transfers of merchandise remained in the 19X8 ending inventory of Mandy. The 19X8 beginning inventory of Mandy included intercompany gross margin of $600.

2. On November 20, 19X8, Sparky sold land costing $16,000 to Mandy for $13,000.

3. Mandy sold equipment with a remaining life of four years to Sparky on July 1, 19X7, for $15,000. At the date of sale, Mandy's records indicated the equipment had a book value of $11,000 (cost, $20,000; accumulated depreciation, $9,000). Straight-line depreciation is applied.

4. On July 1, 19X8, Sparky acquired, in the open market, all the $30,000 par value, 10%, ten-year bonds of Mandy for $33,900. The book value of the bonds on January 1, 19X8, was $28,600. The bonds were issued on January 1, 19X5, with interest payments on June 30 and December 31.

REQUIRED

Prepare a consolidation worksheet for Mandy Company and its subsidiary for the year ended December 31, 19X8.

P6-12 **Consolidation Worksheet: Intercompany Upstream and Downstream Inventory, Land, and Equipment Transfers, Loan and Bond Purchases by Parent, and Bond Purchase by Subsidiary**
Rogers Company acquired 90% of the outstanding common stock of Signet, Inc. on January 1, 19X3, for cash of $111,530. On this date, Signet's common stock and retained earnings balances were $82,000 and $18,000, respectively. The fair values of Signet's net assets were equal to book values except for land, which had a book value of $5,000 and a fair value of $6,700. Any goodwill recognized is to be amortized over ten years.

Financial statements for both companies as of December 31, 19X4, are presented below.

	Rogers Company	Signet, Inc.
Income Statement		
Sales	$239,972	$164,600
Interest revenue	6,000	4,000
Income from subsidiary	8,028	
Gain on sale of land		3,400
Gain on sale of equipment		5,000
Cost of goods sold	(102,000)	(87,000)
Depreciation and amortization expense	(27,000)	(18,000)
Interest expense	(5,000)	(7,000)
Other expenses	(70,000)	(50,000)
Net income	$ 50,000	$ 15,000
Retained Earnings Statement		
Retained earnings, 1-1-X4	$127,000	$ 39,000
Net income	50,000	15,000
Dividends	(12,000)	(6,000)
Retained earnings, 12-31-X4	$165,000	$ 48,000
Balance Sheet		
Cash	$ 14,692	$ 9,300
Accounts receivable	29,000	15,000
Interest receivable	1,500	1,000
Notes receivable	23,000	7,000
Inventory	90,000	50,000
Investment in Signet stock	121,528	
Investment in Signet bonds (net)	9,280	
Investment in Rogers bonds (net)		30,700
Equipment	160,000	100,000
Accumulated depreciation	(60,000)	(35,000)
Land	36,000	32,000
Total assets	$425,000	$210,000
Accounts payable	$ 15,000	$ 11,960
Interest payable	500	1,000
Notes payable	15,000	20,000
Bonds payable (net)	29,500	47,040
Common stock	200,000	82,000
Retained earnings	165,000	48,000
Total liabilities and stockholders' equity	$425,000	$210,000

Additional information:

1. Signet sold merchandise costing $33,000 to Rogers for $42,900 during 19X4. The 19X4 ending inventory of Rogers consisted of 40% of the 19X4 intercompany transfers of merchandise. The 19X4 beginning inventory of Rogers consisted of $3,900 of merchandise purchased from Signet; Signet sells merchandise to Rogers at 30% above cost.

2. Signet purchased $66,000 of merchandise from Rogers during 19X4. Rogers sells merchandise to all customers at 23% above cost. Signet's beginning and ending inventories for 19X4 contained $11,070 and $4,920, respectively, of merchandise purchased from Rogers.

3. During 19X3, Rogers sold land costing $5,000 to Signet for $6,100. Signet sold the land to an unaffiliated firm in 19X4 for $6,500.

4. During 19X4, Signet sold land costing $7,000 to Rogers for $10,000.

5. On July 1, 19X3, Rogers sold Signet equipment that had cost Rogers $27,000. At the time of the equipment sale, accumulated depreciation was $11,500. Signet paid $19,500 for the equipment; its estimated remaining life is eight years, and straight-line depreciation is applied.

6. On January 1, 19X4, Signet sold Rogers equipment that had cost Signet $35,000. At the time of the equipment sale, accumulated depreciation was $15,000. Rogers paid $25,000 for the equipment; its estimated remaining life is five years, and straight-line depreciation is applied.

7. On July 1, 19X4, Rogers transferred $13,000 cash to Signet. In exchange Signet signed a 7%, two-year note. Interest is payable semiannually on January 1 and July 1.

8. On January 1, 19X3, Signet acquired, in the open market, all the $30,000 par value, 8%, six-year bonds of Rogers for $31,400. The book value of the bonds on the date of purchase by Rogers was $29,000. The bonds were issued on January 1, 19X1, with interest payments on December 31.

9. On January 1, 19X4, Rogers acquired, in the open market, one-fourth of the $40,000 par value, 10%, eight-year bonds of Signet for $9,100. The book value of these bonds on January 1, 19X4, was $12,200. The bonds were issued on January 1, 19X1, with interest payments on June 30 and December 31.

REQUIRED
Prepare a consolidation worksheet for Rogers and its subsidiary as of December 31, 19X4.

P6-13   **Consolidation Worksheet: Intercompany Bond Purchase by Parent**   Wells Company acquired
APPENDIX A   a 75% interest in Myers Company on January 1, 19X2, for $34,250. The common stock and retained earnings balances of Myers on January 1, 19X2, were $31,000 and $4,000, respectively. Any excess cost over book value of acquired equity is considered goodwill and amortized over eight years.

Also on January 1, 19X2, Wells acquired in the open market, all the $10,000 par value, 8%, five-year bonds of Myers for $9,676. The book value of the bonds on the date of purchase by Wells was $10,328. The bonds were issued on January 1, 19X1, with interest payments on December 31. The face-value method is used to allocate gains and losses on intercompany debt.

During 19X2, Myers reported net income of $8,000 and dividend payments of $2,000.

The financial statements for both companies as of December 31, 19X3, are presented as follows:

	Wells Company	Myers Company
Income Statement		
Sales	$119,000	$36,000
Interest revenue	1,004	727
Income from subsidiary	2,608	
Cost of goods sold	(78,000)	(24,000)
Interest expense	(500)	(845)
Other expenses	(26,112)	(6,882)
Net income	$ 18,000	$ 5,000
Retained Earnings Statement		
Retained earnings, 1-1-X3	$ 75,000	$10,000
Net income	18,000	5,000
Dividends	(12,000)	
Retained earnings, 12-31-X3	$ 81,000	$15,000
Balance Sheet		
Cash	$ 81,376	$17,085
Notes receivable	70,000	15,000
Inventory	49,000	7,915
Investment in Myers stock	40,786	
Investment in Myers bonds (net)	9,838	
Land	10,000	8,000
Plant and equipment (net)	25,000	20,000
Total assets	$286,000	$68,000
Notes payable	$ 55,000	$11,836
Bonds payable		10,164
Common stock	150,000	31,000
Retained earnings	81,000	15,000
Total liabilities and stockholders' equity	$286,000	$68,000

REQUIRED

a) Show the computations that produced the amounts in the income from subsidiary and the investment in Myers stock accounts on the December 31, 19X3, financial statements of Wells.

b) Prepare a consolidation worksheet for Wells Company and its subsidiary for the year ended December 31, 19X3.

P6-14   **Consolidation Worksheet: Intercompany Loan and Bond Purchase by Subsidiary**   On January
APPENDIX A   1, 19X8, 90% of the outstanding common stock of Eskew Corporation was acquired at a book value
of $126,000 by Jensen Corporation. The following are the financial statements of both companies as
of December 31, 19X8:

	Jensen Corporation	Eskew Corporation
Income Statement		
Sales	$160,000	$ 75,000
Income from subsidiary	21,433	
Interest revenue	300	1,600
Cost of goods sold	(60,000)	(15,000)
Interest expense	(1,733)	(300)
Other expenses	(50,000)	(36,300)
Net income	$ 70,000	$ 25,000
Retained Earnings Statement		
Retained earnings, 1-1-X8	$192,800	$ 75,000
Net income	70,000	25,000
Dividends	(50,000)	(15,000)
Retained earnings, 12-31-X8	$212,800	$ 85,000
Balance Sheet		
Cash	$ 90,000	$ 40,300
Accounts receivable	97,500	40,000
Interest receivable	300	
Notes receivable	10,000	
Inventory	100,000	60,000
Investment in Eskew stock	133,933	
Investment in Jensen bonds (net)		20,000
Total assets	$431,733	$160,300
Interest payable	$	$ 300
Notes payable		10,000
Bonds payable (net)	18,933	
Common stock	200,000	65,000
Retained earnings	212,800	85,000
Total liabilities and stockholders' equity	$431,733	$160,300

Additional information:

1. On July 1, 19X8, Jensen transferred $10,000 cash to Eskew. In exchange, Eskew signed a 6%,
one-year note. Interest is payable on the date the note is due.

2. Eskew acquired in the open market all the outstanding $20,000 par value bonds of Jensen on
January 1, 19X8. Eskew paid par value for the bonds. The book value of the bonds on the date of
purchase by Eskew was $18,800. The 8%, ten-year bonds were initially issued by Jensen on January
1, 19X7; interest is paid on December 31.

3. The face-value method is used to allocate gains and losses on intercompany debt.

REQUIRED
Prepare a consolidation worksheet for Jensen Corporation and its subsidiary for the year ended
December 31, 19X8.

P6-15

APPENDIXES A AND B

Intercompany Debt Purchase and Intercompany Note Discounted by Subsidiary   Young Company acquired an 80% interest in Newman Company on January 1, 19X2, for $260,000. On the date of acquisition, Newman's common stock and retained earnings were $250,000 and $50,000, respectively. Any excess cost over book value of acquired equity is attributable to Newman's building being undervalued. The building has a five-year remaining estimated life at the date of the acquisition.

The following are the financial statements for both companies for the year ended December 31, 19X4. The face-value method is used to allocate gains and losses on intercompany debt.

	Young Company	Newman Company
Income Statement		
Sales	$450,000	$310,000
Interest revenue		1,675
Income from subsidiary	59,914	
Cost of goods sold	(300,000)	(200,000)
Depreciation expense	(40,000)	(20,000)
Interest expense	(1,534)	
Other expenses	(21,380)	(11,675)
Net income	$147,000	$ 80,000
Retained Earnings Statement		
Retained earnings, 1-1-X4	$300,000	$150,000
Net income	147,000	80,000
Dividends	(100,000)	(30,000)
Retained earnings, 12-31-X4	$347,000	$200,000
Balance Sheet		
Cash	$151,484	$160,000
Inventory	100,000	150,000
Investment in Newman stock	368,516	
Investment in Young bonds (net)		18,350
Building (net)	90,000	71,650
Land	100,000	70,000
Total assets	$810,000	$470,000
Accounts payable	$ 23,804	$ 20,000
Notes payable	20,000	
Bonds payable (net)	19,196	
Common stock	400,000	250,000
Retained earnings	347,000	200,000
Total liabilities and stockholders' equity	$810,000	$470,000

Additional information:

1. On January 1, 19X1, Young issued $20,000 par value, 7%, ten-year bonds at a discount. The bonds pay interest on December 31. Newman purchased, in the open market, all the outstanding bonds of Young on January 1, 19X3, for $17,800. The book value of the bonds on the date of purchase by Newman was $18,928.

2. Young borrowed $20,000 from the subsidiary on December 31, 19X4, signing an interest-bearing note in return. On December 31, 19X4, the subsidiary discounted the intercompany note with an unaffiliated party and credited notes receivable.

REQUIRED

a) Show the computations that produced the amount in the income from subsidiary and the investment in Newman's stock accounts on the December 31, 19X4, financial statements of Young.

b) Prepare a consolidation worksheet as of December 31, 19X4, for Young and its subsidiary.

ISSUES IN ACCOUNTING JUDGMENT

I6-1 **Decision to Buy Back Subsidiary Bonds**   Klammer, Inc. has been a 70%-owned subsidiary of Lane Corporation for over seven years. Four years ago, Klammer issued bonds at an effective rate of 14% to finance an expansion of its production facilities. Although it is still too early to know whether the expansion was successful, interest rates on such issues have fallen to 8%, and Lane Corporation has decided to buy as much of the bond issue as possible.

REQUIRED

a) What effect will the purchase have on the consolidated financial statements over the life of the bonds? How would you justify the treatment of gains and losses on such transactions as extraordinary items?

b) Why might the parent decide to buy back these bonds?

I6-2 **Convertible Subsidiary Debt and the Consolidation Decision**   A subsidiary forms a trust that issues debt (with the subsidiary as the sole beneficiary) and uses the proceeds of the debt to buy preferred stock issued by its parent. The preferred stock is cumulative and pays an adjustable dividend pegged in a manner similar to the rate of debt; the preferred stock is also convertible into common but cannot be called while held by the trust. The trust will repay the debt by either selling the preferred stock or converting the preferred stock into common stock and selling the common stock.

REQUIRED

a) What is the economic substance of this transaction from the perspective of the consolidated entity?

b) Why would such a trust be formed? Should the trust be consolidated?

c) How should the subsidiary's debt be classified on the consolidated balance sheet?

Transactions in Subsidiary Common Stock

PARENT'S TRANSACTIONS IN SUBSIDIARY COMMON
STOCK   357

MULTIPLE-STEP STOCK ACQUISITIONS OF
SUBSIDIARIES   357

Changing from Cost to Equity   357   Amortization of
Layered Valuation Differential   359   Interim Purchases and
the Equity Method   359   Consolidation Procedures   360

SALE OF SUBSIDIARY SHARES BY PARENT   361

Impact on Parent's Ownership Percentage   363   Sale of
Portion of Investment in Subsidiary   363   Sale of Entire
Investment in Subsidiary   369

NEW ISSUES OF SUBSIDIARY COMMON STOCK   369

SUBSIDIARY SELLS STOCK TO PARENT   371

Shares Sold to Parent at Book Value   371   Shares Sold to
Parent at More than Book Value   372   Shares Sold to
Parent at Less than Book Value   372

SUBSIDIARY SELLS STOCK TO MINORITY
STOCKHOLDERS   373

Capital-Transaction Method   373   Gain-or-Loss
Method   374

SUBSIDIARY SELLS STOCK TO PARENT AND
MINORITY STOCKHOLDERS   376

SUBSIDIARY TRANSACTIONS IN COMMON TREASURY
SHARES   376

TRANSACTIONS WITH THE PARENT   376

TRANSACTIONS WITH MINORITY
STOCKHOLDERS   377

APPENDIX: OWNERSHIP CHANGES AND INTERCOMPANY
GROSS MARGIN   378

Transactions in subsidiary common stock can be divided into three groups: (1) acquisitions and sales by the parent of outstanding subsidiary shares, (2) issuances of new subsidiary shares, and (3) acquisitions and sales by the subsidiary of its own treasury shares. One-time acquisitions of subsidiaries were considered in earlier chapters; the present chapter begins by extending this discussion to multiple-step or piecemeal acquisitions of subsidiaries and then turns to sales of part or all of an investment in a subsidiary. The second section of the chapter considers new stock issues by subsidiaries and demonstrates that they can affect a parent's records even if the parent does not buy additional shares. The third section of the chapter discusses subsidiary transactions in treasury stock with particular attention to purchases of treasury shares from minority interest stockholders. An appendix to the chapter illustrates the impact of changes in the ownership percentage on intercompany gross margin.

PARENT'S TRANSACTIONS IN SUBSIDIARY COMMON STOCK

Multiple-Step Stock Acquisitions of Subsidiaries

All prior discussion of stock acquisitions assumes that the parent company's interest in its subsidiary is acquired in a very short period of time—in fact, on a single day. Moreover, discussions have not considered sales of subsidiary stock by the parent or transactions in the stock by the subsidiary itself. The paragraphs that follow consider the effect on accounting by the parent company of relaxing both types of restrictions. Let us begin by considering multiple-step stock acquisitions of subsidiaries.

A multiple-step acquisition of a subsidiary involves multiple purchases of the subsidiary's newly or previously issued stock over a fairly long period of time. The acquisition of additional shares by the parent increases the parent's ownership percentage. Consequently, the parent recognizes a higher percentage of income from its subsidiary after the most recent acquisition than before. The acquisition of additional shares at a cost other than their book value to the subsidiary also occasions recognition of an additional valuation differential; the valuation differential associated with each acquisition should be analyzed and amortized separately.

To illustrate, consider an investor, Moyer, Inc., that acquires a controlling interest in Scovill Corporation in three separate purchases of Scovill's stock as described in the following schedule:

Common Stock Acquisitions by Investor

Date	Percent Acquired	Acquisition Cost
12/31/X1	10%	$16,000
12/31/X2	20%	36,000
3/31/X3	50%	89,250

During the three-year period, the total number of Scovill's shares outstanding remained constant, and on March 31, 19X3, Scovill became Moyer's 80%-owned subsidiary. Scovill has a single class of stock, and its financial statements reveal the following information about its total stockholders' equity:

Stockholders' Equity of Investee

	Balance on January 1*	Income	Dividends	Balance on December 31*
19X1	$	$	$	$148,000
19X2	148,000	12,000	3,000	157,000
19X3	157,000	14,000	4,000	167,000

* The balance includes common stock of $100,000, and the remainder is retained earnings.

Assume that all income is earned at a uniform rate throughout each year and that the entire dividend is declared and paid on August 15th of each year.

Changing from Cost to Equity

An analysis of Moyer's investment in Scovill is given in Exhibit 7-1 on the following page. We assume that all valuation differentials ($1,200 for the 10% purchase, $4,600 for the 20% purchase, and $9,000 for the 50% purchase) are in the nature of goodwill and that

EXHIBIT 7-1	ANALYSIS OF PARENT'S INVESTMENT ACCOUNT FOR A MULTIPLE-STEP STOCK ACQUISITION				

		Book Value of Parent's Equity in Subsidiary		Unamortized Valuation Differential	
	Total Investment	Acquired	Earned	Goodwill	Revaluation Increment
Investment, Dec. 31, 19X1	$ 16,000	$ 14,800†	$	$ 1,200	$ –0–
Add: 20% acquisition, Dec. 31, 19X2	36,000	31,400‡		4,600	
Add: Adjustment for change from cost to equity method*	840		900	(60)	
Investment, Dec. 31, 19X2	$ 52,840	$ 46,200	$ 900	$ 5,740	$ –0–
Add: Parent's share of subsidiary net income in excess of dividends for 3 months ending March 31, 19X3 (.30)(3/12 × $14,000)	1,050		1,050		
Less: Parent's amortization of valuation differential for 3 months ending March 31, 19X3 (3/12)($60 + $230)	(73)			(73)	
Subtotal	$ 53,817	$ 46,200	$1,950	$ 5,667	$ –0–
Add: 50% Acquisition, Mar. 31, 19X3	89,250	80,250§		9,000	
Subtotal	$143,067	$126,450	$1,950	$14,667	$ –0–
Add: Parent's share of subsidiary net income in excess of dividends for 9 months ending Dec. 31, 19X3 (.80)[(9/12 × $14,000) − $4,000]	5,200		5,200		
Less: Parent's amortization of valuation differential for 9 months ending Dec. 31, 19X3 (9/12)($60 + $230 + $450)	(555)			(555)	
Investment, Dec. 31, 19X3	$147,712	$126,450	$7,150	$14,112	$ –0–

* The adjustment to the investment account is reduced for any dividends received by the parent prior to the change from cost to equity; no dividends were paid by the subsidiary during 19X1.

† $14,800 = .10 × $148,000

‡$31,400 = .20 × ($148,000 + $12,000 − $3,000)

§ $80,250 = .50 × [$148,000 + $12,000 − $3,000 + (3/12)($14,000)]

each differential is subject to straight-line amortization over the 20-year period following acquisition. During 19X2, the cost method is applied to the investment because the Moyer's ownership percentage is less than 20%. However, on December 31, 19X2, Moyer's ownership percentage passes the 20% mark, and therefore, the equity method of accounting for the investment should be used. The conversion from the cost method to the equity method requires retroactive adjustment of the parent's investment and retained earnings accounts [APB Opinion No. 18, par. 19(m)] to reflect balances that would have existed had the equity method been used since the very inception of the investment. Moyer, the parent, records the retroactive adjustment with the following journal entry:

Parent's entry to record conversion from cost to equity method:

Investment in Scovill 840
          Retained earnings   840

Retroactive adjustment of Moyer's investment in Scovill increases the investment and retained earnings accounts by $840, which represents the excess of the parent's 10% income share for 19X2 ($900 = .10 × $9,000) over the 19X2 amortization of the valuation differential associated with the first purchase ($60 = $1,200 ÷ 20). When comparative income statements are presented, income of prior years must be retroactively restated (for the years the investment was held) as if the equity method were used since the inception of the investment.

Amortization of Layered Valuation Differential

Exhibit 7-1 also demonstrates the amortization of the layered valuation differential—where one layer or differential is added by each purchase. The amortization of the valuation differential in 19X3 ($628 = $73 + $555) includes the amortization of three differentials as shown in the following schedule:

Amortization of Valuation Differential

	Annual Amortization	19X3 First 3 Months	19X3 Last 9 Months	19X3 Total
Acquisition, Dec. 31, 19X1	$ 60	$15	$ 45	$ 60
Acquisition, Dec. 31, 19X2	230	58	172	230
Acquisition, Mar. 31, 19X3	450	—	338	338
Total	$740	$73	$555	$628

The first acquisition (December 31, 19X1) creates a total valuation differential of $1,200, which is amortized at a rate of $60 per year ($1,200 ÷ 20). The second acquisition (December 31, 19X2) creates a total differential of $4,600, which is amortized at a rate of $230 per year ($4,600 ÷ 20). Finally, the third acquisition (March 31, 19X3) creates a total differential of $9,000, which is amortized at a rate of $450 per year ($9,000 ÷ 20). Observe that the 19X3 amortization includes only 9/12, or 3/4, of the annual amortization of the third (March 31, 19X3) layer. When the structure of the valuation differential becomes fairly complex—that is, when it consists not only of layered goodwill but also of layered revaluation increments—it is necessary to construct comprehensive amortization schedules.

Interim Purchases and the Equity Method

In one-step acquisitions, the parent's calculation of acquisition-year income from the subsidiary excludes preacquisition income. In multiple-step acquisitions, subsidiary income earned prior to the most recent acquisition is not excluded, but it must be treated separately because the parent's percentage share in it differs from its percentage share in postacquisition subsidiary income. The following two-part calculation of Moyer's share in Scovill's 19X3 net income demonstrates the procedure for interim purchases:

Moyer's Calculation of Income from Subsidiary for 19X3

	First 3 Months	Last 9 Months
Subsidiary net income for 19X3	$3,500	$10,500
Parent's ownership percentage	×.30	×.80
Parent's share of subsidiary net income	$1,050	$ 8,400
Amortization of goodwill	(73)	(555)
Income from subsidiary	$ 977	$ 7,845

The parent's share of 19X3 net income is $8,822, the sum of its income share from the first three months ($977), which is computed using an ownership percentage of 30% and its income share from the last nine months ($7,845), which is computed using an ownership percentage of 80%.[1]

Consolidation Procedures

An analysis of the investment account is a useful preliminary step in preparing the consolidation worksheet adjustments for multiple-step acquisitions, because such an analysis contains much of the information required for the adjustments. Consider the Moyer-Scovill illustration for which an investment analysis is presented in Exhibit 7-1. On March 31, 19X3, Moyer's ownership percentage rises from 30% to 80% as Moyer acquires control of the subsidiary, Scovill. On that date and thereafter, it is appropriate to prepare consolidated financial statements for the two companies. The following worksheet adjustments are required at the end of 19X3 in order to accomplish the consolidation:

(1) *Reverse parent's recording of subsidiary net income, and eliminate subsidiary dividend to parent for current year:*

Income from subsidiary ($977 + $7,845)	8,822	
Dividend ($4,000 × .80)		3,200
Investment in Scovill		5,622

---

[1] This presentation of multiple-step acquisitions treats each step as a separate acquisition with its own valuation differential and recognizes only purchased goodwill. This procedure, which is followed throughout this book, is in keeping with current practice and is a reflection of proprietary theory. An alternative procedure, which is consistent with entity theory and the economic-unit concept of consolidation, views the date on which the parent acquires control of the subsidiary as "more than just the inauguration date for providing consolidated financial statements or for including a particular subsidiary in consolidated financial statements. It is the critical acquisition date for measuring the assets and liabilities of the subsidiary, including goodwill, that will be reported in the consolidated financial statements" (Pacter, 1991, par. 293). If this procedure were followed, all goodwill associated with the subsidiary (the difference between the fair value of the subsidiary as a whole and the fair value of its identifiable net assets) would be recognized on the date control is acquired. See Chapter 2, Appendix A, for additional discussion of the economic-unit concept of consolidation.

(2) *Eliminate and reclassify beginning-of-the-year balance of parent's investment account (30% ownership):*

Common stock of subsidiary (30% × $100,000)	30,000	
Retained earnings of subsidiary, 1-1-X3 (30% × $57,000) . . .	17,100	
Goodwill	*5,740*	
Investment in Scovill		52,840

(3) *Eliminate and reclassify current period addition of 50% ownership to parent's investment account:*

Common stock of subsidiary (50% × $100,000)	50,000	
Retained earnings of subsidiary, 1-1-X3 (50% × $57,000) . . .	28,500	
Purchased preacquisition subsidiary income	*1,750*	
Goodwill	*9,000*	
Investment in Scovill		89,250

(4) *Amortize valuation differential for current year:*

Amortization expense	628	
Goodwill		628

All four adjustments are familiar forms except for the third adjustment, which eliminates and reclassifies the addition to the investment account during the current period. This new adjustment removes the cost of the 50% interest purchased during the current year ($89,250) from the investment account; $9,000 is reclassified as goodwill, and the remainder is eliminated by being offset against the related equity and income accounts. Notice that $1,750 is eliminated by a debit to purchased preacquisition subsidiary income, which is subtracted on the consolidated income statement.

The acquired 19X3 income is $1,750, which equals 50% of the first-quarter income ($1,750 = .50 × $3,500). Since consolidated revenues and expenses include first-quarter results for the subsidiary (the consolidated income statement follows Form I as described in Chapter 3), the $1,750 must be subtracted as an adjustment on the consolidated income statement. The adjustment to consolidated income is effected by the $1,750 debit to purchased preacquisition subsidiary income. The consolidated worksheet prepared at the end of 19X3 and incorporating the foregoing adjustments is given in Exhibit 7-2 on the following page.

Sale of Subsidiary Shares by Parent

Let us turn now from the parent's acquisition of subsidiary shares to the parent's sale of such shares. When a parent company sells a portion of its investment in a subsidiary, the carrying amount of that stock must be calculated and removed from the investment account. The carrying amount of the stock is its acquisition cost adjusted for subsidiary net income and dividends since its acquisition as well as the amortization of valuation differential. For purposes of measuring the carrying amount of stock, the investment account may be viewed as an inventory in which individual shares (or blocks of identical shares purchased together) are assigned their carrying amounts on a specific identification basis or on the basis of an artificial flow assumption. Any of the standard flow assumptions (FIFO, weighted average) is acceptable under financial accounting standards, but only FIFO and specific identification are allowed for income tax purposes. We use the FIFO method throughout this book unless an alternative method is specifically indicated.

EXHIBIT 7-2	CONSOLIDATION WORKSHEET FOR A MULTIPLE-STEP ACQUISITION WITH AN INTERIM PURCHASE

	Separate Financial Statements		Consolidation Adjustments		Minority Interest	Consolidated Financial Statements
	Moyer	Scovill	Dr.	Cr.		
Income Statement						
Revenue	190,000	46,000				236,000
Income from subsidiary	8,822		(1) 8,822			
Expenses	(150,000)*	(32,000)	(4) 628			(182,628)
Purchased preacquisition subsidiary income			(3) 1,750			(1,750)
Minority interest (.20 × $14,000)					2,800	(2,800)
Net income	48,822	14,000	11,200		2,800	48,822
Retained Earnings Statement						
Retained earnings, 1-1-X3:						
Moyer	140,000					140,000
Scovill		57,000	(2) 17,100 (3) 28,500		11,400	
Net income	48,822	14,000	11,200		2,800	48,822
Dividend	–0–	(4,000)		(3) 3,200	(800)	–0–
Retained earnings, 12-31-X3	188,822	67,000	56,800	3,200	13,400	188,822
Balance Sheet						
Investment in Scovill	147,712			(1) 5,622 (2) 52,840 (3) 89,250		–0–
Goodwill			(2) 5,740 (3) 9,000	(4) 628		14,112
Other assets	341,110	167,000				508,110
Total assets	488,822	167,000				522,222
Common stock:						
Moyer	300,000					300,000
Scovill		100,000	(2) 30,000 (3) 50,000		20,000	
Retained earnings	188,822	67,000	56,800	3,200	13,400	188,822
Minority interest					(33,400)	33,400
Total liabilities and stockholders' equity	488,822	167,000	151,540	151,540	–0–	522,222

* Parentheses indicate decreases.

Impact on Parent's Ownership Percentage

When the sale of subsidiary shares by a parent reduces the parent's ownership percentage below 50% (but not below 20%), then consolidation is no longer appropriate and the remaining investment should be reported as an unconsolidated investee. If a sale causes the parent's ownership percentage to fall below 20%, then financial accounting standards require that the basis of accounting for the remaining investment be changed from the equity method to the cost method. In these cases, the amount remaining in the investment account on the sale date, which now represents less than a 20% interest, is interpreted thereafter as the cost of the investment [*APB Opinion No. 18,* par. 19(1)].

Sale of Portion of Investment in Subsidiary

Let us consider a sale of subsidiary shares. On September 30, 19X4, Alvarez Corporation sold a 15% ownership interest in its 80%-owned subsidiary, Dunham, Inc., for $35,000 in cash. Alvarez acquired the 80% ownership interest in Dunham, Inc., in three separate acquisitions of Dunham's stock as described in the following schedule:

Common Stock Acquisitions by Investor

Date	Percent Acquired	Acquisition Cost	Book Value Acquired	Valuation Differential Total	Valuation Differential Annual Amortization
12/31/X1	10%	$16,000	$ 14,800	$1,200	$ 60
12/31/X2	20%	36,000	31,400	4,600	230
3/31/X3	50%	89,250	79,750	9,500	475
Total			$125,950		$765

On December 31, 19X3, Alvarez's investment in its subsidiary, Dunham, had a balance of $148,194. During the three-year period, the total number of Dunham's shares outstanding remained constant. Dunham has a single class of stock, and its financial statements reveal the following information about its stockholders' equity:

Stockholders' Equity of Investee

	Balance on January 1*	Income	Dividends	Balance on December 31*
19X1	$	$	$	$148,000
19X2	148,000	9,000	–0–	157,000
19X3	157,000	10,000	–0–	167,000
19X4	167,000	12,000	7,500	171,500

* The balance includes common stock of $100,000, and the remainder is retained earnings.

Assume that all income is earned at a uniform rate throughout each year and that dividends (if any) are declared and paid quarterly.

Recording the sale

The calculation of the carrying amount of the 15% interest sold is given in Exhibit 7-3. Under a FIFO flow assumption, the earliest acquisitions are sold first. Consequently, the 15% interest sold consists of the entire block acquired on December 31, 19X1 (100% of the 10% interest), and 25% of the block acquired on December 31, 19X2 (25% of the 20% interest). The calculation in Exhibit 7-3 gives $27,359 as the carrying amount of the stock and is the basis for the entry by the parent company which is shown at the top of the next page.

EXHIBIT 7-3	**ANALYSIS OF FIFO CARRYING AMOUNT OF SUBSIDIARY STOCK SOLD BY PARENT**			
	Total Carrying Amount	Book Value of Parent's Equity in Subsidiary		Unamortized Valuation Differential
		Acquired	Earned	
10% Stock Acquisition on December 31, 19X1				
Acquisition cost	$16,000	$14,800	$	$1,200
Income from subsidiary 19X2 ($900 =	840		900	(60)
.10 × $9,000), 19X3 ($1,000 = .10 × $10,000)	940		1,000	(60)
First 9 months of 19X4 ($900 = .10 × 9/12 × $12,000), ($45 = 9/12 × $60)	855		900	(45)
Subsidiary dividends for the first 9 months of 19X4 (.10 × $7,500)	(750)		(750)	
Carrying amount, Sept. 30, 19X4 (10% interest)	$17,885	$14,800	$2,050	$1,035
Portion sold on Sept. 30, 19X4 (10% interest)	(17,885)	(14,800)	(2,050)	(1,035)
Remainder	$ –0–	$ –0–	$ –0–	$ –0–
20% Stock Acquisition on December 31, 19X2				
Acquisition cost	$36,000	$31,400	$	$4,600
Income from subsidiary 19X3 ($2,000 = .20 × $10,000)	1,770		2,000	(230)
First 9 months of 19X4 ($1,800 = .20 × 9/12 × $12,000), ($173 = 9/12 × $230)	1,627		1,800	(173)
Subsidiary dividends for the first 9 months of 19X4 (.20 × $7,500)	(1,500)		(1,500)	
Carrying amount, Sept. 30, 19X4 (20% interest)	$37,897	$31,400	$2,300	$4,197
Portion sold on Sept. 30, 19X4 (25% of 20% interest)	(9,474)	(7,850)	(575)	(1,049)
Remainder (15% interest)	$28,423	$23,550	$1,725	$3,148
Carrying Amount of Stock Sold on September 30, 19X4				
Acquisition on Dec. 31, 19X1 (10% interest)	$17,885	$14,800	$2,050	$1,035
Acquisition on Dec. 31, 19X2 (5% interest)	9,474	7,850	575	1,049
Carrying amount of stock sold (15% interest)	$27,359	$22,650	$2,625	$2,084

Parent's entry to record sale of subsidiary stock:

Cash..	35,000	
Gain on sale of stock..............................		7,641
Investment in Dunham............................		27,359

Notice that the excess of the proceeds from the sale over the carrying amount of the related investment is recorded as a gain, as required by *APB Opinion No. 18* (par. 19f). Similarly, if the proceeds from the sale had fallen short of the related carrying amount, then a loss on investment would have been recorded.[2] Since such gains or losses are realized in transactions with unaffiliated parties, they are not eliminated in the preparation of consolidated financial statements.

Income from subsidiary

The investment account analysis for 19X4 is presented in Exhibit 7-4 on the following page. Since the sale of stock occurs within the year, the parent's calculation of income from the subsidiary is divided into two parts—a presale part and a postsale part—as shown here:

Parent's Calculation of Income from Subsidiary

	First 9 Months		Last 3 Months	
Subsidiary net income for 19X4		$9,000		$3,000
Parent's ownership percentages		×.80		×.65
Parent's share of subsidiary income		$7,200		$1,950
Amortization of goodwill:				
Acquisition, Dec. 31, 19X1	$ (45)		$ –0–	
Acquisition, Dec. 31, 19X2	(172)		(43)	
Acquisition, Mar. 31, 19X3	(356)	(573)	(119)	(162)
Income from subsidiary		$6,627		$1,788

The amortization of goodwill is influenced by the sale of the 15% interest. The amortization for the first nine months of 19X4 is simply 9/12 of the annual rate of amortization [$573 = (9/12)($60 + $230 + $475)]. The amortization of the last three months of 19X4 must reflect the disposition of the entire block of shares acquired in 19X1 and one-fourth of the block acquired in 19X2. Accordingly, nothing is amortized for the 19X1 block and only $43 is amortized for the 19X2 block [$43 = (3/4)(3/12 × $230)]. Since no part of the 19X3 block was sold, the goodwill amortization equals 3/12 of the annual rate ($119 = 3/12 × $475). Thus, income from the subsidiary for the entire year is $8,415, that is, $6,627 for the first nine months and $1,788 for the last three months.

---

[2] Although such gains and losses must be recognized under current standards, some advocates of entity theory argue that a parent's sales of subsidiary stock should be treated as capital transactions as long as the parent retains control of the subsidiary. In their view, the shares are merely transferred to minority stockholders, who are part of the economic unit. Thus, they advocate adjusting other contributed capital for these gains and losses rather than income unless the parent's ownership interest falls below 50%.

| EXHIBIT 7-4 | ANALYSIS OF PARENT'S INVESTMENT FOR SALE OF STOCK BY PARENT |

| | Total Investment | Book Value of Parent's Equity in Subsidiary | | Unamortized Valuation Differential | |
		Acquired	Earned	Goodwill	Revaluation Increment
Balance, Dec. 31, 19X3	$148,194	$125,950	$7,650	$14,594	$ –0–
Add: Parent's share of subsidiary net income for 9 months ending Sept. 30, 19X4 (.80)(9/12 × $12,000)	7,200		7,200		
Less: Parent's amortization of valuation differential for 9 months ending Sept. 30, 19X4 (9/12 × $765)	(573)			(573)	
Less: Parent's share of subsidiary dividend paid June 30, 19X4 (.80 × $7,500)	(6,000)		(6,000)		
Subtotal	$148,821	$125,950	$8,850	$14,021	$ –0–
Less: Carrying amount of 15% interest sold on Sept. 30, 19X4 (see Exhibit 7-3)	(27,359)	(22,650)	(2,625)	(2,084)	
Balance, Sept. 30, 19X4	$121,462	$103,300	$6,225	$11,937	$ –0–
Add: Parent's share of subsidiary net income for 3 months ending Dec. 31, 19X4 (.65)(3/12 × $12,000)	1,950		1,950		
Less: Parent's amortization of valuation differential for 3 months ending Dec. 31, 19X4 [3/12] [(3/4 × $230) + $475]	(162)			(162)	
Balance, Dec. 31, 19X4	$123,250	$103,300	$8,175	$11,775	$ –0–

Investment account analysis

The foregoing calculation of income from the subsidiary underlies the analysis of the parent's investment account given in Exhibit 7-4. Observe that balances of the investment account are computed immediately before and immediately after the sale of the 15% interest on September 30, 19X4. Note that the sale of the 15% interest reduces earned and acquired book value and the unamortized valuation differential. The total reduction, of course, equals the carrying value of the 15% interest that is sold.

Consolidation worksheet adjustments

Sales of subsidiary stock by a parent do not alter the form of the familiar consolidation worksheet adjustments, but such sales do require an additional adjustment to eliminate the transfer of earned equity to minority interest. The new adjustment is given as adjustment (3) in the following list of consolidation worksheet adjustments for the Alvarez-Dunham illustration:

(1) *Reverse parent's recording of subsidiary net income, and eliminate subsidiary dividend to parent for current year:*

Income from subsidiary ($6,627 + $1,788)	8,415	
Dividend		6,000
Investment in Dunham..........................		2,415

(2) *Eliminate and reclassify beginning-of-the-year balance of parent's investment account:*

Common stock of subsidiary..........................	80,000	
Retained earnings of subsidiary, 1-1-X4 [($125,950* − $80,000) + $7,650*]	53,600	
Goodwill	*14,594*	
Investment in Dunham..........................		148,194

(3) *Reverse foregoing elimination and reclassification of interest in subsidiary sold by parent during current year:*

Investment in Dunham...............................	27,359	
Common stock of subsidiary......................		15,000
Retained earnings of subsidiary, 1-1-X4 [($22,650* − $15,000) + $2,625*]		10,275
Goodwill		2,084

(4) *Amortize valuation differential for current year:*

Amortization expense ($573 + $162)*	735	
Goodwill		735

* See Exhibit 7-4.

Once again, the adjustments follow the form of the investment analysis. The first adjustment (1) reverses the parent's recording of subsidiary net income and eliminates the subsidiary's dividend to the parent. The second adjustment (2) eliminates and reclassifies the beginning-of-the-year balance of the parent's investment account.

The third adjustment (3), which is a new adjustment, reverses the portion of the elimination and reclassification performed by adjustment (2) related to the parent's sale of subsidiary stock during the current year. The final adjustment (4) amortizes the valuation differential for the current year. The related consolidation worksheet for 19X4 is presented in Exhibit 7-5 on the following page.

Minority interest in income

Minority interest in 19X4 subsidiary income ($2,850) accumulates on a 20% equity interest during the first nine months of 19X4 and on a 35% interest during the last three months of 19X4, as shown in the following analysis of minority interest:

Minority Interest in 19X4 Subsidiary Income

	Total	Acquired by Alvarez	Remainder
First 9 Months of 19X4	$3,150	$1,350	$1,800
Last 3 Months of 19X4	1,050		1,050
Minority interest in subsidiary net income	$4,200	$1,350	$2,850

EXHIBIT 7-5	**CONSOLIDATION WORKSHEET FOR AN INTERIM SALE OF SUBSIDIARY SECURITIES**					

	Separate Financial Statements		Consolidation Adjustments		Minority Interest	Consolidated Financial Statements
	Alvarez	**Dunham**	**Dr.**	**Cr.**		
Income Statement						
Revenue	202,359	50,000				252,359
Income from subsidiary	8,415		(1) 8,415			–0–
Gain on sale of stock	7,641					7,641
Expenses	(175,000)†	(38,000)	(4) 735			(213,735)
Minority interest*					2,850	(2,850)
Net income	43,415	12,000	9,150		2,850	43,415
Retained Earnings Statement						
Retained earnings, 1-1-X4:						
Alvarez	186,104					186,104
Dunham		67,000	(2) 53,600	(3) 10,275	23,675	
Net income	43,415	12,000	9,150		2,850	43,415
Dividends		(7,500)		(1) 6,000	(1,500)	
Retained earnings, 12-31-X4	229,519	71,500	62,750	16,275	25,025	229,519
Balance Sheet						
Investment in Dunham	123,250		(3) 27,359	(1) 2,415		–0–
				(2) 148,194		
Goodwill			(2) 14,594	(3) 2,084		11,774
				(4) 735		
Other assets	413,910	171,500				585,410
Total assets	537,160	171,500				597,184
Common stock:						
Alvarez	307,641					307,641
Dunham		100,000	(2) 80,000	(3) 15,000	35,000	
Retained earnings	229,519	71,500	62,750	16,275	25,025	229,519
Minority interest					(60,025)	60,025
Total liabilities and stockholders' equity	537,160	171,500	184,703	184,703	–0–	597,185

* $2,850 = (.20 \times \$9,000) + (.35 \times \$3,000)$

† Parentheses indicate decreases.

The $1,350 acquired interest in the 19X4 subsidiary net income is transferred to the beginning balance of minority interest by the third adjustment; the $1,350 acquired interest in 19X4 income is included in the $2,625 acquired interest in income from 19X4 and all prior years.

Sale of Entire Investment in Subsidiary

When a parent sells part or all of its investment in a subsidiary, the resulting gain or loss is included in the parent's net income for the sale year. The parent's income also includes subsidiary income related to the sold shares earned prior to the sale date during the sale year.[3] If the sale is a *disposal of a segment of a business,* as defined by financial accounting standards, then both the gain or loss and the parent's income from the subsidiary are reported in a separate section of the income statement following the results of recurring operations (*APB Opinion No. 30*). On the other hand, if the sale is not a disposal of a segment of a business, then both the gain or loss and the parent's income from the subsidiary are reported with the results of recurring operations.

To illustrate, consider Garver Corporation, which sells its entire 80% interest in Hansen, Inc., on May 1, 19X7 for $227,000. On January 1, 19X7, the investment in Hansen was carried at $209,000. The valuation differential is amortized at a rate of $1,200 per year, and Hansen reports 19X7 net income of $21,000. Hansen pays no dividend during 19X7, and there are no intercompany transactions during 19X7. Assume that the income is earned at a uniform rate throughout each year. The parent's separate net income must include a $12,800 gain on the sale calculated as follows:

Calculation of Garver's Gain on Sale of Subsidiary

Proceeds for sale of shares		$227,000
Carrying amount of investment on May 1, 19X7:		
Carrying amount, Jan. 1, 19X7	$209,000	
Parent's share of subsidiary income [($21,000 × 4/12) × .80]	5,600	
Amortization of valuation differential ($1,200 × 4/12)	(400)	214,200
Gain on sale of subsidiary		$ 12,800

In addition, the parent's separate net income must include income from the subsidiary (Hansen) for the preacquisition portion of 19X7 in the amount of $5,200 ($5,600 − $400). Of course, the sale of the entire investment in a subsidiary destroys the parent-subsidiary relationship and makes consolidation inappropriate for the sale year.

NEW ISSUES OF SUBSIDIARY COMMON STOCK

We turn now from a parent's transactions in the *outstanding* shares of its subsidiary to a subsidiary's sales of its own newly issued common shares to its parent or to minority stockholders. If a parent acquires a sufficiently high proportion of newly issued subsidiary shares, the parent can increase its ownership percentage. On the other hand, if a sufficiently high proportion of the newly issued shares is acquired by minority stockholders,

[3] When a parent sells a subsidiary but continues to be involved in the business sold—as when the seller retains effective veto power over major contracts or customers or has significant voting power on the company's board—no gain or loss should be recognized. Rather, the seller should segregate on its balance sheet the assets and liabilities of the sold subsidiary under captions such as "assets of business transferred under contractual arrangements" and "liabilities of business transferred." (See *SEC Staff Accounting Bulletin No. 40,* Topic 5-E, for additional discussion.)

the parent's ownership percentage will fall.[4] Since the parent controls the subsidiary, the parent also controls the effect of the new issue on its ownership percentage. Of course, this control is subject to the preemptive rights of minority stockholders to buy additional shares in proportion to their present holdings and limitations on the resources of the parties involved.

The issues section that follows illustrates one possible motivation for a subsidiary stock issue and shows its impact on ownership interests.

Slippery Rock, Inc., which manufactures paper hats and a variety of folded paper products, was founded by George Anderson in 1960 and remained a family company until 1990. In 1990, Mr. Anderson sold 65% of the company's outstanding voting stock to Boulder Corporation, a large manufacturer of paper products, to generate cash required to expand another of his enterprises. Mr. Anderson's remaining 35% interest in Slippery Rock enabled him to elect several directors and remain one of the principal executive officers of the company. In 1993, pressure on prices from competitors made it apparent that the company must invest in new folding equipment. New electronically controlled folding equipment would enable the company to produce hats and a wide variety of other products much more cheaply and to meet the prices of its competitors. The new equipment would cost $5,000,000. Slippery Rock is unable to borrow this amount, and Boulder, which is "borrowed up to the hilt" for its own expansion programs, cannot provide the needed capital through any of its lines of credit. However, Boulder agrees to the issue of new shares of Slippery Rock to raise the $5,000,000—an issue that would reduce Boulder's controlling interest to 55%. Mr. Anderson is in a difficult position. In order to maintain his influence, he would need to exercise his preemptive right and purchase at least 35% of the new stock issue, which would require him to sell other investments. If he does not purchase enough shares, his influence will be diminished and he will probably lose his influential executive position.

This issues section does not present enough information to let us decide what Mr. Anderson should do, but it does illustrate one way in which subsidiary stock issues are used and also shows the importance of understanding the relationship between ownership percentages and the distribution of new subsidiary stock issues between majority and minority stockholders.

In addition to changing the parent's ownership percentage, subsidiary stock issuances may also change the book value of the parent's equity in the subsidiary. To the extent that the new shares are acquired by the *parent,* the transaction does not involve outsiders and should be accounted for at historical cost without adjustment of income or other contributed capital (*AICPA Accounting Interpretation of ABB Opinion No. 16,* Interpretation No. 39); in addition, the parent's unamortized valuation differential may require adjustment. To the extent that the new shares are acquired by *minority stockholders,* an adjustment of

[4] If the percentage of the newly issued subsidiary shares acquired by the parent equals its preissue ownership percentage, then the parent's ownership percentage will be unaffected by the new issue. When new shares are subscribed by one or more interests in the ratio of their preissue holdings, the shares are said to be *ratably subscribed.* If the parent acquires less of the new issue than its preissue ownership percentage, then its ownership percentage will fall; if the parent acquires more, then its ownership percentage will rise.

either other contributed capital or income may be required. When the subsidiary issues shares to both the parent and minority stockholders, it may be necessary to adjust both the valuation differential and either income or other contributed capital.

The effects on a parent's records of stock issuances by its subsidiary are illustrated by reference to the following simple example. Just prior to issuing 200 new shares of its common stock, Whinney, Inc., the 84%-owned subsidiary of Ernst Corporation, reports stockholders' equity as follows:

Common stock (1,000, $100 par shares)	$100,000
Other contributed capital	10,000
Retained earnings	50,000
Total stockholders' equity	$160,000

Ernst's investment account, which is maintained on an equity-method basis, has a balance of $147,000, which includes a $12,600 unamortized valuation differential [$12,600 = $147,000 − (.84 × $160,000)]. We will vary the terms of the 200-share stock issue to illustrate, first, sales of newly issued subsidiary stock to the parent and, then, sales of newly issued subsidiary stock to minority stockholders. In each case, we must decide what effect the subsidiary's stock issue has on the records of its parent.

Subsidiary Sells Stock to Parent

The sale of subsidiary stock to the parent increases the parent's investment balance by the amount paid for the stock. Further, the sale increases the parent's ownership percentage (if the parent buys enough shares) and may alter the unamortized valuation differential depending on the relationship between the price of the new shares and the book value of the already outstanding shares. To illustrate, let us consider three variations of the Ernst and Whinney example. In all three variations, the subsidiary Whinney sells 200 new shares to its parent, Ernst, with the result that Ernst's ownership percentage increases from 84% to 86 2/3% [.86 2/3 = (840 + 200)/1,200].

Shares Sold to Parent at Book Value

Suppose that Whinney issues all 200 new shares to its parent, Ernst, at a price equal to the $160 book value of the already outstanding shares ($160 = $160,000/1,000 shares). As a result, Ernst's investment in Whinney increases by $32,000 ($160 × 200), the amount paid for the shares. Further, the book value of the parent's equity in its subsidiary also increases by $32,000, as the following calculation shows:

Book Value of Parent's Equity in Subsidiary

	Before New Issue	After New Issue
Subsidiary stockholders' equity:		
Common stock	$100,000	$120,000
Other contributed capital	10,000	22,000
Retained earnings	50,000	50,000
Total	$160,000	$192,000
Parent's ownership percentage	×.84	×.86 2/3
Book value of parent's equity	$134,400	$166,400

The $32,000 increase in the book value of the parent's equity ($32,000 = $166,400 − $134,400) is obtained at a cost of $32,000, as the following calculation shows:

Calculation of Change in Valuation Differential

Acquisition cost of new shares (200 × $160)		$32,000
Increase in book value of acquired equity:		
Book value of parent's equity after		
issue [.86 2/3 × ($160,000		
+ $32,000)]	$166,400	
Book value of parent's equity before		
issue (.84 × $160,000)	134,400	32,000
Change in valuation differential		$ –0–

Thus, the valuation differential remains unchanged when a subsidiary issues stock to its parent at a price equal to the book value of the already outstanding stock.

Shares Sold to Parent at More than Book Value

Suppose that Whinney issues all 200 new shares to its parent, Ernst, but this time at a price of $185, which is $25 more than the $160 book value of the already outstanding shares. As a result, Ernst's investment in Whinney increases by $37,000 ($185 × 200), the amount paid for the shares, which exceeds the book value of the acquired equity by $667, as the following calculation shows:

Calculation of Change in Valuation Differential

Acquisition cost of new shares (200 × $185)		$37,000
Increase in book value of acquired equity:		
Book value of parent's equity after		
issue [.86 2/3 × ($160,000		
+ $37,000)]	$170,733	
Book value of parent's equity before		
issue (.84 × $160,000)	134,400	36,333
Change in valuation differential		$ 667

The $667 excess would be assigned to identifiable assets or goodwill and amortized, as appropriate. Thus, a new layer is added to the valuation differential when a subsidiary issues stock to its parent at a price more than the book value of the already outstanding stock. The new layer reflects an implicit transfer of equity in the subsidiary from the parent to minority stockholders.

Shares Sold to Parent at Less than Book Value

Again, suppose that Whinney issues all 200 new shares to its parent, Ernst, but this time at a price of $150, which is $10 less than the $160 book value of the already outstanding shares. As a result, Ernst's investment in Whinney increases by $30,000 ($150 × 200), the amount paid for the shares, which falls short of the book value of the acquired equity by $267, as the following calculation shows:

Calculation of Change in Valuation Differential

Acquisition cost of new shares (200 × $150)		$30,000
Increase in book value of acquired equity:		
Book value of parent's equity after issue [.86 2/3 × ($160,000 + $30,000)]	$164,667	
Book value of parent's equity before issue (.84 × $160,000)	134,400	30,267
Change in valuation differential		$ (267)

The $267 deficiency should be treated like negative goodwill and offset existing valuation differentials as described in Chapter 3; in practice, however, the amount is likely to be simply adjusted to goodwill, particularly if it is viewed as immaterial. Such reductions in the valuation differential arise when a subsidiary issues stock to its parent at a price less than the book value of the already outstanding stock, which reflects an implicit transfer of equity in the subsidiary from minority stockholders to the parent.

Subsidiary Sells Stock to Minority Stockholders

When the subsidiary sells its entire issue to minority stockholders, the parent's ownership percentage falls. In addition, the parent's equity in the subsidiary may change depending on the relationship between the price of the new shares and the book value of the previously outstanding shares. These changes alter the parent's investment in subsidiary account and result in a corresponding adjustment to either contributed capital or income. The traditional method, which we shall call the "capital-transaction method," adjusts the parent's other contributed capital account whereas the alternative "gain-or-loss method" (which is usually permitted by the SEC) adjusts the parent's income.

Capital-Transaction Method

The *capital-transaction method,* which is consistent with the economic-unit concept of consolidation, views sales of subsidiary stock to minority stockholders as capital transactions. *APB Opinion No. 9* (par. 28) excludes from a company's net income the effect of transactions in the company's own stock. If the subsidiary and its parent are viewed as a single entity, then the issuance of subsidiary stock to the public is a transaction by the entity in its own stock. Thus, any resultant change in the parent's investment in subsidiary account should be recorded as an adjustment to other contributed capital, much like the recording of treasury-stock transactions.

To illustrate, let us consider three variations of the Ernst and Whinney example. In all three variations, the subsidiary, Whinney, sells 200 new shares to its minority stockholders and none to its parent, Ernst, with the result that Ernst's ownership percentage decreases from 84% to 70% (.70 = 840/1,200). The three variations differ as to the price at which the new shares are sold to minority stockholders—$160 per share, $185 per share, and $150 per share. The effect on the parent's equity in its subsidiary of varying the issue price is shown in the following schedule:

Book Value of Parent's Equity in Subsidiary			
	Sale at $160	Sale at $185	Sale at $150
Subsidiary stockholders' equity	$192,000	$197,000	$190,000
Parent's ownership percentage	×.70	×.70	×.70
Book value of parent's equity after issue	$134,400	$137,900	$133,000
Book value of parent's equity before issue (.84 × $160,000)	134,400	134,400	134,400
Increase (decrease) in parent's equity	$ –0–	$ 3,500	$ (1,400)

If the shares are sold to minority stockholders at a price equal to the book value of already outstanding shares ($160), then the book value of the parent's equity in its subsidiary is unchanged and the transaction does not affect the parent's records. However, if the shares are sold at $185, which exceeds the book value of already outstanding shares, then the parent's equity in its subsidiary is increased by $3,500, which represents the parent's share of the minority equity contributions in excess of the preissue book value {$3,500 = .70 × [($185 × 200) − ($160 × 200)]}.

Following the capital-transaction method, the parent, Ernst, makes the following entry to recognize the change in the parent's equity in its subsidiary:

Parent's entry to record subsidiary stock issue to minority interest at price over book value:

Investment in Whinney 3,500
      Other contributed capital   3,500

Conversely, if the shares are sold at $150, which is below book value, the parent's equity is decreased by $1,400, which represents the parent's share of the shortfall of minority stockholders' equity contributions relative to preissue book value {−$1,400 = .70 × [($150 × 200) − ($260 × 200)]}. The parent, following the capital-transaction method, would make the following entry to recognize the change in the parent's equity in its subsidiary:

Parent's entry to record subsidiary stock issue to minority interest at price under book value:

Other contributed capital 1,400
      Investment in Whinney   1,400

Under the capital-transaction method, no adjustments are made to the parent's valuation differential; the change in the investment account is viewed as an adjustment of the book-value component of the investment balance.

Gain-or-Loss Method

The *gain-or-loss method,* which is consistent with the parent-company concept of consolidation, views sales of subsidiary stock to minority stockholders as transactions with outside interests; thus, the resultant change in the parent's investment in subsidiary account may give rise to a nonoperating gain or loss to the parent, which is reported on both the parent's separate income statement and the consolidated income statement.[5] The parent, Ernst, is viewed as having sold 16 2/3% of its equity interest in the subsidiary [(84% − 70%)/84%] in exchange for 70% of the proceeds from the subsidiary's sale of stock. The gain or loss on the sale under the three stock prices is calculated as follows:

Gain or Loss to Parent on Issuance of
Subsidiary Stock to Minority Interests

	Sale at $160	Sale at $185	Sale at $150
Parent's share of proceeds:			
Proceeds from sale	$32,000	$37,000	$30,000
Parent's ownership percentage after issuance	×.70	×.70	×.70
	$22,400	$25,900	$21,000
Less: Decrease in parent's investment (.16 2/3 × $147,000)	24,500	24,500	24,500
Gain (loss) to parent	$(2,100)	$ 1,400	$(3,500)

If recognition is permitted and if the parent, Ernst, chooses the gain-or-loss method, then the parent would make the following entry in each of the three examples to recognize the gain or loss and to adjust the parent's investment account:

Parent's entry to record subsidiary stock issue to minority stockholders at price of $160:

Loss on subsidiary stock issue	2,100	
Investment in Whinney		2,100

Parent's entry to record subsidiary stock issue to minority stockholders at price of $185:

Investment in Whinney	1,400	
Gain on subsidiary stock issue		1,400

Parent's entry to record subsidiary stock issue to minority stockholders at price of $150:

Loss on subsidiary stock issue	3,500	
Investment in Whinney		3,500

---

[5] Support for the gain-or-loss method is found in an AICPA "Issues Paper" (AICPA Accounting Standards Executive Committee, 1980; also see Nemec, 1973). The supporting argument is that issuances of subsidiary stock that reduce a parent's ownership percentage are tantamount to sales of already outstanding stock by the parent; since the latter requires gain and loss recognition, the former should as well. The SEC permits (but does not require) gain or loss recognition on an issuance of new common shares by a subsidiary under certain conditions; further, such recognition of gains is specifically precluded if "subsequent capital transactions are contemplated that raise questions about the likelihood of the registrant realizing that gain, such as where the registrant intends to spin-off its subsidiary to shareholders or where reacquisition of shares is contemplated at the time of issuance" (*SEC Staff Accounting Bulletins No. 51* and *No. 84*). For additional discussion of this topic, see Davis and Largay, 1988.

These gains and losses differ from the corresponding capital adjustments under the capital-transaction method by $2,100, which is the portion of the unamortized valuation differential viewed as sold under the gain-or-loss method ($2,100 = .16 2/3 × $12,600). When minority stockholders acquire the new shares at book value, the parent's equity in the subsidiary remains unchanged and the loss equals $2,100. When the minority stockholders acquire the stock at more than book value, the $2,100 valuation differential is more than offset by the $3,500 parent's equity in the excess of the proceeds over book value, which results in a $1,400 gain ($1,400 = $3,500 − $2,100). Similarly, when the minority stockholders acquire the stock at less than book value, the $2,100 valuation differential is added to the $1,400 parent's equity in the shortfall of proceeds relative to book value, which results in a $3,500 loss.

If a parent uses the gain-or-loss method or the capital-transaction method for one subsidiary stock issue, then it should use the same method for all subsidiary stock issues; the methods should not be applied selectively.

Subsidiary Sells Stock to Parent and Minority Stockholders

When both parent and minority stockholders purchase new shares from the subsidiary, the parent's accounting for its purchase depends on whether or not the parent buys enough shares to maintain its ownership percentage. If the parent buys just enough shares to maintain the same ownership percentage (that is, if the new issue is ratably subscribed), then the new issue does not result in any adjustments to the parent's valuation differential, other contributed capital, or income—even if the shares are not sold at book value. On the other hand, if the parent acquires enough shares to increase its ownership percentage, then the valuation differential is adjusted for the difference between (1) the acquisition cost of the parent's new shares and (2) the change in the book value of the parent's equity in its subsidiary; this process is illustrated above. If the parent does not acquire enough shares to maintain its ownership percentage, then the parent should either adjust other contributed capital or recognize a gain or loss on the implied sale of an interest to minority stockholders; the computations follow the same forms illustrated above. In addition, the parent should adjust its valuation differential for the difference between the cost of its new subsidiary shares and the corresponding portion of subsidiary stockholders' equity.

SUBSIDIARY TRANSACTIONS IN COMMON TREASURY SHARES

We turn now to subsidiary transactions in its own *outstanding* common shares, that is, subsidiary transactions in treasury stock. The parent's ownership percentage and equity in a subsidiary are altered by such transactions.

Transactions with the Parent

Transactions between a parent and its subsidiary in the outstanding shares of the subsidiary—whether the parent buys or sells—do not involve outsiders. Hence the parent should account for such transactions at historical cost without adjustment of income or other contributed capital. This procedure parallels accounting for a parent's purchases of newly issued subsidiary shares and may result in adjustment to the unamortized valuation differential. This adjustment reflects the implied transfer of equity in the subsidiary between the parent and minority stockholders and is calculated in the manner illustrated earlier in this chapter.

Transactions with Minority Stockholders

On the other hand, treasury-stock transactions with minority stockholders may require the parent to make adjustments to its contributed capital account for any change in the parent's equity in the subsidiary. Although current standards are not entirely clear on this matter, usually the parent is precluded from recognizing gains and losses on subsidiary stock transactions. This restriction on gain or loss recognition is consistent with the required accounting for a parent's transactions in its own treasury stock and with the entity conception of the parent-subsidiary relationship.

To illustrate, consider Noble Corporation and its 75%-owned subsidiary Karenbrock, Inc. Just prior to purchasing 100 of its outstanding common shares from minority interests, Karenbrock reports stockholders' equity as follows:

Common stock (1,000 $20 par shares)	$20,000
Other contributed capital	6,300
Retained earnings	17,700
Total stockholders' equity	$44,000

Noble's investment account, which is maintained on an equity-method basis, has a balance of $36,000. As a result of the treasury-stock acquisition, Noble's ownership percentage increases from 75% to 83 1/3% [750 ÷ (1,000 − 100)]. In the schedule that follows, we vary the price of the 100-share treasury-stock purchase to illustrate the impact on the parent's equity in its subsidiary [$39,600 = $44,000 − (100 × $44); $38,500 = $44,000 − (100 × $55); and $40,000 = $44,000 − (100 × $39)].

Book Value of Parent's Equity in Subsidiary

	Purchase at $44	Purchase at $55	Purchase at $39
Subsidiary stockholders' equity	$39,600	$38,500	$40,100
Parent's ownership percentage	×.83 1/3	×.83 1/3	×.83 1/3
Book value of parent's equity after purchase	$33,000	$32,083	$33,417
Book value of parent's equity before purchase (.75 × $44,000)	33,000	33,000	33,000
Increase (decrease) in parent's equity	$ −0−	$ (917)	$ 417

If the subsidiary purchases its treasury shares from minority stockholders at book value ($44), then the parent's equity in the subsidiary remains unchanged and no entry is made on the parent's records. If the subsidiary purchases treasury shares at a price above book value, then the parent's equity in the subsidiary falls and other contributed capital must be reduced; Noble, the parent in our example, makes the following entry:

Parent's entry to record purchase of treasury stock by subsidiary from minority stockholders at price over book value:

Other contributed capital	917	
Investment in Karenbrock		917

On the other hand, if the subsidiary purchases its treasury shares at a price less than book value, then the parent's equity in the subsidiary rises and other contributed capital must be increased; Noble, the parent in our example, makes the following entry:

Parent's entry to record purchase of treasury stock by subsidiary from minority stockholders at price under book value:

Investment in Karenbrock 417
    Other contributed capital   417

As the foregoing example illustrates, the calculations underlying the parent's accounting for subsidiary treasury-stock transactions with minority stockholders parallel those for the capital-adjustment method illustrated earlier for sales of new subsidiary stock to minority stockholders. Thus, we shall not illustrate the case in which the subsidiary sells treasury shares to its minority stockholders.

APPENDIX: OWNERSHIP CHANGES AND INTERCOMPANY GROSS MARGIN

Transactions in subsidiary stock alter the parent's ownership percentage, as this chapter demonstrates. When the ownership percentage changes during the year, the subsidiary's reporting year must be partitioned into constant-percentage segments for purposes of calculations required by the equity method and consolidation procedures. The following paragraphs demonstrate the form of these calculations in the presence of gross margin deferrals on upstream merchandise transfers. The deferral of gross margin on downstream merchandise transfers is unaffected by changes in the ownership percentage.

To illustrate, let us consider an interim stock purchase with deferred upstream gross margin. On January 1, 19X1, Pace Corporation organizes a new company, called Koestler, Inc., and acquires 80% of its stock in exchange for $80,000. The remainder of Koestler's stock is issued to minority stockholders for $20,000. Assume that Koestler represents Pace's only source of net income in 19X1 and 19X2. Koestler, Inc., reports net income of $6,000 for 19X1 and pays no dividends. The subsidiary's income includes gross margin of $600 related to upstream merchandise transfers that were not sold by the parent until 19X2.

On September 1, 19X2, Pace acquires an additional 10% interest in Koestler from minority shareholders in exchange for $14,000. Any valuation differential is attributable to land held by the subsidiary and, therefore, is not subject to amortization. Koestler reports net income of $12,000 for 19X2 ($8,000 of which was earned prior to September 1, 19X2) and, again, pays no dividends. Koestler's net income includes gross margin of $1,600 ($400 of which was earned prior to September 1, 19X2) related to upstream merchandise transfers that were not sold by the parent until 19X3. Koestler reported 19X3 net income of $15,000.

The paragraphs that follow demonstrate the equity method of accounting for Pace's investment in Koestler and the procedures required to consolidate the financial statements of Pace and Koestler.

The Equity Method

The acquisition of the additional 10% interest in Koestler changes Pace's ownership percentage on September 1, 19X2, from 80% to 90%. This change complicates the treatment of intercompany gross margin under the equity method.

Income from Subsidiary

A change in the ownership percentage requires that the parent's calculation of income from its subsidiary be partitioned into constant-percentage segments. The partitioned calculation takes the following form for the Pace-Koestler illustration:

Parent's Calculation of Income from Subsidiary

	19X2		19X3	
	80%	90%	80%	90%
Subsidiary net income	$8,000	$4,000	$-0-	$15,000
Add: Deferred gross margin on upstream transfers at beginning of year	600		400	1,200
Less: Deferred gross margin on upstream transfers at end of year	(400)	(1,200)		
Adjusted subsidiary income	$8,200	$2,800	$ 400	$16,200
Parent's ownership percentage	×.80	×.90	×.80	×.90
Income from subsidiary	$6,560	$2,520	$ 320	$14,580

The parent's 19X2 income from the 80% period ($6,560) consists of $6,080 [.80 × ($8,000 − $400)] recorded by the subsidiary during the first eight months of 19X2 and $480 (.80 × $600) recorded by the subsidiary in a prior year ($6,560 = $6,080 + $480). Similarly, the parent's 19X2 income from the 90% period ($2,520) consists entirely of income reported by the subsidiary during the last four months of 19X2. The parent's 19X3 income from the subsidiary consists of the recognition of amounts deferred from 19X2 and the parent's share of $15,000 reported by the subsidiary for 19X3. Care is taken to ensure that amounts deferred across a change in ownership percentage are recognized in the income of the subsequent period at the appropriate ownership rate. Thus, the income calculation is partitioned into segments in both the year of the ownership change (19X2) and the subsequent year.

Calculation of Valuation Differential

The deferral of upstream gross margin across the date of ownership change complicates the calculation of the valuation differential. More precisely, it complicates the calculation of the book value of acquired equity. On September 1, 19X2, the subsidiary's retained earnings balance equals $14,000 ($6,000 + $8,000). Does this mean that retained earnings contribute $1,400 to the book value of the 10% interest acquired by the parent? Or does retained earnings contribute only $1,360 to the book value—$1,360 being 10% of the retained earnings balance adjusted for the $400 deferral of gross margin across the acquisition date [$1,360 = .10 × ($14,000 − $400)]. Financial accounting standards do not resolve the choice, but we proceed as if retained earnings should be adjusted for upstream gross margin deferred across the ownership change date. Under this interpretation, the book value of the 10% interest is $11,360, representing an interest of $1,360 in subsidiary retained earnings and an interest of $10,000 in common stock ($11,360 =

$1,360 + $10,000). Thus, the valuation differential associated with subsidiary land is
$2,640 ($14,000 − $11,360).

Consolidation Procedures

The purchase of additional stock also complicates the treatment of intercompany gross
margin in the context of consolidation procedures.

Investment Analysis

An analysis of the parent's investment account for the Pace-Koestler illustration is given
in Exhibit 7-6. Observe that the equity acquired with the additional 10% interest in the
subsidiary is $11,360, which is 10% of subsidiary ownership equity adjusted for the
deferred gross margin on September 1, 19X2.

Consolidation Worksheet Adjustments

The following consolidation worksheet adjustments are required to produce the consolidated financial statements:

(1) *Reverse parent's recording of subsidiary income for current year:*

Income from subsidiary ($6,560 + $2,520) 9,080
     Investment in Koestler   9,080

EXHIBIT 7-6	ANALYSIS OF PARENT'S INVESTMENT ACCOUNT

| | | Book Value of Parent's Equity in Subsidiary | | Valuation Differential |
	Total	Acquired	Earned	
Acquired 80% interest, Jan. 1, 19X1	$ 80,000	$80,000	$ −0−	$ −0−
Add: Parent's share of subsidiary 19X1 net income [.80 × ($6,000 − $600)]	4,320		4,320	
Balance, Dec. 31, 19X1	$ 84,320	$80,000	$ 4,320	$ −0−
Add: Parent's share of subsidiary's Jan. to Aug. 19X2 net income [.80 × ($8,000 + $600 − $400)]	6,560		6,560	
Subtotal	$ 90,880	$80,000	$10,880	$ −0−
Add: 10% acquisition, Sept. 1, 19X2	14,000	11,360		2,640
Balance, Sept. 1, 19X2	$104,880	$91,360	$10,880	$2,640
Add: Parent's share of subsidiary's Sept. to Dec. 19X2 net income [.90 × ($4,000 − $1,200)]	2,520		2,520	
Balance, Dec. 31, 19X2	$107,400	$91,360	$13,400	$2,640

(2) *Eliminate and reclassify beginning-of-the-year balance of parent's investment account:*

Common stock of subsidiary ($80,000 + $10,000) 90,000
Retained earnings of subsidiary ($4,320 + $540) 4,860
Purchased preacquisition subsidiary income 820
Land *2,640*
    Investment in Koestler   98,320

(3) *Recognize upstream gross margin deferred from prior year:*

Retained earnings, 1-1 600
    Cost of goods sold (income from operations)   600

(4) *Defer upstream gross margin at end of current year:*

Cost of goods sold (income from operations) 1,600
    Inventory, 12-31 (other assets)   1,600

Adjustment (1) reverses the parent's recording of the subsidiary net income for the current year ($9,080). Adjustment (2) eliminates and reclassifies the beginning-of-the-year balance of the parent's investment account ($98,320), which includes both the investment balance held on January 1, 19X2, and the investment balance added by the 10% acquisition on September 1, 19X2, as shown in the following calculation:

Composition of Investment Balance Eliminated by Adjustment (2)

	80%	10%	Total
Common stock	$80,000	$10,000	$90,000
Retained earnings, 1-1	4,320	540	4,860
Purchased preacquisition subsidiary income		820	820
Land (valuation differential)		2,640	2,640
Total	$84,320	$14,000	$98,320

The adjustment to retained earnings ($4,860) represents 90% of the $6,000 January 1, 19X3, balance of retained earnings adjusted for the deferral of the upstream gross margin of $600 [$4,860 = .90 × ($6,000 − $600)]. The purchased preacquisition subsidiary income ($820) represents a 10% interest in the subsidiary income earned during the first eight months of 19X2 adjusted for intercompany merchandise transfers [$820 = .10 × ($8,000 + $600 − $400)]. This 10% equity interest was acquired by the parent on September 1, 19X2, and appears on the consolidated income statement. The third and fourth adjustments are the familiar entries required to defer the gross margin related to upstream merchandise transfers. The related consolidation worksheet for 19X2 is presented in Exhibit 7-7 on the following page.

Minority Interest

Minority interest in 19X2 net income ($1,100) is the *year-end* minority ownership percentage multiplied by subsidiary income *adjusted* for deferrals of the upstream gross margin ($11,000 = $8,200 + $2,800, or $11,000 = $12,000 + $600 − $1,600). Consolidated statements show the beginning balance of the minority interest in retained earnings to be $540 (see Exhibit 7-7), which excludes an equal amount that was transferred to the

EXHIBIT 7-7	CONSOLIDATION WORKSHEET FOR INTERIM PURCHASE OF SUBSIDIARY STOCK WITH DEFERRED UPSTREAM GROSS MARGIN

	Separate Financial Statements		Consolidation Adjustments			Minority Interest	Consolidated Financial Statements
	Pace	Koestler	Dr.		Cr.		
Income Statement							
Income from operations	–0–	12,000	(4) 1,600	(3)	600		11,000
Income from subsidiary	9,080		(1) 9,080				–0–
Purchased preacquisition subsidiary income			(2) 820				(820)
Minority interest						1,100	(1,100)
Net income	9,080	12,000	11,500		600	1,100	9,080
Retained Earnings Statement							
Retained earnings, 1-1-X2:							
Pace	4,320						4,320
Koestler		6,000	(2) 4,860			540	
			(3) 600				
Net income	9,080	12,000	11,500		600	1,100	9,080
Retained earnings, 12-31-X2	13,400	18,000	16,960		600	1,640	13,400
Balance Sheet							
Investment in Koestler	107,400			(1)	9,080		–0–
				(2)	98,320		
Goodwill			(2) 2,640				2,640
Other assets (including inventory)	56,000	118,000		(4)	1,600		172,400
Total assets	163,400	118,000					175,040
Common stock:							
Pace	150,000						150,000
Koestler		100,000	(2) 90,000			10,000	
Retained earnings	13,400	18,000	16,960		600	1,640	13,400
Minority interest						(11,640)	11,640
Total liabilities and stockholders' equity	163,400	118,000	109,600		109,600	–0–	175,040

parent on September 1, 19X2. The beginning balance of minority retained earnings also excludes the minority's share of the $600 deferral of gross margin at December 31, 19X1, which is consistent with the total elimination procedures applied.

SELECTED READINGS

Accountants' International Study Group. *Consolidated Financial Statements: Current Recommended Practices in Canada, the United Kingdom, and the United States.* Plainstow, England: Curwen Press, 1973.

AICPA Accounting Standards Executive Committee. ''Accounting in Consolidation for Issuance of a Subsidiary's Stock,'' Issues Paper (June 3, 1980).

Childs, William Herbert. "Stock Transactions after Original Acquisition," Chap. 7 in *Consolidated Financial Statements: Principles and Procedures.* Ithaca, NY: Cornell University Press, 1949.

Davis, Michael L., and James A. Largay, III. "Reporting Consolidated Gains and Losses on Subsidiary Stock Issuances," *The Accounting Review* (April 1988), pp. 348–363.

Nemec, Marilyn J. "Reporting in Consolidated Statements the Sale of a Subsidiary's Stock," *CPA Journal* (March 1973), pp. 214–217.

Pacter, Paul. *An Analysis of Issues Related to Consolidation Policies and Procedures,* Financial Accounting Standards Board Discussion Memorandum. Norwalk, CT: Financial Accounting Standards Board, September 10, 1991.

Urbancic, Frank R. "Reporting Preferred Stock: Debt or Equity?" *Mergers and Acquisitions* (Spring 1980), pp. 15–20.

QUESTIONS

Q7-1 Rosetta Company acquired 10% of the voting common stock of Shamrock Company in 19X1 and an additional 20% of the outstanding shares in 19X3. What accounting treatment is accorded the investment in Shamrock at the date of the second purchase?

Q7-2 At the beginning of 19X4, Popeyes, Inc. owned 55% of Sentry Company. On June 1, 19X4, Popeyes acquired an additional 25% of Sentry's outstanding common shares. In the 19X4 calculation of income from Sentry, Popeyes excluded the income earned by Sentry prior to June 1. Do you agree with the procedure Popeyes followed in calculating 19X4 income from Sentry? Discuss.

Q7-3 During 19X6, Patterson held a 12% interest in Bloomingdale. In 19X7, Patterson acquired an additional 28% interest in Bloomingdale. How should Patterson's income from Bloomingdale be reported in the comparative income statements of 19X6 and 19X7?

Q7-4 What factors go into determining the carrying value of subsidiary common shares carried in the parent's investment account?

Q7-5 Identify three methods that could be used in assigning a carrying value to subsidiary common shares carried in the parent's investment account. Which of the methods are acceptable for income tax purposes?

Q7-6 When the sales of subsidiary shares by a parent reduce the parent's ownership interest below 20%, the method of accounting for the remaining investment must be changed from the equity method to the cost method. In such cases, how is the cost basis of the remaining investment amount determined?

Q7-7 Where is the parent's gain or loss from the midyear sale of its entire investment in a subsidiary recorded (sale is not considered a disposal of a segment)? How does this affect the parent's income from subsidiary and consolidation process in the year of sale?

Q7-8 Discuss why you agree or disagree with the following statement: If the subsidiary issues all its new shares to minority shareholders for a price equal to the book value of already outstanding shares, the parent's ownership percentage and book value of equity in the subsidiary would decrease.

Q7-9 Under what conditions would the issue of all new shares of subsidiary stock to the parent result in an increase in the valuation differential in the parent's investment account?

Q7-10 Distinguish between the capital-transaction method and the gain-or-loss method used by the parent to account for changes in the parent's investment account resulting from subsidiary stock sales to minority stockholders.

Q7-11   Discuss why you agree or disagree with the following statement: The purchase by the subsidiary of treasury shares from minority shareholders will give rise to gains or losses to the parent.

Q7-12   Discuss why you agree or disagree with the following statement: When a subsidiary acquires shares of its outstanding stock from its parent, both the parent's holdings and the outstanding subsidiary shares are reduced, thus resulting in the parent's ownership percentage falling.

QUESTION FOR APPENDIX

Q7-13   P acquired 70% of S on December 31, 19X1, at book value. On April 1, 19X2, P acquired an additional 20% interest in S at book value. S reported a 19X2 net income of $12,000 ($3,000 of which was earned prior to April 1, 19X2). The net income of S includes upstream inventory gross margin of $2,000 ($500 of which was earned prior to April 1, 19X2), which was not sold by the parent until 19X3. What would be P's income from subsidiary for 19X2?

EXERCISES

E7-1   **Multiple Choice Questions on Multiple-Step Stock Acquisitions of Subsidiaries**

1. Assume that Operating Corporation purchases a 10% common stock interest in Service Corporation for $10,000 on January 1, 19X2, and an additional 20% interest for $22,000 on January 1, 19X3. The balance sheets of Service Corporation, which pays no dividends, are as follows:

	December 31, 19X3	December 31, 19X2	January 1, 19X2
Cash	$130,000	$110,000	$100,000
Total assets	$130,000	$110,000	$100,000
Common stock	$100,000	$100,000	$100,000
Retained earnings	30,000	10,000	–0–
Total stockholders' equity	$130,000	$110,000	$100,000

During 19X2, Operating Corporation carries this investment under the cost method and on January 1, 19X3, adopts the equity method. For 19X3, Operating Corporation should report as income from this 30% investment the single amount of

    a) $9,000   **c)** $6,000

    b) $7,000   **d)** $5,950

2. The investment described in item (1) should be reported as a long-term investment in Operating Corporation's balance sheet at December 31, 19X3, as a single amount of

    a) $41,000   **c)** $38,000

    b) $39,000   **d)** $37,900

3. Company P purchased the outstanding common stock of S as follows:

    10%, January 1, 19X0

    25%, June 1, 19X0

    25%, August 1, 19X0

    40%, September 30, 19X0

The fiscal year of each of the companies ends on September 30. S's stock was acquired by P at book value. Consolidated net income for the fiscal year ended September 30, 19X0, would include the following earnings of the subsidiary:

    a) 10% of earnings, January–May, 19X0

    b) 35% of earnings, June–July, 19X0

    c) 60% of earnings, August–September, 19X0

    d) All of the above

(AICPA adapted)

E7-2   **Multiple-Step Stock Acquisitions of Subsidiary**   On January 1, 19X0, Weeks, Inc., acquired 75% of the outstanding common stock of Monday Company for $175,000. Any excess cost over book value of acquired equity is attributable to the subsidiary's machinery being undervalued. The machinery has an estimated remaining life of 25 years. The stockholders' equity of Monday on the date of acquisition consisted of a common stock of $150,000 and retained earnings of $50,000. Weeks acquired in the open market, on January 1, 19X1, an additional 10% of the common stock of Monday for $25,000. Any difference in cost and acquired equity is again due to machinery being undervalued; its estimated remaining life is 13 years. Net income and dividend payments of Monday for 19X0 and 19X1 are as follows:

	19X0	19X1
Net income	$15,000	$20,000
Dividends	4,000	10,000

REQUIRED

a) Prepare the entry to record the parent's income from subsidiary for 19X0 and 19X1.

b) Calculate the balance in the investment in Monday Company account as of December 31, 19X1.

c) Prepare in journal entry form the 19X1 consolidation worksheet adjustments relating to the above.

E7-3   **Multiple-Step Stock Acquisitions of Subsidiary**   For the past five years Herbert has maintained an investment (properly accounted for and reported upon) in Broome amounting to a 10% interest in the voting common stock of Broome. The purchase price was $700,000 and the underlying net equity in Broome at the date of purchase was $620,000. On January 2 of the current year, Herbert purchased an additional 15% of the voting common stock of Broome for $1,200,000. The underlying net equity of the additional investment at January 2 was $1,000,000. Broome has been profitable and has paid dividends annually since Herbert's initial acquisition.

REQUIRED

Discuss how this increase in ownership affects the accounting for and reporting on the investment in Broome. Include in your discussion adjustments, if any, to the amount shown prior to the increase in investment to bring the amount into conformity with generally accepted accounting principles. Also include how current and subsequent periods would be reported upon.

(AICPA adapted)

E7-4   **Multiple-Step Stock Acquisitions of Subsidiary**   On January 1, 19X8, Jeffries, Inc., paid $700,000 for 10,000 shares of Wolf Company's voting common stock, which was a 10% interest in Wolf. At that date the net assets of Wolf totaled $6,000,000. The fair values of all Wolf's identifiable assets and liabilities were equal to their book values. Jeffries does not have the ability to exercise significant influence over the operating and financial policies of Wolf. Jeffries received dividends of $0.90 per share from Wolf on October 1, 19X8. Wolf reported net income of $400,000 for the year ended December 31, 19X8.

On July 1, 19X9, Jeffries paid $2,300,000 for 30,000 additional shares of Wolf Company's voting common stock, which represents a 30% investment in Wolf. The fair value of all Wolf's identifiable assets net of liabilities was $6,500,000, which equaled the corresponding book value. As a result of this transaction, Jeffries has the ability to exercise significant influence over the operating and financial policies of Wolf. Jeffries received dividends of $1.10 per share from Wolf on April 1, 19X9, and $1.35 per share on October 1, 19X9. Wolf reported net income of $500,000 for the year ended December 31, 19X9, and $200,000 for the six months ended December 31, 19X9. Jeffries amortizes goodwill over a 40-year period.

REQUIRED

a) Prepare a schedule showing the income before income taxes for the year ended December 31, 19X8, that Jeffries should report from its investment in Wolf in its income statement issued in December 31, 19X8.

b) At the end of 19X9, Jeffries issues comparative financial statements for 19X8 and 19X9. Prepare schedules showing the income before taxes for the years ended December 31, 19X8, and 19X9, that Jeffries should report from its investment in Wolf.

(AICPA adapted)

E7-5 **Sale of Subsidiary Shares by Parent**   Valversa acquired an 80% interest in Wellesley several years ago. On May 1, 19X5, Valversa sold 30% of its investment in subsidiary (Wellesley) stock for $57,000 cash. The 80% investment in Wellesley was carried at $150,000 on January 1, 19X5; valuation differential is amortized at a rate of $2,250 per year. Wellesley paid dividends of $7,000 ($5,600 to Valversa) on April 15, 19X5, and reported net income of $33,000 for 19X5; income is earned evenly throughout the year.

REQUIRED

a) Prepare the entry to record the parent's 19X5 income from its subsidiary.

b) Prepare the entry to record the sale of subsidiary stock by the parent. Computations should show the carrying value of the shares sold.

E7-6 **Sale of Subsidiary Shares by Parent**   On January 1, 19X2, Bernstein Company acquired 10% of the outstanding common stock of Dooley Company for $15,000; Dooley's common stock and retained earnings were $70,000 and $40,000, respectively, on this date. Bernstein acquired an additional 80% of the outstanding shares of Dooley on January 1, 19X3, for $105,600. The valuation differential associated with each acquisition is attributable to goodwill and is amortized over eight years.

On April 1, 19X4, Bernstein sold 30% of the shares it held in Dooley for $61,000. Information on the income and dividend payments of Dooley is presented below. All of Dooley's income is earned at a uniform rate throughout each year, and dividends are declared and paid at the end of each quarter.

	19X2	19X3	19X4
Net income	$16,000	$22,000	$36,000
Dividends	4,000	6,000	7,000

REQUIRED

a) Calculate the valuation differential and goodwill associated with each of Bernstein's purchases of Dooley's outstanding common stock.

b) Calculate the annual amortization of valuation differential.

c) Prepare the entry to record income from subsidiary for 19X4.

d) Prepare the entry to record the sale of subsidiary stock by the parent. Computations should show the carrying value of the shares sold.

e) Determine minority interest (acquired and earned) in the 19X4 subsidiary net income.

f) Using the same preceding information, except that Bernstein sold all the shares (and not 30%) it held in Dooley on April 1, 19X4, for $175,000, prepare the entries to record the parent's income from subsidiary and the sale of subsidiary stock. (*Note:* The sale is not considered a disposal of a segment.)

E7-7   **Multiple Choice Questions on New Issues of Subsidiary Common Stock to Parent**   Dart Company owns 90% of the common stock of Hart Company as of January 1, 19X7, at which time Hart's stockholders' equity consisted of common stock of $200,000 ($100 par) and $120,000 of retained earnings. The parent's investment in Hart Company account had a balance of $318,000 on January 1, 19X7. Hart Company is contemplating a new issue of 500 shares of common stock ($100 par). All 500 new shares are to be issued to the parent company.

REQUIRED

1. The parent's ownership percentage in the subsidiary after the new issue would be

a) 90%   c) 92%

b) 75%   d) 80%

2. Assuming all new shares are sold to the parent at a price equal to the book value of outstanding common shares on January 1, 19X7, the valuation differential associated with the change in the parent's ownership percentage would be

a) $-0-   c) $ 900 negative

b) $800 positive   d) $1,000 negative

3. Assuming all new shares are sold to the parent at a price equal to $180 per share, the valuation differential associated with the change in the parent's ownership percentage would be

a) $-0-   c) $ 900 negative

b) $800 positive   d) $1,000 negative

4. Assuming all new shares sold to the parent at a price equal to $135 per share, the valuation differential associated with the change in the parent's ownership percentage would be

a) $-0-   c) $ 900 negative

b) $800 positive   d) $1,000 negative

E7-8   **Multiple Choice Questions on New Issues of Subsidiary Stock to Minority Stockholders**   Dart Company owns 90% of the common stock of Hart Company as of January 1, 19X7, at which time Hart's stockholders' equity consisted of common stock of $200,000 ($100 par) and $120,000 of retained earnings. The parent's investment in Hart Company account had a balance of $318,000 on January 1, 19X7. Hart Company is contemplating a new issue of 400 shares of common stock ($100 par). All 400 new shares are to be issued to minority stockholders.

The parent uses the gain-or-loss method to account for changes in the parent's investment account resulting from subsidiary stock sales to minority stockholders.

REQUIRED

1. The parent's ownership percentage in the subsidiary after the new issue would be

a) 90%   c) 92%

b) 75%   d) 80%

2. Assuming the subsidiary issues all new shares to minority stockholders at a price equal to the book value of outstanding common shares on January 1, 19X7, the parent's gain (or loss) resulting from the new issue would be

a) $4,500 loss	**c)** $5,000 gain
b) $6,000 gain	**d)** $5,000 loss

3. Assuming the subsidiary issues all new shares to minority stockholders at a price equal to $180 per share, the parent's gain (or loss) resulting from the new issue would be

a) $6,000 gain	**c)** $1,000 gain
b) $2,000 loss	**d)** $5,000 loss

4. Assuming the subsidiary issues all new shares to minority stockholders at a price equal to $140 per share, the parent's gain (or loss) resulting from the new issue would be

a) $6,000 loss	**c)** $11,000 loss
b) $8,000 gain	**d)** $ 9,200 gain

E7-9   **New Issues of Subsidiary Stock to Minority Stockholders**   Reaves Company, a 90%-owned subsidiary of Green, Inc., issued 100 new shares of its common stock to minority stockholders on January 1, 19X5. Immediately prior to the new issue, the stockholders' equity of Reaves consisted of common stock of $50,000 ($100 par) and retained earnings of $30,000. Green's investment in Reaves account had a balance of $80,000 just prior to the new issue of common shares.

The parent uses the gain-or-loss method to account for changes in the parent's investment account resulting from subsidiary stock sales to minority stockholders.

REQUIRED

a) Determine the parent's ownership percentage in the subsidiary after the new issue.

b) Prepare the entry by the parent to record the gain (or loss) resulting from each of the following sales of stock:

1. All new shares are sold to minority stockholders at book value of outstanding common shares on January 1, 19X5.

2. All new shares are sold to minority stockholders at $150 per share.

3. All new shares are sold to minority stockholders at $190 per share.

E7-10   **New Issues of Subsidiary Common Stock to Minority Stockholders**   Maxwell Company owns 80% of the common stock of Smart Company as of January 1, 19X6, at which time Smart's stockholders' equity consisted of common stock of $630,000 ($70 par) and $180,000 of retained earnings. The parent's investment in Smart Company account had a balance of $750,000 on January 1, 19X6. Smart Company is contemplating a new issue of 1,000 shares of common stock ($70 par). All 1,000 new shares are to be issued to minority stockholders.

REQUIRED

a) Determine the parent's ownership percentage in the subsidiary after the new issue.

b) Prepare the entry by the parent to record the change in the parent's equity in the subsidiary under each of the conditions listed below. The parent uses the capital-transaction method to record the effect of such transactions.

1. All new shares are sold to minority stockholders at $90 per share.

2. All new shares are sold to minority stockholders at $125 per share.

3. All new shares are sold to minority stockholders at $75 per share.

E7-11 **New Issues of Subsidiary Common Stock to Minority Stockholders** Using the same information in E7-10, complete the following requirements.

REQUIRED

a) Determine the parent's ownership percentage in the subsidiary after the new issue.

b) Assuming the parent uses the gain-or-loss method to account for changes in the parent's investment account resulting from subsidiary stock sales to minority stockholders, prepare the entry by the parent to record the results of each of the following sales of stock:

  1. All new shares are sold to minority stockholders at $90 per share.

  2. All new shares are sold to minority stockholders at $125 per share.

  3. All new shares are sold to minority stockholders at $75 per share.

E7-12 **Purchases of Treasury Shares from Minority Stockholders** As of January 1, 19X2, Bronson Company had 4,000 shares of common stock outstanding—common stock of $400,000 ($100 par value)—and retained earnings of $100,000. On this date, Agnew Company held 75% of Bronson's outstanding stock; investment account balance is $395,000. Bronson is considering acquiring 250 shares of its common stock to hold as treasury stock.

REQUIRED

a) Assuming Bronson acquired all 250 shares of its outstanding common stock from minority stockholders, determine the parent's ownership percentage after the purchase by Bronson of its own stock.

b) Prepare the entry by the parent to record the impact on the parent's equity in the subsidiary resulting from each of the following purchases by Bronson of its own stock.

  1. All 250 subsidiary shares are purchased from minority stockholders at $150 per share.

  2. All 250 subsidiary shares are purchased from minority stockholders at $125 per share.

  3. All 250 subsidiary shares are purchased from minority stockholders at $115 per share.

E7-13 **Purchases of Treasury Shares from Minority Stockholders** Deauville, Inc., decided on January 1, 19X3, to purchase 1,000 shares of its outstanding common stock from minority stockholders to hold as treasury shares. Just prior to the purchase of treasury shares, the stockholders' equity of Deauville appeared as follows:

Common stock ($20 par value)	$200,000
Retained earnings	50,000

Caroline Company owns 81% (8,100 shares) of the outstanding shares of Deauville. Caroline's investment account balance just prior to the treasury-stock transaction was $225,000.

REQUIRED

a) Determine the parent's ownership percentage after the purchase by Deauville of its own stock.

b) Prepare the entry by the parent to record the impact on the parent's equity in the subsidiary resulting from each of the following purchases by Deauville of its own stock.

  1. All subsidiary shares are purchased from minority stockholders at $30 per share.

  2. All subsidiary shares are purchased from minority stockholders at $25 per share.

  3. All subsidiary shares are purchased from minority stockholders at $22 per share.

E7-14 **Multiple-Step Stock Acquisitions and Deferred Upstream Inventory Profits** Sorter Corpora-
APPENDIX tion acquired 60% of the outstanding voting stock of Coe Company on January 1, 19X3, for

$110,000; any valuation differential is attributable to land. At the date of acquisition, Coe's stockholders' equity consisted of common stock of $100,000 and retained earnings of $50,000. On March 31, 19X4, Sorter acquired an additional 20% interest in the subsidiary from minority stockholders in exchange for $40,440. Any valuation differential is attributable to goodwill with an estimated life of 20 years. Information concerning operating performances and dividend payments of the subsidiary is as follows:

Year	Net Income	Deferred Upstream Inventory Gross Margin in Net Income at End of Period	Dividends
19X3	$12,000	$2,000	$4,000
19X4, first 3 months	5,000	800*	—
19X4, last 9 months	10,000	1,400	3,000
19X5	20,000	1,000	—

* Assume that realization occurs in 19X5 and that the $800 is not included in the $1,400.

REQUIRED

a) Determine the valuation differential on the January 1, 19X3, purchase and on the March 31, 19X4, purchase.
b) Prepare the entry to record the parent's income from subsidiary for 19X3, 19X4, and 19X5.
c) Determine the balance in the investment in Coe Company account as of December 31, 19X4. Computations should include a complete analysis of the investment account showing the acquired equity, earned equity, and valuation differential.
d) Prepare in journal entry form the 19X4 consolidation worksheet adjustments relating to the above.

PROBLEMS

P7-1   Multiple-Step Stock Acquisitions of Subsidiary   Macky Corporation acquired 10% of the outstanding common stock of Steward Company on December 31, 19X1, for $32,000. At the date of acquisition, Steward's stockholders' equity consisted of common stock of $200,000 and retained earnings of $96,000. During the next two years, Macky made the following purchases of outstanding shares of Steward:

Date	Purchase Price	Acquired Equity
Dec. 31, 19X2	$ 72,000	20%
Mar. 31, 19X3	178,500	50%

Steward reported net income of $18,000 for 19X2 and $20,000 for 19X3, and paid no dividends during the two-year period. Income is earned evenly throughout the year. Any difference between the cost and book value of acquired equity in each of the purchases is considered goodwill. The estimated life is 20 years.

REQUIRED

a) Prepare the entry to record the parent's income from its subsidiary for 19X3. Support your computation with an amortization of valuation differential schedule.

b) Determine the balance in the investment in Steward Company account as of December 31, 19X3. Prepare an analysis of the parent's investment account using the format shown in the chapter.

c) Prepare in journal entry form the 19X3 consolidation worksheet adjustments relating to the above.

P7-2 **Multiple-Step Stock Acquisitions of Subsidiary** Quarters, Inc., purchased on January 1, 19X6, 15% of the outstanding voting shares of Nickels Ltd., for $60,000. The common stock and retained earnings balances of Nickels at the date of acquisition were $250,000 and $100,000, respectively. Additional purchases of Nickels' stock in the open market by Quarters were as follows:

Date	Cost	Percentage Acquired
1-1-X7	$ 40,000	10%
7-1-X8	211,200	40%

Any valuation differential associated with the purchases of Nickels' stock is attributable to goodwill with an estimated ten-year life. The following is information concerning the net income and dividend payments of Nickels during a three-year period. Income is earned evenly throughout the year, and dividends are declared and paid to stockholders of record on December 31.

	19X6	19X7	19X8
Net income	$50,000	$60,000	$70,000
Dividends	10,000	12,000	15,000

REQUIRED

a) Prepare the entry to record the parent's 19X8 income from subsidiary. Computations should be supported with an amortization of the valuation differential schedule.

b) Determine the balance in the investment in Nickels account as of December 31, 19X8. Prepare an analysis of the parent's investment account using the format shown in the chapter.

c) Prepare the entry on the books of Quarters on January 1, 19X7, to record the change from the cost method to the equity method of accounting for the investment in Nickels.

d) Prepare in journal entry form the 19X8 consolidation worksheet adjustments relating to the above.

P7-3 **Consolidation Worksheet: Multiple-Step Stock Acquisitions of Subsidiary** Marsh Corporation acquired 10% of the outstanding common stock of Dell Company on January 1, 19X4, paying $23,000. Dell's stockholders' equity at the date of acquisition consisted of common stock of $180,000 and retained earnings of $20,000. The net assets of Dell were fairly valued at book value on the date of acquisition, except for land that was appraised at $30,000 above book value. At the end of 19X4, Dell reported a net income of $35,000 and dividend payments of $5,000.

During 19X5, Marsh purchased, in the open market, an additional 20% of Dell's common stock on January 1 for $51,200 and an additional 50% on October 1 for $141,000. Any valuation differential associated with the purchases in 19X5 is attributable to goodwill with an estimated life of 20 years. In 19X5, the income of the subsidiary was earned evenly throughout the year, and no dividends were paid by either company.

Financial statements for both companies as of December 31, 19X5 are as follows:

	Marsh Corporation	Dell Company
Income Statement		
Sales	$151,450	$100,000
Income from subsidiary	20,040	
Cost of goods sold	(40,000)	(32,000)
Operating expenses	(30,000)	(20,000)
Net income	$101,490	$ 48,000
Retained Earnings Statement		
Retained earnings, 1-1-X5	$ 80,000	$ 50,000
Net income	101,490	48,000
Retained earnings, 12-31-X5	$181,490	$ 98,000
Balance Sheet		
Cash	$ 81,400	$ 25,000
Accounts receivable	15,000	36,000
Inventory	70,000	43,000
Investment in Dell	238,240	
Plant and equipment (net)	60,000	135,000
Land	19,600	54,000
Total assets	$484,240	$293,000
Accounts payable	$ 27,750	$ 15,000
Common stock	275,000	180,000
Retained earnings	181,490	98,000
Total liabilities and stockholders' equity	$484,240	$293,000

REQUIRED

Prepare a consolidation worksheet for Marsh Corporation and its subsidiary as of December 31, 19X5.

P7-4   Consolidation Worksheet: Multiple-Step Stock Acquisitions of Subsidiary   Rose Corporation acquired 10% of the outstanding voting stock of Bench, Inc., on January 1, 19X1, for $16,000. At the date of acquisition, the stockholders' equity of Bench consisted of common stock of $100,000 and retained earnings of $60,000. For the year 19X1, Bench reported net income and dividend payments of $25,000 and $5,000, respectively.

In 19X2, Rose acquired, in the open market, an additional 20% of the subsidiary stock on January 1, 19X2, for $40,000 and an additional 60% for $120,000 on April 1. Any valuation differential is attributable to goodwill with an estimated 20 year life. On December 31, 19X2, Bench reported net income of $40,000 (earned evenly throughout the year) and declared dividends on that date of $10,000 payable on January 15, 19X3. Financial statements for both companies for the 12-month period ending December 31, 19X2, are as follows:

	Rose Corporation	Bench, Inc.
Income Statement		
Sales	$120,000	$100,000
Income from subsidiary	27,575	
Cost of goods sold	(60,000)	(40,000)
Operating expenses	(21,000)	(20,000)
Net income	$ 66,575	$ 40,000
Retained Earnings Statement		
Retained earnings, 1-1-X2	$100,000	$ 80,000
Net income	66,575	40,000
Dividends	(25,000)	(10,000)
Retained earnings, 12-31-X2	$141,575	$110,000
Balance Sheet		
Cash	$ 53,300	$ 29,000
Accounts receivable	20,000	18,000
Dividends receivable	9,000	
Inventory	50,000	35,000
Investment in Bench stock	196,575	
Investment in bonds of Rose (net)		27,000
Buildings (net)	67,000	75,000
Land	26,000	37,000
Other assets	22,000	44,000
Total assets	$443,875	$265,000
Accounts payable	$ 32,300	$ 45,000
Dividends payable		10,000
Bonds payable	50,000	
Common stock	220,000	100,000
Retained earnings	141,575	110,000
Total liabilities and stockholders' equity	$443,875	$265,000

Additional information:

1. On December 31, 19X2, Bench acquired one-half ($25,000 par value) of the outstanding bonds of Rose for $27,000. The bonds of Rose were originally issued at par value with interest payments on July 1 and December 30.

2. Rose loaned Bench $10,000 on December 31, 19X2, for use as temporary working capital. Both companies recorded the transaction in their respective accounts receivable and accounts payable accounts.

REQUIRED

a) Prepare an analysis of the parent's "Investment in Bench, Inc." account for 19X1 and 19X2, using the format shown in the chapter.

b) Prepare a consolidation worksheet for Rose and its subsidiary as of December 31, 19X2.

P7-5   Sale of Subsidiary Shares by Parent   St. Johns, Inc., acquired 25% of the outstanding common shares of English Hills Corporation for $30,000 on January 1, 19X2. On this date, the stockholders' equity of English Hills consisted of common stock of $50,000 and retained earnings of $30,000. On January 1, 19X3, St. Johns acquired an additional 50% of the outstanding common stock of English Hills for $53,000. On April 1, 19X4, St. Johns sold 30% of its common shares in English Hills for $70,000. English Hills has always paid dividends of $1,000 at the end of each quarter and earned income at a uniform rate throughout the year. Information on the income of English Hills is as follows:

	Net Income
19X2	$14,000
19X3	16,000
19X4	20,000

Any valuation differential is identified as goodwill and amortized over 20 years.

REQUIRED

a) Prepare the entry to record the parent's 19X4 income from its subsidiary.

b) Prepare the entry to record the sale of subsidiary stock by the parent. Computations should show the carrying value of the shares sold.

P7-6   Sale of Subsidiary Shares by Parent   On January 1, 19X1, Oliver Company acquired 20% of the outstanding voting shares of Dillion Company for $25,000. On the date of purchase, the common stock and retained earnings of Dillion were $70,000 and $30,000, respectively. Oliver increased its interest in Dillion on January 1, 19X2, when it acquired an additional 75% of the outstanding shares of Dillion for $85,000. On July 1, 19X3, Oliver found itself in need of cash, so it sold 35% of the shares it held in Dillion for $50,000. Information on the income and dividend payments of Dillion is as follows:

			19X3	
	19X1	19X2	First 6 Months	Second 6 Months
Net income	$10,000	$12,000	$9,000	$12,000
Dividends	2,000	5,000	4,000	5,000

Any valuation differential is identified as goodwill with an estimated life equal to the maximum period allowed under generally accepted accounting principles.

REQUIRED

a) Prepare the entry to record the parent's 19X3 income from its subsidiary.

b) Prepare the entry to record the sale of subsidiary stock by the parent. Computations should show the carrying value of the shares sold.

c) Determine minority interest (acquired and earned) in the 19X3 subsidiary net income.

d) Using the same preceding information, except that Oliver sold its entire investment in Dillion (and not 35%) on July 1, 19X3, for $130,000, prepare the entries to record the parent's income from its subsidiary and the sale of subsidiary stock. (*Note:* The sale is not considered a disposal of a segment.)

P7-7 **Sale of Subsidiary Shares by Parent** Information concerning the purchases and sales of the voting stock of Subsidiary Company by Parent Company is as follows:

Date	Activity	Purchase/Sale Price	Percentage
1-1-X1	Purchase	$ 8,000	10%
1-1-X2	Purchase	18,000	20%
4-1-X3	Purchase	44,875	50%
10-1-X4	Sale	17,500	15%

At the 1-1-X1 date of acquisition, Subsidiary's common stock and retained earnings balances were $50,000 and $24,000, respectively. Any valuation differential is considered goodwill and amortized over 20 years. Information on the net income of Subsidiary for selected years ending December 31 is presented as follows:

Year	Net Income
19X1	$4,000
19X2	4,500
19X3	5,000
19X4	6,000

No dividends were declared or paid in 19X1, 19X2, or 19X3. A single dividend in the amount of $3,750 was declared in 19X4 and paid on July 1, 19X4.

REQUIRED

a) Determine the balance in the investment in subsidiary account as of December 31, 19X3. Prepare an analysis of the parent's investment account using the format shown in the chapter.

b) Prepare the entry to record the sale of Subsidiary Company stock on October 1, 19X4. Computation should show the carrying value of the shares sold, assuming a FIFO flow is used.

c) Determine the balance in the investment in subsidiary account as of December 31, 19X4. Prepare an analysis of the parent's investment account using the format shown in the chapter.

P7-8   Multiple-Step Stock Acquisitions of Subsidiary; Sale of Subsidiary Shares by Parent   Sterling, Inc., a domestic corporation having a fiscal year ending June 30, has purchased common stock in several other domestic corporations. As of June 30, 19X4, the balance in Sterling's investments account was $870,600, the total cost of stock purchased less the cost of stock sold. Sterling wishes to restate the investments account to reflect the provisions of *APB Opinion No. 18*, ''The Equity Method of Accounting for Investments in Common Stock.'' Data concerning the investments follow:

		Turner, Inc.	Grotex, Inc.	Scott, Inc.
Shares of common stock outstanding		3,000	32,000	100,000
Shares purchased by Sterling	(a)	300	8,000	30,000
	(b)	810		
Date of purchase	(a)	7-1-X1	6-30-X2	6-30-X3
	(b)	7-1-X3		
Cost of shares purchased	(a)	$49,400	$46,000	$670,000
	(b)	$142,000		

Balance sheet at date indicated:

	7-1-X3	6-30-X2	6-30-X3
Assets			
Current assets	$ 362,000	$ 39,600	$ 994,500
Fixed assets (net)	1,638,000	716,400	3,300,000
Patent (net)			148,500
	$2,000,000	$756,000	$4,443,000
Liabilities and Stockholders' Equity			
Liabilities	$1,500,000	$572,000	$2,494,500
Common stock	260,000	80,000	1,400,000
Retained earnings	240,000	104,000	548,500
	$2,000,000	$756,000	$4,443,000
Changes in common stock since July 1, 19X1	None	None	None
Average remaining life of fixed assets at date of balance sheet (above)	12 yrs.	9 yrs.	22 yrs.
Analysis of retained earnings:			
Balance, July 1, 19X1	$234,000		
Net income, 7-1-X1 to 6-30-X2	53,400		
Dividend paid 4-1-X2	(51,000)		
Balance, June 30, 19X2	$236,400	$104,000	
Net income (loss), 7-1-X2 to 6-30-X3	55,600	(2,000)	
Dividend paid 4-1-X3	(52,000)		
Balance, June 30, 19X3	$240,000	$102,000	$548,500
Net income, 7-1-X3 to 6-30-X4	25,000	18,000	330,000
Dividends paid:			
12-28-X3			(150,000)
6-1-X4		(5,600)	
Balance, June 30, 19X4	$265,000	$114,400	$728,500

Sterling's first purchase of Turner's stock was made because of the high rate of return expected on the investment. All later purchases of stock have been made to gain substantial influence over the operations of the various companies. In December 19X3, changing market conditions caused Sterling to revaluate its relation to Grotex. On December 31, 19X3, Sterling sold 6,400 shares of Grotex for $54,000.

For Turner and Grotex the fair values of the net assets did not differ materially from the book values as shown in the preceding balance sheets. For Scott, fair values exceeded book values only with respect to the patent, which had a fair value of $300,000 and a remaining life of 15 years as of June 30, 19X3.

At June 30, 19X4, Sterling's inventory included $48,600 of items purchased from Scott during May and June at a 20% markup over Scott's cost.

REQUIRED

Prepare a worksheet to restate Sterling's investments account as of June 30, 19X4, and its investment income by year for the three years then ended. Amortization of goodwill, if any, is to be over a 40-year period. Income is earned at a uniform rate throughout each year. Use the following columnar headings for your worksheet:

		Investments			. . .
Date	**Description**	**Turner Dr. (Cr.)**	**Grotex Dr. (Cr.)**	**Scott Dr. (Cr.)**	

	Investment Income Year Ended June 30,			Other Accounts	
19X2 Dr. (Cr.)	**19X3 Dr. (Cr.)**	**19X4 Dr. (Cr.)**		**Amount Dr. (Cr.)**	**Account Name**

(AICPA adapted)

P7-9   **Consolidation Worksheet: Two Subsidiaries Involving New Issues of Subsidiary Stock and Multiple-Step Stock Acquisitions; Intercorporate Equipment, Inventory, and Bond Transactions**   After completing the audit of Company P and its subsidiaries for the year ended December 31, 19X2, you have prepared the following trial balances:

	Company P	Company X	Company Y
Debits			
Cash	$ 33,400	$ 41,500	$ 175,200
Accounts receivable	85,000	97,500	105,000
Inventory, Dec. 31, 19X2	137,500	163,000	150,000
Investment in Company X stock	424,750		
Investment in Company Y stock	611,120		
Investment in bonds of Company Y (net)	148,000		
Plant and equipment (net)	298,000	347,000	594,000
Dividends	36,000	30,000	10,000
Cost of goods sold	2,500,000	1,200,000	1,400,000
Operating expenses	427,000	280,000	290,500
Interest expense	16,200	2,500	9,500
	$4,716,970	$2,161,500	$2,734,200
Credits			
Accounts payable	$ 331,500	$ 155,500	$ 90,000
Bonds payable (net)	400,000		199,200
Sales	2,950,400	1,556,000	1,750,000
Interest income on bonds	7,000		
Capital stock, par $50	600,000	250,000	500,000
Capital in excess of par			70,000
Retained earnings	316,200	200,000	125,000
Gain on sale of equipment	2,000		
Gain on subsidiary stock issue	22,000		
Income from subsidiary, Company X	60,750		
Income from subsidiary, Company Y	27,120		
	$4,716,970	$2,161,500	$2,734,200

Your working papers contain the following information:

1. Company P acquired 4,000 shares of Company X common stock for $310,000 on January 1, 19X1, and an additional 500 shares for $40,000 on January 1, 19X2. Any valuation differential is assigned to plant and equipment and amortized over ten years.

2. Company P acquired all of Company Y's 8,000 outstanding shares on January 1, 19X1, for $650,000. Any valuation differential is assigned to goodwill and amortized over ten years. On January 1, 19X2, Company Y issued 2,000 additional shares to the public at $85 per share. Company P has no investments other than the stock of Companies X and Y. The parent uses the gain-or-loss method to account for changes in the parent's investment account resulting from subsidiary stock sales to minority stockholders.

3. Seven years ago, Company Y issued $200,000 of ten-year, 4%, first mortgage bonds at 98. On January 1, 19X2, Company P purchased $150,000 (face value) of these bonds in the open market, for $147,000. Interest is paid on the bonds on June 30 and December 31. The straight-line method of amortization has been employed by both P and Y.

4. Condensed balance sheets for Company X and Company Y at the start of business on January 1, 19X1, and January 1, 19X2, are presented below:

	Company X		Company Y	
	1-1-X2	**1-1-X1**	**1-1-X2**	**1-1-X1**
Current assets	$225,000	$195,000	$205,000	$280,400
Plant and equipment (net)	350,000	305,000	623,800	613,000
Total	$575,000	$500,000	$828,800	$893,400
Current liabilities	$125,000	$100,000	$105,000	$ 95,000
Bonds payable (net)			198,800	198,400
Capital stock ($50 par)	250,000	250,000	400,000	400,000
Retained earnings	200,000	150,000	125,000	200,000
Total	$575,000	$500,000	$828,800	$893,400

5. On June 30, 19X2, Company P sold equipment with a book value of $8,000 to Company X for $10,000. Company X depreciates equipment by the straight-line method based on a ten-year life.

6. Company P consistently sells to its subsidiaries at a price that realizes a gross profit of 25% on sales. Companies X and Y sell to Company P at cost. Prior to 19X2, intercompany sales were negligible, but during 19X2 the following intercompany sales were made:

	Total Sales	Included in Purchaser's Inventory at 12-31-X2
Company P to Company X	$172,000	$20,000
Company P to Company Y	160,000	40,000
Company X to Company P	28,000	8,000
Total	$360,000	$68,000

7. At December 31, 19X2:

Company P owed Company X	$24,000
Company Y owed Company P	12,000
Total	$36,000

REQUIRED

Prepare a consolidation worksheet for Company P and its subsidiaries for the year ended December 31, 19X2.

(AICPA adapted)

P7-10 **Consolidation Worksheet: Multiple-Step Stock Acquisitions and Deferred Downstream Inven-**
APPENDIX **tory Profits; Intercompany Loan and Equipment Sale**   During 19X0, the Products Company
acquired a controlling interest in Designers, Inc. Trial balances of both companies for the 12-month
period ending December 31, 19X0, are presented as follows:

	Products Company	Designers Inc.
Debits		
Cash	$ 129,500	$ 85,000
Notes receivable	75,000	
Accounts receivable	200,000	100,000
Inventories, Dec. 31, 19X0	924,000	125,000
Investment in Designers	459,950	
Plant, property, and equipment (net)	750,000	350,000
Deferred charges	25,000	
Patents		45,000
Dividends		5,000
Cost of goods sold	1,350,000	525,000
Operating expenses	251,000	174,000
Interest expense		1,000
	$4,164,450	$1,410,000
Credits		
Accounts payable	$ 425,000	$ 85,000
Notes payable		75,000
Common stock	300,000	100,000
Retained earnings	1,605,000	400,000
Sales	1,800,000	750,000
Gain on sale of equipment	10,000	
Interest income	1,000	
Income from subsidiary	23,450	
	$4,164,450	$1,410,000

The following information is available regarding transactions and accounts of the companies.

1. The purchases of the subsidiary stock by Products were as follows:

Date	Amount	Interest Acquired
Jan. 1, 19X0	$336,000	70%
Sept. 30, 19X0	105,000	20%
Total	$441,000	90%

2. The net income of Designers, Inc., for the nine months ended September 30, 19X0, was $25,000.

3. Designers paid $5,000 dividends on December 31, 19X0; no dividends were paid by Products.

4. On the January 1, 19X0, acquisition date, the patents of Designers had a book value and a fair
value of $50,000 and $30,000, respectively; estimated remaining life is ten years.

5. On September 30, 19X0, Products loaned its subsidiary $100,000 on a 4% note. Interest and
principal are payable in quarterly installments beginning December 31, 19X0.

6. The subsidiary has made sales to the parent totaling $40,000 since October 1, 19X0; no intercompany sales were made to the parent prior to this date. The subsidiary charges the parent cost plus 50%. As of December 31, 19X0, $16,500 of the transferred merchandise was in the ending inventory of the parent.

7. During the year, parent sales to the subsidiary aggregated $60,000, of which $16,000 remained in the inventory of Designers at December 31, 19X0. Three-fourths of the $16,000 ending inventory was sold to the subsidiary prior to September 30, 19X0, but before January 1, 19X0. The parent's profit on sales to the subsidiary is 25% of the selling price.

8. On October 1, the parent sold equipment costing $15,000 to the subsidiary for $25,000. The subsidiary depreciates such equipment using the straight-line method over a five-year life. One-half year's depreciation is taken in the year of acquisition.

REQUIRED

Prepare a consolidation worksheet for Products Company and its subsidiary as of December 31, 19X0.

(AICPA adapted)

ISSUES IN ACCOUNTING JUDGMENT

I7-1 **Reduction in Ownership of a Subsidiary** In order to finance expansion, Yang Corporation had decided to reduce its ownership in its 100%-owned subsidiary, Imports, Inc. The management of Yang is considering two courses of action to raise the desired amount: (1) sell 20,000 shares of the subsidiary's common stock presently held by Yang (thereby reducing the ownership percentage by 20%), or (2) have the subsidiary issue 20,000 new common shares to minority interests to raise the desired amount. In both cases, the shares are expected to sell below book value of the shares already outstanding. Assume that no gain or loss on either transaction is allowed for tax purposes.

REQUIRED

a) Will the two courses of action result in the same ownership percentage for Yang? Explain.

b) Suppose that you are the controller of Yang and have been asked to recommend a course of action and to support your recommendation with a brief nontechnical presentation to the board of directors. Write a paragraph summarizing what you would say to the board. Would your recommendation differ if the stock were issued at more than book value?

c) Suppose that you are the member of the Securities and Exchange Commission staff who has been asked to review the recommended reporting of this transaction. Write a brief paragraph summarizing the probable reaction of the SEC to the recommendation in item (b) above.

I7-2 **Subsidiary Transactions in Treasury Stock** New-Seal, Inc. is a subsidiary of Container Corporation of America. Several years ago, in order to raise money for research and development activity, New-Seal issued stock to minority stockholders; the new issue sold at a high price, and the Container Corporation recognized a significant gain. The results of the research and development program have been slow in impacting the market, and consequently the price of New-Seal's stock has suffered. Recently, New-Seal bought a large block of treasury stock from minority stockholders, which resulted in a debit to other contributed capital on Container Corporation's records.

REQUIRED

Write a brief analysis and evaluation of the financial reporting for the two subsidiary stock transactions described above.

MULTIPLE SUBSIDIARIES AND INDIRECT
OWNERSHIP 403

MULTIPLE SUBSIDIARIES 403

INDIRECT OWNERSHIP 404

*Ownership Percentages and Indirect Ownership 405
Control and Ownership Percentages 405   The Equity
Method and Indirect Ownership 405   Consolidated Net
Income and Minority Interest 406*

CONSOLIDATION PROCEDURES 406

MUTUAL HOLDINGS 409

MUTUAL HOLDINGS BETWEEN SUBSIDIARIES 409

MUTUAL HOLDINGS BETWEEN PARENT AND
SUBSIDIARY 413

THE TREASURY-STOCK METHOD FOR MUTUAL
HOLDINGS BETWEEN PARENT AND
SUBSIDIARY 414

*Consolidation at Date of Acquisition 415   Accounting by
Subsidiary and Parent after Date of Acquisition 416
Consolidation One Year after Acquisition 417*

THE ALLOCATION METHOD FOR MUTUAL
HOLDINGS BETWEEN PARENT AND
SUBSIDIARY 418

*Consolidation at Date of Acquisition 418   Accounting by
Subsidiary and Parent after Date of Acquisition 419
Consolidation One Year after Acquisition 422*

PARENT'S INVESTMENT IN SUBSIDIARY
PREFERRED STOCK 422

BOOK VALUE OF PREFERRED STOCKHOLDERS'
EQUITY 423

*Preferred Stock Held by Unaffiliated Parties 423
Calculation of Preferred Equity 423   Calculation of the
Book Value of Common Stockholders' Equity Acquired 424*

INTERCOMPANY PREFERRED STOCK INVESTMENT
AND CONSOLIDATED ENTITIES 424

A PARENT INVESTS IN SUBSIDIARY PREFERRED
STOCK 424

CONSOLIDATION AT DATE OF ACQUISITION 424

THE EQUITY METHOD 426

*Income from Common Stock 426   Income from Preferred
Stock 426*

CONSOLIDATION WORKSHEET ADJUSTMENTS 427

CONSOLIDATION WORKSHEET ONE YEAR AFTER
ACQUISITION 427

*Minority Interest in Subsidiary Income 428   Consolidated
and Parent Company Net Incomes 429*

CONSOLIDATION WORKSHEET TWO YEARS AFTER
ACQUISITION 429

JOINT VENTURES 430

ACCOUNTING FOR JOINT VENTURE
INVESTMENTS 431

PROPORTIONATE CONSOLIDATION 431

DEFERRED INCOME TAXES 435

CONSOLIDATED AND SEPARATE TAX RETURNS 435

UNDISTRIBUTED INVESTEE INCOME 435

INTERCOMPANY MERCHANDISE
TRANSACTIONS 436

*Intercompany Transfers and Consolidated Tax Returns 436
Intercompany Transfers and Separate Tax Returns 438*

COMPREHENSIVE EXAMPLE WITH SEPARATE TAX
RETURNS 439

BUSINESS COMBINATIONS 443

*The Equity Method 447   Consolidation Worksheet
Adjustments 447   Deferred Tax Recognition for Taxable
Combinations 448*

Affiliation structures of many companies are vastly more complex than can be illustrated within the confines of a textbook. Many consolidations involve hundreds of subsidiaries including subsidiaries that hold stock in each other as well as subsidiaries that hold stock in the parent. The consolidation environment is also complicated by parents' holdings of subsidiary preferred stock, by stock holdings in joint ventures, and by the intricacies of income tax laws and deferred tax accounting. The sections that follow introduce each of these topics for the purpose of illustrating some general principles to guide consolidation in such complex environments.

MULTIPLE SUBSIDIARIES AND INDIRECT OWNERSHIP

Most consolidated financial statements discussed in earlier chapters are based on a simple single-subsidiary consolidation structure in which a parent company owns a controlling equity interest in a single subsidiary company. As you might suspect, consolidation structures can be far more complex. Consolidations may involve dozens and even hundreds of companies affiliated through a variety of stockholding arrangements. Complications in consolidation structures arise from three principal sources—*multiple subsidiaries, indirect ownership,* and *mutual holdings.* The first section of this chapter considers multiple subsidiaries and indirect ownership; the next section considers mutual holdings.

Multiple Subsidiaries

Diagrams can be used to aid our understanding of consolidation structures. Exhibit 8-1 shows both the single-subsidiary consolidation structure, which is the basis for earlier chapters, and a three-subsidiary structure. Notice that the latter involves direct ownership of voting stock in three subsidiary companies—50% of A's stock, 75% of B's stock, and 90% of C's stock. Accordingly, the consolidated financial statements must reflect the

---

EXHIBIT 8-1   **DIRECT OWNERSHIP**

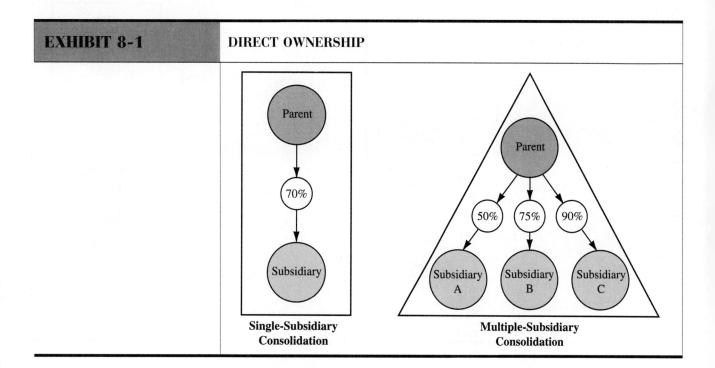

Single-Subsidiary
Consolidation

Multiple-Subsidiary
Consolidation

assets, liabilities, revenues, and expenses of all four companies. The consolidation of multiple subsidiaries requires the insertion of additional columns in the consolidation worksheet, but the consolidation procedures are essentially the same as for single subsidiaries.

Indirect Ownership

Some parent companies control one or more of their subsidiaries indirectly through the stock investments of intermediate companies. For example, Corporation X may control Corporation Y, which, in turn, controls Corporation Z as shown in Exhibit 8-2 by Case I. In this consolidation structure, Corporation X controls Corporation Z *indirectly* through its control of Corporation Y; Corporation X has no direct ownership of Corporation Z. As indicated by the encircling lines of Case I in Exhibit 8-2, two sets of consolidated financial statements can be constructed for the three companies—one consolidating Y and Z and another consolidating all three companies.

In some cases, a company may exercise control through both direct and indirect ownership. Case II in Exhibit 8-2 shows that Corporation T controls Corporation S both

EXHIBIT 8-2	INDIRECT OWNERSHIP

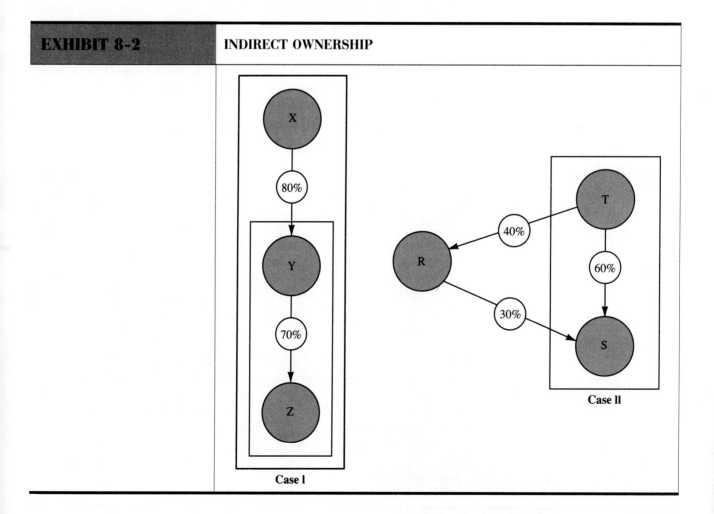

Case I

Case II

directly through ownership of Corporation S stock and *indirectly* through its investment in Corporation R. As indicated in the diagram, it is appropriate to consolidate T and S, but R must be shown as an investment on the consolidated balance sheet because of less than 50% ownership.

Indirect ownership also requires the insertion of additional columns in the consolidation worksheet—one for each of the consolidated companies. However, the basic consolidation procedures are unaltered.

Ownership Percentages and Indirect Ownership

When ownership of voting shares is direct, the ownership percentage is simply the ratio of the number of shares held to the total number of shares outstanding. If ownership of shares is *indirect* through an intermediate company, then the ownership percentage is the product of the affiliated *direct* ownership percentages. For example, referring to Case I in Exhibit 8-2, Corporation X indirectly owns 56% of Corporation Z through its ownership of the intermediate Corporation Y. The indirect ownership percentage of 56% is calculated as the product of the two direct ownership percentages in the chain ($56\% = 80\% \times 70\%$). If ownership is both indirect and direct, then the ownership percentage is the sum of direct and indirect ownership percentages. For example, referring to Case II in Exhibit 8-2, Corporation T owns 60% of Corporation S directly and 12% ($40\% \times 30\%$) indirectly. Hence, T's total ownership percentage is 72% ($60\% + 12\%$).

Control and Ownership Percentages

In purely direct ownership cases, an ownership percentage of over 50% is normally the basis for a controlling financial interest and a parent-subsidiary relationship. In indirect ownership cases, the same test is applied to the ownership percentage calculated as described earlier. In addition, however, a second test must be applied to identify certain parent-subsidiary relationships that are not identified by the 50% test. A less-than-50% investment involving indirect ownership may still be the basis for control of the investee if all direct ownership percentages in the chain of indirect ownership exceed 50%. Suppose that Corporation Alpha owns 60% of Corporation Beta and that Corporation Beta owns 70% of Corporation Gamma. Does Alpha control Gamma? The ownership percentage is 42% ($60\% \times 70\%$), which is less than the required 50%. Yet Alpha controls Beta and Beta controls Gamma. The two control relationships would normally permit Alpha to control Gamma. Accordingly, Gamma is usually treated as a subsidiary of Alpha despite the fact that Alpha's ownership percentage is only 42%.

The Equity Method and Indirect Ownership

In order to illustrate the effect of indirect ownership on the equity method, let us consider the consolidation of Corporations X, Y, and Z shown as Case I in Exhibit 8-2. Assume that the three companies have 19X2 incomes from their own operations (income before income from investments in other companies) as follows:

Corporation X	$46,000
Corporation Y	23,000
Corporation Z	10,000

In addition, assume that no unamortized valuation differential is associated with either Y's 70% interest in Z or X's 80% interest in Y. Using this information, the net incomes of the three companies can be computed as follows:

	X	Y	Z
Income from own operations	$46,000	$23,000	$10,000
Income from Z ($10,000 × .70)		7,000	
Income from Y ($30,000 × .80)	24,000		
Net income	$70,000	$30,000	$10,000

This schedule should be read from right to left. Z has no investment income. Moving to the left, Corporation Y, as a result of its investment in Z, picks up income from Z in the amount of $7,000 under the equity method. Finally, as a result of its investment in Y, X picks up income from Y in the amount of $24,000. Observe that X's share of Y's net income ($24,000) includes net income of Z in the amount of $5,600 ($10,000 × 70% × 80%), reflecting the fact that X owns 56% (70% × 80%) of Z. In other words, the application of X's *direct* ownership percentage to Y's net income provides for X's *indirect* ownership of Z.

Consolidated Net Income and Minority Interest

The net income of Corporation X ($70,000) is also the consolidated net income for the three-company consolidation. A calculation called an *allocation of income* may be used to compute consolidated net income and minority interests in net income. Such a schedule, which begins with each company's income from its own operations, is shown for Corporations X, Y, and Z in Exhibit 8-3. Observe that minority interest in Y's net income ($6,000) includes a portion of the net income of Z.

Consolidation Procedures

Let us illustrate consolidation procedures for indirect holdings by reference to an example. On January 1, 19X2, Kester Corporation acquired 80% of the voting stock of Finney, Inc., by paying cash equal to its book value. One year later, on January 1, 19X3, Finney, Inc., acquired 70% of the voting stock of Miller Corporation paying cash equal to its book value. As a result of these transactions, Kester acquires two subsidiaries. Kester acquires an 80% direct interest in Finney and, through its interest in Finney, a 56% (80% × 70%)

EXHIBIT 8-3 — **ALLOCATION OF INCOME FROM OWN OPERATIONS FOR CONSOLIDATIONS OF CORPORATIONS X, Y, AND Z**

	X	Y	Z
Income from own operations	$46,000	$23,000	$10,000
Allocation of Z's income to Y ($10,000 × .70)		7,000	(7,000)
Subtotal	$46,000	$30,000	$ 3,000
Allocation of Y's income to X ($30,000 × .80)	24,000	(24,000)	
Consolidated net income	$70,000		
Minority interest in net income		$ 6,000	$ 3,000

indirect interest in Miller. The balance sheets of the three companies immediately after Finney acquired 70% of Miller on January 1, 19X3, are as follows:

Balance Sheets at January 1, 19X3, Immediately after 70% Acquisition of Miller by Finney

	Kester	Finney	Miller
Current assets	$ 52,000	$ 37,000	$ 40,000
Investment in Finney (80%)	248,000	—	—
Investment in Miller (70%)	—	98,000	—
Other assets	600,000	265,000	110,000
Total assets	$900,000	$400,000	$150,000
Liabilities	$330,000	$ 90,000	$ 10,000
Common stock	400,000	150,000	60,000
Retained earnings	170,000	160,000	80,000
Total liabilities and stockholders' equity	$900,000	$400,000	$150,000

During 19X3, the three companies reported income from their own operations (i.e., income excluding income from subsidiaries) and paid dividends as follows:

	Kester	Finney	Miller
Income from own operations	$20,000	$12,000	$8,000
Dividends	11,000	5,000	4,500

An analysis of the investments of Kester in Finney and Finney in Miller is presented in Exhibit 8-4. It should be noted that the increase in Kester's investment account is due to its recognition of 80% of Finney's net income. Finney, in turn, recognizes 70% of Miller's net income. Balance sheets for the three companies at December 31, 19X3, are presented in the first three columns of the consolidation worksheet in Exhibit 8-5 on the following page.

EXHIBIT 8-4 | **ANALYSIS OF INVESTMENT ACCOUNTS**

	Kester's Investment in Finney	Finney's Investment in Miller
Balance, January 1, 19X3	$248,000	$ 98,000
Investor's share of investee income:		
Kester's share of Finney's 19X3 income		
.80 × [$12,000 + (.70 × $8,000)]	14,080	
Finney's share of Miller's 19X3 income		
(.70 × $8,000)		5,600
Investor's share of investee dividends:		
Kester's share of Finney's 19X3 dividend		
(.80 × $5,000)	(4,000)	
Finney's share of Miller's 19X3 dividend		
(.70 × $4,500)		(3,150)
Balance, December 31, 19X3	$258,080	$100,450

EXHIBIT 8-5	CONSOLIDATION WORKSHEET WITH INDIRECT OWNERSHIP

	Separate Financial Statements			Consolidation Adjustments		Minority Interest	Consolidated Financial Statements
	Kester	Finney	Miller	Dr.	Cr.		
Income Statements							
Sales	115,000	90,000	54,000				259,000
Income from Finney	14,080			(1) 14,080			
Income from Miller		5,600		(1) 5,600			
Expenses	(95,000)	(78,000)	(46,000)				(219,000)
Minority interest						5,920*	(5,920)
Net income	34,080	17,600	8,000	19,680		5,920	34,080
Retained Earnings Statement							
Retained earnings, 1-1-X3:							
Kester	170,000						170,000
Finney		160,000		(2) 128,000		32,000†	
Miller			80,000	(2) 56,000		24,000‡	
Net income	34,080	17,600	8,000	19,680		5,920	34,080
Dividends	(11,000)	(5,000)	(4,500)		(1) 4,000	(2,350)	(11,000)
					(1) 3,150		
Retained earnings, 12-31-X3	193,080	172,600	83,500	203,680	7,150	59,570	193,080
Balance Sheet							
Current assets	60,000	40,000	35,000				135,000
Investment in Finney	258,080				(1) 10,080		
					(2) 248,000		
Investment in Miller		100,450			(1) 2,450		
					(2) 98,000		
Other assets	625,000	282,150	128,500				1,035,650
Total assets	943,080	422,600	163,500				1,170,650
Liabilities	350,000	100,000	20,000				470,000
Common stock:							
Kester	400,000						400,000
Finney		150,000		(2) 120,000		30,000	
Miller			60,000	(2) 42,000		18,000	
Retained earnings	193,080	172,600	83,500	203,680	7,150	59,570	193,080
Minority interest						(107,570)	107,570
Total liabilities and stockholders' equity	943,080	422,600	163,500	365,680	365,680	–0–	1,170,650

* $5,920 = (30\% \times \$8,000) + (20\% \times \$17,600)$

† $32,000 = 20\% \times \$160,000$

‡ $24,000 = 30\% \times \$80,000$

Consolidation of Kester, Finney, and Miller, as shown in Exhibit 8-5 for our example, does not entail any new consolidation procedures. The two required consolidations are simply performed on the same worksheet: Miller is consolidated with Finney, and Finney is consolidated with Kester. Of course, each consolidation requires a separate set of consolidation adjustments as shown in Exhibit 8-6.

MUTUAL HOLDINGS

A further complication in affiliation structures is presented by mutual holdings, that is, cases in which two companies hold each other's stock. For example, a subsidiary may hold stock of its parent or two subsidiaries may hold each other's stock, as shown in Exhibit 8-7 on the following page. Mutual holdings complicate the attribution of subsidiary income between the majority and minority interests, which affects the application of both the equity method and consolidation procedures. Let us begin by considering mutual holdings among subsidiaries of a single parent.

Mutual Holdings between Subsidiaries

Exhibit 8-7 shows an affiliation structure among the three companies—Rupert, Smith, and Tangle—that involves mutual holdings among subsidiaries. Rupert has two subsidiaries, Smith and Tangle, by virtue of its 80% direct interest in Smith. The two subsidiaries are characterized by mutual ownership because Smith owns a 70% direct interest in Tangle and Tangle owns a 10% direct interest in Smith. The abbreviated 19X7 financial statements of the three companies are shown in the first three columns of Exhibit 8-8 on page 411. Notice that during 19X7, Rupert, Smith, and Tangle earned income from their own operations (before income from affiliates) of $80,000, $56,000, and $34,000, respectively, or a total of $170,000. The reciprocal character of ownership in this affiliation presents an income allocation problem. Smith's income, which includes its share of Tangle's income, cannot be determined unless Tangle's income is known. At the same time, Tangle's in-

		CONSOLIDATION WORKSHEET ADJUSTMENTS WITH INDIRECT OWNERSHIP			
EXHIBIT 8-6					
			Consolidation of Miller (Sub.) and Finney (Parent)		Consolidation of Finney (Sub.) and Kester (Parent)
	(1) *Reverse parent's recording of subsidiary income, and eliminate subsidiary dividend to parent for current year:*				
	Income from subsidiary	5,600		14,080	
	Dividends		3,150		4,000
	Investment in subsidiary		2,450		10,080
	(2) *Eliminate and reclassify beginning-of-the-year balance of parent's investment account:*				
	Common stock of subsidiary	42,000		120,000	
	Retained earnings of subsidiary . . .	56,000		128,000	
	Investment in subsidiary		98,000		248,000

EXHIBIT 8-7	MUTUAL HOLDINGS

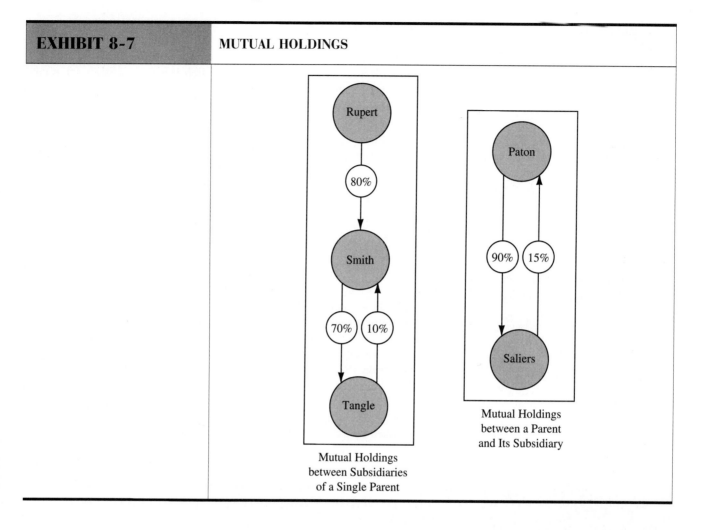

Mutual Holdings
between Subsidiaries
of a Single Parent

Mutual Holdings
between a Parent
and Its Subsidiary

come includes its share of Smith's income and cannot be determined unless Smith's income is known. In order to solve this income allocation problem and distribute the total income of $170,000 among the three groups of stockholders, let us solve the following three equations:

$$R = 80,000 + .80\,S$$
$$S = 56,000 + .70\,T$$
$$T = 34,000 + .10\,S$$

Each equation gives the *total income* for a company as the income from its own operations plus its share of the unknown total income of its subsidiary or investee. The first equation gives the total income of Rupert, denoted by the symbol R, which includes a provision for income on Rupert's 80% interest in Smith. The second equation gives the total income of Smith, denoted by the symbol S, which includes a provision for income on Smith's 70% interest in Tangle. Finally, the third equation gives the total income of Tangle, denoted by the symbol T, which includes a provision for income on Tangle's 10% interest in Smith.

EXHIBIT 8-8	19X7 CONSOLIDATION WORKSHEET WITH MUTUAL HOLDINGS BETWEEN SUBSIDIARIES

	Separate Financial Statements			Consolidation Adjustments			Minority Interest	Consolidated Financial Statements
	Rupert	Smith	Tangle	Dr.		Cr.		
Income Statements								
Income from own operations	80,000	56,000	34,000					170,000
Rupert's income from Smith*	68,645			(1A)	68,645			
Smith's income from Tangle†		29,806		(1B)	29,806			
Tangle's income from Smith‡			800	(1C)	800			
Minority interest§							21,355	(21,355)
Net income	148,645	85,806	34,800		99,251		21,355	148,645
Retained Earnings Statement								
Retained earnings, 1-1-X7:								
Rupert	320,000							320,000
Smith		180,000		(2A)	144,000		18,000	
				(2C)	18,000			
Tangle			115,000	(2B)	80,500		34,500	
Net income	148,645	85,806	34,800		99,251		21,355	148,645
Dividends:								
Rupert	(17,000)							(17,000)
Smith		(8,000)		(1A)		6,400	(800)	
				(1C)		800		
Tangle			(4,700)	(1B)		3,290	(1,410)	
Retained earnings, 12-31-X7	451,645	257,806	145,100		341,751	10,490	71,645	451,645
Balance Sheet								
Other assets	545,400	330,790	202,100					1,078,290
Rupert's investment in Smith	406,245			(1A)		62,245		
				(2A)		344,000		
Smith's investment in Tangle		177,016		(1B)		26,516		
				(2B)		150,500		
Tangle's investment in Smith			43,000	(2C)		43,000		
Total assets	951,645	507,806	245,100					1,078,290
Common stock								
Rupert	500,000							500,000
Smith		250,000		(2A)	200,000		25,000	
				(2C)	25,000			
Tangle			100,000	(2B)	70,000		30,000	
Retained earnings	451,645	257,806	145,100		341,751	10,490	71,645	451,645
Minority interest							(126,645)	126,645
Total liabilities and stockholders' equity	951,645	507,806	245,100		636,751	636,751	–0–	1,078,290

* $68,645 = .80 \times $85,806.451

† $29,806 = .70 \times $42,580.45

‡ $800 = .10 \times $8,000

§ $21,355 = [(.10 \times $85,806.451) + (.30 \times $42,580.645)]

Solving the three equations simultaneously leads to amounts for R, S, and T that make provision for the mutual ownership between Smith and Tangle. The three equations can be solved by substitution as follows:

$$S = 56,000 + .70 \ (34,000 + .10 \ S)$$
$$S = 56,000 + 23,800 + .07 \ S$$
$$.93 \ S = 79,800$$
$$S = 85,806.451$$

$$T = 34,000 + .10 \ (85,806.451)$$
$$T = 34,000 + 8,580.645$$
$$T = 42,580.645$$

$$R = 80,000 + .80 \ (85,806.451)$$
$$R = 80,000 + 68,645.16$$
$$R = 148,645.16$$

Notice that the sum of the three total incomes for R, S, and T ($277,032.25 = $148,645.16 + $85,806.451 + $42,580.645) exceeds the sum of the three incomes from separate operations ($170,000 = $80,000 + $56,000 + $34,000), which is the total amount available for distribution, by $107,032.15. The excess represents a double-counting of income that is necessary to provide for the recognition of the bilateral income transfer between Smith and Tangle. The inclusion of this double-counting in the total income solutions enables us to use the solution amounts in a calculation shown in Exhibit 8-9 that allocates exactly $170,000, the total without double-counting, among majority and minority interests.[1] An allocation is required for each intercompany investment. Since our example pertains to three intercompany investments, three allocations appear in Exhibit 8-9. The investment by Smith in 70% of Tangle's common stock requires an allocation of 70% of Tangle's solution amount (.70 × $42,580.645 = $29,806) from Tangle to Smith. The investment by Tangle in 10% of Smith's common stock requires an allocation of 10% of Smith's solution amount (.10 × $85,806.451 = $8,581) from Smith to Tangle. Finally, the investment by Rupert in 80% of Smith's common stock requires an allocation of 80% of Smith's solution amount (.80 × $85,806.451 = $68,645) from Smith to Rupert. Rupert's income after allocation ($148,645), which includes both the income from Rupert's own operations ($80,000) and its share of income from Smith ($68,645), represents both Rupert's consolidated net income and Rupert's parent-company net income. Rupert's share of income from Smith ($68,645) includes a share of Tangle's net income reflecting Rupert's indirect ownership interest in Tangle through Smith. Since Rupert's ownership of Tangle is entirely indirect, no other provision for Tangle's income needs to be made in the parent-company net income. For purposes of implementing the equity method on Rupert's records, it is sufficient to know that the income from Smith should be recorded at $68,645. Notice that Rupert and Smith use the equity method for their intercompany investments, whereas Tangle, whose investment in Smith represents only a 10%

---

[1] Professor Roman L. Weil has used linear algebra to formulate the mutual holding problem. The use of linear algebra enabled him to prove the correctness of the calculations presented here and to make a precise interpretation of total income. See Roman L. Weil, "Reciprocal or Mutual Holdings: Allocating Earnings and Selecting the Accounting Method," *The Accounting Review* (October 1973), pp. 749–758.

EXHIBIT 8-9	ALLOCATION OF INCOME FROM OWN OPERATIONS FOR CONSOLIDATION OF RUPERT, SMITH, AND TANGLE		
		Rupert	**Smith**	**Tangle**
Income from own operations		$ 80,000	$56,000	$34,000
Allocation of Tangle's income to Smith (.70 × $42,580.645)			29,806	(29,806)
Allocation of Smith's income to Tangle (.10 × $85,806.451)			(8,581)	8,581
Allocation of Smith's income to Rupert (.80 × $85,806.451)		68,645	(68,645)	
Consolidated net income		$148,645		
Minority interest in net income			$ 8,580	$12,775

equity interest, uses the cost method (however, for purposes of determining consolidated income and minority interest, Tangle is allocated 10% of Smith's income, not dividends, as shown in Exhibit 8-9).

For purposes of preparing consolidated financial statements it is also necessary to know the minority interests in the incomes earned by Smith and Tangle. Exhibit 8-9 shows the amount of minority interest in Smith's income to be $8,580, the amount remaining after the allocation from Tangle ($29,806) and the allocations to Tangle ($8,581) and Rupert ($68,645). Similarly, the amount of minority interest in Tangle's net income is $12,775, the amount remaining after the allocation to Smith ($29,806) and the allocation from Smith ($8,581).[2] Accordingly, the total of these two minority interest amounts ($8,580 + $12,775 = $21,355) is subtracted from the combined net income of $170,000 to reach the consolidated net income of $148,645, as shown in Exhibit 8-8. Exhibit 8-8 also shows the familiar worksheet adjustments required to prepare the consolidated statements—three adjustments that reverse income recorded by investors from their investments in affiliated companies (labeled 1A, 1B, and 1C) and three to eliminate the beginning-of-the-period balances of the related investment accounts (labeled 2A, 2B, and 2C).

Mutual Holdings between Parent and Subsidiary

The preceding paragraphs consider mutual holdings between subsidiaries of a single parent. We turn now to mutual holdings between a parent and its subsidiary. As established in earlier chapters, *subsidiary* stock held by the *parent* does not represent outstanding stock from the viewpoint of the consolidated entity, because it is issued and held by the same

---

[2] The minority interest in the incomes of Smith and Tangle can also be calculated more directly by multiplying the minority interest percentage times the corresponding total income solution. For example, the minority interest in Tangle's income ($12,775) can be calculated by multiplying Tangle's minority interest percentage of .30 (100% − 70% owned by Smith) times Tangle's total income solution of $42,580.645 ($12,775 = .30 × $42,580.645). Similarly, the minority interest in Smith's income ($8,580) can be calculated by multiplying Smith's minority interest percentage of 10% (100% − 80% owned by Rupert − 10% owned by Tangle) times Smith's total income solution of $85,806.451 ($8,580 = .10 × $85,806.451).

consolidated entity. For the same reason, financial accounting standards require that the stock of the *parent* held by a *subsidiary* should not be treated as outstanding stock from the consolidated viewpoint (*ARB No. 51,* par. 13). Therefore, neither subsidiary stock held by the parent nor parent stock held by the subsidiary can appear on the consolidated statements as outstanding stock.

Two methods of accounting for the subsidiary's investment in the parent's stock are accepted in practice—the *treasury-stock method* and the *allocation method.* Although either method is acceptable, there is reason to believe that the treasury-stock method is more widely used in practice.[3] The choice of method affects the separate records of the parent as well as the consolidated financial statements. Although the two methods produce different consolidated and parent-company financial statements, both methods satisfy the requirement that parent stock held by a subsidiary should not appear as outstanding on consolidated statements.

Let us illustrate the two methods of accounting for subsidiary investment in parent stock by reference to the Paton-Saliers affiliation that is diagramed in Exhibit 8-7. On January 1, 19X7, Paton Corporation acquired 90% of the outstanding common stock of Saliers, Inc., for $110,000, giving rise to a valuation differential (attributed entirely to goodwill) of $20,000, which is amortized at a rate of $1,000 per year. On the same date, Saliers acquired a 15% interest in Paton for $66,000, which equals its book value. During 19X7 Paton reported income from its own operations of $50,000 and paid dividends of $9,000, including $1,350 (.15 × $9,000) paid to Saliers. During the same year, Saliers reported income from its own operations of $15,000 and paid dividends of $4,000, including $3,600 (.90 × $4,000) paid to Paton. The balance sheets of the two companies prepared immediately after the acquisitions are presented in the first two columns of Exhibit 8-10.

The Treasury-Stock Method for Mutual Holdings between Parent and Subsidiary

The treasury-stock method is predicated on viewing the acquisition of a parent's common stock by its subsidiary as an acquisition of treasury stock that is authorized by the parent.[4] Accordingly, an amount equal to the investment is subtracted from stockholders' equity in the consolidated balance sheet. Since the subsidiary, Saliers, owns less than 20% of its parent, the subsidiary uses the cost method to account for its investment in its parent.[5] The

---

[3] Accountants International Study Group, *Consolidated Financial Statements: Current Recommended Practices in Canada, the United Kingdom, and the United States* (New York: AICPA, 1973), par. 67.

[4] Use of the treasury-stock method is supported by a document issued 40 years ago by the American Accounting Association: Committee on Accounting Concepts and Standards, *Accounting and Reporting Standards for Corporate Financial Statements* (Columbus, OH: American Accounting Association, 1957), p. 44.

[5] When a subsidiary holds 20% or more of the outstanding voting shares of its parent, some accountants argue that the subsidiary can significantly influence the affairs of the parent, and therefore, the subsidiary should apply the equity method to its investment in the parent. Other accountants, however, argue that subsidiaries, by their very nature, cannot exercise significant influence over their parents. How can a subsidiary exercise significant influence over a company that controls the subsidiary? Further, *APB Opinion No. 18* (pars. 16, 17) suggests that the equity method is intended for the "primary reporting company." Professors Petri and Minch argue that this precludes its application by a subsidiary to its investment in its parent. See Enrico Petri and Roland Minch, "The Treasury Stock Method and Conventional Method in Reciprocal Stockholdings—An Amalgamation," *The Accounting Review* (April 1974), pp. 331–332. We assume throughout this book that all subsidiaries with mutually held parents use the cost method to account for investments in their parents.

| EXHIBIT 8-10 | DATE-OF-ACQUISITION CONSOLIDATION WORKSHEET WITH MUTUAL HOLDINGS BETWEEN PARENT AND SUBSIDIARY: TREASURY-STOCK METHOD |

	Separate Financial Statements		Consolidation Adjustments		Minority Interest	Consolidated Financial Statement
	Paton	Saliers	Dr.	Cr.		
Balance Sheet						
Other assets	330,000	34,000				364,000
Investment in Saliers	110,000			(1) 110,000		
Investment in Paton		66,000		(2) 66,000		
Goodwill			(1) 20,000			20,000
Total assets	440,000	100,000				384,000
Common stock:						
Paton	300,000					300,000
Saliers		75,000	(1) 67,500		7,500	
Retained earnings:						
Paton	140,000					140,000
Saliers		25,000	(1) 22,500		2,500	
Treasury stock			(2) 66,000			(66,000)
Minority interest (.10 × $100,000)					(10,000)	10,000
Total liabilities and stockholders' equity	440,000	100,000	176,000	176,000	–0–	384,000

parent, following the equity method, recognizes income from the subsidiary based on its direct interest in the subsidiary without adjustment for the subsidiary's interest in the parent. Thus, the treasury-stock method ignores the equity interest of the parent in itself created by the ownership of stock in its subsidiary, which, in turn, owns stock in the parent. Ignoring this equity interest will usually understate the equity of minority interest in the subsidiary as compared with the allocation method, which is explained later in this chapter.

Consolidation at Date of Acquisition

Let us begin by illustrating the date-of-acquisition consolidation of Paton and Saliers under the treasury-stock method. Consolidation procedures must reclassify the subsidiary's investment in the parent (an asset account) as treasury stock (a contra-equity account). Exhibit 8-10 presents the worksheet for the consolidation of Paton and Saliers immediately following the acquisitions of the mutual holdings. Two worksheet adjustments are required. The reclassification is accomplished by the second adjustment, which debits treasury stock and credits the subsidiary's investment account for $66,000, the cost of the subsidiary's investment in the parent's stock. The first adjustment is the familiar elimination and reclassification of the parent's investment account.

Accounting by Subsidiary and Parent after Date of Acquisition

The financial statements issued by the two companies at the end of 19X7 are shown in the first two columns of Exhibit 8-11. Following the cost method of accounting for its investment in the parent (Paton), the subsidiary (Saliers) recognizes as investment income only its share of the parent's dividend, which is $1,350 (.15 × $9,000). This means that

EXHIBIT 8-11	19X7 CONSOLIDATION WORKSHEET WITH MUTUAL HOLDINGS BETWEEN PARENT AND SUBSIDIARY: TREASURY-STOCK METHOD					
	Separate Financial Statements		Consolidation Adjustments		Minority Interest	Consolidated Financial Statement
	Paton	Saliers	Dr.	Cr.		
Income Statement						
Income from own operations	50,000	15,000				65,000
Income from Saliers	12,365		(1) 12,365			
Income from Paton		1,350	(1) 1,350			
Amortization expense			(3) 1,000			(1,000)
Minority interest (.10 × $16,350)					1,635	(1,635)
Net income	62,365	16,350	14,715		1,635	62,365
Retained Earnings Statement						
Retained earnings, 1-1-X7:						
Paton	140,000					140,000
Saliers		25,000	(2) 22,500		2,500	
Net income	62,365	16,350	14,715		1,635	62,365
Dividends:						
Paton ($9,000 − $1,350)	(7,650)					(7,650)
Saliers		(4,000)		(1) 3,600	(400)	
Retained earnings, 12-31-X7	194,715	37,350	37,215	3,600	3,735	194,715
Balance Sheet						
Other assets	374,600	46,350				420,950
Investment in Saliers	120,115			(1) 10,115		
				(2) 110,000		
Investment in Paton		66,000		(4) 66,000		
Goodwill	—	—	(2) 20,000	(3) 1,000		19,000
Total assets	494,715	112,350				439,950
Common stock:						
Paton	300,000					300,000
Saliers		75,000	(2) 67,500		7,500	
Treasury stock			(4) 66,000			(66,000)
Retained earnings	194,715	37,350	37,215	3,600	3,735	194,715
Minority interest					(11,235)	11,235
Total liabilities and stockholders' equity	494,715	112,350	190,715	190,715	–0–	439,950

Saliers's net income is $16,350 ($15,000 + $1,350). Following the equity method, Paton recognizes 90% of Saliers's net income adjusted for the dividend received from Paton and for amortization of the valuation differential computed as follows:

Parent's Calculation of Income from Subsidiary	
Subsidiary net income [$15,000 + (.15 × $9,000)]	$16,350
Parent's ownership percentage	×.90
Parent's share of subsidiary net income	$14,715
Less: Amortization of valuation differential	(1,000)
Parent's share of subsidiary net income adjusted for amortization of valuation differential	$13,715
Less: Parent's dividend to subsidiary	(1,350)
Income from subsidiary	$12,365

Observe that the parent adjusts its share of subsidiary net income ($14,715) for the entire dividend paid to the subsidiary ($1,350), including the 10% that accrues to the benefit of the minority stockholders in the subsidiary. The following entries by the parent record the parent's 19X7 income and dividends related to its investment in the subsidiary:

Entry on parent's records for income from subsidiary and reclassification of parent's dividend to subsidiary:

Investment in Saliers	13,715	
Dividend ($9,000 × .15)		1,350
Income from Saliers		12,365

Entry on parent's records to record dividend from subsidiary:

Cash	3,600	
Investment in Saliers		3,600

In summary, the parent's investment account balance increases by $13,715 and decreases by $3,600, the parent's share of the subsidiary dividend (.90 × $4,000)—a net increase in the investment account of $10,115.

Consolidation One Year after Acquisition

Exhibit 8-11 presents the worksheet for the consolidation of Paton and Saliers using the treasury-stock method one year after the acquisitions of the mutual holdings. Four worksheet adjustments are required:

(1) *Worksheet adjustment to eliminate income from affiliated companies:*

Income from Saliers	12,365	
Income from Paton	1,350	
Dividend		3,600
Investment in Saliers		10,115

(2) *Worksheet adjustment to eliminate and reclassify beginning-of-the-year balance of parent's investment account:*

Common stock of Saliers 67,500
Retained earnings of Saliers, 1-1 22,500
Goodwill 20,000
    Investment in Saliers   110,000

(3) *Worksheet adjustment to amortize valuation differential for current year:*

Amortization expense................................. 1,000
    Goodwill   1,000

(4) *Worksheet adjustment to reclassify subsidiary's investment in parent as treasury stock:*

Treasury stock...................................... 66,000
    Investment in Paton   66,000

The minority interest in net income ($1,635) is calculated as 10% of the Saliers net income, which ignores the full effect of the mutual holding and understates the minority interest by comparison with the amount calculated using the allocation method, which is illustrated next.

The Allocation Method for Mutual Holdings between Parent and Subsidiary

Unlike the treasury-stock method, the *allocation method* (also called the *conventional method*) recognizes the reciprocal character of the mutual holdings. Under the allocation method, simultaneous equations are applied to determine parent-company and consolidated net income in much the same way as for mutual holdings among subsidiaries. The allocation approach is predicated on the view that a subsidiary's acquisition of its parent's common stock constitutes constructive retirement of the stock from a consolidated viewpoint.

Consolidation at Date of Acquisition

Although the subsidiary's acquisition of its parent's stock is viewed as constructive retirement for purposes of consolidation, the acquisition occasions no entry on the parent's separate records.[6] In consolidation, however, as shown in Exhibit 8-12, the subsidiary's

---

[6] Some accountants argue that the parent should record the constructive retirement on its separate records when a subsidiary acquires its stock; this recording would require the following entry by Paton:

Parent's entry to record subsidiary's acquisition of outstanding stock of parent:
Common stock 45,000
Retained earnings 27,000
    Investment in Saliers   72,000

Such an entry is supported by *APB Opinion No. 18* (par. 19e), which requires that "a transaction of an investee of a capital nature that affects the investor's share of stockholders' equity of the investee should be accounted for as if the investee were a consolidated subsidiary." Other accountants, however, believe that this provision of *APB Opinion No. 18* does not apply to mutual holdings and that the parent should *not* record the subsidiary's acquisition of its parent's stock as a constructive retirement. In the interests of pedagogical simplicity, the latter approach is used in the Paton-Saliers illustration and throughout this text.

EXHIBIT 8-12	CONSOLIDATION WORKSHEET WITH MUTUAL HOLDINGS BETWEEN PARENT AND SUBSIDIARY: ALLOCATION METHOD

	Separate Financial Statements		Consolidation Adjustments		Minority Interest	Consolidated Financial Statement
	Paton	Saliers	Dr.	Cr.		
Balance Sheet						
Other assets	330,000	34,000				364,000
Investment in Saliers	110,000			(1) 110,000		–0–
Investment in Paton		66,000		(2) 66,000		–0–
Goodwill			(1) 20,000			20,000
Total assets	440,000	100,000				384,000
Common stock:						
Paton	300,000		(2) 45,000			255,000
Saliers		75,000	(1) 67,500		7,500	–0–
Retained earnings:						
Paton	140,000		(2) 21,000			119,000
Saliers		25,000	(1) 22,500		2,500	–0–
Minority interest					(10,000)	10,000
Total liabilities and stockholders' equity	440,000	100,000	176,000	176,000	–0–	384,000

investment-in-parent account is offset against the related owners' equity accounts of the parent, giving effect to a constructive retirement of the related stock. This elimination is accomplished by the worksheet adjustment (2) in Exhibit 8-12, which presents the worksheet for the consolidation of Paton and Saliers immediately following the acquisitions of the mutual holdings. Notice that the $45,000 debit to Paton's common stock represents 15% of Paton's common stock balance ($45,000 = .15 × $300,000). The $21,000 remainder ($21,000 = $66,000 − $45,000) is debited to Paton's retained earnings.

Accounting by Subsidiary and Parent after Date of Acquisition

The financial statements issued by the two companies at the end of 19X7 are shown in the first two columns of Exhibit 8-13 on the following page. Since the subsidiary's investment represents only a 15% interest, the subsidiary (Saliers) follows the cost method of accounting for its investment in the parent (Paton).[7] Accordingly, the subsidiary recognizes as investment income only its share of the parent's dividend, which is $1,350 (.15 × $9,000). This means that Saliers's net income is $16,350 ($15,000 + $1,350).

The parent, following the equity method, recognizes 90% of its subsidiary's income adjusted for the subsidiary's share of the parent's net income. Under the allocation method

---

[7] As explained in footnote 5, we assume throughout this book that all subsidiaries with mutually held parents use the cost method to account for investments in their parents–even when the subsidiary owns 20% or more of its parent.

| EXHIBIT 8-13 | 19X7 CONSOLIDATION WORKSHEET WITH MUTUAL HOLDINGS BETWEEN PARENT AND SUBSIDIARY: ALLOCATION METHOD | | | | | |

	Separate Financial Statements		Consolidation Adjustments		Minority Interest	Consolidated Financial Statements
	Paton	Saliers	Dr.	Cr.		
Income Statement						
Income from own operations	50,000	15,000				65,000
Income from Saliers	11,416		(1) 11,416			
Income from Paton		1,350	(1) 1,350			
Amortization expense			(3) 1,000			(1,000)
Minority interest (.10 × 25,838)					2,584	(2,584)
Net income	61,416	16,350	13,766		2,584	61,416
Retained Earnings Statement						
Retained earnings, 1-1-X7:						
Paton	140,000		(4) 21,000			119,000
Saliers		25,000	(2) 22,500		2,500	
Net income	61,416	16,350	13,766		2,584	61,416
Dividends:						
Paton ($9,000 − $1,350)	(7,650)					(7,650)
Saliers		(4,000)		(1) 3,600	(400)	
Retained earnings, 12-31-X7	193,766	37,350	57,266	3,600	4,684	172,766
Balance Sheet						
Other assets	374,600	46,350				420,950
Investment in Saliers	119,166			(1) 9,166		
				(2) 110,000		
Investment in Paton		66,000		(4) 66,000		
Goodwill			(2) 20,000	(3) 1,000		19,000
Total assets	493,766	112,350				439,950
Common stock:						
Paton	300,000		(4) 45,000			255,000
Saliers		75,000	(2) 67,500		7,500	
Retained earnings	193,766	37,350	57,266	3,600	4,684	172,766
Minority interest					(12,184)	12,184
Total liabilities and stockholders' equity	493,766	112,350	189,766	189,766	−0−	439,950

for mutual holdings between the parent and its subsidiary, the parent's calculation of income is based on the solution to the following system of equations:

$$P = 50,000 + (.90\ S - 1,000)$$
$$S = 15,000 + .15\ P$$

Notice that the parent's amortization of goodwill ($1,000) is subtracted in the first equation. These equations, which describe the bilateral income-sharing between parent and subsidiary, may be solved by substitution as follows:

$$P = 50,000 + .90 \ (15,000 + .15 \ P) - 1,000$$
$$P = 50,000 + 13,500 + .135 \ P - 1,000$$
$$.865 \ P = 62,500$$
$$P = 72,254.335$$

$$S = 15,000 + .15 \ (72,254.335)$$
$$S = 25,838.15$$

On the basis of these results, Paton may compute the income from its subsidiary, Saliers, as shown in Exhibit 8-14.

Observe that the parent adjusts its share of subsidiary net income ($23,254) for the subsidiary's share of the parent's total income ($10,838) and for the 19X7 goodwill amortization ($1,000).[8] Paton calculates 19X7 income from its subsidiary by subtracting the parent's income from its own operations from parent-company net income (from Exhibit 8-14) ($61,416 − $50,000 = $11,416) and records it by the following entry:

Entry on parent's records for income from subsidiary (adjusted for subsidiary's income from parent) and reclassification of parent's dividend to subsidiary:

Investment in Saliers	12,766	
Dividend ($9,000 × .15)		1,350
Income from Saliers ($61,416 − $50,000)		11,416

Entry on parent's records to record dividend from subsidiary:

Cash	3,600	
Investment in Saliers		3,600

---

[8] The minority interest in the income of Saliers can also be calculated more directly by multiplying the minority interest percentage times the corresponding total income solution (.10 × $25,838.15 = $2,584).

EXHIBIT 8-14	ALLOCATION OF INCOME FROM OWN OPERATIONS FOR CONSOLIDATION OF PATON AND SALIERS

	Paton	Saliers	Total
Income from own operations	$50,000	$15,000	$65,000
Allocation of Saliers' income to Paton (.90 × $25,838.15)	23,254	(23,254)	
Allocation of Paton's income to Saliers (.15 × $72,254.335)	(10,838)	10,838	
Income after allocation	$62,416	$ 2,584	$65,000
Amortization expense	(1,000)		(1,000)
Parent-company net income	$61,416		
Minority interest in net income		$ 2,584	
Total			$64,000

In summary, the parent's investment account balance increases by $12,766, as a result of the foregoing entry, and decreases by $3,600, the parent's share of the subsidiary dividend (.90 × $4,000)—a net increase in the investment account of $9,166.

Consolidation One Year after Acquisition

Exhibit 8-13 presents the worksheet for the consolidation of Paton and Saliers one year after the acquisition of the mutual holdings. The following worksheet adjustments are required:

(1) *Worksheet adjustment to eliminate income from affiliated companies:*

Income from Saliers	11,416	
Income from Paton	1,350	
Dividend		3,600
Investment in Saliers		9,166

(2) *Worksheet adjustment to eliminate and reclassify beginning-of-the-year balance of parent's investment account:*

Common stock of Saliers	67,500	
Retained earnings of Saliers, 1-1	22,500	
Goodwill	*20,000*	
Investment in Saliers		110,000

(3) *Worksheet adjustment to amortize valuation differential for current year:*

Amortization expense	1,000	
Goodwill		1,000

(4) *Worksheet adjustment to record subsidiary's investment in parent as stock retirement:*

Common stock	45,000	
Retained earnings of Paton, 1-1	21,000	
Investment in Paton		66,000

The minority interest in net income ($2,584) is calculated as shown in Exhibit 8-14 or as the minority interest percentage times the solution amount for Saliers (.10 × $25,838.15).

PARENT'S INVESTMENT IN SUBSIDIARY PREFERRED STOCK

A parent company controls its subsidiary through an investment in the subsidiary's common stock. The basis for the parent's control is the voting rights conferred on the parent by the common stock held. Control, in this sense of the word, is unaffected by a parent's investments in nonvoting equity securities of the subsidiary like preferred stock. However, such investments in preferred stock affect the application of the equity method to the parent's common stock investment and the application of consolidation procedures. The paragraphs that follow review the calculation of preferred stock equity, and demonstrate the impact of a parent's holdings of subsidiary preferred stock on both separate and consolidated financial statements.

Book Value of Preferred Stockholders' Equity

The book value of preferred stockholders' equity ("preferred equity," for short) is measured by the liquidation value of preferred stock. Consequently, preferred equity includes the par value of the preferred shares plus dividends in arrears or other rights of preferred stockholders in retained earnings. In some cases, the liquidation value is a stated dollar amount. However, throughout the remainder of this text, the liquidation value is assumed to be par value plus dividends in arrears.

Preferred Stock Held by Unaffiliated Parties

Newlove Corporation acquires 90% of the outstanding common stock of Bennett, Inc., on January 1, 19X5, when Bennett has the following stockholders' equity balances:

Stockholders' Equity at Acquisition	
Preferred stock ($50 par, 5% cumulative)	$ 50,000
Common stock ($4 par)	100,000
Retained earnings	38,000
Total stockholders' equity	$188,000

The preferred stock of Bennett pays or accumulates a $2,500 annual dividend (.05 × $50,000). On January 1, 19X5, the 19X4 dividend is in arrears. The liquidation value of preferred stock is par value plus dividends in arrears.

Calculation of Preferred Equity

As mentioned, the book value of preferred stock is usually measured by the liquidation value of preferred stock, which may include an equity interest in retained earnings as well as the par value. The book value of preferred stock that is neither cumulative nor participating does not include an interest in retained earnings, but cumulative dividends and participation in earnings may give rise to such an interest. The book value of Bennett's preferred stock equity is $52,500, which equals the sum of the total par value ($50,000) and the dividend in arrears ($2,500). When preferred stock participates in net income, the balance of retained earnings must be divided between preferred stock and common stock interests. If, for example, preferred stock were *fully* participating, as well as cumulative, then the following allocation on the basis of relative par value would be appropriate:

Allocation of Retained Earnings to Cumulative, Fully Participating Preferred Stock	
Dividends in arrears	$ 2,500
Participation in retained earnings ($38,000 − $2,500) × ($50,000 ÷ $150,000)	11,833
Preferred equity in retained earnings	$14,333

In other cases, preferred stock may not be fully participating. If, for example, participation is limited, then the foregoing allocation on the basis of relative par values is replaced by a calculation that properly reflects the limited participation.

Calculation of the Book Value of Common Stockholders' Equity Acquired

The book value of a parent company's common stockholders' equity in a subsidiary excludes all equity of preferred stockholders in retained earnings and other stockholders' equity accounts of the subsidiary. The book value of Newlove's 90% interest in common stockholders' equity is computed as follows:

Common Stockholders' Equity Acquired

Common stock ($4 par)		$100,000
Retained earnings:		
Balance, 1-1-X5	$38,000	
Less: Equity of preferred stockholders in retained earnings (dividend in arrears)	(2,500)	35,500
Total common stockholders' equity		$135,500
Parent's ownership percentage		×.90
Common stockholders' equity acquired		$121,950

The preferred equity is excluded from total stockholders' equity in the calculation of the common stockholders' equity acquired whether the preferred stock is held by the parent or by unaffiliated parties.

Intercompany Preferred Stock Investment and Consolidated Entities

The acquisition by a parent company of the preferred stock of its subsidiary is tantamount to its retirement from the viewpoint of the consolidation. Consequently, consolidation procedures eliminate the preferred stock investment and related preferred stockholders' equity. Any difference between the investment and related preferred equity is regarded as a premium or discount and is credited or debited to other contributed capital of the consolidated entity. The book value of preferred shares held by unaffiliated parties is included in minority interest on the consolidated balance sheet. The illustration that follows demonstrates the parent's separate accounting and the consolidation procedures that are applicable to investments by a parent in the preferred stock of its subsidiary.

A Parent Invests in Subsidiary Preferred Stock

On January 1, 19X1, Turnstead Corporation acquired both common and preferred stock of Ulseth, Inc., in exchange for cash. Immediately after the acquisition, the balance sheets of the two companies appear as in the parent and subsidiary columns of Exhibit 8-15. Turnstead acquired 90% of the outstanding common stock of Ulseth for $99,000, which exactly equals the related common stockholders' equity of the subsidiary [$99,000 = .90 × ($80,000 + $30,000)]. In addition, Turnstead acquired 40% of the subsidiary's (Ulseth's) cumulative, 10%, nonparticipating preferred stock for $14,000, which is $2,000 less than the corresponding equity [$2,000 = (.40 × $40,000) − $14,000]. No preferred dividends are in arrears at January 1, 19X1. Consequently, the acquired preferred equity ($16,000 = .40 × $40,000) includes no part of subsidiary retained earnings.

Consolidation at Date of Acquisition

The consolidation worksheet at the date of acquisition is given by Exhibit 8-15. Two worksheet adjustments are required to produce the consolidated balance sheet. The first (1) is the familiar adjustment to eliminate the acquired equity in common stock accounts

| EXHIBIT 8-15 | CONSOLIDATION WORKSHEET AT DATE OF ACQUISITION: PARENT ACQUIRES PREFERRED STOCK OF SUBSIDIARY |

	Separate Financial Statements		Consolidation Adjustments		Minority Interest	Consolidation Financial Statement
	Turnstead	Ulseth	Dr.	Cr.		
Balance Sheet						
Investment in Ulseth:						
Common stock	99,000			(1) 99,000		
Preferred stock	14,000			(2) 14,000		
Other assets	337,000	150,000				487,000
Total assets	450,000	150,000				487,000
Preferred stock		40,000	(2) 16,000		24,000	–0–
Common stock:						
Turnstead	320,000					320,000
Ulseth		80,000	(1) 72,000		8,000	
Other contributed capital				(2) 2,000		2,000
Retained earnings:						
Turnstead	130,000					130,000
Ulseth		30,000	(1) 27,000		3,000	
Minority interest					(35,000)	35,000
Total liabilities and stockholders' equity	450,000	150,000	115,000	115,000	–0–	487,000

of the subsidiary and the related investment in common stock by the parent. The second adjustment (2) eliminates the acquired equity in preferred stock and the related investment by the parent. This new adjustment takes the following form:

Worksheet adjustment to eliminate acquired preferred stockholders' equity and related investment:

Preferred stock (.40 × $40,000) 16,000
Retained earnings . . . . –0–
      Investment in subsidiary preferred stock 14,000
      Other contributed capital 2,000

Since the preferred equity at acquisition does not include an interest in retained earnings, the foregoing elimination does not affect retained earnings. No part of the subsidiary's preferred stockholders' equity is identified as such on the consolidated balance sheet. Subsidiary preferred stockholders' equity is either eliminated or included in minority interest, as shown by the worksheet (Exhibit 8-15). If a subsidiary has outstanding preferred stock and none of it is owned by the parent, then 100% of the preferred stockholders' equity is included in minority interest.

Any difference between a parent's initial investment in *common* stock and the related equity acquired would be treated as a valuation differential. In contrast, the difference between the investment in *preferred* stock and the related equity acquired is viewed as a premium or discount that reflects changes in the value of the shares since their issuance. When a company retires its own preferred stock, any difference between the acquisition cost and the book value of the retired shares is usually credited or debited to contributed capital. The purchase of intercompany preferred stock is, in effect, a retirement of the stock by the consolidated entity. Consequently, consistency requires the consolidated entity to enter discounts or premiums associated with acquisitions of intercompany preferred stock in other contributed capital. If the acquisition cost exceeds the book value of intercompany preferred shares, then the *premium* should be *debited* against the parent's other contributed capital and, to the extent that the parent's other contributed capital is insufficient to absorb it, against the parent's retained earnings (which will cause consolidated retained earnings to differ from the parent's separate retained earnings). If the book value of intercompany preferred shares exceeds their acquisition cost, then the *discount* should be *credited* to other contributed capital on the consolidated financial statements.

The Equity Method

The following additional information is required to illustrate the equity method. During 19X1, Ulseth (the subsidiary) reports net income of $12,000, but neither the subsidiary nor its parent pays any dividends. Consequently, subsidiary preferred dividends are in arrears in the total amount of $4,000 (.10 × $40,000) at December 31, 19X1. During 19X2, the subsidiary reports net income of $15,000 and pays preferred dividends of $8,000, but no other dividends are paid. The parent and subsidiary trial balances at December 31, 19X1, and December 31, 19X2, are presented in the consolidation worksheets shown in Exhibits 8-17 and 8-18.

Income from Common Stock

Turnstead's calculation of income from its common stock investment in Ulseth is as follows:

Parent's Calculation of Income from Common Stock in Subsidiary

	19X1	19X2
Subsidiary net income	$12,000	$15,000
Preferred dividend	(4,000)	(4,000)
Adjusted subsidiary net income	$ 8,000	$11,000
Parent's ownership percentage	×.90	×.90
Income from subsidiary	$ 7,200	$ 9,900

Since the Ulseth's preferred stock is cumulative, the subsidiary net income is adjusted for the annual dividend whether or not the dividends are paid. No preferred dividend was paid in 19X1, and both 19X1 and 19X2 preferred dividends were paid in 19X2. If preferred stock is noncumulative, then subsidiary net income is usually adjusted for preferred dividends paid during the period.

Income from Preferred Stock

The foregoing calculation yields the parent's (Turnstead's) income from its common stock in the subsidiary but does not give its income from preferred stock. Let us assume that Turnstead recognizes preferred dividends on its separate income statement in the period in which they are received. Following this usual practice, Turnstead reports no income from subsidiary preferred stock in 19X1 and $3,200 in 19X2 ($3,200 = .40 × $4,000 × 2).

Consolidation Worksheet Adjustments

Consolidation worksheet adjustments for the date of acquisition and the two years following the acquisition of Ulseth by Turnstead are given in Exhibit 8-16. The first adjustment reverses the parent's recording of income from its subsidiary related to holdings of both common and preferred stock. Note that preferred stock dividends recorded by the parent are offset against preferred dividends recorded by the subsidiary. The second and third adjustments eliminate the beginning-of-the-year investment balances related to common and preferred stock, respectively. Notice that the elimination for the investment in common stock made at the end of the second year reflects first-year earnings. Observe that no special adjustment is required for the preferred dividend in arrears at December 31, 19X1. However, the arrearage does require modification of the worksheet procedure.

Consolidation Worksheet One Year after Acquisition

The consolidation worksheet prepared one year after the acquisition of Ulseth by Turnstead is presented in Exhibit 8-17 on the following page. Notice that separate accounts are maintained for preferred stock and common stock components of the income from subsidiary, minority interest in subsidiary income, and investment in subsidiary.

EXHIBIT 8-16	CONSOLIDATION WORKSHEET ADJUSTMENTS: PARENT ACQUIRES PREFERRED STOCK OF SUBSIDIARY

Turnstead Corporation

WORKSHEET ADJUSTMENTS FOR CONSOLIDATION OF ULSETH INC.

	Date of Acquisition		One Year after Acquisition		Two Years after Acquisition	
(1) *Worksheet adjustment to reverse parent's recording of subsidiary income and eliminate subsidiary dividends to parent for current year:*						
Income from subsidiary common stock.....			7,200		9,900	
Income from subsidiary preferred stock			–0–		3,200	
Investment in subsidiary common stock				7,200		9,900
Preferred dividend.................				–0–		3,200
(2) *Worksheet adjustment to eliminate beginning-of-the-year balance of parent's investment in subsidiary common stock account:*						
Common stock of subsidiary	72,000		72,000		72,000	
Retained earnings of subsidiary, 1-1	27,000		27,000		34,200	
Investment in subsidiary common stock		99,000		99,000		106,200
(3) *Worksheet adjustment to eliminate beginning-of-the-year balance of parent's investment in subsidiary preferred stock account:*						
Preferred stock	16,000		16,000		16,000	
Investment in subsidiary preferred stock		14,000		14,000		14,000
Other contributed capital		2,000		2,000		2,000

EXHIBIT 8-17	CONSOLIDATION WORKSHEET ONE YEAR AFTER ACQUISITION: PARENT ACQUIRES PREFERRED STOCK OF SUBSIDIARY					

| | Separate Financial Statements | | Consolidation Adjustments | | Minority Interest | Consolidated Financial Statement |
	Turnstead	Ulseth	Dr.	Cr.		
Income Statement						
Revenue	400,000	92,000				492,000
Income from subsidiary:						
Common stock	7,200		(1) 7,200			
Preferred stock	–0–					
Expenses	(340,000)	(80,000)				(420,000)
Minority interest:						
Common stock					800	(800)
Preferred stock					2,400	(2,400)
Net income	67,200	12,000	7,200		3,200	68,800
Retained Earnings Statement						
Retained earnings, 1-1-X1:						
Turnstead	130,000					130,000
Ulseth		30,000	(2) 27,000		3,000	
Net income	67,200	12,000	7,200		3,200	68,800
Retained earnings, 12-31-X1	197,200	42,000	34,200		6,200	198,800
Balance Sheet						
Investment in Ulseth:						
Common stock	106,200			(2) 99,000		–0–
				(1) 7,200		
Preferred stock	14,000			(3) 14,000		–0–
Other assets	397,000	162,000				559,000
Total assets	517,200	162,200				559,000
Preferred stock		40,000	(3) 16,000		24,000	
Common stock						
Turnstead	320,000					320,000
Ulseth		80,000	(2) 72,000		8,000	
Other contributed capital				(3) 2,000		2,000
Retained earnings	197,200	42,000	34,200		6,200	198,800
Minority interest					(38,200)	38,200
Total liabilities and stockholders' equity	517,200	162,000	122,200	122,200	–0–	559,000

Minority Interest in Subsidiary Income

The minority interest in the subsidiary (Ulseth) consists of two groups—nonaffiliated investors in subsidiary common stock and nonaffiliated investors in subsidiary preferred stock. The following schedule shows the structure of the minority interest in consolidated retained earnings at December 31, 19X1:

Minority Interest in Consolidated Retained Earnings

Balance, January 1, 19X1 (.10 × $30,000)	$3,000
Add: Minority common stock interest in 19X1 subsidiary net income [.10 × ($12,000 − $4,000)]	800
Add: Minority preferred stock interest in 19X1 subsidiary net income (.60 × $4,000)	2,400
Balance, December 31, 19X1	$6,200

The minority interest in the 19X1 income associated with common stock ($800) equals the minority ownership percentage for common stock multiplied by the subsidiary net income adjusted for the annual (cumulative) preferred dividend ($800 = .10 × $8,000). The minority interest in the 19X1 income associated with cumulative preferred stock ($2,400) equals the minority ownership percentage for *preferred* stock multiplied by the annual preferred dividend ($2,400 = .60 × $4,000).

Consolidated and Parent Company Net Incomes

Observe that the 19X1 consolidated net income exceeds the parent's (Turnstead's) net income by $1,600 ($1,600 = .40 × $4,000). The reason for the difference is that the parent does not recognize subsidiary earnings associated with cumulative preferred dividends until such dividends are paid. In other words, the parent's net income excludes subsidiary net income associated with dividends in arrears. In contrast, consolidated net income includes the majority interest in all subsidiary net income whether or not it is associated with dividends in arrears. Of course, if the parent applies the equity method to its investment in subsidiary *preferred stock,* then the parent's net income includes subsidiary income associated with dividends in arrears and the difference between the parent's net income and consolidated net income disappears.

Consolidation Worksheet Two Years after Acquisition

The consolidation worksheet prepared two years after the acquisition of Ulseth by Turnstead is presented in Exhibit 8-18 on the following page. The primary difference between this and the previous consolidation worksheet is the treatment of retained earnings at January 1, 19X2. The beginning balance of consolidated retained earnings is $198,800, which includes $1,600 excluded from the parent's beginning balance ($1,600 = $198,800 − $197,200). In order to avoid unnecessary worksheet adjustments, the beginning consolidated balance in retained earnings is represented by two numbers—the parent's beginning balance of retained earnings ($197,200) and the parent's share of preferred dividends in arrears ($1,600). The arrearage equals the remainder of subsidiary retained earnings after consolidated adjustments and the subtraction of the minority interest therein ($1,600 = $42,000 − $27,000 − $7,200 − $6,200). Subsidiary income associated with the preferred dividend in arrears is recognized in 19X2 when the 19X1 dividend is paid. Since the 19X2 preferred dividend is also paid, no dividends are in arrears on December 31, 19X2. Consequently, parent and consolidated retained earnings balances are equal at year-end. Observe that the parent's net income *exceeds* the consolidated net income by the parent's share of the 19X1 preferred dividend paid in 19X2 ($1,600 = $123,100 − $121,500).

EXHIBIT 8-18	CONSOLIDATION WORKSHEET TWO YEARS AFTER ACQUISITION: PARENT ACQUIRES PREFERRED STOCK OF SUBSIDIARY

	Separate Financial Statements		Consolidation Adjustments		Minority Interest	Consolidated Financial Statements
	Turnstead	Ulseth	Dr.	Cr.		
Income Statement						
Revenue	500,000	104,000				604,000
Income from subsidiary:						
Common stock	9,900		(1) 9,900			
Preferred stock	3,200		(1) 3,200			
Expenses	(390,000)	(89,000)				(479,000)
Minority interest:						
Common stock					1,100	(1,100)
Preferred stock					2,400	(2,400)
Net income	123,100	15,000	13,100		3,500	121,500
Retained Earnings Statement						
Retained earnings, 1-1-X2:						
Turnstead	197,200					197,200
Ulseth		42,000	(2) 34,200		6,200	1,600
Net income	123,100	15,000	13,100		3,500	121,500
Preferred dividend		(8,000)		(1) 3,200	(4,800)	
Retained earnings, 12-31-X1	320,300	49,000	47,300	3,200	4,900	320,300
Balance Sheet						
Investment in Ulseth:						
Common stock	116,100			(1) 9,900		–0–
				(2) 106,200		
Preferred stock	14,000			(3) 14,000		–0–
Other assets	510,200	169,000				679,200
Total assets	640,300	169,000				679,200
Preferred stock		40,000	(3) 16,000		24,000	
Common stock:						
Turnstead	320,000					320,000
Ulseth		80,000	(2) 72,000		8,000	
Other contributed capital				(3) 2,000		2,000
Retained earnings	320,300	49,000	47,300	3,200	4,900	320,300
Minority interest					(36,900)	36,900
Total liabilities and stockholders' equity	640,300	169,000	135,300	135,300	–0–	679,200

JOINT VENTURES

A joint venture is an entity owned, operated, and jointly controlled by a small group as a separate business enterprise for the mutual benefit of the owners. Most joint ventures extend or complement the businesses of one or more of the venturers. For example, several companies may collaborate in expensive basic research by forming a research institute as a joint venture, or several companies may form a joint venture to hold land for future expansion of their production facilities. In this way, joint ventures enable the venturers to share the risks and rewards of activities that they may be unable to undertake alone.

Usually all owners or "venturers" participate in the management of their joint venture. Although ownership shares vary widely—from as low as 5% or 10% to as high as 70% or 75%—significant decisions in most joint ventures require the consent of every owner regardless of the size of the related ownership share. Hence, no single owner has unilateral control of the joint venture. For example, even a 10% interest in a joint venture can exercise significant influence over operations. This characteristic, which is called *joint control,* distinguishes joint ventures from subsidiary companies and other entities controlled by a majority of ownership shares.

Accounting for Joint Venture Investments

Joint ventures take the form of (1) corporations, (2) partnerships, or (3) undivided interests (an ownership arrangement in which two or more parties jointly own property and in which title is held individually to the extent of each party's interest). Under current standards, investments in *corporate joint ventures* are accounted for by the equity method (even if ownership exceeds 50%) in both the consolidated financial statements and the separate financial statements of the investor (*APB 18,* par. 16). Further, most joint ventures organized as *partnerships* are accounted for by the equity method in both the consolidated and separate financial statements of the investor.[9]

Although the equity method is applied to most joint ventures, current standards are not completely conclusive and proportionate consolidation is used as an alternative in some cases.[10] For example, joint ventures organized as *undivided interests* may not be appropriately accounted for by the equity method.

If an investor guarantees specific liabilities of the venture, then the equity method is open to criticism. In such cases, the equity method, which represents the investment as a single line on the investor's separate balance sheet, fails to emphasize the investor's share in the venture's liabilities. Critics of the equity method have argued that the one-line balance sheet disclosure enables investors in joint ventures to engage in "off-balance-sheet financing" for the purpose of obscuring the amount of debt for which the investor is liable. By investing in a joint venture that is accounted for by the equity method, a company can secure the advantages of additional borrowing without listing that borrowing among its liabilities.

Proportionate Consolidation

Proportionate consolidation combines just the investor's proportionate share of the venture's assets, liabilities, revenues, and expenses with the corresponding items in both the consolidated and the separate-company financial statements of the investor. In other words, this represents an application of the proprietary concept of financial statement consolidation, which was discussed in the appendix to Chapter 2. In addition, proportionate consolidation is appropriate in the investor's consolidated financial statements, pro-

---

[9] Of course, if the joint venture is controlled by the venturer, then it is really a subsidiary and should be consolidated in the usual way. If the investment in a joint venture is immaterial to the venturer, then it may be accounted for by the cost method.

[10] Proportionate consolidation has been used for many years in the real estate and construction, oil and gas, and utilities industries (AICPA Accounting Standards Executive Committee, 1979).

vided that the investee is not a subsidiary. If the investee is a subsidiary of the investor, then full consolidation is appropriate. We now turn to an illustration of proportionate consolidation for a joint venture.

In order to illustrate proportionate consolidation, let us consider a joint venture formed by Athens Electric Power in collaboration with several other electric utilities. The purpose of the joint venture was to construct and operate under joint control an electric power generation plant called Marietta Station. On January 1, 19X3, the date of formation, Athens Electric Power received a 40% interest in the joint venture in exchange for $4,000,000 cash.[11] On the same date, Marietta Station issued debt in the amount of $7,000,000, 40% of which was guaranteed by Athens Electric. Three years were required to complete the facility that began operating in 19X6.

Athens uses the equity method to account for its investment in Marietta Station on its separate records. Although the equity method is permitted by current financial accounting standards, proportionate consolidation is the preferred method in this case (owing to the debt guarantee) and should be applied in both the separate and consolidated financial statements. Accordingly, a proportionate consolidation procedure is illustrated.

The first four years of operations are given in the analysis of Athens Electric's investment account shown in Exhibit 8-19. Marietta Station sustained operating losses of $25,000, $30,000, and $50,000 in the years 19X3, 19X4, and 19X5, respectively, as a result of noncapitalizable expenditures during the construction period. During this three-year period, there were no intercompany operating transactions between Marietta and any of the venturers. The first sales of electric power to venturers occurred in 19X6. During 19X6, all Marietta's sales, which totaled $250,000, were made to venturers and included $125,000 for sales to Athens.[12] Marietta Station has paid no dividends. Marietta's net income in 19X6 was $40,000.

Proportionate consolidation of Athens and its joint venture interest in Marietta is shown for the year 19X6 in Exhibit 8-20. The financial statements for 19X6 are given in the first two columns of Exhibit 8-20. The consolidation adjustments are shown on page 434.

---

[11] Joint ventures are frequently formed with contributions of identifiable nonmonetary assets by the venturers. If transfer of the assets to the joint venture constitutes a change in ownership, then the assets should be revalued. This approach is supported by the view that the joint venture is a new business entity and that the contributing venturer has exchanged unilateral control over the contributed assets for joint control. Thus the venturer would recognize a gain or loss, and the joint venture would record the assets at their fair value. On the other hand, if the new joint venture does not constitute a change in ownership, then the contributor recognizes neither gain nor loss and the joint venture records the assets at their book value. This approach is supported by the view that control over the transferred assets has not really been transferred to another party. At present, this argument must be resolved in terms of the details of the venture agreement with the result that revaluation or ''new basis accounting'' is used in some cases and not in others. See Chapter 10 for additional discussion of new basis accounting.

[12] Since electric power is not an inventoriable commodity, Marietta's income does not include gross margin that requires deferral for purposes of the equity method or consolidation. All power sold by Marietta to its venturers is almost instantaneously resold to customers of the venturers or used by the venturers themselves. Consequently, the related gross margin is confirmed by a third-party transaction in the period of the intercompany transaction and need not be deferred. Of course, if an inventoriable product is transferred between venturers and their joint venture, then the adjustments described in Chapter 4 are required to defer gross margins that are associated with the transferred product still in inventory at the year-end.

EXHIBIT 8-19	ANALYSIS OF ATHENS ELECTRIC'S INVESTMENT IN MARIETTA STATION			
	19X3	**19X4**	**19X5**	**19X6**
Balance, January 1	$ –0–	$3,990,000	$3,978,000	$3,958,000
Initial investment	4,000,000			
Income (loss) from Marietta (40%)	(10,000)	(12,000)	(20,000)	16,000
Balance, December 31	$3,990,000	$3,978,000	$3,958,000	$3,974,000

EXHIBIT 8-20	PROPORTIONATE CONSOLIDATION OF 19X6 FINANCIAL STATEMENTS					

	Separate Financial Statements		Consolidation Adjustments		Consolidated Financial Statements
	Athens	**Marietta**	**Dr.**	**Cr.**	
Income Statement					
Sales	9,000,000	250,000	(4) 50,000		9,050,000
			(3) 150,000		
Income from Marietta	16,000		(1) 16,000		
Cost of electricity	(6,500,000)	(160,000)		(4) 50,000	(6,514,000)
				(3) 96,000	
Other expenses	(1,700,000)	(50,000)		(3) 30,000	(1,720,000)
Net income	816,000	40,000	216,000	176,000	816,000
Retained Earnings Statement					
Retained earnings, 1-1-X6:					
Athens	25,384,000				25,384,000
Marietta		(105,000)*	(2) 42,000		
			(3) 63,000		
Net income	816,000	40,000	216,000	176,000	816,000
Dividends	(200,000)	–0–			(200,000)
Retained earnings, 12-31-X6	26,000,000	(65,000)	216,000	281,000	26,000,000
Balance Sheet					
Current assets	18,600,000	2,535,000		(3) 1,521,000	19,614,000
Investment in Marietta	3,974,000			(1) 16,000	–0–
				(2) 3,958,000	
Plant and equipment (net)	143,426,000	14,400,000		(3) 8,640,000	149,186,000
Total assets	166,000,000	16,935,000			168,800,000
Liabilities	90,000,000	7,000,000	(3) 4,200,000		92,800,000
Common stock, Athens	50,000,000				50,000,000
Contributed owners' equity, Marietta		10,000,000	(2) 4,000,000		
			(3) 6,000,000		
Retained earnings	26,000,000	(65,000)	216,000	281,000	26,000,000
Total liabilities and stockholders' equity	166,000,000	16,935,000	14,416,000	14,416,000	168,800,000

* ($105,000) = ($25,000) + ($30,000) + ($50,000)

(1) *Reverse investor's recording of investee net income for current year:*

Income from Marietta	16,000	
Investment in Marietta		16,000

(2) *Eliminate beginning-of-the-year balance of investment account:*

Contributed owners' equity, Marietta 4,000,000		
Retained earnings of Marietta (1-1-X6)	42,000	
Investment in Marietta	3,958,000	

(3) *Eliminate pro rata portion of financial statement items related to equity interest of other venturers:*

Sales ($250,000 × .60)	150,000	
Liabilities ($7,000,000 × .60) 4,200,000		
Contributed owners' equity, Marietta 6,000,000		
Current assets ($2,535,000 × .60)...............	1,521,000	
Cost of electricity ($160,000 × .60)	96,000	
Other expenses ($50,000 × .60)	30,000	
Retained earnings of Marietta, 1-1-X6		
($105,000 × .60)	63,000	
Plant and equipment (net) ($14,400,000 × .60)....	8,640,000	

(4) *Eliminate upstream transfer prices from sales and cost of electricity for the current year:*

Sales ($250,000 × .40 × .50)	50,000	
Cost of electricity...........................		50,000

All the foregoing adjustments are familiar except adjustment (3). Adjustment (3) eliminates the proportionate share of the investee's assets, liabilities, owners' equities, revenues, and expenses that are associated with owners other than the investor for whom the proportionate consolidation is prepared. In this case, adjustment (3) eliminates the 60% of Marietta's assets, liabilities, owners' equities, revenues, and expenses that are associated with venturers other than Athens Electric. As a result of these adjustments, Athens Electric's consolidated statements include 40% of the assets, liabilities, revenues, and expenses of Marietta Station. Adjustment (4), which eliminates upstream transfer prices from the income accounts, applies only to the investor's 40% pro rata share of the current year's transfers—the 60% remainder having been eliminated by the preceding adjustment. Accordingly, the amount of the fourth adjustment is calculated by multiplying the total amount of upstream transfers (.50 × $250,000 = $125,000) times the ownership percentage ($50,000 = $125,000 × .40). Notice that the consolidated net income with proportionate consolidation equals the investor's net income with the application of the equity method.

Some accountants believe that proportionate consolidation for joint ventures, although superior to the equity method, may produce misleading balance sheets when applied to certain joint ventures. Suppose, for example, that the investor guarantees a percentage of the venture's debt that differs from the investor's ownership percentage. Proportionate consolidation would include in consolidated liabilities an amount corresponding to the ownership percentage rather than to the guarantee percentage. Although the facts of the matter could be clarified in a footnote, the amount for which the investor is actually liable would not be given on the consolidated statement.

DEFERRED INCOME TAXES

The deferral of income taxes is necessary to match income tax expense with pretax accounting income. Thereby income tax expense consists of the tax effects of income items included in pretax accounting income. Some income items do not enter pretax accounting income and taxable income in the same period. Such differences are called *temporary differences*. Other income items enter one income calculation but not the other. Such differences are called *permanent differences*. The tax effect of a permanent difference is either zero (if it enters pretax accounting income but not taxable income) or reported in the period in which it enters taxable income (if it enters taxable income but not pretax accounting income); in neither case are taxes deferred from one period to another. In contrast, the tax effects of temporary differences require the creation of a deferred tax liability or asset.

Consolidated and Separate Tax Returns

A consolidated entity may file tax returns in one of two ways: (1) the parent and its subsidiary may file *separate tax returns* or (2) the parent and its subsidiary may file a *consolidated tax return*. If separate returns are filed, each corporation pays income taxes on its own income; in addition, as explained below, the parent *may* be required to pay taxes on dividends received from the subsidiary. If a consolidated return is filed, income taxes are paid on the basis of the consolidated taxable income of the group and no taxes are paid by the parent on dividends from its subsidiary or by the subsidiary on dividends from its parent.

Parent and subsidiary corporations *may* file consolidated tax returns if they qualify as an *affiliated group* under the Internal Revenue Code; if parent and subsidiary do not qualify as an affiliated group, they *must* file separate returns. An affiliated group exists when a parent owns at least 80% of the voting stock and at least 80% of the total value of all outstanding stock (voting and nonvoting) of the subsidiary. Even if an affiliated group elects to file separate tax returns, intercorporate dividends are excluded from taxation. Further, domestic corporations that do not qualify as an affiliated group still exclude a portion of intercorporate dividends from their separate tax returns. If the investor corporation owns between 20% and 80% of the investee's voting stock, then 80% of intercorporate dividends are excluded. If the investor owns less than 20%, then 70% is excluded.

Undistributed Investee Income

If parent and subsidiary qualify as an affiliated group, then intercorporate dividends are not taxed and undistributed subsidiary income is not a temporary difference. On the other hand, if parent and subsidiary do not qualify as an affiliated group, then the parent pays tax on its share of subsidiary earnings when those earnings are distributed as dividends. The same is true for investors in nonsubsidiary investees. Thus, such an investor's taxable income includes dividends in the period of their distribution; but the investor's pretax accounting income, under the equity method, includes the investor's share of the net income reported by the investee, whether or not it is distributed as dividends. (Of course, the same may be said of consolidated net income.) The difference between the investor's income share and the dividend payment is a temporary difference resulting in the recognition of a deferred tax liability [see *FASB Statement No. 109,* par. 4(b)].[13] Of course, calculation of the deferred tax liability must take account of the appropriate level of dividend exclusion provided by the tax law.

---

[13] Several exceptions are provided, including one for foreign subsidiaries and foreign joint ventures when the timing difference will not reverse in the foreseeable future (*FASB Statement No. 109,* par. 31).

To illustrate, suppose that a 60%-owned domestic subsidiary of a U.S. parent reports net income of $10,000 and pays total cash dividends of $3,000. The parent's amortization of the valuation differential for the year is $800 (composed entirely of nondeductible goodwill). Assume that the undistributed subsidiary income is the only temporary difference and that the parent pays income taxes at a rate of 40%. Using the equity method, the parent's income share, amortization, and dividend are recorded, without regard to the parent's tax expense, as follows:

Parent's entry to record income, amortization, and dividend for investment in subsidiary:

Investment in subsidiary [($10,000 × .60) − $800 − $1,800] ... 3,400
Cash ($3,000 × .60) 1,800
    Income from subsidiary [($10,000 × .60) − $800]   5,200

Sixty percent ownership cannot qualify as an affiliated group; thus, the parent files a separate tax return. Under this return, 20% of the dividends are included in (80% excluded from) taxable income, with the result that the parent pays taxes of $144 on the dividend from its subsidiary ($144 = $1,800 × .20 × .40). The parent records the deferred tax effects of the $4,200 in undistributed income [$4,200 = ($10,000 × .60) − ($3,000 × .60)] by the following entry:

Parent's entry to record tax effect of subsidiary's undistributed income:

Income tax expense ($4,200 × .20 × .40) 336
    Deferred tax liability   336

Since the parent's income from subsidiary is reported on the income statement before the parent's income tax expense, the tax effect is recorded as part of the parent's income tax expense, and the one-line consolidation approach is not followed.

Intercompany Merchandise Transactions

Intercompany operating transactions result in deferrals of gross margin that affect the calculation of income tax expense in ways that depend on whether consolidated or separate tax returns are filed. The forms of equity-method calculations and consolidation worksheet adjustments are essentially unaltered by the introduction of income taxes.

To illustrate, consider Praha Corporation and its 90%-owned subsidiary, Salvo, Inc. At acquisition, the entire valuation differential was attributed to goodwill, and Praha continues to amortize goodwill at a rate of $2,500 per year. During 19X4, Praha and Salvo had pretax operating incomes (exclusive of investment income as well as taxes) of $100,000 and $50,000, respectively, and Salvo paid a $16,000 cash dividend ($14,400 to Praha). The only intercompany operating transactions affecting 19X4 are (1) an upstream sale of merchandise for $30,000 resulting in unrealized gross margin at year-end of $8,000 and (2) a downstream sale of merchandise for $25,000 resulting in unrealized gross margin at year-end of $6,000. The income tax rate is 40%. There are no changes in temporary differences unless they are specifically mentioned in later development of this example. Let us begin by considering the consolidated tax return case.

Intercompany Transfers and Consolidated Tax Returns

Assume that Praha and Salvo qualify to file a consolidated tax return and elect to do so. The consolidated income tax currently payable would be calculated as follows:

Summary of Consolidated Income Tax Return

Pretax operating income:	
Praha	$100,000
Salvo	50,000
	$150,000
Less: Deferred gross margin on upstream transfers at December 31, 19X4	(8,000)
Less: Deferred gross margin on downstream transfers at December 31, 19X4	(6,000)
	$136,000
Income tax rate	×.40
Consolidated income tax currently payable	$ 54,400

Note that no tax is assessed on the intercompany dividend and that no deduction is allowed for goodwill. In order to prepare separate financial statements, the consolidated income tax expense must be allocated between the affiliates:

Allocation of Consolidated Income Tax Expense

Allocation to Praha:
$$\frac{\$100,000 - \$6,000}{\$136,000} \times \$54,400 = \$37,600$$

Allocation to Salvo:
$$\frac{\$50,000 - \$8,000}{\$136,000} \times \$54,400 = \underline{16,800}$$
$$\$54,400$$

The allocation would be recorded by the two companies by debits to income tax expense and credits to income taxes payable. In addition, the parent would record income from its subsidiary calculated as follows:

Parent's Calculation of Income from Subsidiary

Subsidiary pretax income	$50,000
Less: Income tax expense (allocated)	16,800
Subsidiary net income	$33,200
Less: Deferred gross margin on upstream transfers at December 31, 19X4	(8,000)
	$25,200
Parent's ownership percentage	×.90
	$22,680
Less: Deferred gross margin on downstream transfers at December 31, 19X4	(6,000)
Less: Amortization of valuation differential	(2,500)
Income from subsidiary	$14,180

Note that the parent's calculation of income from subsidiary is unaltered by the introduction of income taxes except to the extent that the allocation of taxes to the subsidiary is subtracted in the determination of subsidiary net income.

Consolidation proceeds in the usual way, and the various worksheet adjustments are prepared without regard to taxes. Consolidated income tax expense is simply the total of the separate (allocated) amounts of income tax expense reported by the parent and its subsidiary.

Intercompany Transfers and Separate Tax Returns

If Praha and Salvo file separate tax returns, then the income taxes currently payable by the two companies would be calculated as follows:

Summary of Separate Income Tax Returns

Parent's (Praha's) separate tax return:	
Pretax operating income	$100,000
Income tax rate	×.40
Separate income tax currently payable	$ 40,000
Subsidiary's (Salvo's) separate tax return:	
Pretax operating income	$ 50,000
Income tax rate	×.40
Separate income tax currently payable	$ 20,000
Total of separate income tax amounts currently payable	$ 60,000

Thus, the amount currently payable is $5,600 higher when separate tax returns are filed because no adjustments are made for intercompany transactions. Again, note that no tax is assessed on the intercompany dividend and that no deduction is allowed for goodwill. Although no adjustments are made to the separate tax returns for intercompany transactions, each company must make such adjustments in the calculation of its separate tax expense:

Calculation of Separate Income Tax Expense Amounts

Parent's (Praha's) separate tax expense:	
Pretax operating income	$100,000
Less: Deferred gross margin on downstream transfers at	
December 31, 19X4	(6,000)
	$ 94,000
Income tax rate	×.40
Parent's income tax expense	$ 37,600
Subsidiary's (Salvo's) separate tax expense:	
Pretax operating income	$ 50,000
Less: Deferred gross margin on upstream transfers at	
December 31, 19X4	(8,000)
	$ 42,000
Income tax rate	×.40
Subsidiary's income tax expense	$ 16,800
Total of separate income tax expense amounts	$ 54,400

Thus, the two companies would make the following entries to record income tax expense for 19X4:

Parent's entry to record tax expense and deferred taxes:

Income tax expense	37,600	
Deferred tax asset ($6,000 × .40)	2,400	
Income taxes payable		40,000

Subsidiary's entry to record tax expense and deferred taxes:

Income tax expense	16,800	
Deferred tax asset ($8,000 × .40)	3,200	
Income taxes payable		20,000

In addition, the parent would record income from its subsidiary calculated as follows:

Parent's Calculation of Income from Subsidiary

Subsidiary pretax income	$50,000
Less: Income tax expense (calculated)	16,800
Subsidiary net income	$33,200
Less: Deferred gross margin on upstream transfers at December 31, 19X4	(8,000)
	$25,200
Parent's ownership percentage	×.90
	$22,680
Less: Deferred gross margin on downstream transfers at December 31, 19X4	(6,000)
Less: Amortization of valuation differential	(2,500)
Income from subsidiary	$14,180

The only difference between the parent's income-from-subsidiary calculation for consolidated tax returns and its income-from-subsidiary calculation for separate tax returns is that subsidiary tax expense is determined by allocation if consolidated returns are filed and calculated separately if separate returns are filed. In both cases, the amount of subsidiary tax expense is the same.

Once again, consolidation proceeds in the usual way, and the various worksheet adjustments are prepared without regard to taxes. Of course, different amounts for taxes payable and deferred taxes are reported in the consolidated statements if separate returns are filed than if consolidated returns are filed; however, the same amounts are reported for income tax expense.

Comprehensive Example with Separate Tax Returns

Chan Corporation acquired a 90% interest in Laser, Inc. in a taxable combination on January 1, 19X1, for $200,000. On the date of acquisition, the stockholders' equity of Laser consisted of common stock of $150,000 and retained earnings of $50,000. The valuation differential of $20,000 {$200,000 − [.90 × ($150,000 + $50,000)]} is entirely attributable to nondeductible goodwill, which is amortized at a rate of $2,000 per year. Although Chan and Laser qualify as an affiliated group, they elect to file separate income tax returns. The tax rate is 40%.

In 19X2, Laser reported net income of $12,000 and paid dividends of $1,000 ($900 to Chan). Financial statements for both companies for the fiscal year ended December 31, 19X2, the second year following acquisition, are shown in Exhibit 8-21. The following information describes intercompany transactions, both upstream and downstream, that are related to 19X2:

1. Laser sold merchandise to its parent during 19X1 at a gross margin of $15,000. Twenty percent of the transferred merchandise was in the parent's 19X1 ending inventory. Consequently, Chan's inventory at *January 1, 19X2,* contains unconfirmed *upstream* gross margin of $3,000 (.20 × $15,000).

2. During 19X2, Laser sold merchandise to its parent (Chan) for $30,000, recognizing gross margin on the transfer of $10,000. One-half of the merchandise transfers remained in the 19X2 ending inventory of the parent representing *upstream* gross margin of $5,000 (.50 × $10,000).

3. On January 1, 19X2, Laser sold a building to its parent (Chan) for $33,000; the estimated remaining life of the building was ten years. On the date of sale, the records of the subsidiary (Laser) indicated original cost of $90,000 and accumulated depreciation of $65,000, or a net book value of $25,000. Consequently, Laser recognized a gain of $8,000 ($33,000 − $25,000) in 19X2, which is taxable at a rate of 40%. In addition, the upstream building transfer created additional depreciation of $800 per year ($8,000 ÷ 10).

4. During 19X2, Chan sold merchandise to its subsidiary (Laser) for $42,000, recognizing gross margin on the transfer of $28,000. At the end of 19X2, 10% of the merchandise remained in the subsidiary's inventory, representing *downstream* gross margin of $2,800 (.10 × $28,000).

Using this information, we can reconstruct the calculation of the parent's income tax *expense* as follows:

Calculation of Parent's Income Tax Expense

Income before income tax	$49,932
Less: Income from subsidiary (not taxed)	(1,032)
Less: Deferred gross margin on downstream merchandise transfers at 12-31-X2	(2,800)
	$46,100
Income tax rate	×.40
Parent's income tax expense	$18,440

On the basis of its separate tax return, the parent is assessed income tax for 19X2 of $19,560 [$19,560 = ($49,932 − $1,032) × .40], all of which is paid during 19X2 except $4,900 still payable at year-end. Thus, the parent's recording of 19X2 income tax expense and related tax payments, tax liabilities, and deferred taxes is summarized in the entry at the top of page 442.

EXHIBIT 8-21	FINANCIAL STATEMENTS FOR COMPREHENSIVE EXAMPLE WITH SEPARATE TAX RETURNS

	Chan	Laser
Income Statements for Year Ended December 31, 19X2		
Sales	$146,000	$ 41,000
Income from subsidiary	1,032	
Gain on sale of building		8,000
Cost of goods sold	(70,100)	(22,000)
Depreciation and amortization expense	(10,000)	(5,000)
Other expenses	(17,000)	(2,000)
Income before income tax	$ 49,932	$ 20,000
Income tax expense	(18,440)	(4,320)
Net income	$ 31,492	$ 15,680
Retained Earnings Statement for Year Ended December 31, 19X2		
Retained earnings, 1-1-X2	$119,300	$ 54,600
Net income	31,492	15,680
Dividends	(14,000)	(1,000)
Retained earnings, 12-31-X2	$136,792	$ 69,280
Balance Sheet at December 31, 19X2		
Cash	$ 55,000	$ 34,000
Accounts receivable	45,000	60,000
Inventory	80,000	42,600
Investment in Laser	200,652	
Deferred tax asset	8,410	5,300
Plant and equipment	620,000	107,000
Accumulated depreciation	(330,000)	(27,000)
Land	11,000	17,380
Total assets	$690,062	$239,280
Accounts payable	$ 29,670	$ 13,700
Taxes payable	4,900	1,800
Deferred tax liability	18,700	4,500
Common stock	500,000	150,000
Retained earnings	136,792	69,280
Total liabilities and stockholders' equity	$690,062	$239,280

Parent's entry to record 19X2 income tax expense and related tax payments, tax liabilities, and deferred taxes:

Income tax expense	18,440	
Deferred tax asset ($2,800 × .40)	1,120	
Cash ($19,560 − $4,900)		14,660
Taxes payable		4,900

The parent's deferred tax asset is increased for the tax effect of the gross margin on downstream merchandise transfers that is deferred at year-end ($1,120 = $2,800 × .40); this tax effect represents taxes the parent pays on the basis of its separate tax return but does not recognize as expense until the related merchandise is sold by the subsidiary.

Similarly, the subsidiary's income tax expense was calculated as follows:

Calculation of Subsidiary's Income Tax Expense

Income before income tax	$20,000
Add: Deferred gross margin on upstream merchandise transfers at 1-1-X2	3,000
Less: Deferred gross margin on upstream merchandise transfers at 12-31-X2	(5,000)
Less: Total deferred gain on 19X2 upstream sale of building	(8,000)
Add: 19X2 recognition of deferred gain on upstream sale of building	800
	$10,800
Income tax rate	× .40
Subsidiary's income tax expense	$ 4,320

On the basis of its separate tax return, the subsidiary is assessed income tax for 19X2 of $8,000 ($8,000 = $20,000 × .40), all of which is paid during 19X2 except $1,800 still payable at year-end. Thus, the subsidiary's recording of 19X2 income tax expense and related tax payments, tax liabilities, and deferred taxes is summarized in the following entry:

Subsidiary's entry to record 19X2 income tax expense and related tax payments, tax liabilities, and deferred taxes:

Income tax expense	4,320	
Deferred tax liability [($5,000 − $3,000) × .40]	800	
Deferred tax asset [($8,000 − $800) × .40]	2,880	
Cash ($8,000 − $1,800)		6,200
Taxes payable		1,800

The subsidiary's deferred tax liability is *decreased* for the $800 tax effect of the change during the year in deferred gross margin on upstream merchandise transfers; the liability is decreased because reversing tax effects exceed originating tax effects. The subsidiary's deferred tax asset is increased for the $2,880 tax effect of the gain on the 19X2 building sale that remains unrecognized at year-end.

The information given also enables us to calculate Chan's income for its subsidiary:

Calculation of Parent's Income from Subsidiary

Subsidiary net income	$15,680
Add: Deferred gross margin on upstream merchandise transfers at 1-1-X2	3,000
Less: Deferred gross margin on upstream merchandise transfers at 12-31-X2	(5,000)
Less: Total deferred gain on 19X2 upstream sale of building	(8,000)
Add: 19X2 recognition of deferred gain on upstream sale of building	800
Adjusted subsidiary net income	$ 6,480*
Parent's ownership percentage	×.90
Parent's share of adjusted subsidiary net income	$ 5,832
Less: Deferred gross margin on downstream merchandise transfers at 12-31-X2	(2,800)
Parent's share of subsidiary net income (adjusted for both upstream and downstream transfers)	$ 3,032
Amortization of valuation differential	(2,000)
Income from subsidiary	$ 1,032

* Minority interest in subsidiary net income, which appears on the consolidated balance sheet, is $648 ($6,480 × .10).

On the basis of this calculation, Chan makes the following entry to record income from its subsidiary for 19X2:

Parent's entry to record income, dividends, and amortization for investment in subsidiary:

Investment in Laser	132	
Cash ($1,000 × .90)	900	
Income from subsidiary		1,032

Note that application of the equity method does not include adjustments for income tax effects; rather the tax effects of investments are recorded in separate tax expense and deferred tax accounts. This, of course, represents a departure from the "one-line consolidation" approach to the equity method.

Exhibit 8-22 on the following page shows the consolidation worksheet adjustments required at December 31, 19X2. The completed consolidation worksheet is given in Exhibit 8-23 on page 445.

Business Combinations

As noted in Chapter 1, we have assumed throughout this book, unless the contrary is specifically indicated, that all combinations are structured so that no deferred taxes are recognized in recording the combination; thus acquisition cost has included no adjustment for deferred tax liabilities or assets, as required by current standards. Specifically, *FASB Statement No. 109* (par. 30) requires recognition of a deferred tax liability or asset for differences between the tax basis of a company acquired in a purchase combination (as adjusted for nontransferable net operating loss carryforwards and revaluations in taxable

EXHIBIT 8-22	CONSOLIDATION WORKSHEET ADJUSTMENTS

Chan Corporation
WORKSHEET ADJUSTMENTS FOR CONSOLIDATION OF LASER, INC.
FOR THE YEAR ENDED DECEMBER 31, 19X2

(1) *Reverse parent's recording of subsidiary income, and eliminate dividend to parent for current year:*

Income from subsidiary	1,032	
Dividends		900
Investment in Laser		132

(2) *Eliminate and reclassify beginning-of-the-year balance of parent's investment account:*

Common stock	135,000	
Retained earnings, 1-1	47,520*	
Goodwill	*18,000*	
Investment in Laser		200,520

    * $47,520 = .90 ($54,600 − $1,800)
            = ($180,000 − $135,000) + $2,520

(3) *Amortize valuation differential for current year:*

Depreciation and amortization expense	2,000	
Goodwill		2,000

(4) *Recognize upstream gross margin on 19X1 merchandise transfers deferred from prior years:*

Retained earnings of Laser, 1-1	3,000	
Cost of goods sold		3,000

(5) *Deferred upstream gross margin on 19X2 merchandise transfers at end of current year:*

Cost of goods sold	5,000	
Inventory		5,000

(6) *Eliminate upstream transfer prices from sales and cost of goods sold for current year:*

Sales	10,000	
Cost of goods sold		10,000

(7) *Eliminate gain on 19X2 upstream building transfer, and restore date-of-transfer cost and depreciation:*

Gain on sale of building	8,000	
Plant and equipment	57,000	
Accumulated depreciation		65,000

(8) *Eliminate additional depreciation created by 19X2 upstream building transfer:*

Accumulated depreciation	800	
Depreciation and amortization expense		800

(9) *Defer downstream gross margin on 19X2 merchandise transfers at end of current year:*

Cost of goods sold	2,800	
Inventory		2,800

(10) *Eliminate downstream transfer prices from sales and cost of goods sold for current year:*

Sales	42,000	
Cost of goods sold		42,000

EXHIBIT 8-23		CONSOLIDATION OF FINANCIAL STATEMENTS TWO YEARS AFTER ACQUISITION					

	Separate Financial Statements		Consolidation Adjustments			Minority Interest	Consolidated Financial Statements
	Chan	Laser	Dr.		Cr.		
Income Statement							
Sales	146,000	41,000	(6) 10,000				135,000
			(10) 42,000				
Income from subsidiary	1,032		(1) 1,032				–0–
Gain on sale of building		8,000	(7) 8,000				–0–
Cost of goods sold	(70,100)	(22,000)	(5) 5,000	(4)	3,000		(44,900)
			(9) 2,800	(6)	10,000		
				(10)	42,000		
Depreciation and amortization expense	(10,000)	(5,000)	(3) 2,000	(8)	800		(16,200)
Other expenses	(17,000)	(2,000)					(19,000)
Income tax expense	(18,440)	(4,320)					(22,760)
Minority interest						648	(648)
Net income	31,492	15,680	70,832		55,800	648	31,492
Retained Earnings Statement							
Retained earnings, 1-1-X2:							
Chan	119,300						119,300
Laser		54,600	(2) 47,520			4,080	
			(4) 3,000				
Net income	31,492	15,680	70,832		55,800	648	31,492
Dividends	(14,000)	(1,000)		(1)	900	(100)	(14,000)
Retained earnings, 12-31-X2	136,792	69,280	121,352		56,700	4,628	136,792
Balance Sheet							
Cash	55,000	34,000					89,000
Accounts receivable	45,000	60,000					105,000
Inventory	80,000	42,600		(5)	5,000		114,800
				(9)	2,800		
Investment in Laser	200,652			(1)	132		–0–
				(2)	200,520		
Deferred tax asset	8,410	5,300					13,710
Plant and equipment	620,000	107,000	(7) 57,000				784,000
Accumulated depreciation	(330,000)	(27,000)	(8) 800	(7)	65,000		(421,200)
Land	11,000	17,380					28,380
Goodwill			(2) 18,000	(3)	2,000		16,000
Total assets	690,062	239,280					729,690
Accounts payable	29,670	13,700					43,370
Taxes payable	4,900	1,800					6,700
Deferred tax liability	18,700	4,500					23,200
Common stock	500,000	150,000	(2) 135,000			15,000	500,000
Retained earnings	136,792	69,280	121,352		56,700	4,628	136,792
Minority interest						(19,628)	19,628
Total liabilities and stockholders' equity	690,062	239,280	332,152		332,152	–0–	729,690

combinations) and the amounts recorded by the acquiring company (usually fair values). Such differences arise in both taxable and nontaxable purchase combinations, although they are apt to be much larger in nontaxable purchase combinations. Exceptions are made for nondeductible goodwill and other permanent differences for which no deferred tax liability or asset should be recognized.

To illustrate a case in which deferred taxes are recognized, let us consider Major Corporation's acquisition of a 60 percent interest in Smallville Product, Inc. on January 1, 19X4, for $25,000 cash; the acquisition is recorded by Major with the following entry:

Parent's entry to record acquisition of subsidiary:

Investment in Smallville 25,000		
Cash...		25,000

On the date of acquisition, Smallville reported common stock of $26,000 and retained earnings of $4,000; thus, the book value acquired by Major equals $18,000 [($26,000 + $4,000) × .60]. Assume that the transaction is a nontaxable combination (hence acquired company's basis transfers to the acquiring company), that the tax basis equals book value, and that the applicable tax rate is 40%. The identifiable net assets of Smallville have a fair value of $27,000. The $9,000 difference between the fair value and the book value of net assets ($9,000 = $27,000 − $18,000) is entirely attributable to (1) a building with a fair value of $16,000 and a book value (tax basis) of $9,000 and (2) a parcel of land with a fair value of $7,000 and a book value (tax basis) of $5,000. Thus the building gives rise to a deferred tax liability of $1,680 [$1,680 = ($16,000 − $9,000) × .60 × .40], and the land gives rise to a deferred tax liability of $480 [$480 = ($7,000 − $5,000) × .60 × .40]. The goodwill associated with the acquisition would be calculated as follows:

Calculation of Valuation Differential and Goodwill		
Acquisition cost		$25,000
Less: Book value acquired [($26,000 + $4,000) × .60]		18,000
Valuation differential		$ 7,000
Less: Revaluation increment—		
Building [($16,000 − $9,000) × .60]	$ 4,200	
Land [($7,000 − $5,000) × .60]	1,200	
Deferred tax liability for taxable temporary differences associated with building [($16,000 − $9,000) × .60 × .40]	(1,680)	
Deferred tax liability for taxable temporary differences associated with land [($7,000 − $5,000) × .60 × .40]	(480)	3,240
Goodwill		$ 3,760

Assume that goodwill is amortized over a 4-year period at a rate of $940 per year ($940 = $3,760 ÷ 4).

The Equity Method

To illustrate application of the equity method, assume that Smallville reported 19X4 net income of $4,800 and paid dividends of $1,200 ($720 to Major). (Since Major owns only 60% of Smallville, the two companies do not meet the 80% affiliated company test for the total exclusion of Smallville's dividends from Major's taxable income; thus, Major must pay tax on 20% of such dividends.) Also assume, for both tax and book purposes, that the building has a remaining life of 4 years, with no salvage value, and is depreciated on a straight-line basis. Thus income from subsidiary will be reduced by $630 per year for the building ($630 = {[($16,000 − $9,000) × .60] − $1,680} ÷ 4). (The land, which is still held by the subsidiary, does not affect income until it is sold.) This information is summarized in the following calculation of income from subsidiary:

Parent's Calculation of Income from Subsidiary

Subsidiary net income	$4,800
Parent's ownership percentage	×.60
Parent's share of subsidiary net income	$2,880
Less: Amortization of valuation differential for building (net of deferred taxes) ({[($16,000 − $9,000) × .60] − $1,680} ÷ 4)	(630)
Less: Amortization of goodwill	(940)
Income from subsidiary	$1,310

On the basis of this calculation and the dividend information, the parent, Major Corporation, would make the following entry:

Parent's entry to record dividends and income from subsidiary:

Cash ($1,200 × .60)	720	
Investment in Smallville	590	
Income from subsidiary		1,310

In addition, the parent's income tax expense would include $58 for taxes on 20% of the $720 cash dividend from Smallville ($57.60 = $720 × .20 × .40).

Consolidation Worksheet Adjustments

The parent's investment account includes a deferred tax component that consolidation worksheet adjustments must reclassify as "Deferred taxes on business combination." The deferred tax component of Major's investment account, which is amortized at $420 per year ($1,680 ÷ 4), has the following composition:

Deferred Taxes in Parent's Investment Account

	Building	Land	Total
Balance, Jan. 1, 19X4	$1,680	$ 480	$2,160
19X4 amortization	420	–0–	420
Balance, Dec. 31, 19X4	$1,260	$ 480	$1,740

To accomplish the required reclassification, the consolidation worksheet adjustments at December 31, 19X4, would be as follows:

Worksheet adjustment to reverse parent's recording of subsidiary income and eliminate subsidiary dividend to parent for current year:

Income from subsidiary	1,310	
Dividends		720
Investment in Smallville		590

Worksheet adjustment to eliminate and reclassify beginning-of-the-year balance of parent's investment account:

Common stock of Smallville ($26,000 × .60)	15,600	
Retained earnings of Smallville ($4,000 × .60)	2,400	
Building (net) [($16,000 − $9,000) × .60]	*4,200*	
Land [($7,000 − $5,000) × .60]	*1,200*	
Goodwill	*3,760*	
Deferred tax liability		*2,160*
Investment in Smallville		25,000

Worksheet adjustment to amortize valuation differential for current year:

Depreciation and amortization expense	2,000	
Building (net) {[($16,000 − $9,000) × .60] ÷ 4}		1,050
Goodwill		950

Worksheet adjustment to adjust deferred tax accounts related to amortization of valuation differential for current year:

Deferred tax liability ($1,680 ÷ 4)	420	
Income tax expense		420

Thus, consolidated income tax expense is reduced by $420 reflecting the reversal of temporary differences between the parent's recorded amounts for subsidiary net assets and the corresponding tax bases.

Deferred Tax Recognition for Taxable Combinations

In taxable business combinations, the acquisition cost is assigned to net assets for both book and tax purposes. However, the amounts assigned to individual identifiable assets and liabilities for book purposes may differ from the corresponding amounts assigned for tax purposes. Such differences may give rise to deferred tax assets and liabilities. For example, part of financial statement goodwill may be assigned for tax purposes to an identifiable asset whose amortization is deductible. The corresponding revaluation increment may give rise to a deferred tax liability or asset at the date of acquisition. The tax effects of amortizing such revaluation increments should be offset against the amortization of goodwill and other noncurrent intangibles and, when that amortization is reduced to zero, against income tax expense. These and other deferred tax recognition procedures for taxable and nontaxable combinations are described and illustrated in *FASB Statement No. 109* (see pars. 260–272).

SELECTED READINGS

AICPA Accounting Standards Executive Committee. "Joint Venture Accounting," Issues Paper (July 17, 1979), 71 pp.

Allison, Terry E., and Paula Bevels Thomas. "Uncharted Territory: Subsidiary Financial Reporting," *Journal of Accountancy* (October 1989), pp. 76–84.

Billings, B. Anthony, and Leonard G. Weld. "Taxable Business Acquisitions: Issues and Answers," *The CPA Journal* (June 1990), pp. 42–48.

Childs, William Herbert. "Indirect and Reciprocal Relationships," Chap. 8 in *Consolidated Financial Statements: Principles and Procedures.* Ithaca, NY: Cornell University Press, 1949.

Deiter, Richard, and Arthur R. Wyatt, "The Expanded Equity Method—An Alternative in Accounting for Investments in Joint Ventures," *Journal of Accountancy* (June 1978), pp. 89–94.

Knechel, W. Robert, and Charles L. McDonald. "Accounting for Income Taxes Related to Assets Acquired in a Purchase Business Combination," *Accounting Horizons* (September 1989), pp. 44–52.

Laibstain, Samuel. "Income Tax Accounting for Business Combinations," *The CPA Journal* (December 1988), pp. 44–52.

Minch, Roland A., and Enrico Petri. "Reporting Income for Reciprocal Parent-Subsidiary Stockholdings," *The CPA Journal* (July 1975), pp. 36–40.

Moonitz, Maurice. "Mutual Stockholdings in Consolidated Statements," *Journal of Accountancy* (October 1939), pp. 227–235.

Petri, Enrico, and Roland A. Minch. "The Treasury Stock Method and Conventional Method in Reciprocal Stockholdings—An Amalgamation," *The Accounting Review* (April 1974), pp. 330–341.

Petri, Enrico, and Clyde P. Stickney. "Business Combinations: Some Unresolved Issues," *Journal of Accountancy* (April 1982), pp. 64–79.

Raiborn, Mitchel H., Michael R. Lane, and D. D. Raiborn. "Purchased Loss Carryforwards: An Unresolved Issue," *Journal of Accountancy* (November 1983), pp. 98–108.

Read, William J., and Robert Bartsch. "How to Account for Acquisitions under FASB 96," *Journal of Accountancy* (May 1989), pp. 54–60.

Reklau, David L. "Accounting for Investments in Joint Ventures—A Reexamination," *Journal of Accountancy* (September 1977), pp. 96–103.

Weil, Roman L. "Reciprocal or Mutual Holdings: Allocating Earnings and Selecting the Accounting Method," *The Accounting Review* (October 1973), pp. 749–758.

Wolk, Harry I., Dale R. Martin, and Virginia A. Nichols. "Statement of Financial Accounting Standards No. 96: Some Theoretical Problems," *Accounting Horizons* (June 1989), pp. 1–5.

QUESTIONS

Q8-1 Describe how the (1) direct ownership percentage and (2) indirect ownership percentage in a company are determined.

Q8-2 T owns 40% of W and 45% of X. W owns 20% of X. Should X be consolidated with T? If so, how should W be presented in the consolidated financial statements of T and X?

Q8-3 Explain why you agree or disagree with the following statement: In both direct and indirect ownership cases, an ownership percentage of over 50% is always necessary in order to have a parent-subsidiary relationship, thus providing the basis for consolidation.

Q8-4   Distinguish between indirect ownership and mutual ownership.

Q8-5   R owns 70% of S, and S owns 60% of T. T owns 20% of S. What are the minority interest percentages in S and T?

Q8-6   Explain why you agree or disagree with the following statement: From the viewpoint of the consolidated entity, subsidiary stock held by a parent does not represent outstanding stock. However, stock of the parent held by the subsidiary is treated as outstanding stock from the consolidated entity viewpoint.

Q8-7   Consolidated procedures for a subsidiary's investment in the parent's common stock can take one of two forms. Identify these alternatives, and briefly distinguish between them.

Q8-8   When a subsidiary has both common and preferred stock outstanding, must the parent have a controlling interest in both groups of stocks before the subsidiary can be included in the consolidated group?

Q8-9   Explain the consolidation treatment of a difference between the parent's acquisition cost of the subsidiary preferred stock and the book value of the preferred stock.

Q8-10   Explain why you agree or disagree with the following statement: Subsidiary preferred stock, whether or not owned by the parent, will not be identified as such on the consolidated balance sheet.

Q8-11   When the parent owns cumulative, nonparticipating preferred stock of the subsidiary and preferred dividends for the current year are in arrears, the parent's net income, under the equity method, will not equal the consolidated net income. Explain the reason for the difference in the two incomes.

Q8-12   When the parent owns cumulative, nonparticipating preferred stock of the subsidiary and preferred dividends in arrears for prior years are paid in the current year, the parent's net income, under the equity method, will not equal the consolidated net income. Explain the reason for the difference in the two incomes.

Q8-13   Define and give an example of a joint venture.

Q8-14   In relation to income taxes, define the terms (a) temporary differences and (b) permanent differences.

Q8-15   Parent and subsidiary companies may file consolidated tax returns if they qualify as an *affiliated group* under the Internal Revenue Code. Describe the conditions that must be met to qualify as an affiliated group.

Q8-16   Explain why you agree or disagree with the following statement: When the parent and subsidiary companies file a consolidated tax return, income taxes are paid on the basis of the consolidated taxable income of the group; in addition, the parent is required to pay taxes on dividends received from the subsidiary.

Q8-17   In situations in which the parent and subsidiary do not qualify as an affiliated group, does the parent pay taxes on its share of subsidiary earnings when reported by the subsidiary or when the subsidiary earnings are distributed as dividends?

EXERCISES

E8-1   **Indirect Ownership and the Equity Method**   Company O owns 90% of Company S, and Company S owns 70% of Company U. The three companies have 19X3 incomes from their own operations as follows:

	Income from Own Operations
Company O	$32,000
Company S	25,000
Company U	20,000

REQUIRED

a) Determine the net income for each of the companies O, S, and U under the equity method.

b) Determine Company O's ownership percentage in Company U.

c) Company O's share of Company S's net income includes what amount of the net income of Company U?

E8-2 **Indirect Ownership: Consolidated Income, Minority Interest Computations** Steven, Inc., owns 60% of Shelia Corporation and 70% of Brad Corporation. Shelia owns 20% of Brad. Incomes of the three companies from their own operations for 19X7 are as follows:

	Income from Own Operations
Steven, Inc.	$70,000
Shelia Corporation	50,000
Brad Corporation	30,000

REQUIRED

Compute the 19X7 consolidated net income for Steven, Inc., and its subsidiaries and the minority interest in the net 19X7 of each of the subsidiaries.

E8-3 **Mutual Holdings between Subsidiaries: Consolidated Income, Minority Interest Computations** Rush owns 75% of Spede, and Spede owns 70% of Taylor. Taylor owns 15% of Spede. During the year 19X9, the three companies had income from their own operations as follows:

	Income from Own Operations
Rush	$ 60,000
Spede	40,000
Taylor	20,000
Total	$120,000

REQUIRED

Compute the 19X9 consolidated net income for Rush and its subsidiaries and the minority interest in the 19X9 net income of each of the subsidiaries.

E8-4 **Mutual Holdings between Parent and Subsidiary (Treasury-Stock Method)** On January 1, 19X1, Previts Corporation acquired an 80% interest in Roberts Corporation for $100,000. The $15,000 paid in excess of acquired equity is identified as goodwill and is to be amortized over ten years. On the same day, Roberts Corporation acquired a 10% interest in Previts Corporation for $50,000, an amount equal to book value.

During the year ended December 31, 19X1, the two companies reported the following income (from their own operations) and dividend payments.

	Income from Own Operations	Dividends
Previts Corporation	$65,000	$10,000
Roberts Corporation	20,000	4,000

REQUIRED

a) Determine the parent's 19X1 income from subsidiary assuming the treasury-stock method of accounting for parent-company stock held by a subsidiary is used.

b) Prepare the entry on the parent's books to record income from subsidiary.

E8-5   **Mutual Holdings between Parent and Subsidiary (Allocation Method)**   Using the information presented in E8-4, complete the following requirements.

REQUIRED

a) Determine the parent's income from its subsidiary assuming the allocation method of accounting for parent-company stock held by a subsidiary is used.

b) Prepare the entry on the parent's books to record the income from its subsidiary.

E8-6   **Multiple Choice Questions on Mutual Holdings between Parent and Subsidiary (Treasury-Stock Method)**   Brown Corporation acquired a 90% interest in Hicks Corporation on January 1, 19X8, for $200,000, which equaled the book value. On the same day, Hicks purchased a 15% interest in Brown for $80,000, which was also equal to the book value of the interest.

During 19X8, Brown and Hicks reported income from their own operations and dividend payments as follows:

	Income from Own Operations	Dividends
Brown Corporation	$70,000	$20,000
Hicks Corporation	30,000	5,000

The treasury-stock method is used to account for the parent-company stock held by the subsidiary, Hicks.

REQUIRED

1. After recording investment income from Brown, Hick's net income for 19X8 would be

a) $30,000   **c)** $33,000

b) $42,000   **d)** $27,000

2. The parent's 19X8 income from subsidiary would be

a) $27,000   **c)** $22,500

b) $26,700   **d)** $25,000

3. The balance in Brown's investment in Hicks account at December 31, 19X8, would be

a) $225,200   **c)** $225,000

b) $222,200   **d)** $222,500

4. Minority interest in the 19X8 subsidiary income would be

a) $3,300   **c)** $2,670

b) $2,970   **d)** $3,000

5. The December 31, 19X8, consolidated retained earnings statement for Brown and its subsidiary would show dividends in the amount of

a) $20,000   **c)** $15,000

b) $17,000   **d)** $25,000

6. The December 31, 19X8, consolidated balance sheet for Brown and its subsidiary would show the treasury stock as a reduction to stockholders' equity in the amount of

a) $83,000   c) $80,000

b) $87,500   d) $90,500

E8-7 **Multiple Choice Questions on Mutual Holdings between Parent and Subsidiary (Allocation Method)** On January 1, 19X9, Olds, Inc. acquired 75% of the outstanding stock of Holley Corporation for $150,000 when Holley's common stock and retained earnings were $160,000 and $40,000, respectively. On this day, Holley acquired a 10% interest in Olds for $50,000. Olds' common stock and retained earnings were $400,000 and $100,000, respectively, on January 1, 19X9.

Olds and Holley earned income from their own operations during 19X9 of $80,000 and $20,000, respectively. Neither company paid dividends in 19X9.

The allocation method is used to account for the parent-company stock held by the subsidiary.

REQUIRED

1. Under the allocation method, stock of the parent company held by the subsidiary is

a) Considered treasury stock and is deducted from consolidated stockholders' equity

b) Considered constructively retired from a consolidation viewpoint

c) Considered outstanding stock of the consolidated entity

d) Considered treasury stock and is deducted from the subsidiary stockholders' equity on its separate financial statements

2. On the consolidated financial statements of Olds and its subsidiary prepared immediately following the mutual acquisitions of parent and subsidiary stock, common stock and retained earnings balances of the parent would be

a) Common stock $400,000; retained earnings $100,000

b) Common stock $350,000; retained earnings $100,000

c) Common stock $360,000; retained earnings $90,000

d) Common stock $400,000; retained earnings $50,000

3. The parent's 19X9 income from subsidiary would be

a) $15,000   c) $12,433

b) $22,703   d) $10,270

4. Minority interest in the 19X9 subsidiary income would be

a) $5,000   c) $5,676

b) $7,568   d) $7,200

5. The balance in Olds' investment in Holley account at December 31, 19X9, would be

a) $112,433   c) $160,270

b) $162,433   d) $120,703

6. The 19X9 consolidated income for Olds and its subsidiary would be

a) $100,000   c) $90,270

b) $ 95,000   d) $92,433

E8-8 **Preferred Stock Impact on Purchase of Common Stock; Parent and Minority Interest in Subsidiary Income** Company X acquired 90% of the common stock (but none of the preferred stock) of Company Y for $275,000 on January 1, 19X7. Any excess investment cost over book value is recognized as goodwill with an estimated 25-year life. Y's stockholders' equity at the date of acquisition appeared as follows:

Preferred stock ($50 par, 5%)	$100,000
Common stock ($100 par)	200,000
Retained earnings	75,000

The preferred stock is cumulative and nonparticipating, with five years of dividends in arrears. For the years 19X7 and 19X8, Y paid no dividends and reported net incomes of $40,000 and $60,000, respectively.

REQUIRED

a) Determine the valuation differential associated with X's investment in the common stock of Y.

b) Determine the parent's share of subsidiary net income for 19X7 and 19X8.

c) Determine the minority interest in the subsidiary net income for 19X7 and 19X8.

E8-9 **Joint Venture and Proportionate Consolidation Adjustments** Chesapeake, Inc., and Union Company agreed to establish as an unincorporated joint venture American Plywood, which is to operate under joint control and produce plywood for the building products divisions of the two firms.

On January 1, 19X2, the date of formation, Chesapeake received a 40% interest in the joint venture by contributing $900,000 of the $2,250,000 contributed owners' equity. On the same day, American Plywood issued a long-term debt in the amount of $500,000. The noncapitalizable cost incurred to construct the facility during 19X2 totaled $25,000.

American Plywood began operating on January 1, 19X3, and during 19X3 had $200,000 of sales (all to venturers), 50% of which were made to Chesapeake. None of the inventory transfers remained in Chesapeake's 19X3 ending inventory. American Plywood's cost of goods sold was $110,000. Accordingly, gross margin on intercompany sales was $90,000.

Other accounts balances of American Plywood at December 31, 19X3, were as follows:

Operating expenses (excluding cost of goods sold)	$ 45,000
Current assets	770,000
Plant and equipment (net)	2,000,000

REQUIRED

a) Determine the December 31, 19X3, balance in the Chesapeake, Inc.'s account, "Investment in American Plywood."

b) Prepare in journal entry form consolidation worksheet adjustments for Chesapeake and its joint venture interest in American Plywood using proportionate consolidation.

E8-10 **Tax Effect of Undistributed Subsidiary Income** Company X acquired 70% of the voting stock of Company Y, paying $10,000 in excess of book value. The excess cost is to be amortized over ten years. At the end of the first full year of operations of the subsidiary, the subsidiary reported net income of $8,000 and paid cash dividends of $3,000. The parent and subsidiary file separate tax returns, each paying income taxes at a rate of 40%.

REQUIRED

a) Prepare the entry on the books of the parent at the end of the first year's operations to record its income and dividends from the subsidiary.

b) Prepare the entry by the parent to record the tax effects of the difference between dividends and parent's income share.

E8-11 **Tax Implications of Upstream/Downstream Inventory Transfers** Perrin Company acquired a 90% interest in Slater Company on January 1, 19X2. At acquisition, the entire valuation differential was attributed to goodwill, which Perrin amortizes at $3,500 per year.

For the year 19X2, Perrin and Slater reported pretax operating incomes (exclusive of investment income as well as taxes) of $170,000 and $110,000, respectively. The subsidiary, Slater, paid dividends of $30,000.

During the year 19X2, upstream transfers of merchandise resulted in unrealized gross margin of $7,500 in the year-end inventory of the parent, and downstream transfers of merchandise resulted in unrealized gross margin of $9,500 in the year-end inventory of the subsidiary.

REQUIRED
Assuming the parent and subsidiary file a consolidated tax return, prepare solutions to the following requirements. The income tax rate is 40%.

a) Calculate the consolidated income tax payable for 19X2.

b) Determine the proper allocation to the parent and subsidiary of the 19X2 consolidated income tax amount calculated in (a) above for purposes of preparing separate financial statements. Prepare the entry by the parent and the subsidiary to record the allocation.

c) Calculate the parent's income from subsidiary for 19X2.

E8-12 **Tax Implications of Upstream/Downstream Inventory Transfers** Using the same information presented in E8-11, complete the following requirements.

REQUIRED
Assuming the parent and subsidiary file separate tax returns, prepare solutions to the following requirements. The income tax is 40%.

a) Calculate the separate income taxes payable for the parent and the subsidiary.

b) Calculate the separate income tax expense for the parent and the subsidiary. Prepare the entry by the parent and the subsidiary to record the tax expense for 19X2.

c) Calculate the parent's income from subsidiary for 19X2.

PROBLEMS

P8-1 **Consolidation Worksheet: Indirect Ownership**   Loeb acquired 75% of the voting stock of Kiger on January 1, 19X3, paying an amount equal to book value of $150,000. One year later, on January 1, 19X4, Kiger acquired 80% of the voting stock of May for $210,000 when May had common stock of $190,000 and retained earnings of $60,000. The difference between the investment cost and acquired equity is goodwill (estimated ten-year life).

For the year 19X3, Kiger reported net income and dividend payments of $60,000 and $20,000, respectively.

Financial statements for Loeb and its subsidiaries for the period ended December 31, 19X4, are as follows:

	Loeb	Kiger	May
Income Statement			
Sales	$300,000	$250,000	$200,000
Income from Kiger	60,750		
Income from May		31,000	
Cost of goods sold	(175,000)	(160,000)	(100,000)
Operating expenses	(55,750)	(40,000)	(60,000)
Net income	$130,000	$ 81,000	$ 40,000
Retained Earnings Statement			
Retained earnings, 1-1-X4	$150,000	$ 90,000	$ 60,000
Net income	130,000	81,000	40,000
Dividends	(40,000)	(30,000)	(10,000)
Retained earnings, 12-31-X4	$240,000	$141,000	$ 90,000
Balance Sheet			
Assets			
Cash	$ 51,750	$ 6,000	$ 35,000
Inventory	80,000	20,000	70,000
Investment in Kiger	218,250		
Investment in May		233,000	
Plant and equipment (net)	200,000	70,000	185,000
Total assets	$550,000	$329,000	$290,000
Liabilities and Stockholders' Equity			
Accounts payable	$ 60,000	$ 38,000	$ 10,000
Common stock	250,000	150,000	190,000
Retained earnings	240,000	141,000	90,000
Total liabilities and stockholders' equity	$550,000	$329,000	$290,000

REQUIRED
Prepare a consolidation worksheet for Loeb and its subsidiaries as of December 31, 19X4.

P8-2   **Mutual Holdings between Subsidiaries: Computations of Income from Investments, Consolidated Income, Minority Interest; Consolidation Worksheet Adjustments**   On January 1, 19X1, Mays paid $144,000 for an 80% interest in Valentine, and Valentine purchased a 70% interest in Flippen for $77,000. On the same day, January 1, 19X1, Flippen acquired a 15% interest in Valentine for $27,000. On the date of acquisition, January 1, 19X1, the stockholders' equity accounts of the three firms were as follows:

	Common Stock	Retained Earnings
Mays	$250,000	$60,000
Valentine	165,000	15,000
Flippen	100,000	10,000

For the year ended December 31, 19X1, the three firms reported the following income (from their own operations) and dividend payments as follows:

	Income from Own Operations	Dividends
Mays	$60,000	$30,000
Valentine	40,000	20,000
Flippen	30,000	10,000

REQUIRED

a) Compute the amount of income for 19X1 that each of the firms Mays, Valentine, and Flippen would report from their respective investment.

b) Compute consolidated net income for Mays and its subsidiaries for the year 19X1.

c) Compute the total minority interest in subsidiary income that would appear in the 19X1 consolidated income statement of Mays and its subsidiaries.

d) Compute the total minority interest that would be reflected in the 19X1 consolidated balance sheet of Mays and its subsidiaries.

e) Prepare in journal entry form the consolidation worksheet adjustments that would appear on the December 31, 19X1, consolidation worksheet of Mays and its subsidiaries.

P8-3 **Consolidation Worksheet: Mutual Holdings between Parent and Subsidiary (Treasury-Stock Method)**   Johnson, Inc., acquired a 90% interest in Dooley Company for $470,000 on January 1, 19X3, when Dooley's common stock and retained earnings were $400,000 and $100,000, respectively. The difference in the cost and book value of acquired equity is attributable to goodwill and is to be amortized over ten years. Dooley purchased a 10% interest in Johnson on January 1, 19X4, paying $100,000. The investment is to be accounted for on the cost basis and consolidated using the treasury-stock method.

Financial statements of Johnson and Dooley for the year ended December 31, 19X4, appear as follows:

	Johnson, Inc.	Dooley Company
Income Statement		
Sales	$317,000	$ 60,000
Income from Dooley	13,000	
Income from Johnson		3,000
Cost of goods sold	(180,000)	(33,000)
Operating expenses	(50,000)	(10,000)
Net income	$100,000	$ 20,000
Retained Earnings Statement		
Retained earnings, 1-1-X4	$200,000	$150,000
Net income	100,000	20,000
Dividends	(27,000)	(5,000)
Retained earnings, 12-31-X4	$273,000	$165,000
Balance Sheet		
Assets		
Cash	$ 65,500	$ 50,000
Investment in Dooley	524,500	
Investment in Johnson		100,000
Plant and equipment (net)	400,000	450,000
Total assets	$990,000	$600,000
Liabilities and Stockholders' Equity		
Accounts payable	$ 17,000	$ 35,000
Common stock	700,000	400,000
Retained earnings	273,000	165,000
Total liabilities and stockholders' equity	$990,000	$600,000

REQUIRED
Prepare a consolidation worksheet as of December 31, 19X4, using the treasury-stock method to account for the parent's stock held by the subsidiary.

P8-4   **Consolidation Worksheet: Mutual Holdings between Parent and Subsidiary (Allocation Method)**   Morris Corporation purchased an 85% interest in Lite Company for $120,000 on January 1, 19X9. Any excess cost over book value of equity acquired is goodwill and is to be amortized over ten years. On the same day, January 1, 19X9, Lite acquired a 15% interest in Morris for $60,000. The allocation method is to be used to account for Lite's investment in Morris.

The stockholders' equity of Morris and Lite just prior to the acquisitions on January 1, 19X9, is as follows:

	Common Stock	Retained Earnings
Morris Corporation	$325,000	$75,000
Lite Company	100,000	25,000

The financial statements of Morris and Lite for the year ended December 31, 19X9, are as follows:

	Morris Corporation	Lite Company
Income Statement		
Sales	$141,000	$ 48,000
Income from Lite	13,546	
Income from Morris		2,250
Cost of goods sold	(54,000)	(18,000)
Operating expenses	(22,000)	(10,000)
Net income	$ 78,546	$ 22,250
Retained Earnings Statement		
Retained earnings, 1-1-X9	$ 75,000	$ 25,000
Net income	78,546	22,250
Dividends	(12,750)	(6,000)
Retained earnings, 12-31-X9	$140,796	$ 41,250
Balance Sheet		
Assets		
Cash	$ 49,304	$ 10,000
Investment in Lite	130,696	
Investment in Morris		60,000
Plant and equipment (net)	300,000	80,000
Total assets	$480,000	$150,000
Liabilities and Stockholders' Equity		
Accounts payable	$ 14,204	$ 8,750
Common stock	325,000	100,000
Retained earnings	140,796	41,250
Total liabilities and stockholders' equity	$480,000	$150,000

REQUIRED
Prepare a consolidation worksheet as of December 31, 19X9, using the allocation method to account for the parent's stock held by the subsidiary.

P8-5 **Parent Holds Common and Preferred Stock of Subsidiary: Compute Income from Subsidiary, Minority Interest; Prepare Worksheet Adjustments** On January 1, 19X3, Company P acquired 80% of the outstanding common stock of Company S for $160,000, which equals the book value of the related equity of the subsidiary. In addition, the parent acquired 50% of the subsidiary cumulative, nonparticipating, 6% preferred stock for $35,000. No preferred dividends are in arrears at

January 1, 19X3. Immediately after acquisition, the balance sheets of the two companies appeared as follows:

	Company P	Company S
Assets		
Assets (various)	$275,000	$280,000
Investments in Company S:		
Common stock	160,000	
Preferred stock	35,000	
	$470,000	$280,000
Liabilities and Stockholders' Equity		
Preferred stock ($10 par)	$	$ 80,000
Common stock ($50 par)	400,000	150,000
Retained earnings	70,000	50,000
	$470,000	$280,000

For the year ended December 31, 19X3, P and S reported net incomes of $40,000 and $20,000, respectively, but no dividends were paid by either company.

On December 31, 19X4, P and S reported net incomes of $50,000 (excluding preferred dividend income) and $30,000, respectively. P paid no dividends, and S paid no dividends to common stockholders and $9,600 dividends to preferred stockholders.

REQUIRED

a) Prepare the entry to record the parent's income from common stock in subsidiary for 19X3 and 19X4.

b) Prepare the entry to record the parent's income from preferred stock in subsidiary for 19X3 and 19X4.

c) Calculate the minority interest in the subsidiary net income for 19X3 and 19X4.

d) Prepare in journal entry form the consolidation worksheet adjustments at the date of acquisition and at the end of years 19X3 and 19X4.

P8-6   **Parent Holds Common and Preferred Stock of Subsidiary: Compute Income from Subsidiary, Minority Interest; Prepare Worksheet Adjustments**   O'Connor Company purchased 75% of the outstanding common stock and 25% of the preferred stock of Jefferson Company on January 1, 19X7, paying $150,000 and $13,000, respectively. Any excess paid for the interest in the common shares is allocated to equipment with a five-year estimated life. No preferred dividends were in arrears at the date of acquisition. The stockholders' equity of Jefferson appeared as follows on the date of acquisition:

Preferred stock ($25 par, 9%, cumulative, nonparticipating)	$ 60,000
Common stock	125,000
Other contributed capital	20,000
Retained earnings	35,000

For the year 19X7, the parent reported net income of $27,000 and paid no dividends, and the subsidiary reported a net income of $10,000 and made dividend payments of $3,400 to preferred stockholders and nothing to common stockholders.

At the end of 19X8, the parent and subsidiary reported net income of $23,000 and $12,000, respectively; neither company paid any dividends.

REQUIRED

a) Prepare the entry to record the parent's income from common stock in subsidiary for 19X7 and 19X8.

b) Prepare the entry to record the parent's income from preferred stock in subsidiary for 19X7 and 19X8.

c) Determine the minority interest that would appear on the 19X7 consolidated balance sheet.

d) Prepare in journal entry form the year-end 19X7 and 19X8 consolidation worksheet adjustments.

P8-7 **Consolidation Worksheet: Preferred Stock**   On January 1, 19X8, Gentry Corporation acquired 90% of the outstanding common stock and 30% of the outstanding preferred stock of Shelton Company for $117,000 and $20,000, respectively. The preferred stock is cumulative and nonparticipating, with two years of dividends in arrears at the date of acquisition by Gentry. The following are the financial statements of both companies as of December 31, 19X8:

	Gentry Corporation	Shelton Company
Income Statement		
Sales	$161,000	$ 75,000
Income from subsidiary common stock	20,250	
Income from subsidiary preferred stock	2,250	
Cost of goods sold	(60,000)	(25,500)
Other expenses	(50,750)	(24,500)
Net income	$ 72,750	$ 25,000
Retained Earnings Statement		
Retained earnings, 1-1-X8	$200,000	$ 75,000
Net income	72,750	25,000
Dividends, common stock	(50,000)	(10,000)
Dividends, preferred stock		(7,500)
Retained earnings, 12-31-X8	$222,750	$ 82,500
Balance Sheet		
Assets		
Cash	$ 57,000	$ 80,000
Accounts receivable	97,500	60,000
Inventory	100,000	60,000
Investment in Shelton common stock	128,250	
Investment in Shelton preferred stock	20,000	
Total assets	$402,750	$200,000
Liabilities and Stockholders' Equity		
Accounts payable	$ 30,000	$ 7,500
Common stock ($20 par)	150,000	60,000
Preferred stock ($50 par, 5%)		50,000
Retained earnings	222,750	82,500
Total liabilities and stockholders' equity	$402,750	$200,000

REQUIRED

Prepare a consolidation worksheet for Gentry and its subsidiary as of December 31, 19X8.

P8-8   **Consolidation Worksheet: Preferred Stock; Upstream Intercompany Land and Equipment Transfers**   Company P purchased, on January 1, 19X2, 90% of the outstanding common stock and 60% of the outstanding preferred stock of Company S for $135,000 and $43,000, respectively. At the date of acquisition, the stockholders' equity of Company S appeared as follows:

Preferred stock ($25 par, 8%)	$ 75,000
Common stock	125,000
Retained earnings	25,000

The preferred stock is cumulative and nonparticipating with no dividends in arrears at the date of acquisition.

Company S reported, for 19X2, net income of $10,000 and preferred dividend payments equal to the preferred's stipulated percentage; no dividends were paid to common stockholders. In 19X2, S sold land costing $10,000 to P for a $5,000 profit.

As of the end of the fiscal year December 31, 19X3, the following financial statements are made available for Companies P and S:

	Company P	Company S
Income Statement		
Sales	$349,100	$121,000
Income from subsidiary	23,400	
Gain on sale of equipment		4,000
Cost of goods sold	(180,000)	(70,000)
Operating expenses	(60,000)	(20,000)
Net income	$132,500	$ 35,000
Retained Earnings Statement		
Retained earnings, 1-1-X3	$107,200	$ 29,000
Net income	132,500	35,000
Dividends	(40,000)	
Retained earnings, 12-31-X3	$199,700	$ 64,000
Balance Sheet		
Assets		
Cash	$ 54,200	$159,000
Inventory	120,000	35,000
Investment in Company S, common stock	157,500	
Investment in Company S, preferred stock	43,000	
Equipment	80,000	100,000
Accumulated depreciation	(20,000)	(25,000)
Land	15,000	10,000
Total assets	$449,700	$279,000
Liabilities and Stockholders' Equity		
Accounts payable	$ 50,000	$ 15,000
Preferred stock		75,000
Common stock	200,000	125,000
Retained earnings	199,700	64,000
Total liabilities and stockholders' equity	$449,700	$279,000

Additional information:

On January 1, 19X3, S sold equipment to P for $40,000. At the date of asset transfer, the subsidiary records showed the cost of the equipment as $54,000 and the accumulated depreciation as $18,000. The equipment is estimated to have a remaining life of four years.

REQUIRED

Prepare a consolidation worksheet for Company P and its subsidiary as of December 31, 19X3.

P8-9 **Consolidation Worksheet: Proportionate Consolidation for a Joint Venture**   On January 1, 19X1, Powhatan Electric and several other electric utilities formed an unincorporated joint venture to construct and operate Tri-County Station, an electric power generation plant. On January 1, 19X1, Powhatan Electric contributed $2,700,000, 30% of the joint venture capital, and received a 30% interest therein. Also, on this date Tri-County Station issued $5,000,000 of long-term debt, 30% of which was guaranteed by Powhatan Electric.

Two years were required to complete Tri-County Station, which began operating on January 1, 19X3. As a result of noncapitalizable expenditures during the 19X1 and 19X2 construction period, Tri-County incurred operating losses of $20,000 and $30,000, respectively.

Financial statements for Powhatan Electric and Tri-County Station for the year ended December 31, 19X3, are presented as follows:

	Powhatan Electric	Tri-County Station
Income Statement		
Sales	$ 850,000	$ 400,000
Income from Tri-County Station	24,000	
Cost of electricity	(510,000)	(220,000)
Operating expenses	(164,000)	(100,000)
Net income	$ 200,000	$ 80,000
Retained Earnings Statement		
Retained earnings, 1-1-X3	$ 5,000,000	$ (50,000)
Net income	200,000	80,000
Dividends	(50,000)	
Retained earnings, 12-31-X3	$ 5,150,000	$ 30,000
Balance Sheet		
Assets		
Cash	$ 641,000	$ 1,030,000
Investment in Tri-County Station	2,709,000	
Plant and equipment (net)	17,000,000	13,000,000
Total assets	$20,350,000	$14,030,000
Liabilities and Stockholders' Equity		
Accounts payable	$ 50,000	$
Long-term debt	150,000	5,000,000
Common stock	15,000,000	
Contributed owners' equity		9,000,000
Retained earnings	5,150,000	30,000
Total liabilities and stockholders' equity	$20,350,000	$14,030,000

Additional information:

1. All sales made by Tri-County Station were to venturers.

2. One-half of Tri-County Station sales were made to Powhatan Electric.

REQUIRED

Prepare a consolidation worksheet as of December 31, 19X3, for Powhatan Electric and its joint venture interest in Tri-County Station using proportionate consolidation.

P8-10 **Separate Tax Return Calculations and Consolidation Worksheet** Ferris Company acquired 90% of the outstanding common stock of VanBreda Inc. in a taxable combination on January 1, 19X3, for cash of $122,430. On this date, VanBreda's common stock and retained earnings balances were $75,000 and $25,000, respectively. The fair values of VanBreda's net assets were equal to book values except for land, which had a book value of $9,000 and a fair value of $11,700. Any goodwill recognized is to be amortized over ten years.

Financial statements for both companies as of December 31, 19X4, are presented below.

	Ferris Company	VanBreda Inc.
Income Statement		
Sales	$272,000	$162,200
Income from subsidiary	6,028	
Gain on sale of land		4,000
Gain on sale of equipment		9,800
Cost of goods sold	(105,000)	(87,000)
Depreciation and amortization expense	(30,000)	(19,000)
Other expenses	(75,000)	(45,000)
Income before income taxes	$ 68,028	$ 32,000
Income tax expense	(24,480)	(7,280)
Net income	$ 43,548	$ 24,720
Statement of Retained Earnings		
Retained earnings, 1-1-X4	$164,480	$ 43,000
Net income	43,548	24,720
Dividends	(16,000)	(4,000)
Retained earnings, 12-31-X4	$192,028	$ 63,720
Balance Sheet		
Assets		
Cash	$ 19,692	$ 4,300
Accounts receivable	52,000	12,500
Inventory	106,750	45,000
Investment in VanBreda	135,958	
Deferred tax asset	6,600	9,200
Plant and equipment	165,000	100,000
Accumulated depreciation	(60,000)	(35,000)
Land	39,000	27,000
Total assets	$465,000	$163,000
Liabilities and Stockholders' Equity		
Accounts payable	$ 12,072	$ 15,280
Taxes payable	3,700	2,900
Deferred tax liability	7,200	6,100
Common stock	250,000	75,000
Retained earnings	192,028	63,720
Total liabilities and stockholders' equity	$465,000	$163,000

Additional information:

1. VanBreda sold merchandise costing $32,000 to Ferris for $40,000 during 19X4. The 19X4 ending inventory of Rogers consisted of 30% of the 19X4 intercompany transfers of merchandise.

The 19X4 beginning inventory of Ferris consisted of $5,000 of merchandise purchased from VanBreda; VanBreda sells merchandise to Ferris at 25% above cost.

2. VanBreda purchased $54,000 of merchandise from Ferris during 19X4. Ferris sells merchandise to all customers at 20% above cost. VanBreda's beginning and ending inventories for 19X4 contained $7,200 and $12,000, respectively, of merchandise purchased from Ferris.

3. During 19X4, VanBreda sold land costing $8,000 to Ferris for $12,000.

4. On January 1, 19X4, VanBreda sold Ferris equipment that had cost VanBreda $24,000. At the time of the equipment sale, accumulated depreciation was $10,000. Ferris paid $23,800 for the equipment; its estimated remaining life is seven years, and straight-line depreciation is applied.

5. Ferris and VanBreda qualify as an affiliated group, and they elect to file separate tax returns. The tax rate is 40%. At 19X2 year-end, Ferris and VanBreda have paid all taxes for 19X2 except $3,700 and $2,900, respectively.

REQUIRED

a) Reconstruct the calculation that produced the amount in the parent's income tax expense account.

b) Prepare the entry, like the one shown in this chapter, made by the parent to record income tax expense, related tax payments, tax liabilities, and deferred taxes.

c) Reconstruct the calculation that produced the amount in the subsidiary's income tax expense account.

d) Prepare the entry, like the one shown in this chapter, made by the subsidiary to record income tax expense, related tax payments, tax liabilities, and deferred taxes.

e) Reconstruct the calculation that produced the amount in the parent's income from subsidiary account.

f) Prepare a consolidation worksheet for Ferris and its subsidiary as of December 31, 19X4.

ISSUES IN ACCOUNTING JUDGMENT

I8-1 **Indirect Ownership and Control** VanWert Corporation has a number of subsidiaries which in turn have investments and subsidiaries of their own. To support its just-in-time manufacturing system, VanWert wishes to gain control of Superba, Inc., which produces components for VanWert's principal product line. Demster Products, Inc., an 80%-owned subsidiary of one of VanWert's 60%-owned subsidiaries, has a 40% interest in Superba among its long-term investments. The remainder of Superba's stock is widely held. Neither VanWert nor any of its other subsidiaries hold Superba stock.

REQUIRED

a) What is VanWert's indirect interest (expressed as a percentage) in Superba?

b) How much Superba stock must VanWert acquire to gain control of Superba? How much additional Superba stock must Demster acquire to give VanWert control of Superba?

c) Evaluate each of the two procedures described in item (b) in terms of the required investment and the nature of the control secured.

I8-2 **Accounting for Joint Ventures** Porter Chemical Corporation has recently formed a joint venture with several other companies to undertake a number of expensive and high-risk research and development projects. The venture is a corporation that is jointly controlled by the venturers; however, Porter holds 65% of the voting stock. Further, Porter expects to be the principal guarantor of the venture's borrowings.

REQUIRED

a) Briefly describe the alternative methods of accounting for ventures on the *separate financial statements of a venturer.* Which method would Porter prefer? Which method should be chosen?

b) Briefly describe the alternative methods of accounting for ventures on the *consolidated financial statements of a venturer.* Which method would Porter prefer? Which method should be chosen?

I8-3   **Income Taxation**   As noted in the chapter, corporations that qualify as affiliated groups may, but need not, file a consolidated tax return.

REQUIRED

a) From the viewpoint of a parent-company taxpayer, what are the advantages and disadvantages of consolidated tax returns for parents and their subsidiaries?

b) Is the choice between consolidated and separate tax returns influenced by the impact of the choice on financial statements?

CHAPTER

9

Reporting Disaggregated Financial Information

HISTORICAL PERSPECTIVE ON THE NEED FOR DISAGGREGATED FINANCIAL INFORMATION   469

REPORTING NONHOMOGENEOUS SUBSIDIARIES   469

SEGMENT REPORTING   470

SEGMENT INFORMATION BY INDUSTRY   473

SEGMENT INFORMATION BY GEOGRAPHIC AREA AND EXPORT SALES   478

SALES TO MAJOR CUSTOMERS   480

DISPOSAL OF A SEGMENT OF A BUSINESS   484

SIGNIFICANT INVESTEES AND JOINT VENTURES   484

PARENT-COMPANY-ONLY FINANCIAL INFORMATION   485

SEPARATELY ISSUED FINANCIAL STATEMENTS FOR SUBSIDIARIES AND PUSH-DOWN ACCOUNTING   486

APPENDIX: INTERIM FINANCIAL REPORTING   491

The discussion of consolidated statements of income, financial position, and cash flows in earlier chapters has been concerned with the aggregation of financial measurements and the disclosures related to those aggregated measurements. *Disaggregated financial information* is financial information about consolidated entities in addition to the aggregated measurements and related disclosures reported in the consolidated financial statements. Disaggregated financial information is the disclosure of financial information in different forms or the disclosure of additional financial information.

As noted in Chapter 2, the aggregated financial measurements and related disclosures do not always meet all the needs for financial information about a consolidated entity. At least four unsatisfied needs for information can be identified: (1) parent-company stockholders need information about the dividend-paying ability of the separate parent company, (2) parent-company stockholders need information about significant operating and geographic differences within the consolidated group, (3) creditors need information about the separate legal entities to which they have lent capital, and (4) minority stockholders need information about subsidiary companies and about the details of their ownership interest in them. Disaggregated financial information is reported to meet these needs for information and to overcome the limitations of consolidated financial statements when conditions indicate that specific information is needed.

Disaggregated financial information takes many different forms: Some is reported in *separate financial statements* of a parent or its investees that are packaged with the consolidated financial statements, some is reported in *separately issued financial statements* of investees,[1] and some is disclosed in the *notes to the consolidated financial statements*. The notes to consolidated financial statements present disaggregated financial information in three principal ways: (1) segment financial information, (2) summary financial information about a parent or its investees, and (3) condensed financial information about a parent or its subsidiaries.

This chapter begins with a brief introduction to the historical development of consolidated financial statements and then turns to consideration of disaggregate financial reporting requirements for nonhomogeneous subsidiaries. This is followed by a section on segment reporting that includes consideration of industry segments, geographic segments, and major customer disclosures. The discussion then turns to consideration of separate financial statements for significant investees and joint ventures, and concludes with a brief discussion of separately issued financial statements for subsidiaries and push-down accounting. An appendix to the chapter presents a discussion of interim financial reporting.

HISTORICAL PERSPECTIVE ON THE NEED FOR DISAGGREGATED FINANCIAL INFORMATION

The need for disaggregated financial information is a result of long-term changes in the nature of the consolidated entity. Consolidated financial reporting developed during the 1930s and 1940s when the primary emphasis of merger and acquisition activity was horizontal or vertical integration. As noted in Chapter 1, horizontal integration refers to expanding the market or market share of a company by combining companies engaged in the same type of production or the sale of the same general product. Vertical integration refers to acquiring customers or suppliers along the production chain by combining companies engaged in different stages of production and distribution of a common product. In contrast, the mergers and acquisitions of the post–World War II period frequently involved firms operating in unrelated industries and resulted in consolidated entities known as *conglomerates*. The international marketing and production activities of U.S. firms also have greatly expanded since the development of consolidated financial reporting. Foreign activities frequently involve far different terms of profitability and risk than those undertaken within the United States.

The diversity of industries included in consolidated financial reports became even greater when the FASB (*Statement No. 94*) removed the exemption from consolidation for nonhomogeneous subsidiaries (such as those involved in lending, insurance, real estate, and leasing operations), large minority interests, and most foreign subsidiaries.

REPORTING NONHOMOGENEOUS SUBSIDIARIES

Even though the FASB removed the exemptions from consolidation for nonhomogeneous subsidiaries, it still requires firms to disclose separate financial information about the now-consolidated nonhomogeneous subsidiaries and foreign operations in the notes to the consolidated statements (*FASB Statement No. 94*, par. 14). The separate financial information may be either (1) "summarized information about the assets, liabilities, and results of

---

[1] Although separately issued financial statements—financial statements of a single affiliate issued under separate cover to the public—are sanctioned for subsidiaries and other investees in certain circumstances, GAAP does not allow separately issued financial statements for a parent. When a parent's separate financial statements are issued, they must accompany the consolidated financial statements.

operations''[2] or (2) ''separate statements.''[3] Further, the separate information may be provided for such subsidiaries either individually or in groups.

Thus, the form and extent of disclosures in annual reports about formerly unconsolidated subsidiaries vary considerably. Exhibit 9-1 shows summarized financial information in the form of separate financial statements for Allstate Insurance Group—the insurance operations of Sears, Roebuck & Co.—which accompany the 1991 consolidated financial statements. Note that the summarized financial information also includes a summary of significant accounting policies and notes specific to the summarized statements of income, financial position, and cash flows. Allstate Insurance Group is one of three summarized financial information presentations in Sears, Roebuck & Co., the others being Dean Witter Financial Services Group and Coldwell Banker Real Estate Group. Disclosures concerning formerly unconsolidated subsidiaries by most companies are far less extensive than those by Sears.

SEGMENT REPORTING

Total performance evaluation of an enterprise relies on consolidated financial reporting. However, the total performance of an enterprise, especially a conglomerate enterprise, is a function of its operations in various industries and locations. *Segment financial information* is the disaggregation of consolidated financial data into the amounts associated with different *industries* and different *geographic areas*. In addition, segment information standards require disclosures about *major customers* and *export sales*. Disclosure rules do not require the disaggregation of all consolidated financial information; it is sufficient to disaggregate revenues, operating profit or loss, and assets identified with particular segments.

Segment disclosures permit the users of financial statements to make better assessments of a company's past performance and future prospects. Segments differ in their profitability, degrees and sources of risk, opportunities for growth, and demands for capital. Disaggregated information provides insight into these differences and thereby enables a better assessment of the uncertainties associated with the amounts and timing of future cash flows.

[2] Rule 1-02(aa)(1) of SEC Regulation S-X provides the following disclosures as being the minimum for meeting the requirement for summarized financial information:

(i) Current assets, noncurrent assets, current liabilities, noncurrent liabilities, and when applicable redeemable preferred stock (see Rule 5-02-28) and minority interests (for specialized industries in which classified balance sheets are not normally presented, information shall be provided as to the nature and amount of the major components of assets and liabilities); and

(ii) Net sales or gross revenues, gross profit (or alternatively, expenses applicable to net sales or gross revenues), income or loss from continuing operations before extraordinary items and cumulative effect of a change in accounting principle, and net income or loss (for specialized industries, other information may be substituted for sales and related costs and expenses if necessary for a more meaningful disclosure).

[3] Separate financial statements are complete sets of financial statements of a subsidiary included with the consolidated financial statements. Contrast this with separately issued financial statements, which are a complete set of financial statements issued separately from the consolidated financial statements. Disclosure requirements differ between the two types of statements.

EXHIBIT 9-1	**REPORTING NONHOMOGENEOUS SUBSIDIARIES: ALLSTATE INSURANCE GROUP**

Summarized Statements of Income

millions	Year Ended December 31		
	1991	**1990**	**1989**
Revenues			
Property-liability insurance premiums earned	**$15,147.0**	$14,280.5	$13,133.0
Life insurance premium income and contract charges	**1,196.9**	1,166.1	1,211.5
Investment income, less investment expense (note 1)	**3,001.4**	2,571.3	2,235.2
Realized capital gains	**4.9**	181.2	223.4
Total revenues	**19,350.2**	18,199.1	16,803.1
Costs and Expenses			
Property-liability insurance claims and claims expense	**12,574.6**	12,198.8	10,873.6
Life insurance policy benefits	**2,121.6**	1,827.2	1,653.7
Policy acquisition costs (note 2)	**3,041.1**	2,870.3	2,678.8
Other operating costs and expenses	**1,074.2**	999.3	912.2
Total costs and expenses	**18,811.5**	17,895.6	16,118.3
Income before income taxes, equity income (loss) and minority interest	**538.7**	303.5	684.8
Income tax benefit			
Current operations	**(183.4)**	(250.8)	(131.5)
Fresh start adjustment from the Revenue Reconciliation Act of 1990	**—**	(139.0)	—
	722.1	693.3	816.3
Equity in net income (loss) of unconsolidated companies and minority interest	**.4**	(2.5)	(1.1)
Income from continuing operations	**722.5**	690.8	815.2
Discontinued operations—gain on disposal, net of tax expense of $5.5	**—**	10.5	—
Group Income	**$ 722.5**	$ 701.3	$ 815.2

See notes to Consolidated and Allstate Insurance Group summarized financial statements.

Only publicly held companies are required to disclose segment information.[4] Further, segment information is not required in financial statements for interim periods (*FASB Statement No. 18*) or for separate financial statements accompanying consolidated statements (*FASB Statement No. 24*).

---

[4] Segment disclosures are not required in the separately issued financial statements of nonpublic enterprises; "a nonpublic enterprise is an enterprise other than one (a) whose debt or equity securities trade in a public market on a foreign or domestic stock exchange or in the over-the-counter market (including securities quoted only locally or regionally) or (b) that is required to file financial statements with the Securities and Exchange Commission. An enterprise is no longer considered a nonpublic enterprise when its financial statements are issued in preparation for the sale of any class of securities in a public market" (*FASB Statement No. 21*, pars. 12–13).

| EXHIBIT 9-1 | REPORTING NONHOMOGENEOUS SUBSIDIARIES: ALLSTATE INSURANCE GROUP (Continued) |

Summarized Statements of Financial Position

millions		December 31
	1991	1990
Assets		
Investments (note 1)		
Bonds and redeemable preferred stocks, at amortized cost (market $27,220.3 and $22,397.1)		
State and municipal	**$15,112.3**	$13,576.8
Other	**10,239.4**	8,444.5
	25,351.7	22,021.3
Mortgage-backed securities (market $4,905.8 and $3,712.1)	**4,534.0**	3,631.4
Mortgage loans	**3,862.8**	3,217.3
Common and preferred stocks, at market (cost $2,876.9 and $2,421.8)	**3,416.5**	2,374.4
Short-term	**860.6**	1,495.8
Other	**835.5**	769.7
Total investments	**38,861.1**	33,509.9
Premium installment receivables	**1,793.6**	1,727.2
Deferred policy acquisition costs (note 2)	**1,422.3**	1,235.4
Property and equipment, net	**948.0**	842.5
Accrued investment income	**669.2**	613.0
Investments in unconsolidated companies	**118.1**	117.5
Deferred income taxes	**618.3**	494.8
Cash	**217.4**	96.8
Other	**1,127.8**	1,313.2
Total Assets	**$45,775.8**	$39,950.3
Liabilities		
Reserve for property-liability insurance claims and claims expense (note 3)	**$12,426.3**	$11,376.3
Reserve for life insurance policy benefits	**17,787.7**	14,367.9
Unearned premiums	**5,094.2**	5,006.0
Claim payments outstanding	**373.7**	342.9
Other liabilities and accrued expenses	**1,942.9**	1,730.5
Total Liabilities	**37,624.8**	32,823.6
Capital (note 1)	**8,151.0**	7,126.7
Total Liabilities and Capital	**$45,775.8**	$39,950.3

See notes to Consolidated and Allstate Insurance Group summarized financial statements.

EXHIBIT 9-1	REPORTING NONHOMOGENEOUS SUBSIDIARIES: ALLSTATE INSURANCE GROUP (Continued)

Summarized Statements of Cash Flows

millions	Year Ended December 31		
	1991	1990	1989
Cash Flows from Operating Activities			
Group income	$ **722.5**	$ 701.3	$ 815.2
Adjustments to reconcile group income to net cash provided by operating activities			
Depreciation, amortization and other noncash items	**76.4**	69.5	106.3
Gains on sales of property and investments	**(4.8)**	(181.2)	(223.4)
Increase in insurance reserves	**1,902.0**	2,004.8	1,470.4
Change in deferred taxes	**(323.2)**	(263.8)	(65.0)
Change in net other operating assets and liabilities	**178.4**	243.4	(177.4)
Net Cash Provided by Operating Activities	**2,551.3**	2,574.0	1,926.1
Cash Flows from Investing Activities			
Proceeds from sales and maturities of investments	**4,754.1**	2,974.1	2,990.8
Purchases of investments	**(8,459.0)**	(6,054.6)	(5,161.5)
Collections on mortgage-backed securities and mortgage loans	**828.5**	312.9	182.7
Purchases and originations of mortgage-backed securities and mortgage loans	**(2,390.9)**	(1,993.3)	(1,749.5)
Net change in short-term investments	**635.2**	(354.7)	303.6
Net purchases of property and equipment	**(256.5)**	(224.2)	(181.1)
Net Cash Used in Investing Activities	**(4,888.6)**	(5,339.8)	(3,615.0)
Cash Flows from Financing Activities			
Payments received under investment contracts	**2,914.9**	2,898.1	1,924.0
Interest credited to investment contracts	**911.0**	707.9	512.3
Payments on maturity of investment contracts and other charges	**(1,258.1)**	(708.4)	(500.0)
Dividends paid to Corporate	**(109.9)**	(108.4)	(330.0)
Net Cash Provided by Financing Activities	**2,457.9**	2,789.2	1,606.3
Net Increase (Decrease) in Cash	$ **120.6**	$ 23.4	$ (82.6)
Cash at Beginning of Year	$ **96.8**	$ 73.4	$ 156.0
Cash at End of Year	$ **217.4**	$ 96.8	$ 73.4

See notes to Consolidated and Allstate Insurance Group summarized financial statements.

Segment Information by Industry

Financial accounting standards define an *industry segment* as a "component of an enterprise engaged in providing a product or service or a group of related products or services primarily to unaffiliated customers (i.e., customers outside the enterprise) for a profit." In other words, segmentation should reflect the disaggregation of the horizontal integrated operations of an enterprise; "the disaggregation of the vertically integrated operations of an enterprise is not required" [*FASB Statement No. 14*, par. 10(a)].

The starting point for the identification of industry segments is a listing of the individual *products and services* from which the enterprise derives its revenue. Next, individ-

EXHIBIT 9-1	REPORTING NONHOMOGENEOUS SUBSIDIARIES: ALLSTATE INSURANCE GROUP (Continued)

Notes to Summarized Financial Statements

Summary of Significant Accounting Policies

Basis of presentation

The summarized financial statements of Allstate Insurance Group include property-liability insurance, life insurance and adjunct business operations such as Allstate Motor Club.

The financial statements have been prepared on the basis of generally accepted accounting principles which vary from statutory accounting principles prescribed or permitted by regulatory authorities. On a statutory basis, capital of the property-liability operations was $5.4 and $4.7 billion and capital of the life operations was $900.3 and $800.4 million at Dec. 31, 1991 and 1990, respectively. Statutory net income of the property-liability operations was $172.9 million and $19.6 million and statutory net income of the life operations was $139.6 million and $150.1 million in 1991 and 1990, respectively.

Investments

Bonds, redeemable preferred stocks and mortgage-backed securities are carried at amortized cost and are intended to be held to maturity; mortgage loans are carried at the outstanding principal balance, net of unamortized premium or discount; other preferred and common stocks are carried at quoted market values; short-term investments are carried at cost; other investments, which include real estate, are primarily accounted for by the equity method.

The difference between cost and market value of common and nonredeemable preferred stocks, less deferred income taxes and minority interest, is reflected in capital. Realized capital gains and losses are determined on a specific identification basis.

Property-liability insurance

Premiums are deferred and earned on a pro rata basis over the terms of the policies. Certain costs of acquiring insurance business, principally agents' compensation and premium taxes, are deferred and amortized to income as premiums are earned.

The reserve for claims and claims expense is an accumulation of the estimated amounts, net of estimated salvage and subrogation recoveries, necessary to settle outstanding claims, based upon the facts in each case and Allstate's experience with similar cases. These estimates are continually reviewed and updated. Any resulting adjustments are reflected in current operations.

Life insurance

Premiums for traditional life and disability insurance are recognized as revenue when due. Revenues on universal life-type contracts are comprised of contract charges and fees which are recognized when assessed against the policyholder account balance. Investment contracts do not involve substantial risk of policyholder mortality and the payments received under such contracts are recorded as interest-bearing liabilities.

Policy benefit reserves for traditional life and disability are computed on the basis of assumptions as to future investment yields, mortality, morbidity and expenses. These assumptions, which for traditional life are applied using the net level premium method, include provisions for adverse deviation and generally vary by such characteristics as plan, year of issue and policy duration. Policy benefit reserves for universal life-type contracts are established using the retrospective deposit method. Under this method, liabilities are equal to the account balance that accrues to the benefit of the policyholder.

Certain costs of acquiring insurance business, principally agents' compensation, certain underwriting costs and direct mail solicitation expenses, are deferred and amortized to income in proportion to the estimated revenues on such business. For universal life-type and investment contracts, the costs are amortized in relation to the estimated profits on such business.

Related party transactions

Insurance premiums include transactions with Sears, Roebuck and Co. and other affiliates. The effect on Group revenues and income is not material.

EXHIBIT 9-1	REPORTING NONHOMOGENEOUS SUBSIDIARIES: ALLSTATE INSURANCE GROUP (Continued)

1. Investments

Investment income by category of investment was as follows:

millions	Year Ended December 31		
	1991	1990	1989
Bonds and redeemable preferred stocks			
State and municipal	$1,164.0	$1,087.1	$1,028.9
Other	891.5	740.2	595.4
	2,055.5	1,827.3	1,624.3
Mortgage-backed securities	398.9	298.2	226.3
Mortgage loans	358.2	277.9	200.8
Common and preferred stocks	80.7	73.5	84.9
Short-term	124.2	139.2	133.1
Other	24.3	9.2	17.2
Investment income, before expense	3,041.8	2,625.3	2,286.6
Investment expense	40.4	54.0	51.4
Investment income, less investment expense	$3,001.4	$2,571.3	$2,235.2

At Dec. 31, 1991, the carrying value of all investments, excluding common and preferred stocks, that were nonincome producing during 1991 was $86.3 million.

Realized capital gains (losses), less income taxes, and changes in unrealized net capital gains, less applicable tax effect and minority interest, for bonds and stocks were as follows:

millions	Year Ended December 31		
	1991	1990	1989
Bonds and redeemable preferred stocks			
Realized	$ 12.4	$ (.4)	$ (2.7)
Change in unrealized	985.3	(245.3)	355.7
Common and preferred stocks			
Realized	32.4	120.3	160.2
Change in unrealized	378.4	(267.9)	85.0

Unrealized capital gains and losses on common and preferred stocks included in capital at Dec. 31, 1991 were as follows:

millions	Cost	Market Value	Gross Unrealized		Net Unrealized Gains (Losses)
			Gains	(Losses)	
Common and preferred stocks	$2,876.9	$3,416.5	$656.6	$(117.0)	$ 539.6
Deferred income tax and other					(174.2)
Total					$ 365.4

2. Deferred policy acquisition costs

Policy acquisition costs deferred and amortized to income were as follows:

millions	Year Ended December 31		
	1991	1990	1989
Costs deferred and amortized			
Amount deferred	$2,006.7	$1,908.6	$1,726.7
Amount amortized to income	1,819.8	1,746.1	1,581.2

EXHIBIT 9-1	REPORTING NONHOMOGENEOUS SUBSIDIARIES: ALLSTATE INSURANCE GROUP (Continued)

3. Reinsurance

Allstate assumes and cedes insurance to participate in the reinsurance market, limit maximum losses and minimize exposure on large risks. Reinsurance ceded arrangements do not discharge Allstate as the primary insurer.

Reserves for insurance claims and policy benefits are shown net of amounts recoverable from other insurers of $1.4 billion at Dec. 31, 1991 and 1990. Insurance premiums assumed totaled $781.7 and $906.3 million in 1991 and 1990, respectively. Insurance premiums ceded totaled $428.8 and $403.3 million for the same periods. Amounts recoverable from pools, associations and facilities on reported losses at Dec. 31, 1991 are $325.6 million. No amount recoverable from any one reinsurer is in excess of $105.8 million at Dec. 31, 1991.

4. Pending legal proceedings

Various regulatory and legal actions are currently pending involving Allstate and specific aspects of the conduct of business in certain states. The following is a summary of the more significant proceedings.

On Nov. 8, 1988 California voters approved Proposition 103, which called for certain changes in the insurance business in the state and for significant rate reductions ("rollback provision") on policies written from Nov. 8, 1988 through Nov. 7, 1989. In the more than three years that have followed, various aspects of this consumer initiative have been tested in the courts, all of which have failed to produce any legally mandated policyholder refunds.

The California Supreme Court upheld most of Proposition 103; however, the Court also ruled that insurers be permitted the opportunity to earn a fair and reasonable rate of return. During 1989 and 1990, the Insurance Commissioner of the State of California undertook a number of administrative actions aimed at facilitating the adjudication of refund liabilities, but no refund order ever was issued to Allstate from that process.

In January 1991, the newly elected Commissioner issued a set of regulations purportedly implementing the rollback provision of Proposition 103. These regulations are also being legally challenged by the insurance industry. On Oct. 16, 1991, the Commissioner issued an order pursuant to those regulations contending that Allstate be required to refund premiums and interest of $243.7 million.

The Superior Court of California has ruled that, before any order requiring rollbacks to be paid may lawfully be finalized, each individual insurer must be granted its due process right to a company-specific hearing as to whether any rollback liability exists, given the circumstances of the particular insurer. Management believes that its rates and practices have been proper, that its position will ultimately be upheld by the courts, and that it will not be required to refund monies to California policyholders.

In North Carolina, Allstate is challenging regulatory actions that would result in refunds of auto premiums to policyholders under certain conditions. The matter is pending review of the North Carolina Supreme Court. In Massachusetts, Allstate is involved in litigation with the Commonwealth Automobile Reinsurers (the auto residual market authority) concerning Allstate's withdrawal from that state. In both cases, management believes its position will be upheld.

The Internal Revenue Service (IRS) has asserted a federal income tax deficiency on Allstate's mortgage insurance subsidiaries by deferring deductions for incurred losses to the time that the insured lender takes title to a mortgagor's property. On Jan. 24, 1991, the Tax Court, in conference proceedings, upheld the IRS position. Allstate is vigorously appealing the lower court decision to the U.S. Court of Appeals. Management believes that Allstate will prevail on this industry-wide issue.

While the aggregate dollar amounts involved in these regulatory and legal actions cannot be determined with certainty, the amounts at issue could have a significant impact on earnings. However, the excess of any liabilities over the amounts currently provided that might result from an adverse final determination in one or more of the above mentioned matters is not expected to have a material effect on liquidity or capital resources.

ual products and services are formed into groups that represent *industry segments* under very general guidelines established by the standards; thus, the determination of industry segments depends "to a considerable extent on the judgment of the management of the enterprise" (*FASB Statement No. 14*, par. 12). Finally, the *reportable industry segments* are identified by the application of quantitative tests specified by the standards.

A reportable segment is any industry segment meeting one of three numerical tests for significance:

1. A *10% revenue test* where the segment's revenues, including both sales to unaffiliated customers and intersegment revenues, are 10% or more of the combined revenues of all industry segments

2. A *10% operating profit or loss test* where the segment's amount of operating profit or loss is 10% or more of the greater in absolute amount of (i) the combined operating profit of all industry segments with operating profits or (ii) the combined operating loss of all industry segments with operating losses[5]

3. A *10% identifiable[6] assets test* where the segment's identifiable assets are 10% or more of the combined identifiable assets of all industry segments

Industry segments that do not meet any of the tests for separate disclosure should be grouped together and reported as a single segment.

The outcome of these tests is subject to four additional criteria. First, no segment reporting is required if more than 90% of revenues, operating profit or loss, and identifiable assets are attributed to one industry segment, referred to as a *dominant segment*, and no other industry segment satisfies any of the 10% tests for a reportable segment. Thus, enterprises that operate almost entirely in a single industry segment do not have to make segment disclosures; however, such enterprises must identify the industry. Second, reportable segments should represent a substantial portion of the enterprise's total operations. When the total revenues from sales to unaffiliated customers of all reportable segments are at least 75% of total revenues from sales to unaffiliated customers of all industry segments, then reportable segments are substantial; however, if unaffiliated revenues for reportable segments are less than 75% of unaffiliated revenues for all industry segments, then additional segments must be identified until the 75% test is met. Generally, the number of reportable segments should not exceed ten. Combining of closely related industry segments into broader reportable segments may be appropriate to achieve the limit of ten. Third, there is a practicality test for assigning revenues, expenses, and assets to segments. When it is impractical to carry out these assignments, the rationale for the impractical nature of the assignments must be disclosed. Finally, enterprises are cautioned

---

[5] It should be noted that this sum does not equal net income by the amount of general corporate expenses, interest expense (except for financial segments), equity method income, gain or loss on discontinued operations, extraordinary items, minority interest, and the cumulative effect of accounting changes. For consolidated statements, the income eliminated in intercompany sales transactions will be used for segment reporting, resulting in recording more income for segments than for operating profit of the consolidated entity.

[6] *Identifiable* as used here means identifiable to the specific industry segment. Thus, goodwill identifiable with a specific industry segment would be recorded as an asset of that segment.

against removing significant segments that have previously been reported and are expected to be reported in the future during a year, or adding a segment which would technically be required to be disclosed because of some one-year change in income.

Developing segment information requires classifying sales, profits, and assets by industry segment. The simplest classification occurs when the parent corporation is a holding company and different industry segments are contained within a single corporation for a consolidated entity and there are no interindustry sales. In such a situation, the data for the segment financial information are available from the consolidation worksheet as the sales for each corporation. Additional complexity is introduced when (1) sales between different industries (termed *intersegment sales*) occur within the consolidated entity (intersegment sales have been eliminated in the preparation of the consolidated financial statements), (2) a parent corporation includes both corporate and operating assets, (3) a single corporation engages in activities in two or more industries, and (4) multiple corporations are engaged in activities in a single industry.[7]

Exhibit 9-2 shows selected information, reclassified for segment reporting, about Rags Corporation. Rags Corporation is a holding company whose only assets are the investments in subsidiary corporations and an office building. Its subsidiaries are engaged in operations in five industries, with each corporation engaging in only one industry. Thus, Rags Corporation introduces only the first additional complexity for segment reporting. To determine which industry segments must be disclosed for Rags Corporation, Exhibit 9-2 shows the following tests: (1) the percentage of total sales in an industry (sales to unaffiliated customers and intersegment sales) to total consolidated sales before eliminations, (2) the industry percentage of operating profit to total consolidated operating profit before eliminations (since all industry segments are profitable), and (3) the total of industry identifiable assets to total industry assets (not including corporate assets since these are not allocated to an industry). The percentages for the five corporations are shown below the various corporations. Using these figures, separate segment disclosures would be required for Rags Auto, Rags Banking, and Rags Gas corporations. Rags Realty and Rags Furniture would be combined into an ''other operations'' segment. It should be noted that total revenues from sales to unaffiliated customers of all reportable segments exceed 75% of total revenues from sales to unaffiliated customers of all segments [($1,000 + $400 + $3,000) ÷ ($4,700) = 93.6%].

Segment Information by Geographic Area and Export Sales

Foreign operations are operations of a consolidated entity domiciled in countries other than the domicile of the parent corporation. Information on foreign operations must be presented when either of the following tests is met: (1) Foreign operation revenues from sales to unaffiliated parties equal 10% or more of sales to unaffiliated parties (consolidated revenue), or (2) foreign operation identifiable assets equal 10% or more of consolidated assets. When foreign operations in the aggregate constitute a substantial portion of the

---

[7] It should be noted that when a parent company includes both operations in one or more industries, its assets must be divided between industry assets and corporate assets and corporate operations must be divided from industry operations. Further, when a corporation operates in more than one industry, its revenue, operating profit, and assets must be divided between the industries. When multiple corporations operate in a single industry, these corporations must be combined into single numbers for revenues, operating profit, and industry assets prior to undertaking the percentage calculations.

EXHIBIT 9-2	INDUSTRY SEGMENTS

SELECTED INFORMATION OF RAGS CORPORATION
ANNUAL CONSOLIDATING STATEMENT OF DECEMBER 31, 19X2

	Rags Auto Corp.	Rags Banking Corp.	Rags Gas Corp.	Rags Reality Corp.	Rags Furniture Corp.	Adjustments & Eliminations	Consolidated
Sales to unaffiliated customers	$1,000	$ 400	$3,000	$ 100	$ 200	$	$ 4,700
Intersegment sales	1,500		500			(2,000)	0
Total revenue	$2,500	$ 400	$3,500	$ 100	$ 200	$(2,000)	$ 4,700
Operating profit	$ 400	$ 200	$ 350	$ 20	$ 15	$ (50)	$ 935
Equity in Rags Insurance Corp. (33% owned)							65
Corporate expenses							(200)
Interest expense							(300)
Income from continuing operations before taxes							$ 500
Identifiable assets	$1,200	$5,000	$7,000	$ 10	$ 100	$ (10)	$13,300
Investment in net assets of Rags Insurance Corp.							600
Corporate assets							500
							$14,400
							Denominator
Revenue percentage	37.3%	6.0%	52.2%	1.5%	3.0%		$ 6,700
Operating profit percentage	40.6	20.3	35.5	2.0	1.5		985
Identifiable assets percentage	9.0	37.6	52.6	0.1	0.8		13,310

enterprise's operations, then separate disclosures for foreign operations must be presented for each significant geographic area (country or group of countries) and, in the aggregate, for all geographic areas that are not significant. A geographic area is considered significant when either of the following tests (which parallel the tests applied to foreign operations) is met for that geographic area: (1) area revenues from sales to unaffiliated parties equals 10% or more of sales to unaffiliated customers (consolidated revenue), or (2) area identifiable assets equal 10% or more of consolidated assets. Note that information on the operating profit and loss of foreign operations is omitted since it is not required to determine significant foreign operations or geographic areas.

Several countries may be grouped in the same geographic area provided they do not differ significantly with respect to such factors as proximity, economic affinity, similarities in business environment, and the nature, scale, and degree of interrelationships of the enterprise's operations in the various countries.

Once the determination of whether to disclose or not is met, the following information about foreign operations would be presented: sales to unaffiliated parties, intergeographic sales, operating profit, and identifiable assets.

Export sales are sales by a company to customers outside the enterprise's home country.[8] Export sales are required to be disclosed when they exceed 10% of sales to unaffiliated customers regardless of whether a company has operations in only one country. When sales in any country or geographic region are greater than 10%, the country or geographic region (or more than one if more than one exceed 10%) of the export sales must also be disclosed.

Exhibit 9-3 shows the Rags Corporation and its subsidiaries by geographic basis. It should be noted in reviewing this exhibit that sales to third parties will be the same as the sum of sales to unaffiliated customers in the industry segment exhibit. These sales are classified by the location of the third party (unaffiliated customer). Intergeographic sales do not total the amount of industry intersegment sales since some sales may be to industry segments in the same geographic region. Further, as illustrated in Exhibit 9-4, intergeographic sales may total more than industry segment sales when an industry segment is located in more than one geographic area. The foreign operations of Rags Corporation represent a substantial portion of its operations since unaffiliated revenue for foreign operations and identifiable assets for foreign operations represent 63% ($3,000 ÷ $4,700) and 33.8% ($4,500 ÷ $13,300), respectively, of the corresponding consolidated amounts.

The percentage calculations in Exhibit 9-3 show that Rags Corporation would have to report three geographic segments: United States, Canada, and Mexico. Europe and South America would be grouped together into an ''other areas'' segment. Individual countries in Europe and South America might have been initially shown separately to determine whether an individual country would require separate geographic disclosure.

Exhibit 9-4 on page 482 shows the industry segment and geographic information for Mobil Corporation from its 1991 Annual Report. Students should especially be aware of the description of the industry segment information and the disclosure of the method of pricing intersegment and intergeographic sales, which is an integral part of this disaggregated financial information.

Sales to Major Customers

''If 10 percent or more of the revenue of an enterprise is derived from sales to any single customer, that fact and the amount of revenue from each such customer shall be disclosed. For this purpose, a group of entities under common control shall be regarded as a single customer, and the federal government, a state government, a local government (for example, a county or municipality), or a foreign government shall each be considered as a single customer. The identity of the customer need not be disclosed, but the identity of the industry segment or segments making the sales shall be disclosed.'' In the case of governments, if sales are concentrated in a particular department or agency, ''disclosure of that fact and the amount of revenue derived from each such source is encouraged'' (*FASB Statement No. 14*, par. 39, as amended by *FASB Statement No. 30*, par. 6). The standards

---

[8] The criteria for export sales and foreign operations in *FASB Statement No. 14* use *domestic* and *foreign* to refer to the country of domicile of the parent corporation. The use of domestic and foreign rather than U.S. and foreign within this standard is to allow non-U.S. domiciled firms to comply with the standard when preparing financial statements to be issued in the United States.

EXHIBIT 9-3	GEOGRAPHIC SEGMENTS

SELECTED INFORMATION OF RAGS CORPORATION
ANNUAL CONSOLIDATING STATEMENT OF DECEMBER 31, 19X2

	U.S.	Canada	Europe	Mexico	South America	Adjustments & Eliminations	Consolidated
Sales: third party	$1,700	$1,600	$ 200	$ 800	$ 400	$	$ 4,700
Sales: intergeographic	1,300			500		(1,800)	
Total revenue	$3,000	$1,600	$ 200	$1,700	$ 400	$(1,800)	$ 4,700
Operating profit	$ 435	$ 250	$ 120	$ 160	$ 20	$ (50)	$ 935
Equity in Rags Insurance Corp. (33% owned)							65
Corporate expenses							(200)
Interest expense							(300)
Income from continuing operations before taxes							500
Identifiable assets	$8,810	$2,500	$ 0	$1,800	$ 200	$ (10)	$13,300
Investment in net assets of Rags Insurance Corp.							600
Corporate assets							500
							$14,400

							Denominator
Revenue percentage	36.2%	34.0%	4.3%	17.0%	8.5%		$ 4,700
Identifiable assets percentage	61.2	17.4	0.0	12.5	1.4		14,400

respecting major customer disclosure should not be interpreted to obviate the need to disclose the economic dependency of an enterprise on one or more parties as necessary for a fair presentation (*FASB Statement No. 21*, par. 9). Disclosure requirements relating to major customers are required even when an enterprise operates only in one industry or has no foreign operations.

Exhibit 9-5 on page 484 shows a portion of the ''Notes to Consolidated Summary of Business Segment Financial Data'' in the 1991 Annual Report of United Technologies Corporation, which has elected to show a three-year summary by segment of sales to the U.S. government. Revenues for United Technologies for 1991 were $21,262 million.

Segment financial information may also be presented in the body of the financial statements (with explanations in the notes) or in separate schedules outside the financial statements within the same cover (referenced as an integral part of the financial statements).

EXHIBIT 9-4	DISAGGREGATED FINANCIAL INFORMATION: MOBIL CORPORATION

Segment and Geographic Information

Year Ended December 31 (in millions)	1989	1990	1991
Revenues by Segment			
Petroleum Operations			
Exploration & Producing—Third Party	$ 4,824	$ 5,833	$ 5,928
—Intersegment	3,799	4,815	4,361
Marketing & Refining —Third Party	46,615	53,882	52,791
—Intersegment	445	517	497
Chemical —Third Party	4,039	4,084	3,953
—Intersegment	166	193	196
Corporate and Other	710	673	555
Intersegment Elimination	(4,410)	(5,525)	(5,054)
Total Revenues	$56,188	$64,472	$63,227
Revenues by Geographic Area			
United States —Third Party	$19,028	$21,006	$20,006
—Intergeographic	163	192	316
Canada —Third Party	993	1,133	1,124
—Intergeographic	65	61	47
Europe —Third Party	17,993	22,146	23,921
—Intergeographic	1,258	1,593	1,418
Other Areas —Third Party	17,464	19,514	17,621
—Intergeographic	4,599	5,931	5,028
Corporate and Other	710	673	555
Intergeographic Elimination	(6,085)	(7,777)	(6,809)
Total Revenues	$56,188	$64,472	$63,227

At December 31 (in millions)			
Identifiable Assets by Segment			
Petroleum Operations			
Exploration & Producing	$16,958	$17,218	$16,500
Marketing & Refining	17,178	19,254	20,789
Chemical	2,702	3,265	3,294
Corporate and Other	2,629	2,385	2,025
Adjustments	(387)	(457)	(421)
Total Assets	$39,080	$41,665	$42,187
Identifiable Assets by Geographic Area			
United States	$16,592	$17,126	$16,871
Canada	2,936	2,766	2,621
Europe	9,246	10,236	10,393
Other Areas	8,195	9,797	10,844
Corporate and Other	2,629	2,385	2,025
Adjustments	(518)	(645)	(567)
Total Assets	$39,080	$41,665	$42,187

The business segment and geographic distribution of Mobil's operations are given above. Petroleum Operations consist of exploration, producing, marketing and refining. Exploration & Producing explores for, develops and produces crude oil and natural gas, and extracts natural gas liquids, sulfur and carbon dioxide. Marketing & Refining is responsible for petroleum refining operations and the marketing of all refined petroleum products. Chemical, another business segment, manufactures and sells various petroleum-based chemical products. Corporate and Other includes the operating results of Real Estate, Mining and Minerals, residual corporate administration costs and other corporate items.

EXHIBIT 9-4	DISAGGREGATED FINANCIAL INFORMATION: MOBIL CORPORATION (Continued)

Year Ended December 31 (in millions)	1989	1990	1991
Earnings by Segment			
Pre-tax Operating Profits			
Petroleum Operations			
Exploration & Producing	$ 2,643	$ 3,840	$ 3,120
Marketing & Refining	1,030	957	1,382
Chemical	751	397	245
Total Pre-tax Operating Profits	4,424	5,194	4,747
Income Taxes	(2,139)	(2,647)	(2,312)
Segment Earnings	2,285	2,547	2,435
Corporate and Other (Net of income taxes)	(69)	(282)	(130)
Net Financing Expense (Net of income taxes)	(407)	(336)	(385)
Net Income	$ 1,809	$ 1,929	$ 1,920
Earnings by Geographic Area (Net of income taxes)			
United States	$ 731	$ 415	$ 334
Canada	95	113	10
Europe	423	692	585
Other Areas	1,036	1,327	1,506
Geographic Earnings	2,285	2,547	2,435
Corporate and Other	(69)	(282)	(130)
Net Financing Expense	(407)	(336)	(385)
Net Income	$ 1,809	$ 1,929	$ 1,920
Capital Expenditures by Segment			
Petroleum Operations			
Exploration & Producing	$ 1,258	$ 1,573	$ 1,768
Marketing & Refining	1,148	1,314	2,041
Chemical	199	402	317
Segment Capital Expenditures	2,605	3,289	4,126
Corporate and Other	259	399	148
Total Capital Expenditures	$ 2,864	$ 3,688	$ 4,274
Depreciation, Depletion and Amortization by Segment			
Petroleum Operations			
Exploration & Producing	$ 1,811	$ 1,902	$ 1,680
Marketing & Refining	525	583	647
Chemical	128	133	156
Segment Depreciation, Depletion and Amortization	2,464	2,618	2,483
Corporate and Other	38	64	106
Total Depreciation, Depletion and Amortization	$ 2,502	$ 2,682	$ 2,589

Significant investments in companies owned 50% or less are accounted for on the equity method. The corporation's share of the net income of such companies is included in Revenues. Information on these affiliates is presented in Note 2 to the Consolidated Financial Statements.

Intersegment and intergeographic revenues are sales within Mobil to other business or geographic segments and are at estimated market prices. These intercompany transactions are eliminated for consolidation purposes. Income taxes are allocated to segments and geographic areas on the basis of operating results.

Effective in 1991 the geographic information presented identifies a European component which was formerly included in Other Areas. Prior year data have been reclassified to conform with the current year presentation.

EXHIBIT 9-5	MAJOR CUSTOMER DISCLOSURE: UNITED TECHNOLOGIES

Revenue by industry segment and geographic area includes intersegment sales and transfers between geographic areas. Generally, such sales and transfers are made at prices approximating those which the selling or transferring entity is able to obtain on sales of similar products to unaffiliated customers.

Revenues include sales under prime contracts and subcontracts to the U.S. government, for the most part Power and Flight Systems products, as follows:

In Millions of Dollars	1991	1990	1989
Power	$1,944	$2,018	$2,339
Flight Systems	$2,479	$2,623	$2,324

Disposal of a Segment of a Business

The disposal of a segment of a business, whether separate disclosure had been made or not, starts with the determination by management of a plan for disposal.[9] The date on which the plan is approved is termed the *measurement date*. Income or loss in the segment prior to the measurement date is disclosed separately from the gain or loss on disposal for all financial statements presented after the measurement date.

On the measurement date, the estimated gain or loss should be determined based on both the disposition of the assets and operations until the disposal date. An estimated net loss from disposal should be recorded at the measurement date. A net gain from disposal should be reported when realized, usually on the *disposal date*.

The disposal of a business segment requires disclosure of (a) the identity of the business segment, (b) the expected disposal date if known, (c) the expected manner of disposal, (d) the assets and liabilities remaining at the balance sheet date, and (e) the income or loss from operations and the proceeds from disposal after the measurement date and a comparison with expectations.

SIGNIFICANT INVESTEES AND JOINT VENTURES

APB Opinion No. 18 [par. 20(d) as amended] states:

When investments in common stock of corporate joint ventures or other investments accounted for under the equity method are, in the aggregate, material in relation to the financial position or results of operations of an investor, it may be necessary for summarized information as to assets, liabilities, and results of operations of the investee to be presented in the notes or in separate statements, either individually or in groups, as appropriate.

The accountant has several judgments to make in such a situation. For SEC registrants (publicly held companies), detailed guidance on when summarized financial information

---

[9] The accounting standards for the disposal of a segment of a business are contained in *APB Opinion No. 30*, pars. 13–17.

can be presented in the notes and when separate financial statements are required is provided [*SEC Accounting Series Release No. 302*, ''Separate Financial Statements Required by Regulation S-X,'' as amended by *Staff Accounting Bulletins Nos. 40, 43, and 44* and codified as Topic 6-K of the Financial Reporting Codification (FRC)]. FRC Topic 6-K describes what is termed a significant subsidiary and a significant investee[10] and focuses on the importance of the investee as a percentage of income and a percentage of consolidated assets to differentiate between conditions of no disclosure, summarized financial information in the notes (generally 10% tests of revenues and assets), and separate financial statements (generally 20% tests). These results represent the interpretation of *APB Opinion No. 18* [par. 20(d)] by the SEC staff.[11]

Disclosures of separate financial information for significant investees exhibit the same variety as disclosures of separate information for formerly unconsolidated subsidiaries. One disclosure option is the inclusion of separate financial statements—a complete set of financial statements, including required notes, like those shown in Exhibit 9-1. Another disclosure option is the reduced disclosures of summarized financial information described in footnote 2.

PARENT-COMPANY-ONLY FINANCIAL INFORMATION

Generally accepted accounting principles do not provide for disclosures to parent-company stockholders that would enable them to assess the dividend-paying ability of the parent. Indeed, *FASB Statement No. 94* specifically prohibits separately issued parent-company financial statements. Consolidated financial statements do not provide full information about the dividend-paying ability of the parent company when there is a restriction on the ability of subsidiaries to pay dividends or otherwise transfer cash (such as through loans or advances) to the parent.

Publicly held companies, registered with the Securities and Exchange Commission (SEC) and filing consolidated financial statements, are required to provide summarized financial information on the parent company when the restricted net assets of consolidated subsidiaries exceed 25% of the consolidated net assets as of the end of the most recent year.[12] The information is provided in a schedule to Form 10-K filed annually with the SEC.

The SEC requires parent-company disclosure only in fairly limited situations, for example, the restriction of cash transfer by third parties. Thus, even this disclosure does not address situations where transfer of cash is limited by business reasons such as capital maintenance or growth possibilities at the subsidiary level. The most common example of

---

[10] The term *investee* means the investee and its consolidated subsidiaries, if appropriate.

[11] There is continuing discussion as to how to identify a significant subsidiary which is not consolidated and a significant investee. Of course, nonconsolidation of the former was eliminated by *FASB Statement No. 94;* however, as explained earlier, there is a summarized financial information requirement for formerly unconsolidated subsidiaries.

[12] This is usually referred to as Schedule III. It is required by Rule 12-04 of *Regulation S-X* of the SEC, which reads in part: ''For purposes of the above test, restricted net assets of consolidated subsidiaries shall mean that amount of the registrant's proportion of net assets of consolidated subsidiaries (after intercompany eliminations) which at the end of the most recent fiscal year may not be transferred to the parent company by subsidiaries in the form of loans, advances or cash dividends without the consent of a third party'' (i.e., lender, regulatory agency, foreign government, etc.).

a requirement for parent-company-only statements is bank holding companies whose subsidiaries do not meet capital requirements of the Financial Institutions Act of 1991.

SEPARATELY ISSUED FINANCIAL STATEMENTS FOR SUBSIDIARIES AND PUSH-DOWN ACCOUNTING

When a parent acquires a subsidiary, the parent revalues the assets and liabilities of the subsidiary for purposes of preparing consolidated financial statements. In general, however, this revaluation is not recorded by the subsidiary and is not reflected in the separate financial statements of the subsidiary. Accordingly, a subsidiary's separately issued financial statements report the subsidiary's assets and liabilities at their preacquisition book values. There are circumstances, however, in which subsidiaries are required to revalue their net assets as of the date of acquisition. In such cases, the values implicit in the parent's acquisition cost are said to be "pushed down" to the subsidiary. Hence, the practice is known as *push-down accounting* for subsidiary assets and liabilities. Of course, the application of push-down accounting alters not only the amounts reported in the subsidiary's separate financial statements but also the worksheet adjustments required to consolidate those statements with the separate statements of the parent.

Although push-down accounting is not addressed in standards issued by the FASB, the SEC requires push-down accounting if a parent owns substantially all (usually 90% or more) of its subsidiary's voting stock and the subsidiary has neither liabilities represented by publicly traded debt nor outstanding preferred stock (*SEC Staff Accounting Bulletin No. 54*, 1983). Despite the existence of this limited requirement, many issues concerning push-down accounting remain to be resolved, including the extent to which push-down accounting should be applied beyond this limited set of cases and the precise form of the revaluation to be pushed down on the subsidiary.

Push-down accounting rarely, if ever, results in changes in the books of the subsidiary. Rather, the adjustments are made on the worksheet used to prepare the financial statements, and the books of the subsidiary are not adjusted. We shall assume throughout this book that push-down accounting has *not* been applied unless its application is specifically indicated.

In general, push-down accounting results in reporting on the subsidiary's separately issued financial statements, the subsidiary asset and liability amounts included in the consolidated financial statements. However, minority interest is not separated. Exhibits 9-6, 9-7, and 9-8 on the following pages show the push-down accounting adjustments for High, Inc., which was discussed in Chapter 3, at the date of consolidation, one year after consolidation, and two years after consolidation. Recall that Broad Corporation acquired an 80% interest in High, Inc. The details of the transaction are captured in the following schedules:

Purchase of High, Inc., by Broad Corporation	
Purchase price	$80,000
Book value of acquired equity	72,000
Valuation differential	$ 8,000
Revaluation increment:	
Building (5-year life)	(5,000)
Goodwill (15-year life)	$ 3,000

Amortization of Valuation Differential

	19X1–X5	19X6–X15
Goodwill ($3,000 ÷ 15)	$ 200	$200
Revaluation increment:		
Building ($5,000 ÷ 5)	1,000	–0–
Amortization of valuation differential	$1,200	$200

Each of the three exhibits (Exhibits 9-6, 9-7, and 9-8) has a column showing the financial statement amounts without push down (prepared from the books), the two columns for adjustments, and a column showing the financial statement amounts with push down for High, Inc.

The date of acquisition push-down worksheet (Exhibit 9-6) adjusts the subsidiary's financial statement (per books) for the valuation differential amounts. The amount of the valuation differential is considered to be an addition to contributed capital from the application of push-down accounting. While only asset valuation differentials are shown in our example, liabilities may be revalued in the purchase business combination. In pushing down the purchase business combination, debt of the parent company may also be pushed

EXHIBIT 9-6   **PUSH-DOWN BALANCE SHEET AT DATE OF ACQUISITION**

HIGH, INC.
SEPARATELY ISSUED FINANCIAL STATEMENTS
(PUSH-DOWN ACCOUNTING)
DATE OF ACQUISITION

	Separate Statements (From Books)	Adjustments Dr.	Cr.	Push-Down Financial Statements
Assets				
Current assets	10,000			10,000
Equipment (net)	70,000			70,000
Building (net)	30,000	(1) 5,000		35,000
Land	10,000			10,000
Goodwill		(1) 3,000		3,000
Total assets	120,000			128,000
Liabilities and Stockholders' Equity				
Current liabilities	5,000			5,000
Long-term liabilities	25,000			25,000
Common stock	60,000			60,000
Contributed capital from push down			(1) 8,000	8,000
Retained earnings	30,000			30,000
Total liabilities and stockholders' equity	120,000	8,000	8,000	128,000

EXHIBIT 9-7	PUSH-DOWN FINANCIAL STATEMENTS ONE YEAR AFTER ACQUISITION

HIGH, INC.
SEPARATELY ISSUED FINANCIAL STATEMENTS
(PUSH-DOWN ACCOUNTING)
ONE YEAR AFTER CONSOLIDATION

	Separate Statements (From Books)	Adjustments		Push-Down Financial Statements
		Dr.	Cr.	
Income Statement				
Revenue	150,000			150,000
Cost of goods sold	(90,000)			(90,000)
Depreciation and amortization	(20,000)	(2) 1,200		(21,200)
Other expense	(31,000)			(31,000)
Net income	9,000			7,800
Retained Earnings				
Retained earnings, 1-1-X1	30,000			30,000
Net income	9,000			7,800
Dividends	(4,000)			(4,000)
Retained earnings, 12-31-X1	35,000			33,800
Assets				
Current assets	32,000			32,000
Equipment (net)	56,000			56,000
Building (net)	24,000	(1) 5,000	(2) 1,000	28,000
Land	10,000			10,000
Goodwill		(1) 3,000	(2) 200	2,800
Total assets	122,000			128,800
Liabilities and Stockholders' Equity				
Current liabilities	8,000			8,000
Long-term liabilities	19,000			19,000
Common stock	60,000			60,000
Contributed capital from push-down			(1) 8,000	8,000
Retained earnings	35,000			33,800
Total liabilities and stockholders' equity	122,000	9,200	9,200	128,800

EXHIBIT 9-8	PUSH-DOWN FINANCIAL STATEMENTS TWO YEARS AFTER ACQUISITION

HIGH, INC.
SEPARATELY ISSUED FINANCIAL STATEMENTS
PUSH-DOWN ACCOUNTING
TWO YEARS AFTER CONSOLIDATION

	Separate Statements (From Books)	Adjustments		Push-Down Financial Statements
		Dr.	Cr.	
Income Statement				
Revenue	170,000			170,000
Cost of goods sold	(94,000)			(94,000)
Depreciation and amortization	(24,000)	(2) 1,200		(25,200)
Other expense	(34,000)			(34,000)
Net income	18,000			16,800
Retained Earnings				
Retained earnings, 1-1-X2	35,000	(1) 1,200		33,800
Net income	18,000			16,800
Dividends	(3,000)			(3,000)
Retained earnings, 12-31-X2	50,000			47,600
Assets				
Current assets	29,000			29,000
Equipment (net)	73,000			73,000
Building (net)	18,000	(1) 4,000	(2) 1,000	21,000
Land	10,000			10,000
Goodwill		(1) 2,800	(2) 200	2,600
Total assets	130,000			135,600
Liabilities and Stockholders' Equity				
Current liabilities	9,000			9,000
Long-term liabilities	11,000			11,000
Common stock	60,000			60,000
Contributed capital from push-down			(1) 8,000	8,000
Retained earnings	50,000			47,600
Total liabilities and stockholders' equity	130,000	9,200	9,200	135,600

down[13] to the subsidiary's financial statements when (a) the debt is secured by assets of the subsidiary, (b) the debt is to be assumed by the subsidiary, or (c) the subsidiary will issue securities whose proceeds will pay off the parent-company debt. When debt is pushed down, a credit for the amount of the debt will replace a credit to contributed capital.[14]

The push-down worksheet adjustments made one year after acquisition and two years after acquisition (Exhibit 9-7) are of two types. First, the assets on the balance sheet are adjusted for the beginning-of-the-period unamortized valuation differential, and the beginning-of-the-period retained earnings is adjusted for the amortization of the valuation differential in prior years. The adjustment to beginning-of-the-period retained earnings is necessary because the amount of contributed capital from push-down accounting, like other forms of contributed capital, cannot be changed by operating results. Thus, the following push-down worksheet adjustment is required:

Worksheet adjustments to prepare the separately issued financial statements on a push-down basis:

	Date of Acquisition	One Year after Acquisition	Two Years after Acquisition
Building (net)	5,000	5,000	4,000
Goodwill	3,000	3,000	2,800
Retained earnings, beginning of year			1,200
Contributed capital from push-down	8,000	8,000	8,000

A second type of worksheet adjustment alters the income statement for amortization of the valuation differential during the current period. In both years, the alterations are made for additional depreciation resulting from the increase in cost of the building and amortization resulting from the recognition of goodwill. Push-down accounting eventually results in the transfer of retained earnings to contributed capital in the amount of the valuation differential (except when the valuation differential is assigned to land).

The separately issued financial statements of subsidiaries are intended to show the results of operations separately; thus intercompany inventory, asset, or liability transactions are not eliminated when preparing these financial statements. Whether the purchase business combination adjustments for the new basis of assets and liabilities are pushed down or not, these intercompany transactions require significant amounts of related party disclosure due to *FASB Statement No. 57*, "Related Party Transactions." An example of related party disclosure is as follows:

Related party transactions: The Company purchased $1,200,000 of inventory from Hoag Corporation, its controlling shareholder, during 1991, of which $78,000 was unsold at the

---

[13] See Staff Accounting Bulletin No. 54, "Push Down Basis of Accounting Required in Certain Limited Circumstances."

[14] While not illustrated here, *FASB Statement No. 109,* "Accounting for Income Taxes," will result in a deferred tax liability in these situations which should be reflected as a deferred tax liability when the tax basis of the assets is unchanged.

end of the year. Hoag Corporation purchased $700,000 of inventory from the Company during 1991 of which $150,000 was unsold at the end of the year. Hoag Corporation has the right to return such inventory which would result in a change in gross profit of $35,000. The Company purchased $250,000 in face value of Hoag Corporation's debt securities on the open market during fiscal year 1990 which are shown on the Company's statement of financial position at an unamortized amount of $255,000.

The amount of gross profit unrealized by the parent on upstream inventory transactions would especially seem to require disclosure since the parent would have the ability to insist upon its right to return the inventories.

APPENDIX: INTERIM FINANCIAL REPORTING

Interim financial reporting is financial information about interim periods within a fiscal year. Interim financial information may be required because the enterprise is publicly held and a registrant of the SEC, or because of some type of lending arrangement with banks or insurance companies. Publicly held companies are required by the SEC to file complete financial statements on Form 10-Q within 45 days of the end of the fiscal quarter;[15] larger companies are required to file a two-year summary of quarterly operating results information as supplementary information in the annual Form 10-K.[16] Banks and insurance companies may require interim financial reports because of the type of lending activities (such as working capital loans) or because of the speed with which they wish to make assessments of a corporation's ability to make payments. Many companies also present quarterly information, either that contained in the Form 10-Q or that summarized income statement information, to their stockholders.

Financial Accounting Standards for Interim Reporting

APB Opinion No. 28 addresses the measurement standards for financial reporting for interim periods. In *APB Opinion No. 28*, the interim period is usually treated as an integral part of an annual period rather than as a distinct accounting period. The exception to this usual treatment is that annual expenses which occur in one interim period should be treated as an expense of that period unless it clearly benefits other interim periods. This leads to the following treatment of various presentations in interim financial statements.

Measurement of Interim Revenue

"Revenue from products sold or services rendered should be recognized during an interim period on the same basis as followed for the full year" (*APB Opinion No. 28*, par. 11). For example, if annual revenues are recognized on the basis of percentage-of-completion, then quarterly revenues should be recognized on the basis of percentage-of-completion. This provision requires interim revenues to reflect seasonal variation from one interim period to another; however, to "avoid the possibility that interim results with material seasonal

---

[15] Securities Exchange Act of 1934, Sections 12(b), 12(g), and 15(d). The specific requirements for disclosure are contained in the Form 10-Q rules.

[16] *SEC Regulation S-K*, Item 302, requires disclosure if the "registrant and consolidated subsidiaries (A) have had a net income after taxes but before extraordinary items and the cumulative effect of a change in accounting of $250,000 for each of the last three fiscal years or (B) had total assets of at least $200,000,000 for at least the last fiscal year."

variations may be taken as indicative of the estimated results for a full fiscal year," *APB Opinion No. 28* (par. 18) also requires disclosure of the seasonal nature of underlying activities.

Two Classes of Cost and Expense

Two classes of costs are distinguished—costs *associated with particular revenues* and costs *not associated with particular revenues*. A cost is associated with revenue if it is *directly related* to revenues (as is the direct cost of merchandise sold) or is *allocated* to the products sold or services rendered (as is depreciation on manufacturing equipment). Costs that are associated with revenues (which are frequently called *product costs*) are taken as expense in the period in which the related revenue is recognized. Costs that are not associated with particular revenues, which are usually called *period costs*, are taken as expense on some basis other than revenue.

Costs and expenses associated with revenue

APB Opinion No. 28 directs that "costs and expenses that are associated directly with or allocated to the products sold or to the services rendered for *annual* reporting purposes . . . should be similarly treated for *interim* reporting purposes" (par. 13, emphasis supplied). Ideally, for example, interim cost of sales should arise from the same inventory costing procedures that generate annual cost of sales; if a periodic inventory system is used to calculate FIFO cost of sales for annual statements, then the same procedures should be used for quarterly statements. The provision for uncollectible accounts is another example of an expense associated with revenue; if the annual provision is established as a percentage of annual revenues, then the quarterly provision should be established as that same percentage of quarterly revenues.

In some cases, feasibility considerations thwart the association of certain costs and expenses with annual and interim revenue by application of the same methods. Cost of sales and other inventory-related costs and losses are especially vulnerable to this inescapable inconsistency. Accordingly, *APB Opinion No. 28* specifically sanctions four inventory-related exceptions to the consistency requirement—one authorizes estimation procedures when an interim physical inventory is not feasible, a second provides for the temporary liquidation of LIFO inventories, and a third sanctions nonrecognition of temporary declines in the market value of inventory. A fourth provision directs the reporting of standard cost variances.

Estimated interim cost of sales

The taking of a physical inventory is a costly process. In some companies, like large merchandising operations, the physical inventory is so costly that quarterly inventories are infeasible. In such cases, *APB Opinion No. 28* sanctions the use of estimated gross profit rates to determine the cost of sales during interim periods. If, for example, the estimated rate of gross profit on sales is 30% for a quarter in which sales total $800,000, then cost of sales in that quarter is estimated to be $560,000 [$800,000 − (.30 × $800,000)]. Of course, the gross profit method is not the only estimation procedure possible; for example, some companies may use sampling experiments to estimate the ending inventory. Whenever interim cost of sales is based on estimates, the estimation procedures should be disclosed together with "any significant adjustments that result from reconciliations with the annual physical inventory" (*APB Opinion No. 28*, par. 14a).

Interim liquidation of LIFO base

When LIFO cost is applied to inventories, inventory cost is apt to include some very old prices. If the inventory falls to an unusually low level during an interim period, then strict application of the LIFO cost method would charge some of these old prices to cost of sales in a "liquidation" of the old LIFO layers. But if the "liquidation of base period inventories at an interim date . . . is expected to be replaced by the end of the annual period" then *APB Opinion No. 28* sanctions a departure from strict LIFO principles. "In such cases the inventory at the interim period should not give effect to the LIFO liquidation, and cost of sales for the interim reporting period should include the expected cost of replacement of the liquidated LIFO base" (*APB Opinion No. 28*, par. 14b). Suppose that the LIFO cost of an inventory on January 1, 19X9, is $1,200, which represents 60 units at the current cost of $10 per unit and 100 units at the 19X1 cost of $6 per unit. During the first quarter of 19X9, no shipments were received owing to a strike by production employees, but 100 units were sold. Strict application of LIFO principles would set the March 31, 19X9, inventory at $360 ($6 × 60 units) and first quarter cost of sales at $840 [$1,200 − $360 or (60 units × $10) + (40 units × $6)]. If the company expects to replenish the inventory at a cost of $10 per unit before year-end, then first-quarter cost of sales should be $1,000 (100 units × $10). Of course, if the company does not expect to replenish the inventory by year-end, then strict LIFO principles should be followed for both interim and annual statements.

Inventory losses

Application of the lower-of-cost-or-market rules (*ARB No. 43*, Ch. 4) at year-end requires the write-down of inventory to market and the recognition of the related loss. The same lower-of-cost-or-market rule must be applied at the end of each interim period with the result that inventory losses from market declines should be reflected in income of the interim period in which the decline occurs. If particular inventory exhibits a market decline in one interim period that is reversed in a later interim period of the same fiscal year, then a gain should be recognized in the later period; but the gain must not exceed the earlier loss on the same inventory. In the special circumstances that "market declines at interim dates . . . can reasonably be expected to be restored" within the same fiscal year, the related loss need not be recognized (*APB Opinion No. 28*, par. 14c).

Standard cost variances

A fourth exception to the consistency requirement applies to certain standard cost variances. In general, the same procedures should be followed "in reporting purchase price, wage rate, usage, or efficiency variances from standard cost at the end of an interim period as followed at the end of a fiscal year. Purchase price variances or volume or capacity cost variances that are planned and expected to be absorbed by the end of the annual period, should ordinarily be deferred at interim reporting dates. The effect of unplanned or unanticipated purchase price or volume variances, however, should be reported at the end of an interim period following the same procedures used at the end of a fiscal year" (*APB Opinion No. 28*, par. 14d).

Period costs and interim expense

Costs and expenses that are *not* associated with particular revenues do not admit the imposition of a straightforward consistency requirement. For some elements of period cost, procedural consistency between quarterly and annual reports does not lead to consistency under the principles of period cost assignment. Moreover, some accountants argue that interim and annual measurements call for fundamentally different principles and that consistency is not an appropriate objective. Both factors complicate the development of financial accounting standards for interim period expense.

Quarterly deferral of costs charged to annual expense as incurred

Charging particular costs to expense as they are incurred may secure a proper association of the costs with the *annual* period of their utilization and yet not secure a proper association of the costs with the *quarterly* periods of their utilization. For example, a cost may be incurred in the second quarter of the year and the related asset subject to use throughout the second, third, and fourth quarters of the year. *APB Opinion No. 28* provides that such a cost should be amortized over the three quarters in which the related asset is used by the company. In short, some costs that are expensed as incurred for annual reporting purposes must be deferred and amortized for quarterly reporting purposes (par. 16a). This procedural difference does not represent an inconsistent treatment of the costs in question. In fact, the procedural difference is *necessary* to ensure a consistent treatment—to ensure the assignment of the costs to both the quarterly and annual periods of their utilization.

Standards for interim period expense

Financial accounting standards offer the following guidelines for interim measurement of costs not associated with revenues (*APB Opinion No. 28*, par. 15):

1. Costs and expenses other than product costs should be charged to income in interim periods as incurred, or be allocated among interim periods based on an estimate of time expired, benefit received, or activity associated with the periods. Procedures adopted for assigning specific cost and expense items to an interim period should be consistent with the bases followed by the company in reporting results of operations at annual reporting dates. However, when a specific cost or expense item charged to expense for annual reporting purposes benefits more than one interim period, the cost or expense item may be allocated to those interim periods.

2. Some costs and expenses incurred in an interim period, however, cannot be readily identified with the activities or benefits of other interim periods and should be charged to the interim period in which incurred. Disclosure should be made as to the nature and amount of such costs unless items of a comparable nature are included in both the current interim period and in the corresponding interim period of the preceding year.

3. Arbitrary assignment of the amount of such costs to an interim period should not be made.

In short, *APB Opinion No. 28* provides that elements of annual expense incurred in one interim period should be charged to expense in that period unless it *clearly benefits* other periods. If an element of annual expense clearly benefits other periods, then it should be amortized among those periods.

Fixed costs and interim expense

The utilization pattern or benefit flow associated with some assets is more or less constant and continuous over periods of several years in length. When period costs are associated with such assets, the cost is appropriately charged to expense on a *time basis*, that is, at a constant rate per year. Rent, insurance, property taxes, administrative salaries, and straight-line depreciation usually have this character. If consistency between annual and interim procedures is maintained, then costs charged at a constant rate to annual expense will also be charged at a constant rate to interim expense.

Annual discretionary costs and interim expense

The utilization or benefit flow associated with some assets may be constant and continuous within each year but vary from year to year at the discretion of management. Research and development costs, major maintenance and repair costs, and advertising costs frequently take this form. Discretionary costs tend to be charged to annual expense in the year of their incurrence. Since the incurrence of such costs does not tend to be uniformly distributed across interim periods, consistency between interim and annual procedures usually produces an erratic interim expense stream. Although a generally applicable standard is lacking for this group of costs, *APB Opinion No. 28* evidences a willingness to both accrue and defer maintenance and repair costs in interim periods and a willingness to defer but not accrue advertising costs.

Gains and Losses

APB Opinion No. 28 (par. 15d) requires that gains and losses be included in annual and interim periods by application of the same principles. "Gains and losses that arise in any interim period similar to those that would *not* be deferred at year end should not be deferred to later interim periods within the same fiscal year." Moreover, losses projected on long-term construction contracts "should be recognized in full during the interim period in which the existence of such losses becomes evident" (*APB Opinion No. 28*, par. 11).

    APB Opinion No. 28 requires that extraordinary items "be disclosed separately and included in the determination of net income for the interim period in which they occur" and that the materiality of such items be assessed relative "to the estimated income for the full fiscal year." The proration of such items over the remainder of the fiscal year is specifically precluded (par. 21).

Accounting for Income Taxes in Interim Periods

For purposes of computing interim income tax expense, pretax accounting income is divided into two parts—ordinary income and nonordinary income. Ordinary income in this context must be distinguished from its use in the income tax context of ordinary income versus capital gains. *Ordinary income* is the "income (or loss) from continuing operations before income taxes (or benefits)." The remainder of pretax accounting income (nonordinary income) consists of unusual or infrequently occurring items—extraordinary items, gains and losses from discontinued operations, and cumulative effects of changes in accounting principles (*FASB Interpretation No. 18*, par. 5a). The income taxes payable and changes in the deferred taxes account related to ordinary income are allocated as expenses reflecting seasonal patterns; the income taxes expense related to discontinued operations, extraordinary items, and cumulative effects of changes in accounting principles are recorded in the interim period of their recognition.

The estimated annual effective tax rate "should reflect anticipated investment tax credits, foreign tax rates, percentage depletion, capital gains rates, and other available tax planning alternatives." Moreover, the estimated rate should be revised, if necessary, to represent "the best *current* estimate" (*FASB Interpretation No. 18*, par. 8; as amended by *FASB Statement No. 109,* par. 288y).

Disclosure of Interim Data in Reports to Security Holders

Publicly traded companies frequently provide less detailed information at interim dates than they provide in annual financial statements; however, *APB Opinion No. 28* (par. 30) requires the following disclosures, as a minimum, in all summarized reports to security holders at interim dates:

1. Sales or gross revenues, provision for income taxes, extraordinary items (including related income tax effects), cumulative effect of a change in accounting principles or practices, and net income

2. Primary and fully diluted earnings per share data for each period presented

3. Seasonal revenue, costs or expenses

4. Significant changes in estimates or provisions for income taxes

5. Disposal of a segment of a business and extraordinary, unusual, or infrequently occurring items

6. Contingent items

7. Changes in accounting principles or estimates

8. Significant changes in financial position

Interim Reporting of Accounting Changes

Changes in accounting principle are of three types: changes in estimate, changes in principle, and changes in the reporting entity.

Changes in estimate are accounted for as a change in the interim period in which the change in estimate is made. Restatement of prior interim periods is prohibited, and the new estimation method should be used for future periods. For example, a company originally estimated its product warranty costs as 1% of sales. During an interim period, the company found that its accrued warranty liability for sales in prior periods was understated. The accrual to bring the estimated warranty liability to the new amount should be recorded in the interim period in which the change in estimate is determined.

Changes in principle include not only changes in principles but also changes in the methods of applying that principle (*APB Opinion No. 20*, par. 7). *APB Opinion No. 20* requires that a change in principle be accounted for either by (1) the cumulative effect adjustment in the income statement or (2) retroactive restatement of financial statements. Interim period reporting follows *APB Opinion No. 20* for retroactive restatements. For situations where a cumulative effect adjustment is required by *APB Opinion No. 20*, the cumulative effect reporting in the income statement should always be shown in the first interim period, even if the decision is not made until subsequent interim periods. When the decision is made in other than the first interim period, the first period shall be restated to show the beginning-of-the-annual-period change in retained earnings resulting from the change in principle (*FASB Statement No. 3*, pars. 9–10).

Changes in the reporting entity impact the comparative financial statements which are provided in interim financial reporting. These changes may occur because of changes (1) from individual company to consolidated financial statements, (2) in the specific subsidiaries included in the consolidated financial statements—including poolings of interests, or (3) in companies included in combined financial statements. Changes in the reporting entity for publicly held companies require special filings under Form 8-K within 15 calendar days after the change.

Disclosure in Quarterly Reports to the SEC

Disclosure of quarterly financial data is made on Form 10-Q, which is filed by registrants following the first, second, and third quarters of each fiscal year. The required disclosures include the following quarterly data:

1. Condensed financial statements
2. A narrative analysis of the results of operations
3. The approval of any accounting changes by the registrant's independent public accountant
4. A signature by the registrant's chief financial officer or chief accounting officer

The condensed financial statements must include (1) comparative income statements for the quarter and year-to-date for the current and preceding year, (2) comparative position statements at the end of the most recent quarter for the current and preceding year, and (3) comparative statements of cash flows for the year-to-date for the current and preceding year.

Condensed Form of Interim Financial Statements

The required financial statements need not be as detailed as the annual statements required in Form 10-K. The quarterly financial statements reported on Form 10-Q are required to include only the major captions specified for the statements on Form 10-K.[17] For example, the subcaptions "Land," "Buildings," and "Equipment" must be reported as separate items on Form 10-K, but the three items may be reported as a single item called "Property, Plant, and Equipment" on Form 10-Q. The only *subcaptions* required on a quarterly basis are for the components of inventory—raw materials, work in process, and finished goods. In addition, major *captions* may be combined provided that specified materiality tests are satisfied.

---

[17] As prescribed by *Regulation S-X*, Article 10. The specific captions are contained in other appropriate articles, for example, Article 5 for commercial and industrial companies.

The detailed footnote disclosures and supporting schedules required on Form 10-K are also not required on Form 10-Q; however, quarterly disclosures should be "adequate to make the information presented not misleading" (*SEC Staff Accounting Bulletin No. 6*). Although the SEC does not completely specify the disclosures required to present misleading quarterly reports, it is clear that the Commission intends that most footnotes be omitted from Form 10-Q. The Commission does specify that business combinations, discontinuances of operations, and accounting changes be fully disclosed in quarterly reports.

Disclosure of Interim Data in Annual Reports to SEC

The SEC requires disclosure of quarterly financial information in a footnote to annual statements included in Form 10-K or in registration statements, which is in addition to the interim disclosures required on Form 10-Q.

Required Footnote Disclosure for Form 10-K

Regulation S-K, item 302, requires disclosure of the following items in an audited note to the annual financial statements:

1. Net sales
2. Gross margin (net sales less costs and expenses associated directly with or allocated to products or services rendered)
3. Income before extraordinary items and cumulative effect of a change in accounting
4. Per share data based upon such income
5. Net income

The foregoing items must be reported "for each full quarter of the two most recent fiscal years and any subsequent interim period for which income statements are presented." In addition, the footnote must describe "the effect of any disposals of segments of a business, and extraordinary, unusual or infrequently occurring items" recognized in a quarter covered by the footnote, "as well as the aggregate effect and the nature of year-end or other adjustments which are material to the results of that quarter."

If the quarterly data disclosed in the footnotes to annual statements differ from corresponding data previously reported in Forms 10-Q, then a reconciliation of the difference must be given and supported by an explanation. For example, quarterly results that precede a pooling of interests should be restated as if the combination had taken place at the beginning of the earliest period presented; such restatements require the inclusion of a reconciliation of the difference between quarterly results as originally reported and restated quarterly results.

SELECTED READINGS

AICPA Accounting Standards Division, Task Force on Consolidation Problems. "'Push Down' Accounting," Issues Paper (October 30, 1979).

Allison, Terry E., and Paula Bevels Thomas. "Uncharted Territory: Subsidiary Financial Reporting," *Journal of Accountancy* (October 1989), pp. 76–84.

Arnold, Jerry, William W. Holder, and M. Herschel Mann. "International Reporting Aspects of Segment Disclosure," *International Journal of Accounting: Education and Research* (Fall 1980), pp. 125–135.

Backer, Morton, and Walter MacFarland. *External Reporting for Segments of a Business*. New York: National Association of Accountants, 1968.

Bagby, John W., and Philip L. Kintzele. "Management Discussion and Analysis: Discretionary Disclosures and the Business Segment," *Accounting Horizons* (March 1987), pp. 51–60.

Colley, J. Ron, and Ara G. Volkan. "Business Combinations: Goodwill and Push-Down Accounting," *Accounting Horizons* (September 1989), pp. 38–43.

Cunningham, Michael E. "Push-Down Accounting: Pros and Cons," *Journal of Accountancy* (June 1984), pp. 3–8.

Dirlam, Joel B., and Richard Vangermeersch. "A Reexamination of Segment Reporting since 1965," *Accounting Inquiries* (February 1992), pp. 294–308.

Doupnik, Timothy S., and Robert J. Rolfe. "Geographic Area Disclosures and the Assessment of Foreign Investment Risk for Disclosure in Accounting Statement Notes," *International Journal of Accounting* (Fall 1990), pp. 252–267.

Edward, James W., Feraldine F. Dominiak, and Thomas V. Hedges. *Interim Financial Reporting* (NAA Research Study). New York: National Association of Accountants, 1972.

Financial Accounting Standards Board Discussion Memorandum. *Financial Reporting for Segments of a Business Enterprise*. Stamford, CT: Financial Accounting Standards Board, May 22, 1974.

Financial Accounting Standards Board Discussion Memorandum. *Interim Financial Accounting and Reporting*. Stamford, CT: Financial Accounting Standards Board, May 25, 1978.

Financial Accounting Standards Board Invitation to Comment. *Reporting Disaggregated Information by Business Enterprises*. Stamford, CT: Financial Accounting Standards Board, May 3, 1993.

Fremgen, James M., and Shu S. Liao. *The Allocation of Corporate Indirect Costs*. New York: National Association of Accountants, 1981.

Goodman, Hortense, and Leonard Lorensen. *Illustrations of "Push Down" Accounting*. New York: American Institute of Certified Public Accountants, 1985.

Gray, Sidney J., and Lee H. Radebaugh. "International Segment Disclosures by U.S. and Multinational Enterprises: A Descriptive Study," *Journal of Accounting Research* (Spring 1984), pp. 351–360.

Horwitz, Bertrand, and Richard Kolodny. "Controversy and Evidence with Respect to the Economic Consequences of Disclosure Rules: Segment Reporting Regulation," Chapter V in *Financial Reporting Rules and Corporate Decisions: A Study of Public Policy*. Greenwich, CT: JAI Press, 1982.

Mautz, Robert K. *Financial Reporting by Diversified Companies*. New York: Financial Executives Research Foundation, 1968.

Mian, Shehzad L., and Clifford W. Smith, Jr. "Incentives for Unconsolidated Financial Reporting," *Journal of Accounting and Economics* (January 1990), pp. 141–171.

Pacter, Paul. *Reporting Disaggregated Information*, Research Report. Norwalk, CT: Financial Accounting Standards Board, 1993.

Puglisi, Joseph A. "Push Down Accounting," *CPA Journal* (February 1984), pp. 61–62.

Rappaport, Alfred. *Segment Reporting for Managers and Investors* (NAA Research Study). New York: National Association of Accountants, 1968.

Thomas, Paula B., and J. Larry Hagler. "Push Down Accounting: A Descriptive Assessment," *Accounting Horizons* (September 1988), pp. 26–31.

QUESTIONS

Q9-1   What is "disaggregated financial information"?

Q9-2   Identify four needs for financial information by the parent-company stockholders, creditors, and minority stockholders that are not satisfied by consolidated financial statements.

Q9-3   Identify three means by which disaggregated financial information might be reported.

Q9-4   Discuss why you agree or disagree with the following statement: One means of providing stockholders of the parent company with information about the separate parent company is to issue separate financial statements for the parent and not consolidated financial statements.

Q9-5   Discuss why you agree or disagree with the following statement: The need for disaggregated financial information is a result of long-term changes in the nature of the consolidated entity.

Q9-6   Even though *FASB Statement No. 94* requires the consolidation of all majority-owned subsidiaries, separate financial information must be provided in consolidated statements about the consolidated nonhomogeneous subsidiaries. Briefly discuss the type of financial information required to be disclosed about nonhomogeneous subsidiaries and the forms of presentation that might be used.

Q9-7   What is "segment financial information"?

Q9-8   Discuss three tests used in identifying a reportable segment. How is a segment that does not qualify as a reportable segment reported?

Q9-9   What determines if a customer of an enterprise is a "major customer"?

Q9-10 Identify three alternative methods for presenting segment information in the financial statements.

Q9-11 Financial accounting standards require that a substantial portion of an enterprise's operations be explained by its segment information. What test is applied to ensure that this exists?

Q9-12 What tests are applied to determine if an industry segment of an enterprise is a dominant segment? What disclosures are required concerning a dominant segment?

Q9-13 When foreign operations represent a substantial portion of enterprise operations, separate disclosures must be made for foreign operations. In addition, when foreign operations can be partitioned into significant geographic areas, then separate disclosure for each significant area is required. State the conditions that must be met for each of the above to be operative.

Q9-14 Under what conditions would an investor provide summarized information as to assets, liabilities, and results of operations of significant investees and joint ventures accounted for under the equity method?

Q9-15 Under what conditions would publicly held companies registered with the SEC and filing consolidated financial statements be required to provide summarized financial information on the parent company?

Q9-16 Briefly describe "push-down accounting."

Q9-17 Under what conditions would the SEC require the use of push-down accounting?

QUESTIONS FOR APPENDIX

Q9-18 Define the term *interim financial reporting*.

Q9-19 Discuss how interim revenue is recognized.

Q9-20 State how costs that are directly associated with interim revenue are treated in interim periods, and discuss four inventory-related exceptions to the general treatment of direct costs.

Q9-21 Discuss how costs that are not directly associated with interim revenue are treated in interim periods.

Q9-22 Discuss the accounting treatment of extraordinary items in the determination of net income for interim periods in which they occur. How is the materiality of such extraordinary items assessed?

Q9-23 For purposes of computing interim income tax expense, pretax accounting income is divided into two parts. Identify and define the two parts of pretax income, and indicate how the income tax expense (or benefit) relating to each part of pretax income is computed.

Q9-24 Describe the financial information that is required by financial accounting standards to be reported to security holders at interim dates.

EXERCISES

E9-1 **Changes in the Nature of the Consolidated Entity** It has been advocated that the need for disaggregated financial information is a result of changes in the nature of the consolidated entity.

REQUIRED
Briefly discuss how the nature of the consolidated entity has changed over the last 60 years or so.

E9-2 **Disclosures about Consolidated Nonhomogeneous Subsidiaries** Ready Cool Inc., a manufacturer of air conditioners, has two subsidiaries. One subsidiary manufactures components used in the production of air conditioners, and the other subsidiary is a lending institution.

In a recent meeting that you had with the accountant in charge of preparing the consolidated financial statements for Ready Cool Inc. and its subsidiaries, the accountant made the statement that "since *FASB Statement No. 94* was issued several years ago requiring the consolidation of all majority-owned subsidiaries, there is no requirement to disclose additional information in the consolidated statements about now-consolidated nonhomogeneous subsidiaries."

REQUIRED
Discuss whether you agree or not with the statement made by the accountant and why.

E9-3 **Segment Reporting** The controller of the publicly held company Goodie Inc. has requested your assistance in developing segment financial information for presentation in the notes to the company's consolidated financial statements. The controller would like your response to the following:

a) What does segment information include?

b) What is an industry segment, and what procedure would be followed in identifying Goodie's reportable industry segments?

c) What are the general requirements for reporting information on foreign operations and geographic areas?

d) What constitutes a major customer?

REQUIRED
Prepare responses for the controller to each of the items (a) through (d) listed above.

E9-4 **Terminology** Terms (1) through (9) are related to the reporting of disaggregated financial information.

REQUIRED
For each of the following terms, select the best phrase or description from the answers listed A through I below.

Term	Descriptions
1. Disaggregated financial information	**A.** A group of entities under common control that accounts for 10% or more of the revenue of a company.
2. Segment financial information	**B.** A component of an enterprise whose sales to unaffiliated customers and intersegment sales constitute 10% of total consolidated sales before eliminations.
3. Industry segment	**C.** A consolidation of Alvin Company, a manufacturer of electric space heaters, with Interface Inc., a manufacturer of thermostats used in manufacturing electric space heaters.
4. Major customer	**D.** The practice whereby subsidiaries, at the date of acquisition, revalue their net assets.
5. Push-down accounting	
6. Reportable segment	**E.** Data on the various industries and geographic areas of operations, as well as major customers and export sales of a consolidated entity.
7. Horizontal integration	
8. Vertical integration	**F.** Financial information about a consolidated entity in addition to the aggregated measurements and related disclosures reported in the consolidated financial statements.
9. Conglomerates	**G.** Combining companies engaged in the same type of production or the sale of the same general product.
	H. A component of an enterprise that provides a product or service to unaffiliated customers for a profit.
	I. The acquisition by one company of another company that operates in an unrelated industry.

E9-5 **Analysis of Comments on Reporting Disaggregated Financial Information**   Indicate whether you agree or disagree with each of the following statements. If you disagree with a statement, provide an explanation as to why.

1. Both publicly held and nonpublic companies are required to disclose segment information.

2. There are some who contend that the need for disaggregated financial information is a result of long-term changes in the nature of the consolidated entity.

3. The diversity of industries included in consolidated financial statements was lessened as a result of a recent FASB pronouncement allowing the exemption from consolidation of nonhomogeneous subsidiaries.

4. Segment information is not required to be reported in financial statements for interim periods.

5. Segment information should reflect the disaggregation of the vertically integrated operations of the enterprise.

6. The determination of a company's industry segments depend, to a considerable extent, on the judgment of the management of the enterprise.

7. Segment reporting is not required if more than 90% of revenues, operating profit or loss, and identifiable assets is attributed to one industry segment.

8. The limitation of consolidated financial statements to provide information about the dividend-paying ability to parent-company stockholders is a restriction on the ability of subsidiaries to pay dividends or otherwise transfer cash to the parent.

9. Push-down accounting generally results in reporting on the separately issued financial statements of the subsidiary different amounts from the subsidiary amounts included in the consolidated financial statements.

10. Push-down financial statements of the subsidiary reflect the new basis of certain assets and liabilities based on the purchase by the parent and reflect all adjustments for intercompany transactions.

11. In the application of push-down accounting, the amount of the valuation differential is considered to be an addition to contributed capital.

E9-6 **Segment Reporting** Barnet Co. has several reportable industry segments that account for 90% of its operations. It has no foreign operations, sales, or major individual customers. On August 1, 19X1, Barnet signed a formal agreement to sell its boating segment for considerably less than its carrying amount. Small profits were realized on the boating segment throughout 19X1 and are expected to continue until final disposition on February 28, 19X2. The sum of the 19X1 and 19X2 boating profits is expected to be less than the disposal loss.

REQUIRED

a) What is the purpose of segment disclosure?

b) What tests should Barnet apply in determining its reportable segments?

c) How should Barnet report discontinued boating operations on its 19X1 income statement?

(AICPA adapted)

E9-7 **Identifying and Disclosing Segment Information** Hughes Company is developing, for the first time, segment information to present in its annual financial statements to shareholders. Hughes activities involve both domestic and foreign operations. The management of Hughes has hired you as a consultant to assist them in presenting appropriate segment disclosures. Hughes derived 12% of the current period's revenue from the unaffiliated firm of Martin, Inc.

REQUIRED

a) Describe the procedures that Hughes might follow in identifying its industry segments.

b) Describe the tests used in identifying reportable segments.

c) Describe the tests that Hughes would use in determining if its foreign operations constitute a substantial portion of its operations, thus requiring separate disclosures.

d) In presenting segment information, must Hughes make any disclosures in relation to its customer, Martin, Inc.? Explain.

E9-8 **Identifying Reportable Segments** Webster, Inc., is a conglomerate entity with operations in four industry segments. The revenues, operating profits and losses, and identifiable assets attributable to each segment are as follows:

	Industry Segment			
	A	B	C	D
Revenues:				
Sales to unaffiliated parties	$ 75	$ 20	$ 10	$ 100
Intersegment sales	20		5	25
Operating profit (loss)	25	(5)	(15)	35
Identifiable assets	800	300	200	1,200

REQUIRED

Determine which of the industry segments of Webster are reportable segments.

E9-9   **Foreign Operations and Geographic Areas**   In addition to doing business in the United States, Rubber Band, Inc., has operations in Israel, Egypt, and China. The revenues, operating profits and losses, and identifiable assets attributable to each of the four countries for the year ended December 31, 19X1, are presented below.

| | Operations in | | | |
	United States	China	Israel	Egypt
Revenues:				
Unaffiliated domestic customers	$200	$ 80	$ 50	$ 15
Unaffiliated foreign customers	20			
Transfers between countries		10	5	10
Operating profit (loss)	40	20	(10)	(25)
Identifiable assets	900	600	300	100

The management of Rubber Band has identified two geographic areas within its foreign operations—the China Area and the Israel-Egypt Area.

REQUIRED

a) Do the foreign operations of Rubber Band represent a substantial portion of the enterprise's operations? Discuss and show appropriate computations.

b) Are Rubber Band's geographic areas within its foreign operations significant, and thus do they require separate disclosures? Discuss and show appropriate computations.

 E9-10   **Identifying Reportable Segments**   Busch, Inc., is preparing segment information for disclosure in its year-end financial statements. Busch has identified five industry segments. Selective information on these segments is presented below.

| | Industry Segment | | | | |
	A	B	C	D	E
Revenues:					
Sales to unaffiliated					
customers	$ 500	$ 145	$ 80	$ 60	$ 20
Intersegment sales		40			5
Operating profit (loss)	100	50	(10)	(20)	15
Identifiable assets	4,000	1,800	700	600	400

REQUIRED

a) Determine which of the above industry segments are reportable segments.

b) Do the reportable segments represent a substantial portion (the 75% test) of the enterprise's total operations? Discuss and show appropriate computations for the 75% test.

c) Are any of the industry segments identified as a dominant segment? Discuss.

 E9-11   **Push-Down Accounting Adjustment**   On October 1, 19X5, Stull Company purchased 85% of the common stock of Wootton Company for $160,000. The balances in Wootton's common stock and retained earnings were $45,000 and $125,000, respectively. The book values of Wootton's assets and liabilities reflected fair values except for land, which had a book value of $10,000 and a fair value of $16,000.

REQUIRED

Prepare in journal entry form the worksheet adjustment to prepare separate subsidiary financial statements on a push-down basis at October 1, 19X5.

E9-12 **Push-Down Accounting Adjustments**   On January 1, 19X7, Cady Company acquired 80% of Kagel Corporation for $101,200 cash. Kagel's stockholders' equity consisted of common stock, $80,000, and retained earnings, $40,000. Book values equal fair values of all assets and liabilities of Kagel except for equipment which has a fair value that is $4,000 more than book value. The equipment has a remaining life of eight years, and any intangibles are to be amortized over ten years. During the years 19X7 and 19X8, Kagel earned a net income and paid dividends as follows:

	19X7	19X8
Net income	$8,000	$13,000
Dividends	3,000	6,000

REQUIRED

a) Prepare in journal entry form the worksheet adjustments to prepare separate subsidiary financial statements on a push-down basis at January 1, 19X7, December 31, 19X7, and December 31, 19X8.

b) Determine the amount of net income and the amount of retained earnings that would be reported on the separate subsidiary income statement and balance sheet on a push-down basis at December 31, 19X7, and December 31, 19X8.

E9-13
APPENDIX

Interim Reporting   Interim financial reporting has become an important topic in accounting. There has been considerable discussion as to the proper method of reflecting results of operations at interim dates. Accordingly, the Accounting Principles Board issued an opinion clarifying some aspects of interim financial reporting.

REQUIRED

a) Discuss generally how revenue should be recognized at interim dates. Discuss specifically how revenue should be recognized for industries subject to large seasonal fluctuations in revenue and for long-term contracts, using the percentage-of-completion method at annual reporting dates.

b) Discuss generally how product and period costs should be recognized at interim dates. Also discuss how inventory and cost of goods sold may be afforded special accounting treatment at interim dates.

c) Discuss how the provision for income taxes is computed and reflected in interim financial statements.

(AICPA adapted)

E9-14
APPENDIX

Interim Reporting   Listed below are six independent cases on how accounting facts might be reported on an individual company's interim financial reports. For the six cases, state whether the method proposed to be used for interim reporting would be acceptable under generally accepted accounting principles applicable to interim financial data. Support each answer with a brief explanation.

1. Coe Company was reasonably certain it would have an employee strike in the third quarter. As a result, it shipped heavily during the second quarter but plans to defer the recognition of the sales in excess of the normal sales volume. The deferred sales will be recognized as sales in the third quarter when the strike is in progress. Coe Company management thinks this is more nearly representative of normal second- and third-quarter operations.

2. Day Company takes a physical inventory at year-end for annual financial statement purposes. Inventory and cost of sales reported in the interim quarterly statements are based on estimated gross profit rates because a physical inventory would result in a cessation of operations. Day Company does have reliable perpetual inventory records.

3. Ball Company is planning to report one-fourth of its pension expense each quarter.

4. Fragle Company wrote inventory down to reflect lower of cost or market in the first quarter of 19X5. At year-end, the market exceeds the original acquisition cost of this inventory. Consequently, management plans to write the inventory back up to its original cost as a year-end adjustment.

5. Good Company realized a large gain on the sale of investments at the beginning of the second quarter. The company wants to report one-third of the gain in each of the remaining quarters.

6. Jay Company has estimated its annual audit fee. It plans to prorate this expense equally over all four quarters.

(CMA adapted)

E9-15

APPENDIX

Multiple Choice Questions on Interim Reporting

1. In considering interim financial reporting, how should such reporting be viewed?

a) As a "special" type of reporting that need *not* follow generally accepted accounting principles.

b) As useful only if activity is evenly spread throughout the year so that estimates are unnecessary.

c) As reporting for a basic accounting period.

d) As reporting for an integral part of an annual period.

2. During the second quarter of 19X8, Buzz Company sold a piece of equipment at a $12,000 gain. What portion of the gain should Buzz report in its income statement for the second quarter of 19X8?

a) $12,000

b) $ 6,000

c) $4,000

d) $0

3. For external reporting purposes, it is appropriate to use estimated gross profit rates to determine the cost of goods sold for

	Interim Financial Reporting	Year-End Financial Reporting
a)	Yes	Yes
b)	Yes	No
c)	No	Yes
d)	No	No

4. An inventory loss from a market price decline occurred in the first quarter. The loss was not expected to be restored in the fiscal year. However, in the third quarter the inventory had a market price recovery that exceeded the market decline that occurred in the first quarter. For interim financial reporting, the dollar amount of net inventory should

a) Decrease in the first quarter by the amount of the market price decline and increase in the third quarter by the amount of the market price recovery.

b) Decrease in the first quarter by the amount of the market price decline and increase in the third quarter by the amount of decrease in the first quarter.

c) Not be affected in the first quarter and increase in the third quarter by the amount of the market price recovery that exceeded the amount of the market price decline.

d) Not be affected in either the first quarter or the third quarter.

5. A planned volume variance in the first quarter, which is expected to be absorbed by the end of the fiscal period, ordinarily should be deferred at the end of the first quarter if it is

	Favorable	**Unfavorable**
a)	Yes	No
b)	No	Yes
c)	No	No
d)	Yes	Yes

6. For interim financial reporting, an extraordinary gain occurring in the second quarter should be

a) Recognized ratably over the last three quarters.

b) Recognized ratably over all four quarters with the first quarter being restated.

c) Recognized in the second quarter.

d) Disclosed by footnote only in the second quarter.

7. On June 30, 19X1, Mill Corp. incurred a $100,000 net loss from disposal of a business segment. Also, on June 30, 19X1, Mill paid $40,000 for property taxes assessed for the calendar year 19X1. What amount of the foregoing items should be included in the determination of Mill's net income or loss for the six-month interim period ended June 30, 19X1?

a) $140,000   **c)** $90,000

b) $120,000   **d)** $70,000

8. For interim financial reporting, a company's income tax provision for the second quarter of 19X1 should be determined using the

a) Statutory tax rate for 19X1.

b) Effective tax rate expected to be applicable for the second quarter of 19X1.

c) Effective tax rate expected to be applicable for the full year of 19X1 as estimated at the end of the first quarter of 19X1.

d) Effective tax rate expected to be applicable for the full year of 19X1 as estimated at the end of the second quarter of 19X1.

9. For interim financial reporting, the computation of a company's second quarter provision for income taxes uses an effective tax rate expected to be applicable for the full fiscal year. The effective tax rate should reflect anticipated

	Foreign Tax Rates	**Available Tax Planning Alternatives**
a)	No	Yes
b)	No	No
c)	Yes	No
d)	Yes	Yes

(AICPA adapted)

PROBLEMS

P9-1   **Reporting Segment Information**   The operations of Swingline are confined to the United States, with all operations conducted in four significant industry segments. The revenue and operating profit of each industry segment for the year ended December 31, 19X5, are as follows:

Industry	Revenue	Operating Profit
Segment A	$ 3,000	$1,200
Segment B	4,200	1,600
Segment C	2,500	800
Segment D	1,200	300
Total	$10,900	$3,900

During 19X5, intersegment sales occurred as follows:

1. Segment B sold merchandise costing $400 to Segment A for a selling price of $700; 20% of this merchandise remains in the inventory of Segment A at year-end.

2. Segment C sold merchandise costing $200 to Segment D for a selling price of $350; 30% of this merchandise remains in the inventory of Segment D.

The only intersegment transfer in inventory on January 1, 19X5, is carried in the inventory of Segment A at $100 and was produced by Segment B during 19X4 at a cost of $50.

Swingline's identifiable assets by segment as of December 31, 19X5, together with each segment's 19X5 depreciation and amortization expense and capital expenditures, are presented as follows:

Industry	Identifiable Assets	Depreciation and Amortization	Capital Expenditures
Segment A	$ 3,800	$ 300	$ 600
Segment B	4,500	400	800
Segment C	4,200	325	150
Segment D	1,500	175	50
Total	$14,000	$1,200	$1,600

Corporate assets as of December 31, 19X5, totaled $2,000; corporate depreciation and amortization and capital expenditures during 19X5 were $100 and $125, respectively.

Additional Information:

1. During 19X5, Swingline recorded income from investments of $350. This amount included income from a 35% ownership interest in Boston, Inc., which is located in the United States and supplies raw materials to operations in Segment A. The investment in Boston, Inc., is carried at $1,500, which is included in total investments of $2,500 as of December 31, 19X5. The $100 remainder ($350 − $250) of income from investments represents dividends from small stock holdings in corporations.

2. General corporate expenses and interest expense for 19X5 totaled $300 and $100, respectively.

REQUIRED

For the year ended December 31, 19X5, present information about Swingline's operations in different industries. Follow the format illustrated in Exhibit 9-2 in the text.

P9-2 **Reporting Segment Information** While the major operations of Sweepstakes, Inc., are located in the United States, Sweepstakes also has significant foreign operations located in two significant geographic areas. The revenue and operating profit of each geographic area for the year ended December 31, 19X3, are presented below:

Geographic Area	Revenue	Operating Profit
United States	$4,500	$1,800
Foreign operations:		
Geographic Area I	2,000	900
Geographic Area II	1,500	300
Total	$8,000	$3,000

During 19X3, a U.S. operations sold merchandise costing $700 to affiliated foreign operations in Geographic Area II for $1,200; 25% of the merchandise remains in Area II ending inventory. The only interarea transfer in inventory on January 1, 19X3, is carried in the inventory of Area II at $400 and was produced by the U.S. operations during 19X2 at a cost of $250. U.S. operations during 19X3 recorded sales of $800 to unaffiliated foreign customers in Area I.

As of December 31, 19X3, the identifiable assets of each geographic area are as follows:

Geographic Area	Identifiable Assets
United States	$ 8,000
Foreign operations:	
Geographic Area I	3,800
Geographic Area II	3,200
Total	$15,000

Additional Information:

1. Corporate assets as of December 31, 19X3, totaled $2,500.

2. General corporate expenses and interest expense for 19X3 totaled $350 and $150, respectively.

3. During 19X3, Sweepstakes recognized income from unconsolidated subsidiaries of $200. The investments are carried at $1,000.

REQUIRED

Present information about Sweepstake's operations in different geographic areas as of December 31, 19X3. Follow the format illustrated in Exhibit 9-3 in the text.

P9-3 **Identifying Reportable Segments** Hilton, Inc., operations are divided into five industry segments. As of December 31, 19X7, the following information was made available concerning each segment:

	Industry Segment				
	A	B	C	D	E
Revenues:					
Sales to unaffiliated customers	$4,000	$2,000	$3,000	$1,000	$ 500
Intersegment sales	1,200				
Operating profit (loss)	1,800	800	(1,000)	200	(150)
Identifiable assets	6,500	4,700	5,000	1,800	1,500

During the year 19X7, Industry Segment A sold merchandise to Industry Segments C and D at a selling price of $720 and $480, respectively; Segment A bills all customers at 20% above cost. Thirty percent of the related intersegment transfers of merchandise remains in the inventory of Segment C, and 40% remains in the inventory of Segment D. The only intersegment transfers in inventory on January 1, 19X7, are carried in the inventory of Segment C at $840; these intersegment purchases were made from Segment A during 19X6 at A's normal 20% markup on cost.

The 19X7 depreciation and amortization expense and 19X7 capital expenditures for each segment are as follows:

| | Industry Segment | | | | |
	A	B	C	D	E
Depreciation and amortization	$ 600	$700	$500	$300	$200
Capital expenditures	2,000	800	200	600	400

Additional Information:

1. Corporate assets of Hilton totaled $4,500 as of December 31, 19X7; and 19X7 depreciation and amortization expenses and capital expenditures totaled $750 and $500, respectively.

2. Hilton's 19X7 income from investments in small stock holdings of corporations—each representing less than a 20% ownership interest—totaled $300. These investments are carried on the books at $1,600.

3. General corporate expenses and interest expense were $200 and $50, respectively.

REQUIRED

a) Determine which of the industry segments of Hilton, Inc., are reportable segments.

b) Do the reportable segments of Hilton, Inc., represent a substantial portion of the enterprise's total operations? Discuss and show appropriate calculations.

P9-4 **Foreign Operations and Geographic Areas** Selected information as of December 31, 19X9, concerning the revenues, operating profits, and identifiable assets of the domestic and foreign operations of Imperial Company is as follows:

	Revenue	Operating Profit	Identifiable Assets
United States	$375	$125	$3,000
Foreign operations:			
Germany	365	100	2,500
Japan	60	25	225
Korea	50	10	150
Total	$850	$260	$5,875

During 19X9, U.S. operations sold merchandise costing $75 to affiliated foreign operations in Germany for $100; 40% of this merchandise remains in the ending inventory of affiliate firms in Germany. In addition, revenues of U.S. operations for 19X9 include sales to unaffiliated foreign customers in Germany of $200.

Corporate assets and expenses of Imperial totaled $2,000 and $100, respectively, as of December 31, 19X9. Neither U.S. inventories nor the inventories of foreign operations contain interarea transfers at January 1, 19X9.

The management of Imperial identifies two geographic areas within its foreign operations—the Germany Area and the Japan-Korea Area.

REQUIRED

a) Do the foreign operations of Imperial represent a substantial portion of the enterprise's operations? Discuss and show appropriate calculations.

b) Are Imperial's geographic areas within its foreign operations significant, thus requiring separate disclosures? Discuss and show appropriate computations.

P9-5 **Reporting Segment Information** Gleim, Inc., is based in the United States and has manufacturing operations in the United States and foreign countries. For the year ended December 31, 19X3, Gleim presented the following information concerning its various industry segments:

	Industry Segment			
	A	B	C	D
Revenues:				
Sales to unaffiliated customers	$1,400	$ 100	$1,800	$ 300
Intersegment sales		225	200	
Interest revenue	25			
Income from investments	300			
Operating profit (loss)—before allocation of common costs	600	100	397	200
Assets:				
Identifiable assets	5,000	1,500	2,500	1,000
Investments in stock	3,000			
Depreciation and amortization	900	150	200	100
Capital expenditures	500	300	100	50

Additional Information:

1. Income from investments of $300 includes $200 from a 20% ownership interest in Leer, Inc.; Leer's operations are located in the United States and supply raw materials to operations in Industry Segment C. At December 31, 19X3, the investment in Leer is carried at $2,000, which is included in total investments of $3,000. The remainder of income from investments represents dividends from small stock holdings in corporations.

2. Selling and administrative expenses of Gleim total $1,500, of which $1,000 is identified as common cost (nontraceable costs) and attributable to individual segments and $500 as corporate expenses. Gleim allocates common costs based on the ratio of a segment's sales (unaffiliated and intersegment) to total sales (unaffiliated and intersegment).

3. Intersegment transfers during 19X3:

a) Segment B sold merchandise costing $150 to Segment C for $225; 40% of the merchandise remains in the inventory of Segment C.

b) Segment C sold merchandise costing $100 to Segment D for $200; 10% of the merchandise remains in the inventory of Segment D.

4. The only intersegment transfers in inventory on January 1, 19X3, are carried in the inventory of Segment C at $250 and were produced by Segment A during 19X2 at a cost of $150.

5. Corporate assets as of December 31, 19X3, totaled $4,000; corporate depreciation and amortization and capital expenditures during 19X3 were $500 and $300, respectively.

6. Geographic areas of the operations of Gleim are as follows:

United States Area (consisting of Segment A)
Canada Area (consisting of Segment C)
Mediterranean Area (consisting of Segments B and D)

7. During 19X3, operations in the United States made sales of $400 to unaffiliated foreign customers in the Mediterranean Area.

REQUIRED

a) Determine which of the industry segments of Gleim are reportable segments.

b) Prepare information about Gleim's operations in different industries as of December 31, 19X3. Follow the format illustrated in Exhibit 9-2 in the text.

c) Prepare information about Gleim's operations in different geographic areas as of December 31, 19X3. Follow the format illustrated in Exhibit 9-3 in the text. (*Note:* All geographic areas are significant.)

P9-6 **Push-Down Accounting Worksheet**   On July 1, 19X6, Garner Corporation acquired 90% of the common stock of Murphy, Inc., for cash of $415,000. The balance sheets for both companies immediately after acquisition are presented here. Also shown are the agreed-upon fair values of the assets of Murphy; liabilities are fairly valued as shown:

	Garner Corporation	Murphy, Inc.	
	Book Value	Book Value	Fair Value
Assets			
Cash	$ 290,000	$100,000	$100,000
Accounts receivable (net)	30,000	20,000	15,000
Notes receivable	10,000*		
Inventories	100,000	50,000	58,000
Investment in Murphy	415,000		
Property, plant and equipment (net)	500,000	400,000	455,000
Total assets	$1,345,000	$570,000	$628,000
Liabilities and Stockholders' Equity			
Accounts payable	$ 20,000	$ 85,000	
Notes payable		10,000*	
Long-term liabilities	40,000	90,000	
Common stock	685,000	245,000	
Retained earnings	600,000	140,000	
Total liabilities and stockholders' equity	$1,345,000	$570,000	

* Murphy owed Garner $10,000 (notes payable) due to a cash loan on the date of acquisition.

REQUIRED
Prepare a worksheet at the date of acquisition, July 1, 19X6, to prepare separate subsidiary financial statements on a push-down basis.

P9-7 **Push-Down Accounting Worksheet**   Medlin Company acquired, on January 1, 19X1, all the outstanding common stock of Parsley Company for $50,000. Parsley's net asset book values equal fair values on this date except for land which had a fair value of $2,000 more than book value. At the date of acquisition, the common stock and retained earnings balances of Parsley were $30,000 and $14,000, respectively. Both companies amortize intangible assets over a four-year period. Financial statements for the two companies as of December 31, 19X1, are as follows:

	Medlin Company	Parsley Company
Income Statement		
Sales	$120,000	$100,000
Income from subsidiary	9,000	
Cost of goods sold	(60,000)	(75,000)
Operating expenses	(35,000)	(15,000)
Net income	$ 34,000	$ 10,000
Statement of Retained Earnings		
Retained earnings, 1-1-X1	$ 60,000	$ 14,000
Net income	34,000	10,000
Dividends	(20,000)	(5,000)
Retained earnings, 12-31-X1	$ 74,000	$ 19,000
Balance Sheet		
Assets		
Cash	$ 45,000	$ 15,000
Notes receivable	25,000	17,000
Inventory	70,000	23,000
Investment in Parsley	54,000	
Land	30,000	20,000
Total assets	$224,000	$ 75,000
Liabilities and Stockholders' Equity		
Accounts payable	$ 25,000	$ 26,000
Common stock	125,000	30,000
Retained earnings	74,000	19,000
Total liabilities and stockholders' equity	$224,000	$ 75,000

REQUIRED

Prepare a worksheet at December 31, 19X1, to prepare separate subsidiary financial statements on a push-down basis.

P9-8   **Push-Down Accounting Worksheet**   Haydon Company acquired a 90% interest in Ladd Company on January 1, 19X4, for $125,000. On this date, common stock and retained earnings of Ladd Company totaled $75,000 and $25,000, respectively. Financial statements of Haydon and Ladd for the year ending December 31, 19X5, are as follows:

	Haydon Company	Ladd Company
Income Statement		
Sales	$ 75,000	$ 50,000
Income from subsidiary	11,300	
Cost of goods sold	(30,000)	(25,000)
Operating expenses	(15,000)	(10,000)
Net income	$ 41,300	$ 15,000
Statement of Retained Earnings		
Retained earnings, 1-1-X5	$ 71,000	$ 50,000
Net income	41,300	15,000
Dividends	(10,000)	(5,000)
Retained earnings, 12-31-X5	$102,300	$ 60,000
Balance Sheet		
Assets		
Cash	$ 25,500	$ 18,000
Accounts receivable	25,000	20,000
Inventory	40,000	35,000
Investment in Ladd	145,500	
Equipment (net)	45,000	32,000
Building (net)	30,000	20,000
Land	30,000	30,000
Total assets	$341,000	$155,000
Liabilities and Stockholders' Equity		
Accounts payable	$ 38,700	$ 20,000
Common stock	200,000	75,000
Retained earnings	102,300	60,000
Total liabilities and stockholders' equity	$341,000	$155,000

Additional Information:

1. All the assets and liabilities of Ladd are recorded at their fair values except for the following:

	Book Value	Fair Value
Land	$30,000	$35,000
Equipment	40,000	50,000
Building	25,000	30,000

2. On the date of acquisition, Ladd's equipment and building had a remaining life of 10 years; all intangibles are amortized over a 20-year period.

REQUIRED

Prepare a worksheet at December 31, 19X5, to prepare separate subsidiary financial statements on a push-down basis.

P9-9   **Interim Reporting**   Carllock Corporation, a publicly traded company, is preparing the interim
APPENDIX   financial data that it will issue to its stockholders and the Securities and Exchange Commission
(SEC) at the end of the first quarter of the 19X7–X8 fiscal year. Carllock's financial accounting
department has compiled the following summarized revenue and expense data for the first quarter of
the year:

Sales	$10,000,000
Cost of goods sold	6,000,000
Variable selling expenses	300,000
Fixed selling expenses	500,000

Included in the fixed selling expenses was the single lump sum payment of $400,000 for television
advertisements for the entire year.

REQUIRED

a) Carllock Corporation must issue its quarterly financial statements in accordance with generally
accepted accounting principles regarding interim financial reporting. State how the sales, cost of
goods sold, and fixed selling expenses would be reflected in Carllock Corporation's quarterly report
prepared for the first quarter of the 19X7–X8 fiscal year. Briefly justify your presentation.

b) Carllock Corporation also must file a quarterly report, Form 10-Q, with the SEC. Companies
must comply with the SEC rules regarding quarterly reports when filing Form 10-Q. According to
current SEC pronouncements,

   1. What financial statement(s) must be presented, and what period of time must the statement(s)
   represent?

   2. What additional nonfinancial statement information must Carllock Corporation submit to the
   SEC with Form 10-Q?

(CMA adapted)

P9-10   **Interim Reporting**   The Anderson Manufacturing Company, a California corporation listed on the
APPENDIX   Pacific Coast Stock Exchange, budgeted activities for 19X5 as follows:

	Amount	Units
Net sales	$6,000,000	1,000,000
Cost of goods sold	3,600,000	1,000,000
Gross margin	$2,400,000	
Selling, general, and administrative expenses	1,400,000	
Operating earnings	$1,000,000	
Nonoperating revenues and expenses	–0–	
Earnings before income taxes	$1,000,000	
Estimated income taxes (current and deferred)	550,000	
Net earnings	$ 450,000	
Earnings per share of common stock	$ 4.50	

Anderson has operated profitably for many years and has experienced a seasonal pattern of
sales volume and production similar to the following ones forecasted for 19X5. Sales volume is
expected to follow a quarterly pattern of 10%, 20%, 35%, 35%, respectively, because of the season-
ality of the industry. Also, because of production and storage capacity limitations, it is expected that
production will follow a pattern of 20%, 25%, 30%, 25% per quarter, respectively.

At the conclusion of the first quarter of 19X5, the controller of Anderson has prepared and issued the following interim report for public release:

	Amount	Units
Net sales	$ 600,000	100,000
Cost of goods sold	360,000	100,000
Gross margin	$ 240,000	
Selling, general, and administrative expenses	275,000	
Operating loss	$ (35,000)	
Loss from warehouse fire	(175,000)	
Loss before income taxes	$(210,000)	
Estimated income taxes	–0–	
Net loss	$(210,000)	
Loss per share of common stock	$ (2.10)	

The following additional information is available for the first quarter just completed but was not included in the public information released:

1. The company uses a standard cost system in which standards are set at currently attainable levels on an annual basis. At the end of the first quarter, there was underapplied fixed factory overhead (volume variance) of $50,000 that was treated as an asset at the end of the quarter. Production during the quarter was 200,000 units, of which 100,000 were sold.

2. The selling, general, and administrative expenses were budgeted on a basis of $900,000 fixed expenses for the year plus $0.50 variable expenses per unit of sales.

3. Assume that the warehouse fire loss met the conditions of an extraordinary loss. The warehouse had an undepreciated cost of $320,000; $145,000 was recovered from insurance on the warehouse. No other gains or losses are anticipated this year from similar events or transactions, nor has Anderson had any similar losses in preceding years; thus, the full loss will be deductible as an ordinary loss for income tax purposes.

4. The effective income tax rate, for federal and state taxes combined, is expected to average 55% of earnings before income taxes during 19X5. There are no permanent differences between pretax accounting earnings and taxable income.

REQUIRED

a) Without reference to the specific situation described above, what are the standards of disclosure for interim financial data (published interim financial reports) for publicly traded companies? Explain.

b) Identify the weaknesses in form and content of Anderson's interim report without reference to the additional information.

c) For each of the four items of additional information, indicate the preferable treatment for each item for interim-reporting purposes and explain why that treatment is preferable.

(AICPA adapted)

ISSUES IN ACCOUNTING JUDGMENT

I9-1   Disclosures for Discontinued Operations Malamar Corporation determined just before its December 31, 19X3, year-end that it would dispose of its appliance business. The measurement date would be December 31, 19X3. After extensive discussions with its investment bankers, Malamar Corporation expected that the time of disposal would be July 1, 19X4, which became the disposal date. Malamar then presented the following on its income statement:

Malamar Corporation
Partial Income Statement
Period Ending December 31, 19X3

Income from continuing operations	$22,550
Loss from operations of discontinued segment (net of tax effect of $340)	(660)
Loss on disposal of segment (net of tax effect of $644)	(3,756)
Net income	$18,084

The $660 loss from operations before taxes for 19X3 was $1,000 less the tax impact at the marginal rate of 34%. The $3,756 loss on disposal was calculated as follows:

	Gross	Tax Effect
Expected loss 1-1-X4 to 7-1-X4	$1,200	$408
Write-down of nonmonetary assets to fair value (book)	2,800	100
Expected loss on disposal	400	136
Total	$4,400	$644

The reason for the small tax effect on the write-down was the difference between the book value and the tax basis of these assets.

During May 19X4, the research and production departments made some discoveries that would lead to the ability of Malamar Corporation to be very competitive in the appliance business. The purchase of new assets to start this production would be significantly more than modifying the production line of the existing appliance business.

REQUIRED

a) What are the financial disclosure implications for the 19X4 financial statements of Malamar Corporation if management determines that it will not dispose of the appliance business?

b) What should comparative disclosures between 19X4 and 19X3 be like if Malamar Corporation earns $1,000,000 in the appliance segment and $22,000 in other segments during 19X4?

19-2 **Related Party Disclosure** Bland Corporation acquired 200,000 shares of nonvoting common stock and 100,000 shares of voting common stock of Pierpont Spice Corporation by transferring assets to Pierpont Spice Corporation for a new issue of stock. The assets transferred constituted 75% of the assets of Bland. After the purchase by Bland, Pierpont had outstanding 200,000 shares of nonvoting and 200,000 shares of voting common stock.

Bland also executed a contract with Pierpont which required that Pierpont purchase all spices directly from Bland, that Pierpont participate in all advertising campaigns with Bland based on their percentage of Bland's spice sales, and that Pierpont purchase accounting and data processing services on a cost-plus basis from Bland. The contract between Bland and Pierpont covers a period of ten years unless Bland sells all of its securities and provides 90-day notice to Pierpont.

REQUIRED

Bland Corporation's director of financial reporting has asked you to assist her in drafting an analysis of the implications of the purchase and the contract for financial reporting and for the information to be received by Bland's shareholders.

Reporting under New Basis Accounting

FOUR RATIONALES FOR NEW BASIS ACCOUNTING   519

PURCHASE BUSINESS COMBINATIONS AND PUSH-DOWN ACCOUNTING   520

LEVERAGED BUYOUTS   520

RECORDING LBOs WITHOUT NEW BASIS ACCOUNTING   520

RECORDING LBOs USING NEW BASIS ACCOUNTING   521

GUIDANCE FROM THE EMERGING ISSUES TASK FORCE   523

STOCKHOLDERS' EQUITY IN THE LBO   525

LBO FINANCIAL STATEMENTS   525

ANALYZING LBOs   525

REORGANIZATION ACCOUNTING   526

RESTRUCTURING-RECAPITALIZATION   526

QUASI REORGANIZATION   526

BANKRUPTCY   527

REORGANIZATION UNDER THE BANKRUPTCY CODE   528

ACCOUNTING WHEN THE PETITION IS FILED   529

ACCOUNTING DURING THE BANKRUPTCY   532

ACCOUNTING WHEN EMERGING FROM BANKRUPTCY   533

NEW BASIS ACCOUNTING FOR THE EMERGING ENTITY   534

ACCOUNTING FOR ENTERPRISES EMERGING FROM BANKRUPTCY WHEN NEW BASIS IS NOT ALLOWED   535

SUMMARY   536

New basis accounting is the revaluation of an entity as the result of some event, or series of events, judged to be so significant that financial statements using prior financial statement valuations are no longer considered relevant. New basis accounting results in the revaluation of assets and liabilities to reflect fair value at the date of the event (or the last in the series of events). New basis accounting takes two different forms—revaluation accounting and fresh-start accounting. *Revaluation accounting* adjusts income for the revaluation and reports prior-year data on a comparable basis. *Fresh-start accounting* adjusts other contributed capital (rather than income) for the revaluation, resets retained earnings to zero, and reports no prior-year data. Fresh-start accounting is restricted to cases in which a substantially new entity is created.

This chapter begins with an overview of four rationales for new basis accounting and then turns to an analysis of the new basis decision under different conditions. The chapter begins by considering new basis accounting in relation to purchase business combinations and push-down accounting. The chapter then turns to a discussion of the new basis decision for leveraged buyouts (LBOs) and reorganizations. The chapter concludes with a discussion of accounting for reorganizations under the bankruptcy code.

FOUR RATIONALES FOR NEW BASIS ACCOUNTING

The fundamental question of what transactions or events trigger a new basis of accounting remains to be resolved.[1] As a first step in resolving this complex question, the FASB has issued a discussion memorandum entitled "An Analysis of Issues Related to New Basis Accounting" that develops four rationales for recognizing a new basis of accounting (*FASB Discussion Memorandum*, December 18, 1991, par. 18):

1. *Stock purchase transactions.* "A new basis of accounting should be recognized when an external party or group values the entity in conjunction with the purchase of a majority residual interest in it." This rationale supports new basis accounting in the form of *purchase accounting for business combinations, push-down accounting,* and certain *leveraged buyouts.*

2. *Significant borrowing transactions.* "A new basis of accounting should be recognized when a third-party lender values the entity in conjunction with a borrowing transaction in which the lender puts a substantial amount of debt capital at risk to the entity's performance." This rationale supports new basis accounting in certain *leveraged buyouts.*

3. *Reorganizations.* "A new basis of accounting should be recognized when related parties value the entity in conjunction with a capital restructuring or reorganization in which the entity's stockholders exchange one configuration of the entity's assets or rights for another." This rationale includes but is not limited to *reorganizations and restructurings under bankruptcy laws.*

4. *Corporate joint ventures.* "A new basis of accounting should be recognized when participants in a corporate joint venture value the entity in conjunction with its formation or the subsequent sale of interests therein." This rationale supports new basis accounting for the *formation and sale of joint ventures.*

Each of the four rationales might be applicable in a number of different and frequently complex cases. Our discussion in this chapter will emphasize the simplest cases and will be restricted to the cases in which the first and third rationales may be applicable.[2]

---

[1] Although financial accounting standards do not prescribe the domain of new basis accounting, it is clear that new basis accounting is neither current value accounting nor inflation adjusted accounting. It is not current value accounting because the triggering event is not the ending of an accounting period at which a new set of financial statements must be prepared. It is not inflation adjusted accounting because the triggering event is not a change in the purchasing power or other measure of change in monetary value.

[2] Two issues of increasing importance in discussions of new basis accounting will not be dealt with here: (1) the question of whether majority voting control represents the only definition of control; and (2) the question of what to do in situations where majority voting control is separated from residual equity ownership such as might occur in situations (a) where voting control is held by preferred shareholders or (b) where there is a substantial amount of nonvoting common stock. Chapter 2 of this text discusses the definition of control. See FASB Discussion Memorandum (December 18, 1991), Chapter 6, for additional exploration of these unresolved issues.

PURCHASE BUSINESS COMBINATIONS AND PUSH-DOWN ACCOUNTING

The stock purchase rationale for new basis accounting is based on a ''change in control'' argument. A stock purchase results in the transfer of voting equity interests from one shareholder or group of shareholders to another shareholder or group of shareholders. When the transfer of voting equity interests constitutes a transfer of control to the acquiring company and when the acquiring company has substantive other operations, then the first rationale supports new basis accounting. The application of new basis accounting to such *purchase business combinations* is discussed in the first eight chapters of this book. Even if the purchasing company borrows to accomplish the combination, the transaction is still considered a purchase business combination for accounting purposes as long as the purchaser has substantive other operations and is not merely an investment company.

Like purchase accounting for business combinations, the use of push-down accounting in the separately issued financial statements of a subsidiary acquired in a purchase business combination is an example of new basis accounting under the first rationale. Of course, the use of push-down accounting in current practice is limited to special circumstances (see Chapter 9); consequently, new basis accounting may not be applied to the separately issued statements of all purchased subsidiaries.

LEVERAGED BUYOUTS

Some, but not all, leveraged buyouts also result in a change in control. When a change in control occurs, the first rationale supports the use of new basis accounting. A *leveraged buyout* (LBO) is the purchase of controlling interest in a single corporation by one shareholder (who cannot be a corporation with substantive other operations) or a group of shareholders (who may or may not have substantive other operations), in which substantial leverage is used to effect the purchase of the controlling interest. *Leveraging* means borrowing against the future cash flows of the purchased corporation—sometimes with the assignment of security interests in assets being purchased.[3]

Two methods of accounting for LBOs are illustrated by reference to the case of Potter Manufacturing, Inc., which is described in Exhibit 10-1. The first method records the LBO without recognizing a new basis of accounting (see Exhibit 10-2). The second method records the LBO using new basis accounting (see Exhibit 10-3).

Recording LBOs without New Basis Accounting

Exhibit 10-2 on page 522 demonstrates the concerns of Ed White, the vice-president of Potter Manufacturing in Exhibit 10-1. If no new basis of accounting is recognized, the pro forma balance sheet includes negative stockholders' equity. Yet, many accountants would argue that recording the LBO of Potter Manufacturing in the manner shown in Exhibit 10-2 provides appropriate disclosure of reliable information under the historical cost framework. These accountants feel that cases like Potter Manufacturing represent financial restructuring-recapitalizations for which no change in basis is appropriate. In effect, these accountants feel that purchase of the controlling interest—whether by individuals or a holding company—is irrelevant. These accountants believe that a holding company without substantive other operations (like BGW Acquisition, Inc., suggested in Exhibit 10-1) should be treated as transparent for accounting purposes, that is, treated as if the holding company did not exist.

---

[3] A *leveraged purchase business combination* is like a leveraged buyout in which the purchaser is a single corporate shareholder *except* that the purchaser in a leveraged purchase business combination has substantive operations other than those of the purchased company.

EXHIBIT 10-1	POTTER MANUFACTURING, INC.

Potter Manufacturing, Inc.

Mr. Glenn Potter was 68 years old and had owned and operated Potter Manufacturing, Inc., for 32 years. The latest balance sheet showed the following:

Potter Manufacturing, Inc.

BALANCE SHEET
JULY 1, 19X2

Cash	$ 200,000	Current liabilities	$1,000,000
Other current assets	800,000	Common stock, no par	250,000
Long-term assets	2,000,000	Retained earnings	1,750,000
Total assets	$3,000,000	Total liabilities and stockholders' equity	$3,000,000

Mr. Potter had wanted to retire for three years, but his specialized manufacturing concern was valuable only if the right managers were involved. Three managers who worked for Mr. Potter—vice-presidents Tom Brown, Julie Green, and Ed White—wanted to purchase the business. The three vice-presidents, their investment banker Boyd & Llewellyn, and Mr. Potter all agreed that the correct price was $3,500,000. A proposal had been explored with the various parties and the National Bank of Columbia for the following:

1. Tom Brown, Julie Green, and Ed White would each purchase 100,000 shares of common stock (no par) for $100,000.

2. Boyd & Llewellyn would find one or more investors and form a limited partnership called B&L Potter Partners, LP, to purchase 300,000 shares of common stock for $300,000 and accept a short-term note of $100,000.

3. The National Bank of Columbia would lend $2,800,000, with the manufacturing plant building, the land on which the plant building sat, and the equipment in the manufacturing plant as collateral.

4. Mr. Potter would receive $3,500,000 in cash for his common stock in Potter Manufacturing.

Ed White, the vice-president for finance, was a little worried. "Sure," he said to Julie Green, "it looks like the cash goes the right way. But the financial statements might not be very pretty. All those conservative bankers down at National Bank of Columbia might not be very happy if they thought the company to whom they were going to make a $2,800,000 loan would have a deficit equity account." Julie Green responded, "Would it help us in this regard to form a holding company called, say, BGW Acquisition, Inc.?"

Recording LBOs Using New Basis Accounting

Other accountants, however, believe that the LBO described in Exhibit 10-1 results in a change in control that requires new basis accounting. In other words, the transaction constitutes the sale of Potter Manufacturing, Inc., by Mr. Potter to the three vice-presidents and the limited partnership, and this sale calls for a new historical cost. These accountants believe that the leveraged buyout calls for the same redetermination of historical cost that would have been required by *APB Opinion No. 16* if Potter Manufacturing had been purchased by another operating company in a leveraged purchase business combination. They also believe that the identity of the owners, as long as they constitute a control group, is irrelevant to that determination.

EXHIBIT 10-2	LEVERAGED BUYOUT OF POTTER MANUFACTURING WITH NO NEW BASIS OF ACCOUNTING: ENTRIES BY POTTER MANUFACTURING (NO HOLDING COMPANY) AND RESULTING BALANCE SHEETS

Entry to record sale of 300,000 shares in Potter Manufacturing to Brown, Green, and White:

Cash	300,000	
Common stock, no par		300,000

Entry to record sale of 300,000 shares in Potter Manufacturing to B&L Potter Partners, LP:

Cash	300,000	
Common stock, no par		300,000

Entry to record short-term loan to be repaid using cash of Potter Manufacturing, Inc.:

Cash	100,000	
Note payable to B&L Potter Partners, LP		100,000

Entry to record loan from National Bank of Columbia secured by plant, land, and equipment:

Cash	2,800,000	
Mortgage payable to National Bank of Columbia		2,800,000

Entry to record purchase of shares in Potter Manufacturing from Glenn Potter (assuming the shares remain in the treasury and are not retired):

Treasury stock	3,500,000	
Cash		3,500,000

Potter Manufacturing, Inc.

PRO FORMA BALANCE SHEET
ASSUMING TRANSACTIONS ABOVE TOOK PLACE
JULY 1, 19X2

Cash	$ 200,000	Current liabilities	$1,100,000
Other current assets	800,000	Mortgage payable	2,800,000
Long-term assets	2,000,000	Total liabilities	$3,900,000
		Common stock, no par	$ 850,000
		Retained earnings	1,750,000
		Treasury stock	(3,500,000)
		Total stockholders' equity	$ (900,000)
Total assets	$3,000,000	Total liabilities and stockholders' equity	$3,000,000

Guidance from the Emerging Issues Task Force

The Emerging Issues Task Force reached the consensus that the purchase of a controlling interest by a new group of shareholders in a single transaction, or series of coordinated transactions, was an event that allowed a new basis of accounting.[4] If an LBO results in a ''change in control,'' then new basis accounting should be applied, although its application is subject to a number of limitations. *EITF Issue 88-16* provides for a new basis of accounting when three conditions are met: (1) a control group which did not have control prior to the LBO obtains control; (2) the change in control is substantive, genuine, and other than temporary; and (3) at least 80% of the purchase price must be monetary consideration (cash and unsubordinated debt securities) for fair value treatment of the transaction. *EITF Issue 88-16* applies to LBOs using a holding company with no substantive operations to carry out the acquisition. An analysis of the use of this holding company under the terms of *EITF Issue 88-16* determines whether or not the LBO transaction, or series of coordinated transactions, effects a change in control and thereby warrants new basis accounting. LBOs exhibit many complexities that are not illustrated in the Potter Manufacturing example, which was constructed to focus on the fundamental structure of new basis accounting.[5]

Exhibit 10-3 on the following page shows the transactions as they would be recorded by the holding company, BGW Acquisition, Inc., formed by the three vice-presidents and the limited partnership, B&L Potter Partners, LP, formed by the investment banking firm Boyd & Llewellyn.

Under *EITF Issue 88-16,* all employees and members of management who have an equity interest in the holding company are treated as a single shareholder for purposes of determining a control group. Since BGW Acquisition, Inc., is owned 50% by management and 50% by B&L Potter Partners, LP, the two must jointly constitute a control group that went from no ownership position to a 100% residual equity interest ownership. It should be noted that if the vice-presidents had an ownership interest prior to the LBO, then that prior interest would receive predecessor basis treatment, which is similar to the treatment of prior ownership in a purchase business combination carried out using the step-acquisition method. When the equity interest of some stockholders receives predecessor basis treatment, the change in basis of net assets is limited, and therefore, new basis accounting is only partial.

---

[4] The original consensus was in *EITF Issue 86-16,* which was later replaced by the consensus in *EITF Issue 88-16.* The primary difference between the two consensus positions concerns the valuation of the equity interests for owners whose ownership percentage declines or remains the same as a result of the leveraged buyout. This issue was not addressed in *EITF Issue 86-16,* which discussed accounting only for owners whose ownership percentage increased as a result of the leveraged buyout. *EITF Issue 88-16* recommended treatment of equity interests of owners whose ownership percentage does not increase is discussed later in this chapter.

[5] Specifically, the following complexities are not represented in the Potter Manufacturing example: (1) no shareholders in BGW Acquisition, Inc., had a prior equity interest in Potter Manufacturing, Inc.; (2) the equity interests of all prior shareholders are being purchased; (3) there are no side agreements concerning future compensation including options, warrants, or convertible debt; and (4) all consideration is cash, thus removing determination of monetary or nonmonetary consideration for more complex securities or additional accounting when less than 80% of the consideration is monetary.

EXHIBIT 10-3	LEVERAGED BUYOUT OF POTTER MANUFACTURING WITH NEW BASIS ACCOUNTING: ENTRIES BY BGW ACQUISITION, INC. (A HOLDING COMPANY), AND RESULTING BALANCE SHEETS

Entry to record sale of 300,000 shares in BGW Acquisition to Brown, Green, and White:

Cash	300,000	
Common stock, no par		300,000

Entry to record sale of 300,000 shares in BGW Acquisition to B&L Potter Partners, LP:

Cash	300,000	
Common stock, no par		300,000

Entry to record short-term loan to be repaid using cash of Potter Manufacturing, Inc.:

Cash	100,000	
Note payable to B&L Potter Partners, LP		100,000

Entry to record loan from National Bank of Columbia secured by plant, land, and equipment:

Cash	2,800,000	
Mortgage payable to National Bank of Columbia		2,800,000

Entry to record purchase of shares in Potter Manufacturing from Glenn Potter (assuming formation of a holding company):

Investment in stock of Potter Manufacturing, Inc.	3,500,000	
Cash		3,500,000

This would leave the balance sheet of BGW Acquisition, Inc., as

BGW Acquisition, Inc.
PRO FORMA BALANCE SHEET
JULY 1, 19X2

Investment in Potter Manufacturing	$3,500,000	Note payable	$ 100,000
		Mortgage payable	2,800,000
		Common stock	600,000
	$3,500,000		$3,500,000

The transactions could then be pushed down to the Potter Manufacturing, Inc., statement replacing the former equity of the purchased corporation with the debt and equity of BGW Acquisition.

Potter Manufacturing, Inc.
PRO FORMA BALANCE SHEET
TRANSACTIONS IN BGW ACQUISITION PUSHED DOWN
JULY 1, 19X2

Cash	$ 200,000	Current liabilities	$1,100,000
Other current assets	800,000	Mortgage payable	2,800,000
Long-term assets	3,500,000*	Total liabilities	$3,900,000
		Common stock, no par	$ 600,000[†]
Total assets	$4,500,000	Total liabilities and stockholders' equity	$4,500,000

* The additional amount of step-up in basis is treated as a revaluation of property, plant, and equipment since a bank normally lends only some percentage of fair value. If the fair value of the property, plant, and equipment were less than $3,500,000, then some amount might be treated as an unidentified intangible, goodwill.

[†] The $3,500,000 total investment, since there was no prior investment, less the $2,900,000 financed or paid using cash of the investee.

It should be noted that similar pro forma balance sheets would result if the LBO were structured in any of the following other ways: (1) the consolidation of BGW Acquisition, Inc., and its subsidiary, Potter Manufacturing, Inc.; (2) the statutory merger of Potter Manufacturing, Inc., into BGW Acquisition, Inc.; and (3) the statutory merger of BGW Acquisition, Inc., into Potter Manufacturing, Inc.

Stockholders' Equity in the LBO

Accounting for LBOs results in the substitution of the fair value for new ownership interests (the fair value of both equity investment and debt investment utilized by the new owners), when the monetary consideration test is met, and the predecessor basis of continuing ownership interests for the equity portion of the balance sheet. Any debt investment is then classified as a liability on the balance sheet. For Potter Manufacturing, this results in the equity valuation of the purchase being $3,500,000, composed of the following:

Mortgage note	$2,800,000
Loan from B&L Potter Partners, LP	100,000
Stockholders' investment	600,000
Total	$3,500,000

Of the total $3,500,000, $2,900,000 would be classified as debt and $600,000 would be classified as stockholders' equity.[6] The entire amount of the new investment can be valued at fair value because the monetary consideration (in this case, cash) was greater than 80%.[7]

LBO Financial Statements

Essentially the same pro forma balance sheet as shown in Exhibit 10-3 for the push-down interpretation of the LBO of Potter Manufacturing would result from any of the following four alternative LBO structures for the Potter case: (1) consolidated statements for BGW Acquisition, Inc., and its subsidiary, Potter Manufacturing, Inc.; (2) the financial statements of Potter Manufacturing, Inc., using push-down accounting; (3) the financial statements of BGW Acquisition, Inc., as the surviving corporation after the statutory merger of BGW Acquisition, Inc. and its wholly owned subsidiary with a name change to Potter Manufacturing, Inc.; or (4) the financial statements of Potter Manufacturing, Inc., as the surviving corporation after a statutory merger with its parent. The reason for all four situations being the same is that the holding company, BGW Acquisition, Inc., is a parent company with no other substantive operations.

Analyzing LBOs

LBO transactions are among the most complex of all transactions. LBO transactions, at least in situations where a substantive change in control using monetary consideration occurs, have been held to be situations where new basis accounting can be utilized under *EITF Consensus 88-16*. LBO transactions require careful analysis to ensure (1) that a change in control has occurred, (2) that appropriate distinction is made between new investment and continuing investment, and (3) that appropriate distinction is made between fair value and book basis determinations when less than 80% monetary consideration is paid in the change in control transaction or series of transactions.

When no change in control occurs *or* when the change in control is not substantive, genuine, and other than temporary, LBOs are accounted for as restructuring-recapitalizations for which new basis accounting is not appropriate. When the 80% monetary consid-

---

[6] If there had been any continuing stockholder interests, the stockholders' equity part of the above schedule would be for fair value for new interests and predecessor basis for continuing interests.

[7] If the monetary consideration had been less than 80% (such as preferred stock or some other nonmonetary consideration), only the percentage of monetary consideration of fair value could have been used in the above calculation of the purchase price.

eration test is not met, the percent of monetary consideration establishes the limit of step-up in basis. For example, only 75% of the difference in fair value and book value could represent a change in basis if monetary consideration constituted 75% of the consideration in the stock purchase transaction.

The analysis of individual LBO transactions required for a particular new basis determination is significantly more complex than that illustrated for the Potter Manufacturing case. *EITF Consensus 88-16* provides a number of examples that aid in the analysis of a specific LBO transaction.

REORGANIZATION ACCOUNTING

A firm in financial difficulty may be forced to seek concessions from its stockholders and debt holders. Stockholders may be asked to agree to changes in par value and the offsetting of losses against paid-in capital. Debt holders may be asked to agree to changes in payment schedules, interest rates, or other characteristics of its liabilities—in order to continue its operations. In this process, which is called *reorganization,* debt holders and stockholders exchange one configuration of ownership interests for another. In cases of extreme financial distress, the firm may be forced to terminate its operations and sell all its assets in a process called *liquidation.* In cases of liquidation, a going concern assumption is no longer appropriate and the basis of accounting changes to one of liquidation values. Cases of reorganization also call for revaluations and may require some form of new basis accounting.

Generally accepted accounting principles recognize three types of accounting for reorganizations: restructuring-recapitalization, quasi reorganization, and bankruptcy.

Restructuring-Recapitalization

Since a restructuring-recapitalization is a transaction between related parties, no new basis of accounting is recognized. Rather, each transaction in a restructuring-recapitalization is treated separately. Assets may be reduced under impairment principles but not increased in value. No new assets may be recorded. New debt is valued at fair value. Payments for securities are valued at book value of the debt when the exchange involves existing debt and at fair value when the exchange involves new debt. Purchases of equity securities are treated as treasury-stock transactions. Other payments of cash to shareholders (without equity security purchase) are treated as dividends. Exchanges of security interests by other parties are not recorded by the enterprise.

Exhibit 10-2 presents an example of a restructuring-recapitalization. New basis accounting is not used in restructuring-recapitalizations because the impairment of assets to their fair value represents *only a limited change in basis* for an enterprise. Further, an impairment results in the reporting of a loss on the income statement.[8] In contrast, new basis accounting involves a completely new basis of valuation for the enterprise.

Quasi Reorganization

Quasi reorganizations provide companies that are accumulating substantial losses with a fresh start by securing concessions from stockholders. Usually debt holders are not directly involved in quasi reorganizations, and liabilities remain unaltered. Quasi reorgani-

---

[8] The loss can be reported as a discontinued operation if a part of an enterprise meeting the requirements of *APB Opinion No. 30* is being impaired and the company intends to discontinue the operation of that segment. Otherwise, the loss resulting from a restructuring-recapitalization is reported as a separate component of earnings from continuing operations because it is an unusual item.

zations involve write-downs of assets and restructurings of stockholders' equity including offsetting retained earnings deficits against paid-in capital resulting in a zero value for retained earnings.

Under *ARB No. 43,* the first step in a quasi reorganization is the revaluation of all assets to a lower-of-cost-or-market value—an "impairment determination" on all assets. The loss from the impairment of assets is charged to retained earnings prior to charging the retained deficit against contributed capital accounts. The retained earnings after a quasi reorganization are dated for a reasonable period to indicate that they represent earnings accumulated after the quasi reorganization.[9]

Quasi reorganizations, like restructuring-recapitalizations, do not represent a new basis of accounting since assets can only decrease and no new asset values can be recorded. The impairment charge reduces the amount of stockholders' equity. However, quasi reorganizations differ from restructuring-recapitalizations in that the impairment charge does not enter income but is charged directly to retained earnings and, when retained earnings is reduced to zero, offset against other paid-in capital.

Bankruptcy

Bankruptcy is a judicial action carried out under the U.S. Bankruptcy Code (the current code is largely the result of the Bankruptcy Reform Act of 1978). Either debtors or creditors may petition the bankruptcy court for assistance under the bankruptcy code. As debtors, business enterprises seek judicial action under two chapters of the bankruptcy code: (1) Chapter 11 provides for *reorganizations* in which the court system protects debtor and creditor interests while the enterprise attempts to reorganize itself to return to profitable operations, and (2) Chapter 7 provides for *liquidations* in which the court system protects debtor and creditor interests while the enterprise's assets are sold and the proceeds distributed to claimants.

Enterprises in reorganization under the bankruptcy code are those attempting to survive during the time they are under the protection of the court system and reorganize so as to exist afterward. Reorganization may result in a new basis of accounting for the enterprise as it emerges from bankruptcy. As explained below, new basis accounting should be used if the emerging enterprise has both negative net worth and a new controlling shareholder group.

Enterprises in liquidation under the bankruptcy code are not eligible for new basis accounting since no enterprise will emerge from the administration by the court system. In fact, accounting for enterprises in liquidation will not follow GAAP since there is no going concern. Instead of financial statements, an *accounting statement of affairs* showing expected realizations from assets and expected payments to claimants is utilized. This report will not be illustrated.

Bankruptcy accounting involves new terminology because the accounting for firms under the control of the court system must be responsive to the legal procedures and documents used. Four such terms are of particular importance. A *petition* is a filing by a party to a civil lawsuit, and filings under the bankruptcy code are civil lawsuits. *Prepetition transactions* are transactions that occur before the filing of the bankruptcy petition, while *postpetition transactions* are transactions that occur after the filing (but prior to

---

[9] Quasi reorganizations do require that a company have positive retained earnings prior to carrying out a quasi reorganization. Reclassification of stockholders' equity accounts may be necessary in quasi reorganizations where common stock has a par or stated value so that charging the retained deficit to contributed capital results in properly stating the par or stated value amounts.

emergence from bankruptcy at which time the distinction between the two types of transactions is no longer made). A *plan of reorganization* is a particular type of petition which is the basis of the ruling, the confirmation, by the bankruptcy judge. Our treatment of bankruptcy accounting in the remainder of this chapter emphasizes accounting for reorganizations rather than liquidations.

REORGANIZATION UNDER THE BANKRUPTCY CODE

AICPA Statement of Position (SOP) No. 90-7, ''Financial Reporting by Entities in Reorganization under the Bankruptcy Code,'' provides accounting and disclosure requirements for enterprises during the time that such enterprises are subject to the provisions of the bankruptcy code. *SOP No. 90-7* (par. 2) provides the following description of this process:

> An entity enters reorganization under Chapter 11 by filing a petition with the Bankruptcy Court, an adjunct of the United States District Courts. The filing of the *petition* starts the *reorganization proceeding.* The goal of the proceeding is to maximize recovery by creditors and shareholders by preserving it as a viable entity with going concern value. For that purpose, the entity prepares a *plan of reorganization* intended to be confirmed by the court. The plan provides for the treatment of all the assets and liabilities of the debtor, which might result in forgiveness of debt. For the plan to be confirmed and the reorganization thereby concluded, the consideration to be received by parties in interest under the plan must exceed the consideration they otherwise would receive on liquidation of the entity under *Chapter 7* of the Bankruptcy Code. The court may confirm a plan even if some classes of creditors or some of the stockholders have not accepted it, provided that it meets standards of fairness required by Chapter 11 to the dissenting class of creditors or the dissenting shareholders.

SOP No. 90-7 provides accounting for enterprises in reorganization at the time of the filing of the petition, during the time the enterprise is subject to the control of the bankruptcy court, and at the time that the enterprise emerges from the bankruptcy proceedings after confirmation of the reorganization plan by the bankruptcy court. The basic principles established by *SOP No. 90-7* are:

1. Unsecured and undersecured prepetition claims shall be reported at the amount of the claim allowed by the bankruptcy court.

2. Prepetition liabilities subject to compromise (unsecured and undersecured claims) shall be separated from prepetition liabilities not subject to compromise (secured claims), and both shall be separated from postpetition liabilities.

3. Operating items related to the reorganization (interest income on cash from nonpayment of debt, professional fees, realized gains and losses from asset sales or asset impairment, and other restructuring and reorganization losses) shall be separately disclosed from other operations.

The reporting of an allowed claim under *SOP No. 90-7,* as described in item (1) above, differs from the usual reporting of liabilities at present value under *APB Opinion No. 21.* An *allowed claim* is the amount allowed by the court as a claim against the enterprise which may differ from the actual *settlement amount.* The settlement amount will be determined by the court considering cash availability, future operating ability, and fairness to all creditors.

Accounting When the Petition Is Filed

Aberdeen Corporation (see Exhibit 10-4) will be used to illustrate the types of issues in accounting at the filing of the petition and during the time the enterprise is subject to the control of the bankruptcy court. Exhibit 10-5 on page 531 shows a series of columns concerning the various balance sheets and adjustments to these balance sheets. The first column shows the balance sheet of Aberdeen Corporation immediately prior to filing the petition. The second column shows the adjustments to that balance sheet at the time of filing[10] the petition: (1) the adjustment of the account payable to its allowed claim value[11] and (2) the separation of the undersecured amount of the claim and the impairment of the asset. These two adjustments appear at the top of page 532.

---

[10] These are adjustments at the time of the filing of the petition. The Aberdeen Corporation simply recognizes that it may take time to determine the adjustments necessary at the time of the filing of the petition.

[11] The bankruptcy court will continue to make decisions about allowed amounts of claims during the time the enterprise is under the control of the bankruptcy court for both liabilities already recorded on the balance sheet and for previously unrecorded liabilities. Each decision of the bankruptcy court will change the value of a liability, but this is not further illustrated in this example.

EXHIBIT 10-4	ABERDEEN CORPORATION

On July 1, 19X1, Aberdeen Corporation filed a bankruptcy petition with the Bankruptcy Court for the Northern District of Ohio. On June 30, 19X1, Aberdeen Corporation showed the following balance sheet in accordance with GAAP.

Aberdeen Corporation
BALANCE SHEET
JUNE 30, 19X1

Cash	$ 50,000	Accounts payable	$1,000,000
Accounts receivable	2,200,000	Unsecured loans	3,000,000
Inventory	3,000,000	Accruals	1,200,000
		Secured loans	1,800,000
Property, plant, and equipment	2,200,000	Common equity	450,000
Total assets	$7,450,000	Total liabilities and stockholders' equity	$7,450,000

The following schedule shows the rates of interest for interest-bearing debt on the 6-30-X1 balance sheet.

Unsecured Loans
First National Bank of Twinsburg, originally due 11-1-X1, 9% $2,000,000
Ohio Bank of Commerce, originally due 7-1-X1, 10% 1,000,000
$3,000,000

Secured Loans
First National Bank of Twinsburg, with five years remaining, next payment of $50,000 due on 7-1-X1, plus interest at 12% (*Note:* Part of this loan becomes undersecured.) $1,000,000
Ebersole Finance Corporation, with eight years remaining, next payment of $25,000 due 7-15-X1, plus interest at 14% 800,000
$1,800,000

EXHIBIT 10-4	ABERDEEN CORPORATION (Continued)

After entering bankruptcy, the creditors of the company filed their claims with the bankruptcy court. During the period July 1, 19X1, to July 10, 19X1, Aberdeen Corporation and the bankruptcy court made the following judgments:

1. The account payable to Bates Corporation, shown on the June 30, 19X1, books at $50,000, was allowed as a claim for only $30,000.

2. The collateral for the secured loan of First National Bank of Twinsburg was determined to have a value of $500,000. The amount of the loan of the First National Bank of Twinsburg was $1,000,000; and the book value of the property, plant, and equipment securing the loan was $1,200,000.

During the six months from July 1 to December 31, 19X1, the following operations were performed:

1. The company had sales of $3,000,000 and collected all but $1,000,000.

2. The company collected $2,000,000 of its June 30 receivables and deemed the remainder to be uncollectible.

3. The company had written off $500,000 of inventory as obsolete on July 10. The company had sold $1,500,000 of its inventory in a bulk sale on July 21 for $1,000,000. The company had purchased $1,000,000 in additional inventory and had cost of goods sold of $1,500,000. The company owed $200,000 for the new inventory on December 31, 19X1, with the remainder of the new purchases having been paid for prior to the end of the year.

4. The company had normal operating expenses composed of cash expenses of $1,000,000, accrued expenses of $200,000, and depreciation of $200,000 during the period.

5. The company accrued the following expenses in connection with the bankruptcy: court costs of $20,000, attorney fees of $50,000, and accountant fees of $20,000.

On December 15, 19X1, a disclosure statement had been prepared by investment bankers concerning the value of the firm. The reorganization value was determined to be $6,530,000 including excess cash ($2,930,000) and the value of the reorganized entity ($3,600,000). On January 1, 19X2, the bankruptcy court approved a plan whereby the following actions would take place. The bankruptcy costs would be paid in cash. The allowed claims for prepetition accounts payable, unsecured or undersecured amounts of loans, and accrued expenses would be settled as follows:

1. Fifty percent of the face value of the allowed claim would be paid in cash.

2. Twenty-five percent of the face value of the allowed claim would be settled by giving the holder $1 in face value of a new class of 4%, ten-year debentures due in equal payments of principal each December 31 plus interest on the unpaid principal at the beginning of the period. The interest rate for similar types of credit was 12%.

3. Twenty-five percent of the face value of the allowed claims would be settled by giving the holder one share of common stock for each $1 in face value of allowed claim being settled. These shares would constitute 80% of the common shares outstanding.

The prior shareholders would turn in their shares of common stock and would receive a distribution of newly issued shares of common stock based upon their pro rata holdings such that their total holdings equal 20% of the total common shares outstanding.

The amounts recorded for identifiable assets (cash, accounts receivable, inventory, and property, plant, and equipment) and the uncompromised liabilities (postpetition accounts payable, postpetition accruals, and secured loans) on December 31, 19X1, after adjustments approximate fair market value.

EXHIBIT 10-5	WORKSHEET SHOWING BALANCE SHEET AMOUNTS AND ADJUSTMENTS FOR REORGANIZATION

Aberdeen Corporation

WORKSHEET SHOWING REORGANIZATION BALANCE SHEETS AND ADJUSTMENTS
(ALL AMOUNTS IN THOUSANDS)

Account	Balance Sheet 6-30-X1	Entering Bankruptcy Adjustments Dr. (Cr.)	Adjusted Balance Sheet 6-30-X1	Period Changes Dr. (Cr.)	Balance Sheet 12-31-X1	Reorganization Adjustments Dr. (Cr.)	Emerging from Reorganization Balance Sheet (New Basis) 12-31-X1
Assets							
Cash	50		50	3,200**	3,250	(2,930)	320
Accounts receivable	2,200		2,200	(1,200)	1,000		1,000
Inventory	3,000		3,000	(2,500)	500		500
Property, plant, and equipment	2,200	(700)	1,500	(200)	1,300		1,300
Reorganization value						480	480
Total assets	7,450		6,750		6,050		3,600
Postpetition Liabilities							
Accounts payable				(200)	200		200
Accrued operating expenses				(200)	200		200
Accrued bankruptcy costs				(90)	90	90	0
Debentures						(1,008)	1,008
Prepetition Secured Loans	1,800	500	1,300		1,300		1,300
Liabilities Subject to Compromise							
Accounts payable	1,000	20	980		980	980	0
Unsecured loans	3,000		3,000		3,000	3,000	0
Undersecured loans		(500)	500		500	500	0
Accruals	1,200		1,200		1,200	1,200	0
Total liabilities	7,000		6,980		7,470		2,708
Common stockholders' equity	450	680*	(230)	1,190	(1,420)	(2,312)	892
Total liabilities and stockholders' equity	7,450	–0–	6,750	–0–	6,050	–0–	3,600

Note: Parentheses indicate credits.

* 680 = 700 − 20

** 3,200 = 2,000 + 2,000 + 1,000 − 800 − 1,000

Worksheet adjustment to record account payable at allowed claim value (7-1-X1):

Accounts payable 20,000
    Common stockholders' equity[12]   20,000

Worksheet adjustment to record impairment of property and plant and to record undersecured portion of mortgage loan (7-1-X1):

Common stockholders' equity 700,000
Secured loans 500,000
    Undersecured loans   500,000
    Property and plant   700,000

The third column of Exhibit 10-5 shows the adjusted balance sheet for Aberdeen Corporation immediately after the time of filing of the petition.

Accounting during the Bankruptcy

Exhibit 10-6 shows the income statement for Aberdeen Corporation during the period of the bankruptcy (July 1, 19X1, to December 31, 19X1), including the distinction between continuing operations and bankruptcy-related expenses.[13] During this period, a tremendous amount of cash is being built up within the company from collections of receivables and sales of assets which is not being paid to debtors because the enterprise is under the control of the bankruptcy court.

The "period changes" column of Exhibit 10-5 shows the changes in the balance sheet that result from the asset sales, collections of receivables, and operating items during

---

[12] Common stockholders' equity is shown as a single account here to simplify our presentation.

[13] For simplicity, there is no recognition of interest income in the Aberdeen Corporation example from the investing of the cash.

EXHIBIT 10-6	INCOME STATEMENT FOR REORGANIZATION: NEW BASIS ACCOUNTING

Aberdeen Corporation

INCOME STATEMENT
FOR THE SIX MONTHS ENDING DECEMBER 31, 19X1
(ALL AMOUNTS IN THOUSANDS)

Continuing Operations	
Sales	$ 3,000
Cost of sales	(1,500)
Operating expenses	(1,400)
Income from operations before bankruptcy-related gains, losses, and expenses	$ 100
Bankruptcy-Related Gains, Losses, and Expenses	
Loss on bulk sale	$ (500)
Write-off of obsolete inventory	(500)
Bad debts	(200)
Bankruptcy expenses	(90)
Total bankruptcy-related losses and expenses	$(1,290)
Net income	$(1,190)

the six-month period. Both the income statement and the balance sheet changes are the result of the following worksheet entries from the items in the Aberdeen Corporation example.

Worksheet adjustment to record sales:

Accounts receivable	1,000,000	
Cash	2,000,000	
Sales revenue		3,000,000

Worksheet adjustment to record collection and write-off of prepetition accounts receivable:

Cash	2,000,000	
Bad debt expense	200,000	
Accounts receivable		2,200,000

Worksheet adjustment to write off obsolete inventory and record bulk sale of inventory:

Cash	1,000,000	
Loss on bulk sale	500,000	
Write-off of obsolete inventory	500,000	
Inventory		2,000,000

Worksheet adjustment to record purchase of new inventory:

Inventory	1,000,000	
Cash		800,000
Accounts payable		200,000

Worksheet adjustment to record cost of goods sold:

Cost of goods sold	1,500,000	
Inventory		1,500,000

Worksheet adjustment to record operating and bankruptcy expenses:

Operating expenses	1,400,000	
Bankruptcy expenses	90,000	
Accrued operating expenses		200,000
Accrued bankruptcy expenses		90,000
Cash		1,000,000
Property, plant, and equipment		200,000

Accounting When Emerging from Bankruptcy

A reorganization value must be established for enterprises emerging from bankruptcy. The *reorganization value* is the value of a reorganized enterprise's assets as a going concern. It includes excess cash held by the enterprise as it emerges from bankruptcy and is not reduced for any liabilities. The reorganization value is an important part of the plan of reorganization confirmed by the bankruptcy court. Experts in business valuation, usually investment bankers, analyze the future cash flows of the reorganized entity and prepare this valuation, which is presented in a report called the *disclosure statement.* The disclosure statement presents the reorganization value, the *value of the reorganized entity,* and the excess cash to be paid to satisfy liabilities upon emergence from bankruptcy. The value of the reorganized entity is the reorganization value reduced for the excess cash. The disclosure statement becomes part of the plan of reorganization.

An enterprise emerging from bankruptcy can use new basis (fresh-start) accounting when two conditions are met:

(1) the reorganization value is less than the postpetition liabilities, the prepetition secured liabilities, and the prepetition allowed claims (unsecured and undersecured liabilities), and
(2) the former shareholders immediately before the petition is filed have less than 50% of the voting shares after emergence from reorganization.

In Aberdeen, the former shareholders receive 20% and the former debt holders receive 80% of the shares upon emergence from bankruptcy. The $6,530,000 reorganization value (see disclosure statement information in Exhibit 10-4) is less than the $7,470,000 amount of postpetition and prepetition liabilities at the date of emergence from bankruptcy (see total liabilities in column 5, 12-31-X1 balance sheet, Exhibit 10-5). Thus, Aberdeen Corporation qualifies for new basis accounting.

New Basis Accounting for the Emerging Entity

Effectively, this means that the total assets after paying out the excess cash will be $3,600,000 regardless of the fair value of the *individual identified assets* because $3,600,000 is the value of the reorganized entity. Since the fair value of the identified assets is $3,120,000 (assets of $6,050,000 in column 5 of Exhibit 10-5 less $2,930,000 in excess cash; see last paragraph of Exhibit 10-4), an unidentified intangible account, "reorganization value in excess of amounts allocable to identified assets," is used to bring the total asset value to $3,600,000.

Part of the excess cash will be used to pay for bankruptcy expenses, which have been accrued as a postpetition liability in the amount of $90,000. The remaining $2,840,000 in excess cash will be paid to claimants whose liabilities are being compromised. The holder of $100 in compromised liabilities will receive $50 in cash, $25 face value of debentures, and 25 shares of common stock. The value of the common stock will be dependent upon the value of the liabilities. Since in total there are $5,840,000 in compromised liabilities, $1,420,000 face value of new debentures will be issued which have a fair value of $1,008,000 (rounded) at an effective rate of 12%. This means the liabilities of the emerging entity will be:

Formerly postpetition liabilities	$ 400,000
Secured loans	1,300,000
Debentures	1,008,000
Total liabilities	$2,708,000

The value of the common equity must be $892,000 to make the total liabilities and shareholders' equity equal the total assets. The worksheet entries at December 31, 19X1, to record the payment of cash, the issuance of the debentures, and the issuance of stock are as follows:

Worksheet adjustment to record payment of excess cash:

Accrued bankruptcy costs	90,000	
Accounts payable	490,000	
Unsecured loans	1,500,000	
Undersecured loans	250,000	
Accruals	600,000	
Cash		2,930,000

Worksheet adjustment to establish the unidentified intangible assets:

Reorganization value in excess of identifiable assets ...	480,000	
Common stockholders' equity.................		480,000

Worksheet adjustment to record issuing debentures and new stock for compromised securities and amount of compromise:

Accounts payable............................	490,000	
Unsecured loans...............................	1,500,000	
Undersecured loans	250,000	
Accruals	600,000	
Debentures		1,008,000
Common stockholders' equity.................		714,000
Gain on compromise		1,118,000

It should be noted that the book value of the common equity of the former shareholders equals $178,000 after these entries, which is 20% (rounded) of the common equity of Aberdeen Corporation using new basis accounting.

Accounting for Enterprises Emerging from Bankruptcy When New Basis Is Not Allowed

When new basis accounting is not allowed, the entity emerging from reorganization must account for the debt compromise without asset revaluation. This means that the assets are maintained at their cost basis immediately before emerging from reorganization. Consider as an example that all of the Aberdeen Corporation illustration is the same except that the shareholders immediately before the petition receive 60% of the stock of the emerging corporation. Then, assuming that the fair value of the stock received by former debt holders is 40% of the $892,000 value determined by the bankruptcy court, the entries to record emergence would be:

Entry to record payment of excess cash:

Accrued bankruptcy costs	90,000	
Accounts payable	490,000	
Unsecured loans................................	1,500,000	
Undersecured loans	250,000	
Accruals	600,000	
Cash......................................		2,930,000

Entry to record issuing debentures and new stock for compromised securities and amount of compromise:

Accounts payable	490,000	
Unsecured loans................................	1,500,000	
Undersecured loans	250,000	
Accruals	600,000	
Debentures		1,008,000
Common stockholders' equity.................		357,000
Gain on compromise		1,475,000

For companies *not* in bankruptcy, *FASB Statement No. 15,* ''Accounting by Debtors and Creditors for Troubled Debt Restructurings,'' requires limited recognition of gains on forgiveness of *specific* debt. In contrast, the compromise of debts under Chapter 11 bankruptcy in the no-new-basis situation recognizes such gains because the reorganization under the bankruptcy court is a *general determination* of forgiveness rather than a single, specific debt.

The forgoing entries would result in total assets of $3,120,000 and total common equity of:

Amount prior to emergence	$(1,420,000)
Gain on compromise	1,475,000
New common equity issued to former debt holders	357,000
Total	$ 412,000

The above entries would then be used in column 6 of Exhibit 10-5 to prepare the December 31, 19X1, emerging from bankruptcy balance sheet (no new basis). The income statement for the six months in reorganization for the no-new-basis situation would also change. See Exhibit 10-7.

The difference in common stockholders' equity between the entity with this accounting and the entity under new basis accounting is the inability to recognize the reorganization value in excess of identifiable assets. If there had been a fair value of identifiable assets in excess of the recorded cost prior to emergence from bankruptcy, then such fair value excess for identifiable assets would also have resulted in a difference.

SUMMARY

The FASB's consideration of new basis accounting issues may result in additional situations where such accounting becomes part of generally accepted accounting principles. Presently, only three events have been deemed pervasive enough to result in new basis

---

EXHIBIT 10-7 | **INCOME STATEMENT DURING REORGANIZATION: NO NEW BASIS ACCOUNTING**

Aberdeen Corporation

INCOME STATEMENT
FOR THE SIX MONTHS ENDING DECEMBER 31, 19X1
(ALL AMOUNTS IN THOUSANDS)

Continuing Operations	
Sales	$ 3,000
Cost of sales	(1,500)
Operating expense	(1,400)
Income from operations before bankruptcy-related gains, losses, and expenses	$ 100
Bankruptcy-Related Gains, Losses, and Expenses	
Loss on bulk sale	$ (500)
Write-off of obsolete inventory	(500)
Bad debts	(200)
Bankruptcy expenses	(90)
Gain on compromise of debts in reorganization	1,475
Income from bankruptcy-related gains, losses, and expenses	$ 185
Net income	$ 285

accounting within GAAP: (1) purchase business combinations, (2) leveraged buyouts (LBOs), and (3) reorganizations under the bankruptcy code when change of control occurs and the reorganization value is less than the liabilities recorded prior to emergence.

SELECTED READINGS

AICPA Accounting Standards Executive Committee. "Quasi-reorganizations," Issues Paper 88-1 (1988).

Crooch, G. Michael, and James A. Largay III. "Understanding the FASB's New Basis Project," *Journal of Accountancy* (May 1992), pp. 85–90.

Financial Accounting Standards Board Discussion Memorandum. *New Basis Accounting*. Norwalk, CT: Financial Accounting Standards Board, December 18, 1991.

Gibson, Charles. "Quasi-reorganizations in Practice," *Accounting Horizons* (September 1988), pp. 83–89.

Gorman, Jerry. "Pooling of Interests: Accounting for the New LBO Exit Strategy," *Journal of Accountancy* (March 1991), pp. 60–68.

Jensen, Michael. "The Eclipse of the Public Corporation," *Harvard Business Review* (September–October 1989), pp. 61–75.

Newton, Grant W. "Bankruptcy," Chapter 33 in *Accountants' Handbook,* 7th ed., D. R. Carmichael, S. B. Lilien, and M. Mellman (eds.). New York: Wiley, 1991.

Patterson, George F., and Grant W. Newton. "Accounting for Bankruptcies: Implementing SOP 90-7," *Journal of Accountancy* (April 1993), pp. 46–53.

Rappaport, Alfred. "The Staying Power of the Public Corporation," *Harvard Business Review* (January–February 1990), pp. 96–104.

Robbins, John, Al Goll, and Paul Rosenfield. "Accounting for Companies in Chapter 11 Reorganization," *Journal of Accountancy* (January 1991), pp. 74–80.

Yockey, Dennis W. "Bankruptcy: An Introductory Lesson," *Business Planning* (vol. 2, no. 3, 1986), pp. 22–24.

QUESTIONS

Q10-1 Identify the four rationales being considered for new basis accounting which are currently accepted under GAAP.

Q10-2 What are the three criteria for fully recognizing new basis accounting in leveraged buyouts?

Q10-3 What are the two criteria for using new basis accounting when emerging from reorganization under Chapter 11 of the bankruptcy code?

Q10-4 What is the distinguishing factor for a corporation that purchases the common stock of another corporation which determines whether purchase business combination accounting or leveraged buyout accounting will be considered?

Q10-5 What is the difference between recording a liability under *APB Opinion No. 21* (the present value of the future cash flows using the issuer's discount rate) and an allowed claim under *SOP No. 90-7?*

Q10-6 *FASB Statement No. 15* requires nonrecognition of a gain when accounting for forgiveness of a specific debt. What differentiates compromise of debts under Chapter 11 bankruptcy when new basis accounting is not used from *FASB Statement No. 15?*

Q10-7   What is the difference between the reorganization value and the value of the reorganized entity?

Q10-8   What is the difference between a restructuring-recapitalization and a quasi reorganization?

Q10-9   What will be the form of accounting when a change in control does not occur during a leveraging transaction and purchase of shares of common stock of a corporation by another corporation with no substantive operations? When the change in control is not substantive, genuine, or other than temporary?

Q10-10   What is monetary consideration in a leveraged buyout? Why is monetary consideration important in leveraged buyout accounting?

EXERCISES

E10-1   **Determination of Change in Control**   The following information is available about the leveraged buyout of Kennesaw Manufacturing Corporation ("Manufacturing") by Kennesaw Acquisition Company ("Acquisition"). The stockholders of Kennesaw Acquisition Company are:

	Percentage Held in Manufacturing	Percentage Held in Acquisition
Management	10%	25%
ABC Investment Partners	0	30
EFG Investment Bank	0	45
Public shareholders	90	0

REQUIRED
Has a change in control occurred? Which shareholders could constitute a control group?

E10-2   **Determination of Change in Control**   The following information is available about the leveraged buyout of Park Stores Corporation ("Stores") by Park Acquisition Company ("Acquisition"). The stockholders of Park Acquisition Company are:

	Percentage Held in Stores	Percentage Held in Acquisition
Management	20%	25%
Park Investment Partners	0	30
New York Investment Bank	20	45
Public shareholders	60	0

REQUIRED
Has a change in control occurred? Which shareholders could constitute a control group?

E10-3   **Determination of Change in Control**   The following information is available about the leveraged buyout of Park Stores Corporation ("Stores") by Park Acquisition Company ("Acquisition"). The stockholders of Park Acquisition Company are:

	Percentage Held in Stores	Percentage Held in Acquisition
Management	20%	35%
ABC Investment Partners	0	20
EFG Investment Bank	0	25
Louis Corporation	80	20

REQUIRED

Has a change in control occurred? Which shareholders could constitute a control group?

E10-4 **Calculation of Monetary Consideration** Alexander Acquisition Corporation (''Acquisition''), a corporation formed exclusively to carry out the acquisition, purchased 100% of the common shares of Alexander Foods Corporation (''Foods''). On January 2, 19X1, the day prior to the leveraged buyout, shares of Foods were selling for $100 each. Each selling shareholder of Alexander Foods Corporation received the following for each 100 share block of common shares of Foods owned prior to the acquisition:

Cash from loan secured by assets of Alexander Foods Corporation	$ 6,000.00
4% debenture bonds, par value $1,000, due in 20 years at current market value of similar securities, 2 bonds (10% interest rate)	978.28
7% subordinated notes, par value $1,000, due in 20 years at current market value of similar securities (10% rate), with attached warrant for purchase of 10 shares of common stock at $15.00	744.55
3% preferred shares, par value $100, convertible into common stock at $12.50 (10 shares)	1,000.00
Common stock, no par, 100 shares	1,277.17
Total	$10,000.00

REQUIRED

What was the percentage of monetary consideration in this leveraged buyout transaction?

E10-5 **Determination of Liabilities and Stockholders' Equity Value (No Predecessor Basis) in a Leveraged Buyout** Makar Acquisition Corporation was formed as a corporation to carry out a leveraged buyout of Makar Foods Corporation. Makar Acquisition funded the leveraged buyout with the following:

Proceeds from mortgage loans to Makar Acquisition Corporation secured by land and buildings of Makar Foods Corporation	$6,000,000
Debenture bonds payable, par value and fair market value	2,000,000
Purchase of 60% of the common shares by Makar Partners, LP	1,000,000
Purchase of 40% of the common shares by management of Makar Foods Corporation	300,000

Makar Acquisition purchased 100% of the common shares of Makar Foods Corporation.

REQUIRED

What will be (a) the total liabilities and (b) the total stockholders' equity of Makar Acquisition Corporation?

E10-6 **Accounting on Entering Bankruptcy under Chapter 11** Anderson Company sought protection under Chapter 11 of the bankruptcy code when a major loan payment came due at a time when inventories had increased dramatically. At the date of entering bankruptcy, its balance sheet was as follows:

Anderson Company
Balance Sheet
As of July 18, 19X3

Assets

Cash	$ 50,000
Accounts receivable	800,000
Inventory	2,500,000
Property, plant, and equipment (net)	500,000
Total assets	$3,850,000

Liabilities and Stockholders' Equity

Current payables and accruals	$1,300,000
Current notes payable	1,200,000
Bonds payable (fully secured)	1,000,000
Common stock, no par value	200,000
Retained earnings	150,000
Total liabilities and stockholders' equity	$3,850,000

On July 18, 19X3, Anderson Company received a report from its business valuation specialists which indicated that $100,000 of accounts receivable was not collectible, that $600,000 of its inventory was obsolete, and that the fair market value of its plant and equipment was at least $2,800,000. Immediately after Anderson filed a petition for bankruptcy protection, two suppliers of Anderson filed claims for amounts not recorded on the financial statements totaling $60,000 which were allowed by the court.

REQUIRED

Prepare any entry or entries that Anderson Company should make upon entering bankruptcy.

E10-7   Classification of Expenses and Revenues during Bankruptcy   Brimfield Manufacturing Corporation had entered bankruptcy on May 15, 19X4. During the period from May 15, 19X4, to December 31, 19X4, Brimfield Manufacturing Corporation recorded the following:

Brimfield Manufacturing Corporation
Income Statement
For the Period May 15, 19X4, to December 31, 19X4

Sales revenue	$4,300,000
Interest revenue on cash deposited in interest-bearing accounts rather than making loan payments	60,000
Cost of goods sold	(3,800,000)
Loss from impairment of equipment	(40,000)
Accounting costs for normal audit	(20,000)
Legal costs for defending a lawsuit	(40,000)
Legal costs for bankruptcy petition and pleadings	(100,000)
Gain on sale of excess equipment	20,000
Write-off of uncollectible accounts from special valuation	(40,000)
Recording of payables as allowed claim	(300,000)
Net income	$ 40,000

REQUIRED

Prepare a classified income statement to separate the amounts for continuing operations and the bankruptcy-related gains, losses, and expenses.

E10-8 **Determination of Reorganization Value**   Marbury & Sands was analyzing the Anderson Company, currently under the protection of the bankruptcy court. On June 30, 19X8, Anderson Company was expected to emerge from bankruptcy. Marbury & Sands had estimated that Anderson Company would have $2,300,000 in cash on that date. Marbury & Sands had estimated that the smaller reorganized entity would need operating cash of $300,000 and that the company would produce cash flows distributable to debt holders and shareholders averaging $600,000 per year for the next ten years. Similar companies were requiring a risk-adjusted return of 12%.

REQUIRED

What is the amount of the reorganization value for Anderson Company?

E10-9 **Determination of New Basis Accounting in Reorganization**   Parrot Industries, Inc., emerged from bankruptcy on December 19, 19X6. On that date, the following information is available:

Excess cash	$2,200,000
Value of the reorganized entity	3,000,000
Fair value of identifiable assets after payment of excess cash	2,200,000
Book value of identifiable assets after payment of excess cash	1,900,000
Secured claims	1,000,000
Postpetition accruals and payables	1,300,000
Prepetition allowed claims	4,200,000
Bankruptcy accruals	200,000
Claims not allowed	520,000

The disclosure statement showed that the debt holders would receive 85% of the common equity of the reorganized corporation.

REQUIRED

Prepare an accounting which shows whether Parrot Industries will be allowed to use new basis accounting in reorganization.

E10-10 **Determination of Gain (New Basis Accounting Not Allowed) in Reorganization**   Simpkins Corporation emerged from bankruptcy on December 1, 19X7. On that date, the following information is available:

Reorganization value	$5,400,000
Total of secured claims, prepetition and postpetition liabilities and accruals	5,200,000
Excess cash	1,400,000
Fair value of identifiable assets after payment of excess cash	3,000,000
Book value of identifiable assets after payment of excess cash	2,200,000
Liabilities at fair value after payment of excess cash	1,600,000

The disclosure statement showed that the debt holders would receive 60% of the common equity of the reorganized corporation.

REQUIRED

What amount of gain on reorganization will be recorded by Simpkins Corporation?

PROBLEMS

P10-1   **Determination of Liabilities and Stockholders' Equity Value (No Predecessor Basis) in an LBO**
Aurora Acquisition Corporation was formed as a corporation to carry out a leveraged buyout of
Aurora Foods Corporation. Aurora Acquisition funded the leveraged buyout with the following:

Proceeds from mortgage loans to Aurora Acquisition Corporation	
secured by land and buildings of Aurora Foods Corporation	$3,000,000
Debenture bonds payable, par value and fair market value	2,000,000
Purchase of 600,000 common shares, $1 par, by Aurora	
Partners, LP	2,000,000
Purchase of 400,000 common shares, $1 par, by management of	
Aurora Foods Corporation	600,000

Aurora Acquisition purchased 100% of the common shares of Aurora Foods Corporation on July 1,
19X1. On that date, Aurora Foods Corporation had existing debt of $4,000,000, which was un-
changed by the leveraged buyout, and total assets of $6,000,000 prior to the acquisition.

REQUIRED
a) What will be the (a) total liabilities and (b) total stockholders' equity of Aurora Acquisition
Corporation?

b) What will be the valuation differential for the purchase of Aurora Foods Corporation by Aurora
Acquisition Corporation?

c) If the book value of all assets of Aurora Foods Corporation approximates fair value, prepare the
financial statements of Aurora Acquisition Corporation and its consolidated subsidiary at the date of
acquisition.

P10-2   **Restructuring-Recapitalization**   Omni Industries, Inc., had the following balance sheet on October 1, 19X3:

Omni Industries, Inc.
Balance Sheet
As of October 1, 19X3

Assets	
Current assets	$ 750,000
Investments (at cost)	100,000
Property, plant, and equipment (net)	2,200,000
Intangibles (primarily patents)	100,000
Total assets	$3,150,000
Liabilities and Stockholders' Equity	
Current liabilities	$ 350,000
Common stock, $1 par	500,000
Retained earnings	2,300,000
Total liabilities and stockholders' equity	$3,150,000

On October 1, 19X3, Omni Industries, Inc., sold $4,000,000 of 20-year, 11% bonds payable in a
private placement for $4,000,000 in cash. A portion of the proceeds of the bond issue ($3,000,000)
was used to purchase the 300,000 shares of common stock owned by its largest shareholder, which
would be held in the treasury for use in a stock purchase plan. The remaining $1,000,000 proceeds

of the bond issue were used to pay a special $5 per share dividend to the remaining shareholders using a special state law which allowed directors to pay dividends beyond the amount of unrestricted retained earnings.

REQUIRED

a) Prepare the journal entries to record the issuance of the bonds, the purchase of the treasury stock, and the payment of the special cash dividend.

b) Prepare a balance sheet for Omni Industries, Inc., after these transactions.

P10-3 **Accounting for a Leveraged Buyout Transaction; Push Down to Separate Financial Statements** Carpenter Hardware, Inc., had the following balance sheet on October 1, 19X3:

Carpenter Hardware, Inc.
Balance Sheet
As of October 1, 19X3

Assets

Current assets	$ 750,000
Investments (at cost)	100,000
Property, plant, and equipment (net)	2,200,000
Intangibles (primarily patents)	100,000
Total assets	$3,150,000

Liabilities and Stockholders' Equity

Current liabilities	$ 350,000
Common stock, $5 par	500,000
Retained earnings	2,300,000
Total liabilities and stockholders' equity	$3,150,000

The management and a limited partnership, Echo Partners, decided to undertake a leveraged purchase of Carpenter Hardware, Inc., using a newly formed corporation, Carpenter Acquisitions, Inc. On October 1, 19X3, Carpenter Acquisitions, Inc., sold $4,000,000 of 20-year, 11% mortgage bonds payable in a private placement for $4,000,000 in cash. These bonds were secured by the plant and equipment of Carpenter Hardware, valued at $3,500,000, and the patent rights, valued at $950,000. All other balance sheet amounts approximated fair value. The management invested $100,000 for 25% of the common shares (2,500 shares with a par value of $5), and Echo Partners invested $300,000 for 75% (7,500 shares with a par value of $5) of the common equity of Carpenter Acquisitions. Echo Partners also invested $600,000 in Carpenter Acquisitions to purchase 60,000 shares of 5% convertible preferred stock, par $100 (conversion price $100 per share). The entire $5,000,000 was utilized to purchase 100% of the common shares of Carpenter Hardware, Inc.

REQUIRED

a) Prepare the journal entries to record the issuance of the bonds, common stock, and preferred stock by Carpenter Acquisitions, Inc.

b) Prepare a balance sheet for Carpenter Hardware, Inc., after the leveraged buyout using push-down accounting to account for the debt and stockholders' equity of the parent, Carpenter Acquisitions, on the balance sheet of the subsidiary.

P10-4 **Liquidation of Acquisition Corporation** Using the information in Problem 10-3, prepare the journal entries necessary to merge Carpenter Acquisition, Inc., with Carpenter Hardware, Inc., with Carpenter Hardware, Inc., being the surviving corporation on October 1, 19X3.

P10-5   Determination of Stockholders' Equity in a Leveraged Buyout with Predecessor Basis   Shook & Company, a Chicago investment banking firm, had purchased 100,000 common shares of Palance Stores, Inc., on October 1, 19X1, when Palance Stores, Inc., had issued stock. The cost of the common shares had been $12 per share when the stock had a book value of $6 per share. Shook & Company had used the cost method of accounting for the stock. The assets of Palance Stores, Inc., had been so recently purchased when Shook & Company bought the common stock that their book values approximated their fair market value. Shook & Company believed that Palance Stores, Inc., was a good name for a western clothing store and that the management was excellent. Thus, Shook & Company believed that the name had a permanent value. On October 1, 19X9, Palance Stores, Inc., had a book value per share of $15.

On October 1, 19X9, Shook & Company was involved with two investment partnerships in a leveraged buyout of Palance Stores, Inc. Palance Acquisition Corporation sold $2,000,000 in subordinated debentures and $8,000,000 in mortgage bonds secured by assets of Palance Stores, Inc. Shook exchanged its 100,000 common shares of Palance Stores, Inc., for 50% (100,000 common shares, no par value) of Palance Acquisition Corporation. Each of the investment partnerships, Palance Partners I and Palance Partners II, paid $2,500,000 for 50,000 shares of common stock, no par value, of Palance Acquisition Corporation.

All the cash received by Palance Acquisition Corporation went to purchase the 900,000 shares of Palance Stores, Inc., not owned by Shook & Company.

REQUIRED
Prepare a schedule showing the total amount of liabilities and stockholders' equity which will be attributed in the leveraged buyout transaction.

P10-6   Journal Entries for Emerging from Bankruptcy (No New Basis Accounting)   The balance sheet for Shumate Corporation on October 31, 19X4, is presented below:

Shumate Corporation
Balance Sheet
October 31, 19X4

Assets	
Cash	$3,050,000
Other current assets	1,500,000
Investments (at cost)	200,000
Property, plant, and equipment (net)	2,200,000
Intangibles (primarily patents)	50,000
Total assets	$7,000,000
Liabilities and Stockholders' Equity Postpetition Liabilities	
Current liabilities	$1,350,000
Bankruptcy accruals	250,000
Prepetition Liabilities	
Mortgage bonds	1,000,000
Unsecured liabilities	2,800,000
Total liabilities	$5,400,000
Stockholders' Equity	
Common stock, $5 par	1,500,000
Retained earnings	100,000
Total liabilities and stockholders' equity	$7,000,000

On October 31, 19X4, the bankruptcy court approved the plan of reorganization based on the reorganization value submitted by Black & White Investment Banking Company of $6,600,000, which included excess cash of $2,800,000. Black and White also estimated the following fair market values:

Other current assets	$1,800,000
Investments (at cost)	300,000
Property, plant, and equipment (net)	3,500,000
Intangibles (primarily patents)	100,000

The following took place as Shumate Corporation emerged from bankruptcy:

1. The excess cash was used to (a) pay $650,000 of the other current liabilities, (b) pay the bankruptcy accruals, and (c) make payments of $500,000 to the mortgage bondholders and $1,400,000 to the unsecured liability holders.

2. Shumate Corporation changed the par value of its common stock to $1 per share.

3. The unsecured liability holders also received (a) subordinated notes at the current market rate with a face value of $600,000 and (b) $30,000 in newly issued common shares of Shumate Corporation in full payment of their claims.

REQUIRED

Prepare the journal entries necessary to account for the emergence from bankruptcy.

P10-7 **Journal Entries for Emerging from Bankruptcy (New Basis Accounting; Balance Sheet of the Reorganized Entity)**   The balance sheet for Walker Leathers, Inc., on July 1, 19X1, is presented below:

Walker Leathers, Inc.
Balance Sheet
As of July 1, 19X1

Assets	
Cash	$3,550,000
Other current assets	1,000,000
Property, plant, and equipment (net)	2,450,000
Intangibles (primarily patents)	100,000
Total assets	$7,100,000
Liabilities and Stockholders' Equity Postpetition Liabilities	
Current liabilities	$1,250,000
Bankruptcy accruals	500,000
Prepetition Liabilities	
Mortgage bonds	1,000,000
Unsecured liabilities	5,000,000
Total liabilities	$7,750,000
Stockholders' Equity	
Common stock, $5 par	1,500,000
Retained earnings	(2,150,000)
Total liabilities and stockholders' equity	$7,100,000

On July 1, 19X1, the bankruptcy court approved the plan of reorganization based on the reorganization value submitted by Redding & King, investment bankers, of $7,500,000, which included excess cash of $3,050,000. Redding & King also estimated the following fair market values for the assets remaining in the reorganized entity:

Cash	$ 500,000
Other current assets	1,000,000
Property, plant, and equipment (net)	2,450,000
Intangibles (primarily patents)	300,000

The following took place as Walker Leathers, Inc., emerged from bankruptcy:

1. The excess cash was used to (a) pay $650,000 of the other current liabilities, (b) pay the bankruptcy accruals, and (c) make payments of $500,000 to the mortgage bondholders and $1,400,000 to the unsecured liability holders.

2. Walker Leathers, Inc., changed the par value of its common stock to $1 per share.

3. The unsecured liability holders also received (a) subordinated notes at the current market rate with a face value of $1,000,000 and (b) 900,000 in newly issued common shares of Walker Leathers, Inc., in full payment of their claims.

REQUIRED
Prepare the journal entries necessary to account for the emergence from bankruptcy and the balance sheet of the reorganized entity Walker Leathers, Inc.

P10-8   Preparation of Income Statements during Reorganization   The following revenue and expense information is available from the trial balances of Williams Bakeries, Inc.

Williams Bakeries, Inc.
Partial Trial Balances
For the Periods Ending December 31, 19X1, and 19X2
(DR)/CR

Account	19X1	19X2
Sales revenues	$3,800,000	$2,900,000
Cost of goods sold	(3,900,000)	(2,300,000)
Operating expenses	(800,000)	(600,000)
Bankruptcy expenses	(50,000)	(150,000)
Loss from allowed claims	(100,000)	(200,000)
Interest revenue	200,000	200,000
Interest revenue from cash not paid to debt holders	50,000	350,000
Loss on sale of excess assets	(80,000)	
Loss from impairments	(180,000)	(90,000)
Loss from settlement of lawsuit		(250,000)
Change in accounting method for recording pensions		(1,200,000)

Williams Bakeries, Inc., entered bankruptcy on January 2, 19X1, and is still under the protection of the bankruptcy court on December 31, 19X2. Williams Bakeries is still negotiating with the debtors concerning the reorganization of the entity.

REQUIRED
Prepare properly classified comparative income statements for the fiscal years ending December 31, 19X1, and 19X2.

P10-9   Comprehensive Problem on Leveraged Buyouts   Miriam Lane, president of Ravenna Manufacturing Corporation, had persuaded three other managers to join her in initiating a leveraged buyout of Ravenna Manufacturing Corporation from its parent, Ohio Steel & Foundry, Inc.

Ohio Steel & Foundry, Inc., had wanted to get out of the manufacturing business for several months but had been unable to find a buyer because Miriam Lane and the other managers would not commit to remain for a large corporate buyer. The investment banker Redding & King approached the managers with a buyout proposal. The managers and Ohio Steel & Foundry all agreed that the correct price was $4,000,000 based on discounting the future cash flows of Ravenna Manufacturing Corporation ($200 per share). A proposal had been made concerning financing to the National Bank of Ravenna. The following conditions were accepted by all parties:

1. Miriam Lane would form a new corporation, RMC Acquisition, Inc. RMC Acquisition would be authorized to issue 1,000,000 shares of no par value common stock and 10,000 shares of $100 par value 5% convertible preferred stock with a conversion price of $1.

2. Lane would then purchase 100,000 shares of RMC Acquisition common stock for $100,000. The other three managers would purchase 100,000 shares of RMC Acquisition common stock for $100,000. Lane would receive another 100,000 shares of RMC Acquisition common stock for her 1,000 shares of Ravenna Manufacturing Corporation common stock. Lane had been allowed to purchase these shares at book value less than 90 days ago; thus her cost of $60,000 approximated predecessor basis.

3. Redding & King would form a limited partnership, RMC Partners, which would purchase 300,000 shares of RMC Acquisition common stock for $600,000.

4. Redding & King would purchase 200,000 shares of RMC Acquisition common stock for $200,000 and would receive 2,000 shares of the convertible preferred stock as payment of its investment banking fee of $200,000.

5. Ohio Steel & Foundry, Inc., would exchange 2,000 shares of Ravenna Manufacturing Corporation common stock for 100,000 shares of RMC Acquisition common stock. The predecessor basis was the book value per share of Ravenna Manufacturing Corporation.

6. The National Bank of Ravenna would lend $2,400,000 with the manufacturing plant building, the land on which the plant building sat, and the equipment in the manufacturing plant as collateral. The appraisers estimated the fair value of these assets as $3,000,000. They also estimated that the company had unrecorded patents valued at $60,000 and that the value of other patents was $50,000 versus their book value of $10,000.

7. Ohio Steel & Foundry would receive $3,400,000 in cash for its remaining 17,000 shares of Ravenna Manufacturing Corporation common stock.

The transaction was to be completed on December 31, 19X1. The balance sheet of Ravenna Manufacturing Company on December 31, 19X1, is presented below:

Ravenna Manufacturing Company
Balance Sheet
As of December 31, 19X1

Assets	
Current assets	$ 550,000
Property, plant, and equipment (net)	1,440,000
Intangibles (patents)	10,000
Total assets	$2,000,000
Liabilities and Stockholders' Equity	
Current liabilities	$ 600,000
Notes payable	200,000
Common stock, $5 par	100,000
Retained earnings	1,100,000
Total liabilities and stockholders' equity	$2,000,000

REQUIRED

a) Show that the series of coordinated transactions meets the requirements for leveraged buyout accounting.

b) Prepare the journal entries to record the transaction of the leveraged buyout by RMC Acquisition, Inc.

c) Prepare the December 31, 19X1, balance sheet for RMC Acquisition, Inc., and its consolidated subsidiary.

d) Prepare the journal entries to merge Ravenna Manufacturing Corporation into RMC Acquisition, Inc.

e) If the name of RMC Acquisition were changed to Ravenna Manufacturing Corporation after the merger, what would be the change in the postmerger balance sheet from that prepared in item (c) above?

P10-10   **Comprehensive Reorganization Accounting Problem**   On July 1, 19X1, Cartwright Corporation filed a bankruptcy petition with the Bankruptcy Court for the Northern District of Ohio. On June 30, 19X1, Cartwright Corporation showed the following balance sheet in accordance with GAAP.

Cartwright Corporation
Balance Sheet
As of June 30, 19X1
(thousands)

Assets		**Liabilities and Stockholders' Equity**	
Cash	$ 100	Accounts payable	$ 5,000
Accounts receivable	2,400	Unsecured loans	3,000
Inventory	6,000	Accruals	1,500
		Secured loans	4,400
Property, plant, and		Common stock, no par	500
equipment	5,500	Retained earnings	(400)
		Total liabilities and	
Total assets	$14,000	stockholders' equity	$14,000

The following schedule shows the rates of interest for interest-bearing debt on the 6-30-X1 balance sheet.

Unsecured Loans

$1,000,000	Home State Bank, originally due 11-1-X1, 9%
1,000,000	Ohio Bank of Commerce, originally due 7-1-X1, 10%
1,000,000	Stockbridge Bank, originally due 6-15-X1, 10%
$3,000,000	Total unsecured loans

Secured Loans

$2,000,000	First National Bank of Xavier, with ten years remaining, next quarterly payment of $50,000 due on 7-1-X1, plus interest at 12% (*Note:* Part of this loan becomes undersecured.)
2,400,000	Consolidated Finance Corporation, with eight years remaining, next payment of $25,000 due 7-15-X1, plus interest at 14%
$4,400,000	Total secured loans

After entering bankruptcy, some of the creditors of the company filed their claims with the bankruptcy court. During the period July 1, 19X1, to July 10, 19X1, Cartwright Corporation and the bankruptcy court made the following judgments:

1. The accounts payable to various corporations, shown on the June 30, 19X1, books at $600,000, were allowed as claims for $900,000.

2. The collateral for the secured loan of First National Bank of Xavier was determined to have a value of $1,500,000. The amount of the loan of the First National Bank of Xavier was $2,000,000, and the book value of the property, plant, and equipment securing the loan was $600,000.

During the six months from July 1 to December 31, 19X1, the following operations were performed:

1. The company had sales of $6,000,000 and collected all but $1,500,000.

2. The company collected $2,000,000 of its June 30, 19X1, receivables and deemed the remainder to be uncollectible.

3. The company had written off $500,000 of inventory as obsolete on July 10. The company had sold $1,500,000 of its inventory in a bulk sale on July 21 for a selling price of $300,000. The company had purchased $2,000,000 in additional inventory and had cost of goods sold of $3,500,000. The company had paid cash for all purchases of inventory after seeking the protection of the bankruptcy court.

4. The company had normal operating expenses composed of cash expenses of $1,800,000, accrued expenses of $200,000, and depreciation of $400,000 during the period.

5. The company accrued the following expenses in connection with the bankruptcy: court costs of $20,000, attorney fees of $150,000, and accountant fees of $40,000.

During the seven months from January 1, 19X2, to August 1, 19X2, the following transactions occurred:

1. In January 19X2, the company sold property, plant, and equipment in a series of transactions. The selling prices totaled $3,000,000; and the net book value of property, plant, and equipment sold was $3,500,000. The bankruptcy court authorized the payment of $1,500,000 to First National Bank of Xavier and $500,000 to Consolidated Finance Corporation (both secured lenders) from the proceeds of these sales. First National Bank of Xavier was no longer a secured creditor.

2. Cartwright collected all December 31, 19X1, accounts receivable and paid all December 31, 19X1, postpetition liabilities.

3. The company had sales of $3,000,000 of which $2,600,000 was collected by August 1, 19X2.

4. The company purchased $1,000,000 of inventory and paid $800,000. The cost of goods sold was $1,700,000. In addition, the company made a bulk sale of inventory with a book value of $800,000 for $300,000 on June 15, 19X2.

5. As a result of a special study completed in May 19X2, the company recorded impairments in property, plant, and equipment of $200,000.

6. The company had operating expenses of $900,000 of which $600,000 was paid in cash, $200,000 was accrued, and $100,000 was depreciation.

7. Bankruptcy costs of $320,000 were accrued.

8. With the sale of the property, plant, and equipment, the company terminated part of its labor force. The released workers filed for benefits under the labor agreement in the amount of $400,000, which the bankruptcy court treated as a postpetition liability.

9. Various contractual defaults and the interest on secured debt, previously not accrued, were allowed as claims by the bankruptcy court in the amount of $1,800,000.

During July 19X2, a disclosure statement had been prepared by investment bankers concerning the value of the firm. The reorganization value was determined to be $11,560,000 including excess cash ($5,960,000) and the value of the reorganized entity ($5,600,000). The investment bankers identified only one asset, a parcel of land, where the fair value was not approximated by the book value. The fair value of the parcel of land was $900,000 in excess of the book value. On August 1, 19X2, the bankruptcy court approved a plan whereby the following actions would take place. All postpetition liabilities would be paid in cash, including the accrual for worker claims. No change would occur in the secured claims. The liabilities subject to compromise would receive for each dollar of allowed claim (1) $0.40 in cash, (2) $0.20 in face value of a subordinated debenture carrying the current rate of interest of 12%, and (3) 1/10th share of common stock. The former holders of liabilities subject to claim would hold 80% of the common shares after the reorganization.

REQUIRED

a) Prepare a worksheet during reorganization showing the changes on entering bankruptcy, the adjusted balance sheet on 6-30-X1, the period changes from 7-1-X1 to 12-31-X1, the period changes from 1-1-X2 to 8-1-X2, the balance sheet as of 8-1-X2, the reorganization adjustment, and the postreorganization balance sheet.

b) Prepare income statements during reorganization for the periods 7-1-X1 to 12-31-X1 and 1-1-X2 to 8-1-X2.

c) Since no interest is being accrued during the bankruptcy, how much interest expense is not being accrued that would require disclosure in the financial statements of the period 7-1-X1 to 12-31-X1?

ISSUES IN ACCOUNTING JUDGMENT

I10-1 **New Basis Accounting** Elliott Stores, Inc., is a retailer of clothing and accessories. Elliott Stores also has a long history of owning its own stores and warehouses or investing in the corporations which operate shopping centers in which its stores are located in addition to operating as a retailer. In 19X8, Elliott needed additional capital for expansion and undertook a major financing. A group of banks agreed to lend Elliott Stores $300,000,000 secured by the land and buildings owned by Elliott Stores.

Elliott Stores was considering the financial implications of this type of financing. The director of financial reporting had written the following draft note for the financial statements to describe the financing if it occurred:

The Company has obtained a $300,000,000 revolving line of credit for expansion purposes with a group of banks. The line of credit will be secured by land and buildings with an original cost of $120,000,000 and a book value of $76,000,000 at December 31, 19X8. The line of credit will expire on December 1, 19X3, at which time any unpaid balance will be paid in equal monthly installments of principal and interest over a period of seven years.

The chief financial officer wondered about this note: "Why doesn't this financing show that the amounts on the books for land and buildings should be revalued? After all, banks usually lend only 80% of the market value of real property. The loan would indicate that the market value of these assets was at least $375,000,000. What would happen if we decided to purchase treasury stock with the amount if the expansion falls through? Are you aware that the banks are talking about asking for the stocks in the shopping center companies as additional collateral?"

REQUIRED
Write a brief essay explaining whether or not you believe implementation of the proposal should qualify for new basis accounting.

I10-2 **LBO Accounting** Boston Manufacturing Company engaged in operations in both steel products and chemical products. The chemical products segment realized the same return on investment as the steel products segment. Boston Manufacturing decided to sell the wholly owned chemical products subsidiary, BMC Chemicals, which had a book value of $65,000,000. Two investment bankers and the managers of the chemical products subsidiary, approached the company about a leveraged buyout of the subsidiary.

The assets of BMC Chemicals would be leveraged using loans from a group of banks and insurance companies. Boston Manufacturing would receive $50,000,000 in cash and $100,000,000 in face value of bonds, and would own 40% of the common equity of BMC Chemical Acquisition Corporation, a newly formed company. The managers would receive 15% of the common equity of BMC Chemical Acquisition Corporation for an investment of $1,500,000. The two investment bankers would create investment partnerships which would own 25% and 20% of the common equity, plus each would receive $10,000,000 in book value of preferred stock for investments of $12,500,000 and $12,000,000, respectively.

REQUIRED

The chief financial officer of BMC Chemical Acquisition Corporation, the former chief financial officer of BMC Chemicals, wishes to prepare the financial statements using leveraged buyout accounting. Does the above transaction meet the requirements for a change in control? Can something be done to ensure that a change in control has occurred?

Researching Accounting Principles

RESEARCHING FINANCIAL ACCOUNTING PRONOUNCEMENTS 553

ACCOUNTING MEASUREMENTS 553

ACCOUNTING PRESENTATION AND DISCLOSURE 554

THE HIERARCHY OF GAAP 554

FRAMEWORK OF THE HIERARCHY 554

PARALLEL HIERARCHIES FOR PRIVATE AND PUBLIC SECTORS 555

IMPACT OF REGULATORY AGENCIES 556

BANKING REGULATORS AND THE CALL REPORT 556

SECURITIES AND EXCHANGE COMMISSION 558
Form 10-K 559   Form 10-Q 560   Other Forms 560

INSURANCE AND UTILITY REGULATORS 561

THE RESEARCH PROCESS 561

TERMINOLOGY AND RESEARCH 561

STANDARDS AND INTERPRETATIVE GUIDANCE 562

ITERATION AND CONSULTATION 562

A RESEARCH EXAMPLE 562

SUMMARY 565

Research is undertaken by auditors, controllers, and regulators to resolve questions about the financial statements of particular companies. As accounting becomes increasingly subject to rules and regulations, this research activity assumes a larger role in the day-to-day activity of practicing accountants. Of course, financial reporting research need not be confined to the financial reports of a particular company. Regulatory agencies and professional groups undertake research to answer more general questions about the nature of accounting practice and alternative accounting policies. Accounting academics are frequently involved in this research activity. In addition, accounting academics undertake research on more general questions about accounting phenomena. This chapter, however, emphasizes the day-to-day research of accounting practice that seeks to identify accounting alternatives, to document authoritative support for those alternatives, and to determine a preferred alternative.

This research may be undertaken to determine the measurement, presentation, and disclosure requirements for financial information in the statements of a particular enterprise. *Measurement* is the process of determining a quantitative amount that appears in the body of the financial statements. *Presentation* is the form of the information in the body of the financial statements. *Disclosure* is the measurement and presentation of information beyond that appearing in the body of the financial statements.

Research is also necessary to determine the nonfinancial information required to accompany the financial statements. Nonfinancial information includes: (1) management's discussion and analysis of financial condition and results of operations; (2) the names of directors and executive officers, their principal occupation or employment, and the name and principal business of their respective employers; and (3) market data on common stock including the price and dividend information and the number of common stockholders. Such nonfinancial information must accompany the financial statements when companies issue proxies to stockholders, make filings with regulators, and issue financial statements when publicly held. Professional pronouncements, securities laws and regulations, industry laws and regulations (such as those for utilities, banking, and insurance), and writings by expert accountants all constitute guidance available for determining measurements, presentation, and disclosure for financial statements and the requirements for accompanying nonfinancial information.

The purpose of this chapter is to describe the professional and regulatory literatures that underlie professional research. In addition, the chapter characterizes the regulatory institutions that issue and rely upon those literatures to control the dissemination of accounting information.

RESEARCHING FINANCIAL ACCOUNTING PRONOUNCEMENTS

Financial statements are presented to aid users in estimating future cash flows. The Financial Accounting Standards Board (FASB) has defined the class of users to whom the standard-setting process should be responsive as those who (1) are reasonably informed about business and economic matters and (2) are willing to study the financial statements with reasonable diligence (*FASB Concepts Statement No. 1,* par. 34). Users meeting these criteria are sometimes referred to as ''sophisticated users'' in contrast to ''naive users'', or those who lack a reasonable understanding of business or who lack the willingness to study the information with reasonable diligence. Sophisticated users demand additional disclosure in order to understand the uncertainty and estimation used in financial statements. The demand for this information is met by accountants working under the guidance of an extensive literature of professional pronouncements and scholarly writing.

Accounting Measurements

Accounting measurements are responsive to both general theories and specific principles. At one level, accounting theory describes and organizes the basic concepts to be used in accounting measurements. At another level, however, specific measurement principles are developed for different types of transactions. Advances in business and information technology coupled with the development of new financial markets have produced a vast array of new, complex business transactions. These transactions reflect the diversity of different industries, regions, or countries. The complexity and diversity of transactions executed by modern businesses require that careful attention be given to both the substance and form of transactions in order to meaningfully capture their impacts on the financial statements. In an environment of new and developing transaction forms, measurement principles tied to the specific transaction can produce misleading results; thus, the accountant must be aware of the theories and concepts that describe more general reporting objectives.

Accounting Presentation and Disclosure

Accounting measurements are numbers that should be viewed as estimates of aggregated economic phenomena. Accounting must enable the users of financial statements to understand the uncertainty associated with these estimates and the nature of the underlying estimation process. Accountants in the United States have a well-developed literature that provides guidance on presentations and disclosures to accomplish this objective. This guidance is documented in the publications of accounting experts and both private-sector standard-setting bodies (like the FASB and the American Institute of Certified Public Accountants, or AICPA) and public-sector regulatory agencies (like the Securities and Exchange Commission, or SEC). We turn now to a useful way to view the literature that guides measurement, presentation, and disclosure of financial information.

THE HIERARCHY OF GAAP

A "hierarchy of generally accepted accounting principles (GAAP)" has been constructed to identify the sources of guidance on accounting measurements, presentation, and disclosure and to show the relative authoritativeness of the different sources of guidance. The current hierarchy was promulgated in 1991 by the Auditing Standards Board of the AICPA in *Statement of Auditing Standards (SAS) No. 69* to help auditors decide in issuing an audit opinion whether financial statements "present fairly in accordance with generally accepted accounting principles." Auditors' need for such a hierarchy is also supported by the AICPA's ethics rules[1] and by court decisions that have applied these rules to accountants. Finally, and most important for our purposes, the Auditing Standards Board hierarchy of GAAP is recognized by both the FASB and the Government Accounting Standards Board (GASB) as the appropriate way to apply their pronouncements. Thus, it provides a framework for professional accounting research.

Framework of the Hierarchy

SAS No. 69 establishes a five-part hierarchy (par. 5; *Codification of Statements on Auditing Standards,* sec. AU411):

> A. Standards issued by the body designated by the AICPA Council for that type of entity: (1) business and nonprofit enterprises and (2) state and local governments and governmental bodies.
>
> B. Pronouncements issued by other bodies of expert accountants following a due process[2] and cleared[3] by the appropriate body designated by the AICPA Council.

---

[1] Rule 203, "Accounting Principles," of the *AICPA Code of Professional Conduct* states: "A member shall not (1) express an opinion or state affirmatively that the financial statements or other financial data of any entity are presented in conformity with generally accepted accounting principles or (2) state that he or she is not aware of any material modifications that should be made to such statements or data in order for them to be in conformity with generally accepted accounting principles, if such statements or data contain any departure from an accounting principle promulgated by bodies designated by Council to establish such principles that has a material effect on the statements or data taken as a whole. If, however, the statements or data contain such a departure and the member can demonstrate that due to unusual circumstances the financial statements or data would otherwise have been misleading, the member can comply with the rule by describing the departure, its approximate effects, if practicable, and the reason why compliance with the principle would result in a misleading statement."

[2] *Due process* means that the body of expert accountants issues an exposure draft for public comment prior to issuing a final standard and that public comments are considered in the determination of the final standard.

[3] *Cleared* means that the body designated by the AICPA Council has issued a letter saying that it does not object to the issuance of the pronouncement. In some cases, this is implicit, such as pronouncements of the FASB staff (Technical Bulletins) and the Emerging Issues Task Force.

C. Pronouncements issued by other bodies of expert accountants who do not follow due process but which have been cleared by the appropriate body designated by the AICPA Council.

D. Practices or pronouncements which are widely recognized as being generally accepted because they represent prevalent practice in an industry (usually referred to as "industry practice") or the knowledgeable application to specific circumstances (pronouncements of other bodies of expert accountants not cleared by the body designated by the AICPA Council).

E. Other writings by expert accountants.

Technically, only categories A through D are covered by Rule 203 of the *AICPA Code of Professional Conduct.* The last category, E, is allowed for situations not covered by a pronouncement by a body of expert accountants or a prevalent industry practice, such as instances of new types of business operations or transactions.

SAS No. 69 establishes a preference ordering among accounting pronouncements. Accountants and auditors are required to prefer a pronouncement at the highest level at which a pronouncement exists when determining what constitutes GAAP.[4] Thus, an accountant or auditor must be able to justify a client's financial reporting practices by reference to the highest level pronouncement concerning that area of practice. Individual accountants have the right to determine that an alternative measurement, presentation, or disclosure is preferable; however, such a determination requires a modification of their audit opinion or accountant's report and special disclosure of the preferability determination, which is referred to as a "Rule 203 exception."

Parallel Hierarchies for Private and Public Sectors

Accounting practices and principles in the private and public sectors have developed separately and exhibit significant differences. Further, accounting systems serve somewhat different objectives in the private and public sectors. Thus, the regulatory pronouncements that meet the requirements of *SAS No. 69* for inclusion in the hierarchy are stated separately for private-sector entities (business enterprises and nonprofit organizations) and public-sector entities (state and local governments).

The hierarchy of pronouncements for business enterprises and nonprofit organizations is described in Exhibit 11-1 on the following page. Documents issued by agencies other than the FASB must be submitted to the FASB for review and "cleared," that is, given informal approval. FASB pronouncements are issued as the *Codification of Accounting Standards,* which contains references to the pronouncements of other organizations. Abstracts of Emerging Issues Task Force (EITF) consensus positions are also indexed and published by the FASB. Accounting Standards Executive Committee (AcSEC) and other AICPA pronouncements are published separately by the AICPA.

The pronouncements of regulatory agencies that meet the requirements of *SAS No. 69* for inclusion in the hierarchy for state and local governments and governmental organizations are described in Exhibit 11-2 on page 557. A codification of GASB pronouncements, *Codification of Governmental Accounting and Financial Reporting Standards,* is published by the GASB with references to the pronouncements of other organizations. The pronouncements are discussed in Chapters 17, 18, and 19.

---

[4] This requirement for using the pronouncement in the highest category in *SAS No. 69* differs dramatically from the requirement which existed prior to the issuance of *SAS No. 69.* Previously, an accountant was required to consider such preferability only when an enterprise changed accounting principles and a preferability judgment was required under *APB Opinion No. 20.*

EXHIBIT 11-1	HIERARCHY OF GENERALLY ACCEPTED ACCOUNTING PRINCIPLES FOR BUSINESS ENTERPRISES AND NONPROFIT ORGANIZATIONS

Category	Pronouncements Included
A	FASB Statements and Interpretations APB Opinions AICPA Accounting Research Bulletins
B	FASB Technical Bulletins* Cleared AICPA Industry Audit and Accounting Guides** Cleared AICPA (AcSEC) Statements of Position
C	FASB EITF consensus positions Cleared AICPA (AcSEC) Practice Bulletins
D	AICPA Accounting Interpretations (to APB Opinions) FASB "Question and Answer" publications* Industry practices widely recognized and prevalent Noncleared pronouncements from categories B and C
E	FASB Concepts Statements APB Statements AICPA Issues Papers International Accounting Standards Committee Statements GASB pronouncements Pronouncements of other associations and regulatory agencies AICPA Technical Practice Aids Accounting textbooks, handbooks, and articles

* Issued by the FASB staff, not the FASB.

** Usually issued jointly by the Auditing Standards Board, the Accounting Standards Executive Committee (AcSEC), and the particular industry committee of the AICPA.

IMPACT OF REGULATORY AGENCIES

Various federal and state regulatory agencies have influenced the development of GAAP and the format and amount of the disclosure—especially in special industries. In some instances, the accounting prescribed by these regulators has been so different from the conceptual basis of GAAP that enterprises in these industries prepare two sets of financial statements—one conforming to GAAP and one following regulatory accounting principles (RAP). Let us consider three important examples of regulatory domains that interact with the accounting profession: banking, securities, and insurance.

Banking Regulators and the Call Report

Regulatory agencies invariably determine the timing and distribution of financial information of enterprises subject to their regulation. For example, banking regulators (the Office of the Comptroller of the Currency for national banks, the Federal Reserve System for state member banks, and the state banking commissions for nonmember state banks) require the issuance of quarterly call reports (a type of abbreviated balance sheet showing types of assets, types of deposits and other liabilities, and capital accounts) and require their publication in newspapers in areas served by the banking institution.

EXHIBIT 11-2	**HIERARCHY OF GENERALLY ACCEPTED ACCOUNTING PRINCIPLES FOR STATE AND LOCAL GOVERNMENTS AND GOVERNMENT ORGANIZATIONS**

Category	Pronouncements Included
A	GASB Statements and Interpretations AICPA* and FASB pronouncements if specifically made applicable to state and local governments by the GASB**
B	GASB Technical Bulletins AICPA Industry Audit and Accounting Guides and AICPA (AcSEC) Statements of Position if specifically made applicable to state and local governments by the AICPA
C	GASB EITF consensus positions# AICPA (AcSEC) Practice Bulletins specifically made applicable to state and local governments by the AICPA
D	GASB ''Questions and Answers'' Industry practices widely recognized and prevalent
E	GASB Concepts Statements Pronouncements in categories A, B, C, and D of the business and nonprofit hierarchy when not specifically made applicable to state and local governments APB Statements FASB Concepts Statements AICPA Issues Papers International Accounting Standards Committee Statements Pronouncements of other professional associations and regulatory agencies AICPA Technical Practice Aids Accounting textbooks, handbooks, and articles

* This includes APB Opinions and AICPA Accounting Research Bulletins.

** This change was made in *SAS No. 69* to remove the need for ''negative pronouncements'' by the GASB (pronouncements exempting state and local governments from an FASB Statement), which was required by the former hierarchy.

No GASB EITF exists at present.

Banking regulators are concerned with the appropriateness of transactions undertaken by banks, the maintenance of capital adequacy, and (in some instances) the insurance of bank deposits. On occasion, different regulatory objectives produce conflicting operating requirements. For example, the need for income to maintain capital may conflict with the need for uncertainty reduction in future returns to reduce the costs of insurance. In a misguided effort to resolve such conflicts with accounting rules, banking regulators have sometimes fostered accounting principles designed to give the illusion of capital adequacy or, more precisely, have allowed bank management to undertake transactions which were then accounted for in a way that masked their impact on capital. Nonearning assets (loans not earning interest but on which the loss of implied interest is not recorded), loan splitting (dividing one loan into a nonearning asset and an earning asset), and cherry picking (selling investments whose market value is above cost to record gains but holding investments whose market value is below cost without recording the loss in value) are examples of transactions for which special accounting practices have been fostered by bank regulators.

Securities and Exchange Commission

The Securities and Exchange Commission (SEC), an independent regulatory agency of the federal government, was established to administer the federal securities laws. The federal securities laws require filings of both financial statements and nonfinancial information (1) when companies wish to issue securities to the public (termed a *public offering* or *registration of securities*) and (2) when securities are traded on stock exchanges or over the counter after securities are registered (termed *publicly traded*).

The SEC filings are of two types: (1) filings to register securities under the Securities Act of 1933, and (2) periodic filings under the Securities Exchange Act of 1934. In addition, the SEC regulates information in annual reports to stockholders and proxy statements, the latter being information sent by corporations to obtain the votes of stockholders.

Each form to be filed with the SEC specifies both the financial statement information and the nonfinancial information to be reported. Filings by U.S. companies to register securities are made using Forms S-1 to S-16, although not all numbers are used.[5] Periodic filings are made annually (Form 10-K), quarterly for the first three quarters (Form 10-Q), and soon after certain events occur (Form 8-K), such as a business combination or change in independent accountants.

The SEC has the authority under the federal securities laws to establish accounting standards. The SEC has rarely exercised that authority, having adopted the position that private-sector standard setting was a preferable way of establishing accounting standards (*Accounting Series Release (ASR) No. 4,* ''Administrative Policy on Financial Statements,'' April 1938). In *ASR No. 150,* ''Statement of Policy as to the Establishment and Improvement of Accounting Principles and Standards'' (December 1973), the SEC reaffirmed the policy in *ASR No. 4* and formally acknowledged the FASB.

The SEC has developed its own presentation and disclosure rules relating to the content and form of financial statements *(Regulation S-X)* and to the type and content of nonfinancial statement information *(Regulation S-K)* to be contained in registration filings, periodic filings, annual reports, and proxy statements. Furthermore, the SEC staff often interprets GAAP when it issues Staff Accounting Bulletins (SABs). The SEC also interprets its own rules through Financial Reporting Releases (FRRs) and requires specific additional disclosures for industries like banking, real estate, and insurance, which are described in a series of Industry Guides.

The nonfinancial statement information required by the SEC to accompany the financial statement information is extremely detailed. For example, the ''Management Discussion and Analysis'' section for filings and annual reports requires registrant enterprises to discuss liquidity, capital resources, results of operations, and other information necessary to an understanding of a registrant's financial condition, changes in financial condition,

---

[5] Foreign private registrants and smaller U.S. registrants (maximum $25,000,000 in sales and market value of securities) use other forms which are not discussed here for both registration of securities and continuous reporting.

and results of operations [*Regulation S-K,* Item 303(a); see also *FRR No. 36*]. Another example is the ''Executive Compensation'' section of the proxy statement that requires registrant enterprises to disclose compensation of its executive managers (*Regulation S-K,* Item 402).

The types of forms and the relationship of SEC regulations and other guidance are shown in Exhibit 11-3. The information to be included on a form is specified by the instructions that accompany the form. As shown in Exhibit 11-3, filings on 1933 Act forms are *transactional,* that is, required each time securities are to be publicly offered or registered. The filings on 1934 Act forms are *continuous,* that is, required periodically as long as publicly traded securities are outstanding. The exhibit also indicates that Regulation S-X and Regulation S-K—together with the related Industry Guides, FRRs, and SABs—determine the form and content of the information included.

Form 10-K

Form 10-K is an extensive document on which registrants report annually to the SEC. It contains four parts requiring the following 14 items of information:

Part I

1. Description of the business
2. Description of properties (principal plants, buildings, natural resource deposits, etc.)

EXHIBIT 11-3	THE SEC INTEGRATED DISCLOSURE SYSTEM

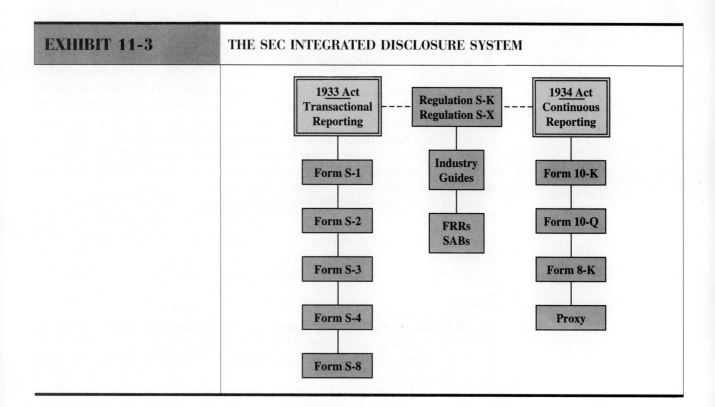

3. Description of legal proceedings in which the company is involved

4. Description of matters submitted to a vote of stockholders

Part II

5. Market price of common stock, dividends, and other matters related to stockholders

6. Selected financial data (five-year summary of annual operating revenues, total and per-share income or loss from continuing operations, total assets, long-term debt, and cash dividends per share)

7. Management's discussion and analysis of financial condition and results of operations (typically includes discussion of liquidity, funding and acquisition of assets, trends and unusual events affecting operations)

8. Financial statements and supplementary data (from the registrant's annual report to stockholders)

9. Changes in and disagreements with accountants on accounting and financial disclosure

Part III

10. List of directors and executive officers of the registrant

11. Description of executive compensation and transactions with executives

12. Security ownership of certain beneficial owners and management

13. Certain relationships and related transactions

Part IV

14. Various exhibits, financial statement schedules, and reports on Form 8-K which disclose changes in firm policies or financial condition

The SEC requires the financial statements and supplementary data in item (8) to conform with *Regulation S-X*. In most cases, the financial statements and notes presented in the annual report to stockholders meet this requirement and are simply "incorporated by reference" into Form 10-K. This is a consequence of the SEC efforts to construct an "integrated disclosure system" that homogenizes the financial report requirements of both the 1933 and 1934 acts and brings annual report information and disclosures into line with SEC requirements.

Form 10-Q

Form 10-Q is required for quarterly reporting to the SEC in the first three quarters of each year. Although 10-Q follows generally accepted accounting principles, it presents unaudited information and is much less extensive than the annual reporting on Form 10-K.

Other Forms

Form 8-K, the "current report," is required to report significant changes in a firm's policies or financial position within a few days of their occurrence. Proxy solicitations, which must include virtually the same financial information included in the annual report, must be filed with the SEC.

    The 1933 Act form provides for the registration of securities under different circumstances. Form S-1 is the most commonly used; it can be used whenever no other form is prescribed except that it cannot be used by foreign governments. Forms S-2 and S-3 provide a short-form registration for issuers meeting specified requirements. Form S-4 is used for securities issued in connection with business combinations. Form S-8 is used for securities issued to employees under certain circumstances including stock options. Many other forms are defined and available to issuers of securities, but this list is sufficient to indicate their general character. The choice of an appropriate form under the 1933 Act is a decision requiring expert legal and financial advice.

Insurance and Utility Regulators

Insurance and utility regulators establish the rates that can be charged for services in the industries they regulate. They use financial statements to ensure that the regulated industries charge fairly for those services within the parameters established by the enabling legislation. Insurance regulators also ensure that insurance companies can meet their commitments.

Insurance and utility regulators have developed accounting rules that must be followed in reports filed by regulated companies. Such reports are frequently so different from those prepared under GAAP that regulated companies effectively have two conceptually distinct sets of financial statements. Even if multiple financial statements are prepared, the regulatory statements may influence the GAAP statements. For example, the method of revenue determination in such regulated companies may influence the accounting for some financial statement items under GAAP.

THE RESEARCH PROCESS

The research process involves two activities: (1) searches for guidance on situations already covered by the pronouncements and (2) searches for analogous situations when guidance does not exist within the GAAP hierarchy. Since the latter situation is not always known when the research process begins, research on accounting principles should begin with a search for guidance on situations already covered by pronouncements.

Terminology and Research

Individuals researching accounting principles will need to understand several different uses of terminology that have developed in accounting:

1. The word *should* when encountered in accounting pronouncements means that the accounting specified in the pronouncement is required.

2. The word *encouraged* when encountered in accounting pronouncements means that the accounting is recommended but not required.

3. When more than one method of accounting is specified as required in an accounting pronouncement, the two or more methods are termed *allowed alternatives* and any one can be used in the financial statements. *APB Opinion No. 22* requires that the method used be disclosed in the Summary of Significant Accounting Policies.[6]

4. When an enterprise ''changes'' from one allowed alternative method to another, the accountant is required to make a preferability judgment in accordance with *APB Opinion No. 20*. If the accountant does not make such a judgment, then the financial statements do not conform to GAAP.

---

[6] *FASB Interpretation No. 40*, ''Applicability of Generally Accepted Accounting Principles to Mutual Life Insurance Companies and Other Enterprises'' (April 1993), notes the requirement to disclose when exempted and when one or more specialized industry practices are used.

Standards and Interpretative Guidance

The expanding number of accounting pronouncements can be divided into two classes: standards and interpretative guidance. The hierarchy of GAAP in *SAS No. 69* recognizes this difference in that standards always have higher status than interpretative guidance in the GAAP hierarchy. For example, the standard for pension accounting *(FASB Statement No. 87)* is further interpreted in *A Guide to Implementation of SFAS No. 87 on Employers' Accounting for Pensions: Questions and Answers* (FASB Special Report, 1986). Thus, while searches for guidance on situations already covered by pronouncements will start at the highest level of the GAAP hierarchy, additional research will be necessary at lower levels to see if interpretative guidance exists at that level.

Iteration and Consultation

Researching accounting principles requires careful attention to each suggested solution from every stage of the research. Especially in complex transactions, two or more answers may seem appropriate depending upon a specific judgment made during the research. In effect, researching accounting principles requires developing a preliminary solution, researching additional pronouncements based on the preliminary solution, and repeating this process.

Accounting practice does not require an individual accountant to research accounting principles without assistance. *AICPA Statement of Quality Control Standards (SQCS) No. 1* provides for consultation as an integral part of accounting practice. Consultation as used in *SQCS No. 1* means that the accountant should develop his or her solution to the measurement, presentation, and disclosure issues and then consult with other knowledgeable accountants concerning the adequacy of that solution. *SQCS No. 1* requires that the results of the consultation process concerning accounting measurements, presentations, and disclosures should be documented.

This research process, integrated with adequate consultation,[7] allows accountants to prepare financial statements in accordance with generally accepted accounting principles.

A RESEARCH EXAMPLE

An example of the research process will be illustrated using Ark Milling Company in Exhibit 11-4. The research process should start with a careful reading of *APB Opinion No. 16* since it is a level-A pronouncement covering business combinations. The researcher should conclude that two different purchase price allocation schedules can be prepared for this purchase business combination from the Noah Milling Company consolidated financial statements, which are shown below and at the top of page 564.

Purchase Price Allocation Schedule I

Purchase price		$3,000,000
Purchased equity:		
Common stock	$ 100,000	
Retained earnings	1,300,000	(1,400,000)
Valuation differential		$1,600,000
Revaluation increment:		
Milling assets	$ 500,000	
Trucking assets	100,000	(600,000)
Goodwill		$1,000,000

---

[7] While SQCS No. 1 applies to public accounting firms, research and consultation are also applicable to an enterprise's accountants engaged in the preparation of financial statements.

EXHIBIT 11-4	A RESEARCH PROBLEM: ARK MILLING COMPANY

Ark Milling Company, which owned over 50 corn milling operations, acquired Noah Milling Company in a business combination accounted for as a purchase. Ark Milling had borrowed $3,000,000 from a local bank at an 8% rate of interest payable over ten years in equal payments of principal to acquire all of the common stock of Noah Milling Company. Prepayments will be allowed at any time. Noah Milling Company owned six corn milling operations and had a wholly owned subsidiary, Pullman & Harris Trucking Corporation, engaged in transporting cotton from Arkansas farms to cotton ginning locations. Ark Milling Company had decided that it did not intend to operate the Pullman & Harris Trucking Corporation; the trucking operation would be sold as soon as possible immediately after the business combination was completed. The consolidation worksheet of Noah Milling Company at the date of the acquisition of Noah by Ark is shown below:

Noah Milling Company

CONSOLIDATION WORKSHEET
NOVEMBER 16, 19X3
(AMOUNTS IN THOUSANDS)

	Noah Milling	Pullman & Harris Trucking	Worksheet Adjustments Dr. (Cr.)	Consolidated
Assets				
Millings assets	1,500			1,500
Trucking assets		1,500		1,500
Investment in Pullman & Harris	500		(500)	–0–
Total assets	2,000	1,500		3,000
Liabilities and Stockholders' Equity				
Liabilities	600	1,000		1,600
Common stock	100	100	100	100
Retained earnings	1,300	400	400	1,300
Total stockholders' equity	1,400	500		1,400
Total liabilities and stockholders' equity	2,000	1,500		3,000

An independent appraisal company hired by Ark Milling Company had estimated that the milling assets had a fair market value of $2,000,000 and that the trucking assets had a fair market value of $1,600,000. The independent appraisal company also estimated that the Pullman & Harris Trucking Corporation could be sold as a going operation for $1,000,000 approximately six months after completion of the business combination.

The chief financial officer of Ark Milling is uncertain how to account for the purchase business combination because the transaction includes the purchase of the operations of Noah Milling with an anticipated sale of the Pullman & Harris Trucking Corporation. Furthermore, the business combination was completed on November 30 and the chief financial officer is concerned how the operations of Pullman & Harris should be presented in the December 31 annual financial statements, which will have to be prepared prior to the anticipated sale date. Ark Milling intends to use the proceeds from the sale of Pullman & Harris Trucking to reduce the $3,000,000 in bank debt taken on to finance the purchase of Noah Milling.

Purchase Price Allocation Schedule II

Purchase price		$3,000,000
Purchased equity:		
Common stock	$ 100,000	
Retained earnings	1,300,000	(1,400,000)
Valuation differential		$1,600,000
Revaluation increment:		
Milling assets	$ 500,000	
Estimated receivable*	500,000	(1,000,000)
Goodwill		$ 600,000

* Investment in subsidiary ($500,000) becomes an estimated receivable ($1,000,000) from sale of Pullman & Harris Trucking.

However, even the second schedule does not capture the entire situation because the estimated receivable from the sale of the trucking operation would be stated at $1,000,000, the estimated proceeds six months after the date of acquisition. Stating the receivable at $1,000,000 would violate *APB Opinion No. 21* on the valuation of receivables. Furthermore, some amount of the debt was undertaken to temporarily hold Pullman & Harris during the time that it took to sell the subsidiary of Noah Milling. Further research should lead to *EITF Issue 87-11,* which addresses these issues; this EITF consensus provides that the estimated cash flows from the subsidiary, the interest expense on the debt used to carry the subsidiary during the time until sale, and the proceeds from the sale should not affect earnings of the unconsolidated subsidiary except when events occur after the purchase date. Thus, the estimated receivable would be recorded at $1,000,000 less the amount of the interest on the debt, which would be added to the amount of the receivable over the six-month period such that there should be no gain or loss at the anticipated time of sale. The allocation of the purchase price, assuming no cash flows are expected from Pullman & Harris Trucking Corporation by the acquiring company in the six-month period, would be:

Purchase Price Allocation Schedule III

Purchase price		$3,000,000
Purchased equity:		
Common stock	$ 100,000	
Retained earnings	1,300,000	(1,400,000)
Valuation differential		$1,600,000
Revaluation increment:		
Milling assets	$ 500,000	
Estimated receivable*	460,000	(960,000)
Goodwill		$ 640,000

* Investment in subsidiary ($500,000) becomes net assets held for sale composed of the estimated amount to be received ($1,000,000) from sale of Pullman & Harris Trucking less the amount of interest, $40,000 (8% × 1/2 × $1,000,000), which will be added to the estimated receivable over the six-month period.

Following the provisions of *EITF Issue 87-11,* any income of Pullman & Harris subsequent to the date of the business combination would not affect the consolidated net income of Ark Milling Company and Consolidated Subsidiaries except in very special circumstances, since the consensus would also require reallocation of the purchase price if the sales proceeds differed from the amount of the net assets held for sale (the amount would increase or decrease goodwill).

SUMMARY

The literature of accounting pronouncements is sufficiently large and volatile so that, to be effective, even experts must specialize in industry or transactions segments of accounting practice. The best way to develop a facility for working with this literature is to research some specific accounting questions. Opportunities for such research are provided at the end of this chapter. These assignments require you to visit your reference library and search the pronouncements. Most require you to identify alternative measurements, presentations, or disclosures; to document authoritative support; to recommend a most preferred alternative for the case at hand; and to justify that recommendation.

SELECTED READINGS

Accountants SEC Practice Manual. Chicago: Commerce Clearing House, regularly updated.

American Institute of Certified Public Accountants. *International Accounting and Auditing Standards.* Chicago: Commerce Clearing House, regularly updated.

Auditing Standards Board. *Codification of Statements on Auditing Standards.* New York: American Institute of Certified Public Accountants, regularly updated.

Craig, James L., Jr. ''The AICPA Accounting Standards Executive Committee: An interview with Chairman Norman Strauss,'' *The CPA Journal* (April 1993), pp. 44–50.

Financial Accounting Standards Board. *Accounting Standards: Original Pronouncements.* Norwalk, CT: Governmental Accounting Standards Board, regularly updated.

Financial Accounting Standards Board. *Accounting Standards: Statements of Financial Accounting Concepts.* Norwalk, CT: Financial Accounting Standards Board, updated as necessary.

Financial Accounting Standards Board. *Codification of Accounting Standards.* Norwalk, CT: Financial Accounting Standards Board, regularly updated (cited FASB Codification).

Financial Accounting Standards Board. *EITF Abstracts: A Summary of Proceedings of the FASB Emerging Issues Task Force.* Norwalk, CT: Financial Accounting Standards Board, regularly updated.

Governmental Accounting Standards Board. *Codification of Governmental Accounting and Financial Reporting Standards.* Norwalk, CT: Governmental Accounting Standards Board, regularly updated (cited GASB Codification).

Governmental Accounting Standards Board. *Governmental Accounting and Financial Reporting Standards: Original Pronouncements.* Norwalk, CT: Governmental Accounting Standards Board, regularly updated.

Magill, Harry T., and Gary John Previts. *CPA Professional Responsibilities.* Cincinnati, OH: South-Western, 1991.

Sauter, Douglas P. ''The New GAAP Hierarchy: Important Changes Affecting Audits, Reviews, and Compilations,'' *The CPA Journal* (January 1993), pp. 52–58.

SEC Compliance (loose-leaf service). Englewood Cliffs, NJ: Prentice-Hall, regularly updated.

Securities Regulations. Englewood Cliffs, NJ: Prentice-Hall, regularly updated.

Shohet, Jack, and Richard Rikert (eds.). *Accounting Trends and Techniques.* New York: American Institute of Certified Public Accountants, published annually.

Skousen, K. Fred. *An Introduction to the SEC,* 5th ed. Cincinnati, OH: South-Western, 1991.

Soldano, Joseph J., Jr. (ed.). *Local Government Accounting Trends and Techniques.* New York: American Institute of Certified Public Accountants, issued annually.

QUESTIONS

Q11-1 Why is research necessary in the practice of accounting?

Q11-2 Describe measurement, presentation, and disclosure as they relate to financial reporting.

Q11-3 What is the hierarchy of generally accepted accounting principles? How does it influence financial reporting?

Q11-4 Why does the hierarchy of generally accepted accounting principles consist of two parallel hierarchies?

Q11-5 What are the principal codifications of pronouncements listed in the two parts of the hierarchy of GAAP?

Q11-6 Identify three sources of regulatory influence on financial reporting.

Q11-7 Describe the two situations in which federal securities laws require financial reports to be filed with the Securities and Exchange Commission.

Q11-8 Discuss what is meant by ''Rule 203 exception.''

Q11-9 Banking regulators require banks to issue quarterly call reports. What are quarterly call reports and where are they required to be published?

Q11-10 Explain why you agree or disagree with the following statement: The SEC has the authority under the federal securities laws to establish accounting standards, and it consistently exercises that authority.

Q11-11 List some examples of nonfinancial statement information required by the SEC to accompany the financial statement information.

Q11-12 What is the purpose of the SEC's ''integrated disclosure system?''

Q11-13 Identify the fourteen items of information provided in Form 10-K filed with the SEC.

Q11-14 Describe the research process that one might follow in researching accounting principles.

EXERCISES

E11-1 **Terminology** Terms 1 through 11 are related to researching accounting principles.

REQUIRED

For each of the following terms, select the best phrase or description from the answers listed A through K below.

Terms	Descriptions

Terms

1. Call report
2. Disclsoure
3. Hierarchy of GAAP
4. Measurement
5. Naive users
6. Presentation
7. Proxy statement
8. Securities and Exchange Commission
9. Sophisticated users
10. Public offering
11. Publicly traded

Descriptions

A. The process of determining a quantitative amount that appears in the body of the financial statements.

B. Those who lack a reasonable understanding of business and economic matters or who lack the willingness to study the financial statements with due diligence.

C. An independent regulatory agency of the federal government established to administer the federal securities laws.

D. Information sent by corporations to stockholders to obtain the vote of stockholders.

E. The form of the information in the body of the financial statements.

F. Those who are reasonably informed about business and economic matters and are willing to study the financial statements with reasonable diligence.

G. A type of abbreviated balance sheet for a bank showing types of assets, types of deposits and other liabilities, and capital accounts.

H. The measurement and presentation of information beyond that appearing in the body of the financial statements.

I. A ranking of the different sources of guidance on accounting measurements, presentation, and disclosure that assist accountants and auditors in determining what constitutes GAAP.

J. The issuance of securities to the public.

K. The buying and selling of registered securities on stock exchanges or over-the-counter.

E11-2 **Analysis of Comments on Researching Accounting Principles** Indicate whether you agree or disagree with each of the following statements. If you disagree with a statement, provide an explanation as to why.

1. Quantitative amounts that appear in the body of the financial statements should be viewed as exact amounts and not estimates of aggregate economic phenomena.

2. When a pronouncement has been issued to guide practice in a particular area, that pronouncement must be followed, without exception, by the accountant or auditor in the client's financial reporting.

3. Banking regulators require banks to issue quarterly call reports and require their publication in newspapers in areas served by the bank.

4. The Securities and Exchange Commission is the primary rule-making body for the accounting profession in the private sector.

5. A publicly traded company would file Form 8-K with the SEC when certain events occur such as a change in independent accountants.

6. Insurance and utility regulators develop accounting rules to be followed in reports filed by regulated companies; however, such reports seldom, if ever, differ from those prepared under generally accepted accounting principles.

7. The word ''should'' when used in accounting pronouncements means that the accounting specified in the pronouncement is required.

8. When the accountant or auditor selects one method of accounting over an "allowed alternative," it is not necessary that the method used be disclosed.

9. The word "encouraged" when used in accounting pronouncements means that the accounting specified in the pronouncement is recommended but not required.

10. Research on accounting principles involves (1) searches for guidance on situations already covered by pronouncements and (2) searches for analogous situations when guidance does not exist. Since the latter is not always known when the research is undertaken, research on accounting principles should start with a search for guidance on situations already covered by pronouncements.

E11-3 **The SEC** The U.S. Securities and Exchange Commission (SEC) was created in 1934. The primary objective of the SEC is to support fair securities markets. The SEC also strives to foster enlightened shareholder participation in corporate decisions of publicly traded companies. The SEC has a significant presence in financial markets, the development of accounting practices, and corporation-shareholder relations, and has the power to exert influence on entities whose actions lie within the scope of its authority.

REQUIRED

a) Explain where the Securities and Exchange Commission receives its authority.

b) Describe the official role of the Securities and Exchange Commission in the development of financial accounting theory and practices.

c) Discuss the interrelationship between the Securities and Exchange Commission and the Financial Accounting Standards Board with respect to the development and establishment of financial accounting theory and practices.

(CMA adapted)

PROBLEMS

P11-1 **Securities and Exchange Commission** The Securities and Exchange Commission, an independent regulatory agency of the federal government, was established to administer the federal securities laws.

REQUIRED

a) Distinguish between when a company would file with the SEC under the Securities Act of 1933 and when it would file under the Securities and Exchange Act of 1934.

b) Briefly describe the following types of filings associated with the Securities Act of 1933.

  1. Form S-1

  2. Form S-2

  3. Form S-3

  4. Form S-4

  5. Form S-8

c) Briefly describe the following types of filings associated with the Securities and Exchange Act of 1934.

  1. Form 10-K

  2. Form 10-Q

  3. Form 8-K

  4. Proxy

d) Filings on 1933 Act forms are considered transactional, whereas filings on 1934 Act forms are considered continuous. What is meant by the terms transactional and continuous?

e) The form and content of information filed by companies with the SEC under the Securities Act of 1933 and the Securities and Exchange Act of 1934, are determined by the items listed below. Briefly describe the contents of each of the items.

1. Regulation S-X
2. Regulation S-K
3. Financial Reporting Releases
4. Staff Accounting Bulletins
5. Industry Guides

P11-2 **Measurement of Building Value in a Business Combination** Thomas Corporation had purchased 60% of the voting common equity of Timothy Corporation for $1,000,000 on July 1, 19X1, when Timothy Corporation had a book value of stockholders' equity of $900,000. The building housing the retail facility had a net book value of $250,000, and a real estate appraiser had estimated its fair value at $750,000 a month before the purchase. Book value approximated fair value for all other assets. Thomas believed that any goodwill in the purchase of Timothy would have a life of 20 years. On the day after the purchase took place, the architectural firm hired by Timothy Corporation to make the renovations required to handle ''Thomas'' brand merchandise due to the new relationship found that the building had an asbestos problem. The architectural firm's engineer estimated that it would cost an additional $300,000 to take care of the asbestos problem in the building.

REQUIRED
How should Thomas Corporation allocate the valuation differential for this purchase business combination? What is the source of GAAP for the allocation?

P11-3 **Determination of Pooling of Interests or Purchase Business Combination in Accounting for a Merger** DL Corporation and ER Corporation agreed to merge and wished to account for the merger as a pooling of interests. DL Corporation would be the parent company and would exchange 1.2 shares of its common stock for each share of ER Corporation. This ratio was the ratio of market values of the common shares on the date that the agreement was reached. Edward Roberts, the largest shareholder in ER Corporation, held 22% of the voting common shares. Edward Roberts read the pooling rules and agreed to exchange 14% of the voting common shares of ER Corporation. All other shareholders of ER Corporation agreed to exchange their shares. Would the fact that Edward Roberts continues to own 8% of the common shares of ER Corporation as a minority shareholder violate one of the conditions for a pooling of interests and require accounting for this merger as a purchase business combination? All other conditions for a pooling of interests have been met.

P11-4 **Disclosure for Annual Financial Statement When a Company Is under the Protection of the Bankruptcy Court (Chapter 11)** Using the information in Problem 10-10, prepare the note disclosure for the December 31, 19X1, financial statements. What is the source of the required disclosure?

P11-5 **Presentation of Gain When Emerging from Chapter 11 Bankruptcy** Geauga Stores, Inc., had emerged from bankruptcy on December 1, 19X3. The Bankruptcy Court for the Northern District of Illinois had confirmed (1) that all postpetition liabilities would be paid in cash, (2) that all secured liabilities would continue at their face amount with interest to the date of bankruptcy being paid in cash, (3) that no changes in common stock ownership would occur, and (4) that the $3,000,000 in unsecured allowed claims would receive the right to 50% of net income for the next ten years to a maximum of $3,000,000. Based on the projections for the disclosure statement prepared by the investment banking firm of McHardie & Eaton, the present value of the current estimates of net income was $1,000,000. Geauga Stores, Inc., therefore, recorded the following entry in its books on 12-1-X3:

Unsecured liabilities	2,000,000	
Estimated reduction in liabilities from approval of petition by the bankruptcy court		2,000,000

REQUIRED

a) How should the $2,000,000 estimated reduction in liabilities from approval of the petition by the bankruptcy court be presented in the income statement of Geauga Stores, Inc.? What is the source of the appropriate GAAP?

b) How should Geauga Stores, Inc., present any change in its estimate in the income statement due to earning being higher than projected in fiscal year 19X5? What is the source of the appropriate GAAP?

P11-6   **Determination of Gain or Loss by Selling Shareholder in LBO Transaction**   Tucker Corporation received $4,000,000 in cash, $2,000,000 in par value of 8%, 20-year debentures, and $1,000,000 in par value of 4%, 20-year convertible subordinated debentures from Aurora Acquisition, Inc., in exchange for all of Tucker Corporation's common shares of Aurora Manufacturing, Inc. The exchange took place on July 1, 19X1. Prior to this exchange, Aurora Manufacturing, Inc., had been a wholly owned subsidiary of Tucker Corporation. Aurora Acquisition, Inc., was a new corporation formed by managers and investment banking partnerships to carry out a leveraged buyout of Aurora Manufacturing, Inc. The forecast of cash flow and income for the next five years prepared by the investment bankers indicated that excess cash flow will be low and that net losses will occur unless cost savings can be implemented. Primarily this is due to the amount of interest payments and expense which Aurora Manufacturing will have to pay. The Investment in Aurora Manufacturing account on the books of Tucker Corporation had a balance of $6,500,000 on July 1, 19X1, before the exchange. Tucker Corporation common stock and preferred stock trades on the New York Stock Exchange.

REQUIRED

What amount of gain from sale of the investment in Aurora Manufacturing, Inc., can Tucker Corporation recognize on July 1, 19X1? How should this be presented on the income statement? What are the sources of GAAP?

P11-7   **Disclosure for a Purchase Business Combination: Partially Owned Subsidiary, Valuation Differential, Interim Acquisition**   On May 1, 19X2, Company P acquired a 75% interest in Company S for $35,250. Financial statements for both companies for the 12-month period ending December 31, 19X2, are as follows:

	Company P	Company S
Income Statement		
Sales	$ 88,000	$44,000
Income from subsidiary	5,000	
Cost of goods sold	(30,000)	(22,000)
Operating expenses	(20,000)	(10,000)
Net income	$ 43,000	$12,000
Statement of Retained Earnings		
Retained earnings, 1-1-X2	$ 32,000	$16,000
Net income	43,000	12,000
Dividends	(8,000)	(4,000)
Retained earnings, 12-31-X2	$ 67,000	$24,000
Balance Sheet		
Assets		
Cash	$ 19,000	$ 7,000
Accounts receivable	12,000	4,000
Inventory	24,000	4,000
Investment in Company S	38,000	
Plant and equipment (net)	84,000	34,000
Total assets	$177,000	$49,000
Liabilities and Stockholders' Equity		
Accounts payable	$ 11,000	$ 5,000
Common stock	99,000	20,000
Retained earnings	67,000	24,000
Total liabilities and stockholders' equity	$177,000	$49,000

Additional information:

1. Both companies paid their respective dividends in equal amounts each quarter.

2. Income of the subsidiary is earned at a constant rate throughout the year.

Company P prepared the following schedule showing the analysis of the valuation differential:

Company P
SCHEDULE OF VALUATION DIFFERENTIAL
PURCHASE OF 75% INTEREST IN COMPANY S
MAY 1, 19X2

Acquisition cost		$35,250
Less: Book value of net assets acquired:		
Common stock (.75 × $20,000)	$15,000	
Retained earnings 1-1-X2 (.75 × $16,000)	12,000	
Income from January 1–April 30 (.75 × $4,000)	3,000	
Less: Dividends paid 3-31-X2 (.75 × $1,000)	(750)	29,250
Valuation differential		$ 6,000
Less: Revaluation increment		–0–
Goodwill		$ 6,000

Company P had also prepared the consolidated worksheet for the year ended December 31, 19X2, as follows:

Company P and Subsidiary
CONSOLIDATION WORKSHEET
FOR THE YEAR ENDED DECEMBER 31, 19X2

	Separate Financial Statements		Consolidation Adjustments		Minority Interest	Consolidated Financial Statements
	P	S	Dr.	Cr.		
Income Statement						
Sales	88,000	44,000				132,000
Income from subsidiary	5,000		(1) 5,000			
Cost of goods sold	(30,000)	(22,000)				(52,000)
Operating expenses	(20,000)	(10,000)	(3) 1,000			(31,000)
Purchased preacquisition subsidiary income			(2) 3,000			(3,000)
Minority interest .25($12,000)					3,000	(3,000)
Net income	43,000	12,000	9,000	–0–	3,000	43,000
Statement of Retained Earnings						
Retained earnings, 1-1-X2:						
Company P	32,000					32,000
Company S		16,000	(2) 12,000		4,000	
Net income	43,000	12,000	9,000		3,000	43,000
Dividends	(8,000)	(4,000)		(1) 2,250		
				(2) 750	(1,000)	(8,000)
Retained earnings, 12-31-X2	67,000	24,000	21,000	3,000	6,000	67,000
Balance Sheet						
Cash	19,000	7,000				26,000
Accounts receivable	12,000	4,000				16,000
Inventory	24,000	4,000				28,000
Investment in S	38,000			(1) 2,750		
				(2) 35,250		
Plant and equipment (net)	84,000	34,000				118,000
Goodwill			(2) 6,000	(3) 1,000		5,000
Total assets	177,000	49,000				193,000
Accounts payable	11,000	5,000				16,000
Common stock:						
Company P, $1 par	99,000					99,000
Company S, $1 par		20,000	(2) 15,000		5,000	
Retained earnings	67,000	24,000	21,000	3,000	6,000	67,000
Minority interest					(11,000)	11,000
Total liabilities and stockholders' equity	177,000	49,000	42,000	42,000	–0–	193,000

Note: Parentheses indicate decreases.

Company P was engaged in the manufacture of shoemaking equipment with its principal location in Cleveland, Ohio. Company S was also manufacturing shoemaking equipment with its principal location in Fall River, Massachusetts. The common stock of Company P is traded in the over-the-counter market. Company S is a nonpublic company.

REQUIRED

Prepare any disclosures required to be included as notes to the consolidated financial statements for Company P and its consolidated subsidiary for the period ending December 31, 19X2.

ISSUES IN ACCOUNTING JUDGMENT

I11-1 **Explaining Different Accounting Practices** A staff accountant has been working on the financial statements of Oakmont Clinic, which is owned and operated by the City of Oakmont. The hospital establishes its cost of services for reimbursement by the City of Oakmont by determining a cost for the use of the building housing the clinic. This clinic serves the eastern portion of the city. A similar clinic run by a nonprofit corporation, Westside Clinic, Inc., serves the western portion of the city and receives a similar reimbursement from the city for services rendered. The staff accountant knows that Westside Clinic, Inc., reports depreciation on its statement of revenues and expenses. No depreciation was reported on the financial statement of the Oakmont Clinic for the previous year.

REQUIRED

Explain the difference in accounting practices.

I11-2 **Accounting for International Investment** Key Largo Entertainment Company received $1,000,000 from the Cascade Bank. The $1,000,000 was the U.S. dollar equivalent of Mexican pesos received from a group of Mexican investors. Key Largo Entertainment Company built an entertainment complex in Mexico. It sold the complex to a subsidiary of Mexententa, a Mexican corporation, named Mexententa Key Largo, SA. At the time of the sale of the complex, Key Largo Entertainment expensed all costs of the complex.

Mexententa Key Largo, SA, also obtained the right to use the Key Largo name. The Key Largo name had value because of its association with a famous motion picture, and the entertainment complex was designed to trade on that association. Key Largo Entertainment Company received 10% of the after-tax profits of Mexententa Key Largo, SA, the operator of the entertainment complex, for the use of the trade name, which Key Largo Entertainment used on three U.S. entertainment complexes.

Key Largo Entertainment agreed to give the Mexican investors 40% of the amounts received from Mexententa Key Largo, SA, for a period of ten years for the $1,000,000. The estimate by Key Largo Entertainment at the date of sale had been that the present value of 40% of the expected future receipts from Mexententa Key Largo, SA, was $1,000,000. Various executives had described the transaction as the sale of future revenues or as variable rate debt to be repaid from future amounts to be received from Mexententa Key Largo, SA.

REQUIRED

a) How should Key Largo Entertainment treat the amount received from the Mexican investors? Can it be treated as a sale? Should it be shown as a liability? Should it be treated as deferred income? If it is shown as a liability, what will be the impact of changing exchange rates?

b) Would your answer change if Key Largo Entertainment had to make a minimum payment? If there was a maximum amount that the Mexican investors could receive from Key Largo Entertainment?

PART TWO

Multinational Companies

12

Restatement of Foreign Financial Statements

FOREIGN CURRENCY RESTATEMENT 577

RESTATEMENT AND CONVERSION 577

CURRENCY EXCHANGE RATES 578

MEASUREMENT ISSUES IN FOREIGN STATEMENT RESTATEMENT 578

CONFORMITY WITH U.S. GENERALLY ACCEPTED ACCOUNTING PRINCIPLES 578

HISTORICAL RATE AND CURRENT RATE RESTATEMENT 579

Current Rate Restatement 579   Historical Rate Restatement 580

TREATMENT OF RESTATEMENT ADJUSTMENTS 581

THE FUNCTIONAL CURRENCY CONCEPT 582

TRANSLATION 584

TRANSLATION AT DATE OF ACQUISITION 584

TRANSLATION ONE YEAR AFTER ACQUISITION 585

Translation Procedures 586   Balancing-Figure Calculation of Translation Adjustment 587   Preparation of Subsidiary's Financial Statements 587

TRANSLATION TWO YEARS AFTER ACQUISITION 587

REMEASUREMENT 590

REMEASUREMENT PROCEDURES 593

Remeasurement of Cost of Goods Sold 596 Remeasurement of Plant and Equipment and Accumulated Depreciation 596   Remeasurement of Retained Earnings 598   Balancing-Figure Calculation of Remeasurement Gain 598

REMEASURED FINANCIAL STATEMENTS 598

TRANSLATION OF REMEASURED TRIAL BALANCES 599

INVENTORY REMEASUREMENT AND THE LOWER-OF-COST-OR-MARKET ADJUSTMENT 601

SUBSIDIARIES IN HIGHLY INFLATIONARY ECONOMIES 602

SUMMARY 603

APPENDIX A: EQUITY-METHOD AND CONSOLIDATION PROCEDURES FOR FOREIGN SUBSIDIARIES 603

APPENDIX B: COMPOSITION OF TRANSLATION ADJUSTMENT 616

Our economy is increasingly involved in international business transactions including investments in foreign entities as well as transactions with foreign buyers and sellers. When an investment by a domestic company in a foreign entity enables an investor to influence significantly the affairs of the foreign entity, then the investor must use the equity method to account for the investment. When an investment in a foreign entity enables the investor to control the affairs of the foreign entity, then the financial statements of the two entities should be consolidated. Neither the equity method nor consolidation procedures can proceed for an affiliated foreign entity until the financial statements of the foreign entity are restated in the reporting currency of the investor. For U.S. investors this usually means restating the financial statements of the foreign affiliate into U.S. dollars. The present chapter discusses restating the financial statements of foreign affiliates to permit use of the equity method and consolidation procedures.[1] The next chapter considers accounting for transactions with foreign buyers and sellers.

FOREIGN CURRENCY RESTATEMENT

Amounts reported in one currency cannot be combined with amounts reported in another currency unless one of the amounts is adjusted by a process called *restatement*.[2] A foreign currency amount is restated into another currency simply by multiplying the foreign currency amount by the appropriate currency exchange rate:

$$\begin{array}{ccc} \text{Restated} & & \text{Foreign} & & \text{Currency} \\ \text{currency} & = & \text{currency} & \times & \text{exchange} \\ \text{amount} & & \text{amount} & & \text{rate} \end{array}$$

For example, consider the Japanese subsidiary of a U.S. company that reports accounts receivable of 1,000,000 yen (abbreviated ¥) when the exchange rate for the yen is $.004945. In order to produce consolidated financial statements, the U.S. company would restate the receivable as $4,945 ($4,945 = $.004945 × ¥ 1,000,000). This would enable the U.S. company to combine the restated Japanese receivables with its own receivables on the consolidated balance sheet.

Restatement and Conversion

Conversions of foreign currency must be distinguished from restatements of foreign currency. *Foreign currency conversions* are transactions in which one currency is exchanged for another. For example, a U.S. enterprise might go to its bank and convert dollars into the number of French francs required to pay a debt to a French supplier. In contrast, *foreign currency restatement* is the process of expressing foreign currency amounts in another currency by the use of a currency exchange rate. Unlike conversions, restatements are not transactions. Although restatements may be viewed as *hypothetical* conversions, foreign currency restatement is an adjustment process and not a transaction.

---

[1] Foreign affiliates may be either incorporated (foreign investee corporations or subsidiary corporations) or unincorporated (unincorporated foreign branches). This chapter emphasizes the restatement of financial statements issued by incorporated foreign affiliates. However, the restatement of financial statements issued by unincorporated foreign branches follows the same general principles.

[2] Later in the chapter, two types of restatement are identified—one called translation and the other called remeasurement. Sometimes the word *translation* is used to refer both to this special type of restatement and to the general restatement calculation described in this paragraph. The authors find this practice confusing and therefore restrict the use of the word *translation* to the special type of restatement that is described later in this chapter.

Currency Exchange Rates

A currency exchange rate is the price of one currency in terms of another. More precisely, it is the rate at which one currency may be converted into another under certain conditions. For example, if a bank quotes a rate for the French franc of $.2235, it means that the bank is willing to sell 100 francs for $22.35. Of course, the rate may change from one time to another owing to changes in market conditions. All the exchange rates considered in this chapter pertain to conversions on the date of the rate—that is, immediate or on-the-spot conversions—and are therefore called *spot rates*. Of course, we may have occasion to refer to past or historical spot rates as well as to the current spot rate for a given currency. Consequently, it is important to know the date of a spot rate.

Spot rates can be stated either directly in units of local currency or indirectly in units of foreign currency. A *direct exchange rate* gives the price of the foreign currency in terms of the local currency; an *indirect exchange rate* gives the price of the local currency in terms of the foreign currency. From the U.S. viewpoint, the direct exchange rate tells us how much one unit of foreign currency costs in terms of U.S. dollars. Thus, the direct exchange rate implied by a bank's willingness to sell 100 French francs for $22.35 is $.2235 per franc ($22.35 ÷ Fr 100). Conversely, the indirect exchange rate, from the U.S. viewpoint, tells us how much one U.S. dollar costs in terms of the foreign currency. Thus, a bank's willingness to sell 100 French francs for $22.35 implies an indirect rate of Fr 4.474 per dollar (Fr 100 ÷ $22.35).[3] Since most accounting calculations use direct rates, the words *exchange rate* are usually synonymous with direct exchange rate.

MEASUREMENT ISSUES IN FOREIGN STATEMENT RESTATEMENT

The restatement of foreign financial statements raises several measurement issues: The first concerns adjustments to the foreign statements that are made necessary by variations in accounting principles from one country to another. The second concerns the choice of the exchange rate that is used to restate foreign statement items. The third concerns the treatment of adjustments that arise from the restatement process. These issues are discussed in the paragraphs that follow.

Conformity with U.S. Generally Accepted Accounting Principles

The accounting principles applied in foreign countries differ from the accounting principles applied in the United States. For example, few countries require comprehensive interperiod income tax allocation or permit the LIFO inventory method. Financial accounting standards require that foreign financial statements be adjusted to conform with U.S. generally accepted accounting principles prior to restatement (*FASB Statement No. 52*, par. 4b). Such adjustments frequently raise complex measurement problems. Such measurement problems must be resolved by an accounting specialist with a thorough understanding of both U.S. generally accepted accounting principles and the accounting principles and procedures that are used by the foreign entity. The development of such an understanding is beyond the scope of this chapter. Accordingly, our discussions assume that foreign statements have already been adjusted to conform with U.S. accounting principles.

---

[3] Of course, from a French viewpoint, the dollar is the foreign currency and the identification of the rates as direct and indirect is reversed. The direct exchange rate is Fr 4.474 per dollar, and the indirect rate is $.2235 per franc.

Historical Rate and Current Rate Restatement

Additional adjustments are required to restate each item on the foreign entity's statements from the foreign currency into dollars. The central measurement issue is whether each statement item and the activity in the corresponding account should be restated using current exchange rates or historical exchange rates. Let us illustrate these two approaches to restatement.

Current Rate Restatement

When an account is restated using current rates, the beginning and ending balances are multiplied by the exchange rates in effect on the dates of each balance. Activity in the account is multiplied by the rate in effect on the date of the related transaction. The imbalance created in accounts by this procedure is offset by a restatement adjustment. To illustrate, consider the restatement of a cash account at current rates. Restatement at the current rates implies that all receipts and disbursements of foreign currency should be multiplied by the rate in effect on the date of receipt or disbursement. The following balances, events, and exchange rates describe a cash account maintained by a Swiss subsidiary during 19X4 (Swiss franc is abbreviated SFr):

Chronology of Balances, Events, and Exchange Rates

Date	Balance or Event	Rate
Jan. 1, 19X4	Balance is SFr 1,000	$.5000
Mar. 1, 19X4	Receive SFr 6,000	.5100
July 1, 19X4	Disburse SFr 5,800	.5150
Dec. 31, 19X4	Balance is SFr 1,200	.5200

The following T-accounts show the cash account in both Swiss francs and restated dollars:

Cash (SFr)					Cash ($)			
Balance	1,000				Balance	500		
Receive	6,000	Pay	5,800		Receive	3,060	Pay	2,987
					Adjustment	51		
Balance	1,200				Balance	624		

Beginning and ending cash balances are multiplied by the beginning and ending current rates, respectively ($500 = $.5000 × SFr 1,000, and $624 = $.5200 × SFr 1,200). The single cash receipt of SFr 6,000 occurs when the rate was $.5100. Accordingly, the receipt is multiplied by that rate ($3,060 = $.5100 × SFr 6,000). The single cash disbursement of SFr 5,800 occurred when the rate was $.5150 and is restated using that rate ($2,987 = $.5150 × SFr 5,800). If these restated amounts are entered in a T-account, the account is out of balance by $51 ($500 + $3,060 − $2,987 − $624)—that is, the restated account requires an additional debit of $51. The balancing debit is a restatement adjustment, which is recorded as a debit to cash, as shown in the foregoing T-account, and a credit to either income or a special equity account, as explained later in this chapter.

Our cash account illustration makes possible an *exact* restatement because the precise date and amount of each receipt and disbursement is known. Frequently, we know only the total amount of transactions during a period without knowing how much occurred on each day. As an approximation in such cases, the transaction total is simply multiplied by the average exchange rate for the period of the transactions. The approximation is valid under the assumption that the transactions occur continuously and that their cumulative total rises at a uniform rate. For example, suppose that sales of a Swiss subsidiary amount to SFr 100,000 during 19X3. The exact restatement of sales at historical rates is infeasible, but individual sales are fairly uniform in amount and occur at a uniform rate throughout the year (no seasonal variation). Under these conditions, it is appropriate to restate sales by multiplying the *average* exchange rate during 19X3 (say, $.5010) times sales in Swiss francs (SFr 100,000). Thus, the approximate restatement of sales at historical rates is $50,100 ($.5010 × SFr 100,000). In practice, this approximation is frequently applied on a quarterly basis using the average rate for each quarter.

Historical Rate Restatement

When an account is restated at historical rates, no restatement adjustment is necessary because amounts are multiplied by the same rate when they leave an account as when they enter it. For example, when plant and equipment are restated during historical rates, the balance of plant and equipment should be divided into segments according to the date of its acquisition and each segment should be multiplied by the corresponding date-of-acquisition rate. Accumulated depreciation and depreciation expense are also segmented by the date of acquisition, and each segment is multiplied by the corresponding date-of-acquisition rate. The following balances, events, and exchange rates describe a building owned by a Spanish subsidiary of a U.S. corporation:

Chronology of Balances, Events, and Exchange Rates

Date	Balance or Event	Rate
Jan. 1, 19X1	Acquire building with ten-year life and no salvage value for 500,000 pesetas (abbreviated Pta)	$.0100
Dec. 31, 19X5	Net book value of building is Pta 250,000	.0140
19X6	Straight-line depreciation is Pta 50,000 per year	.0145 average
Dec. 31, 19X6	Net book value of building is Pta 200,000	.0150

The following T-accounts describe the building for 19X6 in both Spanish pesetas and dollars:

Historical Rate Restatement of Building Account

Building, Net (Pta)		Building, Net ($)	
Balance 250,000		Balance 2,500	
	Depreciation 50,000		Depreciation 500
Balance 200,000		Balance 2,000	

Beginning and ending balances are multiplied by the historical (date-of-acquisition) rate ($2,500 = $.0100 × Pta 250,000, and $2,000 = $.0100 × Pta 200,000). Annual depreciation is also multiplied by the acquisition date rate ($500 = $.0100 × 50,000 Pta). In other words, the restated asset is diminished by depreciation, which is restated at the same rate that restated the asset's acquisition. As a result, no restatement adjustment is created.[4]

Treatment of Restatement Adjustments

As noted previously, the restatement of accounts using current rates creates remeasurement adjustments. Some have argued that this adjustment should be included in net income in the period in which it arises. Others have argued that the adjustment should bypass net income (at least until the foreign affiliate is sold or liquidated) and be recorded in a special equity account. The theoretical aspects of this debate over the two treatments are described by the following issues section.

ISSUES

Restatement Adjustments as Income Elements or Direct Equity Adjustments

Two accounting students—John Swan and Jane Lake—are discussing the theoretical merits of different treatments of adjustments arising from the restatement of foreign financial statements.

John argues that an investor in a foreign entity gains or loses money every time the exchange rate changes. If the exchange rate increases, the restated net investment goes up and the investor gains. If the exchange rate falls, the restated net investment goes down and the investor loses. Further, such gains and losses should be included in the net income in the period in which they occur.

Jane does not agree. She argues that the investor in a foreign entity does not gain or lose unless the investment is actually converted into dollars and that this does not occur until the investment is sold or liquidated. Prior to that time, the effect of exchange rate movements on the investor's reporting entity is too remote and uncertain to be recognized. Further, the operations of the foreign entity, which are presumably conducted in the foreign currency, are not directly affected by movements in the exchange rate. In other words, the adjustments are unrealized from the viewpoint of the investor and meaningless from the viewpoint of the foreign entity. Therefore, they should not be included in the investor's net income. Instead, they should merely be accumulated in a separate equity account on the balance sheet until the foreign entity is sold or liquidated. Further, Jane notes that exchange rates are subject to wide variation from year to year. It is quite likely that "gains" in one year will be offset by "losses" in subsequent years—particularly if the investment is held for many years. To include such unrealized gains and losses in income would be very misleading.

The principal official pronouncement on accounting matters pertaining to foreign currency is *FASB Statement No. 52*. This statement resolves the dispute described in the

---

[4] When plant and equipment are restated at current rates, each event that alters plant and equipment accounts is multiplied by the rate in effect when the event occurs. Acquisitions during the current year are multiplied by the rate in effect on the acquisition date, retirements during the year are multiplied by the rate in effect on the retirement date, and depreciation for the current year is multiplied by the average rate for the year. Balances at the beginning of the year are multiplied by the beginning-of-the-year rate, and balances at the end of the year are multiplied by the end-of-the-year rate. Of course, restatement of plant and equipment accounts at current rates produces restatement adjustments.

foregoing issues section by requiring different treatments of the restatement adjustment under different circumstances. Under some circumstances, all asset and liability accounts are restated at current rates and the adjustment enters equity directly without affecting income. This restatement procedure is called *translation.* Under other circumstances, some asset and liability accounts are restated at current rates, whereas others are restated at historical rates, and the resulting adjustment is included in net income. This restatement procedure is called *remeasurement.* The functional currency concept, which is defined by *FASB Statement No. 52,* guides the determination of whether translation or remeasurement is appropriate.

THE FUNCTIONAL CURRENCY CONCEPT

The currency of the primary economic environment in which an entity generates and expends cash is called the *functional currency of the entity.* It is the currency of the economic system that determines the prices of the goods and services that are bought and sold by the entity. Accordingly, the functional currency of an entity is the most meaningful measurement unit for its assets, liabilities, and operations.[5]

When the operations of the foreign entity are relatively self-contained and integrated in the economic environment of its foreign location (as when the day-to-day operations of a foreign subsidiary generate and expend its local currency and are not dependent on either the U.S. parent's functional currency or any currency other than its local currency), the identification of the foreign entity's local currency as its functional currency is a straight-forward matter. On the other hand, when a foreign entity transacts significant amounts of business in several currencies, the determination of the functional currency is a more subjective task.

Despite the guidelines established by the FASB—including criteria related to the nature of the foreign entity's cash flows, sales prices, sales markets, expenses, financing, and intercompany transactions (*FASB Statement No. 52,* par 42)—the judgment remains subjective. The standards also note that management, rather than the external auditor or accountant, "is in the best position to obtain the pertinent facts and weigh their relative importance in determining the functional currency of each operation" (*FASB Statement No. 52,* par. 41).

Usually, an entity's functional currency is the same as the local currency in which the entity keeps records and issues financial statements, which is called the reporting currency. This is true for most of the entities with which we are concerned in this chapter. Thus, unless contrary indication is given, we will assume that the U.S. dollar is both the reporting currency and the functional currency for all U.S. investors in foreign entities. However, we will consider some foreign investees that exhibit different functional and reporting currencies. For example, a U.S. company's Philippine subsidiary, which keeps records and issues financial statements in the local Philippine currency, might conduct most of its business in U.S. dollars.

Although the functional currency of some foreign subsidiaries of U.S. parents (like the Philippine subsidiary mentioned in the preceding paragraph) is the U.S. dollar, the functional currency of most foreign subsidiaries differs from the reporting currency of

---

[5] An exception exists when the functional currency is unstable as when it is subject to a very high rate of inflation. Such exceptions are discussed later in this chapter.

their U.S. parent. Consequently, the foreign investee's functional currency financial statements must be restated in the parent's reporting currency before the equity method or consolidation procedures can be applied. This restatement process, which is described later in this chapter, is called *translation*. The objective of translation is to restate the functional currency information so as to maintain the same economic results and relationships that exist in the functional currency financial statements.

In most situations where the foreign investee's functional currency is not its local currency, the foreign investee's functional currency is the same as the investor's functional currency, as in the case of the Philippine subsidiary whose functional currency is the U.S. dollar. When a foreign investee's functional currency differs from its local currency, its financial statements must be restated in its functional currency to obtain the best measure of the foreign investee's assets, liabilities, and operations. This restatement process is distinguished from translation and is called *remeasurement*. The objective of remeasurement is to produce the same financial information as if the foreign investee's records had been maintained in its functional currency. The equity method and consolidation procedures can then be applied to the remeasured information because the dollar is both the foreign investee's functional currency and the investor's reporting currency.

In some unusual situations, the functional currency of a foreign investee differs from *both* the investee's local currency and the investor's reporting currency. In such situations, remeasurement into the investee's functional currency must be followed by translation of the remeasured information into the reporting currency of the investor before the equity method and consolidation procedures can be applied. In most situations, however, the foreign investee's functional currency is either its local currency or the parent's functional currency (the U.S. dollar for most U.S. investors).

To illustrate the use of remeasurement and translation, let us consider the three independent situations depicted in Exhibit 12-1. Each situation represents a different currency structure for a U.S. parent and its foreign subsidiary and requires a different remeasurement and translation procedure. Situation I, for example, requires no remeasurement because the Swiss subsidiary's local currency is the functional currency; however, the Swiss franc financial statements of the subsidiary must be translated into U.S. dollars (the parent's reporting currency). In situation II, the subsidiary's financial information must be remeasured from Swiss francs (the subsidiary's local currency) to U.S. dollars (the subsidiary's functional currency). Since the U.S. dollar is the reporting currency of the parent, no translation is required. Finally, in situation III, both remeasurement and translation are

EXHIBIT 12-1	REMEASUREMENT AND TRANSLATION				
	Reporting Currency of Parent	Subsidiary Local Currency	Functional Currency	Remeasurement	Translation
Situation I	U.S.$	SFr	SFr	None	SFr to U.S.$
Situation II	U.S.$	SFr	U.S.$	SFr to U.S.$	None
Situation III	U.S.$	SFr	DM	SFr to DM	DM to U.S.$

required: first, the subsidiary financial information is remeasured from Swiss francs (its local currency) into Deutsche marks (its functional currency); then, the Deutsche mark information is translated into U.S. dollars (the parent's reporting currency).

Translation and remeasurement represent different restatement processes for the financial information of a foreign entity. Translation is the process of restating functional currency measurements in the reporting currency. Remeasurement is the process of restating local currency in functional currency. Since all accounting measurements are made in functional currency *before* translation, remeasurement always precedes translation. Mechanically, the two restatement processes differ in that translation restates all assets and liabilities using current rates, whereas the remeasurement restates some assets and liabilities using historical rates and others using current rates. Also, as noted earlier, restatement adjustments arising under translation are made to a special equity account (bypassing net income), whereas restatement adjustments arising under remeasurement are included in net income. First, let us illustrate the restatement procedures that are required by translation and then turn to the restatement procedures that are required by remeasurement.

TRANSLATION

Translation restates all asset and liability accounts at current rates and all owners' equity accounts at historical rates. (Accordingly, translation is sometimes called the *current rate method* of restatement.) In translation, beginning-of-the-year balances are multiplied by the beginning-of-the-year exchange rate, and all end-of-the-year balances are multiplied by the end-of-the-year rate. Further, all transactions during the year are restated using the rate in effect on the transaction date, the date on which the transaction amount is recognized. Typically, this means that revenues and expenses are multiplied by an average exchange rate for the period, as an approximation. Restatement adjustments arising from translation, which are called *translation adjustments,* are excluded from the determination of net income. Rather, they are reported separately and accumulated in a separate equity account (*FASB Statement No. 52,* par. 13). This procedure is appropriate because the translation adjustments are artifacts of the translation process that have no direct effect on the reporting currency cash flows. Although such adjustments have an indirect effect on the amount to be realized when the foreign investment is sold or liquidated, that effect is remote, uncertain, and unrelated to operations (see *FASB Statement No. 52,* pars. 111–115).

Translation at Date of Acquisition

Let us illustrate translation by reference to the financial statements of Gerhardt Manufacturing, the German subsidiary of EXN, Inc., a U.S. corporation. The subsidiary was acquired by EXN on December 31, 19X0, and recorded as a purchase. The subsidiary's balance sheet (in trial balance form) on the date of acquisition, stated in the subsidiary's local currency (which is also its functional currency) and adjusted to conform with U.S. generally accepted accounting principles, is shown in the first column of Exhibit 12-2. Exhibit 12-2 also shows the translation of the functional currency (DM) financial statement into the reporting currency of the parent (U.S. dollars). Notice that all accounts are restated using the date-of-acquisition exchange rate, including the equity accounts. From the parent's viewpoint, the date of acquisition is the beginning of the subsidiary's history for purchase accounting purposes. Accordingly, the historical rate that is applicable to equity accounts equals the date-of-acquisition rate. Since all accounts are restated at the

EXHIBIT 12-2	TRANSLATION AT DATE OF ACQUISITION

Gerhardt Manufacturing (Subsidiary of EXN, Inc.)

TRANSLATION WORKSHEET
DECEMBER 31, 19X0

	Subsidiary's Adjusted Trial Balance (Marks)	Exchange Rate		Subsidiary's Translated Adjusted Trial Balance (Dollars)
		Date	Amount	
Debits				
Cash	DM 50,000	12-31-X0	$.3000	$ 15,000
Accounts receivable	35,000	12-31-X0	.3000	10,500
Inventory, 12-31-X0	65,000	12-31-X0	.3000	19,500
Plant and equipment	350,000	12-31-X0	.3000	105,000
Total debits	DM 500,000			$150,000
Credits				
Accumulated depreciation	DM 80,000	12-31-X0	.3000	$ 24,000
Accounts payable	20,000	12-31-X0	.3000	6,000
Common stock	300,000	12-31-X0	.3000	90,000
Retained earnings	100,000	12-31-X0	.3000	30,000
Total credits	DM 500,000			$150,000

date-of-acquisition exchange rate, there is no accumulated translation adjustment on the translated date-of-acquisition balance sheet of the subsidiary.[6]

Translation One Year after Acquisition

In order to demonstrate translation one year after acquisition, let us extend our EXN-Gerhardt illustration to the year following acquisition. Gerhardt's trial balance at December 31, 19X1, stated in the subsidiary's functional currency and adjusted to conform with U.S. accounting principles, is shown in the first column of Exhibit 12-3 on the following page. The relevant direct exchange rates for the Deutsche mark are as follows:

Direct Exchange Rates for Deutsche Mark

Dec. 31, 19X0	$.3000
19X1 Average	.3400
Dec. 31, 19X1	.3800

---

[6] In poolings of interests, the subsidiary's history from the parent's viewpoint extends back beyond the date of acquisition, and the historical rates that are applicable to equity accounts are the historical rates as of the dates of the subsidiary's various equity transactions. Of course, assets and liabilities of pooled companies are restated at current rates just as they are for purchased companies. Consequently, a cumulative translation adjustment, an element of equity, must be recognized as the amount required to balance the translated date-of-acquisition balance sheet.

EXHIBIT 12-3	TRANSLATION ONE YEAR AFTER ACQUISITION

Gerhardt Manufacturing (Subsidiary of EXN, Inc.)

TRANSLATION WORKSHEET
DECEMBER 31, 19X1

	Subsidiary's Adjusted Trial Balance (Marks)	Exchange Rate		Subsidiary's Translated Adjusted Trial Balance (Dollars)
		Date	Amount	
Debits				
Cash	DM 41,000	12-31-X1	$.3800	$ 15,580
Accounts receivable	94,000	12-31-X1	.3800	35,720
Inventory	60,000	12-31-X1	.3800	22,800
Plant and equipment	350,000	12-31-X1	.3800	133,000
Cost of goods sold	175,000	19X1 average	.3400	59,500
Depreciation expense	27,000	19X1 average	.3400	9,180
Other expense	25,000	19X1 average	.3400	8,500
Total debits	DM 772,000			$284,280
Credits				
Accumulated depreciation	DM 107,000	12-31-X1	.3800	$ 40,660
Accounts payable	25,000	12-31-X1	.3800	9,500
Common stock	300,000	12-31-X0	.3000	90,000
Retained earnings, 1-1-X1	100,000	12-31-X0	.3000	30,000
Sales	240,000	19X1 average	.3400	81,600
Translation adjustment				32,520
Total credits	DM 772,000			$284,280

Unless there is evidence to the contrary, assume throughout this chapter (and in exercises and problems) that all revenues, expenses, and inventory purchases arise at a uniform rate throughout the year. Exhibit 12-3 shows the translation of the Gerhardt's financial statements for the first year following acquisition by EXN, Inc.

Translation Procedures

The worksheet in Exhibit 12-3 shows the translation of the functional currency (DM) financial statements into the reporting currency of the parent (dollars). The first step in completing the worksheet is to select the appropriate exchange rate or rates to translate each item of the foreign currency trial balance and enter it in the central columns of the worksheet. Then the selected rates must be multiplied by the corresponding amounts in DM to obtain the translated amounts in dollars, which are entered in the right-most column of the worksheet. In translation, all asset and liability accounts are restated at current exchange rates, and all owners' equity accounts are restated at historical rates. Accordingly, all year-end asset and liability balances accounts are multiplied by the year-end

(12-31-X1) exchange rate of $.3800. Purchases, expenses, and revenues, which arise uniformly throughout the year, are multiplied by the average exchange rate for 19X1 of $.3400. Owners' equity accounts are restated using appropriate historical rates. The date-of-acquisition rate is the appropriate historical rate for both common stock and the beginning-of-the-year balance of retained earnings.

Balancing-Figure Calculation of Translation Adjustment

The third step is the calculation of the translation adjustment. The translation adjustment may be calculated as the figure that is required to balance the translated trial balance. In Exhibit 12-3, a credit of $32,520 is required to balance the schedule. Accordingly, a translation adjustment of $32,520 is entered on the worksheet.[7] Recall that the translation adjustment is not included in net income. Instead, it is reported separately and accumulated as a separate component of owners' equity, as we will demonstrate subsequently. The accumulated translation adjustment is not removed from the balance sheet until the foreign affiliate is sold or liquidated. Appendix B shows an alternative calculation of the translation adjustment. Although the alternative calculation is more difficult to perform, it shows clearly the composition of the translation adjustment.

Preparation of Subsidiary's Financial Statements

The translated financial statements for the German subsidiary prepared from the translated trial balance are shown in Exhibit 12-4 on the following page. In some cases, the subsidiary's translated statements may not be issued. Instead, the translated results serve only as the basis for the parent's equity method entries, consolidation procedures, and required disaggregated disclosures. The equity method and consolidation procedures for EXN, Inc., are shown in Appendix A.

Translation Two Years after Acquisition

To illustrate translation two years after acquisition, we will extend the EXN-Gerhardt illustration into a second year by introducing the trial balance shown in the first column of Exhibit 12-5 on page 589 and the following additional information:

1. The subsidiary purchased additional equipment on January 1, 19X2, for DM 50,000. Depreciation on plant and equipment for 19X2 is DM 40,000, including DM 13,000 related to the newly purchased equipment.

2. The subsidiary borrowed DM 77,000 from a German bank on January 1, 19X2. Interest at 10% per annum is payable at each year-end, and the principal is payable on December 31, 19X5.

3. The subsidiary declared and paid a dividend of DM 20,000 on December 31, 19X2.

---

[7] If a periodic inventory system is employed, then the trial balance includes the beginning inventory and purchases as debits and the ending inventory as both a debit (representing the asset) and a credit (representing an element of the cost of goods sold calculation). In this case, the excess of the translated beginning inventory and purchases over the translated ending inventory includes the translation adjustment as well as the cost of goods sold. Consequently, the total translation adjustment ($32,520 in the Gerhardt example) is calculated in two parts: (1) the amount required to balance the trial balance ($27,520) and (2) an additional amount that is associated with the periodic inventory ($5,000).

| EXHIBIT 12-4 | SUBSIDIARY'S TRANSLATED FINANCIAL STATEMENTS |

Gerhardt Manufacturing (Subsidiary of EXN, Inc.)

BALANCE SHEET
DECEMBER 31, 19X1

Assets

Cash		$ 15,580
Accounts receivable		35,720
Inventory		22,800
Plant and equipment	$133,000	
Less: Accumulated depreciation	40,660	92,340
Total assets		$166,440

Liabilities and Stockholders' Equity

Accounts payable		$ 9,500
Common stock		90,000
Cumulative translation adjustment		32,520
Retained earnings		34,420
Total liabilities and stockholders' equity		$166,440

Gerhardt Manufacturing (Subsidiary of EXN, Inc.)

INCOME STATEMENT
FOR THE YEAR ENDED DECEMBER 31, 19X1

Sales		$ 81,600
Cost of goods sold		59,500
Gross margin		$ 22,100
Depreciation expense	$ 9,180	
Other expense	8,500	17,680
Net income		$ 4,420

Gerhardt Manufacturing (Subsidiary of EXN, Inc.)

STATEMENT OF RETAINED EARNINGS
FOR THE YEAR ENDED DECEMBER 31, 19X1

Retained earnings, 1-1-X1	$ 30,000
Net income	4,420
Retained earnings, 12-31-X1	$ 34,420

EXHIBIT 12-5	TRANSLATION TWO YEARS AFTER ACQUISITION

Gerhardt Manufacturing (Subsidiary of EXN, Inc.)
TRANSLATION WORKSHEET
DECEMBER 31, 19X2

	Subsidiary's Adjusted Trial Balance (Marks)	Exchange Rate		Subsidiary's Translated Adjusted Trial Balance (Dollars)
		Date	Amount	
Debits				
Cash	DM 72,000	12-31-X2	$.4200	$ 30,240
Accounts receivable	130,000	12-31-X2	.4200	54,600
Inventory	77,000	12-31-X2	.4200	32,340
Plant and equipment	400,000	12-31-X2	.4200	168,000
Cost of goods sold	170,000	19X2 average	.4000	68,000
Depreciation expense	40,000	19X2 average	.4000	16,000
Interest expense	7,700	19X2 average	.4000	3,080
Other expense	42,300	19X2 average	.4000	16,920
Dividends	20,000	12-31-X2	.4200	8,400
Total debits	DM 959,000			$397,580
Credits				
Accumulated depreciation	DM 147,000	12-31-X2	.4200	$ 61,740
Accounts payable	32,000	12-31-X2	.4200	13,440
Notes payable	77,000	12-31-X2	.4200	32,340
Common stock	300,000	12-31-X0	.3000	90,000
Retained earnings, 1-1-X2	113,000	Various		34,420
Sales	290,000	19X2 average	.4000	116,000
Translation adjustment				49,640
Total credits	DM 959,000			$397,580

4. The relevant exchange rates for the Deutsche mark are as follows:

Direct Exchange Rates for Deutsche Mark

Dec. 31, 19X0	$.3000
Dec. 31, 19X1	.3800
19X2 Average	.4000
Dec. 31, 19X2	.4200

The translation of Gerhardt Manufacturing's financial information for the second year following its acquisition by EXN, Inc., is summarized in Exhibit 12-5. The general procedure is the same as that used for the first year's financial statements. The subsidiary's functional currency trial balance is adjusted to accord with U.S. accounting principles and entered in the left-most column of the worksheet. Next, the appropriate exchange rates are selected, and each item is translated into dollars. Finally, the translation adjustment is obtained as the figure that is required to balance the translated trial balance. The translated financial statements of the subsidiary prepared from the translated trial balance are presented in Exhibit 12-6. The parent's equity method and consolidation procedures for 19X2 are shown in Appendix A.

The translation of retained earnings and dividends deserves a word of explanation. Retained earnings, like other elements of equity, is translated at historical rates. Accordingly, the beginning balance of translated retained earnings represents the accumulation of translated net income offset by translated dividends for all prior years. Translated retained earnings at January 1, 19X2, in our illustration ($34,420) may be calculated from the worksheet prepared at the end of 19X1 (the translated December 31, 19X0, balance of $30,000 plus the translated net income of $4,420) or may be obtained from the translated financial statements prepared at the end of 19X1 (from the balance sheet or the statement of retained earnings).[8] The dividend is also translated at historical rates, that is, the rates in effect on the dates of dividend declaration. Gerhardt paid a dividend on December 31, 19X2. Thus, the dividend is translated at the end-of-19X2 rate, which happens to be the current rate as well as the appropriate historical rate.

Once the translated beginning-of-the-year balance of retained earnings has been obtained, the accumulated translation adjustment may be calculated as the amount required to balance the translation worksheet ($49,640). This amount includes the translation adjustment that is associated with both the current year and all prior years. Since the prior year's portion was $32,520, the current year's portion is $17,120 ($49,640 − $32,520).

REMEASUREMENT

We turn now to the remeasurement of a foreign subsidiary's financial statements. Recall that *FASB Statement No. 52* requires remeasurement whenever the foreign investee's functional currency is not the local currency. The objective of remeasurement is to restate the foreign investee's local currency results and relationships as if they had been conducted in the functional currency environment.[9] Consequently, some balance sheet elements are remeasured using historical exchange rates, and others are remeasured using current exchange rates. For example, remeasurement restates foreign inventories at the current rate when they are reported at market (under a lower-of-cost-or-market rule) and at the historical rate when they are reported at historical cost. In general, accounts reported at approximately current or future values (including cash, accounts receivable, accounts payable, and notes payable) are restated at current rates. Amounts reported at past or historical values (like plant and equipment, advances from customers for goods or services, and stockholders' equity accounts) are restated at historical rates. Revenues, expenses, and gains and losses related to assets or liabilities remeasured at historical rates should be remeasured at the historical date-of-acquisition or date-of-incurrence rate, re-

---

[8] If the previous year's worksheet is not available, it may be possible to translate all elements of the *beginning-of-the-year* balance sheet *except* retained earnings and to derive translated retained earnings as the figure that is required to balance the translated beginning-of-the-year balance sheet.

[9] In addition, remeasurement to the parent's reporting currency is required when the subsidiary's functional currency is subject to hyperinflation as explained later in this chapter.

EXHIBIT 12-6	SUBSIDIARY'S TRANSLATED FINANCIAL STATEMENTS

Gerhardt Manufacturing (Subsidiary of EXN, Inc.)

BALANCE SHEET
DECEMBER 31, 19X2

Assets

Cash		$ 30,240
Accounts receivable		54,600
Inventory		32,340
Plant and equipment	$168,000	
Less: Accumulated depreciation	61,740	106,260
Total assets		$223,440

Liabilities and Stockholders' Equity

Accounts payable	$ 13,440
Notes payable	32,340
Common stock	90,000
Cumulative translation adjustment	49,640
Retained earnings	38,020
Total liabilities and stockholders' equity	$223,440

Gerhardt Manufacturing (Subsidiary of EXN, Inc.)

INCOME STATEMENT
FOR THE YEAR ENDED DECEMBER 31, 19X2

Sales		$116,000
Cost of goods sold		68,000
Gross margin		$ 48,000
Depreciation expense	$ 16,000	
Interest expense	3,080	
Other expense	16,920	36,000
Net income		$ 12,000

Gerhardt Manufacturing (Subsidiary of EXN, Inc.)

STATEMENT OF RETAINED EARNINGS
FOR THE YEAR ENDED DECEMBER 31, 19X2

Retained earnings, 1-1-X2	$ 34,420
Net income	12,000
Dividends	(8,400)
Retained earnings, 12-31-X2	$ 38,020

spectively. On the other hand, revenues, expenses, and gains and losses related to assets or liabilities remeasured at current rates should be remeasured at the rate in effect on the date that the revenue, expense, and gain or loss is recognized—that is, the transaction date rate. As noted earlier, this means that most revenues and expenses are multiplied by an average exchange rate for the period as an approximation. Exhibit 12-7 summarizes the restatement procedure followed in both translation and remeasurement for a variety of accounts.

Restatement adjustments arising from remeasurement are called *remeasurement gains or losses* and, unlike translation adjustments, are included in remeasured income. Since the objective of remeasurement is to restate the subsidiary's local currency results, as if they had occurred in the functional currency environment, remeasurement restatement adjustments are part of operating results and are appropriately included in remeasured income.

EXHIBIT 12-7	**SUMMARY OF RESTATEMENT PROCEDURES FOR REMEASUREMENT AND TRANSLATION**		
		Restatement Procedure	
	Balance Sheet Account	**Remeasurement**	**Translation**
	Assets		
	Cash on hand, demand and time deposits	Current	Current
	Marketable securities:		
	Carried at cost	Historical	Current
	Carried at current market	Current	Current
	Accounts and notes receivable and related unearned discounts	Current	Current
	Allowances for doubtful accounts or notes	Current	Current
	Inventories:		
	Carried at cost	Historical	Current
	Carried at current market	Current	Current
	Prepaid expenses	Historical	Current
	Refundable deposits	Current	Current
	Property, plant, and equipment	Historical	Current
	Accumulated depreciation on property, plant, and equipment	Historical	Current
	Cash surrender value of life insurance	Current	Current
	Deferred income tax charges	Current	Current
	Patents, trademarks, licenses, and formulas	Historical	Current
	Goodwill and other intangible assets	Historical	Current
	Liabilities		
	Accounts and notes payable and overdrafts	Current	Current
	Accrued expenses payable	Current	Current
	Deferred income tax credits	Current	Current
	Deferred income and other deferred credits	Historical	Current
	Bonds payable and other long-term debt	Current	Current
	Stockholders' Equity (all accounts)	Historical	Historical

Remeasurement Procedures

Remeasurement is assisted by a worksheet procedure like that used for translation. We will demonstrate this procedure by reference to the same example used previously to demonstrate translation. Accordingly, we must alter the assumption that the functional currency of Gerhardt Manufacturing is the Deutsche mark. Instead, let us assume that Gerhardt's functional currency is the U.S. dollar. This means that most of Gerhardt's operations are conducted in dollars despite its German location.[10]

In addition to the information presented earlier for the Gerhardt-EXN illustration, the following is added:

1. The FIFO-cost inventory at each year-end is composed entirely of purchases that are made uniformly throughout the most recent quarter-year.

2. In order to accommodate historical translation of the inventories, the average exchange rate for the last three months of each year is required in addition to the rates presented earlier. A complete list of the exchange rates that are necessary to complete the remeasurement follows:

Direct Exchange Rates for Deutsche Mark	
Dec. 31, 19X0	$.3000
19X1 average	.3400
Last quarter 19X1 average	.3700
Dec. 31, 19X1	.3800
19X2 average	.4000
Last quarter 19X2 average	.4100
Dec. 31, 19X2	.4200

The remeasurement of Gerhardt's three trial balances at December 31, 19X0, December 31, 19X1, and December 31, 19X2 is presented in Exhibit 12-8 on the following pages. Cash, accounts receivable, accounts payable, notes payable, and bonds payable—all of which are carried at current prices—are remeasured at current exchange rates. All other items on the trial balance are remeasured at historical rates, as described here:

1. All items related to plant and equipment (plant and equipment, depreciation expense, and accumulated depreciation) are remeasured at the rate in effect when the plant and equipment were acquired.

2. Common stock is remeasured at the rate in effect when the subsidiary was acquired. (The same rate is used to translate common stock under the current rate method.)

3. The year-end inventory cost is remeasured at the last-quarter average rate, which reflects the fact that the inventory consists of purchases made uniformly throughout the last quarter of each year. Assume that market exceeds cost for all inventories.

---

[10] In order to record transactions denominated in dollars, Gerhardt must restate the dollar amounts in marks. This restatement process, which is described in Chapter 13, gives rise to gains and losses measured in marks and included in Gerhardt's net income. Such gains and losses should be remeasured into dollars using the average rate for the period in which they are recorded. To simplify our illustration, we assume here that restatement gains are exactly offset by restatement losses in every period.

4. Purchases, other expenses, and sales are remeasured at the annual average rate, reflecting the assumption that each item arose at a uniform rate throughout each year.

5. Retained earnings, like common stock, is restated at historical rates under both remeasurement and translation. As under translation, indirect calculation procedures obviate the need for remeasurement using explicit historical rates.

Notice that all accounts on the December 31, 19X0, balance sheet are remeasured at the date-of-acquisition exchange rate. From the parent's viewpoint in a purchase combination, the date of acquisition is the beginning of the subsidiary's history. Accordingly, the historical rate equals the current rate at the date of acquisition; and all assets, liabilities, and

---

EXHIBIT 12-8   **REMEASUREMENT AT DATE OF ACQUISITION, ONE YEAR AFTER ACQUISITION, AND TWO YEARS AFTER ACQUISITION**

Gerhardt Manufacturing (Subsidiary of EXN, Inc.)

REMEASUREMENT WORKSHEETS
DECEMBER 31, 19X0, DECEMBER 31, 19X1, AND DECEMBER 31, 19X2

	December 31, 19X0			
	Subsidiary's Adjusted Trial Balance (Marks)	Exchange Rate		Subsidiary's Remeasured Adjusted Trial Balance (Dollars)
		Date	Amount	
Debits				
Cash	DM 50,000	12-31-X0	$.3000	$ 15,000
Accounts receivable	35,000	12-31-X0	.3000	10,500
Inventory	65,000	12-31-X0	.3000	19,500
Plant and equipment	350,000	12-31-X0	.3000	105,000
Cost of goods sold				
Depreciation expense				
Interest expense				
Other expense				
Dividends				
Total debits	DM 500,000			$150,000
Credits				
Accumulated depreciation	DM 80,000	12-31-X0	.3000	$ 24,000
Accounts payable	20,000	12-31-X0	.3000	6,000
Notes payable				
Common stock	300,000	12-31-X0	.3000	90,000
Retained earnings, 1-1	100,000	12-31-X0	.3000	30,000
Sales				
Remeasurement gain				
Total credits	DM 500,000			$150,000

equities (whether calling for current or historical rate remeasurement) are multiplied by the date-of-acquisition rate in the remeasurement of the date-of-acquisition balance sheet.[11]

---

[11] In poolings of interests, the subsidiary's history from the parent's viewpoint extends back beyond the date of acquisition; and the historical rates that are applicable to asset, liability, and equity accounts are the historical rates as of the dates of the subsidiary's various asset, liability, and equity transactions. In other words, the accounts are remeasured as if the company had always been a subsidiary of the parent. Consequently, an accumulated translation adjustment, as an element of equity, must be recognized as the amount that is required to balance the translated date-of-acquisition balance sheet.

	December 31, 19X1				December 31, 19X2		
Subsidiary's Adjusted Trial Balance (Marks)	Exchange Rate Date	Amount	Subsidiary's Remeasured Adjusted Trial Balance (Dollars)	Subsidiary's Adjusted Trial Balance (Marks)	Exchange Rate Date	Amount	Subsidiary's Remeasured Adjusted Trial Balance (Dollars)
DM 41,000	12-31-X1	$.3800	$ 15,580	DM 72,000	12-31-X2	.4200	$ 30,240
94,000	12-31-X1	.3800	35,720	130,000	12-31-X2	.4200	54,600
60,000	Last quarter 19X1	.3700	22,200	77,000	Last quarter 19X2	.4100	31,570
350,000	12-31-X0	.3000	105,000	400,000	Various		124,000
175,000	Various		55,100	170,000	Various		65,430
27,000	12-31-X0	.3000	8,100	40,000	Various		13,040
				7,700	19X2 average	.4000	3,080
25,000	19X1 average	.3400	8,500	42,300	19X2 average	.4000	16,920
				20,000	12-31-X2	.4200	8,400
DM 772,000			$250,200	DM 959,000			$347,280
DM 107,000	12-31-X0	.3000	$ 32,100	DM 147,000	Various		$ 45,140
25,000	12-31-X1	.3800	9,500	32,000	12-31-X2	.4200	13,440
				77,000	12-31-X2	.4200	32,340
300,000	12-31-X0	.3000	90,000	300,000	12-31-X0	.3000	90,000
100,000	Various		30,000	113,000	Various		46,900
240,000	19X1 average	.3400	81,600	290,000	19X2 average	.4000	116,000
			7,000				3,460
DM 772,000			$250,200	DM 959,000			$347,280

Once the appropriate exchange rate or rates are selected for each account, the remeasured U.S. dollar amount of each item is obtained by multiplying the selected rates and corresponding amount in marks. Several elements of Gerhardt's trial balance are translated at multiple exchange rates—cost of goods sold, depreciation expense, accumulated depreciation, and retained earnings. Let us consider remeasurement of each of these items.

Remeasurement of Cost of Goods Sold

Cost of goods sold is remeasured at the historical rates that are associated with the goods sold. Under a FIFO inventory assumption, these are the rates that are associated with the oldest purchases included in the cost of goods available for sale. Since rates in our example are not identified with specific purchases, it is not possible to remeasure the cost of goods sold by multiplying historical rates times specific amounts sold and then summing the products. Instead, the remeasured cost of goods sold is calculated by reference to the remeasured inventories and purchases. The foreign currency amounts of inventories are given on the adjusted trial balance, but the foreign currency amount of purchases must be calculated by reference to the foreign currency amounts of inventories and the cost of goods sold. For example, Gerhardt's purchases in 19X1 and 19X2 can be calculated as follows:

Calculation of Foreign Currency Amount of Purchases

	19X1	19X2
Cost of goods sold	DM 175,000	DM 170,000
Add: Ending inventory	60,000	77,000
Subtotal	DM 235,000	DM 247,000
Less: Beginning inventory	65,000	60,000
Purchases	DM 170,000	DM 187,000

The foregoing information can then be used to calculate the remeasured amount of cost of goods sold as shown in Exhibit 12-9.

Remeasurement of Plant and Equipment and Accumulated Depreciation

The measurement of plant and equipment is shown in Exhibit 12-10 on page 598. The balances of the plant and equipment account on December 31, 19X0, and December 31, 19X1, are remeasured using the date-of-acquisition rate of $.3000 as shown in Exhibit 12-8. The balance of the plant and equipment account on December 31, 19X2, however, includes the acquisition on January 1, 19X2, in addition to the original acquisition. Accordingly, remeasurement of this balance requires two exchange rates—the date-of-acquisition rate and the rate on the date of the subsequent addition—as shown in Exhibit 12-10.

The remeasurement of related accumulated depreciation is shown in Exhibit 12-11 on page 599. Remeasured 19X2 depreciation expense and the balance of accumulated depreciation at December 30, 19X2, also require two exchange rates as shown in the exhibit. An alternative calculation of accumulated depreciation is as follows:

Alternative Calculation of Accumulated Depreciation		
Remeasured accumulated depreciation, 1-1-X0		$24,000
19X1 remeasured depreciation expense:		
1-1-X0 acquisition (DM 27,000 × $.3000)		8,100
Remeasured accumulated depreciation, 12-31-X1		$32,100
19X2 remeasured depreciation expense:		
1-1-X0 acquisition (DM 27,000 × $.3000)	$8,100	
1-1-X2 acquisition (DM 13,000 × $.3800)	4,940	13,040
Remeasured accumulated depreciation, 12-31-X2		$45,140

Although the calculation of remeasured accumulated depreciation shown in Exhibit 12-11 is instructive, it is usually easier to calculate remeasured accumulated depreciation as shown earlier—simply by adding remeasured depreciation expense to the remeasured beginning-of-the-period balance of accumulated depreciation obtained from the prior period's remeasured financial statements.

EXHIBIT 12-9	REMEASUREMENT OF COST OF GOODS SOLD

Gerhardt Manufacturing (Subsidiary of EXN, Inc.)

CALCULATION OF REMEASURED COST OF GOODS SOLD
FOR THE YEARS ENDED DECEMBER 31, 19X1, AND DECEMBER 31, 19X2

	Subsidiary's Inventory Account (Marks)	Exchange Rate		Subsidiary's Remeasured Inventory Account (Dollars)
		Date	Amount	
19X1 Cost of Goods Sold				
Inventory, 12-31-X0	DM 65,000	12-31-X0	$.3000	$19,500
Add: 19X1 purchases	170,000	19X1 average	.3400	57,800
Subtotal	DM 235,000			$77,300
Less: Inventory, 12-31-X1	60,000	Last quarter 19X1	.3700	22,200
Cost of goods sold	DM 175,000			$55,100
19X2 Cost of Goods Sold				
Inventory, 12-31-X1	DM 60,000	Last quarter 19X1	$.3700	$22,200
Add: 19X2 purchases	187,000	19X2 average	.4000	74,800
Subtotal	DM 247,000			$97,000
Inventory, 12-31-X2	77,000	Last quarter	.4100	31,570
Cost of goods sold	DM 170,000			$65,430

EXHIBIT 12-10	REMEASUREMENT OF PLANT AND EQUIPMENT

Gerhardt Manufacturing (Subsidiary of EXN, Inc.)

CALCULATION OF REMEASURED PLANT AND EQUIPMENT
FOR THE YEARS ENDED DECEMBER 31, 19X1, AND DECEMBER 31, 19X2

	Total	1-1-X0 Acquisition	1-1-X2 Acquisition
Plant and Equipment at December 31, 19X1			
Plant and equipment, 1-1-X0	DM 350,000	DM 350,000	
Add: 19X1 acquisitions	–0–	–0–	
Less: 19X1 retirements	–0–	–0–	
Plant and equipment, 12-31-X1	DM 350,000	DM 350,000	
Historical rate		×.3000	
Remeasured plant and equipment, 12-31-X1	$105,000	$105,000	
Plant and Equipment at December 31, 19X2			
Plant and equipment, 12-31-X1	DM 350,000	DM 350,000	
Add: 19X2 acquisitions:			
Equipment acquired 1-1-X2	50,000		DM 50,000
Less: 19X2 retirements	–0–	–0–	–0–
Plant and equipment, 12-31-X2	DM 400,000	DM 350,000	DM 50,000
Historical rate		×.3000	×.3800
Remeasured plant and equipment, 12-31-X2	$124,000*	$105,000	$19,000

* $124,000 = $105,000 + $19,000

Remeasurement of Retained Earnings

Retained earnings is both remeasured and translated at historical rates. Accordingly, the same procedures are followed in the remeasurement of retained earnings as in the translation of retained earnings. These procedures are described earlier in this chapter.

Balancing-Figure Calculation of Remeasurement Gain

The final step in the remeasurement procedure is the calculation of the remeasurement gain or loss. The remeasurement gain or loss may be calculated as the figure required to balance the remeasured trial balance. In Exhibit 12-8, $7,000 is required to balance the 19X1 schedule and $3,460 is required to balance the 19X2 schedule.

Remeasured Financial Statements

Gerhardt's remeasured financial statements for 19X1 and 19X2 are presented in Exhibit 12-12 on page 600. Notice the treatment of the remeasurement gain. Unlike translation adjustments, which are excluded from net income and recorded as a separate component

EXHIBIT 12-11	REMEASUREMENT OF ACCUMULATED DEPRECIATION

Gerhardt Manufacturing (Subsidiary of EXN, Inc.)

CALCULATION OF REMEASURED ACCUMULATED DEPRECIATION
FOR THE YEARS ENDED DECEMBER 31, 19X1, AND DECEMBER 31, 19X2

	Total	1-1-X0 Acquisition	1-1-X2 Acquisition
Accumulated Depreciation at December 31, 19X1			
Accumulated depreciation, 1-1-X0	DM 80,000	DM 80,000	
Add: 19X1 depreciation expense	27,000	27,000	
Less: Depreciation on retirements	–0–	–0–	
Accumulated depreciation, 12-31-X1	DM 107,000	DM 107,000	
Historical rate		×.3000	
Remeasured accumulated depreciation, 12-31-X1	$24,000*	$32,100	
Accumulated Depreciation at December 31, 19X2			
Accumulated depreciation, 12-31-X1	DM 107,000	DM 107,000	
Add: 19X1 depreciation expense:			
Equipment acquired, 1-1-X0	27,000	27,000	
Equipment acquired, 1-1-X2	13,000		DM 13,000
Less: Depreciation on retirements	–0–	–0–	–0–
Accumulated depreciation, 12-31-X2	DM 147,000	DM 134,000	DM 13,000
Historical rate		×.3000	×.3800
Remeasured accumulated depreciation, 12-31-X2	$45,140	$40,200	$4,940

* $24,000 = DM 80,000 × $.3000

of stockholders' equity, remeasurement gains and losses are included in remeasured net income and ultimately closed to retained earnings. Accordingly, remeasurement gains of $7,000 and $3,460 are included in remeasured net income for 19X1 and 19X2, respectively. Further, the January 1, 19X2, balance of retained earnings includes the remeasurement gain recognized in 19X1. These remeasured financial statements serve as the basis for application of the equity method and consolidation procedures, which are discussed in Appendix A.

Translation of Remeasured Trial Balances

When the subsidiary's functional currency differs from the parent's reporting currency, translation of the subsidiary's financial information is required, even if the subsidiary's financial information has been remeasured into its functional currency. Consider a U.S. subsidiary corporation located in Japan that maintains its records in Japanese yen but conducts most of its operating transactions in Deutsche marks, which is its functional currency. The financial information of this Japanese subsidiary is first remeasured into its functional currency (Deutsche marks), and then the remeasured financial information is translated into the parent's reporting currency (dollars). (Any remeasurement gains or

EXHIBIT 12-12	SUBSIDIARY'S REMEASURED FINANCIAL STATEMENTS

Gerhardt Manufacturing (Subsidiary of EXN, Inc.)
BALANCE SHEET
DECEMBER 31, 19X2, AND DECEMBER 31, 19X1

	12-31-X2	12-31-X1
Assets		
Cash	$ 30,240	$ 15,580
Accounts receivable	54,600	35,720
Inventory	31,570	22,200
Plant and equipment	124,000	105,000
Less: Accumulated depreciation	(45,140)	(32,100)
Total assets	$195,270	$146,400
Liabilities and Stockholders' Equity		
Accounts payable	$ 13,440	$ 9,500
Notes payable	32,340	–0–
Common stock	90,000	90,000
Retained earnings	59,490	46,900
Total liabilities and stockholders' equity	$195,270	$146,400

Gerhardt Manufacturing (Subsidiary of EXN, Inc.)
INCOME STATEMENT
FOR THE YEARS ENDED DECEMBER 31, 19X2, AND DECEMBER 31, 19X1

	19X2	19X1
Sales	$116,000	$ 81,600
Cost of goods sold	(65,430)	(55,100)
Gross margin	$ 50,570	$ 26,500
Depreciation expense	(13,040)	(8,100)
Interest expense	(3,080)	–0–
Other expense	(16,920)	(8,500)
Remeasurement gain	3,460	7,000
Net income	$ 20,990	$ 16,900

Gerhardt Manufacturing (Subsidiary of EXN, Inc.)
STATEMENT OF RETAINED EARNINGS
FOR THE YEARS ENDED DECEMBER 31, 19X2, AND DECEMBER 31, 19X1

	19X2	19X1
Retained earnings, 1-1	$ 46,900	$ 30,000
Net income	20,990	16,900
Dividend	(8,400)	–0–
Retained earnings, 12-31	$ 59,490	$ 46,900

losses created by the remeasurement of yen into Deutsche marks are translated into dollars using the average rate for the period.) On the other hand, when the subsidiary's functional currency is the same as the parent's reporting currency, as in the EXN-Gerhardt illustration, no translation is required. Since the U.S. dollar is both EXN's reporting currency and Gerhardt's functional currency, the remeasurement of Gerhardt's Deutsche mark financial information into U.S. dollars need not be followed by translation. The equity method or consolidation procedures can be applied to the remeasured U.S. dollar information.

Inventory Remeasurement and the Lower-of-Cost-or-Market Adjustment

The lower-of-cost-or-market rule requires special application when the subsidiary's local and functional currencies differ, as in the EXN-Gerhardt illustration. The remeasurement of inventory at historical rates is predicated on a lower-of-cost-or-market analysis that finds cost to be lower than market. When the market is lower than cost, inventory must be written down to a market value that is remeasured at the current exchange rate.[12] The standards require that the lower-of-cost-or-market test must be applied in units of functional currency. This means that the three candidates for market value (replacement cost, net realizable value, and net realizable value reduced by a normal profit allowance) and the cost as well must be remeasured into units of functional currency before the test can be applied. This requirement is consistent with the guiding principle of remeasurement, which requires that past prices be restated at historical rates and that current and future prices be restated at current rates. Further, write-downs of foreign inventories from remeasured cost to remeasured market should enter the current income and should not be treated as part of the remeasurement gain or loss. This can result in market write-downs in a U.S. investor's statements that do not appear in the local currency statement of the foreign investee.

To illustrate, let us consider a Japanese subsidiary of a U.S. corporation; most of the subsidiary's transactions are denominated in U.S. dollars. Accordingly, the subsidiary's functional currency is the U.S. dollar. Exhibit 12-13 on the following page shows the data that are necessary to apply the lower-of-cost-or-market rule to the subsidiary's inventory that was purchased uniformly throughout the last quarter of 19X3. The cost and the three candidates for market are determined in the local currency (yen) and then remeasured into the functional currency—using the historical exchange rate for cost and the current rate for the three market candidates. Since the remeasured inventory market value ($2,691) is lower than its remeasured cost ($2,752), the remeasured inventory equals the remeasured market. Notice that no write-down is appropriate for reports issued by the subsidiary in its reporting currency since cost (¥ 640,000) is lower than market (¥ 690,000). Although the write-down adjustment of $61 ($2,752 − $2,691) is not recorded by the subsidiary, it does alter two remeasured amounts on the remeasurement worksheet—remeasured inventory, which is entered at market, and a write-down adjustment, which is entered as an element of remeasured net income. Sometimes, a write-down is required in the local currency but not in the functional currency. In such cases, the remeasurement must reverse the write-down made in the reporting currency. Both write-downs and write-down reversals in remeasured statements are given effect in the remeasurement worksheet by entering the

---

[12] Financial accounting standards require that inventories be reported at the lower of their cost or market, and the requirement extends to translated foreign inventories (*FASB Statement No. 52,* pars. 49–53). Recall that market is either (1) replacement cost, (2) net realizable value, or (3) net realizable value reduced by a normal profit allowance. More precisely, the market equals whichever of the three values falls between the other two.

EXHIBIT 12-13	REMEASUREMENT AND THE LOWER-OF-COST-OR-MARKET RULE

	Subsidiary's Local Currency (Yen)	Exchange Rate		Subsidiary's Functional Currency (Dollar)
		Date	Amount	
Inventory at cost	¥ 640,000*	Last quarter 19X3 average	$.0043	$2,752
Inventory at replacement cost	560,000	12-31-X3	.0039	2,184
Inventory at net realizable value	770,000	12-31-X3	.0039	3,003
Inventory at net realizable value less normal profit margin	690,000†	12-31-X3	.0039	2,691‡

* Designated as the lower of the cost or market.

† Designated as market value by lower-of-cost-or-market rule.

‡ Designated as both the market value by the lower-of-cost-or-market rule and the lower of the cost or market.

appropriate amount for inventory and inventory write-down. No entry is made by the subsidiary.

SUBSIDIARIES IN HIGHLY INFLATIONARY ECONOMIES

Inflation is the increase in the general level of prices in an economy. Under *FASB Statement No. 52* (par. 109) an economy that experiences cumulative inflation of approximately 100% or more over a three-year period is identified as a highly inflationary economy.[13] In highly inflationary economies, historical cost grossly understates the value of plant and equipment purchased at earlier times. When a subsidiary's functional currency is highly inflationary, the translation at current rates of its plant and equipment may produce a significantly understated amount for plant and equipment. To avoid such understatements, the standards do not permit *translation* when the subsidiary's functional currency is highly inflationary. Instead, *FASB Statement No. 52* requires that the subsidiary's highly inflationary functional currency information be *remeasured* into the parent's reporting currency.[14] In effect, the required procedure substitutes the stable reporting currency of the parent for the unstable functional currency of its subsidiary.[15]

[13] *International Financial Statistics,* which is published monthly by the Bureau of Statistics of the International Monetary Fund, reports inflation statistics by country on a regular basis.

[14] The alternative of adjusting the functional currency amount for general price-level changes and then applying the current rate method was rejected by the FASB. The alternative was rejected because reliable, timely general price indexes are not always available and because the procedure would mix price-level adjusted amounts from the subsidiary with unadjusted amounts from the parent in the consolidated financial statements. For additional discussion, see *FASB Statement No. 52,* pars. 102–109.

[15] When an economy ceases to be highly inflationary, the change in the functional currency from the reporting currency to the local currency (the change from remeasurement to translation) should be in accordance with *EITF Issue 92-4.* This pronouncement states that "the reporting currency amounts at the date of change should be translated into the local currency at current exchange rates and those amounts should become the new function currency accounting basis for the nonmonetary assets and liabilities." *EITF Issue 92-8* addresses related income tax matters.

SUMMARY

Exhibit 12-14 on the following page presents a diagrammatic summary of a foreign statement restatement under *FASB Statement No. 52*. In order to determine whether translation, remeasurement, or both are required, we need to answer three questions or tests. The first is a hyperinflation test. If the subsidiary's functional currency is subject to hyperinflation, then *remeasurement* is necessary to restate the subsidiary's unstable functional currency into the parent's stable reporting currency. The restated subsidiary financial statements may then be used as the basis for equity method entries by the parent and consolidation. If the subsidiary's functional currency is not subject to hyperinflation, then two additional tests are required. The first asks if the subsidiary's local currency and functional currency are the same. If they are not the same, then the subsidiary's financial statements must be *remeasured* from the subsidiary's local currency into its functional currency. Following remeasurement or a decision that the subsidiary's reporting and functional currency are the same, a second test must be applied. The second test asks whether or not the subsidiary's functional currency and the parent's reporting currency are the same. If they are the same, then no further adjustment is required and the subsidiary's (possibly remeasured) statements are the basis for equity-method entries by the parent and consolidation. If, however, the subsidiary's functional currency differs from the parent reporting currency, then the subsidiary's statements must be translated into the parent's reporting currency before proceeding to equity-method entries and consolidation.

APPENDIX A: EQUITY-METHOD AND CONSOLIDATION PROCEDURES FOR FOREIGN SUBSIDIARIES

This appendix describes the application of the equity-method and consolidation procedures to restated foreign financial statements. These procedures are demonstrated by reference to the EXN-Gerhardt illustration considered earlier in this chapter, for which the following additional information is given:

1. EXN acquired 100% of the outstanding stock of Gerhardt for $135,000 cash on December 31, 19X0.

2. Gerhardt's identifiable net assets had a fair value equal to their book value of DM 400,000 on December 31, 19X0.

We begin by considering the equity method and then turn to consolidation. Although our illustrations of the equity method are restricted to wholly owned foreign subsidiaries, the same general principles are applicable to a partially owned foreign investee to which an investor must apply the equity method.

The Equity Method for Translated Foreign Subsidiaries

The equity method is applicable to both translated and remeasured foreign financial statements. We begin with a discussion of the equity method for translated foreign statements, which is followed by a discussion of the equity method for remeasured financial statements.

Date-of-Acquisition Analysis and Entries

Turning to the EXN-Gerhardt illustration, since the exchange rate for the Deutsche mark was $.30 on the date of acquisition, the analysis of the valuation differential as presented on page 605 is appropriate.

EXHIBIT 12-14   SUMMARY OF FOREIGN STATEMENT RESTATEMENT

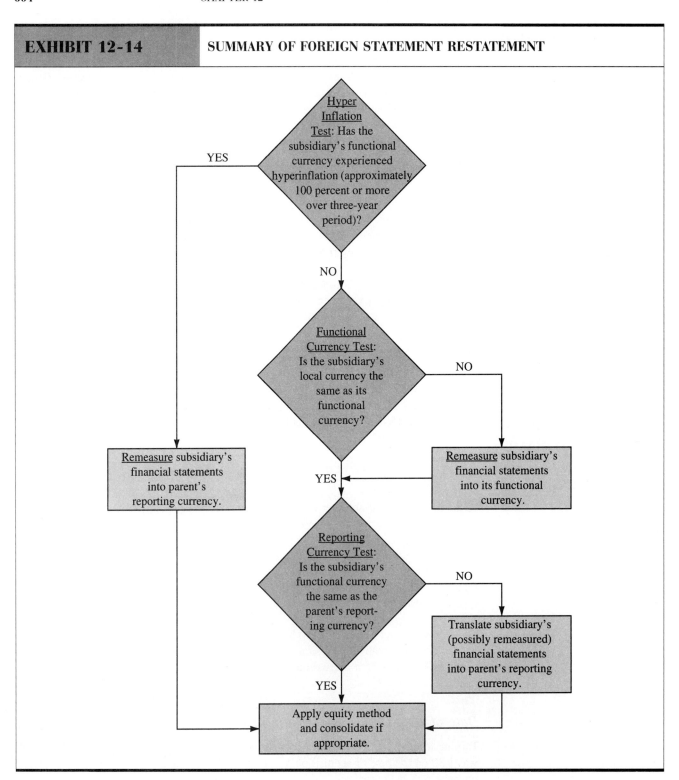

Analysis of the Valuation Differential under Translation

	Deutsche Marks		U.S. Dollars
Acquisition cost	DM 450,000*		$135,000
Book value of net assets acquired	400,000	× $.30 =	120,000
Valuation differential	DM 50,000		$ 15,000
Revaluation increments	–0–	× $.30 =	–0–
Goodwill	DM 50,000		$ 15,000

* DM 450,000 = $135,000 ÷ $.30

The fair value of Gerhardt's identifiable net assets should be measured by reference to their value in Germany, the economic environment of the functional currency, rather than their value in the United States. Hence, revaluation increments, if any, are measured in the functional currency and translated into U.S. dollars. Of course, if the acquisition is treated as a pooling of interests, then the subsidiary's assets and liabilities are not revalued and no valuation differential is recognized. The acquisition is recorded by EXN with the following entry:

Parent's entry to record acquisition of subsidiary:

Investment in Gerhardt 135,000
     Cash..   135,000

Of course, the investment account includes the $15,000 valuation differential that is subject to amortization on the parent's records over subsequent periods (estimated to be ten years for the EXN-Gerhardt illustration).

Analysis and Entries One Year after Acquisition

During 19X1, the first year following acquisition, Gerhardt's translated net income is $4,420, as shown in Exhibit 12-4. Since the average exchange rate for the mark during 19X1 is $.3400, EXN calculates its share of Gerhardt net income as follows:

Parent's Calculation of Income from Subsidiary

Subsidiary's (translated) net income	$4,420
Parent's ownership percentage	×1.00
Parent's share of subsidiary net income	$4,420
Less: Amortization of valuation differential [(50,000 DM ÷ 10 years) × $.3400]	1,700
Income from subsidiary	$2,720

Notice that the amortization of valuation differential (here composed entirely of goodwill) is calculated in the functional currency and then translated into the reporting currency at current rates (here the average rate for the current period).

The valuation differential, like other assets, is translated at the current rate. The following T-accounts show the goodwill account both before and after translation for the EXN-Gerhardt illustration in which the entire valuation differential is goodwill:

Current Rate Translation of Goodwill Account

Goodwill (DM)			Goodwill ($)		
Balance	50,000		Balance	15,000	
		Amortization 5,000			Amortization 1,700
			Translation adjustment 3,800		
Balance	45,000		Balance	17,100	

The beginning balance is translated at the 12-31-X0 rate ($15,000 = DM 50,000 × $.3000), the ending balance is translated at the 12-31-X1 rate ($17,100 = DM 45,000 × $.3800), and the amortization is translated at the average 19X1 rate ($.3400). The translation adjustment of $3,800 is calculated as the amount that is required to balance the account in dollars after other translated amounts have been determined ($3,800 = $17,100 − $15,000 + $1,700).

Since the valuation differential is not recorded by the subsidiary, the translation adjustment related to the valuation differential ($3,800) is not included in the translation adjustment ($32,520) arising from the subsidiary's financial statements. Accordingly, the cumulative translation adjustment, which is reported on the parent's balance sheet, must be calculated as the sum of its two parts:

Calculation of Change in Cumulative Translation Adjustment for Equity Method

Adjustment from translation of subsidiary's 19X1 financial statements (see Exhibits 12-3 and 12-4)	$32,520
Adjustment from translation of subsidiary's date-of-acquisition financial statements (see Exhibit 12-2; date-of-acquisition translation never gives rise to a translation adjustment)	–0–
Change cumulative translation adjustment reported by subsidiary during 19X1	$32,520
Parent's ownership percentage	×1.00
Parent's share of change in translation adjustment reported by subsidiary during 19X1	$32,520
19X1 adjustment from translation of valuation differential	3,800
Increase in cumulative translation adjustment during 19X1	$36,320

When the subsidiary is partially rather than wholly owned by the parent, only the fraction of total translation adjustment that is associated with the parent's ownership percentage is included in the accumulated translation adjustment. The remainder of the cumulative translation adjustment represents the share of stockholders other than the investor in the adjustment. For consolidation purposes, this amount is combined with minority interest by a worksheet adjustment.[16]

---

[16] Of course, if push-down accounting is followed, then the subsidiary will have recorded the valuation differential on its records. In that case, the cumulative translation adjustment computed in translating the subsidiary's foreign financial statements will include the translation adjustment related to the valuation differential, and a separate adjustment will not be required for purposes of the equity method. The parent need only apply its ownership percentage to the cumulative translation adjustment determined in the translation of the subsidiary's statements.

On the basis of the foregoing calculations, the parent makes the following entry:

Parent's entry to record income from subsidiary and cumulative translation adjustment:

Investment in Gerhardt 39,040		
Income from subsidiary		2,720
Cumulative translation adjustment		36,320

As the following paragraphs show, the cumulative translation adjustment recorded by the parent must be adjusted in subsequent periods to reflect the impact of future translation adjustments.

Analysis and Entries Two Years after Acquisition

During 19X2, the second year following acquisition, Gerhardt's translated net income is $12,000 and pays a cash dividend of 20,000 marks (translated as $8,400) at year-end, as shown in Exhibit 12-6. Since the average exchange rate for the mark during 19X2 is $.4000, EXN calculates its share of Gerhardt net income as follows:

Parent's Calculation of Income from Subsidiary

Subsidiary's (translated) net income	$12,000
Parent's ownership percentage	×1.00
Parent's share of subsidiary net income	$12,000
Less: Amortization of valuation differential [(DM 50,000 ÷ 10 years) × $.4000]	2,000
Income from subsidiary	$10,000

Note that the amortization varies with changes in the exchange rate. The following T-accounts describe goodwill over the two-year period, in terms of both Deutsche marks and translated dollars:

Current Rate Translation of Goodwill Account

Goodwill (DM)				Goodwill ($)				
Balance, 1-1-X1	50,000			Balance, 1-1-X1	15,000			
		19X1 amortization	5,000	Translation adjustment	3,800	19X1 amortization		1,700
Balance, 12-31-X1	45,000			Balance, 12-31-X1	17,100			
		19X2 amortization	5,000	Translation adjustment	1,700	19X2 amortization		2,000
Balance, 12-31-X2	40,000			Balance, 12-31-X2	16,800			

Each foreign currency balance is multiplied by the exchange rate for the date of the balance ($15,000 = DM 50,000 × $.3000; $17,100 = DM 45,000 × $.3800; and $16,800 = DM 40,000 × $.4200), and each amortization is multiplied by the average rate for the year of the amortization ($1,700 = DM 5,000 × $.3400, and $2,000 = DM 5,000 × $.4000). In both years, the translation adjustment is calculated as the amount that is required to balance the account in dollars after other translated amounts have been determined.

As in the previous year, the translation adjustment arising from the subsidiary's financial statements does not include the translation adjustment arising from the valuation differential. Accordingly, the total translation adjustment must be calculated as follows:

Calculation of Change in Cumulative Translation Adjustment for Equity Method

Adjustment from translation of subsidiary's 19X2 financial statements (see Exhibits 12-5 and 12-6)	$49,640
Adjustment from translation of subsidiary's 19X1 financial statements (see Exhibits 12-3 and 12-4)	32,520
Change cumulative translation adjustment reported by subsidiary during 19X2	$17,120
Parent's ownership percentage	×1.00
Parent's share of adjustment from translation of subsidiary's financial statements	$17,120
19X2 adjustment from translation of valuation differential	1,700
Increase in cumulative translation adjustment during 19X2	$18,820

On the basis of the foregoing calculations, the parent makes the following entries:

Parent's entry to record income from subsidiary and cumulative translation adjustment:

Investment in Gerhardt	28,820	
Income from subsidiary		10,000
Cumulative translation adjustment		18,820

Parent's entry to record dividend from subsidiary:

Cash	8,400	
Investment in Gerhardt		8,400

Disclosure Rules for Cumulative Translation Adjustment

Investors required to use the equity method or consolidation for translated foreign investees must disclose an analysis of the cumulative translation adjustment in a separate statement, a note, or as part of a statement of changes in equity (*FASB Statement No. 52*, par. 141). The analysis should include (1) the beginning and ending balances of the cumulative translation adjustment, (2) the aggregate translation adjustment for the current period resulting from the translation of the foreign investee's financial statements and from certain transactions described in Chapter 13, (3) the amount of income taxes for the period allocated to translation adjustments, and (4) any amount transferred from cumulative translation adjustments and included in determining net income for the period as a result of the sale or liquidation of all or part of an investment in a foreign entity.

The Equity Method for Remeasured Foreign Subsidiaries

Recall that restatement adjustments arising in remeasurement are included in the net income of the investee. Consequently, remeasurement does not give rise to a separate cumulative adjustment in the equity section of the investor's balance sheet. Let us illustrate the equity method for remeasured foreign subsidiaries by reference to the EXN-

Gerhardt illustration under the assumption that Gerhardt's functional currency is the U.S. dollar rather than its local currency (the Deutsche mark).

Date-of-Acquisition Analysis and Entries

Under remeasurement, the valuation differential is restated at historical rates. Since the spot rate is $.3000 on the date of EXN's acquisition of Gerhardt, the following analysis of the valuation differential is appropriate:

Analysis of the Valuation Differential under Remeasurement

	Deutsche Marks		U.S. Dollars
Acquisition cost	DM 450,000*		$135,000
Book value of net assets acquired	400,000	× $.30 =	120,000
Valuation differential	DM 50,000		$ 15,000
Revaluation increment	–0–	× $.30 =	–0–
Goodwill	DM 50,000		$ 15,000

* DM 450,000 = $135,000 ÷ $.30

The fair value of Gerhardt's identifiable net assets should be measured by reference to their value in the United States, the economic environment of the functional currency, rather than their value in Germany. Hence, revaluation increments, if any, should be measured relative to fair values of comparable assets and liabilities in the United States. We assume here that Gerhardt's assets and liabilities have fair values equal to their book values. The acquisition is recorded by EXN with this entry:

> *Parent's entry to record acquisition of subsidiary:*
>
> Investment in Gerhardt 135,000
>   Cash..   135,000

Of course, the investment account includes the $15,000 valuation differential that is subject to amortization on the parent's records over subsequent periods. As previously discussed, the amount of the valuation differential changes from year to year under translation owing to the required restatement at current rates. However, under remeasurement the amount of the valuation differential remains the same from year to year owing to the required restatement at historical rates, as shown in the parent's equity method entries that follow.

Analysis and Entries One and Two Years after Acquisition

The parent's entries under the equity method are based on the remeasured financial statements of the subsidiary shown in Exhibit 12-12, the supporting worksheet shown in Exhibit 12-8, and the supporting calculations shown in Exhibits 12-9, 12-10, and 12-11. EXN's share of Gerhardt's income in 19X1 and 19X2 is calculated as follows:

Parent's Calculation of 19X1 and 19X2 Income from Subsidiary

	19X1	19X2
Subsidiary (remeasured) net income	$16,900	$20,990
Parent's ownership percentage	×1.00	×1.00
Parent's share of subsidiary net income	$16,900	$20,990
Less: Amortization of valuation differential [(DM 50,000 ÷ 10 years) × $.3000]	1,500	1,500
Income from subsidiary	$15,400	$19,490

Since the remeasured valuation differential does not change from year to year, the related amortization remains unchanged. Further, the remeasurement of the valuation differential does not give rise to a separate restatement adjustment. Recall from our previous discussion that translation of the valuation differential contributes to the cumulative translation adjustment reported in the parent's balance sheet. The remeasured financial statements and the foregoing calculations are the basis for the equity-method entries by the parent shown in Exhibit 12-15.

We turn now from the equity method for translated and remeasured subsidiaries to consolidation procedures for such subsidiaries. We begin with the consolidation of translated subsidiaries and then turn to the consolidation of remeasured subsidiaries.

Consolidation Procedures for Translated Foreign Subsidiaries

This section of the appendix describes consolidation procedures that are applicable to translated foreign subsidiaries by reference to the consolidation of EXN and its subsidiary, Gerhardt, both one year and two years after acquisition. The related consolidation adjustments in journal entry form are shown in Exhibit 12-16. The end-of-19X1 and end-of-19X2 financial statements of EXN, Inc. (representing previously unstated information),

---

EXHIBIT 12-15

PARENT'S EQUITY-METHOD ENTRIES FOR SUBSIDIARY UNDER REMEASUREMENT

EXN, Inc.

EQUITY-METHOD ENTRIES FOR INVESTMENT IN GERHARDT MANUFACTURING

	Year Ended December 31, 19X0		Year Ended December 31, 19X1		Year Ended December 31, 19X2	
Parent's entry to record acquisition of subsidiary:						
Investment in Gerhardt	135,000					
Cash		135,000				
Parent's entry to record income from subsidiary:						
Investment in Gerhardt	–0–		15,400		19,490	
Income from subsidiary		–0–		15,400		19,490
Parent's entry to record 19X2 dividend from subsidiary:						
Cash	–0–		–0–		8,400	
Investment in Gerhardt		–0–		–0–		8,400

EXHIBIT 12-16	CONSOLIDATION WORKSHEET ADJUSTMENTS FOR TRANSLATION

EXN, Inc.

WORKSHEET ADJUSTMENTS FOR CONSOLIDATION OF GERHARDT MANUFACTURING

	Year Ended December 31, 19X1		Year Ended December 31, 19X2	
(1) *Reverse parent's recording of subsidiary income, and eliminate subsidiary dividend to parent for the current year:*				
Income from subsidiary	2,720		10,000	
Dividends		–0–		8,400
Investment in Gerhardt		2,720		1,600
(2) *Eliminate and reclassify beginning-of-the-year balance of parent's investment account (except for portion related to cumulative translation adjustment and valuation differential translation adjustment):*				
Common stock of Gerhardt	90,000		90,000	
Retained earnings of Gerhardt	30,000		34,420*	
Goodwill	*15,000*		*17,100*	
Investment in Gerhardt		135,000		141,520
(3) *Eliminate subsidiary's cumulative translation adjustment, and reclassify translation adjustment related to valuation differential:*				
Goodwill	3,800		1,700	
Cumulative translation adjustment	32,520		49,640	
Investment in Gerhardt		36,320		51,340
(4) *Record amortization valuation of differential for current year:*				
Depreciation and amortization expense	1,700		2,000	
Goodwill		1,700		2,000

* $34,420 = $30,000 + $4,420

and the corresponding translated financial statements of its subsidiary, Gerhardt Manufacturing, are shown in the first two columns of Exhibits 12-17 and 12-18 on page 613.

The first, second, and fourth adjustments represent familiar forms. The third adjustment, however, requires a word of explanation. The third adjustment performs two functions. First, it eliminates the subsidiary's cumulative translation adjustment ($32,520 at the end of 19X1 and $49,640 at the end of 19X2) by offsetting it against the reciprocal portion of the investment account. Second, it reclassifies the translation adjustment related to the valuation differential ($3,800 at the end of 19X1 and $1,700 at the end of 19X2; here all of it is related to goodwill) from the investment account to the goodwill account. Note that only the current year's portion of the goodwill-related adjustment needs to be reclassified. Prior year's goodwill-related translation adjustments are appropriately reclassified by the second adjustment. When the subsidiary is partially rather than wholly owned by the parent, the minority interest's share of the total translation adjustment must be included in the minority interest column of the worksheet.

EXHIBIT 12-17	CONSOLIDATION WORKSHEET FOR PARENT AND TRANSLATED FOREIGN SUBSIDIARY ONE YEAR AFTER ACQUISITION

	Separate Financial Statements		Consolidation Adjustments		Consolidated Financial Statements
	EXN	Gerhardt	Dr.	Cr.	
Income Statement					
Sales	950,000	81,600			1,031,600
Income from subsidiary	2,720		(1) 2,720		–0–
Cost of goods sold	(430,000)*	(59,500)			(489,500)
Depreciation and amortization expense	(87,000)	(9,180)	(4) 1,700		(97,880)
Other expense	(395,000)	(8,500)			(403,500)
Net income	40,720	4,420	4,420		40,720
Retained Earnings Statement					
Retained earnings, 1-1-X1	222,000	30,000	(2) 30,000		222,000
Net income	40,720	4,420	4,420		40,720
Dividends	(12,500)				(12,500)
Retained earnings, 12-31-X1	250,220	34,420	34,420		250,220
Balance Sheet					
Cash	120,000	15,580			135,580
Accounts receivable	310,000	35,720			345,720
Inventory	477,000	22,800			499,800
Investment in Gerhardt	174,040			(1) 2,720	–0–
				(2) 135,000	
				(3) 36,320	
Goodwill			(2) 15,000	(4) 1,700	17,100
			(3) 3,800		
Plant and equipment	637,500	133,000			770,500
Accumulated depreciation	(279,000)	(40,660)			(319,660)
Total assets	1,439,540	166,440			1,449,040
Accounts payable	103,000	9,500			112,500
Bonds payable	400,000				400,000
Common stock:					
EXN	650,000				650,000
Gerhardt		90,000	(2) 90,000		–0–
Translation adjustment:					
EXN	36,320				36,320
Gerhardt		32,520	(3) 32,520		–0–
Retained earnings	250,220	34,420	34,420		250,220
Total liabilities and stockholders' equity	1,439,540	166,440	175,740	175,740	1,449,040

* Parentheses indicate decreases.

EXHIBIT 12-18	CONSOLIDATION WORKSHEET FOR PARENT AND TRANSLATED FOREIGN SUBSIDIARY TWO YEARS AFTER ACQUISITION

	Separate Financial Statements		Consolidation Adjustments		Consolidated Financial Statements
	EXN	Gerhardt	Dr.	Cr.	
Income Statement					
Sales	997,000	116,000			1,113,000
Income from subsidiary	10,000		(1) 10,000		–0–
Cost of goods sold	(450,000)*	(68,000)			(518,000)
Depreciation and amortization expense	(92,000)	(16,000)	(4) 2,000		(110,000)
Interest expense	(40,000)	(3,080)			(43,080)
Other expense	(348,000)	(16,920)			(364,920)
Net income	77,000	12,000	12,000		77,000
Retained Earnings Statement					
Retained earnings, 1-1-X2	250,220	34,420	(2) 34,420		250,220
Net income	77,000	12,000	12,000		77,000
Dividends	(15,000)	(8,400)		(1) 8,400	(15,000)
Retained earnings, 12-31-X2	312,220	38,020	46,420	8,400	312,220
Balance Sheet					
Cash	142,000	30,240			172,240
Accounts receivable	329,500	54,600			384,100
Inventory	542,000	32,340			574,340
Investment in Gerhardt	194,460			(1) 1,600	–0–
				(2) 141,520	
				(3) 51,340	
Goodwill			(2) 17,100	(4) 2,000	16,800
			(3) 1,700		
Plant and equipment	670,400	168,000			838,400
Accumulated depreciation	(366,000)	(61,740)			(427,740)
Total assets	1,512,360	223,440			1,558,140
Accounts payable	95,000	13,440			108,440
Notes payable		32,340			32,340
Bonds payable	400,000				400,000
Common stock:					
EXN	650,000				650,000
Gerhardt		90,000	(2) 90,000		–0–
Translation adjustment:					
EXN	55,140				55,140
Gerhardt		49,640	(3) 49,640		–0–
Retained earnings	312,220	38,020	46,420	8,400	312,220
Total liabilities and stockholders' equity	1,512,360	223,440	204,860	204,860	1,558,140

* Parentheses indicate decreases.

Consolidation Procedures for Remeasured Foreign Subsidiaries

The consolidation worksheet adjustments made by EXN, Inc., at the end of 19X1 and 19X2 are given in Exhibit 12-19. The consolidation worksheet for 19X2 is shown in Exhibit 12-20. Since the 19X1 worksheet is very similar to the 19X2 worksheet, it is not presented. However, several of the parent's balances that relate to the 19X1 worksheet deserve a word of explanation. First, the parent's balance of retained earnings at January 1, 19X2, can be calculated as follows:

Calculation of Parent's Retained Earnings Balance at January 1, 19X2		
Parent's retained earnings, 1-1-X1		$222,000
Parent's income before income from subsidiary ($40,720 − $2,720; see Exhibit 12-17)	$38,000	
Income from subsidiary (see Exhibit 12-15)	15,400	53,400
Subtotal		$275,400
Dividends (see Exhibit 12-17)		12,500
Parent's retained earnings, 1-1-X2		$262,900

The schedule presented at the top of page 616 summarizes activity in the parent's investment account that is recorded by the journal entries shown in Exhibit 12-15.

EXHIBIT 12-19	CONSOLIDATION WORKSHEET ADJUSTMENTS FOR REMEASUREMENT

EXN, Inc.

WORKSHEET ADJUSTMENTS FOR CONSOLIDATION OF GERHARDT MANUFACTURING

	Year Ended December 31, 19X1		Year Ended December 31, 19X2	
(1) *Reverse parent's recording of subsidiary income, and eliminate subsidiary dividend to parent for the current year:*				
Income from subsidiary	15,400		19,490	
Dividends		–0–		8,400
Investment in Gerhardt		15,400		11,090
(2) *Eliminate and reclassify beginning-of-the-year balance of parent's investment account:*				
Common stock of Gerhardt	90,000		90,000	
Retained earnings of Gerhardt	30,000		46,900*	
Goodwill	*15,000*		*13,500*	
Investment in Gerhardt		135,000		150,400
(3) *Record amortization of valuation differential for current year:*				
Depreciation and amortization expense	1,500		1,500	
Goodwill		1,500		1,500

* $46,900 = $30,000 + $16,900; that is, the 1-1-X1 balance of subsidiary retained earnings plus the change in retained earnings during 19X1, which in this case equals the subsidiary's 19X1 net income.

EXHIBIT 12-20	CONSOLIDATION WORKSHEET FOR PARENT AND REMEASURED FOREIGN SUBSIDIARY TWO YEARS AFTER ACQUISITION

	Separate Financial Statements		Consolidation Adjustments		Consolidated Financial Statements
	EXN	Gerhardt	Dr.	Cr.	
Income Statement					
Sales	997,000	116,000			1,113,000
Income from subsidiary	19,490		(1) 19,490		–0–
Cost of goods sold	(450,000)*	(65,430)			(515,430)
Depreciation and amortization expense	(92,000)	(13,040)	(3) 1,500		(106,540)
Interest expense	(40,000)	(3,080)			(43,080)
Other expense	(348,000)	(16,920)			(364,920)
Remeasurement gain		3,460			3,460
Net income	86,490	20,990	20,990		86,490
Retained Earnings Statement					
Retained earnings, 1-1-X2	262,900	46,900	(2) 46,900		262,900
Net income	86,490	20,990	20,990		86,490
Dividends	(15,000)	(8,400)		(1) 8,400	(15,000)
Retained earnings, 12-31-X2	334,390	59,490	67,890	8,400	334,390
Balance Sheet					
Cash	142,000	30,240			172,240
Accounts receivable	329,500	54,600			384,100
Inventory	542,000	31,570			573,570
Investment in Gerhardt	161,490			(1) 11,090 (2) 150,400	–0–
Goodwill			(2) 13,500	(3) 1,500	12,000
Plant and equipment	670,400	124,000			794,400
Accumulated depreciation	(366,000)	(45,140)			(411,140)
Total assets	1,479,390	195,270			1,525,170
Accounts payable	95,000	13,440			108,440
Notes payable		32,340			32,340
Bonds payable	400,000				400,000
Common stock:					
EXN	650,000				650,000
Gerhardt		90,000	(2) 90,000		–0–
Retained earnings	334,390	59,490	67,890	8,400	334,390
Total liabilities and stockholders' equity	1,479,390	195,270	171,390	171,390	1,525,170

* Parentheses indicate decreases.

Summary of Parent's Investment Account

Investment in subsidiary, 1-1-X1	$135,000
19X1 income from subsidiary	15,400
19X1 dividend from subsidiary	–0–
Investment in subsidiary, 12-31-X1	$150,400
19X2 income from subsidiary	19,490
19X2 dividend from subsidiary	(8,400)
Investment in subsidiary, 12-31-X2	$161,490

Of course, neither the beginning balance of the parent retained earnings nor the ending balance of the parent's investment account needs to be calculated in practice. It will appear in the accounts of the parent and can be taken directly from the parent's adjusted trial balance.

APPENDIX B: COMPOSITION OF TRANSLATION ADJUSTMENT

Recall that restatement adjustments arise from accounts restated at current rates; accounts restated at historical rates do not give rise to restatement adjustments. Translation, as demonstrated in Exhibit 12-3, restates all assets and liabilities at current rates. Accordingly, the composition of the translation adjustment is revealed by an analysis of the restated activity in all asset and liability accounts. Although such an analysis of restated activity is much more cumbersome than the balancing figure calculation, it enhances our understanding of the translation adjustment. This analysis is performed for the EXN-Gerhardt illustration in Exhibit 12-21 and is summarized as follows:

Composition of 19X1 Translation Adjustment

Translation adjustment for cash	$ 3,640
Translation adjustment for accounts receivable	5,160
Translation adjustment for inventory	5,000
Translation adjustment for plant and equipment	28,000
Translation adjustment for accumulated depreciation	(7,480)
Translation adjustment for accounts payable	(1,800)
Net translation adjustment (a credit)	$32,520

Observe that translation adjustments requiring debits to an asset or liability account require balancing credit adjustments to equity. Similarly, translation adjustments requiring credits to an asset or liability account require balancing debit adjustments to equity.

SELECTED READINGS

Alleman, Raymand H. "Why ITT Likes FAS 52," *Management Accounting* (July 1982), pp. 23–29.

Choi, Frederick D. S. (ed.). *Handbook of International Accounting.* New York: Wiley, 1991.

Evans, Thomas G, and Timothy S. Doupnik. *Determining the Functional Currency under Statement 52,* Research Report. Stamford, CT: Financial Accounting Standards Board, 1986.

EXHIBIT 12-21	ANALYSIS OF ASSETS AND LIABILITIES BEFORE AND AFTER TRANSLATION

Gerhardt Manufacturing (Subsidiary of EXN, Inc.)

COMPARATIVE T-ACCOUNT ANALYSIS OF ASSETS AND LIABILITIES
FOR THE YEAR ENDED DECEMBER 31, 19X1

Accounts in Deutsche Marks

Cash (DM)

Balance	50,000		
Collect	181,000	Other expense	25,000
		Pay accounts	165,000
Balance	41,000		

Accounts Receivable (DM)

Balance	35,000		
Sales	240,000	Collect	181,000*
Balance	94,000		

Inventory (DM)

Balance	65,000		
Purchases	170,000*	Cost of goods sold	175,000
Balance	60,000		

Plant and Equipment (DM)

Balance	350,000		
Balance	350,000		

Accumulated Depreciation (DM)

		Balance	80,000
		Depreciation	27,000
		Balance	107,000

Accounts Payable (DM)

		Balance	20,000
Pay accounts	165,000*	Purchase	170,000
		Balance	25,000

Accounts in U.S. Dollars

Cash ($)

Balance	15,000		
Collect	61,540	Other expense	8,500
		Pay accounts	56,100
Translation adjustment	3,640		
Balance	15,580		

Accounts Receivable ($)

Balance	10,500		
Sales	81,600	Collect	61,540
Translation adjustment	5,160		
Balance	35,720		

Inventory ($)

Balance	19,500		
Purchases	57,800	Cost of goods sold†	59,500
Translation adjustment	5,000		
Balance	22,800		

Plant and Equipment ($)

Balance	105,000		
Translation adjustment	28,000		
Balance	133,000		

Accumulated Depreciation ($)

		Balance	24,000
		Depreciation	9,180
		Translation adjustment	7,480
		Balance	40,660

Accounts Payable ($)

		Balance	6,000
Pay accounts	56,100	Purchase	57,800
		Translation adjustment	1,800
		Balance	9,500

* Calculated as the amount required to balance the account.

† $59,500 = $175,000 × $.3400

Griffin, Paul A., and Richard P. Castanias II. *Accounting for the Translation of Foreign Currencies: The Effects of Statement 52 on Equity Analysis,* Research Report. Stamford, CT: Financial Accounting Standards Board, 1987.

Hepworth, Samuel R. *Reporting Foreign Operations.* Ann Arbor: Bureau of Business Research, Univ. of Michigan, 1956.

Huefner, Ronald J., J. Edward Ketz, and James A. Largay III. "Foreign Currency Translation and the Cash Flow Statement," *Accounting Horizons* (June 1989), pp. 66–75.

Largay, James A., III. "SFAS 52: Expediency or Principle?" *Journal of Accounting, Auditing and Finance* (Fall 1983), pp. 44–53.

Lorensen, Leonard. *Reporting Foreign Operations of U.S. Companies in U.S. Dollars,* Accounting Research Study No. 12. New York: American Institute of Certified Public Accountants, 1972.

Lowe, Howard D. "Shortcomings of Japanese Consolidated Financial Statements," *Accounting Horizons* (September 1990), pp. 1–9.

Rayburn, Frank R., and G. Michael Crooch. "Currency Translation and the Funds Statement: A New Approach," *Journal of Accountancy* (October 1983), pp. 51–62.

Rezaee, Zabihollah. "The Impact of New Accounting Rules on the Consolidation of Financial Statements of Multinational Companies," *International Journal of Accounting* 26:3 (1991), pp. 206–219.

Survey of International Accounting Practices. New York: Arthur Andersen, Coopers & Lybrand, Deloitte & Touche, Ernst & Young, KPMG Peat Marwick, and Price Waterhouse, 1991.

QUESTIONS

Q12-1 Distinguish between *foreign currency conversion* and *foreign currency restatement.*

Q12-2 Define *currency exchange rate.*

Q12-3 Distinguish between direct and indirect currency exchange rates.

Q12-4 Explain why you agree or disagree with the following statement: Financial accounting standards do not require that foreign financial statements be adjusted to conform with U.S. generally accepted accounting principles prior to restatement in dollars.

Q12-5 Explain the concept of functional currency.

Q12-6 A U.S. company desires to restate the financial statements of its Canadian subsidiary into U.S. dollars. The Canadian subsidiary maintains its records in Canadian dollars. Indicate whether translation, remeasurement, or remeasurement and translation would be required under each of the following circumstances:

a) The functional currency of the Canadian subsidiary is the Canadian dollar.

b) The functional currency of the Canadian subsidiary is the French franc.

c) The functional currency of the Canadian subsidiary is the U.S. dollar.

Q12-7 What is a *highly inflationary economy?* Can a highly inflationary currency serve as an entity's functional currency?

Q12-8 Translation procedures are used to restate foreign currency financial statements that are measured in a foreign affiliate's functional currency into the parent's reporting currency. What is the objective of translation?

Q12-9   Using translation procedures, what exchange rate is used to restate the assets and liabilities in foreign currency financial statements?

Q12-10   Using translation procedures, what exchange rate is used to restate the revenues, expenses, gains, and losses in foreign currency financial statements?

Q12-11   How are translation adjustments that result from the application of translation procedures reported?

Q12-12   Remeasurement of a foreign subsidiary's financial statements is required whenever the subsidiary's functional currency differs from its reporting currency. What is the objective of the remeasurement process?

Q12-13   What exchange rate(s) is used to restate the assets and liabilities in foreign currency financial statements under remeasurement?

Q12-14   What exchange rate(s) is used to restate the revenues, expenses, gains, and losses in foreign currency financial statements under remeasurement?

Q12-15   How are remeasurement gains and losses arising from remeasurement reported?

Q12-16   Explain why you agree or disagree with the following statement: When a subsidiary's local and functional currencies differ under remeasurement, the local currency should be used in applying the lower-of-cost-or-market test to the subsidiary inventory.

Q12-17   The U.S. firm Noland Company includes two wholly owned foreign subsidiaries in its consolidated financial statements, Big Ben Company in England and Black Forest, Inc., in Germany. The U.S. dollar is the functional currency for Big Ben, and the German mark is the functional currency for Black Forest. Identify the process that Noland would use to restate the financial statements of each subsidiary, and discuss how the restatement adjustments for each would be reported.

Q12-18   Describe a situation in which a subsidiary's foreign currency financial statements would have to be remeasured and translated before consolidation procedures could be applied by the U.S. parent company.

QUESTIONS FOR APPENDIX A

Q12-19   Explain why you agree or disagree with the following statement: At the date of acquisition of a foreign subsidiary by a U.S. parent, the fair value of the subsidiary's net assets should be measured in U.S. dollars even if the U.S. dollar is not the functional currency of the subsidiary.

Q12-20   A U.S. firm acquires a foreign subsidiary paying $10,000 in excess of the fairly valued net assets of the foreign subsidiary. The $10,000 is identified as goodwill and is amortized over ten years. Discuss how accounting for goodwill would differ under translation procedures versus remeasurement procedures.

QUESTION FOR APPENDIX B

Q12-21   Explain why you agree or disagree with the following statement: The translation adjustment that is associated with the translation of a subsidiary's financial statements arises from accounts being restated at historical rates; accounts restated at current rates do not give rise to translation adjustments.

EXERCISES

E12-1   **Terminology**   Terms (1) through (9) are related to the restatement of foreign financial statements.

REQUIRED
For each of the following terms, select the best phrase or description from the answers listed A through I below.

Terms	**Descriptions**
1. Currency exchange rate	**A.** The currency of the primary economic environment in which an entity generates and expends cash.
2. Foreign currency restatement	**B.** The restatement rate that, when used to restate an account, results in a restatement adjustment.
3. Translation	**C.** The restatement procedure in which all asset and liability accounts are restated at current rates and all owners' equity accounts are restated at historical rates, and the resulting adjustment is reported in a separate equity account.
4. Remeasurement	
5. Reporting currency	
6. Functional currency	
7. Historical rate restatement	**D.** An economy in which the cumulative inflation rate over a three-year period is approximately 100% or more.
8. Current rate restatement	
9. Highly inflationary economy	**E.** The process of expressing foreign currency amounts in another currency by the use of a currency exchange rate.
	F. The currency in which the entity keeps records and issues financial statements.
	G. The price of one currency in terms of another currency.
	H. The restatement rate that, when used to restate an account, results in no restatement adjustment.
	I. The restatement procedure in which some asset and liability accounts are restated at current rates, whereas others are restated at historical rates, and the resulting adjustment is included in net income.

 E12-2 **Identification of Exchange Rates for Translation and Remeasurement**   Harper Company, a U.S. parent company, includes the financial results of its foreign subsidiary in Australia in the consolidated statements of the parent. Following are selected accounts from the adjusted trial balance of the Australian subsidiary, which maintains its records in the Australian dollar.

1. Inventory (at cost)
2. Marketable securities (at market, which is below cost)
3. Prepaid expenses
4. Machinery
5. Buildings
6. Accumulated depreciation
7. Goodwill
8. Accounts payable

9. Bonds payable
10. Unamortized premium on bonds payable
11. Common stock
12. Sales
13. Advertising expense
14. Depreciation expense
15. Amortization of goodwill
16. Retained earnings (beginning of year)

REQUIRED
Indicate the exchange rate (e.g., current exchange rate, historical exchange rate) that would be used to restate each of the preceding accounts if the

a) Foreign subsidiary's local currency is its functional currency
b) Foreign subsidiary's functional currency is the U.S. dollar

E12-3 **Analysis of Comments on Translation and Remeasurement** Indicate whether you agree or disagree with each of the following statements. If you disagree with a statement, provide an explanation as to why.

1. The conversion of foreign currency is the exchange of one currency for another, whereas the translation of foreign currency is the process of expressing in one currency amounts that are denominated or measured in a different currency by the use of a currency exchange rate.

2. From a U.S. viewpoint, if a bank offers to sell 1,000 Hong Kong dollars for $128.20, the implied direct exchange rate is $.1282.

3. An entity's functional currency and reporting currency are always the same.

4. A French subsidiary of a U.S. firm that keeps its records in the French franc but has the U.S. dollar as its functional currency must remeasure its financial information from the franc to the dollar before inclusion in the consolidated statements of the U.S. firm.

5. The translation adjustments resulting from the translation of a foreign firm's financial statements from the functional currency to U.S. dollars should be included in the foreign firm's remeasured net income.

6. An economy would have to incur an inflation rate of about 20% per year for three consecutive years to be considered a highly inflationary economy.

7. Remeasurement of a foreign subsidiary's financial statements restates the subsidiary's local currency results and relationships as though they had been conducted in the functional currency environment.

8. Restatement of stockholders' equity accounts in foreign currency financial statements is accomplished the same way for both remeasurement and translation (that is, capital stock and other paid-in capital accounts are restated at the historical rates, and the beginning retained earnings for the period is restated at the dollar value determined at the end of the prior period).

9. When the inventory of a foreign subsidiary is to be valued at the lower of cost or market, the comparison of cost and market must be made in units of the functional currency.

E12-4 **Multiple Choice Questions on Restatement of Foreign Currency Financial Statements**

1. Remeasurement gains and losses resulting from remeasuring foreign currency financial statements into U.S. dollars should be included as

    a) A deferred item in the balance sheet

    b) An extraordinary item in the income statement for the period in which the rate changes

    c) An ordinary item in the income statement for losses but deferred for gains

    d) An ordinary item in the income statement for the period in which the rate changes

2. A wholly owned subsidiary of Ward, Inc., has certain expense accounts for the year ended December 31, 19X4, stated in local currency units (LCU) as follows:

	LCU
Depreciation of equipment (related assets were purchased January 1, 19X2)	120,000
Provision for doubtful accounts	80,000
Rent	200,000
	400,000

The exchange rates at various dates are as follows:

	Dollar Equivalent of 1 LCU
December 31, 19X4	$.40
Average for year ended 12-31-X4	.44
January 1, 19X2	.50

Assume that the LCU is the subsidiary's functional currency and that the charges to the expense accounts occurred approximately evenly during the year. What total dollar amount should be included in the 19X4 restated income statement of the subsidiary to reflect these expenses?

a) $160,000   **c)** $176,000

b) $168,000   **d)** $183,200

3. A company is translating account balances from another currency into dollars for its December 31, 19X9, balance sheet and its calendar-year 19X9 earnings statement and statement of cash flows. The average exchange rate for the year 19X9 should be used to translate

a) Cash at December 31, 19X9   **c)** Retained earnings at January 1, 19X9

b) Land purchased in 19X7   **d)** Sales for 19X9

4. At December 31, 19X8, Jem Company had foreign subsidiaries with 1,500,000 local currency units (LCU) in long-term receivables and 2,400,000 LCU in long-term debt. The rate of exchange in effect when the specific transactions occurred involving those foreign currency amounts was 2 LCU to $1. The rate of exchange in effect at December 31, 19X8, was 1.5 LCU to $1. Assuming the functional currency is the local currency of the foreign entity, the translation of the preceding foreign currency amounts into U.S. dollars would result in long-term receivables and long-term debt, respectively, of

a) $750,000 and $1,200,000   **c)** $1,000,000 and $1,200,000

b) $750,000 and $1,600,000   **d)** $1,000,000 and $1,600,000

5. Tree Company acquired 80% of the outstanding stock of Limb Company, a foreign company. In the preparation of consolidated statements, the paid-in capital of Limb Company should be translated into dollars at the

a) Exchange rate effective when Limb Company was organized

b) Current exchange rate

c) Average exchange rate for the period Tree Company has held the Limb Company stock

d) Exchange rate effective at the date Tree Company purchased the Limb Company stock

6. At what exchange rates should the following balance sheet accounts in the statements of a foreign subsidiary be reflected in the restated subsidiary's statements if the U.S. dollar is the subsidiary's functional currency?

	Equipment	Accumulated Depreciation of Equipment
a)	Current	Current
b)	Current	Average for year
c)	Historical	Current
d)	Historical	Historical

7. The Dease Company owns a foreign subsidiary with 3,600,000 local currency units (LCU) of property, plant, and equipment before accumulated depreciation at December 31, 19X5. Of this amount, 2,400,000 LCU were acquired in 19X3 when the rate of exchange was 1.6 LCU to $1, and 1,200,000 LCU were acquired in 19X4 when the rate of exchange was 1.8 LCU to $1. The rate of exchange in effect at December 31, 19X5, was 2 LCU to $1. The weighted average of exchange rates in effect during 19X5 was 1.92 LCU to $1.

Assuming that the property, plant, and equipment are depreciated using the straight-line method over a ten-year period with *no* salvage value, how much depreciation expense relating to the foreign subsidiary's property, plant, and equipment would appear in the restated subsidiary's income statement for 19X5 if the subsidiary's functional currency is the U.S. dollar?

a) $180,000   **c)** $200,000

b) $187,500   **d)** $216,667

8. Certain balance sheet accounts in a foreign subsidiary of the Brogan Company at December 31, 19X7, have been restated into U.S. dollars as follows:

	Restated	
	Current Rates	**Historical Rates**
Marketable equity securities carried at cost	$100,000	$110,000
Marketable equity securities carried at current market price	120,000	125,000
Inventories carried at cost	130,000	132,000
Inventories carried at net realizable value	80,000	84,000
	$430,000	$451,000

What amount should be shown in the subsidiary's restated balance sheet at December 31, 19X7, as a result of the previous information if the functional currency of the foreign entity is the U.S. dollar?

a) $430,000   **c)** $442,000

b) $436,000   **d)** $451,000

9. A balance arising from the translation or remeasurement of a subsidiary's foreign currency financial statements is reported in the consolidated income statement when the subsidiary's functional currency is the

	Foreign Currency	**U.S. Dollar**
a)	No	No
b)	No	Yes
c)	Yes	No
d)	Yes	Yes

10. A foreign subsidiary's functional currency is its local currency, which has not experienced significant inflation. The weighted average exchange rate for the current year would be the appropriate exchange rate for translating

	Sales to Customers	**Wages Expense**
a)	No	No
b)	Yes	Yes
c)	No	Yes
d)	Yes	No

(AICPA adapted)

E12-5   Identification of Exchange Rates for Remeasurement   Dhia Products Company was incorporated in the state of Florida in 19X0 to do business as a manufacturer of medical supplies and equipment. Since incorporating, Dhia has doubled in size every year and is now considered one of the leading medical supply companies in the country.

During January 19X5, Dhia established a subsidiary, Ban, Ltd., in the emerging nation of Shatha. Dhia owns 90% of the outstanding capital stock of Ban; the remaining 10% of Ban's outstanding capital stock is held by Shatha citizens, as required by Shatha constitutional law. The investment in Ban, accounted for by Dhia by the equity method, represents about 18% of the total assets of Dhia at December 31, 19X8, the close of the accounting period for both companies. Ban's functional currency is the U.S. dollar.

REQUIRED

Assume it has been appropriate for Dhia and Ban to prepare consolidated financial statements for each year 19X5 through 19X8, but before consolidated financial statements can be prepared, the individual account balances in Ban's December 31, 19X8, adjusted trial balance must be remeasured into the appropriate number of U.S. dollars. For each of the ten accounts listed below, taken from Ban's adjusted trial balance, specify what exchange rate (for example, average exchange rate for 19X8, current exchange rate at December 31, 19X8) should be used to remeasure the account balances into dollars, and explain why that rate is appropriate.

1. Cash in Shatha National Bank

2. Trade accounts receivable (all from 19X8 revenues)

3. Supplies inventory (all purchased during the last quarter of 19X8)

4. Land (purchased in 19X5)

5. Short-term note payable to Shatha National Bank

6. Capital stock (no par or stated value and all issued in January 19X5)

7. Retained earnings, January 1, 19X8

8. Sales revenue

9. Depreciation expense (on buildings)

10. Salaries expense

(AICPA adapted)

E12-6 **Restatement of Subsidiary's Balance Sheet at Date of Acquisition**   To enhance its foreign sales territory, Shelton Corporation acquired on December 31, 19X6, all the capital stock of LeBrone Company located in Kenya. The December 31, 19X6, balance sheet (in shillings) of LeBrone Company is as follows:

Assets	
Cash	110,000
Accounts receivable	150,000
Notes receivable	200,000
Inventory, 12-31-X6	350,000
Plant and equipment (net)	500,000
	1,310,000
Liabilities and Stockholders' Equity	
Accounts payable	240,000
Notes payable	250,000
Accrued liabilities	100,000
Capital stock	450,000
Paid-in capital	90,000
Retained earnings	180,000
	1,310,000

The current exchange rate for the shilling on December 31, 19X6, the date of acquisition, was $.20.

REQUIRED

a) Prepare a worksheet to restate the amounts in the December 31, 19X6, balance sheet of LeBrone Company into U.S. dollars, assuming LeBrone's functional currency is its local currency.

b) If Shelton Corporation paid book value for the net assets of LeBrone Company, what U.S. dollar amount would Shelton have paid?

c) Would the restated balance sheet amounts in part (a) have been different had LeBrone's functional currency been the U.S. dollar or some other currency?

E12-7 **Application of Lower-of-Cost-or-Market Rule in Remeasurement of Inventory** A Hong Kong subsidiary of a U.S. corporation reported ending inventory of 600,000 Hong Kong dollars (HK$) on its December 31, 19X2, financial statements. The inventory was acquired during the last quarter of 19X2 when the exchange rate for the Hong Kong dollar was $.13. Relevant information as of December 31, 19X2, relating to the inventory follows:

	HK$
Replacement cost	570,000
Net realizable value	700,000
Net realizable value less normal profit margin	660,000

The subsidiary's functional currency is the U.S. dollar. The exchange rate for the Hong Kong dollar was $.11 on December 31, 19X2.

REQUIRED

Applying the lower-of-cost-or-market rule, determine the dollar value that would be assigned the inventory of the subsidiary when it is remeasured into U.S. dollars.

E12-8 **Determination and Application of the Functional Currency** A U.S. company's subsidiary operating in Italy acquired land on April 1, 19X1. In the subsidiary's financial statements dated December 31, 19X4, the land was reported at 7,200,000 lira to reflect a 20% increase in general inflation since the date the land was acquired.

The functional currency of the Italian subsidiary is the French franc. The following exchange rates are presented:

	Lira to Dollar	Franc to Dollar	Franc to Lira
April 1, 19X1	$.004	$.12	30
December 31, 19X4	.006	.15	25

REQUIRED

a) Determine the amount at which the land would be presented in the subsidiary's restated financial statements by completing the following:

1. Restate the land on December 31, 19X4, to reflect the carrying value in U.S. generally accepted accounting principles (historical cost).

2. Remeasure the land on December 31, 19X4, in the functional currency of the subsidiary.

3. Translate the land on December 31, 19X4, into the currency of the U.S. parent company.

b) Independent of the requirements in part (a), determine the amount at which the land would be presented in the restated financial statements of the subsidiary if the French economy had experienced a cumulative inflation of over 100 percent in the last three years.

E12-9
APPENDIX A

Apply the Equity Method to Translated Financial Statements of Partially Owned Subsidiary Peat Company, a U.S. company, acquired, at book value, a 90% interest in Marwick Company of France on January 1, 19X3.

Marwick Company's functional currency is the French franc. The translation of Marwick's 19X3 financial statements resulted in translated net income of $6,000 and translation adjustment of $23,500.

During 19X4, the second year following acquisition, Marwick's translated net income was $7,000 and the translation adjustment arising from its financial statements was $36,200.

REQUIRED

a) Prepare the entry on the books of Peat Company for 19X3 to record income from subsidiary and cumulative translation adjustment.

b) Assuming Marwick Company paid a cash dividend in 19X3 of 10,000 francs (translated as $2,000), prepare the entry on the books of Peat Company to record the dividends from the subsidiary.

c) Prepare the entry on the books of Peat Company for 19X4 to record the income from subsidiary and cumulative translation adjustment.

E12-10
APPENDIX A

Apply the Equity Method to Translated Financial Statements of Wholly Owned Subsidiary, Valuation Differential; Prepare Consolidation Worksheet Adjustments Right Company, a Virginia-based firm, acquired all the outstanding common stock of Guard, Inc., of Pakistan for $70,000 cash on January 1, 19X1, when the exchange rate for the Pakistan rupee was $.10. Guard's net assets had a fair value equal to their book value of 660,000 rupees on January 1, 19X1; any valuation differential is amortized over five years. Guard's stockholders' equity at the date of acquisition consisted of common stock of 400,000 rupees and retained earnings of 260,000 rupees.

The functional currency of Guard, Inc., is the rupee. For the year 19X1, Guard's translated net income was $8,500. The average exchange rate for the rupee during 19X1 was $.12, and the December 31, 19X1, current rate for the rupee was $.14. The translation adjustment arising from Guard's 19X1 financial statements was $16,250.

REQUIRED

a) Prepare the journal entry on the books of Right Company to record the acquisition of Guard, Inc.

b) Prepare an analysis of the parent's valuation differential as of the date of acquisition, January 1, 19X1.

c) Calculate the parent's income from subsidiary for 19X1.

d) Calculate the translation adjustment for 19X1 that is related to the valuation differential. Construct T-accounts (in rupees and dollars) showing the goodwill account both before and after translation.

e) Prepare the journal entry on the books of Right Company for 19X1 to record the income from subsidiary and cumulative translation adjustment.

f) Prepare in journal entry form the consolidation adjustments that would appear on the December 31, 19X1, consolidated worksheet of Right Company and its subsidiary.

E12-11
APPENDIX A

Apply the Equity Method to Translated Financial Statements of Wholly Owned Subsidiary, Valuation Differential; Prepare Consolidation Worksheet Adjustments Using the information in Exercise 12-10 and the following information about Guard, Inc., during 19X2, the second year following acquisition, complete the following requirements.

For the year 19X2, Guard's translated net income was $15,000. The average exchange rate for the Pakistan rupee was $.20, and the December 31, 19X2, current rate for the rupee was $.24. The translation adjustment arising from Guard's 19X2 financial statements was $25,400.

REQUIRED

a) Calculate the parent's income from subsidiary for 19X2.

b) Calculate the translation adjustment for 19X2 related to the valuation differential. Construct T-accounts (in rupees and dollars) showing the goodwill account both before and after translation.

c) Prepare the journal entry on the books of Right Company for 19X2 to record income from subsidiary and cumulative translation adjustment.

d) Prepare a journal entry from the consolidation adjustments that would appear on the December 31, 19X2, consolidated worksheet of Right Company and its subsidiary.

E12-12
APPENDIX A
Apply the Equity Method to Remeasured Financial Statements of Partially Owned Subsidiary, Valuation Differential; Prepare Consolidation Worksheet Adjustments   Smith Company of East Lansing, Michigan, acquired 80% of the outstanding common stock of Beal Company, a Canadian-based firm, on January 1, 19X7, for $180,000 cash; the exchange rate on this date was $.90. Any valuation differential is considered goodwill with a ten-year life. On the date of acquisition, Beal Company's common stock and retained earnings had balances of 187,500 Canadian dollars and 25,000 Canadian dollars, respectively.

The remeasured net income and dividend payments of the Canadian subsidiary, Beal Company, for 19X7 and 19X8 are as follows:

	19X7	19X8
Net income	$15,800	$17,200
Dividends	—	8,000

REQUIRED

a) Prepare the journal entry on the books of Smith Company to record the acquisition of Beal Company.

b) Prepare an analysis of the parent's valuation differential as of the date of acquisition.

c) Prepare the journal entries on the books of Smith Company to record income and dividends from subsidiary for 19X7 and 19X8.

d) Prepare in journal entry form the consolidation adjustments that would appear on the December 31, 19X7, and 19X8 consolidation worksheets of Smith Company and its subsidiary.

PROBLEMS

P12-1
Subsidiary Functional Currency Is U.S. Dollar: Restate Trial Balances, Prepare Restated Financial Statement   Commonwealth Corporation of Virginia acquired a Singapore subsidiary on December 31, 19X7. The adjusted trial balance of the subsidiary in Singapore dollars as of December 31, 19X7, is presented as follows:

	Debit	Credit
Cash	9,000	
Accounts receivable	15,000	
Allowance for uncollectible accounts		2,000
Inventory, December 31, 19X7	14,000	
Plant and equipment	60,000	
Accumulated depreciation—plant and equipment		13,000
Accounts payable		8,000
Notes payable		5,000
Common stock		45,000
Retained earnings		25,000
	98,000	98,000

Additional information:

1. The subsidiary's ending inventory was acquired when the exchange rate was $.57.

2. The subsidiary purchased plant and equipment when the exchange rate was $.55.

3. The exchange rate on the date of acquisition, December 31, 19X7, was $.60.

REQUIRED

a) Prepare a worksheet to restate the adjusted trial balances of the Singapore subsidiary into U.S. dollars on December 31, 19X7, assuming that the U.S. dollar is the subsidiary's functional currency.

b) Using the restated dollar amounts in the worksheet, prepare the balance sheet for the Singapore subsidiary on December 31, 19X7.

P12-2 **Subsidiary Functional Currency Is Its Local Currency: Restate Trial Balances; Prepare Restated Financial Statement** Using the information in Problem 12-1, complete the following requirements.

REQUIRED

a) Prepare a worksheet to restate the adjusted trial balances of the Singapore subsidiary into U.S. dollars on December 31, 19X7, assuming that the Singapore dollar is the subsidiary's functional currency.

b) Using the restated dollar amounts in the worksheet, prepare the balance sheet for the Singapore subsidiary on December 31, 19X7.

P12-3 **Subsidiary Functional Currency Is U.S. Dollar: Restate Trial Balances; Prepare Restated Financial Statements** Kessler Company, a U.S. firm, acquired Aussie Company of Australia on December 31, 19X3, when the exchange rate for the Australian dollar ($A) was $.49. The adjusted trial balance of Aussie Company on December 31, 19X4, in Australian dollars is as follows:

	Australian Dollars	
	Debit	**Credit**
Cash	40,000	
Accounts receivable	20,000	
Allowance for uncollectible accounts		1,000
Inventory, 12-31-X4	42,000	
Plant and equipment (net)	100,000	
Accounts payable		18,000
Notes payable		30,000
Common stock		100,000
Retained earnings, 1-1-X4		40,000
Dividends	10,000	
Sales		90,000
Cost of goods sold	50,000	
Depreciation expense	8,000	
Other expenses	10,000	
	280,000	280,000

Additional information:

1. Aussie's ending inventory is composed entirely of purchases made uniformly throughout the last quarter of 19X4 when the exchange rate for the Australian dollar averaged $.53.

2. The December 31, 19X3, inventory of $A 40,000 was acquired in 19X3 when the exchange rate was $.50. Purchases of inventory totaling $A 52,000 were acquired uniformly throughout 19X4.

3. Dividends were declared and paid on July 30, 19X4, when the exchange rate was $.51.

4. Plant and equipment were acquired in 19X1 when the exchange rate was $.47.

5. Other exchange rates for the Australian dollar are as follows:

19X4 average	$.54
December 31, 19X4	.58

REQUIRED

a) Prepare a worksheet to restate the adjusted trial balance of Aussie company into U.S. dollars on December 31, 19X4, assuming that the U.S. dollar is the functional currency of Aussie Company.

b) Using the restated dollar amounts in the worksheet, prepare an income statement, statement of retained earnings, and balance sheet for Aussie Company as of December 31, 19X4.

P12-4 **Subsidiary Functional Currency Is Its Local Currency: Restate Trial Balance; Prepare Restated Financial Statements** Using the information in Problem 12-3, complete the following requirements.

REQUIRED

a) Prepare a worksheet to restate the adjusted trial balance of Aussie Company into U.S. dollars on December 31, 19X4, assuming that the Australian dollar is the functional currency of Aussie Company.

b) Using the restated dollar amounts in the worksheet, prepare an income statement, statement of retained earnings, and balance sheet for Aussie Company as of December 31, 19X4.

P12-5 **Subsidiary Functional Currency is U.S. Dollar: Restate Trial Balances; Prepare Restated Financial Statements** Cardinal Company, a U.S. company, acquired, at book value, an 80% interest in Blue Jay Company of France on January 1, 19X2, when the exchange rate for the French franc was $.12. On the date of acquisition, the book values of Blue Jay's assets and liabilities were equal to their fair values.

The adjusted trial balance of Blue Jay Company, as of December 31, 19X4, is presented as follows:

	French Francs	
	Debit	**Credit**
Cash	65,000	
Accounts receivable	100,000	
Allowance for uncollectible accounts		15,000
Inventory (FIFO), 12-31-X4	180,000	
Equipment	300,000	
Accumulated depreciation—equipment		160,000
Building	900,000	
Accumulated depreciation—building		450,000
Land	200,000	
Accounts payable		320,000
Common stock		500,000
Retained earnings, 1-1-X4		215,000
Dividends	60,000	
Sales		600,000
Cost of goods sold	250,000	
Depreciation expense, equipment	35,000	
Depreciation expense, building	90,000	
Other expenses	80,000	
	2,260,000	2,260,000

Additional information:

1. The December 31, 19X4, ending inventory of 180,000 French francs was acquired in the latter part of 19X4 when the exchange rate was $.20.

2. The January 1, 19X4, beginning inventory of 130,000 Franch francs was acquired in 19X3 when the exchange rate was $.15. Purchases of 300,000 French francs were acquired uniformly throughout the year 19X4.

3. All fixed assets were on the books when the subsidiary was acquired except for 50,000 francs of equipment that was acquired on January 1, 19X4, when the exchange rate was $.16. The newly acquired equipment of 50,000 francs is depreciated over a five-year life, 10,000 francs per year.

4. Dividends were declared and paid in mid-19X4 when the exchange rate was $.17.

5. Other exchange rates for the French franc are as follows:

December 31, 19X4	$.21
Average for 19X4	.18

REQUIRED

a) Prepare a worksheet to restate the adjusted trial balances of Blue Jay Company into U.S. dollars on December 31, 19X4, assuming that the U.S. dollar is the functional currency of Blue Jay. (*Note:* The December 31, 19X3, retained earnings that appeared in Blue Jay's restated financial statements was $25,450.)

b) Using the restated dollar amounts in the worksheet, prepare an income statement, statement of retained earnings, and balance sheet for Blue Jay Company as of December 31, 19X4.

P12-6 **Subsidiary Functional Currency Is Its Local Currency: Restate Trial Balance; Prepare Restated Financial Statements; Apply Equity Method**   Using the information in Problem 12-5, complete the following requirements.

REQUIRED

a) Prepare a worksheet to restate the adjusted trial balance of Blue Jay Company into U.S. dollars on December 31, 19X4, assuming that the French franc is the functional currency of Blue Jay. (*Note:* The December 31, 19X3, retained earnings that appeared in Blue Jay's restated financial statements was $19,886, and the cumulative translation adjustment at December 31, 19X3, was $10,000.)

b) Using the restated dollar amounts in the worksheet, prepare the income statement, statement of retained earnings, and balance sheet for Blue Jay Company as of December 31, 19X4.

P12-7 **Subsidiary Functional Currency Is U.S. Dollar; Restate Selected Balance Sheet Accounts** On January 1, 19X7, the Franklin Company formed a foreign subsidiary that issued all its currently outstanding common stock on that date. Selected captions from the balance sheets, all of which are shown in local currency units (LCU), are as follows:

	December 31	
	19X8	**19X7**
Accounts receivable (net allowances for uncollectible accounts of 2,200 LCU at Dec. 31, 19X8, and 2,000 LCU at Dec. 31, 19X7)	40,000 LCU	35,000 LCU
Inventories, at cost	80,000	75,000
Property, plant, and equipment (net of allowance for accumulated depreciation of 31,000 LCU at Dec. 31, 19X8, and 14,000 LCU at Dec. 31, 19X7)	163,000	150,000
Long-term debt	100,000	120,000
Common stock, authorized 10,000 shares par value 10 LCU per share, issued and outstanding 5,000 shares at Dec. 31, 19X8, and Dec. 31, 19X7	50,000	50,000

Additional information:

1. Exchange rates are as follows:

Jan. 1, 19X7, to July 31, 19X7	2 LCU to $1
Aug. 1, 19X7, to Oct. 31, 19X7	1.8 LCU to $1
Nov. 1, 19X7, to June 30, 19X8	1.7 LCU to $1
July 1, 19X8, to Dec. 31, 19X8	1.5 LCU to $1
Average monthly rate for 19X7	1.9 LCU to $1
Average monthly rate for 19X8	1.6 LCU to $1

2. An analysis of the accounts receivable balance is as follows:

	19X8	**19X7**
Accounts Receivable		
Balance at beginning of year	37,000 LCU	–0– LCU
Sales (36,000 LCU per month in 19X8 and 31,000 LCU per month in 19X7)	432,000	372,000
Collections	(423,600)	(334,000)
Write-offs (May 19X8 and December 19X7)	(3,200)	(1,000)
Balance at end of year	42,200 LCU	37,000 LCU
Allowance for Uncollectible Accounts		
Balance at beginning of year	2,000 LCU	–0– LCU
Provision for uncollectible accounts	3,400	3,000
Write-offs (May 19X8 and December 19X7)	(3,200)	(1,000)
Balance at end of year	2,200 LCU	2,000 LCU

3. An analysis of inventories, for which the first-in, first-out (FIFO) inventory method is used, is as follows:

	19X8	19X7
Inventory at beginning of year	75,000 LCU	–0– LCU
Purchases (June 19X8 and June 19X7)	335,000	375,000
Goods available for sale	410,000	375,000
Inventory at end of year	(80,000)	(75,000)
Cost of goods sold	330,000 LCU	300,000 LCU

4. On January 1, 19X7, Franklin's foreign subsidiary purchased land for 24,000 LCU and plant and equipment for 140,000 LCU. On July 4, 19X8, additional equipment was purchased for 30,000 LCU. Plant and equipment are being depreciated on a straight-line basis over a ten-year period with no salvage value. A full year's depreciation is taken in the year of purchase.

5. On January 15, 19X7, 7% bonds with a face value of 120,000 LCU were sold. These bonds mature in six years, and interest is paid semiannually on July 15 and January 15. The first payment was made on January 15, 19X8.

6. The functional currency of the foreign subsidiary is the U.S. dollar.

REQUIRED

Prepare a schedule remeasuring the previous selected balance sheet captions (accounts receivable; inventories; property, plant, and equipment; long-term debt; and common stock) into U.S. dollars at December 31, 19X8, and December 31, 19X7, respectively.

(AICPA adapted)

P12-8   **Subsidiary Functional Currency Is U.S. Dollar: Restate Trial Balances**   The Wiend Corporation acquired The Dieck Corporation on January 1, 19X3, by the purchase at book value of all outstanding capital stock. The Dieck Corporation is located in a Central American country whose monetary unit is the peso. The Dieck Corporation's accounting records were continued without change; a trial balance, in pesos, of the balance sheet accounts at the purchase date follows:

The Dieck Corporation
Trial Balance (in pesos)
January 1, 19X3

	Debit	Credit
Cash	3,000	
Accounts receivable	5,000	
Inventories	32,000	
Machinery and equipment	204,000	
Allowance for depreciation		42,000
Accounts payable		81,400
Capital stock		50,000
Retained earnings		70,600
	244,000	244,000

The Dieck Corporation's trial balance, in pesos, at December 31, 19X4, follows:

The Dieck Corporation
Trial Balance (in pesos)
December 31, 19X4

	Debit	Credit
Cash	25,000	
Accounts receivable	20,000	
Allowance for uncollectible accounts		500
Due from Wiend Corporation	30,000	
Inventories, 12-31-X4	110,000	
Prepaid expenses	3,000	
Machinery and equipment	210,000	
Allowance for depreciation		79,900
Accounts payable		22,000
Income taxes payable		40,000
Notes payable		60,000
Capital stock		50,000
Retained earnings		100,600
Sales—domestic		170,000
Sales—foreign		200,000
Cost of goods sold	207,600	
Depreciation expense	22,400	
Selling and administration expense	60,000	
Gain on sale of assets		5,000
Provision for income taxes	40,000	
	728,000	728,000

Additional information:

1. All The Dieck Corporation's export sales are made to its parent company and are accumulated in an account, sales—foreign. The balance in the account, due from Wiend Corporation, is the total of unpaid invoices. All foreign sales are billed (denominated) in U.S. dollars. The reciprocal accounts on the parent company's books show total 19X4 purchases as $471,000 and the total of unpaid invoices as $70,500.

2. Depreciation is computed by the straight-line method over a ten-year life for all depreciable assets. Machinery costing 20,000 pesos was purchased on December 31, 19X3, and no depreciation was recorded for this machinery in 19X3. There have been no other depreciable assets acquired since January 1, 19X3, and no assets are fully depreciated.

3. Certain assets that were in the inventory of fixed assets at January 1, 19X3, were sold on December 31, 19X4. For 19X4, a full year's depreciation was recorded before the assets were removed from the books. Information (in pesos) regarding the sale follows:

Cost of assets	14,000
Accumulated depreciation	4,900
Net book value	9,100
Proceeds from sale	14,100
Gain on sale	5,000

4. Notes payable are long-term obligations that were incurred on December 31, 19X3.

5. No entries have been made in the retained earnings of the subsidiary since its acquisition other than the net income for 19X3. The retained earnings per the December 31, 19X3, restated financial statements was $212,000.

6. The December 31, 19X4, inventory is composed of purchases made uniformly throughout the year. There was no January 1, 19X4, inventory.

7. Prepaid expenses were paid on December 31, 19X3.

8. The prevailing exchange rates were:

	Dollars per Peso
January 1, 19X3	$2.00
19X3 average	2.10
December 31, 19X3	2.20
19X4 average	2.30
December 31, 19X4	2.40

REQUIRED
Prepare a worksheet to restate the December 31, 19X4, adjusted trial balance of The Dieck Corporation into U.S. dollars, assuming that the U.S. dollar is Dieck's functional currency.

(AICPA adapted)

P12-9 **Subsidiary Functional Currency Is Neither Its Local Currency Nor U.S. Dollar but That of a Third Country: Restate Trial Balances; Prepare Restated Financial Statements**   On January 1, 19X1, American Company, a U.S. company, acquired all the outstanding common stock of Swiss Company, a company based in Switzerland. The purchase price was equal to book value. The subsidiary's manufactured goods are primarily marketed and sold in Germany. The adjusted trial balance of Swiss Company, as of December 31, 19X1, is presented as follows:

	Swiss Francs	
	Debit	Credit
Cash	25,000	
Accounts receivable	24,000	
Allowance for uncollectible accounts		4,000
Inventory	30,000	
Plant and equipment	105,000	
Accumulated depreciation		20,000
Accounts payable		10,000
Notes payable		8,000
Common stock		90,000
Retained earnings, 1-1-X1		40,000
Sales		100,000
Cost of goods sold	60,000	
Depreciation expense	10,000	
Other expenses	18,000	
	272,000	272,000

Additional information:

1. The December 31, 19X1, inventory is composed of purchases made uniformly throughout the year. There was no January 1, 19X1, inventory.

2. The management of Swiss Company has identified the German mark as its functional currency. The following direct exchange rates are presented:

	Swiss Franc to German Mark	German Mark to U.S. Dollar
January 1, 19X1	1.20	$.25
19X1 average	1.22	.32
December 31, 19X1	1.25	.40

REQUIRED

a) Prepare a worksheet using the column headings that follow to restate the adjusted trial balances of Swiss Company into U.S. dollars on December 31, 19X1, assuming that the German mark is Swiss Company's functional currency.

Subsidiary's Adjusted Trial Balance (Swiss Francs)	Exchange Rate Date Amount	Subsidiary's Adjusted Trial Balance (German Marks)	Exchange Rate Date Amount	Subsidiary's Adjusted Trial Balance (U.S. Dollars)

b) Using the restated dollar amounts in the worksheet, prepare an income statement, statement of retained earnings, and balance sheet for Swiss Company as of December 31, 19X1.

P12-10
APPENDIX A

Subsidiary Functional Currency Is U.S. Dollar: Restate Trial Balances; Prepare Restated Financial Statements; Apply Equity Method Consolidated Products, a Florida-based firm, acquired on January 1, 19X6, a 100% interest in Oriental Goods, Inc., of Hong Kong, when the exchange rate for the Hong Kong dollar was $.22. Consolidated Products' cash payment of $99,000 for the 100% interest in Oriental Goods exceeded the book value of the equity acquired by $11,000; the excess is attributable to goodwill with an estimated life of ten years.

The adjusted trial balance of Oriental Goods, Inc., as of December 31, 19X6, is presented as follows. Oriental Goods maintains its inventory on the perpetual basis.

	Hong Kong Dollars Debit	Credit
Cash	100,000	
Accounts receivable	80,000	
Allowance for uncollectible accounts		10,000
Inventory (FIFO), 12-31-X6	138,000	
Plant and equipment	250,000	
Accumulated depreciation—plant and equipment		75,000
Accounts payable		30,000
Notes payable		40,000
Common stock		300,000
Retained earnings, 1-1-X6		100,000
Dividends	9,000	
Sales		180,000
Cost of goods sold	110,000	
Depreciation and amortization expense	12,500	
Other expenses	35,500	
	735,000	735,000

Additional information:

1. Current period purchases (of 208,000 Hong Kong dollars), sales, and operating expenses were made uniformly throughout the year.

2. The beginning inventory of 19X6 consisted of 40,000 Hong Kong dollars; ending inventory was acquired on November 1, 19X6, when the exchange rate was $.26.

3. Dividends were declared and paid in mid-19X6, when the exchange rate was $.27.

4. Other exchange rates for the Hong Kong dollar were $.30 on December 31, 19X6, and $.25 average for 19X6.

REQUIRED

a) Prepare a worksheet to restate the adjusted trial balances of Oriental Goods, Inc., into U.S. dollars on December 31, 19X6, assuming that the U.S. dollar is Oriental's functional currency.

b) Using the restated dollar amounts in the worksheet, prepare an income statement, statement of retained earnings, and balance sheet for Oriental Goods, Inc., as of December 31, 19X6.

c) Prepare the necessary entries on the books of Consolidated Products to apply the equity method to its investment in Oriental Goods, Inc.

d) Determine the balance in the Investment in Oriental Goods, Inc., account on the books of Consolidated Products at December 31, 19X6.

P12-11
APPENDIX A

Subsidiary Functional Currency Is U.S. Dollar: Prepare Consolidation Worksheet (End of First Year), Wholly Owned Subsidiary, Valuation Differential   Using the information in Problem 12-10 and the following December 31, 19X6, financial statements for Consolidated Products (the U.S. parent company in Problem 12-10), prepare a consolidation worksheet as of December 31, 19X6, for Consolidated Products and its subsidiary, Oriental Goods, Inc. The financial statements of Consolidated Products reflect all entries that are necessary to account for the investment in Oriental Goods, Inc., under the equity method.

		Consolidated Products
Income Statement		
Sales		$180,000
Income from subsidiary		17,710
Cost of goods sold		(100,000)
Depreciation and amortization expense		(12,000)
Other expenses		(40,250)
Net income		$ 45,460
Statement of Retained Earnings		
Retained earnings, 1-1-X6		$110,000
Net income		45,460
Dividends		(12,000)
Retained earnings, 12-31-X6		$143,460
Balance Sheet		
Assets		
Cash		$ 90,000
Accounts receivable	$ 70,000	
Less: Allowance for uncollectible accounts	15,000	55,000
Inventory		85,000
Investment in Oriental Goods		114,280
Plant and equipment	$155,000	
Less: Accumulated depreciation—plant and equipment	25,000	130,000
Total assets		$474,280
Liabilities and Stockholders' Equity		
Accounts payable		$ 30,820
Common stock		300,000
Retained earnings		143,460
Total liabilities and stockholders' equity		$474,280

P12-12
APPENDIX A

Functional Currency Is Its Local Currency: Restate Trial Balances; Prepare Restated Financial Statements; Apply Equity Method   The following information is the same as that presented in Problem 12-10; it is reproduced here to assist the student in referring to information needed to solve new requirements.

Consolidated Products, a Florida-based firm, acquired on January 1, 19X6, a 100% interest in Oriental Goods, Inc., of Hong Kong, when the exchange rate for the Hong Kong dollar was $.22. Consolidated Products' cash payment of $99,000 for the 100% interest in Oriental Goods exceeded the book value of the equity acquired by $11,000. The excess is attributable to goodwill with an estimated life of ten years.

The adjusted trial balance of Oriental Goods, Inc., as of December 31, 19X6, is presented as follows. Oriental Goods maintains its inventory on a perpetual basis.

	Hong Kong Dollars	
	Debit	Credit
Cash	100,000	
Accounts receivable	80,000	
Allowance for uncollectible accounts		10,000
Inventory (FIFO), 12-31-X6	138,000	
Plant and equipment	250,000	
Accumulated depreciation—plant and equipment		75,000
Accounts payable		30,000
Notes payable		40,000
Common stock		300,000
Retained earnings, 1-1-X6		100,000
Dividends	9,000	
Sales		180,000
Cost of goods sold	110,000	
Depreciation and amortization expense	12,500	
Other expenses	35,500	
	735,000	735,000

Additional information:

1. Current period purchases of 208,000 Hong Kong dollars, sales, and operating expenses were made uniformly throughout the year.

2. The beginning inventory of 19X6 consisted of 40,000 Hong Kong dollars; ending inventory was acquired on November 1, 19X6, when the exchange rate was $.26.

3. Dividends were declared and paid in mid-19X6, when the exchange rate was $.27.

4. Other exchange rates for the Hong Kong dollar were $.30 on December 31, 19X6, and $.25 average for 19X6.

REQUIRED

a) Prepare a worksheet to restate the adjusted trial balances of Oriental Goods, Inc., into U.S. dollars on December 31, 19X6, assuming that the Hong Kong dollar is Oriental's functional currency.

b) Using the restated dollar amounts in the worksheet, prepare the income statement, statement of retained earnings, and balance sheet for Oriental Goods, Inc., as of December 31, 19X6.

c) Prepare the necessary entries on the books of Consolidated Products to apply the equity method to its investment in Oriental Goods, Inc.

d) Determine the balance in the Investment in Oriental Goods, Inc., account on the books of Consolidated Products at December 31, 19X6.

e) Determine the amount of the accumulated translation adjustment that Consolidated Products would show as a special component of stockholders' equity in its separate balance sheet on December 31, 19X6.

P12-13
APPENDIX A

Subsidiary Functional Currency Is Its Local Currency: Prepare Consolidation Worksheet (End of First Year), Wholly Owned Subsidiary, Valuation Differential   Using the information in Problem 12-12 and the following December 31, 19X6, financial statements for Consolidated Products (the U.S. parent company in Problem 12-12), prepare a consolidation worksheet as of December 31, 19X6, for Consolidated Products and its subsidiary, Oriental Goods, Inc. The financial statements of Consolidated Products reflect all entries that are necessary to account for the investment in Oriental Goods, Inc., under the equity method.

		Consolidated Products
Income Statement		
Sales		$180,000
Income from subsidiary		4,250
Cost of goods sold		(100,000)
Depreciation and amortization expense		(12,000)
Other expenses		(40,250)
Net income		$ 32,000
Statement of Retained Earnings		
Retained earnings, 1-1-X6		$110,000
Net income		32,000
Dividends		(12,000)
Retained earnings, 12-31-X6		$130,000
Balance Sheet		
Assets		
Cash		$ 90,000
Accounts receivable	$ 70,000	
Less: Allowance for uncollectible accounts	15,000	55,000
Inventory		85,000
Investment in Oriental Goods		137,400
Plant and equipment	$155,000	
Less: Accumulated depreciation—plant and equipment	25,000	130,000
Total assets		$497,400
Liabilities and Stockholders' Equity		
Accounts payable		$ 30,820
Common stock		300,000
Accumulated translation adjustment		36,580
Retained earnings		130,000
Total liabilities and stockholders' equity		$497,400

P12-14
APPENDIX A

Subsidiary Functional Currency Is U.S. Dollar: Prepare Consolidation Worksheet (End of Third Year), Partially Owned Subsidiary, Acquired at Book Value   Using the information in Problem 12-5 above and the following December 31, 19X4, financial statements for Cardinal Company (the U.S. parent company in Problem 12-5), prepare a consolidation worksheet as of December

31, 19X4, for Cardinal Company and its subsidiary, Blue Jay Company. The financial statements of Cardinal reflect all entries that are necessary to account for the investment in Blue Jay under the equity method.

	Cardinal Company
Income Statement	
Sales	$324,000
Income from subsidiary	17,160
Cost of goods sold	(115,000)
Depreciation expense, equipment	(14,000)
Depreciation expense, building	(32,000)
Other expenses	(45,160)
Net income	$135,000
Statement of Retained Earnings	
Retained earnings, 1-1-X4	$140,000
Net income	135,000
Dividends	(15,000)
Retained earnings, 12-31-X4	$260,000
Balance Sheet	
Assets	
Cash	$ 56,640
Accounts receivable	63,000
Allowance for uncollectible accounts	(10,000)
Inventory	108,000
Investment in Blue Jay	77,360
Equipment	90,000
Accumulated depreciation, equipment	(40,000)
Building	280,000
Accumulated depreciation, building	(75,000)
Land	60,000
Total assets	$610,000
Liabilities and Stockholders' Equity	
Accounts payable	$150,000
Common stock	200,000
Retained earnings	260,000
Total liabilities and stockholders' equity	$610,000

ISSUES IN ACCOUNTING JUDGMENT

I12-1 **Functional Currency and Remeasurement** Ulseth Corporation has a subsidiary located in Hong Kong. The subsidiary contracts with a number of small manufacturers to produce a large fraction of the products Ulseth sells in the United States. In recent months, as a result of economic development initiatives of the Indonesian government, the Hong Kong subsidiary has been shifting a number of its production contracts from Hong Kong companies to Indonesian companies. Assume that the Hong Kong dollar has tended to be very stable in relation to the U.S. dollar but that the Indonesian rupiah has a much more variable relationship.

REQUIRED

As controller for Ulseth, write a brief analysis of the potential impact of these changes on Ulseth's net income.

I12-2   **Sale of Foreign Subsidiaries**   As a result of a worldwide economic slowdown, Ardmore Products, Inc., faces the prospect of reporting a net loss for the first time in over two decades. Ardmore is a U.S. corporation with worldwide manufacturing operations. These operations are organized as subsidiary corporations for which the local currency is the functional currency. Several of the older foreign subsidiaries are located in countries whose currencies have substantially weakened with respect to the dollar in recent years. The management group is giving serious consideration to selling one or more of these older operations.

REQUIRED

What incentives might the management group have to sell these older operations? Do financial reporting rules play any part in this decision?

FOREIGN CURRENCY RESTATEMENT 644

CURRENCY EXCHANGE RATES **644**

Spot and Forward Exchange Rates 644   Direct and Indirect Exchange Rates 644   Free and Fixed Exchange Rates 645

RECORDING FOREIGN SALES AND PURCHASES 645

TRANSACTION AND SETTLEMENT DATES **645**

RESTATEMENTS AND EXCHANGE RATE MOVEMENTS **646**

RECORDING FOREIGN SALES **647**

Recording Sale to Foreign Customer 647   Calculation of Transaction Gain 647   Recognition of Transaction Gain at Year-End 649   Recording Collection and Conversion of Foreign Currency 649

RECORDING FOREIGN PURCHASES **649**

Recording Purchase of Foreign Shipment 650   Calculation of Transaction Gain 651   Recognition of Transaction Gain at Year-End 651   Recording Acquisition and Payment of Foreign Currency 651

HEDGES AND FOREIGN CURRENCY 652

FORWARD CONTRACTS **653**

Premiums and Discounts on Forward Contracts 653 Gains and Losses on Forward Contracts 654

HEDGING EXPOSURE TO FOREIGN CURRENCY ASSETS AND LIABILITIES **655**

Recording the Purchase and Related Forward Contract 655

Recording Year-End Adjustments 657   Recording the Exercise of the Forward Contract 657

HEDGES OF IDENTIFIABLE FOREIGN CURRENCY COMMITMENTS **658**

Recording the Forward Contract 659   Transaction Gain on Forward Contract 661   Deferral of Transaction Gain at Midyear 661   Accounting for Premium at Midyear 661   Recording Receipt of Foreign Shipment 662   Recognition of Transaction Gains and Losses at Year-End 662   Amortization of Premium at Year-End 663   Recording Exercise of Forward Exchange Contract 663   Recording the Payment of Foreign Currency 663   Recording Amortization of Remaining Premium 663   Alternatives to Forward Contracts 664

HEDGES OF NET INVESTMENT POSITIONS **664**

DISCLOSURE RULES FOR TRANSACTION GAINS AND LOSSES **665**

SPECULATIVE FORWARD EXCHANGE CONTRACTS 665

RECORDING THE SPECULATIVE FORWARD CONTRACT **666**

TRANSACTION GAIN ON FORWARD CONTRACT **666**

RECOGNITION OF TRANSACTION GAIN AT YEAR-END **667**

RECORDING EXERCISE OF THE SPECULATIVE FORWARD CONTRACT **667**

SUMMARY 667

Entities involved in international business frequently enter transactions wherein they agree to make or accept payment in a *foreign currency* that differs from the local currency in which they transact most of their business and in which they keep records and issue financial statements. Transactions in which payment of a foreign currency is made or accepted are said to be denominated in a foreign currency and are called *foreign currency transactions.* For example, a U.S. firm might sell electronic computing equipment to an Italian buyer in exchange for Italian lira, or a U.S. firm might buy foreign currency from a U.S. bank in exchange for U.S. dollars in order to pay a foreign debt.[1] Both transactions are foreign currency transactions from the viewpoint of the U.S. firm. Notice that the conversion of one currency into another is a foreign currency transaction despite the fact that both parties to the transaction are located in the United States. In other words, it is the use of a foreign currency that distinguishes a foreign currency transaction rather than the location of the transacting parties.[2]

This chapter describes the special measurement and accounting procedures that are used for foreign currency transactions. In order to record foreign currency transactions, we need to transform foreign currency amounts into the local currency amounts through a process called *foreign currency restatement.* We begin with a discussion of the restatement process. For students who have read the preceding chapter, this discussion will be largely a review.[3] We then examine the accounting procedures for foreign sales and purchases and the associated gains and losses that result from changes in the value of foreign currency. Next, we discuss a special class of foreign currency transactions, called *hedges,* which are designed to reduce the risk of such gains and losses. Finally, we

---

[1] Foreign currency transactions often result in the sale or purchase of foreign currency in exchange for the local currency. Consider a U.S. seller of merchandise who accepts payment in Italian lira and subsequently sells the lira to a bank or foreign currency dealer in exchange for U.S. dollars. Similarly, a U.S. buyer of merchandise that makes payment in French francs may find it necessary to buy francs from a bank or foreign currency dealer in exchange for U.S. dollars. Such sales and purchases of one currency for another are a special kind of foreign currency transaction called *foreign currency conversions.*

[2] The currency in which an entity conducts most of its business—or, more precisely, the currency of the primary economic environment in which an entity generates and expends cash—is called the *functional currency* of the entity. (The functional currency concept is discussed in greater detail in Chapter 12.) Strictly speaking, a currency is viewed a foreign by an entity if it is any currency other than its functional currency. Thus, a foreign currency transaction is any transaction that is denominated in a currency other than the entity's *functional currency* (*FASB Statement No. 52,* par. 162). For most entities the local currency, in which they keep records and issue financial statements, is the same as their functional currency. Consequently, most functional currency transactions are accurately described as being denominated in a currency other than the local currency. In order to simplify discussion and avoid references to the functional currency concept, we will frequently speak of foreign currency transactions as being denominated in currency other than the local currency. This accurately identifies foreign currency transactions from the viewpoint of virtually all entities located in the United States. In addition, it accurately identifies foreign currency transactions from the viewpoint of most foreign entities as well. However, some foreign entities conduct most of their business in a currency other than their local currency. For example, a U.S. company's Philippine subsidiary might conduct most of its business in Japanese yen (its functional currency) yet keep records and issue financial statements in the Philippine currency. Transactions by the subsidiary denominated in the Philippine currency, U.S. dollars, or any currency other than the Japanese yen would be foreign currency transactions from the viewpoint of the subsidiary.

[3] An introduction to the restatement process is included in both Chapters 12 and 13 to permit instructors to cover Chapter 13 before Chapter 12 if they wish to do so.

consider speculative foreign currency transactions entered in anticipation of gains from changes in the value of a foreign currency.

FOREIGN CURRENCY RESTATEMENT

In order to record foreign currency transactions, we must restate amounts that are denominated in foreign currency into local currency amounts. Amounts denominated in one currency cannot be recorded in that currency on records maintained in another currency. For example, a U.S. company cannot record a sale to be collected in Canadian dollars until the selling price stated in Canadian dollars has been restated into U.S. dollars.

A foreign currency amount is restated into another currency simply by multiplying the foreign currency amount by the appropriate currency exchange rate, which gives the price of one currency in terms of another:

$$\text{Restated currency amount} = \text{Foreign currency amount} \times \text{Currency exchange rate}$$

For example, if a U.S. firm sells merchandise to a Japanese buyer on March 1, 19X8, for 1,000,000 yen (abbreviated ¥) when the yen is $.004945 in terms of the dollar, the U.S. firm records a sale and receivable of $4,945 ($.004945 × ¥ 1,000,000), as shown in the following entry:

Entry by seller to record foreign sale:

Accounts receivable 4,945
    Sales 4,945

The dollar amount of the sale and receivable represents a statement of a foreign currency amount.

Currency Exchange Rates

A currency exchange rate is the price of one currency in terms of another currency. More precisely, it is the rate at which one currency may be converted into another under certain conditions. For example, if a bank quotes a rate for the French franc of $.2235, it means that the bank is willing to sell 100 francs for $22.35 under specified conditions.

Spot and Forward Exchange Rates

The date of the quotation and the date on which the exchange takes place are two of the conditions that must be specified. When the date of the quotation and the date of the anticipated exchange are the same, the rate is called a *spot rate* to indicate that an immediate or on-the-spot conversion is contemplated. In other cases, a rate may be quoted for a conversion at some future date. Such rates are called *forward rates* to indicate that the contemplated exchange date follows the quotation date. Exchange rate is synonymous with spot rate unless a forward rate is specifically indicated.

Direct and Indirect Exchange Rates

Currency exchange rates can be stated in two ways. The price of the foreign currency in terms of the local currency is called the *direct* exchange rate; the price of the local currency in terms of the foreign currency is called the *indirect* exchange rate. If the U.S.

dollar is the local currency, the direct exchange rate (U.S. dollars per foreign currency unit) implied by a bank's willingness to sell 100 French francs for $22.35 is $.2235 per franc ($22.35 ÷ Fr 100), and the indirect rate (foreign currency unit per U.S. dollar) is 4.474 francs per dollar (Fr 100 ÷ $22.35). (Of course, to the French, the dollar is the foreign currency and the identification of the rates as direct and indirect is reversed. The direct exchange rate is 4.74 francs per dollar, and the indirect rate is $.2235 per franc.) Since most accounting calculations use direct rates, the words *exchange rate* are usually synonymous with direct exchange rate.[4]

Free and Fixed Exchange Rates

Exchange rates are either determined by free market forces or established by government-controlled markets. Rates determined by the free market for foreign currency are called *free rates* or *floating rates* and are subject to continual change in response to the supply of currencies and the demand for currencies. Rates established by governments are called *fixed rates* or *official rates.* Fixed or official rates are controlled by a government to further various economic policies of the government.[5]

RECORDING FOREIGN SALES AND PURCHASES

Currency exchange rates vary over time in response to changes in international monetary markets. Variations cause changes in the recorded amounts of restated assets and liabilities related to foreign currency transactions. Before we illustrate the accounting procedures for foreign currency transactions, let us consider the various dates at which exchange rates may be required to record a foreign currency transaction and then turn to illustrations of such recordings.

Transaction and Settlement Dates

A foreign currency transaction, like other exchange transactions, may be characterized in terms of its transaction and settlement dates. The date of each entry respecting a transaction is called a *transaction date,* and the transaction date of the last entry respecting a

---

[4] A distinction also is made between *buying rates* and *selling rates,* the different rates at which the bank or dealer will buy or sell currency. Typically, the selling rate is higher than the buying rate. For example, on a certain day, a New York bank quotes a rate for the Swiss franc (abbreviated SFr) of $.5446/$.5451. The buying rate is quoted first. The quotation means that the bank will buy SFr 1,000 for immediate delivery for $544.60 (SFr 1,000 × $.5446) and that the bank will sell SFr 1,000 for immediate delivery for $545.10 (SFr 1,000 × $.5451). A receivable resulting from a foreign currency transaction should be restated at the buying rate, since its collection will produce foreign currency that is likely to be sold to (bought by) a bank or broker. Similarly, a payable resulting from a foreign currency transaction should be restated at the selling rate, since its payment will require foreign currency that is likely to be bought from (sold by) a bank or broker. When problems and exercises present a single rate, as most do, you may assume that the buying and selling rates are equal.

[5] Some governments establish different official rates for different classes of transactions. In addition, the various classes of transactions may be subject to various restrictions, including requirements for notification of a government agency and approval by the agency. For example, a country that wishes to build productive capacity and to retard distributions of income to foreign investors may establish a more favorable exchange rate for the acquisition of capital equipment than for the payment of dividends or branch profits to owners in other countries. In addition, the payment of foreign dividends may require the approval of a central bank or another agency of the government. When different exchange rates are available, translation should use the rate at which the transaction under consideration could be settled at the date of the translation (*FASB Statement No. 52,* par. 27a).

transaction is called the *settlement date.* The period over which a transaction occasions entries on the accounting records—the period from the first transaction date to the settlement date—is called the *transaction period.* The currency exchange rate corresponding to each transaction and settlement date may be required to effect the required accounting for a foreign currency transaction. In addition, the exchange rate corresponding to the end of each accounting period will also be required.

Restatements and Exchange Rate Movements

A restatement is predicated on a particular exchange rate. When the rate changes, so do the restated amounts that are used to record a foreign currency transaction. Consider the ¥ 1,000,000 sale recorded earlier in this chapter at $4,945 based on the exchange rate of $.004945 on the date of sale, March 1, 19X8. Suppose that the account is collected on April 5, 19X8 (the settlement date), when the rate is $.005000. Accordingly, the collection date restatement of the ¥ 1,000,000 price is $5,000. Clearly, the receivable must be raised to $5,000 by a debit of $55. But what account does the seller credit? Financial accounting standards view the $55 as a foreign currency transaction gain that is included in the determination of net income as a transaction gain (*FASB Statement No. 52,* pars. 15, 123–124). Consequently, the seller must make the following entries to record the change in the exchange rate during the transaction period and the collection on the settlement date:

Entry by seller to record transaction gain on foreign sale:

Accounts receivable	55	
Transaction gain		55

Entry by seller to record collection of foreign sale:

Cash (foreign currency)	5,000	
Accounts receivable		5,000

In general, any asset or liability denominated in a foreign currency gives rise to an exchange gain or loss whenever the related exchange rate changes. Such exchange gains and losses are recorded at the end of every accounting period and at the transaction settlement date. Assets and liabilities denominated in a foreign currency are adjusted to reflect exchange rate movements since the last adjustment, and the corresponding gains and losses are recorded in an income account. Suppose, for example, that the $55 gain described in the foregoing example has occurred in two accounting periods—say, $25 in one accounting period and $30 in the next accounting period. Then a gain of $25 would be included in the first period's income and a gain of $30 in the second period's income.

The historical development of standards for transaction gain or loss recognition illustrates alternative ways of viewing accounting for such gains and losses as the following issues section explains.

ISSUES

Historical Perspective on Foreign Currency Standards

Prior to the issuance of *FASB Statement No. 8* in 1975, the principal authoritative statement on foreign currency restatement was Chapter 12 of *Accounting Research Bulletin (ARB) No. 43,* issued in 1953. Under *ARB No. 43,* transaction *losses* entered net income of the period in which the related exchange rate movements occurred, but transaction *gains* did not enter net income until *realized.* An exception provided that unrealized transaction gains might *offset* transaction losses included in net income. The deferral of transaction gains to the time of their realization required criteria to separate realized from unrealized gains. Chapter 12 of *ARB No. 43* did not specify realization criteria, and practices varied considerably from one firm to another. *FASB Statement No. 8* secured uniformity by requiring that *transaction gains as well as transaction losses enter net income of the period in which the related exchange rate movements occur*. However, *FASB Statement No. 8* sanctioned the deferral of certain transaction gains and losses that arise during the commitment periods of related transactions. Such gains and losses could be deferred to the transaction date and included in the amount recorded for the transaction at that time. The current authoritative pronouncement on foreign currency restatement is *FASB Statement No. 52*, which was issued in 1981 to supersede *FASB Statement No. 8*. Like its predecessor, *FASB Statement No. 52*, requires that most transaction gains and losses be included in net income of the period in which the related exchange rate movements occur. The statement also sanctions deferrals of transaction gains for certain transactions, although these transactions are defined somewhat differently from how they are defined in *FASB Statement No. 8*. The specific exceptions are described later in this chapter.

Recording Foreign Sales

Suppose that a U.S. company (an exporter) sells a quantity of its product costing $31,000 to a German buyer for 160,000 marks (abbreviated DM). The following dates, events, and exchange rates characterize the foreign currency transaction:

Chronology of Foreign Currency Transaction

Date	Event	Direct Rate
Dec. 1, 19X7	Date of sale	$.4000
Dec. 31, 19X7	Year-end	.4120
Feb. 1, 19X8	Collect foreign currency, and convert into dollars	.4200

Accounting procedures for the U.S. company, which issues statements on a calendar-year basis, are described in the following paragraphs. The related journal entries are shown in Exhibit 13-1 on the following page.

Recording Sale to Foreign Customer

The seller records the sale of the product on December 1, 19X7, by entries (1) and (2) in Exhibit 13-1. In order to record the revenue effect of the shipment, the selling price, which is stated (denominated) in marks (DM 160,000), must be restated in dollars. The restatement is accomplished by multiplying the date-of-sale (December 1, 19X7) exchange rate times the selling price in marks ($64,000 = $.4000 × DM 160,000). No restatement is required to record the cost-of-goods-sold effect ($31,000) because it is denominated in dollars. If an end-of-chapter exercise or problem omits information about the cost of goods sold, then entry (2) is omitted from the solution.

Calculation of Transaction Gain

The seller's records display an account receivable denominated in marks throughout the transaction period, that is, from the date of sale to the date of collection. During the transaction period, the exchange rate for the mark rises, with the result that the receivable,

---

EXHIBIT 13-1	**RECORDING A FOREIGN SALE**

December 1, 19X7: U.S. company sells goods to German buyer for DM 160,000.

(1) *Entry by seller to record revenue on sale to foreign customer:*

Accounts receivable	64,000	
Sales		64,000

(2) *Entry by seller to record cost of goods sold on sale to foreign customer:*

Cost of goods sold	31,000	
Inventory		31,000

December 31, 19X7: The U.S. company adjusts foreign currency receivable at year-end.

(3) *Adjusting entry by seller to recognize transaction gain on receivable at year-end:*

Accounts receivable	1,920	
Transaction gain		1,920

February 1, 19X8: The U.S. company collects DM 160,000 from the German customer and converts it into U.S. dollars.

(4) *Entry by seller to recognize transaction gain on receivable since year-end:*

Accounts receivable	1,280	
Transaction gain		1,280

(5) *Entry by seller to record collection of foreign currency on account:*

Foreign currency	67,200	
Accounts receivable		67,200

(6) *Entry by seller to record conversion of foreign currency into U.S. dollars:*

Cash	67,200	
Foreign currency		67,200

---

which is denominated in marks, has a larger dollar value at the date of collection than at the date of sale. Specifically, the exchange rate increases from $.4000 on the sale date to $.4200 on the collection date, which gives rise to a foreign currency transaction gain of $3,200 calculated as follows:

Calculation of Foreign Currency Transaction Gain	
Dollar value of foreign receivable on collection date ($.4200 × DM 160,000)	$67,200
Dollar value of foreign receivable on sale date ($.4000 × DM 160,000)	64,000
Transaction gain	$ 3,200

Observe that the transaction gain can also be calculated as the increase in the exchange rate multiplied by the foreign currency selling price in marks [$3,200 = ($.4200 − $.4000) × DM 160,000]. Since the seller's year-end falls within the transaction period, part of the gain will enter 19X7 net income and the remainder will enter 19X8 net income as shown in the paragraphs that follow.

Recognition of Transaction Gain at Year-End

On December 31, 19X7, the U.S. seller adjusts the receivable to its year-end dollar equivalent and recognizes the related transaction gain by recording entry (3) as shown in Exhibit 13-1. Remeasurement is required to adjust the receivable to its dollar equivalent. At year-end, the receivable has a dollar value of $65,920 ($65,920 = $.4120 × DM 160,000), which exceeds its date-of-sale value by $1,920 ($1,920 = $65,920 − $64,000). The increase in the receivable occasions a credit to an income account, transaction gain, which represents the gain that is associated with the first month of the transaction period. The remainder of the transaction gain ($1,280 = $3,200 − $1,920) is included in the next year's net income.

Recording Collection and Conversion of Foreign Currency

The seller records the collection and conversion of the DM 160,000 receivable on February 1, 19X8, by making entries (4), (5), and (6) as shown in Exhibit 13-1. The restated dollar value of the receivable just before settlement is $67,200 ($.4200 × DM 160,000). This represents a $1,280 increase in the receivable's dollar value since year-end, which is recorded by entry (4). Entry (5) records the receipt of DM 160,000 at its dollar equivalent ($67,200 = $64,000 + $1,920 + $1,280), and entry (6) records the conversion of the German currency into U.S. dollars. Of course, if conversion does not coincide with the collection date and the foreign currency is held by the seller for an additional period, then additional transaction gains or losses should be recorded for movement in the exchange rate during this additional holding period.

When collection and conversion occur simultaneously and are processed by the same bank or foreign currency dealer, the three entries for collection and conversion may be combined as follows:

Entry by seller to recognize transaction gain, record collection of account, and record conversion of foreign currency:

Cash. 67,200		
Account receivable.	65,920	
Transaction gain	1,280	

Combination of the entries for collection and conversion eliminates the use of a foreign currency account on the seller's records.

Recording Foreign Purchases

A U.S. company (an importer) purchases a quantity of wine from a French seller for 100,000 French francs (abbreviated Fr). The following date, events, and exchange rates characterize the foreign currency transaction:

Chronology of Foreign Currency Transaction

Date	Event	Direct Rate
Dec. 15, 19X4	Date of purchase	$.2195
Dec. 31, 19X4	Year-end	.2150
Jan. 15, 19X5	Convert dollars into foreign currency, and pay account	.2185

Accounting procedures for the U.S. importer, which issues statements on a calendar-year basis, are described next. The related journal entries are shown in Exhibit 13-2.

Recording Purchase of Foreign Shipment

The buyer records the purchase of the wine from the French seller on December 15, 19X4, by entry (1) in Exhibit 13-2. The purchase is recorded at the dollar equivalent of its cost in francs restated at the date of its purchase ($21,950 = $.2195 × Fr 100,000).

EXHIBIT 13-2

RECORDING A FOREIGN PURCHASE

December 1, 19X4: U.S. company buys goods from French seller for Fr 100,000.

(1) *Entry by purchaser to record purchase from foreign supplier:*

Inventory	21,950	
Accounts payable		21,950

December 31, 19X4: The U.S. company adjusts its foreign currency payable at year-end.

(2) *Adjusting entry by purchaser to recognize transaction gain on accounts payable at year-end:*

Accounts payable	450	
Transaction gain		450

January 15, 19X5: The U.S. company acquires Fr 100,000 and pays the account with the French supplier.

(3) *Entry by purchaser to record conversion of dollars into foreign currency:*

Foreign currency	21,850	
Cash		21,850

(4) *Entry by purchaser to recognize transaction loss on payable since year-end:*

Transaction loss	350	
Accounts payable		350

(5) *Entry by purchaser to record payment to foreign seller:*

Accounts payable	21,850	
Foreign currency		21,850

Calculation of Transaction Gain

Throughout the transaction period, the purchaser's records display accounts payable denominated in francs. During the transaction period, the exchange rate for the franc falls from $.2195 on the date of purchase to $.2185 on the settlement date. The decrease in the exchange rate gives rise to a transaction gain of $100, which is calculated as follows:

Calculation of Foreign Currency Transaction Gain

Dollar value of foreign payable on date of purchase	
($.2195 × Fr 100,000)	$21,950
Dollar value of foreign payable on payment date	
($.2185 × Fr 100,000)	21,850
Transaction gain	$ 100

The transaction gain can also be calculated as the decrease in the exchange rate multiplied by the purchase price in francs [$100 = ($.2195 − $.2185) × Fr 100,000]. The decrease in the dollar value of the accounts payable represents a gain because a lesser number of dollars satisfy the debt on the payment date than would have satisfied the debt on the date of purchase. In general, transaction *gains* are associated with decreases in the dollar value of foreign currency liabilities (liabilities denominated in a foreign currency) and increases in the dollar value of foreign currency assets (assets denominated in a foreign currency). Transaction *losses* are associated with increases in the dollar value of foreign currency liabilities and decreases in the dollar value of foreign currency assets.

Recognition of Transaction Gain at Year-End

On December 31, 19X4, the U.S. buyer adjusts the foreign currency payable to its year-end dollar equivalent and recognizes the related transaction gain by recording entry (2) as shown in Exhibit 13-2. At year-end, the payable has a dollar value of $21,500 ($21,500 = $.2150 × Fr 100,000), which is $450 less than its dollar value on the date of purchase ($450 = $21,950 − $21,500). The decrease in the payable occasions a $450 credit to an income amount, transaction gain, which represents the gain that is associated with the first 15 days of the transaction period. Since the gain for the entire transaction period is only $100, a $350 *loss* must be included in next year's income ($350 = $450 − $100).

Recording Acquisition and Payment of Foreign Currency

The purchaser records the acquisition and payment of the Fr 100,000 on January 15, 19X5, by making entries (3), (4), and (5) as shown in Exhibit 13-2. Since the account payable is denominated in French francs, the purchaser must acquire French currency in order to pay the account. The buyer acquires the French currency by converting U.S. dollars into francs on January 15, 19X5, when the exchange rate is $.2185 dollars per franc. Hence, $21,850 is exchanged for Fr 100,000, which is recorded by entry (3). The restated value of the payable just before payment is $21,850 ($.2185 × Fr 100,000). Entry (4) recognizes a $350 increase in the payable's dollar value since year-end ($350 = $21,850 − $21,500). Entry (5) records the payment of Fr 100,000 at its dollar equivalent.

Note that the $100 transaction gain that is associated with the foreign purchase is reflected in net income as a $450 gain in 19X4 and a $350 loss in 19X5.

When conversion and payment occur simultaneously and are processed by the same bank or foreign currency dealer, the last three entries may be combined as follows:

> *Entry by purchaser to recognize transaction loss, record conversion of dollars, and record payment of account:*
>
> Account payable 21,500
> Transaction loss   350
>   Cash.   21,850

Combination of the entries for conversion and payment eliminates the use of a foreign currency account on the purchaser's records.

HEDGES AND FOREIGN CURRENCY

Any asset or liability denominated in a foreign currency exposes an entity to changes in the value of foreign currency. A company holding assets denominated in a foreign currency loses when the value of the foreign currency falls and gains when it rises. Conversely, a company holding liabilities denominated in a foreign currency gains when the value of the foreign currency falls and loses when it rises. In order to escape the risk of loss that is associated with exposure to changes in the value of foreign currency, an entity may enter a transaction called a *hedge*. For example, an entity fearing a decline in the value of a foreign currency receivable might incur an equal foreign currency liability. Then, if the value of the foreign currency falls, the loss on the receivable will be exactly offset by the gain on the hedge liability. Of course, hedges eliminate the risk of gain as well as the risk of loss. Accordingly, if the value of the foreign currency rises, the gain on the receivable will be exactly offset by the loss of the hedge liability.[6]

In general terms, a foreign currency hedge is any transaction whose purpose is to offset gain or loss arising from exchange rate fluctuations. Hedges are entered to accomplish three business purposes:

1. To hedge exposure to foreign currency assets and liabilities arising from foreign currency transactions

2. To hedge identifiable foreign currency commitments arising from future foreign currency transactions

3. To hedge net investment positions arising from investments in foreign entities

The accounting for hedge transactions varies with the purpose for which the hedge is entered. Before illustrating accounting for the three types of hedges, let us consider one of the principal vehicles for hedge transactions—the forward contract.

---

[6] We will not discuss other instruments for hedging foreign currency risk such as *purchased options* in all their forms (see *EITF Issue 90-17*) or *synthetic instruments* (see *EITF Issues 91-1 and 91-4*). It should be noted that members of a consolidated group may hedge the foreign currency risk of *intercompany* transactions in certain circumstances (*see EITF Issue 91-1*).

Forward Contracts

As previously noted, a firm hedges a foreign currency receivable by entering a transaction that creates a foreign currency liability of equal amount. Similarly, a firm hedges a foreign currency liability by entering a transaction that creates an equal foreign currency receivable. Although hedge transactions that create the required liabilities and receivables take a variety of forms, one of the most frequently used hedge transactions is a foreign currency transaction called a forward exchange contract.

A *forward exchange contract* (forward contract) is "an agreement to exchange different currencies at a specified future date and at a specified rate" (*FASB Statement No. 52,* par. 17). The specified future date is typically one, two, three, six, or twelve months hence. The specified rate of exchange is called the *forward rate.* Forward rates should be distinguished from spot rates. When a company wishes to buy or sell foreign currency, it secures exchange rate quotations from one or more banks or foreign currency dealers. If the foreign currency is to be transferred immediately to or from the bank, then the relevant exchange rate is called a *spot rate.* If the foreign currency is to be transferred to or from the bank at some future date, then the relevant exchange rate is called a *forward rate.*

Let us consider an example of a forward contract. On December 31, 19X5, Richmond Corporation, a U.S. company, sells merchandise to a Norwegian customer for 100,000 Norwegian kroner (NKr) to be paid on January 20, 19X6. To hedge the exposure to changes in the value of the Norwegian krone, Richmond Corporation on December 31, 19X5, enters a forward contract with its bank to exchange, on January 20, 19X6, NKr 100,000 for $18,450. In other words, the bank agrees to buy NKr 100,000 from Richmond on January 20, 19X6, for a price of $18,450. The forward exchange rate implied by the contract is $.1845 per krone ($.1845 = $18,450 ÷ NKr 100,000). From the viewpoint of Richmond, the forward contract fixes the January 20, 19X6, exchange rate at $.1845 per Norwegian krone and thereby avoids any risk of loss that is associated with changes in the value of the krone.

Premiums and Discounts on Forward Contracts

The difference between the forward rate of a forward contract and the spot rate at the start of the contract gives rise to a premium or discount on the contract. If the forward rate exceeds the spot rate, then the foreign currency costs more for delivery in the future than for delivery today and the currency is said to be trading at a *premium.* On the other hand, if the forward rate is less than the spot rate, then the foreign currency costs less for delivery in the future than for delivery today and the currency is said to be trading at a *discount.* The issues section that follows provides insight into the nature of forward contracts and the forces that determine forward rates.[7]

---

[7] Forward rates are frequently quoted as the difference between the spot rate and the forward rate. For example, a 30-day forward rate quoted as $.0010/$.0012, together with a spot rate of $.4565/$.4570, tells us that the foreign currency is trading at a premium and that the bank or dealer will buy the foreign currency in 30 days for $.4575 ($.4575 = $.4565 + $.0010) and will sell the foreign currency for $.4582 ($.4582 = $.4570 + $.0012). Whenever the currency is trading at a *premium,* the buying rate differential ($.0010) is less than the selling rate differential ($.0012). Since $.0010 is less than $.0012, the currency in question must be trading at a premium. Whenever a foreign currency is trading at a premium, the differential must be *added* to the spot rate to calculate the forward rate. If the bank quotes a forward rate of $.0012/$.0010 in conjunction with a spot rate of $.4565/$.4570, then the currency is trading at a *discount,* the differential must be *subtracted,* and the forward buying and forward selling rates are $.4553 ($.4553 = $.4565 − $.0012) and $.4560 ($.4560 = $.4570 − $.0010), respectively.

The premium or discount that is associated with a forward rate usually equals the approximate difference between the interest rates available for the two currencies involved. Suppose a U.S. importer needs 100,000 French francs (abbreviated Fr) in 30 days to pay a French supplier. Since the exchange rate changes over time, the cost of acquiring Fr 100,000 in 30 days may be substantially different from the cost of doing so today. If the U.S. importer wishes to fix the cost of paying the French debt at today's exchange rate, he or she might acquire Fr 100,000 today and simply hold the foreign currency for 30 days. But such a plan forgoes all income not only on the U.S. currency given up but also on the French currency held. A better plan invests the French currency in France for 30 days, until it is transferred to the French supplier. The cost (or benefit) to the importer of fixing the exchange rate is then only the difference between the French interest earned and the U.S. interest sacrificed for the 30-day period.

Still another plan uses a forward contract. The U.S. importer can enter a forward contract with a bank whereby the bank or foreign currency dealer will deliver Fr 100,000 in 30 days in exchange for a price fixed in U.S. dollars. The forward contract forces the bank or dealer to choose between (1) buying Fr 100,000 in 30 days and (2) buying Fr 100,000 now and investing that amount in France for 30 days. In other words, the forward contract transfers the cost of fixing the exchange rate to the bank. Accordingly, the bank passes the cost on to the U.S. importer by requiring a larger or smaller payment of U.S. dollars in 30 days than would buy Fr 100,000 today. The difference between the payment of U.S. dollars required by the forward contract and the price of Fr 100,000 at the spot rate is called the *premium* or *discount.* The premium or discount should approximately equal the 30-day interest differential between France and the United States. If the U.S. interest rate is higher than the French interest rate, then the forward contract will involve a premium to compensate the bank for the interest it would lose by buying now and investing in France. On the other hand, if the U.S. interest rate is lower than the French rate, then the forward contract will involve a discount to reflect the additional interest available in France.

Gains and Losses on Forward Contracts

Changes in the spot rate during the period of a forward contract give rise to gains or losses. The gain or loss on a forward contract is computed by multiplying the foreign currency amount by the change in the spot rate during the period of the contract. Consider an example. On February 1, 19X5, Moore Corporation entered a forward contract with its bank to buy 200,000 Australian dollars ($A) on April 1, 19X5. The following exchange rates are necessary to account for the forward contract:

Chronology of Forward Contract

Date	Event	Spot Rate	Two-Month Forward Rate
Feb. 1, 19X5	Enter forward contract	$.2150	$.2181
Apr. 1, 19X5	Give U.S. dollars for Australian dollars	.2162	

The gain on the forward contract is $240 [$A 200,000 × ($.2162 − $.2150)], which represents the increase (measured in U.S. dollars) in the value of $A 200,000 during the period of the forward contract. Moore Corporation paid a premium of $620 [$A 200,000 × ($.2181 − $.2150)] for the forward contract. Accordingly, it cost Moore an extra $380 ($620 − $240) for having purchased the forward contract rather than waiting until April 1 and simply buying the foreign currency at the then current spot rate.

Hedging Exposure to Foreign Currency Assets and Liabilities

Although *FASB Statement No. 52* sanctions important exceptions, the basic method of accounting for hedges of foreign currency exposure requires that (1) all gains and losses on forward contracts (or other foreign currency transactions designed to hedge foreign currency exposure) be included in the determination of net income for the period in which the related exchange rate movement occurs and (2) any premium or discount be accounted for separately from the gain or loss and be amortized and included in net income over the life of the contract. Forward contracts are foreign currency transactions. Accordingly, it is appropriate that the basic method of accounting for gains and losses on forward contracts is the same as the method of accounting for gains and losses on other foreign currency transactions described earlier in this chapter. Exceptions to this basic method are made for (1) hedges of identifiable foreign currency commitments and (2) hedges of net investments in foreign entities. In addition, distinctive accounting procedures are required for forward contracts that are entered for speculative reasons rather than to hedge foreign currency exposure. Let us begin by illustrating the basic method of accounting for hedges of foreign currency exposure and then turn to a discussion of the exceptions to the basic method.

Forward contracts operate as hedges by fixing the amount at which foreign currency will be bought to satisfy a foreign currency liability or sold upon liquidation of a foreign currency receivable. Consider the following hedge of exposure to a foreign currency liability. On November 1, 19X7, Downright, Inc., purchased merchandise inventory from a Swiss supplier for 850,000 Swiss francs (SFr). The amount is to be paid in francs on February 1, 19X8. In order to hedge the foreign currency exposure resulting from the foreign currency liability, Downright entered a forward contract for the purchase of SFr 850,000 on February 1, 19X8. The following exchange rates are required to account for the forward contract:

Chronology of Forward Contract

Date	Event	Spot Rate	Three-Month Forward Rate
Nov. 1, 19X6	Enter forward contract	$.3255	$.3271
Dec. 31, 19X6	Year-end	.3260	
Feb. 1, 19X7	Give U.S. dollars for Swiss francs	.3180	

Accounting procedures for the U.S. firm, which issues statements annually, are described in the paragraphs that follow. The related journal entries are shown in Exhibit 13-3 on the following page.

Recording the Purchase and Related Forward Contract

The purchase of the merchandise and the entering of the forward contract are recorded on November 1, 19X6, by entries (1) and (2) as shown in Exhibit 13-3. The purchase is recorded at the foreign currency amounts restated at the spot rate for the date of purchase

| EXHIBIT 13-3 | RECORDING A FOREIGN PURCHASE AND RELATED FORWARD CONTRACT |

November 1, 19X6: Downright, Inc., purchases merchandise from a Swiss supplier for SFr 850,000 and enters a forward contract to acquire SFr 850,000 on February 1, 19X7.

(1) *Entry by purchaser to record purchase from foreign supplier:*

Inventory 276,675
    Accounts payable   276,675

(2) *Entry by purchaser to record forward exchange contract to purchase foreign currency:*

Receivable for foreign currency purchased 276,675
Premium on forward exchange contract 1,360
    Payable for foreign currency purchased   278,035

December 31, 19X6: Downright records adjusting entries at year-end.

(3) *Adjusting entry by purchaser to recognize transaction loss on accounts payable at year-end:*

Transaction loss   425
    Accounts payable   425

(4) *Adjusting entry by purchaser to recognize transaction gain on foreign currency receivable at year-end:*

Receivable for foreign currency purchased   425
    Transaction gain   425

(5) *Adjusting entry by purchaser to amortize premium at year-end:*

Premium amortization expense   907
    Premium on forward exchange contract   907

February 1, 19X7: Downright exchanges U.S. dollars for foreign currency under the forward contract and pays foreign currency to supplier.

(6) *Entry by purchaser to record payment of liability under forward exchange contract:*

Payable for foreign currency purchased 278,035
    Cash   278,035

(7) *Entry by purchaser to recognize transaction loss (since last balance sheet date) and record receipt of foreign currency under forward exchange contract:*

Foreign currency 270,300
Transaction loss 6,800
    Receivable for foreign currency purchased   277,100

(8) *Entry by purchaser to recognize transaction gain (since last balance sheet date) and record payment of account payable to foreign seller:*

Accounts payable 277,100
    Transaction gain   6,800
    Foreign currency   270,300

(9) *Entry by purchaser to amortize remainder of premium on forward contract:*

Premium amortization expense   453
    Premium on forward exchange contract   453

($276,675 = SFr 850,000 × $.3255). The recording of the forward contract establishes a receivable denominated in a foreign currency. The amount of the receivable is calculated as the amount of foreign currency provided by the forward contract multiplied by the spot rate at the inception of the contract ($276,675 = SFr 850,000 × $.3255). The recording of the forward contract also establishes a liability that is fixed in dollars and equal to the foreign currency provided by the contract multiplied by the forward exchange rate specified by the contract ($278,035 = SFr 850,000 × $.3271). The excess of the fixed dollar liability over the foreign currency receivable represents a cost to Downright of the hedge transaction and is called the premium on the forward contract ($1,360 = $278,035 − $276,675). Alternatively, the premium can be calculated as the excess of the forward rate over the spot rate multiplied by the amount of foreign currency provided by the forward contract [$1,360 = ($.3271 − $.3255) × SFr 850,000].[8]

Recording Year-End Adjustments

The basic method of accounting for forward contracts requires entries (3), (4), and (5) at year-end. Entry (3) adjusts the accounts payable in foreign currency, and entry (4) adjusts the foreign currency receivable under the forward contract to reflect the increase in the exchange rate between November 1 and December 31 [$425 = (SFr 850,000 × $.3260) − (SFr 850,000 × $.3255)]. Entry (5) amortizes the premium on the forward contract on a straight-line basis. Accordingly, two-thirds of the total premium is assigned to the period November 1 through December 31 ($907 = $1,360 × 2/3).

Recording the Exercise of the Forward Contract

On February 1, 19X7, the forward contract directs Downright, Inc., to pay $278,035 to its bank or foreign currency dealer in exchange for the foreign currency needed to pay the Swiss supplier, which occasions entries (6), (7), (8), and (9). Entry (6) records the payment of cash that discharges Downright's liability under the forward exchange contract. The contract also directs the bank or dealer to deliver SFr 850,000 to the U.S. firm, which results in entry (7). The transaction loss of $6,800 recorded by entry (7) is the result of the drop in the spot rate since December 31, 19X6, which reduces the value of the foreign currency receivable [$6,800 = ($.3260 − $.3180) × SFr 850,000]. Entry (8) records the payment of the foreign currency to satisfy the liability to the Swiss supplier. The transaction gain of $6,800 is also the result of the drop in the spot rate since December 31, 19X6, which reduces the amount of Downright's liability. Finally, entry (9) charges to income the unamortized one-third of the premium on the forward contract associated with the period January 1 through February 1, 19X7 ($453 = $1,360 × 1/3). These four entries at the end of the forward contract's transaction period complete Downright's accounting for

---

[8] At its inception, the forward contract is an *executory contract* because neither party has given up currency as required by the contract. The forward contract remains executory until the two parties exchange currency on February 1, 19X7. The recognition of forward contracts and related gains and losses during their executory periods is an exception to the usual prohibition against recording executory contracts. The accounting for forward contracts illustrated here is one of several possible procedures. As explained in Bierman, Johnson, and Peterson (1991), hedge accounting is a complex and unsettled area, and a variety of procedures are used in practice.

its forward contract and the related credit purchase following the general method of accounting.[9]

The Downright example illustrates the hedging of an exposure to a foreign currency liability. The accounting for exposure to a foreign currency asset position, which arises when an entity sells to foreign customers and accepts payment in foreign currency, follows the same general principles and is therefore not illustrated. Of course, hedging exposure to a foreign currency asset requires a hedge transaction that creates a liability denominated in the foreign currency.

We turn now to several exceptions to this basic method of accounting for hedges of exposure to foreign currency assets and liabilities: (1) hedges of identifiable foreign currency commitments and (2) hedges of net investments in foreign entities. The chapter concludes with a discussion of speculative forward contracts, which also require distinctive accounting procedures.

Hedges of Identifiable Foreign Currency Commitments

An entity may commit itself to a foreign currency transaction long before the transaction is recorded by the entity. The period between the commitment date and the transaction date (on which the transaction is first recorded) is called the *foreign currency commitment period*. Throughout this period, the company is committed to pay or receive a known amount of foreign currency at a future date—and thereby be exposed to risk of loss through changes in the value of that foreign currency—even though the amount is not recorded in its records. The entity can hedge this foreign currency exposure by entering a forward contract that fixes the dollar effect of the unrecorded future commitment to pay or to receive foreign currency.

Hedges of foreign currency commitments should be distinguished from hedges of foreign currency transactions. Hedges of transactions, discussed in the preceding section, give rise to offsetting gains and losses. The gain or loss from the hedge's foreign currency payable or receivable offsets the gain or loss from the transaction's foreign currency receivable or payable. Hedges of foreign currency commitments, however, do not give rise to offsetting gains and losses. Since the foreign currency commitment is not recorded, only the gain or loss from the hedge's payable or receivable is a matter of record.

Under certain conditions, the gains and losses from hedges of foreign currency commitments are not included in the income of the period in which they occur. Instead, they are deferred until the transaction related to the hedged commitment is recorded and included as adjustments to the amount recorded for the transaction. This special treatment is accorded hedges of foreign currency commitments that satisfy both of the following conditions (*FASB Statement No. 52,* par. 21):

1. The hedge transaction (e.g., the forward contract) is designated as, and is effective as, a hedge of a foreign currency commitment.

2. The foreign currency commitment associated with the hedge is firm.

---

[9] In the illustration, the amount of the forward contract equals the amount of the hedged liability, which means that gains or losses on the forward contract exactly offset gains or losses on the hedged liability. If the amount of the forward contract is less than the amount of the hedged liability or asset, then the accounting entries take the same form but the hedge will not be completely effective in offsetting transaction gains and losses that are related to the hedged asset or liability. Further, if the amount of the forward contract is greater than the amount of the hedged liability or asset, then the excess should be accounted for as a speculative hedge following procedures described later in this chapter.

Such hedges are called *hedges of identifiable foreign currency commitments,* or simply "qualified hedges."

The accounting for qualified hedges differs from the basic method of accounting for forward contracts in two respects. First, as noted previously, gains and losses on hedges of identifiable foreign currency commitments are deferred to the date on which the hedged transaction is first recorded and included in the amount recorded for the transaction.[10] However, as illustrated earlier, gains and losses on nonqualified hedges are included in the determination of net income over the life of the contract. Second, premiums and discounts that are associated with identifiable foreign currency commitments are treated in one of two ways, at the option of the reporting firm. Premiums and discounts *related to the commitment period* may be deferred along with related transaction gains or losses and included in the amount recorded for the transaction. Alternatively, premiums and discounts may be amortized over the life of the forward contract and included in net income, as required for nonqualified hedges.

An illustration will demonstrate the accounting for hedges of identifiable foreign currency commitments. On May 15, 19X2, a U.S. distributor of foreign motorcycles agrees to purchase a quantity of Japanese vehicles for 100,000,000 yen (abbreviated ¥); delivery is expected in November, and payment is due on January 15, 19X3. On the commitment date (May 15, 19X2), the U.S. firm enters a forward contract with a bank to receive ¥ 100,000,000 on January 15, 19X3, in exchange for $445,000. Hence, the eight-month forward rate is $.004450 ($.004450 = $445,000 ÷ ¥ 100,000,000). The following dates, events, and exchange rates characterize the foreign currency transaction and the related forward contract:

Chronology of Foreign Currency Transaction and Related Forward Contract

Date	Event	Spot Rate
May 15, 19X2	Sign purchase agreement, and hedge foreign currency commitment	$.004200
June 30, 19X2	Midyear closing	.004500
Nov. 15, 19X2	Receive shipment	.004720
Dec. 31, 19X2	Year-end	.005100
Jan. 15, 19X3	Exercise forward contract, and pay account	.005200

Assume that the forward contract qualified as a hedge of an identifiable foreign currency commitment. Accounting procedures for the U.S. firm, which issues statements semiannually, are described in the paragraphs that follow, and the related journal entries are shown in Exhibit 13-4 on the following page for both allowable treatments of the premium.

Recording the Forward Contract

The signing of the purchase agreement on May 15, 19X2, does not alter the purchaser's records, but the forward contract entered on the same day results in entry (1) shown in Exhibit 13-4. Since the eight-month forward rate on May 15, 19X2 ($.004450), is higher

---

[10] An exception is made for certain losses; if it is estimated that deferral of a loss would lead to recognizing losses in later periods, then the loss is included in net income in the period in which it occurs (*FASB Statement No. 52,* par. 21).

EXHIBIT 13-4	RECORDING IDENTIFIABLE FOREIGN CURRENCY COMMITMENT AND RELATED FOREIGN PURCHASE

	Premium Deferred	Premium Amortized

May 15, 19X2: U.S. company signs purchase agreement for ¥ 100,000,000 worth of motorcycles (which does not alter accounting records) and enters forward contract for amount of agreement.

(1) *Entry by purchaser to record forward exchange contract to purchase foreign currency:*

Receivable for foreign currency purchased	420,000		420,000
Premium on forward exchange contract	25,000		25,000
Payable for foreign currency purchased		445,000	445,000

June 30, 19X2: U.S. company records adjusting entries at midyear.

(2) *Adjusting entry by purchaser to defer transaction gain on hedge of identifiable foreign currency commitment at midyear:*

Receivable for foreign currency purchased	30,000		30,000
Deferred transaction gain		30,000	30,000

(3) *Adjusting entry by purchaser to record amortization of premium on forward exchange contract at midyear:*

Premium amortization expense	—		4,688
Premium on forward exchange contract		—	4,688

November 15, 19X2: U.S. company receives motorcycles from Japanese supplier.

(4) *Entry by purchaser to record remaining transaction gain:*

Receivable for foreign currency purchased	22,000		22,000
Deferred transaction gain		22,000	22,000

(5) *Entry by purchaser to record receipt of goods from foreign supplier:*

Inventory	438,750		420,000
Deferred transaction gain	52,000		52,000
Premium on forward exchange contract		18,750	—
Accounts payable		472,000	472,000

December 31, 19X2: U.S. company records adjusting entries at year-end.

(6) *Adjusting entry by purchaser to recognize transaction gain on foreign currency receivable at year-end:*

Receivable for foreign currency purchased	38,000		38,000
Transaction gain		38,000	38,000

(7) *Adjusting entry by purchaser to recognize transaction loss on foreign currency payable at year-end:*

Transaction loss	38,000		38,000
Accounts payable		38,000	38,000

(8) *Adjusting entry by purchaser to amortize premium at year-end:*

Premium amortization expense	4,688		18,750
Premium on forward exchange contract		4,688	18,750

January 15, 19X3: U.S. company receives foreign currency under forward contract and pays Japanese supplier.

(9) *Entry by purchaser to record payment of liability under forward exchange contract:*

Payable for foreign currency purchased	445,000		445,000
Cash		445,000	445,000

(10) *Entry by purchaser to recognize transaction gain (since last balance sheet date) and record receipt of foreign currency under forward exchange contract:*

Foreign currency	520,000		520,000
Transaction gain		10,000	10,000
Receivable for foreign currency purchased		510,000	510,000

(11) *Entry by purchaser to recognize transaction loss (since last balance sheet date) and record payment of account payable to foreign seller:*

Accounts payable	510,000		510,000
Transaction loss	10,000		10,000
Foreign currency		520,000	520,000

(12) *Entry by purchaser to amortize remainder of premium on forward contract:*

Premium amortization expense	1,562		1,562
Premium on forward exchange contract		1,562	1,562

than the spot rate on that date ($.004200), the yen is trading at a premium. The amount of the recorded premium ($25,000) is simply the difference between the fixed liability in dollars under the forward contract and the foreign currency receivable valued at the currency spot rate [$25,000 = $445,000 − ($.004200 × ¥ 100,000,000)].

Transaction Gain on Forward Contract

Over the entire term of the forward contract, the receivable increases from $420,000 on May 15, 19X2, to $520,000 on January 15, 19X3 ($520,000 = $.005200 × ¥ 100,000,000), which generates a total transaction gain of $100,000. The transaction gain on the forward contract is divided into two segments—one segment is caused by the exchange rate movement during the six-month commitment period (May 15, 19X2, to November 15, 19X2) and the other by the exchange rate movement during the two-month transaction period (November 15, 19X2, to January 15, 19X3). The following calculation shows the composition of the transaction gain on the forward contract:

Composition of Transaction Gain on Forward Exchange Contract

Segment of gain for commitment period [($.004720 − $.004200) × ¥ 100,000,000]	$ 52,000
Segment of gain for transaction period [($.005200 − $.004720) × ¥ 100,000,000]	48,000
Total transaction gain	$100,000

Since the forward contract qualifies as a hedge of an identifiable foreign currency commitment, the segment of the gain that is associated with the commitment period is deferred to the transaction date and adjusted to the dollar value of the inventory acquired in the related foreign currency transaction. The segment of the gain that is associated with the transaction period must be recognized in income as it arises.

Deferral of Transaction Gain at Midyear

The U.S. firm issues statements on June 30, 19X2, which is 1.5 months after the commitment date. Consequently, the foreign currency receivable must be adjusted for the movement in the exchange rate during the first 1.5 months of the forward contract. Since this period is entirely within the commitment period, the resulting gain is deferred and therefore appears as a liability on the balance sheet. On June 30, 19X2, the spot rate for the yen is $.004500, and the receivable is adjusted upward by $30,000 [$30,000 = ($.004500 − $.004200) × ¥ 100,000,000] by entry (2) shown in Exhibit 13-4. As previously indicated, the deferral of transaction gains and losses on hedges of identifiable foreign currency commitments is an exception to the general requirement that transaction gains and losses on hedges be included in net income of the period in which the related rate change occurs. As explained later in this chapter, another exception is provided for hedges of net investments in foreign entities.

Accounting for Premium at Midyear

If the premium related to the six-month commitment period is deferred until the transaction date (November 15, 19X2), then ''premium on forward exchange contracts,'' a deferred debit (asset) account, does not require adjustment at June 30, 19X2. On the other hand, if the premium is amortized over the eight-month life of the forward contract, then entry (3) shown in Exhibit 13-4 is appropriate at June 30, 19X2. The total premium of $25,000 is amortized at a rate of $3,125 per month ($3,125 = $25,000 ÷ 8). Since midyear falls 1.5 months after the commitment date, the amortization at midyear is $4,688 ($4,688 = $3,125 × 1.5).

Recording Receipt of Foreign Shipment

Upon receipt of the Japanese motorcycles by the U.S. firm on November 15, 19X2, the transaction gain on the receivable since the last financial statements were issued on June 30, 19X2 ($22,000 = $52,000 − $30,000), is recognized by an adjustment to the receivable. Receipt of the motorcycles also increases both the inventory and accounts payable. The entry to accounts payable equals the purchase price translated at the current spot rate ($472,000 = .004720 × ¥ 100,000,000). The entry to inventory equals the purchase price translated at the current spot rate with adjustments for deferred transaction gains (or losses) and premiums (or discounts) that are associated with the related forward contract, provided that the premium (or discount) is deferred and not amortized. Thus, the charge to inventory depends on the treatment of the premium (or discount) for the related forward contract, as the following calculation shows:

Calculation of Purchase Cost at November 15, 19X2

	Premium Deferred	Premium Amortized
Translated purchase price ($.004720 × ¥ 100,000,000)	$472,000	$472,000
Transaction gain on forward exchange contract during commitment period	(52,000)	(52,000)
Premium on forward exchange contract ($3,125 × 6)	18,750	—
Debit to inventory	$438,750	$420,000

If the premium is amortized, then it is charged to income over the life of the forward contract (at a rate of $3,125 per month). Alternatively, six months' worth of the premium ($18,750 = $3,125 × 6) is deferred to the transaction date and included in the cost of purchases. The foregoing calculations lead to the entries numbered (4) and (5) in Exhibit 13-4, which are shown for both deferral and amortization of premium. Entry (4) recognizes the transaction gain on the foreign currency receivable since the last balance sheet date (the total transaction gain is $52,000 = $22,000 + $30,000), and entry (5) records the dollar value of the Japanese vehicles received on November 15, 19X2.

Recognition of Transaction Gains and Losses at Year-End

Once the receipt of the shipment is recorded, the records of the U.S. firm display two items denominated in a foreign currency—a foreign currency receivable under the forward exchange contract and a foreign currency account payable under the related foreign currency transaction. Both items are fixed at ¥ 100,000,000, and both are restated at the current spot rate. Consequently, the receivable and payable exhibit the same amount at November 15, 19X2 ($472,000 = $.004720 × ¥ 100,000,000). Moreover, as the spot rate changes, the two items move together, one giving rise to a gain and the other to an offsetting loss. Entries (6) and (7) present the adjustments at year-end when the spot rate is $.005100. The $38,000 adjustment represents the effect of the spot rate movement between November 15, 19X2, and December 31, 19X2, on the dollar value of ¥ 100,000,000.

Amortization of Premium at Year-End

In addition to these adjustments for the offsetting transaction gains and losses, an adjustment is also required to amortize premium on the forward contract at year-end. If the commitment-period premium is deferred, the portion of the premium on the forward contract that is associated with the 1.5-month period since the end of the commitment period on November 15, 19X2 ($4,688 = $3,125 × 1.5), must be amortized and charged to expense by entry (8) in Exhibit 13-4. If the commitment-period premium is amortized to expense, then $18,750 ($3,125 × 6) must be amortized at December 31, 19X2. Regardless of the treatment accorded the commitment period's portion of the premium or discount, the transaction period's portion must be amortized and charged to expense during the transaction period.

Recording Exercise of Forward Exchange Contract

On January 15, 19X3, the forward exchange contract directs the U.S. firm to pay $445,000 to the bank, which occasions entry (9) in Exhibit 13-4. The payment of cash discharges the liability of the purchaser under the forward exchange contract. The contract also directs the bank to deliver ¥ 100,000,000 to the U.S. firm, which results in entry (10) by the U.S. firm. The spot rate for the yen is $.005200 on January 15, 19X3, which means that the foreign currency received has a dollar value of $520,000. The transaction gain of $10,000 [($.005200 − $.005100) × ¥ 100,000,000] is the result of an advance in the spot rate since December 31, 19X2, and a corresponding advance in the dollar value of the foreign currency receivable.

Recording the Payment of Foreign Currency

Payment of ¥ 100,000,000 to the Japanese supplier is recorded by entry (11) in Exhibit 13-4. The transaction loss of $10,000 [($.005200 − $.005100) × ¥ 100,000,000] is the result of an advance in the spot rate since December 31, 19X2, and a corresponding advance in the dollar amount of the foreign currency payable. This loss exactly offsets the gain recorded upon receipt of the foreign currency.

Recording Amortization of Remaining Premium

The portion of the premium that is related to the period since the last financial statements were issued (the period December 31, 19X2, to January 15, 19X3) is $1,562 ($3,125 × 1/2), and its amortization is recorded by entry (12) in Exhibit 13-4.

Alternatives to Forward Contracts

Forward contracts are not the only way to hedge a foreign currency commitment. Further, any hedge transaction that satisfies the two conditions stated by *FASB Statement No. 52* and stated earlier in this chapter (on pages 658–659) qualifies for the special accounting treatment previously described. For example, a company engaged to construct a bridge in Mexico and agreeing to accept payment in pesos could hedge the anticipated receipt of pesos by borrowing pesos in Mexico to finance the construction project and designating the borrowing to be a hedge of the anticipated receivable. Similarly, a U.S. company committed to purchasing inventory from a South Korean manufacturer in exchange for won could convert dollars into won, designate the transaction as a hedge of the purchase, and then hold or invest the Korean currency until it is used to satisfy the commitment. Although the accounting for these hedges differs somewhat from the accounting for a forward contract, the same general principles are followed. The commitment period must be distinguished from the transaction period, transaction gains and losses that are associated with the commitment period must be deferred (subject to the detailed rule of *FASB Statement No. 52*), and transaction gains and losses that are associated with the transaction period must be recognized as they occur.

Hedges of Net Investment Positions

Many U.S. companies have investments in foreign entities including investments in foreign subsidiaries and branch operations. Movements in exchange rates can produce significant changes in the restated dollar value of these investments. In order to escape the risk of significant declines in restated value in response to anticipated exchange rate movements, companies may enter transactions that hedge such foreign investments. For example, consider a U.S. parent of an Australian subsidiary doing business in Australian dollars. The assets of the subsidiary are hedged by its liabilities to the extent of its liabilities, but its net assets (the excess of assets over liabilities) are exposed to the risk of exchange rate losses. In order to hedge against an anticipated decline in the value of the Australian dollar, which would reduce the net investment in the subsidiary, the U.S. parent might borrow Australian dollars in the amount of the subsidiary's net assets.[11] If such transactions are designated and are effective as hedges of a net investment in a foreign entity, then any exchange gains or losses on foreign currency assets or liabilities created by such transactions are excluded from the net income and accumulated in a separate stockholders' equity account called *cumulative translation adjustment.* As explained in Chapter 12, this account also receives translation adjustments that are associated with the restatement of the foreign entity's financial statements into dollars. If the hedge is effective, these latter translation adjustments will be offset by the gains and losses arising from the hedge transaction. The premium or discount on forward contracts that are used in this way may be included with the translation adjustments in a separate component of stockholders' equity (*FASB Statement No. 52,* par. 18) or amortized to the net income over the life of the contract.

---

[11] Hedges of investments in foreign entities should be denominated in the same currency as the functional currency of the foreign investee. Consequently, such hedges are not applicable to foreign investees subject to remeasurement. (See Chapter 12 for a discussion of translation and remeasurement of foreign financial statements.) When a hedge in the functional currency is not practical or feasible, however, a hedge denominated in another currency that moves in tandem with the functional currency of the investee may be allowable (*FASB Statement No. 52,* par. 130).

Disclosure Rules for Transaction Gains and Losses

FASB Statement No. 52 (par. 30) requires disclosure of the net transaction gain or loss included in the determination of the current net income. This net gain or loss, which includes translation gains and losses related to forward contracts as well as gains and losses related to other foreign currency transactions, may be disclosed in either the financial statements or the related notes. In addition, if the effect of postbalance sheet exchange rate changes on unsettled foreign currency transactions is significant, then the amount of the effect must be disclosed. Recall that hedges of net investments in foreign entities are recorded in a separate stockholders' equity account, called cumulative translation adjustment, along with adjustments arising from the translation of foreign investee financial statements (as discussed in Chapter 12). Companies must disclose an analysis of the cumulative translation adjustment account that specifies, among other things, the amount of current year adjustments related to hedges of investments in foreign entities (see Appendix A of Chapter 12 for additional discussion of this analysis).

SPECULATIVE FORWARD EXCHANGE CONTRACTS

Forward contracts may be entered for purely speculative reasons (i.e., in anticipation of possible gains) rather than as hedges of assets or liabilities denominated in foreign currency. For example, a U.S. speculator might enter a forward contract to purchase 10,000 pounds sterling in 90 days for a given dollar price in the hope that the pound sterling will strengthen against the dollar and that the dollar value of 10,000 pounds in 90 days will exceed the given dollar price. The distinctive feature of accounting for speculative forward contracts is that the receivable for foreign currency purchased or the payable for foreign currency sold is valued at the current forward rate for the remaining life of the forward contract period instead of the current spot rate. Thus, a premium or discount is never recorded. The current forward rate for the remaining life of the contract usually provides a better indication than the current spot rate of the amount to be received when the contract expires. Gains and losses on speculative forward contracts resulting from changes in the current forward rate for the contract's remaining life are included in the net income. In other words, the treatment of speculative gains and losses follows the general method of accounting for forward contracts except that the basis for valuing the contract is the current forward rate for the contract's remaining life rather than the current spot rate.

To illustrate, consider a U.S. speculator who enters a three-month forward contract on November 1, 19X1, to purchase 10,000 pounds sterling in the expectation of an exchange gain. The following dates, events, and exchange rates characterize the forward contract:

Chronology of Speculative Forward Contract

Date	Event	Spot Rate	One-Month Forward Rate	Three-Month Forward Rate
Nov. 1, 19X1	Enter speculative forward contract	$1.7800	$	$1.7900
Dec. 31, 19X1	Year-end	1.8120	1.8115	
Feb. 1, 19X2	Exercise forward contract	1.8160		

The recording of these events by the U.S. speculator, who prepares statements on a calendar-year basis, is described in the paragraphs that follow, and the related entries are shown in Exhibit 13-5 on the following page.

EXHIBIT 13-5	RECORDING SPECULATIVE FORWARD CONTRACTS

November 1, 19X1: U.S. speculator enters three-month speculative contract to buy 10,000 pounds sterling.

(1) *Entry by speculator to record forward contract to purchase foreign currency:*

Receivable for foreign currency purchased	17,900	
Payable for foreign currency purchased		17,900

December 31, 19X1: U.S. speculator records entry to adjust foreign currency receivable at year-end.

(2) *Adjusting entry by speculator to recognize transaction gain on foreign currency receivable at year-end:*

Receivable for foreign currency purchased	215	
Transaction gain		215

February 1, 19X2: U.S. speculator acquires foreign currency under forward contract.

(3) *Entry by speculator to record payment of local currency under forward contract:*

Payable for foreign currency purchased	17,900	
Cash		17,900

(4) *Entry by speculator to recognize transaction gain on foreign currency receivable since last balance sheet date and record receipt of foreign currency under forward contract:*

Foreign currency	18,160	
Transaction gain		45
Receivable for foreign currency purchased		18,115

Recording the Speculative Forward Contract

The U.S. speculator records the forward contract by making entry (1) shown in Exhibit 13-5. The liability is recorded at its fixed dollar value, and the receivable is restated at the forward rate ($17,900 = $1.7900 × 10,000 pounds). If the purpose of the forward contract to purchase pounds had been to hedge rather than to speculate, then the receivable would have been translated at the spot rate ($1.7800) and a premium would have been recorded.

Transaction Gain on Forward Contract

The transaction gain on the speculative forward contract is the difference between the cash paid on February 1, 19X2, and the dollar value of the pounds received on that date. The gain is calculated as follows:

Calculation of Gain on Forward Contract to Purchase Foreign Currency	
Dollar value of foreign currency purchased ($1.8160 × 10,000 pounds)	$18,160
Dollars paid to acquire foreign currency ($1.7900 × 10,000 pounds)	17,900
Transaction gain	$ 260

Since the contract period covers the year-end, part of the $260 gain is recognized in 19X1 and the remainder is recognized in 19X2.

Recognition of Transaction Gain at Year-End

At year-end the dollar value of the foreign currency receivable is adjusted using the year-end forward rate for the one-month remainder of the forward contract as shown in entry (2) in Exhibit 13-5. On December 31, 19X1, the speculative contract has one month before it expires. The $18,115 dollar value of the foreign currency receivable is determined by multiplying the foreign currency amount of the contract (10,000 pounds) by the one-month forward rate of $1.8115 ($18,115 = $1.8115 × 10,000 pounds). The year-end adjustment raises the receivable by $215 ($215 = $18,115 − $17,900) and results in a gain.

Recording Exercise of the Speculative Forward Contract

On February 1, 19X2, the forward contract directs the U.S. speculator to pay $17,900 to the bank, which is recorded by entry (3) in Exhibit 13-5. The payment of cash discharges the U.S. speculator's liability under the forward contract. The contract also directs the bank to deliver 10,000 pounds sterling to the speculator, which results in entry (4) by the U.S. speculator. The spot rate for the pound is $1.8160 on February 1, 19X2, which means that the foreign currency received has a value of $18,160 ($1.8160 × 10,000 pounds). The source of the exchange gain ($45) is the difference between the current spot rate and the one-month forward rate used to value the foreign currency receivable on December 31, 19X1 [$45 = ($1.8160 − $1.8115) × 10,000 pounds].

Of course, one can also speculate by entering a forward contract to sell foreign currency. The accounting for such speculative forward contracts follows the same principles as those illustrated for forward contracts to buy foreign currency and therefore is not illustrated.

SUMMARY

Foreign currency transactions are defined as transactions whose amounts are denominated in foreign currency, that is, a currency other than the currency in which the reporting entity keeps records. Since the amounts of such transactions are denominated in foreign currency, they must be restated into the reporting currency. The principal accounting issue concerns proper treatment of the gains and losses (called transaction gains and losses) that arise from changes in foreign currency exchange rates. Recall that such changes also change the amounts of assets and liabilities. Although exceptions are sanctioned, the general principle requires that such transaction gains and losses be recognized in the period in which the related exchange rates change.

This chapter describes accounting for three classes of foreign currency transactions. The first is sales and purchases denominated in foreign currency. These transactions give rise to assets and liabilities that are denominated in foreign currency that, in turn, give rise to transaction gains and losses in response to exchange rate movements. The second class of transactions is designed to hedge various kinds of exposure to exchange rate movements (by holding foreign currency assets or owing foreign currency liabilities) and thereby avoid the risk of the gains and losses that are associated with exchange rate movements. The third class of foreign currency transactions is speculative forward contracts that are intended to secure gains from exchange rate movements.

Foreign currency hedges and speculation may be accomplished through forward exchange contracts, whereby the entity agrees to buy or sell foreign currency at a fixed rate of exchange on some future date, or through other foreign currency transactions that achieve the same objective. Accounting for forward exchange contracts is summarized in Exhibit 13-6 on the following page. The required accounting treatment specified by *FASB*

| EXHIBIT 13-6 | SUMMARY OF ACCOUNTING FOR FORWARD EXCHANGE CONTRACTS |

Item	Hedge of Exposure to Foreign Currency Asset or Liability*	Hedge of Identifiable Foreign Currency Commitment†	Hedge of Net Investment in Foreign Entity	Speculative Forward Contracts
Accounting for transaction gains and losses	Include in net income of period in which exchange rate changes	Defer to transaction date,‡ and adjust to amount recorded	Record in separate equity account called *cumulative translation adjustments*	Include in net income of period in which exchange rate changes
Valuation of foreign currency receivable or payable	Value at current spot rate	Value at current spot rate	Value at current spot rate	Value at current forward rate for remainder of forward contract period
Accounting for premium and discount	Amortize to income over life of contract	*Either* (1) amortize to income over life of contract *or* (2) defer to transaction date and adjust to amount recorded	*Either* (1) amortize to income over life of contract *or* (2) combine with translation adjustment and record in separate equity account	No separate accounting for premium or discount because none is recognized

* Accounting for hedges of exposure to foreign currency assets or liabilities may be viewed as the basic method of accounting for hedges. Accounting for hedges of identifiable foreign currency commitments and of net investments in foreign entities can then be viewed as exceptions to the basic method.

† Hedges of identifiable foreign currency commitments must meet the two conditions set forth in *FASB Statement No. 52* and identified on pages 658–659.

‡ An exception is made for certain losses. If deferral of a loss would lead to recognizing losses in later periods, then the loss is included in the net income in the period in which it occurs.

Statement No. 52 varies according to the hedging or speculative objective of the forward contract. Each column in Exhibit 13-6 indicates a different objective. In some cases, a hedging or speculating objective can be secured by a foreign currency transaction that does not involve a forward contract. When this occurs, the same accounting principles are followed with respect to the treatment of resultant gains and losses and the valuation of related foreign currency assets and liabilities.

SELECTED READINGS

Bierman, Harold, Jr., L. Todd Johnson, and D. Scott Peterson. *Hedge Accounting: An Exploratory Study of the Underlying Issues,* Research Report. Norwalk, CT: FInancial Accounting Standards Board, 1991.

Bindon, Kathleen R., and Edward J. Schnee. "Forward Contracts: Accounting and Tax Implications," *The CPA Journal* (September 1986), pp. 38–50.

Bridges, Tim. "Foreign Exchange Exposure Management," *The CPA Journal* (August 1988), pp. 77–79.

Evans, Thomas G., and Timothy S. Doupnik. *Foreign Exchange Risk Management under Statement 52,* Research Report. Stamford, CT: Financial Accounting Standards Board, 1986.

Feskoe, Gaffney. "Reducing Currency Risks in a Volatile Foreign Exchange Market," *Management Accounting* (September 1980), pp. 19–24.

Houston, Carol O., and Gerhard G. Mueller. "Foreign Exchange Rate Hedging and SFAS No. 52—Relatives or Strangers?" *Accounting Horizons* (December 1988), pp. 50–57.

Piteo, Thomas A. "Forward Contracts—Free Market Tools," *Journal of Accountancy* (August 1982), pp. 72–82.

Stewart, John E. "The Challenges of Hedge Accounting," *Journal of Accountancy* (November 1989), pp. 48–56.

QUESTIONS

Q13-1 Define *foreign currency transactions.*

Q13-2 Define *currency exchange rate.*

Q13-3 Describe the following types of currency exchange rates:

a) Spot exchange rate

b) Forward exchange rate

c) Free exchange rate

d) Fixed exchange rate

e) Direct exchange rate

f) Indirect exchange rate

Q13-4 Explain how transaction gains and losses result from import and export transactions.

Q13-5 When are transaction gains and losses resulting from import and export transactions included in net income?

Q13-6 Explain why you agree or disagree with the following statement: Financial accounting standards currently governing the treatment of transaction gains and losses are presented in *FASB Statement No. 8.*

Q13-7 What is the purpose of hedge transactions?

Q13-8 Define the term *forward exchange contract.* Identify four circumstances in which a firm might enter into a forward exchange contract.

Q13-9 Describe the conditions that must be satisfied for a hedge of a foreign currency commitment to be classified as a hedge of an identifiable foreign currency commitment (qualified hedge). What special accounting treatment is given for exchange gains and losses on such hedges?

Q13-10 The premiums and discounts associated with forward exchange contracts that qualify as a hedge of an identifiable foreign currency commitment may be accounted for in one of two ways. Describe these two ways.

Q13-11 The difference between the forward rate of a forward exchange contract and the spot rate at the start of the contract gives rise to a premium or discount on the contract. Discuss what causes this premium or discount to exist.

Q13-12 Explain why you agree or disagree with the following statement: A company that has liabilities denominated in foreign currency units gains when the value of the foreign currency units increases.

Q13-13 The U.S. firm Pacific Corp. has an accounts receivable that is denominated in 75,000 Singapore dollars. If the exchange rate for the Singapore dollar decreased from $.60 to $.57, would Pacific Corp. incur a transaction gain or loss?

Q13-14 Explain why you agree or disagree with the following statement: In a forward exchange contract, if the forward rate exceeds the spot rate, the foreign currency is said to be trading at a discount.

Q13-15 Explain why you agree or disagree with the following statement: A premium or discount is never recorded on a forward contract that is entered into for purely speculative reasons.

EXERCISES

E13-1 **Terminology** Terms (1) through (9) are related to foreign currency transactions.

REQUIRED
For each of the following terms, select the best phrase or description from the answers listed A through I below.

Terms	Descriptions
1. Foreign currency transactions	**A.** The exchange rate for immediate conversion of one currency for another currency.
2. Direct exchange rate	
3. Indirect exchange rate	**B.** Hedges that (1) are designated as, and are effective as, hedges of foreign currency commitments and (2) are associated with foreign currency commitments that are firm.
4. Floating exchange rate	
5. Spot exchange rate	**C.** Transactions of a company that are denominated in a currency other than the company's local currency.
6. Forward exchange contract	
7. Forward exchange rate	**D.** The price of the foreign currency in terms of the local currency.
8. Hedges of identifiable foreign currency commitments	**E.** The exchange rate that is determined by the free market for foreign currency, and is subject to continual changes in response to the supply and demand for currencies.
9. Foreign currency commitment period	**F.** The exchange rate for conversion of one currency for another currency at a future date.
	G. An agreement to exchange different currencies at a specified future date and at a specified rate.
	H. The period between the date an entity commits itself to a foreign currency transaction and the date the transaction is recorded by the entity.
	I. The price of the local currency in terms of the foreign currency.

E13-2 **Importing Transaction; Intervening Balance Sheet Date** On November 25, 19X8, Ameritech Company, a Chicago-based firm, acquired equipment from a foreign supplier. The invoice price is to be paid in 40,000 units of a foreign currency on February 1, 19X9. Ameritech prepares financial statements on December 31 of each year. Exchange rates for the foreign currency are as follows: November 25, 19X8—$2.50; December 31, 19X8—$2.25; February 1, 19X9—$2.35.

REQUIRED

a) Prepare the entries to be made by Ameritech Company on November 25, 19X8, December 31, 19X8, and February 1, 19X9.

b) What is the amount of transaction gain or loss identified with the years 19X8 and 19X9?

E13-3 **Exporting Transaction; Intervening Balance Sheet Date** On December 1, 19X2, Borland International, a U.S. firm, sold merchandise to a foreign firm for 100,000 units of the local currency of the foreign firm. The invoice price is due on January 15, 19X3. Borland prepares financial statements on December 31 of each year. Spot rates for the foreign currency are as follows: December 1, 19X2—$.30; December 31, 19X2—$.28; January 15, 19X3—$.33.

REQUIRED

a) Prepare the entries to be made by Borland International on December 1, 19X2, December 31, 19X2, and January 15, 19X3.

b) What is the amount of transaction gain or loss identified with the years 19X2 and 19X3?

E13-4 **Analysis of Comments on Foreign Currency Transactions** Indicate whether you agree or disagree with each of the following statements. If you disagree with a statement, provide an explanation as to why.

1. Foreign currency transactions are those transactions that are denominated in a foreign currency.

2. Transaction amounts denominated in one currency can be recorded in that currency on records maintained in another currency.

3. A company holding assets denominated in a foreign currency loses when the value of the foreign currency falls and gains when it rises. Conversely, a company holding liabilities denominated in a foreign currency gains when the value of the foreign currency falls and loses when it rises.

4. Transaction gains and losses of a U.S. firm resulting from import and export activities denominated in foreign currencies should be included in determining the net income for the period in which the exchange rate changes.

5. An agreement to exchange different currencies at a specified future date and at a specified rate is referred to as a forward exchange contract.

6. If the forward rate quoted in a forward contract is less than the current spot rate, then the foreign currency is said to be trading at a premium.

7. Gains and losses from hedges of identifiable foreign currency commitments are not included in the income of the period in which they occur but are deferred and included as adjustments to the amount recorded for the transaction.

8. Premiums and discounts on forward exchange contracts qualifying as hedges of identifiable foreign currency commitments may be either amortized over the life of the forward contract or deferred and included as an adjustment to the amount recorded for the transaction.

9. In speculative forward contracts, the receivable for foreign currency purchased or the payable for foreign currency sold is valued at the current spot exchange rate, and the resulting premium or discount is amortized over the life of the forward contract.

E13-5 **Multiple Choice Questions on Foreign Currency Transactions**

1. U.S. Importers, Inc., bought 5,000 dolls from Latin American Exporters, S.A., at 12.5 pesos each, when the rate of exchange was $.08 per peso. How much should U.S. Importers record on its books as the total dollar cost for the merchandise purchased?

    a) $400   **c)** $5,000

    b) $625   **d)** $6,250

2. On July 1, 19X1, Stone Company lent $120,000 to a foreign supplier, evidenced by an interest-bearing note due on July 1, 19X2. The note is denominated in the currency of the borrower and was equivalent to 840,000 local currency units (LCU) on the loan date. The note principal was appropriately included at $140,000 in the receivables section of Stone's December 31, 19X1, balance sheet. The note principal was repaid to Stone on the July 1, 19X2, due date, when the exchange rate was 8 LCU to $1. In its income statement for the year ended December 31, 19X2, what amount should Stone include as a foreign currency transaction gain or loss?

a) $–0–   c) $25,000 gain

b) $15,000 loss   d) $35,000 loss

3. Dale, Inc., a U.S. corporation, bought machine parts from Kluger Company of Germany on March 1, 19X1, for 30,000 marks, when the spot rate for marks was $.4895. Dale's year-end was March 31, 19X1, when the spot rate for marks was $.4845. Dale bought 30,000 marks and paid the invoice on April 20, 19X1, when the spot rate was $.4945. How much should be shown in Dale's income statements as the transaction gain or loss for the years ended March 31, 19X1, and 19X2?

	19X1	19X2
a)	$–0–	$–0–
b)	$–0–	$150 loss
c)	$150 loss	$–0–
d)	$150 gain	$300 loss

4. On November 30, 19X0, Tyrola Publishing Company, located in Colorado, executed a contract with Ernest Blyton, an author from Canada, providing for payment of 10% royalties on Canadian sales of Blyton's book. Payment is to be made in Canadian dollars each January 10 for the previous year's sales. Canadian sales of the book for the year ended December 31, 19X1, totaled $50,000 Canadian. Tyrola paid Blyton his 19X1 royalties on January 10, 19X2. Tyrola's 19X1 financial statements were issued on February 1, 19X2. Spot rates for Canadian dollars were as follows:

November 30, 19X0	$.87
January 1, 19X1	.88
December 31, 19X1	.89
January 10, 19X2	.90

How much should Tyrola accrue for royalties payable at December 31, 19X1?

a) $4,350   c) $4,450

b) $4,425   d) $4,500

5. The Marvin Company has a receivable from a foreign customer that is payable in the local currency of the foreign customer. The amount receivable for 900,000 local currency units (LCU) has been restated into $315,000 on Marvin's December 31, 19X5, balance sheet. On January 15, 19X6, the receivable was collected in full and converted when the exchange rate was 3 LCU to $1. What journal entry should Marvin make to record the collection of this receivable?

a) Cash 300,000
    Accounts receivable 300,000

b) Cash 300,000
    Transaction loss 15,000
    Accounts receivable 315,000

c) Cash...	300,000	
Deferred transaction loss	15,000	
Accounts receivable		315,000

| d) Cash .... | 315,000 | |
| Accounts receivable .... | | 315,000 |

(AICPA adapted)

E13-6 **Exporting Transaction; Intervening Balance Sheet Date** On June 30, 19X4, Macintosh, Inc., a U.S. manufacturer, sold merchandise costing $75,000 to Sharp Company located in Mexico, taking a note payable denominated in Sharp's local currency, which at the current rate of exchange on the date of sale had a fair market value of $100,000. On December 31, 19X4, the note was worth $75,000 due to a change in the exchange rate. On March 15, 19X5, the note was paid in full, and when immediately converted to U.S. dollars, received $125,000.

REQUIRED

a) Prepare the entries to be made by Macintosh, Inc., on June 30, 19X4, December 31, 19X4, and March 15, 19X5.

b) What is the amount of transaction gain or loss identified with the years 19X4 and 19X5?

(AICPA adapted)

E13-7 **Importing and Exporting Transactions; Intervening Balance Sheet Date** Zero Corporation, a U.S. multinational company with a December 31 fiscal year, had the following foreign transactions during December 19X4. All transactions are denominated in the respective foreign currency. Zero prepares financial statements each December 31.

December 3 Purchased machinery on account from La Siesta, Inc., of Mexico for $1,500 when the spot rate for the peso was $.05. The invoice is denominated in the foreign currency.

11 Sold merchandise on account to Hitachi, Ltd., of Japan to be paid in 400,000 yen. The spot rate for the yen on this date was $.003.

15 Paid La Siesta, Inc., of Mexico in full. The spot rate for the peso on this date was $.07.

21 Purchased $1,800 of merchandise on account from Patel Company of India, when the spot rate for the rupee was $.12. The invoice is denominated in the foreign currency.

REQUIRED

a) Prepare entries on the books of Zero Corporation to record the above December transactions.

b) Prepare entries on the books of Zero Corporation to value properly accounts receivable and payable as of December 31, 19X4, assuming the current rates for the yen and rupee were $.002 and $.10, respectively.

E13-8 **Hedge Exposure to Foreign Currency Liability** On September 1, 19X7, Bartles Company of Delaware purchased merchandise from Jaymes Company of Pakistan for 350,000 rupees; the exchange rate on this date for the rupee was $.12. The invoice is payable in rupees and is due on November 1, 19X7.

To hedge exposure to the foreign currency liability, Bartles negotiated a forward exchange contract on September 1 to purchase 350,000 rupees for delivery on November 1; the two-month forward rate for the rupee was $.15. The spot rate for the rupee on November 1 was $.16.

Bartles issues financial statements each December 31.

REQUIRED

a) Prepare entries for Bartles Company on September 1 and November 1, 19X7.

b) What is the amount of transaction gain or loss and amortization expense that Bartles Company would present on its 19X7 financial statements?

E13-9   Multiple Choice Questions on Foreign Currency Transactions

1. On September 1, 19X0, Cano & Co., a U.S. corporation, sold merchandise to a foreign firm for 250,000 francs. Terms of the sale require payment in francs on February 1, 19X1. On September 1, 19X0, the spot exchange rate was $.20 per franc. At December 31, 19X0, Cano's year-end, the spot rate was $.19, but the rate increased to $.22 by February 1, 19X1, when payment was received. How much should Cano report as foreign exchange gain or loss in its 19X1 income statement?

   a) $0   **c)** $5,000 gain

   b) $2,500 loss   **d)** $7,500 gain

2. On November 15, 19X8, Celt, Inc., a U.S. company, ordered merchandise FOB shipping point from a German company for 200,000 marks. The merchandise was shipped and invoiced to Celt on December 10, 19X8. Celt paid the invoice on January 10, 19X9. The spot rates for marks on the respective dates are as follows:

November 15, 19X8	$.4955
December 10, 19X8	.4875
December 31, 19X8	.4675
January 10, 19X9	.4475

In Celt's December 31, 19X8 income statement, the foreign exchange gain is

   a) $9,600   **c)** $4,000

   b) $8,000   **d)** $1,600

3. Ball Corp. had the following foreign currency transactions during 19X7:

• Merchandise was purchased from a foreign supplier on January 20, 19X7, for the U.S. dollar equivalent of $90,000. The invoice was paid on March 20, 19X7, at the U.S. dollar equivalent of $96,000.

• On July 1, 19X7, Ball borrowed the U.S. dollar equivalent of $500,000 evidenced by a note that was payable in the lender's local currency on July 1, 19X9. On December 31, 19X7, the U.S. dollar equivalents of the principal amount and accrued interest were $520,000 and $26,000, respectively. Interest on the note is 10% per annum.

In Ball's 19X7 income statement, what amount should be included as foreign exchange loss?

   a) $0   **c)** $21,000

   b) $6,000   **d)** $27,000

4. On April 8, 19X7, Day Corp. purchased merchandise from an unaffiliated foreign company for 10,000 units of the foreign company's local currency. Day paid the bill in full on March 1, 19X8 when the spot rate was $.45. The spot rate was $.60 on April 8, 19X7 and was $.55 on December 31, 19X7. For the year ended December 31, 19X8, Day should report a transaction gain of

   a) $1,500   **c)** $500

   b) $1,000   **d)** $0

5. Shore Co. records its transactions in U.S. dollars. A sale of goods resulted in a receivable denominated in Japanese yen, and a purchase of goods resulted in a payable denominated in French francs. Shore recorded a foreign exchange gain on collection of the receivable and an exchange loss on settlement of the payable. The exchange rates are expressed as so many units of foreign currency to one dollar. Did the number of foreign currency units exchangeable for a dollar increase or decrease between the contract and settlement dates?

Yen Exchangeable for $1	Francs Exchangeable for $1
a) Increase	Increase
b) Decrease	Decrease
c) Decrease	Increase
d) Increase	Decrease

6. The following information pertains to Flint Co.'s sale of 10,000 foreign currency units under a forward contract dated November 1, 19X1, for delivery on January 31, 19X2:

	11/1/X1	12/31/X1
Spot rates	$0.80	$0.83
30-day future rates	0.79	0.82
90-day future rates	0.78	0.81

Flint entered into the forward contract in order to speculate in the foreign currency. In Flint's income statement for the year ended December 31, 19X1, what amount of loss should be reported from this forward contract?

a) $400   c) $200
b) $300   d) $0

(AICPA adapted)

E13-10 **Hedge of an Identifiable Foreign Currency Commitment; Intervening Balance Sheet Date**
On October 1, 19X1, Dalmatian, Inc., a U.S. distributor of fire protection equipment and supplies, signed an agreement to purchase a quantity of fire protection supplies from a foreign supplier for 10,000 foreign currency units. The spot rate for the foreign currency unit on October 1, 19X1, was $.35. The delivery date is January 15, 19X2, with payment due on February 1, 19X2. Dalmatian prepares financial statements each December 31.

On the commitment date (October 1, 19X1), Dalmatian entered into a forward exchange contract to receive 10,000 foreign currency units on February 1, 19X2, at a current forward rate of $.40. Subsequent spot rates for the foreign currency unit were

December 31, 19X1	$.45
January 15, 19X2	.43
February 1, 19X2	.47

REQUIRED
Assuming the forward exchange contract is a hedge of an identifiable foreign currency commitment, prepare entries to be recorded by Dalmatian, Inc., on October 1, 19X1, December 31, 19X1, January 15, 19X2, and February 1, 19X2. Dalmatian amortizes any premium or discount on the forward exchange contract.

E13-11 **Speculative Forward Exchange Contract; Intervening Balance Sheet Date** A U.S. speculator enters a forward contract on December 1, 19X1 to purchase 50,000 German marks for delivery in two months. On December 1, the spot rate for the mark was $.49, and the two-month forward rate was $.51.

The U.S. speculator's fiscal period ends December 31, 19X1, at which time the spot rate for the mark was $.50 and the forward rate for a one-month delivery was $.53. On February 1, 19X2, the spot rate for the mark was $.52.

REQUIRED
Prepare entries to be recorded by the U.S. speculator on December 1, 19X1, December 31, 19X1, and February 1, 19X2.

E13-12   **Summary of Accounting for Forward Exchange Contracts**   For the four types of forward exchange contracts indicated here, describe the required accounting for exchange gains and losses, the required valuation of foreign currency receivable or payable, and the required accounting for premium and discount.

a) To hedge exposure to foreign currency assets and liabilities

b) To hedge an identifiable foreign currency commitment

c) To hedge a net investment in a foreign entity

d) To speculate in foreign currency price movements

PROBLEMS

P13-1   **Importing and Exporting Transactions; Intervening Balance Sheet Date**   During December 19X7, Robins, Inc., a U.S. corporation, incurred the following foreign transactions. All transactions are denominated in the respective foreign currency. Robins prepares financial statements each December 31.

December 1 Sold $2,600 of merchandise on account to X Company of Egypt. The spot rate for the pound was $2.60.

6 Purchased merchandise on account from Y Company of France for 10,000 francs. On this date, the spot rate for the franc was $.20.

15 Purchased $4,000 of merchandise on account from Z Company of Pakistan. The spot rate for the rupee was $.10.

20 Received full settlement from X Company of Egypt. On this date, the spot rate for the pound was $2.75.

23 Paid Y Company of France for one-half of the merchandise purchased on December 6. The current rate for the franc was $.18.

REQUIRED
a) Prepare entries on the books of Robins, Inc., to record the above December transactions.

b) Prepare entries on the books of Robins, Inc., to value properly accounts receivable and payable as of December 31, 19X7, assuming the current rates for the rupee and franc were $.13 and $.22, respectively.

c) Determine the amount of transaction gain or loss that Robins, Inc., would report in 19X7.

P13-2   **Importing and Exporting Transactions; No Intervening Balance Sheet Date**   During April 19X4, the following foreign transactions were contracted by Frasier, Inc., a Chicago-based firm:

April 1 Sold $2,160 of merchandise to Company A of Japan. The exchange rate for the yen was $.36 on this date.

5 Purchased merchandise for $450 from Company B of Mexico. The exchange rate for the peso was $.045 on this date.

15 Sold merchandise for $3,400 to Company C of Great Britain. The exchange rate for the pound was $1.70 on this date.

25 Received payment from Company A of Japan (April 1 transaction) when the exchange rate for the yen was $.38.

28 Paid Company B of Mexico (April 5 transaction) when the exchange rate for the peso was $.048.

30 Received payment from Company C of Great Britain (April 15 transaction) when the exchange rate for the British pound was $1.72.

REQUIRED

Record the preceding transactions on the books of Frasier under each of the following circumstances:

a) All transactions are denominated in U.S. dollars.

b) All transactions are denominated in the foreign currency.

P13-3 **Hedge Exposure to Foreign Currency Asset; Intervening Balance Sheet Date** On October 1, 19X7, Ferris and Company of Chicago sold merchandise to A Company of Sweden for 300,000 Swedish kronor. The spot rate on October 1, 19X7, was $.24. The invoice is due on February 1, 19X8, and is payable in kronor.

To hedge exposure to the foreign currency asset, Ferris engaged in a forward exchange contract on October 1 to sell 300,000 Swedish kronor to be delivered on February 1, 19X8; the future rate for delivery was $.23.

Spot rates for the krona on December 31, 19X7, and February 1, 19X8, were $.21 and $.20, respectively. Ferris's fiscal period ends December 31.

REQUIRED

Record the entries on the books of Ferris and Company for the following dates: October 1, 19X7, December 31, 19X7, and February 1, 19X8.

P13-4 **Hedge Exposure to Foreign Currency Liability; Intervening Balance Sheet Date** For many years, Pier V, a U.S. firm dealing in imported goods, has acquired merchandise from various British exporters. On December 1, 19X2, Pier V purchased merchandise from a British firm for 20,000 pounds; the spot rate on the date was $1.70. The invoice is payable in pounds and is due on February 1, 19X3.

Pier V hedged the exposure to the foreign currency liability by negotiating a forward exchange contract on December 1 to purchase pounds for delivery on February 1, 19X3, to pay the British exporter in full. The future rate for delivery in two months is $1.72.

Spot rates for the pound on other dates were as follows: December 31, 19X2—$1.75; February 1, 19X3—$1.74.

REQUIRED

Prepare entries for Pier V on December 1, 19X2, December 31, 19X2, and February 1, 19X3.

P13-5 **Hedge Exposure to Foreign Currency Liability; Intervening Balance Sheet Date** Dorfman Inc., a U.S.-based firm, purchased a supply of natural gas from Pancho Ltd. of Mexico on November 1, 19X6, for 1,000,000 pesos. The invoice is to be paid in pesos on February 1, 19X7. Dorfman prepares financial statements on December 31 of each year.

To hedge exposure to its foreign currency liability position, Dorfman entered into a forward contract on November 1, 19X6, to purchase 1,000,000 pesos for delivery on February 1, 19X7; the future rate for delivery in three months is $.40.

Relevant spot exchange rates for the peso are:

November 1, 19X6	$.33
December 31, 19X6	.32
February 1, 19X7	.38

REQUIRED

a) Prepare entries for Dorfman Inc. on November 1, 19X6, December 31, 19X6, and February 1, 19X7.

b) What amount of transaction gain or loss and amortization expense would Dorfman Inc. present on its 19X6 income statement?

P13-6

Hedge of an Identifiable Foreign Currency Commitment; Intervening Balance Sheet Date
Previts, Inc., placed an order on November 1, 19X3, to purchase for its inventory radios manufactured by Lee Company of India. Due to the size of the order, Lee has promised delivery in seven months (on June 1, 19X4), just in time for Previts's busy season. On the day the merchandise is delivered, the purchase price is to be paid in 700,000 rupees.

To avoid the risk of fluctuations in foreign exchange rates, Previts entered into a forward exchange contract on November 1, 19X3, to receive 700,000 rupees in seven months (on June 1, 19X4) at a current forward rate of $.15. On November 1, 19X3, the spot rate for the rupee was $.14.

Subsequent spot rates for the rupee were $.17 on December 31, 19X3 (end of Previts's fiscal period) and $.18 on June 1, 19X4.

REQUIRED
Prepare the entries to be recorded by Previts, Inc., on the following dates, assuming the forward exchange contract is a hedge of an identifiable foreign currency commitment. Previts defers any premium or discount on the forward exchange contract.

a) November 1, 19X3

b) December 31, 19X3

c) June 1, 19X4

P13-7
Nonqualified Hedge of a Foreign Currency Commitment; Intervening Balance Sheet Date
Using the same information as in Problem 13-6, and assuming that the forward exchange contract *does not* qualify as a hedge of an identifiable foreign currency commitment, prepare the entries that would be recorded by Previts, Inc., on

a) November 1, 19X3

b) December 31, 19X3

c) June 1, 19X4

P13-8
Speculative Forward Exchange Contract; Intervening Balance Sheet Date   The foreign currency division of Casey, Inc., of Boston speculates in foreign currencies. On November 1, 19X7, a forward exchange contract was consummated to purchase 20,000 Barbados dollars (Bds$) for delivery in three months. On this date, the spot rate for the Bds$ was $.50, and the three-month forward rate was $.45.

On December 31, 19X7 (end of Casey's fiscal period), the spot rate for the Bds$ was $.45 and the forward rate for a one-month delivery was $.48. The spot rate on February 1, 19X8, was $.46.

REQUIRED
Prepare entries to be recorded by Casey, Inc., on November 1, 19X7, December 31, 19X7, and February 1, 19X8.

P13-9 **Hedging a Net Investment Position** On January 1, 19X1, SMU Technologies, a U.S. parent company, has a $575,000 net investment in a Canadian subsidiary with a local currency (Canadian dollar) functional currency. The management of SMU expects that the Canadian dollar will weaken over the next nine months. Accordingly, on January 1, 19X1, management entered into a nine-month forward exchange contract to sell 600,000 Canadian dollars to be delivered on October 1, 19X1. SMU's fiscal year ends June 30.

The following exchange rates relate to 19X1:

	Spot Rate	Six-month Forward Rate
January 1, 19X1	$.92	$.90
June 30, 19X1	.91	
October 1, 19X1	.88	

REQUIRED

a) Prepare entries on the books of SMU Technologies to record the forward exchange contract. SMU amortizes any premium or discount that is associated with the forward contract.

b) Determine the amount that would be deferred and charged or credited to the special component of SMU's stockholders' equity on June 30, 19X1.

P13-10 **Importing and Exporting Transactions; Hedge of Identifiable Foreign Currency Commitment; Speculative Forward Exchange Contract; Intervening Balance Sheet Date** Birmingham Company of Alabama conducts all its foreign operations with a Canadian firm and a British firm. The understanding with the foreign firms is that all transactions are denominated in the currency of the respective foreign firm. Birmingham reported the following foreign currency transactions during the first six months of its calendar year. The company prepares financial statements on June 30 and December 31 of each year.

February 1 Purchased equipment from the British firm for 50,000 pounds. The exchange rate for the pound was $1.80 on this date. Invoice price is due in 45 days.

25 Sold merchandise to the Canadian firm. Payment is due in 30 days in 30,000 Canadian dollars. The current exchange rate for the Canadian dollar is $1.10.

March 15 Paid in full the British firm for the purchase of equipment on February 1. The exchange rate for the pound was $1.78 on March 15.

25 Received full settlement from the Canadian firm for merchandise purchased on February 25. The exchange rate for the Canadian dollar on March 25 was $1.13.

April 1 Signed a purchase agreement with the British firm to purchase merchandise from the foreign supplier. The merchandise is to be delivered on June 1 with payment of 100,000 British pounds due on July 1.

1 On April 1, Birmingham Company entered into a forward exchange contract to receive 100,000 British pounds on July 1 at a current forward exchange rate of $1.86. Any premium or discount on this hedge of an identifiable foreign currency commitment is deferred. The spot rate for the British pound on April 1 was $1.81.

15 Birmingham Company speculated in the Canadian dollars by entering into a forward exchange contract to purchase 10,000 Canadian dollars for de-

livery in two months. The current spot rate was $1.08, and the two-month future rate was $1.09.

June   1   Received the merchandise ordered in the April 1 transaction. The current exchange rate for the British pound was $1.84.

       15   Fulfilled the term of the speculative forward exchange contract entered into on April 15. The current exchange rate for the Canadian dollar was $1.15.

       25   Sold merchandise to the British firm. Payment is due in one month in 15,000 British pounds. The current exchange rate for the pound is $1.85.

REQUIRED

a) Prepare entries on the books of Birmingham Company to record the preceding transactions.

b) Prepare entries on the books of Birmingham Company to value properly accounts receivable and payable and any other accounts for presentation on midyear financial statements of June 30, assuming the current exchange rates for the British pound and Canadian dollar were $1.83 and $1.14, respectively.

P13-11   **Importing and Exporting Transactions; Hedges of Exposed Foreign Currency Asset and Liability Positions; Identifiable Foreign Currency Commitment; Speculative Forward Exchange Contract; Intervening Balance Sheet Date**   Reynolds Corporation has extensive dealings with foreign suppliers and buyers. During the first six months of the fiscal year 19X5, Reynolds reported the following foreign transactions, all of which are denominated in the local currency of the respective foreign firm. Reynolds prepares financial statements on June 30 and December 31 of each year.

January   1   Sold merchandise to Company T of Denmark for 200,000 kroner; payment is due in 60 days. The exchange rate at the time was $.15 per krone. On this date, Reynolds entered into a forward exchange contract with a local bank to sell 200,000 kroner to be delivered on March 1. The exchange rate for future delivery was $.14.

       15   Signed an agreement with Company U of India to purchase merchandise for 500,000 rupees; merchandise is to be delivered on August 1. The spot rate for the rupee was $.18. To avoid the risk of fluctuation in foreign exchange rates, Reynolds entered into a forward exchange contract to receive 500,000 rupees on August 1 at a current forward exchange rate of $.19. The forward exchange contract qualifies as a hedge of an identifiable foreign currency commitment. Any premium or discount on the forward exchange contract is deferred.

       25   Purchased equipment from Company V of Canada for 50,000 Canadian dollars when the exchange rate was $.98 for the Canadian dollar. The invoice price is to be paid on March 25.

March   1   Received payment from Company T of Denmark. Delivered 200,000 kroner to the bank in accordance with terms of the forward exchange contract (January 1 transaction). The spot rate for the krone on March 1 was $.16.

       25   Paid in full Company V of Canada. The exchange rate for the Canadian dollar was $1.02 on this date.

May   1   Entered into a forward exchange contract to speculate in British pounds. Terms of the forward exchange contract call for Reynolds to purchase 30,000 British pounds for delivery in three months. The current spot rate for the British pound was $1.75, and the three-month future rate was $1.72.

       20   Sold merchandise to Company W of France for 200,000 French francs;

payment is due in one month. The current exchange rate for the franc was $.20.

June   1   Purchased merchandise from Company X of Mexico for 1,000,000 pesos. The exchange rate for the peso was $.06. The invoice price is to be paid on August 1.

       20   Received full settlement from Company W of France. On this date, the exchange rate for the franc was $.19.

REQUIRED

a) Prepare entries on the books of Reynolds Corporation to record the preceding transactions.

b) Prepare entries on the books of Reynolds Corporation to value properly the accounts receivable and payable for midyear financial statements of June 30, 19X5, assuming the current exchange rates were as follows:

Rupee	$ .20
Peso	.05
One-month forward rate for British pound	1.70

ISSUES IN ACCOUNTING JUDGMENT

I13-1   **Effects of Stronger Dollar**   Houston Manufacturing, Inc., is a U.S. company that acquires merchandise from a profitable, wholly owned Mexican subsidiary. Late last year, the U.S. dollar had weakened against the Mexican peso, but recently the dollar has begun to rise against the peso, a trend that is expected to continue. Houston's balance sheet has significant payables denominated in pesos that resulted from large year-end shipments from its subsidiary. In addition, the subsidiary is able to pay a dividend in pesos.

REQUIRED

If you were controller of Houston Manufacturing, what advice would these facts lead you to give company management? Give reasons for the advice you would offer.

I13-2   **Hedging Foreign Commitments**   Ansonia Products, Inc., a U.S. company, has entered a contract denominated in Turkish lira to purchase goods for resale. The contract must be paid in 60 days. At present, a 60-day forward contract for Turkish lira involves a significant discount.

REQUIRED

What factors should Ansonia consider in deciding whether or not to hedge the contract?

THREE

Partnerships and Branches

Partnerships: Formation, Operation, and Ownership Changes

PARTNERSHIPS AS ORGANIZATIONS **685**

PARTNERSHIP AGREEMENTS **685**

DISTINCTIVE CHARACTERISTICS **686**

OWNERSHIP EQUITY ACCOUNTS FOR PARTNERSHIPS **686**

INITIAL CAPITAL BALANCES **687**

PARTNERS' DRAWING ACCOUNTS **688**

Recording Withdrawals and Closing Drawing Accounts **688**
Excessive Withdrawals Charged to Capital **689**

OTHER PAYMENTS TO PARTNERS **690**

ALLOCATION OF PARTNERSHIP INCOME OR LOSS **690**

BASES FOR THE ALLOCATION OF INCOME AND LOSS **690**

SPECIFIED NUMERICAL RATIO **691**

CAPITAL INVESTMENT BASES **691**

Allocation in Proportion to Beginning-of-the-Year Capital Balances **691** *Allocation of Interest on Beginning-of-the-Year Capital Balances and Remainder in Specified Ratio* **692** *Allocation of Interest on Average Capital Balances and Remainder in Specified Ratio* **692**

SERVICE CONTRIBUTIONS BASES **694**

Bonus Based on Partnership Income **694** *Partners' Salaries* **694**

DEFICIENCIES OF INCOME RELATIVE TO SALARIES AND INTEREST **695**

PARTNERS' SALARIES AND INTEREST IN THE INCOME STATEMENT **697**

CORRECTION OF PRIOR YEARS' NET INCOME **698**

FINANCIAL REPORTING AND TAXATION **698**

FINANCIAL STATEMENTS OF PARTNERSHIPS **698**

FEDERAL INCOME TAX LAW AND PARTNERSHIPS **699**

CHANGES IN OWNERSHIP **701**

ADMISSION OF A NEW PARTNER **702**

Admission by Investment and by Purchased Interest **702**
The Revaluation Decision **703**

ADMISSION BY INVESTMENT **705**

The Goodwill Method **705** *The Bonus Method* **709**

ADMISSION BY A PURCHASED INTEREST **711**

The Goodwill Method **711** *The Bonus Method* **714**
Distribution of Proceeds among Partners **716**

WITHDRAWAL OR DEATH OF A PARTNER **717**

Equity Fixed at Book Value **717** *Equity Valued at More Than Book Value: Bonus versus Implied Goodwill* **718**

SUMMARY **719**

Partnerships, together with corporations and single proprietorships, constitute the principal forms of business organization. An "association of two or more persons to carry on as co-owners a business for profit" is called a *partnership,* where the word *person* may refer to individuals, corporations, or other partnerships. This definition is given by the Uniform Partnership Act, which has been adopted by most states. Although the single proprietorship is the most numerous form of business organization, and although the corporate form of organization accounts for by far the largest volume of business, the partnership form is widely used by smaller business entities and in professional fields such as law, medicine, and accounting.[1]

This chapter discusses the characteristics of partnerships and illustrates the distinctive features of partnership accounting. After describing the features of partnership organizations, we describe and illustrate the accounting for ownership equity of partnerships, including the distinctive form of ownership equity accounts, the allocation of partnership income or loss, and the treatment of changes in ownership. Chapter 15 considers accounting procedures for the liquidation of partnerships.

PARTNERSHIPS AS ORGANIZATIONS

Partnership Agreements

Unlike corporations, partnerships can be formed without the express approval of the state government. Indeed, a partnership can be formed without a written partnership agreement, although it is unwise to do so. A carefully written partnership agreement (also called ''articles of partnership'') is advisable because it can remove doubts as to important points such as the following:

1. The initial investment by each partner

2. The rights, duties, and authorities of each partner

3. The formula by which income and loss are allocated among the partners

4. Provisions for partners' salaries and withdrawals

5. Provisions for arbitration of disputes among partners, for addition and withdrawal of partners, and for liquidation of the partnership

6. Provisions that direct the treatment of errors in the net income of prior periods

7. Provisions that direct the treatment of special gains and losses

If the partnership agreement is not clear on these points, disputes between partners are resolved by the provisions of the Uniform Partnership Act. If, for example, the partnership agreement fails to specify a formula for the allocation of income and loss among the partners, the act provides for an equal allocation.[2]

---

[1] A new form of organization, called *limited liability corporations (LLC),* combines aspects of partnerships and corporations. As in corporations (including ''professional corporations,'' which may be formed in some states) the *personal* assets of ''innocent'' LLC members are protected from litigation arising from the misdeeds of a fellow member; the liability of innocent members is limited to their investment in the LLC. As in partnerships, LLCs can be treated (under certain conditions) as a ''pass-through entity'' for federal income tax purposes and thereby avoid double taxation of business profits. (This tax benefit may not be available to professional corporations.) The LLC also has an advantage over ''limited partnerships''; limited partners usually cannot participate in partnership management and thereby lose certain tax benefits.

[2] If, however, the partnership agreement states a formula for the division of income but is silent on the formula for the distribution of a loss, then the law provides that the stated income allocation formula should be used for both income and loss. Most partnership agreements specify that the same formula be used for the allocation of both income and loss. However, some agreements specify that income and loss be allocated differently.

Distinctive Characteristics

Partnerships, in contrast to other forms of business organization, exhibit a number of distinctive characteristics including (1) limited life, (2) mutual agency, (3) unlimited liability, and (4) co-ownership of partnership assets and income. Each characteristic is now considered.

Limited life refers to the life of the partnership as a legal entity, which should be distinguished from the life of a partnership as a business entity. Partnership law specifies that the legal entity is dissolved when any of a number of events occurs. These events include the death, retirement, withdrawal, bankruptcy, or incapacity of an existing partner, and the admission of a new partner. In addition, partnership agreements may specify conditions under which dissolution occurs including limiting the life of the partnership to a specified time period. These limitations on the life of partnerships might suggest that they are unstable, short-lived organizations, but such need not be the case. A partnership agreement can provide for a succession of legal partnership entities that provides a framework for a smooth continuity of operations.

Mutual agency means that the partnership is bound by the acts of individual partners that are within their express or implied authority. *Unlimited liability* means that a partner's responsibility for partnership liabilities is not limited by his or her ownership equity in the partnership. When a partnership is insolvent, the personal assets of a partner may be used to settle partnership liabilities. The responsibility of some partners for partnership liabilities may be limited to their partnership investments by the partnership agreement when such agreements are allowed by state statute, but such partnerships must publicly identify themselves as *limited partnerships*. In addition, at least one partner in a limited partnership must have unlimited liability for all partnership debts. Limited partnerships are distinguished from *general partnerships* in which each partner has unlimited liability.

Co-ownership of assets means ownership in common. A partner holds no ownership rights in specific partnership assets even though he or she may have contributed such assets. Instead, each partner holds *equity* in all assets of the partnership. Of course, this does not mean that the *amount* of the equity held is not derived from the *value* of specific assets contributed. In a similar way, no component of partnership income is earmarked for particular partners except to the extent that the partnership agreement establishes priorities in the distribution of *all* income.

OWNERSHIP EQUITY ACCOUNTS FOR PARTNERSHIPS

Accounting for ownership equity in a partnership requires a separate capital account for each partner. The ownership equity structure of partnerships differs from that of corporations as the following issues section explains.

ISSUES

Partnership versus Corporate Ownership Equity

The organizing principle of corporate ownership equity is the distinction between *contributed* capital and *earned* capital. Capital stock accounts record the capital contributed by stockholders upon issuance of the shares, and retained earnings accounts record the earnings of the corporation that have not been distributed to owners in the form of dividends. While it is possible to distinguish and measure contributed and earned capital of partnerships, the two are not usually recorded in separate accounts. Instead, the organizing principle of partnership ownership equity is the identities of the partners. Ownership equity for a partnership usually consists of a single, separate capital account for each partner.

In corporate accounting, dividends and net income are closed to retained earnings, and the year-end (postclosing) balance of retained earnings represents undistributed income belonging to all stockholders. In partnership accounting, a partner's withdrawals and income share are closed to the partner's capital account, and the year-end (postclosing) balance of the capital account represents the undistributed income and contributed capital belonging to the particular partner.

The reason that partnership ownership equity is partitioned among individual partners is that income allocation rules frequently vary from one partner to another. In contrast, every corporate voting share receives the same allocation of income, and the allocation to each shareholder is always directly proportional to the number of shares held. Consequently, it is unnecessary to maintain an account for the equity of each shareholder; that equity can be easily calculated by multiplying the number of shares held by a per-share amount which is the same for all voting shareholders.

The establishment of initial capital balances and the subsequent changes in capital are directed by provisions of the partnership agreement. The paragraphs that follow discuss a variety of such provisions—including initial capital balances, partners' drawing accounts, and other payments to partners—by reference to the James-Thorn Partnership formed on January 1, 19X1, by W. C. James and H. L. Thorn.

Initial Capital Balances

The initial capital balances are usually stated in the partnership agreement. Under the James-Thorn Partnership agreement, each partner's initial (January 1, 19X1) capital balance equals the net assets contributed by that partner as shown on the following schedule, which appears in the agreement:

Schedule of Contributed Net Assets

	James	Thorn
Cash	$ 10,000	$50,000
Inventory	40,000	
Land and building	70,000	
Total	$120,000	$50,000
Mortgage on building	20,000	
Contributed net assets	$100,000	$50,000

Such schedules are frequently the outcome of negotiations and discussions in which an accountant participates, and the end result should reflect the fair value of the assets and liabilities presented. In keeping with the terms of the James-Thorn Partnership agreement, the accounts of the partnership are opened with the following entries:

Entry to establish capital balance for James:

Cash	10,000	
Inventory	40,000	
Land and building	70,000	
Mortgage payable		20,000
James, capital		100,000

Entry to establish capital balance for Thorn:

Cash. 50,000

       Thorn, capital 50,000

Immediately following organization, the partnership has total ownership equity or total partnership capital of $150,000 ($100,000 + $50,000). James has a two-thirds *interest in partnership capital,* and Thorn has a one-third interest in partnership capital. Thus, the percentage shares of the partners' capital (67%, 33%) do not equal the income-and-loss-sharing percentages (50%, 50%) agreed upon by the partners.

    The James-Thorn Partnership agreement did not specify the initial percentage interest of each partner in the partnership capital. Rather, the initial percentage interest of each partner in the partnership capital was inferred from the fair values of contributed net assets, as stated in the partnership agreement. In some cases, however, a partnership agreement may specify initial percentage interests in capital, and those percentages may differ from the percentages implied by the fair value of contributed net assets. When such a difference occurs, the partners must choose between two accounting procedures for the establishment of their capital accounts—one is called the bonus method and the other, the goodwill method. Suppose that Spock and Minton form a new partnership by contributing net assets with fair values of $12,000 and $8,000, respectively, but that the partnership agreement specifies that they should have equal capital shares. Under the *bonus method,* total net assets of $20,000 ($12,000 + $8,000) are recorded and each partner is given an initial capital balance of $10,000. In effect, Spock gives Minton a $2,000 ($12,000 − $10,000, or $10,000 − $8,000) capital bonus. Under the *goodwill method,* Minton is viewed as contributing intangible assets of $4,000 ($12,000 − $8,000), which are recorded by the partnership as contributed goodwill. Accordingly, total net assets of $24,000 are recorded and each partner is given an initial capital balance of $12,000. The decision to use the bonus or goodwill method is up to the partners, and it depends on how the partners feel about recording goodwill on the books and how Spock feels about receiving a reduction in capital of $2,000 under the bonus method. Unless otherwise indicated, a partner's initial capital balance should equal the fair value of the net assets contributed by that partner.

Partners' Drawing Accounts

Drawing accounts are temporary owners' equity accounts. A drawing account is established for each partner to record withdrawals of cash and other assets by the partner. Withdrawals of cash or other assets are recorded by a debit to the appropriate partner's drawing account and a credit to the appropriate asset account. Drawing accounts may also accumulate miscellaneous credits and debits for transactions entered into by the partnership on behalf of the partner. For example, the partnership may collect a note due to the partner as an individual and credit the partner's drawing account. Or the partnership might pay for services or merchandise purchased by the partner as an individual and charge such amounts to the partner's drawing account. At year-end, the drawing account of each partner is closed to his or her capital account.

Recording Withdrawals and Closing Drawing Accounts

The amount of withdrawals by partners is regulated by the partnership agreement. The typical partnership agreement sets an upper limit on withdrawals by each partner. For example, the James-Thorn Partnership agreement authorizes withdrawals by James and

Thorn up to a maximum of $12,000 per year. Withdrawals in excess of $12,000 per year are charged to the partner's capital account by an adjustment to the partner's drawing account, as illustrated later in this chapter. During 19X1 James withdraws $5,000 from the partnership, and Thorn withdraws nothing. The entries to record the cash withdrawals by James from the James-Thorn Partnership during 19X1 and the closing of the drawing accounts are as follows:

Entry to record withdrawals by James:

James, drawing	5,000	
Cash		5,000

Entry to close James's drawing account to capital:

James, capital	5,000	
James, drawing		5,000

Of course, if Thorn had made withdrawals during the year, similar entries would be made for Thorn.

Excessive Withdrawals Charged to Capital

Investments of partnership capital subsequent to the formation of the partnership are credited to the capital accounts of the appropriate partners as soon as they are received by the partnership. Similarly, withdrawals of capital in excess of amounts authorized by the partnership agreement should be debited to the partner's capital account as soon as they are detected. To illustrate using the James-Thorn example, suppose that James withdraws a total of $12,650 during 19X2 ($11,150 on September 1 and $1,500 on December 31). These withdrawals result in a balance of $650 in excess of the $12,000 limit as the following T-account shows:

James, Drawing

Withdrawal	11,150		
Withdrawal	1,500		
Balance	12,650		
		Adjustment	650
Balance	12,000		

The adjustment is recorded by the following entry at December 31, 19X2:

Adjustment for excess over maximum allowable withdrawal by James:

James, capital	650	
James, drawing		650

The $650 excessive charge to drawing should be transferred to capital as soon as it is detected. For example, if withdrawals by James pass the $12,000 maximum during October of some future year, then the excess should be adjusted to capital at the end of October and additional withdrawals during November and December should be charged directly to capital. Charges to capital may influence a partner's share of partnership income under certain income allocation plans described later in this chapter.

Other Payments to Partners

Partnerships make cash payments to partners for reasons other than the withdrawals initiated by partners under the partnership agreement, as the following list indicates:

1. A partner may *borrow money* from the partnership, giving a note in exchange. The amount borrowed should be recorded by the partnership as a debit to notes receivable rather than the partner's drawing account. Interest should be recorded as income to the partnership.

2. If a partner *lends money* to the partnership, the partnership pays *interest and principal* on the note to the partner. Such payments should be recorded by the partnership as debits to interest expense and notes payable rather than the partner's drawing account.

The distinction among withdrawals, capital charges, liability reductions, and expenses may be difficult to make for particular payments to partners. In the final analysis, the joint decision of the partners determines the character of particular payments.

We turn now to a discussion of the allocation of partnership income or loss among the partners' capital accounts.

ALLOCATION OF PARTNERSHIP INCOME OR LOSS

Partners are free to allocate partnership income among their capital accounts in any agreed-upon manner. But in the interest of avoiding disputed distributions, the distribution formula should be carefully spelled out by the partnership agreement. If the agreement does not do so, then the Uniform Partnership Act specifies that income and loss be allocated equally among the partners. The usual objective of income-and-loss-sharing arrangements is to allocate partnership income and loss among the partners in a way that reflects each partner's contribution to the success of the firm. A partner's contribution is influenced by several factors, including capital investment in the firm and time devoted to the firm as well as the partner's experience and ability.

Bases for the Allocation of Income and Loss

Bases for the allocation of income and loss among partners usually take one or a combination of the following three forms:

1. Allocation in a *specified numerical ratio* (called an *income-and-loss-sharing ratio*)

2. Allocation in proportion to *capital investments* of partners

3. Allocation in proportion to *service contributions* by partners

Partnership agreements often partition the income or loss into segments and specify allocation of the different segments on different bases. For example, $20,000 of annual income may be allocated as salaries to reflect relative service contributions by partners, and the remainder may be shared equally. The number of possible allocation procedures is myriad, and those demonstrated in the paragraphs that follow are merely examples, Whatever procedure is selected, it is essential that the procedure be clearly spelled out by the partnership agreement.

As a vehicle for illustration and discussion of several income-and-loss-sharing agreements, consider the Able-Baker Partnership, which has been operating for a number of years. Able and Baker begin 19X5 with capital balances of $130,000 and $120,000, respectively, and on April 30, 19X5, Baker makes an additional capital contribution of

$48,000 cash. During 19X5 the two partners make withdrawals as follows:

Withdrawals by Partners During 19X5

	Able	Baker
Withdrawal, 6-30-X5	$ 6,000	$
Withdrawal, 8-30-X5		6,000
Withdrawal, 12-31-X5	6,000	
Total	$12,000	$6,000

Let us begin by illustrating the allocation of income on the basis of a specified numerical ratio before showing the allocation of income on the basis of capital investments and service contributions.

Specified Numerical Ratio

In previous years, Able and Baker have allocated partnership net income in the income-and-loss-sharing ratio of 4:2. For example, the 19X4 partnership net income was $10,000. Accordingly, $6,667 was allocated to Able ($6,667 = 4/6 × $10,000) and $3,333 to Baker ($3,333 = 2/6 × $10,000). The 19X4 allocation would have been recorded by the following closing entry at year-end:

Entry to record allocation of 19X4 partnership income:

Income summary	10,000	
Able, capital		6,667
Baker, capital		3,333

For purposes of illustrating alternative allocation methods, let us suppose that Able and Baker are contemplating a revision of their income allocation agreement shortly after the end of 19X4. In the paragraphs that follow, several alternative allocation arrangements are demonstrated using the partnership net income for 19X5 of $40,000. Let us begin with several allocation arrangements using capital investment bases.

Capital Investment Bases

Income allocations on the basis of capital balances reward partners in proportion to their respective investments in the partnership. Since partners' capital balances change over time, periodic income allocations on the basis of capital investment may take several computational forms. Allocations of income at the end of each year may be in proportion to partners' capital balances at the partnership's inception, at the beginning or end of the year in which income is earned, or at any other agreed-upon time. Alternatively, the allocation of income may be tied to the average capital balances during the year in which the income is earned. Three capital investment bases are demonstrated subsequently, using the Able-Baker data: (1) allocation in proportion to beginning-of-the-year capital balances, (2) allocation of interest on beginning-of-the-year capital balances and remainder in specified ratio, and (3) allocation of interest on average capital balances and remainder in specified ratio.

Allocation in Proportion to Beginning-of-the-Year Capital Balances

One allocation procedure under consideration by Able and Baker assigns the entire income in proportion to capital balances at the beginning of the year. Able's beginning capital balance is $130,000, and Baker's is $120,000. Consequently, 52% (.52 =

$130,000 \div \$250,000$) of the current year's income is distributed to Able and 48% (.48 = $120,000 \div \$250,000$) to Baker. Assuming the the 19X5 partnership income is $40,000, Able is allocated $20,800 (.52 × $40,000) and Baker is allocated $19,200 (.48 × $40,000). This allocation of income would be recorded by the following closing entry at year-end:

Entry to record allocation of 19X5 partnership income:

Income summary	40,000	
Able, capital		29,800
Baker, capital		19,200

Alternative allocations could be obtained by dividing income in proportion to the end-of-the-year capital balance or in proportion to the average capital balance.

Allocation of Interest on Beginning-of-the-Year Capital Balances and Remainder in Specified Ratio

Another allocation procedure under consideration by Able and Baker calls for allocating an 8% interest allowance based on *January 1st capital balances* with an equal allocation of any remainder (whether income or loss). Using this procedure, $20,400 of the $40,000 income for 19X5 would be credited to Able's capital account, and the remaining $19,600 would be credited to Baker's capital account. The allocation is calculated as follows:

Able-Baker Partnership Income Allocation* for the Year Ended December 31, 19X5

	Able	Baker	Total
Interest:			
8% × $130,000	$10,400	$	$10,400
8% × $120,000		9,600	9,600
Total interest	$10,400	$ 9,600	$20,000
Remainder shared equally	10,000	10,000	20,000
Allocation of income	$20,400	$19,600	$40,000

* Interest is allocated based on the beginning-of-the-year capital balances, and the remainder of partnership income is allocated in specified ratio.

Allocation of Interest on Average Capital Balances and Remainder in Specified Ratio

A third allocation procedure under consideration by Able and Baker calls for allocation of an 8% interest allowance based on the *weighted average of beginning-of-the-month capital balances* without regard to drawing account transactions. Any remainder is divided in the ratio of 2:3. Able's weighted average capital balance would be $130,000, the initial balance that was maintained throughout the entire year. Since Baker made an additional capital contribution of $48,000 on April 30, 19X5, his weighted average capital balance would be $152,000 calculated as follows:[3]

Calculation of Baker's Weighted Average Capital Balance

$120,000 × 4/12	=	$ 40,000
$168,000 × 8/12	=	112,000
Weighted average capital balance		$152,000

Computing 8% interest on these balances and allocating the remainder in the ratio 2:3 results in the following allocation of partnership income:

Able-Baker Partnership Income Allocation* for the Year Ended December 31, 19X5

	Able	Baker	Total
Interest:			
8% × $130,000	$10,400	$	$10,400
8% × $152,000		12,160	12,160
Total interest	$10,400	$12,160	$22,560
Remainder shared in ratio 2:3			
2/5 × $17,440	6,976		
3/5 × $17,440		10,464	17,440
Allocation of income	$17,376	$22,624	$40,000

* Interest is allocated based on average capital balances, and the remainder of partnership income is allocated in specified ratio.

This allocation procedure will credit $17,376 to Able's capital account and $22,624 to Baker's capital account.

When interest is allowed on capital balances, the partnership agreement should specify the interest rate, the calculation of the capital base (e.g., beginning, average, or ending balances), the procedure to be used when a loss occurs, the procedure to be used when the

[3] The following alternative computation of the weighted average capital balance may also be employed, but it is somewhat more cumbersome:

ALTERNATIVE CALCULATION OF WEIGHT AVERAGE CAPITAL BALANCE FOR BAKER

Period	Capital Balance	Number of Months	Weighted Amount
January 1 to April 30	$120,000	4	$ 480,000
May 1 to December 31	168,000	8	1,344,000
Total		12	$1,824,000
Divide by total number of months			÷ 12
Weighted average capital balance			$ 152,000

Of course, both computations of the weighted average balance yield the same result.

interest allowance exceeds partnership income, and any restrictions on investment of capital considered necessary by the partners.

Service Contributions Bases

We turn now to income allocation arrangements based on service contributions by partners. When one partner contributes substantial personal services that are not contributed by other partners, it may be appropriate to award that partner a bonus, a salary, or some combination of the two. Allocations of income, whether in the form of bonuses or salaries, must be distinguished from withdrawals of assets. For example, partnership agreements may provide for salary allocations but limit withdrawals so that less than the full salary is payable. Consequently, it is important that the partnership agreement clearly and separately specify provisions for allocations and withdrawals.

Bonus Based on Partnership Income

When a particular partner's services are reflected in income, the partnership may award that partner a bonus calculated as a specified percentage of partnership income. For example, a partner might be awarded a bonus equal to 20% of the partnership income after subtraction of the bonus. If the letter B represents the unknown bonus and if income for the current year is $40,000, then the bonus can be calculated using the following equation.

$$B = 0.20 \ (\$40,000 - B)$$
$$B = \$8,000 - 0.20 \ B$$
$$1.20 \ B = \$8,000$$
$$B = \$6,667$$

The first equation simply states that the unknown bonus, B, equals 20% of the income after subtraction of the unknown bonus. Solving the equation for B gives the bonus of $6,667. If the bonus is to be calculated after salary and interest allocations (but before subtraction of the bonus), then the $40,000 income figure in the first equation should be replaced by $40,000 less salary and interest allocations. The partnership agreement should provide for the treatment of bonus provisions when the income is not sufficient to provide a specified bonus and when the partnership incurs a loss. Bonus provisions are usually inoperative when the partnership incurs a loss.

Partners' Salaries

Able and Baker are contemplating a salary provision in their new income-and-loss-sharing agreement since Baker contributes full-time to the partnership while Able contributes only occasional periods of time. The proposal under consideration is a three-stage allocation. First, Baker is awarded a salary of $15,000 annually. Second, both partners receive an 8% interest allowance computed on average capital balances. And finally, the remainder would be divided equally. The proposal also specifies that Baker's salary be provided *before* any interest is allowed. The application of this arrangement results in the following allocation of income:

Able-Baker Partnership Income Allocation* for the Year Ended December 31, 19X5

	Able	Baker	Total
Salary	$	$15,000	$15,000
Interest:			
8% × $130,000	10,400		10,400
8% × $152,000		12,160	12,160
Total salary and interest	$10,400	$27,160	$37,560
Remainder shared equally	1,220	1,220	2,440
Allocation of income	$11,620	$28,380	$40,000

* A salary is allowed, interest is allocated based on average capital balances, and the remainder of partnership income is allocated in specified ratio.

Note that the $15,000 salary allowance to Baker provides a $15,000 advantage to Baker in all allocations of income and loss, unless allowances for salaries are made only to the extent that profits provide them. This point is discussed in a later section of the chapter.

Deficiencies of Income Relative to Salaries and Interest

Ordinarily, partnerships expect net income to exceed provisions for salaries and interest, and it is customary to allocate the excess in the income-and-loss-sharing ratio. However, when net income falls short of the provision for salaries and interest, partnership agreements may handle the deficiency in at least two different ways. The first method allocates the deficiency in the income-and-loss-sharing ratio. Thus, under the first method, any remainder of income after salaries and interest—whether the remainder is an excess or a deficiency—is allocated in the income-and-loss-sharing ratio. The second method allocates an excess in the income-and-loss-sharing ratio but treats a deficiency differently. Rather than allocating the deficiency, the procedure allocates salaries and interest only to the extent that income is sufficient to provide them.

To illustrate the two methods of handling deficiencies of income relative to salaries and interest, consider the following provisions for salaries and interest, which represent one of the agreements under considerations by Able and Baker:

Proposed Salaries and Interest Provisions for Able-Baker Partnership

	Able		Baker		Total	
	Amount	Percent	Amount	Percent	Amount	Percent
Salary	$	0.0%	$15,000	100.0%	$15,000	100.0%
Interest	10,400	46.1	12,160	53.9	22,560	100.0
Total	$10,400		$27,160		$37,560	

Under such an agreement, any excess or deficiency would be measured relative to total salaries and interest of $37,560. If the income were only $30,000 for 19X5, the first method would divide the $7,560 deficiency ($7,560 = $37,560 − $30,000) between the partners in the income-and-loss-sharing ratio (50% to each partner in our example) subtracting $3,780 (.50 × $7,560) from each partner's credit for salary and interest as shown in the schedule on the following page.

Able-Baker Partnership Income Allocation* for the Year Ended December 31, 19X5

	Able	Baker	Total
Salary	$	$15,000	$15,000
Interest	10,400	12,160	22,560
Total salary and interest	$10,400	$27,160	$37,560
Deficiency allocated in income-and-loss-sharing ratio	(3,780)	(3,780)	(7,560)
Allocation of income	$ 6,620	$23,380	$30,000

* A salary is allowed and interest is allocated based on average capital balances; the deficiency of *income* relative to salaries and interest is allocated in the income-and-loss-sharing ratio.

Thus, under the first method, Able would receive a net credit of $6,620 and Baker a net credit of $23,380.

Continuing consideration of the first method of handling deficiencies, suppose the partnership were to register a loss of $5,000 for 19X5. The $42,560 deficiency is the *sum* of the loss and the provision for interest and salaries ($42,560 = $5,000 + $37,560). The allocation of the loss by the first method is as follows:

Able-Baker Partnership Income Allocation* for the Year Ended December 31, 19X5

	Able	Baker	Total
Salary	$	$15,000	$15,000
Interest	10,400	12,160	22,560
Total salary and interest	$ 10,400	27,160	$37,560
Deficiency allocated in income-and-loss-sharing ratio	(21,280)	(21,280)	(42,560)
Allocation of income	$(10,880)	$ 5,880	$ (5,000)

* A salary is allowed and interest is allocated based on average capital balances; the *loss and deficiency of income* are allocated in the income-and-loss-sharing ratio.

Notice that division of the deficiency in the income-and-loss-sharing ratio results in a *credit* to Baker's capital account of $5,880 but a *debit* to Able's capital account of $10,880, an amount that exceeds the loss reported by the partnership. The prospect of such perverse allocations leads some partnerships to specify different treatments for deficiencies from those for excesses. One such treatment is the second method to which we now turn.

Instead of allocating full salaries and interest allowances as if income were sufficient to provide them, the second method creates allowances for salaries and interest only to the extent that the income is sufficient to provide them. Such a procedure assigns the $30,000 income considered earlier as follows:

Able-Baker Partnership Income Allocation* for the Year Ended December 31, 19X5

	Able	Baker	Total
Salary	$	$15,000	$15,000
Interest	6,915†	8,085‡	15,000
Allocation of income	$6,915	$23,085	$30,000

* A salary is allowed and interest is allocated based on average capital balances; salary and interest are allocated to the extent provided by income with salary allocated before interest.

† $6,915 = .461 × $15,000

‡ $8,085 = .539 × $15,000

The income of $30,000 is sufficient for the full salary of $15,000, but the $15,000 remainder of the income is short of the $22,560 total of interest credits. Consequently, the $15,000 remainder is allocated in the *ratio* of the full individual interest credits. Able receives $6,915, or 46.1% of $15,000 (46.1% = $10,400 ÷ $22,560); and Baker receives $8,085, or 53.9% of $15,000 (53.9% = $12,160 ÷ $22,560).

Under the second method, the *order of allocation may affect the result.* The foregoing schedule shows the result if salaries are provided before interest; the following schedule shows the result if interest is provided before salary:

Able-Baker Partnership Income Allocation* for the Year Ended December 31, 19X5

	Able	Baker	Total
Interest	$10,400	$12,160	$22,560
Salary		7,440	7,440
Allocation of income	$10,400	$19,600	$30,000

* A salary is allowed and interest is allocated based on average capital balances; salary and interest are allocated to the extent provided by income with interest allocated before salary.

In the latter case, the $30,000 income provides for the full interest credit but for only part of Baker's salary.[4] Partnership agreements should specify any limitations on allocating full salary, interest, and bonus allowances. Otherwise the full allowance is allocated for such items, and the deficiency is divided on the basis of the ratio specified by the income-and-loss-sharing arrangement (the first method).

Partners' Salaries and Interest in the Income Statement

A question arises as to how salaries and interest to partners are to be treated on the partnership income statement. Should partners' salary and interest allowances be shown as expense, or should they be treated as distributions of income? In our example at the top of page 695, is partnership income $40,000, with all interest and salary treated as a distribu-

---

[4] If the income were only $20,000, then Baker would receive no salary when interest credits were created before salaries. The entire $20,000 would be allocated as interest with $9,220 going to Able ($9,220 = .461 × $20,000) and $10,780 going to Baker ($10,780 = .539 × $20,000). If a loss had been incurred, the loss would have been divided in the income-and-loss-sharing ratio without regard to salaries and interest.

tion of income, or is partnership income $2,440, with all interest and salary treated as expenses? The answer depends on one's view of the partnership organization. Some accountants argue that the payment of salaries and interest to partners does not differ from payments of salaries and interest to anyone else. Therefore, all salaries and interest should have the same impact on income and should be treated as expenses. Moreover, it is argued that this procedure makes partnership income comparable to corporation income, which treats salaries and interest paid to stockholders as expenses. But the dominant view rejects this argument and treats salaries and interest as allocations of income on the grounds that a partner, by definition, cannot be an employee of the partnership. A partnership is usually viewed as an association in which partners have only a proprietary or residual equity interest. Hence, all salaries and interest payments are allocations of income. The same view is reflected in the Internal Revenue Code and in most laws respecting partnerships. Consequently, the generally used procedure reports income of $40,000 for the Able-Baker Partnership and treats all salaries and interest on capital as allocations of that income.

Correction of Prior Years' Net Income

An error in the computation of a prior period's net income requires correction. The central issue is whether the correction should alter the net income of the current year (the year in which the error is discovered) or the net income of the prior year (the year in which the error occurred). When an error is corrected by adjustment of a prior year's income, the allocation of income for the prior year should be recalculated using the corrected net income and the income-and-loss-sharing procedure in effect during the prior year. When an error is corrected by adjustment of the current year's net income, the error is allocated among capital accounts using the current year's income-and-loss-sharing procedure. The two adjustment methods produce different capital balances if the income-and-loss-sharing procedure or the identity of partners changes while the error remains undiscovered.

Financial accounting standards restrict the adjustment of prior periods' net income to the effects of a few transactions. Consequently, most corrections to published financial statements alter current net income (see *APB Opinions No. 9 and No. 20* and *FASB Statement No. 16*). In general, the standards should be followed for partnerships, but when a partnership agreement specifies that particular items be treated as prior-period adjustments, the partnership agreement should be followed—particularly when application of the standards would result in a different allocation of income among the partners.

FINANCIAL REPORTING AND TAXATION

Financial Statements of Partnerships

The balance sheets and income statements prepared for partnerships are similar to those prepared for corporations. The primary difference between partnership and corporate balance sheets is that the partnership ownership equity section consists of the partners' capital accounts rather than capital stock and retained earnings accounts. In other words, partnership balance sheets do not maintain a distinction between contributed and earned capital as do corporate balance sheets. The primary difference between partnership and corporate income statements is the usual practice in partnerships of excluding salaries, interest, and bonuses that are paid to partners from expenses.

The 19X5 income statement for Able-Baker is shown in Exhibit 14-1 and is based on data that were not previously introduced. Note that salaries and wages reported on the income statement *exclude* amounts earned by partners, yet interest on amounts borrowed from partners is included in expenses. The income statement usually discloses the detailed

EXHIBIT 14-1	PARTNERSHIP INCOME STATEMENT

Able-Baker Partnership

INCOME STATEMENT
FOR THE YEAR ENDED DECEMBER 31, 19X5

Sales			$500,000
Cost of goods sold			280,000
Gross margin			$220,000
Operating expenses:			
Salaries and wages to nonpartners		$96,000	
Interest on loans from Able		2,000	
Other expenses		82,000	180,000
Net income			$ 40,000

Allocation of income to partners:

	Able	Baker	Total
Salary	$	$15,000	$15,000
Interest	10,400	12,160	22,560
Remainder allocated in income- and-loss-sharing ratio	1,220	1,220	2,440
Allocation of income	$11,620	$28,380	$40,000

allocation of income in the form of a footnote or a computations schedule appended to the income statement. The allocation schedule shown in Exhibit 14-1 is based on the income allocation plan presented at the top of page 695.

In place of the statement of retained earnings used by corporations, partnerships prepare a statement of partners' capital. Using the information contained in the income statement in Exhibit 14-1 and the previously established capital balances and withdrawals, the statement of partners' capital is presented in Exhibit 14-2 on the following page.

A partnership may prepare a statement of cash flows. The preparation of this statement for a partnership would parallel that for other profit-oriented entities and is therefore not illustrated here.

Federal Income Tax Law and Partnerships

Partnerships report their income to the Internal Revenue Service on information tax returns, but they do not pay federal income tax. Instead, the tax is paid by the individual partners on their respective shares of the income. Moreover, partners pay the tax as the income is earned, whether or not it is withdrawn by partners. This fact may create a cash flow problem for partners who invest a significant part of their income allocation in the partnership. (Under federal income tax laws, certain small, closely held corporations—called ''subchapter S corporations''—may elect to be taxed as partnerships.)

| EXHIBIT 14-2 | STATEMENT OF PARTNERS' CAPITAL BALANCES |

Able-Baker Partnership

STATEMENT OF PARTNERS' CAPITAL BALANCES
FOR THE YEAR ENDED DECEMBER 31, 19X5

	Able	Baker	Total
Capital, January 1, 19X5	$130,000	$120,000	$250,000
Add: Additional investments		48,000	48,000
Net income	11,620	28,380	40,000
Subtotal	$141,620	$196,380	$338,000
Less: Withdrawals	12,000	6,000	18,000
Capital, December 31, 19X5	$129,620	$190,380	$320,000

When partners transfer assets to the partnership, the Internal Revenue Code does not recognize any gain or loss. Instead, the tax "basis" of the assets to the partner is merely transferred to the partnership. This means that the tax basis of a partner's capital interest may differ from the accounting basis and that depreciation and amortization for tax purposes will differ from depreciation and amortization for accounting purposes. Consequently, taxable income of the partnership will differ from reported net income and may be calculated by adjusting accounting income for differences in depreciation and amortization expense owing to differences between the tax and accounting bases of contributed assets. Moreover, the *taxable gain or loss* from the disposition of a partnership interest is calculated relative to the tax basis of the interest rather than to the capital account balance.

To illustrate, suppose that Gordon and Howell form a partnership. Gordon contributes $12,000 cash, and Howell contributes $2,000 cash and a building with a fair value of $16,000 subject to a $6,000 mortgage. The mortgage is transferred to the partnership. The partners agree to allocate income and loss equally and to record equal initial capital shares. The following entries establish the partnership accounts:

Entry to establish capital balance for Gordon:

Cash... 12,000
       Gordon, capital   12,000

Entry to establish capital balance for Howell:

Cash.. 2,000
Building... 16,000
       Mortgage payable   6,000
       Howell, capital   12,000

Suppose further that the tax basis of Howell in the building is only $11,000, which is $5,000 less than its fair value. This means that the tax bases of the partners' interests are not equal to the initial balances of the capital accounts. The tax bases are calculated as follows:

Schedule of Tax Bases of Partners' Capital Interests in the Gordon-Howell Partnership

	Gordon	Howell
Tax bases of contributed assets:		
Cash	$12,000	$ 2,000
Building		11,000
Subtotal	$12,000	$13,000
Adjustment to bases for $6,000 mortgage transferred to partnership by Howell and assumed by the partnership	3,000	(3,000)
Tax bases of capital interests	$15,000	$10,000

For tax purposes, the initial basis of the equity interest is $15,000 for Gordon and $10,000 for Howell, instead of the balances reflected in the capital accounts. Howell's transferred basis is $11,000 rather than the cost to the partnership of $16,000. The assumption of partner Howell's mortgage by the partnership is viewed by tax law as a constructive payment to Howell by Gordon; Howell is better off to the extent that the transfer reduces his responsibility for the mortgage. The constructive payment is calculated by multiplying Gordon's profit-and-loss-sharing ratio by the amount of the mortgage and is recorded as an increase in Gordon's basis (treating the constructive payment as an additional capital contribution) and a decrease in Howell's basis (treating the constructive payment as a return of capital).

In general, the *tax basis of a partner's ownership interest* in the partnership is the sum of the tax bases of assets contributed by the partner, decreased by any personal liabilities of the partner that are assumed by other partners, and increased by any personal liabilities of other partners that are assumed by the partner in question. Observe that the *total tax basis* of *all* partners' ownership interests in a partnership ($25,000) may be computed without reference to personal liabilities transferred to the partnership. That is, it may be computed as the sum of the tax bases of all contributed assets ($25,000 = $12,000 + $2,000 + $11,000).

CHANGES IN OWNERSHIP

The admission of a new partner and the withdrawal of an existing partner are analogous to the sale of shares of corporate stock. The essence of both transactions is a change in the identity of ownership. A partnership's records include a separate account for the owner's equity of each partner. Consequently, any change in the identity of the partners or the size of their capital interests occasions an entry in the owners' equity accounts. In contrast, a corporation's records do not include a separate account for each stockholder. Rather, owners' equity consists of capital stock and retained earnings accounts. Consequently, a change in the identity of stockholders in response to the sale of its outstanding stock occasions no entry by the corporation; the corporation merely makes a memorandum entry in its list of stockholders.

Admission of a New Partner

The admission of new partners and the withdrawal or death of existing partners change the identity of the partnership group. Whenever the identity of one or more partners changes, the legal partnership entity is dissolved and a new legal partnership entity is created.[5] Dissolution of the legal entity, however, does not imply liquidation or destruction of the business entity. For example, the admission of a new partner legally dissolves the old partnership and creates a new one. A new partnership agreement must be reached—including agreement on a new income-and-loss-sharing ratio—but the old business entity may continue its operations undisturbed. On the other hand, when liquidation accompanies dissolution, the assets of the partnership are sold and the proceeds are used to satisfy claims against the partnership by creditors and partners. Thus, liquidation destroys both the legal entity and the business entity. Liquidation of a partnership is discussed in the next chapter.

A new partner gains admission to an existing partnership in one of two ways: (1) by investing assets directly in the partnership or (2) by purchasing an interest from one or more existing partners. The following section describes and illustrates these two forms of admission.

Admission by Investment and by Purchased Interest

When a new partner is admitted by investment, the new partner transfers assets (and sometimes liabilities) directly to the partnership, which increases the physical quantity of partnership assets. To illustrate, suppose that Cook secures a 25% interest (meaning a 25% capital interest and a 25% share of income and losses) in the McLean-George Partnership by investing $40,000; the investment consists of a building valued at $90,000 subject to a mortgage of $50,000. Just prior to the investment by Cook, the partnership has total capital of $120,000. The admission of the new partner would be recorded by the following entry:

Entry to record investment and establish new partner's capital account:

Building.	90,000	
Mortgage payable		50,000
Cook, capital		40,000

Notice that the $40,000 contributed by Cook raises the total capital of the partnership to $160,000 ($120,000 + $40,000) and that Cook's capital of $40,000 represents exactly

---

[5] The precise legal meaning of dissolution varies somewhat from one state to another, owing to modifications of the Uniform Partnership Act enacted by individual states. In general, it means that the terms of the original partnership agreement are not binding on the new legal partnership entity and that a new partnership agreement must be created. Frequently, however, the creation of the new partnership agreement is anticipated and guided by the terms of the original agreement. Although the possible causes of dissolution vary somewhat from state to state, dissolution of a partnership is either the result of action by the partners themselves or a response to the law. Partners may cause dissolution (1) by including a termination date in the partnership agreement, (2) by agreeing to change their membership, (3) by agreeing to end their association, or (4) by withdrawal of a partner. The Uniform Partnership Act brings dissolution in the event of the death or bankruptcy of any partner. In addition, a court of law may decree dissolution in a variety of special circumstances, as when a partner "is shown to be of unsound mind" (Uniform Partnership Act, Sec. 31).

25% of this total ($40,000 = .25 × $160,000), as required by the new partnership agreement in this example.

We turn now to admission by purchased interest. The Uniform Partnership Act permits any partner to sell his or her interest in a partnership to a third party. However, the third party is not entitled to participate in the management of the partnership unless the remaining partners agree to admit the third party.[6] When a new partner gains admission by purchasing an interest from existing partners, the assets given up by the new partner pass directly to the original partner or partners and the physical quantity of partnership assets is unaltered. To illustrate, suppose that Weber secures a 25% interest in the Joyce-Kline Partnership by acquiring half of Kline's 50% interest for $15,000 cash, which is paid directly to Kline. The partnership has total capital of $60,000; accordingly, Weber receives a capital interest of $15,000 (.25 × $60,000). The admission of the new partner is recorded by the following entry on the partnership records:

Entry to establish new partner's capital account:

Kline, capital	15,000	
Weber, capital		15,000

Notice that the physical quantity of partnership assets is unaffected by the admission of Weber; equity is merely transferred from one capital account to another.

In some cases, the admission of a new partner may require the revaluation of the old partnership's assets and liabilities. We turn now to this revaluation decision and the related accounting procedures.

The Revaluation Decision

As previously mentioned, the admission of a new partner creates a new legal entity for the partnership, but it does not always create a new business entity. For example, the admission of a new partner to a large public accounting firm usually does not create a new business entity. On the other hand, the admission of an influential partner to a small research and development partnership may create a new business entity. Although accountants are reluctant to revalue the assets of a business entity unless the case for a new business entity is very strong, financial accounting standards do not set forth criteria for the identification of a new partnership entity. Thus, the decision on whether or not a new basis of accounting is created by the admission of a new partner is made by partners in consultation with accountants and lawyers on a case-by-case basis. (See Chapter 10 for additional discussion of new basis accounting.)

---

[6] If the remaining partners agree to admit the third party, then the old partnership is dissolved and the third party assumes the role of the partner or partners that he or she replaces in a new partnership. If the other partners do not agree to admit the third party to the partnership, as occasionally happens, but wish to continue the existing partnership, then no dissolution occurs and the third party is entitled to receive partnership income and, in the event of liquidation, any assets that would flow to the original partner's interest. These provisions of the act modify the common-law rule that a partner cannot sell his or her interest without the approval of all the partners. Throughout the remainder of this chapter (and in the exercises and problems), the purchaser of all or part of the capital interest from one or more partners is assumed to be admitted to the partnership by the remaining partners unless otherwise specified.

When the admission of a new partner creates a new business entity, all assets and liabilities (including assets and liabilities contributed to the partnership, if any, by the new partner) should be adjusted to fair value. *Fair value* is the value that would be agreed upon by well-informed buyers and sellers; it is often estimated by reference to appraisals and current market prices. To illustrate, suppose that the admission of Dodd to the Edwards-Gamble Partnership creates a new business entity and that the assets and liabilities of the old partnership are all recorded at fair value except for a building that is undervalued by $10,000 and land that is overvalued by $3,000. If Edwards and Gamble share income and loss equally, the following entry is required to revalue the assets:

Entry to write up assets of old partnership:

Building	10,000	
Land		3,000
Edwards, capital		3,500
Gamble, capital		3,500

Notice that the $7,000 revaluation adjustment ($10,000–$3,000) is divided between the old partners, Edwards and Gamble, in their income-and-loss-sharing ratios. Throughout this book we assume that partners agree to share revaluation adjustments in the income-and-loss-sharing ratio, unless a contrary indication is given. As long as the admission of Dodd creates a new business entity—whether the admission is by investment or by purchased interest—the foregoing entry is required to revalue the net assets of the old partnership. In contrast, when admission of a new partner does not create a new business entity, the book values of the old partnership's assets and liabilities are not adjusted. However, any assets or liabilities contributed by the new partner are recorded at fair value, as would be any newly acquired assets or liabilities. Unlike partnerships, corporations are not permitted to revalue their assets in response to changes in the identity of the owners, as the following issues section explains.

ISSUES

Revaluation and Ownership Changes— Corporations and Partnerships

The admission of a new partner by investment is analogous to the issuance of new shares of corporate stock. A corporation exchanges new shares for assets with the result that both assets and ownership equity increase by the fair value of assets that are received. Similarly, the admission of a new partner by investment also increases both assets and ownership equity by the fair value of assets contributed. But there is an important difference between the two expansions of ownership equity: admission of a new partner may dissolve the old partnership business entity and replace it with a new one, whereas the issuance of additional shares does not disrupt the corporate business entity. Consequently, *all* assets of a new partnership are revalued and reported at fair value, but only the newly invested assets of the corporation are reported at fair value.[7]

The admission of a new partner by purchased interest is analogous to the sale of already outstanding stock. Although admission by purchased interest may lead to the

[7] In exceptional cases, discussed in earlier chapters, the corporation does not revalue the assets received when stock is issued; instead, net assets are recorded at their book values. Such cases are called *poolings of interests.*

revaluation of the partnership assets and liabilities, transactions in the outstanding stock of a corporation (like sales of newly issued stock) cannot lead to the revaluation of assets and liabilities on that corporation's records.[8]

Of course, whether or not the assets and liabilities of the old partnership are revalued, their fair values are usually considered an important input to the negotiation of the new partnership agreement. For the sake of simplicity, problem materials at the end of this chapter do not require a judgment on revaluation but simply indicate whether or not to revalue assets and liabilities upon dissolution.

Admission by Investment

When a new partner is admitted by investment, the fair value of the identifiable assets and liabilities contributed by the new partner is credited to the new partner's capital account. If the admission creates a new business entity, then the old partnership's assets and liabilities must be revalued and the old partner's capital accounts adjusted. After these entries have been made, the balance of the new partner's capital account must equal the agreed-upon fraction of the total of all capital balances. If the new partner's capital balance does not equal his or her agreed-upon fraction of total capital, then additional adjustments are required. This section illustrates two methods of accomplishing these adjustments—the goodwill method and the bonus method. Of course, the particular adjustments recorded must be approved by the partners. Thus, although accountants and lawyers may advise partners on such matters, the form and amount of the adjustment are decided by the partners.

The Goodwill Method

Under the goodwill method, the partners agree to an adjustment recognizing an intangible asset called goodwill. Goodwill reflects the value of intangibles that cannot be identified with particular assets on the records of the new partnership. Goodwill may represent intangibles that are associated with the old partnership, such as its reputation for quality services. Alternatively, goodwill may represent intangibles—such as special skills, knowledge, or experience of the new partner—that cannot be identified with assets invested by the new partner. In the latter case, goodwill may be called *contributed goodwill.* The form of the goodwill adjustment depends on a comparison of two amounts: (1) the cost to the new partner, that is, the fair value of identifiable assets and liabilities invested in the partnership by the new partner, and (2) the new partner's share of the new partnership's assets and liabilities, measured at their fair value.[9] If the cost to the new partner

---

[8] As explained in earlier chapters, however, one corporation may acquire all or most of the stock of another corporation, which requires the assets and liabilities of the acquired corporation to be revalued in preparing financial statements for the acquiring corporation.

[9] Equivalently, one can compare (1) the total value of the new partnership implied by dividing the cost to the new partner by the new partner's acquired capital share and (2) the total value of the new partnership implied by dividing the fair value of the old partnership's identifiable assets and liabilities by the old partner's total capital share in the new partnership.

exceeds the acquired share in the new partnership, then goodwill is credited to the old partners. On the other hand, if the cost to the new partner is less than the acquired share in the new partnership, then the goodwill is credited to the new partner. Let us illustrate each case.

Cost exceeds acquired share (goodwill to old partners)

We begin with the case in which the cost to the new partner—the fair value of assets and liabilities invested by the new partner—exceeds that partner's share of the new partnership's identifiable assets and liabilities measured at their fair value. Consider the admission of Jones to the Nelson-Voss Partnership, which is assumed to create a new business entity. Nelson and Voss share *equally* in all income and loss and have capital balances, just before the admission of Jones, as follows:

Nelson, Capital	$ 30,000
Voss, Capital	70,000
Total	$100,000

In all exercises and problems, we shall assume that the book values of partnership assets equal their fair values unless the contrary is indicated. All the identifiable assets and liabilities of the old Nelson-Voss Partnership are recorded at fair value except for a parcel of land that is undervalued by $16,000. Assuming that the admission of Jones creates a new business entity, the following entry is made to revalue the assets of the old partnership:

Entry to write up assets of old partnership:

Land	16,000	
Nelson, capital		8,000
Voss, capital		8,000

Suppose that Jones acquires a 20% interest by investing equipment with a fair value of $30,000, which is recorded by the following entry:

Entry to record investment and establish new partner's capital account:

Equipment	30,000	
Jones, capital		30,000

Jones's acquired share in the identifiable assets and liabilities of the new partnership is $29,200 [.20 × ($100,000 + $16,000 + $30,000)]. Thus, the cost to Jones exceeds the acquired share of assets and liabilities by $800 ($30,000 − $29,200). Why did Jones pay $800 more than the acquired share of the assets and liabilities? The answer may be that the fair value of the new partnership's identifiable assets and liabilities understates the total value of the new partnership by an amount of unrecorded goodwill associated with the old partnership. Further, Jones is buying for $800 a 20% share in this goodwill which totals $4,000 ($800 ÷ .20).[10] This goodwill is recorded as an asset of the new partnership and

[10] Alternatively, goodwill can be calculated by using the new partner's cost ($30,000) to impute a total value to the new partnership of $150,000 ($30,000 ÷ .20) and subtracting the fair value of the new partnership's identifiable assets and liabilities [$4,000 = $150,000 − ($100,000 + $16,000 + $30,000)].

divided between the old partners by the following entry:

Entry to record goodwill to old partners:

```
Goodwill . . . . . . . . . . . . . . . . . . . . . . . . . . . . . . . . . . . . . . . . . . . . . . . . . . . 4,000
        Newton, capital . . . . . . . . . . . . . . . . . . . . . . . . . . . . . . . . . . . . .        2,000
        Voss, capital . . . . . . . . . . . . . . . . . . . . . . . . . . . . . . . . . . . . . . .        2,000
```

Unless specifically indicated otherwise, we assume throughout this book (as assumed in the foregoing entry) that goodwill attributed to the old partners is divided in their income-and-loss-sharing ratio. The following schedule shows the impact of the three adjustments on the partners' capital accounts:

The Goodwill Method for an Admission by Investment with Goodwill to Old Partners

	Capital Accounts			
	Newton	Voss	Jones	Total
Original capital balances	$30,000	$70,000	$	$100,000
Revaluation of land	8,000	8,000		16,000
Adjusted capital balances	$38,000	$78,000		$116,000
Investment by Jones			30,000	30,000
Adjusted capital balances	$38,000	$78,000	$30,000	$146,000
Goodwill	2,000	2,000		4,000
Capital balances after admission of Jones	$40,000	$80,000	$30,000	$150,000

The adjustments result in capital balances that give Jones a 20% interest in total capital ($30,000 = .20 × $150,000).

Another explanation for Jones's willingness to pay $800 more than the acquired share of the assets and liabilities in the new partnership is that Jones receives a particularly favorable income-sharing arrangement. Perhaps Jones's income share exceeds Jones's capital share, and the additional $800 payment compensates the old partners for this arrangement. However, if this explanation is correct, it would not be appropriate to record goodwill. Rather, a capital bonus should be allocated among the old partners following the bonus method described later in this chapter.

Cost less than acquired share (goodwill to new partner)

We now turn to a case in which the cost to the new partner is less than the new partner's share of the new partnership's identifiable assets and liabilities measured at fair value. Let us reconsider the admission of Jones to the Nelson-Voss Partnership using the same facts that were previously given, except that Jones invests equipment valued at only $27,000 in exchange for his 20% interest. As before, the revaluation of the old partnership's assets and the investment by Jones are recorded by the following entries (only the amount of the new investment differs):

Entry to record revaluation of assets:

```
Land . . . . . . . . . . . . . . . . . . . . . . . . . . . . . . . . . . . . . . . . . . . . . . . . . . 16,000
        Nelson, capital . . . . . . . . . . . . . . . . . . . . . . . . . . . . . . . . . . . . .        8,000
        Voss, capital . . . . . . . . . . . . . . . . . . . . . . . . . . . . . . . . . . . . . . .        8,000
```

Entry to record investment and establish new partner's capital account:

Equipment 27,000
      Jones, capital   27,000

Jones's acquired share in the identifiable assets and liabilities of the new partnership is $28,600 [.20 × ($100,000 + $16,000 + $27,000)]. Thus, the cost to Jones is less than the acquired share of assets and liabilities by $1,600 ($28,600 − $27,000). Why did Jones pay $1,600 less than the acquired share of the assets and liabilities? The answer may be that the fair value of Jones's total contribution to the partnership is more than the fair value of the identifiable assets invested (equipment valued at $27,000) and that Jones is contributing goodwill in the form of special skills, knowledge, or experience. The goodwill contributed by the new partner can be calculated by reference to the $1,600 deficiency of cost to the new partner relative to the share acquired in the fair value of identifiable assets and liabilities. Since the old partners have an 80% interest in the new partnership, including the goodwill contributed by Jones, the $1,600 deficiency represents only 80% of the total contributed goodwill. Therefore, the total amount of goodwill contributed by Jones must be $2,000 ($1,600 ÷ .80).[11] This goodwill is recorded as an asset of the new partnership and credited to the new partner's capital accounting by the following entry:

Entry to record goodwill to new partner:

Goodwill 2,000
      Jones, capital   2,000

The following schedule shows the impact of these adjustments on the partners' capital accounts:

The Goodwill Method for an Admission by Investment with Goodwill to New Partner

	Capital Accounts			
	Newton	Voss	Jones	Total
Original capital balances	$30,000	$70,000	$	$100,000
Revaluation of land	8,000	8,000		16,000
Adjusted capital balances	$38,000	$78,000		$116,000
Investment by Jones			27,000	27,000
Adjusted capital balances	$38,000	$78,000	$27,000	$143,000
Goodwill			2,000	2,000
Capital balances after admission of Jones	$38,000	$78,000	$29,000	$145,000

The schedule shows the impact of these adjustments on the partners' capital accounts. Crediting the entire amount of contributed goodwill to Jones's capital account raises its balance to $29,000, which equals 20% of the total partnership capital as required by the partnership agreement ($29,000 = .20 × $145,000). The goodwill is credited to the new

---

[11] Alternatively, the amount of goodwill ($2,000) can be calculated by using the fair value of the old partnership's assets and liabilities ($116,000) to impute a total value to the new partnership of $145,000 ($116,000 ÷ .80) and subtracting the fair value of the new partnership's identifiable assets and liabilities [$2,000 = $145,000 − ($100,000 + $16,000 + $27,000)].

partner's capital account because the new partner is viewed as contributing goodwill. In contrast, when goodwill is viewed as contributed by the old partners, as in the earlier illustration, goodwill is credited to the old partners' capital accounts.

Another explanation for the old partners' willingness to accept $1,600 less than the acquired share of the assets and liabilities in the new partnership is that the income-sharing arrangement granted to Jones is less favorable than the capital share granted to Jones. However, if this explanation is correct, it would not be appropriate to record goodwill. Rather, a capital bonus should be given to Jones following the bonus method described later in this chapter.

If the partners had not viewed the admission of Jones as creating a new business entity, then the revaluation of the old partnership's net assets would not be appropriate under generally accepted accounting principles. Nor would it be appropriate to recognize goodwill that is associated with the old partnership. On the other hand, the partners could appropriately agree to recognize contributed goodwill that is associated with Jones's admission (and not associated with the old partnership) whether or not a new business entity is created. Of course, the assets that are invested by Jones would be recorded at their fair value whether or not the admission of Jones creates a new business entity.

The Bonus Method

In contrast to the goodwill method, the bonus method neither revalues the assets or liabilities of the old partnership nor results in the recognition of goodwill. Accordingly, the bonus method is applicable to cases in which a new business entity has not been created. Of course, assets invested in the partnership by a new partner are recorded at the fair value whether the bonus method or the goodwill method is used. Rather than revalue the old partnership and recognize related goodwill, the bonus method adjusts capital balances so that the new partner's capital equals the acquired fraction of total capital in the new partnership. As before, the identity of the capital accounts adjusted depends on a comparison of the cost to the new partner and the new partner's share in the new partnership. If the cost to the new partner exceeds the acquired share in the new partnership, then a capital bonus is transferred from the new partner's capital account to the capital accounts of the old partners. If the cost to the new partner is less than the acquired share in the new partnership, then a capital bonus is transferred from the old partners' capital accounts to the capital account of the new partner. Let us illustrate each case.

Cost exceeds acquired share (bonus to old partners)

We begin with the case in which the investment by the new partner exceeds the acquired share in the new partnership. Suppose that Burton invests land with a fair value of $30,000 in exchange for a 20% interest in the Osborn-Rossi Partnership. Osborn and Rossi share income and loss equally and have capital balances, just before Burton's investment, of $30,000 and $70,000, respectively, which total $100,000. Assume that the admission of Burton does not call for the revaluation of the assets and liabilities of the old partnership. Instead, the book values of the old partnership's assets and liabilities are simply carried forward, and the fair value of Burton's contribution is recorded by the following entry:

Entry to record investment and establish new partner's capital account:

Land 30,000
       Burton, capital   30,000

Since the assets are not revalued, the capital of the new partnership totals $130,000 ($100,000 + $30,000) and Burton's acquired share is $26,000 (.20 × $130,000). In other words, Burton paid $4,000 more than the amount of the acquired share ($30,000 − $26,000). Under the bonus method, Burton's capital balance is reduced to the acquired share of $26,000 (.20 × $130,000) and the $4,000 reduction is transferred as a capital bonus to Osborn and Rossi. Unless specifically indicated otherwise, we shall assume throughout this book that partners agree to share the bonus in the income-and-loss-sharing ratio. This leads to an equal division of the bonus between Osborn and Rossi, as shown in the following entry:

Entry to transfer capital bonus from new partner to old partners:

Burton, capital	4,000	
Osborn, capital		2,000
Rossi, capital		2,000

The following schedule shows the effect of these adjustments on the partners' capital accounts:

The Bonus Method for an Admission by Investment with Bonus to Old Partners

	Capital Accounts			Total
	Osborn	Rossi	Burton	
Original capital balances	$30,000	$70,000	$	$100,000
Investment by Burton			30,000	30,000
Distribution of bonus	2,000	2,000	(4,000)	
Capital balances after admission of Burton	$32,000	$72,000	$26,000	$130,000

The bonus compensates the original partners for the noncapital consideration given to the new partner. For example, Burton may receive a larger percentage interest in income than in capital, or Burton may benefit from intangibles associated with the old partnership (e.g., good reputation or above normal earnings prospects) that are not recorded on the new partnership records.

Cost less than acquired share (bonus to new partner)

When the new partner invests less than the acquired share in the new partnership, the bonus method results in a capital bonus to the new partner. To illustrate, suppose that Burton acquires a 20% interest in the Osborn-Rossi Partnership by investing land valued at only $22,000. Burton's contribution is recorded by the following entry:

Entry to record investment and establish new partner's capital account:

Land	22,000	
Burton, capital		22,000

The capital of the new partnership totals $122,000 ($100,000 + $22,000), and Burton's acquired share is $24,400 (.20 × $122,000). In other words, Burton paid $2,400 less than the amount of the acquired share ($24,400 − $22,000). Under the bonus method, Burton's capital balance is increased to the acquired share of $24,400 (.20 × $122,000) and the $2,400 increase is transferred as a capital bonus from Osborn and Rossi. The bonus is recorded by the following entry:

Entry to transfer capital bonus from old partners to new partner:

Osborn, capital 1,200
Rossi, capital 1,200
     Burton, capital   2,400

The following schedule shows the effect of these adjustments on the partners' capital accounts:

The Bonus Method for an Admission by Investment with Bonus to New Partner

	Capital Accounts			
	Osborn	Rossi	Burton	Total
Original capital balances	$30,000	$70,000	$	$100,000
Investment by Burton			22,000	22,000
Distribution of bonus	(1,200)	(1,200)	2,400	
Capital balances after admission of Burton	$28,800	$68,800	$24,400	$122,000

The bonus compensates the new partner for the contribution of special skills, knowledge, or experience.

Admission by a Purchased Interest

When a new partner gains admission by purchasing an equity interest from one or more of the old partners, the new partner transfers assets directly to the old partners rather than to the partnership. As a result, the physical assets of the partnership are not increased. Our illustrations of admission by purchased interest parallel those for admission by investment. We illustrate both the goodwill and bonus methods of recording the new partner's admission.

The Goodwill Method

Recall that under the goodwill method, the partners agree to recognize an intangible asset called goodwill. The form of the goodwill adjustment depends on a comparison of the cost to the new partner and the new partner's share in the new partnership's assets and liabilities, measured at their fair value. If the cost to the new partner (the fair value of identifiable assets and liabilities paid to one or more of the old partners) exceeds the acquired share in the new partnership, then goodwill is credited to the older partners. On the other hand, if the cost to the new partner is less than the acquired share, then goodwill is credited to the new partner.

Cost exceeds acquired share (goodwill to old partners)

Let us begin with a case in which the cost to the new partner exceeds the acquired share of the new partnership's identifiable assets and liabilities measured at their fair value. Consider the admission of Beck to the Harris-McLeod Partnership, which is assumed to create a new business entity. Harris and McLeod share income and loss in the ratio of 2:3 and have capital balances of $30,000 and $70,000, respectively, at the admission of a new partner, Beck. The assets and liabilities of the old partnership are recorded at fair value except for a parcel of land that is undervalued by $17,000. Since the admission of Beck creates a new business entity, the following entry is made to revalue the assets of the old partnership:

Entry to write up assets of old partnership:

Land	17,000	
Harris, capital ($17,000 × 2/5)		6,800
McLeod, capital ($17,000 × 3/5)		10,200

Beck purchases a 20% interest in the Harris-McLeod partnership by paying McLeod $24,000 in cash. Since Beck pays this amount directly to McLeod, no entry is made on the partnership records to record the payment. However, entries must be made to transfer a portion of McLeod's capital balance to Beck and to recognize any implied goodwill. Beck's acquired share in the identifiable assets and liabilities of the new partnership is $23,400 [.20 × ($100,000 + $17,000)]. Thus, the cost to Beck exceeds the acquired share by $600 ($24,000 − $23,400). The implication is that the fair value of the new partnership's identifiable assets and liabilities understates its total value by goodwill in the amount of $3,000 ($600 ÷ .20).[12] This goodwill is recorded as an asset of the new partnership and is divided between the old partners by the following entry:

Entry to record goodwill to old partners:

Goodwill	3,000	
Harris, capital ($3,000 × 2/5)		1,200
McLeod, capital ($3,000 × 3/5)		1,800

The revaluation of land and the recognition of goodwill raise the total capital of the partnership to $120,000 ($100,000 + $17,000 + $3,000). Beck's 20% interest in this capital is recorded by the following entry:

Entry to establish new partner's capital account:

McLeod, capital	24,000	
Beck, capital		24,000

The following schedule shows the impact of these adjustments on the partners' capital accounts:

---

[12] Alternatively, goodwill can be calculated by using the new partner's cost ($24,000) to impute a total value to the new partnership of $120,000 ($24,000 ÷ .20) and subtracting the fair value of the new partnership's identifiable assets and liabilities [$3,000 = $120,000 − ($100,000 + $17,000)].

The Goodwill Method for an Admission by Purchased Interest with Goodwill to Old Partners

	Capital Accounts			
	Harris	McLeod	Beck	Total
Original capital balances	$30,000	$70,000	$	$100,000
Revaluation of land	6,800	10,200		17,000
Goodwill	1,200	1,800		3,000
Adjusted capital balances	$38,000	$82,000		$120,000
Purchase of 20% interest		(24,000)	24,000	
Capital balances after admission of Beck	$38,000	$58,000	$24,000	$120,000

Cost less than acquired share (goodwill to new partner)

We now turn to a case in which the cost to the new partner is less than the new partner's share of the new partnership's identifiable assets and liabilities measured at fair value. We reconsider the admission of Beck to the Harris-McLeod Partnership using the same facts as given earlier, except that Beck pays McLeod only $22,000 for a 20% interest. As before, the revaluation of the old partnership's assets requires the following entry:

Entry to write up assets of old partnership:

Land 17,000
        Harris, capital ($17,000 × 2/5)   6,800
        McLeod, capital ($17,000 × 3/5)   10,200

Since Beck pays McLeod directly, no entry is made on the partnership records for the payment. However, entries must be made to transfer a portion of McLeod's capital balance to Beck and to recognize any implied goodwill. Beck's acquired share in the identifiable assets and liabilities of the new partnership is $23,400 [.20 × ($100,000 + $17,000)], as before. Thus, the cost to Beck is less than the acquired share by $1,400 ($23,400 − $22,000). Since the partners have agreed to record goodwill, the $1,400 difference tells us that Beck contributes special skills, knowledge, and experience to the partnership. Accordingly, goodwill is recognized and credited to Beck's capital account. Since the old partners have an 80% interest in the new partnership, including the goodwill contributed by Beck, the $1,400 deficiency of cost relative to acquired share represents only 80% of the total contributed goodwill. Therefore, the total amount of goodwill contributed by Beck must be $1,750 ($1,400 ÷ 80).[13] This goodwill is recorded as an asset of the new partnership and credited to Beck's capital account by the following entry:

Entry to record goodwill to new partner:

Goodwill 1,750
        Beck, capital   1,750

---

[13] See footnote 11 for an alternative calculation.

The revaluation of land and the recognition of goodwill raise the total capital of the partnership to $118,750 ($100,000 + $17,000 + $1,750). The remainder of Beck's 20% interest in this capital is recorded by the following entry:

Entry to record remainder of new partner's capital:

McLeod, capital 22,000
       Beck, capital   22,000

The following schedule shows the impact of these adjustments on the partners' capital accounts:

The Goodwill Method for an Admission by Purchased Interest with Goodwill to New Partner

	Capital Accounts			
	Harris	McLeod	Beck	Total
Original capital balances	$30,000	$70,000	$	$100,000
Revaluation of land	6,800	10,200		17,000
Goodwill			1,750	1,750
Adjusted capital balances	$36,800	$80,200	$ 1,750	$118,750
Purchase of 20% interest		(22,000)	22,000	
Capital balances after admission of Beck	$36,800	$58,200	$23,750	$118,750

The Bonus Method

Under the bonus method, goodwill is not recognized. Rather, capital balances are simply adjusted so that the new partner's capital equals the agreed-upon fraction of total capital in the new partnership. The form of the adjustment depends on a comparison of the cost to the new partner and the new partner's share in the new partnership. If the cost to the new partner exceeds the acquired share in the new partnership, then a capital bonus is transferred from the new partner's capital account to the capital accounts of the old partners. If the cost to the new partner is less than the acquired share in the new partnership, then a capital bonus is transferred from the old partners' capital accounts to the capital account of the new partner. Let us illustrate each case.

Cost exceeds acquired share (bonus to old partners)

We begin with the case in which the cost to the new partner exceeds the acquired share in the new partnership. Suppose that Jackson pays Lacey $23,000 in cash for a 20% interest in the Lacey-Rubin Partnership. Lacey and Rubin share income and loss equally and have capital balances, just before Jackson's admission, of $30,000 and $70,000, respectively. Assume that the admission of Jackson does not create a new business entity. Accordingly, revaluation of the assets and liabilities of the old partnership is not appropriate. Instead, the book values of the old partnership's assets and liabilities, which total $100,000, are simply carried forward and the new partner's capital account is established by the following transfer from Lacey's to Jackson's capital account:

Entry to establish new partner's capital account:

Lacey, capital 23,000
    Jackson, capital   23,000

Under the partnership agreement, Jackson's share of the new partnership's capital should be only $20,000 (.20 × $100,000). In other words, Jackson paid $3,000 more than the amount of the acquired share ($23,000 − $20,000). Under the bonus method, Jackson's capital balance is reduced to the acquired share of $20,000 and the $3,000 reduction is transferred as a capital bonus to Lacey and Rubin, as shown in the following entry:

Entry to transfer capital bonus from new partner to old partners:

Jackson, capital 3,000
    Lacey, capital   1,500
    Rubin, capital   1,500

The following schedule shows the impact of these adjustments on the partners' capital accounts:

The Bonus Method for an Admission by Purchased Interest with Bonus to Old Partners

	Capital Accounts			
	Lacey	Rubin	Jackson	Total
Original capital balances	$30,000	$70,000	$	$100,000
Purchase of 20% interest	(23,000)		23,000	
Distribution of bonus	1,500	1,500	(3,000)	
Capital balances after admission of Jackson	$ 8,500	$71,500	$20,000	$100,000

Cost less than acquired share (bonus to new partner)

When the new partner pays less than the acquired share in the new partnership, the bonus method results in a capital bonus to the new partner. To illustrate, suppose that Jackson acquires a 20% interest in the Lacey-Rubin Partnership by paying Lacey only $19,000. Jackson's capital account is established by the following transfer from Lacey's to Jackson's capital account:

Entry to establish new partner's capital account:

Lacey, capital 19,000
    Jackson, capital   19,000

Under the partnership agreement, Jackson's share of the new partnership's capital should be $20,000 (.20 × $100,000). In other words, Jackson paid $1,000 less than the amount of the acquired share ($20,000 − $19,000). Under the bonus method, Jackson's capital balance is increased to the acquired share of $20,000 and the $1,000 increase is transferred as a capital bonus from Lacey and Rubin, as shown in the following entry:

Entry to transfer capital bonus from old partners to new partner:

Lacey, capital 500
Rubin, capital 500
    Jackson, capital...................................... 1,000

The following schedule shows the impact of these adjustments on the partners' capital accounts:

The Bonus Method for an Admission by Purchased Interest with Bonus to New Partner

| | Capital Accounts | | | |
	Lacey	Rubin	Jackson	Total
Original capital balances	$30,000	$70,000	$	$100,000
Purchase of 20% interest	(19,000)		19,000	
Distribution of bonus	(500)	(500)	1,000	
Capital balances after admission of Jackson	$10,500	$69,500	$20,000	$100,000

Distribution of Proceeds among Partners

When a partner is admitted by the purchase of an interest from *several* partners, a question arises as to the distribution of the proceeds among the partners. Suppose that Kindig acquires a 20% interest in the Skillman-Wilcox Partnership by paying $30,000 in cash to Skillman and Wilcox, jointly. Just prior to Kindig's admission, Skillman and Wilcox, who share income and loss equally, have capital balances of $30,000 and $70,000, respectively. The old partners agree to relinquish 20% of their respective capital balances or a total of $20,000 [(.20 × $30,000) + (.20 × $70,000)]. How should the $30,000 cash payment be distributed? A frequently applied method is shown in Exhibit 14-3, which uses

EXHIBIT 14-3

DISTRIBUTION OF PROCEEDS FROM SALE OF CAPITAL INTEREST: EXCESS OF PROCEEDS OVER BOOK VALUE ACQUIRED DISTRIBUTED IN INCOME-AND-LOSS-SHARING RATIO

| | Capital Accounts | | |
	Skillman	Wilcox	Total
Capital relinquished to Kindig:			
By Skillman (.20 × $30,000)	$ 6,000	$	$ 6,000
By Wilcox (.20 × $70,000)		14,000	14,000
Subtotal	$ 6,000	$14,000	$20,000
Excess of proceeds over book value acquired (distributed in income-and-loss-sharing ratio):			
To Skillman (.50 × $10,000)	5,000		5,000
To Wilcox (.50 × $10,000)		5,000	5,000
Distribution of proceeds	$11,000	$19,000	$30,000

the income-and-loss-sharing ratio to distribute the payment in excess of the relinquished book value. In the final analysis, the distribution is a matter for negotiation among the partners, but in the early stages of negotiation, the schedule in Exhibit 14-3 offers a reasonable starting point.

Withdrawal or Death of a Partner

Withdrawal from a partnership should be distinguished from the sale of a capital interest to a party outside the partnership. In both cases, the old partner is divested of his or her ownership equity in the partnership. But there is an important difference. The sale of a capital interest to an outside party results in the admission of a new partner. The withdrawal or death of a partner reduces the number of partners and requires the partnership to liquidate the withdrawing or deceased partner's ownership equity.[14]

Most partnership agreements make provision for the withdrawal and death of partners. From an accounting viewpoint, it is particularly important that the partnership agreement set forth the manner in which the equity of a withdrawing or deceased partner should be valued. For example, the agreement may specify that book values be the basis for repayment of equity or that current market values be the basis. If the partnership agreement is silent on the matter, then the basis for valuation is open to negotiation between the partnership and the withdrawn partner or his or her estate. Such negotiations, which can be difficult and protracted affairs, are subject to the applicable provisions of state partnership laws.

The paragraphs that follow present two illustrations of partnership withdrawal: (1) a case in which the withdrawing partner is paid an amount equal to the book value of his or her capital interest and (2) a case in which the withdrawing partner is paid an amount in excess of the book value of his or her capital interest. Both cases are demonstrated by reference to RST Partnership with partners named Randall, Stone, and Tobin. Suppose that RST Partnership has the following capital balances at the date of Tobin's withdrawal from the partnership:

Randall, capital	$20,000
Stone, capital	20,000
Tobin, capital	20,000
Total capital	$60,000

The withdrawal of Tobin dissolves the partnership, and Randall and Stone continue as a new partnership. The circumstances of Tobin's withdrawal will be varied throughout this section of the chapter to demonstrate the principal accounting issues.

Equity Fixed at Book Value

If RST Partnership agreement specified that Tobin's withdrawal requires repayment of the book value of Tobin's equity, then the entry on the following page is appropriate on the records of the continuing partnership:

---

[14] If a partner withdraws from a partnership in violation of the partnership agreement, then the withdrawing partner is liable for damages to the other partners and, thereby, may impair the value of his or her interest in the organization. But in the absence of an explicit agreement to the contrary, a partner may withdraw from a partnership at any time and expect to be paid his or her equity in the organization.

Entry to record withdrawal of partner:

Tobin, capital	20,000	
Payable to withdrawn partner		20,000

The entry closes Tobin's capital account and creates a liability for the continuing partnership. If the repayment is made on an installment basis, then interest may be paid in addition to the principal of $20,000.

Equity Valued at More Than Book Value: Bonus versus Implied Goodwill

Suppose that the continuing partners agree to pay $25,000 to Tobin for his or her capital interest and that this amount is also acceptable to Tobin. Why does the payment exceed the book value of Tobin's equity by $5,000? The answer depends on the intentions of the partners in reaching the settlement, and at least two sets of intentions are consistent with the $5,000 excess.

Recording capital bonus

First, the continuing partners may view the excess as a capital bonus paid to Tobin. If this view is accepted, then the following recording of the withdrawal is appropriate:

Entry to record withdrawal of partner with capital bonus:

Tobin, capital	20,000	
Randall, capital	2,500	
Stone, capital	2,500	
Payable to withdrawn partner		25,000

The $5,000 bonus is divided in the income-and-loss-sharing ratio (here it is assumed to be an equal split) between the continuing partners. Some partnership agreements make explicit provision for the payment of such bonuses and also for the manner in which they are divided among the capital accounts of continuing partners.

Recording implied goodwill and revaluation increments

A second possibility is that the $5,000 excess is evidence of the existence of incorrectly valued assets and/or unrecorded goodwill in the total amount of $15,000 ($5,000 ÷ 1/3). If the total amount of the revaluation is recognized, then the following entries record the withdrawal:

Entry to revalue net assets of partnership:

Revaluation of assets and/or goodwill (various accounts)	15,000	
Randall, capital		5,000
Stone, capital		5,000
Tobin, capital		5,000

Entry to record withdrawal of partner:

Tobin, capital	25,000	
Payable to withdrawn partner		25,000

Some partnerships prefer to recognize just that portion of the revaluation of assets and/or goodwill that is related to Tobin's equity. In such cases, the following entries record the withdrawal:

Entry to revalue withdrawing partner's equity

Revaluation of assets and/or goodwill (various accounts)	5,000	
Tobin, capital		5,000

Entry to record withdrawal of partner:

Tobin, capital	25,000	
Payable to withdrawn partner		25,000

The final choice between recognizing all or just part of the implied revaluation depends on the preferences of continuing partners and the financial reporting conventions applied by the continuing partnership. In both cases, the withdrawing partner receives $25,000.

Conservative valuation practices may result in book values for inventories, plant and equipment, and other recorded assets that cannot be used to calculate the equity of a withdrawing partner. The partnership agreement or negotiation among the partners may call for revaluation of recorded assets as well as for recognition of unrecorded assets and goodwill. The choice between recognizing the entire valuation increment (total revaluation) and recognizing just the portion that is associated with the withdrawn partner's equity (fractional revaluation) raises fundamental questions of financial reporting for the continuing partnership, as the following issues section illustrates.

ISSUES

Total versus Fractional Revaluation

Suppose that RST Partnership holds an inventory that is maintained on a LIFO basis and is undervalued by $3,000 as a result. If just Tobin's $1,000 share of the valuation increment is recognized, then the financial statements of the continuing partnership display only as much of the write-up as was paid out in the withdrawal of Tobin. Some theorists argue that this treatment is consistent with cost valuation rules and with the principle that only purchased assets be recorded in the financial statements. They argue that recognition of the entire $3,000 increment would introduce an unrealized profit into the financial statements of the continuing partnership.

Other theorists disagree and point out that the old partnership is dissolved and that the statements are prepared for a new business entity whose assets should be entered at their current values. In small partnerships, withdrawal of a partner may indeed occasion a new entity, but in large partnerships withdrawal is received in the ordinary course of events with nominal effect on the organization. Whether or not withdrawal of a partner creates a new business entity, as distinguished from a new legal entity, is an open question, and the partners must make a separate determination in each case. Consequently, the choice between total and fractional revaluation also remains open.

SUMMARY

Partnerships require special accounting procedures that reflect the distinctive aspects of the partnership organization. The principal differences between partnership and corporate accounting concern owners' equity. Partnership owners' equity is composed of a capital account for each partner, whereas corporate owners' equity is composed of capital stock and retained earnings accounts. More fundamentally, the accounting differences reflect the great flexibility partnerships have in allocating and distributing income to partners. Withdrawals of cash and other assets by partners are recorded in temporary equity accounts called drawing accounts. Allocations of income to partners are recorded directly in partners' capital accounts and may reflect any factors upon which the partners agree. Typical allocation arrangements include interest and salary allowances as well as distributions based on an income-and-loss-sharing ratio. The partnership agreement records the allocation arrangement and other agreed-upon terms of the partnership with which the accountants must be familiar to prepare financial statements and tax returns for the partnership.

Ownership changes in partnerships occur in response to the admission of new partners and the withdrawal or death of previously admitted partners. A new partner may gain admission to an existing partnership in two ways—by investing directly in the partnership or by purchasing an interest from one or more of the existing partners. In the latter case, the physical quantity of the partnership's assets is unchanged. Of course, the dollar valuation of the partnership's assets and liabilities may be changed if the admission of the new partner is judged to create a new business entity. In that case, assets and liabilities may be revalued, and following the goodwill method, an intangible asset called goodwill may be recognized. If a new business entity is not created, then no revaluation of assets is appropriate, but following the bonus method, it may be necessary to make transfers among the partners' capital accounts to accomplish the agreed-upon percentage interests in capital.

An equitable payment to a withdrawing partner or to a former partner's estate may occasion a revaluation of all or part of the partnership's assets and liabilities. In other cases, equity may be secured by recording a capital bonus without revaluing the assets.

SELECTED READINGS

Berryman, R. Glen. "Partnership Accounting," Chap. 30 in *Handbook of Modern Accounting,* 3rd ed., Sidney Davidson and Roman L. Weil, eds. New York: McGraw-Hill, 1983.

Corwin, Leslie D. "What's a Partner to Do?" *CPA Journal* (April 1991), pp. 22–27, 30.

Kay, Robert S., and D. Gerald Searfoss. "Smaller and Emerging Businesses," Chap. 39 in *Handbook of Accounting and Auditing.* Boston: Warren, Gorham & Lamont, 1989.

Patten, Ronald J. "Partnerships," Chap. 30 in *Accountants Handbook,* D. R. Carmichael, S. B. Lilien, M. Mellman, eds. New York: John Wiley, 1991.

Segal, Robert E. "Take a Careful Look at Your Partnership Agreement," *CPA Journal* (April 1991), pp. 28, 29.

Talwar, Akshay K. "Profit Allocations in CPA Firm Partnership Agreements," *Journal of Accountancy* (March 1986), pp. 91–95.

QUESTIONS

Q14-1 Define a *partnership*.

Q14-2 Discuss four distinct characteristics of the partnership form of organization.

Q14-3 What are *articles of partnership?* List five items that should be included in the articles of partnership.

Q14-4   Describe how the ownership equity structure of partnerships differs from that of corporations.

Q14-5   If Partner A and Partner B have capital interests in the partnership of 75% and 25%, respectively, does this mean that the partners also share income of the partnership in this ratio? Discuss.

Q14-6   When a partner's initial percentage interest in capital is not the same as that partner's percentage contribution of net assets, the partners must choose between two accounting procedures for the establishment of their capital balances. Identify and illustrate these two accounting procedures. What factors would the partners consider in deciding which procedure to use?

Q14-7   What is the fundamental objective of the income-and-loss-sharing arrangements of a partnership? List three bases for the distribution of income and loss among partners.

Q14-8   Partners Conroy and Farmer treat partners' salaries as an expense in computing partnership income. Income after salaries is divided between Conroy and Farmer in a ratio of 4:1, respectively. Conroy insists that her capital account is understated because salaries are treated as an expense and not as an allocation of income. Comment on whether you agree or disagree with Conroy.

Q14-9   Partners Cole and Bishop agreed to a new income-and-loss-sharing ratio of 4:2 beginning with the current year. In previous years, they allocated income and loss equally. At the end of the current year, it was discovered that an error was made in computing last year's net income. Discuss how the correction of the error could be treated.

Q14-10   The tax basis of a partner's capital interest in a partnership may differ from his or her accounting basis. Describe how the tax basis of a partner's capital interest is determined.

Q14-11   Identify two ways a new partner might obtain an ownership interest in an existing partnership, and indicate the impact each of these methods has on the physical quantity of partnership assets.

Q14-12   Discuss how the admission of a new partner by purchased interest is analogous to the sale of already outstanding shares of corporate stock.

Q14-13   The admission of a new partner creates a new legal entity for the partnership, but it may or may not create a new business entity. What is the significance of whether or not the admission of a partner creates a new business entity?

Q14-14   Discuss how the admission of new partners by investment is analogous to the issuance of new shares of corporate stock.

Q14-15   When a new partner is admitted to a partnership under the bonus method, what basis is used in allocating the bonus to the capital accounts of the old partners?

Q14-16   When a new partner is admitted to a partnership under the goodwill method and goodwill is to be allocated to the old partners, what basis is used in allocating goodwill to their capital accounts?

Q14-17   Discuss why the continuing partners of a partnership would pay a withdrawing partner $10,000 more than the book value of his 40% capital interest.

EXERCISES

E14-1   Accounting Basis versus Tax Basis of Partners' Capital Interest   Homburger and Andrews formed a partnership. The fair values of the assets contributed by each partner were as follows:

	Homburger	Andrews
Cash	$15,000	$10,000
Equipment	8,000	
Building		30,000

A $10,000 mortgage on the building contributed by Andrews is transferred to the partnership. The tax bases of the equipment and building are $6,000 and $20,000, respectively. The income and loss of the partnership are to be divided equally.

REQUIRED

a) Prepare the journal entries to record the investments of Homburger and Andrews in the partnership.

b) Homburger and Andrews did not mention in the partnership agreement the basis for allocating the income and loss of the partnership. Does this mean that income and loss are to be allocated on the basis of the relative capital investments of the partners?

c) Prepare a schedule showing the tax bases of the partners' capital interest.

E14-2 **Record Initial Capital Investment: Net Assets Invested, Bonus, Goodwill** Alley and Harvey established a partnership on December 1, 19X4. They agreed that each would make the following contributions:

	Alley	Harvey
Cash	$20,000	$30,000
Land	15,000	
Building	50,000	
Furniture and fixtures		25,000

Accounts payable of Alley totaling $10,000 are to be assumed by the partnership.

REQUIRED

Prepare the entries on December 1, 19X4, to record investments in the partnership by Alley and Harvey under each of the following independent assumptions:

1. Each partner is credited for the full amount of net assets invested.

2. Each partner initially should have an equal interest in partnership capital with no contribution of intangible assets (bonus method).

3. Each partner initially should have an equal interest in partnership capital, and any contributed goodwill should be recognized (goodwill method).

E14-3 **Discussion of Income Allocation Plan and Income Statement Treatment of Partners' Salary and Bonus** Partnership agreements usually specify an income-and-loss-sharing ratio. They may also provide for additional income-and-loss-sharing features such as salaries, bonuses, and interest allowances on invested capital.

REQUIRED

a) What is the objective of income-and-loss-sharing arrangements? Why may there be a need for features in addition to the income-and-loss-sharing ratio? Discuss.

b) Discuss the arguments for recording salary and bonus allowances to partners as charges to operations.

c) What are the arguments against treating partnership salary and bonus allowances as expenses? Discuss.

d) In addition to its other income-and-loss-sharing features, a partnership agreement may state that "interest is to be allowed on invested capital." List the additional provisions that should be included in the partnership agreement so that "interest to be allowed on invested capital" can be computed.

(AICPA adapted)

E14-4 **Income Allocation: Interest on Capital, Salary Allowances, and Bonuses; Prepare Entry to Record Allocation**   Laurel and Hardy formed a partnership on January 1, 19X1. The activity in their respective capital accounts during the fiscal year ended December 31, 19X1, is presented here. During the year the partnership earned a net income of $36,000.

	Laurel				Hardy		
Oct. 31	3,000	Jan. 1	18,000	June 30	4,000	Jan. 1	22,000
		May 31	5,000			Oct. 31	7,000

REQUIRED

a) Determine the allocation of the net income to Laurel and Hardy under each of the following situations:

1. Each partner receives 8% interest on beginning-of-the-year capital balances, and the remainder is divided between Laurel and Hardy in a ratio of 3:1, respectively.

2. Laurel and Hardy are given salaries of $7,000 and $13,000, respectively, 12% interest on the end-of-the-year capital balances, and the remainder divided equally.

3. Laurel and Hardy are given salaries of $14,500 and $18,500, respectively, 12% interest on weighted average of beginning-of-the-month capital balances, and the remainder divided between Laurel and Hardy in a ratio of 3:1, respectively.

4. Laurel and Hardy earn salaries of $5,000 and $10,000, respectively, and 10% interest on the weighted average of beginning-of-the-month capital balances. The remainder is divided in the following ratio: Laurel, 40%; Hardy, 60%.

5. Each partner receives 5% interest on beginning-of-the-year capital balances and a salary of $5,000; Laurel receives a bonus of 10% of the net income after deducting interest and salaries; and the remainder is divided between Laurel and Hardy in a ratio of 2:3, respectively.

b) Prepare the entry to record the allocation of the partnership net income to individual capital accounts for situations (1) through (5) in part (a).

E14-5 **Income (Loss) Allocation: Interest on Capital, Salary Allowances, and Bonuses; Prepare Entry to Record Allocation**   Kirk and Sibley have operated a partnership for several years. Kirk and Sibley had capital balances at the beginning of the current year of $30,000 and $40,000, respectively.

On October 1 of the current year, Sibley contributed $10,000 more permanent capital to the partnership. The partnership net income for the current year is $30,000. The partners are contemplating a change in the way they allocate partnership income.

REQUIRED

a) Determine the allocation of partnership income under each of the following independent situations:

1. Kirk and Sibley are given salaries of $12,000 and $15,000, respectively, interest of 9% on beginning-of-the-year capital balances, and the remainder divided equally.

2. Kirk and Sibley are given salaries of $14,000 and $12,500, respectively, interest of 10% on beginning-of-the-year capital balances, and the remainder divided equally. Salaries of partners and interest on capital should be made only to the extent that income provides them.

3. Each partner receives a salary of $10,000 and interest of 5% on end-of-the-year capital balances; Kirk receives a bonus of 10% of net income before deduction of salaries, interest, and bonus; and any remainder is divided between Kirk and Sibley in a ratio of 2:1, respectively.

4. Kirk and Sibley are given salaries of $8,000 and $6,000, respectively, and interest of 6% on end-of-the-year capital balances; Kirk receives a bonus of 10% of net income after deducting bonus but before deducting salaries and interest; and any remainder is divided between Kirk and Sibley in the ratio 1:3, respectively.

5. Each partner receives a salary of $7,000 and interest of 5% on beginning-of-the-year capital balances; Kirk receives a bonus of 10% of net income after deducting salaries, interest, and bonus; and any remainder is divided between Kirk and Sibley in the ratio 1:3, respectively.

b) Assuming that the partnership incurred a net loss of $2,500 (and not a net income of $30,000), determine the allocation of the partnership loss to the partners if each partner receives a salary of $7,000 and interest of 5% on beginning-of-the-year capital balances; Kirk receives a bonus of 10% of net income before deduction of salaries, interest, and bonus; and any remainder is divided in the ratio 1:3, respectively.

E14-6   Multiple Choice Questions on Formation and Operation of a Partnership

1. Partners C and K share income and loss equally after each has been credited in all circumstances with annual salary allowances of $15,000 and $12,000, respectively. Under this arrangement, C will benefit by $3,000 more than K in which of the following circumstances?

   a) Only if the partnership has earnings of $27,000 or more for the year

   b) Only if the partnership does not incur a loss for the year

   c) In all earnings or loss situations

   d) Only if the partnership has earnings of at least $3,000 for the year

2. Arthur Plack, partner in the Brite Partnership, has a 30% participation in partnership income and loss. Plack's capital account had a net decrease of $60,000 during the calendar year 19X4. During 19X4, Plack withdrew $130,000 (charged against his capital account) and contributed property valued at $25,000 to the partnership. What was the net income of the Brite Partnership for 19X4?

   a) $150,000   **c)** $350,000

   b) $233,333   **d)** $550,000

3. Partners Hatton and Elsner share income in a 2:1 ratio, respectively. Each partner receives an annual salary allowance of $6,000. If the salaries are recorded in the accounts of the partnership as an expense rather than treated as an allocation of income, the total amount allocated to each partner for salaries and net income would be

   a) Less for both Hatton and Elsner

   b) Unchanged for both Hatton and Elsner

   c) More for Hatton and less for Elsner

   d) More for Elsner and less for Hatton

4. The partnership agreement of Reid and Simm provides that interest at 10% per year is to be credited to each partner on the basis of weighted-average capital balances. A summary of Simm's capital account for the year ended December 31, 19X9, is as follows:

Balance, January 1	$140,000
Additional investment, July 1	40,000
Withdrawal, August 1	(15,000)
Balance, December 31	165,000

What amount of interest should be credited to Simm's capital account for 19X9?

   a) $15,250   **c)** $16,500

   b) $15,375   **d)** $17,250

5. Geller and Harden formed a partnership on January 2, 19X4, and agreed to share income 90%, 10%, respectively. Geller contributed a capital of $25,000. Harden contributed no capital but has a specialized expertise and manages the firm full-time. There were no withdrawals during the year. The partnership agreement provides for the following:

a) Capital accounts are to be credited annually with interest at 5% of beginning capital.

b) Harden is to be paid a salary of $1,000 a month.

c) Harden is to receive a bonus of 20% of income calculated before deducting his bonus, his salary, and interest on both capital accounts.

d) Bonus, interest, and Harden's salary are to be considered partnership expenses.

The partnership's 19X4 income statement follows:

Revenues	$96,450
Expenses (including salary, interest, and bonus)	49,700
Net income	$46,750

What is Harden's 19X4 bonus?

a) $11,688   **c)** $15,000

b) $12,000   **d)** $15,738

6. The partnership of Wayne and Ellen was formed on February 28, 19X3. At that date the following assets were contributed:

	Wayne	Ellen
Cash	$25,000	$ 35,000
Merchandise		55,000
Building		100,000
Furniture and equipment	15,000	

The building is subject to a mortgage loan of $30,000, which is to be assumed by the partnership. The partnership agreement provides that Wayne and Ellen share an income and loss of 25% and 75%, respectively. Ellen's capital account at February 28, 19X3, would be

a) $190,000   **c)** $172,500

b) $160,000   **d)** $150,000

7. Based on the same facts as described in item (6), if the partnership agreement provides that the partners initially should have an equal interest in partnership capital with no contribution of intangible assets, Wayne's capital account on February 28, 19X3, would be

a) $100,000   **c)** $200,000

b) $115,000   **d)** $230,000

8. Hayes and Jenkins formed a partnership, each contributing assets to the business. Hayes contributed inventory with a current market value in excess of its carrying amount. Jenkins contributed real estate with a carrying amount in excess of its current market value. At what amount should the partnership record each of the following assets?

	Inventory	Real estate
a)	Market value	Market value
b)	Market value	Carrying amount
c)	Carrying amount	Market value
d)	Carrying amount	Carrying amount

(AICPA adapted)

E14-7 Correction of Prior Years' Net Income On January 1, 19X0, Carson and Mann formed a partnership with capital contributions of $50,000 and $75,000, respectively. The partners agreed that income and loss would be allocated as follows: $6,000 salary to each partner, 3% interest on initial capital contributions, the remainder divided in the ratio of 3:2 to Carson and Mann, respectively. As of January 1, 19X4, the partnership agreement was amended so that income and loss would be allocated as follows: 8% interest on initial capital contributions, the remainder divided equally. During 19X4 the following partnership errors were discovered:

1. In 19X3, a purchase of a piece of equipment costing $10,000 was expensed. The equipment has an estimated life of ten years with equal service potential each year.

2. On December 31, 19X2, inventory was understated by $8,000.

3. On December 31, 19X3, inventory was overstated by $12,000.

The partnership agreement specifies that errors of the preceding nature are to be treated as prior-period adjustments. Net income of the partnership for 19X3 was $20,000.

REQUIRED

a) Prepare a schedule showing the adjustments needed to the capital account of each partner as a result of the errors.

b) Prepare the necessary correcting entry or entries on the books of the partnership concerning the errors.

E14-8 Admission by Purchased Interest Partners Duck and Quail of Wildfowl Carving are considering the admission of Pheasant to the partnership. Duck and Quail share income and loss in the ratio of 2:4, respectively. Duck's capital balance totals $48,000, and Quail's capital balance totals $36,000.

REQUIRED

Prepare entries to record the admission of Pheasant to the partnership under each of the following independent situations:

1. Pheasant acquired a one-fourth interest in the partnership from Duck paying $24,900. The assets and liabilities of the partnership are fairly valued except for land that is undervalued by $6,000. Partnership assets are to be revalued, and Pheasant is to be admitted under the goodwill method.

2. Pheasant acquired a one-third interest in the partnership from Duck, paying $26,000. Net assets of the partnership are fairly valued except for land that is overvalued by $6,000. Partnership assets are to be revalued, and Pheasant is to be admitted.

3. Pheasant acquired a one-fourth interest in the partnership from Quail, paying $18,000. The net assets of the partnership are fairly valued. Contributed goodwill is to be recorded by the partnership.

4. Pheasant acquired a one-fifth interest in the partnership from Duck, paying $12,000. The net assets of the partnership are fairly valued. Pheasant is to be admitted under the bonus method.

5. Pheasant acquired a one-fourth interest in the partnership from Quail, paying $24,600. The net assets of the partnership are fairly valued. Pheasant is to be admitted under the bonus method.

E14-9 Admission by Purchased Interest with Proceeds Distribution Schedule Taylor and Byrd are partners in TR Partnership. Their capital balances and income-and-loss-sharing ratio are as follows:

	Capital Balance	Income-and-Loss-Sharing Ratio
Taylor	$60,000	3
Byrd	40,000	2

Taylor and Byrd are contemplating several alternative plans for selling a part of their capital interest to Jones.

REQUIRED

a) Prepare entries to record the admission of Jones to the partnership under each of the following independent situations. Net assets of the partnership are fairly valued.

    1. Jones purchases one-fifth of the capital interest of each partner, paying Taylor $12,000 and Byrd $8,000.

    2. Jones purchases one-fourth of the capital interest of each partner, paying Taylor and Byrd a total of $35,000. Goodwill implied by the purchase price is to be recorded by the partnership.

    3. Jones purchases a one-fourth capital interest in the partnership from Taylor for $30,000. The bonus method is to be used in admitting Jones.

    4. Jones purchases a one-fourth capital interest in the partnership from Taylor, paying $22,000. Jones is to be admitted using the bonus method.

    5. Jones purchases a one-fifth capital interest in the partnership from Byrd for $18,000. Goodwill implied by the purchase price is to be recorded by the partnership.

b) Assuming Jones purchased one-fourth of the capital balances of both Taylor and Byrd, paying a total of $40,000, prepare a schedule to assist in determining the cash to be transferred to Taylor and Byrd. Net assets of the partnership are fairly valued.

E14-10   **Retirement of a Partner**   Butts, Croaker, Evans, and Taylor are partners in South Hill Surveying Services. They have equal capital balances and share income and loss equally. The partners agreed that Evans, upon retirement next month, is to receive $71,000 cash from the partnership for her $50,000 capital interest in the fairly valued net assets of the partnership.

REQUIRED

Prepare journal entries to show three possible methods of recording the retirement of Evans. State the conditions under which each method would be appropriate.

E14-11   **Admission by Investment: Comparison of Bonus and Goodwill Methods**   The capital balances and the income-and-loss-sharing ratio of the partners of Do-It-Yourself Ceramics are as follows:

	Capital Balance	Income-and-Loss- Sharing Ratio
Harris	$75,000	2
Stephens	25,000	1
West	50,000	2

The partnership has not been as successful as originally forecasted. To assist in rectifying certain problems of the partnership, Sperry has been admitted to the partnership with a one-third capital interest for a cash investment of $60,000. The partnership's net assets are carried on the books at their fair value.

REQUIRED

Prepare the entries to record the admission of Sperry under the (1) bonus method and (2) goodwill method. Give reasons to support each of these accounting treatments.

E14-12   **Admission by Investment: Comparison of Bonus and Goodwill Methods**   Willis and Williams are partners in W & W Catering Services, with capital balances of $30,000 and $40,000, respectively. Income and loss are distributed between Willis and Williams in the ratio of 3:2, respectively. They decided to admit Wingfield with a one-third interest for a cash investment of $50,000. Net assets of the partnership are presented on the books at their fair value.

(Continued on next page)

REQUIRED

Prepare the entries to record the admission of Wingfield under the (1) bonus method and (2) good-will method. Give reasons to support each of these accounting treatments.

E14-13   Multiple Choice Questions on Admission and Withdrawal of Partners

1. At December 31, 19X4, Arno and Dey are partners with capital balances of $80,000 and $40,000, respectively, and they share profit and loss in the ratio of 2:1, respectively. On this date West invests $36,000 cash for a one-fifth interest in the partnership. The partners agree that the net assets of the partnership are fairly valued and that the implied partnership goodwill is to be recorded simultane-ously with the admission of West. The total implied goodwill of the firm is:

a) $4,800   c) $24,000

b) $6,000   d) $30,000

Items (2) and (3) are based on the following information: Presented here is the condensed balance sheet of the partnership of Kane, Clark, and Lane, who share income and loss in the ratio of 6:3:1, respectively:

Cash	$ 85,000
Other assets	415,000
Total assets	$500,000
Liabilities	$ 80,000
Capital, Kane	252,000
Capital, Clark	126,000
Capital, Lane	42,000
Total liabilities and capital	$500,000

2. The assets and liabilities on the preceding balance sheet are fairly valued, and the partnership wishes to admit Bayer with a 25% interest *without* recording goodwill or bonus. How much should Bayer invest in the partnership?

a) $ 70,000   c) $125,000

b) $105,000   d) $140,000

3. Assume that the partners agree instead to sell Bayer 20% of their respective interests in the partnership for a total payment of $90,000. The payment by Bayer is to be made directly to the individual partners. The partners agree that goodwill is to be recorded prior to the admission of Bayer. What are the capital balances of Kane, Clark, and Lane, respectively, immediately after the admission of Bayer?

a) $198,000; $ 99,000; $33,000

b) $201,600; $100,800; $33,600

c) $216,000; $108,000; $36,000

d) $255,600; $127,800; $42,600

4. Cicci and Arias are partners who share income and loss in the ratio of 7:3, respectively. On October 5, 19X0, their respective capital accounts are as follows:

Cicci	$35,000
Arias	30,000
Total capital	$65,000

On that date, they agreed to admit Soto as a partner with a one-third interest in the partnership upon his investment of $25,000. The new partnership will begin with a total capital of $90,000. Immediately after Soto's admission, what are the capital balances of Cicci, Arias, and Soto, respectively?

a) $30,000; $30,000; $30,000

b) $31,500; $28,500; $30,000

c) $31,667; $28,333; $30,000

d) $35,000; $30,000; $25,000

5. James Dixon, a partner in an accounting firm, decided to withdraw from the partnership. Dixon's share of the partnership income and loss was 20%. Upon withdrawing from the partnership, he was paid $74,000 in final settlement for his interest. The total of the partners' capital accounts before recognition of partnership goodwill prior to Dixon's withdrawal was $210,000. After his withdrawal the remaining partners' capital accounts, excluding their share of goodwill, totaled $160,000. The total agreed-upon goodwill of the firm was

a) $120,000   c) $160,000

b) $140,000   d) $250,000

6. On June 30, 19X1, the balance sheet for the partnership of Coll, Maduro, and Prieto, together with their respective income-and-loss-sharing ratios, was as follows:

Assets (at cost)	$180,000
Coll, loan	$ 9,000
Coll, capital (20%)	42,000
Maduro, capital (20%)	39,000
Prieto, capital (60%)	90,000
Total	$180,000

Coll has decided to retire from the partnership. By mutual agreement, the assets are to be adjusted to their fair value of $216,000 at June 30, 19X1. It was agreed that the partnership would pay Coll $61,200 cash for Coll's partnership interest, including Coll's loan, which is to be repaid in full. No goodwill is to be recorded. After Coll's retirement, what is the balance of Maduro's capital account?

a) $36,450   c) $45,450

b) $39,000   d) $46,200

7. The partnership of Metcalf, Petersen, and Russell shared profits and losses equally. When Metcalf withdrew from the partnership, the partners agreed that there was unrecorded goodwill in the partnership. Under the bonus method, the capital balances of Petersen and Russell were

a) Not affected

b) Each reduced by one-half of the total amount of the unrecorded goodwill

c) Each reduced by one-third of the total amount of the unrecorded goodwill

d) Each reduced by one-half of Metcalf's share of the total amount of the unrecorded goodwill

(AICPA adapted)

E14-14 **Admission by Purchased Interest**   Mitchell, Miller, and Mead are partners in 3M Partnership with capital balances of $60,000, $40,000, and $50,000, respectively. The partners share income and loss equally. In recent months, several offers have been received by the partners from persons interested in acquiring an interest in the partnership.

REQUIRED

Prepare entries to record the admission of the new partner under each of the following independent situations:

1. Kemp acquired a one-fifth interest in the partnership directly from Mitchell, paying $30,000. Net assets of the partnership are properly valued.

2. Spring paid Miller, as an individual, $13,500 for a one-tenth interest in the partnership. The net assets of the partnership are fairly valued except for a building that is overvalued by $15,000. Partnership assets are to be revalued, and Spring is to be admitted.

3. West acquired a one-third interest in the partnership from Mead, paying $47,000. West is to be admitted under the goodwill method. Net assets of the partnership are fairly valued.

4. Wood acquired a one-fourth interest in the partnership from Miller for $34,500. Wood is to be admitted under the bonus method. Net assets of the partnership are fairly valued.

5. Howard acquired a one-fifth interest in the partnership from Mead for $13,200. Howard is to be admitted under the goodwill method. Net assets of the partnership are properly valued.

6. Hill paid Mitchell, as an individual, $39,000 for a one-fourth interest in the partnership. Hill is to be admitted under the bonus method. Partnership net assets are fairly valued.

E14-15 **Admission by Investment** Grady and Broad are partners who share income and loss in the ratio 2:3, respectively. The partners agree to admit Barr as a partner. The capital accounts of Grady and Broad are $45,000 and $30,000 respectively.

REQUIRED

Prepare the entries to record the admission of Barr under each of the following independent situations:

1. Barr invests $25,000 cash for a one-fourth interest; partnership net assets are fairly valued.

2. Upon investing $30,000 cash, Barr receives a one-third interest under the bonus method. Net assets of the partnership are properly valued.

3. Barr invests $15,000 cash for a one-fifth interest. Assets of the partnership are fairly valued except for a parcel of land that is overvalued by $15,000. Net assets of the partnership are to be revalued, and Barr is to be admitted.

4. Upon investing $60,000 cash, Barr receives a two-fifths interest under the goodwill method. Partnership net assets are fairly valued.

5. Barr invests $23,000 cash for a one-fourth interest under the goodwill method. Net assets of the partnership are properly valued.

6. Upon investing $22,000 cash, Barr receives a one-fifth interest under the bonus method. Net assets of the partnership are properly valued.

PROBLEMS

P14-1 **Record Initial Capital Investments; Allocate Income, and Prepare Entry to Record Allocation; Close Drawing Accounts; Discuss Financial Statements**   Bishop and Street formed JMU Partnership on January 1, 19X4. Bishop and Street had been operating as sole proprietors. The book values and the fair values of the contributions to be made by each of the partners, as agreed upon by the partners, are as follows:

	Bishop	
	Book Value	Fair Value
Cash	$ 5,000	$ 5,000
Accounts receivable (net)	12,000	14,000
Inventory	15,000	16,000
Machinery and equipment (net)	10,000	10,000

	Street	
	Book Value	Fair Value
Cash	$10,000	$10,000
Accounts receivable (net)	4,000	5,000
Inventory	30,000	35,000
Land	8,000	10,000
Building	30,000	30,000

The partnership is to assume accounts payable of Bishop and Street in the amounts of $10,000 and $20,000, respectively.

The partnership reported net income of $40,000 for the year ended December 31, 19X4.

REQUIRED

a) Prepare the entries to record the investments of Bishop and Street in the partnership, with each partner credited for the full amount of net assets invested.

b) Determine the allocation of income to the partners assuming Bishop and Street are paid salaries of $14,000 and $10,000, respectively; interest of 8% on initial capital contribution; and any remainder divided in the ratio of 3:2, respectively.

c) Prepare the entry to record the allocation of partnership net income to individual capital accounts for part (b).

d) Assuming the partners withdrew cash equal to 60% of their salary allowances, prepare entries to record the cash withdrawals by Bishop and Street during 19X4 and to record the closing of the drawing accounts.

e) Discuss the primary differences between the financial statement that may be prepared at year-end for JMU Partnership and those prepared for corporations.

P14-2 **Record Initial Capital Investments, Determine Tax Bases of Partners' Capital, and Allocate Income**   On January 1, 19X1, Parks and Duke combined their individual accounting practices to form the partnership of Parks and Duke, Certified Public Accountants. On this date, the book values and fair values of the contributions of each partner were as follows:

	Parks	
	Book Value	**Fair Value**
Assets		
Cash	$10,000	$10,000
Furniture and fixtures (net)	6,000	10,000
Equipment (net)	5,000	4,000
Total assets	$21,000	
Equities		
Accounts payable	$ 6,000	6,000
Parks, capital	15,000	
Total equities	$21,000	

	Duke	
	Book Value	**Fair Value**
Assets		
Cash	$12,000	$12,000
Furniture and fixtures (net)	2,000	2,500
Equipment (net)	500	1,500
Library materials	3,000	4,000
Total assets	$17,500	
Equities		
Accounts payable	$10,000	10,000
Duke, capital	7,500	
Total equities	$17,500	

Additional information:

1. The partnership is to assume the total accounts payable of Parks and Duke. Tax bases of the assets contributed by the partners equal their book values.

2. On June 30, 19X1, Parks withdrew $2,000 of permanent capital from the partnership. Duke invested in the partnership additional capital of $6,000 on September 30, 19X1.

3. For the first year of operations ending December 31, 19X1, the partnership reported net income of $15,000.

REQUIRED

a) Prepare the entry to record the investments of Parks and Duke, assuming Duke's contributed capital is to represent one-third the total partnership capital; any contributed goodwill is to be recognized.

b) Prepare a schedule showing the tax bases of the partners' capital interests. The liabilities of the individual partners are assumed by the partnership, and each partner agrees to assume one-half the other partner's liabilities.

c) Determine the allocation of income to Parks and Duke under each of the following independent situations being considered by the partners:

  1. Parks and Duke are to be paid salaries of $4,000 and $6,000, respectively; 10% interest on the weighted average of beginning-of-the-month capital balances; and the remainder divided between Parks and Duke in a ratio of 2:1, respectively.

2. Parks and Duke are to be paid salaries of $8,000 and $5,000, respectively; 8% interest on the original capital investment; bonus to Parks of 10% of net income after deducting bonus but before deducting salaries and interest; and the remainder divided equally. Any deficiency between these allocations and net income is to be divided equally.

P14-3 **Allocate Income and Prepare Entry to Record Allocation, Close Drawing Accounts, and Prepare Financial Statements**   Several years ago Killough and Seago formed Hokie Partnership. The partnership agreement states that each partner is to receive a salary of $1,000 per month and 5% interest on beginning-of-the-year capital balances; any remainder would be divided between Killough and Seago in the ratio of 2:3, respectively. The *unadjusted* trial balance of Hokie Partnership as of December 31, 19X6, appears as follows:

Debits		**Credits**	
Cash	$ 50,000	Accounts payable	$ 35,000
Accounts receivable	30,000	Notes payable	20,000
Inventory, 1-1-X6	40,000	Killough, capital	75,000
Furniture and fixtures (net)	15,000	Seago, capital	62,000
Building (net)	30,000	Sales	80,000
Killough, drawing	10,000		
Seago, drawing	12,000		
Purchases	60,000		
Operating expenses	25,000		
Total	$272,000	Total	$272,000

Additional information:

1. December 31, 19X6, inventory was $55,000. 19X6 purchases of $60,000 were recorded using the periodic inventory method.

2. Depreciation for 19X6 on furniture and fixtures and building is determined to be 10% and 20%, respectively, of net valuations.

3. On July 1, 19X6, the partnership recorded a $10,000 additional capital contribution by Seago. Killough made no additional capital contributions during the year.

REQUIRED

a) Prepare a partnership income statement as of December 31, 19X6.

b) Determine the allocation of partnership income or loss for 19X6 to Killough and Seago, and prepare the entry to record the income allocation to individual capital accounts.

c) Prepare entries to close the partners' drawing accounts as of December 31, 19X6.

d) Prepare a statement of partners' capital and a balance sheet for the partnership as of December 31, 19X6.

P14-4 **Allocate Income, and Prepare Entry to Record Allocation and Statement of Partners' Capital**   The partnership of Flesher, Mills, and Parker was formed on January 1, 19X7. The original investments were as follows:

Flesher	$100,000
Mills	120,000
Parker	150,000

According to the partnership agreement, net income or loss is to be allocated among the partners as follows:

1. Salaries of $14,000 for Flesher, $10,000 for Mills, and $15,000 for Parker.

2. Interest of 9% on initial capital contribution

3. Remainder divided equally

Additional information:

1. Net income of the partnership for the year ended December 31, 19X7, was $75,000.

2. Flesher invested additional capital of $20,000 in the partnership on July 1, 19X7.

3. Mills withdrew $25,000 of permanent capital from the partnership on November 1, 19X7.

4. Flesher, Mills, and Parker made regular drawings of $9,000 each against their shares of net income during 19X7.

REQUIRED

a) Determine the allocation of net income for 19X7 among the three partners, and prepare the entry to record the income allocation to individual capital accounts.

b) Prepare a statement of partners' capital as of December 31, 19X7.

P14-5   **Income Allocation: Alternative Methods, Prepare Entry to Record Allocation**   Partners Bitner and Haverty have operated Tortilla Flat Partnership for five years with partnership income and loss allocated equally. Bitner and Haverty are contemplating a revision of their income-and-loss-sharing agreement. For the current period just ended, the partnership earned $38,000. Beginning-of-the-year capital balances for Bitner and Haverty were $100,000 and $150,000, respectively.

REQUIRED

a) Determine the allocation of partnership income to Bitner and Haverty under each of the following independent situations:

> **1.** Interest of 6% is allocated on beginning-of-the-year capital balances; salaries of $8,000 and $13,000 are allocated to Bitner and Haverty, respectively; and any remainder is divided between Bitner and Haverty in a ratio of 1:3, respectively.
>
> **2.** Salaries of $12,000 and $16,000 are allocated to Bitner and Haverty, respectively; interest is allocated at a rate of 5% on the excess capital investment of one partner over the other at the beginning of the year; and any remainder is divided between Bitner and Haverty in a ratio of 4:1, respectively. Bitner's total allocation of income is not to exceed $17,000.
>
> **3.** Bitner is paid a bonus of 12% of net income after deducting bonus. Any remainder is divided equally.
>
> **4.** Salaries of $15,000 and $20,000 are allocated to Bitner and Haverty, respectively; interest is allocated at a rate of 3% on beginning-of-the-year capital balances; and any remainder is divided between Bitner and Haverty in the ratio of 1:2, respectively. Any deficiency of net income relative to salary and interest credits is divided between Bitner and Haverty in the ratio 3:2, respectively.
>
> **5.** Bitner and Haverty share income in a ratio of 4:1, respectively, after salaries of $10,000 to each and 8% interest on beginning-of-the-year capital balances. Partners' salaries and interest on capital should be allocated only to the extent that net income provides them.
>
> **6.** Salaries of $10,000 and $12,000 are allocated to Bitner and Haverty, respectively; interest is allocated at a rate of 4% on beginning-of-the-year capital balances; a bonus is allocated to Bitner of 20% of net income after deducting interest on capital and bonus but before deducting salaries; and any remainder is divided equally.

b) Prepare the entry to record the allocation of partnership net income to individual capital accounts for situations (1) through (6) in part (a) above.

P14-6 **Record Investments and Transactions, Prepare Income Statement, Allocate Income (Loss), and Prepare Entry to Record Allocation** On January 1, 19X1, sole proprietors Wright and Woolley formed a partnership to bear their names. A schedule of the book values and fair values of the net assets contributed by each partner appears as follows:

	Wright	
	Book Value	**Fair Value**
Cash	$ 20,000	$20,000
Inventory	15,000	22,000
Machinery and equipment	30,000	60,000
Building	40,000	50,000
Land	15,000	25,000
	$120,000	
Mortgage on building	27,000	27,000
Contributed net assets	$ 93,000	

	Woolley	
	Book Value	**Fair Value**
Cash	$100,000	$100,000
Inventory	5,000	8,000
Machinery and equipment	10,000	20,000
Contributed net assets	$115,000	

The partnership agreement specifies that the partners' initial capital balances should be equal and any contributed goodwill should be recognized.

Partners Wright and Woolley agree that the income-and-loss-sharing arrangement should be as follows: interest of 5% on beginning-of-the-year capital balances; salaries to Wright and Woolley of $16,000 and $12,000, respectively; bonus to Wright of 5% of partnership income after subtraction of the bonus, and any remainder divided between Wright and Woolley in the ratio of 1:3, respectively. Accounting records are to be maintained on the accrual method of accounting.

During the year 19X1 the following partnership transactions took place:

1. Sales totaling $165,900 on account were made.

2. The partnership received $5,000 from Woolley on July 1, signing a one-year, 8% note in exchange. Interest to be paid in equal installments on December 31, 19X1, and July 1, 19X2.

3. The partnership purchased $60,000 of merchandise on account. The periodic inventory system is used.

4. The partnership collected account receivables totaling $75,000.

5. Operating expenses incurred and paid during the period were as follows:

Salaries and wages to nonpartners	$23,000
Interest on loan from Woolley	200
Other expenses	10,000

6. Withdrawals by partners in anticipation of income were as follows:

Wright	$16,000
Woolley	12,000

7. Partnership paid $200 to an accounting firm for services performed for Wright as an individual.

8. Partnership collected from an outsider $500 on a note due to Woolley as an individual.

Additional information:

1. The machinery and equipment have an estimated life of ten years, and the building has an estimated life of 20 years.

2. Goodwill is amortized over an estimated life of ten years.

3. Inventory on December 31, 19X1, totaled $20,000.

REQUIRED

a) Prepare entries on January 1, 19X1, to record the investments in the partnership by Wright and Woolley.

b) Prepare entries to record transactions (1) through (8) for 19X1.

c) Prepare an income statement for the year ended December 31, 19X1.

d) Determine the allocation of partnership income/loss for 19X1 to Wright and Woolley, and prepare the entry to record the income allocation to individual capital accounts.

P14-7 **Admission by Investment and by Purchased Interest with Schedule for Distribution of Proceeds to Partners** In 19X2, Sherwood and Estes established Up-and-Ready Ski Resort in Michigan. As a very successful partnership, Sherwood and Estes have increased their capital balances to $112,000 and $168,000, respectively. Since Sherwood devotes full-time to the business and Estes part-time, they share in the income and loss in the ratio of 7:3, respectively. Eastman, a ski instructor at the resort, has approached the partners about buying an interest in the partnership. Net assets as presented on the partnership books are fairly valued.

REQUIRED

a) Prepare entries to record the admission of Eastman to the partnership under each of the following independent situations:

    1. Eastman invests $70,000 cash for a one-fifth interest in net assets.

    2. Eastman invests $100,000 cash for a one-fourth interest in net assets; bonus method is to be used.

    3. Eastman invests $140,000 cash for a one-fourth capital interest; goodwill method is to be used.

    4. Eastman pays Sherwood and Estes a total of $110,000 for one-third of their respective capital balances; goodwill implied by the purchase price is not to be recorded by the partnership.

    5. Eastman pays Sherwood and Estes a total of $70,000 for one-fifth of their respective capital balances; goodwill implied by the purchase price is to be recorded by the partnership.

b) Assuming Eastman paid a total of $120,000 to Sherwood and Estes for two-fifths of their respective capital balances, prepare a schedule to assist in determining the cash to be transferred to Sherwood and Estes. Net assets of the partnership are fairly valued.

P14-8 **Admission by Purchased Interest** Partners Ray and Davis have capital balances of $25,000 and $15,000, respectively, and they share income and loss in the ratio of 4:1. The partners are considering the admission of Doyle.

REQUIRED

Prepare the entries to record the admission of Doyle to the partnership under each of the following independent situations:

1. Doyl acquires a one-fifth interest in the partnership from Ray, paying $8,000. Net assets of the partnership are fairly valued.

2. Doyle acquires a one-fifth interest in the partnership from Ray, paying $10,000. Net assets of the partnership are fairly valued. Doyle is to be admitted under the bonus method.

3. Doyle acquires a one-fourth interest in the partnership from Ray, paying $14,000. The assets and liabilities of the partnership are fairly valued except for a building that is undervalued by $12,000. Partnership assets are to be revalued, and Doyle is to be admitted under the goodwill method.

4. Doyle acquires a one-fifth interest in the partnership from Ray, paying $7,000. Net assets of the partnership are fairly valued except for land that is overvalued by $5,000. Land is to be adjusted on the books of the partnership, and Doyle is to be admitted.

5. Doyle acquires a one-fourth interest in the partnership from Ray, paying $8,800. Net assets of the partnership are fairly valued. Doyle is to be admitted under the goodwill method.

6. Doyle acquires a one-fourth interest in the partnership from Ray, paying $7,600. Net assets of the partnership are fairly valued. Doyle is to be admitted under the bonus method.

P14-9

Admission by Investment   Brewer and Light have operated a successful partnership for the last ten years. They agree that a new partner should be admitted to the partnership in order that he may be trained to be the managing partner upon their retirement. Brewer and Light share income and loss 60% and 40%, respectively. Brewer's capital is $200,000, and Light's capital is $160,000.

REQUIRED

Prepare the entries to record the admission of the new partner, Mitchell, under each of the following independent situations:

1. Mitchell invests $120,000 cash in the partnership for a one-fourth interest. Partnership net assets are fairly valued.

2. Mitchell invests $140,000 cash in the partnership for a one-fourth interest. Mitchell is to be admitted under the goodwill method. Net assets of the partnership are fairly valued.

3. Mitchell invests $204,000 cash in the partnership for a one-third interest. Mitchell is to be admitted under the bonus method. Net assets of the partnership are fairly valued.

4. Mitchell invests $80,000 cash in the partnership for a one-fifth interest. Net assets of the partnership are fairly valued except for land that is overvalued by $40,000. Land is to be revalued, and Mitchell is to be admitted to the partnership.

5. Mitchell invests $100,000 cash in the partnership for a one-fourth interest. Net assets of the partnership are fairly valued. The goodwill method is to be used in admitting Mitchell.

6. Mitchell invests $85,000 cash in the partnership for a one-fifth interest. Net assets of the partnership are fairly valued. Mitchell is to be admitted using the bonus method.

P14-10

Multiple Choice Questions on Admission and Withdrawal of Partners

1. Frank and Moore are partners who share income and losses equally in a highly successful partnership. The capital accounts of Frank and Moore have tripled in five years and at present stand at $90,000 and $60,000, respectively. Swoop desires to join the firm and offers to invest $50,000 for a one-third interest in capital and in income and loss of the firm. Frank and Moore declined this offer but extended a counteroffer to Swoop of $70,000 for a one-fourth interest in capital and in income and loss of the firm. If Swoop accepted this offer and goodwill is recorded, what should be the balances in the capital accounts of Frank and Moore after Swoop's admission?

    a) Frank, $90,000; Moore, $60,000

    b) Frank, $97,500; Moore, $67,500

    c) Frank, $100,000; Moore, $70,000

    d) Frank, $120,000; Moore, $90,000

2. William desires to purchase a one-fourth capital and income-and-loss interest in the partnership Eli, George, and Dick. The three partners agree to sell William one-fourth of their respective capital and income-and-loss interest in exchange for a total payment of $40,000. The capital accounts and the respective percentage interest in income and losses immediately before the sale to William follow:

	Capital Accounts	Income-and-Loss-Sharing Ratio
Eli	$ 80,000	60%
George	40,000	30%
Dick	20,000	10%
Total	$140,000	100%

All other assets and liabilities are fairly valued, and implied goodwill is to be recorded prior to the acquisition by William. Immediately after William's acquisition, what should be the capital balances of Eli, George, and Dick, respectively?

a) $60,000; $30,000; $15,000

b) $69,000; $34,500; $16,500

c) $77,000; $38,500; $19,500

d) $92,000; $46,000; $22,000

3. The capital accounts for the partnership of Lance and Dey at October 31, 19X5, are as follows:

Lance, capital	$ 80,000
Dey, capital	40,000
	$120,000

The partners share income and loss in the ratio of 6:4, respectively. The partnership is in desperate need of cash, and the partners agree to admit Carey as a partner with a one-third interest in capital and in income and loss, upon his investment of $30,000. Immediately after Carey's admission, what should be the capital balances of Lance, Dey, and Carey, respectively, assuming goodwill is not to be recognized?

a) $50,000; $50,000; $50,000

b) $60,000; $60,000; $60,000

c) $66,667; $33,333; $50,000

d) $68,000; $32,000; $50,000

4. Partners Allen, Baker, and Coe share income and loss 50:30:20, respectively. The balance sheet at April 30, 19X5, follows:

Assets	
Cash	$ 40,000
Other assets	360,000
Total assets	$400,000

Liabilities and Capital	
Accounts payable	$100,000
Allen, capital	74,000
Baker, capital	130,000
Coe, capital	96,000
Total liabilities and capital	$400,000

The assets and liabilities are recorded and presented at their respective fair values.

Jones is to be admitted as a new partner with a 20% capital interest and a 20% income-and-loss-sharing ratio in exchange for a cash investment. No goodwill or bonus is to be recorded. How much cash should Jones invest in the partnership?

a) $60,000   c) $75,000

b) $72,000   d) $80,000

5. Pat, Helma, and Diane are partners with capital balances of $50,000, $30,000, $20,000, respectively. The partners share income and loss equally. For an investment of $50,000 cash, Mary Ann is to be admitted as a partner with a one-fourth interest in capital and income. Based on this information, the amount of Mary Ann's investment can best be justified by which of the following?

a) Mary Ann will receive a bonus from the other partners upon her admission to the partnership.

b) Assets of the partnership were overvalued immediately prior to Mary Ann's investment.

c) The book value of the partnership's net assets was less than their fair value immediately prior to Mary Ann's investment.

d) Mary Ann is apparently bringing goodwill into the partnership, and her capital account will be credited for the appropriate amount.

6. The total of the partners' capital accounts was $110,000 before the recognition of partnership goodwill in preparation for the withdrawal of a partner whose income-and-loss-sharing ratio is 2/10. He was paid $28,000 by the firm in final settlement for his interest. The remaining partners' capital accounts, excluding their share of the goodwill, totaled $90,000 after his withdrawal. The total goodwill of the firm agreed upon was

a) $40,000   c) $20,000

b) $28,000   d) $ 8,000

7. The balance sheet for the partnership of Lang, Monte, and Newton at April 30, 19X5, follows. The partners share income and loss in the ratio of 2:2:6, respectively.

Assets, at cost	$100,000
Notes payable, Lang	$ 9,000
Lang, capital	15,000
Monte, capital	31,000
Newton, capital	45,000
Total liabilities and capital	$100,000

Lang is retiring from the partnership. By mutual agreement, the assets are to be adjusted to their fair value of $130,000 at April 30, 19X5. Monte and Newton agree that the partnership will pay Lang $37,000 cash for his partnership interest, exclusive of his loan, which is to be paid in full. No goodwill is to be recorded. What is the balance of Newton's capital account after Lang's retirement?

a) $51,000   c) $59,000

b) $53,400   d) $63,000

8. The capital accounts of the partnership of Newton, Sharman, and Jackson on June 1, 19X7, are presented as follows with their respective income-and-loss-sharing ratios:

	Capital Balance	Income-and-Loss-Sharing Ratio
Newton	$139,200	1/2
Sharman	208,800	1/3
Jackson	96,000	1/6
	$444,000	

On June 1, 19X7, Sidney was admitted to the partnership when he purchased, for $132,000, a proportionate interest from Newton and Sharman in the net assets and income of the partnership. As a result of this transaction, Sidney acquired a one-fifth interest in the net assets and in income and loss of the firm. Assuming that implied goodwill is not to be recorded, what is the combined gain realized by Newton and Sharman upon the sale to Sidney of a portion of their interest in the partnership?

a) $-0-

c) $62,400

b) $43,200

d) $82,000

9. If E is the total capital of a partnership before the admission of a new partner, F is the total capital of the partnership after the admission of the new partner, G is the amount of the new partner's investment, and H is the amount of capital credited to the new partner, then there is

a) Goodwill to the new partner if $F > (E + G)$ and $H < G$

b) Goodwill to the old partners if $F = E + G$ and $H > G$

c) A bonus to the new partner if $F = E + G$ and $H > G$

d) Neither bonus nor goodwill if $F > (E + G)$ and $H > G$

10. When Dee retired from the partnership of Dee, Ken, and Ned, the final settlement of Dee's partnership interest exceeded Dee's capital balance. Under the bonus method, the excess

a) Reduced the capital balances of Ken and Ned

b) Had no effect on the capital balances of Ken and Ned

c) Was recorded as goodwill

d) Was recorded as an expense

(AICPA adapted)

P14-11 **Admission by Purchased Interest with Preparation of Income Statement and Statement of Partners' Capital** Abbott and Barnes, equal partners in the A & B Grocery Stores, sold one-third of their interest in Store No. 3 to Costello, manager of that store, for cash on January 1, 19X4. The new partnership will operate as the ABC Grocery Company. Abbott and Barnes will continue to operate other stores. The balance sheet of Store No. 3 at January 1, 19X4, was as follows:

Assets		
Merchandise		$63,000
Fixtures and equipment	$22,000	
Less: Allowance for depreciation	10,000	12,000
Prepaid expenses		3,900
Utility deposits		1,100
Total assets		$80,000
Liabilities and Capital		
Accounts payable		$20,000
Capital:		
Abbott	$30,000	
Barnes	30,000	60,000
Total liabilities and capital		$80,000

Fixtures and equipment, which have an estimated remaining life of five years, were revalued at $18,000, according to the agreement of sale. All depreciable assets are depreciated using the straight-line method of depreciation. The following transactions for the year 19X4 were all in cash:

Sales	$620,000
Merchandise purchases	493,000
Salaries and wages (including salary of $9,000 to Costello, as manager)	77,000
Expenses (excluding depreciation expense)	25,400
New equipment purchased July 1, 19X4 (estimated life ten years)	3,000

You are also given the following additional information:

| Merchandise inventory, December 31, 19X4 | $ 60,000 |
| Prepaid expenses, December 31, 19X4 | 3,000 |

The check record was kept open until all 19X4 bills were paid before closing the books as of December 31, 19X4. The books of the partnership are maintained on the accrual basis. The partnership agreement provides for a salary of $750 monthly to Costello. All remaining income is divided equally. Partners' drawing accounts each show a net debit balance of $3,000.

REQUIRED

a) Determine the cash payment that Costello made to Abbott and Barnes, as individuals, for a one-third interest in Store No. 3, assuming the purchase price was equal to one-third of the adjusted partners' capital on January 1, 19X4.

b) Prepare an income statement for ABC Grocery Company for the year ended December 31, 19X4, including a schedule attached to the income statement showing the allocation of income to the partners.

c) Prepare a statement of partners' capital as of December 31, 19X4.

(AICPA adapted)

P14-12 **Retirement of a Partner** Fertig, Stanley, and Scott have been partners in the Executive Development Partnership for over 20 years, sharing income and loss equally. Fertig is scheduled to retire from the partnership. As the partnership agreement does not make any provisions for the retirement of a partner, several alternative payments for Fertig's interest are being considered. The net assets of the partnership are correctly valued. The capital balances of the partners are Fertig, $40,000; Stanley, $50,000; Scott, $30,000.

REQUIRED
Under each of the following independent circumstances, record the entries for the retirement of Fertig:

1. Fertig is paid cash equal to the book value of his interest.

2. Fertig is paid $64,000 cash for his interest; excess payment over book value is treated as a bonus.

3. Fertig is paid $64,000 cash for his interest; excess payment over book value is treated as goodwill. Total implied goodwill is to be recorded by the partnership.

4. Fertig is paid $64,000 cash for his interest; excess payment over book value is treated as goodwill. Only implied goodwill relating to Fertig's equity is recorded by the partnership.

5. Fertig is paid $36,000 cash for his interest; excess capital interest over payment is treated as a bonus.

P14-13 **Admission by Investment and by Purchased Interest with Preparation of Schedule for Distribution of Proceeds** The trial balance of AB Partnership appeared as follows on January 1, 19X6:

	Debit	Credit
Cash	$ 70,000	
Accounts receivable	50,000	
Notes receivable	40,000	
Merchandise inventories	35,000	
Land	85,000	
Buildings and equipment (net)	15,000	
Temporary investments at cost	35,000	
Prepaid insurance	4,500	
Office supplies	3,000	
Bank loans		$ 45,000
Accounts payable		60,000
Accrued taxes		2,500
Notes payable		55,000
A, capital		100,000
B, capital		75,000
	$337,500	$337,500

Income and loss are shared equally by A and B. As of December 31, 19X6, C purchased, for $80,000 in cash from partners A and B, a third interest in the partnership's capital and income. Each partner agreed to transfer one-third of his individual capital account to C. Prior to C's admission, it was decided that a valuation allowance of $5,000 should be established with respect to temporary investments, that an allowance for uncollectible accounts should be established in the amount of $10,000, and that the valuation of buildings and equipment should be reduced to $11,000. Income sharing by C commenced on January 1, 19X7.

As of December 31, 19X7, D was admitted to the partnership for a one-fourth interest and contributed the following assets from a business previously operated by her as a sole proprietor:

Cash	$33,000
Accounts receivable	20,000
Investments	10,000

The following liabilities incurred by D in her previous business were assumed by the new partnership:

Accounts payable	$20,500

As an inducement to merge her enterprise with the ABC Partnership, D was admitted under the goodwill method. Income is to be shared equally by A, B, C, and D in the new firm, commencing January 1, 19X8.

Additional data are as follows:

| | Year Ended December 31 ||
	19X6	19X7
Income of the firm	$19,000	$27,000
Drawings:		
A	10,000	7,500
B	7,000	6,000
C	—	14,000

For the purpose of simplicity, it is assumed that income for each year was realized in cash and that the balance sheet of the firm on January 1, 19X6, did not change during the two-year period, except as indicated in the terms of this problem.

REQUIRED

a) Prepare the entry on the books of the partnership to admit C on December 31, 19X6.

b) Prepare a schedule to assist in determining the distribution of the cash paid by C to A and B.

c) Determine capital balances of A, B, and C as of December 31, 19X7.

d) Prepare the entry on the books of the partnership to admit D on December 31, 19X7.

(AICPA adapted)

P14-14 **Admission of Partners: Death and Retirement of Partners** A, B, and C decide to practice law together starting January 1, 19X1. They enter into an agreement under which they share income and loss in the ratio of 50%, 25%, and 25%, respectively, and agree to contribute $50,000 in cash in these same proportions to provide working capital. They decide to keep their books on a cash basis.

On January 1, 19X2, B died; and the remaining partners agreed to admit D, giving him a 20% share in income and loss with a minimum guarantee of $10,000 per year whether or not operations are profitable. A and C have income-sharing percentages and capital interests of 45% and 35%, respectively. On December 31, 19X2, C decides to retire but permits the use of his name on future partnerships, subject to the payment to him of $5,000 per annum, to be treated as an expense of the partnership.

As of January 1, 19X3, a partnership is formed in which C's name is utilized in accordance with his proposal and to which E is admitted. The partners' capital interests in this partnership are as follows: A, 55%; D, 30%; and E, 15%.

Since there were no substantial accruals at the end of the year, disbursements for expenses made during any one period were treated as expenses of the then current partnership. These disbursements were $70,000 in 19X1, $80,000 in 19X2, and $90,000 in 19X3.

Receipts of fees were as follows:

	Earned by Partnership		
	No. 1	**No. 2**	**No. 3**
19X1	$ 80,000		
19X2	145,000	$40,000	
19X3		50,000	$70,000

Each new partnership agreement provided for the newly created partnership to purchase from the old partnership the $50,000 capital that was originally paid in by A, B, and C. The agreements also provided that the partners should bear the cost of acquisition of this amount in the proportion in which they shared income and loss. However, it was agreed that an incoming partner, or one acquiring an increased percentage, need not make his contribution in cash immediately but could have the same charged to his drawing account. All such partners availed themselves of this privilege. Partners selling all or a part of their interest in capital are credited through their drawing accounts and immediately withdraw the amount of such credit. In addition to drawings made under this agreement, the partners or their heirs made cash drawings as follows:

	A	B	C	D	E
19X1	$10,500	$27,750	$13,750		
19X2	40,000	4,750	5,000	$7,000	
19X3	10,000	5,000	15,000	2,500	$5,000

REQUIRED

Prepare statements showing the details of transactions in the partners' drawing accounts and capital accounts for each of the years involved. These accounts should be prepared in such a form so that the balance at the end of each year that was available for withdrawal by each partner is shown in that partner's drawing account. The partners' capital accounts should reflect only the $50,000 original investment.

(AICPA adapted)

P14-15   **Admission of Partners: Income Allocation**   You have been engaged to prepare financial statements for the partnership of Alexander, Randolph, and Ware as of June 30, 19X2. You have obtained the following information from the partnership agreement as amended and from the accounting records:

1. The partnership was formed originally by Alexander and Barnes on July 1, 19X1. At that date

   a) Barnes contributed $400,000 cash.

   b) Alexander contributed land, building, and equipment with fair market values of $110,000, $520,000, and $185,000, respectively. The land and building were subject to a mortgage securing an 8% per annum note (interest rate of similar notes at July 1, 19X1). The note is due in quarterly payments of $5,000 plus interest on January 1, April 1, July 1, and October 1 of each year. Alexander made the July 1, 19X1, principal and interest payment personally. The partnership then assumed the obligation for the remaining $300,000 balance.

   c) The agreement further provided that Alexander had contributed a certain intangible benefit to the partnership due to his many years of business activity in the area to be serviced by the new partnership. The assigned value of this intangible asset, plus the net tangible assets he contributed, gave Alexander a 60% initial capital interest in the partnership.

   d) Alexander was designated the only active partner at an annual salary of $24,000, plus an annual bonus of 4% of net income after deducting his salary but before deducting interest on his partners' capital investments (see below). Both the salary and the bonus are operating expenses of the partnership.

   e) Each partner is to receive a 6% return on his weighted average of the beginning-of-the-month capital balance; such interest is to be an expense of the partnership.

   f) All remaining income or loss is to be shared equally.

2. On October 1, 19X1, Barnes sold his partnership interest and rights, as of July 1, 19X1, to Ware for $370,000. Alexander agreed to accept Ware as a partner if he would contribute sufficient cash to meet the October 1, 19X1, principal and interest payment on the mortgage note. Ware made the payment from personal funds.

3. On January 1, 19X2, Alexander and Ware admitted a new partner, Randolph. Randolph invested $150,000 cash for a 10% capital interest based on the initial investments at July 1, 19X1, of Alexander and Barnes. At January 1, 19X2, the book value of the partnership's assets and liabilities approximated their fair market values. Randolph contributed no intangible benefit to the partnership. Similar to the other partners, Randolph is to receive a 6% return on his weighted average of the beginning-of-the-month capital balance. His investment also entitled him to 20% of the partnership's income or loss as defined earlier. However, for the year ended June 30, 19X2, Randolph would receive one-half of his pro rata share of the income or loss.

4. The accounting records show that on February 1, 19X2, "other miscellaneous expenses" had been charged $3,600 in payment of hospital expenses incurred by Alexander's 8-year-old daughter.

5. All salary payments to Alexander have been charged to his personal account. On June 1, 19X2, Ware made a $33,000 withdrawal. These are the only transactions recorded in the partners' personal accounts.

6. Presented here is a trial balance that summarizes the partnership's general ledger balances at June 30, 19X2. The general ledger has not been closed.

	Debits	Credits
Current assets	$ 307,100	
Fixed assets (net)	1,285,800	
Current liabilities		$ 157,000
8% mortgage note payable (net)		290,000
Alexander, capital		515,000
Randolph, capital		150,000
Ware, capital		400,000
Alexander, personal	24,000	
Randolph, personal	–0–	
Ware, personal	33,000	
Sales		872,600
Cost of goods sold	695,000	
Administrative expenses	16,900	
Other miscellaneous expenses	11,100	
Interest expense	11,700	
	$2,384,600	$2,384,600

REQUIRED

Prepare a worksheet to adjust the net income (loss) and partners' capital accounts for the year ended June 30, 19X2, and to close the net income (loss) to the partners' capital accounts at June 30, 19X2. Amortization of goodwill, if any, is to be over a ten-year period. Use the following column headings, and begin with balances per books as shown here:

Description	Net Income (Loss) Cr. (Dr.)	Partners' Capital			Other Accounts	
		Alexander Cr. (Dr.)	Randolph Cr. (Dr.)	Ware Cr. (Dr.)	Amount Dr. (Cr.)	Name
Book balances at 6-30-X2	$137,900	$515,000	$150,000	$400,000		

(AICPA adapted)

ISSUES IN ACCOUNTING JUDGMENT

I14-1   Profit and Loss Sharing   Ms. Pankov and Mr. Hermann are preparing to form a partnership that will provide management consulting services to small and medium-sized businesses. Ms. Pankov has taken early retirement from a management position in a large manufacturing business and plans to spend most of her time on client relations and generating new consulting engagements. Mr. Hermann is a midcareer management consultant with ten years of experience with a large well-known consulting firm. Although Pankov and Hermann view themselves as "equal partners," they are prepared to have the income-and-loss-sharing arrangement constructed to accommodate personal differences.

REQUIRED

Describe an income-and-loss-sharing arrangement for the new partnership, and state why you think it would be suitable.

I14-2 **Analysis of Alternative Forms of Partnership Admission** Saxton & Benchley, a small public accounting partnership, has requested you to consult with them about revising their partnership admission rules in connection with plans to admit several new partners. The existing partners, one of whom is close to retirement, are considering changing from the bonus method to the goodwill method for admitting new partners, each of whom will make a small capital contribution in exchange for a 10% interest in the partnership. The partnership agreement specifies that upon retirement, partners are paid the book value of their capital interest. The fair value of the existing partnership is significantly larger than the recorded book values.

REQUIRED

a) Which method do you believe the existing partners would prefer? Write a paragraph supporting your opinion.

b) Which method do you believe the new partners would prefer? Write a paragraph supporting your opinion.

I14-3 **Evaluation of Promotion Criteria** Adams & Reston is a small public accounting partnership that has grown significantly in recent years and hopes to continue to grow. Next year, several members of the firm will be reviewed for promotion to partner. In preparation for this review, the existing partners have hired you to consult with them in the revision of promotion criteria which haven't been changed for over ten years. The present criteria state that a candidate for promotion to partner should have "at least 5,000 chargeable hours per year under his or her direction," "at least $450,000 per year in collected fees," and "a high level of industry and integrity."

REQUIRED

Write a brief paragraph describing how and why you would propose revising the present criteria.

15

Partnerships: Liquidation

STATEMENT OF PARTNERSHIP LIQUIDATION   749

LIQUIDATION TRANSACTIONS   749

Gains and Losses on Realization of Assets   750
Liquidation Expenses   750   Revenues and Expenses from
Partnership Operations   750   Distribution of Realization
Proceeds   750

SINGLE-STEP AND INSTALLMENT
DISTRIBUTIONS   751

SINGLE-STEP DISTRIBUTIONS   752

DEBIT BALANCES IN CAPITAL ACCOUNTS   752

Collection of Cash   754   Offset against Liabilities   754
Treatment as a Liquidation Loss   754

INSOLVENCY AND DISTRIBUTION PRIORITIES   754

LIQUIDATION OF INSOLVENT PARTNERSHIPS   755

INSTALLMENT DISTRIBUTIONS   756

A TWO-INSTALLMENT DISTRIBUTION TO
PARTNERS   756

THE SAFE-PAYMENT CALCULATION   756

INSTALLMENT DISTRIBUTION SCHEDULES   759

Maximum Absorbable Loss   759   Impact of Possible Losses
on Equity Balances   760   Calculation of Installment
Distribution Schedule   761   Use of the Installment
Distribution Schedule   763

SUMMARY   763

A liquidation winds up all operations of the partnership, converts all partnership assets into cash (or another distributable form), and distributes the cash to creditors of the partnership and to the partners. Thus, liquidation terminates both the legal and the business entities that are represented by a partnership. In some cases, a partnership may be sold as a going concern to another entity in a single transaction. In other cases, a partnership may be sold piecemeal in several transactions to a variety of entities. Whether the assets of a partnership are sold to one or several parties, a liquidation officer is usually appointed to oversee the sale of the assets and their distribution to creditors and partners.

The purpose of this chapter is to discuss the accounting and asset distribution procedures for partnership liquidations—procedures that are specified by the provisions of state and federal bankruptcy acts, as well as provisions of the partnership agreement and the Uniform Partnership Act. The chapter begins with a discussion of the statement of partnership liquidation and then turns to a discussion of distribution procedures and their impact on the statement of partnership liquidation.

STATEMENT OF PARTNERSHIP LIQUIDATION

The detailed accounting records that underlie a partnership liquidation vary according to the complexity and scale of the liquidation, but all liquidation records may be summarized in a *statement of partnership liquidation,* sometimes called a statement of realization and liquidation. The statement of partnership liquidation is issued by the liquidation officer upon completion of the liquidation. It summarizes all liquidation transactions that are recorded in the partnership records and shows the impact of these transactions on the liquidating partnership's balances of assets, liabilities, and owners' equity. A statement of partnership liquidation is shown in Exhibit 15-1. Notice that all postdistribution account balances are shown to be zero, indicating that the liquidation is complete. The liquidation officer may also issue *statements of partial liquidation* before the liquidation process is complete. Such statements display nonzero current balances for asset, liability, and owners' equity accounts.

Liquidation Transactions

The principal liquidation transactions can be characterized as *realizations* and *distributions.* Realizations are transactions that convert noncash assets of the partnership into cash. Distributions are transactions that distribute the realized proceeds to creditors and partners. Other liquidation transactions pay and collect various amounts that are associated with the winding up of partnership operations; for example, fees must be paid to accountants and lawyers for services rendered in connection with the liquidation.

EXHIBIT 15-1	STATEMENT OF PARTNERSHIP LIQUIDATION

GH Partnership
STATEMENT OF PARTNERSHIP LIQUIDATION

	Assets		Liabilities		Capital	
	Cash	Noncash Assets	Outside Creditors	Partner H	Partner G	Partner H
Income-and-loss-sharing ratio					50%	50%
Balances before realization	$ –0–	$50,000	$(21,000)	$(4,000)	$(15,000)	$(10,000)
Realization and loss	40,000	(50,000)*			5,000	5,000
Balances before distribution	$40,000	$ –0–	$(21,000)	$(4,000)	$(10,000)	$ (5,000)
Liquidation expenses	(1,000)				500	500
Subtotal	$39,000	$ –0–	$(21,000)	$(4,000)	$ (9,500)	$ (4,500)
Distribution of cash:						
Liabilities	(21,000)		21,000			
Partner's loan	(4,000)			4,000		
Partner's capital	(14,000)				9,500	4,500
Balances after distribution	$ –0–	$ –0–	$ –0–	$ –0–	$ –0–	$ –0–

* Parentheses indicate credits.

Gains and Losses on Realization of Assets

As noted earlier, realizations convert partnership assets into cash (or another distributable form). Usually, the amount of cash realized does not equal the book value of partnership assets; the difference between the cash realized and the related book value is a *liquidation gain or loss*. In the absence of an agreement to the contrary, liquidation gains and losses are distributed in the income-and-loss-sharing ratio. This means that provisions of the partnership agreement for salaries, interest on capital, and bonuses are typically ignored in the distribution of liquidation gains and losses. Consider the liquidation described in Exhibit 15-1. Noncash assets with a book value of $50,000 realize only $40,000 cash in liquidation. The two partners, who shared operating income and loss equally, also share the $10,000 liquidation loss equally, and capital balance of each partner is reduced by $5,000.

Liquidation Expenses

Costs (expenses) incurred by the liquidation process must be paid out of realization proceeds and are distributed among partners' capital accounts in the income-and-loss-sharing ratio. For example, the statement of partnership liquidation in Exhibit 15-1 shows liquidation expenses as a $1,000 reduction of cash and as a $500 reduction of each partner's capital balance. Liquidation expenses include sales commissions, shipping costs, title transfer fees, legal fees, costs of dismantling and removing equipment, and costs of completing work in process inventory.

Revenues and Expenses from Partnership Operations

Ideally, all revenue and expense accounts should be closed at the start of the liquidation process to establish the balances for which the liquidation officer is responsible. When a partnership liquidation commences in the middle of the partnership's fiscal year, however, revenues and expenses of the partially completed year may not have been closed to partners' capital accounts. In other cases, partnership assets may continue to generate revenues and incur expenses as operations gradually come to a conclusion. Although such revenues and expenses should be distinguished from liquidation transactions, they may be recorded by the liquidation officer along with the liquidation transactions and reported on the statement of partnership liquidation. As long as liquidation gains, losses, and expenses are distributed in the same ratio as operating income and loss, the distinction between such operating items and liquidation items is of little importance.

Distribution of Realization Proceeds

Under partnership law, the claims of outside creditors against partnership assets have priority over the claims of partners against those assets. The Uniform Partnership Act gives the following rank order of the payment of claims against a partnership in liquidation:

1. Amounts owed to creditors other than partners
2. Amounts owed to partners other than for capital and income

3. Amounts owed to partners with respect to their capital and income[1]

In other words, the only partnership assets available for distribution to partners are those that are not required to pay the full claims of *outside* creditors. Further, amounts owed to partners respecting loans to the partnership have priority over amounts owed to partners respecting their capital and income; however, this does not mean that loans from partners are always repaid before capital distributions (see discussion of debit balances in capital accounts).

    To be completely safe, some liquidation officers make no distributions to partners until all outside creditors have been satisfied. If payments are made to partners before all outside creditors have been satisfied, future realizations may not provide amounts that are sufficient to satisfy outside creditors, and the liquidation officer may be held personally liable to the creditors, as the following issues section illustrates.

 Personal Liability of Liquidation Officer	John Lightner, a certified public accountant, was engaged to serve as the liquidation officer for the Stulz-Tanner Partnership. Lightner oversaw the sale of the partnership's assets and the payment of the partnership's creditors. Lightner planned to charge a fee of $3,000 for his services and estimated that other liquidation expenses would total $2,000. Accordingly, he held back a $5,000 cash reserve to pay his fees and other liquidation expenses and distributed the entire remainder to Stulz and Tanner following procedures to be described later in this chapter. Following this distribution, Lightner received a bill for legal services in the amount of $800 that he neglected to include in his estimate of other liquidation expenses. Although Lightner may have a claim for $800 against the partners for the distribution in excess of the amount needed for liquidation expenses, such a claim is apt to be very difficult to collect. If the claim proves to be uncollectible, Lightner is personally liable for the unpaid liquidation expenses, which, in this case, would reduce his fee by $800.

Techniques for calculating the amount of safe reserves are described later in this chapter.

Single-Step and Installment Distributions

In some liquidations, all distributions are made at a single time following the realization of all partnership assets. Liquidation officers are apt to prefer such *single-step distributions* because they minimize the risk of overpaying one partner at the expense of another. Frequently, however, the realization process proceeds slowly, and partners press for partial distributions of assets. Distributions of partnership assets that occur at several times are called *installment distributions*. Of course, single-step and installment distributions are two methods of accomplishing the same thing; unless distribution errors are made under one method and not the other, the two methods produce the same total distribution to each

---

[1] Technically, the Uniform Partnership Act accords a lower priority to amounts owed partners for income than amounts owed for capital. However, the priority of a partner's capital over a partner's income has no practical significance unless capital balances are insufficient to absorb losses of the partnership. Since such unabsorbed losses rarely occur, we shall assume throughout this chapter that capital and income have the same status.

partner. We turn now to a discussion of single-step distributions. Later in the chapter we consider the somewhat more complicated procedures that are associated with installment distributions.

SINGLE-STEP DISTRIBUTIONS

Since partners have unlimited liability for partnership debt, a partner's personal assets may be taken to satisfy liabilities of the partnership in liquidation. As the following issues section explains, this is in marked contrast to the limited liability characteristic of corporations.

ISSUES

Limited and Unlimited Liability

In corporate liquidations, realization losses fall equally on each share of common stock. If such losses eliminate more than the recorded owners' equity, no claim arises against the shareholders for the deficiency. Since shareholders' liability is limited to their owners' equity, unsatisfied creditors may not proceed against the stockholders' personal assets. In contrast, partners' responsibility for partnership debt is not limited to recorded owners' equity or capital. Unsatisfied creditors of the partnership may proceed against the personal assets of individual partners. Indeed, if only one partner has personal resources, that partner may be required to pay the entire amount sought by partnership creditors. New partners, however, have some protection against the unlimited liability provisions. The personal liability of partners is limited by the date of their admission to the partnership. When a new partner is admitted, whether by purchased interest or by investment in the partnership, the new partner has no *personal* liability for the obligations of the partnership incurred prior to admission. Section 17 of the Uniform Partnership Act states that a "person admitted as a partner into an existing partnership is liable for all the obligations of the partnership arising before his admission as though he had been a partner when such obligations were incurred, *except* that this liability shall be satisfied only out of partnership property." Throughout this chapter, however, we shall assume that all partnership liabilities are incurred subsequent to the admission of every partner.

In the paragraphs that follow, single-step distributions are used to illustrate liquidations in the presence of debit capital balances and insolvency.

Debit Balances in Capital Accounts

When losses or other amounts charged to a partner's capital account exceed its credit balance, the partner is said to have a debit balance. Debit capital balances represent a claim of the partnership against the individual partner. Ordinarily, a partner may be expected to satisfy such a claim by payment to the partnership or by offsetting the claim against liabilities of the partnership owed to the partner. If a partner fails to satisfy his or her debit balance, the debit balance is equivalent to a loss and is charged against the other partners' capital balances in the income-and-loss-sharing ratio. In summary, a debit balance in a partner's capital account may be disposed of in three ways: (1) by collection of cash from the partner, (2) by offset against liabilities owed to the partner by the partnership, or (3) by treatment as a liquidation loss.

To illustrate, consider the information for the liquidating CDE Partnership presented in the top portion of Exhibit 15-2. The liquidation of $70,000 of noncash assets for $50,000 resulted in a $20,000 liquidation loss. Allocation of the $20,000 loss among the

EXHIBIT 15-2	ALTERNATIVE DISPOSITIONS OF DEBIT CAPITAL BALANCES: THREE ILLUSTRATIONS

	Assets		Liabilities		Capital		
	Cash	Noncash Assets	Outside Creditors	Part-ners	Partner C	Partner D	Partner E
Information for Three Illustrations:							
Income-and-loss-sharing ratio					50%	30%	20%
Balances before realization	$ 5,000	$70,000	$(10,000)	$(5,000)	$(40,000)	$(17,000)	$(3,000)
Realization and loss	50,000	(70,000)*			10,000	6,000	4,000
Balances after realization	$55,000	$ –0–	$(10,000)	$(5,000)	$(30,000)	$(11,000)	$ 1,000
Illustration A: Collection of Debit Balance from Partner:							
Balances after realization	$55,000	$ –0–	$(10,000)	$(5,000)	$(30,000)	$(11,000)	$ 1,000
Collection of debit balance	1,000						(1,000)
Balances before distribution	$56,000	$ –0–	$(10,000)	$(5,000)	$(30,000)	$(11,000)	$ –0–
Illustration B: Offset of Debit Balance against Liabilities Owed to Partner:							
Balances after realization	$55,000	$ –0–	$(10,000)	$(5,000)	$(30,000)	$(11,000)	$ 1,000
Offset of debit balance against liability owed to Partner E				1,000			(1,000)
Balances before distribution	$55,000	$ –0–	$(10,000)	$(4,000)	$(30,000)	$(11,000)	$ 1,000
Illustration C: Charged as Liquidation Loss to Other Partners:							
Balances after realization	$55,000	$ –0–	$(10,000)	$(5,000)	$(30,000)	$(11,000)	$ 1,000
Absorption of debit balance by Partners C and D					625	375	(1,000)
Balances before distribution	$55,000	$ –0–	$(10,000)	$(5,000)	$(29,375)	$(10,625)	$ –0–

* Parentheses indicate credits.

partners using their income-and-loss-sharing ratio results in a $1,000 debit capital balance for Partner E. Let us use this information as a basis for three *independent* illustrations—each representing a different disposition of Partner E's debit balance.

Collection of Cash

In the first illustration, Illustration A, let us assume that the partnership collects cash from Partner E in the amount of his or her debit balance. The collection of cash is entered on the statement of partnership liquidation as illustrated in Exhibit 15-2 (in the segment labeled Illustration A); the cash column is increased by a debit of $1,000, and E's debit capital balance is reduced to zero by a credit of $1,000.

Offset against Liabilities

In the second illustration, Illustration B, let us assume that liabilities to partners ($5,000) include $1,000 payable to Partner E; hence, the debit capital balance may be offset against liabilities such as those shown in the Illustration B section of Exhibit 15-2. If the partnership offsets the $1,000 debit capital balance against the $5,000 due to partners, then both the amount due to E and the debit capital balance are eliminated.[2]

Treatment as a Liquidation Loss

In the final illustration, let us assume that Partner E is insolvent and that, consequently, the debit balance cannot be collected from Partner E. Further, assume that no amounts are owed to Partner E by the partnership. Accordingly, the debit balance must be treated as a liquidation loss and distributed among the capital accounts of the partners with credit capital balances in proportion to their income-and-loss-sharing ratios. Exhibit 15-2 (Illustration C) shows the effect of this disposition on the partners' capital balances; E's debit capital balance is reduced to zero by a $1,000 credit, and a $1,000 loss is distributed among the capital accounts of C and D in proportion to their income-and-loss-sharing ratios—62.5% (.50 ÷ .80) to C and 37.5% (.30 ÷ .80) to D. In all three cases, illustrated earlier, the partnership has had sufficient resources to pay its outside creditors in liquidation. We turn now to consider cases in which the partnership's resources are insufficient to meet outside liabilities.

Insolvency and Distribution Priorities

When the assets of a partnership are not sufficient to satisfy completely the claims of outside creditors, then the *partnership is insolvent.*[3] When assets of a partner are not sufficient to satisfy completely his or her personal creditors, then the *partner is insolvent.*

[2] In some cases, amounts owed by a partnership to a partner may not be available to offset the debit balance. For example, if Partner E is insolvent, E's personal creditors may have a prior claim to the partnership liability. Throughout the remainder of this chapter, however, we assume that a partner's debit capital balances may be offset against partnership liabilities owed to the individual partner even if the partner is insolvent.

[3] As a basis for determining personal solvency, partners are usually asked to prepare personal financial statements including a personal balance sheet and a personal income statement (or statement of changes in net worth). Under *AICPA Statement of Position 82-1,* ''Accounting and Financial Reporting for Personal Financial Statements'' (1982), personal assets are stated at estimated current values (rather than historical costs) and personal liabilities are stated at the lower of the discounted value of future cash payments or the current cash settlement amount. Further, liabilities must include an amount for the estimated taxes to be paid upon liquidation of all assets and liabilities.

If a partnership is insolvent but the individual partners are solvent, then the outside creditors of the partnership may proceed against the personal assets of the solvent partners—but only to the extent of personal assets remaining after personal creditors have been completely satisfied. If an insolvent partnership has just one solvent partner, then partnership creditors may proceed against the solvent partner's personal assets for the entire unsatisfied partnership liabilities and may be limited only by the priority granted to the partner's personal creditors. Of course, if both the partnership and all its partners are insolvent, then the claims of partnership creditors cannot be completely satisfied. In general, outside creditors of the partnership have priority over partners in the distribution of partnership assets, and a partner's *personal* creditors have priority over the partnership's creditors in the distribution of a partner's *personal* assets.

Liquidation of Insolvent Partnerships

Let us consider the liquidation of an insolvent partnership shown in Exhibit 15-3. The liquidation of partnership assets results in a $13,200 loss ($18,000 − $4,800), which reduces both partners' capital accounts to debit balances and provides cash that is $1,200 short ($6,000 − $4,800) of the amount required to satisfy partnership liabilities. If both partners are solvent, the $1,200 would be recovered from both partners—$280 from X and $920 from Y. Let us assume, however, that while Partner Y is solvent, Partner X is insolvent and is forced to liquidate, with the result that realization of his personal assets provides $1,000 less than the amount that is required to satisfy his personal creditors. Consequently, the debit capital balance of Partner X is uncollectible and allocated to the capital account of Partner Y, which increases her debit balance to $1,200. Since Partner Y

				Capital	
EXHIBIT 15-3	**LIQUIDATION OF INSOLVENT PARTNERSHIP WITH ONE INSOLVENT PARTNER**				

XY Partnership
STATEMENT OF PARTNERSHIP LIQUIDATION

	Assets			Capital	
	Cash	Noncash assets	Liabilities	Partner X	Partner Y
Income-and-loss-sharing ratio				40%	60%
Balances before realization	$ –0–	$18,000	$(6,000)	$(5,000)	$(7,000)
Realization and loss	4,800	(18,000)*		5,280	7,920
Balances after realization	$4,800	$ –0–	$(6,000)	$ 280	$ 920
Absorption of X's debit balance by Y				(280)	280
Balances	$4,800	$ –0–	$(6,000)	$ –0–	$ 1,200
Collection of debit balance from Y	1,200				(1,200)
Balances before distribution	$6,000	$ –0–	$(6,000)	$ –0–	$ –0–
Distribution of cash to creditors	(6,000)		6,000		
Balances after distribution	$ –0–	$ –0–	$ –0–	$ –0–	$ –0–

* Parentheses indicate credits.

is solvent, the partnership creditors may proceed against her personal assets for recovery of the entire $1,200 deficiency. Once Partner Y pays the $1,200 to the partnership, partnership liabilities are paid in full.

INSTALLMENT DISTRIBUTIONS

The foregoing discussion of liquidation has assumed that all liquidation losses—including uncollectible debit capital balances—are distributed among partners' capital accounts *before* any liquidating payments are made to partners. Frequently, however, the realization process may proceed slowly, and partners may press for partial distributions of assets. Care must be exercised in partial distributions to avoid distributing more to a partner than he or she should ultimately receive. The problem is that partial distributions are made *before* the amount that a partner should ultimately receive is known—before the realization process is complete. When the liquidation experiences unanticipated losses or expenses, the liquidation officer may be placed in the difficult position of having to reclaim amounts that are distributed to certain partners. If efforts to reclaim earlier distributions fail, the liquidation officers may be personally liable for such amounts. Consequently, it is necessary to make assumptions about the unrealized portion of noncash assets that prevent erroneous distributions. We illustrate this procedure by reference to a partnership liquidation that entails a two-installment distribution.

A Two-Installment Distribution to Partners

Let us consider the liquidation of GH Partnership, which is shown in the statement of partnership liquidation illustrated in Exhibit 15-4. The statement of partnership liquidation shows that the assets are sold in two segments and that a partial distribution is made to creditors and partners following the first sale of assets. Early in the year, $45 is realized from the sale of assets with a book value of $60, and the $15 loss ($60 − $45) is distributed between the partners' capital accounts. The liquidation officer distributes a total of $38 ($3 to outside creditors and $35 to Partner G). The reasons for this distribution are discussed subsequently. The remaining noncash assets are sold later in the year for $30, and the resultant loss of $10 is distributed between the partners' capital accounts. Finally, the remaining outside creditors are paid and each partner is paid an amount of cash equal to his or her adjusted capital balance. The paragraphs that follow offer a rationale for the particular cash distribution chosen by the liquidation officer. The rationale supports two *equivalent* methods for determining partial distributions: (1) a method based on a series of *safe-payment calculations* and (2) a method based on a predetermined *installment distribution schedule*.

The Safe-Payment Calculation

As noted earlier, the objective in installment distributions to partners is to avoid paying more to a partner than he or she should ultimately receive, which depends on the impact of future, unknown liquidation losses on the partner's capital balance. If future liquidation losses were known, a partner could be safely paid any amount up to the partner's capital balance that is adjusted for the partner's share of the known future losses. In contrast, when future liquidation losses are unknown, as they invariably are, liquidation officers typically make two very conservative assumptions: (1) that the *maximum* possible future loss, which we shall call the *maximum unrealized loss,* will occur and (2) that every partner is *personally* insolvent. The maximum unrealized loss on noncash assets is usually set equal to the book value of remaining noncash assets. This rough estimation procedure is equivalent to assuming that nothing will be realized from the noncash assets that remain

EXHIBIT 15-4	STATEMENT OF PARTNERSHIP LIQUIDATION

GH Partnership

STATEMENT OF PARTNERSHIP LIQUIDATION

	Assets		Liabilities		Capital	
	Cash	Noncash Assets	Outside Creditors	Partner H	Partner G	Partner H
Income-and-loss-sharing ratio					60%	40%
Balances before realization	$-0-	$ 100	$ (10)	$ (3)	$ (70)	$ (17)
Partial realization and loss	45	(60)*			9	6
Balances before distribution	$ 45	$ 40	$ (10)	$ (3)	$ (61)	$ (11)
Partial distribution to partners	(38)		3		35	
Balances after partial distribution to partners	$ 7	$ 40	$ (7)	$ (3)	$ (26)	$ (11)
Final realization and loss	30	(40)			6	4
Balances before final distribution	$ 37	$-0-	$ (7)	$ (3)	$ (20)	$ (7)
Final distribution	(37)		7	3	20	7
Balances after final distribution	$-0-	$-0-	$-0-	$-0-	$-0-	$-0-

* Parentheses indicate credits.

to be sold. If nothing is realized, a liquidation loss equal to the book value of the noncash assets is incurred.[4] If, as the second assumption states, all partners are insolvent, then no amounts are recoverable from the partners as individuals and the entire liquidation loss must be absorbed by the partners' credit-balance capital and loan accounts. Following these conservative assumptions, the liquidation officer may calculate safe payments to partners that do not risk erroneous distributions that are difficult and costly to correct.

The safe-payment calculation subtracts the book value of remaining noncash assets, which equals the assumed maximum unrealized loss, from the net amount currently owed to partners (the partner's capital balance plus any partnership liabilities payable to the partner and less any partnership receivables due from the partner). Assuming that all claims of outside creditors (including amounts reserved to pay liquidation expenses) have

---

[4] Setting the maximum unrealized loss equal to the noncash book value has a computational advantage. When the current capital balances are reduced for the noncash book value, the sum of the adjusted capital and liability balances equals the amount of cash on hand, and each adjusted capital and liability balance equals the safe payment to the party to whom the balance is owed. In contrast, if the maximum unrealized loss is set equal to something less than the book value of noncash assets, then the sum of capital balances adjusted for that maximum loss will *exceed* the cash on hand and additional criteria are required to determine the safe distribution of cash among the partners. If the maximum unrealized loss is more than the noncash book value (as when nothing is realized and, in addition, disposal costs are incurred), then cash on hand should be reserved by the liquidation officer to pay disposal costs and other prior claims.

been recorded and charged against the partners' capital accounts, the remainder of the balance owed to each partner represents a safe distribution to that partner—a distribution that will not exceed the amount that the partner should ultimately receive.

A separate safe-payment calculation is made for each distribution to partners. The safe-payment calculation for the first of two distributions to partners of GH Partnership is shown in Exhibit 15-5. The calculation begins with the combined capital and liability-to-partner balances[5] immediately after the first realization of assets, which is shown in Exhibit 15-4. The liability balances of outside creditors (including amounts owed for liquidation expenses) are excluded from the safe-payment calculation because cash is always reserved to pay outside creditors whose claims have priority over the claims of partners. Only the excess of cash available over such reserves ($45 − $10 = $35) is available for distribution to partners. Next the balances owed to partners are adjusted for the maximum unrealized loss ($40), which is distributed between the partners in the income-and-loss-sharing ratio (60% or $24 to Partner G, and 40% or $16 to Partner H). Subtracting the assumed maximum unrealized loss of $40 from the partners' balances

---

[5] As noted earlier, we assume here and throughout this chapter that partnership liabilities owed to partners are payable directly to the partner and not to his or her creditors. If the $3 liability were payable to creditors of Partner H rather than to Partner H directly, then that liability should not be combined with the capital balance owed to Partner H. Rather, the liability to Partner H should be treated like a liability to an outside creditor. The result would be that an additional $3 would be charged against the balance of Partner G, who would receive $32 rather than $35.

EXHIBIT 15-5	**SAFE-PAYMENT CALCULATION**

GH Partnership
SAFE-PAYMENT CALCULATION FOR FIRST DISTRIBUTION TO PARTNERS

	Total Partners' Equity	Equity Partner G	Equity Partner H
Income-and-loss-sharing ratio		60%	40%
Current capital balances per Exhibit 15-4 (after first realization of assets)	$(72)*	$(61)	$ (11)
Current liability-to-partner balances per Exhibit 15-4	(3)		(3)
Total current equity	$(75)	$(61)	$ (14)
Maximum unrealized loss on noncash assets	40	24	16
Subtotal	$(35)	$(37)	$ 2
Maximum unrealized loss on debit capital balance		2	(2)
Safe payment of cash on hand	$(35)	$(35)	$–0–

* Parentheses indicate credits.

leaves a credit remainder of $37 for Partner G and a debit remainder of $2 for Partner H. Under the assumption that Partner H is insolvent, the $2 debit balance is charged against Partner G's balance, reducing it to $35, as shown in Exhibit 15-5. The implication of this calculation is that H should receive no payment in the partial distribution and the entire $35 should be paid to G.

Installment Distribution Schedules

The approach to installment distributions illustrated previously requires a separate safe-payment calculation for each distribution of cash to partners. If partners are paid at three different times, then three safe-payment calculations of the form shown in Exhibit 15-5 are required—one as the basis for each distribution. Alternatively, it is possible to prepare, prior to any realization of assets, a schedule that indicates the appropriate distribution of every dollar to be realized from the liquidation of partnership assets. The schedule, which replaces the repeated safe-payment calculation, is called an *installment distribution schedule;* and it shows, prior to the liquidation, how all cash will be distributed among creditors and partners as it becomes available.

The paragraphs that follow explain the calculations that underlie an installment distribution schedule by reference to the liquidation of KLM Partnership, which has the following balance sheet just prior to liquidation:

Preliquidation Balance Sheet of KLM Partnership

Assets		Liabilities and Capital	
Cash	$ 10	Liabilities to outside creditors	$ 15
Noncash assets	125	Liability to Partner K	10
		Capital of Partner K	30
		Capital of Partner L	60
		Capital of Partner M	20
Total assets	$135	Total liabilities and capital	$135

Partners K, L, and M have income-and-loss-sharing percentages of 50%, 30%, and 20%, respectively.

To derive the installment distribution schedule, two supporting schedules must first be constructed—a schedule of maximum absorbable loss and a schedule of possible losses and equity balances. The paragraphs that follow consider each schedule in turn.

Maximum Absorbable Loss

Preparation of a schedule of maximum absorbable loss is the first step in the construction of an installment distribution schedule. The *maximum absorbable loss* is the maximum loss to the partnership that a given partner's equity can absorb. The maximum absorbable loss is calculated for each partner by dividing that partner's equity (the partner's capital balance plus any partnership liabilities payable to the partner and less any partnership receivables due from the partner) by the partner's income-and-loss-sharing ratio. For example, Partner K has a $40 credit equity balance ($30 + $10) and receives 50% of income and loss. The maximum loss to the partnership that K's equity balance can absorb is $80 ($40 ÷ .50). If 50% of an $80 loss is charged against K's equity balance, the balance is brought to zero. A similar calculation can be made for the remaining partners as shown in Exhibit 15-6 on the following page.

EXHIBIT 15-6	SCHEDULE OF MAXIMUM ABSORBABLE LOSS FOR KLM PARTNERSHIP

Partner	Equity Balance		Income-and-Loss-Sharing Ratio		Maximum Absorbable Loss
K	$40	÷	50%	=	$ 80
L	60	÷	30%	=	200
M	20	÷	20%	=	100

Impact of Possible Losses on Equity Balances

The maximum loss absorbable by each partner's equity balance is used to calculate the impact of possible losses on equity balances, which is the second supporting schedule for the installment distribution schedule. The schedule of possible losses on equity balances for the KLM Partnership is shown in Exhibit 15-7. Preparation of such a schedule requires the following four steps:

Step I. Prepare a schedule with one column for each partner. Enter the income-and-loss-sharing ratios and the equity balance for each partner. Each partner's equity balance is calculated as the partner's capital balance increased for any partnership liabilities payable to the partner and decreased for any partnership receivables due from the partner. (This is the same equity balance calculated as the basis for the maximum absorbable loss.)

EXHIBIT 15-7	SCHEDULE OF POSSIBLE LOSSES ON EQUITY BALANCES

KLM Partnership

SCHEDULE OF POSSIBLE LOSSES ON EQUITY BALANCES

		Adjusted Equity Balances		
	Total	Partner K	Partner L	Partner M
Income-and-loss-sharing ratio		50%	30%	20%
Balances before distribution to partners	$(120)*	$ (40)	$ (60)	$ (20)
Loss to eliminate K	80	40	24	16
Balances after elimination of K	$ (40)	$–0–	$ (36)	$ (4)
Additional loss to eliminate M	10		6	4
Balances after elimination of M	$ (30)	$–0–	$ (30)	$–0–
Additional loss to eliminate L	30		30	
Balances after elimination of all partners	$–0–	$–0–	$–0–	$–0–

* Parentheses indicate credits.

Step II. Using the information in the schedule of maximum absorbable loss, identify the partner with the *smallest* maximum absorbable loss and enter that loss in the schedule, distributing it among the partners in the income-and-loss-sharing ratio.

Step III. Identify the partner with the *next smaller* maximum absorbable loss, and calculate the *additional loss* required to bring that partner's remaining equity balance to zero. Remember that partners with zero equity balances are assumed to bear no part of this additional loss. Distribute the additional loss among the partners with nonzero balances in proportion to their income-and-loss-sharing ratios.

Step IV. Repeat step III until only one partner's balance is nonzero, and enter the additional loss to reduce that balance to zero.

Remember that the schedule generated by this procedure is merely an intermediate step on the way to an installment distribution schedule.

Consider the performance of the four-step procedure for KLM Partnership as shown in Exhibit 15-7. Partner K exhibits the smallest maximum absorbable loss, which is $80. This means that all three equity balances can absorb liquidation losses of $80 and that Partner K's equity balance goes to zero with the absorption of an $80 liquidation loss to the partnership. Partner M has the second smallest maximum absorbable loss, which indicates that M's equity balance is the next to go to zero as the loss increases from a level of $80. M's balance after an $80 loss is $4; consequently, an additional loss of $10 ($4 ÷ .40) is sufficient to bring the remaining balance to zero. Observe that M receives 40% (.20 ÷ .50) of the loss once K's balance goes to zero. The increase in M's income-and-loss-sharing ratio is a consequence of assuming that the debit balance in K's equity for losses in excess of $80 is uncollectible and is absorbed by partners whose equity balances are credits. Also observe that M's equity balance goes to zero when the loss reaches $90, which is $10 less than M's maximum absorbable loss. The reason for the $10 discrepancy is that K's debit balance is treated as uncollectible. Partner L exhibits the largest maximum absorbable loss, which indicates that L's equity is the last to go to zero. An additional loss of $30, which is absorbed entirely by L's remaining equity, will reduce that balance to zero.

Calculation of Installment Distribution Schedule

The installment distribution schedule gives the appropriate distribution of cash that is realized from liquidation of the partnership. The installment distribution schedule presented in Exhibit 15-8 on the following page is calculated from the schedule of possible losses on equity balances (Exhibit 15-7). The calculation takes the form of the following five-step procedure:

Step I. Prepare a schedule with one column for each partner, a column for liabilities, and a column for the cash distribution increment.

Step II. Enter the amount of liabilities as the first increment to be distributed, and indicate that 100% of this increment is distributed to satisfy liabilities.

Step III. Enter the loss increment that just eliminates the last equity balance in the schedule of possible losses on equity balances. Indicate that 100% of this increment is distributed to the partner whose balance was last to be eliminated.

EXHIBIT 15-8	INSTALLMENT DISTRIBUTION SCHEDULE

KLM Partnership
INSTALLMENT DISTRIBUTION SCHEDULE

		To Partners		
Cash Distributed	**To Outside Creditors**	**Partner K**	**Partner L**	**Partner M**
First $15	100%	0%	0%	0%
Next $30	0	0	100	0
Next $10	0	0	60	40
Additional amounts	0	50	30	20

Step IV. Enter the loss increment that just eliminates the previously eliminated equity balance in the schedule of possible losses on equity balances. Enter, as the distribution percentages, the ratios in which the increment was applied against equity.

Step V. Repeat step IV—working from bottom to top in the schedule of possible losses on equity balances—until the loss increment is applied against all equity balances. Enter the income-and-loss-sharing ratios as the distribution percentages for this and all additional increments.

Consider the application of the foregoing five-step procedure to calculate the installment distribution schedule for KLM Partnership shown in Exhibit 15-8. The first $15 realized from liquidation of the partnership should be paid to outside creditors as required by law. Additional amounts realized may be paid to partners. Since Partner L has the last equity balance to be eliminated by a rising liquidation loss, as shown in Exhibit 15-7, Partner L should receive 100% of the first $30 paid to partners. If liquidation losses are so large that only $30 is distributed to partners, then Partner L should receive the entire $30. Partners K and M should receive no part of this distribution because the related liquidation loss eliminates their equity balances. A rising liquidation loss eliminates Partner M's equity balance just prior to the elimination of Partner L's equity balance. Consequently, the next $10 distributed to partners in excess of $30 should be divided between L and M in the ratio of their income-and-loss-sharing ratios (30% and 20%). If liquidation losses are so large that only $40 is distributed to partners, then $36 should be paid to L ($36 = $30 + 3/5 of $10) and $4 should be distributed to M ($4 = 2/5 of $10). Partner K should receive no part of this distribution because the related loss entirely eliminates K's equity balance. If more than $40 is available for distribution to partners, then the excess over $40 should be distributed in the partners' income-and-loss-sharing ratios. For example, if $60 is distributed to partners, then L should receive $42 ($30 + 3/5 of $10 + 30% of $20), M should receive $8 (2/5 of $10 + 20% of $20), and K should receive $10 (50% of $20). In essence, once all partners are paid some amount, however small, all subsequent distributions are divided in the income-and-loss-sharing ratio. At this point, the ratio of each partner's capital balance to total capital is the same as the partner's income-and-loss-sharing ratio.

Use of the Installment Distribution Schedule

The reasoning presented in the foregoing paragraph underlies the construction of the installment distribution schedule shown in Exhibit 15-8. The objective of an installment distribution is to pay each dollar as if it were the last dollar to be realized from the liquidation of noncash assets. In other words, the division among the partners of each dollar that is realized equals their equity balances, under the assumption that the unrealized loss will equal the book value of remaining noncash assets. The installment distribution schedule in Exhibit 15-8 specifies that the first $15 available for distribution should be paid to outside creditors. The next $30 realized should be paid to Partner L. The next $10 should be divided between L and M with 60% (.30 ÷ .50) of each dollar paid to L and 40% (.20 ÷ .50) of each dollar paid to M. Each dollar of any additional amounts that are realized should be distributed 50% to K, 30% to L, and 20% to M. In other words, if the liquidation officer has previously distributed $35 according to the schedule and wishes to distribute an additional $20, Partner L should receive $16 ($10 plus 60% of the remaining $10) and Partner M should receive $4 (40% of $10). In this way, the installment distribution schedule and knowledge of past distributions are combined to determine the appropriate distribution of any amount that is available for distribution.

SUMMARY

Partnership liquidations convert all partnership assets into cash (or another distributable form) and distribute the cash to creditors and partners. The claims of outside creditors, including creditors whose claims are created by the liquidation process, have priority over the claims of partners. Since partnership assets are frequently insufficient to pay the full amount of claims against the partnership by both outside creditors and partners, liquidation officers must take care to reserve a sufficient amount of cash to pay claims that have priority over the claims of partners. The job of liquidation officers is particularly complex when partnership assets are distributed in several installments. In order to avoid paying more to a partner than he or she will ultimately receive, the liquidation officer must perform safe-payment calculations or construct an installment distribution schedule.

QUESTIONS

Q15-1 Define the following terms:

a) Liquidation

b) Realizations

c) Liquidation gain or loss

d) Insolvent partnership

e) Insolvent partner

Q15-2 Describe what the liquidation process generally entails.

Q15-3 How are liquidation gains and losses distributed among the partners' capital balances?

Q15-4 What information is normally shown in the "statement of partnership liquidation"?

Q15-5 During partnership liquidation, the allocation of a liquidation loss produces a debit balance in a partner's capital account. Assuming the partner is personally insolvent, how is the partner's debit balance distributed among the capital accounts of the remaining partners?

Q15-6   Discuss why you agree or disagree with the following statement: When a new partner is admitted to the partnership, the new partner is *personally* liable for all partnership obligations incurred prior to his or her admission.

Q15-7   When partnership assets are insufficient to cover liabilities to outside creditors of the partnership, what claim would the partnership creditors have to the personal assets of (a) the solvent partner and (b) the insolvent partner? Discuss.

Q15-8   When making partial distributions during liquidation, care must be exercised to avoid distributing more to a partner than he or she should ultimately receive. To avoid this occurrence, what assumption is made concerning the unrealized portion of partnership noncash assets?

Q15-9   What are the benefits of preparing an installment distribution schedule before the start of liquidation?

Q15-10   Discuss the steps followed in preparing the installment distribution schedule and in preparing the two supporting schedules: the schedule of maximum absorbable loss and the schedule of possible losses on equity balances.

EXERCISES

E15-1   **Liquidation: Single-Step Distribution with One Insolvent Partner, Prepare Statement of Liquidation**   On June 1, 19X4, Harris and Tweed, partners of Sportswear Partnership, decided to liquidate their partnership. At the time of liquidation, the balance sheet accounts consisted of cash, $5,000; noncash assets, $12,000; liabilities to outsiders, $25,000; and capital balances of Harris, $45,000, and Tweed, $55,000.

Harris and Tweed share income and loss in the ratio 3:2, respectively. Harris is personally insolvent. Noncash assets were sold for $30,000.

REQUIRED
Prepare a statement of partnership liquidation.

E15-2   **Safe-Payment Calculation**   It is anticipated that it will take several years to liquidate May Partnership. After selling some of the noncash assets, the accounts of the partnership were as follows:

Assets		Liabilities and Capital	
Cash	$103,000	Accounts payable	$ 38,000
Loan to May	12,000	Loan from Hatfield	10,000
Noncash assets	60,000	May, capital	87,000
		Hatfield, capital	40,000
Total assets	$175,000	Total liabilities and capital	$175,000

May and Hatfield share income and loss in the ratio 1:3, respectively.

REQUIRED
Prepare the safe-payment calculation for the distribution of cash to each partner at this time.

E15-3   **Multiple Choice Questions on Partnership Liquidation**

1. In a partnership liquidation, the final cash distribution to the partners would be made in accordance with the:

a) Partners' income-and-loss-sharing ratio

b) Balances of the partners' capital accounts

c) Ratio of the capital contributions by the partners

d) Ratio of capital contributions less withdrawals by the partners

2. The following balance sheet is for the AdGemDa Partnership. The partners Ad, Gem, and Da share income and losses in the ratio of 5:3:2, respectively.

Cash	$ 30,000
Other assets	270,000
	$300,000
Liabilities	$ 70,000
Ad, capital	140,000
Gem, capital	80,000
Da, capital	10,000
	$300,000

Assuming the original partners agreed to liquidate the partnership by selling the other assets, what should each of the respective partners receive if the other assets are sold for $200,000?

a) Ad, $102,500; Gem, $57,500; Da, $0

b) Ad, $103,000; Gem, $57,000; Da, $0

c) Ad, $105,000; Gem, $59,000; Da, $4,000

d) Ad, $140,000; Gem, $80,000; Da, $10,000

3. Q, R, S, and T are partners sharing income and loss equally. The partnership is insolvent and is to be liquidated. The status of the partnership and each partner is as follows:

	Partnership Capital Balance	Personal Assets (Exclusive of Partnership Interest)	Personal Liabilities (Exclusive of Partnership Interest)
Q	$ 15,000	$100,000	$40,000
R	10,000	30,000	60,000
S	(20,000)	80,000	5,000
T	(30,000)	1,000	28,000
Total	$(25,000)		

Assuming the Uniform Partnership Act applies, the partnership creditors

a) Must first seek recovery against S because he is solvent personally and he has a negative capital balance

b) Will not be paid in full regardless of how they proceed legally because the partnership assets are less than the partnership liabilities

c) Will have to share, with R's personal creditors, R's interest in the partnership on a pro rata basis

d) Have first claim to the partnership assets before any partner's personal creditors have rights to the partnership assets

4. The following condensed balance sheet is presented for the partnership of Lever, Polen, and Quint, who share profits and losses in the ratio of 4:3:3, respectively:

Cash	$ 90,000
Other assets	830,000
Loan to Lever	20,000
	$940,000

Accounts payable	$210,000
Loan from Quint	30,000
Lever, capital	310,000
Polen, capital	200,000
Quint, capital	190,000
	$940,000

Assume the partners decide to liquidate the partnership. If the other assets are sold for $700,000, how much of the available cash should be distributed to Lever?

a) $230,000   c) $258,000

b) $238,000   d) $310,000

5. The partnership of Jenson, Smith, and Hart share profits and losses in the ratio of $5:3:2$, respectively. The partners voted to dissolve the partnership when its assets, liabilities, and capital were as follows:

Assets	
Cash	$ 40,000
Other assets	210,000
Total assets	$250,000

Liabilities and Capital	
Accounts payable	$ 60,000
Jenson, capital	48,000
Smith, capital	72,000
Hart, capital	70,000
Total liabilities and capital	$250,000

The partnership will be liquidated over a prolonged period of time. As cash is available, it will be distributed to the partners. The first sale of noncash assets having a book value of $120,000 realized $90,000. How much cash should be distributed to each partner after this sale?

a) Jenson $0; Smith $28,800; Hart $41,200

b) Jenson $0; Smith $30,000; Hart $40,000

c) Jenson $35,000; Smith $21,000; Hart $14,000

d) Jenson $45,000; Smith $27,000; Hart $18,000

(AICPA adapted)

E15-4   Prepare an Installment Distribution Schedule   Partners Flippen, Banton, and Nelson of Contractors Partnership have capital balances of $45,000, $40,000, and $15,000, and they share income and loss in the ratio of 40%, 40%, and 20%, respectively. The partners have decided to liquidate the partnership. The partnership has no liabilities other than a $15,000 loan from Flippen.

REQUIRED
Prepare an installment distribution schedule, showing how cash will be distributed to the partners as it becomes available.

E15-5   **Liquidation: Single-Step Distribution with One Insolvent Partner, Prepare a Statement of Liquidation**   The balance sheet of Creative Games Partnership immediately prior to liquidation is as follows. Figures shown parenthetically beside the partners' capital accounts reflect the partners' respective income and loss percentage.

Creative Games Partnership
Balance Sheet
March 31, 19X9

Assets		Liabilities and Capital	
Cash	$10,000	Accounts payable	$35,000
Other assets	73,000	Loan from Murdock	10,000
		Fox, capital (30%)	6,000
		Murdock, capital (50%)	30,000
		Hunt, capital (20%)	2,000
Total assets	$83,000	Total liabilities and capital	$83,000

Fox's personal assets exceed his personal liabilities by $30,000; however, Hunt is personally insolvent after paying her creditors. Other assets of the partnership were sold for $43,000 cash.

REQUIRED
Prepare a statement of partnership liquidation.

E15-6   **Safe-Payment Calculation**   Partners A, B, C, and D have been operating ABCD Partnership for ten years. Due to a significant reduction in the demand for their product over recent years, the partners have agreed to liquidate the partnership. At the time of liquidation, balance sheet accounts consisted of cash, $69,000; noncash assets, $200,000; liabilities to outsiders, $40,000; capital credit balances for partners A, B, and C, $60,000, $100,000, and $80,000, respectively; and a debit capital balance for partner D of $11,000. Partners share equally in income and loss. It is estimated that the administrative cost of liquidation will total $3,000. While preparing for liquidation, an unrecorded liability of $5,000 was discovered.

REQUIRED
Prepare the safe-payment calculation for the distribution of cash to each partner at this time.

E15-7   **Prepare an Installment Distribution Schedule**   The partners of Rent-A-Pet Partnership find it financially infeasible to continue operations and have agreed to liquidate the partnership. The balance sheet just prior to the start of liquidation appears here. Partners Collie, Poodle, and Beagle share income and loss in the ratio of 5:3:2, respectively.

Assets		Liabilities and Capital	
Cash	$ 20,000	Accounts payable	$ 30,000
Noncash assets	130,000	Loan from Collie	5,000
		Collie, capital	35,000
		Poodle, capital	60,000
		Beagle, capital	20,000
Total assets	$150,000	Total liabilities and capital	$150,000

REQUIRED
a) Prepare an installment distribution schedule showing how cash will be distributed to the partners as it becomes available.

(Continued on next page)

b) If the first sale of noncash assets having a book value of $75,000 realizes $50,000 and all available cash is distributed, determine the amount of cash to be distributed to each partner.

E15-8   **Multiple Choice Questions on Installment Distributions**   Questions (1) through (3) are based on the following information: The following balance sheet is for the partnership of Able, Boyer, and Cain, who share income and loss in the ratio of 4:4:2, respectively.

Assets		Liabilities and Capital	
Cash	$ 20,000	Liabilities	$ 50,000
Other assets	180,000	Able, capital	37,000
		Boyer, capital	65,000
		Cain, capital	48,000
Total assets	$200,000	Total liabilities and capital	$200,000

1. The firm is dissolved and liquidated by selling assets in installments. If the first sale on noncash assets having a book value of $90,000 realizes $50,000 and all cash available after settlement with creditors is distributed, the respective partners would receive (to the nearest dollar)

a) Able, $8,000; Boyer, $8,000; Cain, $4,000

b) Able, $6,667; Boyer, $6,667; Cain, $6,666

c) Able, $0; Boyer, $13,333; Cain, $6,667

d) Able, $0; Boyer, $3,000; Cain, $17,000

2. If the facts are as in question (1) except that $3,000 cash is to be withheld, the respective partners would then receive (to the nearest dollar)

a) Able, $6,800; Boyer, $6,800; Cain, $3,400

b) Able, $5,667; Boyer, $5,667; Cain, $5,666

c) Able, $0; Boyer, $11,333; Cain, $5,667

d) Able, $0; Boyer, $1,000; Cain, $16,000

3. If each partner properly received some cash in the distribution after the second sale, the cash to be distributed amounts to $12,000 from the third sale, and unsold assets with an $8,000 book value remain [ignore questions (1) and (2)], the respective partners would receive

a) Able, $4,800; Boyer, $4,800; Cain, $2,400

b) Able, $4,000; Boyer, $4,000; Cain, $4,000

c) Able, 37/150 of $12,000; Boyer, 65/150 of $12,000; Cain, 48/150 of $12,000

d) Able, $0; Boyer, $8,000; Cain, $4,000

(AICPA adapted)

E15-9   **Multiple Choice Questions on Installment Distributions**   Questions (1) through (4) are based on the following information: Partners Blake, Pulley, and Reed, who share income and loss in the ratio 3:5:2, respectively, have decided to liquidate their partnership. At the time of liquidation, the balance sheet of the partnership consisted of the following:

Assets		Liabilities and Capital	
Cash	$ 40,000	Accounts payable	$ 31,000
Other assets	120,000	Loan from Pulley	10,000
		Blake, capital	36,000
		Pulley, capital	40,000
		Reed, capital	43,000
Total assets	$160,000	Total liabilities and capital	$160,000

The partners desire to prepare an installment distribution schedule showing how cash would be distributed to partners as assets are realized.

1. In the schedule of maximum absorbable loss, the maximum absorbable loss for each partner would be

    a) Blake, $120,000; Pulley, $ 80,000; Reed, $215,000

    b) Blake, $100,000; Pulley, $200,000; Reed, $ 75,000

    c) Blake, $150,000; Pulley, $175,000; Reed, $125,000

    d) Blake, $120,000; Pulley, $100,000; Reed, $215,000

2. The schedule of possible losses on capital balances would indicate that the first cash distributed, after the payment of outside creditors, would be distributed to (and in the amount of)

    a) Blake in the amount of $16,000

    b) Pulley in the amount of $20,000

    c) Reed in the amount of $19,000

    d) Reed in the amount of $10,000

3. If the first sale of other assets having a book value of $50,000 realized $15,000 and all available cash is distributed, the respective partners would receive

    a) Blake, $0; Pulley, $6,000; Reed, $18,000

    b) Blake, $3,000; Pulley, $0; Reed, $21,000

    c) Blake, $8,000; Pulley, $8,000; Reed, $8,000

    d) Blake, $21,000; Pulley, $0; Reed, $3,000

4. If the second sale of other assets (assume previous first sale facts) having a book value of $30,000 realized $40,000 and all available cash is distributed, the respective partners would receive

    a) Blake, $13,500; Pulley, $17,500; Reed, $9,000

    b) Blake, $6,000; Pulley, $0; Reed, $4,000

    c) Blake, $3,000; Pulley, $5,000; Reed, $2,000

    d) Blake, $0; Pulley, $6,000; Reed, $4,000

E15-10 **Prepare an Installment Distribution Schedule** The Walker, Wilson, and Winston Partnership is being liquidated. All liabilities have been paid. The balance of assets on hand is being realized gradually. The following are details of partners' accounts:

	Capital Account Balances	Drawing Account Balances	Loans to Partnership	Income-and- Loss-Sharing Ratio
Walker	$20,000	$1,500 Cr.	$15,000	4
Wilson	25,000	2,000 Dr.	—	4
Winston	10,000	1,000 Cr.	5,000	2

REQUIRED

Prepare an installment distribution schedule, showing how cash should be distributed to the partners as it becomes available.

(AICPA adapted)

PROBLEMS

P15-1 **Liquidation: Single-Step Distribution with One Insolvent Partner, Prepare a Statement of Liquidation** The Larimore-Bailey Partnership has just completed a very unprofitable year. The partners agree to liquidate. The financial statements of the partnership have been prepared for the fiscal year ending December 31, 19X2, and the year-end balance sheet appears as follows:

Assets

Cash		$ 1,000
Accounts receivable	$ 80,000	
Less: Allowance for uncollectibles	20,000	60,000
Merchandise inventory		50,000
Prepaid advertising		2,000
Machinery and equipment	$100,000	
Less: Accumulated depreciation	60,000	40,000
Total assets		$153,000

Liabilities and Capital

Accounts payable	$ 20,000
Notes payable (due 19X4)	86,000
Larimore, capital	30,000
Bailey, capital	17,000
Total liabilities and capital	$153,000

The partners desired to complete the liquidation process as quickly as possible. Information concerning liquidation:

1. Accounts receivable equal to the net carrying value plus 20% of the estimated uncollectibles were collected.

2. Merchandise inventory realized $25,000 of its carrying value.

3. The prepaid advertising contract has a cancellation value of $800.

4. Machinery and equipment realized 60% of its book value.

5. Unrecorded accounts payable totaling $2,000 were discovered.

6. The bank charged $1,000 for paying the note earlier than the due date; the amount is added to the note.

Larimore is personally insolvent. However, Bailey's personal assets exceed her personal liabilities by $4,000. Larimore and Bailey share an income and loss in the ratio of 4:6, respectively.

REQUIRED

a) Prepare a schedule showing the net amount of liquidation gain or loss.

b) Prepare a statement of partnership liquidation.

P15-2 **Liquidation: Single-Step Distribution with Partnership and One Partner Insolvent, Prepare a Statement of Liquidation** X, Y, and Z partners share an income and loss in the ratio of 4:3:2, respectively. Two of the partners, Y and Z, are currently unable to pay their personal creditors in full. The firm's balance sheet and the personal status of the partners are as follows:

X, Y, Z Partnership
Balance Sheet

Assets		Liabilities and Capital	
Cash	$ 500	Accounts payable	$37,000
Other assets	60,500	X, capital	10,000
		Y, capital	6,000
		Z, capital	8,000
Total assets	$61,000	Total liabilities and capital	$61,000

PERSONAL STATUS OF PARTNERS
(EXCLUDING PARTNERSHIP INTERESTS)

Partner	Cash and Cash Value of Personal Assets	Liabilities
X	$31,000	$20,000
Y	9,450	11,900
Z	4,000	5,000

REQUIRED

a) Assuming "other assets" of the partnership are sold for $33,500, prepare a statement of partnership liquidation.

b) Prepare a schedule showing the settlement of partners with their personal creditors according to provisions of the Uniform Partnership Act.

c) Determine the minimum amount that would have to be realized from the sale of "other assets" to allow the personal creditors of Partner Y to receive full settlement of their claims.

(AICPA adapted)

P15-3 **Liquidation: Installment Distributions, Determine Safe-Payment Calculations, and Prepare Partial Statement of Liquidation** Partners Hall, Lambert, and Sheffield of Partlow Communications Center have decided to liquidate their partnership. At the time of liquidation, balance sheet amounts consisted of cash, $10,000; other assets, $100,000; accounts payable, $8,000; and partners' accounts as follows:

Loan from Hall	$ 5,000
Loan from Sheffield	2,000
Hall, capital	30,000
Lambert, capital	40,000
Sheffield, capital	25,000

The partners agreed to distribute partnership cash as it becomes available. Hall, Lambert, and Sheffield share income and loss in the ratio of 3:2:5, respectively. In the first sale of other assets, one-fourth of the assets were sold for $10,000. In the second sale of other assets, a gain of $10,000 was realized. Other assets on hand, after the preceding sales, totaled $45,000. All partners are personally insolvent.

REQUIRED

Prepare a partial statement of partnership liquidation with supporting safe-payment calculations showing the amount of cash to be distributed to each partner after each of the two sales of other assets. Accounts payable are paid in full after the first sale of assets.

P15-4 **Liquidation: Installment Distributions with All Partners Insolvent, Determine Safe-Payment Calculations, Prepare Partial Statement of Liquidation** Partners Cates, Flowers, and Talley, who share income and loss in the ratio of 30%, 20% and 50%, respectively, have decided to liquidate their partnership. At the time of liquidation, balance sheet amounts consisted of cash, $20,000; other assets, $220,000; accounts payable, $35,000; and partners' accounts as follows:

Loan from Cates	$10,000
Loan from Talley	5,000
Cates, capital	60,000
Flowers, capital	80,000
Talley, capital	50,000

In the first sale of other assets, one-fourth of the assets were sold for $25,000. In the second sale of other assets, a $90,000 loss was incurred. Other assets on hand, after the preceding sales, totaled $30,000. All partners are personally insolvent.

REQUIRED
Prepare a partial statement of partnership liquidation with supporting safe-payment calculations showing the amount of cash that can be distributed to each partner after each of the two sales of other assets.

P15-5   **Record Initial Capital Investments, Allocate Income and Prepare Entry to Record Allocation, Admission of Partner by Investment, and Prepare Installment Distribution Schedule and Distribute Cash**   Jordan and Bird formed Sports Unlimited Partnership on January 1, 19X4. Jordan and Bird had been operating as sole proprietors. The book values and the fair values of the contributions to be made by each of the partners, as agreed upon by the partners, are as follows:

	Jordan	
	Book Value	**Fair Value**
Cash	$15,000	$15,000
Accounts receivable (net)	22,000	20,000
Inventory	45,000	66,000
Machinery and equipment (net)	70,000	90,000

	Bird	
	Book Value	**Fair Value**
Cash	$ 7,000	$ 7,000
Accounts receivable (net)	5,000	5,000
Inventory	30,000	38,000
Machinery and equipment (net)	28,000	35,000
Building	32,000	65,000

The partnership is to assume accounts payable of Jordan and Bird in the amounts of $16,000 and $25,000, respectively.

Partners Jordan and Bird agree that partnership income is to be divided as follows: salaries of $19,000 and $26,000 to Jordan and Bird, respectively; a 5% interest on the partners' beginning-of-the-year capital balances; a bonus to Bird of 10% of net income (after deducting the bonus but before deducting salaries and interest); and the remainder divided between Jordan and Bird in a ratio of 5:3, respectively.

During the first year of operations ending December 31, 19X4, the partnership reported net income of $55,000.

During the years subsequent to the year of formation of the partnership, the growth in sales of the partnership did not meet the partners' expectations. By September 1, 19X7, the partnership was in desperate need of cash. In light of this, the partners agreed to admit Thomas as a partner with a one-fifth interest in the partnership upon his investment of $30,000. The balance sheet of the partnership at September 1, 19X7, was as presented below. On September 1, 19X7, the assets and liabilities of the partnership were fairly valued except for land that is undervalued by $8,000. Partnership assets are to be revalued, and Thomas is to be admitted under the goodwill method.

Sports Unlimited Partnership
Balance Sheet
September 1, 19X7

Assets

Cash	$ 10,000
Land	40,000
Other assets	205,000
Total assets	$255,000

Liabilities and Capital

Accounts payable	$100,000
Jordan, capital	96,500
Bird, capital	58,500
Total liabilities and capital	$255,000

After the admission of Thomas to the partnership, it was agreed by the partners that all income and loss of the partnership would be allocated to Jordan, Bird, and Thomas in the ratio 5:3:2, respectively. The partners continued to operate the partnership for several more years; however, due to a significant reduction in the demand for their product, the partners decided on October 15, 19X9, to liquidate the partnership. At the time of liquidation, balance sheet accounts consisted of the following balances:

Assets		Liabilities and Capital	
Cash	$ 10,000	Accounts payable	$ 30,500
Loan to Thomas	4,000	Loan from Bird	10,000
Noncash assets	166,000	Jordan, capital	70,500
		Bird, capital	50,000
		Thomas, capital	19,000
Total assets	$180,000	Total liabilities and capital	$180,000

Since the partnership is to be liquidated over a prolonged period of time, the partners agreed to prepare an installment distribution showing how cash would be distributed to partners as assets are realized.

REQUIRED

a) Prepare the entries on January 1, 19X4, to record investments in the partnership by Jordan and Bird with each partner's capital credited for the full amount of net assets invested.

b) Determine the allocation of partnership net income for the year ended December 31, 19X4, to Jordan and Bird; and prepare the entry to record the allocation to individual capital accounts.

c) Prepare the entries on the books of the partnership on September 1, 19X7, to record the revaluation of the land and the admission of Thomas to the partnership.

d) Prepare an installment distribution schedule as of October 15, 19X9, showing how cash will be distributed to the partners as it becomes available.

e) Assuming that during liquidation the first sale on October 20, 19X9, of noncash assets having a book value of $48,000 brought in $42,000 and assuming that all cash available is distributed, determine the amount of cash, if any, that each partner would receive.

P15-6   Prepare an Installment Distribution Schedule, and Distribute Cash under Varying Conditions
Partners Dascher, Benjamin, and DePaul of DePaul Partnership have decided to dissolve their partnership. All partners are personally insolvent. Due to the specialized nature of the activities of the partnership, it is expected to take eight months to complete liquidation. The partners agree that partnership cash is to be distributed among partners when it becomes available. The partnership balance sheet prior to the start of liquidation follows. Figures shown parenthetically beside the partners' capital accounts reflect the income-and-loss-sharing ratio.

Assets		*Liabilities and Capital*	
Cash	$ 30,000	Accounts payable	$ 40,000
Noncash assets	146,000	Loan from Dascher	10,000
		Dascher, capital (40%)	30,000
		Benjamin, capital (30%)	60,000
		DePaul, capital (30%)	36,000
Total assets	$176,000	Total liabilities and capital	$176,000

REQUIRED

a) Prepare an installment distribution schedule showing how cash will be distributed to the partners as it becomes available.

b) Prepare answers to each of the following independent questions:

1. DePaul received $2,000 on the first distribution of cash. How much cash did Dascher and Benjamin receive?

2. Dascher received $4,000 from the total liquidation. How much was the gain or loss on realization of noncash assets?

3. Benjamin received $39,000 from total liquidation. How much cash did Dascher and DePaul receive?

4. If $156,000 was realized from noncash assets, how much cash did each partner receive from total liquidation?

P15-7   Prepare an Installment Distribution Schedule, and Distribute Cash   The partners of Able, Bright, Cool, and Dahl have decided to dissolve their partnership. They plan to sell the assets gradually in order to minimize losses. They share income and loss as follows: Able, 40%; Bright, 35%; Cool, 15%; Dahl, 10%. Presented here is the partnership's trial balance as of October 1, 19X1, the date on which liquidation begins.

	Debit	Credit
Cash	$ 200	$
Receivables	25,900	
Inventory, Oct. 1, 19X1	42,600	
Equipment (net)	19,800	
Accounts payable		3,000
Loan from Able		6,000
Loan from Bright		10,000
Able, capital		20,000
Bright, capital		21,500
Cool, capital		18,000
Dahl, capital		10,000
	$88,500	$88,500

REQUIRED

a) Prepare an installment distribution schedule as of October 1, 19X1, showing how cash will be distributed to partners as it becomes available.

b) On October 31, 19X1, cash of $12,700 became available to creditors and partners. How should it be distributed?

(AICPA adapted)

P15-8 **Liquidation: Installment Distributions, Prepare an Installment Distribution Schedule and a Partial Statement of Liquidation** The partners of Sims and Company agreed to dissolve their partnership and to begin liquidation on February 1, 19X3. Rowe was designated as the partner in charge of liquidation. It was agreed that distributions of cash to the partners were to be made on the last day of each month during liquidation, providing that there was sufficient cash available. The partnership agreement provided that income and loss were to be shared on the following basis: Quinn, 20%; Rowe, 30%; Sims, 30%; and Tot, 20%. The firm's condensed balance sheet as of February 1, 19X3, was as follows:

Assets		Liabilities and Capital	
Cash	$33,440	Accounts payable	$ 7,120
Goodwill	20,000	Loan from Quinn	5,000
Other assets	44,510	Quinn, capital	8,040
		Rowe, capital	32,160
		Sims, capital	36,340
		Tot, capital	9,290
Total assets	$97,950	Total liabilities and capital	$97,950

The liquidating transactions for February and March other than cash disbursements to partners are summarized by months as follows:

	February	March
Liquidation of assets with book value of:		
$22,020	$16,440	
14,950		$16,110
Paid liquidation expenses	2,740	2,460
Paid creditors on account (excluding partner loan)	5,910	1,210

REQUIRED

Prepare a partial statement of partnership liquidation showing the amount of cash distributed to each partner at the end of February and March. Also prepare a supporting installment distribution schedule. Round all amounts to the nearer dollar.

(AICPA adapted)

P15-9   Prepare an Installment Distribution Schedule, and Distribute Cash   The partners Adams, Baker, and Crane have called upon you to assist them in winding up the affairs of their partnership. You are able to gather the following information:

1. The trial balance of the partnership at June 30, 19X2, is as follows:

	Debit	Credit
Cash	$ 6,000	$
Accounts receivable	22,000	
Inventory	14,000	
Plant and equipment (net)	99,000	
Loan to Adams	12,000	
Loan to Crane	7,500	
Accounts payable		17,000
Adams, capital		67,000
Baker, capital		45,000
Crane, capital		31,500
	$160,500	$160,500

2. The partners share income and loss as follows: Adams, 50%; Baker, 30%; and Crane, 20%.

3. The partners are considering an offer of $100,000 for the accounts receivable, inventory, and plant and equipment as of June 30. The $100,000 would be paid to the partners in installments, the number and amounts of which are to be negotiated.

REQUIRED

a) Prepare an installment distribution schedule as of June 30, 19X2, showing how the $100,000 would be distributed as it becomes available.

b) Assume the same facts as in part (a) except that the partners have decided to liquidate their partnership instead of accepting the offer of $100,000. Cash is distributed to the partners at the end of each month. A summary of the liquidation transactions follows:

July:

    $16,500—collected on accounts receivable, balance is uncollectible
    $10,000—received for the entire inventory
    $ 1,000—liquidation expenses paid
    $ 8,000—cash retained in the business at end of the month

August:

    $1,500—liquidation expenses paid
    As a part of his capital, Crane accepted a piece of special equipment he had developed, which had a book value of $4,000. The partners agreed that a value of $10,000 should be placed on the machine for liquidation purposes.
    $2,500—cash retained in the business at the end of the month

September:

    $75,000—received on sale of remaining plant and equipment
    $ 1,000—liquidation expenses paid
    No cash retained in the business

Prepare a schedule showing the amount of cash distributed to each partner at the end of July, August, and September.

(AICPA adapted)

P15-10 **Liquidation: Installment Distributions with All Partners Solvent, Determine Safe Calculations, Prepare Statement of Liquidation** On January 1, 19X2, the partners of Allen, Brown, and Cox, who share profits and losses in the ratio of 5:3:2, respectively, decide to liquidate their partnership. The partnership trial balance at this date is as follows:

	Debit	Credit
Cash	$ 18,000	$
Accounts receivable	66,000	
Inventory	52,000	
Machinery and equipment (net)	189,000	
Loan to Allen	30,000	
Accounts payable		53,000
Loan from Brown		20,000
Allen, capital		118,000
Brown, capital		90,000
Cox, capital		74,000
	$355,000	$355,000

The partners plan a program of piecemeal conversion of assets in order to minimize liquidation losses. All available cash, less an amount retained to provide for future expenses, is to be distributed to the partners at the end of each month. A summary of the liquidation transactions is as follows:

January:
   a) $51,000 was collected on accounts receivable; the balance is uncollectible.
   b) $38,000 was received for the entire inventory.
   c) $ 2,000 liquidation expenses were paid.
   d) $50,000 was paid to outside creditors, after offset of a $3,000 credit memorandum received on January 11, 19X2.
   e) $10,000 cash was retained in the business at the end of the month for potential unrecorded liabilities and anticipated expenses.

February 19X2:
   f) $ 4,000 liquidation expenses were paid.
   g) $ 6,000 cash was retained in the business at the end of the month for potential unrecorded liabilities and anticipated expenses.

March 19X2:
   h) $146,000 was received on sale of all items of machinery and equipment.
   i) $ 5,000 liquidation expenses were paid.
   j) No cash was retained in the business.

REQUIRED
Prepare a statement of partnership liquidation with supporting safe-payment calculations showing the amount of cash to be distributed to each partner at the end of January, February, and March.

(AICPA adapted)

ISSUES IN ACCOUNTING JUDGMENT

I15-1 **Recovery under Conditions of Insolvency** The insolvent partnership of Comstock, Bowman, and Glassey is undergoing liquidation. All noncash assets have been converted into cash, and the resulting loss has been distributed equally among the partners' capital accounts. The liquidation officer prepares the following schedule of balances from the partnership liquidation records and the personal financial statements of the partners:

	Partnership Capital Balance	Personal Balance Sheet	
		Assets	Liabilities
Mr. Comstock	$(26,000)	$ 50,000	$72,000
Mr. Bowman	(38,000)	96,000	70,000
Ms. Glassey	27,000	120,000	54,000

No liabilities of the partnership are owed to partners. The amounts taken from the partners' personal financial statements are current values and include no partnership assets or liabilities.

REQUIRED

a) Discuss the partnership creditors' prospects for collecting the amounts they are owed.

b) Discuss the partner creditors' prospects for collecting the amounts they are owed.

c) How much will Ms. Glassey lose as a result of this partnership liquidation?

I15-2 **Liquidation Provisions in Partnership Agreement**   Jane Berghoff and Alex Fritzel are negotiating an agreement as the basis for forming a new partnership to operate a restaurant. Berghoff has considerably greater personal resources than Fritzel and would invest twice as much capital in the partnership as Fritzel. The two partners have agreed to pay a generous rate of interest on capital balances and to share all remaining income or loss equally. In addition, they have agreed to the same dollars-per-period restriction on their drawing accounts. The partners have not been able to agree on a provision for the distribution of liquidation gains and losses. Distribution in the income-and-loss-sharing ratio and distribution in the ratio of capital balances are both under discussion. Assume that the partners hold the same view of the future prospects for the partnership and that both expect the partnership will be profitable and result in the distribution of gains at liquidation.

REQUIRED

a) How do you think Ms. Berghoff would want liquidation gains or losses distributed? Explain.

b) How do you think Mr. Fritzel would want liquidation gains or losses distributed? Explain.

c) If you were an accountant advising the two partners, what would you propose to resolve this dispute?

CHAPTER 16

Accounting for Branches

BRANCH ACCOUNTING SYSTEMS 781

ACCOUNTING FOR BRANCH TRANSACTIONS 782

BRANCH INVESTMENT AND HOME OFFICE ACCOUNTS 782

TRANSFERS FROM HOME OFFICE TO BRANCH 783
Transfers of Cash 783 Transfers of Merchandise 783 Freight on Transferred Merchandise 785 Fixed Asset Transfers 785 Transfers of Expense 786

BRANCH OPERATING TRANSACTIONS AND TRANSFERS TO HOME OFFICE 787

END-OF-PERIOD REPORTING BY BRANCH AND CLOSING PROCEDURES 787
Branch Reporting and Closing Procedures 787 Recording Branch Income by Home Office 788

PREPARATION OF COMBINED FINANCIAL STATEMENTS 790

WORKSHEET FOR COMBINED FINANCIAL STATEMENTS 790
Elimination of Current Year's Branch Income 792 Elimination of Branch Investment and Home Office Accounts 792 Completion of Worksheet 792 Worksheet Adjustments for Omitted Entries and Errors 793

COMBINED FINANCIAL STATEMENTS 794

MERCHANDISE TRANSFERS BILLED IN EXCESS OF COST 794

RECORDING MERCHANDISE TRANSFERS FROM HOME OFFICE TO BRANCH BILLED IN EXCESS OF COST 796
Entries by Home Office to Record Merchandise Transfers 796 Year-End Adjustments by Home Office of Allowance for Unrealized Gross Margin in Branch Inventory 797 Merchandise Transfers Billed at Selling Price 798

COMBINATION WORKSHEET WHEN MERCHANDISE TRANSFERS ARE BILLED IN EXCESS OF COST 798
Elimination of Current Year's Branch Income 800 Elimination of Branch Investment and Home Office Accounts 800 Elimination of Unrealized Gross Margin in Branch Inventory 801 Combined Financial Statements 801 Separate Financial Statements 801 Treatment of the Beginning Branch Inventory 801

MULTIPLE BRANCHES 804

INTERBRANCH TRANSFERS 804

SUMMARY 805

A company may establish branches for a variety of reasons. Branches provide a way to decentralize operations without conferring a high level of autonomy on the branches. Further, branches may be used to expand the firm's sales efforts into new markets. Branches are frequently seen as alternatives to the establishment of a traveling sales force operated from a corporate headquarters or to the acquisition of firms already operating in the new market.

When a company is composed of a home office and branches, a distinct accounting system is frequently maintained for each branch as well as for the home office. Such accounting systems are characterized by two levels of financial reporting. Reports may be prepared to reflect the records of the home office or branch as separate entities, or reports may be prepared to reflect the aggregate of all records for the entire company. The preparation of such a company's financial statements presents a variety of aggregation problems with which this chapter is concerned.

Following a description of some of the possible variations in branch accounting systems, this chapter describes accounting for branch transactions on the records of both the home office and its branch. The chapter then turns to the preparation of financial statements for the home office and its branches, both as separate entities and as a single, combined entity. Next, the chapter illustrates accounting for merchandise transfers to branches that are billed in excess of cost. The chapter concludes with brief discussions of multiple branch systems and interbranch transfers.

BRANCH ACCOUNTING SYSTEMS

Branch accounting systems range from simple memorandum records to complete double-entry accounting systems. The structure of particular systems depends on the autonomy and transactions authority given to a branch by its home office. The degree of autonomy granted a branch varies greatly from one company to another and even from one branch to another within the same company. Some branches are empowered to enter virtually any operating transaction without the express approval or involvement of the home office and to report to the home office on a monthly, quarterly, or even annual basis. In contrast, other branches are authorized to enter only specified operating transactions, and most such transactions may require the express approval or direct involvement of the home office. In addition, the branch may be required to report its transactions to the home office on a weekly or even daily basis. A branch accounting system must accommodate the particular set of transactions that the branch is authorized to enter and must also enable the home office to implement financial controls over branch activities. Branch accounting policies for receivables, inventories, and fixed assets are subject to a particularly wide variation. The following issues section describes such variations in branch accounting systems and also a special kind of branch called a sales agency.

ISSUES

Variations in Branch Accounting Systems

ACCOUNTING FOR RECEIVABLES

The role of the branch in credit sales and collections on account may be restricted in a variety of ways. Some branches must secure home office approval for each credit sale, and all collections on account are made by the home office. In such cases, the branch does not maintain accounts receivable records. Other branches may be authorized to sell and collect on account, provided that customers' names are on an approved-customer list; such branches must maintain accounts receivable records.

ACCOUNTING FOR INVENTORIES

The role of the branch in transfers of merchandise may also be restricted. Some branches carry a line of samples but are precluded from carrying an inventory of merchandise. In such cases, merchandise is shipped to branch customers directly from the home office and the branch does not maintain inventory records. Other branches may carry an inventory of merchandise for shipment to customers. In that case, the branch must maintain inventory records.

ACCOUNTING FOR FIXED ASSETS

A branch may or may not be authorized to purchase fixed assets. Further, a branch may or may not be authorized to maintain fixed asset accounts. A highly autonomous branch will have authority both to purchase fixed assets and to maintain fixed asset accounts. On the other hand, if the home office dominates the acquisition of fixed assets, then branch fixed assets are not apt to be maintained by the branch. Instead, the branch fixed assets are recorded in the fixed asset accounts of the home office.

SALES AGENCIES

Sales agencies represent a special class of branches whose authority to enter transactions is so restricted that a complete double-entry accounting system is not required to record them. A typical sales agency is restricted to carrying samples of the merchandise inventoried by the home office and to taking orders, which are forwarded to the home office for delivery to customers. Thus, the home office collects all cash from customers and approves all customer credit. The home office provides cash to the agency for operating expenses. This cash is replenished when necessary, sometimes on an imprest basis. The accounting records of a sales agency may be a simple cash record with a provision for requesting reimbursements from the home office. In addition, a sales register may be useful, but complete double-entry records are not required. Except for a year-end adjustment to record unreimbursed expenditures by the agency, the financial position and operating results of the agency are fully reflected by the home office records. The remainder of this chapter is devoted to branches for which complete double-entry records are required.

ACCOUNTING FOR BRANCH TRANSACTIONS

A branch and its home office represent two accounting systems but just one accounting entity. All transactions entered in the accounting system of the branch are also entered, at least in summary form, in the accounting system of the home office. Further, although separate financial statements can be prepared for the home office and its branch for internal management purposes, only the combined financial statements of the entire entity are issued to parties outside the company.

Branch Investment and Home Office Accounts

Branch and home office records are linked together by two accounts: the investment in branch account, which appears on the home office records, and the home office account, which appears on the branch records. The *home office account,* on the branch records, is like an ownership equity account in that it represents the equity of the home office in the net assets of the branch. The home office account reflects all transfers from the branch to the home office and vice versa. In addition, branch net income (loss) is closed to the home office account. The *investment in branch account,* on the home office records, is an asset account that is reciprocal to the corresponding home office account on the branch records. For example, when the home office transfers cash to the branch, the home office credits cash and debits *investment in branch.* Correspondingly, the branch debits cash and credits *home office.* In this way, the home office account and investment in branch account are *reciprocal accounts,* which means that they display the same numerical balance, although one balance is a debit and the other is a credit. Of course, reciprocal accounts may display different numerical balances temporarily, owing to omitted recordings or errors, but reciprocity must be restored at the end of the accounting period before the preparation of financial statements. When combined (corporate) financial statements are prepared for the home office and its branch, the home office account and the investment in branch account are offset against one another and thereby eliminated from the combined statements.

The relationship between the separate branch and home office records and their year-end combination is demonstrated by reference to an illustration. Consider Wilsonville Branch established in Wilsonville, New York, on January 1, 19X1, by Storr Manufacturing, Inc., whose home office is located in Newark, New Jersey. Exhibit 16-1 on the following page summarizes all events affecting the Wilsonville Branch during 19X1 and shows their effect on both the branch and home office records. For purposes of emphasizing the general character of these events, we have divided them into four groups: (1) transfers from the home office to the branch, (2) operating transactions of the branch, (3) transfers from the branch to the home office, and (4) end-of-period reporting by the branch and closing entries. Each group has distinctive accounting characteristics that the following paragraphs explain.

Transfers from Home Office to Branch

Transfers of monetary or physical assets, like cash or merchandise, from the home office to the branch are recorded by both accounting systems as the transfers occur. Transfers of services or other intangible benefits, like insurance coverage and depreciation expense, are usually recorded by the branch upon notification from the home office.

Transfers of Cash

The Wilsonville Branch is established by a cash transfer of $3,000 from the home office of Storr Manufacturing. The recording of the transfer is shown as entry (1) in Exhibit 16-1. As a result of the transfer, the home office establishes a branch investment account and the branch establishes a home office account.

Transfers of Merchandise

The home office in our illustration also transfers merchandise to the branch that augments the branch investment account and the home office account as shown by entry (2) in Exhibit 16-1. Storr bills Wilsonville Branch for the cost of transferred merchandise, and both the home office and branch use a perpetual inventory system. Accordingly, the home office credits inventory for the cost of $12,000 and the branch debits inventory for the $12,000 cost billed to it by the home office. A perpetual inventory system is assumed throughout this chapter unless otherwise stated.[1]

---

[1] If the home office had used a periodic inventory system, then the home office would credit a *shipments to branch account* rather than an inventory account. In the calculation of home office cost of goods sold, the shipments to branch account is subtracted along with the ending inventory. Similarly, if the branch had used a periodic inventory system, the branch would debit a *shipments from home office account* rather than an inventory account. In the calculation of branch cost of goods sold, the shipments from home office account is added along with purchases from sources outside the company and beginning inventory. In order to simplify the presentation of both branch and combined financial statements, we have restricted illustrations, exercises, and problems throughout this book to perpetual inventory systems.

EXHIBIT 16-1	RECORDING BRANCH TRANSACTIONS ON BRANCH AND HOME OFFICE RECORDS

Transactions of Wilsonville Branch

(BRANCH OF STORR MANUFACTURING, INC.)
FOR THE YEAR ENDED DECEMBER 31, 19X1

Home Office Records			Branch Records		

Transfers from Home Office to Branch

(1) *Home office sends $3,000 cash to branch:*

Home Office Records			Branch Records		
Investment in branch	3,000		Cash	3,000	
Cash		3,000	Home office		3,000

(2) *Home office ships merchandise with a cost of $12,000 to branch; the merchandise is billed at cost:*

Investment in branch	12,000		Inventory (shipments from home office)	12,000	
Inventory (shipments to branch)		12,000	Home office		12,000

(3) *Home office purchases equipment for $3,600 cash and transfers it to the branch; branch does not maintain fixed asset accounts:*

Equipment	3,600		No entry		
Cash		3,600			

(4) *Home office incurs and notifies the branch of operating expenses totaling $900 to benefit the branch; $250 represents depreciation on branch equipment, and the remainder represents cash outlays for various operating expenses:*

Investment in branch	900		Depreciation expense	250	
Accumulated depreciation		250	Other expenses	650	
Cash		650	Home office		900

Operating Transactions of Branch

(5) *Branch sells merchandise for $16,000 on account; merchandise costs branch $8,000:*

No entry			Accounts receivable	16,000	
			Sales		16,000
			Cost of goods sold	8,000	
			Inventory		8,000

(6) *Branch collects $11,000 on account:*

No entry			Cash	11,000	
			Accounts receivable		11,000

(7) *Branch pays operating expenses of $2,500 in cash:*

No entry			Other expenses	2,500	
			Cash		2,500

(8) *Branch purchases equipment for $800 and notifies home office of purchase; branch does not maintain fixed asset accounts:*

Equipment	800		Home office	800	
Investment in branch		800	Cash		800

(9) *Branch determines that ending inventory has a cost of $4,000:*

No entry			No entry		

Transfers from Branch to Home Office

(10) *Branch transfers $10,000 cash to home office:*

Cash	10,000		Home office	10,000	
Investment in branch		10,000	Cash		10,000

End-of-Period Reporting by Branch to Home Office and Closing Entries

(11) *Branch reports operating income of $4,600 for the period to the home office:*

Investment in branch	4,600		No entry		
Income from branch		4,600			

(12) *Home office and branch prepare closing entries for period:*

Income from branch	4,600		Sales	16,000	
Income summary		4,600	Cost of goods sold		8,000
			Depreciation expense		250
			Other expenses		3,150
			Income summary		4,600
			Income summary	4,600	
			Home office		4,600

Freight on Transferred Merchandise

Transfers of merchandise from the home office to the branch frequently occasion freight costs. Although the treatment of such freight costs on shipments to branches varies in practice, we will assume throughout this chapter and in problems and exercises that branches debit a freight-in account for freight costs incurred on shipments from its home office. In other words, we assume that branches do not debit such freight costs to inventory. Similarly, when the home office incurs freight costs on shipments to a branch, we assume that the freight costs are not to be recorded in the inventory. Instead, the home office debits the investment in branch account for the freight costs and credits the means of payment. If the home office bills freight to its branch, then the branch should debit its freight-in account for the freight cost incurred and billed by the home office and credit the home office account. The freight-in account is reported among the expenses. Although it may be technically correct to allocate some portion of freight-in cost to the ending inventory, we will assume throughout this chapter that it is not necessary to do so.[2]

Fixed Asset Transfers

The purchase of equipment by the home office for use by the branch is recorded in the usual way by the home office, except that branch equipment may be entered in a separate account (e.g., ''Equipment-Branch''). If a branch does not maintain fixed asset accounts, then the transfer of the equipment to the branch occasions no entry by either the branch or the home office. If a branch maintains fixed asset accounts, however, then the transfer of equipment to the branch occasions entries by both the home office and its branch. To illustrate, suppose that a home office acquires new equipment for its branch that maintains fixed asset accounts. The equipment is purchased for $22,000 cash, and the following entries are appropriate:

Home office entry to record transfer of new equipment to a branch that maintains fixed asset accounts:

Investment in branch	22,000	
Cash		22,000

Branch entry to record receipt of new equipment from home office:

Equipment	22,000	
Home office		22,000

If a home office transfers used rather than new equipment to its branch, then the entries are somewhat different. To illustrate, suppose that a home office transfers used equipment

---

[2] We would also assume that branches using periodic systems would debit freight costs to a freight-in account for freight costs incurred on shipments from its home office and would not debit such freight costs to the shipments from home office account. Similarly, we would assume that home offices using periodic systems would debit the investment in branch account rather than shipments to branch account. If the home office bills freight to its branch, then the branch should debit its freight-in account for such amounts and credit its home office account. The freight-in account should be added along with purchases in the calculation of cost of goods sold if a periodic system is used.

with a cost of $10,000 and accumulated depreciation of $4,000 to its branch. The following entries record the transfer:

Home office entry to record transfer of used equipment to a branch that maintains fixed asset accounts:

Investment in branch	6,000	
Accumulated depreciation	4,000	
Equipment		10,000

Branch entry to record receipt of used equipment from home office:

Equipment	10,000	
Accumulated depreciation		4,000
Home office		6,000

Since the equipment is simply moved from one segment of the accounting entity to another, the book values are simply transferred and no revaluation is appropriate.

In some cases, a branch that does not maintain fixed asset accounts may be authorized to purchase equipment. For example, suppose that such a branch purchases equipment for $9,200 cash and notifies its home office of the purchase. The following entries are appropriate:

Home office entry to record purchase of new equipment by a branch that does not maintain fixed asset accounts:

Equipment	9,200	
Investment in branch		9,200

Branch entry to record purchase of new equipment where branch does not maintain fixed asset accounts:

Home office	9,200	
Cash		9,200

Of course, if the branch maintained fixed asset records, then the branch would debit an equipment account rather than the home office account and no entry by the home office would be appropriate.

Transfers of Expense

Since separate income statements are usually prepared for each branch, it is appropriate that all expenses incurred by the home office on behalf of the branch be reported to the branch and recorded in branch accounts. The recording of such expenses by the branch is based on a report from the home office. When branch income statements are prepared by the home office and not by the branch itself, then such expense transfers are unnecessary, although communication with branch managers may be impaired without them. Entry (4) in Exhibit 16-1 records the incurrence and transfer of such expenses in our illustration. Observe that depreciation expense is transferred by entry (4); if all fixed asset accounts are maintained by a branch, the transfer of depreciation expenses does not occur. Entry (4) assumes that the various expenses incurred on behalf of the branch are segregated from other expenses and recorded in the investment in branch account at the point of incurrence. This assumption is made throughout all materials relating to this chapter.[3]

Branch Operating Transactions and Transfers to Home Office

Operating transactions entered into by the branch with parties other than the home office are recorded by the branch as they occur. Since the branch has a separate accounting system, such transactions are not recorded by the home office until the branch reports to the home office at the end of the accounting period. The branch must also transfer cash to the home office at regular intervals. Such transfers reduce both the home office account and the investment in branch account as illustrated by entry (10) in Exhibit 16-1.

End-of-Period Reporting by Branch and Closing Procedures

At the end of the accounting period, the branch reports the result of its operations to the home office. On the basis of this report, the home office records the branch income. These reports and the related closing procedures are discussed in the two sections that follow.

Branch Reporting and Closing Procedures

The report by the branch to its home office may take the form of branch financial statements or simply a trial balance of branch accounts. The adjusted (preclosing) trial balance at December 31, 19X1, for Wilsonville Branch, which reflects the 19X1 operating transactions shown in Exhibit 16-1, is presented in Exhibit 16-2 on the following page. On the basis of this information, Wilsonville Branch prepares financial statements for its home office. In addition, Exhibit 16-2 gives the adjusted (preclosing) trial balance of Storr Manufacturing, the home office. The trial balances include additional information that is not presented in the foregoing discussion. We assume here and throughout the text that such trial balances incorporate all adjusting entries by both the home office and branch except those related to items in transit between the home office and branch or those related to errors. Exhibit 16-3 on page 789 shows the branch and home office financial statements prepared from these trial balances.

Closing entries by the branch, which are illustrated in Exhibit 16-1, transfer the balances of all revenue and expense accounts to an income summary account and transfer the income summary account balance to the home office account. After closing, the home office account has the appearance of the following T-account:

		Home Office	
		Balance	0
(8)	800	(1)	3,000
(10)	10,000	(2)	12,000
		(4)	900
		Balance	5,100
		(12)	4,600
		Balance	9,700

[3] Some home office accounting systems may not segregate expenses incurred on behalf of the branch until the year-end. Such systems record branch-related expenses in the same accounts as other home office expenses as they are incurred, and require a year-end adjusting entry to transfer branch-related expenses from the home office expense accounts to the branch investment account.

| EXHIBIT 16-2 | HOME OFFICE AND BRANCH ADJUSTED TRIAL BALANCES |

Storr Manufacturing, Inc.
ADJUSTED TRIAL BALANCES* FOR HOME OFFICE AND WILSONVILLE BRANCH
AT DECEMBER 31, 19X1

	Home Office		Branch	
	Dr.	Cr.	Dr.	Cr.
Cash	$ 2,100	$	$ 700	$
Accounts receivable	9,800		5,000	
Inventory	15,000		4,000	
Investment in branch	5,100			
Other assets	131,000			
Liabilities		25,000		
Common stock		100,000		
Retained earnings, 1-1-X1		30,000		
Home office				5,100
Sales		120,000		16,000
Cost of goods sold	70,000		8,000	
Depreciation	12,400		250	
Other expenses	19,600		3,150	
Dividends	10,000			
Totals	$275,000	$275,000	$21,100	$21,100

* Adjusted trial balances include all adjusting entries by the home office and branch except those related to items in transit and errors.

The year-end balance of the home office account ($9,700) represents the equity of the home office in the branch at year-end, and it is reported on the branch balance sheet shown in Exhibit 16-3. In our simple example, the home office account is the only equity account on the branch balance sheet. If a branch is authorized to incur liabilities, then the year-end balance sheet may also reflect accounts payable as well as the home office equity.

Recording Branch Income by Home Office

Upon receipt of the financial statement or trial balance from its branch, a home office records the branch income by crediting a single income account and debiting the branch investment account. For example, when Storr Manufacturing receives the income statement shown in Exhibit 16-3 from its Wilsonville Branch, Storr records $4,600 in its income from branch account using entry (11) shown in Exhibit 16-1. Thus, the detailed revenues and expenses of the branch are not recorded on the records of the home office. In addition, as part of its closing entries, the home office must close its income from branch

| EXHIBIT 16-3 | SEPARATE FINANCIAL STATEMENTS |

Storr Manufacturing, Inc.

**SEPARATE INCOME STATEMENTS FOR HOME OFFICE AND WILSONVILLE BRANCH
FOR THE YEAR ENDED DECEMBER 31, 19X1**

	Home Office	Branch
Sales	$120,000	$16,000
Cost of goods sold	(70,000)	(8,000)
Gross margin	$ 50,000	$ 8,000
Depreciation expense	(12,400)	(250)
Other expenses	(19,600)	(3,150)
Income from home office	$ 18,000	
Income from branch	4,600	
Net income	$ 22,600	$ 4,600

Storr Manufacturing, Inc.

**SEPARATE BALANCE SHEETS FOR HOME OFFICE AND WILSONVILLE BRANCH
AT DECEMBER 31, 19X1**

	Home Office	Branch
Assets		
Cash	$ 2,100	$ 700
Accounts receivable	9,800	5,000
Inventory	15,000	4,000
Investment in branch ($5,100 + $4,600)	9,700	
Other assets	131,000	
Total assets	$167,600	$ 9,700
Equities		
Liabilities	$ 25,000	$
Home office ($5,100 + $4,600)		9,700
Common stock	100,000	
Retained earnings	42,600	
Total liabilities and stockholders' equity	$167,600	$ 9,700

account to its income summary. Immediately after closing, the investment in branch
account has the following appearance:

Investment in Branch

Balance	0		
(1)	3,000	(8)	800
(2)	12,000	(10)	10,000
(4)	900		
Balance	5,100		
(11)	4,600		
Balance	9,700		

Observe that the $800 payment by the branch for equipment [entry (8)] has the same effect
on the investment account as the $10,000 transfer of cash from the branch [entry (10)].
The investment in branch account is a control account for the net assets of the branch. The
investment in branch account balance of $9,700 in our illustration represents the cash,
accounts receivable, and inventory balances ($700 + $5,000 + $4,000 = $9,700) reported on the branch's balance sheet at the year-end.

   This completes our discussion of accounting for branch transactions and their impact
on the separate financial statements of the branch and its home office. We now turn to a
discussion of the combined financial statements of the home office and its branch.

PREPARATION OF COMBINED FINANCIAL STATEMENTS

As previously noted, a branch and its home office represent two accounting systems but
just one accounting entity. Since home office records do not reflect branch records in full
detail, the account balances of the branch and its home office must be combined to
produce fully detailed financial statements for the single accounting entity. It is customary
to prepare the combined statements that merge the accounts of the home office and branch
accounting systems. Combined (corporate) financial statements are used by both internal
management and interested parties outside the entity—stockholders, creditors, bankers,
and government agencies—to answer questions related to the entity as a whole. Although
the separate financial statements of the home office and its branches are not issued to
outsiders, they are useful to internal management in evaluating the progress and position
of the individual components that form the entity.

   The preparation of combined financial statements is demonstrated by reference to the
Wilsonville-Storr illustration considered earlier. Recall that Wilsonville Branch was established on January 1, 19X1, and that Storr bills its branch for the cost of transferred
merchandise. The adjusted (preclosing) trial balances at December 31, 19X1, for both
Storr Manufacturing and its only branch, Wilsonville, were presented earlier in Exhibit
16-2 and were used as a basis for the separate home office and branch financial statements
presented in Exhibit 16-3.

Worksheet for Combined Financial Statements

The combined financial statements are prepared with the aid of a worksheet, based on the
separate financial statements of the home office and branch. Such a worksheet is shown
for the Wilsonville-Storr illustration in Exhibit 16-4. The worksheet facilitates the preparation of combined financial statements by providing a systematic format for the combination of like accounts and the making of required adjustments.

EXHIBIT 16-4	COMBINATION WORKSHEET FOR HOME OFFICE AND BRANCH

Storr Manufacturing, Inc.

COMBINATION WORKSHEET FOR HOME OFFICE AND WILSONVILLE BRANCH
FOR THE YEAR ENDED DECEMBER 31, 19X1

	Separate Financial Statements		Adjustments		Combined Financial Statements
	Home Office	Branch	Dr.	Cr.	
Income Statement					
Sales	120,000	16,000			136,000
Income from branch	4,600		(1) 4,600		
Cost of goods sold	(70,000)	(8,000)			(78,000)
Depreciation	(12,400)	(250)			(12,650)
Other expenses	(19,600)	(3,150)			(22,750)
Net income	22,600	4,600	4,600		22,600
Retained Earnings and Home Office					
Retained earnings, 1-1-X1	30,000				30,000
Home office, preclosing		5,100	(2) 5,100		
Net income	22,600	4,600	4,600		22,600
Dividends	(10,000)				(10,000)
Retained earnings/home office, 12-31-X1	42,600	9,700	9,700		42,600
Balance Sheet					
Cash	2,100	700			2,800
Accounts receivable	9,800	5,000			14,800
Inventory	15,000	4,000			19,000
Investment in branch	9,700			(1) 4,600	
				(2) 5,100	
Other assets	131,000				131,000
Total assets	167,600	9,700			167,600
Liabilities	25,000				25,000
Common stock	100,000				100,000
Retained earnings/home office	42,600	9,700	9,700		42,600
Total liabilities and stockholders' equity	167,600	9,700	9,700	9,700	167,600

Note: Parentheses indicate decreases.

The separate financial statements are entered in the home office and branch columns on the left-hand side of the worksheet, with the various accounts grouped according to the financial statement with which they are associated.[4] Completion of the worksheet requires the entry of several adjustments on the worksheet before the combined results can be calculated. These worksheet adjustments, which are not recorded on either the home office or the branch records, are discussed in the paragraphs that follow.

Elimination of Current Year's Branch Income

The first adjustment shown in Exhibit 16-4 reverses the entry made by the home office to record branch income for the current year and has the following form:

(1)   *Worksheet adjustment to eliminate current year's branch income:*

Income from branch 4,600
       Investment in branch   4,600

The foregoing adjustment is entered as adjustment (1) on the worksheet, but as noted earlier, it is not entered on either the home office or the branch records. The elimination is necessary to avoid double-counting of the branch income when the two financial statements are added together.

Elimination of Branch Investment and Home Office Accounts

The second adjustment eliminates the preclosing home office balance from the branch's home office account and the home office's investment in branch account. The elimination is accomplished by offsetting one balance against the other with the following worksheet entry:

(2)   *Worksheet adjustment to eliminate branch investment and home office accounts:*

Home office 5,100
       Investment in branch   5,100

The foregoing adjustment is entered as adjustment (2) on the worksheet but is not entered on either the home office or the branch records. If the foregoing elimination were not made, the combined balance sheet would exhibit an investment represented by its own equity, which is contrary to fundamental accounting measurement rules. The same rules preclude the reporting of treasury stock as an asset. Taken together, adjustments (1) and (2) eliminate the entire (postclosing) balance ($9,700) of both the investment in branch account and the home office account.

Completion of Worksheet

The worksheet is completed section-by-section beginning with the income statement section. We begin the income statement section by simply adding across each row and entering the sum in the combined financial statements column. For example, combined

---

[4] The home office and branch columns of the worksheet can also be completed by reference to the adjusted trial balance provided that its balances are adjusted for all errors and items in transit before they are introduced into the worksheet.

sales (\$136,000) is the sum of home office and branch sales balances (\$136,000 = \$120,000 + \$16,000). The combined income from branch is zero because the debit adjustment of \$4,600 eliminates the income recorded by the home office. The cost of goods sold, depreciation, and other expenses rows are completed in the same way. Finally, the net income row is completed by summing the amounts in each column.

Notice that the home office net income equals the combined net income. The worksheet procedure has merely substituted the detailed revenues and expenses of the branch for the single item income from branch item on the home office income statement. The home office income statement shows the branch income as a single item (\$4,600), whereas the combined income statement shows the branch income appropriately integrated with the elements of the home office income. Similarly, with reference to the balance sheets, although home office net assets (\$142,600 = \$167,600 − \$25,000) equal combined net assets, home office and combined net assets exhibit different compositions. The home office balance sheet shows branch net assets in a single item (investment in branch), whereas the combined balance sheet shows branch net assets in full detail and appropriately integrated with the assets and liabilities of the home office.

Returning to our worksheet procedure, next, we carry forward the net income totals, entering them in the net income row of the retained earnings and home office section. As before, we complete the retained earnings and home office section by summing across its rows and entering the totals on the last line of the section.

Next, we carry forward the retained earnings/home office totals, entering them in the retained earnings/home office row of the balance sheet section. The balance sheet section is completed by summing across its rows and forming the column totals for total assets, total liabilities, and stockholders' equity.

Worksheet Adjustments for Omitted Entries and Errors

An important part of the closing process is the reconciliation of the investment in branch and home office accounts, which are reciprocal accounts and thus must display the same numerical balance. Any discrepancy between the two accounts is evidence of omitted recordings or erroneous recordings by either the home office, the branch, or both. Accordingly, the discrepancy must be fully explained and properly recorded or adjusted. The trial balances for the Wilsonville-Storr illustration incorporate all appropriate adjusting entries by the home office and branch. In other cases, however, a branch or home office may omit an adjusting entry that is discovered during the process of worksheet preparation. For example, a branch may fail to adjust for merchandise, shipped to the branch from the home office, that is in transit at year-end. In order to bring the home office account and investment in branch account into agreement and to state ending inventory correctly, the following worksheet adjustment is required:[5]

> *Worksheet adjustment to record merchandise, in transit from home office to branch, that has not been recorded by branch:*
>
> Inventory XX
>   Home office XX

---

[5] When the merchandise in transit is billed in excess of cost, as demonstrated later in this chapter, a worksheet adjustment is required to eliminate intracompany markup from the ending inventory of the branch [see adjustment (3) in the Dover-Palmer illustration presented later in this chapter]. Such eliminations should include intracompany markup on the inventory in transit as well as the inventory on hand.

Unrecorded cash in transit at the year-end is another example of an omitted adjustment requiring a worksheet adjustment. If the home office has not recorded cash in transit from the branch, then the following worksheet adjustment is required:

Worksheet adjustment to record cash, in transit from branch to home office, that has not been recorded by home office:

Cash..	XX	
Investment in branch		XX

It is appropriate to enter such adjustments on the worksheet, but they should also be entered on the branch or home office records from which they were omitted—particularly if separate branch and home office financial statements are prepared. Note that the reconciliation process may occasion adjustments to branch records as well as to home office records. This possibility may cause the branch to delay its formal closing entries until after the reconciliation is complete.

Combined Financial Statements

The worksheet enables the preparation of the combined financial statements for Storr Manufacturing shown in Exhibit 16-5. Notice that the combined statements portray the company as a single accounting entity and that all traces of the separate branch and home office accounting systems have been removed.

MERCHANDISE TRANSFERS BILLED IN EXCESS OF COST

When a branch is billed for the cost of merchandise transferred from the home office, as in the Storr-Wilsonville illustration discussed earlier in this chapter, the entire gross margin on the merchandise enters branch income upon its sale by the branch. Home office income (exclusive of branch income) does not include the gross margin on merchandise transferred to a branch. If the company wishes to allocate the entire gross margin to the home office rather than to the branch, then merchandise transfers are billed at their selling prices to outside customers. In this case, the branch reports a gross margin of zero. An intermediate procedure establishes a billing or transfer price that allocates the gross margin on transferred merchandise between the home office and the branch. Following this intermediate method, the transferred goods are billed at an amount between their cost to the home office and their selling price to outside customers. In choosing among the three methods of billing merchandise transfers to a branch, the home office should consider the control and measurement objectives of the branch accounting system, as the following issues section indicates.

ISSUES

Branch Versus Home Office Margin

Billing transfers at cost has the advantage of simplicity because the billing or transfer price is derived directly from the cost records and because the procedure does not require the special gross margin accounts used when merchandise transfers are billed in excess of cost. However, the branch and home office gross margins produced by transfers at cost may distort the relative contribution of the various company segments to the income of the whole company. To illustrate, consider Newark Distributors, Inc., a distributor of building supplies with a home office located in Newark, New Jersey, and branches located in several middle-Atlantic states. All building supplies are inventoried and shipped by the home office. Supplies are sold by both the home office and the branches. Supplies sold by

EXHIBIT 16-5	COMBINED FINANCIAL STATEMENTS

Storr Manufacturing, Inc.
INCOME STATEMENT
FOR THE YEAR ENDED DECEMBER 31, 19X1

Sales	$136,000
Cost of goods sold	(78,000)
Gross margin	$ 58,000
Depreciation	(12,650)
Other expenses	(22,750)
Net income	$ 22,600

Storr Manufacturing, Inc.
STATEMENT OF RETAINED EARNINGS
FOR THE YEAR ENDED DECEMBER 31, 19X1

Retained earnings, 1-1-X1	$30,000
Net income	22,600
Subtotal	$52,600
Dividends	(10,000)
Retained earnings, 12-31-X1	$42,600

Storr Manufacturing, Inc.
BALANCE SHEET
AT DECEMBER 31, 19X1

Assets

Cash	$ 2,800
Accounts receivable	14,800
Inventory	19,000
Other assets	131,000
Total assets	$167,600

Liabilities and Stockholders' Equity

Liabilities	$ 25,000
Common stock	100,000
Retained earnings	42,600
Total liabilities and stockholders' equity	$167,600

the branches are billed to the branches at cost. Middle management is paid an annual bonus that is allocated among the home office and its branches in proportion to their reported gross margin. In recent years, the volume of sales by the branches has increased substantially while home office sales have remained fairly stable. As a result, the largest bonuses in recent years have been paid to branch managers despite the fact that home office managers are responsible for inventory functions as well as for selling. Home office managers have recently appealed to Newark's president to change the policy of billing the branches for the cost of the merchandise they sell. They request that they be billed for cost plus an additional amount to compensate the home office for carrying and shipping the inventory, which would reduce branch margins and, in their view, result in a more suitable allocation of the annual bonus.

As this illustration shows, the intermediate method of pricing may give the home office a better means of evaluating the effectiveness of branch and home office operations. The intermediate method is particularly appropriate if the billing price is based on an appropriate measure of the cost to the home office of providing the goods to the branch or reflects the amount the branch would have paid for the merchandise if acquired from an outside supplier.

Recording Merchandise Transfers from Home Office to Branch Billed in Excess of Cost

The accounting procedures used when transfers are billed at a price in excess of cost are demonstrated by reference to the case of Queensland Distributors, which operates a newly established branch in Comport, Indiana. The Comport Branch receives all its merchandise from the home office, which bills the branch at cost plus 40% of cost. During 19X3, merchandise costing the home office $30,000 is transferred to Comport. The merchandise will be sold by the Comport branch for a total price of $50,000 and is billed to the branch at $42,000 [$30,000 + (.40 × $30,000)]. On January 1, 19X3, the branch has no inventory of merchandise, and during 19X3 the branch sells 75% of the merchandise transferred from the home office. In addition, the branch incurs operating expenses of $2,500 during 19X3. Accordingly, the branch reports income for 19X3 as follows:

Branch Income Statement for 19X3

Sales (.75 × $50,000)	$37,500
Cost of goods sold (.75 × $42,000)	31,500
Gross margin	$ 6,000
Other expenses	2,500
Branch net income	$ 3,500

The paragraphs that follow demonstrate the recording of merchandise transfers by the home office and the branch when the home office bills the branch in excess of cost by reference to the Queensland-Comport illustration.

Entries by Home Office to Record Merchandise Transfers

When merchandise transfers are billed to the branch at cost plus a markup, the home office must record the markup separately. The transfers described in the Queensland-Comport illustration and the related billings are recorded by the following entries:

Home office entry to record shipment to branch of merchandise costing $30,000 and billing to branch at cost plus 40%:

Investment in branch 42,000
    Inventory (shipments to branch) 30,000
    Allowance for unrealized gross margin in branch
      inventory 12,000

Branch entry to record receipt of merchandise billed at cost plus 40%:

Inventory (shipments from home office) 42,000
    Home office 42,000

Since the selling price of 19X3 transfers to the branch is $50,000, the combined gross margin to be realized by the branch and home office is $20,000 ($50,000 − $30,000). If the transferred merchandise had been billed at cost ($30,000), the entire gross margin of $20,000 would be reflected in the branch income upon the sale of the merchandise. If the transferred merchandise had been billed at its selling price ($50,000), the branch would realize no gross margin upon the sale of the merchandise. But the merchandise was transferred at $12,000 over cost. Consequently, gross margin of $8,000 ($20,000 − $12,000) will be realized by the branch upon the sale of the merchandise, and the $12,000 remainder of total gross margin is realized by adjustments to the *allowances for unrealized gross margin in branch inventory* on the home office records.

Year-End Adjustments by Home Office of Allowance for Unrealized Gross Margin in Branch Inventory

The allowance for unrealized gross margin in branch inventory is a contra-asset account that is subtracted from the investment in branch account to reduce the inventory component of its balance to cost. Accordingly, the allowance must be reduced at year-end for the markup associated with transferred merchandise sold by the branch during the year. During 19X3, the Comport branch sells 75% of the transferred merchandise, which occasions realization of 75% of the total gross margin, or $15,000 (.75 × $20,000). The branch realizes gross margin of $6,000 (.75 × $8,000), as shown on its income statement. The home office must transfer the $9,000 remainder of the realized gross margin ($9,000 = $15,000 − $6,000) from its allowance account to its income from branch account. When the branch buys all its merchandise from the home office, the amount of the transfer can be determined from the branch's cost of goods sold and the markup percentage on cost [$9,000 = $31,500 − ($31,500 ÷ 1.40)]. The home office records the transfer with the following year-end adjusting entry:

Home office entry to adjust allowance for unrealized gross margin in branch inventory:

Allowance for unrealized gross margin in branch inventory 9,000
    Income from branch 9,000

The foregoing adjusting entry adds $9,000 to the reported branch income of $3,500, raising the branch income account on the home office records to $12,500, ($9,000 +

$3,500).[6] The foregoing adjustment also reduces the allowance for unrealized gross margin in the branch inventory to $3,000 ($12,000 − $9,000), which equals the markup on the branch's ending inventory—the cost of the inventory to the branch ($10,500) less the cost of the inventory to the home office ($7,500 = .25 × $30,000). The allowance for unrealized gross margin in branch inventory account is subtracted from the investment account balance, which includes $10,500 for the branch inventory at the year-end.

The year-end adjustment to the allowance for unrealized gross margin in branch inventory, which appears on the home office records, represents the portion of the intracompany markup over cost that is associated with branch sales during the year. If branch sales include sales from a beginning branch inventory, then the amount of the adjustment will include the markup on transfers made in prior years as well as transfers made during the current year. For example, if the Comport branch sells its entire December 31, 19X3, inventory during the following year, then the adjustment of the allowance for unrealized gross margin in branch inventory at the end of 19X4 will include the intracompany markup of $3,000 that is associated with transfers made during 19X3.

Merchandise Transfers Billed at Selling Price

When merchandise transfers to a branch are billed at selling price, the branch's gross margin is equal to zero, or if not equal to zero, it reflects deviations from anticipated or standard selling prices. Further, when merchandise is transferred to a branch at selling prices, the entire anticipated gross margin is credited to the allowance for unrealized gross margin in branch inventory, which requires adjustments similar to those previously demonstrated. It is important to understand that the allowance represents gross margin in the branch's ending inventory which is carried at the selling price. When all merchandise sold by the branch is transferred from its home office at the selling price, and if all selling prices are correctly anticipated, then the branch will report a loss equal to its operating expenses.

Billing transfers at selling prices facilitates inventory control. If the merchandise selling prices are correctly anticipated and all branch merchandise is transferred from its home office, then the year-end physical inventory taken by the branch must equal the beginning branch inventory, plus shipments from the home office, minus branch sales. This relationship may be used to check the accuracy of the year-end branch inventory.

Combination Worksheet When Merchandise Transfers Are Billed in Excess of Cost

When merchandise transfers are billed to the branch in excess of their cost to the home office, additional worksheet adjustments are required to produce combined financial statements. Further, the separate income statements of the home office and its branch articulate in a somewhat different way. Let us demonstrate these differences by reference to Dover Branch, which is the only branch of Palmer Products, Inc. Dover Branch is billed for 140% of the cost of all merchandise transferred from its home office. The branch was organized on January 1, 19X1, and the worksheet in Exhibit 16-6 is based on the separate financial statements prepared for the home office and branch at December 31, 19X1.

---

[6] Although the procedure is not followed by this text, the $9,000 credit may be entered in a separate income account, (e.g., ''Income from Branch—Home Office Share'') rather than the branch income account, to indicate that it represents an allocation of gross margin to the home office.

EXHIBIT 16-6	COMBINATION WORKSHEET FOR HOME OFFICE AND BRANCH WITH MERCHANDISE TRANSFERS BILLED IN EXCESS OF COST

Palmer Products, Inc.

COMBINATION WORKSHEET FOR HOME OFFICE AND DOVER BRANCH
FOR THE YEAR ENDED DECEMBER 31, 19X1

	Separate Financial Statements		Adjustments		Combined Financial Statements
	Home Office	Branch	Dr.	Cr.	
Income Statement					
Sales	120,000	16,000			136,000
Income from branch	4,600		(1) 4,600		
Cost of goods sold	(70,000)	(11,200)		(1) 3,200	(78,000)
Depreciation	(12,400)	(250)			(12,650)
Other expenses	(19,600)	(3,150)			(22,750)
Net income	22,600	1,400	4,600	3,200	22,600
Retained Earnings and Home Office					
Retained earnings, 1-1-X1	30,000				30,000
Home office, preclosing		9,900	(2) 9,900		
Net income	22,600	1,400	4,600	3,200	22,600
Dividends	(10,000)				(10,000)
Retained earnings/home office, 12-31-X1	42,600	11,300	14,500	3,200	42,600
Balance Sheet					
Cash	2,100	700			2,800
Accounts receivable	9,800	5,000			14,800
Inventory	15,000	5,600		(3) 1,600	19,000
Investment in branch	11,300			(1) 1,400	
				(2) 9,900	
Allowance for unrealized gross margin in branch inventory	(1,600)		(3) 1,600		
Other assets	131,000				131,000
Total assets	167,600	11,300			167,600
Liabilities	25,000				25,000
Common stock	100,000				100,000
Retained earnings/home office	42,600	11,300	14,500	3,200	42,600
Total liabilities and stockholders' equity	167,600	11,300	16,100	16,100	167,600

Note: Parentheses indicate decreases.

During 19X1, the branch was billed $16,800 for merchandise transfers during that year, with a total cost of $12,000 ($16,800 = 1.40 × $12,000), a $4,800 markup. By the end of 19X1, two-thirds of the transferred merchandise had been sold to unaffiliated parties. The home office makes the following entry at the year-end to record the branch income and adjust the allowance for unrealized gross margin in branch inventory:

> *Home office entry to record branch income and to adjust allowance for unrealized gross margin in branch inventory:*
>
> Investment in branch 1,400
> Allowance for unrealized gross margin in branch inventory 3,200
>   Income from branch ($1,400 + $3,200)   4,600

By making this entry, the home office reduces its allowance account for the portion of the $4,800 markup on transfers that is *realized* (associated with branch sales) during the period [$3,200 = $11,200 − ($11,200 ÷ 1.40)]. Also note that the investment in branch account is increased by the branch income as recorded on branch records ($1,400), which does not include the gross margin reserved for the home office on transfers billed in excess of cost. Except for the $4,800 markup on merchandise transfers, the 19X1 transactions for Palmer Products and its Dover Branch are identical to the 19X1 transactions in the Wilsonville-Storr illustration considered earlier in this chapter (where merchandise was billed to the branch at cost to the home office). This contrived coincidence enables a comparison of the two illustrations, showing clearly the impact of markups on intracompany transfers.

Elimination of Current Year's Branch Income

The worksheet in Exhibit 16-6 incorporates three adjustments. The first adjustment removes the home office's income from branch account to zero:

(1) *Worksheet adjustment to eliminate current year's branch income:*

> Income from branch..................................... 4,600
>   Cost of goods sold   3,200
>   Investment in branch   1,400

The portion of total branch income recognized by the branch ($1,400) is credited against the investment account, and the portion recognized by the home office ($3,200 = $4,600 − $1,400) is credited against the branch's cost of goods sold. The home office share of total branch income ($3,200) equals the portion of the markup over cost on the merchandise transferred during the current year that was sold to unaffiliated parties. Recall that the home office transferred this amount at the year-end from its allowance for unrealized gross margin in branch inventory account to its income from branch account.

Elimination of Branch Investment and Home Office Accounts

The second adjustment eliminates the reciprocal balances of the investment in the branch account and the home office account by the following worksheet entry:

(2) *Worksheet adjustment to eliminate branch investment and home office accounts:*

> Home office 9,900
>   Investment in branch   9,900

Both the home office account and the branch account reflect the $4,800 markup on intracompany transfers. Since the markup on intracompany transfers is the only difference between the Dover-Palmer and Wilsonville-Storr illustrations, the reciprocal home office and branch investment account balances in the Dover-Palmer illustration exceed those in the Wilsonville-Storr illustration by the amount of the markup ($4,800 = $9,900 − $5,100).

Elimination of Unrealized Gross Margin in Branch Inventory

The third adjustment offsets the allowance for unrealized gross margin in the branch inventory against the branch inventory:

(3) *Worksheet adjustment to eliminate unrealized gross margin in branch inventory:*

Allowance for unrealized gross margin in branch inventory 1,600
     Inventory   1,600

The foregoing worksheet adjustment reduces the recorded branch inventory to its $4,000 cost to the company as a whole, which is the appropriate basis for its representation in the combined financial statements.

Combined Financial Statements

Since the intracompany markup is the only difference between the Dover-Palmer and Wilsonville-Storr illustrations, the combined financial statements for the two illustrations are identical. In other words, the worksheets in Exhibits 16-4 and 16-6 lead to the same combined financial statements.

Separate Financial Statements

Although the combined financial statements in the Dover-Palmer and Wilsonville-Storr illustrations are identical, the separate home office and branch financial statements differ. The separate financial statements for the Dover-Palmer illustration are shown in Exhibit 16-7 on the following page. Observe that the Dover branch's net income is only $1,400 as compared with $4,600 for the Wilsonville branch. The $3,200 difference ($4,600 − $1,400) represents the portion of gross margin on branch sales that is recognized on the home office income statement but not on the branch income statement. Also note that the inventory account and the home office account on the branch balance sheet include markup of $1,600, which represents the unrealized gross margin from the combined, or company, viewpoint. The investment in branch account on the home office records also reflects the unrealized gross margin of $1,600, but it is offset by the allowance for unrealized gross margin in the branch inventory account.

Treatment of the Beginning Branch Inventory

An extension of the Dover-Palmer illustration into a second year (19X2) demonstrates the preparation of a combination worksheet in the presence of intracompany markup and beginning branch inventories. The extension takes the form of the assumed amounts entered in the separate financial statement columns of Exhibit 16-8 on page 803. During 19X2, Palmer transfers merchandise costing $20,000 to its Dover Branch and bills the

EXHIBIT 16-7	SEPARATE FINANCIAL STATEMENTS

Palmer Products, Inc.

SEPARATE INCOME STATEMENTS FOR HOME OFFICE AND DOVER BRANCH
FOR THE YEAR ENDED DECEMBER 31, 19X1

	Home Office	Branch
Sales	$120,000	$16,000
Cost of goods sold	(70,000)	(11,200)
Gross margin	$ 50,000	$ 4,800
Other expenses	(32,000)	(3,400)
Income from home office	$ 18,000	
Income from branch	4,600	
Net income	$ 22,600	$ 1,400

Palmer Products, Inc.

SEPARATE BALANCE SHEETS FOR HOME OFFICE AND DOVER BRANCH
AT DECEMBER 31, 19X1

	Home Office	Branch
Assets		
Cash	$ 2,100	$ 700
Accounts receivable	9,800	5,000
Inventory	15,000	5,600
Investment in branch	11,300	
Allowance for unrealized gross margin in branch inventory	(1,600)	
Other assets	131,000	
Total assets	$167,600	$11,300
Liabilities and Stockholders' Equity		
Liabilities	$ 25,000	$
Home office ($9,000 + $1,400)		11,300
Common stock	100,000	
Retained earnings	42,600	
Total liabilities and stockholders' equity	$167,600	$11,300

branch a total of $28,000 ($20,000 × 1.40). The branch's FIFO inventory at the year-end consists of one-quarter of the merchandise transferred during 19X2. The home office makes the following year-end entry to record the branch income and adjust the allowance for unrealized gross margin in branch inventory:

> *Home office entry to record branch income and to adjust allowance for unrealized gross margin in branch inventory:*

Investment in branch 4,000
Allowance for unrealized gross margin in branch inventory . . 7,600
    Income from branch ($4,000 + $7,600)   11,600

EXHIBIT 16-8	COMBINATION WORKSHEET FOR HOME OFFICE AND BRANCH WITH MERCHANDISE TRANSFERS BILLED IN EXCESS OF COST (BEGINNING INVENTORY AT BRANCH)

Palmer Products, Inc.
COMBINATION WORKSHEET FOR HOME OFFICE AND DOVER BRANCH
FOR THE YEAR ENDED DECEMBER 31, 19X2

	Separate Financial Statements		Adjustments		Combined Financial Statements
	Home Office	Branch	Dr.	Cr.	
Income Statement					
Sales	150,000	35,000			185,000
Income from branch	11,600		(1) 11,600		
Cost of goods sold	(86,000)	(26,600)		(1) 7,600	(105,000)
Other expenses	(40,000)	(4,400)			(44,400)
Net income	35,600	4,000	11,600	7,600	35,600
Retained Earnings and Home Office					
Retained earnings, 1-1-X2	42,600				42,600
Home office, preclosing		11,800	(2) 11,800		
Net income	35,600	4,000	11,600	7,600	35,600
Dividends	(15,000)				(15,000)
Retained earnings/home office, 12-31-X2	63,200	15,800	23,400	7,600	63,200
Balance Sheet					
Cash	28,700	600			29,300
Accounts receivable	12,700	8,200			20,900
Inventory	19,000	7,000		(3) 2,000	24,000
Investment in branch	15,800			(1) 4,000	
				(2) 11,800	
Allowance for unrealized gross margin in branch inventory	(2,000)		(3) 2,000		
Other assets	116,000				116,000
Total assets	190,200	15,800			190,200
Liabilities	27,000				27,000
Common stock	100,000				100,000
Retained earnings/home office	63,200	15,800	23,400	7,600	63,200
Total liabilities and stockholders' equity	190,200	15,800	25,400	25,400	190,200

Note: Parentheses indicate decreases.

The allowance account is reduced for the portion of the markup on transfers (whether transfers during the current year, 19X2, or the preceding year, 19X1) that is *realized* (associated with branch sales) during the current year. This consists of gross margin of $1,600 on 19X1 transfers sold during 19X2 and gross margin of $6,000 on 19X2 transfers sold during 19X2 ($6,000 = $8,000 × 3/4).

The three worksheet adjustments for 19X2, which take the same general form as in the preceding year (19X1), have the following appearance:

(1) *Worksheet adjustment to eliminate for current year's branch income:*

Income from branch..	11,600	
Cost of goods sold................................		7,600
Investment in branch		4,000

(2) *Worksheet adjustment to eliminate branch investment and home office accounts:*

Home office	11,800	
Investment in branch		11,800

(3) *Worksheet adjustment to eliminate unrealized gross margin in branch inventory:*

Allowance for unrealized gross margin in branch inventory ..	2,000	
Inventory..		2,000

The foregoing adjustments are entered in the adjustment columns of the worksheet in Exhibit 16-8, which serves as the basis for the preparation of the combined financial statements.

MULTIPLE BRANCHES

When a company is composed of a home office and several branches, the home office records include a separate investment account and a separate allowance for unrealized gross margin in branch inventory account for each branch. Multiple branches are accommodated on the combination worksheet by a separate pair of trial balance columns for each branch and by a separate set of worksheet adjustments for each branch.

INTERBRANCH TRANSFERS

The transfer of assets from one branch to another does not create interbranch payables or receivables. Instead, credits and debits enter the home office account in each branch. In effect, the transferor branch *reverses* the entry to record the transfer from the home office, and the transferee branch *enters* a transfer as if from the home office.

Suppose that Branch X transfers merchandise to Branch Y. The merchandise was previously transferred from the home office and billed to Branch X at its cost to the home office of $7,000 plus freight of $250. The freight on the merchandise shipment from Branch X to Branch Y is $170, which is paid by Branch X. If the merchandise had been shipped directly from the home office to Branch Y, the freight would have been $300, which establishes an upper limit on the amount of freight chargeable to Branch Y. One might be tempted to create a liability—"Due to Branch X"—on Branch Y's records and an asset—"Due from Branch Y"—on Branch X's records, but the correct recording, which follows, does not create such interbranch accounts:

Branch X entry to record transfer of merchandise to Branch Y:

Home office 7,420		
Inventory (shipments from home office)	7,000	
Freight-in	250	
Cash.	170	

Branch Y entry to record receipt of merchandise from Branch X:

Inventory (shipments from home office) 7,000		
Freight-in. 300		
Home office	7,300	

Home office entry to record transfer of merchandise from Branch X to Branch Y:

Investment in Branch Y. 7,300		
Inventory (shipments to Branch X) 7,000		
Freight expense ($250 + $170 − $300) 120		
Inventory (shipments to Branch Y)	7,000	
Investment in Branch X.	7,420	

Observe that the charge to freight expense by the home office represents the expenditure on freight in excess of that required for a direct shipment to Branch Y. In effect, the $120 charge represents the cost of the management error of having shipped merchandise to X instead of Y ($120 = $250 + $170 − $300), which is treated by the home office as an operating expense of the current period.

SUMMARY

The division of a firm into a home office and branches is a convenient way to decentralize its accounting for operations. The foregoing chapter illustrates the distinctive accounting procedures required to account for transactions between a home office and its branches. The recording of such transactions on the records of the home office and its branches gives rise to equal and offsetting or *reciprocal* account balances. Although branches may maintain separate double-entry accounting systems for which separate financial statements can be prepared, branches do not represent separate accounting entities for purposes of financial reporting. Accordingly, the financial information from the records of a home office and its branches must be combined before the financial statements for the company can be prepared. The combination procedure, which is accomplished on a worksheet, requires that reciprocal account balances be offset against one another and eliminated before the branch and home office financial information is combined. The combination worksheet procedure varies somewhat depending on whether the home office bills its branches for the cost of transferred merchandise or for an amount above cost. Both cases are illustrated in the foregoing chapter.

QUESTIONS

Q16-1   Discuss why a company might establish branches.

Q16-2   Discuss the nature of the home office account on the books of the branch and the investment in branch account on the books of the home office.

Q16-3   What are three pricing methods used by a home office in billing the branch for merchandise transferred from the home office? Discuss the reasons for the use of each of these methods.

Q16-4   Under what conditions might the home office and the branch desire to (a) prepare separate financial statements and (b) prepare combined financial statements?

Q16-5   Discuss the purpose of worksheets in preparing combined financial statements of the home office and branch.

Q16-6   Describe two potential types of worksheet adjustments made when preparing combined financial statements for the home office and branch, and indicate whether each of the respective types of adjustments is formally recorded in the home office and/or branch records.

Q16-7   What are reciprocal accounts? Give an example of reciprocal accounts in a home office/branch relationship.

Q16-8   Branch A transferred merchandise to Branch B; both branches purchase all their merchandise from the home office. Describe the general guidelines governing the amount of freight cost recorded by Branch B for the interbranch transfer of merchandise.

Q16-9   Describe how the allowance for unrealized gross margin in branch inventory account is used by a company that wishes to allocate the gross margin on transferred merchandise between the home office and the branch.

Q16-10   Assuming the home office and branch prepare separate financial statements, in whose financial statements would each of the following accounts appear and where in the respective financial statements would the account be reported?

a) Allowance for unrealized gross margin in branch inventory

b) Home office

c) Investment in branch

Q16-11   Prepare entries on the books of the home office and the branch to record the following independent purchases of furniture and fixtures for use by a branch. Use an X to indicate amounts.

a) The home office purchases furniture and fixtures for cash and transfers them to the branch; the branch does not maintain fixed asset accounts.

b) The branch purchases furniture and fixtures for cash; the branch does not maintain fixed asset accounts.

c) The home office purchases furniture and fixtures for cash and transfers them to the branch; the branch maintains fixed asset accounts.

d) The branch purchases furniture and fixtures for cash; the branch maintains fixed asset accounts.

Q16-12   Explain why you agree or disagree with the following statement: The pricing method used by the home office in billing the branch for merchandise transfers will affect the amounts in the combined financial statements.

Q16-13   How should freight costs on merchandise transferred from Branch C to Branch D in excess of that required for a direct transfer to Branch D be treated?

EXERCISES

E16-1   **Journal Entries for Home Office and Branch**   Brockwell Company is located in Virginia and operates a branch in North Carolina. Transactions related to the branch operations are as follows:

1. The home office transferred $1,000 of cash to the branch.

2. The merchandise costing the home office $2,000 was transferred to the branch; the merchandise is billed at cost.

3. The sales on account totaling $1,000 were made by the branch; merchandise cost the branch $500.

4. The branch collected accounts receivable of $300.

5. The home office paid and notified the branch that it had incurred $500 of general and administrative expenses to benefit the branch.

6. The branch remitted $100 of cash to the home office.

7. Returned to the home office $300 of the merchandise received in transaction (2) above.

8. The home office purchased equipment for $900 cash and transferred it to the branch; the branch does not maintain fixed asset accounts.

9. The branch paid operating expenses of $400.

10. The branch purchased equipment for $700 cash and notified the home office of the purchase; the branch does not maintain fixed asset accounts.

REQUIRED
Prepare journal entries to record the preceding transactions for the home office and the branch.

E16-2 **Home Office and Branch Journal Entries for Intracompany Transfers of Inventory at Various Billing Rates** The Franklin Coin Company, a Washington-based company dealing in the buying and selling of rare coins, operates several branches in Washington and northern Virginia. Franklin transfers merchandise to its various branches at different billing rates. The following are transfers of merchandise from the home office to its branches:

1. The merchandise costing the home office $7,000 was transferred to the branch at cost.

2. The merchandise costing the home office $6,000 was transferred to the branch at a billed price of cost plus 25% of cost.

3. The home office transferred merchandise to the branch at a billed price of $5,400, which is the price the home office sells to its outside customers. The home office sells its merchandise at 120% of the cost.

4. The home office ordered and paid for $2,000 of merchandise and had it shipped directly from the supplier to the branch. A freight cost of $200 is to be paid by the branch upon arrival of the merchandise. The home office policy is to sell merchandise to the branch at cost.

5. The merchandise costing the home office $1,000 was billed to the branch at 110% of the cost. The home office paid the freight cost of $50 for the branch.

REQUIRED
Prepare entries for the home office and the branch to record each of the preceding independent transactions.

E16-3 **Analysis of Comments on Branch Accounting** Indicate whether you agree or disagree with each of the following statements. If you disagree with a statement, provide an explanation as to why.

1. The division of a firm into a home office and branches is a convenient way to centralize its operations without conferring a high level of autonomy on the branches.

2. Branches may be used to expand a firm's sales efforts into new markets.

3. A home office and a branch represent two accounting systems but one accounting entity for purposes of financial reporting.

4. The investment in branch account and the home office account are reciprocal accounts that appear in the combined financial statement for the home office and branch.

5. The allowance for unrealized gross margin in branch inventory account is a contra-asset account that is subtracted from the investment in branch account on the separate financial statements of the home office.

6. The entry on the books of the home office to record the transfer of $25,000 of new equipment to a branch that does not maintain fixed asset accounts would be

Investment in branch 25,000
      Equipment   25,000

7. If cash transferred from the home office to a branch is in transit and has not been recorded on the branch books, the balance of the home office account exceeds the balance of the investment in branch account.

8. Home office net income (including income from branch) presented on its separate financial statements equals net income presented on combined financial statements of the home office and branch.

9. Freight costs of transferring merchandise from the Sarasota Branch to the Orono Branch in excess of that required for a direct transfer of merchandise from the home office to the Orono Branch should be treated as an operating expense of the home office for the current period.

10. Separate financial statements of the home office and its branches are useful for internal management purposes; however, only the combined financial statements of the entity are issued to parties outside the entity.

E16-4   **Adjust the Allowance for Unrealized Gross Margin in Branch Inventory**   On January 1, 19X5, Ginger Company established the Ale Branch. Ale, while operating very much as an independent entity, acquires all its merchandise from Ginger at 120% of cost. Ginger records the markup on merchandise transfers to the branch in an *allowance for unrealized gross margin in branch inventory* account.

    During 19X5, Ginger shipped merchandise to the Ale Branch at a billing price of $9,000. For the fiscal year ended December 31, 19X5, Ale sold 75% of the merchandise transferred from the home office and reported a net income of $5,500.

REQUIRED

a) Prepare the entry on the books of the home office to record branch income and to adjust the *allowance for unrealized gross margin in branch inventory* account for the markup on transfers realized (associated with branch sales) during the year.

b) What type of account is the *allowance for unrealized gross margin in branch inventory,* and how would this account be presented in the separate financial statements of the home office?

E16-5   **Reconciliation of Home Office and Branch Accounts**   On January 1, 19X1, Taylor Company established a branch in a nearby city. At the close of the fiscal year ended December 31, 19X1, the investment in branch account on the books of the home office had a balance of $6,600, and the home office account on the books of the branch had a balance of $4,500. The difference in the balances in the reciprocal accounts is due to the following data:

1. Cash of $1,000 forwarded to the home office by the branch is in transit and has not been recorded on the home office books.

2. Merchandise costing the home office $800 was transferred to the branch at a billing price of $900. The merchandise is in transit and has not been recorded on the branch books.

3. Notification sent by the home office to the branch, informing the branch of $500 of operating expenses that the home office paid on behalf of the branch, has not been received by the branch and thus has not been recorded by the branch.

4. Cash of $200 received by the branch from the home office was erroneously recorded by the branch as $2,000.

5. The branch purchased, for cash, $1,500 of equipment for its use; fixed asset accounts of the branch are maintained at the home office. Notification sent to the home office by the branch, informing the home office of the branch's action, has not been received by the home office and thus has not been recorded by the home office.

REQUIRED

a) Prepare entries on the books of the home office or the branch for items (1) through (5).

b) Prepare a reconciliation of the investment in branch and home office accounts, showing the corrected book balances.

E16-6   **Multiple Choice Questions on Home Office/Branch Accounting**

1. The home office account on the books of the branch is comparable to

    a) An asset account

    b) An ownership equity account

    c) A liability account

    d) All of the above

2. The Hopalong Branch receives all its inventory from the home office at a billing price equal to the retail selling price of the inventory. If selling prices are correctly anticipated, then the branch income statement for the year will show

    a) A net income or loss depending on the sales volume

    b) A net loss equal to the amount of operating expenses

    c) A net loss due to operating expenses being overstated

    d) A net income due to the cost of goods sold being correctly stated

3. The adjustments (excluding those adjustments for in-transit items and errors) appearing on the worksheet used in preparing combined financial statements of the home office and the branch

    a) Are recorded in the accounting records of both the home office and the branch

    b) Are recorded in the accounting records of the home office only

    c) Are not recorded in the accounting records of the home office or the branch

    d) Are recorded in the accounting records of the branch only

4. Branch A and Branch B receive all inventories from the home office at cost to the home office plus 10% to cover freight charges of the home office. The home office instructed Branch A to transfer $1,000 of merchandise to Branch B. Freight cost of shipping inventory from A to B was $120. The $20 excess freight cost of transferring inventory from A to B over the freight cost of a direct shipment to B from the home office should be treated as

    a) An increase in the value of the inventory of Branch B

    b) A decrease in the value of the inventory of Branch A

    c) An operating expense of the current period by Branch A

    d) An operating expense of the current period by the home office

5. The home office bills its branch for merchandise transfers at a price in excess of cost. When the home office prepares separate financial statements, the allowance for unrealized gross margin in branch inventory account would appear in the financial statements of the home office as

    a) An operating expense of the current period

    b) Deduction from the cost of goods sold

    c) Addition to the cost of goods sold

    d) Deduction from the investment in branch account

6. In home office/branch merchandise transfers, the use of a *shipment to branch* account by the home office and the use of a *shipment from home office* account by the branch indicates that the inventory system employed

    a) Is a perpetual inventory system

    b) Is a periodic inventory system

    c) Is neither perpetual nor periodic

    d) Cannot be determined from the information provided

7. Which of the following accounts would be shown on the combined financial statements of the home office and branch?

    a) Investment in branch account

    b) Allowance for unrealized gross margin in branch inventory

    c) Home office account

    d) None of the above

8. Corporation A established several branches in a neighboring city. Which of the following would be possible reasons for Corporation A establishing the branches?

    a) The branches may be a suitable way to expand the firm's sales efforts into new markets.

    b) The branches may provide Corporation A certain benefits of decentralized operations without conferring a high level of autonomy on the various components of the firm.

    c) The branches may have been a favorable alternative to establishing a traveling sales force operated from corporate headquarters or to the acquisition of firms already operating in the new markets.

    d) All of the above.

9. The home office sells merchandise to its branch at 120% of cost. The branch was established several years ago with the policy that all its merchandise would be acquired from the home office. Information from the records of the home office and branch reveals the following for the current year ended:

	Home Office	Branch
Allowance for unrealized gross margin in branch inventory	$4,600	
Inventory, beginning		$3,600
Inventory, ending		6,000

The balance that would appear in the *allowance for unrealized gross margin in branch inventory* account on the home office books, after adjusting and closing entries have been prepared by the home office, would be

    a) $1,000   **c)** $2,000

    b) $ 400   **d)** $2,400

E16-7   **Journal Entries for Home Office and Branch; Branch Income Statement and Closing Entries**

The Knicks Sporting Goods, Inc., located in New York, established a branch in Alabama on January 1, 19X7. The home office transferred $3,000 of cash and $10,000 of merchandise (cost) to the branch. During the year, the branch sold 51% of the merchandise transferred from the home office on account for $7,800. The branch collected cash of $4,500 from accounts receivable during the year and allowed $325 in sales discounts. The branch paid $1,200 of operating expenses incurred for the year and remitted cash of $1,000 to the home office. Ending inventory of the branch as of December 31, 19X7, was $4,900.

REQUIRED

a) Prepare journal entries for the preceding 19X7 transactions on the books of the home office and branch.

b) Prepare a 19X7 income statement for the branch.

c) Prepare closing entries for the branch as of December 31, 19X7.

E16-8 **Journal Entries for Home Office and Adjustment of the Allowance for Unrealized Gross Margin in Branch Inventory** Elm Company, a manufacturer and distributor of toys, established a branch in Florida on December 1, 19X1. Earlier during the year, a branch had been established in Atlanta. Both branches acquire all their merchandise from the home office at 110% of the cost to the home office. All long-lived assets used by the branches are recorded on the books of the home office. As of December 31, 19X1, the Florida branch's cost of goods sold was $5,500 and its home office account consisted of the following:

Home Office Account

19X1				19X1			
Dec. 16	Purchased long-lived asset (equipment) on account	350		Dec. 1	Received cash from home office	5,000	
20	Forwarded cash to home office	500		5	Merchandise transfers from home office (excluding freight)	5,720	
25	Transferred merchandise to Atlanta Branch (no freight involved)	220		31	Notification by home office of insurance expense it paid on behalf of the branch	75	
				31	Net income	955	

REQUIRED

a) For each of the preceding December postings in the branch's home office account, prepare the journal entry that the home office would have recorded on its books.

b) Record the entry for the home office to adjust its allowance for unrealized gross margin in branch inventory account for the markup on transfers realized (associated with branch sales) during the year.

E16-9 **Combination Worksheet Adjustments** Presented here is selected information from the separate financial statements of the home office and the branch at the end of the fiscal year, December 31, 19X1. The home office bills merchandise to the branch at cost plus 15% of cost. The branch was established five years ago and buys all its merchandise from the home office.

	Home Office	Branch
Allowance for unrealized gross margin in branch inventory	$ 900	
Income from branch	5,000	
Cost of goods sold		$23,000
Merchandise inventory, 12-31-X1		6,900
Home office, preclosing		50,000
Net income		2,000

(Continued on page 812)

REQUIRED

Prepare in journal entry form the adjustments that would appear on the worksheet to prepare combined financial statements for the home office and the branch as of December 31, 19X1.

E16-10 **Adjust the Allowance for Unrealized Gross Margin in Branch Inventory** At the beginning of 19X1, Samco Video established a Regency Branch and a Cloverleaf Branch in order to provide wider distribution of its merchandise. Merchandise is transferred to the branches at a price 30% above cost. All branch merchandise is acquired from the home office. At the end of 19X1, the Regency Branch and the Cloverleaf Branch reported net income and ending inventory balances as follows:

	Net Income	Ending Inventory
Regency Branch	$45,500	$65,000
Cloverleaf Branch	52,000	78,000

The year-end balances in the home office account's *allowance for unrealized gross margin in branch inventory* are $48,750 for the Regency Branch and $58,500 for the Cloverleaf Branch.

REQUIRED

Prepare entries on the home office books to record the income from the branches and to adjust the allowance for unrealized gross margin in branch inventory accounts for the markups on transfers realized (associated with branch sales) during the year.

E16-11 **Journal Entries for Home Office and Branch Relating to Fixed Asset Transactions** The following are several home office/branch transactions relating to fixed assets:

1. The branch purchased equipment for $5,000 cash. The asset is to be used by the branch but carried on the home office books.

2. The branch forwarded to the home office $1,000 of equipment purchased in transaction (1) above because it was no longer needed for its operations.

3. The home office purchased, on account, $2,000 of furniture and fixtures for the branch. The items were forwarded to the branch, where all records for assets used by the branch are maintained.

4. The branch purchased, on account, $1,200 of equipment to be used in its operations. Assets used by the branch are carried on the books of the branch.

5. The home office forwarded machinery costing originally $10,000, with accumulated depreciation of $7,500, to the branch for use in its operations. Assets used by the branch are carried on the books of the branch.

6. The home office recorded and notified the branch of $700 of depreciation expense on fixed assets used by the branch; assets used by the branch are carried on the books of the home office.

7. The branch acquired, on account, $2,500 of equipment for its use. The branch agrees to pay for the equipment within 60 days; fixed assets used by the branch are carried on the home office books.

8. The branch pays for the equipment acquired in item (7).

REQUIRED

Prepare the journal entries on the books of the home office and the branch for each of the preceding transactions.

PROBLEMS

P16-1 **Journal Entries for Home Office and Branch** KPMG Design recently established a branch in a very popular shopping center in the Washington-Baltimore area. Following are selected transactions of the home and branch during the first year of operations.

1. The home office transferred $20,000 cash to the branch.

2. The branch purchased $8,000 of merchandise on account from outside suppliers.

3. Machinery costing the home office $30,000, with accumulated depreciation of $13,000, is transferred by the home office to the branch. Assets used by the branch are carried on the books of the branch.

4. The home office shipped merchandise costing the home office $18,000 to the branch at a billed price of cost plus 30% of cost.

5. The branch sold merchandise on account for $19,600; the merchandise cost the branch $14,000.

6. The branch paid operating expenses of $3,500.

7. Accounts receivable of $6,000 were collected by the branch.

8. The home office paid and notified the branch of operating expenses of $1,800 that had been incurred on behalf of the branch.

9. The branch transferred $1,200 cash to the home office.

10. The branch purchased $3,200 of equipment on account to be used in its operations. Assets used by the branch are carried on the books of the branch.

REQUIRED
Prepare journal entries on the books of the home office and the branch for the above transactions.

P16-2 **Journal Entries and Closing Entries for Home Office and Branch** In 19X1, James River Company opened a branch in a neighboring state. The branch acquires all its merchandise from the home office at a billing price of 120% of the cost to the home office. During 19X3, the following transactions concerning the home office and branch occurred:

1. The home office shipped merchandise to the branch and billed the branch for $14,400.

2. The home office purchased $40,000 of merchandise on account.

3. The home office and branch made sales on account totaling $70,000 and $40,000, respectively. Cost of the goods sold for the home office and branch was $20,000 and $14,400, respectively.

4. The home office purchased, for cash, $8,000 of equipment and forwarded it to the branch for the branch's use; fixed asset accounts are maintained at the home office.

5. The home office and branch paid operating expenses totaling $45,000 and $25,000, respectively.

6. The home office recorded and notified the branch of $300 of depreciation expense relating to the equipment the branch is using.

7. The branch forwarded $2,000 cash to the home office.

8. The branch returned $2,400 (billing price) of the merchandise shipped to it by the home office in item (1).

Additional information:

1. The ending inventory on the books of the home office and branch was $25,000 and $3,600, respectively.

2. The allowance for unrealized gross margin in the branch inventory account on the home office books had a balance of $3,000 before the adjustment for the portion of markup on transfers that were realized (associated with branch sales) during 19X3.

(Continued on page 814)

REQUIRED

a) Prepare journal entries on the books of the home office and the branch for transactions (1) through (8).

b) Prepare closing entries for the branch as of December 31, 19X3.

c) Prepare the entry on the home office books to record the income from the branch, and adjust the allowance for unrealized gross margin in branch inventory account for the portion of markup on transfers realized (associated with branch sales) during 19X3.

d) Prepare closing entries for the home office as of December 31, 19X3.

P16-3 **Combination Worksheet (End of First Year, Inventory Transferred at Cost); Combined Financial Statements**   Layfield, a well-known department store in the Chicago area, established a branch in a nearby city on January 1, 19X2. Layfield buys all merchandise for the branch and bills the branch at cost to the home office. The financial statements of each company as of December 31, 19X2, are presented as follows:

	Home Office	Branch
Income Statement		
Sales	$100,000	$30,000
Cost of goods sold	(28,000)	(20,000)
Gross margin	$ 72,000	$10,000
Other expenses	(18,000)	(7,000)
Income from home office	$ 54,000	
Income from branch	3,000	
Net income	$ 57,000	$ 3,000
Statement of Retained Earnings and Home Office		
Retained earnings, 1-1-X2	$ 25,000	$
Home office, preclosing		52,000
Net income	57,000	3,000
Retained earnings/home office, 12-31-X2	$ 82,000	$55,000
Balance Sheet		
Assets		
Cash	$ 29,000	$22,000
Accounts receivable	50,000	16,000
Inventory	28,000	12,000
Investment in branch	55,000	
Other assets	30,000	15,000
Total assets	$192,000	$65,000
Liabilities and Stockholders' Equity		
Accounts payable	$ 18,000	$10,000
Home office		55,000
Common stock	92,000	
Retained earnings	82,000	
Total liabilities and stockholders' equity	$192,000	$65,000

REQUIRED

a) Prepare a combination worksheet for Layfield and its branch as of December 31, 19X2.

b) Prepare a combined income statement and balance sheet for Layfield and its branch as of December 31, 19X2.

P16-4 **Journal Entries for Home Office and Branches, Branch Closing Entry, Home Office Adjustment to Allowance for Unrealized Gross Margin in Branch Inventory** Top Forty, Inc., a distributor of record albums, cassette tapes, compact discs, and related hardware equipment, operates two branches—Cary Branch and Lee Branch. Top Forty and its branches prepare monthly financial statements. The following are selected transactions between the home office and its branches during the month ended December 31, 19X2.

1. Home office transferred $5,000 cash to Cary Branch.

2. Merchandise costing the home office $8,000 was shipped to Cary Branch at a billing price of cost plus 10% of cost. Freight cost on the transfer of $200 was paid by the home office and billed to the branch in this amount.

3. Cary Branch purchased furniture and fixtures for $1,000 cash; records of fixed assets are maintained on the books of the home office.

4. Cary Branch purchased $4,000 of merchandise for cash from outside entities.

5. The home office paid and notified Cary Branch of expenses for insurance of $100 and advertising of $150 that had been incurred on behalf of the branch.

6. Cary Branch recorded $12,000 of sales on account; cost of goods sold is $8,400, consisting of $4,000 of merchandise purchased from outsiders and $4,400 of merchandise from the home office.

7. The home office incurred and notified Cary Branch of a $100 depreciation expense on the furniture and fixtures used by the branch and carried on the books of the home office.

8. At the request of the home office, Cary Branch sent $1,000 cash to Lee Branch.

9. Cary Branch paid rent and utility expenses of $400 and $125, respectively.

10. Upon notification from the home office, Cary Branch shipped one-fourth of the merchandise received in item (2) to Lee Branch. Cary Branch paid the freight cost of $75 to transfer the merchandise to Lee Branch. Freight cost on shipments of this kind, when sent directly from the home office, is normally $60.

11. Cary Branch remitted $1,000 cash to the home office.

The inventory of Cary Branch on December 31, 19X2, was $2,200 (composed entirely of merchandise acquired from the home office); Cary Branch did not have any beginning inventory.

REQUIRED

a) Prepare entries on the books of the home office and Cary Branch and Lee Branch for the preceding transactions.

b) Prepare an income statement for Cary Branch for the month ended December 31, 19X2.

c) Prepare closing entries for Cary Branch for the month ended December 31, 19X2.

d) Prepare the entry on the books of the home office to record the net income from Cary Branch for the month of December, and adjust the allowance for unrealized gross margin in branch inventory account for the portion of markups on transfers realized (associated with branch sales) during the month ended December 31, 19X2.

P16-5 **Combination Worksheet (End of First Year, Inventory Transferred above Cost), Home Office and Branch Closing Entries**   In an effort to expand its sales into a new market, Banner Ideas Inc. established a branch in an adjacent state on January 1, 19X2. The branch acquires all its merchandise from the home office at 125% of the cost to the home office. As of December 31, 19X2, the financial statements of the home office and the branch appeared as follows:

	Home Office	Branch
Income Statement		
Sales	$125,000	$40,000
Cost of goods sold	(54,200)	(16,000)
Gross margin	$ 70,800	$24,000
Other expenses	(35,000)	(25,000)
Income from home office	$ 35,800	
Income from branch	2,200	
Net income (loss)	$ 38,000	$(1,000)
Statement of Retained Earnings and Home Office		
Retained earnings, 1-1-X2	$ 30,000	$
Home office, preclosing		25,000
Net income (loss)	38,000	(1,000)
Retained earnings/home office, 12-31-X2	$ 68,000	$24,000
Balance Sheet		
Assets		
Cash	$ 20,000	$10,000
Accounts receivable	30,000	18,000
Inventory	45,000	10,000
Investment in branch	24,000	
Allowance for unrealized gross margin in branch inventory	(2,000)	
Furniture and fixtures (net)	40,000	
Other assets	15,000	9,000
Total assets	$172,000	$47,000
Liabilities and Stockholders' Equity		
Liabilities	$ 14,000	$23,000
Home office		24,000
Common stock	90,000	
Retained earnings	68,000	
Total liabilities and stockholders' equity	$172,000	$47,000

REQUIRED

a) Prepare a combination worksheet for Banner Ideas Inc. and its branch as of December 31, 19X2.

b) Prepare closing entries for the branch as of December 31, 19X2.

c) Prepare closing entries for the home office as of December 31, 19X2.

P16-6   **Combination Worksheet for Two Branches (End of Second Year, Inventory Transferred above Cost)**   In 19X4, the Goodlife Corporation expanded its sales operations by establishing two branches, Bigtime and Anytime. The branches acquire their merchandise from the home office at 110% of cost. The financial statements for the home office and the two branches, as of December 31, 19X5, are listed as follows:

	Home Office	Bigtime Branch	Anytime Branch
Income Statement			
Sales	$267,000	$136,000	$62,850
Cost of goods sold	(199,000)	(176,000)	(44,000)
Gross margin (loss)	$ 68,000	$ (40,000)	$18,850
Other expenses	(25,000)	(5,000)	(7,750)
Income from home office	$ 43,000		
Income (loss) from Bigtime Branch	(29,000)		
Income from Anytime Branch	15,100		
Net income (loss)	$ 29,100	$ (45,000)	$11,100
Statement of Retained Earnings and Home Office			
Retained earnings, 1-1-X5	$486,500	$	$
Home office, preclosing		200,000	92,000
Net income (loss)	29,100	(45,000)	11,100
Retained earnings/home office, 12-31-X5	$515,600	$155,000	$103,100
Balance Sheet			
Assets			
Cash	$150,000	$ 5,000	$ 3,500
Accounts receivable	175,000	3,600	1,200
Inventory	100,000	77,000	55,000
Investment in Bigtime Branch	155,000		
Allowance for unrealized gross margin in branch inventory, Bigtime	(7,000)		
Investment in Anytime Branch	103,100		
Allowance for unrealized gross margin in branch inventory, Anytime	(5,000)		
Furniture and fixtures (net)	150,000	20,000	
Other assets	125,000	60,000	55,000
Total assets	$946,100	$165,600	$114,700
Liabilities and Stockholders' Equity			
Accounts payable	$ 51,000	$ 3,600	$ 5,750
Other liabilities	25,850	7,000	5,850
Home office		155,000	103,100
Common stock	353,650		
Retained earnings	515,600		
Total liabilities and stockholders' equity	$946,100	$165,600	$114,700

REQUIRED
Prepare a combination worksheet for Goodlife Corporation and its branches as of December 31, 19X5.

P16-7 **Combination Worksheet (End of Second Year, Inventory Transferred above Cost), Home Office and Branch Closing Entries and Financial Statements**   Two years ago Rose Company established the Bud Branch in Short Pump, Virginia. The branch acquires all its merchandise from the home office at cost plus 10% of cost to the home office. Trial balances of the home office and branch as of December 31, 19X7, appear as follows:

	Home Office	Branch
Debits		
Cash	$ 2,000	$ 500
Accounts receivable	9,000	4,000
Inventory	20,000	5,500
Investment in branch	15,000	
Other assets	83,400	20,000
Cost of goods sold	36,000	20,900
Other expenses	30,000	4,500
Dividends	12,000	
	$207,400	$55,400
Credits		
Allowance for unrealized gross margin in branch inventory	$ 2,400	$
Liabilities	15,000	10,400
Common stock	75,000	
Retained earnings	25,000	
Home office, preclosing		15,000
Sales	90,000	30,000
	$207,400	$55,400

REQUIRED

a) Prepare an income statement and a balance sheet for the branch as of December 31, 19X7.

b) Prepare entries on the home office books to record income from the branch and to adjust the *allowance for unrealized gross margin in branch inventory* account for the portion of markup on transfers realized (associated with branch sales) during the year.

c) Prepare an income statement and a balance sheet for the home office as of December 31, 19X7.

d) Prepare a combination worksheet for Rose Company and its branch as of December 31, 19X7.

e) Prepare a combined income statement and balance sheet for Rose Company and its branch as of December 31, 19X7.

P16-8 **Combination Worksheet (End of First Month, Inventory Transferred above Cost), Items in Transit**   On December 1, 19X7, Beauty Mark Corporation opened a branch to sell various types of contemporary jewelry. To assist in the planning of future expansion, Beauty Mark prepares monthly financial statements. The trial balances of the home office and its branch as of December 31, 19X7, appear as follows:

	Home Office	Branch
Debits		
Cash	$ 25,000	$ 33,000
Accounts receivable	16,000	40,000
Inventory	16,000	12,000
Investment in branch	84,000	
Furniture and fixtures (net)	80,000	
Cost of goods sold	34,000	24,000
Other expenses	10,000	11,000
	$265,000	$120,000
Credits		
Allowance for unrealized gross margin in branch inventory	$ 4,000	$
Accounts payable	35,000	15,000
Common stock	75,000	
Retained earnings	50,000	
Home office, preclosing		65,000
Sales	92,000	40,000
Income from branch	9,000	
	$265,000	$120,000

Additional information:

1. Items in transit:

a) The home office shipped merchandise on December 29, 19X7, at a billed price of $12,000 to the branch, but the branch has not received the merchandise.

b) On December 30, 19X7, the branch forwarded $1,250 cash to the home office, but the home office has not received the cash.

c) The branch purchased display cases for $750 cash. Notification of the branch's action has been forwarded to the home office but has not yet been received. Accounts for fixed assets used by the branch are maintained at the home office.

2. All merchandise sold at the branch is received from the home office. Billings to the branch are at cost plus 20% of cost to the home office. The $12,000 inventory of the branch at December 31, 19X7, does not include the inventory transfer in transit from the home office at the end of December.

The preceding trial balances for the home office and branch incorporate all appropriate adjusting entries by the home office and branch except those relating to items in transit.

REQUIRED

a) Prepare a combination worksheet for Beauty Mark Corporation and its branch for the month ended December 31, 19X7. Enter the preceding trial balances in the home office and branch columns on the left-hand side of the worksheet, with the various accounts grouped according to the financial statements with which they are associated. Then enter the adjustments for items in transit on the worksheet before making the combination worksheet adjustments.

b) Prepare the entries to record the adjustments for items in transit on the respective books of the home office or branch.

P16-9 **Combination Worksheet (End of Third Year, Inventory Transferred above Cost), Items in Transit, Combined Financial Statements**   The Havens Company, a prominent retail clothing firm, established a branch three years ago to provide a distribution channel for its merchandise in a rapidly growing area of the country. The trial balances of the Havens Company and its branch at the end of the fiscal period, December 31, 19X3, appear as follows:

	Home Office	Branch
Debits		
Cash	$ 17,000	$ 750
Inventory	30,000	15,400
Investment in branch	66,200	
Other assets	200,000	48,450
Cost of goods sold	77,000	105,600
Other expenses	48,000	29,800
	$438,200	$200,000
Credits		
Allowance for unrealized gross margin in branch inventory	$ 2,000	$
Liabilities	36,000	8,500
Common stock	200,000	
Retained earnings	31,000	
Home office, preclosing		51,500
Sales	155,000	140,000
Income from branch	14,200	
	$438,200	$200,000

Additional information:

1. The branch deposits all cash receipts in a local bank to the account of the home office. Deposits of this nature included the following:

Amount	Date Deposited by Branch	Date Recorded by Home Office
$1,050	December 27, 19X3	December 31, 19X3
1,100	December 30, 19X3	January 2, 19X4
600	December 31, 19X3	January 3, 19X4
300	January 2, 19X4	January 6, 19X4

2. The branch pays expenses incurred locally from an imprest bank account that is maintained with a balance of $2,000. Checks are drawn once a week on this imprest account, and the home office is notified of the amount needed to replenish the account. At December 31, an $1,800 reimbursement check was mailed to the branch; the check was not received by the branch until January 19X4.

3. The branch receives all its merchandise from the home office. The home office bills merchandise to the branch at 110% of the cost to the home office. At December 31, 19X3, a shipment with a billing value of $6,600 was in transit to the branch.

The preceding trial balances for the home office and branch incorporate all appropriate adjusting entries by the home office and branch except those relating to items in transit.

REQUIRED

a) Prepare a combination worksheet for the Havens Company and its branch for the year ended December 31, 19X3. Enter the preceding trial balances in the home office and branch columns on the left-hand side of the worksheet, with the various accounts grouped according to the financial statements with which they are associated. Then enter the adjustments for items in transit on the worksheet before making the combination worksheet adjustments.

b) Prepare a combined income statement, statement of retained earnings, and balance sheet for Havens Company and its branch as of December 31, 19X3.

(AICPA adapted)

P16-10 **Combination Worksheet (Inventory Transferred above Cost), Errors and Items in Transit**
The trial balances of the Baltimore Wholesale Company and its Atlanta Branch at December 31, 19X5, are shown as follows:

Accounts	Home Office Dr. (Cr.)	Branch Dr. (Cr.)
Cash	$ 36,000	$ 8,000
Accounts receivable	35,000	12,000
Inventory	55,000	20,000
Investment in branch	35,000	
Allowance for unrealized gross margin in branch inventory	(3,500)	
Property, plant and equipment (net)	92,600	
Accounts payable	(50,000)	(16,000)
Home office, preclosing		(9,000)
Common stock	(50,000)	
Retained earnings	(42,500)	
Sales	(392,000)	
Income from branch	(24,600)	
Cost of goods sold	265,000	64,000
Other expenses	44,000	16,000
	$ –0–	$ –0–

Additional information:

1. Errors and items in transit:

a) On December 23, the branch manager purchased $4,000 of furniture and fixtures for cash, but failed to notify the home office. The accountant, knowing that all fixed assets are carried on the home office books, recorded the proper entry on the branch records. It is the company's policy not to take any depreciation on assets acquired in the last half of the year.

b) On December 27, a branch customer erroneously paid his account of $2,000 to the home office. The accountant made the correct entry on the home office books but did not notify the branch.

c) On December 30, the branch remitted cash of $5,000. It was received by the home office in January 19X6.

d) On December 31, the branch erroneously recorded the December allocated expenses from the home office as $500 instead of $1,500.

e) On December 31, the home office shipped merchandise billed at $3,000 to the branch. The merchandise was received in January 19X6.

2. The branch may acquire its merchandise from outside suppliers or the home office. The branch's cost of goods sold and its inventory at December 31, 19X5, excluding the shipment in transit from the home office, are comprised of 10% of merchandise acquired from outside suppliers.

3. The home office consistently bills shipments to the branch at 120% of the cost.

The preceding trial balances for the home office and branch incorporate all appropriate adjusting entries by the home office and branch except those relating to items in transit and errors.

REQUIRED

Prepare a combination worksheet for the Baltimore Wholesale Company and its branch for the year ended December 31, 19X5. Enter the preceding trial balance in the home office and branch columns on the left-hand side of the worksheet, with the various accounts grouped according to the financial statements with which they are associated. Then enter the adjustments on the worksheet for items in transit and errors before making the combination worksheet adjustments.

(AICPA adapted)

P16-11 **Combination Worksheet (Inventory Transferred above Cost), Items in Transit** You have been hired by the Terrific Corporation to assist the controller in preparing year-end financial data. In addition to selling its merchandise through its home office, Terrific sells its products through a branch. The trial balances of the home office and branch at December 31, 19X6, follow:

	Home Office	Branch
Debits		
Cash	$ 15,000	$ 2,000
Accounts receivable	20,000	17,000
Inventory	30,000	8,000
Investment in branch	60,000	
Other assets (net)	150,000	
Cost of goods sold	136,000	93,000
Other expenses	70,000	41,000
	$481,000	$161,000
Credits		
Allowance for unrealized gross margin in		
branch inventory	$ 3,600	$
Accounts payable	73,000	2,000
Common stock	100,000	
Retained earnings	24,800	
Home office, preclosing		9,000
Sales	245,000	150,000
Income from branch	34,600	
Total	$481,000	$161,000

Additional information:

1. The branch receives all its merchandise from the home office. The home office bills merchandise to the branch at 125% of cost.

2. Items in transit:

a) At December 31, 19X6, merchandise with a billing value of $10,000 was in transit to the branch.

b) The home office billed the branch for $12,000 on December 31, 19X6, representing the branch's share of expenses paid at the home office. The branch has not recorded this billing.

c) All cash collections made by the branch are deposited in a local bank to the account of the home office. Deposits of this nature included the following:

Amount	Date Deposited by Branch	Date Recorded by Home Office
$5,000	December 28, 19X6	December 31, 19X6
3,000	December 30, 19X6	January 2, 19X7
7,000	December 31, 19X6	January 3, 19X7
2,000	January 2, 19X7	January 5, 19X7

d) Expenses incurred locally by the branch are paid from an imprest bank account, which is reimbursed periodically by the home office. Just prior to the end of the year, the home office forwarded a reimbursement check in the amount of $3,000, which was not received by the branch until January 19X7.

The preceding trial balances for the home office and branch incorporate all appropriate adjusting entries by the home office and branch except those relating to items in transit.

REQUIRED
Prepare a combination worksheet for the Terrific Corporation and its branch for the year ended December 31, 19X6. Enter the preceding trial balance in the home office and branch columns on the left-hand side of the worksheet, with the various accounts grouped according to the financial statements with which they are associated. Then record the adjustments for items in transit on the worksheet before making the combination worksheet adjustments.

(AICPA adapted)

ISSUES IN ACCOUNTING JUDGMENT

I16-1   Proposed Capitalization of New Branch Operating Loss   Early in 19X7, Evansville Products established a branch in Columbus to distribute its line of household cleaning products and to provide customer service and regional advertising. The branch has reported a significant loss for 19X7, and Evansville's controller argues that the loss is really an investment in starting a branch that should be capitalized and amortized over three or four years.

REQUIRED
Write a brief evaluation of the controller's argument.

I16-2   Transferring Merchandise at Price above Cost   Sanchez Manufacturing, Inc., is located in a state that levies no corporate income tax; however, the company is in the process of establishing branches in several states that levy significant corporate income taxes. The branches will maintain inventories, distribute the company's products to customers, and provide customer service. Your consulting firm has been hired to design the branch accounting system.

REQUIRED
Write a paragraph giving your recommendations for the segment of the accounting system concerned with the transfer of merchandise to the new branches.

I16-3   Branches versus Wholly Owned Subsidiaries   Marple Manufacturing, Inc., is planning to establish several sales offices at several distant locations and is debating whether to make them branches or wholly owned subsidiary corporations. All merchandise sold at these locations will be supplied by the central manufacturing facility on a just-in-time basis and will be billed at full standard cost plus a profit margin.

REQUIRED
Write a brief analysis of the accounting differences between branches and wholly owned subsidiary corporations in this context.

PART

FOUR

Governmental and Nonprofit Entities

17

Accounting for Governments

FUNDAMENTALS AND THE GENERAL FUND

ACCOUNTING FOR GOVERNMENTS   827

ACCOUNTING STANDARDS FOR STATE AND LOCAL GOVERNMENTS   828

Governmental Accounting Standards Board   829   GAAP and Legal Compliance   829

THE FINANCIAL REPORTING ENTITY   830

FUND ACCOUNTING SYSTEMS   831

Definition of a Fund   831   Types of Funds   832 Account Groups for General Fixed Assets and General Long-Term Debt   833

MEASUREMENT AND RECOGNITION   833

Measurement and Recognition of Revenue   834 Measurement and Recognition of Expenditures   836

BUDGETS AND EXPENDITURES CONTROL   839

Recording the Annual Budget   840   Recording Actual Sources and Uses of Funds   841   Closing Entries   841

ENCUMBRANCE ACCOUNTING   842

Recording Encumbrances   842   Reporting Encumbrances   843   Reporting a Fund Balance Reserved for Encumbrances   843   Recording Expenditures Related to Encumbrances of Prior Year   844

ACCOUNTING FOR THE GENERAL FUND   845

RECORDING GENERAL FUND BUDGET   848

RECORDING GENERAL FUND REVENUES AND OTHER FINANCIAL SOURCES   848

Recording Levy of Property Taxes   848   Recording Collection and Write-Off of Delinquent Property Taxes   849 Recording Tax Anticipation Notes Payable   849   Recording Collection and Write-Off of Current Property Taxes   851

Recording Delinquent Taxes and Related Allowance   852 Recording Interest and Penalties Receivable on Taxes   852 Delinquency Date after Year-End   852   Delinquent Property Taxes and Tax Liens   852   Recording Other Revenues   852

RECORDING GENERAL FUND ENCUMBRANCES AND EXPENDITURES   853

Recording Encumbrances   853   Recording Expenditures   853   Year-End Adjustment to Establish Fund Balance Reserved for Encumbrances   853   Recording Payment of Vouchers   853   Year-End Adjustment to Record Significant Supplies Inventories   856   Recording Permanent Petty Cash Funds   856   Recording Interfund Loan   856 Disposal of General Fixed Assets   856

GENERAL LEDGER ACCOUNTS AND CLOSING ENTRIES   856

FINANCIAL REPORTING FOR THE GENERAL FUND   857

INTERFUND TRANSACTIONS   858

QUASI-EXTERNAL TRANSACTIONS AND REIMBURSEMENTS   858

TRANSFERS   860

INTERFUND LOANS   861

ACCOUNTING FOR GRANTS, ENTITLEMENTS, AND SHARED REVENUES   863

SUMMARY   864

An ever-growing segment of our nation's resources is allocated to nonbusiness activities—the activities of federal, state, and local governments; of public educational systems; of nonprofit organizations like hospitals, research foundations, and social service organizations. Such organizations differ from business organizations in a number of ways. Perhaps the most striking difference is that the activities of nonbusiness organizations are not profit-seeking to any significant degree. Indeed, the direct charges for services delivered by nonbusiness organizations usually do not cover the full cost of those services. In some cases, in fact, no direct charge is made upon the recipients of the service and the entire cost is paid by others. Rather than being profit-oriented, nonbusiness organizations pursue goals that are defined in terms of the particular activities of the organization. For instance, education systems seek to instill and produce knowledge; hospitals seek to provide health care through training, research, and service; governments provide diverse programs, each with its own goals. Furthermore, resource contributions to nonbusiness organizations usually do not result in ownership equity interests in the organization. For example, taxpayers do not receive ownership shares in their government. These differences between nonbusiness and business organizations are reflected in the distinctive characteristics of the accounting and reporting systems of nonbusiness organizations, which are described in this and the next two chapters.

Nonbusiness organizations are divided into two basic groups—governments and nonprofit organizations. *Governments* perform a wide variety of functions and are funded substantially through taxes levied by formulas that may not reflect the benefits received by individual taxpayers. Some *nonprofit organizations,* like universities and hospitals, perform specified functions and are funded substantially by charges imposed on the direct beneficiaries of their services. Other nonprofit organizations, like charities and religious organizations, are funded substantially by donations. As a consequence of differences in objectives and activities, governments and nonprofit organizations employ somewhat different accounting systems. In addition, a separate rule-making organization issues authoritative accounting standards for governments. Although the FASB has primary standard-setting authority for nonprofit and business organizations, the Governmental Accounting Standards Board (GASB) is the primary standard-setter for state and local governments.

This and the following chapter present an introduction to governmental accounting. Accounting for nonprofit organizations is discussed in Chapter 19. We begin with a discussion of the fundamentals of governmental accounting; the latter part of the chapter is devoted to a discussion and illustration of common transactions of the general fund, which is one component of the governmental accounting system. The chapter concludes with a discussion of interfund transactions and accounting for grants, entitlements, and shared revenues.

ACCOUNTING FOR GOVERNMENTS

The objectives of external financial reporting by governments reflect the information needs of those who use these reports and the distinctive character of governmental operations. The principal users of external financial reports by governments are (1) the citizenry, (2) legislative and other oversight bodies, and (3) creditors and investors in securities issued by governments. Citizens, legislators, and other oversight officials use financial reports to assess accountability, that is, to assess whether the government has operated in a responsible manner. Creditors and investors in government securities use financial reports to assess a government's financial condition and its compliance with finance-related laws and regulations. In addition to these specific information needs, of course, governmental financial reports are influenced by the basic characteristics that are sought for any financial reporting system—understandability, reliability, relevance, timeliness, consistency, and comparability. *GASB Concepts Statement No. 1* (GASB Codification, Sec. 100.177–100.179) sets forth the financial reporting objectives that are summarized in the following issues section.

ISSUES

Financial Reporting Objectives

1. Financial reporting should assist in fulfilling government's duty to be publicly accountable and should enable users to assess that accountability by:

   a) Providing information to determine whether current year revenues were sufficient to pay for current year services

   b) Demonstrating whether resources were obtained and used in accordance with the entity's legally adopted budget, and demonstrating compliance with other finance-related legal or contractual requirements

   c) Providing information to assist users in assessing the service efforts, costs, and accomplishments of the governmental entity

2. Financial reporting should assist users in evaluating the operating results of the governmental entity for the year by:

   a) Providing information about sources and uses of financial resources

   b) Providing information about how it financed its activities and met its cash requirements

   c) Providing information necessary to determine whether its financial position improved or deteriorated as a result of the year's operations

3. Financial reporting should assist users in assessing the level of services that can be provided by the governmental entity and its ability to meet its obligations as they become due by:

   a) Providing information about its financial position and condition

   b) Providing information about its physical and other nonfinancial resources having useful lives that extend beyond the current year, including information that can be used to assess the service potential of those resources

   c) Disclosing legal or contractual restrictions on resources and the risk of potential loss of resources

Such objectives guide the determination of accounting standards for state and local governments, to which we now turn.

Accounting Standards for State and Local Governments

Although accounting by state and local governments is subject to standards and directives from many sources—including the Congress, state and local lawmaking bodies, the Governmental Accounting Standards Board, and the American Institute of Certified Public Accountants (AICPA)—the principal accounting and rule-making agency for state and local governments is the Governmental Accounting Standards Board.[1]

---

[1] All governmental units within the United States are not subject to the GASB. Accounting within the federal government and its many agencies is ultimately the responsibility of the Congress. The Congress

Governmental Accounting Standards Board

The Governmental Accounting Standards Board (GASB) was established in 1984. Like the Financial Accounting Standards Board (FASB), the GASB is under the general oversight of the Financial Accounting Foundation. The GASB succeeded the National Council on Governmental Accounting (NCGA) as the principal rule-making body for state and local governments. NCGA was a part-time body affiliated with the Government (formerly Municipal) Finance Officers Association and, during its lifetime, issued NCGA Statements and NCGA Interpretations. NCGA pronouncements together with various pronouncements of the AICPA and other organizations were incorporated into the standards of the GASB.

The GASB publishes *Governmental Accounting and Financial Reporting Standards* in two forms: original pronouncements and a codification that organizes the pronouncements into a cohesive framework incorporating revisions and additions. Both publications are regularly updated and reissued. Throughout this chapter and the next, pronouncements are referenced both to their original form (e.g., *GASB Concepts Statement No. 1*) and to the codification (e.g., *GASB Codification,* sec. 100.177). All the codified pronouncements do not carry equal weight. Rather, as noted in Chapter 11, there is a hierarchy of generally accepted accounting principles for state and local governments that must be observed in applying the pronouncements to real situations.

GAAP and Legal Compliance

Standards promulgated by the GASB require that governmental accounting systems make it possible to report in conformity with generally accepted accounting principles (GAAP) and to "determine and demonstrate compliance with finance-related legal and contractual provisions" (*NCGA Statement No. 1,* par. 2; *GASB Codification,* sec. 1200). Occasionally, legal provisions require accounting practices that differ from GAAP. For example, statutes may require a municipal water treatment facility to maintain its records on a cash basis, whereas GAAP require financial reporting on the accrual basis. Such conflicts are frequently the result of outmoded or poorly conceived statutes, which are, nonetheless, difficult to change. Moreover, compliance with the legal provisions is essential. Fortunately, it is usually possible to satisfy both the law and GAAP by supplementing the legally required records with additional records to permit reporting under GAAP. Usually, the primary financial statements could be prepared in accordance with GAAP, as required,

---

has established several agencies that direct accounting within the federal government. The Office of Management and Budget (OMB), an agency of the executive branch, assists the President in the preparation of the annual federal budget, which is submitted to Congress for approval. The Congressional Budget Office assists the Congress in its work with the budget. The General Accounting Office, an agency of the Congress under the direction of the Comptroller General of the United States, establishes and reviews the accounting systems and procedures applied in all departments of the federal government. Recent interest in improving federal accounting and budgeting systems produced the Federal Managers' Financial Integrity Act of 1982 and the Chief Financial Officer (CFO) Act of 1990. The latter established an office of federal financial management within the OMB, headed by a controller appointed by the President, and required each major department to have a CFO and a deputy CFO. For additional discussion of federal government accounting practices, see Larry Eisenhart and William Rita, "Federal Government Accounting Principles and Practices," Chapter 3 in Apostolou and Crumbley (1988), pp. 1-77 to 1-103.

and supplementary notes and schedules can be prepared to comply with divergent statutory reporting requirements. In extreme cases, the divergence of GAAP and statutory reporting directives may require the issuance of two sets of financial statements—one that satisfies GAAP and a second that satisfies the statutes.

The Financial Reporting Entity

The *financial reporting entity* for a state or local government consists of a primary government and its component units (*GASB Statement No. 14; GASB Codification,* sec. 2100). The financial reporting entity also includes related organizations that do not qualify as component units; they are "other organizations for which the nature and significance of their relationship with the primary government are such that exclusion would cause the reporting entity's financial statements to be misleading or incomplete" (par. 20). A *primary government* has a separately elected governing body; it is both legally separate and fiscally independent from other state and local governments. The *component units* of a primary government include organizations for which the primary government is *financially accountable*. A primary government is *accountable* for an organization if the primary government appoints a majority of the organization's governing body. The primary government is *financially accountable* if, in addition, either the government is able to impose its will on the organization *or* the organization is capable of providing specific financial benefits to or imposing specific financial burdens on the primary government. Although *GASB Statement No. 14* provides fairly detailed guidance, the determination of the financial reporting entity can be a complicated and subjective task, as the following issues section demonstrates.

ISSUES

A City's Reporting Entity

In addition to other operations of a municipality, Capital City is associated with a university located in the city. The university was once a city college wholly owned and operated by the city. Twenty years ago, the state added the university to its higher education system and began subsidizing the university according to a formula applied to all universities in the state system. The state subsidy represents about 60% of the university's total revenue. The remaining 40% is split about equally between student tuition and endowment income. The university is administered by a board of nine trustees—three elected by residents of the city, three appointed by the mayor, and three appointed by the state governor. The university operates several bookstores organized as a separate nonprofit corporation; they are wholly owned by the university, and the considerable profits are invested in a scholarship endowment fund.

One could argue that the university is a component unit of the city and, therefore, should be included in the city's financial reporting entity because six of the nine trustees come from the city. However, one could also argue that only three of the trustees really come from the city government (the other three come from the electorate), making control of the board by the government far from assured. Thus, although the university is related to the city, it is not a component organization of the city. We lack sufficient information to resolve this matter, and the university may be either a component unit of the city or merely a related organization. In either case, however, it is likely that the nonprofit corporation operating the bookstores would be a component unit of the university.

The reporting entity also includes organizations that do not qualify as component units but whose governing board members are appointed, entirely or in part, by the primary government. The relationship with all such organizations should be appropriately disclosed in the notes to the financial statements. If the primary government has an equity interest (including equity interests conferred by joint ventures) in the organization, then that interest should be reported as an asset of the fund that holds the interest. If the "investor" is a proprietary fund, then a variation of the equity method is employed; if the "investor" is a government fund, then the cost of the equity interest is reported in the general fixed asset account group and also in the government fund to the extent that the equity interest generates revenues and expenditures. Of course, if the primary government's equity interest is a majority or controlling interest, then the organization is apt to qualify as a component unit.

Elected officials must be accountable to their constituents for their actions, and the financial reports of governments should enable constituents to assess the accountability of their elected officials. Thus, the financial statements "should allow users to distinguish between the primary government and its component units" and should not create "the perception that the primary government and all of its component units are one legal entity" (*GASB Statement No. 14,* par. 11). This is accomplished by both disaggregate reporting of fund types, account groups, and component units and aggregate reporting to give an overview of the entire financial reporting entity. Although most component units should be reported separately ("discretely presented"), some may be combined ("blended") with a primary government of which they are an integral part. The way in which these financial reporting objectives are accomplished is discussed in the next chapter. The present chapter emphasizes the structure of the underlying accounting and budgetary system.

Fund Accounting Systems

The accounts of a governmental unit are partitioned into segments called *funds,* and separate financial statements are prepared for each fund. A *fund accounting system* is a collection of distinct entities or funds in which each fund reflects the financial aspects of a particular segment of the organization's activities. Separate funds are used to segregate activities by function because of the diverse nature of the services offered and because it is necessary to comply with legal provisions regarding activities of a governmental unit. Although funds are separate entities, the structure of funds is such that a single transaction may occasion entries in the accounts of several funds.

Definition of a Fund

A fund is defined as a distinct accounting entity "with a self-balancing set of accounts recording cash and other financial resources, together with all related liabilities and residual equities or balances, and changes therein" (*NCGA Statement No. 1,* par. 16; *GASB Codification,* sec. 1300). In other words, a fund is a segregated collection of both asset and equity accounts, together with related revenue and expenditure (or expense) accounts that describe a particular aspect of the organization. Each fund is established to account for specific activities or objectives in accordance with applicable regulations and restrictions. In some cases, particular funds are required by law or as a condition of receiving resources from another organization or government. Since each fund represents a distinct reporting entity, separate financial statements are prepared for each fund; in addition, combined financial statements may also be prepared.

Types of Funds

The accounting system of a government is composed of as many funds as are required by law or deemed appropriate by the government itself for sound financial administration. In general, it is desirable to avoid the creation of funds in the absence of a clear reason for doing so. Although the structure of fund accounting systems varies from one government to another, most state and local governments employ one or more funds in each of the seven *types* of funds described in Exhibit 17-1. The seven fund types are arranged in three *classes*—governmental funds, proprietary funds, and fiduciary funds. *Governmental funds* are established to account for the receipt and disbursement of financial resources to

EXHIBIT 17-1	TYPES OF FUNDS*

Governmental Funds

1. *General Fund*—to account for all financial resources except those required to be accounted for in another fund.

2. *Special Revenue Funds*—to account for the proceeds of specific revenue sources (other than expendable trusts, or for major capital projects) that are legally restricted to expenditure for specified purposes.

3. *Capital Projects Funds*—to account for financial resources to be used for the acquisition or construction of major capital facilities (other than those financed by proprietary funds and trust funds).

4. *Debt Service Funds*—to account for the accumulation of resources for, and the payment of, general long-term debt principal and interest.

Proprietary Funds

5. *Enterprise Funds*—to account for operations (a) that are financed and operated in a manner similar to private business enterprises—where the intent of the governing body is that the cost (expenses, including depreciation) of providing goods or services to the general public on a continuing basis be financed or recovered primarily through user charges; or (b) where the governing body has decided that periodic determination of revenues earned, expenses incurred, and/or net income is appropriate for capital maintenance, public policy, management control, accountability, or other purposes.

6. *Internal Service Funds*—to account for the financing of goods or services provided by one department or agency to other departments or agencies of the governmental unit, or to other governmental units, on a cost-reimbursement basis.

Fiduciary Funds

7. *Trust and Agency Funds*—to account for assets held by a governmental unit in a trustee capacity or as an agent for individuals, private organizations, other governmental units, and/or other funds. These include (a) expendable trust funds, (b) nonexpendable trust funds, (c) pension trust funds, and (d) agency funds.

* NCGA Statement No. 1, par. 18, as modified by subsequent GASB pronouncements; GASB Codification, sec. 102.

provide services to the general public. Accordingly, *governmental funds* are subject to distinct accounting principles that focus on the determination of financial position and changes in financial position and not on the measurement of income. *Proprietary funds* are established to account for the delivery of goods and services to the general public (enterprise funds) or to other departments or agencies of the government (internal service funds). Essentially the same generally accepted accounting principles are applicable to proprietary funds as to similar businesses in the private sector. *Fiduciary funds* are established to account for assets held by the governmental unit as a trustee or agent for another organization or an individual. Accounting for fiduciary funds may take the form of accounting for either governmental or proprietary funds, depending on the nature of the fiduciary fund. Expendable fiduciary funds are accounted for as governmental funds, whereas nonexpendable fiduciary funds are treated as proprietary funds for accounting purposes.

Account Groups for General Fixed Assets and General Long-Term Debt

The definition of a fund requires that all assets and equities included therein be devoted to the specific purpose of the fund. In general, only proprietary and nonexpendable trust funds exhibit fixed assets among their assets, and long-term liabilities among their equities. Fixed assets and long-term debt included in fund accounts are called *fund fixed assets* and *fund long-term debt* to distinguish them from *general fixed assets* and *general long-term debt*.

General fixed assets are not recorded as assets in any fund despite the fact that they are acquired by, and used in the operations of, the government. Similarly, general long-term capital debt is not recorded as a liability in any fund despite the fact that it represents obligations that are to be repaid from governmental funds. Although general fixed assets and general long-term capital debt are not included in the accounts of any fund, such assets and debt are recorded in the *general fixed assets account group* and the *general long-term debt account group*, respectively. An account group is a collection of self-balancing accounts and is not regarded as a fund. Further discussion of account groups is presented in Chapter 18.

Measurement and Recognition

Two questions must be answered in order to describe an accounting system: (1) what resources are measured, and (2) when are the effects of transactions on those resources recognized? Accounting for governmental funds has a much narrower focus than accounting for businesses. Whereas the focus of business accounting is all resources or assets of a business, the focus of governmental fund accounting, which is called *the flow of financial resources focus,* is just the financial resources of the fund:

Cash

Claims to cash (securities and receivables)

Claims to goods or services (prepayments)

Consumable goods (supplies inventories)

Equity securities

This restricted focus reflects the importance of short-term budgeting and financial control in most governments. However, as explained below, some government activities—like the operation of government-owned public utilities—require a more comprehensive perspective and a broader measurement focus.

On the recognition side, governmental funds, like businesses, use accrual accounting and recognize the effects of most transactions when they occur rather than when the related cash is received or paid. Of course, the transactions of governmental funds are distinctive, and recognition principles must be carefully specified.

These recognition and measurement issues are addressed in *GASB Statement No. 11,* which clarifies and redefines accounting for governmental funds, known as *modified accrual accounting.* Although implementation of this statement has been delayed, all state and local governments may eventually be required to apply it.[2] Accordingly, this chapter introduces general aspects of *GASB Statement No. 11* and illustrates some of the points at which it departs from current practice. We begin by considering recognition and measurement for governmental fund revenues and then turn to governmental fund expenditures.

Measurement and Recognition of Revenue

Recall that business organizations recognize revenue when it is (1) realized or realizable and (2) earned (*FASB Concepts Statement No. 5,* par. 83). Business revenue is *realized* when goods or services are exchanged for cash or receivables, and *realizable* when other assets received in exchange are readily convertible into known amounts of cash or receivables. Business revenue is earned when the business has performed substantially all the effort related to the exchange.

In contrast, most government fund revenues do not arise from exchange transactions; consequently, a different revenue recognition principle is required. Most government fund revenues arise from taxation and other nonexchange transactions including fines, license fees, and donations. Such revenues are typically recognized when they become *measurable* and *available* for expenditure.

Tax revenues

Under *GASB Statement No. 11,* tax revenues should be recognized when (1) the underlying transaction or event has taken place and (2) the government has demanded the taxes from the taxpayer by establishing a due date; "these two conditions (taken together) are evidence that the government has obtained financial resources, regardless of when cash is received" (*GASB Statement No. 11,* pars. 40 and 144).[3]

---

[2] Implementation of *GASB Statement No. 11* is delayed to provide additional time for the Board to complete several closely related projects. Since the Board believes that the standards arising from all of these projects should be implemented simultaneously, early implementation of *GASB Statement No. 11* is not permitted. It should be noted, however, that much of present accounting and reporting for governmental funds is consistent with the basic perspective of *GASB Statement No. 11.*

[3] Prior to the issuance of *GASB Statement No. 11,* the modified accrual method was usually interpreted to require revenue recognition when the accrued amounts were (1) *available* to satisfy obligations of the government that are related to the year of the accrual and (2) *measurable* in amount with a high degree of certainty. Although the new criteria are much clearer—particularly in relation to tax revenues—their application may not materially alter amounts recognized in the majority of cases.

For purposes of revenue recognition, the relevant underlying transaction or event depends on the nature of the tax. For example, the sale of goods underlies sales taxes, the earning of income underlies income taxes, and the passage of time underlies property taxes. The demand date is the date on which the taxes are due without regard to administrative lead times under two months. For example, a tax calculated on the basis of events during the year ended December 31, 19X1, but allowed a two-month administrative lead time for taxpayer calculation and payment should be recognized as revenue in 19X1; the tax is viewed as demanded by the government at year-end despite the fact that the tax calculation and payment is not required to be made until as much as two months after year-end.

Sales and income tax revenue

Application of these criteria to sales and income taxes results in the recognition of tax revenues in the period during which the related sales or income earning occurs. For example, a state with a 5% sales tax would recognize sales taxes of $4.5 billion in a year in which taxable sales transactions totaled $90 billion, provided that taxes are due within two months of year-end. Similarly, a state with a flat 10% income tax on annual incomes over $20,000 would recognize income tax revenue of $2.7 billion in a year in which taxable incomes totaled $27 billion, provided that taxes are due within two months of year-end.[4] In addition to recognizing tax revenues, an accrual should also be made for related delinquent taxes based on both known data and historical trends. In practice, many governments do not accrue "taxpayer-assessed" taxes (like sales and income taxes)—particularly if they are collected by another governmental unit—because the information needed to make the accrual is not readily available; rather, such governments recognize sales and income taxes as received.[5] Illustrations, exercises, and problems throughout this book will assume that sales and income tax revenues are recognized on a cash basis unless the contrary is specifically indicated.

Property tax revenue

Application of these criteria to property taxes usually results in recognition of tax revenues in the period in which the taxes are billed.

For example, suppose a county government bills property taxes in the total amount of $2,000,000 that are used to pay for the maintenance of roads and other services. The county estimates that about 7% of this amount will never be collected. Following the modified accrual method, the county would record the following entry when the property tax bills are mailed:

---

[4] *GASB Statement No. 11* (Appendix C) illustrates tax revenue accrual calculations under a variety of assumptions.

[5] *GASB Statement No. 11* (par. 50) would severely restrict the applicability of cash basis of revenues collected by another government. When *taxpayer-assessed* tax revenues (e.g., sales taxes or income taxes) are administered or collected by another government and the required accrual information cannot be obtained, the government for which the taxes are assessed could recognize the tax revenue on a modified cash basis (cash collected during the year plus cash received during the first month following year-end), but it would be discouraged from doing so. Furthermore, alternative recognition criteria would *not* be sanctioned for *government-assessed* tax revenues (e.g., property taxes).

County's entry to accrue property taxes in advance of collection:

```
Taxes receivable . . . . . . . . . . . . . . . . . . . . . . . . . . . . . . . 2,000,000
        Allowance for uncollectible taxes . . . . . . . . . . . . . .           140,000
        Tax revenue  . . . . . . . . . . . . . . . . . . . . . . . . . . . . . .         1,860,000
```

Under *GASB Statement No. 11,* property tax revenue should be recognized in the period for which the taxes are levied provided that the government has demanded the taxes on or before the end of that period. "The demand date for property taxes is the date those taxes are due. For purposes of recognizing revenue and reporting receivables, the due date is the last day before penalties or interest begin to accrue" (*GASB Statement No. 11,* par. 51). If property taxes are due after the period for which they are levied, they should be recognized as revenue in the period due. If property taxes are received or receivable before the period for which they are levied, they should be reported as deferred revenue with a provision for uncollectible receivables. In practice, governments employ a variety of revenue recognition methods for property taxes. In illustrations, exercises, and problems throughout this book, we shall assume that property tax revenue is appropriately recognized when levied or billed, unless the contrary is specifically indicated.

Nontax revenues

Nontax revenues arising in nonexchange transactions—including revenues from fines, licenses and permits, and donations—should be recognized "when the underlying event takes place and the government has an enforceable legal claim to the amounts, regardless of when received" (*GASB Statement No. 11,* par. 54). On the other hand, if government fund revenues arise from exchange transactions—such as charges for services, investments, and operating leases—they are subject to the same recognition criteria as business revenues; that is, "they should be recognized when earned, regardless of when cash is received" (*GASB Statement No. 11,* par. 62). Again, the revenue recognition practices of governments for nontax revenues exhibit considerable variation. Currently, cash basis recognition is probably most widely used.

Measurement and Recognition of Expenditures

As a consequence of the flow of financial resources measurement focus, governmental funds use expenditure accounting rather than expense accounting. Unlike expense accounting, expenditure accounting does not entail the matching of expenditures with related revenues. In general, expenditures are "recognized when transactions or events that result in claims against the financial resources take place, regardless of when cash is paid" (*GASB Statement No. 11,* par. 73). In most cases, a government recognizes an expenditure when it receives goods or services to be paid for at a later time. Thus, expenditures for salaries should be recognized when the related work is performed, and expenditures for utilities should be recognized when utility services are used.

Prepayments

Under *GASB Statement No. 11,* goods or services (but not capital assets) that are paid for in advance of their use should be recorded as financial resources (assets or prepayments), and the related expenditures should be recognized when the good is used or the service is received (*GASB Statement No. 11,* pars. 75–76). To illustrate, consider the following entries to record the payment of a $3,200 insurance premium, of which $1,700 pertains to coverage of the current year:

General fund entry to record payment of insurance premium:

Prepaid insurance	3,200	
Cash		3,200

General fund adjusting entry to record insurance expenditure:

Expenditures control	1,700	
Prepaid insurance		1,700

General fund adjusting entry to establish fund balance reserve for prepaid insurance:

Unreserved fund balance	1,500	
Fund balance reserved for prepaid insurance		1,500

These entries record insurance premiums as prepayments and recognize the related expenditure over the term of the coverage. The entry to record the "fund balance reserved for prepaid insurance" is reported as an element of fund equity to indicate that the related prepayment is not available for unrestricted future expenditure. In current practice, most governments do not accrue prepayments of insurance or other expenditures, although some may record a fund balance reserve for prepayments.

Supplies

In parallel fashion, *GASB Statement No. 11* requires that supplies purchased for later use in operations be recorded in a supplies inventory and recognized as expenditures when used in operations, as the following paragraph explains. In current practice, however, the recognition of supplies expenditures follows one of two methods. Under the *consumption method,* which meets the requirements of *GASB Statement No. 11,* the expenditure is recognized as supplies are used in operations and an inventory account is maintained. Under the *purchases method,* the expenditure is recognized when the supplies are purchased regardless of when they are actually consumed. To illustrate the entries for these two methods, consider a $10,000 expenditure on account for supplies by the general fund, of which $2,000 remains on hand at year-end; the entries are as follows:

Purchases Method		**Consumption Method**	

General fund entry to record purchase of inventory:

Expenditures control......10,000		Expenditures control..... 10,000	
Vouchers payable	10,000	Vouchers payable ...	10,000

General fund adjusting entries to record supplies on hand and reservation of fund balance at end of year:

Inventory of supplies 2,000		Inventory of supplies 2,000	
Fund balance reserved for inventory of supplies	2,000	Expenditures control.	2,000
		Unreserved fund balance . 2,000	
		Fund balance reserved for inventory of supplies	2,000

The foregoing entries assume the use of an expenditure control account and a subsidiary ledger for expenditures. If, instead, individual expenditure accounts appear in the general ledger, then general ledger entries would debit the individual expenditure accounts rather than a control account.

Whichever method is used, a consistent budgetary provision should be made. Supplies accounted for by the purchases method should be budgeted on the basis of usage; supplies accounted for by the consumption method should be budgeted on an acquisition basis. In either case, significant inventory amounts should be shown on the fund's balance sheet. The account entitled "fund balance reserved for inventory of supplies" is reported as an element of fund equity in order to indicate that the related inventory is not available for expenditure.

Capital expenditures

Capital expenditures result from the acquisition of capital assets through purchase, construction, or capital lease. Such expenditures should be recognized when the capital asset is acquired. Thus, the full cost of an asset is included in expenditures for the period of its acquisition.

Interest and principal on operating debt

Debt issued to fund the operations of the government (rather than to purchase capital assets) and repaid from governmental fund revenues is called *operating debt*. Operating debt includes revenue and tax anticipation notes and other short-term and long-term debt issued to finance operations. The expenditure for interest on operating debt is recognized as the interest accrues. Furthermore, the receipt and payment of principal are currently treated as revenues and expenditures.

Under *GASB Statement No. 11*, receipt and payment of operating debt principal would *not* be treated as operating revenues and expenditures. This change is justified because operating debt provides no benefit to future-year citizens. To report receipt and payment of principal on the operating statement would distort the statement as a measure of the extent to which operating expenditures were covered by operating revenues (*GASB Statement No. 11*, par. 31).

Interest and principal on long-term capital debt

In contrast, the treatment of interest and principal on long-term capital debt follows the financial resources measurement focus. Debt issued to purchase capital assets is called *long-term capital debt* and is usually accounted for in a capital projects fund. The face amount of such debt is recognized as an "other financing source" in the period received. Thus, the face amount of such debt is not reported as a liability of the fund but is reported in the general long-term debt account group. Interest (adjusted for amortized premium or discount) and principal, which may be accounted for in debt service funds, are recognized as expenditures in the period in which they are *due*. Consequently, interest that accrues in the current period may not be recorded until the subsequent period in which it is due to be paid. This, of course, represents an exception to the accrual basis of accounting. Since resources to pay interest and other debt charges are usually appropriated in the period of the payment, recognition of such charges in earlier periods, as the related resources are used, is considered to be misleading. However, if resources are appropriated in the period of the expenditure accrual, then the related expenditures should be recognized in that same period. The details of accounting for long-term capital debt are illustrated later in this chapter and in the next.

Budgets and Expenditures Control

Governmental accounting systems frequently record *budgeted* revenues and expenditures as well as *actual* revenues and expenditures. The dual recording makes possible a continuing comparison of actual and budgeted items throughout the year, thus serving as an aid to effective budgetary control and accountability. Control of expenditures is particularly important in governments, as the following issues section indicates.

ISSUES

Appropriations and Expenditures

Capital City, population 200,000, employs a widely used budgetary process to control expenditures. The process begins with preparation of a budget. The city's budget officer assembles the budget requests and prepares the budget document, which is submitted to the city council for possible modification, adoption, and final enactment. The budget includes estimates of revenues from such sources as property taxes, income taxes, licenses and permits, fines and forfeitures, intergovernmental grants, and shared revenue. The expenditure budget, once modified and adopted by the council, is enacted into law by the passage of an appropriation ordinance. The appropriation authorizes the various city departments to make expenditures and to incur obligations up to the maximum level specified by the appropriation. Expenditures in excess of the appropriation are illegal unless a supplemental appropriation to cover the excess is later approved by the council. Statutes applicable to Capital City direct that unexpected appropriations lapse at the end of the budget period. In some cities, however, unexpended appropriations do not lapse and continue as authority to make expenditures in the subsequent period.

In some governmental accounting systems, the budgeted amount is merely entered as a memorandum in each subsidiary revenue and expenditure account. In other systems, the budgeted amount is entered in the general ledger control accounts by a formal journal entry at the beginning of the fiscal year. At the same time, budgeted amounts are entered in the subsidiary revenue and expenditure records. During the year, actual revenues and expenditures are also recorded in the subsidiary revenue and expenditure records (as well as in their respective control accounts). Consequently, the balance of each subsidiary expenditure account represents the unexpended residual of budgeted expenditure, and the balance of each subsidiary revenue account represents the uncollected (or unrecognized) residual of budgeted revenue. The following example demonstrates the general ledger entries for recording the budget and the actual revenues and expenditures. The form of subsidiary records is shown later in Exhibit 17-3 for expenditures and in Exhibit 17-4 for revenues.

To illustrate, assume that a general fund begins 19X8 with no assets or liabilities. The budget for 19X8 shows estimated revenues of $100,000 and other financing sources (operating transfers in) of $20,000, and authorizes expenditures of $95,000 and estimated other financing uses (operating transfers out) of $10,000. To simplify our illustration, assume that all revenues of the fund are received in cash and all expenditures are paid in cash. Actual revenues and expenditures for 19X8 were $96,000 and $94,500, respectively. The actual operating transfers in and out were equal to the budgeted amounts.

Recording the Annual Budget

The 19X8 budget is recorded by the following entry:

(1) *General fund entry to record annual budget on January 1, 19X8:*

Estimated revenues control	100,000	
Estimated other financing sources control	20,000	
Appropriations control		95,000
Estimated other financing uses control		10,000
Budgetary fund balance		15,000

The foregoing entry, which is made at the beginning of 19X8, is shown as entry (1) in the T-accounts in Exhibit 17-2. Observe that estimated revenues and other financing sources are recorded as a *debit* and appropriations (authorized expenditures) and other financing uses are recorded as a *credit*. The excess of estimated revenues and estimated other

---

EXHIBIT 17-2 **T-ACCOUNTS FOR BUDGETED AND ACTUAL REVENUES AND FOR BUDGETED AND ACTUAL EXPENDITURES**

Cash

Balance	–0–		
(2)	116,000	(3)	104,500
Balance	11,500		

Appropriations Control

(4)	95,000	(1)	95,000

Estimated Revenues Control

(1)	100,000	(4)	100,000

Estimated Other Financing Uses Control

(4)	10,000	(1)	10,000

Estimated Other Financing Sources Control

(1)	20,000	(4)	20,000

Expenditures Control

(3)	94,500	(5)	94,500

Revenues Control

(5)	96,000	(2)	96,000

Other Financing Uses Control

(3)	10,000	(5)	10,000

Other Financing Sources Control

(5)	20,000	(2)	20,000

Budgetary Fund Balance

(4)	15,000	(1)	15,000

Unreserved Fund Balance

		(5)	11,500
		Balance	11,500

financing sources over appropriations and estimated other financing uses is a credit to the budgetary fund balance. The budgetary fund balance represents the anticipated increase (or decrease) in the unreserved fund balance at the end of the current budget year.

Recording Actual Sources and Uses of Funds

The recording of actual 19X8 revenues, other financing sources, expenditures, and other financing uses is summarized by the following entries:

(2) *General fund entry to summarize recording of actual revenues and other financing sources during 19X8:*

Cash.	116,000	
Revenues control		96,000
Other financing sources control		20,000

(3) *General fund entry to summarize recording of actual expenditures and other financing uses during 19X8:*

Expenditures control.	94,500	
Other financing uses control	10,000	
Cash.		104,500

The foregoing entries, which are also entered in Exhibit 17-2, summarize the recording of receipts and disbursements during the year. Throughout the year, the excess of the estimated revenues control account over the revenues control account represents the portion of budgeted revenue that remains to be collected. Similarly, the excess of the appropriations control account over the expenditures control account represents the portion of authorized expenditures that remains to be spent.

Closing Entries

In order to prepare the accounts for the next year, the current year's budget must be removed from the records and the accounts for actual sources and uses of resources must be closed to the unreserved fund balance. This two-step closing process is accomplished by the following entries:

(4) *General fund entry to close budgetary accounts at December 31, 19X8:*

Appropriations control	95,000	
Estimated other financing uses control	10,000	
Budgetary fund balance	15,000	
Estimated revenues control		100,000
Estimated other financing sources control		20,000

(5) *General fund entry to close actual revenues, other financing sources, expenditures, and other financing uses accounts to unreserved fund balance at December 31, 19X8:*

Revenues control	96,000	
Other financing sources control	20,000	
Expenditures control.		94,500
Other financing uses control		10,000
Unreserved fund balance		11,500

Entry (4) simply reverses entry (1). Entry (5) transfers the balances of all actual revenues and other financing sources accounts and all expenditure and other financing uses accounts to the unreserved fund balance account.

We turn now to another aid in the expenditure control: a method known as encumbrance accounting.

Encumbrance Accounting

A governmental unit often makes a commitment to future expenditures prior to the time it is legally obligated to pay the expenditures. Such commitments, which are called *encumbrances,* take the form of purchase orders, purchase agreements, or other unperformed (executory) contracts for goods and services. The amount available for future expenditure is the excess of the appropriations over the sum of both encumbrances and expenditures. In order to avoid exceeding appropriation limits, encumbrances are recorded in the expenditure subsidiary accounts as well as in the encumbrances control account. The recording of encumbrances is particularly appropriate in general funds, special revenue funds, and capital projects funds.

Recording Encumbrances

Encumbrances are frequently recorded before the amount of the related future expenditure is known with precision. Consequently, the recording of encumbrances does not replace the recording of expenditures. Consider a purchase in the general fund of police department supplies; the 19X4 budget for such supplies is $1,200. On January 15, 19X4, a purchase order is issued for the acquisition of supplies with an estimated cost of $500. On February 20, 19X4, the supplies are received, together with an invoice giving their cost as $512. The following entries record the encumbrance for the purchase order, the reversal of this encumbrance, and the related expenditure in the accounts of the general fund:[6]

General fund entry to record encumbrances—January 15, 19X4:

Encumbrances control—Police Department supplies	500	
Fund balance reserved for encumbrances		500

General fund entry to record reversal of encumbrances—February 20, 19X4:

Fund balance reserved for encumbrances	500	
Encumbrances control—Police Department supplies		500

General fund entry to record expenditures—February 20, 19X4:

Expenditures control—Police Department supplies	512	
Vouchers payable		512

The foregoing entries utilize two control accounts—one for encumbrances and one for expenditures. The subsidiary records may be designed so that the two control accounts correspond to different segments of a joint subsidiary record, as illustrated in Exhibit 17-3.

---

[6] Governmental units make extensive use of control and subsidiary accounts for revenues, expenditures (or expenses), encumbrances, and budgetary accounts. Throughout this chapter and the following one, the use of control and subsidiary accounts will be indicated by the use of the word *control* in the account title followed, when appropriate, by a dash and the name of the subsidiary account (e.g., Revenues Control—Property Taxes).

EXHIBIT 17-3	ACCOUNT FROM JOINT SUBSIDIARY RECORD FOR ENCUMBRANCES AND EXPENDITURES

Account: Police Department Supplies   **Account No. 117**

			Encumbrances			Expenditures		Appropria- tions	Unencumbered Balance (Credit)
Date	Item	Ref.	Debit	Credit	Balance	Debit	Total	Credit	
1-1-X4	Appropriation							1,200	1,200
1-15-X4	Purchase order		500		500				700
2-20-X4	Invoice			500	–0–	512	512		688

Observe that the joint record displays the unencumbered balance (the excess of the appropriation over the sum of *both* encumbrances and expenditures) as well as the balance of encumbrances and the total of expenditures.

When expenditures are made at a fairly uniform rate per period and are subject to long-standing, continuing commitments, encumbrances related to such expenditures are frequently not recorded. For example, encumbrances for salaries of the governmental unit's personnel are not usually recorded. Instead, salaries are simply recorded as expenditures when incurred. In other words, a fund may record encumbrances for some expenditures and not for others.

Reporting Encumbrances

Encumbrances are not expenditures. Encumbrances lead to expenditures, but the two amounts must be distinguished from one another. The balance of encumbrances at year-end should *not* be combined with expenditures in operating statements. Rather, expenditures related to encumbrances at year-end should not be reported until the subsequent period in which the liability is incurred. However, comparison of budget appropriations and the sum of expenditures and outstanding encumbrances *may* be presented as supplementary information to the statement of revenues, expenditures, and changes in fund balance—budget and actual.

Reporting a Fund Balance Reserved for Encumbrances

At year-end, the debit balance of the *encumbrances control* account equals the credit balance of the *fund balance reserved for encumbrances* account. Moreover, the reciprocal balances are artifacts of the budgetary control system; and, strictly speaking, neither account is reported in the financial statements of the related fund. Although neither account is reported, as such, a segregation of the fund's equity balance, under the circumstances described subsequently, may be required in the amount of the outstanding encumbrances. For example, when appropriations do not lapse (or when the unencumbered portion of the appropriation lapses), the encumbered portion of the appropriation continues to be effective after year-end and confers authority on the governmental unit to complete transactions in process at year-end. In such cases, a fund balance reserved for encumbrances should be established to indicate a commitment to make an expenditure in the subsequent year.

The reciprocal balances in the *encumbrances control* and the *fund balance reserved for encumbrances* accounts are offset against each other, and an additional entry is then made to reserve a portion of the fund balance, as shown as follows for the general fund that had outstanding encumbrances of $30,000 for supplies at the end of year 19X1:

General fund entry to close encumbrances control and fund balance reserved for encumbrances at end of year 19X1:

Fund balance reserved for encumbrances 30,000
        Encumbrances control—supplies   30,000

General fund entry to reserve a portion of unreserved fund balance for outstanding encumbrances at end of year 19X1:

Unreserved fund balance 30,000
        Fund balance reserved for encumbrances   30,000

This procedure emphasizes that the amount of the encumbrance is a reservation of the fund balance.

It appears to be usual practice for encumbered appropriations not to lapse at year-end. However, if all appropriations, including those encumbered, lapse at year-end, then completion of the transactions in process at year-end should be authorized by next year's appropriation, and a reservation of fund equity for outstanding encumbrances at year-end is not appropriate. In such cases, the reciprocal balances in *encumbrances control* and *fund balance reserved for encumbrances* are simply offset against one another (by debiting *fund balance reserved for encumbrances* and crediting *encumbrances control*) in the closing process, leaving no balance in either account at year-end. Throughout this chapter and the next, and in related exercise and problem materials, it is assumed that encumbered appropriations do not lapse unless otherwise stated.

Recording Expenditures Related to Encumbrances of Prior Year

As indicated in the previous section, when the appropriations related to year-end encumbrances do not lapse, or only unencumbered appropriations lapse, the fund balance reserved for encumbrances is appropriately carried forward to the next year as a segregation of the fund balance. On the first day of the subsequent year (19X2), the encumbrances control account for the $30,000 encumbrances shown in the above example should be reestablished by the following entries:

General fund entry to reverse entry reserving a portion of unreserved fund balance for outstanding encumbrances at end of year 19X1:

Fund balance reserved for encumbrances 30,000
        Unreserved fund balance   30,000

General fund entry to reestablish encumbrances control and fund balance reserved for encumbrances accounts at beginning of year 19X2:

Encumbrances control 30,000
        Fund balance reserved for encumbrances   30,000

As a result of these entries, the *encumbrances control* and the *fund balance reserved for encumbrances* accounts once again have reciprocal balances of $30,000.

When the invoice was received in 19X2 for the supplies, the reversal of the encumbrance of $30,000 and the actual cost of $31,000 would be recorded in the general fund by the following entries:

General fund entry to record reversal of encumbrances in 19X2:

Fund balance reserved for encumbrances 30,000
         Encumbrances control—supplies   30,000

General fund entry in 19X2 to record expenditures related to previous year:

Expenditures control—supplies 31,000
         Vouchers payable   31,000

Thus, in recording the transactions and in the operating statement of the year 19X2 there is no distinction made between expenditures that were encumbered in 19X1 and paid in 19X2 and those that were encumbered and paid in 19X2.

The remainder of the chapter illustrates the application of governmental accounting procedures with particular attention to the general fund.

ACCOUNTING FOR THE GENERAL FUND

The general fund accounts for the general operations of a governmental unit; that is, the general fund accounts for all financial resources that are not accounted for in another fund. The accounting system for every governmental unit contains at least one general fund. In addition, of course, the governmental unit may also employ other funds for specific purposes. The general fund is normally the largest and is usually considered to be the most important of the governmental unit's funds. Most of the basic services provided by the governmental unit are financed by the general fund. These services would normally include, but not be restricted to, the following: police, fire, parks, courts, and general administration. Typical revenue sources for providing these services are property taxes, sales taxes, state and federal aid, fees, licenses and permits, and fines.

Let us illustrate the accounting entries and financial statements prepared for a general fund by reference to the City of Fisherville. Fisherville was incorporated in 1936, and its accounting system includes the following funds and account groups:

General fund

Capital projects fund

Debt service fund

General fixed assets account group

General long-term debt account group

Utility fund (an enterprise fund)

Central garage fund (an internal service fund)

Scholarship trust funds (nonexpendable and expendable scholarship trust funds)

In this chapter and the following one, the 19X6 activities related to the various funds of Fisherville are used to illustrate accounting for a local government. The remaining sec-

846

CHAPTER 17

tions of this chapter illustrate the accounting transactions for the City of Fisherville's general fund for the fiscal year ended December 31, 19X6.

On December 15, 19X5, the city council of Fisherville adopted the 19X6 budget for the city government. The budgeted estimated revenues, authorized expenditures, and estimated other financing uses are as follows:

General Fund Budget for 19X6

Estimated revenues:		
Property taxes (net)		$258,000
Interest and penalties on delinquent taxes (net)		400
Other		63,600
Total estimated revenues		$322,000
Appropriations—expenditures:		
Supplies	$ 21,000	
Salaries	122,000	
Transportation equipment	14,300	
Interest	250	
Other	150,450	
	$308,000	
Estimated other financing uses—operating transfers out (to debt service fund)	10,000	
Total appropriations and estimated other financing uses		318,000
Excess of estimated revenues over appropriations and estimated other financing uses		$ 4,000

In addition to providing for estimated revenues and appropriating amounts for various expenditures, the budget provides for a transfer of cash from the general fund to the debt service fund. The transfer to the debt service fund will be used to pay matured principal and interest on long-term debt. Interfund transfers are discussed later in this chapter; debt service funds are considered in Chapter 18.

On December 31, 19X5, the general fund had the following balance sheet:

City of Fisherville

GENERAL FUND BALANCE SHEET
AT DECEMBER 31, 19X5

Assets		
Cash		$8,400
Taxes receivable—delinquent	$2,400	
Less: Allowance for uncollectible delinquent taxes	1,000	1,400
Total assets		$9,800
Liabilities and Fund Balance		
Vouchers payable		$ 420
Unreserved fund balance		9,380
Total liabilities and unreserved fund balance		$9,800

The city has a small inventory of supplies at December 31, 19X5, that is not judged to be material in amount. There were no encumbrances at December 31, 19X5. Fisherville's unencumbered appropriations lapse at year-end, but encumbered appropriations do not lapse.

The following items summarize all transactions in the general fund during 19X6:

1. On January 1, 19X6, property taxes are levied in the total amount of $272,000, which includes $14,000 estimated to be uncollectible.

2. Delinquent property taxes in the amount of $1,500 are collected on January 12, 19X6, and the remainder of prior years' delinquent taxes is judged to be uncollectible.

3. To provide operating resources prior to collection of the 19X6 tax levy, the general fund borrows $50,000 from a local bank on a tax anticipation note payable on January 15, 19X6. The face of the note and $250 in interest are paid to the bank on July 15, 19X6.

4. Current property taxes in the amount of $255,600 are collected, and current taxes in the amount of $9,900 are written off as uncollectible. Uncollected taxes become delinquent at December 5 of each year. An allowance for uncollectible delinquent taxes in the amount of $3,280 is provided at December 5, 19X6.

5. At December 31, 19X6, interest and penalties accrued on delinquent taxes amount to $450; of this amount, $50 is estimated to be uncollectible.

6. Revenues other than property taxes are collected in the total amount of $56,000.

7. Encumbrances for supplies and other expenditures are recorded in the amount of $176,250.

8. Vouchers are approved for payment as follows:

Expenditures related to encumbrances:		
Supplies	$ 20,000	
Transportation equipment	15,000	
Other	140,000	
Subtotal		$175,000
Expenditures not related to encumbrances:		
Salaries	$120,000	
Other	12,000	
Subtotal		132,000
Operating transfer to debt service fund		10,000
Total approved for payment		$317,000

Expenditures related to encumbrances of $175,000 are associated with purchase orders that were encumbered for a total of $175,800. Consequently, outstanding encumbrances at the end of the fiscal year, December 31, 19X6, total $450 {$176,250 [item (7)] − $175,800}.

9. Vouchers totaling $315,200 are paid, including vouchers payable at January 1, 19X6.

10. At December 31, 19X6, supplies on hand total $3,800; the inventory is judged to be

material, and the fund balance is reserved in the amount of $3,800. The general fund uses the purchases method of accounting for inventories.

11. On December 31, 19X6, the general fund establishes a petty cash fund in the amount of $2,000.

12. On June 15, the general fund borrows $15,000 from the utility (enterprise) fund. This amount is repaid on August 15 together with $250 interest (no purchase order or voucher is prepared for this payment).

13. On December 31, 19X6, equipment carried in the general fixed assets account group at a cost of $7,500 is sold as scrap for $100.

14. The general fund books are closed at December 31, 19X6.

The city follows the modified accrual method of accounting for its general fund. Property taxes are accrued when levied, but all other revenues are recognized when the related cash is collected. Salaries are not encumbered, but all expenditures for supplies require a purchase order, which is recorded as an encumbrance. Purchase orders are required for some but not all of the remaining expenditures.

Exhibit 17-5 on pages 850–851 shows the general fund entries to record Fisherville's budget and transactions for 19X6. The entry to record the budget is identified by the letter B. The entries to record the various transactions are identified with the foregoing list of transactions by the parenthetical number that accompanies the related entries. In some cases, more than one entry is required to record a transaction.

Recording General Fund Budget

The following entry in the general ledger accounts of the general fund records the budget for 19X6:

(B) *General fund entry to record budget for 19X6:*

Estimated revenues control	322,000	
Appropriations control		308,000
Estimated other financing uses control		10,000
Budgetary fund balance		4,000

In addition, appropriate entries are made in underlying subsidiary records for estimated revenues and appropriations. For example, the $258,000 property tax component of the $322,000 estimated revenues is recorded as a debit in the property tax account of the revenue subsidiary ledger as shown in Exhibit 17-4.

Recording General Fund Revenues and Other Financial Sources

The revenue and other financial sources transactions involving Fisherville's general fund during 19X6 are described by items (1) through (6) in the list of transactions on page 847. The journal entries by the general fund to record these transactions are shown in Exhibit 17-5.

Recording Levy of Property Taxes

Since Fisherville accrues property taxes, a receivable of $272,000 is established in the general fund when property taxes are levied as shown by entry (1) in Exhibit 17-5. The 19X6 subsidiary ledger accounts of individual taxpayers also receive debits that total

EXHIBIT 17-4	ACCOUNT FROM SUBSIDIARY RECORD FOR REVENUE: FISHERVILLE GENERAL FUND

Account: Property Taxes Account No. 601

Date	Item	Ref.	Estimated Revenue (Debit)	Revenue (Credit)	Balance Debit (Credit)
19X6					
1-1	Budget estimate	B	258,000		258,000
1-1	Tax levy less allowance for uncollectible current taxes	1		258,000	–0–
1-12	Adjustment to allowance for uncollectible delinquent taxes	2c		100	(100)
12-5	Adjustment to allowance for uncollectible current taxes	4d		820	(920)

$272,000. In addition, the property taxes account in the revenue subsidiary ledger (an example of which is shown in Exhibit 17-4) receives a credit of $258,000. (If the governmental unit is required to recognize revenues on the cash basis, then no entries are made in advance of the collection of the taxes and revenues are simply recorded as the taxes are received.) The amount of property taxes estimated to be uncollectible is treated as a reduction of revenue, thus avoiding the use of an uncollectible tax expense account. The use of an uncollectible tax expense account would not be appropriate since governmental funds are concerned with expenditures rather than expenses.

Recording Collection and Write-Off of Delinquent Property Taxes

Fisherville's collection and write-off of delinquent property taxes (property taxes levied in prior years) is accomplished using three entries—(2a), (2b), and (2c)—as shown in Exhibit 17-5. If delinquent taxes are potentially collectible, then the delinquent taxes receivable and the offsetting allowance should be carried forward for at least one more year. Consequently, a balance sheet may exhibit delinquent taxes receivable and the related allowance for several prior years. Observe that changes in the *allowance for uncollectible delinquent taxes,* for reasons other than the write-off of taxes receivable, result in credits (or debits) to revenues of the current period because changes in estimates related to uncollectible receivables of prior years are not treated as prior-period adjustments.

Recording Tax Anticipation Notes Payable

Governmental units sometimes need to make cash disbursements prior to the collection of their tax levies. In anticipation of tax collections later in the fiscal year, they could borrow money from banks or other lenders by issuing tax anticipation notes. Fisherville's issuance and repayment of such obligations are recorded using two entries—(3a) and (3b)—as shown in Exhibit 17-5.

EXHIBIT 17-5	GENERAL FUND ENTRIES TO RECORD REVENUES AND OTHER FINANCIAL SOURCES

City of Fisherville

GENERAL FUND ENTRIES TO RECORD REVENUES AND OTHER FINANCIAL SOURCES
FOR THE YEAR ENDED DECEMBER 31, 19X6

Transaction (1): On January 1, 19X6, property taxes are levied in the total amount of $272,000, which includes $14,000 estimated to be uncollectible.

(1) *General fund entry to record property tax levy:*

Taxes receivable—current 272,000		
Revenues control—property taxes		258,000
Allowance for uncollectible current taxes		14,000

Transaction (2): Delinquent property taxes in the amount of $1,500 are collected on January 12, 19X6, and the remainder of prior years' delinquent taxes is judged to be uncollectible.

(2a) *General fund entry to record collection of delinquent property taxes:*

Cash 1,500		
Taxes receivable—delinquent		1,500

(2b) *General fund entry to write off delinquent taxes:*

Allowance for uncollectible delinquent taxes	900	
Taxes receivable—delinquent		900

(2c) *General fund entry to adjust allowance for uncollectible delinquent taxes:*

Allowance for uncollectible delinquent taxes	100	
Revenues control—property taxes		100

Transaction (3): To provide operating resources prior to collection of the 19X6 tax levy, the general fund borrows $50,000 from a local bank on a tax anticipation note payable on January 15, 19X6. The face of the note and $250 in interest are paid to the bank on July 15, 19X6.

(3a) *General fund entry to record issuance of tax anticipation note on January 15, 19X6:*

Cash 50,000		
Tax anticipation notes payable		50,000

(3b) *General fund entry to record repayment of tax anticipation note and interest on July 15, 19X6:*

Tax anticipation notes payable	50,000	
Expenditures control—interest	250	
Cash		50,250

EXHIBIT 17-5	GENERAL FUND ENTRIES TO RECORD REVENUES AND OTHER FINANCIAL SOURCES (Continued)

Transaction (4): Current property taxes in the amount of $255,600 are collected, and current taxes in the amount of $9,900 are written off as uncollectible. Uncollected taxes become delinquent at December 5 of each year. An allowance for uncollectible delinquent taxes in the amount of $3,280 is provided at December 5, 19X6.

(4a) *General fund entry to record collection of current property taxes:*

Cash	255,600	
Taxes receivable—current		255,600

(4b) *General fund entry to record write-off of current property taxes:*

Allowance for uncollectible current taxes	9,900	
Taxes receivable—current		9,900

(4c) *General fund entry to reclassify current taxes receivable as delinquent:*

Taxes receivable—delinquent	6,500	
Taxes receivable—current		6,500

(4d) *General fund entry to establish allowance for uncollectible delinquent taxes:*

Allowance for uncollectible current taxes	4,100	
Revenues control—property taxes		820
Allowance for uncollectible delinquent taxes		3,280

Transaction (5): At December 31, 19X6, interest and penalties accrued on delinquent taxes amount to $450; of this amount, $50 is estimated to be uncollectible.

(5) *General fund entry to record interest and penalties accrued on delinquent taxes at December 31, 19X6:*

Interest and penalties receivable on taxes	450	
Allowance for uncollectible interest and penalties		50
Revenues control—interest and penalties on delinquent		
taxes		400

Transaction (6): Revenues other than property taxes are collected in the total amount of $56,000.

(6) *General fund entry to summarize recording of other revenues as collected:*

Cash	56,000	
Revenues control—other		56,000

Recording Collection and Write-Off of Current Property Taxes

The collection and write-off of current property taxes (property taxes levied in the current year) are recorded using two general fund entries—(4a) and (4b)—as shown in Exhibit 17-5. Entry (4b) reduces the balance of *allowance for uncollectible current taxes* from $14,000, which was recorded by entry (1), to $4,100 ($14,000 − $9,900). (If the write-off exceeds the balance of *allowance for uncollectible current taxes,* then the excess represents an overstatement of revenues and should be charged to revenue.)

Recording Delinquent Taxes and Related Allowance

Since Fisherville's uncollected current taxes become delinquent on December 5, the entire balance of *taxes receivable—current* ($6,500 = $272,000 − $255,600 − $9,900) is reclassified as *taxes receivable—delinquent* on that date. In addition, the balance in *allowance for uncollectible current taxes* is reclassified as *allowance for uncollectible delinquent taxes*. A review of taxes receivable may result in a revised estimate of the uncollectible taxes. Fisherville reclassifies current taxes receivable as delinquent with entry (4c) and establishes the allowance for uncollectible delinquent taxes with entry (4d) as shown in Exhibit 17-5. Since the estimated uncollectible amount on December 5 is $820 less than the balance of *allowance for uncollectible current taxes* ($820 = $4,100 − $3,280), revenues for 19X6 are understated by $820 and are adjusted upward by entry (4d). If the estimated uncollectible amount had been more than the balance of the allowance, then revenues would have been overstated and the adjustment would have decreased the amount of revenue.

Recording Interest and Penalties Receivable on Taxes

Delinquent property taxes usually incur interest and penalty charges. Penalties are a flat percentage imposed on the taxpayers on the date on which the taxes become delinquent, whereas interest charges continue to accumulate until the delinquent taxes and other charges are paid in full. Some governmental units accrue interest and penalty charges, whereas others do not record them until they are collected. Entry (5) in Exhibit 17-5 records Fisherville's accrual of interest and penalties and the related estimated uncollectible amount.

Delinquency Date after Year-End

Since taxes levied by Fisherville become delinquent before the end of the fiscal year in which they are levied, *taxes receivable—current* never appears on Fisherville's annual balance sheet. When the delinquency date comes after the year-end, *taxes receivable—current,* together with the *allowance for uncollectible current taxes,* must be reported at year-end.

Delinquent Property Taxes and Tax Liens

When property tax payments remain delinquent for the period specified by law, the governmental unit may post a lien against the property. The tax liens are recorded by transferring the taxes receivable, the related *allowance for uncollectible delinquent taxes* account, and any accrued interest and penalties receivable on taxes to tax lien accounts. The City of Fisherville has no tax liens against any property. More detailed discussion of tax liens is provided in texts devoted entirely to governmental and nonprofit accounting.

Recording Other Revenues

Fisherville accrues property taxes but does not accrue other revenues. Consequently, other revenues are recorded at the time of cash collection as summarized by entry (6) in Exhibit 17-5. Of course, various revenue accounts in subsidiary revenue records should also receive credits totaling $56,000. Amounts collected in advance of the normal collection time should be credited to *deferred revenues* at the time of collection and recognized at the normal collection time (by debiting deferred revenues and crediting revenues). No part of the $56,000 collected by Fisherville was collected in advance of the normal collection time.

Recording General Fund Encumbrances and Expenditures

The expenditures transactions and the related encumbrances involving Fisherville's general fund during 19X6 are described by items (7) through (13) in the list of transactions shown on pages 847–848. The journal entries made by the general fund to record these transactions are shown in Exhibit 17-6 on the following page.

Recording Encumbrances

An encumbrance is recorded when a purchase order is approved by the governmental unit. Entry (7) in Exhibit 17-6 summarizes the recording of all general fund encumbrances by Fisherville during 19X6. Encumbrances totaling $176,250 should also be recorded in the underlying joint subsidiary record for encumbrances and expenditures as demonstrated earlier in this chapter in Exhibit 17-3.

Recording Expenditures

Expenditures are recorded when the related liabilities are incurred (and vouchers are approved for payment) by the governmental unit. Expenditures are recorded in the usual way except that expenditures associated with encumbrances also occasion reversal of the related encumbrances. Expenditures and related transactions by Fisherville during 19X6 are recorded by entries (8a) through (8e) in Exhibit 17-6. Both the reversal of encumbrances and the recording of expenditures occasion entries in the underlying joint subsidiary record for encumbrances and expenditures. Note that the fixed asset, transportation equipment, is recorded as an expenditure in the general fund when acquired. Since fixed assets are not carried in the general fund, the transportation equipment should be recorded in the general fixed assets account group as demonstrated in the next chapter.

Year-End Adjustment to Establish Fund Balance Reserved for Encumbrances

At December 31, 19X6, Fisherville's *fund balance reserved for encumbrances* and *encumbrances control* accounts display reciprocal balances of $450 ($176,250 − $175,800), representing outstanding purchase orders for which the city is not yet liable. Since Fisherville's encumbered appropriation does not lapse, a portion of the unreserved fund balance should be segregated in a fund balance reserved for encumbrances. The closing of the encumbrances control and fund balance reserved for encumbrances and the reservation of the unreserved fund balance are recorded as entries (14c) and (14d) under closing entries discussed later in this chapter.

Recording Payment of Vouchers

The payment of approved vouchers by Fisherville's general fund is summarized in entry (9) in Exhibit 17-6, which includes payments of $420 of vouchers that were unpaid at the end of the preceding year.

EXHIBIT 17-6	GENERAL FUND ENTRIES TO RECORD ENCUMBRANCES, EXPENDITURES, AND SALE OF OLD EQUIPMENT

City of Fisherville

GENERAL FUND ENTRIES TO RECORD ENCUMBRANCES AND EXPENDITURES
FOR THE YEAR ENDED DECEMBER 31, 19X6

Transaction (7): Encumbrances for supplies and other expenditures are recorded in the amount of $176,250

(7) *General fund entry to summarize recording of encumbrances:*

Encumbrances control 176,250
     Fund balance reserved for encumbrances   176,250

Transaction (8): During 19X6 vouchers totaling $175,000 (these had been encumbered for $175,800) were approved for payments of encumbered expenditures as follows: supplies, $20,000; transportation equipment, $15,000; and other expenditures, $140,000. Vouchers totaling $132,000 were approved for payment of unencumbered expenditures as follows: salaries, $120,000, and other expenditures of $12,000. In addition, cash of $10,000 was transferred to the debt service fund.

(8a) *General fund entry to summarize reversal of encumbrances:*

Fund balance reserved for encumbrances 175,800
     Encumbrances control   175,800

(8b) *General fund entry to summarize recording of expenditures related to encumbrances:*

Expenditures control 175,000
     Vouchers payable   175,000

(8c) *General fund entry to summarize recording of expenditures not related to encumbrances:*

Expenditures control 132,000
     Vouchers payable   132,000

(8d) *General fund entry to record operating transfer:*

Other financing uses control—operating transfers out (to debt
    service fund) 10,000
     Due to debt service fund   10,000

(8e) *General fund entry to record approval of voucher for operating transfer:*

Due to debt service fund 10,000
     Vouchers payable   10,000

Transaction (9): Vouchers totaling $315,200 are paid, including vouchers payable at January 1, 19X6.

(9) *General fund entry to summarize recording of vouchers payments:*

Vouchers payable 315,200
     Cash   315,200

EXHIBIT 17-6	GENERAL FUND ENTRIES TO RECORD ENCUMBRANCES, EXPENDITURES, AND SALE OF OLD EQUIPMENT (Continued)

Transaction (10): At December 31, 19X6, supplies on hand total $3,800; the inventory is judged to be material, and the fund balance is reserved in the amount of $3,800. The general fund uses the purchases method of accounting for inventories.

(10) *General fund adjustment to record significant inventory using purchases method:*

Inventory of supplies	3,800	
Fund balance reserved for inventory of supplies		3,800

Transaction (11): On December 31, 19X6, the general fund establishes a petty cash fund in the amount of $2,000.

(11a) *General fund entry to record establishment of petty cash fund:*

Petty cash	2,000	
Cash		2,000

(11b) *General fund entry to record fund balance reserved for petty cash fund:*

Unreserved fund balance	2,000	
Fund balance reserved for petty cash fund		2,000

Transaction (12): On June 15, the general fund borrows $15,000 from the utility (enterprise) fund; this amount is repaid on August 15 together with $250 interest (no purchase order or voucher is prepared for this payment).

(12a) *General fund entry to record loan from utility fund:*

Cash	15,000	
Due to utility fund		15,000

(12b) *General fund entry to record repayment to utility fund of loan and related interest:*

Due to utility fund	15,000	
Expenditures control—interest	250	
Cash		15,250

Transaction (13): On December 31, 19X6, equipment carried in the general fixed assets account group at a cost of $7,500 is sold as scrap for $100.

(13) *General fund entry to record proceeds from sale of old equipment as scrap:*

Cash	100	
Revenues control—other		100

Year-End Adjustment to Record Significant Supplies Inventories

Fisherville follows the *purchases method* of accounting for governmental fund inventories. Under the purchases method, inventoried goods are recorded as expenditures upon acquisition, and significant inventories on hand at year-end are entered among both assets and equities with entry (10) in Exhibit 17-6. The *fund balance reserved for inventory* is reported as an element of fund equity and indicates that the related inventory listed among the assets is not available for expenditures. The inventory and related reserve should be adjusted at each year-end to equal the cost of supplies on hand.

Recording Permanent Petty Cash Funds

When a general fund establishes a permanent petty cash fund, it is appropriate to credit the amount of the fund to a *fund balance reserved for petty cash fund,* which represents a reservation of the general fund's fund balance. The reserve should be established to indicate that the petty cash fund must be maintained permanently. Establishment of a petty cash fund of $2,000 by the general fund is recorded by entries (11a) and (11b) in Exhibit 17-6.

Recording Interfund Loan

Fisherville makes entries (12a) and (12b) in its general fund to record the short-term loan to the general fund by the utility (enterprise) fund. Payment of the interest is a quasi-external transaction, as discussed later in this chapter. Thus, the debit to expenditures is appropriate. The recording of the interfund loan by the utility (enterprise) fund is discussed in the next chapter.

Disposal of General Fixed Assets

When general fixed assets are disposed of (e.g., sold or scrapped), the proceeds, if any, from the disposal are recorded in a general or special revenue fund (usually the general fund) by a debit to cash and a credit to *revenues control—other,* as shown in entry (13) in Exhibit 17-6. The disposal is also recorded in the general fixed assets account group by a debit to the *investment in general fixed assets* account and a credit to the appropriate fixed asset account, as discussed in the next chapter.

General Ledger Accounts and Closing Entries

The recording of Fisherville's 19X6 transactions in the ledger accounts of the general fund is summarized in the T-accounts shown in Exhibit 17-7 on pages 858–859. The year-end balances shown represent balances before closing entries. Fisherville records the following closing entries of the general fund on December 31, 19X6:

(14a) *General fund entry to close budgetary accounts at December 31, 19X6:*

Appropriations control	308,000	
Estimated other financing uses control	10,000	
Budgetary fund balance	4,000	
Estimated revenues control		322,000

(14b) *General fund entry to close actual revenues, expenditures, and other financing uses accounts to unreserved fund balance at December 31, 19X6:*

Revenues control 315,420		
Unreserved fund balance	2,080	
Expenditures control...........................		307,500
Other financing uses control—operating transfers		
out (to debt service fund)		10,000

(14c) *General fund entry to close encumbrances control and fund balance reserved for encumbrances at December 31, 19X6:*

Fund balance reserved for encumbrances...............	450	
Encumbrances control		450

(14d) *General fund entry to reserve a portion of unreserved fund balance for outstanding encumbrances at December 31, 19X6:*

Unreserved fund balance	450	
Fund balance reserved for encumbrances............		450

As a result of the foregoing closing entries, the unreserved fund balance account of Fisherville's general fund has the following appearance:

Unreserved Fund Balance

		Balance	9,380
(11b)	2,000		
(14b)	2,080		
(14d)	450		
		Balance	4,850

It should be noted that the $4,850 balance in the unreserved fund balance account is the amount that is available for future appropriations.

Financial Reporting for the General Fund

The basic financial statements for the general fund are the (1) *balance sheet,* (2) *statement of revenues, expenditures, and changes in fund balance,* and (3) *statement of revenues, expenditures, and changes in fund balance—budget and actual.* The basic financial statements should be accompanied by appropriate footnotes and supplementary schedules of detailed financial data. Fisherville's general fund balance sheet at December 31, 19X6, is shown in Exhibit 17-8 on page 860. Observe that the total fund balance ($11,100) shown in the balance sheet at year-end includes both reserved and unreserved fund balances and is the bottom line of the statement of revenues, expenditures, and changes in fund balance. Fisherville's statement of revenues, expenditures, and changes in fund balance for the general fund for 19X6 is displayed in Exhibit 17-9 on page 861. The statement of revenues, expenditures, and changes in fund balance—budget and actual represents a comparison of actual and budgeted results of operations. Such a comparison is demonstrated for Fisherville's general fund in Exhibit 17-10 on page 862. The form of the statement parallels the form of the basic financial statement, statement of revenues, expenditures, and changes in fund balance illustrated in Exhibit 17-9. Notice that the *actual* column of Exhibit 17-10 contains the same information as that presented in Exhibit 17-9.

EXHIBIT 17-7 — GENERAL FUND ACCOUNTS FOR THE CITY OF FISHERVILLE

Cash

Balance	8,400	(3b)	50,250
(2a)	1,500	(9)	315,200
(3a)	50,000	(11a)	2,000
(4a)	255,600	(12b)	15,250
(6)	56,000		
(12a)	15,000		
(13)	100		
Balance	3,900		

Petty Cash

(11a)	2,000		

Taxes Receivable—Current

(1)	272,000	(4a)	255,600
		(4b)	9,900
		(4c)	6,500
Balance	–0–		

Allowance for Uncollectible Current Taxes

(4b)	9,900	(1)	14,000
(4d)	4,100		
		Balance	–0–

Taxes Receivable—Delinquent

Balance	2,400	(2a)	1,500
(4c)	6,500	(2b)	900
Balance	6,500		

Allowance for Uncollectible Delinquent Taxes

(2b)	900	Balance	1,000
(2c)	100	(4d)	3,280
		Balance	3,280

Interest and Penalties Receivable on Taxes

(5)	450		

Allowance for Uncollectible Interest and Penalties on Taxes

		(5)	50

Inventory of Supplies

(10)	3,800		

Vouchers Payable

(9)	315,200	Balance	420
		(8b)	175,000
		(8c)	132,000
		(8e)	10,000
		Balance	2,220

Due to Debt Service Fund

(8e)	10,000	(8d)	10,000
		Balance	–0–

Tax Anticipation Notes Payable

(3b)	50,000	(3a)	50,000
		Balance	–0–

Due to Utility Fund

(12b)	15,000	(12a)	15,000
		Balance	–0–

INTERFUND TRANSACTIONS

Interfund transactions are discussed in this section under three broad categories: quasi-external transactions and reimbursements, transfers (residual equity and operating), and interfund loans.

Quasi-External Transactions and Reimbursements

Quasi-external transactions are interfund transactions that would be treated as revenues or expenditures if they involved an entity external to the governmental unit. Accordingly, these quasi-external transactions should be accounted for as revenues, expenditures, or expenses in the funds involved. An example of such a transaction would be a payment by

	Budgetary Fund Balance			Fund Balance Reserved for Petty Cash Fund			Fund Balance Reserved for Inventory of Supplies	
		(B)	4,000		(11b)	2,000		(10)	3,800

Fund Balance Reserved for Encumbrances				Unreserved Fund Balance				Estimated Revenues Control	
(8a)	175,800	(7)	176,250	(11b)	2,000	Balance	9,380	(B)	322,000
		Balance	450						

Revenues Control			Other Financing Uses Control—Operating Transfers Out (to Debt Service Fund)			Appropriations Control	
	(1)	258,000	(8d)	10,000		(B)	308,000
	(2c)	100					
	(4d)	820					
	(5)	400					
	(6)	56,000					
	(13)	100					
	Balance	315,420					

Estimated Other Financing Uses Control			Encumbrances Control			Expenditures Control	
	(B)	10,000	(7)	176,250	(8a)	175,800	(3b)	250
			Balance	450			(8b)	175,000
							(8c)	132,000
							(12b)	250
							Balance	307,500

the general fund to the electric utility (enterprise) fund for electrical power used by the governmental unit. This transfer would be accounted for as an *expenditure* by the general fund and as *revenue* by the enterprise fund.

Reimbursements are repayments by one fund to another for expenditures made (or expenses incurred) on behalf of the reimbursing fund. The reimbursement should be recorded as an expenditure or expense, as appropriate, by the reimbursing fund, and as a reduction of an expenditure or expense by the fund that is reimbursed.

EXHIBIT 17-8	GENERAL FUND BALANCE SHEET

City of Fisherville

GENERAL FUND BALANCE SHEET
AT DECEMBER 31, 19X6

Assets

Cash		$ 3,900
Petty cash		2,000
Taxes receivable—delinquent	$6,500	
Less: Allowance for uncollectible delinquent taxes	3,280	3,220
Interest and penalties receivable on taxes	$ 450	
Less: Allowance for uncollectible interest and penalties on taxes	50	400
Inventory of supplies		3,800
Total assets		$13,320

Liabilities and Fund Balance

Vouchers payable		$ 2,220
Fund balance:		
Reserved for encumbrances	$ 450	
Reserved for inventory of supplies	3,800	
Reserved for petty cash	2,000	
Unreserved	4,850	11,100
Total liabilities and fund balance		$13,320

Transfers

Transfers are interfund transactions by which resources are shifted from the fund that initially received the resources to another fund that will expend them. There are two major types of interfund transfers—residual equity transfers and operating transfers. Nonroutine or nonrecurring transfers between funds are residual equity transfers. Examples include a contribution of capital from the general fund for the establishment of an enterprise fund or an internal service fund, the return of such a capital contribution to the general fund, and transfers of the residual equities of discontinued funds to some other fund. Transactions involving such transfers will result in debits to *residual equity transfers out* for the transferring funds and credits to *residual equity transfers in* for the receiving funds.

Operating transfers are all other legally authorized transfers of resources from one fund (frequently the general fund) to another fund that will expend the resources. An example is a transfer of tax revenues from the general fund to the debt service fund to be expended for debt retirement and interest. Another example would be an operating subsidy transfer from the general fund to a special revenue fund or to an enterprise fund. Operating transfers result in debits to *other financing uses control—operating transfers out* for the transferring funds and credits to *other financing sources control—operating transfers in* for the receiving funds.

EXHIBIT 17-9	**GENERAL FUND STATEMENT OF REVENUES, EXPENDITURES, AND CHANGES IN FUND BALANCE**	

City of Fisherville
GENERAL FUND STATEMENT OF REVENUES, EXPENDITURES,
AND CHANGES IN FUND BALANCE
FOR THE YEAR ENDED DECEMBER 31, 19X6

Revenues:
Property taxes ($258,000 + $100 + $820)	$258,920	
Interest and penalties on delinquent taxes	400	
Other ($56,000 + $100)	56,100	
Total revenues		$315,420

Expenditures:
Supplies	$ 20,000	
Salaries	120,000	
Transportation equipment	15,000	
Interest ($250 + $250)	500	
Other ($140,000 + $12,000)	152,000	
Total expenditures		307,500
Excess of revenues over expenditures		$ 7,920
Other financing sources (uses):		
Operating transfer to debt service fund		(10,000)
Excess (deficiency) of revenues over expenditures and other uses		$ (2,080)
Fund balance, January 1, 19X6		9,380
Increase in reserve for inventory		3,800
Fund balance, December 31, 19X6		$ 11,100

The balances in both the residual equity transfer accounts and the operating transfer accounts are closed at year-end to the unreserved fund balance. However, they appear in different sections of the annual operating statement. Operating transfers are shown as other financing sources (uses) and added to (or subtracted from) the excess (deficiency) of revenues over expenditures. The residual equity transfers are, on the other hand, treated as direct additions to or deductions from the beginning balance of the fund equity.

Interfund Loans Short-term receivables from and payables to other funds are recorded in accounts called *due from other funds* or *due to other funds*. A cash loan from one fund to another would be recorded as follows: The receiving fund would debit *cash* and credit *due to other funds;* the fund making the disbursement would debit *due from other funds* and credit *cash.* Upon repayment of the loan, the preceding entries would be reversed in the respective funds.

Long-term receivables from and payables to other funds are recorded in accounts called *advances to other funds* or *advances from other funds.* Following is an illustration of a long-term advance of $5,000 from the general fund to an enterprise fund. Because

EXHIBIT 17-10	GENERAL FUND STATEMENT OF REVENUES, EXPENDITURES, AND CHANGES IN FUND BALANCE: BUDGET AND ACTUAL

City of Fisherville

GENERAL FUND STATEMENT OF REVENUES, EXPENDITURES, AND
CHANGES IN FUND BALANCE: BUDGET AND ACTUAL
FOR THE YEAR ENDED DECEMBER 31, 19X6

	Budget	Actual	Variance—Favorable (Unfavorable)
Revenues:			
Property taxes	$258,000	$258,920	$ 920
Interest and penalties on delinquent taxes	400	400	
Other	63,600	56,100	(7,500)
Total revenues	$322,000	$315,420	$(6,580)
Expenditures:			
Supplies	$ 21,000	$ 20,000	$ 1,000
Salaries	122,000	120,000	2,000
Transportation equipment	14,300	15,000	(700)
Interest	250	500	(250)
Other	150,450	152,000	(1,550)
Total expenditures	$308,000	$307,500	$ 500
Excess (deficiency) of revenues over expenditures	$ 14,000	$ 7,920	$(6,080)
Other financing sources (uses): Operating transfers out (to debt service fund)	(10,000)	(10,000)	
Excess (deficiency) of revenues over expenditures and other uses	$ 4,000	$ (2,080)	$(6,080)
Fund balances, January 1, 19X6	9,380	9,380	
Increase in reserve for inventory		3,800	3,800
Fund balances, December 31, 19X6	$ 13,380	$ 11,100	$(2,280)

such an advance represents an asset to the general fund that is not spendable, a fund balance reserve must also be recorded:

General fund entry to record long-term interfund loan:

```
Advances to enterprise fund ............................. 5,000
      Cash..............................................        5,000
```

General fund entry to reserve a portion of unreserved fund balance for long-term interfund loan:

```
Unreserved fund balance ................................. 5,000
      Fund balance reserved for advances to enterprise fund  ....        5,000
```

Enterprise fund entry to record long-term interfund loan:

Cash.. 5,000
    Advances from general fund 5,000

ACCOUNTING FOR GRANTS, ENTITLEMENTS, AND SHARED REVENUES

Grants, entitlements, and shared revenues are intergovernmental revenues from other governments (e.g., federal and/or state government). These three forms of intergovernmental revenues are defined as follows:

A *grant* is a contribution or gift of cash or other assets from another government to be used or expended for a specified purpose, activity, or facility. *Capital grants* are restricted by the grantor for the acquisition and/or construction of fixed (capital) assets. All other grants are *operating grants.*

An *entitlement* is the amount of payment to which a state or local government is entitled as determined by the federal government (e.g., the Director of the Office of Revenue Sharing) pursuant to an allocation formula contained in applicable statutes. A *shared revenue* is a revenue levied by one government but shared on a predetermined basis, often in proportion to the amount collected at the local level, with another government or class of government. (*NCGA Statement No. 2,* pars. 3–4; *GASB Codification,* sec. G60. 501–505)

Grants, entitlements, and shared revenues should be recognized as revenue in the period in which they meet the criteria for accrual, that is, when they become measurable and available. If such revenues are unrestricted as to usage, or where they are restricted more in form than in substance, such as resources given to the general fund for operating purposes (usually entitlements and shared revenues), they should be recognized as revenue when susceptible to accrual. For resources (usually grants) where expenditure is the primary factor in determining eligibility (i.e., where the grant is for a specified purpose such as the purchase of a new fire truck), revenue should be recognized when the expenditure is made. In the latter case, the following is the appropriate entry in the general fund upon receipt or accrual of a federal grant in the amount of $200,000:

General fund entry to record receipt or accrual of a federal grant:

Cash or grants receivable 200,000
    Deferred revenue 200,000

Assuming that the general fund has satisfied the grant restrictions and expenditures of $150,000 have been made for special equipment, the following entries are appropriate:

General fund entry to record grant expenditures:

Expenditures control—equipment 150,000
    Vouchers payable 150,000

General fund entry to recognize revenue as a result of grant expenditures:

Deferred revenues.................................. 150,000
    Revenues control—federal grants 150,000

The remaining $50,000 would be left in the deferred revenue account until expended for the intended purpose.

SUMMARY

The principal distinguishing characteristic of nonbusiness organizations is the absence of a profit orientation. Nonbusiness organizations are established as governments and nonprofit organizations to pursue goals defined in terms of the particular activities of the organization. The accounting systems of governments reflect this distinctive orientation in many ways. Governmental accounting systems are composed of multiple, distinct accounting entities called funds. Although proprietary funds (enterprise funds and internal service funds) follow essentially the same accrual accounting procedures as businesses, governmental funds (general funds, special revenue funds, capital projects funds, and debt service funds) follow a narrower "flow of financial resources" measurement focus. In addition, the emphasis on accountability and expenditure control in governmental accounting systems leads to the recording of budgets and encumbrances in the accounting records. These distinctive characteristics of governmental accounting are illustrated in the foregoing chapter by reference to the general fund.

SELECTED READINGS

American Institute of Certified Public Accountants. *Audits of State and Local Government Units.* Audit and Accounting Guide, rev. ed. New York: American Institute of Certified Public Accountants, 1986.

Anthony, Robert N. *Financial Accounting in Nonbusiness Organizations: An Exploratory Study of Conceptual Issues.* Research Report. Stamford, CT: Financial Accounting Standards Board, 1978.

Apostolou, Nicholas G., and D. Larry Crumbley. *Handbook of Governmental Accounting and Finance.* New York: Wiley, 1988.

Chan, James L. "The Birth of the Governmental Accounting Standards Board: How? Why? What Next?" *Research in Governmental and Nonprofit Accounting* (1985), pp. 20–36.

Chaney, Barbara A. "The Governmental Financial Reporting Entity: Inclusion and Display," *The CPA Journal* (January 1993), pp. 40–46.

Drebin, Allan R., James L. Chan, and Lorna C. Ferguson. *Objectives of Accounting and Financial Reporting for Governmental Units: A Research Study* (nine vols.). Chicago: National Council on Government Accounting, 1981.

Governmental Accounting Standards Board. *Codification of Governmental Accounting and Financial Reporting Standards.* Norwalk, CT: Governmental Accounting Standards Board, regularly updated (cited GASB Codification).

Governmental Accounting Standards Board. *Governmental Accounting and Financial Reporting Standards: Original Pronouncements.* Norwalk, CT: Governmental Accounting Standards Board, regularly updated.

Governmental Accounting Standards Board. *Implementation of GASB Statement No. 11,* "Measurement Focus and Basis of Accounting—Governmental Fund Operating Statements," Preliminary Views. Norwalk, CT: Governmental Accounting Standards Board, April 30, 1992.

Governmental Accounting Standards Board. *Service Efforts and Accomplishments Reporting,* Preliminary Views. Norwalk, CT: Governmental Accounting Standards Board, December 18, 1992.

Hatry, Harry P., James R. Fountain, Jr., Jonathan M. Sullivan, and Lorraine Kremer. *Service Efforts and Accomplishments Reporting: Its Time Has Come—An Overview,* Research Report. Norwalk, CT: Governmental Accounting Standards Board, 1990.

Hay, Leon E., and Earl R. Wilson. *Accounting for Governmental and Nonprofit Entities,* 9th ed. Homewood, IL: Irwin, 1992.

Holder, William. "Expenditure and Liability Recognition in Government," *Journal of Accountancy* (September 1983), pp. 79–84.

Ingram, Robert W., Russel J. Petersen, and Susan Work Martin. *Accounting and Financial Reporting for Governmental and Nonprofit Organizations: Basic Concepts.* New York: McGraw-Hill, 1991.

Leonard, Herman B. "Measuring and Reporting the Financial Condition of Public Organizations," *Research in Governmental and Nonprofit Accounting* (1985), pp. 117–148.

Lorensen, Leonard, and Richard J. Haas. "Governmental Accounting: Time for an Accommodation," *Journal of Accountancy* (March 1982), pp. 56–62.

Mautz, Robert K. "Financial Reporting: Should Government Emulate Business?" *Journal of Accountancy* (August 1981), pp. 53–60.

Mautz, Robert K. "Monuments, Mistakes, and Opportunities," *Accounting Horizons* (June 1988), pp. 123–128.

Meyer, Dan W., Albert C. Kiser, L. Leanne Whitaker, and Thomas A. Gavin. "How GASB 11 Will Affect Municipal Governments' Financial Reporting," *Journal of Accountancy* (January 1993), pp. 53–59.

Pallot, June. "The Nature of Public Assets: A Response to Mautz," *Accounting Horizons* (June 1990), pp. 79–85.

Roberts, Robin W., and James M. Kurtenbach. "An Analysis of Lobbying Activities before the Governmental Accounting Standards Board," *Research in Governmental and Nonprofit Accounting* (1992), pp. 25–40.

Wallace, Wanda A. "Objectives for the Governmental Accounting Standards Board," *Research in Governmental and Nonprofit Accounting* (1985), pp. 33–76.

QUESTIONS

Q17-1 Define the term *fund* as used in governmental accounting.

Q17-2 Distinguish among governmental funds, proprietary funds, and fiduciary funds.

Q17-3 Identify and briefly describe the purpose of each of the seven types of funds used by governmental units.

Q17-4 Discuss why you agree or disagree with the following statement: All funds exhibit fixed assets among their assets and long-term liabilities among their equities.

Q17-5 Distinguish between expense accounting and expenditure accounting.

Q17-6 What would be the main benefit(s) of recording budgeted revenues and expenditures in governmental accounting systems?

Q17-7 Define *encumbrances,* and briefly discuss the purpose of a system of encumbrances.

Q17-8 Describe the function of the general fund, and identify the basic financial statements for the general fund.

Q17-9 Distinguish between the purchases method and the consumption method of accounting for governmental fund inventories. What is the relationship between the method of accounting for inventory and the budget process?

Q17-10 Under what conditions should a governmental unit using the modified accrual method of accounting accrue revenues?

Q17-11   Identify and briefly describe three broad categories of interfund transactions.

Q17-12   Discuss why you agree or disagree with the following statement: General fund encumbrances outstanding at year-end should be combined with expenditures and the total presented in the general fund's statement of revenues, expenditures, and changes in fund balance.

Q17-13   Discuss why you agree or disagree with the debit to "bad debts expense" in the following entry recorded in the general fund when property taxes were levied:

Taxes receivable—current	250,000	
Bad debts expense	10,000	
Revenues control		250,000
Allowance for uncollectible current taxes		10,000

Q17-14   Describe the financial reporting entity for a government.

Q17-15   Discuss the objectives of financial reporting for a government.

EXERCISES

E17-1   **Multiple Choice Questions on Fundamentals of Governmental Units**

1. When used in fund accounting, the term *fund* usually refers to

  a) A sum of money designated for a special purpose

  b) A liability to other governmental units

  c) The equity of a municipality in its own assets

  d) A fiscal and accounting entity having a set of self-balancing accounts

2. In governmental accounting, an encumbrance is defined as

  a) A claim that a governmental unit has upon property until taxes levied against it have been paid

  b) An obligation that is chargeable to an appropriation and for which a part of the appropriation is reserved

  c) A proportionate share of debts of local governmental units located wholly or in part within the limits of the reporting government that must be borne by property within the government

  d) Indebtedness represented by outstanding bonds

3. Authority granted by a legislative body to make expenditures and to incur obligations during a fiscal year is the definition of an

  a) Appropriation   **c)** Encumbrance

  b) Authorization   **d)** Expenditure

4. When reporting for governmental units, what type of costs should be presented in the basic financial statements?

  a) Historical

  b) Historical adjusted for price-level changes

  c) Current appraisal

  d) Historical and current presented in two separate columns

5. The primary authoritative body for determining the measurement focus and basis of accounting standards for governmental fund operating statements is the

  a) Governmental Accounting Standards Board (GASB)

  b) National Council on Governmental Accounting (NCGA)

    c) Government Accounting and Auditing Committee of the AICPA (GAAC)

    d) Financial Accounting Standards Board (FASB)

6. One feature of state and local government accounting and financial reporting is that fixed assets used for general governmental activities

    a) Often are *not* expected to contribute to the generation of revenues

    b) Do *not* depreciate as a result of such use

    c) Are acquired only when direct contribution to revenues is expected

    d) Should *not* be maintained at the same level as those of businesses so that current financial resources can be used for other government services

7. What is the underlying reason a governmental unit uses separate funds to account for its transactions?

    a) Governmental units are so large that it would be unduly cumbersome to account for all transactions as a single unit.

    b) Because of the diverse nature of the services offered and legal provisions regarding activities of a governmental unit, it is necessary to segregate activities by functional nature.

    c) Generally accepted accounting principles require that not-for-profit entities report on a funds basis.

    d) Many activities carried on by governmental units are short-lived, and their inclusion in a general set of accounts could cause undue probability of error and omission.

8. Which of the following terms refers to an actual cost rather than an estimate?

    a) Expenditure

    b) Appropriation

    c) Budget

    d) Encumbrance

9. What is *not* a major concern of governmental units?

    a) Budgets

    b) Funds

    c) Legal requirements

    d) Consolidated statements

(AICPA adapted)

E17-2   **Comparison of Municipal and Commercial Accounting**   William Bates is executive vice-president of Mavis Industries, Inc., a publicly held industrial corporation. Bates has just been elected to the city council of Gotham City. Prior to assuming office as a city councilman, he asks you, as his CPA, to explain the major differences that exist in accounting and financial reporting for a large city when compared with a large industrial corporation.

REQUIRED

a) Describe the major differences that exist in the purpose of accounting and financial reporting and in the types of financial reports of a large city when compared with a large industrial corporation.

b) Why are inventories often ignored in accounting for local governmental units? Explain.

c) Under what circumstances should depreciation be recognized in accounting for local governmental units? Explain.

(AICPA adapted)

E17-3   **Budgetary Accounting**   Governmental accounting gives substantial recognition to budgets, with those budgets being recorded in the accounts of the governmental unit.

REQUIRED

a) What is the purpose of a governmental accounting system, and why is the budget recorded in the accounts of a governmental unit? Include in your discussion the purpose and significance of appropriations.

b) Describe when and how a governmental unit records its budget and closes it out.

(AICPA adapted)

E17-4   Multiple Choice Questions on Budgetary Accounting

1. Which of the following accounts is a budgetary account in governmental accounting?

   a) Fund balance reserved for inventory of supplies

   b) Unreserved fund balance

   c) Appropriations control

   d) Allowance for uncollectible property taxes

2. Which of the following steps in the acquisition of goods and services occurs first?

   a) Appropriation   **c)** Budget

   b) Encumbrance   **d)** Expenditure

3. If a credit was made to the budgetary fund balance in the process of recording a budget for a governmental unit, it can be assumed that

   a) Estimated revenues exceed appropriations

   b) Estimated expenses exceed actual revenues

   c) Actual expenses exceed estimated expenses

   d) Appropriations exceed estimated revenues

4. Which of the following accounts of a governmental unit is credited when the budget is recorded?

   a) Encumbrances control

   b) Fund balance reserved for encumbrances

   c) Estimated revenues control

   d) Appropriations control

5. The Board of Commissioners of the City of Rockton adopted its budget for the year ending July 31, 19X2, which indicated revenues of $1,000,000 and appropriations of $900,000. If the budget is formally integrated into the accounting records, what is the required journal entry?

	Debit	Credit
a) Memorandum entry only		
b) Appropriations control	900,000	
General fund	100,000	
Estimated revenues control		1,000,000
c) Estimated revenues control	1,000,000	
Appropriations control		900,000
Budgetary fund balance		100,000
d) Revenues receivable	1,000,000	
Expenditures payable		900,000
General fund unreserved balance		100,000

6. The estimated revenues control account of a governmental unit is credited when

   a) The budget is closed out at the end of the year

   b) The budget is recorded

   c) Property taxes are recorded

   d) Property taxes are collected

Items (7) through (9) are based on the following data:

The Board of Commissioners of Vane City adopted its budget for the year ending July 31, 19X5, consisting of revenues of $30,000,000 and appropriations of $29,000,000. Vane formally integrates its budget into the accounting records.

7. What entry should be made for budgeted revenues?

   a) Memorandum entry only

   b) Debit estimated revenues receivable control, $30,000,000

   c) Debit estimated revenues control, $30,000,000

   d) Credit estimated revenues control, $30,000,000

8. What entry should be made for budgeted appropriations?

   a) Memorandum entry only

   b) Credit estimated expenditures payable control, $29,000,000

   c) Credit appropriations control, $29,000,000

   d) Debit estimated expenditures control, $29,000,000

9. What entry should be made for the budgeted excess of revenues over appropriations?

   a) Memorandum entry only

   b) Credit budgetary fund balance, $1,000,000

   c) Debit estimated excess revenues control, $1,000,000

   d) Debit excess revenues receivable control, $1,000,000

10. The budget of a governmental unit, for which the appropriations exceed the estimated revenues, was adopted and recorded in the general ledger at the beginning of the year. During the year, expenditures and encumbrances were less than appropriations, whereas revenues equaled estimated revenues. The budgetary fund balance account is

   a) Credited at the beginning of the year and debited at the end of the year

   b) Credited at the beginning of the year and *not* changed at the end of the year

   c) Debited at the beginning of the year and credited at the end of the year

   d) Debited at the beginning of the year and *not* changed at the end of the year

(AICPA adapted)

E17-5   Multiple Choice Questions on Encumbrance Accounting

   1. The encumbrances control account of a governmental unit is debited when

   a) A purchase order is approved

   b) Goods are received

   c) A voucher payable is recorded

   d) The budget is recorded

   2. Which of the following accounts of a governmental unit is credited when a purchase order is approved?

   a) Fund balance reserved for encumbrances

   b) Encumbrances control

c) Vouchers payable

d) Appropriations control

3. Which of the following accounts of a governmental unit is debited when supplies previously ordered are received?

   a) Encumbrances control

   b) Fund balance reserved for encumbrances

   c) Vouchers payable

   d) Appropriations control

4. When supplies ordered by a governmental unit are received at an actual price that is less than the estimated price on the purchase order, the encumbrances control account is

   a) Credited for the estimated price on the purchase order

   b) Credited for the actual price for the supplies received

   c) Debited for the estimated price on the purchase order

   d) Debited for the actual price of the supplies received

5. The following balances are included in the subsidiary records of Burwood Village's Parks and Recreation Department at March 31, 19X2:

Appropriations—supplies	$7,500
Expenditures—supplies	4,500
Encumbrances—supply orders	750

How much does the department have available for additional purchases of supplies?

   a) $–0–   **c)** $3,000

   b) $2,250   **d)** $6,750

Items (6) and (7) are based on the following data:

Albee Township's fiscal year ends on June 30. Albee uses encumbrance accounting. On April 5, 19X4, an approved $1,000 purchase order was issued for supplies. Albee received these supplies on May 2, 19X4, and the $1,000 invoice was approved for payment.

6. What journal entry should Albee make on April 5, 19X4, to record the approved purchase order?

		Debit	Credit
a)	Memorandum entry only		
b)	Encumbrances control....................................	1,000	
	Fund balance reserved for encumbrances		1,000
c)	Supplies	1,000	
	Vouchers payable		1,000
d)	Encumbrances control....................................	1,000	
	Appropriations control		1,000

7. What journal entry or entries should Albee make on May 2, 19X4, upon receipt of the supplies and approval of the invoice?

		Debit	Credit
a)	Appropriations control	1,000	
	Encumbrances control		1,000
	Supplies	1,000	
	Vouchers payable		1,000
b)	Supplies	1,000	
	Vouchers payable		1,000
c)	Fund balance reserved for encumbrances	1,000	
	Encumbrances control		1,000
	Expenditures control	1,000	
	Vouchers payable		1,000
d)	Encumbrances control	1,000	
	Appropriations control		1,000
	Unreserved fund balance	1,000	
	Vouchers payable		1,000

8. At December 31, 19X9, Midlothian Township's committed appropriations that had not been expended in 19X9 totaled $10,000. These appropriations do not lapse at year-end. Midlothian reports on a calendar-year basis. On its December 31, 19X9, balance sheet, the $10,000 should be reported as

    a) Vouchers payable—prior year

    b) Deferred expenditures

    c) Fund balance reserved for encumbrances

    d) Budgetary fund balance—reserved for encumbrances

(AICPA adapted)

E17-6   **Encumbrance Accounting**   The general fund of Townsville has $3,000 of encumbrances outstanding at year-end. Prepare the necessary entries in Townsville's general fund relating to encumbrances outstanding at year-end if (a) the encumbrances do not lapse at year-end and (b) the encumbrances do lapse at year-end.

E17-7   **Multiple Choice Questions on Analyzing General Fund Transactions**

1. Repairs that have been made for a governmental unit, and for which a bill has been received, should be recorded in the general fund as a debit to

    a) Expenditures control

    b) Encumbrances control

    c) Expense control

    d) Appropriations control

2. Which of the following accounts of a governmental unit is credited when taxpayers are billed for property taxes?

    a) Estimated revenues control

    b) Revenues control

    c) Appropriations control

    d) Fund balance reserved for encumbrances

3. Which of the following types of revenue would generally be recorded directly in the general fund of a governmental unit?

a) Receipts from a city-owned parking structure

b) Interest earned on investments held for retirement of employees

c) Revenues from internal service funds

d) Property taxes

4. When fixed assets purchased from general fund revenues were received, the appropriate journal entry was made in the general fixed assets account group. What account, if any, should have been debited in the general fund?

a) No journal entry should have been made in the general fund

b) Fixed assets

c) Expenditures control

d) Due from general fixed assets account group

5. What account should be debited in the general fund for wages that have been earned by the employees of a governmental unit, but *not* paid?

a) Appropriations control

b) Encumbrances control

c) Expenditures control

d) Expense control

6. Kingsford City general fund incurred $100,000 of salaries and wages for the month ended March 31, 19X2. How should this be recorded at that date?

		Debit	Credit
a)	Expenditures control—salaries and wages	100,000	
	Vouchers payable		100,000
b)	Salaries and wages expense	100,000	
	Vouchers payable		100,000
c)	Encumbrances control—salaries and wages	100,000	
	Vouchers payable		100,000
d)	Unreserved fund balance	100,000	
	Vouchers payable		100,000

7. When goods that have been previously approved for purchase are received by a governmental unit but *not* yet paid for, what account is credited?

a) Fund balance reserved for encumbrances

b) Vouchers payable

c) Expenditures control

d) Appropriations control

(AICPA adapted)

E17-8   Multiple Choice Questions on Closing Entries of Governmental Units

1. Which of the following accounts of a governmental unit is credited to close it out at the end of the fiscal year?

a) Appropriations control

b) Revenues control

c) Fund balance reserved for encumbrances

d) Encumbrances control

2. Which of the following accounts of a governmental unit is closed out at the end of the fiscal year?

a) Unreserved fund balance

b) Property taxes receivable—current

c) Appropriations control

d) Vouchers payable

3. Which of the following accounts of a governmental unit is (are) closed out at the end of the fiscal year?

Estimated Revenues Control	Unreserved Fund Balance
a) No	No
b) No	Yes
c) Yes	Yes
d) Yes	No

4. When the accounts of a governmental unit are closed out at the end of the fiscal year, the excess of the revenues control over the expenditures control is

a) Debited to unreserved fund balance

b) Debited to fund balance reserved for encumbrances

c) Credited to unreserved fund balance

d) Credited to fund balance reserved for encumbrances

5. What journal entry should be made at the end of the fiscal year to close out encumbrances (that do not lapse) for which goods and services have *not* been received?

a) Debit fund balance reserved for encumbrances, and credit expenditures control.

b) Debit fund balance reserved for encumbrances, and credit unreserved fund balance.

c) Debit fund balance reserved for encumbrances, and credit encumbrances control.

d) Debit encumbrances control, and credit fund balance reserved for encumbrances.

6. Which of the following accounts is closed out at the end of the fiscal year?

a) Unreserved fund balance

b) Expenditures control

c) Vouchers payable

d) Taxes receivable—delinquent

7. The following information pertains to Pine City's general fund for 19X9:

Appropriations	$6,500,000
Expenditures	5,000,000
Other financing sources	1,500,000
Other financing uses	2,000,000
Revenues	8,000,000

After Pine's general fund accounts were closed at the end of 19X9, the fund balance increased by

a) $3,000,000

b) $2,500,000

c) $1,500,000

d) $1,000,000

(AICPA adapted)

E17-9   Multiple Choice Questions on Financial Reporting for the General Fund

1. On December 31, 19X1, Madrid Township paid a contractor $2,000,000 for the total cost of a new firehouse built in 19X1 on Township-owned land. Financing was by means of a $1,500,000 general obligation bond issue sold at face amount on December 31, 19X1, with the remaining $500,000 transferred from the general fund. What should be reported on Madrid's 19X1 financial statements for the general fund?

    a) Expenditures, $500,000

    b) Other financing uses, $500,000

    c) Revenues, $1,500,000; expenditures, $2,000,000

    d) Revenues, $1,500,000; other financing uses, $2,000,000

2. The following items were among Kew Township's expenditures from the general fund during the year ended July 31, 19X1:

    Minicomputer for tax collector's office $22,000
    Furniture for Township Hall 40,000

How much should be classified as fixed assets in Kew's general fund balance sheet at July 31, 19X1?

    a) $–0–   **c)** $40,000

    b) $22,000   **d)** $62,000

3. During the year ended December 31, 19X1, Leyland City received a state grant of $500,000 to finance the purchase of buses and an additional grant of $100,000 to aid in the financing of bus operations in 19X1. Only $300,000 of the capital grant was used in 19X1 for the purchase of buses, but the entire operating grant of $100,000 was spent in 19X1.

    If Leyland's bus transportation system is accounted for as part of the city's general fund, how much should Leyland report as grant revenues for the year ended December 31, 19X1?

    a) $100,000   **c)** $400,000

    b) $300,000   **d)** $500,000

                               (AICPA adapted)

E17-10   Recording the Budget, Revenues, Expenditures, and Closing Entries The City of Flat Rock had the following transactions pertaining to its general fund for the fiscal period ending June 30, 19X9:

1. A budget that estimated revenues of $150,000 and authorized expenditures of $145,000 was adopted.

2. Revenues totaling $148,000 were received in cash.

3. Expenditures totaling $140,000 were paid in cash.

REQUIRED

a) Prepare journal entries to record budget, revenues, and expenditures.

b) Prepare closing entries as of June 30, 19X9.

E17-11   Encumbrance Accounting Following are selected activities relating to the general fund of the town of Short Pump during the fiscal period ending December 31, 19X3:

1. Encumbrances for supplies and two microcomputers were recorded in the amounts of $5,000 and $15,000, respectively. Each microcomputer is estimated to cost $7,500.

2. Supplies ordered in part (1) are received together with an invoice giving their cost as $4,900. The invoice is to be paid at a later date.

3. One of the microcomputers ordered in part (1) is received. The accompanying invoice totaling $7,700 was paid upon delivery of equipment.

4. The invoice for the supplies received in part (2) is paid.

No encumbrances were outstanding at the end of December 31, 19X2.

REQUIRED

a) Prepare journal entries relating to the preceding transactions.

b) Prepare the necessary entries relating to encumbrances outstanding at the end of 19X3 if (1) encumbrances do not lapse at year-end and (2) encumbrances do lapse at year-end.

c) Assuming that year-end encumbrances do not lapse, prepare (1) the entry to reestablish the encumbrances control account on January 1, 19X4, for encumbrances that were outstanding at the end of 19X3 and (2) prepare the entry or entries in 19X4 to record receipt of the microcomputer ordered in 19X3 (the accompanying invoice totaled $7,400 and is to be paid at a later date).

E17-12 **Accounting for Property Taxes** On December 31, 19X3, the general fund presented the following information in its balance sheet in relation to property taxes:

Taxes receivable—delinquent	$5,000	
Less: Allowance for uncollectible delinquent taxes	1,000	$4,000

The following information relates to property tax transactions in the general fund during 19X4:

1. Early in the year, property taxes are levied in the total amount of $300,000, which includes $20,000 estimated to be uncollectible.

2. Delinquent property taxes in the amount of $3,500 are collected, and the remainder of the prior years' delinquent taxes is considered uncollectible.

3. Current property taxes of $268,000 are collected.

4. Current taxes in the amount of $14,000 are written off as uncollectible. Uncollectible taxes become delinquent at December 31 of each year. An allowance for uncollectible taxes in the amount of $7,000 is provided at December 31, 19X4.

REQUIRED

a) Prepare journal entries to record the four preceding transactions. List the transaction numbers (1) through (4) and give the necessary entry or entries for each.

b) Indicate how information relating to property taxes would be presented in the December 31, 19X4, balance sheet of the general fund.

E17-13 **General Fund: Balance Sheet and Closing Entries** The general fund adjusted trial balance of the Town of South Hill for the fiscal year ending June 30, 19X9, is presented as follows:

	Debit	Credit
Cash	$ 4,000	$
Petty cash	1,000	
Taxes receivable—delinquent	7,200	
Allowance for uncollectible delinquent taxes		1,200
Interest and penalties receivable on taxes	350	
Allowance for uncollectible interest and penalties on taxes		50
Due from other funds	1,500	
Inventory of supplies	2,000	
Vouchers payable		3,400
Due to other funds		600
Fund balance reserved for petty cash		1,000
Fund balance reserved for inventory of supplies		2,000
Unreserved fund balance		5,300
Budgetary fund balance		2,000
Estimated revenues control	10,000	
Appropriations control		8,000
Revenues control		12,000
Expenditures control	9,500	
Encumbrances control	700	
Fund balance reserved for encumbrances		700
Total	$36,250	$36,250

REQUIRED

a) Prepare closing entries for the general fund as of June 30, 19X9.

b) Prepare a general fund balance sheet as of June 30, 19X9.

E17-14   General Fund: Statement of Revenues, Expenditures, and Changes in Fund Balance   Following is selected information from the financial records of the general fund of the City of Crew at December 31, 19X6, the end of its fiscal year:

Fund balance, January 1, 19X6 (including both reserved and unreserved fund balance)	$ 7,500
Revenues:	
Property taxes	150,000
Interest and penalties on delinquent taxes	475
Other	40,125
Residual equity transfers in (from internal service fund)	2,500
Expenditures:	
Supplies	12,000
Salaries	90,000
Transportation equipment	19,500
Other	60,100
Operating transfers out (to special revenue fund)	8,000

REQUIRED

Prepare a statement of revenues, expenditures, and changes in fund balance for the general fund for the year ended December 31, 19X6.

PROBLEMS

P17-1 General Fund: Journal Entries The following transactions are related to the general fund of the Town of New Kent during the fiscal year ending June 30, 19X3.

1. The annual budget was adopted; it provided for estimated revenues of $550,000 and appropriations of $545,000.

2. The general fund borrowed $25,000 from a local bank on a tax anticipation note payable.

3. A $10,000 residual equity transfer was made from the general fund to an internal service fund to establish and operate a central purchasing department for the benefit of all departments of the municipality.

4. Property taxes were levied in the total amount of $490,000, which includes $20,000 estimated to be uncollectible.

5. Property taxes in the amount of $440,000 were collected, and $15,000 of property taxes was written off as uncollectible.

6. The face ($25,000) of the tax anticipation note in item (2) and $875 in interest were paid to the bank.

7. Encumbrances were recorded for purchase orders placed for supplies (estimated cost $4,000) and patrol cars (estimated cost $15,000) to be used by the Police Department.

8. Vouchers were approved for the payment of the salaries for the governmental unit's personnel in the amount of $12,000.

9. The supplies and patrol cars ordered in item (7) were received, together with invoices giving their total cost as $19,200. The invoices are to be paid at a later date.

10. Equipment used by the Parks and Recreation Department and carried in the general fixed asset account group at a cost of $3,500 was sold for $500.

11. At the end of the current fiscal year, uncollected property taxes become delinquent, and an allowance for uncollectible delinquent taxes in the amount of $5,500 was provided.

12. The $2,000 year-end inventory of supplies of the general fund is considered significant. The general fund uses the consumption method of accounting for supplies inventory.

REQUIRED
Prepare journal entries in the general fund to record the preceding activities. Number the activities 1 through 12, and give the necessary entry or entries.

P17-2 General Fund: Journal and Closing Entries The following financial activities relate to the City of Oilville's general fund during the fiscal year ending June 30, 19X7.

1. The budget was adopted: estimated revenues, $950,000; appropriations, $925,000.

2. Property taxes are levied in the amount of $700,000, which includes $50,000 estimated to be uncollectible.

3. Property taxes in the amount of $600,000 were collected, and $30,000 of property taxes was written off as uncollectible during the year.

4. All uncollected property taxes at year-end become delinquent. There were no delinquent property taxes at June 30, 19X6. An allowance for uncollectible taxes of $40,000 is desired at June 30, 19X7.

5. Revenues other than property taxes of $250,000 are collected.

6. Encumbrances of $400,000 were recorded for purchase orders placed with vendors.

7. Three-fourths, or $300,000, of the goods and services on encumbered purchase orders in item (6) was received; total billing was $310,000. Encumbrances outstanding at year-end do not lapse. There were no encumbrances outstanding at June 30, 19X6.

(Continued on page 878)

8. Expenditures of $540,000 not related to encumbrances (i.e., payroll, etc.) were recorded. Of this amount, $440,000 was paid.

9. The city received a donation of a building; the cost of the building to the donor was $20,000, and its estimated fair value was $60,000 at the date of the gift to the city.

REQUIRED

a) Prepare journal entries in the general fund to record the preceding activities. Number the activities 1 through 9, and give the necessary entry or entries.

b) Prepare closing entries for the general fund as of June 30, 19X7.

c) Prepare the entry to reestablish the encumbrances control account on July 1, 19X7, for encumbrances that were outstanding as of June 30, 19X7.

d) Prepare the entry or entries in the general fund on November 1, 19X7, to record the receipt of the remaining goods and services related to the encumbered purchase orders outstanding at June 30, 19X7. Assume expenditures related to these encumbrances totaled $95,000.

P17-3 **General Fund: Journal and Closing Entries, and Financial Statement**   The following information relates to the operations of the general fund of the City of King and Queen during the fiscal year ending June 30, 19X7. No encumbrances were outstanding at the beginning or end of the current fiscal year.

1. The following budget for the year was adopted:

Estimated revenues:		
Property taxes (net)	$335,000	
Licenses, permits, and fines	90,000	
Other	5,000	$430,000
Appropriations:		
Supplies	$ 53,000	
Salaries	162,000	
Office equipment	20,000	
Other	88,000	
	$323,000	
Estimated other financing uses—operating transfers out (to debt service fund for payment of principal and interest)	45,000	368,000
Excess of estimated revenues over appropriations and estimated other financing uses		$ 62,000

2. Property taxes were levied in the amount of $350,000. Of this amount $15,000 was estimated to be uncollectible. There were no delinquent taxes outstanding at the beginning of the current fiscal year.

3. Property taxes of $310,000 were collected, and taxes in the amount of $6,000 were written off as uncollectible. Uncollectible current taxes become delinquent at year-end. An allowance for uncollectible delinquent taxes of $12,000 is desired at year-end.

4. Revenues from licenses, permits, and fines totaled $80,000.

5. Vouchers were approved for payment for the following expenditures not related to encumbrances: salaries, $160,000; other, $85,000.

6. Vouchers were approved for payment of purchase orders for supplies, $54,000, and office equipment, $18,000. Encumbrances had been established for these two items in the current year in the amounts of $55,000 for supplies and $20,000 for office equipment. The city uses the purchases method of accounting for supplies inventory. The supplies inventory was insignificant at June 30, 19X7.

7. A transfer of $45,000 was made to the debt service fund to be expended for principal and interest payments on the general long-term debt of the city.

8. The remaining fund balance of $17,000 of the discontinued special revenue fund was transferred to the general fund.

9. The general fund sold equipment for $7,000. The equipment is carried in the general fixed assets account group at $10,000.

REQUIRED

a) Prepare journal entries in the general fund to record the preceding activities.

b) Prepare closing entries for the general fund as of June 30, 19X7.

c) Prepare a statement of revenues, expenditures, and changes in fund balance—budget and actual for the general fund for the year ended June 30, 19X7. (Assume that the general fund's total fund balance on July 1, 19X6, was $67,000.)

P17-4 **General Fund: Journal Entries and Financial Statements** The general fund trial balance of the City of Solna at December 31, 19X2, was as follows:

	Debit	**Credit**
Cash	$ 62,000	
Taxes receivable—delinquent	46,000	
Allowance for uncollectible delinquent taxes		$ 8,000
Stores inventory—program operations	18,000	
Vouchers payable		28,000
Fund balance reserved for stores inventory		18,000
Fund balance reserved for encumbrances		12,000
Unreserved undesignated fund balance		60,000
	$126,000	$126,000

Collectible delinquent taxes are expected to be collected within 60 days after the end of the year. Solna uses the "purchases" method to account for stores inventory. The following data pertain to 19X3 general fund operations:

1. Budget adopted:

Revenues and other financing sources

Taxes	$220,000
Fines, forfeits, and penalties	80,000
Miscellaneous revenues	100,000
Share of bond issue proceeds	200,000
	$600,000

Expenditures and other financing uses

Program operations	$300,000
General administration	120,000
Stores—program operations	60,000
Capital outlay	80,000
Periodic transfer to debt service fund	20,000
	$580,000

2. Taxes were assessed at an amount that would result in revenues of $220,800, after deduction of 4% of the tax levy as uncollectible.

3. Orders placed but not received:

Program operations	$176,000
General administration	80,000
Capital outlay	60,000
	$316,000

4. The city council designated $20,000 of the unreserved undesignated fund balance for possible future appropriation for capital outlay.

5. Cash collections and transfer:

Delinquent taxes	$ 38,000
Current taxes	226,000
Refund of overpayment of invoice for purchase of equipment	4,000
Fines, forfeits, and penalties	88,000
Miscellaneous revenues	90,000
Share of bond issue proceeds	200,000
Transfer of remaining fund balance of a discontinued fund	18,000
	$664,000

6. Approved vouchers for expenditures related to encumbrances:

	Estimated	Actual
Program operations	$156,000	$166,000
General administration	84,000	80,000
Capital outlay	62,000	62,000
	$302,000	$308,000

7. Additional vouchers approved for payment:

Program operations	$188,000
General administration	38,000
Capital outlay	18,000
Transfer to debt service fund	20,000
	$264,000

8. Albert, a taxpayer, overpaid his 19X3 taxes by $2,000. He applied for a $2,000 credit against his 19X4 taxes. The city council granted his request.

9. Vouchers paid amounted to $580,000.

10. Stores inventory on December 31, 19X3, amounted to $12,000.

REQUIRED

a) Prepare journal entries in the general fund to record the effects of the foregoing data.

b) Prepare closing entries for the general fund as of December 31, 19X3.

c) Prepare a balance sheet for the general fund as of December 31, 19X3.

(Continued on page 881)

d) Prepare a statement of revenues, expenditures, and changes in the fund balance for the general fund for the year ended December 31, 19X3.

(AICPA adapted)

P17-5 **General Fund: Journal Entries and Financial Statement** The following financial activities affecting Judbury City's general fund took place during the year ended June 30, 19X1:

1. The following budget was adopted:

Estimated revenues:	
Property taxes	$4,500,000
Licenses and permits	300,000
Fines	200,000
Total	$5,000,000
Appropriations:	
General government	$1,500,000
Police services	1,200,000
Fire department services	900,000
Public works services	800,000
Acquisition of fire engines	400,000
Total	$4,800,000

2. Property tax bills totaling $4,650,000 were mailed. It was estimated that $300,000 of this amount will be delinquent; in addition, $150,000 will be uncollectible.

3. Property taxes totaling $3,900,000 were collected. The $150,000 previously estimated to be uncollectible remained unchanged, but $750,000 was reclassified as delinquent. It is estimated that delinquent taxes will be collected soon enough after June 30, 19X1, to make these taxes available to finance obligations incurred during the year ended June 30, 19X1. There was no balance of uncollected taxes at July 1, 19X0.

4. Tax anticipation notes in the face amount of $300,000 were issued.

5. Other cash collections were as follows:

Licenses and permits	$270,000
Fines	200,000
Sale of public works equipment (original cost, $75,000)	15,000
Total	$485,000

6. The following purchase orders were executed:

	Total	Outstanding at 6/30/X1
General government	$1,050,000	$ 60,000
Police services	300,000	30,000
Fire department services	150,000	15,000
Public works services	250,000	10,000
Fire engines	400,000	—
Totals	$2,150,000	$115,000

No encumbrances were outstanding at June 30, 19X0.

7. The following vouchers were approved for payment:

General government	$1,440,000
Police services	1,155,000
Fire department services	870,000
Public works services	700,000
Fire engines	400,000
Total	$4,565,000

8. Vouchers totaling $4,600,000 were paid, including those outstanding at June 30, 19X0.

9. The $300,000 tax anticipation notes [item (4)] and $2,000 interest were paid.

REQUIRED

a) Prepare journal entries to record the foregoing financial activities in the general fund.

b) Prepare a statement of revenues, expenditures, and changes in fund balance—budget and actual for the year ended June 30, 19X1, for the general fund. (Assume that the general fund's total fund balance on July 1, 19X0, was $110,000.)

(AICPA adapted)

P17-6   **General Fund: Reconstruct Transactions and Closing Entries**   The following information was abstracted from the accounts of the general fund of the City of Rom after the books had been closed for the fiscal year ended June 30, 19X0:

	Postclosing Trial Balance June 30, 19X9	Transactions July 1, 19X9, to June 30, 19X0 Debit	Transactions July 1, 19X9, to June 30, 19X0 Credit	Postclosing Trial Balance June 30, 19X0
Cash	$700,000	$1,820,000	$1,852,000	$668,000
Taxes receivable—current	40,000	1,870,000	1,828,000	82,000
	$740,000			$750,000
Allowance for uncollectible				
current taxes	$ 8,000	8,000	10,000	$ 10,000
Vouchers payable	132,000	1,852,000	1,840,000	120,000
Fund balance:				
Reserved for				
encumbrances				
Item No. 1	—	1,000,000	1,070,000	70,000
Item No. 2	—	70,000	70,000	-0-
Unreserved	600,000	70,000	20,000	550,000
Budgetary fund balance		60,000	60,000	
	$740,000			$750,000

Additional information:

The budget for the fiscal year ended June 30, 19X0, provided for estimated revenues of $2,000,000 and appropriations of $1,940,000.

REQUIRED

Prepare journal entries to record the budgeted and actual transactions, and prepare closing entries for the fiscal year ended June 30, 19X0.

(AICPA adapted)

P17-7 **General Fund: Closing Entries and Financial Statements** The following information relates to the operations of a municipal general fund for the fiscal year ended April 30, 19X8:

1. Unreserved fund balance at May 1, 19X7, consisting entirely of cash $ 2,350
2. Budget estimate of revenue 185,000
3. Budget appropriations 178,600
4. Tax levy $115,620, which includes $4,000 estimated to be uncollectible
5. Tax receipts, $112,246; penalties on taxes, $310
6. Receipts from temporary loans $20,000, all of which were repaid during period with interest of $300
7. Fund balance reserved for encumbrances at April 30, 19X8 3,250
8. Vouchers approved for operating expenditures 146,421
9. Vouchers approved for capital expenditures 28,000
10. Miscellaneous revenue received 74,319
11. Rebate of current year's taxes collected in error 240
12. Payments of vouchers 169,400
13. Refund on an expenditures voucher on which an excess payment was made 116
14. All outstanding taxes receivable at year-end become delinquent and are estimated to be uncollectible

REQUIRED

a) Construct general fund T-accounts showing year-end balances at April 30, 19X8, after adjusting entries but before closing entries.

b) Prepare closing entries for the general fund for the year ended April 30, 19X8.

c) Prepare a balance sheet for the general fund as of April 30, 19X8.

d) Prepare a statement of revenues, expenditures, and changes in fund balance for the year ended April 30, 19X8.

(AICPA adapted)

P17-8 **General Fund: Adjusting and Closing Entries, and Financial Statement** You have been engaged to examine the financial statements of the town of Workville for the year ended June 30, 19X7. Your examination disclosed that due to the inexperience of the town's bookkeeper all transactions were recorded in the general fund even though other funds and account groups were involved. The following general fund trial balance as of June 30, 19X7, was furnished to you:

Town of Workville
GENERAL FUND TRIAL BALANCE
JUNE 30, 19X7

	Debit	Credit
Cash	$ 16,800	
Short-term investments	40,000	
Accounts receivable	11,500	
Taxes receivable—current	30,000	
Tax anticipation notes payable		$ 50,000
Appropriations control		400,000
Expenditures control	382,000	
Estimated revenues control	320,000	
Revenues control		360,000
General property	85,400	
Bonds payable	52,000	
Unreserved fund balance		207,700
Budgetary fund balance	80,000	
	$1,017,700	$1,017,700

Your audit disclosed the following additional information:

1. The accounts receivable of $11,500 includes $1,500 due from the town's water utility for the sale of scrap iron sold on its behalf. Accounts for the municipal water utility operated by the town are maintained in a separate fund.

2. The balance in taxes receivable—current is now considered delinquent, and the town estimates that $24,000 will be uncollectible.

3. On June 30, 19X7, the town retired, at face value, 6% general obligation serial bonds totaling $40,000. The bonds were issued on July 1, 19X2, at face value of $200,000. Interest paid during the year ended June 30, 19X7, was also charged to bonds payable. The town maintains a debt service fund for this bond issue.

4. In order to service other municipal departments, the town at the beginning of the year authorized the establishment of a central supplies warehouse. During the year supplies totaling $128,000 were purchased and charged to expenditures. The town chose to conduct a physical inventory of supplies on hand at June 30, 19X7, and this physical count disclosed that supplies totaling $84,000 were used. The town uses the consumption method of accounting for inventories.

5. Expenditures for the year ended June 30, 19X7, included $11,200 that was applicable to purchase orders issued in the prior year. Outstanding purchase orders at June 30, 19X7, that were not recorded amounted to $17,500.

6. On June 28, 19X7, the State Revenue Department informed the town that its share of a state-collected locally shared tax would be $34,000.

7. During the year, equipment with a book value of $7,900 was removed from service and sold for $4,600. In addition, new equipment costing $90,000 was purchased. The transactions were recorded in the general property account.

8. During the year, 100 acres of land were donated to the town for use as an industrial park. The land had a value of $125,000. No recording of this donation has been made.

REQUIRED

a) Prepare the necessary reclassification and adjusting entries for the general fund pertaining to the preceding transactions. (Do not prepare entries for any fund or account group other than the general fund.)

(Continued on page 885)

b) Prepare closing entries for the general fund as of June 30, 19X7.

c) Prepare a balance sheet for the general fund as of June 30, 19X7.

(AICPA adapted)

P17-9 **General Fund: Reconstruct Journal Entries** The following summary of transactions was taken from the accounts of the Annaville School District general fund before the books had been closed for the fiscal year ended June 30, 19X5:

	Postclosing Balances (June 30, 19X4)	Preclosing Balances (June 30, 19X5)
Cash	$400,000	$ 700,000
Taxes receivable—current	150,000	170,000
Allowance for uncollectible current taxes	(40,000)	(70,000)
Estimated revenues control		3,000,000
Expenditures control		2,900,000
Encumbrances control		91,000
	$510,000	$6,791,000
Vouchers payable	$ 80,000	$ 408,000
Due to other funds	210,000	142,000
Fund balance reserved for encumbrances	60,000	91,000
Unreserved fund balance	160,000	220,000
Budgetary fund balance		20,000
Revenues control—taxes		2,800,000
Revenues control—miscellaneous		130,000
Appropriations control		2,980,000
	$510,000	$6,791,000

Additional information:

1. Current tax levy for the year ended June 30, 19X5, was $2,870,000 and taxes collected during the year totaled $2,810,000.

2. An analysis of the transactions in the vouchers payable account for the year ended June 30, 19X5, follows:

	Debit (Credit)
Current expenditures	$(2,700,000)
Expenditures for prior year	(58,000)
Vouchers for payment to other funds	(210,000)
Cash payments during year	2,640,000
Net change	$ (328,000)

3. Current expenditures were encumbered at $2,700,000.

4. During the year the general fund was billed $142,000 for services performed on its behalf by other city funds.

5. On May 2, 19X5, commitment documents were issued for the purchase of new textbooks at a cost of $91,000.

REQUIRED

Based on the preceding data, reconstruct the original detailed journal entries that were required to record all transactions for the fiscal year ended June 30, 19X5, including the recording of the current year's budget. Do not prepare closing entries at June 30, 19X5.

(AICPA adapted)

P17-10 **General Fund: Journal and Closing Entries, and Financial Statements** The accounts of the general fund of the City of Lightfoot had the following balances as of January 1, 19X3:

	Debit	Credit
Cash	$1,300	
Taxes receivable—delinquent	3,500	
Allowance for uncollectible delinquent taxes		$ 300
Vouchers payable		800
Fund balance reserved for encumbrances		1,100
Unreserved fund balance		2,600
Totals	$4,800	$4,800

The following data pertain to the operations of the general fund during 19X3:

1. The encumbrances control account is reestablished at the beginning of the year.

2. The cash receipts for the year were:

From delinquent taxes	$ 3,200
From taxes of the current year	76,000
Other current revenues	16,000
Sale of old equipment	600
Temporary loans	20,000
Total	$115,800

3. The disbursements for the year were as follows:

Vouchers payable of preceding year	$ 800
Payment of current expenditures and interest:	
a) Covering all encumbered orders and contracts outstanding at	
beginning of year	1,200
b) Incurred during year	80,000
Payment of bonds falling due during year (the municipality does not	
have a debt service fund)	10,000
Purchase of fixed assets	4,000
Permanent petty cash advance made to city finance office	500
Supplies purchased for central storeroom established during year	
(the inventory is to be maintained on general fund books)	4,000
Payment of temporary loans	15,000
Total	$115,500

4. During the year, $1,600 of supplies purchased was issued to departments whose expenses are met from the general fund. The balance of stock on hand at the end of the year represents a minimum

inventory, which the municipality proposes to maintain in the storeroom. The consumption method is used in accounting for inventories.

5. The only taxes considered collectible at the end of 19X3 were those of the current year amounting to $7,000.

6. The only item encumbered during 19X3 was a $900 order placed for office equipment. The order is still outstanding at the end of 19X3.

REQUIRED

a) Prepare journal entries to record the six preceding sets of facts in the general fund. List the transaction numbers (1 through 6) and give the necessary entry or entries.

b) Prepare closing entries for the general fund for the year 19X3.

c) Prepare a balance sheet for the general fund at the end of 19X3 showing the amount available for future appropriation.

d) Prepare a statement of revenues, expenditures, and changes in the fund balance for the general fund for the year 19X3.

(AICPA adapted)

ISSUES IN ACCOUNTING JUDGMENT

I17-1   **Revenue Recognition**   Robert Norton, a new member of the Stockwood Town Council, was really confused. For years, the Town of Stockwood had hosted a major outdoor music concert. The 19X1 festival had occurred almost six months ago and the town had yet to record the revenues from this festival. The town council had talked of the revenues generated as a major reason for continuing to let the promoter operate the outdoor music concert. Last year, the Mayor had been quoted as saying, "The Stockwood Music Concert has allowed our fair city to have many things. While the amounts taken in by the town have varied considerably over the years, the Town of Stockwood has been pleased by the tax revenues generated by the festival. The Town Council treats these as special revenues and funds special projects when the amount is known."

     The Town of Stockwood collected a tax of 15% of the ticket revenue. The promoter would reduce this amount on a complicated sliding scale that provided multiple-dollar reductions in the amount to which the percentage would be applied for every dollar lost and a reduction to the percentage for every dollar of income less than $100,000. The town recorded the revenue only when the promoter filed its tax statements concerning the concert, usually on the last day to file each year (April 30).

     "Am I missing something about when the town can record the revenue?" asked Mr. Norton. "Surely the town's accountant can do better than this."

REQUIRED

a) Discuss the problems created by the town's revenue recognition practice.

b) How would you recommend that the town handle this situation?

I17-2   **Infrastructure and Depreciation**   Elaine Johnson tried to control her temper as the tax bill moved toward passage. "Mr. Chairperson, I simply don't understand what happened. For several years, the Village of Pericles has had one of the lowest tax rates in the entire state. Everyone in this room ran for office on the basis of keeping taxes low. Now, you want to raise taxes substantially to cover the cost of a new sewage system. Hasn't this been anticipated?"

     The Village of Pericles had been one of the first towns in the state to install a complete sewage system. It had been a wonder in the 1890s. As the 20th Century drew to a close, however, the system was falling apart. The system was still recorded at its original cost of $27,500 and no depreciation had been recorded. The lowest bidder to replace the system had submitted a bid of $1,400,000.

''Perhaps we should have been depreciating the cost and setting aside money to cover a new system years ago,'' responded the chairperson.

REQUIRED

If the village had done as the chairperson now suggests, would the current political problem have been avoided?

Accounting for Governments

SPECIFIC PURPOSE FUNDS, ACCOUNT GROUPS, AND ANNUAL FINANCIAL REPORTING

ACCOUNTING FOR SPECIAL REVENUE FUNDS 891

ACCOUNTING FOR CAPITAL PROJECTS FUNDS 891

BOND PREMIUM AND DISCOUNT 892

BUDGETS AND ENCUMBRANCES 892

RECORDING CAPITAL PROJECTS FUND TRANSACTIONS 892

Recording the Issuance of Bonds and the State Grant 892 Recording the State Grant and First-Year Encumbrances and Expenditures 892   First-Year Closing of Capital Projects Fund 896   Reestablishment of Encumbrances Closed at End of Preceding Year 896   Recording Receipt of Remaining State Grant and Second-Year Encumbrances and Expenditures 896 Recording Transfer of Unexpended Cash to Debt Service Fund 896   Second-Year Closing Entry 896

FINANCIAL REPORTING FOR THE CAPITAL PROJECTS FUND 897

ACCOUNTING FOR DEBT SERVICE FUNDS 898

RECORDING DEBT SERVICE FUND TRANSACTIONS 899

Recording Revenues, Other Financial Sources, Residual Equity Transfers In, and Investment Transactions 900 Recording Expenditures 900   Recording Closing Entries 903

FINANCIAL REPORTING FOR DEBT SERVICE FUND 903

ACCOUNTING FOR SERIAL BONDS AND INTEREST IN DEBT SERVICE FUND 904

GENERAL FIXED ASSETS ACCOUNT GROUP 905

CLASSIFICATION OF FIXED ASSETS 907

RECORDING GENERAL FIXED ASSETS 907

FINANCIAL REPORTING FOR GENERAL FIXED ASSETS ACCOUNT GROUP 907

GENERAL LONG-TERM DEBT ACCOUNT GROUP 907

RECORDING TRANSACTIONS IN THE LONG-TERM DEBT ACCOUNT GROUP 910

Recording Issuance of Long-Term Debt 910   Recording the Provision of Funds for Debt Retirement 911   Recording the Retirement of Debt 911

FINANCIAL REPORTING FOR GENERAL LONG-TERM DEBT ACCOUNT GROUP 911

ACCOUNTING FOR PROPRIETARY FUNDS 911

DISTINCTIVE ASPECTS OF ENTERPRISE FUNDS 913

DISTINCTIVE ASPECTS OF INTERNAL SERVICE FUNDS 916

ACCOUNTING FOR SPECIAL ASSESSMENTS 917

SERVICES FINANCED BY SPECIAL ASSESSMENTS 918

CAPITAL IMPROVEMENTS FINANCED BY SPECIAL ASSESSMENTS 918

ACCOUNTING FOR FIDUCIARY FUNDS 919

RECORDING AGENCY FUND TRANSACTIONS 920

RECORDING TRUST FUND TRANSACTIONS 921

Recording Contribution of Principal, Investment, and Investment Income 922

FINANCIAL REPORTING FOR NONEXPENDABLE AND EXPENDABLE TRUST FUNDS 924

ANNUAL FINANCIAL REPORTING 924

LEVEL 1: GENERAL PURPOSE FINANCIAL STATEMENTS 926

Combined Balance Sheet—All Fund Types and Account Groups 926   Combined Statement of Revenues, Expenditures, and Changes in Fund Balances—All Governmental Fund Types 926   Combined Statement of Revenues, Expenditures, and Changes in Fund Balances—Budget and Actual—General and Special Revenue Fund Types 930   Combined Statement of Revenues, Expenses, and Changes in Retained Earnings—All Proprietary Fund Types 930   Combined Statement of Changes in Financial Position—All Proprietary Fund Types 930

LEVEL 2: COMBINING STATEMENTS BY FUND TYPE 930

LEVEL 3: INDIVIDUAL FUND AND ACCOUNT GROUP STATEMENTS 931

LEVEL 4: SCHEDULES 933

SUMMARY 934

As indicated in the previous chapter, the general fund is used to account for the general operations of a governmental unit; that is, the general fund accounts for all financial resources that are not required to be accounted for in another fund. These other funds are often called specific or special purpose funds because they account for resources that must be kept separate to comply with legal, contractual, or sound administration requirements. Every governmental unit will have at least one fund—a general fund. A governmental unit may have one of each of the account groups and one or more of the special purpose funds, the exact number depending on the number of types of financial resources the governmental unit may have that require separate funds.

The remainder of this chapter will be a discussion of the six types of special purpose funds and the two account groups. The special purpose governmental-type funds—special revenue, capital projects, and debt service—will be discussed first because they have much in common with the general fund that was just covered in the preceding chapter. The two account groups—general fixed assets and general long-term debt—will then be considered because they are closely related to the governmental-type funds. Next to be covered will be the proprietary funds—enterprise and internal service funds—followed by discussions of special assessments and fiduciary funds—agency funds, and nonexpendable, expendable, and pension trust funds. The last section of this chapter will deal with annual financial reporting requirements for governmental units.

ACCOUNTING FOR SPECIAL REVENUE FUNDS

Special revenue funds are established to account for the proceeds of specific revenue sources that are restricted by law or administrative action to be expended for specified purposes. Special revenue funds account for activities like libraries, parks, and schools, for which the principal revenues do not represent charges for the service provided. Resources to support the activities of special revenue funds may be provided by specific tax levies, grants from other governments (e.g., state or federal grants), operating transfers from the general (or other) fund, and so on. When the principal revenues of a fund represent charges for services or goods provided, the fund is a proprietary fund and not a special revenue fund. Fund accounting and financial reporting for special revenue funds use modified accrual accounting (accrual accounting with a flow of financial resources measurement focus) and are essentially the same as they are for the general fund. Thus, accounting for general fund transactions (discussed in the preceding chapter), including budgetary and encumbrance accounting for expenditure control, is equally applicable to special revenue funds. For this reason, further discussion of special revenue fund accounting is not necessary.

ACCOUNTING FOR CAPITAL PROJECTS FUNDS

Capital projects funds account for financial resources that are set aside for the acquisition or construction of major fixed assets (e.g., a library or a civic center). Capital projects funds do not account for the acquisition of fixed assets that are financed by proprietary or nonexpendable trust funds; the acquisition or construction of such assets is accounted for by the fund that finances them. The financial resources of capital projects funds are derived from sources such as general obligation long-term debt, transfers from the general fund, and grants from state and federal governments. Bond issue proceeds and transfers from the general fund are classified as other financing sources; whereas grants from federal, state, or other governmental units are classified as revenues (intergovernmental).

Accounting for capital projects funds, like accounting for all governmental-type funds, is primarily concerned with available, spendable resources. Thus, it uses modified accrual accounting (accrual accounting with a flow of financial resources measurement focus).

Bond Premium and Discount

When bonds are issued at a premium, the premium is usually recorded as a part of the bond issue proceeds. In theory, the bond premium is a factor in determining interest expense. Since the bond interest and principal are repaid by the debt service fund, the premium should be transferred to such a fund. Bond discounts, on the other hand, reduce the bond proceeds, and thus reduce the amount that is available for the capital project unless the resources to cover this deficiency are available from some other source (e.g., the general fund).

Budgets and Encumbrances

It is generally not necessary to use budgetary accounting for capital projects funds unless more than one project is being accounted for in a single capital projects fund. In such a case, budgetary accounting could help avoid the spending of resources for one project that are intended for another project. However, budgetary accounting would be necessary in any case if required by law. In the absence of a formal journal entry to record the budget, a memorandum entry may be made of the project authorization. Proper control of capital projects requires the recording of encumbrances and the annual closing of the accounts of the capital projects fund.

Recording Capital Projects Fund Transactions

We illustrate the accounting entries and financial statements for a capital projects fund by reference to a capital projects fund established by the City of Fisherville. Fisherville's capital projects fund was established in 19X5 to account for the construction of a bridge that is estimated to cost $110,000. Construction is financed by general obligation bonds of $100,000 and a $10,000 irrevocable capital grant received from the state. Construction begins in 19X5 and is completed in 19X6. The transactions affecting the capital projects fund during 19X5 and 19X6 are shown in Exhibit 18-1. The journal entries made by Fisherville's capital projects fund to record these transactions are also shown in Exhibit 18-1 and are discussed in the following paragraphs.

Recording the Issuance of Bonds and the State Grant

The issuance of $100,000 in bonds at a premium of $7,711 is recorded in the capital projects fund by entry (1a) in Exhibit 18-1 on April 1, 19X5 (the entry to record the bonds payable in the general long-term debt account group is discussed later in this chapter). Entry (1b) records the transfer of the premium to the debt service fund (the entry to record receipt of this amount in the debt service fund is discussed later in this chapter). When bonds are issued at a discount, no transfers are required. However, the general fund may be required to provide resources to complete the related capital project if the proceeds from the bond issue are insufficient to do so.

Recording the State Grant and First-Year Encumbrances and Expenditures

The state grant and the receipt of $4,000 is recorded by entry (2) in Exhibit 18-1. The entire $10,000 grant is recorded, and a receivable is established for the $6,000 portion not

EXHIBIT 18-1	CAPITAL PROJECTS FUND ENTRIES

City of Fisherville
CAPITAL PROJECTS FUND ENTRIES
FOR THE YEARS ENDED DECEMBER 31, 19X5, AND DECEMBER 31, 19X6

Transaction (1): On April 1, 19X5, Fisherville issues general obligation ten-year, 6% term bonds with a par value of $100,000 for cash of $107,711. Following the usual practice, the premium on the bond issue is transferred to the debt service fund.

(1a) *Capital projects fund entry to record the issuance of bonds:*

Cash 107,711
    Other financing sources control—proceeds of
      bond issue 107,711

(1b) *Capital projects fund entry to record transfer of premium to debt service fund:*

Other financing uses control—operating transfers out
    (to debt service fund) 7,711
      Cash 7,711

Transaction (2): The state grant was recorded on April 10, 19X5; $4,000 was received, and the remaining amount is to be received later.

(2) *Capital projects fund entry to record state grant:*

Cash 4,000
Due from state government 6,000
    Revenues control—intergovernmental (state grant) 10,000

Transaction (3): On May 1, 19X5, a contract was entered into with Farmington Construction Company for the major part of the project for $65,000. This amount is encumbered. Expenditures during 19X5, all of which are related to progress billings under the preceding construction contract, total $34,000 (including $29,500 paid in cash and $4,500 that remains unpaid at year-end in accordance with the percentage retention clause in the contract).

(3a) *Capital projects fund entry to record first-year encumbrances for construction contract:*

Encumbrances control................................ 65,000
    Fund balance reserved for encumbrances 65,000

(3b) *Capital projects fund entry to record first-year encumbrance reversals:*

Fund balance reserved for encumbrances 34,000
    Encumbrances control............................. 34,000

(3c) *Capital projects fund entry to record first-year expenditures:*

Expenditures control 34,000
    Contracts payable 29,500
    Contracts payable—retained percentage 4,500

EXHIBIT 18-1	CAPITAL PROJECTS FUND ENTRIES (Continued)

(3d) *Capital projects fund entry to record first-year payments to contractor:*

Contracts payable	29,500	
Cash		29,500

Transaction (4): Fund accounts are closed at December 31, 19X5.

(4a) *Capital projects fund entry to close actual revenues, other financing sources, expenditures, and other financing uses accounts to unreserved fund balance at December 31, 19X5:*

Revenues control—intergovernmental (state grant)	10,000	
Other financing sources control—proceeds of bond issue.....	107,711	
Expenditures control		34,000
Other financing uses control—operating transfers out (to debt service fund)		7,711
Unreserved fund balance		76,000

(4b) *Capital projects fund entry to close encumbrances control and fund balance reserved for encumbrances at December 31, 19X5:*

Fund balance reserved for encumbrances	31,000	
Encumbrances control ($65,000 − $34,000)		31,000

(4c) *Capital projects fund entry to reserve a portion of unreserved fund balance for outstanding encumbrances at December 31, 19X5:*

Unreserved fund balance	31,000	
Fund balance reserved for encumbrances		31,000

Transaction (5): Encumbrances are reestablished on January 1, 19X6.

(5a) *Capital projects fund entry to reverse entry reserving a portion of fund balance at December 31, 19X5:*

Fund balance reserved for encumbrances	31,000	
Unreserved fund balance		31,000

(5b) *Capital projects fund entry to reestablish encumbrances control and fund balance reserved for encumbrances accounts at January 1, 19X6:*

Encumbrances control.................................	31,000	
Fund balance reserved for encumbrances		31,000

Transaction (6): On January 5, 19X6, the remaining $6,000 was received from the state.

(6) *Capital projects fund entry to record receipt of remaining balance of state grant:*

Cash	6,000	
Due from state government		6,000

EXHIBIT 18-1	CAPITAL PROJECTS FUND ENTRIES (Continued)

Transaction (7): Additional encumbrances in the total amount of $40,000 for construction costs are recorded in 19X6. Expenditures during 19X6 total $71,000, of which $31,000 pertains to 19X5 encumbrances and $40,000 pertains to 19X6 encumbrances. After inspection of the bridge by the city engineer all amounts for construction of the bridge are paid by year-end, including the contracts payable—retained percentage.

(7a) *Capital projects fund entry to record second-year encumbrances for construction contract:*

Encumbrances control	40,000	
Fund balance reserved for encumbrances		40,000

(7b) *Capital projects fund entry to record second-year encumbrance reversals:*

Fund balance reserved for encumbrances	71,000	
Encumbrances control		71,000

(7c) *Capital projects fund entry to record second-year expenditures:*

Expenditures control	71,000	
Contracts payable		71,000

(7d) *Capital projects fund entry to record second-year payment to contractor:*

Contracts payable	71,000	
Contracts payable—retained percentage	4,500	
Cash		75,500

Transaction (8): The $5,000 cash balance of the capital projects fund is transferred to the debt service fund.

(8) *Capital projects fund entry to record transfer of unexpended cash to debt service fund:*

Residual equity transfers out (to debt service fund)	5,000	
Cash		5,000

Transaction (9): Fund accounts are closed at December 31, 19X6.

(9) *Capital projects fund entry to close actual expenditures, and residual equity transfers out accounts to unreserved fund balance at December 31, 19X6:*

Unreserved fund balance	76,000	
Expenditures control		71,000
Residual equity transfers out (to debt service fund)		5,000

yet received. Encumbrances, reversal of encumbrances, and expenditures during 19X5 are recorded by entries (3a) through (3d).

First-Year Closing of Capital Projects Fund

Although the capital projects fund is project-oriented, proper accounting for operations and financial status at year-end requires the periodic closing of its accounts. Fisherville's capital projects fund makes closing entries at December 31, 19X5, as shown in Exhibit 18-1 by entries (4a) through (4c). The closing entry for expenditures in the capital project fund is accompanied by the recording of assets in the general fixed assets account group. Accordingly, Fisherville records $34,000 in the *construction in progress* account in the general fixed assets account group on December 31, 19X5. Accounting for the general fixed assets account group is discussed later in this chapter.

Reestablishment of Encumbrances Closed at End of Preceding Year

In order to maintain uniform entries for recording expenditures and related encumbrance reversals, and because expenditure authorization of capital projects funds does not expire at year-end, one needs to reestablish the encumbrances control account at the beginning of the next year. Entries (5a) and (5b) accomplish the reestablishment of encumbrances for Fisherville on January 1, 19X6. Recall that such an entry was also made in the period-oriented general fund in the previous chapter. In both cases, outlays related to the prior year's encumbrances are charged to the current year's expenditures account.

Recording Receipt of Remaining State Grant and Second-Year Encumbrances and Expenditures

Receipt of the remaining amount of the state grant is recorded by entry (6) in Exhibit 18-1. Encumbrances, reversal of encumbrances, and expenditures during 19X6 are recorded by entries (7a) through (7d).

Recording Transfer of Unexpended Cash to Debt Service Fund

The total expenditures for a project rarely equal the amount authorized for expenditure on the project. In general, applicable statutes, ordinances, and governmental policies should be consulted to determine the appropriate handling of the difference. An unexpended balance is frequently transferred to a related debt service fund. Fisherville transfers the $5,000 ($110,000 − $29,500 − $75,500) remainder to its debt service fund using entry (8) (the entry that records receipt of this amount in the debt service fund is discussed later in this chapter). When expenditures exceed the amount authorized, the general fund is typically required to provide the difference by an operating transfer to the capital projects fund.

Second-Year Closing Entry

Once a capital project is completed and all related payments and transfers have been made, expenditure, transfer, and revenue balances may be offset against the unreserved fund balance, which eliminates the unreserved fund balance. At the end of 19X6, Fisherville accomplishes this closing process by entry (9) in Exhibit 18-1. Entry (9) exactly eliminates the Fisherville's capital projects unreserved fund balance. Accounting for the cost of the completed project in the general fixed assets account group will be discussed later in this chapter.

The cash proceeds of a bond issue are seldom expended immediately. Any excess cash is normally invested in short-term high-grade securities. The interest earnings on such investments should be credited to revenues. Such revenues may be made available for expenditure in case the actual cost of the project exceeds the original estimate. In many cases, the capital projects fund will be required to transfer such earnings to a debt service fund or other appropriate fund.

Financial Reporting for the Capital Projects Fund

The capital projects fund has two basic financial statements: (1) a *balance sheet* and (2) a *statement of revenues, expenditures, and changes in fund balance*. A *statement of revenues, expenditures, and changes in fund balance—budget and actual* is also required if an annual budget is legally adopted for a capital projects fund. Fisherville's capital projects fund balance sheet at December 31, 19X5, is shown in Exhibit 18-2. One year later, the project is completed, and all resources are distributed at December 31, 19X6. Consequently, the capital projects fund does not exist at that date, and all of its balance sheet accounts equal zero. Fisherville's statement of revenues, expenditures, and changes in fund balance for the capital projects fund is presented in Exhibit 18-3 for both 19X5 and 19X6. As mentioned in the previous chapter, operating transfers and residual equity transfers are classified differently in the statement of revenues, expenditures, and changes in fund balance. Operating transfers are treated as other financing sources (uses) and added to (or subtracted from) the excess (deficiency) of revenues over expenditures. Residual equity transfers are, on the other hand, treated as direct additions to or deductions from the beginning balance of the fund equity.

EXHIBIT 18-2	CAPITAL PROJECTS FUND BALANCE SHEET

City of Fisherville

CAPITAL PROJECTS FUND BALANCE SHEET
AT DECEMBER 31, 19X5

Assets

Cash		$74,500
Due from state government		6,000
Total assets		$80,500

Liabilities and Fund Balance

Contracts payable—retained percentage		$ 4,500
Fund balances:		
Reserved for encumbrances	$31,000	
Unreserved	45,000	76,000
Total liabilities and fund balance		$80,500

EXHIBIT 18-3	CAPITAL PROJECTS FUND STATEMENT OF REVENUES, EXPENDITURES, AND CHANGES IN FUND BALANCE

City of Fisherville

CAPITAL PROJECTS FUND STATEMENT OF REVENUES, EXPENDITURES,
AND CHANGES IN FUND BALANCE
FOR YEARS ENDED DECEMBER 31, 19X6, AND DECEMBER 31, 19X5

	12-31-X6	12-31-X5
Initial project authorization	$110,000	$110,000
Revenues:		
Intergovernmental (state grant)	$	$ 10,000
Expenditures:		
Construction contract	71,000	34,000
Excess (deficiency) of revenues over expenditures	$ (71,000)	$ (24,000)
Other financing sources (uses):		
Proceeds of general obligation bonds		107,711
Operating transfers out (to debt service fund)		(7,711)
Excess (deficiency) of revenues and other sources over expenditures and other uses	$ (71,000)	$ 76,000
Fund balance, January 1	76,000	
Residual equity transfers out (to debt service fund)	(5,000)	
Fund balance, December 31	$ –0–	$ 76,000

ACCOUNTING FOR DEBT SERVICE FUNDS

Debt service funds account for the accumulation of resources for, and the payments of, general long-term debt principal and interest. Debt service funds are required only when legally or contractually mandated, and/or when resources are being accumulated for future maturities of debt (term bonds) and interest. Debt service fund resources are derived largely from tax revenues either by transfer from the general fund or, in some cases, by direct tax levy by the debt service funds. Resources are accumulated and invested by the debt service fund until they are required to make interest and principal payments. Since the terms of bond issues vary from one issue to another, a separate debt service fund is frequently established for each major issue. Accounting for debt service funds follows modified accrual accounting (accrual accounting with a financial resource measurement focus). Budgetary accounting may be used but is not often required in debt service funds because spending for these funds is controlled, for the most part, through bond indenture provisions. Encumbrance accounting is not normally used by debt service funds. Revenue from investments is accrued as earned, but interest on indebtedness need not be recognized as an expenditure until the due date. However, if resources for the payment of interest have been appropriated during the period of interest accrual, then the interest expenditure and related fund liability should be recorded in that same period. In other words, the expenditure is recorded in the same period in which the appropriation is recorded for such expenditure.

Recording Debt Service Fund Transactions

Because Fisherville has issued term bonds (rather than serial bonds), Fisherville must establish a debt service fund to service the future maturity and interest on these bonds. Fisherville's debt service fund is related to the $100,000 issue of 6%, ten-year term bonds issued on April 1, 19X5, to finance construction of a bridge. The bonds were issued for cash of $107,711 to yield an effective interest rate of 5% and require a $6,000 interest coupon payment on March 31 of each year. The bond indenture requires the general fund to contribute $10,000 annually to the debt service fund, which is to be invested in specified securities and, together with the earnings thereon, used to pay interest and principal. The general fund must make the full contribution even when taxes levied for that purpose do not yield the required $10,000 contribution.

In order to accumulate the $100,000 to retire the $100,000 in term bonds at the end of ten years, it is essential to meet the additions and earnings required by the actuarial calculations. If the actual accumulations fall short of the actuarial requirements, then additional transfers will be required from the general fund to make up the shortage. If actual earnings exceed the earnings required by the actuarially assumed rate, then the general fund may reduce its future transfers accordingly. The actuarial requirement for the amount of the fund balance reserved for debt service should be disclosed in a note to the annual financial statements.

Fisherville's debt service fund is assumed to have the balance sheet shown in Exhibit 18-4 at December 31, 19X5. Neither the proceeds from the bond issue nor the unmatured bond liability is recorded in the accounts of the debt service fund. The bond liability accounts are recorded in the general long-term debt account group, and the proceeds from the bond issue are recorded in a capital projects fund. In Fisherville, the law requires that premiums on bond issues be transferred from the capital projects fund to the debt service fund; the transfer occurred during 19X5 and was recorded by the following entry:

Debt service fund entry to record receipt of bond premium from capital project fund in 19X5:

Cash.. 7,711
    Other financing sources control—operating transfers in
      (from capital projects fund)........................ 7,711

EXHIBIT 18-4 | **DEBT SERVICE FUND BALANCE SHEET**

City of Fisherville

DEBT SERVICE FUND BALANCE SHEET
AT DECEMBER 31, 19X5

Assets
Cash	$ 200
Interest receivable	150
Investment in securities	17,300
Total assets	$17,650

Fund Balance
Fund balance reserved for debt service	$17,650

Exhibit 18-5 shows the entries to record transactions in the debt service fund for 19X6. The 19X6 budget for Fisherville's debt service fund is as follows:

Debt Service Fund Budget for 19X6

Estimated revenues and other financing sources:		
Estimated other financing sources—operating transfers in (from general fund)		$10,000
Estimated revenues—earnings		1,500
Total estimated revenues and other financing sources		$11,500
Appropriations:		
Interest payments	$6,000	
Investment fees	100	6,100
Excess of estimated revenues and other financing sources over appropriations		$ 5,400

The following budget entry in the debt service fund records the required additions from the general fund and the required earnings on the investments of the debt service fund:

Debt service fund entry to record budget for 19X6:

Estimated other financing sources control	10,000	
Estimated revenues control	1,500	
Appropriations control		6,100
Budgetary fund balance		5,400

Recording Revenues, Other Financial Sources, Residual Equity Transfers In, and Investment Transactions

Entries (1a) through (4) in Exhibit 18-5 record debt service fund revenues, transfers in, and investment transactions.

Recording Expenditures

Entries (5a) through (6) record debt service fund expenditures for interest coupons and fees paid to brokers and bankers. The entry to record the retirement of the $100,000 face value of bonds at maturity in the debt service fund requires a debit to *expenditures control* and a credit to *matured term bonds payable*. A subsequent entry would then be made debiting *matured term bonds payable* and crediting *cash* for $100,000. At the same time, the bonds payable are removed from the general long-term debt account group as illustrated later in this chapter. Observe that interest on indebtedness since the last interest payment date of March 31, 19X6, is not accrued at December 31, 19X6, because interest on general long-term debt is recorded as a liability when it is legally due (March 31 of each year in this example). The appropriation for this expenditure will be made in 19X7, the following year. Such a procedure records the expenditure in the period in which the appropriation is made.

If the City of Fisherville employs a fiscal agent to handle bond interest coupon payments, transaction (5) would be handled in the following manner. Cash of $6,000

EXHIBIT 18-5	DEBT SERVICE FUND ENTRIES

City of Fisherville

DEBT SERVICE FUND ENTRIES
FOR THE YEAR ENDED DECEMBER 31, 19X6

Transaction (1): The general fund transfers cash of $10,000 to the debt service fund, as required by the bond indenture, and the entire amount is invested in securities.

(1a) *Debt service fund entry to record amount due from general fund at January 1, 19X6:*

Due from general fund	10,000	
Other financing sources control—operating transfers in (from general fund)		10,000

(1b) *Debt service fund entry to record the collection of amount due from general fund:*

Cash	10,000	
Due from general fund		10,000

(1c) *Debt service fund entry to record investment of cash transferred from general fund:*

Investments	10,000	
Cash		10,000

Transaction (2): Securities with a cost of $9,000 are sold for $9,500, which includes $500 interest of which $150 was accrued at December 31, 19X5; $3,200 is reinvested in other securities. No other sales or reinvestments occur during 19X6.

(2a) *Debt service fund entry to record sale of investments:*

Cash	9,500	
Investments		9,000
Interest receivable		150
Revenues control—interest		350

(2b) *Debt service fund entry to record reinvestment of proceeds from sale of investment:*

Investments	3,200	
Cash		3,200

Transaction (3): Interest earned and uncollected at December 31, 19X6, is $1,200.

(3) *Debt service fund entry to record accrued interest revenue at December 31, 19X6:*

Interest receivable	1,200	
Revenues control—interest		1,200

EXHIBIT 18-5	DEBT SERVICE FUND ENTRIES (Continued)

Transaction (4): The debt service fund received a transfer of $5,000 cash from the capital projects fund, which represents the amount of unexpended cash upon completion of the bridge construction project.

(4) *Debt service fund entry to record transfer from capital projects fund:*

Cash	5,000	
Residual equity transfers in (from capital		
projects fund)		5,000

Transaction (5): Bond interest coupons in the amount of $6,000 are paid on March 31.

(5a) *Debt service fund entry to record matured interest coupons:*

Expenditures control—interest	6,000	
Matured interest payable		6,000

(5b) *Debt service fund entry to record payment of interest coupons:*

Matured interest payable	6,000	
Cash		6,000

Transaction (6): Investment fees of $95 are paid to brokers and banks.

(6) *Debt service fund entry to record payment of fees to brokers and bankers:*

Expenditures control—investment fees	95	
Cash		95

Transaction (7): Fund accounts are closed at December 31, 19X6.

(7a) *Debt service fund entry to close budgetary accounts:*

Appropriations control	6,100	
Budgetary fund balance	5,400	
Estimated other financing sources control		10,000
Estimated revenues control		1,500

(7b) *Debt service fund entry to close actual revenues, other financing sources, residual equity transfers, and expenditures accounts to fund balance at December 31, 19X6:*

Revenues control—interest	1,550	
Other financing sources control—operating transfers in		
(from general fund)	10,000	
Residual equity transfers in (from capital projects fund)	5,000	
Expenditures control		6,095
Fund balance reserved for debt service		10,455

would be transferred to the fiscal agent, and an entry would be made debiting *cash with fiscal agent* and crediting *cash* for $6,000. On the interest due date, *expenditures control* would be debited for $6,000 and *matured interest payable* would be credited for $6,000. Upon notification by the fiscal agent that the interest coupons had been redeemed, *matured interest payable* would be debited for $6,000 and *cash with fiscal agent* would be credited for $6,000. When financial statements are prepared after the transfer of cash to a fiscal agent, but before all the matured coupons have been presented for payment, the amount held for payment of the remaining coupons should be reported on the balance sheet as an asset, *cash held by fiscal agent,* and as a liability of the same amount, *matured interest payable.*

Recording Closing Entries

Closing entries for the debt service fund for 19X6 are shown in entries (7a) and (7b) in Exhibit 18-5. As discussed later in this chapter, the $10,455 increase in fund balance reserved for debt service would be recorded in the general long-term debt account group by debiting (to increase) the account *amount available in debt service fund—term bonds* and crediting (to decrease) the account *amount to be provided for retirement of term bonds.*

Financial Reporting for Debt Service Fund

The two basic financial statements for the debt service fund are the (1) *balance sheet* and (2) *statement of revenues, expenditures, and changes in fund balance.* The basic statements for Fisherville's debt service fund are shown in Exhibits 18-6 and 18-7. The *statement of revenues, expenditures, and changes in fund balance—budget and actual* presented in Exhibit 18-8 on page 905 is required for the debt service fund only when the budget is legally adopted, which was the case with the City of Fisherville.

EXHIBIT 18-6 — **DEBT SERVICE FUND BALANCE SHEET**

City of Fisherville
DEBT SERVICE FUND BALANCE SHEET
DECEMBER 31, 19X6

Assets
Cash	$ 5,405
Interest receivable	1,200
Investment in securities	21,500
Total assets	$28,105

Fund Balance
Fund balance reserved for debt service ($17,650 + $10,455)	$28,105

EXHIBIT 18-7	DEBT SERVICE FUND STATEMENT OF REVENUES, EXPENDITURES, AND CHANGES IN FUND BALANCE

City of Fisherville

DEBT SERVICE FUND STATEMENT OF REVENUES, EXPENDITURES, AND CHANGES
IN FUND BALANCE
FOR YEAR ENDED DECEMBER 31, 19X6

Revenues:		
Interest ($350 + $1,200)		$ 1,550
Expenditures:		
Interest	$6,000	
Fees to brokers and bankers	95	
Total expenditures		6,095
Excess (deficiency) of revenues over expenditures		$ (4,545)
Other financing sources (uses):		
Operating transfers in (from general fund)		10,000
Excess of revenues and other financing sources over expenditures		$ 5,455
Fund balance, January 1, 19X6		17,650
Residual equity transfers in (from capital projects fund)		5,000
Fund balance, December 31, 19X6		$28,105

Accounting for Serial Bonds and Interest in Debt Service Fund

If Fisherville had issued serial bonds instead of term bonds, establishment of the debt service fund would not have been required unless mandated by law or by the terms of the bond indenture. As you will recall, term bonds are bonds for which the entire maturity value becomes due at one date, whereas serial bonds arc those whose principal is repaid in periodic installments over the life of the bond issue. If the use of a debt service fund is not so mandated, serial bond principal and interest payments may be made directly from the general fund. In any event, when the matured portion of the bonds payable is recorded in the fund that is to pay the liability (the general fund or the debt service fund), the face value of the matured liability is removed from the general long-term debt account group.

To illustrate the servicing of serial bonds and interest thereon through a debt service fund, assume the following: Harbor City has serial bonds outstanding in the amount of $100,000, payable in equal amounts at the end of each of the next ten years, with interest at 6% per annum on the unpaid balance payable at the end of each year. Amounts to pay the matured principal and interest each year are to be transferred from the general fund to the debt service fund. Transactions for the first year, 19X5, would be recorded as shown in Exhibit 18-9 on page 906.

The general long-term debt account group entries for 19X5, which are shown in Exhibit 18-9, record the increase in resources in the debt service fund and the matured serial bonds payable.

EXHIBIT 18-8	DEBT SERVICE FUND STATEMENT OF REVENUES, EXPENDITURES, AND CHANGES IN FUND BALANCE: BUDGET AND ACTUAL

City of Fisherville

DEBT SERVICE FUND STATEMENT OF REVENUES, EXPENDITURES, AND CHANGES
IN FUND BALANCE—BUDGET AND ACTUAL
FOR YEAR ENDED DECEMBER 31, 19X6

	Budget	Actual	Variance— Favorable (Unfavorable)
Revenues:			
Interest	$ 1,500	$ 1,550	$ 50
Expenditures:			
Interest	$ 6,000	$ 6,000	$
Fees to brokers and bankers	100	95	(5)
Total expenditures	$ 6,100	$ 6,095	$ (5)
Excess (deficiency) of revenues over expenditures	$ (4,600)	$ (4,545)	$ 55
Other financing sources (uses):			
Operating transfers in (from general fund)	$10,000	$10,000	
Excess of revenues and other financing sources over expenditures	$ 5,400	$ 5,455	$ 55
Fund balance, January 1, 19X6	17,650	17,650	
Residual equity transfers in (from capital projects fund)		5,000	5,000
Fund balance, December 31, 19X6	$23,050	$28,105	$5,055

GENERAL FIXED ASSETS ACCOUNT GROUP

"General fund fixed assets do not represent financial resources available for expenditure, but are items for which financial resources have been used and for which accountability should be maintained" (NCGA Statement No. 1, par. 39; and GASB Codification, sec. 1400.107). Further general fixed assets are accounted for in an account group rather than a fund. The general fixed assets group represents a record of all general fixed assets of the governmental unit except those accounted for in proprietary funds (enterprise funds and internal service funds) and nonexpendable trust funds.[1] General fixed assets may be acquired by purchase, lease-purchase, construction, donation, eminent domain, and foreclosure. The asset accounts are maintained on a cost basis except that donated assets are

---

[1] Although the general fixed asset account group should include all fixed assets, inclusion of assets used directly in the public domain ("infrastructure assets")—assets such as roads, bridges, sidewalks, and lighting systems—is optional (NCGA Statement No. 1, par. 40; and GASB Codification, sec. 1400.109).

EXHIBIT 18-9	DEBT SERVICE FUND AND GENERAL LONG-TERM DEBT ACCOUNT GROUP ENTRIES FOR SERIAL BONDS AND INTEREST

Harbor City

ENTRIES FOR SERIAL BONDS AND INTEREST
FOR YEAR ENDED DECEMBER 31, 19X5

Debt Service Fund Entries for Year Ended December 31, 19X5:

Debt service fund entry to record budget for 19X5:

Estimated other financing sources control	16,000	
Appropriations control		16,000

Debt service fund entry to record amount due from general fund:

Due from general fund	16,000	
Other financing sources control—operating transfers in (from general fund)		16,000

Debt service fund entry to record receipt of amount due from general fund:

Cash	16,000	
Due from general fund		16,000

Debt service fund entry to record bond principal and interest due:

Expenditures control—principal and interest	16,000	
Matured bonds payable		10,000
Matured interest payable		6,000

Debt service fund entry to record payment of bond principal and interest due:

Matured bonds payable	10,000	
Matured interest payable	6,000	
Cash		16,000

Debt service fund entry to close budgetary accounts at year-end:

Appropriations control	16,000	
Estimated other financing sources control		16,000

Debt service fund entry to close actual other financing sources and expenditures accounts at end of 19X5:

Other financing sources control—operating transfers in (from general fund)	16,000	
Expenditures control		16,000

General Long-Term Debt Account Group Entries for the Year Ended December 31, 19X5:

General long-term debt account group entry to record increase in assets available for retirement of serial bonds:

Amount available in debt service fund—serial bonds	10,000	
Amount to be provided for retirement of general long-term debt—serial bonds		10,000

General long-term debt account group entry to record maturity of serial bonds:

Serial bonds payable	10,000	
Amount available in debt service fund—serial bonds		10,000

recorded at their fair value at the time of receipt of the gift. Depreciation on general fixed assets may be recorded in the general fixed assets account group but should not be recorded as an expense in the accounts of governmental-type funds. Few governmental units record depreciation on general fixed assets.

Classification of Fixed Assets

General fixed assets of governments may be classified into land, buildings, improvements other than buildings, equipment, and construction in progress. In addition, the equity in general fixed assets should be identified with the source of moneys from which the general fixed assets are acquired; that is, an equity account should be maintained for each fund that provides general fixed assets as well as for gifts and other sources. Furthermore, the equity account *investment in general fixed assets—capital projects fund* is usually subdivided into the portions arising from general obligation bonds, grants from other governments, and so on. For instance, the equity in the bridge constructed in the capital projects fund is subdivided into the portion arising from general obligation bonds and the portion arising from state grants.

Recording General Fixed Assets

To illustrate, consider the additions to the general fixed assets of Fisherville, which are described in Exhibit 18-10 on the following page.

Financial Reporting for General Fixed Assets Account Group

A summary of changes in general fixed assets must be presented as a part of the governmental unit's annual financial statements either as a separate statement or in the notes to the financial statements.

In addition, a *schedule of general fixed assets* at year-end is frequently prepared. The City of Fisherville includes the schedules shown in Exhibits 18-11 and 18-12 on page 909 as a part of its 19X6 annual financial statements. The amounts shown in both schedules are assumed except for those developed in this chapter and the preceding one.

GENERAL LONG-TERM DEBT ACCOUNT GROUP

General long-term liabilities or debt, like general fixed assets, is accounted for in an account group rather than a fund. The general long-term debt account group represents a record of all general long-term debt of the governmental unit except for the long-term debt recorded in the proprietary funds (enterprise funds and internal service funds) and nonexpendable trust funds. General long-term liabilities are not secured by the general fixed assets or resources of specific funds but, rather, are secured by the general credit rating and revenue-raising powers of the governmental unit. Fisherville's general long-term debt account group includes the general obligation bonds issued to finance construction of capital projects (bridge) but does not include long-term debt of the utility fund (enterprise fund). The general long-term debt account group may also include noncurrent liabilities on lease-purchase agreements, judgments, and similar commitments. (For additional discussions, see *GASB Codification,* sec. 1500.)

The long-term debt account group is a self-balancing set of accounts. Liabilities (term bonds payable or serial bonds payable) are carried at par or face value with a debit to an account entitled *amount to be provided for retirement of bonds* (term or serial) that indicates the amount required to retire the related par or face value. In subsequent periods, when amounts accumulate in debt service funds for bond retirement, the *amount to be provided for retirement of bonds* (term or serial) account is reduced (credited) by an

EXHIBIT 18-10   **GENERAL FIXED ASSETS ACCOUNT GROUP ENTRIES**

City of Fisherville

GENERAL FIXED ASSETS ACCOUNT GROUP ENTRIES
FOR THE YEARS ENDED DECEMBER 31, 19X5, AND DECEMBER 31, 19X6

Transaction (1): Transportation equipment costing $15,000 is purchased by the general fund [item (8), page 854, under the general fund transactions in the preceding chapter].

(1) *General fixed assets account group entry to record purchase of transportation equipment by general fund:*

Equipment	15,000	
Investment in general fixed assets—general fund revenues		15,000

Transaction (2): On November 10, 19X6, the city received a donation of land; the cost of the land to the donor was $2,800, and its fair value at date of donation was $8,100.

(2) *General fixed assets account group entry to record donation of land:*

Land	8,100	
Investment in general fixed assets—gifts		8,100

Transaction (3): Equipment carried as a general fixed asset with a cost of $7,500 was sold as scrap in 19X6 [item (13), page 855, under the general fund transactions in the preceding chapter]. The equipment was originally purchased by the general fund.

(3) *General fixed assets account group entry to record sale of equipment:*

Investment in general fixed assets—general fund revenues	7,500	
Equipment		7,500

Transaction (4): A bridge is constructed during 19X5 and 19X6 with a total cost of $105,000, of which $34,000 is related to 19X5 and $71,000 is related to 19X6 expenditures of the capital projects fund. (Because the state grant was irrevocable, the total amount credited to *investment in general fixed assets—state grants* equals $10,000, and the remainder of the total cost is credited to *investment in general fixed assets—general obligation bonds.* The $5,000 residual equity transfer to the debt service fund is considered to have come from the proceeds of the bond issue.)

(4a) *General fixed assets account group entry to record partial completion of project at December 31, 19X5:*

Construction in progress	34,000	
Investment in general fixed assets—capital projects fund—general obligation bonds ($100,000/$110,000 × $34,000)		30,909
Investment in general fixed assets—state grants ($10,000/$110,000 × $34,000)		3,091

(4b) *General fixed assets account group entry to record completion of capital project at December 31, 19X6:*

Improvements other than buildings	105,000	
Investment in general fixed assets—capital projects fund—general obligation bonds ($105,000 − $10,000 − $30,909)		64,091
Investment in general fixed assets—state grants ($10,000 − $3,091)		6,909
Construction in progress		34,000

EXHIBIT 18-11	SCHEDULE OF GENERAL FIXED ASSETS

City of Fisherville

SCHEDULE OF GENERAL FIXED ASSETS—BY SOURCES
AT DECEMBER 31, 19X6

General Fixed Assets

Land	$ 800,000
Buildings	1,300,000
Improvements other than buildings	1,500,000
Equipment	380,000
Construction in progress	56,000
Total general fixed assets	$4,036,000

Investment in General Fixed Assets from:

Capital projects funds:	
General obligation bonds	$1,760,000
Federal grants	800,000
State grants	540,000
County grants	366,000
Special assessments	72,000
General fund revenues	330,000
Special revenue fund revenues	140,000
Gifts	28,000
Total investment in general fixed assets	$4,036,000

EXHIBIT 18-12	SCHEDULE OF CHANGES IN GENERAL FIXED ASSETS

City of Fisherville

SCHEDULE OF CHANGES IN GENERAL FIXED ASSETS
FOR YEAR ENDED DECEMBER 31, 19X6

	General Fixed Assets 1/1/X6	Additions	Deductions	General Fixed Assets 12/31/X6
Assets				
Land	$ 791,900	$ 8,100	$	$ 800,000
Buildings	1,300,000			1,300,000
Improvements other than buildings	1,395,000	105,000		1,500,000
Equipment	372,500	15,000	7,500	380,000
Construction in progress	90,000		34,000	56,000
Total general fixed assets	$3,949,400	$128,100	$41,500	$4,036,000

amount equal to the increase in the debit service fund, and an account entitled *amount available in debt service fund* (term or serial) is increased (debited).

Recording Transactions in the Long-Term Debt Account Group

Exhibit 18-13 shows the City of Fisherville transactions for 19X5 and 19X6 that affect the general long-term debt account group.

Recording Issuance of Long-Term Debt

Entry (1) in Exhibit 18-13 records Fisherville's 19X5 issuance of general obligation bonds with a face value of $100,000 for $107,711 in cash, which was accounted for in the capital projects fund; the $7,711 premium was transferred from the capital projects fund to the debt service fund. Observe that the debt is recorded at its par value ($100,000) and not at the amount of cash received. General long-term debt should be classified according to its nature, that is, term bonds, serial bonds, lease-purchase agreements, and so on.

EXHIBIT 18-13	**GENERAL LONG-TERM DEBT ACCOUNT GROUP ENTRIES**

City of Fisherville

GENERAL LONG-TERM DEBT ACCOUNT GROUP ENTRIES
FOR THE YEARS ENDED DECEMBER 31, 19X5, AND DECEMBER 31, 19X6

Transaction (1): On April 1, 19X5, Fisherville issues general obligation ten-year, 6% term bonds with a par value of $100,000 for cash of $107,711; the premium is transferred to the debt service fund.

(1) *General long-term debt account group entry to record issuance of bonds in 19X5:*

Amount to be *provided* for retirement of term bonds	100,000	
Term bonds payable		100,000

Transaction (2): The fund balance in Fisherville's debt service fund increased by $17,650 during 19X5.

(2) *General long-term debt account group entry to record increase in related debt service fund balance at December 31, 19X5:*

Amount *available* in debt service fund—term bonds	17,650	
Amount to be *provided* for retirement of term bonds		17,650

Transaction (3): The fund balance in Fisherville's debt service fund increased by $10,455 during 19X6.

(3) *General long-term debt account group entry to record increase in related debt service fund balance at December 31, 19X6:*

Amount *available* in debt service fund—term bonds	10,455	
Amount to be *provided* for retirement of term bonds		10,455

Recording the Provision of Funds for Debt Retirement

Increases in the debt service fund balance, which represent amounts that are available for the retirement of general long-term debt, result in the reduction of the *amount to be provided for retirement of bonds* and an increase in the *amount available in debt service fund.* Fisherville's debt service fund increased by $17,650 during 19X5 and by $10,455 during 19X6 ($10,455 = $5,455 + $5,000—see Exhibit 18-6). Consequently, entries (2) and (3) are made in the general long-term debt account group. The foregoing entry (3) is the only entry made in Fisherville's general long-term debt account group during 19X6. Over the term of the bonds, the total amount charged to the *amount available in debt service fund* should not exceed the related bond par value.

Recording the Retirement of Debt

The retirement of bonds is recorded in both the debt service fund and the general long-term debt account group. The expenditure recorded in the debt service fund for the bonds retired reduces the assets and fund balance of the debt service fund. In addition, the par value of the bonds is removed from the general long-term debt accounts. For example, when Fisherville retires the ten-year term bonds that were issued in 19X5 for a total par value of $100,000, the following entry will be made in the general long-term debt account group:

> *General long-term debt account group entry to record retirement of debt:*
>
> Term bonds payable 100,000
>   Amount available in debt service fund—term bonds . . .   100,000

If the balance of the *amount available in debt service fund* is less than the par value, then the deficiency is credited to the *amount to be provided for retirement of bonds.* The debt service fund would record the preceding transaction by a debit to *expenditures* and a credit to *matured term bonds payable* or *cash.*

Financial Reporting for General Long-Term Debt Account Group

A summary of the changes in general long-term debt must be presented as a part of the annual financial statements either as a separate statement or in notes to the financial statements. In addition, a schedule of general long-term debt at year-end is frequently prepared. The City of Fisherville includes the schedules shown in Exhibits 18-14 and 18-15 on the following page as a part of its 19X6 annual financial statements.

ACCOUNTING FOR PROPRIETARY FUNDS

There are two types of proprietary funds: *enterprise funds* and *internal service funds.* They are established to account for the delivery of goods and services to the general public (enterprise funds) or to other departments of the governmental unit or to other governments (internal service funds).

Unlike governmental funds, which follow accrual accounting with a flow of financial resources measurement focus, proprietary funds follow accrual accounting focusing on resources broadly defined. In fact, the records of a proprietary fund parallel the records of a similar business enterprise. Revenues are accrued when earned. Prepayments are recorded and deferred as appropriate. Fixed assets and long-term debt of a proprietary fund are recorded in the proprietary fund accounts, and periodic depreciation is charged against

EXHIBIT 18-14	SCHEDULE OF LONG-TERM DEBT

City of Fisherville

SCHEDULE OF GENERAL LONG-TERM DEBT
AT DECEMBER 31, 19X6

Amount available and to be provided for retirement of general
long-term debt—term bonds:

Amount available in debt service fund ($17,650 + $10,455)	$ 28,105
Amount to be provided for retirement of long-term debt	71,895
Total amount available and to be provided for the retirement of general long-term debt	$100,000

General long-term debt payable:

Ten-year, 6% term bonds maturing in 8¼ years	$100,000
Total general long-term debt payable	$100,000

fund revenues. Encumbrances and budgets are not recorded in the accounts of a proprietary fund. Proprietary funds, however, should use flexible budgets that are similar to those prepared for private enterprise.

Enterprise funds are used to account for operations that are similar to business enterprises. They should be used where the intent of the governing body is to cover all costs of operations, including depreciation expenses, primarily through user charges to those benefiting from the goods or services provided. For example, electric and water utilities owned and operated by a governmental unit are accounted for in enterprise funds. Enterprise funds may also be used where the governing body wishes to determine periodic revenues earned, expenses incurred (including depreciation), and net income for purposes of accountability, capital maintenance, public policy, management control, and the like, even though user charges may not provide the primary source of resources.

EXHIBIT 18-15	SCHEDULE OF CHANGES IN GENERAL LONG-TERM DEBT

City of Fisherville

SCHEDULE OF CHANGES IN GENERAL LONG-TERM DEBT
FOR YEAR ENDED DECEMBER 31, 19X6

	Amount Payable 1-1-X6	New Debt Issued	Debt Retired	Amount Payable 12-31-X6
General obligation term bonds	$100,000	$	$	$100,000
Total bonded debt	$100,000	$	$	$100,000

Examples of such operations that may be accounted for as enterprise funds are municipally owned airports, public transportation systems, swimming pools, and similar publicly owned activities. If such periodic income determination is not deemed necessary or appropriate, these operations may be accounted for in special revenue funds where user charges do not constitute the primary source of resources. After the decision is made to account for an operation in an enterprise fund or a special revenue fund, the accounting practice adopted should be followed consistently from year to year because of the substantial differences in the accounting methods of enterprise (proprietary) funds and special revenue (governmental-type) funds.

Internal service funds are used to account for operations that provide, on a cost-reimbursement basis, goods or services to other departments and funds of the same governmental unit or, in some cases, to other governmental units. Their revenues derive primarily from charges for goods or services provided to the other departments, funds, or governmental units. Examples of operations that may be accounted for in internal service funds are central purchasing departments, data processing departments, central garages or transportation facilities, and similar operations.

Distinctive Aspects of Enterprise Funds

Although enterprise funds and private-sector enterprises have much in common, enterprise funds exhibit several distinctive characteristics. For example, distributions of private-sector net income take the form of dividends, whereas distributions of enterprise fund net income take the form of *cash transfers to other funds.* Enterprise funds also establish *retained earnings reserves* that equal cash and investments restricted to the payment of revenue bond interest and principal. Such reserves are rarely found in private-sector accounts. (Revenue bonds are those bonds whose principal and interest are payable exclusively from the earnings of an enterprise fund.) Equity capital contributions to private-sector enterprises are recorded in capital stock accounts, whereas equity capital contributions to enterprise funds are recorded in *contributed capital accounts* that identify the source of the contributions (e.g., contributed capital—general fund). Such capital transfers from other funds are considered to be residual equity transfers.

Enterprise funds sometimes receive grants from other governmental units, such as the federal or state governments. Operating grants are usually restricted by the grantor to operating purposes, but sometimes may be used by the grantee for either capital or operating purposes. Such operating grants should be recognized as revenue in the period in which they become available for expenditure, regardless of whether they are used for capital or operating purposes. Capital grants are restricted to the acquisition or construction of fixed assets. When accrued or received, these capital grants should be recorded as *contributed capital—capital grants.*

The records of some enterprise funds (notably utility funds) are also distinctive in that they exhibit a number of *restricted assets* that are available only for specified purposes.

Typical restricted asset and related liability and reserve accounts that may appear in an enterprise fund (especially a utility fund) balance sheet are as follows:

Restricted Assets:

1. *Customer deposits*—Customer deposits that must be refunded to customers upon termination of service.

2. *Revenue bond construction account*—Revenue bond proceeds earmarked for enterprise fund fixed asset construction as required by bond indenture.

3. *Revenue bond current debt service account*—Each month, one-twelfth of the annual bond principal and interest due during the next year is accumulated in this account, and used to pay current debt service requirements as specified by bond indenture.

4. *Revenue bond future debt service account*—Moneys accumulated over the first 60 months, more or less as required by the bond indenture, earmarked to pay matured bonds and interest in the event of a deficiency in the revenue bond current debt service account. Typically, the moneys accumulated are used upon the final retirement of the bond issue.

5. *Revenue bond contingency (renewal and replacement) account*—Moneys accumulated for unforeseen expenditures and/or asset renewals and replacements. Specific requirements for the accounts are set forth in the bond indenture.

Liabilities and Retained Earnings Reserved to Offset Preceding Restricted Asset Balances:

1. Customer deposits payable from restricted assets

2. Construction contracts payable from restricted assets

3. Revenue bonds payable (due within one year)
Accrued revenue bond interest payable
Retained earnings reserved for revenue bond current debt service account

4. Retained earnings reserved for revenue bond future debt service account

5. Retained earnings reserved for revenue bond contingency account

Journal entries are not illustrated for the transactions of the Fisherville utility fund because of the similarity between the transactions of a government-owned enterprise fund and those of a similar business enterprise. The 19X6 financial statements for Fisherville's utility fund (an enterprise fund) are presented in Exhibits 18-16 and 18-17; the figures shown in both statements are assumed amounts. The statements illustrate the distinctive characteristics of enterprise funds in relation to restricted assets, current liabilities that are payable from restricted assets, retained earnings reserves, and contributed capital accounts. The utility has issued revenue bonds to pay for construction of an electricity distribution plant on several occasions. The proceeds of the most recent issue have been entirely expended except for $47,700, which is reported as a restricted asset. Observe that $10,000 of this amount is about to be paid to contractors as indicated by current liabilities that are payable from restricted assets. A second restricted cash balance of $8,400 is provided for the debt service on outstanding revenue bonds. Moneys are accumulated each month in this account that are equal to one-twelfth of the annual principal and interest payments, and current debt service payments are made from this account. A sinking fund has been established to provide for principal payments that are related to outstanding revenue bonds. At December 31, 19X6, the sinking fund amounts to $77,000, which is reported as a restricted asset; and principal payments of $30,000 are scheduled for the coming year, as shown by current liabilities that are payable from restricted assets. Cus-

EXHIBIT 18-16	ENTERPRISE FUND BALANCE SHEET: UTILITY FUND

City of Fisherville

UTILITY FUND BALANCE SHEET
DECEMBER 31, 19X6

Assets			Liabilities and Fund Equity		
Current assets:			Current liabilities (payable from current assets):		
Cash	$ 93,000		Vouchers payable		$ 6,100
Accounts receivable	40,000		Current liabilities (payable from restricted assets):		
Allowance for uncollectible accounts	(2,000)		Construction contracts payable	$10,000	
Inventories	4,200		Accrued interest payable on revenue bonds	4,900	
Prepaid expenses	8,100	$143,300	Current portion of revenue bonds payable	30,000	
			Customer deposits	14,600	59,500
Restricted assets:			Long-term liabilities:		
Cash from revenue bonds restricted to construction payments	$ 47,700		Revenue bonds payable (net of current portion)		320,000
Cash restricted to current debt service on revenue bonds	8,400		Fund equity:		
Revenue bond sinking fund, investments	77,000		Contributed capital— municipality		60,000
Customer deposits, investments	14,600	147,700	Retained earnings:		
Utility plant in service:			Reserved for revenue bond current debt service	$ 8,400	
Land	$ 73,000		Reserved for revenue bond retirement	77,000	
Buildings, improvements, and equipment	260,000		Unreserved	25,000	110,400
Less: Accumulated depreciation	(110,000)	223,000			
Construction in progress		42,000			
Total assets		$556,000	Total liabilities and fund equity		$556,000

tomer deposits in the amount of $14,600 are held by the utility fund and are ultimately returnable to customers, as indicated by the related current liability payable from restricted assets. In addition to the *balance sheet* and the *statement of revenues, expenses, and changes in retained earnings,* the financial statements of Fisherville's utility fund should also include a *statement of cash flows* prepared in accordance with *GASB Statement No. 9* (*GASB Codification,* sec. 2450). This cash flow statement is similar to the cash flow statement prepared by businesses except that proprietary fund financing activities are

EXHIBIT 18-17	ENTERPRISE FUND STATEMENT OF REVENUES, EXPENSES, AND CHANGES IN RETAINED EARNINGS

City of Fisherville

UTILITY FUND (ENTERPRISE FUND)
STATEMENT OF REVENUES, EXPENSES, AND CHANGES IN RETAINED EARNINGS
FOR YEAR ENDED DECEMBER 31, 19X6

Operating revenues:		
Sales of electricity	$265,000	
Other	11,000	
Total operating revenues		$276,000
Operating expenses:		
Cost of purchased power	$120,000	
Depreciation	86,000	
Materials	3,200	
Heat, light, and power	6,000	
Other	16,000	
Total operating expenses		231,200
Operating income		$ 44,800
Nonoperating revenues (expenses):		
Operating grants	$ 18,000	
Interest and fiscal charges	(50,000)	
Total nonoperating revenues (expenses)		(32,000)
Net income		$ 12,800
Retained earnings, January 1, 19X6		97,600
Retained earnings, December 31, 19X6		$110,400

divided into two sections: capital financing activities (borrowing for the acquisition, construction, or improvement of capital assets) and noncapital financing activities (borrowing for other purposes). Cash flow statements for proprietary funds and businesses use similar forms and preparation procedures; hence, the proprietary fund cash flow statement does not receive further attention in this chapter.

Distinctive Aspects of Internal Service Funds

Internal service funds, like enterprise funds, apply accrual accounting principles. Internal service funds usually operate on a cost-reimbursement basis and charge other funds for the estimated cost of goods and services provided. However, the terms *net income* and *retained earnings* are used in the same manner as in business enterprises. As in the case of enterprise funds, equity capital contributions to internal service funds are recorded in *contributed capital accounts* that identify the sources of the contributions.

The City of Fisherville maintains a central garage (internal service) fund that serves as a motor pool for the other departments of the city. The user departments are billed on a mileage basis for their usage of automotive equipment for conducting city business. The fees charged are based on the cost of service provided, so it is necessary for the central garage fund to measure the full costs incurred (including depreciation) in providing the services in order to determine how much to charge the user departments.

The 19X6 financial statements of the central garage fund presented in Exhibits 18-18 and 18-19 illustrate the similarities (and minor differences) between internal service funds and their counterparts in business; both statements contain amounts not previously presented. Journal entries are not illustrated for the transactions of the internal service fund because of the similarity between the transactions of a government-owned internal service fund and those of a similar business enterprise. In addition to the *balance sheet* and *the statement of revenues, expenses, and changes in retained earnings,* internal service funds should also present a *statement of cash flows* in accordance with the provisions of *GASB Statement No. 9.*

ACCOUNTING FOR SPECIAL ASSESSMENTS

Local governments may provide services or make capital improvements that primarily benefit particular property owners or groups of property owners rather than the general community. For example, residential streets, sidewalks, or storm sewers may be paid for wholly or in part by the owners of property that is adjacent to the improvements. The payments by property owners are called *special assessments,* and they are frequently paid in installments over a period of years. When assessments are based on estimated costs, refunds or additional assessments may be required when the cost is determined.

EXHIBIT 18-18   **INTERNAL SERVICE FUND BALANCE SHEET**

City of Fisherville

CENTRAL GARAGE (INTERNAL SERVICE FUND) BALANCE SHEET
AT DECEMBER 31, 19X6

Assets		*Liabilities and Fund Equity*	
Current assets:		Current liabilities:	
Cash	$10,000	Vouchers payable	$ 7,000
Due from other funds	5,000	Due to other funds	3,000
Total current assets	$15,000	Total current liabilities	$10,000
Property, plant, and equipment:		Long-term liabilities:	
Land	$10,000	Advance from general fund	5,000
Buildings	50,000	Total liabilities	$15,000
Improvements other than buildings	15,000	Fund equity:	
Machinery and equipment	20,000	Contributed capital—	
		general fund	$50,000
Total	$95,000	Retained earnings	10,000
Less: Accumulated depreciation	35,000	Total fund equity	$60,000
Net property, plant, and equipment	$60,000		
Total assets	$75,000	Total liabilities and fund equity	$75,000

EXHIBIT 18-19	INTERNAL SERVICE FUND STATEMENT OF REVENUES, EXPENSES, AND CHANGES IN RETAINED EARNINGS

City of Fisherville

CENTRAL GARAGE (INTERNAL SERVICE FUND)
STATEMENT OF REVENUES, EXPENSES, AND CHANGES IN RETAINED EARNINGS
FOR YEAR ENDED DECEMBER 31, 19X6

Operating revenues:		
Charges for services		$50,000
Operating expenses:		
Personal services	$20,000	
Contractual services	5,000	
Supplies	3,000	
Materials	2,000	
Heat, light, and power	6,000	
Depreciation	10,000	
Total operating expenses		46,000
Net income		$ 4,000
Retained earnings, January 1, 19X6		6,000
Retained earnings, December 31, 19X6		$10,000

Services Financed by Special Assessments

When special assessments are made for services rendered by a local government, the assessments and related expenditures should be recorded in the general fund, a special revenue fund, or an enterprise fund, depending on which fund best fits the nature of the transactions. For example, special assessments might be made for street cleaning or snow plowing in areas that are not normally provided such services. It would be reasonable to account for such transactions in the same fund that accounts for similar services provided without special assessments. Revenues from service-type special assessments should be recognized in the period that the services are provided regardless of when the assessment is billed or collected. Expenditures (or expenses) related to service-type special assessments should be recognized on the same basis as other expenditures (or expenses) of the fund used.

Capital Improvements Financed by Special Assessments

Special assessments may also provide for capital improvements. The revenues from such assessments (including interest revenues) should be recognized when the government demands the amounts from the assessed property owners (i.e., the due date of the property owners' installment payment), regardless of when the cash is received.

When the special assessment capital improvement is financed initially by existing governmental resources, the fund providing the financing must establish a special assessments receivable account. The City of Fisherville has not used special assessment to finance either services or capital improvements. To illustrate, however, suppose that the general fund of the City of Granville transfers $400,000 to a capital projects fund to pay for the construction of new sidewalks to be paid for by special assessments. The following entries would be appropriate in the general fund:

General fund entry to record transfer of cash for special assessments improvements:

Other financing uses control—operating transfers out
  (to capital project fund) 400,000
    Cash   400,000

General fund entry to record special assessment levy:

Special assessments receivable 400,000
    Deferred revenues   400,000

In some cases, a local government issues bonds (frequently serial bonds) to provide financing for a special assessment project; such bonds are then retired as assessments are collected. If the government is obligated to pay (or stands ready to assume) such a debt in the event of default by the property owners (even if the obligation is for part of the total debt), then the transactions related to the capital improvement are recorded in a capital projects fund just like any other capital improvement. Furthermore, the fixed assets related to the project should be recorded in the general fixed assets account group. Debt service transactions related to special assessments are recorded in a debt service fund just like any other debt service transaction. In addition, the outstanding long-term debt should be recorded in the general long-term debt account group. To illustrate, suppose that a municipality issues $5,000,000 in bonds to pay for street improvements of which $3,000,000 (plus interest) is to be repaid by special assessments and the remainder is to be repaid by the general fund. The debt would be recorded in the general long-term debt account group by the following entry:

General long-term debt account group entry to record issuance of debt to finance special assessments improvements:

Amount to be provided by special assessments 3,000,000
Amount to be provided for general obligation debt 2,000,000
    Special assessment debt with government
      commitment   3,000,000
    General obligation debt   2,000,000

On the other hand, if the government is not obligated in any manner to pay the special assessments debt, then the debt should be reported in an agency fund rather than in a debt service fund and no entries would be appropriate in the general long-term debt account group. The construction or acquisition of the special assessments assets would still be recorded in a capital projects fund, and the resultant assets would still be recorded in the general fixed assets account group.

ACCOUNTING FOR FIDUCIARY FUNDS

Fiduciary funds account for assets that are held by a governmental unit as trustee or agent for an individual, private organization, or another governmental unit. Agency funds account for assets, frequently cash, that are collected and held by a governmental unit for a brief period before disbursal to authorized recipients; for example, county governments use agency funds to account for property taxes that are collected on behalf of cities. In contrast, trust funds, which are of three types—nonexpendable, expendable, and pension trust funds—account for assets that are held for longer periods of time. In fact, assets or principal contributed to *nonexpendable trusts* must be held indefinitely; only the income from the principal of nonexpendable trusts is subject to expenditure. On the other hand, all the assets of *expendable trusts* are subject to expenditure. The transactions of a trust fund must satisfy the terms of the trust agreement, statutes, and ordinances as well as appropriate accounting standards. As is true with other governmental-type funds, budgetary and encumbrance accounting may be used in expendable trust funds. However, budgetary and encumbrance accounting are not applicable to nonexpendable trust funds because they are treated as proprietary funds.

    Pension trust funds account for resources that are accumulated for employee retirement purposes, and for the payment of benefits to retirees. Pension trust funds are considered to have characteristics of both nonexpendable and expendable trusts and are often the largest trust fund of a governmental unit. In their investment activities, they are like nonexpendable trust funds, whereas in their pension payment activities, they are like expendable trust funds. Accounting for pension trust funds is on an accrual basis. Students desiring a more detailed discussion of pension trust funds should refer to a text devoted entirely to governmental and nonprofit accounting.

Recording Agency Fund Transactions

Agency funds are used to account for cash and/or other assets that are collected for, and paid to, other funds, other governmental units, individuals, or organizations. All the assets of an agency fund are owed to whatever entity they were collected for. Thus, there is no fund balance account in an agency fund.

    The City of Fisherville does not have an agency fund. To illustrate transactions for such a fund, however, assume the County of Michelin collects its property taxes as well as those for the City of Uniroyal. Property taxes were levied in 19X2 in the amount of $75,000 ($750 estimated to be uncollectible) for Michelin and $25,000 ($250 estimated to be uncollectible) for Uniroyal. During 19X2, $48,000 of the $100,000 tax levy is collected and disbursed to the authorized recipients. Michelin charges Uniroyal a fee of 2% of taxes collected for its services. Entries to record these events in a tax agency fund are as follows:

Tax agency fund entry to record taxes receivable for other fund and governmental unit:

Taxes receivable for other fund and governmental unit	100,000	
Due to general fund (75%)		75,000
Due to City of Uniroyal (25%)		25,000

The information in the preceding entry would also be recorded in the general fund of Michelin and Uniroyal as follows:

General fund entry to record property tax levy:

	Michelin		Uniroyal	
Taxes receivable—current	75,000		25,000	
Revenues control—property taxes		74,250		24,750
Allowance for uncollectible current taxes		750		250

The estimated uncollectible portion of the tax levy is recorded in the accounts of the taxing units, but not in the tax agency fund. Tax collections and distributions are recorded as follows:

Tax agency fund entry to record collection of taxes receivable:

Cash...	48,000	
Taxes receivable for other fund and governmental unit ..		48,000

Tax agency fund entry to record collection fee charged the City of Uniroyal:

Due to City of Uniroyal	240	
Due to general fund [.02 × .25($48,000)]		240

Tax agency fund entry to record distribution of cash collected:

Due to general fund [.75($48,000) + $240]...............	36,240	
Due to City of Uniroyal [.25($48,000) − $240]	11,760	
Cash...		48,000

The distribution of cash in the preceding entry would also be recorded in the general fund of Michelin and Uniroyal as follows:

General fund entry to record collection of current property taxes:

	Michelin	Uniroyal
Cash.................................	36,240	11,760
Expenditures control.....................		240
Taxes receivable—current	36,000	12,000
Revenues control	240	

Since agency funds do not have revenues and expenditures, the only financial statement that is required would be a balance sheet. The balance sheet at the end of the 19X2 fiscal year for the tax agency fund of the County of Michelin illustrated previously would consist of *assets* (taxes receivable for other fund and governmental unit for $52,000) and *liabilities* (due to general fund $39,000, and due to City of Uniroyal $13,000) only. As mentioned earlier, there is no fund balance account in an agency fund.

Recording Trust Fund Transactions

The accounting for nonexpendable and expendable trusts is illustrated by reference to Fisherville's scholarship trust funds, which were established on January 1, 19X6, to provide scholarships for students at a nearby state-supported university. The city maintains a nonexpendable trust fund to account for the principal and an expendable trust fund to account for the income to be expended for the scholarship grants. Expendable trust funds are governmental-type funds and accordingly follow modified accrual accounting (accrual accounting with a flow of financial resources measurement focus), whereas nonexpendable trust funds are treated as proprietary funds and follow accrual accounting for financial resources broadly defined. Since the principal of Fisherville's scholarship fund is not expendable, the accounting records must enable a precise determination of revenues and expenses to ensure maintenance of principal in accordance with the trust indenture. Investment earnings become a part of the expendable trust fund, while gains and losses on sale or disposal of investments are increases or decreases in nonexpendable trust fund principal. The events affecting Fisherville's scholarship funds during 19X6 are described in Exhibit 18-20 on the following pages. The paragraphs that follow discuss the recording of these events.

EXHIBIT 18-20	TRUST FUND ENTRIES

City of Fisherville
SCHOLARSHIP TRUST FUND ENTRIES
FOR THE YEAR ENDED DECEMBER 31, 19X6

Transaction (1): Nonexpendable scholarship trust fund—On January 1, 19X6, cash in the amount of $50,000 is received in trust from an individual to establish the scholarship fund. The trust indenture directs that the assets be invested in certain securities and that only the income from the trust be expended.

(1) *Nonexpendable scholarship trust fund entry to record contribution of principal:*

Cash	50,000	
Revenues control—gifts		50,000

Transaction (2): Nonexpendable scholarship trust fund—On January 1, 19X6, $42,684 is invested in 9%, ten-year bonds with a total face value of $40,000; the effective interest rate is 8%. Interest coupons are due on December 31 of each year; on December 31, 19X6, a coupon payment of $3,600 is received.

(2a) *Nonexpendable scholarship trust fund entry to record investment in bonds:*

Investment in bonds	40,000	
Unamortized premium on bond investment	2,684	
Cash		42,684

(2b) *Nonexpendable scholarship trust fund entry to record interest revenue on bonds and amortization of premium:*

Cash	3,600	
Unamortized premium on bond investment		185
Revenues control—interest (.08 × $42,684)		3,415

Transaction (3): Nonexpendable scholarship trust fund—An additional $5,000 is invested in certificates of deposit that pay quarterly interest at a rate of 6% per annum; $225 is received during 19X6, and an additional $75 is due on January 1, 19X7.

(3a) *Nonexpendable scholarship trust fund entry to record investment in certificates of deposit:*

Investment in certificates of deposit	5,000	
Cash		5,000

(3b) *Nonexpendable scholarship trust fund entry to record interest collected and accrued on certificate of deposit:*

Cash	225	
Interest receivable	75	
Revenues control—interest		300

Recording Contribution of Principal, Investment, and Investment Income

The contribution of principal to Fisherville's scholarship fund is recorded by entry (1) in Exhibit 18-20. Fisherville's scholarship fund investments in bonds and certificates of deposit, together with the related investment income, are recorded by entries (2a) through (3b). Note that entry (2b) credits *unamortized premium on bond investment* for the portion

EXHIBIT 18-20	TRUST FUND ENTRIES (Continued)

Transaction (4): Nonexpendable and expendable scholarship trust funds—Revenues from investments are transferred to the expendable trust fund.

(4a) *Nonexpendable scholarship trust fund entry to record transfer of revenues to expendable scholarship trust fund:*

Other financing uses control—operating transfers out (to expendable scholarship trust fund) ($3,415 + $300)	3,715	
Cash		3,640
Due to expendable scholarship trust fund		75

(4b) *Expendable scholarship trust fund entry to record transfer of revenues from nonexpendable scholarship trust fund:*

Cash	3,640	
Due from nonexpendable scholarship trust fund	75	
Other financing sources control—operating transfers in (from nonexpendable scholarship trust fund)		3,715

Transaction (5): Expendable scholarship trust fund—Expenditures paid during 19X6 representing grants to students totaled $3,200.

(5) *Expendable scholarship trust fund entry to record expenditures:*

Expenditures control—grants to students	3,200	
Cash		3,200

Transaction (6): Nonexpendable and expendable scholarship trust funds—Closing entries are recorded at December 31, 19X6.

(6a) *Nonexpendable scholarship trust fund entry to close actual revenues and operating transfers out accounts to fund balance at December 31, 19X6:*

Revenues control—gifts	50,000	
Revenues control—interest	3,715	
Other financing uses control—operating transfers out (to expendable scholarship trust fund)		3,715
Fund balance reserved for scholarship endowment		50,000

(6b) *Expendable scholarship trust fund entry to close actual operating transfers in and expenditures accounts to fund balance at December 31, 19X6:*

Other financing sources control—operating transfers in (from nonexpendable scholarship trust fund)	3,715	
Expenditures control		3,200
Fund balance reserved for scholarships		515

of bond coupons that is associated with the premium ($185) and credits *revenues control—interest* with the effective interest earned ($3,415). This procedure is necessary to ensure maintenance of the principal. (In contrast, if there had been a $185 *discount* amortization instead of a *premium* amortization, the $3,600 debit to cash would be accompanied by a debit of $185 to *unamortized discount on bond investment* and a $3,785 credit to *revenues control—interest.*) The recording of expenditures and related cash disbursements in

Fisherville's expendable scholarship trust fund during 19X6 is summarized by entry (5) in Exhibit 18-20. Entries (6a) and (6b) close the accounts of the scholarship trust funds at year-end.

Financial Reporting for Nonexpendable and Expendable Trust Funds

The basic financial statements of nonexpendable trust funds are the (1) *balance sheet,* (2) *statement of revenues, expenses, and changes in fund balance,* and (3) *statement of cash flows.* These statements, except for the statement of changes in financial position, for Fisherville's nonexpendable scholarship trust fund are shown in Exhibits 18-21 and 18-22. The statement of changes in financial position is not discussed here because of its similarity to such statements prepared for business enterprises. The basic financial statements for expendable trust funds are the (1) *balance sheet* and (2) *statement of revenues, expenditures, and changes in fund balance.* The statement of changes in financial position is not required for expendable trust funds because they are governmental-type funds. Financial statements for Fisherville's expendable trust fund are presented in Exhibits 18-23 and 18-24.

ANNUAL FINANCIAL REPORTING

As discussed in Chapter 17, the *financial reporting entity* for a state or local government consists of a primary government and its component units. The official annual report of such a governmental entity is the *comprehensive annual financial report* (CAFR). A CAFR should be prepared and published as a matter of public record by governmental entities. Like the annual report of a business enterprise, the introductory section of the CAFR includes the table of contents, letter(s) of transmittal, and other information that is deemed appropriate by management.

EXHIBIT 18-21 — NONEXPENDABLE TRUST FUND BALANCE SHEET

City of Fisherville
NONEXPENDABLE SCHOLARSHIP TRUST FUND BALANCE SHEET
AT DECEMBER 31, 19X6

Assets
Cash		$ 2,501
Interest receivable		75
Investment in certificate of deposit		5,000
Investment in bonds	$40,000	
Unamortized premium on bonds investment	2,499	42,499
Total assets		$50,075

Liabilities and Fund Balance
Due to expendable scholarship trust fund		$ 75
Fund balance reserved for scholarship endowment		50,000
Total liabilities and fund balance		$50,075

EXHIBIT 18-22	NONEXPENDABLE TRUST FUND STATEMENT OF REVENUES, EXPENSES, AND CHANGES IN FUND BALANCE

City of Fisherville

NONEXPENDABLE SCHOLARSHIP TRUST FUND
STATEMENT OF REVENUES, EXPENSES, AND CHANGES IN FUND BALANCE
FOR YEAR ENDED DECEMBER 31, 19X6

Revenues:	
Gift to establish scholarship fund	$50,000
Interest	3,715
Total revenues	$53,715
Expenses	–0–
Excess of revenues over expenses	$53,715
Other financing sources (uses):	
Operating transfers out (to expendable scholarship trust fund)	(3,715)
Excess of revenues over expenses and other uses	$50,000
Fund balance, January 1, 19X6	–0–
Fund balance, December 31, 19X6	$50,000

The detail of the financial reporting included in the CAFR can be compared to the "reporting pyramid" presented in Exhibit 18-25 on page 927. The levels of the pyramid include condensed summary data, general purpose financial statements (combined statements—overview), combining statements—by fund type, individual fund and account group statements, schedules, and transaction data (the accounting system).

The top of the pyramid represents highly condensed, consolidated financial statements, whereas the base of the pyramid represents highly detailed transaction data. Both extremes should be distinguished from the requirements for a CAFR. Condensed sum-

EXHIBIT 18-23	EXPENDABLE TRUST FUND BALANCE SHEET

City of Fisherville

EXPENDABLE SCHOLARSHIP TRUST FUND BALANCE SHEET
AT DECEMBER 31, 19X6

Assets	
Cash	$440
Due from nonexpendable scholarship trust fund	75
Total assets	$515
Fund Balance	
Fund balance reserved for scholarships	$515

EXHIBIT 18-24	EXPENDABLE TRUST FUND STATEMENT OF REVENUES, EXPENDITURES, AND CHANGES IN FUND BALANCE

City of Fisherville

EXPENDABLE SCHOLARSHIP TRUST FUND
STATEMENT OF REVENUES, EXPENDITURES, AND CHANGES IN FUND BALANCE
FOR YEAR ENDED DECEMBER 31, 19X6

Revenues	$ –0–
Expenditures:	
Grants to students	3,200
Excess (deficiency) of revenues over expenditures	$(3,200)
Other financing sources:	
Operating transfers in (from nonexpendable scholarship trust fund)	3,715
Excess of revenues and other financing sources over expenditures	$ 515
Fund balance, January 1, 19X6	–0–
Fund balance, December 31, 19X6	$ 515

mary data are not sufficiently detailed to constitute a CAFR. Transaction data are too detailed to be included in a CAFR. Rather, a CAFR includes the four levels between the extremes. These four levels are now discussed.

Level 1: General Purpose Financial Statements

The general purpose financial statements (level 1 on the reporting pyramid) are combined statements and notes that present an overview of the governmental unit's financial position and reporting results. Combined financial statements present each fund type and account group in a separate column. The general purpose financial statements have five components, which are described in the paragraphs that follow. Of course, footnotes to the statements in these five components may be used to present additional information concerning the statements.

Combined Balance Sheet—All Fund Types and Account Groups

The combined balance sheet for all fund types and account groups presents the assets and equities of all funds and account groups. A separate column is provided for each fund type and account group. A total column may be shown and labeled ''memorandum only.'' Current rules for governments permit but do not require the elimination of interfund transactions. The combined balance sheet for the City of Fisherville is presented in Exhibit 18-26 on page 928. (Note that this combined balance sheet does not have a column for the capital projects fund because all of this fund's resources had been distributed and its balance sheet accounts equal zero at the reporting date.)

Combined Statement of Revenues, Expenditures, and Changes in Fund Balances—All Governmental Fund Types

The combined statement of revenues, expenditures, and changes in fund balances for all governmental fund types displays the operating results for each type of governmental fund

EXHIBIT 18-25	THE FINANCIAL REPORTING PYRAMID

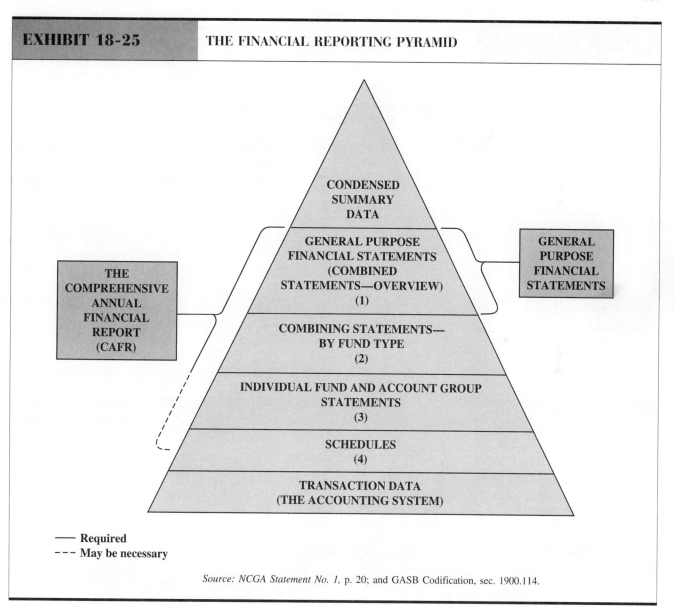

CONDENSED SUMMARY DATA

GENERAL PURPOSE FINANCIAL STATEMENTS (COMBINED STATEMENTS—OVERVIEW) (1)

COMBINING STATEMENTS— BY FUND TYPE (2)

INDIVIDUAL FUND AND ACCOUNT GROUP STATEMENTS (3)

SCHEDULES (4)

TRANSACTION DATA (THE ACCOUNTING SYSTEM)

THE COMPREHENSIVE ANNUAL FINANCIAL REPORT (CAFR)

GENERAL PURPOSE FINANCIAL STATEMENTS

—— Required
- - - May be necessary

Source: NCGA Statement No. 1, p. 20; and GASB Codification, sec. 1900.114.

in a separate column. Expendable trust funds using accrual accounting with a flow of financial resources measurement focus may be reported as a part of the operating statement for governmental-type funds or as a part of the operating statement for fiduciary funds. A "memorandum only" total column that displays the combined amounts for all funds included in the statement may be shown. Such a statement for the City of Fisherville is presented in Exhibit 18-27 on page 929.

EXHIBIT 18-26 — COMBINED BALANCE SHEET

City of Fisherville
COMBINED BALANCE SHEET—ALL FUND TYPES AND ACCOUNT GROUPS
AT DECEMBER 31, 19X6

	Governmental Fund Types		Proprietary Fund Types		Fiduciary Fund Types	Account Groups		Totals (Memorandum Only)
	General	Debt Service	Enterprise	Internal Services	Nonexpendable and Expendable Trust	General Fixed Assets	General Long-Term Debt	
Assets								
Cash	$ 5,900	$ 5,405	$ 93,000	$10,000	$ 2,941	$	$	$ 117,246
Investment in securities		21,500			47,499			68,999
Receivables:								
Current taxes (net)								
Delinquent taxes (net)	3,220							3,220
Interest and penalties on taxes (net)	400							400
Accounts (net)			38,000					38,000
Interest		1,200			75			1,275
Due from other funds				5,000	75			5,075
Inventories, at cost	3,800		4,200					8,000
Prepaid expenses			8,100					8,100
Restricted assets:								
Cash and investments			147,700					147,700
Land			73,000	10,000		800,000		883,000
Buildings, improvements, and equipment			260,000	85,000		3,180,000		3,525,000
Accumulated depreciation			(110,000)	(35,000)				(145,000)
Construction in progress			42,000			56,000		98,000
Amount available in debt service fund							28,105	28,105
Amount to be provided for retirement of general long-term debt							71,895	71,895
Total assets	$13,320	$28,105	$556,000	$75,000	$50,590	$4,036,000	$100,000	$4,859,015
Liabilities								
Vouchers payable	$ 2,220	$	$ 6,100	$ 7,000	$		$	$ 15,320
Construction contracts payable			10,000					10,000
Accrued interest payable			4,900					4,900
Due to other funds				3,000	75			3,075
Bonds payable (net)			350,000				100,000	450,000
Advances from other funds				5,000				5,000
Customer deposits			14,600					14,600
Total liabilities	$ 2,220	$	$385,600	$15,000	$ 75		$100,000	$ 502,895
Fund Equity								
Contribution from municipality	$	$	$ 60,000	$50,000	$	$		$ 110,000
Investment in general fixed assets						4,036,000		4,036,000
Retained earnings:								
Reserved for revenue current bond debt service			8,400					8,400
Reserved for revenue bond retirement			77,000					77,000
Unreserved			25,000	10,000				35,000
Fund balance:								
Reserved for encumbrances	450							450
Reserved for petty cash	2,000							2,000
Reserved for inventory	3,800							3,800
Reserved for debt service		28,105						28,105
Reserved for scholarships					50,515			50,515
Unreserved	4,850							4,850
Total fund equity	$11,100	$28,105	$170,400	$60,000	$50,515	$4,036,000		$4,356,120
Total liabilities and fund equity	$13,320	$28,105	$556,000	$75,000	$50,590	$4,036,000	$100,000	$4,859,015

EXHIBIT 18-27	COMBINED STATEMENT OF REVENUES, EXPENDITURES, AND CHANGES IN FUND BALANCES

City of Fisherville

COMBINED STATEMENT OF REVENUES, EXPENDITURES, AND CHANGES IN
FUND BALANCES—ALL GOVERNMENTAL FUND TYPES AND EXPENDABLE TRUST FUNDS
FOR THE YEAR ENDED DECEMBER 31, 19X6

	Governmental Fund Types			Fiduciary Fund Types	Totals (Memorandum Only)
	General	Capital Projects	Debt Service	Expendable Trust (Scholarship)	
Revenues:					
Property taxes	$258,920		$		$258,920
Interest and penalties on taxes	400				400
Interest revenue			1,550		1,550
Other	56,100				56,100
Total revenues	$315,420		$ 1,550		$316,970
Expenditures:					
Supplies	$ 20,000	$	$	$	$ 20,000
Salaries	120,000				120,000
Transportation equipment	15,000				15,000
Interest	500				500
Grants to students				3,200	3,200
Construction		71,000			71,000
Debt service					
Interest			6,000		6,000
Brokerage fees			95		95
Other	152,000				152,000
Total expenditures	$307,500	$ 71,000	$ 6,095	$ 3,200	$387,795
Excess (deficiency) of revenues over expenditures	$ 7,920	$(71,000)	$ (4,545)	$(3,200)	$ (70,825)
Other financing sources (uses):					
Operating transfers in (out)	$ (10,000)		$10,000	$ 3,715	$ 3,715
Total other financing sources (uses)	$ (10,000)		$10,000	$ 3,715	$ 3,715
Excess (deficiency) of revenues and other financing sources over expenditures and other uses	$ (2,080)	(71,000)	$ 5,455	$ 515	$ (67,110)
Fund balance, January 1, 19X6	9,380	76,000	17,650		103,030
Residual equity transfer in (out)		(5,000)	5,000		
Increase in reserve for inventory	3,800				3,800
Fund balance, December 31, 19X6	$ 11,100	$ –0–	$28,105	$ 515	$ 39,720

Combined Statement of Revenues, Expenditures, and Changes in Fund Balances—Budget and Actual—General and Special Revenue Fund Types

The combined statement of revenues, expenditures, and changes in fund balance showing budgeted and actual results for general and special revenue funds (and similar governmental fund types for which annual budgets have been legally adopted) provides a comparison of actual revenues and expenditures with the budgeted amounts. The differences represent favorable and unfavorable variances from the budget. The annual budget was adopted by two of Fisherville's governmental-type funds—the general fund and the debt service fund. Such a statement for the City of Fisherville is presented in Exhibit 18-28.

Combined Statement of Revenues, Expenses, and Changes in Retained Earnings—All Proprietary Fund Types

The combined statement of revenues, expenses, and changes in retained earnings (or equity) for all proprietary funds displays the operating results for each type of proprietary fund and similar trust fund. A total "memorandum only" column is presented. Nonexpendable and pension trust funds that are maintained on an accrual basis may also be presented in this statement for proprietary funds or as a part of the operating statement for fiduciary funds. This combined statement for the City of Fisherville is presented in Exhibit 18-29 on page 932.

Combined Statement of Changes in Financial Position—All Proprietary Fund Types

The combined statement of changes in financial position for all proprietary funds provides information on the financing and investment activities of these funds. A total "memorandum only" column is presented. Nonexpendable and pension trust funds that are maintained on an accrual basis may also be presented in this statement for proprietary funds or as a part of the statement of changes in financial position for fiduciary funds. This statement is not illustrated for the City of Fisherville since a statement of changes in financial position was not prepared for any of the proprietary fund types because of the similarity of such statements to those prepared for business enterprises.

Level 2: Combining Statements by Fund Type

Combining statements (level 2 on the reporting pyramid) are presented when the governmental unit has several funds of the same type—several capital projects funds or several debt service funds, for example. Combining statements show individual amounts for each such fund and the total amount for all such funds in separate columns. For instance, a governmental unit with two capital projects funds would prepare a three-column combining financial statement for its capital projects funds with one column for each capital projects fund and one column for the total amounts for both funds. The total column should agree with the capital projects funds column in the combined (level 1) statements. If the governmental unit has only one fund of each fund type, as does the City of Fisherville, then combining statements would not be necessary.

EXHIBIT 18-28	COMBINED STATEMENT OF REVENUES, EXPENDITURES, AND CHANGES IN FUND BALANCES: BUDGET AND ACTUAL

City of Fisherville

COMBINED STATEMENT OF REVENUES, EXPENDITURES, AND CHANGES IN
FUND BALANCES—BUDGET AND ACTUAL—GENERAL AND DEBT SERVICE FUND TYPES
FOR THE YEAR ENDED DECEMBER 31, 19X6

	General Fund			Debt Service Fund		
	Budget	Actual	Variance—Favorable (Unfavorable)	Budget	Actual	Variance—Favorable (Unfavorable)
Revenues:						
Property taxes	$258,000	$258,920	$ 920	$	$	$
Interest and penalties on delinquent taxes	400	400				
Interest				1,500	1,550	50
Other	63,600	56,100	(7,500)			
Total revenues	$322,000	$315,420	$(6,580)	$ 1,500	$ 1,550	$ 50
Expenditures:						
Supplies	$ 21,000	$ 20,000	$ 1,000	$	$	$
Salaries	122,000	120,000	2,000			
Transportation equipment	14,300	15,000	(700)			
Interest	250	500	(250)	6,000	6,000	
Fees to brokers and bankers				100	95	(5)
Other	150,450	152,000	(1,550)			
Total expenditures	$308,000	$307,500	$ 500	$ 6,100	$ 6,095	$ (5)
Excess (deficiency) of revenues over expenditures	$ 14,000	$ 7,920	$(6,080)	$ (4,600)	$ (4,545)	$ 55
Other financing sources (uses):						
Operating transfers in (out)	(10,000)	(10,000)		10,000	10,000	
Excess (deficiency) of revenues and other financing sources over expenditures and other uses	$ 4,000	$ (2,080)	$(6,080)	$ 5,400	$ 5,455	$ 55
Fund balance, January 1, 19X6	9,380	9,380		17,650	17,650	
Residual equity transfers in					5,000	5,000
Increase in reserve for inventory		3,800	3,800			
Fund balance, December 31, 19X6	$ 13,380	$ 11,100	$(2,280)	$23,050	$28,105	$5,055

Level 3: Individual Fund and Account Group Statements

Individual fund financial statements and account group statements (level 3 on the reporting pyramid) present information for each fund of a particular fund type and for the account groups (general fixed assets and general long-term debt). The City of Fisherville's individual fund statements and account group schedules are not shown here because they are presented in this chapter and the previous one with the related discussion of the

EXHIBIT 18-29	COMBINED STATEMENT OF REVENUES, EXPENSES, AND CHANGES IN RETAINED EARNINGS OR FUND BALANCES

City of Fisherville

COMBINED STATEMENT OF REVENUES, EXPENSES, AND CHANGES IN RETAINED EARNINGS OR
FUND BALANCES—ALL PROPRIETARY FUND TYPES AND SIMILAR TRUST FUNDS
FOR THE YEAR ENDED DECEMBER 31, 19X6

	Proprietary Fund Types		Fiduciary Fund Types	Totals (Memorandum Only)
	Enterprise	Internal Service	Nonexpendable Trust	
Operating revenues:				
Sales of electricity	$265,000	$	$	$265,000
Charges for services		50,000		50,000
Interest			3,715	3,715
Gifts			50,000	50,000
Other	11,000			11,000
Total operating revenues	$276,000	$50,000	$53,715	$379,715
Operating expenses:				
Cost of purchased power	$120,000	$		$120,000
Personal services		20,000		20,000
Contractual services		5,000		5,000
Supplies		3,000		3,000
Materials	3,200	2,000		5,200
Heat, light, and power	6,000	6,000		12,000
Depreciation	86,000	10,000		96,000
Other	16,000			16,000
Total operating expenses	$231,200	$46,000		$277,200
Operating income	$ 44,800	$ 4,000	$53,715	$102,515
Nonoperating revenues (expenses):				
Operating grants	$ 18,000			$ 18,000
Interest and fiscal charges	(50,000)			(50,000)
Total nonoperating revenues (expenses)	$(32,000)			$(32,000)
Income before operating transfers	$ 12,800	$ 4,000	$53,715	$ 70,515
Other financing sources (uses):				
Operating transfers in (out)			(3,715)	(3,715)
Net income	$ 12,800	$ 4,000	$50,000	$ 66,800
Retained earnings or fund balance, 1-1-X6	97,600	6,000	–0–	103,600
Retained earnings or fund balance, 12-31-X6	$110,400	$10,000	$50,000	$170,400

particular fund or account group. The inclusion of such statements in a CAFR is appropriate when the (level 1) statement does not present sufficiently detailed information. Usually a level 3 statement will not be needed if a combining (level 2) statement is presented.

Level 4: Schedules

Additional information may be presented in schedules (level 4 on the reporting pyramid) (1) to demonstrate compliance with finance-related legal and contractual provisions, (2) to present information spread throughout the statements that can be brought together and shown in greater detail, and (3) to present greater detail for information reported in the statements.

The governmental unit does not need to report at all levels shown on the pyramid, but it should report as as many levels as necessary to provide adequate disclosure. For some governmental units, adequate disclosure may be accomplished by reporting at only one or two levels on the pyramid, whereas adequate disclosure for other governmental units may require reporting at all four levels.

The financial statements of some governmental units are audited by a state audit agency, whereas others are audited by independent certified public accountants. In either case, the auditor's opinion should be reproduced in the CAFR.

The CAFR should also include any statistical tables that are felt necessary to provide information to the reader who has more than a casual interest in the financial statements (e.g., economic and social data, financial trends, and the fiscal capacity of the government).

Although our Fisherville illustration is simplified, it serves to demonstrate the extreme complexity of reporting for an entity that is composed of multiple funds, each of which must be addressed in external financial reports. (See Exhibits 18-26 through 18-29.) Still, our simplified illustration does not call attention to the importance of detailed information within funds. In particular, detailed classifications of revenues and expenditures within funds are frequently useful for internal if not for external reporting purposes. The following issues section describes the principles that guide the design of such classification systems for governmental funds.

ISSUES

Classification of Revenues and Expenditures

REVENUE CLASSIFICATION

Accounting records and financial statements for governmental funds should classify each fund's revenues by the source from which the revenue was obtained. The principal sources of governmental funds revenues are taxes, licenses and permits, intergovernmental revenues, charges for services, fines and forfeits, and miscellaneous. For purposes of management control and accountability, governments may classify revenues by organizational unit (departments, bureaus, divisions, or other administrative agencies), but such classifications "should supplement rather than supplant the classifications by fund and source" (*NCGA Statement No. 1,* par. 110; and *GASB Codification,* sec. 1800.114).

EXPENDITURES CLASSIFICATION

"Multiple classification of governmental fund expenditure data is important from both internal and external management control and accountability standpoints. It facilitates the aggregation and analysis of data in different ways for different purposes and in manners that cross fund and organization lines, for internal evaluation, external reporting, and intergovernmental comparison purposes. The major accounting classifications of expenditures are by fund, function (or program), organization unit, activity, character, and object class.'' Expenditures classified by character are classified on the basis of the period receiving the benefit of the expenditure; for example, current expenditures should be separated from capital outlays and debt service expenditures. Expenditures classified by object class are classified by the type of service or object obtained by an expenditure (e.g., personal services, supplies, and capital expenditures). Excessively detailed object classifications should be avoided because they are of limited use in financial management and needlessly complicate the accounting and reporting system (*NCGA Statement No. 1*, pars. 111–116; and *GASB Codification*, secs. 1800.115–1800.120).

SUMMARY

Chapters 17 and 18 survey the distinctive characteristics and accounting procedures of the various types of funds and account groups that constitute the accounting system for a state or local government. These distinctive characteristics and procedures, which are summarized in Exhibit 18-30, greatly complicate the preparation of comprehensive financial reporting for governmental units as the concluding section of this chapter demonstrates.

EXHIBIT 18-30   CHARACTERISTICS OF INDIVIDUAL FUNDS AND ACCOUNT GROUPS

Characteristics	Governmental Funds				Proprietary Funds	
	General	Special Revenue	Capital Project	Debt Service	Enterprise	Internal Service
Purpose: To account for	Basic services; resources not accounted for in other funds	Resources restricted to specific purposes	Construction or acquisition of major capital facilities	Accumulation of resources and payments on general long-term debt and interest	Goods or services sold to public	Goods or services provided to governmental departments or agencies
Sources of financial resources	Property tax, sales tax, state/federal government aid, fees, fines, special assessments, etc.	Specific taxes, government grants, transfers from other funds, etc.	Bond issues, government grants, transfers from general fund	Transfers from other funds, interest earned, special tax levy, special assessments	Charges to users	Charges to users
Use of financial resources	Administration, police, fire, parks, courts, etc.	Particular operations	Buildings, equipment, major improvements	Payment of debt principal and interest	Operations	Operations
Length of life	Year to year	Year to year	Life of project	Life of general obligation debt	Going concern	Going concern

SELECTED READINGS

Baber, William R., and Pradyot K. Sen. "The Role of Generally Accepted Reporting Methods in the Public Sector: An Empirical Test," *Journal of Accounting and Public Policy* (Summer 1984), pp. 91–106.

Berne, Robert. *The Relationships between Financial Reporting and the Measurement of Financial Condition,* Research Report. Norwalk, CT: Governmental Accounting Standards Board, 1992.

Carpenter, Francis H., and Florence C. Sharp. *Popular Reporting: Local Government Financial Reports to the Citizenry,* Research Report. Norwalk, CT: Governmental Accounting Standards Board, 1992.

Dye, Kenneth M., and Charles A. Bowsher. "Financial Statements for a Sovereign State: The Federal Government Reporting Study," *Accounting Horizons* (March 1987), pp. 17–24.

Freeman, Robert J., and Craig D. Shoulders. "Defining the Governmental Reporting Entity," *Journal of Accountancy* (October 1982), pp. 50–63.

Freeman, Robert J., and Craig D. Shoulders. "Governmental Fund Operating Results: 3 Formats," *Journal of Accountancy* (November 1985), pp. 110–121.

Fiduciary Funds				Account Groups	
Expendable Trust	**Nonexpendable Trust**	**Pension Trust**	**Agency**	**General Fixed Assets**	**General Long-Term Debt**
Expendable resources held under trust	Nonexpendable resources held under trust	Public employee retirement systems	Assets held as agent for others	Fixed assets—control account for fixed assets	Long-term debt—control account for long-term debts
Grants, gifts, endowment earnings	Grants (endowments)	Contributions from employer and/or employees, investment earnings	—	—	—
Expenditure according to agreement	Invested to produce earnings	Retirement benefits	—	—	—
Duration of trust	Duration of trust	Going concern	Duration of agency	Life of general fixed assets	Life of general obligation debt

EXHIBIT 18-30	CHARACTERISTICS OF INDIVIDUAL FUNDS AND ACCOUNT GROUPS (Continued)

| | Governmental Funds | | | | Proprietary Funds | |
Characteristics	General	Special Revenue	Capital Project	Debt Service	Enterprise	Internal Service
Record budget	Yes	Yes	No*	No*	No	No
Record encumbrances	Yes	Yes	Yes	No	No	No
Accounting method	Modified accrual**	Modified accrual**	Modified accrual**	Modified accrual**	Full accrual#	Full accrual#
Record assets:						
Current	Yes	Yes	Yes	Yes	Yes	Yes
Fixed	No	No	No	No	Yes	Yes
Record depreciation	No	No	No	No	Yes	Yes
Record liabilities	Current	Current	Current	Current	Current & long-term with premium or discount	Current & long-term with premium or discount
Equity account titles	Fund balance	Fund balance	Fund balance	Fund balance	Contributed capital, retained earnings	Contributed capital, retained earnings
Basic financial reports issued:						
Balance sheet	Yes	Yes	Yes	Yes	Yes	Yes
Statement of revenues, expenditures, and changes in fund balance	Yes	Yes	Yes	Yes	No	No
Statement of revenues, expenditures, and changes in fund balance—budget and actual	Yes	Yes	No*	No*	No	No
Statement of revenues, expenses, and changes in retained earnings (or fund balance)	No	No	No	No	Yes	Yes
Statement of cash flows	No	No	No	No	Yes	Yes

* Record budget, and prepare statement comparing budget with actual only if a budget is legally adopted.
** Accrual accounting with a financial resources measurement focus.
# Accrual accounting with a measurement focus on resources broadly defined, as used in business enterprises.

	Fiduciary Funds			Account Groups	
Expendable Trust	**Nonexpendable Trust**	**Pension Trust**	**Agency**	**General Fixed Assets**	**General Long-Term Debt**
No*	No	No	—	—	—
Yes	No	No	—	—	—
Modified accrual**	Full accrual#	Full accrual#	—	—	—
Yes	Yes	Yes	Yes	No	No
No	Yes	Yes	No	Yes	No
No	May	Yes	No	May	—
Current	Current & long-term	Current	Current	No	Long-term at par
Fund balance	Fund balance	Fund balance	None	Investment in general fixed assets	—
Yes	Yes	Yes	Yes	No (but schedule of general fixed assets required)	No (but schedule of general long-term debt required)
Yes	No	No	—	—	—
No*	No	No	—	—	—
No	Yes	Yes	—	—	—
No	Yes	Yes	—	—	—

Gaffney, Mary Anne. "Consolidated versus Fund-Type Accounting Statements," *Journal of Accounting and Public Policy* (Fall 1986), pp. 167–189.

Hay, Leon E., and James F. Antonio. "What Users Want in Government Financial Reports," *Journal of Accountancy* (August 1990), pp. 91–98.

Hwang, Yuhchang, and James M. Patton. "An Economic Analysis of Interperiod Equity in Governmental Financial Reporting," *Research in Governmental and Nonprofit Accounting* (1992), pp. 3–23.

Parry, Robert W., Jr. "Defining the Municipal Entity," *Management Accounting* (September 1982), pp. 50–55.

Patton, James M. "An Experimental Investigation of Some Effects of Consolidating Municipal Financial Reports," *The Accounting Review* (April 1978), pp. 402–414.

Patton, James M. "The Governmental Financial Reporting Entity: A Review and Analysis," *Research in Governmental and Nonprofit Accounting* (1985), pp. 85–116.

Sharp, Florence C. "The Effects of Governmental Accounting Methods on Asset-Acquisition Decisions: A Theoretical Model and Three Case Studies," *Journal of Accounting and Public Policy* (Winter 1985), pp. 251–276.

Soldano, Joseph J., Jr. (ed.). *Local Government Accounting Trends and Techniques.* New York: American Institute of Certified Public Accountants, issued annually.

QUESTIONS

Q18-1   What is the purpose of a special revenue fund? Given an example of a special revenue fund.

Q18-2   Discuss why you agree or disagree with the following statement: The capital projects funds account for financial resources that are set aside for the acquisition of fixed assets for all funds of a governmental unit.

Q18-3   The state authorized $200,000 for the construction of a state court building. If the bonds issued to finance the capital project are issued at a premium of $20,000 ($200,000 par value), is the project authorization also automatically increased by $20,000?

Q18-4   Expenditures of $100,000 were recorded in the capital projects fund relating to partial construction of a city hall building financed by general obligation bonds. In what other fund or account group would this information be recorded, and what entry would be made?

Q18-5   What is the relationship between debt service funds and the general long-term debt account group?

Q18-6   What is the purpose of the general fixed assets account group and the general long-term debt account group?

Q18-7   Discuss three distinctive characteristics of enterprise funds, and contrast these characteristics with those of private-sector enterprises.

Q18-8   Distinguish between nonexpendable trusts and expendable trusts.

Q18-9   Distinguish between *combined* financial statements and *combining* financial statements.

Q18-10   What is the title of the official annual report of a governmental unit?

Q18-11   List the five financial statements that constitute the general purpose financial statements of a governmental unit.

EXERCISES

E18-1 **Multiple Choice Questions on Budgetary and Encumbrance Accounting**

1. Which of the following funds of a governmental unit integrates budgetary accounts into the accounting system?

a) Enterprise

b) Special revenue

c) Internal service

d) Nonexpendable trust

2. Encumbrances would *not* appear in which fund?

a) General

b) Enterprise

c) Capital projects

d) Special revenue

3. Which of the following funds requires the use of the encumbrance system?

a) Capital projects

b) Debt service

c) General fixed assets account group

d) Enterprise

(AICPA adapted)

E18-2 **Multiple Choice Questions on Special Revenue Fund**

1. The accounting for special revenue funds is most similar to which type of fund?

a) Capital projects

b) Enterprise

c) General

d) Debt service

2. The following financial resources were among those received by Seco City during 19X9:

For acquisition of major capital facilities	$6,000,000
To create an expendable trust	2,000,000

With respect to the foregoing resources, what amount should be recorded in special revenue funds?

a) $–0–

c) $6,000,000

b) $2,000,000

d) $8,000,000

3. Revenues that are legally restricted to expenditures for specified purposes should be accounted for in special revenue funds, including

a) Accumulation of resources for payment of general long-term debt principal and interest

b) Pension trust fund revenues

c) Gasoline taxes to finance road repairs

d) Proprietary fund revenues

4. Lake County received the following proceeds that are legally restricted to expenditure for specified purposes:

Levies on affected property owners to install sidewalks	$500,000
Special property taxes to finance public library operations	900,000

What amount should be accounted for in Lake's special revenue funds?

a) $1,400,000   **c)** $500,000

b) $ 900,000   **d)** $–0–

(AICPA adapted)

E18-3   **Multiple Choice Questions on Capital Projects Fund**

1. A capital projects fund of a municipality is an example of what type of fund?

   a) Internal service

   b) Proprietary

   c) Fiduciary

   d) Governmental

2. When a capital project is financed entirely from a single bond issue and the proceeds of the bond issue equal the par value of the bonds, the capital projects fund would record this transaction by debiting cash and crediting

   a) Other financing sources control—bond issue proceeds

   b) Unreserved fund balance

   c) Appropriations control

   d) Bonds payable

(AICPA adapted)

E18-4   **Multiple Choice Questions on Debt Service Fund**

1. A debt service fund of a municipality is an example of which of the following types of funds?

   a) Fiduciary

   b) Governmental

   c) Proprietary

   d) Internal service

2. Interest on bonds payable should be recorded in a debt service fund as an expenditure

   a) At the end of the fiscal period if the interest due date does *not* coincide with the end of the fiscal period

   b) When bonds are issued

   c) When legally payable

   d) When paid

3. Ariel Village issued the following bonds during the year ended June 30, 19X3:

For installation of street lights, to be assessed against properties benefited (the village must pay these bonds in the event of default)	$300,000
For construction of public swimming pool; bonds to be paid from pledged fees collected from pool users	400,000

How much should be accounted for through debt service funds for payments of principal over the life of the bonds?

   a) $–0–   **c)** $400,000

   b) $300,000   **d)** $700,000

Items (4) and (5) are based on the following information:

The following events relating to the City of Albury's debt service funds occurred during the year ended December 31, 19X1:

Debt principal matured	$2,000,000
Unmatured (accrued) interest on outstanding debt at January 1, 19X1	50,000
Matured interest on debt	900,000
Unmatured (accrued) interest on outstanding debt at December 31, 19X1	100,000
Interest revenue from investments	600,000
Cash transferred from general fund for retirement of debt principal	1,000,000
Cash transferred from general fund for payment of matured interest	900,000

All principal and interest due in 19X1 were paid on time.

4. What is the total amount of expenditures that Albury's debt service fund should record for the year ended December 31, 19X1?

a) $900,000

b) $950,000

c) $2,900,000

d) $2,950,000

5. How much revenue should Albury's debt service fund record for the year ended December 31, 19X1?

a) $ 600,000

b) $1,600,000

c) $1,900,000

d) $2,500,000

6. Tott City's serial bonds are serviced through a debt service fund with cash provided by the general fund. In a debt service fund's statements, how are cash receipts and cash payments reported?

	Cash Receipts	**Cash Payments**
a)	Revenues	Expenditures
b)	Revenues	Operating transfers
c)	Operating transfers	Expenditures
d)	Operating transfers	Operating transfers

(AICPA adapted)

E18-5 **Multiple Choice Questions on Proprietary Funds**

1. An enterprise fund would be used when the governing body requires that

I. Accounting for the financing of an agency's services to other government departments be on a cost-reimbursement basis

II. User charges cover the costs of general public services

III. Net income information be provided for an activity

a) I only

b) I and II

c) I and III

d) II and III

2. Long-term liabilities of an enterprise fund should be accounted for in the

	Enterprise Fund	**Long-Term Debt Account Group**
a)	No	No
b)	No	Yes
c)	Yes	Yes
d)	Yes	No

3. Gem City's internal service fund received a residual equity transfer of $50,000 cash from the general fund. This $50,000 transfer should be reported in Gem's internal service fund as a credit to

a) Revenues

b) Other financing sources

c) Accounts payable

d) Contributed capital

4. Through an internal service fund, Wood County operates a centralized data processing center to provide services to Wood's other governmental units. In 19X9, this internal service fund billed Wood's parks and recreation fund $75,000 for data processing services. What account should Wood's internal service fund credit to record this $75,000 billing to the parks and recreation fund?

a) Operating revenues control

b) Interfund exchanges

c) Intergovernmental transfers

d) Data processing department expenses

5. During 19X9, Spruce City reported the following receipts from self-sustaining activities paid for by users of the services rendered:

Operation of water supply plant	$5,000,000
Operation of bus system	900,000

What amount should be accounted for in Spruce's enterprise funds?

a) $–0–

b) $ 900,000

c) $5,000,000

d) $5,900,000

(AICPA adapted)

E18-6 **Multiple Choice Questions on Identification of Types of Funds and Account Groups**

1. An expenditures account appears in

a) The general fixed assets account group

b) The general long-term debt account group

c) A special revenue fund

d) An internal service fund

2. In 19X9, a state government collected income taxes of $8,000,000 for the benefit of one of its cities that imposes an income tax on its residents. The state remitted these collections periodically to the city. The state should account for the $8,000,000 in the

a) General fund

b) Agency funds

c) Internal service funds

d) Special assessment funds

3. Dale City is accumulating financial resources that are legally restricted to payments of general long-term debt principal and interest maturing in future years. At December 31, 19X1, $5,000,000 has been accumulated for principal payments and $300,000 has been accumulated for interest payments. These restricted funds should be accounted for in the

	Debt Service Fund	General Fund
a)	$–0–	$5,300,000
b)	$ 300,000	$5,000,000
c)	$5,000,000	$ 300,000
d)	$5,300,000	$–0–

4. Fixed assets utilized in a city-owned utility are accounted for in which of the following?

	Enterprise Fund	**General Fixed Assets Account Group**
a)	No	No
b)	No	Yes
c)	Yes	No
d)	Yes	Yes

5. Which of the following funds of a governmental unit would account for depreciation in the accounts of the fund?

a) General

b) Internal service

c) Capital projects

d) Debt service

6. Lisa County issued $5,000,000 of general obligation bonds at 101 to finance a capital project. The $50,000 premium was to be used for payment of principal and interest. This transaction should be accounted for in the

a) Capital projects fund, debt service fund, and general long-term debt account group

b) Capital projects fund and debt service fund only

c) Debt service fund and general long-term debt account group only

d) Debt service fund only

7. Which of the following funds of a governmental unit would account for long-term liabilities in the accounts of the fund?

a) Enterprise

b) Special revenue

c) Capital projects

d) Debt service

8. Which of the following funds of a governmental unit could use the general fixed assets account group to account for fixed assets?

a) Internal service

b) Enterprise

c) Nonexpendable trust

d) Capital projects

9. Which of the following funds should account for the payment of interest and principal on revenue bond debt?

a) Capital projects

b) Enterprise

c) Expendable trust

d) Debt service

10. Which of the following funds of a governmental unit would account for long-term debt in the accounts of the fund?

a) Special revenue

b) Capital projects

c) Internal service

d) General

11. *Investment in general fixed assets* accounts would appear in which fund or account group?

    a) General fixed assets

    b) Enterprise

    c) Capital projects

    d) General

(AICPA adapted)

E18-7   **Identify and Record Entries in Appropriate Funds and Account Groups**   Listed here are four independent transactions or events that relate to a local government:

1. $25,000 was disbursed from the general fund for the cash purchase of new equipment.

2. An unrestricted cash gift of $100,000 was received from a donor.

3. Listed common stocks with a total carrying value of $50,000, exclusive of any allowance, were sold by an endowment fund for $55,000, before any dividends were earned on these stocks. There are no restrictions on the gain.

4. $1,000,000 face amount of general obligation bonds payable were sold at par, with the proceeds required to be used solely for construction of a new building. This building was completed at a total cost of $1,000,000, and the total amount of bond issue proceeds was disbursed in connection therewith. Disregard interest capitalization.

REQUIRED

For each of the preceding transactions or events, prepare journal entries specifying the affected funds and account groups and showing how these transactions or events should be recorded by a local government whose debt is serviced by general tax revenues.

(AICPA adapted)

E18-8   **Multiple Choice Questions on General Fixed Assets and General Long-Term Debt Account Groups**

1. The general fixed assets account group would be used for the fixed assets of the

    a) Capital projects fund

    b) Enterprise fund

    c) Nonexpendable trust fund

    d) Internal service fund

2. The following assets are among those owned by the City of Foster:

Apartment building (part of the principal of a nonexpendable trust fund)	$ 200,000
City Hall	800,000
Three fire stations	1,000,000
City streets and sidewalks	5,000,000

How much should be included in Foster's general fixed assets account group?

    a) $1,800,000 or $6,800,000

    b) $2,000,000 or $7,000,000

    c) $6,800,000, without election of $1,800,000

    d) $7,000,000, without election of $2,000,000

3. Which of the following funds of a governmental unit would use the general long-term debt account group to account for unmatured general long-term liabilities?

a) Enterprise	c) Nonexpendable trust
b) Capital projects	d) Internal service

4. Fixed assets should be accounted for in the general fixed assets account group for

	Governmental Funds	Proprietary Funds
a)	No	Yes
b)	No	No
c)	Yes	No
d)	Yes	Yes

5. Elkton Village issued the following bonds during the year ended June 30, 19X1:

Revenue bonds to be repaid from admission fees collected by the Elkton Zoo enterprise fund	$200,000
General obligation bonds issued for the Elkton water and sewer enterprise fund that will service the debt	300,000

How much of these bonds should be accounted for in Elkton's general long-term debt account group?

a) $–0–	c) $300,000
b) $200,000	d) $500,000

6. Fred Bosin donated a building to Palma City in 19X3. Bosin's original cost of the property was $100,000. Accumulated depreciation at the date of the gift amounted to $60,000. Fair market value at the date of the gift was $300,000. In the general fixed assets account group, at what amount should Palma record this donated fixed asset?

a) $300,000	c) $40,000
b) $100,000	d) $–0–

7. On June 28, 19X1, Silver City's debt service fund received funds for the future repayment of bond principal. As a consequence, the general long-term debt account group reported

a) An increase in the amount available in debt service funds and an increase in the fund balance

b) An increase in the amount available in debt service funds and an increase in the amount to be provided for bonds

c) An increase in the amount available in debt service funds and a decrease in the amount to be provided for bonds

d) No changes in any amount until the bond principal is actually paid

8. Lori Township received a gift of an ambulance having a market value of $180,000. What account in the general fixed assets account group should be debited for this $180,000 gift?

a) None (memorandum entry only)

b) Investment in general fixed assets from gifts

c) Machinery and equipment

d) General fund assets

9. Old equipment, which is recorded in the general fixed assets account group, is sold for less than its carrying amount. The sale reduces the investments in general fixed assets balance by the

a) Difference between the cost of the equipment and the sales price

b) Difference between the carrying amount of the equipment and the sales price

c) Selling price of the equipment

d) Carrying amount of the equipment *(AICPA adapted)*

E18-9   **Multiple Choice Questions on Financial Reporting for Various Funds, Account Groups, and Governmental Units**

1. Which of the following accounts could be included in the balance sheet of an enterprise fund?

	Fund Balance Reserved for Encumbrances	Revenue Bonds Payable	Retained Earnings
a)	No	No	Yes
b)	No	Yes	Yes
c)	Yes	Yes	No
d)	No	No	No

2. Customers' meter deposits that cannot be spent for normal operating purposes would be classified as restricted cash in the balance sheet of which fund?

a) Internal service
b) Trust
c) Agency
d) Enterprise

3. Which of the following funds of a governmental unit would include retained earnings in its balance sheet?

a) Pension trust
b) Internal service
c) Special revenue
d) Capital projects

4. Which of the following accounts would be included in the asset section of the combined balance sheet of a governmental unit for the general long-term debt account group?

	Amount Available in Debt Service Funds	Amount to Be Provided for Retirement of General Long-Term Debt
a)	Yes	Yes
b)	Yes	No
c)	No	Yes
d)	No	No

5. The comprehensive annual financial report (CAFR) of a governmental unit should contain a combined statement of cash flows for

	Governmental Funds	Proprietary Funds
a)	No	No
b)	No	Yes
c)	Yes	No
d)	Yes	Yes

6. Which of the following would be included in the combined statement of revenues, expenditures, and changes in fund balances—budget and actual in the comprehensive annual financial report (CAFR) of a governmental unit?

	Enterprise Fund	General Fixed Assets Account Group
a)	Yes	Yes
b)	Yes	No
c)	No	Yes
d)	No	No

7. On December 31, 19X1, Madrid Township paid a contractor $2,000,000 for the total cost of a new firehouse built in 19X1 on Township-owned land. Financing was by means of a $1,500,000 general obligation bond issue sold at face amount on December 31, 19X1, with the remaining $500,000 transferred from the general fund. What should be reported on Madrid's 19X1 financial statements for the capital project fund?

   a) Revenues, $1,500,000; expenditures, $1,500,000

   b) Revenues, $1,500,000; other financing sources, $500,000; expenditures, $2,000,000

   c) Revenues, $2,000,000; expenditures, $2,000,000

   d) Other financing sources, $2,000,000; expenditures, $2,000,000

8. During the year ended December 31, 19X1, Leyland City received a state grant of $500,000 to finance the purchase of buses and an additional grant of $100,000 to aid in the financing of bus operations in 19X1. Only $300,000 of the capital grant was used in 19X1 for the purchase of buses, but the entire operating grant of $100,000 was spent in 19X1. If Leyland's bus transportation system is accounted for as an enterprise fund, how much should Leyland report as grant revenues for the year ended December 31, 19X1?

   a) $100,000   **c)** $400,000

   b) $300,000   **d)** $500,000

9. The City of Rover has two debt service funds. In the preparation of the balance sheet for these funds as of the end of the fiscal year, these funds may be reported on

   a) A combining basis that shows the total for both funds and has separate columns to present account balances for each fund

   b) A consolidated basis after eliminating the effects of interfund transactions

   c) A separate basis but never together in the same statement

   d) A consolidated basis with the general fund after eliminating the effects of interfund transactions

10. What will be the balance sheet effect of recording $50,000 of depreciation in the accounts of a utility, an enterprise fund, owned by Brockton City?

   a) Reduce total assets of the utility fund and the general fixed assets account group

   b) Reduce total assets of the utility fund by $50,000 but have no effect on the general fixed assets account group

   c) Reduce total assets of the general fixed assets account group by $50,000 but have no effect on assets of the utility fund

   d) Have no effect on total assets of either the utility fund or the general fixed assets account group

11. In a government's comprehensive annual financial report (CAFR), account groups are included in which of the following combined financial statements?

	Balance Sheet	**Statement of Revenues, Expenditures, and Changes in Fund Balances**
a)	Yes	No
b)	No	Yes
c)	Yes	Yes
d)	No	No

12. The Town of Boyd electric utility fund, which is an enterprise fund, had the following:

Prepaid insurance paid in December 19X6	$ 43,000
Depreciation for 19X6	129,000
Provision for doubtful accounts for 19X6	14,000

What amount should be reflected in the statement of revenues and expenses (income statement) of the Town of Boyd electric utility fund for the preceding items?

    a) $(43,000)   **c)** $129,000

    b) $–0–   **d)** $143,000

13. Clover City's comprehensive annual financial report contains both combining and combined financial statements. Total columns are

    a) Required for both combining and combined financial statements

    b) Optional, but commonly shown, for combining financial statements and required for combined financial statements

    c) Required for combining financial statements and optional, but commonly shown, for combined financial statements

    d) Optional, but commonly shown, for both combining and combined financial statements

14. At December 31, 19X1, the following balances were due from the state government to Clare City's various funds:

Capital projects	$300,000
Trust and agency	100,000
Enterprise	80,000

In Clare's December 31, 19X1, combined balance sheet for all fund types and account groups, what amount should be classified under governmental funds?

    a) $100,000   **c)** $300,000

    b) $180,000   **d)** $480,000

(AICPA adapted)

E18-10   **Multiple Choice Questions on Identification of Types of Funds and Account Groups**

    1. Which type of fund can be either expendable or nonexpendable?

        a) Debt service

        b) Enterprise

        c) Trust

        d) Special revenue

    2. The activities of a municipal employees' retirement and pension system should be recorded in

        a) A general fund

        b) A special revenue fund

        c) An internal service fund

        d) A trust fund

    3. Which fund of a governmental unit would account for fixed assets in a manner similar to a "for-profit" organization?

        a) Enterprise

        b) Capital projects

        c) General fixed assets account group

        d) General

    4. Activities of a central print shop offering printing services at cost to various city departments should be accounted for in

        a) The general fund   **c)** A special revenue fund

        b) An internal service fund   **d)** A capital projects fund

5. Sanders County collects property taxes for the benefit of the state government and the local school districts and periodically remits collections to these units. These activities should be accounted for in

    a) An agency fund

    b) The general fund

    c) An internal service fund

    d) A special revenue fund

6. In order to provide for retirement of general obligation bonds, the City of Osborn invests a portion of its receipts from general property taxes in marketable securities. This investment activity should be accounted for in

    a) A capital projects fund

    b) A debt service fund

    c) A trust fund

    d) The general fund

7. The operations of a public library receiving the majority of its support from property taxes levied for that purpose should be accounted for in

    a) The general fund

    b) A special revenue fund

    c) An enterprise fund

    d) An internal service fund

8. The construction activities of a street improvement project that is being financed by requiring each owner of property facing the street to pay a proportionate share of the total cost should be accounted for in the

    a) Capital projects fund

    b) General fund

    c) Debt service fund

    d) Special revenue fund

9. Recreational facilities run by a governmental unit and financed on a user-charge basis would be accounted for in which fund?

    a) General

    b) Trust

    c) Enterprise

    d) Capital projects

10. A transaction in which a municipality issued general obligation serial bonds to finance the construction of a fire station requires accounting recognition in the

    a) General fund

    b) Capital projects and general funds

    c) Capital projects fund and the general long-term debt account group

    d) General fund and the general long-term debt account group

11. Expenditures of $200,000 were made during the year on the fire station in item (10). This transaction requires accounting recognition in the

    a) General fund

    b) Capital projects fund and the general fixed assets account group

    c) Capital projects fund and the general long-term debt account group

    d) General fund and the general fixed assets account group

12. Fixed and current assets are not accounted for in the same fund, with the exception of the

a) General fund

b) Internal service fund

c) Debt service fund

d) Special revenue fund

(AICPA adapted)

E18-11   Identification of Accounts with Types of Funds and Account Groups   The following accounts *frequently* appear in municipal accounting records.

Accounts	Municipal Accounting Funds and Account Groups
1. Bonds payable	**a)** General fund
2. Fund balance reserved for encumbrances	**b)** Special revenue fund
3. Equipment	**c)** Capital projects fund
4. Appropriations control	**d)** Agency fund
5. Estimated revenues control	**e)** Debt service fund
6. Taxes receivable—current	**f)** Internal service fund
7. Contracts payable—retained percentage	**g)** Nonexpendable trust fund
	h) Enterprise fund
	i) General fixed assets account group
	j) General long-term debt account group

REQUIRED

List the letter(s) next to the account indicating the municipal funds and/or account groups in which these accounts might properly appear. An account might appear in more than one fund and/or account group.

(AICPA adapted)

E18-12   Identify Funds and Account Groups Affected by Transactions   The Town of Blackwell uses budgetary accounts and separates its accounts into the following funds and account groups.

Identification Letter	Funds and Account Groups
A	General fund
B	Stores fund—an internal service fund
C	Agency and trust funds
D	Capital projects fund
E	Debt service fund
F	General fixed assets account group
G	General long-term debt account group

During 19X9 the following 14 transactions were among those taking place:

1. The 19X9 budget providing for $398,000 of appropriations and $400,000 of estimated revenues was approved.

2. The two approved construction of streets that were to cost $60,000 and be financed by special assessments bonds payable, which were to be repaid by a levy on the adjacent property.

3. Purchase orders of $7,000 for the Fire Department were entered into.

4. Current taxes of $350,000 were levied.

5. Taxes written off in 19X5 in the amount of $1,000 were collected.

6. Serial bonds in the amount of $25,000 matured and were paid. This payment was contemplated by the appropriations for the year.

7. A general bond issue of $50,000 was authorized; the proceeds were to be expended for a building.

8. The bonds in item (7) were sold for cash at par.

9. Property costing $30,000 was retired with a cash salvage of $500 received.

10. The purchase orders of $7,000 referred to in item (3) were filled at a cost of $7,200.

11. Stores were issued to the town clerk's office in the amount of $220.

12. The building referred to in item (7) was completed at a cost of $49,500.

13. Salaries of the Police Department amounting to $3,700 were paid after deducting $200 to go into the police pension fund.

14. Collections of taxes belonging to the county amounted to $17,400.

REQUIRED
Write down the numbers 1 through 14 and opposite each number show, by use of the appropriate letter or letters, the fund(s) and/or account group(s) that are affected by each of the transactions. If more than one fund is affected, be sure to show all of them.

(AICPA adapted)

PROBLEMS

P18-1 **Capital Projects Fund: Journal and Closing Entries, Financial Statements** The following information pertains to Eden Township's construction and financing of a new administration center:

Estimated total cost of project	$9,000,000
Project financing:	
State entitlement grant	3,000,000
General obligation bonds:	
Face amount	6,000,000
Stated interest rate	6%
Issue date	December 1, 19X1
Maturity date	November 30, 19X9

During Eden's year ended June 30, 19X2, the following events occurred that affect the capital projects fund established to account for this project:

July 1, 19X1—The capital projects fund borrowed $300,000 from the general fund for preliminary expenses.

July 9, 19X1—Engineering and planning costs of $200,000, for which no encumbrance had been recorded, were paid to Napp Associates.

December 1, 19X1—The bonds were sold at 101. Total proceeds were retained by the capital projects fund.

December 1, 19X1—The entitlement grant was formally approved by the state.

April 30, 19X2—A $7,000,000 contract was executed with Caro Construction Corp., the general contractors, for the major portion of the project. The contract provides that Eden will withhold 4% of all billings pending satisfactory completion of the project.

May 9, 19X2—$1,000,000 of the state grant was received.

June 10, 19X2—The $300,000 borrowed from the general fund was repaid.

June 30, 19X2—Progress billing of $1,200,000 was received from Caro.

Eden uses encumbrance accounting for budgetary control. Unencumbered appropriations lapse at the end of the year.

REQUIRED

a) Prepare journal entries in the administration center capital projects fund to record the foregoing transactions.

b) Prepare the June 30, 19X2, closing entries for the administration center capital projects fund.

c) Prepare the administration center capital projects fund balance sheet at June 30, 19X2.

(AICPA adapted)

P18-2 **Capital Projects Fund: Journal and Closing Entries, Financial Statements** The City of Westgate's fiscal year ends on June 30. During the fiscal year ended June 30, 19X8, the city authorized the construction of a new library and sale of general obligation term bonds to finance the construction of the library. The authorization imposed the following restrictions: construction cost was not to exceed $5,000,000, and annual interest rate was not to exceed 8-1/2%.

The city maintains budgetary accounts for the capital projects fund. The following transactions relating to the financing and constructing of the library occurred during the fiscal year beginning July 1, 19X8, and ending June 30, 19X9:

1. The budget was adopted by the city as follows: Estimated bond proceeds $5,000,000; estimated interest earnings on temporary investments $140,000 (which must be transferred to the library debt service fund); authorized construction cost for the library $5,000,000; and estimated transfers to library debt service fund $140,000.

2. On July 1, 19X8, the city issued $5,000,000 of 30-year 8% general obligation bonds for $5,100,000. The semiannual interest dates are December 31 and June 30. The premium of $100,000 was transferred to the library debt service fund.

3. On July 3, 19X8, the library capital projects fund invested $4,900,000 in short-term commercial paper. These purchases were at face value with no accrued interest. As noted earlier, interest on cash invested by the library capital projects fund must be transferred to the library debt service fund.

4. On July 5, 19X8, the city signed a contract with F&A Construction Company to build the library for $4,980,000.

5. On January 15, 19X9, the library capital projects fund received $3,040,000 from the maturity of short-term notes purchased on July 3. The cost of these notes was $3,000,000. The interest of $40,000 was transferred to the library debt service fund.

6. On January 20, 19X9, F&A Construction Company properly billed the city $3,000,000 for work performed on the new library. The contract calls for 10% retention until final inspection and acceptance of the building. The library capital projects fund paid F&A $2,700,000.

7. On June 30, 19X9, the library capital projects fund made adjusting entries to record accrued interest receivable of $103,000 and to record the interfund payable of the same amount to the library debt service fund.

8. The library capital projects fund made closing entries on June 30, 19X9.

REQUIRED

a) Prepare journal entries to record the eight preceding sets of facts in the library capital projects fund. List the transaction numbers (1 through 8) and give the necessary entry or entries. Do not record journal entries in any other fund or account group.

b) Prepare a balance sheet for the City of Westgate—library capital projects fund as of June 30, 19X9.

c) Prepare a statement of revenues, expenditures, and changes in the fund balance for the City of Westgate—library capital projects fund for the year ended June 30, 19X9.

(AICPA adapted)

P18-3 **Debt Service Fund Emphasis: Journal and Closing Entries, Financial Statement**   Selected transactions for the City of Sleepy Hollow for the fiscal year ended December 31, 19X4, are presented as follows:

1. The city issued $2,000,000 of general obligation term bonds for $2,050,000. The bond proceeds are to be used to construct a new police station, which is estimated to cost $2,000,000. The premium of $50,000 was transferred to the debt service fund.

2. The general fund transferred $12,000 to the debt service fund as required by a serial bond indenture.

3. Bond interest coupons in the amount of $8,000 were paid by the debt service fund.

4. General obligation serial bonds with a face value of $12,000 matured and were retired by the debt service fund. This installment completes the repayment of all serial bonds.

5. Accrued interest on unmatured bond indebtedness as of December 31, 19X4, was $4,000. However, the amount is not due until next year when the appropriation for interest will be made.

6. The debt service fund received a $2,000 transfer from a discontinued special revenue fund.

7. Investments of the debt service fund with a cost of $5,000 are sold for $5,300, which includes $300 of interest.

8. The city's enterprise fund issued $500,000 of revenue bonds at par value.

9. The police station in item (1) was completed on November 15, 19X4, at a cost of $2,000,000. The contractor properly billed the city $2,000,000 for the work performed on the new station. After inspection of the building the full $2,000,000 was paid to the contractor.

10. Special assessment bonds were issued for par value of $200,000 for the construction of residential storm sewers. The governmental unit stands ready to assume this debt in the event of default by the property owners.

REQUIRED

a) Prepare journal entries to record each of the preceding transactions in the appropriate fund(s) or account groups of the City of Sleepy Hollow for the fiscal year ended December 31, 19X4. Your answer sheet should be organized as follows:

Transaction No.	Fund or Account Group	Account Title and Explanation	Amount	
			Debit	Credit

b) Prepare closing entries for the debt service fund as of December 31, 19X4, and prepare the necessary entry in the general long-term debt account group to record the increase in the debt service fund balance.

c) Prepare a statement of revenues, expenditures, and changes in the fund balance for the debt service fund as of December 31, 19X4. (Assume that the amount in the fund balance account of the debt service fund was $9,500 on January 1, 19X4.)

P18-4 **Capital Projects Fund: Journal and Closing Entries, Financial Statements**   In a special election held on May 1, 19X7, the voters of the City of Nicknar approved a $10,000,000 issue of 6% general obligation bonds maturing in 20 years. The proceeds of this sale will be used to help finance the construction of a new civic center. The total cost of the project was estimated at $15,000,000. The remaining $5,000,000 will be financed by an irrevocable state grant that has been awarded. A capital projects fund was established to account for this project and was designated the civic center construction fund. The formal project authorization was appropriately recorded in a memorandum entry.

The following transactions occurred during the fiscal year beginning July 1, 19X7, and ending June 30, 19X8:

1. On July 1, the general fund loaned $500,000 to the civic center construction fund for defraying engineering and other expenses.

2. The state grant was recorded.

3. Preliminary engineering and planning costs of $320,000 were paid to Akron Engineering Company. There had been no encumbrance for this cost.

4. On December 1, the bonds were sold at 101. The premium on the bonds was transferred to the debt service fund.

5. On March 15, a contract for $12,000,000 was entered into with Candu Construction Company for the major part of the project.

6. Orders were placed for materials estimated to cost $55,000.

7. On April 1, a partial payment of $2,500,000 was received from the state.

8. The materials that were previously ordered in item (6) were received at a cost of $51,000 and paid for.

9. On June 15, a progress billing of $2,000,000 was received from Candu Construction for work done on the project. As per the terms of the contract, the city will withhold 6% of any billing until the project is completed.

10. The general fund was repaid the $500,000 previously loaned.

REQUIRED

a) Prepare journal entries to record the transactions in the civic center construction fund for the period July 1, 19X7, through June 30, 19X8, and the appropriate closing entries at June 30, 19X8. Do not record journal entries in any other fund or account group.

b) Prepare a balance sheet of the civic center construction fund as of June 30, 19X8.

c) Prepare a statement of revenues, expenditures, and changes in fund balance for the civic center construction fund for the year ended June 30, 19X8.

(AICPA adapted)

P18-5 **Identify and Record Entries in Appropriate Funds and Account Groups (Emphasis on Special Assessments)**   On January 1, 19X8, the City of Urbanna established a capital projects fund and a debt service fund to account for the financing and construction of sidewalks and sewers in a certain section of the city. The $125,000 estimated cost of the improvements will be collected from certain property owners: $25,000 is due immediately in 19X8 (to be used for the construction project), and the remainder (to be used to retire special assessments serial bonds) is due in four equal annual installments beginning January 1, 19X9. The assessments of $100,000 due in future years will carry interest of 10%, and the interest will be paid semiannually each July 1 and January 1.

Special assessment serial bonds with a par value of $100,000 (9% coupon rate) were approved for issuance. Interest on the bonds is paid semiannually each July 1 and January 1, and the bond principal is to be repaid in four equal installments beginning January 1, 19X9.

The following events related to the city's special assessment transactions during the fiscal year ended December 31, 19X8.

1. Special assessment bonds of $100,000 were issued at par value on January 1, 19X8.

2. Special assessment receivables are levied on January 1, 19X8.

3. Current assessments in the amount of $25,000 are collected when due in 19X8.

4. A construction contract for the sidewalk and sewer improvements was signed for $120,000.

5. Billings of $90,000 were presented to the city by the contractor, and payments of $80,000 were made.

6. On July 1, 19X8, interest expense on special assessment bonds is paid. On the same date, interest revenue earned on the deferred special assessments is collected.

7. Deferred special assessments of $25,000 that are scheduled for collection on January 1, 19X9, are reclassified, and an equal amount of deferred revenue is recognized as revenue.

REQUIRED

a) Prepare journal entries in the capital projects fund, the debt service fund, and the general long-term debt account group to record the preceding transactions during the fiscal year ended December 31, 19X8.

b) Prepare closing entries for the capital projects fund and the debt service fund at December 31, 19X8.

c) Prepare balance sheets for the capital projects fund and the debt service fund at December 31, 19X8.

d) Prepare statements of revenues, expenditures, and changes in fund balance for the capital projects fund and the debt service fund for the fiscal year ended December 31, 19X8.

e) Assuming that the City of Urbanna accounts for the construction of sidewalks and sewers in its general fixed assets account group, prepare the necessary entry in the general fixed assets group as of December 31, 19X8.

f) Prepare all necessary journal entries for the capital projects fund and the debt service fund as of January 1, 19X9.

P18-6   **Enterprise Fund: Journal and Closing Entries, Financial Statements**   The City of Outer Banks provides electric energy to its citizens through the electric utility fund. The electric utility fund is supported by revenue from the sale of energy. Plant expansion is financed by the issuance of bonds, which are repaid out of revenues.

Presented here is the balance sheet of the electric utility fund as of the end of its fiscal year ended June 30, 19X6.

Assets

Current assets:		
Cash	$ 90,000	
Accounts receivable	50,000	
Less: Allowance for uncollectible accounts	(4,000)	
Due from other funds	10,000	
Materials and supplies	3,000	$ 149,000
Restricted assets:		
Cash from revenue bonds restricted to		
construction payments	$ 70,000	
Cash and investments for customer deposits	16,000	86,000
Utility plant in service:		
Land	$210,000	
Plant and equipment	800,000	
Less: Accumulated depreciation	(120,000)	890,000
Construction in progress		175,000
Total assets		$1,300,000

Liabilities and Fund Equity

Current liabilities (payable from current assets):		
Vouchers payable	$ 20,000	
Accrued interest payable	6,000	$ 26,000
Current liabilities (payable from restricted assets):		
Construction contracts payable	$ 23,000	
Customer deposits	16,000	39,000
Long-term liabilities:		
Revenue bonds payable		188,000
Fund equity:		
Contributed capital—municipality		800,000
Retained earnings		247,000
Total liabilities and fund equity		$1,300,000

During the year ended June 30, 19X7, the following transactions were related to the electric utility fund.

1. Billings to citizens and to other departments of the City of Outer Banks for electric energy that was provided totaled $756,000 and $150,000, respectively.

2. Materials and supplies in the amount of $2,000 are acquired on account. The periodic inventory system is used to account for materials and supplies.

3. A progress billing of $20,000 was received from the contractors for the construction of a steam boiler; this amount will be paid later from the proceeds of the revenue bonds.

4. Accounts receivable that were collected totaled $750,000, and $140,000 of the amount due from other funds was collected.

5. The following operating expenses were paid:

Cost of power purchased from a neighboring utility	$360,000
Salaries and wages	250,000
Heating and lighting	51,000
Other	90,000
	$751,000

6. Interest of $18,000 was paid on the bonds; this included the accrued interest of $6,000 on the June 30, 19X6, balance sheet.

7. Steam-generating equipment under construction at the beginning of the year is placed in service; construction costs incurred on this project totaled $68,000.

8. Vouchers payable totaling $12,000 were paid.

9. $400,000 of 15-year 9% electric revenue bonds was sold at face value on May 31, 19X7.

10. Accrued interest on revenue bonds payable as of June 30, 19X7, totaled $9,000.

11. Inventory of materials and supplies as of June 30, 19X7, totaled $1,000.

12. Depreciation on the electric utility plant and equipment totaled $80,000 for the year ended June 30, 19X7.

13. Construction contracts payable of $40,000 were paid out of the proceeds from the revenue bonds; this included the construction contracts payable of $23,000 on the June 30, 19X6, balance sheet.

14. Deposits amounting to $2,000 were returned to customers who discontinued their service.

REQUIRED

a) For the period July 1, 19X6, through June 30, 19X7, prepare journal entries to record the preceding transactions in the electric utility fund.

b) Prepare closing entries for the electric utility fund at June 30, 19X7.

c) Prepare a balance sheet for the electric utility fund at June 30, 19X7.

d) Prepare a statement of revenues, expenses, and changes in retained earnings for the electric utility fund for the year ended June 30, 19X7.

P18-7 **Internal Service Fund: Journal and Closing Entries, Financial Statements** The City of Merlot operates a central garage through an internal service fund to provide garage space and repairs for all city-owned and city-operated vehicles. The central garage fund was established by a contribution of $200,000 from the general fund on July 1, 19X6, at which time the building was acquired. The after-closing trial balance at June 30, 19X8, was as follows:

	Debit	Credit
Cash	$150,000	
Due from general fund	20,000	
Inventory of materials and supplies	80,000	
Land	60,000	
Building	200,000	
Allowance for depreciation—building		$ 10,000
Machinery and equipment	56,000	
Allowance for depreciation—machinery and equipment		12,000
Vouchers payable		38,000
Contributed capital—general fund		200,000
Retained earnings		306,000
	$566,000	$566,000

The following information applies to the fiscal year ended June 30, 19X9.

1. Materials and supplies were purchased on account for $74,000. The fund uses the perpetual inventory method.

2. The inventory of materials and supplies at June 30, 19X9, was $58,000, which agreed with the physical count taken.

3. Salaries and wages paid to employees totaled $230,000, including related fringe benefits.

4. A billing was received from the enterprise fund for utility charges totaling $30,000 and was paid.

5. Depreciation of the building was recorded in the amount of $5,000. Depreciation of the machinery and equipment amounted to $8,000.

6. Billings to other departments for services rendered to them were as follows:

General fund	$262,000
Water and sewer fund	84,000
Special revenue fund	32,000

7. Unpaid interfund receivable balances at June 30, 19X9, were as follows:

General fund	$ 6,000
Special revenue fund	16,000

8. Vouchers payable at June 30, 19X9, were $14,000.

REQUIRED

a) For the period July 1, 19X8, through June 30, 19X9, prepare journal entries to record all the transactions in the central garage fund accounts.

b) Prepare closing entries for the central garage fund at June 30, 19X9.

c) Prepare a balance sheet for the central garage fund at June 30, 19X9.

d) Prepare a statement of revenues, expenses, and changes in retained earnings for the central garage fund for the year ended June 30, 19X9.

(AICPA adapted)

P18-8 **Nonexpendable and Expendable Trust Funds: Journal Entries and Financial Statements** On March 1, 19X3, $100,000 in cash was donated by Mary Pickens to the City of Parkhill for the establishment of the Pickens scholarship endowment (nonexpendable trust) fund to support city residents attending a local university. The terms of the trust agreement are that the principal of $100,000 is to be maintained intact and the earnings from the trust are to be used for scholarships that are to be accounted for in the scholarship awards (expendable trust) fund.

The following events relate to the establishment and operations of these funds during the year 19X3.

1. The city received the $100,000 donation from Mary Pickens on March 1, 19X3.

2. The entire $100,000 was invested on March 1, 19X3, in 11% bonds with a total face value of $100,000; the city acquired the bonds at par value. Interest is paid on the bonds each September 1 and March 1.

3. Interest on the bonds is received on September 1 and recorded in the Pickens scholarship endowment fund.

4. Revenues on the bonds in item (3) are transferred to the scholarship awards fund.

5. Scholarships totaling $5,000 were awarded to students.

6. Bonds held for investment were sold on December 31 at par value of $50,000 plus $1,833 interest accrued since September 1.

7. Revenue on the bonds sold in item (6) is transferred to the scholarship awards fund.

8. Accrued interest on the bond investments is recorded as of December 31, 19X3, in the Pickens scholarship endowment fund and reflected in the scholarship awards fund.

REQUIRED

a) Prepare the necessary journal entries in the Pickens scholarship endowment fund and the scholarship awards fund to record the preceding transactions.

b) Prepare closing entries for the Pickens scholarship endowment fund and the scholarship awards fund as of December 31, 19X3.

c) Prepare a balance sheet and a statement of revenues, expenses, and changes in fund balance for the Pickens scholarship endowment fund for the fiscal year ended December 31, 19X3.

d) Prepare a balance sheet and a statement of revenues, expenditures, and changes in fund balance for the scholarship awards fund for the fiscal year ended December 31, 19X3.

P18-9 **Agency and General Fund: Journal Entries** In compliance with a newly enacted state law, Dial County assumed the responsibility of collecting all property taxes levied within its boundaries as of July 1, 19X5. A composite property tax rate per $100 of net assessed valuation was developed for the fiscal year ending June 30, 19X6, and is presented as follows:

Dial County general fund	$ 6.00
Eton City general fund	3.00
Bart Township general fund	1.00
	$10.00

All property taxes are due in quarterly installments and, when collected, are then distributed to the governmental units that are represented in the composite rate. In order to administer collection and distribution of such taxes, the county has established a tax agency fund.

Additional information:

1. In order to reimburse the county for estimated administrative expenses of operating the tax agency fund, the tax agency fund is to deduct 2% from the tax collections each quarter for Eton City and Bart Township. The total amount deducted is to be remitted to the Dial County general fund.

2. Current year tax levies to be collected by the tax agency fund are as follows:

	Gross Levy	Estimated Amount to Be Collected
Dial County	$3,600,000	$3,500,000
Eton City	1,800,000	1,740,000
Bart Township	600,000	560,000
	$6,000,000	$5,800,000

3. As of September 30, 19X5, the tax agency fund has received $1,440,000 in first-quarter payments. On October 1, this fund made a distribution to the three governmental units.

REQUIRED

For the period July 1, 19X5, through October 1, 19X5, prepare journal entries to record the preceding transactions for the following funds: Dial County tax agency fund, Dial County general fund, Eton City general fund, and Bart Township general fund. Your answer sheet should be organized as follows:

	Dial County Tax Agency Fund		Dial County General Fund		Eton City General Fund		Bart Township General Fund	
Accounts	Debit	Credit	Debit	Credit	Debit	Credit	Debit	Credit

(AICPA adapted)

P18-10 **Identify and Record Entries in Appropriate Funds and Account Groups** The Village of Dexter was recently incorporated and began financial operations on July 1, 19X8, the beginning of its fiscal year.

The following transactions occurred during this first fiscal year, July 1, 19X8, to June 30, 19X9:

1. The village council adopted a budget for general operations during the fiscal year ending June 30, 19X9. Revenues were estimated at $400,000. Legal authorizations for budgeted expenditures were $394,000.

2. Property taxes were levied in the amount of $390,000; it was estimated that 2% of this amount would prove to be uncollectible. These taxes are available as of the date of levy to finance current expenditures.

3. During the year a resident of the village donated marketable securities valued at $50,000 to the village under the terms of a trust agreement. The terms of the trust agreement stipulated that the principal amount is to be kept intact. Use of revenue generated by the securities is restricted to financing college scholarships for needy students. Revenue earned and received on these marketable securities amounted to $5,500 through June 30, 19X9.

4. A general fund transfer of $5,000 was made to establish an internal service fund to provide for a permanent investment in inventory.

5. The village decided to install lighting in the village park, and a special assessment project was authorized to install the lighting at a cost of $75,000; $72,000 is to be provided by special assessments, and $3,000 is to be provided by the general fund. The appropriation was formally recorded.

6. The assessments were levied for $72,000, with the village contributing $3,000 out of the general fund. All assessments were collected during the year, including the village's contribution.

7. A contract for $75,000 was let for the installation of the lighting. At June 30, 19X9, the contract was completed but not approved. The contractor was paid all but 5%, which was retained to ensure compliance with the terms of the contract. Encumbrances and other budgetary accounts are maintained.

8. During the year the internal service fund purchased for cash various supplies at a cost of $1,900. The fund uses the perpetual inventory method.

9. Cash collections recorded by the general fund during the year were as follows:

Property taxes	$386,000
Licenses and permits	7,000

10. The village council decided to build a village hall at an estimated cost of $500,000 to replace space occupied in rented facilities. The village does not record project authorizations. It was decided that general obligation bonds bearing interest at 6% would be issued. On June 30, 19X9, the bonds were issued at their face value of $500,000, payable at the end of 20 years. No contracts have been signed for this project, and no expenditures have been made.

11. A fire truck was purchased for $15,000, and the voucher was approved and paid by the general fund. This expenditure was previously encumbered for $15,000.

REQUIRED
Prepare journal entries to record each of the preceding transactions in the appropriate fund(s) or

account groups of Dexter Village for the fiscal year ended June 30, 19X9. Use the following funds and account groups.

General fund	Expendable trust fund
Capital projects fund	General long-term debt account group
Internal service fund	General fixed assets account group
Nonexpendable trust fund	

Each journal entry should be numbered to correspond with the preceding transactions. Do *not* prepare closing entries for any fund.

Your answer sheet should be organized as follows:

Transaction Number	Fund or Account Group	Account Title and Explanation	Amounts Debit Credit

(AICPA adapted)

P18-11 **Identify and Record Entries in Appropriate Funds and Account Groups** The following transactions represent practical situations frequently encountered in accounting for municipal governments. Each transaction is independent of the others.

1. The city council of Bernardville adopted a budget for the general operations of the government during the new fiscal year. Revenues were estimated at $695,000. Legal authorizations for budgeted expenditures were $650,000.

2. Taxes of $160,000 were levied for the special revenue fund of Millstown. One percent was estimated to be uncollectible.

3. a) On July 25, 19X3, office supplies estimated to cost $2,390 were ordered for the city manager's office of Bullersville. Bullersville, which operates on the calendar year, does not maintain an inventory of such supplies.

b) The supplies ordered July 25 were received on August 9, 19X3, accompanied by an invoice for $2,500.

4. On October 10, 19X3, the general fund of Washingtonville repaid to the utility fund a loan of $1,000 plus $40 interest. The loan had been made earlier in the fiscal year.

5. A prominent citizen died and left 10 acres of undeveloped land to Harper City for a future school site. The donor's cost of the land was $55,000. The fair value of the land was $85,000.

6. a) On March 6, 19X3, Dahlstrom City issued 4% special assessment bonds payable March 6, 19X8, at face value of $90,000. Interest is payable annually. Dahlstrom City, which operates on the calendar year, will use the proceeds to finance a curbing project. The city is obligated to pay these bonds in case of default by the property owners.

b) On October 29, 19X3, the full $84,000 cost of the completed curbing project was accrued. Also, appropriate closing entries were made with regard to the project.

7. a) Conrad Thamm, a citizen of Basking Knoll, donated common stock valued at $22,000 to the city under a trust agreement. Under the terms of the agreement, the principal amount is to be kept intact. Use of revenue from the stock is restricted to financing academic college scholarships for needy students.

b) On December 14, 19X3, dividends of $1,100 were received on the stock donated by Mr. Thamm.

8. a) On February 23, 19X3, the town of Lincoln, which operates on the calendar year, issued 4%, ten-year general obligation bonds with a face value of $300,000 to finance the construction of an addition to the city hall. Total proceeds were $308,000.

b) On December 31, 19X3, the addition to the city hall was officially approved, the full cost of $297,000 was paid to the contractor, and appropriate closing entries were made with regard to the project. (Assume that no entries have been made with regard to the project since February 23, 19X3.)

REQUIRED

For each transaction, prepare the necessary journal entries for all the funds and account groups involved. Use the following headings for your workpaper:

Transaction Number	Journal Entries	Amount		Fund or Account Group
		Debit	Credit	

In the far-right column, indicate in which fund or account group each entry is to be made, using the following coding:

Funds:

General	G
Special revenue	SR
Capital projects	CP
Debt service	DS
Enterprise	E
Internal service	IS
Nonexpendable trust	NT
Expendable trust	ET
Agency	A

Account groups:

General fixed assets	GFA
General long-term debt	LTD

(AICPA adapted)

P18-12   Identify and Record Entries in Appropriate Funds (Other Than General Fund) and Account Groups   Your examination of the accounts of your new client, the City of Delmas, as of June 30, 19X1, revealed the following:

1. On December 31, 19X0, the city paid $115,000 out of general fund revenues for a central garage to service its vehicles, with $67,500 being applicable to the building, which has an estimated life of 25 years; $14,500 to land; and $33,000 to machinery and equipment, which have an estimated life of 15 years. A $12,200 cash contribution was received by the garage from the general fund on the same date.

2. The garage maintains no records, but a review of deposit slips and canceled checks revealed the following:

Collections for services to city departments financed from the general fund	$30,000
Office salaries	6,000
Utilities	700
Mechanics' wages	11,000
Materials and supplies	9,000

3. The garage had uncollected billings of $2,000, accounts payable for materials and supplies of $500, and an inventory of materials and supplies of $1,500 at June 30, 19X1.

4. On June 30, 19X1, the city issued $200,000 in special assessment bonds at par to finance a street improvement project estimated to cost $225,000. The project is to be paid by a $25,000 levy against the city (payable in fiscal year 19X1–X2) and $200,000 against property owners (payable in five equal annual installments beginning October 1, 19X1). The levy was made on June 30. A $215,000 contract was let for the project on July 2, 19X1, but work had not begun. The city is obligated to pay this debt in the event of default by the property owners.

5. On July 1, two years ago, the city issued $400,000 in 30-year, 6% general obligation term bonds of the same date at par to finance the construction of a public health center. Construction was completed and the contractors fully paid a total of $397,500 in fiscal year 19X0–X1.

6. For the health center bonds, the city sets aside general fund revenues that are sufficient to cover interest (payable semiannually on July 1 and January 1 of each year) and $5,060 to provide for the retirement of the bond principal, the latter transfer being made at the end of each fiscal year and invested at the beginning of the next. Your investigation reveals that such investments earned $304 during fiscal year 19X0–X1, the exact amount budgeted. This $304 was received in cash and will be invested at the beginning of the next year.

REQUIRED

The preceding information disclosed by your examination was recorded only in the general fund. Prepare the formal entries as of June 30, 19X1, to adjust the funds other than the general fund. Entries should be classified into clearly labeled groups for each fund, and fund titles should be selected from the following list:

Special revenue fund
Capital projects fund
Debt service fund
Trust fund (endowment fund)
Agency fund
Internal service fund
Enterprise fund
General fixed assets account group
General long-term debt account group

(AICPA adapted)

ISSUES IN ACCOUNTING JUDGMENT

I18-1   **Recording Expenditures and Access to Cash**   The Vice President-Finance of Town University was in a quandary. The University President was proposing that the general fund borrow temporarily $1,000,000 from the capital projects fund for current expenditures due to a short-fall in tuition revenues for the current year. The money in the capital projects fund had been received from special revenue bonds whose proceeds were dedicated to paying for a new dormitory under construction. The President and the Vice President-Finance both knew that the dormitory construction would not be completed until the next fiscal year when the University would have received additional funds and expenditure authority. The difficulty, the Vice President-Finance knew, was not in borrowing the cash, but in reporting that expenditures exceeded revenues by the $1,000,000. The excess of expenditures over revenues reported in the current fiscal year would place the general fund balance in a deficit position.

REQUIRED

Discuss the accounting and management issues raised by this case.

I18-2   **The Reporting Entity**   Mercy Hospital was formed by the City of Cleopolis almost fifty years ago. Mercy Hospital operates under a charter issued by the City Council and is run by a thirteen-member board of trustees, seven appointed by the City Council and six elected by doctors authorized to practice at Mercy Hospital. The trustees appointed by the City Council are appointed for seven-year terms, one each year. However, City Council can replace any trustee under emergency legislation for failing to carry out their duties in a prudent manner. Mercy Hospital has been partially supported by a special appropriation by the City Council for each of the past nine years. The City Council deems this in the interest of the city because Mercy Hospital operates a special emergency medical operation in the downtown area. The hospital's other revenues come from private insurance (35%) and medical benefits from other governmental units (55%).

REQUIRED

How should the relationship with Mercy Hospital be disclosed in the City of Cleopolis's Comprehensive Annual Financial Report?

CHAPTER 119

Accounting for Nonprofit Organizations

ACCOUNTING STANDARDS FOR NONPROFIT ORGANIZATIONS 968

HISTORICAL DEVELOPMENT 968

THE GAAP HIERARCHY 968

NONPROFIT ACCOUNTING PRACTICES 969

COLLEGES AND UNIVERSITIES 971

FUND STRUCTURE 971

Current Funds 971   Board-Designated Funds 972

ACCOUNTING METHODS OF COLLEGES AND UNIVERSITIES 972

Accrual Accounting and Depreciation 972   Summer Terms 973   Mandatory and Nonmandatory Transfers 973 Budgetary and Encumbrance Accounting 973

ACCOUNTING FOR COLLEGE AND UNIVERSITY CURRENT FUNDS 974

ACCOUNTING FOR COLLEGE AND UNIVERSITY LOAN FUNDS 978

ACCOUNTING FOR COLLEGE AND UNIVERSITY ENDOWMENT AND SIMILAR FUNDS 978

ACCOUNTING FOR COLLEGE AND UNIVERSITY ANNUITY AND LIFE INCOME FUNDS 980

ACCOUNTING FOR COLLEGE AND UNIVERSITY PLANT FUNDS 982

Unexpended Plant Fund 982   Renewal and Replacement Plant Fund 982   Retirement of Indebtedness Plant Fund 984   Investment in Plant Fund 984   Physical Plant and Depreciation 985

ACCOUNTING FOR COLLEGE AND UNIVERSITY AGENCY FUNDS 985

CLOSING ENTRIES FOR FUNDS OTHER THAN CURRENT FUNDS 985

ANNUAL FINANCIAL STATEMENTS OF COLLEGES AND UNIVERSITIES 990

HOSPITALS 990

FUND STRUCTURE 993

CLASSIFICATION AND RECOGNITION OF HOSPITAL REVENUES 993

Patient Service Revenues 993   Other Operating Revenues 997   Nonoperating Revenues 998

CLASSIFICATION OF OPERATING EXPENSES 998

ACCOUNTING FOR HOSPITAL UNRESTRICTED AND RESTRICTED FUNDS 998

Specific Purpose Funds 999   Plant Replacement and Expansion Fund 1004   Endowment Funds 1005

NO CLOSING ENTRIES FOR RESTRICTED FUNDS 1007

ANNUAL FINANCIAL STATEMENTS OF HOSPITALS 1007

VOLUNTARY HEALTH AND WELFARE ORGANIZATIONS 1010

ACCOUNTING METHODS OF VOLUNTARY HEALTH AND WELFARE ORGANIZATIONS 1010

Public Support and Revenue 1010   Expenses 1010 Donated Services, Materials, and Facilities 1011

FUND STRUCTURE 1011

Current Funds 1011   Land, Building, and Equipment Fund (Plant Fund) 1012   Endowment Funds 1012 Custodian and Other Funds 1013

ACCOUNTING FOR VHWO FUNDS 1013

ANNUAL FINANCIAL STATEMENTS 1013

OTHER NONPROFIT ORGANIZATIONS 1013

ACCOUNTING METHODS OF OTHER NONPROFIT ORGANIZATIONS 1022

Revenues, Public Support, and Capital Additions 1022 Expenses 1022   Donated Services, Materials, and Facilities 1022

FUND STRUCTURE 1023

Operating Funds 1023   Plant (Land, Building, and Equipment) Funds 1023   Endowment and Other Funds 1024

ANNUAL FINANCIAL STATEMENTS 1024

SUMMARY 1025

This chapter discusses the accounting and reporting principles and practices for *nonprofit* organizations including colleges and universities, hospitals, voluntary health and welfare organizations, and other nonprofit organizations. Nonprofit organizations, which are also called *not-for-profit organizations,* are distinguished by the following characteristics (*FASB Concepts Statement No. 4,* par. 6):

1. Contributions of significant amounts of resources from resource providers who do not expect commensurate or proportionate pecuniary return

2. Operating purposes other than to provide goods or services at a profit

3. Absence of ownership interests like those of business enterprises

The following issues section explores the distinctive character of nonprofit organizations.

ISSUES

Objectives, Revenues, and Governance of Nonprofit Organizations

As their name suggests, nonprofit organizations are not established to earn a profit. Rather, they are established to deliver some product or service to their members or to the community in which they reside without regard to the relationship between the fee charged and the cost of the product or service to the organization. Thus, the objectives of nonprofit organizations are defined in terms of particular products or services rather than the economic impact of those products or services on the organization.

It is not surprising, therefore, that fees charged the recipients of services or products provided by nonprofit organizations are frequently insufficient to cover the entire cost of providing the services. Frequently, nonprofit organizations provide services that aid governments, social agencies, and charitable interests. As a result, additional revenues are frequently provided by governments, foundations, and other organizations or individuals that are interested in supporting the work of the nonprofit organization. For example, private colleges aid governments in carrying out their responsibilities for education. Consequently, private colleges are supported by student loan programs and research grants that are sponsored by the federal government in addition to student tuition and fees and alumni donations.

Nonprofit organizations like other organizations are run by managers and other administrative personnel who are responsible to a governing board. In profit-oriented organizations, the governing board is responsible, in turn, to a group of owners who view their equity in the organization as an investment for profit. In nonprofit organizations, in contrast, the governing board may be responsible to a group of owners or members but they usually view their equity interest as a commitment to producing the service or product rather than as an investment for profit. In addition, the governing boards of many nonprofit organizations represent recipients of the service provided, funding agencies, or segments of the general public without any relationship to an ownership interest in the net assets of the organization.

These differences between businesses and nonprofit organizations lead to distinctive accounting standards and practices. Indeed, even within nonprofit organizations, significant differences in accounting standards and practices can be observed for different types of nonprofit organizations. For this reason, it is necessary to divide nonprofit organizations into four groups—colleges and universities, hospitals, voluntary health and welfare organizations, and other nonprofit organizations—and to consider each group separately. Before discussing accounting for these four major groups, let us consider the principal sources of nonprofit accounting standards and the general structure of nonprofit accounting systems.

ACCOUNTING STANDARDS FOR NONPROFIT ORGANIZATIONS

Although the jurisdiction of the Financial Accounting Standards Board (FASB) and the Governmental Accounting Standards Board (GASB) over nonprofits is clearly specified, this jurisdictional division does not follow institutional lines. Hospitals and universities, for example, exist in both the public and private sectors. If the GASB and FASB issue different standards, then accounting and reporting will differ for very similar organizations simply because one is in the private sector and the other is in the public sector. Furthermore, industry and professional groups are frequently organized along institutional lines that cut across both sectors, making it difficult to organize support for improvement in accounting and reporting standards.

Historical Development

Authoritative pronouncements of accounting and reporting standards for nonprofit organizations have come from a number of sources. The first accounting and reporting standards were issued by industry and professional organizations devoted to colleges and universities, hospitals, and various other nonprofit organizations. Later, the AICPA, FASB, and GASB also issued standards.[1]

Under a 1984 agreement between the FASB and the GASB, generally accepted accounting principles applicable to public-sector utilities, hospitals, colleges and universities, pension plans, and other similar nonprofit organizations were to be "guided by standards of the FASB except in circumstances where the GASB has issued a pronouncement applicable to such entities or activities" (*FASB Statement No. 93,* par. 45). Under this agreement, the pronouncements of the GASB applied only to state and local governmental units (including governmental hospitals, universities, etc.) and were *not* applicable to other types of nonprofit organizations; however, entities subject to the GASB were also subject to the FASB in matters not addressed by the GASB.

The GAAP Hierarchy

In 1992, the AICPA Auditing Standards Board issued *Statement of Auditing Standards No. 69* to clarify the meaning of the phrase "present fairly in conformity with generally accepted accounting principles" in the independent auditor's report. As explained in Chapter 11, *SAS No. 69* created two separate hierarchies of pronouncements: one for nongovernmental entities and one for state and local governments. Furthermore, the highest authority in the state and local government hierarchy was given to GASB Statements

---

[1] It was not until 1979 that the Financial Accounting Standards Board (FASB) assumed responsibility for setting accounting and reporting standards for all nonprofit organizations except governments. In 1979, the FASB issued *Statement No. 32,* "Specialized Accounting and Reporting Principles and Practices in AICPA Statements of Position and Guides on Accounting and Auditing Matters." While *Statement No. 32* stopped short of endorsing the AICPA statements of position (SOPs) and accounting and auditing guides as generally accepted accounting principles, it did state that the AICPA SOPs and guides were "preferable" accounting principles for purposes of justifying a change in principles under *APB Opinion No. 20,* "Accounting Changes." More recently, the AICPA Auditing Standards Board *SAS No. 69* has clarified the status of the various pronouncements in determining generally accepted accounting principles.

and Interpretations and "AICPA and FASB pronouncements specifically made applicable by GASB Statements and Interpretations" (*SAS No. 69,* par. 12a). Thus, the hierarchy removes the need for the GASB to issue "negative standards" that exempt governmental nonprofits from the effects of FASB pronouncements on matters until the GASB has an opportunity to consider the matter.[2]

The hierarchy also identifies the GASB and the FASB as the primary sources of authoritative pronouncements on nonprofit accounting and reporting within their respective jurisdictions. Of course, the hierarchy does not prevent the FASB and GASB from issuing different standards for nongovernmental and governmental organizations.

NONPROFIT ACCOUNTING PRACTICES

The accounting systems and practices of nonprofit organizations are similar, in some respects, to those of government accounting; their major similarity is their use of fund accounting. Fund accounting usage is justified by restrictions on the uses of financial resources because it permits accounting and reporting for these resources according to their specified use.

These nonprofit organizations (colleges and universities, hospitals, voluntary health and welfare organizations, and all other nonprofit organizations) also have similarities among themselves, notably their service-oriented objectives, lack of profit motive, use of fund accounting, and use of accrual accounting for fair presentation of their financial statements in accordance with generally accepted accounting principles. The fund structures frequently found in these organizations are shown in Exhibit 19-1.

Despite their similarities, the differences among nonprofits warrant separate treatment under the following four headings: colleges and universities, hospitals, voluntary health and welfare organizations, and other nonprofit organizations. In recent years, both the FASB and the GASB have worked to create standards that improve the accounting and reporting for these groups of organizations. In 1993, for example, the FASB issued two new standards, *FASB Statements No. 117 and 116:* one containing broad general standards for general purpose financial statements of nonprofits, and the other reforming accounting for contributions. The purpose of the financial reporting standards is to foster reporting of basic information that focuses on the entity as a whole and thereby better serves the needs of external users of the statements. The following issues section illustrates several aspects of accounting for contributions.

ISSUES

Revenue from Contributions

Contributions are unconditional, voluntary, nonreciprocal transfers of assets (or cancellations of liabilities) by a donor. Traditionally, nonprofit organizations have recorded contributions on a cash basis and have not recognized pledges as receivables; further, most nonprofit organizations under GASB jurisdiction will continue to account for contributions on a cash basis. Under *FASB Statement No. 116,* however, pledges that represent unconditional promises to transfer assets should be recognized as revenue when the pledge is received and measured at their fair value. (Although the fair value of pledges is nor-

---

[2] *GASB Statement No. 8* is an example of a "negative standard." It exempts governmental universities and certain other governmental nonprofits from the requirement of *FASB Statement No. 93* that all nonprofits recognize depreciation on long-lived tangible assets (other than works of art and historical treasures).

EXHIBIT 19-1	**FUND STRUCTURES FOR NONPROFIT ORGANIZATIONS**	

Colleges and Universities

1. Current funds
   —Unrestricted current funds
   —Restricted current funds

2. Loan funds

3. Endowment and similar funds

4. Annuity and life income funds

5. Plant funds
   —Unexpended plant fund
   —Renewal and replacement plant fund
   —Retirement of indebtedness plant fund
   —Investment in plant fund

6. Agency funds

Hospitals

1. Unrestricted funds (including board-designated funds and property, plant and equipment funds)

2. Restricted funds
   —Specific purpose funds
   —Plant replacement and expansion funds
   —Endowment funds

Voluntary Health and Welfare Organizations

1. Current funds
   —Current unrestricted funds
   —Current restricted funds

2. Land, building, and equipment fund (plant fund)

3. Endowment funds

4. Custodian funds

5. Loan funds

6. Annuity funds

Other Nonprofit ("78–10") Organizations

1. Operating funds
   —Unrestricted operating funds
   —Restricted operating funds

2. Plant funds

3. Endowment funds

4. Custodian (agency) funds

5. Loan funds

6. Annuity and life income funds

mally the present value of the estimated future cash flow, net realizable value is an acceptable approximation to present value for pledges to be collected within the next year.) Thus, nonprofits under the jurisdiction of the FASB must record the fair value of pledges received as revenue and a receivable.

FASB Statement No. 116 makes exceptions to the revenue recognition requirement for contributed services and contributed museum collection items. Contributed services should not be recognized as revenue unless they replace services that would otherwise be purchased. Contributed works of art and historical treasures added to the collections of nonprofit institutions should not be recognized as revenue unless the museum capitalizes its collection. If a museum capitalizes *acquired* (purchased) collection items, as the FASB encourages them to do, then *contributed* items should also be capitalized and the fair value should be recognized as revenue. If a museum does not capitalize its collection, then contributed items should not be recognized as revenue.

Although contributions must be unconditional (in that the transfer is not conditional on specified future events), the use of contributed assets may be restricted by the donor. Restrictions may also arise from circumstances surrounding the receipt of a contribution, as when pledged resources are not available for use until future years because they have yet to be transferred by (collected from) the donor. Under *FASB Statement No. 116,* pledges to be collected in future years are viewed as *temporarily restricted,* and nonprofits subject to FASB jurisdiction are required to report temporarily restricted funds and activities separately (see *FASB Statement No. 117* for additional details).

As efforts to develop accounting standards move forward, we should expect greater uniformity of accounting practices and financial reporting in this important segment of economic and social activity.

COLLEGES AND UNIVERSITIES

Two distinct but similar accounting and reporting models are available to colleges and universities. The first, called "the AICPA audit guide model," is set forth in the AICPA's *Audits of Colleges and Universities* as amended by *SOP No. 74-8* and various FASB pronouncements. The second, called "the governmental model," is set forth in *NCGA Statement No. 1* as amended by various NCGA and GASB pronouncements. Nongovernmental (private sector) colleges and universities must use the AICPA model under FASB direction as required by *SAS No. 69.* Governmental colleges and universities may use either model (*GASB Statement No. 15,* par. 4); however, the majority of governmental colleges and universities use the AICPA model.[3] The presentation that follows emphasizes the AICPA model as applied by many colleges and universities under GASB jurisdiction.

Fund Structure

Most colleges and universities employ the following fund types: current funds, loan funds, endowment funds, annuity and life income funds, plant funds, and agency funds. These funds are discussed in the following paragraphs.

Current Funds

The current funds of a college or university (which are similar to general funds) are used to account for resources that are expendable in carrying out the operating purposes of the educational institution on a day-to-day basis. Such activities usually relate to the instructional, research, and public service activities of the institution. Current funds consist of two subgroups: unrestricted current funds and restricted current funds.

An *unrestricted current fund* is used to account for resources that have no restrictions as to the operating purposes for which they may be expended. Typical sources of revenues for unrestricted current funds include student tuition and fees; government appropriations, grants, and contracts; private gifts and grants; unrestricted income from endowment funds; auxiliary enterprise revenue (residence halls, food services, intercollegiate athletics, bookstores, and the like); expired term endowments; and so on. Typical operating expenditures are for instructional costs (such as faculty salaries), research (both departmental and sponsored), public service, library costs, student services, operation and maintenance of plant, general administration, student aid, and so on.

It is customary to record tuition remissions (e.g., remissions granted to faculty mem-

---

[3] Some governmental colleges and universities use the AICPA model without conforming completely to its requirements—particularly its requirements concerning endowment fund revenue, gift pledges, and reporting for separate organizations such as foundations, athletic organizations, and research units. However, *GASB Statement No. 15,* states that governmental colleges and universities should use one model or the other.

bers' families) and tuition waivers (e.g., student scholarships and fellowships) as both a debit to expenditures and a credit to revenues, even though no resources are actually expended or received. Tuition refunds (e.g., due to class cancellations or student withdrawals) are debited to revenues and credited to cash or accounts receivable.

A *restricted current fund* is used to account for resources to be expended for operating purposes that are specified by an outside donor or grantor. Resources for restricted current funds are typically derived from private gifts that are restricted to specified operating purposes (e.g., scholarship aid to students, purchase of library books); government and private grants and contracts for research, training, or other sponsored programs; governmental appropriations for specific operating purposes; restricted income from endowment funds; and so on. Expenditure of these resources would be for whatever operating purpose (e.g., scholarship aid to students) that has been specified by the outside donor or grantor. It is important to note that *resources of restricted current funds are recognized as revenues only upon expenditure for the specified purpose.* Upon receipt or accrual, these resources are credited to restricted current fund balance. The expenditure for the specified purpose would be recorded by an entry debiting the appropriate expenditures account and crediting cash, and, at the same time, debiting the restricted current fund balance and crediting the appropriate revenue account.

Revenues and expenditures are recorded *only* in the current funds (both unrestricted and restricted). In all other funds that are used by colleges and universities, sources and uses of resources are recorded by credits or debits directly to the appropriate fund balance accounts.

Board-Designated Funds

Board-designated funds are unrestricted current funds that are designated by the governing board to serve as loan or quasi-endowment funds, or to be expended or appropriated for plant purposes. Such funds are *not* accounted for in the current funds but are transferred to other funds. For example, quasi-endowment funds are accounted for in the same manner as endowment or term endowment funds, and amounts set aside for plant purposes are accounted for in the plant funds. In the financial statements, a clear distinction must be made between externally restricted and internally restricted (board-designated) funds.

Accounting Methods of Colleges and Universities

Colleges and universities use fund accounting; accordingly, their accounting systems emphasize measuring and reporting the sources and uses of resources rather than the determination of income. The paragraphs that follow consider several distinctive aspects of college and university fund accounting systems.

Accrual Accounting and Depreciation

Colleges and universities use accrual accounting. Most revenues are recognized when earned and most expenditures are recognized when incurred without regard to when the related amounts of cash are received or paid. As noted earlier, *FASB Statement No. 93* requires private-sector nonprofit organizations to record depreciation on long-lived tangible assets (other than works of art and historical treasures).[4] However, *GASB Statement No. 8* exempts (at least temporarily) governmental colleges and universities and certain other governmental nonprofits from this requirement. Thus some colleges and universities recognize depreciation and others do not.

Summer Terms

A summer or other term that overlaps two fiscal years presents distinctive accounting problems for educational institutions. All revenues and expenditures of such a term should be reported in the fiscal year in which the term is predominantly conducted.

Mandatory and Nonmandatory Transfers

Transfers from unrestricted or restricted current funds to other fund groups may be either mandatory transfers or nonmandatory transfers. *Mandatory transfers* arise from (1) binding legal agreements related to the financing of the educational plant (e.g., debt retirement, interest on indebtedness, and required provisions for plant renewal and replacement) and (2) agreements with donors (e.g., federal or state government, private donors, or other organizations) to match grants to loan funds or other funds. *Nonmandatory transfers* are transfers from current funds to other funds made at the discretion of the governing board for such purposes as prepayment of debt principal, plant renewal and replacement, plant acquisition, additions to quasi-endowment funds, and so on. Nonmandatory transfers may include retransfers back to the current funds.

In the current funds, such transfers are *not* treated as expenditures, but are debited to a mandatory or nonmandatory transfer account and credited to cash (or due to other fund). The receiving fund would debit cash (or due from current funds) and credit fund balance. A retransfer would require a reversal of the preceding entries in the affected funds.

Budgetary and Encumbrance Accounting

Budgetary accounting is recommended for colleges and universities and may be used for either or both the current unrestricted and the current restricted funds. The following entry illustrates the recording of the annual budget for the current funds of an educational institution.

Current funds (unrestricted and restricted) entry to record annual budget:

Estimated revenues	2,500,000	
Budget allocations for expenditures and other fund balance changes		2,450,000
Unallocated budget balance		50,000

---

[4] The FASB statement does not provide guidance on how depreciation expense should be displayed in financial reports in addition to that already provided in the three AICPA audit guides and SOP 78-10. Thus, for example, the FASB permits colleges and universities to report depreciation expense "in a statement of changes in the balance of the investment-in-plant fund subsection of the plant funds group" (*FASB Statement No. 93,* par. 43). Consequently, colleges and universities need not report depreciation in either their statements of current funds revenues, expenditures, and other changes or their statements of changes in unrestricted current funds balance.

It should be noted that the difference between estimated revenues and budget allocations for expenditures is recorded in an *unallocated budget balance* account rather than in the *current fund balance*. The preceding entry would be reversed at the end of the fiscal year. Except for minor differences in terminology, budgetary accounting for colleges and universities parallels that of the general fund in governmental accounting, discussed in Chapter 17, and is not illustrated further in this section.

Encumbrance accounting is frequently used for either or both the current unrestricted and the current restricted funds of colleges and universities. Encumbrance accounting for educational institutions parallels that used in governmental-type funds of governmental units, as discussed in the two previous chapters. Thus, encumbrance accounting is not discussed further in this section.

Accounting for College and University Current Funds

Exhibit 19-2 gives the transactions and related journal entries for the current funds, both unrestricted and restricted, of Regional University for the year ended June 30, 19X6. Expenditures of the unrestricted and restricted current funds fall into two major categories: *expenditures—educational and general,* and *expenditures—auxiliary enterprises.* To save space and avoid repetition, we will omit the words *educational* and *general* in the journal entries affecting this control account and will indicate only the subsidiary account (e.g., instructional and departmental research). However, for entries affecting auxiliary enterprise expenditures, the account *expenditures—auxiliary enterprises* will be indicated. For similar reasons, the words educational and general have been omitted from revenue accounts that are related to educational and general operations. However, revenues from auxiliary enterprises and expired terms endowments will be so titled.

Closing entries at June 30, 19X6, for the unrestricted and restricted current funds of Regional University are presented as follows. It should be noted that revenues and expenditures in the restricted current funds are equal because restricted resources are not recognized as revenue until they are expended for the specified purpose.

Unrestricted current fund closing entry at June 30, 19X6:

Revenue—tuition and fees	1,100,000	
Revenue—federal appropriations	200,000	
Revenue—state appropriations	300,000	
Revenue—governmental grants	50,000	
Revenue—private gifts	150,000	
Revenue—endowment income	75,000	
Revenue—auxiliary enterprises	305,000	
Revenue—expired term endowment	40,000	
Fund balance	74,000	
Expenditures—instruction and departmental research		1,300,000
Expenditures—provision for uncollectible accounts		25,000
Expenditures—public service		150,000
Expenditures—libraries		110,000
Expenditures—student services		95,000
Expenditures—operation and maintenance of plant		75,000
Expenditures—general administration		74,000

(Entries continue on page 978)

Expenditures—student aid		17,000
Expenditures—auxiliary enterprises		207,000
Mandatory transfers to retirement of indebtedness plant fund		126,000
Mandatory transfers to renewal and replacement plant fund		35,000
Nonmandatory transfers to loan fund		5,000
Nonmandatory transfers to quasi-endowment fund		50,000
Nonmandatory transfer to unexpended plant fund		25,000

Restricted current funds closing entry at June 30, 19X6:

Revenue—governmental grants	716,000	
Revenue—endowment income	37,000	
Expenditures—instruction and departmental research		448,000
Expenditures—sponsored research		268,000
Expenditures—student aid		37,000

Accounting for College and University Loan Funds

Loan funds are used to account for resources that are available for making loans to students, faculty, and staff. The sources of loan funds (e.g., gifts and bequests, government advances, income and gains on investments held by loan funds, interest on outstanding loan receivables, and interfund transfers) are credited to the loan fund balance. Loan fund administrative and collection costs and interfund transfers out are debited to the loan fund balance. Loans are recorded as debits to loans (notes) receivable and credits to cash. The assets of these funds usually consist of cash, loans receivable, and temporary investments. Loans receivable are shown as assets in the loan fund section of the balance sheet at face value, less an allowance for uncollectible loans. The provision for uncollectible loans is charged to the loan fund balance. The fund balance is divided into restricted (by outside donors or grantors) and unrestricted (including board-designated) accounts. Exhibit 19-3 shows the transactions and related journal entries for the loan funds of Regional University for the year ended June 30, 19X6.

Accounting for College and University Endowment and Similar Funds

Endowment funds are closely related to term endowment funds and quasi-endowment funds. Thus, the latter are included in the endowment funds group (and referred to as similar funds). *Endowment funds* are used to account for resources where the outside donor or grantor has specified, as a condition of the gift or bequest, that the principal is to remain intact in perpetuity and is to be invested to produce income that may be expended (e.g., for operating purposes) or added to the principal. *Term endowment funds* are similar to endowment funds, except that after a specified period of time has passed, a specific event has occurred, or a condition has been fulfilled, the governing board may expend all or part of the principal in accordance with the provisions under which the term endowment was established. *Quasi-endowment funds,* which function as endowment funds, consist of resources that are set aside by the governing board (board-designated funds), rather than by an outside donor or grantor, to be retained and invested. They are accounted for in the same manner as endowment funds and term endowment funds. However, since these resources are internally designated, they may retransfer to unrestricted current funds and be expended at any time by the governing board.

Each endowment, term endowment, and quasi endowment is accounted for in a

EXHIBIT 19-2	UNRESTRICTED AND RESTRICTED CURRENT FUNDS ENTRIES

Regional University

UNRESTRICTED AND RESTRICTED CURRENT FUND ENTRIES
FOR THE YEAR ENDED JUNE 30, 19X6

Transaction (1): Student tuition and fees billed amounted to $1,100,000. Of this amount, $883,000 was collected in cash, $17,000 of tuition was waived for students holding scholarships, $200,000 has not yet been collected (of which it is estimated that $25,000 will be uncollectible).

(1) *Unrestricted current fund entry to record tuition and fees revenues:*

Cash	883,000	
Accounts receivable	200,000	
Expenditures—student aid	17,000	
Expenditures—provision for uncollectible accounts	25,000	
Revenue—tuition and fees		1,100,000
Allowance for uncollectible accounts		25,000

Transaction (2): Unrestricted government appropriations received were as follows: federal, $200,000; state, $300,000.

(2) *Unrestricted current fund entry to record unrestricted government appropriations:*

Cash	500,000	
Revenue—federal appropriations		200,000
Revenue—state appropriations		300,000

Transaction (3): Federal grants received in cash amount to $826,000. Of this amount, $50,000 was unrestricted and $776,000 was restricted for biological research.

(3a) *Unrestricted current fund entry to record unrestricted federal grants received:*

Cash	50,000	
Revenue—governmental grants		50,000

(3b) *Restricted current fund entry to record restricted federal grants received:*

Cash	776,000	
Fund balance—restricted		776,000

Transaction (4): Of the amount ($776,000) received as a restricted federal grant for biological research, $716,000 was expended as follows: expenditures—instruction and departmental research, $448,000, and sponsored research, $268,000.

(4a) *Restricted current fund entry to record expenditure of restricted federal grants:*

Expenditures—instruction and departmental research	448,000	
Expenditures—sponsored research	268,000	
Cash		716,000

(4b) *Restricted current funds entry to recognize revenue as a result of expenditure of restricted federal grants:*

Fund balance—restricted	716,000	
Revenue—governmental grants		716,000

EXHIBIT 19-2	UNRESTRICTED AND RESTRICTED CURRENT FUNDS ENTRIES (Continued)

Transaction (5): Unrestricted private gifts received in cash were $150,000.

(5) *Unrestricted current fund entry to record unrestricted private gifts received:*

Cash	150,000	
Revenue—private gifts		150,000

Transaction (6): Unrestricted income from endowment funds was received in the amount of $75,000. (Note that this income is recorded directly in the unrestricted current fund rather than in the endowment fund.)

(6) *Unrestricted current fund entry to record unrestricted endowment income:*

Cash	75,000	
Revenue—endowment income		75,000

Transaction (7): Restricted income (for student aid) from endowments in the amount of $48,000 was received. Of this amount $37,000 was expended for student aid in accordance with the terms of the endowment gift. (Note that this income is recorded directly in the restricted current funds rather than in the endowment fund.)

(7a) *Restricted current funds entry to record restricted endowment income:*

Cash	48,000	
Fund balance—restricted		48,000

(7b) *Restricted current funds entry to record expenditure of restricted endowment income:*

Expenditures—student aid	37,000	
Cash		37,000

(7c) *Restricted current funds entry to recognize revenue as a result of expenditure of restricted endowment income:*

Fund balance—restricted	37,000	
Revenue—endowment income		37,000

Transaction (8): Auxiliary enterprise operations (residence halls, bookstore, intercollegiate athletics) provided cash revenue from sales and services in the amount of $305,000. Auxiliary enterprise expenditures—consisting of salaries, supplies, and so on—amounted to $207,000, all of which was paid in cash.

(8a) *Unrestricted current fund entry to record revenue from auxiliary enterprises:*

Cash	305,000	
Revenue—auxiliary enterprises		305,000

(8b) *Unrestricted current fund entry to record expenditures of auxiliary enterprises:*

Expenditures—auxiliary enterprises	207,000	
Cash		207,000

Transaction (9): Mandatory transfers (related to auxiliary enterprises) from the unrestricted current fund to other funds were as follows: to retirement of indebtedness plant fund for principal and interest, $126,000, and to the renewal and replacement plant fund, $35,000. [See related entry (7) in the plant funds section discussed later.]

(9) *Unrestricted current fund entry to record mandatory transfers:*

Mandatory transfers to retirement of indebtedness plant fund	126,000	
Mandatory transfers to renewal and replacement plant fund	35,000	
Cash		161,000

EXHIBIT 19-2	UNRESTRICTED AND RESTRICTED CURRENT FUNDS ENTRIES (Continued)

Transaction (10): Unrestricted gifts (nonmandatory transfers) were allocated, but not paid, from the unrestricted current fund to other funds as follows: loan fund, $5,000; quasi-endowment fund, $50,000; and unexpended plant fund, $25,000. [See related entry (5) in the loan fund section, entry (5) in the endowment and similar funds section, and entry (8) in the plant funds section discussed later.]

(10) *Unrestricted current fund entry to record allocation of unrestricted gifts to other funds:*

Nonmandatory transfer to loan fund	5,000	
Nonmandatory transfer to quasi-endowment fund	50,000	
Nonmandatory transfer to unexpended plant fund	25,000	
Due to other funds		80,000

Transaction (11): Additional unrestricted current fund expenditures were incurred and paid as follows: instruction and departmental research, $1,270,000; public service, $150,000; libraries, $110,000; student services, $95,000; operation and maintenance of plant, $75,000; general administration, $74,000.

(11) *Unrestricted current fund entry to record expenditures:*

Expenditures—instruction and departmental research	1,270,000	
Expenditures—public service	150,000	
Expenditures—libraries	110,000	
Expenditures—student services	95,000	
Expenditures—operation and maintenance of plant	75,000	
Expenditures—general administration	74,000	
Cash		1,774,000

Transaction 12: The unrestricted current fund purchased $127,000 of instructional and research materials and supplies, which were charged to inventory. Of this amount, $30,000 of materials was used for instruction and departmental research.

(12a) *Unrestricted current fund entry to record purchases of materials and supplies:*

Inventory	127,000	
Cash		127,000

(12b) *Unrestricted current fund entry to record usage of materials and supplies:*

Expenditures—instruction and departmental research	30,000	
Inventory		30,000

Transaction (13): The time period expired for a term endowment fund. Upon expiration of this time period, the principal amount of $40,000 became available for use as unrestricted current funds. [See related entry (4) in the endowment and similar funds section discussed later.]

(13) *Unrestricted current fund entry to record receipt of expired endowment principal:*

Cash	40,000	
Revenue—expired term endowment		40,000

| **EXHIBIT 19-3** | **LOAN FUNDS ENTRIES** |

Regional University
LOAN FUNDS ENTRIES
FOR THE YEAR ENDED JUNE 30, 19X6

Transaction (1): The loan funds received in cash are the following amounts: gifts and bequests to be used to make loans to students. $50,000; income on investments held by the loan funds, $10,000; interest earnings on outstanding loans receivable, $14,000.

(1) *Loan funds entry to record cash received:*

Cash	74,000	
Fund balance—restricted—gifts and bequests		50,000
Fund balance—restricted—investment income		10,000
Fund balance—restricted—interest on loans receivable		14,000

Transaction (2): Investments were purchased at a cost of $15,000.

(2) *Loan funds entry to record purchase of investments:*

Investments	15,000	
Cash		15,000

Transaction (3): Investments with a cost of $10,000 were sold for $11,000.

(3) *Loan funds entry to record sale of investments:*

Cash	11,000	
Investments		10,000
Fund balance—restricted—realized gain on investments		1,000

Transaction (4): Loans totaling $70,000 were made to students, faculty, and staff.

(4) *Loan funds entry to record loans made:*

Loans receivable	70,000	
Cash		70,000

Transaction (5): There was a nonmandatory transfer of $5,000 that became due to the loan funds from the unrestricted current fund. [Refer to related entry (10) in the current funds section discussed earlier.]

(5) *Loan funds entry to record nonmandatory transfer from the unrestricted current fund:*

Due from unrestricted current fund	5,000	
Fund balance—unrestricted—nonmandatory transfer		
from unrestricted current fund		5,000

Transaction (6): A provision for uncollectible loans was recorded in the amount of $7,000.

(6) *Loan funds entry to record provision for uncollectible loans:*

Fund balance—restricted—provision for uncollectible loans	7,000	
Allowance for uncollectible loans		7,000

Transaction (7): Loans written off as uncollectible totaled $2,000.

(7) *Loan funds entry to record loan write-offs:*

Allowance for uncollectible loans	2,000	
Loans receivable		2,000

Transaction (8): Administrative and collection costs incurred and paid by the loan funds amounted to $5,000.

(8) *Loan funds entry to record costs incurred:*

Fund balance—restricted—administrative and collection costs	5,000	
Cash		5,000

separate fund, although their assets and liabilities are combined for balance sheet presentation. However, the balance sheet reflects separate fund balances for endowment, term endowment, and quasi-endowment funds. Assets of these funds typically include cash and investments of various types (e.g., securities and real estate), and liabilities consist of payables that are related to fund assets (e.g., mortgages payable). Increases in the principal of endowments and similar funds are recognized by a debit to cash (or other appropriate asset) and a credit to the appropriate fund balance account.

Accounting treatment of income from endowment and similar funds depends on the terms of the documents under which the funds are established. If the income may be used, without restrictions, for operating purposes, it is recognized as revenue in the unrestricted current fund. If the income is to be used for specified operating purposes, it is credited to the fund balance of the restricted current funds until expended for the specified purpose, at which time it is recognized as revenue in the restricted current funds. In some cases, restrictions on the use of endowment income require that it be added to the fund balance of an endowment, loan, or plant fund. In the determination of income for endowment and similar funds, depreciation of endowment fixed assets and amortization of premiums and discounts on investment securities should be recognized to differentiate between the principal and income of these funds.

The assets of various endowments are frequently pooled for purposes of investments. Such pooling requires that the earnings from these investments be allocated among the individual endowments. Allocation of earnings on the basis of fair market values of the pooled assets at the date of their pooling is generally viewed as the preferred allocation basis.

Exhibit 19-4 shows the transactions and related journal entries for the endowment and similar funds of Regional University for the year ended June 30, 19X6.

Accounting for College and University Annuity and Life Income Funds

Annuity funds are used to account for resources given to a college or university with the provision that specified dollar amounts will be paid to designated individuals over a specified period of time. After the lapse of such time period, the principal of the annuity fund would be transferred to the fund specified by the donor, or to the unrestricted current fund in the absence of such designation. The contributed assets are recorded at their fair value on the date contributed. The present value of the amounts to be paid to designated individuals in the future should be recorded in the annuities payable account (based on life expectancy tables), and the balance should be credited to the annuity fund balance account.

Life income funds are used to account for resources that are given to the institution with the provision that the income earned on the assets will be paid to a designated individual over his or her lifetime, or some other specified period of time. Upon termination, the principal of the life income fund would be transferred to the fund designated by the donor, or to the unrestricted current fund in the absence of such a designation.

The essential difference between annuity and life income funds is that the distribution to the beneficiary from an annuity fund is a fixed amount each period, whereas the distribution to the beneficiary from a life income fund, which maintains the principal intact, is the income of the period that may vary from period to period. The assets of both annuity and life income funds usually consist of cash and investments of various types. Liabilities of annuity funds usually consist of debts that are related to the fund assets (e.g., mortgages payable) and annuities payable. Liabilities of life income funds usually consist of debts that are related to fund assets and life income payments that are currently due to

EXHIBIT 19-4	ENDOWMENT AND SIMILAR FUNDS ENTRIES

Regional University
ENDOWMENT AND SIMILAR FUNDS ENTRIES
FOR THE YEAR ENDED JUNE 30, 19X6

Transaction (1): Restricted cash gifts and bequests to the endowment funds totaled $85,000.

(1) *Endowment funds entry to record cash receipts from gifts and bequests:*

Cash	85,000	
Fund balance—endowment—gifts and bequests		85,000

Transaction (2): Investments totaling $100,000 were purchased by the endowment funds.

(2) *Endowment funds entry to record investments purchased:*

Investments	100,000	
Cash		100,000

Transaction (3): Investments held by the term endowment funds with a cost of $50,000 were sold for $60,000. Investments held by the quasi-endowment funds with a cost of $35,000 were sold by $40,000.

(3a) *Term endowment funds entry to record sales of investments:*

Cash	60,000	
Investments		50,000
Fund balance—term endowment—realized gains on investments		10,000

(3b) *Quasi-endowment funds entry to record sales of investments:*

Cash	40,000	
Investments		35,000
Fund balance—quasi endowment—realized gains on investments		5,000

Transaction (4): The principal of a term endowment of $40,000 has been held for ten years in accordance with the terms of the bequest, which established the term endowment. This principal became available for unrestricted operating purposes. [Refer to related entry (13) in the current funds section discussed earlier.]

(4) *Term endowment funds entry to record expired term endowment:*

Fund balance—term endowment—expired term endowment	40,000	
Cash		40,000

Transaction (5): There was a nonmandatory transfer of $50,000 that became due to the quasi-endowment funds from the unrestricted current fund. [Refer to related entry (10) in the current funds section discussed earlier.]

(5) *Quasi-endowment funds entry to record nonmandatory transfer from the unrestricted current fund:*

Due from unrestricted current fund	50,000	
Fund balance—quasi endowment—nonmandatory transfer from unrestricted current fund		50,000

the beneficiary. The fund balance of an annuity fund may be increased by the receipt of new gifts in excess of the actuarial amount of the related annuities payable. Decreases in fund balance result from the transfer of resources to other funds upon termination of annuity funds. The annuities payable account of an annuity fund is credited with the actuarially determined amount of new gifts, and is also credited with investment income and gains (or debited with investment losses). Annuity payments are debited to the annuities payable account. Adjustments resulting from changes in life expectancy of the beneficiary may result in an increase or decrease in annuities payable with a corresponding decrease or increase in the annuity fund balance.

The fund balance of a life income fund may be increased by new gifts and by investment gains. It may be decreased by investment losses or by transfers to other funds upon termination of the life income fund. Investment income is credited to income payable and does not affect the fund balance. Life income payments are debited to the income payable accounts.

Exhibit 19-5 shows the transactions and related journal entries for Regional University's annuity and life income funds.

Accounting for College and University Plant Funds

The plant funds for colleges and universities consist of the following subgroups: (1) unexpended plant fund, (2) renewal and replacement plant fund, (3) retirement of indebtedness plant fund, and (4) investment in plant fund. Colleges and universities subject to FASB standards are required to account for plant assets and long-term debt in the manner illustrated for hospitals later in this chapter. The accounting shown for Regional University in the following paragraphs and exhibits illustrates an alternative accounting for plant assets and related long-term debt that is currently acceptable for nonprofit organizations subject to GASB standards.

Unexpended Plant Fund

The *unexpended plant fund* accounts for the acquisition or construction of fixed assets. Acquisitions of plant assets are charged to the fund balance of the *unexpended plant fund* and credited to cash or appropriate payable. At the same time, the acquisitions are recorded as a debit to the asset account and a credit to the net investment in plant account (not fund balance) in the *investment in plant fund*. Construction outlays are charged to construction in progress accounts in the unexpended plant fund; at year-end (before the issuance of the balance sheet), construction in progress accounts are transferred to the *investment in plant fund*. The issuance of debt to finance new plant assets is recorded in the *unexpended plant fund* accounts by debiting appropriate asset accounts for the proceeds and by crediting long-term liability accounts. At year-end (before the issuance of the balance sheet), the long-term liabilities are transferred to the *investment in plant fund* to the extent that the proceeds are expended at year-end. As a consequence of these transfers, the assets section of the balance sheet of the *unexpended plant fund* does not display plant assets. However, it usually consists of cash, due from other funds, and investments. The liabilities usually consist of accounts payable, due to other funds, and long-term liabilities (bonds, notes, and/or mortgages payable) to the extent that the proceeds of such long-term debt are unexpended at year-end.

Additions to the fund balance of the unexpended plant fund (resources) typically include private donations that are restricted to plant acquisition, government grants or

EXHIBIT 19-5	**ANNUITY AND LIFE INCOME FUNDS ENTRIES**

Regional University

ANNUITY AND LIFE INCOME FUNDS ENTRIES
FOR THE YEAR ENDED JUNE 30, 19X6

Transaction (1): Gifts and bequests of securities received amounted to $130,000 ($105,000 to the annuity funds and $25,000 to the life income funds). For the gift of $105,000, the present value of future annuity payments to the recipient amounted to $90,000.

(1a) *Annuity funds entry to record gifts and bequests received:*

Investments	105,000	
Annuities payable		90,000
Fund balance—gifts and bequests		15,000

(1b) *Life income funds entry to record gifts and bequests received:*

Investments	25,000	
Fund balance—gifts and bequests		25,000

Transaction (2): Investment income received amounted to $75,000 ($15,000 for the annuity funds and $60,000 for the life income funds).

(2a) *Annuity funds entry to record investment income received:*

Cash	15,000	
Annuities payable		15,000

(2b) *Life income funds entry to record investment income received:*

Cash	60,000	
Income payable		60,000

Transaction (3): Realized gains on investments sold amounted to $15,000, determined as follows: Annuity funds investments that cost $35,000 were sold for $40,000, and life income funds investments that cost $60,000 were sold for $70,000.

(3a) *Annuity funds entry to record sale of investments:*

Cash	40,000	
Investments		35,000
Annuities payable		5,000

(3b) *Life income funds entry to record sale of investments:*

Cash	70,000	
Investments		60,000
Fund balance—realized gain on investments		10,000

Transaction (4): Recipients of annuities were paid $55,000.

(4) *Annuity funds entry to record payments to recipients of annuities:*

Annuities payable	55,000	
Cash		55,000

Transaction (5): Life income recipients were paid $50,000.

(5) *Life income funds entry to record payments to life income recipients:*

Income payable	50,000	
Cash		50,000

Transaction (6): Recomputation of annuities payable that was based on revised life expectancies of annuitants resulted in a reduction of the liability in the amount of $8,000.

(6) *Annuity funds entry to record actuarial gains resulting from revised life expectancies of annuitants:*

Annuities payable	8,000	
Fund balance—actuarial gain		8,000

appropriations that are restricted to plant acquisition, income and gains from unexpended plant fund investments, and transfers from current (or other) funds. Deductions from the fund balance of the unexpended plant fund include plant asset (including construction) costs, losses on investments, retransfers to unrestricted current funds, and fund-raising costs that are related to plant acquisition. The fund balance is divided into restricted (by outside donors or grantors) and unrestricted (including board-designated) accounts.

Renewal and Replacement Plant Fund

The *renewal and replacement plant fund* accounts for resources that are set aside for the renewal and replacement of plant assets. Some amounts that are expended from this fund are capitalized (e.g., replacement and upgrading of computer facilities) and are also accounted for in the investment in plant fund. Other amounts expended for renewal and replacement do not require capitalization (e.g., major repairs to roof) and thus are not accounted for in the investment in plant fund. The assets of this fund typically consist of cash, due from other funds, and investments. Liabilities typically consist of accounts payable and due to other funds. Additions to the fund balance (resources) may include transfers (mandatory and nonmandatory) from current funds, investment income and gains, government appropriations and grants, and private gifts and grants. Deductions from the fund balance typically include renewal and replacement costs, investment losses, and retransfers to unrestricted current funds. The fund balance is divided into restricted (by outside grantors and donors) and unrestricted (board-designated) accounts.

Retirement of Indebtedness Plant Fund

The *retirement of indebtedness plant fund* accounts for the payment of interest and principal on long-term debt that is related to plant assets. However, the face values of the related long-term liabilities (e.g., mortgages payable) are included in the *investment in plant fund* and not in the *retirement of indebtedness plant fund.* The assets of this latter fund usually consist of cash, cash on deposit with others (trustees), due from other funds, and investments. Liabilities usually include accounts payable (for trustees' fees, etc.). Additions to the fund balance (resources) normally include transfers (mandatory and nonmandatory) from current funds for interest and principal payments, investment income and gains, governmental appropriations and grants that are restricted to debt retirement, private gifts and grants that are restricted to debt retirement, and transfers from other fund groups as specified by donors (e.g., expired term endowment). These additions are recorded as credits to the fund balance account. Deductions from the fund balance typically include debt principal and interest payments, trustees' fees and expenses, and investment losses. These deductions are recorded as debits to the fund balance account (debt principal payments also require an entry, debiting the long-term liability account and crediting the net investment in plant account in the *investment in plant fund,* as indicated in the next paragraph). The fund balance is divided into restricted (by outside donors or grantors) and unrestricted (including board-designated) accounts.

Investment in Plant Fund

The *investment in plant fund* accounts for plant assets (land, buildings, improvements other than buildings, equipment, and library books) and for liabilities that are related to amounts *expended* for plant assets. Construction in progress is included in this fund unless it is included in the unexpended plant funds. (As indicated previously, construction in progress is normally carried in the unexpended plant fund until the end of the fiscal year, at which time it is transferred along with the related long-term liability to the investment in plant fund.) The liabilities typically consist of accounts payable and long-term debt (bonds, notes, and mortgages payable) that are related to the acquisition or construction of the plant assets. The excess of plant assets over related liabilities represents the net investment in plant rather than a fund balance. Additions to the net investment in plant account arise from capital outlays from unexpended plant funds, capital outlays from renewal and replacement plant funds, equipment expenditures by current funds, gifts of plant assets (books, equipment, art collections, etc.), and reduction of debt by the retirement of indebtedness plant fund. Deductions from the net investment in plant account include asset disposals through sale, abandonment, or otherwise, which require removal of the asset cost from the plant asset accounts.

Physical Plant and Depreciation

Plant assets are recorded and shown in the balance sheet at cost or, in the case of donated assets, at the fair market value at the date of the gift. College and university plant assets are not normally depreciated. However, if they are depreciated, the depreciation would be recorded in the investment in plant fund by a debit to the *net investment in plant* account and a credit to the *allowance for depreciation* account. Note that depreciation expense is not reflected in the accounts of any funds of a college or university, other than certain endowment funds.

Exhibit 19-6 shows the transactions and related entries for Regional University's plant funds for the year ended June 30, 19X6.

Accounting for College and University Agency Funds

Agency funds are used to account for resources that are held by the institution as a fiscal agent for students, campus organizations, or faculty members. Assets of these funds usually consist of cash, investments, and sometimes interfund or other receivables. Liabilities consist of payables to the person or organization for whom the institution is acting as custodian, and sometimes interfund payables and payables to third parties. An agency fund has no fund balance account since the institution has no equity in such a fund.

The following journal entry shows the activity in the agency funds of Regional University during the year ended June 30, 19X6.

Transaction: Earnings on agency fund investments amounted to $2,000.

Agency funds entry to record earnings on investments:

Cash	2,000	
Deposits held in custody for others		2,000

Closing Entries for Funds Other Than Current Funds

Closing entries at June 30, 19X6, for the unrestricted and restricted current funds of Regional University were recorded and discussed earlier. However, closing entries for other funds (i.e., loan funds, endowment, and similar funds; annuity and life income funds; and plant funds) for Regional University are not required because all resource receipt and disbursement transactions for which closing entries might otherwise be required are credited or debited directly to the appropriate fund balance account.

| EXHIBIT 19-6 | PLANT FUNDS ENTRIES |

Regional University

PLANT FUNDS ENTRIES
FOR THE YEAR ENDED JUNE 30, 19X6

Transaction (1): Bonds payable in the amount of $200,000 were issued at par for the purpose of adding a wing to the business administration building. This amount was immediately invested in marketable securities until the construction was started.

(1a) *Unexpended plant fund entry to record issuance of bonds:*

| Cash | 200,000 | |
| Bonds payable | | 200,000 |

(1b) *Unexpended plant fund entry to record investment of bond proceeds:*

| Investments | 200,000 | |
| Cash | | 200,000 |

Transaction (2): Restricted cash gifts and bequests received amounted to $103,000. Of this amount, $70,000 was restricted for use in purchasing laboratory equipment for the chemistry department, and $33,000 was given for the purpose of repaying a portion of the long-term debt.

(2a) *Unexpended plant fund entry to record receipt of restricted gift:*

| Cash | 70,000 | |
| Fund balance—restricted—gifts and bequests | | 70,000 |

(2b) *Retirement of indebtedness plant fund entry to record receipt of restricted gift:*

| Cash | 33,000 | |
| Fund balance—restricted—gifts and bequests | | 33,000 |

Transaction (3): Microcomputers with a value of $20,000 were given to the business administration department by a computer manufacturer.

(3) *Investment in plant fund entry to record receipt of microcomputers:*

| Equipment | 20,000 | |
| Net investment in plant | | 20,000 |

Transaction (4): $25,000 was received from the state as an appropriation to purchase special equipment for the school of education.

(4) *Unexpended plant fund entry to record receipt of restricted state appropriation:*

| Cash | 25,000 | |
| Fund balance—restricted—government appropriations | | 25,000 |

EXHIBIT 19-6	PLANT FUND ENTRIES (Continued)

Transaction (5): Restricted investment income was received in cash in the amount of $15,000 as follows: income from unexpended plant fund investments, $5,000; income from renewal and replacement fund investments, $10,000.

(5a) *Unexpended plant fund entry to record restricted investment income:*

Cash	5,000	
Fund balance—restricted—investment income		5,000

(5b) *Renewal and replacement fund entry to record restricted investment income:*

Cash	10,000	
Fund balance—restricted—investment income		10,000

Transaction (6): Realized gains on restricted plant fund investments sold amounted to $15,000, determined as follows: unexpended plant fund investments that cost $40,000 were sold for $50,000; and renewal and replacement fund investments that cost $30,000 were sold for $35,000.

(6a) *Unexpended plant fund entry to record sale of investments:*

Cash	50,000	
Investments		40,000
Fund balance—restricted—realized gains on investments		10,000

(6b) *Renewal and replacement fund entry to record sale of investments:*

Cash	35,000	
Investments		30,000
Fund balance—restricted—realized gains on investments		5,000

Transaction (7): Mandatory transfers (related to auxiliary enterprises) from the unrestricted current fund to the plant funds amounted to $161,000 as follows: for renewals and replacements, $35,000, and for payment of principal and interest on indebtedness, $126,000. [Refer to related entry (9) in the current funds section discussed earlier.]

(7a) *Renewal and replacement fund entry to record mandatory transfer from unrestricted current fund:*

Cash	35,000	
Fund balance—restricted—mandatory transfers for renewals and replacements		35,000

(7b) *Retirement of indebtedness fund entry to record mandatory transfer from unrestricted current fund:*

Cash	126,000	
Fund balance—restricted—mandatory transfers for principal and interest		126,000

EXHIBIT 19-6	PLANT FUNDS ENTRIES (Continued)

Transaction (8): There was a nonmandatory transfer of $25,000 that became due to the unexpended plant fund from the unrestricted current fund. [Refer to related entry (10) in the current funds section discussed earlier.]

(8) *Unexpended plant fund entry to record nonmandatory transfer from unrestricted current fund:*

Due from unrestricted current fund	25,000	
Fund balance—unrestricted—nonmandatory		
transfer from unrestricted current fund		25,000

Transaction (9): Administrative costs of $1,000 were paid out of unrestricted moneys of the retirement of indebtedness fund.

(9) *Retirement of indebtedness fund entry to record payment of administrative costs:*

Fund balance—unrestricted—administrative costs	1,000	
Cash		1,000

Transaction (10): A new building was constructed at a cost of $500,000, which was paid by the unexpended plant fund (this building was partly financed by $100,000 from bonds issued last year).

(10a) *Unexpended plant fund entry to record construction of new building:*

Construction in progress	500,000	
Cash		500,000

(10b) *Unexpended plant fund entry to record completion of building:*

Bonds payable	100,000	
Fund balance—restricted—plant facilities	400,000	
Construction in progress		500,000

(10c) *Investment in plant fund entry to record cost of building and related liability:*

Buildings	500,000	
Bonds payable		100,000
Net investment in plant..........................		400,000

Transaction (11): The renewal and replacement fund expended $150,000 ($85,000 of which was for rehabilitation of an old building that was capitalized, and $65,000 was for repairs that were not capitalized).

(11a) *Renewal and replacement fund entry to record cost of plant facilities:*

Fund balance—restricted—plant facilities	150,000	
Cash		150,000

(11b) *Investment in plant fund entry to record capitalized cost of rehabilitation:*

Buildings	85,000	
Net investment in plant		85,000

| EXHIBIT 19-6 | PLANT FUNDS ENTRIES (Continued) |

Transaction (12): Obsolete laboratory equipment with no resale value was scrapped. Cost of the equipment was $110,000. (If the old equipment had been sold instead of scrapped, the proceeds would be recorded as revenue in the unrestricted current fund or as an addition to the fund balance of the unexpended plant (or some other) fund, depending on the intended use of the proceeds.)

(12) *Investment in plant fund entry to record disposal of old equipment:*

| Net investment in plant | 110,000 | |
| Equipment | | 110,000 |

Transaction (13): Interest on long-term indebtedness paid amounted to $25,000.

(13) *Retirement of indebtedness plant fund entry to record payment of interest on long-term debt:*

| Fund balance—restricted—interest on indebtedness | 25,000 | |
| Cash | | 25,000 |

Transaction (14): Long-term debt retired amounted to $150,000, consisting of the following payments: bonds payable, $50,000, and mortgages payable, $100,000.

(14a) *Retirement of indebtedness fund entry to record retirement of long-term indebtedness:*

| Fund balance—restricted—retirement of indebtedness | 150,000 | |
| Cash | | 150,000 |

(14b) *Investment in plant fund entry to record retirement of long-term indebtedness:*

Bonds payable	50,000	
Mortgages payable	100,000	
Net investment in plant		150,000

Transaction (15): The unexpended plant fund expended $15,000 for equipment for the biology laboratory.

(15a) *Unexpended plant fund entry to record expenditure for equipment:*

| Fund balance—unrestricted | 15,000 | |
| Cash | | 15,000 |

(15b) *Investment in plant fund entry to record capitalization of equipment:*

| Equipment | 15,000 | |
| Net investment in plant | | 15,000 |

Annual Financial Statements of Colleges and Universities

The structure of the financial statements for a college or university depends on whether the institution is subject to FASB or GASB standards. *FASB Statement No. 117* requires three financial statements: (1) a *statement of financial position* or balance sheet, (2) a *statement of activities* including revenues, expenses, and changes in fund balances, and (3) a *statement of cash flows*. The structure of financial statements for colleges and universities under GASB standards varies considerably. The financial statements presented below for Regional University illustrate one such variation. They include (1) a *balance sheet,* (2) *statement of changes in fund balances,* and (3) a *statement of current funds revenues, expenditures, and other changes.*

The balance sheet for nonprofit organizations under the GASB may be presented in either the layered (''pancake'') form illustrated in Exhibit 19-7 for Regional University or the columnar form illustrated for hospitals and other nonprofit organizations later in this chapter. A weakness of the layered form is that it does not display the sum of similar items across all funds. The balance sheets for nonprofit organizations under the FASB must use the columnar form.

Educational institutions often derive income from endowment-type resources that are held in trust and administered by outside fiscal agents, where such resources are neither possessed nor controlled by the institution. These resources should not be included in the institution's balance sheet but, rather, should be included parenthetically (e.g., in the endowment fund section of the balance sheet) or in notes to the financial statements. However, if the college or university has legally enforceable rights, as to either principal or income, these funds may be reported as assets in the financial statements.

A statement of changes in fund balances is prepared that includes a column for each fund group except for agency funds that do not have fund balances. The statement of changes in fund balances shows the additions (sources of financial resources), deductions (uses of financial resources), net increase or decrease for the year, beginning fund balances, and ending fund balances.

The statement of current funds revenues, expenditures, and other changes reflects the financial activities of the current funds for the reporting period. This statement is unique to educational and similar institutions because it does not purport to present the results of operations or net income or loss for the institution. Note that this statement relates only to the current funds and that it reflects expenditures rather than expenses. Thus such a statement is not prepared for any other funds. For the period covered, this statement provides the reader with information concerning the details of current funds revenues by source, current funds expenditures by function, and all other changes in current funds.

The annual financial statements for Regional University are presented in Exhibits 19-7, discussed earlier, and in Exhibits 19-8 and 19-9. The amounts reflected in Exhibit 19-8 (statement of changes in fund balances) and Exhibit 19-9 (statement of current funds revenues, expenditures, and other changes) result solely from the transactions that were previously recorded for Regional University. The amounts reflected in Exhibit 19-7 (the balance sheet) result from the transactions that were previously recorded and the beginning balance sheet figures. These beginning figures are not given in the illustration; therefore, the ending figures cannot be determined solely from the transactions that were previously recorded.

HOSPITALS

Many hospitals are operated as investor-owned business enterprises, whereas others are nonbusiness organizations and are owned and operated by a governmental body or by a nonprofit corporation. The ensuing discussion relates only to nonprofit hospitals and em-

EXHIBIT 19-7	UNIVERSITY BALANCE SHEET

Regional University
BALANCE SHEET
AT JUNE 30, 19X6

CURRENT FUNDS

Unrestricted Fund

Cash	$ 60,000	Accounts payable	$ 112,000
Investments	90,000	Due to other funds	80,000
Accounts receivable (less allowance		Fund balance	246,000
of $25,000)	175,000		
Inventory	97,000		
Prepaid expenses	16,000		
Total unrestricted	$ 438,000	Total unrestricted	$ 438,000

Restricted Fund

Cash	$ 100,000	Accounts payable	$ 16,000
Investments	460,000	Fund balance	584,000
Accounts receivable (less allowance			
of $5,000)	40,000		
Total restricted	$ 600,000	Total restricted	$ 600,000
Total current funds	$1,038,000	Total current funds	$1,038,000

LOAN FUNDS

Cash	$ 25,000	Fund balances:	
Due from unrestricted current fund	5,000	Restricted	$ 100,000
Investments	25,000	Unrestricted	50,000
Loans to students, faculty, and staff			
(less allowance of $5,000)	95,000		
Total loan funds	$ 150,000	Total loan funds	$ 150,000

ENDOWMENT AND SIMILAR FUNDS

Cash	$ 242,000	Fund balances:	
Due from unrestricted current fund	50,000	Endowment, restricted	$ 750,000
Investments	610,000	Term endowment, restricted	100,000
		Quasi endowment, unrestricted	52,000
Total endowment and similar funds	$ 902,000	Total endowment and similar funds	$ 902,000

EXHIBIT 19-7	UNIVERSITY BALANCE SHEET (Continued)

ANNUITY AND LIFE INCOME FUNDS
Annuity Funds

Cash	$ 115,000	Annuities payable	$ 275,000
Investments	400,000	Fund balances	240,000
Total annuity funds	$ 515,000	Total annuity funds	$ 515,000

Life Income Funds

Cash	$ 120,000	Income payable	$ 15,000
Investments	500,000	Fund balances	605,000
Total life income funds	620,000	Total life income funds	$ 620,000
Total annuity and life income funds	$ 1,135,000	Total annuity and life income funds	$ 1,135,000

PLANT FUNDS
Unexpended Plant Fund

Cash	$ 190,000	Accounts payable	$ 46,000
Due from unrestricted current fund	25,000	Bonds payable	200,000
Investments	505,000	Fund balances:	
		Restricted	400,000
		Unrestricted	74,000
Total unexpended	$ 720,000	Total unexpended	$ 720,000

Renewal and Replacement Fund

Cash	$ 41,000	Fund balances:	
Investments	110,000	Restricted	$ 30,000
		Unrestricted	121,000
Total renewal and replacement	$ 151,000	Total renewal and replacement	$ 151,000

Retirement of Indebtedness Fund

Cash	$ 75,000	Fund balances:	
		Restricted	$ 35,000
		Unrestricted	40,000
Total retirement of indebtedness	$ 75,000	Total retirement of indebtedness	$ 75,000

Investment in Plant Fund

Land	$ 290,000	Notes payable	$ 230,000
Buildings	12,000,000	Bonds payable	300,000
Equipment	8,000,000	Mortgages payable	1,400,000
Library books	210,000	Net investment in plant	18,570,000
Total investment in plant	$20,500,000		$20,500,000
Total plant funds	$21,446,000	Total plant funds	$21,446,000

AGENCY FUND

Cash	$ 5,000	Deposits held in custody for others	$ 25,000
Investments	20,000		
Total agency funds	$ 25,000	Total agency funds	$ 25,000

phasizes the accounting and reporting practices of hospitals under FASB jurisdiction. The major sources of accounting principles for hospitals are the AICPA's *Hospital Audit Guide* (1972), various AICPA statements of position, which are reprinted in the guide, and various FASB pronouncements.

Fund Structure

The *AICPA Hospital Audit Guide* provides that all funds that are used in hospital accounting fall under two major categories: unrestricted funds and restricted funds. *Unrestricted funds* are used to account for resources that may be used at the discretion of the governing board. The unrestricted funds are used to account for the normal operating transactions of a hospital and consist of all unrestricted resources, including board-designated funds (for quasi endowment and other purposes), and property, plant, and equipment. On the other hand, *restricted funds* are used to account for resources that are externally restricted; that is, their usage is restricted by the third-party donor or grantor. Hospitals subject to FASB rules must also segregate *temporarily restricted funds* from *permanently restricted funds* for financial reporting purposes.

A *board-designated fund* accounts for resources that are designated by the governing board to be used for special purposes (e.g., for expansion of outpatient facilities, quasi endowment). Board-designated funds usually consist of cash and marketable securities that are set aside until they are used for the intended purpose. They are accounted for as unrestricted funds because the board can rescind its action by which it set aside the funds and can direct the resources to general operating or other uses. They are not classified as restricted funds because the latter includes only resources that are restricted by the outside grantor or donor.

Property, plant, and equipment of a hospital, with related liabilities (e.g., mortgages payable), are accounted for as unrestricted funds because to do otherwise would imply that there are restrictions on the use of such assets. Property, plant, and equipment are accounted for at historical cost (or, in the case of donated assets, at the fair market value at the date of receipt of the asset) by debiting the asset account and crediting the fund balance. All hospitals, whether under FASB or GASB jurisdiction, depreciate their property, plant, and equipment (excluding land) over their estimated useful lives. As is true with business enterprises, hospital fixed asset depreciation is cost-based and is a process of allocation, not of valuation.

Classification and Recognition of Hospital Revenues

Hospitals follow accrual accounting in their fund accounting systems. Sources of revenues for hospitals are classified as daily patient service revenue, other operating revenue, and nonoperating revenue. Exhibit 19-10 illustrates the types of items that would be included under each of these revenue classifications.

Patient Service Revenues

Patient service revenues, consisting of nursing services revenues and other professional services revenues, is the major revenue source for a hospital. Such revenues should be recorded at the gross amount of the established charge, regardless of whether or not the hospital expects to collect the full amount of such charges. Charity allowances, contractual adjustment arrangements with third-party payors (e.g., Blue Cross/Blue Shield, other insurance companies, Medicare) allowing them to pay less than the established charges, and the provision for uncollectible accounts should be reported separately from gross revenues as *deductions from gross revenues,* rather than as operating expenses.

EXHIBIT 19-8 UNIVERSITY STATEMENT OF CHANGES IN FUND BALANCES

Regional University
STATEMENT OF CHANGES IN FUND BALANCES
FOR THE YEAR ENDED JUNE 30, 19X6

	Current Funds		Loan Funds	Endowment and Similar Funds
	Unrestricted	Restricted		
Revenues and other additions:				
Educational and general revenues	$1,875,000	$	$	$
Auxiliary enterprise revenues	305,000			
Expired term endowment revenues	40,000			
Gifts and bequests—restricted			50,000	85,000
Grants and contracts—restricted		776,000		
Government appropriations—restricted				
Investment income—restricted		48,000	10,000	
Realized gains on investments—unrestricted				5,000
Realized gains on investments—restricted			1,000	10,000
Interest on loans receivable			14,000	
Expended for plant facilities				
Retirement of indebtedness				
Total revenues and other additions	$2,220,000	$824,000	$ 75,000	$100,000
Expenditures and other deductions:				
Educational and general expenditures	$1,846,000	$753,000	$	$
Auxiliary enterprise expenditures	207,000			
Provision for uncollectible loans			7,000	
Administrative and collection costs			5,000	
Expended for plant expenditures (including noncapitalized expenditures of $50,000)				
Retirement of indebtedness				
Interest on indebtedness				
Disposal of plant facilities				
Expired term endowments				40,000
Total expenditures and other deductions	$2,053,000	$753,000	$ 12,000	$ 40,000
Transfers among funds—additions (deductions):				
Mandatory:				
Principal and interest	$ (126,000)		$	$
Renewals and replacements	(35,000)			
Nonmandatory:				
Loan fund	(5,000)		5,000	
Quasi-endowment funds	(50,000)			50,000
Unexpended plant fund	(25,000)			
Total transfers	$ (241,000)		$ 5,000	$ 50,000
Net increase (decrease) for the year	$ (74,000)	$ 71,000	$ 68,000	$110,000
Fund balance at July 1, 19X5	320,000	513,000	82,000	792,000
Fund balance at June 30, 19X6	$ 246,000	$584,000	$150,000	$902,000

Annuity and Life Income Funds	Plant Funds			
	Unexpended	Renewal and Replacement	Retirement of Indebtedness	Investment in Plant
$	$	$	$	$
40,000	70,000		33,000	20,000
	25,000			
	5,000	10,000		
10,000				
	10,000	5,000		
				500,000
				150,000
$ 50,000	$ 110,000	$ 15,000	$ 33,000	$ 670,000
	$	$	$	$
			1,000	
	415,000	150,000		
			150,000	
			25,000	
				110,000
	$ 415,000	$ 150,000	$176,000	$ 110,000
	$	$	$126,000	
		35,000		
	25,000			
	$ 25,000	$ 35,000	$126,000	
$ 50,000	$(280,000)	$(100,000)	$ (17,000)	$ 560,000
795,000	754,000	251,000	92,000	18,010,000
$845,000	$ 474,000	$ 151,000	$ 75,000	$18,570,000

EXHIBIT 19-9	UNIVERSITY STATEMENT OF CURRENT FUNDS REVENUES, EXPENDITURES, AND OTHER CHANGES

Regional University

STATEMENT OF CURRENT FUNDS REVENUES, EXPENDITURES, AND OTHER CHANGES
FOR THE YEAR ENDED JUNE 30, 19X6

	Unrestricted	Restricted	Total
Revenues:			
Educational and general:			
Student tuition and fees	$1,100,000	$	$1,100,000
Governmental appropriations:			
Federal	200,000		200,000
State	300,000		300,000
Governmental grants	50,000	716,000	766,000
Private gifts	150,000		150,000
Endowment income	75,000	37,000	112,000
Total educational and general revenues	$1,875,000	$753,000	$2,628,000
Auxiliary enterprises	305,000		305,000
Expired term endowment	40,000		40,000
Total revenues	$2,220,000	$753,000	$2,973,000
Expenditures and mandatory transfers:			
Educational and general:			
Instruction and departmental research	$1,300,000	$448,000	$1,748,000
Sponsored research		268,000	268,000
Public service	150,000		150,000
Libraries	110,000		110,000
Student services	95,000		95,000
Operation and maintenance of plant	75,000		75,000
General administration	74,000		74,000
Provision for uncollectible accounts	25,000		25,000
Student aid	17,000	37,000	54,000
Total educational and general expenditures	$1,846,000	$753,000	$2,599,000
Auxiliary enterprises:			
Expenditures	$ 207,000		$ 207,000
Mandatory transfers for:			
Principal and interest	126,000		126,000
Renewals and replacements	35,000		35,000
Total auxiliary enterprises	$ 368,000		$ 368,000
Total expenditures and mandatory transfers	$2,214,000	$753,000	$2,967,000
Excess of revenues over expenditures and mandatory transfers	$ 6,000	$ –0–	$ 6,000
Other transfers and additions/(deductions):			
Excess of restricted receipts over transfers to revenues		71,000*	71,000
Nonmandatory transfers to:			
Loan fund	$ (5,000)		
Quasi-endowment fund	(50,000)		
Unexpended plant fund	(25,000)		
Total nonmandatory transfers to other funds	(80,000)		(80,000)
Net increase/(decrease) in fund balance	$ (74,000)	$ 71,000	$ (3,000)

* This amount is the excess of resources received by the current restricted funds over the amount expended and subsequently recognized as revenue in the current restricted funds (see the net increase in fund balance for the restricted current funds in Exhibit 19-8).

EXHIBIT 19-10	ILLUSTRATIONS OF HOSPITAL REVENUES CLASSIFICATIONS*

Patient Service Revenues

1. Revenue from daily patient services
(routine care)
    Medical
    Surgical
    Pediatrics
    Intensive care
    Psychiatric
    Obstetric
    Newborn nurseries
    Premature nurseries
    Other

2. Revenue from other nursing services
    Operating room
    Recovery room
    Delivery and labor room
    Central services and supply
    Intravenous therapy
    Emergency service
    Other

3. Revenue from other professional
services (ancillary services)
    Laboratories
    Blood bank
    Electrocardiology
    Radiology
    Pharmacy
    Anesthesiology
    Physical therapy
    Other

Other Operating Revenues

1. Tuition revenue from educational programs

2. Research and other specific purpose grants
(recognized as revenue at time of expenditure)

3. Miscellaneous
    Donated supplies
    Rental revenues from hospital space, etc.
    Accommodation sales of supplies to doctors,
      nurses, etc.
    Fees for transcripts of medical and billing
      records
    Sales of cafeteria meals to staff and visitors
    Recovery of charges for personal telephone
      calls
    Sale of scrap, waste materials, etc.
    Revenues from gift shops, newsstands, parking
      lots, television rentals, etc.

Nonoperating Revenues

1. Unrestricted gifts, grants, and bequests

2. Unrestricted income from endowment funds

3. Miscellaneous
    Income and gains from investments of unrestricted
      funds
    Donated services
    Gain on sale of hospital properties
    Rentals from facilities not used in hospital
      operations
    Term endowment funds upon termination of
      restrictions

* American Institute of Certified Public Accountants, *Hospital Audit Guide*, pp. 29–30, 33–34.

Other Operating Revenues

Other operating revenues include revenue from nonpatient care services to patients (e.g., television rentals), sales and activities to persons other than patients, tuition revenue from educational programs, research and other specific purpose grants, and miscellaneous (see Exhibit 19-10). There is nothing unusual in the recording of these resources except for donated supplies, shown under miscellaneous in Exhibit 19-10. Hospitals often receive donated supplies (e.g., bed linens, medicines, office supplies) that would normally be purchased. These donated supplies are recorded at fair market value by debiting inventory or expense and crediting *other operating revenue.*

Nonoperating Revenues

Nonoperating revenue is not directly related to the care of patients, to other services rendered to patients, or to sales of goods related to patient care (see Exhibit 19-10). There is nothing unusual about the accounting treatment of most of these types of revenues. A few of these revenue sources do require further discussion, however, including unrestricted gifts, grants, and bequests; investment income and gains or losses; and donated services.

Unrestricted gifts, grants, and bequests may be expended for purposes that are designated by the governing board. Thus, they are recognized as nonoperating revenue in the unrestricted funds. Unrestricted pledges are accounted for in the unrestricted funds by a debit to pledges receivable and a credit to nonoperating revenue. An appropriate amount for uncollectible pledges should be recorded by a debit to nonoperating revenue and a credit to the estimated uncollectible pledges account. See the issues section earlier in this chapter for additional discussion of revenue from contributions.

Investment income should be recognized as nonoperating revenue in the statement of revenues and expenses, if such revenue derives from the investment of unrestricted funds (including board-designated funds), or if it is unrestricted income from endowment funds. Realized gains (or losses) from the sale of investments of unrestricted funds (including board-designated funds) should also be included as nonoperating revenue in the hospital's statement of revenues and expenses. "Gains or losses on investment trading between unrestricted and restricted funds should be recognized [as nonoperating revenue] and separately disclosed in the financial statements. Gains or losses resulting from transactions between designated portions of the unrestricted fund should not be recognized."[5]

Donated services are frequently received by hospitals. Such donated services are recorded by nonprofits under FASB jurisdiction if the "services received (a) create or enhance nonfinancial assets or (b) require specialized skills, are provided by individuals possessing those skills, and would typically need to be purchased if not provided by donation."[6] If either test is met, the fair value of such services should be debited to the appropriate expense account and credited to nonoperating revenue.

Classification of Operating Expenses

Operating expenses of hospitals are divided into the following categories: nursing services, other professional services, general services, fiscal services, administrative services, and depreciation. Exhibit 19-11 shows how these categories can be subdivided into object classifications.

Accounting for Hospital Unrestricted and Restricted Funds

Exhibit 19-12 shows the transactions and related journal entries for the unrestricted funds of Buffalo Gap Municipal Hospital during the year ended December 31, 19X6. Exhibits 19-13, 19-14, and 19-15 show the transactions and related journal entries for the unrestricted funds of Buffalo Gap Hospital during the year ended December 31, 19X6.

---

[5] American Institute of Certified Public Accountants, *Hospital Audit Guide,* p. 10. See *FASB Statement No. 117,* pars. 22–23 and 120–132 for additional discussion of gain and loss classification.

[6] *FASB Statement No. 116,* par. 9.

| EXHIBIT 19-11 | ILLUSTRATIONS OF HOSPITAL EXPENSES CLASSIFICATIONS* |

Operating Expenses
  Nursing services
  Other professional services
  General services
  Fiscal services
  Administrative services
  Provision for depreciation

Further Classification by Object or Nature of Each of the Above Types of Operating Expenses (Except Provision for Depreciation)
  Salaries and wages
  Employee benefits
  Fees to individuals and organizations
  Supplies
  Purchased services
  Other expenses

* American Institute of Certified Public Accountants, *Hospital Audit Guide,* pp. 35–36.

When a hospital receives gifts, bequests, grants, and restricted income from endowment funds that are restricted as to use by the third-party grantor or donor, such resources are accounted for in the restricted funds. However, the restricted funds do not ultimately expend the resources for the intended purpose. The resources are expended by the unrestricted funds, at which time an amount equal to the expense is transferred from the restricted to unrestricted funds. Restricted resources are generally of three types: (1) funds for specific operating purposes; (2) funds for additions to property, plant, and equipment; and (3) endowment funds.[7] (In addition, hospitals sometimes make use of other restricted funds—loan funds, annuity funds, and life income funds. Where these funds are used, the accounting would be essentially identical with comparable funds, which were discussed earlier in the chapter under college and university accounting. For this reason, they are not discussed here.)

Specific Purpose Funds

Specific purpose funds consist of resources (e.g., cash, pledges receivable, or investments) that were given to the hospital for specific operating purposes, except for plant replacement and expansion (e.g., for heart disease research). At the time of the receipt of these resources, they are credited to the fund balance of the specific purpose fund. The resources are held in this fund until operating expenses are incurred for the intended purpose in the unrestricted funds, at which time an amount equal to the expense is transferred to the unrestricted funds from the specific purpose fund, by debiting the fund balance of the

[7] American Institute of Certified Public Accountants, *Hospital Audit Guide,* pp. 8–9.

EXHIBIT 19-12	UNRESTRICTED FUNDS ENTRIES

Buffalo Gap Municipal Hospital

UNRESTRICTED FUNDS ENTRIES
FOR THE YEAR ENDED DECEMBER 31, 19X6

Transaction (1): Billing for patient service revenues amounted to $1,500,000: daily patient services, $900,000; other nursing services, $450,000; and other professional services, $150,000.

Unrestricted funds entry to record patient service revenues:

Accounts and notes receivable	1,500,000	
Patient service revenues—daily patient services		900,000
Patient service revenues—other nursing services		450,000
Patient service revenues—other professional services		150,000

Transaction (2): Estimated deductions from patient service revenues were as follows: contractual adjustments for third-party payers, $75,000; charity service adjustments, $35,000; provision for uncollectible accounts, $25,000.

Unrestricted funds entry to record deductions from patient service revenues:

Contractual adjustments	75,000	
Charity service	35,000	
Provision for uncollectible accounts	25,000	
Estimated uncollectibles and allowances		135,000

Transaction (3): Accounts and notes receivable collected amount to $1,200,000:

Unrestricted funds entry to record collections of accounts and notes receivable:

Cash	1,200,000	
Accounts and notes receivable		1,200,000

Transaction (4): Actual write-offs of uncollectibles and adjustments of $115,000 were as follows: contractual adjustments, $70,000; charity service, $30,000; and uncollectible accounts, $15,000.

Unrestricted funds entry to record write-offs of actual uncollectibles and adjustments:

Estimated uncollectibles and allowances	115,000	
Accounts and notes receivable		115,000

Transaction (5): Unrestricted gifts and bequests of $15,000 were received in 19X6 in the form of pledges to be collected in future years.

Unrestricted funds entry to record revenues from uncollected pledges:

Pledges receivable	15,000	
Nonoperating revenues—temporarily restricted gifts		15,000

| EXHIBIT 19-12 | UNRESTRICTED FUNDS ENTRIES (Continued) |

Transaction (6): Other operating revenues collected include cafeteria sales, $10,000, and television rentals, $5,000.

Unrestricted funds entry to record cafeteria sales and television rentals:

Cash	15,000	
Other operating revenues—cafeteria sales		10,000
Other operating revenues—television rentals		5,000

Transaction (7): The unrestricted funds incurred expenses amounting to $400,000 for nursing services for which they are entitled to reimbursement by the specific purpose fund; $120,000 has been collected in cash, and $280,000 is still due from the specific purpose fund. [See related entry (2) in the specific purpose funds section discussed later.]

Unrestricted funds entry to record expenditures to be reimbursed by the specific purpose fund:

Operating expenses—nursing services	400,000	
Cash		400,000

Unrestricted funds entry to record transfers from specific purpose funds:

Cash	120,000	
Due from specific purpose fund	280,000	
Other operating revenues—transfers from specific purpose fund		400,000

Transaction (8): Operating expenses incurred that have been or will be paid in cash included the following: nursing services, $230,000; other professional services, $596,000; general services, $330,000; fiscal services, $48,000; administrative services, $99,000; and interest, $20,000. The amount paid was $1,223,000, and accounts payable were increased by $100,000.

Unrestricted funds entry to record operating expenses:

Operating expenses—nursing services	230,000	
Operating expenses—other professional services	596,000	
Operating expenses—general services	330,000	
Operating expenses—fiscal services	48,000	
Operating expenses—administrative services	99,000	
Operating expenses—interest	20,000	
Accounts payable		100,000
Cash		1,223,000

Transaction (9): Receipts of nonoperating revenues include unrestricted gifts, $20,000; income from board-designated investments, $25,000; and unrestricted income from endowments, $30,000.

Unrestricted funds entry to record nonoperating revenues:

Cash	75,000	
Nonoperating revenues—unrestricted gifts		20,000
Nonoperating revenues—income from board-designated investments		25,000
Nonoperating revenues—unrestricted income from endowments		30,000

EXHIBIT 19-12	UNRESTRICTED FUNDS ENTRIES (Continued)

Transaction (10): Donated services were nursing services, $35,000, and general services, $15,000.

Unrestricted funds entry to record donated services:

Operating expenses—nursing services	35,000	
Operating expenses—general services	15,000	
Nonoperating revenues—donated services		50,000

Transaction (11): The depreciation expense provision amounted to $75,000.

Unrestricted funds entry to record provision for depreciation:

Operating expenses—provision for depreciation	75,000	
Accumulated depreciation		75,000

Transaction (12): Materials and supplies inventories acquired for cash amounted to $25,000.

Unrestricted funds entry to record acquisition of inventories:

Inventories	25,000	
Cash		25,000

Transaction (13): Materials and supplies inventories were used for the following operating purposes:

Nursing services	$10,000
Other professional services	4,000
General services	5,000
Fiscal services	2,000
Administrative services	1,000
Total	$22,000

Unrestricted funds entry to record materials and supplies withdrawn from inventories:

Operating expenses—nursing services	10,000	
Operating expenses—other professional services	4,000	
Operating expenses—general services	5,000	
Operating expenses—fiscal services	2,000	
Operating expenses—administrative services	1,000	
Inventories		22,000

Transaction (14): A loss on disposal of assets in the amount of $5,000 resulted from the sale of major movable equipment with a cost of $55,000 and accumulated depreciation of $40,000; the equipment was sold for $10,000 cash.

Unrestricted funds entry to record sale of equipment:

Cash	10,000	
Accumulated depreciation	40,000	
Operating expenses—loss on disposal of assets	5,000	
Major movable equipment		55,000

Transaction (15): The unrestricted funds received $75,000 cash from the plant replacement and expansion fund to finance property, plant, and equipment acquisitions. [See related entry (2) in the plant replacement and expansion funds section discussed later.]

EXHIBIT 19-12	UNRESTRICTED FUNDS ENTRIES (Continued)

Unrestricted funds entry to record transfer from plant replacement and expansion fund to finance property, plant, and equipment expenditures:

Cash	75,000	
Fund balance—unrestricted—transfer from plant		
replacement and expansion fund......................		75,000

Transaction (16): The unrestricted funds expended $80,000 for major movable equipment. This included the $75,000 received from the plant replacement and expansion fund, along with $5,000 from the unrestricted funds.

Unrestricted funds entry to record acquisition of plant assets:

Major movable equipment	80,000	
Cash		80,000

Transaction (17): In the unrestricted funds, $20,000 cash was paid on the mortgage payable:

Unrestricted funds entry to record payment on mortgage:

Mortgage payable	20,000	
Cash		20,000

Closing entries: Closing entries for the unrestricted funds are made at December 31, 19X6.

Unrestricted funds closing entries at December 31, 19X6:

Patient service revenues—daily patient services	900,000	
Patient service revenues—other nursing services	450,000	
Patient services revenues—other professional services..........	150,000	
Other operating revenues—cafeteria sales	10,000	
Other operating revenues—television rentals	5,000	
Other operating revenues—transfers from specific purpose fund ..	400,000	
Nonoperating revenues—unrestricted gifts	35,000	
Nonoperating revenues—income from board-		
designated investments	25,000	
Nonoperating revenues—unrestricted income from endowments...	30,000	
Nonoperating revenues—donated services....................	50,000	
Contractual adjustments..........................		75,000
Charity service		35,000
Provision for uncollectible accounts.....................		25,000
Operating expenses—nursing services		675,000
Operating expenses—other professional services		600,000
Operating expenses—general services		350,000
Operating expenses—fiscal services		50,000
Operating expenses—administrative services		100,000
Operating expenses—provision for depreciation............		75,000
Operating expenses—loss on disposal of assets		5,000
Operating expenses—interest		20,000
Excess of revenues over expenses		45,000
Excess of revenues over expenses	45,000	
Unrestricted fund balance		45,000

EXHIBIT 19-13	SPECIFIC PURPOSE FUNDS ENTRIES

Buffalo Gap Municipal Hospital

SPECIFIC PURPOSE FUNDS ENTRIES
FOR THE YEAR ENDED DECEMBER 31, 19X6

Transaction (1): The specific purpose funds received the following: restricted gifts and bequests, $125,000; research grants, $280,000 ($20,000 of which has not been collected in cash); and income from investments, $35,000.

Specific purpose funds entry to record amounts received:

Cash	420,000	
Grants receivable	20,000	
Specific purpose fund balance—restricted gifts and bequests .		125,000
Specific purpose fund balance—research grants		280,000
Specific purpose fund balance—income from investments ...		35,000

Transaction (2): The unrestricted funds incurred expenses amounting to $400,000 for which they are entitled to reimbursement by the specific purpose fund; $120,000 has been paid, and $280,000 is still due to the unrestricted funds. [Refer to related entry (7) in the unrestricted funds section discussed earlier.]

Specific purpose funds entry to record transfers to unrestricted funds:

Specific purpose funds balance—transfers to unrestricted funds ...	400,000	
Cash		120,000
Due to unrestricted funds		280,000

Transaction (3): Specific purpose fund cash invested in securities amounted to $290,000.

Specific purpose fund entry to record investments:

Investments	290,000	
Cash		290,000

specific purpose fund and crediting cash. These resources are recognized as *other operating revenue* in the unrestricted funds at the time of such a transfer by a debit to cash and a credit to *other operating revenue*. The assets of this fund would normally consist of cash and investments and would sometimes include pledges receivable and/or grants receivable. Normally the only liability listed would be amounts due to the unrestricted funds.

Exhibit 19-13 shows the transactions and related journal entries for the specific purpose funds of Buffalo Gap Municipal Hospital during the year ended December 31, 19X6.

Plant Replacement and Expansion Fund

The plant replacement and expansion fund consists of donor-restricted resources (e.g., cash, pledges receivable, or investments) intended for additions to property, plant, and equipment. Such resources are debited to cash, pledges receivable, or investments and are

EXHIBIT 19-14	PLANT REPLACEMENT AND EXPANSION FUNDS

Buffalo Gap Municipal Hospital

PLANT REPLACEMENT AND EXPANSION FUNDS ENTRIES
FOR THE YEAR ENDED DECEMBER 31, 19X6

Transaction (1): The plant replacement and expansion funds received the following amounts in 19X6: restricted gifts and bequests, $80,000, of which $5,000 has not yet been collected; and income from investments, $25,000.

Plant replacement and expansion funds entry to record amounts received:

Cash	100,000	
Pledges receivable	5,000	
Plant replacement and expansion fund balance—		
restricted gifts and bequests		80,000
Plant replacement and expansion fund balance—		
income from investments		25,000

Transaction (2): The plant replacement and expansion funds paid $75,000 to the unrestricted funds to finance property, plant, and equipment acquisitions. (Refer to related entry (15) in the unrestricted funds section discussion earlier.)

Plant replacement and expansion funds entry to record transfer to unrestricted funds:

Plant replacement and expansion fund balance—transfer		
to unrestricted funds	75,000	
Cash		75,000

credited to the plant replacement and expansion fund balance. These resources are considered to be contributions to the hospital's permanent capital. Thus, they are *not* recognized as revenue. When an appropriate capital outlay is made in the unrestricted funds for the purpose intended by the donor, resources equal to the outlay are transferred to the unrestricted fund. This transfer is recorded in the plant replacement and expansion fund by a debit to fund balance and a credit to cash. At the same time, the unrestricted funds would debit cash and credit fund balance [see entry (15) in Exhibit 19-12]. The assets of the plant replacement and expansion fund typically include cash and investments and sometimes pledges receivable. This fund would normally have no liabilities. However, it could sometimes have a liability for the amount due to the unrestricted funds for unreimbursed capital outlays.

Exhibit 19-14 shows the transactions and related journal entries for the plant replacement and expansion fund of Buffalo Gap Municipal Hospital during the year ended December 31, 19X6.

Endowment Funds

A hospital may have endowment funds (the governing board may not expend the principal) and term endowment funds (the governing board may expend the principal after the passage of a specified period of time, after a specific event has occurred, or after a

EXHIBIT 19-15	ENDOWMENT FUNDS

Buffalo Gap Municipal Hospital

ENDOWMENT FUNDS ENTRIES
FOR THE YEAR ENDED DECEMBER 31, 19X6

Transaction (1): The endowment funds received permanently restricted gifts and bequests in the amount of $75,000 cash, and the term endowment funds had a gain on the sale of investments in the amount of $5,000 which by the terms of the endowment remains part of the endowment balance (cost of investments sold, $60,000).

Endowment fund entry to record receipt of restricted gifts and bequests:

Cash	75,000	
Endowment fund balance—restricted gifts and bequests		75,000

Term endowment fund entry to record gain on sale of investments:

Cash	65,000	
Investments		60,000
Term endowment fund balance—gain on sale of investments		5,000

Transaction (2): Endowment fund cash invested in securities amounted to $115,000.

Endowment fund entry to record investments:

Investments	115,000	
Cash		115,000

condition has been fulfilled). Both kinds of endowments should be accounted for as restricted funds.

If the term endowment funds principal becomes available for unrestricted purposes, the amount available should be recognized in the unrestricted funds by a debit to cash and a credit to *nonoperating revenue* at the time it becomes available. However, if such funds become available for some specified purpose, they should be transferred to and accounted for in a specific purpose fund (if intended for a specified operating purpose) or in a plant replacement and expansion fund (if intended for capital expenditures) or in some other appropriate restricted fund (e.g., a loan fund). Upon expiration of the term endowment, the term endowment fund debits fund balance and credits cash. The receiving restricted fund would record the transaction by debiting cash and crediting fund balance. Once transferred, these resources are accounted for in the usual manner for the particular funds to which the transfers are made.

Income from investments of endowment funds may be unrestricted or restricted. If unrestricted, it should be accounted for in the unrestricted funds as *nonoperating revenue*. If restricted, it should be accounted for as a credit to fund balance in a specific purpose fund or in a plant replacement and expansion fund or in some other appropriate restricted fund depending on the type of restriction. *Realized gains (or losses)* from the sale of investments of endowment funds are added to (or deducted from) the endowment fund principal unless such gains or losses under the terms of the endowment gift should be added to or deducted from some other fund.

It should be noted that unlike colleges and universities, hospitals do not include quasi endowments (board-designated funds) among their endowment funds. Instead, the assets of the quasi endowment are included among the assets of the unrestricted funds with an explanatory note to the financial statements to indicate the purpose for which they are designated.

Exhibit 19-15 shows the transactions and related journal entries for the endowment funds of Buffalo Gap Municipal Hospital during the year ended December 31, 19X6.

No Closing Entries for Restricted Funds

Closing entries for the restricted funds are not required because all transactions in incoming and outgoing resources for which closing entries might be otherwise required are credited or debited directly to the appropriate fund balance accounts.

Annual Financial Statements of Hospitals

The basic statements that are required of hospitals are the (1) *balance sheet,* (2) *statement of activities,* and (3) *statement of cash flows.* In addition, appropriate notes to the financial statements are required as illustrated in *FASB Statement No. 117.*

Balance sheet accounts for hospitals under GASB jurisdiction are segregated by funds (one balance sheet for the unrestricted funds and one for *each* of the restricted funds) and may be presented in columnar form or in the widely used layered ("pancake") format illustrated in Exhibit 19-7 for colleges and universities. In contrast, balance sheets for hospitals under FASB jurisdiction must report total assets, liabilities, and net assets which precludes the layered balance sheet.

Sometimes hospitals have endowment-type resources that are held in trust and administered by outside parties, where such resources are not directly or indirectly controlled by the hospital. Such resources should not be included in the hospital's balance sheet. However, their existence should be disclosed parenthetically (e.g., in the endowment fund section of the balance sheet) or in the notes to the financial statements. But if the hospital has legally enforceable rights, as to either principal or income, these funds may be reported as assets in the financial statements. Distributions of income to the hospital from endowment funds that are held in trust by others should be recognized by the hospital as endowment income. Such endowment income may be either unrestricted or restricted and should be accounted for accordingly.

The operating statement of all organizations under FASB jurisdiction (including hospitals under FASB jurisdiction) is the *statement of activities.* The statement of activities is prepared on the accrual basis and describes the revenues, expenses (including depreciation), gains, and losses that change each of three classes of net assets— *unrestricted net assets, temporarily restricted net assets,* and *permanently restricted net assets.* Further, all expenses are reported as decreases in unrestricted net assets (*FASB Statement No. 117,* par. 20); thus, restricted net assets do not give rise to expenses until the related restrictions expire or are satisfied.

The statement of activities for Buffalo Gap Municipal Hospital is shown in Exhibit 19-17. Exhibit 19-18 shows supplementary disclosures that explain the calculation of net patient service revenues. As shown in the net assets section of the balance sheet in Exhibit 19-16, Buffalo Gap's temporarily restricted net assets are pledges receivable, specific purpose funds, plant replacement and expansion funds, and term endowment funds; Buffalo Gap's permanently restricted net assets are permanent endowment funds. Notice that the ending net asset balances appear both in the net asset section of the balance sheet and at the bottom on the statement of activities. Also notice that all expenses and losses are

EXHIBIT 19-16	HOSPITAL BALANCE SHEET

Buffalo Gap Municipal Hospital
BALANCE SHEET
AT DECEMBER 31, 19X6

Assets

Current assets:

Cash (including board-designated funds of $10,000)			$ 30,000
Investments (all board-designated funds)			250,000
Accounts and notes receivable (net of estimated uncollectibles allowances of $20,000)			300,000
Pledges receivable (temporarily restricted)			15,000
Due unrestricted funds from specific-purpose funds			280,000
Inventories			50,000
Prepaid expenses			10,000
Restricted assets—specific purpose funds:			
Cash		$ 10,000	
Investments		350,000	
Grants receivable		20,000	380,000
Restricted assets—plant replacement and expansion fund:			
Cash		$ 25,000	
Investments		235,000	
Pledges receivable		5,000	265,000
Total current assets			$1,580,000
Noncurrent assets:			
Land		$ 500,000	
Buildings		800,000	
Fixed equipment		100,000	
Major movable equipment		40,000	
Total property, plant, and equipment		$1,440,000	
Less: Accumulated depreciation		740,000	
Net property, plant, and equipment			700,000
Restricted assets—endowment funds:			
Cash		$ 25,000	
Investments		250,000	275,000
Total assets			$2,555,000

Liabilities

Current liabilities:

Notes payable			$ 75,000
Accounts payable			110,000
Due unrestricted funds from specific purpose funds			280,000
Total current liabilities			$ 465,000
Long-term liabilities:			
Mortgage payable			300,000
Total liabilities			$ 765,000

Net assets

Unrestricted		$1,135,000	
Temporarily restricted:			
Pledges receivable	$ 15,000		
Specific purpose funds	100,000		
Plant replacement and expansion funds	265,000		
Term endowment funds	100,000	480,000	
Permanently restricted:			
Endowment funds		175,000	1,790,000
Total liabilities and net assets			$2,555,000

EXHIBIT 19-17   HOSPITAL STATEMENT OF ACTIVITIES

Buffalo Gap Municipal Hospital
STATEMENT OF ACTIVITIES
FOR YEAR ENDED DECEMBER 31, 19X6

	Unrestricted	Temporarily Restricted	Permanently Restricted	Total
Revenues, gains, and other support				
Net patient service revenues (see Exhibit 19-18)	$1,365,000			$1,365,000
Other operating revenues:				
Cafeteria sales	10,000			10,000
Television rental	5,000			5,000
Total operating revenue	$1,380,000			$1,380,000
Nonoperating revenues:				
Unrestricted gifts	$ 20,000	$ 15,000[1]	$	$ 35,000
Restricted gifts and bequests		205,000[2]	75,000	280,000
Research grants		280,000		280,000
Income from board-restricted funds	25,000			25,000
Income from endowments	30,000			30,000
Other income from investments		60,000[3]		60,000
Gain on sale of investments		5,000		5,000
Donated services	50,000			50,000
Total nonoperating revenue	$ 125,000	$ 565,000	$ 75,000	$ 765,000
Net assets released from restrictions:				
Satisfaction of specific purpose fund restrictions	$ 400,000	$(400,000)		
Satisfaction of equipment acquisition restrictions	75,000	(75,000)		
Total net assets released from restrictions	$ 475,000	$(475,000)		
Total revenues, gains, and other support	$1,980,000	$ 90,000	$ 75,000	$2,145,000
Expenses and losses				
Nursing services	$ 675,000			$ 675,000
Other professional services	600,000			600,000
General services	350,000			350,000
Fiscal services	50,000			50,000
Administrative services	100,000			100,000
Provision for depreciation	75,000			75,000
Loss on disposal of assets	5,000			5,000
Interest	20,000			20,000
Total expenses and losses	$1,875,000			$1,875,000
Change in net assets	$ 105,000	$ 90,000	$ 75,000	$ 270,000
Net assets at beginning of year	1,030,000	390,000	100,000	1,520,000
Net assets at end of year	$1,135,000	$ 480,000	$175,000	$1,790,000

[1] Pledges receivable recorded in the unrestricted fund; see transaction (5) in Exhibit 19-12.

[2] $205,000 = $125,000 from special purpose funds + $80,000 from plant replacement and expansion fund.

[3] $60,000 = $35,000 from special purpose funds + $25,000 from plant replacement and expansion fund.

recorded in the unrestricted column; resources cannot be expensed until any restrictions attached to them expire or are satisfied. All activities data in Exhibits 19-17 and 19-18 derive from the Buffalo Gap transactions for 19X6 recorded earlier. Beginning-of-the-year account balances necessary to complete the balance sheet in Exhibit 19-16 and the fund balance calculations in Exhibit 19-17 were not given earlier but are presented for the first time in these financial statements.

Hospitals under GASB jurisdiction may prepare a two-part statement of activities. One part is a statement of unrestricted funds revenues and expenses that is less inclusive than that required by the FASB. The other part is a statement of changes in fund balances that includes summarized revenues and expenses for unrestricted funds and detailed revenues and expenses for each restricted fund or fund group.

The statement of cash flows is not illustrated here because of its similarity to such statements that are prepared for business enterprises. The statement of cash flows must report net cash used by *operating activities,* net cash used by *investing activities,* and net cash used by *financing activities*. The statement may use either the indirect or the direct method.

VOLUNTARY HEALTH AND WELFARE ORGANIZATIONS

Voluntary health and welfare organizations are nonprofit entities (e.g., Red Cross, The United Way, local child welfare organizations) that use their resources in their efforts to solve health and welfare problems of society and/or specific individuals. The major source of accounting principles for voluntary health and welfare organizations under FASB jurisdiction is the AICPA audit guide entitled *Audits of Voluntary Health and Welfare Organizations,* related statements of position, and various FASB pronouncements.

Accounting Methods of Voluntary Health and Welfare Organizations

The accrual basis of accounting is required for voluntary health and welfare organizations (hereafter referred to as VHWOs). However, the cash basis of accounting is acceptable if it results in financial statements that do not differ materially from those prepared on the accrual basis. Fund accounting should be used by VHWOs that have significant amounts of restricted resources. The records of VHWOs without significant amounts of restricted resources usually resemble the records of business enterprises.

Public Support and Revenue

VHWOs derive *revenue* from a variety of sources: membership dues, investment income, ticket sales, and so on. For many such organizations, their revenue is insufficient to cover operating costs. Therefore, they often solicit outside *public support,* such as contributions and gifts, bequests, grants, donated services, and so on, from foundations, corporations, governmental units, and individuals. Pledges of support that are legally enforceable should be recorded as assets and as public support at their net realizable value.

Expenses

Each of the various funds of VHWOs incurs expenses to carry out its operations in providing program services and supporting services. Program services expenses are the costs of providing the programs for which the organization was established to provide. Supporting services expenses include management and general costs and fund-raising costs.

EXHIBIT 19-18	SUPPLEMENTARY DISCLOSURE FOR HOSPITAL REVENUES

Buffalo Gap Municipal Hospital
SCHEDULE OF PATIENT SERVICE REVENUES AND DEDUCTIONS
FOR THE YEAR ENDED DECEMBER 31, 19X6

Patient service revenues:		
Daily patient services		$ 900,000
Other nursing services		450,000
Other professional services		150,000
Total patient service revenues		$1,500,000
Less: Deductions from patient service revenues		
Contractual adjustments	$75,000	
Charity service	35,000	
Provision for uncollectible accounts	25,000	135,000
Net patient service revenues		$1,365,000

Donated Services, Materials, and Facilities

Donated services should be recorded as public support (contributions) in the statement of activities, with an equivalent amount recorded as an expense when the "services received (a) create or enhance nonfinancial assets or (b) require specialized skills, are provided by individuals possessing those skills, and would typically need to be purchased if not provided by donation" (*FASB Statement No. 117,* par. 9). Significant amounts of donated materials and free use of facilities should be recorded at their fair value as public support (contributions) and as an asset or expense of the same amount. Normally such contributed services, materials, and facilities are unrestricted; in such cases, they would be recorded in the current unrestricted fund. Contributed capital assets are recorded in the land, building, and equipment fund.

Fund Structure   Like other nonprofit organizations, VHWOs use fund accounting systems. The paragraphs that follow briefly describe the types of funds that are frequently used by VHWOs.

Current Funds

The current funds of VHWOs are used to account for resources that are expendable in carrying out the operating purposes of the organization on a day-to-day basis. Current funds consist of two subgroups: the current unrestricted fund and current restricted funds.

The *current unrestricted fund* is used to account for resources (including board-designated funds) over which the governing board has discretionary control, that is, resources that are unrestricted and available for general operations. These resources come from public support or revenues. Plant assets acquired with current unrestricted funds are recorded in the unrestricted fund (by debiting fund balance and crediting cash) and also recorded in the plant fund (by debiting an asset account and crediting fund balance).

The *current restricted funds* are used to account for resources that are currently available but are restricted to certain operating purposes as specified by the outside donor or grantor. These resources may come from gifts, bequests, grants, income from endowments, or other sources.

Land, Building, and Equipment Fund (Plant Fund)

This fund is used to account for the following: (1) resources restricted by donors for the acquisition or replacement of operating assets—land, buildings, and equipment; (2) land, buildings, and equipment that are currently used in the operations of the organization; (3) any related allowance for depreciation on these plant assets; (4) mortgages or other long-term debt that is associated with these assets; and (5) the net investment in plant— land, buildings, and equipment.

Plant assets of VHWOs are recorded at cost or, in the case of donated assets, at the fair market value at the date of the gift. The use of fixed assets by VHWOs represents a cost of providing their services. Thus, it is appropriate to show depreciation as a cost of providing services to the community, in order to enable contributors and managers to evaluate the efficiency of the use of their resources. Depreciation of fixed assets of VHWOs is accounted for over the useful lives of assets in essentially the same manner as it is in business enterprises; and it is recorded in the *land, buildings, and equipment fund* by a debit to depreciation expense and a credit to accumulated depreciation.

Endowment Funds

The principal of endowment funds of VHWOs is to remain intact in perpetuity and is to be invested to produce income. The principal of term endowment funds is to be invested and remain intact for a specified period or until the occurrence of a specified event, at which time the principal is to be transferred to the current unrestricted fund or to a restricted fund, depending on the provisions set forth by the donor. If the income from endowment funds and term endowment funds is unrestricted, it goes directly to and is accounted for as revenue in the current unrestricted fund. If such income is donor-restricted, it goes directly to and is accounted for as revenue in the appropriate restricted fund. However, some VHWOs follow the practice of recording investment income as revenue in the endowment fund and later transferring it to the appropriate current fund. In such a case, the transfer-in is shown as an addition to the fund balance in the recipient fund, and the transfer-out is shown as a deduction from the fund balance in the endowment fund.

Custodian and Other Funds

VHWOs sometimes make use of other funds, such as custodian (agency) funds, loan funds, and annuity funds. The accounting for these funds parallels that described in the first part of this chapter dealing with comparable funds for colleges and universities.

Accounting for VHWO Funds

Exhibit 19-19 presents the transactions and related journal entries for a voluntary health and welfare organization for the year ended December 31, 19X6. The VHWO illustrated (Columbus Home Health Support) receives significant amounts of public support and restricted resources. Because of these restricted resources, it uses fund accounting.

Annual Financial Statements

The basic financial statements of VHWOs are the (1) *balance sheet,* (2) *statement of activities,* (3) *statement of functional expenses* and (4) *cash flow statement.* The statement of cash flows is not illustrated here because of its similarity to such statements that are prepared for business enterprises.

Although VHWOs under GASB jurisdiction may issue balance sheets in the layered ("pancake") format shown for a university earlier in this chapter (see Exhibit 19-7), VHWOs under FASB jurisdiction must use the columnar form shown in Exhibit 19-20 for Columbus Home Health Support. The presentation of net assets in Exhibit 19-20 requires an allocation of the land, building, and equipment fund balance between unrestricted net assets and temporarily restricted net assets. This fund includes the cost (less depreciation) of land, buildings, and equipment ($220,000) that should be classified as unrestricted assets. (Although donor-restrictions on the use of donated assets may require them to be treated as restricted assets, the assets in question here are assumed to be acquired by the nonprofit in the normal course of its operations or donated without restrictions.) In addition, the fund includes a mortgage payable ($55,000) that should be classified as unrestricted. Thus, $165,000 ($220,000 − $55,000) of the land, building, and equipment fund balance must be classified as unrestricted; the $125,000 remainder corresponding to the fund's cash, investments, pledges receivable is classified as temporarily restricted.

The statement of activities for Columbus Home Health Support is shown in Exhibit 19-21. The related statement of functional expenses is shown in Exhibit 19-22. Unlike other nonprofit organizations, VHWOs are required to report their expenses disaggregated both by natural and functional classifications.

As shown in the net assets section of the balance sheet in Exhibit 19-20, Columbus Home Health Support's temporarily restricted net assets are accounted for in the current restricted fund and the land, building, and equipment fund. The VHWO's's permanently restricted net assets are accounted for in the endowment fund which is assumed to include no term endowments. All the activity data in Exhibits 19-21 and 19-22 derive from the Columbus Home Health Support transactions for 19X6 recorded earlier. Beginning-of-the-year account balances necessary to complete the balance sheet in Exhibit 19-20 were not given earlier but are presented for the first time in these financial statements.

OTHER NONPROFIT ORGANIZATIONS

The major sources of accounting principles for other nonprofit organizations include an AICPA audit guide—*Audits of Certain Nonprofit Organizations* (1987)—and several position statements—notably *Statement of Position 78-10,* "Accounting Principles and Reporting Practices for Certain Nonprofit Organizations." *Statement of Position 78-10* was issued by the AICPA in 1978 to recommend accounting principles and reporting

EXHIBIT 19-19	VOLUNTARY HEALTH AND WELFARE ORGANIZATION FUNDS ENTRIES

Columbus Home Health Support

FUND ENTRIES
FOR THE YEAR ENDED DECEMBER 31, 19X6

Transaction (1): The annual fund drive resulted in cash contributions as follows: $690,000 is not restricted in any way; $15,000 is to be used in 19X7 for unrestricted purposes (but recorded as temporarily restricted until then); $75,000 is restricted to specified operating purposes; $10,000 is restricted for use in purchasing new equipment; and $10,000 is to be used as an addition to the principal of the endowment fund.

Current unrestricted fund entry to record contributions received:

Cash	705,000	
Public support—contributions		690,000
Public support—temporarily restricted contributions		15,000

Current unrestricted fund entry to record contributions received:

Cash	75,000	
Public support—contributions		75,000

Land, building, and equipment fund entry to record contributions for new equipment:

Cash	10,000	
Public support—contributions		10,000

Endowment fund entry to record contributions received:

Cash	10,000	
Public support—contributions		10,000

Transaction (2): In addition to the cash contributions in transaction (1), the annual fund drive resulted in unpaid pledges as follows: $119,000 for unrestricted purposes, to be paid in early 19X7, of which $9,000 is expected to be uncollectible; and $16,000 restricted to the purchase of new equipment, to be paid in early 19X7, of which $1,000 is expected to be uncollectible.

Current unrestricted fund entry to record uncollected pledges:

Pledges receivable	119,000	
Allowance for uncollectible pledges		9,000
Public support—contributions		110,000

Land, building, and equipment fund entry to record uncollected pledges:

Pledges receivable	16,000	
Allowance for uncollectible pledges		1,000
Public support—contributions		15,000

Transaction (3): A special fund-raising banquet resulted in unrestricted cash receipts of $90,000 (after deducting direct costs of $20,000).

Current unrestricted fund entry to record receipts of fund-raising events:

Cash	90,000	
Public support—special events		90,000

EXHIBIT 19-19	VOLUNTARY HEALTH AND WELFARE ORGANIZATION FUND ENTRIES (Continued)

Transaction (4): Bequests received in cash were as follows: unrestricted, $50,000; designated to be added to the endowment fund principal, $5,000.

Current unrestricted fund entry to record bequests received:

Cash	50,000	
Public support—bequests		50,000

Endowment fund entry to record bequests received:

Cash	5,000	
Public support—bequests		5,000

Transaction (5): Membership dues, all of which were collected in cash, amounted to $8,000.

Current unrestricted fund entry to record membership dues received:

Cash	8,000	
Revenues—membership dues		8,000

Transaction (6): Investment earnings received were as follows: unrestricted, $25,000, and restricted to specified operating purposes, $20,000.

Current unrestricted fund entry to record investment earnings:

Cash	25,000	
Revenues—investment earnings		25,000

Current restricted fund entry to record investment earnings:

Cash	20,000	
Revenues—investment earnings		20,000

Transaction (7): Gains on sales of investments amounted to $15,000, determined as follows: current unrestricted fund investments that cost $75,000 were sold for $85,000, and endowment fund investments that cost $25,000 were sold for $30,000. The endowment fund gain is available for expenditure in future years (temporarily restricted).

Current unrestricted fund entry to record sale of investments:

Cash	85,000	
Investments		75,000
Revenues—gain on sale of investments		10,000

Endowment fund entry to record sale of investments:

Cash	30,000	
Investments		25,000
Revenues—gain on sale of investments		5,000

Transaction (8): Educational materials purchased for cash amounted to $75,000. Of this amount, $50,000 was used in connection with public health education activities.

Current unrestricted fund entry to record purchases of educational materials:

Inventories of educational materials	75,000	
Cash		75,000

Current unrestricted fund entry to record use of educational materials:

Program services expenses—public health education	50,000	
Inventories of educational materials		50,000

| EXHIBIT 19-19 | VOLUNTARY HEALTH AND WELFARE ORGANIZATION FUND ENTRIES (Continued) |

Transaction (9): Program services expenses paid from unrestricted funds were as follows: research expenses, $374,500; public health education expenses, $73,000; professional education and training expenses, $197,500; and community services expenses, $99,800. Research expenses paid from current restricted funds were $90,000.

Current unrestricted fund entry to record program services expenses:

Program services expenses—research 374,500
Program services expenses—public health education 73,000
Program services expenses—professional education and training 197,500
Program services expenses—community services... 99,800
    Cash 744,800

Current restricted fund entry to record program services expenses:

Program services expenses—research 90,000
    Cash 90,000

Transaction (10): Supporting services expenses paid by the current unrestricted fund were as follows: management and general expenses, $72,700, and fund-raising expenses, $97,500.

Current unrestricted fund entry to record supporting services expenses:

Supporting services expenses—management and general 72,700
Supporting services expenses—fund-raising 97,500
    Cash 170,200

Transaction (11): Current unrestricted funds expended $5,000 for new equipment.

Current unrestricted fund entry to record purchase of new equipment:

Fund balance—unrestricted—undesignated 5,000
    Cash 5,000

Land, building, and equipment fund entry to record purchase of new equipment from current unrestricted fund:

Land, building, and equipment 5,000
    Fund balance—restricted—expended 5,000

Transaction (12): $5,000 cash was paid on the mortgage payable by the land, building, and equipment fund.

Land, building, and equipment fund entry to record mortgage payment:

Mortgage payable 5,000
Fund balance—restricted—unexpended... 5,000
    Cash 5,000
    Fund balance—restricted—expended 5,000

Transaction (13): Of the $490,000 current unrestricted fund balance at the end of 19X6, $200,000 was designated by the governing board to be expended for future research grants.

Current unrestricted fund entry to record designation of unrestricted fund balance by governing board on December 31, 19X6:

Fund balance—unrestricted—undesignated 200,000
    Fund balance—unrestricted—designated for research grants................................. 200,000

EXHIBIT 19-19	VOLUNTARY HEALTH AND WELFARE ORGANIZATION FUND ENTRIES (Continued)

Transaction (14): Depreciation of buildings and equipment was $10,000, allocated as follows: (1) for program services expenses, research, $500; public health education, $2,000; professional education and training, $2,500; community services, $200; and (2) for supporting services expenses, management and general, $2,300; fund-raising, $2,500.

Land, building, and equipment fund entry for record depreciation:

Program services expenses—research	500	
Program services expenses—public health education	2,000	
Program services expenses—professional education and training	2,500	
Program services expenses—community services	200	
Supporting services expenses—management and general	2,300	
Supporting services expenses—fund-raising	2,500	
Accumulated depreciation		10,000

Closing Entries: At December 31, 19X6, closing entries are made for the public support, revenue, and expense accounts of the health and welfare organization.

Current unrestricted fund entries to record closing of public support, revenue, and expense accounts at December 31, 19X6:

Public support—contributions	815,000	
Public support—special events	90,000	
Public support—bequests	50,000	
Revenues—membership dues	8,000	
Revenues—investment earnings	25,000	
Revenues—gain on sale of investments	10,000	
Program services expenses—research		374,500
Program services expenses—public health education		123,000
Program services expenses—professional education and training		197,500
Program services expenses—community services		99,800
Supporting services expenses—management and general		72,700
Supporting services expenses—fund-raising		97,500
Excess of public support and revenues over expenses		33,000
Excess of public support and revenues over expenses	33,000	
Fund balance—unrestricted—undesignated		33,000

Current restricted fund entries to record closing of public support, revenue, and expense accounts at December 31, 19X6:

Public support—contributions	75,000	
Revenues—investment earnings	20,000	
Program services expenses		90,000
Excess of public support and revenues over expenses		5,000
Excess of public support and revenues over expenses	5,000	
Fund balance—restricted		5,000

EXHIBIT 19-19	VOLUNTARY HEALTH AND WELFARE ORGANIZATION FUND ENTRIES (Continued)

Land, building, and equipment fund entries to record closing of public support and depreciation expenses accounts at December 31, 19X6:

Public support—contributions...25,000		
Program expenses—research		500
Program expenses—public health education		2,000
Program expenses—professional education and training		2,500
Program expenses—community services...........................		200
Supporting services expenses—management and general		2,300
Supporting services expenses—fund-raising		2,500
Excess of public support and revenues over expenses		15,000
Excess of public support and revenues over expenses.........................15,000		
Fund balance—restricted—unexpended...............................		15,000

Endowment fund entries to record closing of public support and revenue accounts at December 31, 19X6:

Public support—contribution 10,000		
Public support—bequests 5,000		
Revenues—gain on sale of investments 5,000		
Excess of public support and revenues over expenses		20,000
Excess of public support and revenues over expenses.......................20,000		
Fund balance—restricted.................................		20,000

practices for nonprofit organizations that were not covered by previously issued audit guides. In addition, these other nonprofit organizations (hereafter referred to as "78-10 organizations") are subject to the various FASB pronouncements concerning nonprofits including *FASB Statement No. 116* and *FASB Statement No. 117*. "78-10 organizations" include, but are not limited to, the following:[8]

Cemetery organizations	Private and community foundations
Civic organizations	Private elementary and secondary schools
Fraternal organizations	Professional associations
Labor unions	Public broadcasting stations
Libraries	Religious organizations
Museums	Research and scientific organizations
Other cultural institutions	Social and country clubs
Performing arts organizations	Trade associations
Political parties	Zoological and botanical societies

---

[8] American Institute of Certified Public Accountants, *Statement of Position 78-10,* p. 62.

EXHIBIT 19-20	VHWO BALANCE SHEET

Columbus Home Health Support
BALANCE SHEET
AT DECEMBER 31, 19X6

Assets
Current assets:

Cash		$ 230,000
Investments		230,000
Accounts receivable (net of estimated uncollectibles, $9,000)		110,000
Inventories of educational materials at cost		25,000
Prepaid expenses		5,000
Temporarily restricted assets—current funds:		
Cash	$ 5,000	
Investments	45,000	50,000
Temporarily restricted assets—land, building, and equipment fund:		
Cash	$ 10,000	
Investments	100,000	
Pledges receivable (less allowance for uncollectibles, $1,000)	15,000	125,000
Total current assets		$ 775,000
Noncurrent assets:		
Land, buildings, and equipment	$330,000	
Less: Accumulated depreciation	110,000	220,000
Permanently restricted assets—endowment funds:		
Cash	$ 5,000	
Investments	150,000	155,000
Total assets		$1,150,000

Liabilities

Accounts payable		$ 95,000
Mortgage payable		55,000
Total liabilities		$ 150,000

Net assets
Unrestricted:

Designated for research grants	$200,000	
Undesignated	470,000	$670,000
Temporarily restricted:		
Current funds	$ 50,000	
Land, building, and equipment fund	125,000	180,000
Permanently restricted:		
Endowment funds		150,000	1,000,000
Total liabilities and net assets		$1,150,000

EXHIBIT 19-21	VHWO STATEMENT OF SUPPORT, REVENUE, EXPENSES, AND CHANGES IN FUND BALANCES

Columbus Home Health Support

STATEMENT OF ACTIVITIES
FOR YEAR ENDED DECEMBER 31, 19X6

	Unrestricted	Temporarily Restricted	Permanently Restricted	Total
Revenues, gains, and other support				
Public Support:				
Contributions	$ 815,000	$ 100,000[1]	$ 10,000	$ 925,000
Special events (net of direct costs, $20,000)	90,000			90,000
Bequests	50,000		5,000	55,000
Total public support	$ 955,000	$ 100,000	$ 15,000	$1,070,000
Other revenues:				
Membership dues	$ 8,000	$		$ 8,000
Investment earnings	25,000	20,000		45,000
Gain on sale of investments	10,000	5,000		15,000
Total other revenues	$ 43,000	$ 25,000		$ 68,000
Net assets released from restrictions:				
Satisfaction of current fund restrictions	$ 90,000	$ (90,000)		
Satisfaction of land, building, and equipment fund restrictions	10,000	(10,000)		
Total net assets released from restrictions	$ 100,000	$(100,000)		
Total revenues, gains, and other support	$1,098,000	$ 25,000	$ 15,000	$1,138,000
Expenses and losses				
Program services:				
Research	$ 465,000			$ 465,000
Public health education	125,000			125,000
Professional education and training	200,000			200,000
Community services	100,000			100,000
Total program services	$ 890,000			$ 890,000
Supporting services:				
Management and general	$ 75,000			$ 75,000
Fund-raising	100,000			100,000
Total supporting services	$ 175,000			$ 175,000
Total expenses and losses	$1,065,000			$1,065,000
Change in net assets	$ 33,000	$ 25,000	$ 15,000	$ 73,000
Net assets at beginning of year	637,000	155,000	135,000	927,000
Net assets at end of year	$ 670,000	$ 180,000	$150,000	$1,000,000

[1] $100,000 = $75,000 from restricted current funds + $27,000 from land, building, and equipment fund.

EXHIBIT 19-22 VHWO STATEMENT OF FUNCTIONAL EXPENSES

Columbus Home Health Support
STATEMENT OF FUNCTIONAL EXPENSES*
FOR YEAR ENDED DECEMBER 31, 19X6

	Program Services					Supporting Services			Total Expense
	Research	Public Health Education	Professional Education and Training	Community Services	Total	Management and General	Fund-Raising	Total	
Salaries	$ 40,900	$ 70,700	$ 81,000	$ 65,400	$258,000	$30,500	$ 89,500	$120,000	$ 378,000
Employee health and retirement benefits	1,000	3,400	3,400	3,400	11,200	5,300	3,500	8,800	20,000
Payroll taxes	500	3,800	3,800	3,800	11,900	4,000	3,100	7,100	19,000
Total salaries and related expenses	$ 42,400	$ 77,900	$ 88,200	$ 72,600	$281,100	$39,800	$ 96,100	$135,900	$ 417,000
Professional fees	$ 500	$ 1,000	$ 3,000	$ 500	$ 5,000	$ 3,000	$	$ 3,000	$ 8,000
Supplies	500	2,000	8,000	2,000	12,500	3,500	100	3,600	16,100
Telephone and telegraph	500	2,000	4,000	1,000	7,500	2,500	100	2,600	10,100
Postage and shipping	300	2,500	5,000	500	8,300	2,000	100	2,100	10,400
Occupancy	1,000	3,000	3,000	1,000	8,000	5,000	100	5,100	13,100
Rental of equipment	500	4,000	2,000	1,000	7,500	2,000		2,000	9,500
Conferences, conventions, meetings	500	3,000	20,000	4,000	27,500	9,000		9,000	36,500
Printing and publications	1,000	25,000	10,000	2,000	38,000	4,000	1,000	5,000	43,000
Awards and grants	416,800	2,000	50,000	15,000	483,800				483,800
Miscellaneous	500	600	4,300	200	5,600	1,900		1,900	7,500
Total expenses before depreciation	$464,500	$123,000	$197,500	$ 99,800	$884,800	$72,700	$ 97,500	$170,200	$1,055,000
Depreciation of buildings and equipment	500	2,000	2,500	200	5,200	2,300	2,500	4,800	10,000
Total expenses	$465,000	$125,000	$200,000	$100,000	$890,000	$75,000	$100,000	$175,000	$1,065,000

* The amounts of the functional expenses shown here are assumed and cannot be determined from the journal entries that are recorded in this section of the chapter.

"78-10 organizations" do not include nonprofit entities that operate essentially as business enterprises for the benefit of members or stockholders, such as mutual insurance companies, mutual banks, and farm cooperatives.

Accounting Methods of Other Nonprofit Organizations

The accrual basis of accounting is required for "78-10 organizations." As was the case with VHWOs, the cash basis of accounting is acceptable if it results in financial statements that do not differ materially from those prepared on the accrual basis. Fund accounting is recommended for "78-10 organizations" that have significant amounts of restricted resources. Some "78-10 organizations" have only unrestricted funds. In such a case, there is no need to use fund accounting. The financial statements of such organizations would resemble those of business enterprises.

Revenues, Public Support, and Capital Additions

"78-10 organizations" derive *revenues* from several sources: membership dues, investment income, ticket sales, sales of goods and services, and so on. Some of these organizations, such as museums and cultural institutions, often solicit outside *public support,* such as contributions and gifts, bequests, grants, donated services, and so on, from foundations, corporations, governmental units, and individuals. The operating statements of these organizations show two sources of operating resources—revenues and public support. Some "78-10 organizations," such as social and country clubs and professional associations, show only one source of operating resources—revenues—in their operating statements.

"78-10 organizations" often have a third source of revenues—capital additions. *Capital additions* are contributions and gifts, grants, and bequests that are restricted by the donors to endowment, plant, or loan funds (they do not include donor-restricted gifts for program or supporting services). Also included in capital additions are income and gains and losses from investments where such income, gains, and losses are legally restricted and must be added to the principal of endowment, plant, or loan funds.

For "78-10 organizations," capital additions (sometimes called *nonexpendable additions*) are reported as revenue when received under the caption "capital additions" in the statement of activity. The credit to the revenue account is accompanied by a corresponding debit to cash, investments, or pledges receivable.

Expenses

In "78-10 organizations" that receive significant support from contributions from the general public, expenses are divided into two major categories: (1) program services expenses, which show the cost of providing the programs for which the organizations were established, and (2) supporting services expenses, including management and general costs and fund-raising costs. All other "78-10 organizations" would have only one category of expenses, classified on a functional basis.

Donated Services, Materials, and Facilities

As noted earlier, donated services are recorded by nonprofit organizations if either of two criteria is met:[9]

---

[9] *FASB Statement No. 116,* par. 9.

1. The services create or enhance nonfinancial assets.
2. The services require specialized skills, are provided by individuals possessing those skills, and would typically need to be purchased if not provided by donation.

Donated services that meet either criterion are recorded by a debit to an expense account and a credit to public support (contributions). Donated materials and free use of facilities should be recorded at their fair value. An exception to the recording requirement is made for contributed works of art and historical treasures provided that the museum does not capitalize purchases of such items and that appropriate disclosures are made in the notes to the financial statements. See *FASB Statement No. 116,* pars. 11–13 and 26–27 for additional discussion of contributed collection items.

Fund Structure

"78-10 organizations" that do not have significant amounts of restricted resources do not usually use fund accounting. The financial statements are similar to those of business enterprises, except that the equity of "78-10 organizations" is referred to as *net assets.* Those organizations having significant amounts of restricted resources use fund accounting; their funds fall under two major categories, unrestricted and restricted. In practice, the specific titles of such funds vary widely. However, following is a brief description of the kinds of funds that are frequently used by "78-10 organizations."

Operating Funds

The operating funds of "78-10 organizations" are used to account for resources that are expendable in carrying out the operating purposes of the organization on a day-to-day basis. Operating funds consist of two subgroups: the unrestricted operating fund and restricted operating funds. The *unrestricted operating fund* is used to account for resources that are unrestricted and available for general operations. These resources may come from revenues and from public support. The *restricted operating funds* are used to account for resources that are currently available but are restricted to certain operating purposes as specified by the outside donor or grantor. These resources may come from gifts, bequests, grants, income from endowments, or other sources.

Plant (Land, Building, and Equipment) Funds

These funds are used to account for the following: (1) resources available for the acquisition or replacement of operating assets—land, buildings, and equipment; (2) land, buildings, and equipment that are currently used in the operations of the organization; (3) any related allowance for depreciation on these plant assets; (4) mortgages or other long-term debt that is associated with these assets; and (5) the net investment in plant—land, buildings, and equipment.

Plant assets of "78-10 organizations" are recorded at cost or, in the case of donated assets, at the fair market value at the date of the gift. These plant assets may be classified as exhaustible or inexhaustible. *Exhaustible plant assets,* such as buildings and equipment, should be depreciated over their useful lives. Depreciation of fixed assets of "78-10 organizations" is accounted for in essentially the same manner as in business enterprises.

Depreciation is recorded in the *plant fund* by a debit to depreciation expense and a credit to accumulated depreciation.

Inexhaustible assets—such as historical treasures, monuments, landmarks, paintings, art objects, rare books, and so on—are not subject to depreciation. *FASB Statement No. 93* requires all nonprofit (not-for-profit) organizations to recognize depreciation in general purpose external financial statements. An exception is provided for inexhaustible plant assets, which are particularly important to libraries and museums: "Consistent with the accepted practice for land used as a building site, depreciation need not be recognized on individual works of art or historical treasures whose economic benefit or service potential is used up so slowly that their estimated useful lives are extraordinarily long. A work of art or historical treasure shall be deemed to have that characteristic only if verifiable evidence exists demonstrating that (a) the asset individually has cultural, aesthetic, or historical value that is worth preserving and (b) the holder has the technological and financial ability to protect and preserve essentially undiminished the service potential of the asset and is doing that" (*FASB Statement No. 93*, par. 6.).

Endowment and Other Funds

Other nonprofit organizations often use endowment funds, and less frequently custodian (agency) funds, loan funds, and annuity and life income funds. Accounting for endowment funds parallels that for endowment funds for VHWOs, described in the preceding section of this chapter. Accounting for custodian (agency) funds, loan funds, and annuity and life income funds parallels that described in the first part of this chapter dealing with comparable funds for colleges and universities. For this reason, they are not discussed here.

Annual Financial Statements

The basic financial statements that are generally required of "78-10 organizations" are the (1) *balance sheet,* (2) *statement of activities,* and (3) *statement of cash flows.*

Each of the types of nonprofit organizations covered in the AICPA audit guide *(Audits of Certain Nonprofit Organizations)* and *Statement of Position 78-10* has its own unique characteristics that affect the content of its annual financial statements. However, they all use accrual accounting, they all match revenues and expenses (rather than revenue and expenditures), they all depreciate their fixed assets, and fund accounting is used by those with significant amounts of restricted resources.

The specific format for the balance sheet varies among different types of "78-10 organizations," depending on the degree of complexity of the organization, on whether or not the organization receives material amounts of restricted resources, and on whether or not the organization uses fund accounting. The balance sheets of "78-10 organizations" that receive significant amounts of restricted resources, will be similar to the balance sheets presented earlier in this chapter for hospitals and voluntary health and welfare organizations. The balance sheet for an organization that does not receive restricted resources in material amounts and that does not use fund accounting would be quite similar to that of a business enterprise; however, the net worth would be called net assets or equity.

The format of activity statements differs according to the type of "78-10 organization." Those organizations whose resources derive primarily from fee revenues of various kinds usually summarize expenses on a functional basis. Those that receive significant amounts of public support for operations and/or capital projects, in addition to various revenues, usually divide their expenses into two major categories: program services expenses and supporting services expenses.

''78-10 organizations'' that receive significant public support and that have significant restricted resources would present a balance sheet and a statement of activities that are similar in format to the statements shown for voluntary health and welfare organizations in Exhibits 19-20 and 19-21. Because of the similarity in format to the statements for VHWOs, a balance sheet and a statement of support, revenue, expenses, and changes in fund balances for ''78-10 organizations'' with significant amounts of public support and restricted resources are not shown here.

The balance sheet presented in Exhibit 19-23 and the statement of activities presented in Exhibit 19-24 for a country club are representative of financial statements prepared for ''78-10 organizations'' that do not receive significant amounts of public support and do not have significant restricted resources, and thus do not use fund accounting.

SUMMARY

This chapter surveys accounting principles and recommended reporting practices of nonprofit organizations—colleges and universities, hospitals, voluntary health and welfare organizations, and ''78-10 organizations.'' All nonprofit organizations with significant restricted resources use fund accounting systems. However, the fund structure differs from one type of nonprofit organization to another, as shown in Exhibit 19-1 early in this chapter. Although all nonprofit organizations use a current or operating fund (similar in purpose to the general fund used by governmental organizations), the name and precise structure vary from one type of nonprofit organization to another. For example, colleges and universities account for plant and equipment and related liabilities in separate plant funds, whereas hospitals account for plant and equipment and related liabilities in unrestricted (current operating) funds. Nonprofit organizations also differ in their use of depreciation. Whereas most nonprofit organizations recognize depreciation, most colleges and universities do not recognize depreciation (although those under FASB jurisdiction are required to do so). Colleges and universities are also distinctive in that they include board-designated (quasi-endowment) funds in endowment funds, whereas other nonprofit organizations include only externally restricted funds among endowment funds. Nonprofit organizations also issue different forms of financial statements. Recent FASB pronouncements (especially *FASB Statement No. 116* on accounting for contributions and *FASB Statement No. 117* on financial reporting by nonprofit organizations) will secure a high degree of uniformity among nonprofit financial statements under FASB jurisdiction. However, nonprofit organizations under GASB jurisdiction are not directly affected by these pronouncements. To some degree, the differences among the accounting practices of nonprofit organizations reflect the distinctive objectives and operations of the different types of nonprofit organizations. However, greater uniformity in accounting for nonprofit organizations is undoubtedly possible.

EXHIBIT 19-23	BALANCE SHEET FOR "78-10 ORGANIZATION"

North River Country Club
BALANCE SHEET
AT DECEMBER 31, 19X6

Assets

Current assets:		
Cash		$ 40,000
Investments		200,000
Accounts receivable	$75,000	
Less: Allowance for uncollectible accounts	5,000	70,000
Inventories		20,000
Prepaid expenses		10,000
Total current assets		$ 340,000
Property and equipment:		
Land		$ 500,000
Buildings		1,300,000
Furniture and equipment		200,000
		$2,000,000
Less: Accumulated depreciation		800,000
Total property and equipment		$1,200,000
Other assets:		
Beverage license		$ 5,000
Total assets		$1,545,000

Liabilities and Membership Equity

Current liabilities:	
Accounts payable	$ 75,000
Accrued expenses	10,000
Deferred revenues— initiation fees	15,000
Due to resigned members	5,000
Taxes payable	20,000
Total current liabilities	$ 125,000
Long-term liabilities:	
Five-year note payable	$ 100,000
Membership equity:	
Proprietary certificates, 600 @ $1,500 each	$ 900,000
Cumulative excess of revenues over expenses	420,000
Total membership equity	$1,320,000
Total liabilities and membership equity	$1,545,000

SELECTED READINGS

American Institute of Certified Public Accountants. *Audits of Certain Nonprofit Organizations,* 2nd ed. New York: American Institute of Certified Public Accountants, 1987.

American Institute of Certified Public Accountants. *Audits of Colleges and Universities,* 2nd ed. New York: American Institute of Certified Public Accountants, 1975.

American Institute of Certified Public Accountants. *Audits of Voluntary Health and Welfare Organizations,* 2nd ed. New York: American Institute of Certified Public Accountants, 1988.

American Institute of Certified Public Accountants. *Hospital Audit Guide,* 6th ed. New York: American Institute of Certified Public Accountants, 1987.

American Institute of Certified Public Accountants. *Statement of Position No. 74-8.* "Financial Accounting and Reporting by Colleges and Universities." New York: American Institute of Certified Public Accountants, 1974.

| EXHIBIT 19-24 | STATEMENT OF ACTIVITIES FOR A "78-10 ORGANIZATION" |

North River Country Club

STATEMENT OF ACTIVITIES
FOR YEAR ENDED DECEMBER 31, 19X6

Revenues:	
Membership dues	$ 500,000
Restaurant and bar charges	250,000
Greens fees	175,000
Tennis and swimming fees	80,000
Initiation fees	60,000
Locker rentals	50,000
Golf cart rentals	25,000
Interest	20,000
Gains on investments	30,000
Total revenues	$1,190,000
Expenses:	
House	$ 225,000
Restaurant and bar	135,000
Greens	210,000
Tennis and swimming	65,000
General and administrative	510,000
Total expenses	$1,145,000
Excess of revenues over expenses before capital additions	$ 45,000
Capital additions:	
Membership assessments for capital improvements (temporarily restricted)	25,000
Change in membership equity	$ 70,000
Membership equity at beginning of period	350,000
Membership equity at end of period	$ 420,000

American Institute of Certified Public Accountants. *Statement of Position No. 78-1.* "Accounting by Hospitals for Certain Marketable Equity Securities." New York: American Institute of Certified Public Accountants, 1978.

American Institute of Certified Public Accountants. *Statement of Position No. 78-7.* "Financial Accounting and Reporting by Hospitals Operated by a Governmental Unit." New York: American Institute of Certified Public Accountants, 1978.

American Institute of Certified Public Accountants. *Statement of Position 78-10.* "Accounting Principles and Reporting Practices for Certain Nonprofit Organizations." New York: American Institute of Certified Public Accountants, 1978.

American Institute of Certified Public Accountants. *Statement of Position 81-2.* "Reporting Practices Concerning Hospital-Related Organizations. New York: American Institute of Certified Public Accountants, 1981.

American Institute of Certified Public Accountants. *Statement of Position 85-1.* "Financial Reporting by Not-for-Profit Health Care Entities for Tax-Exempt Debt and Certain Funds Whose Use Is Limited." New York: American Institute of Certified Public Accountants, 1985.

American Institute of Certified Public Accountants. *Statement of Position No. 87-1.* "Accounting for Asserted and Unasserted Medical Malpractice Claims of Health Care Providers and Related Issues." New York: American Institute of Certified Public Accountants, 1987.

American Institute of Certified Public Accountants. *Statement of Position No. 89-5.* "Financial Accounting and Reporting by Providers of Prepaid Health Care Services." New York: American Institute of Certified Public Accountants, 1989.

Anthony, Robert N. *Financial Accounting in Nonbusiness Organizations: An Exploratory Study of Conceptual Issues* (Research Report). Stamford, CT: Financial Accounting Standards Board, 1978.

Anthony, Robert N., and David W. Young. *Management Control in Nonprofit Organizations.* Homewood, IL: Irwin, 1984.

Fetterman, Allen L. "Update on Not-for-Profit Organizations," *The CPA Journal* (March 1990), pp. 26–30.

Financial Accounting Standards Board. *Statement of Financial Accounting Concepts No. 4.* "Objectives of Financial Reporting by Nonbusiness Organizations." Stamford, CT: Financial Accounting Standards Board, 1980.

Hay, Leon E., and Earl R. Wilson. *Accounting for Governmental and Nonprofit Entities,* 9th ed. Homewood, IL: Irwin, 1992.

Henke, Emerson O., and Lucian G. Conway, Jr. "A Recommended Format for College and University Financial Statements," *Accounting Horizons* (June 1989), pp. 49–65.

Herzlinger, Regina E., and H. David Sherman. "Advantages of Fund Accounting in 'Nonprofits,'" *Harvard Business Review* (May–June 1980), pp. 95–105.

Mautz, R. K. "Not-for-Profit Financial Reporting: Another View," *Journal of Accountancy* (August 1989), pp. 60–66.

Mautz, R. K. "Why Not-for-Profits Should Report Their Commitments," *Journal of Accountancy* (June 1990), pp. 92–98.

National Association of College and University Business Officers, *College and University Business Administration,* 4th ed. Washington, D.C.: National Association of College and University Business Officers, 1982.

National Center for Higher Education Management Systems. *Higher Education Finance Manual.* Washington, D.C.: U.S. Government Printing Office, 1980.

Vatter, William J. "State of the Art—Non-Business Accounting," *The Accounting Review* (July 1979), pp. 574–584.

Weiss, Susan E. "FASB Statements on Not-for-Profit Issues," *The CPA Journal* (July 1993), pp. 40–75.

QUESTIONS

19-1   Discuss why you agree or disagree with the following statement: The Governmental Accounting Standards Board (GASB) is the primary source of accounting standards for nonprofit organizations.

19-2   The current funds of colleges and universities consist of two subgroups. Identify these subgroups and the distinguishing characteristic between them.

19-3 Identify and explain the differences in three types of endowment funds that may be included in the endowment and similar funds of a college or university.

19-4 Identify the four subgroups that constitute the plant funds of colleges and universities, and explain the purpose of each of the four subgroups.

19-5 List the three basic financial statements that are prepared by colleges and universities under GASB jurisdiction.

19-6 When are the resources (e.g., federal research grants) of restricted current funds of colleges and universities recognized as revenues under FASB rules? under GASB rules?

19-7 Explain why a fiscal period's revenues and expenditures are equal in the restricted current funds of a college or university.

19-8 Funds used in hospitals subject to FASB rules are categorized as either unrestricted, temporarily restricted, or permanently restricted. Discuss the types of activities that are accounted for in each of the three categories, and identify the subgroups of resources included in each category.

19-9 What are board-designated funds of hospitals? Explain why such funds are accounted for as unrestricted funds and not as restricted funds.

19-10 Identify the three basic financial statements that are normally required of hospitals under FASB rules.

19-11 In order for donated services (e.g., nursing services) to be recorded by a hospital either of two tests must be met. Describe these two tests.

19-12 Discuss why you agree or disagree with the following statement: All revenues and expenses of a hospital are reflected in the unrestricted funds under FASB rules.

19-13 Discuss why you agree or disagree with the following statement: Donor-restricted resources for additions to a hospital's property, plant, and equipment are recognized as revenue in the unrestricted funds.

19-14 Describe the differences between "78-10 organizations" and voluntary health and welfare organizations.

EXERCISES

E19-1 **Multiple Choice Questions on College and University Accounting**

1. Which of the following is utilized for current expenditures by a not-for-profit university under FASB jurisdiction?

	Unrestricted Current Funds	Restricted Current Funds
a)	No	No
b)	No	Yes
c)	Yes	No
d)	Yes	Yes

2. The temporarily restricted net assets of a not-for-profit private university includes which of the following funds?

	Term Endowment Funds	Life Income Funds
a)	No	No
b)	No	Yes
c)	Yes	Yes
d)	Yes	No

3. Which of the following receipts is properly recorded as restricted current funds on the books of a university?

a) Tuition

b) Student laboratory fees

c) Housing fees

d) Research grants

4. In the loan fund of a college or university, each of the following types of loans would be found *except*

a) Student

b) Staff

c) Building

d) Faculty

5. Which of the following should be included in the current funds revenues of a not-for-profit private university?

	Tuition Waivers	Unrestricted Bequests
a)	Yes	No
b)	Yes	Yes
c)	No	Yes
d)	No	No

6. A college's plant funds group includes which of the following subgroups?

I. Renewals and replacement plant fund

II. Retirement of indebtedness plant fund

III. Restricted current fund

a) I and II

b) I and III

c) II and III

d) I only

(AICPA adapted)

E19-2   Multiple Choice Questions on College and University Accounting

1. Tuition waivers for which there is *no* intention of collection from the student should be classified by a not-for-profit university as

	Revenue	Expenditure
a)	No	No
b)	No	Yes
c)	Yes	Yes
d)	Yes	No

2. During the years ended June 30, 19X2, and 19X3, Sonata University conducted a cancer research project financed by a $2,000,000 gift from an alumnus. This entire amount was pledged by the donor on July 10, 19X1, although he paid only $500,000 at that date. The gift was restricted to the financing of this particular research project. During the two-year research period Sonata's related gift receipts and research expenditures were as follows:

	Year Ended June 30	
	19X2	**19X3**
Gift receipts	$1,200,000	$ 800,000
Cancer research expenditures	900,000	1,100,000

Under FASB rules how much gift revenue should Sonata report for this project in its statement of activities for the year ended June 30, 19X3?

a) $–0–   **c)** $1,100,000

b) $800,000   **d)** $2,000,000

3. The following funds were among those on Kery University's books at April 30, 19X4:

Funds to be used for acquisition of additional properties for university purposes (unexpended at 4/30/X4)	$3,000,000
Funds set aside for debt service charges and for retirement of indebtedness on university properties	5,000,000

How much of the aforementioned funds should be included in plant funds?

a) $–0–   **c)** $5,000,000

b) $3,000,000   **d)** $8,000,000

4. On January 2, 19X2, John Reynolds established a $500,000 trust, the income from which is to be paid to Mansfield University for general operating purposes. The Wyndham National Bank was appointed by Reynolds as trustee of the fund. What journal entry is required on Mansfield's books?

	Debit	Credit
a) Memorandum entry only		
b) Cash	500,000	
Endowment fund balance		500,000
c) Nonexpendable endowment fund	500,000	
Endowment fund balance		500,000
d) Expendable funds	500,000	
Endowment fund balance		500,000

5. For the fall semester of 19X1, Cranbrook College assessed its students $2,300,000 for tuition and fees. The net amount realized was only $2,100,000 because of the following revenue reductions:

(continues on next page)

Refunds occasioned by class cancellations and student withdrawals	$ 50,000
Tuition remissions granted to faculty members' families	10,000
Scholarships and fellowships	140,000

How much should Cranbrook report for the period for unrestricted current funds revenues from tuition and fees?

a) $2,100,000   c) $2,250,000

b) $2,150,000   d) $2,300,000

6. The following funds were among those held by State College at December 31, 19X1:

Principal specified by the donor as nonexpendable	$500,000
Principal expendable after the year 19X9	300,000
Principal designated by the governing board from current funds	100,000

What amount should State College classify as permanently restricted?

a) $100,000   c) $500,000

b) $300,000   d) $900,000

(AICPA adapted)

E19-3 **Analysis of Comments on Accounting Principles and Procedures of Colleges and Universities**
Indicate whether you agree or disagree with each of the following statements. If you disagree with a statement, provide an explanation as to why.

1. The unrestricted current fund of a college or university accounts for resources that have been released from restrictions as to the operating purpose for which they may be expended.

2. In college and university accounting, transfers from unrestricted or restricted current funds to other funds, whether mandatory transfers or nonmandatory transfers, are treated as expenditures in the current funds.

3. The university's fiscal year ends June 30, 19X5. However, it is offering a five-week summer term from June 3 through July 5. Revenues and expenditures that are associated with this summer term should be prorated between the two fiscal years.

4. The assets of various endowments (e.g., endowments, term endowments) are frequently pooled for purposes of investments. Allocation of the earnings on such investments on the basis of the fair market value of the pooled assets at the date of their pooling is generally viewed as a preferred allocation basis.

5. At year-end (before the issuance of the balance sheet), plant asset accounts and construction in progress accounts of the unexpended plant fund of a college or university are transferred to the investment in plant fund.

6. The retirement of indebtedness plant fund of a college or university accounts for the payment of interest and principal on the long-term debt related to plant assets. The related liability accounts are also included in the retirement of indebtedness plant fund.

7. Colleges and universities, like commercial enterprises, never use budgetary accounting or encumbrance accounting.

8. A college or university's statement of current funds revenues, expenditures, and other changes presents the net income or loss for the institution.

9. Resources received by a university that are to be expended for operating purposes specified by the grantor (e.g., accounting history research) should be recorded as revenue in the period they are received even though the expenditures for the specified purposes will take place over the next several fiscal years.

10. A primary difference between annuity and life income funds is that distributions to designated individuals are fixed under annuity funds, whereas such distributions under life income funds vary with the income earned on the funds.

E19-4. **Analysis of Comments on Accounting Principles and Procedures of Hospitals** Indicate whether you agree or disagree with each of the following statements. If you disagree with a statement, provide an explanation as to why.

1. Restricted funds of a hospital are used to account for resources that are restricted in their usage by the third-party donor or grantor.

2. Hospitals follow full accrual accounting in their fund accounting systems.

3. Although each hospital fund could have its own balance sheet, hospitals under FASB jurisdiction must issue a balance sheet that presents the amounts and descriptions of the entire organization's assets, liabilities, and net assets.

4. Hospitals account for property, plant, and equipment, along with related liabilities, as restricted funds.

5. Hospitals do not depreciate their fixed assets.

6. Donor-restricted resources of hospitals that are held for future acquisition of property, plant, and equipment are accounted for in the plant replacement and expansion fund.

7. Unrestricted income from a hospital's endowment fund should be recognized as nonoperating revenue in the statement of revenues and expenses.

8. Endowment funds of a hospital that are held in trust by outside parties, where the principal is not controlled by the hospital, should be included in the hospital's balance sheet at the fair market value of the investments.

9. When resources that are held in a hospital's specific purpose fund are expended for the intended purpose, the appropriate expense accounts in the specific purpose fund are increased and the fund balance is reduced.

10. In hospital accounting, the provision for bad debts should be treated as a deduction from gross patient service revenues, rather than as an operating expense.

E19-5 **Multiple Choice Questions on Hospital Accounting**

1. Donated medicines that would normally be purchased by a hospital should be recorded at the fair market value and should be credited directly to

    a) Other operating revenue

    b) Nonoperating revenue

    c) Fund balance

    d) Deferred revenue

2. On July 1, 19X1, Lilydale Hospital's Board of Trustees designated $200,000 for the expansion of outpatient facilities. The $200,000 is expected to be expended in the fiscal year ending June 30, 19X4. In Lilydale's balance sheet at June 30, 19X2, this cash should be classified as a $200,000

    a) Restricted current asset

    b) Restricted noncurrent asset

    c) Unrestricted current asset

    d) Unrestricted noncurrent asset

3. Which of the following would normally be included in other operating revenues of a voluntary not-for-profit hospital?

a) Unrestricted interest income from an endowment fund

b) An unrestricted gift

c) Donated services

d) Tuition received from an educational program

4. During the year ended December 31, 19X1, Melford Hospital received the following donations stated at their respective fair values:

Employee services from members of a religious group	$100,000
Medical supplies from an association of physicians. These supplies were restricted for indigent care and were used for such a purpose in 19X1.	30,000

How much revenue (both operating and nonoperating) from donations should Melford report in its 19X1 statement of revenues and expenses?

a) $–0–	**c)** $100,000
b) $ 30,000	**d)** $130,000

5. Glenmore Hospital's property, plant, and equipment (net of depreciation) consists of the following:

Land	$ 500,000
Buildings	10,000,000
Movable equipment	2,000,000

What amount should be included in the restricted fund grouping?

a) –0–	**c)** $10,500,000
b) $ 2,000,000	**d)** $12,500,000

6. Depreciation must be recognized in the financial statements of

a) Proprietary (for-profit) hospitals only

b) Both proprietary (for-profit) and not-for-profit hospitals

c) Both proprietary (for-profit) and not-for-profit hospitals, only when they are affiliated with a college or university

d) All hospitals, as a memorandum entry not affecting the statement of revenues and expenses

Items (7) and (8) are based on the following information pertaining to Lori Hospital for the year ended May 31, 19X9:

In March 19X9, a $300,000 unrestricted bequest and a $500,000 permanent endowment grant were received.

7. Lori should record the $300,000 unrestricted bequest as

a) Nonoperating revenue

b) Other operating revenue

c) A direct credit to the fund balance

d) A credit to operating expenses

8. The $500,000 permanent endowment grant

a) May be expended by the governing board only to the extent of the principal since the income from this fund must be accumulated

b) Should be reported as nonoperating revenue when the full amount of principal is expended

c) Should be recorded as a memorandum entry only

d) Should be accounted for as restricted funds upon receipt

(AICPA adapted)

E19-6   **Multiple Choice Questions on Hospital Accounting**

1. Which of the following would be included in the unrestricted funds of a not-for-profit hospital?

a) Permanent endowments

b) Term endowments

c) Board-designated funds originating from previously accumulated income

d) Plant expansion and replacement funds

2. On May 1, 19X4, Lila Lee established a $50,000 endowment fund, the income from which is to be paid to Waller Hospital for general operating purposes. Waller does not control the fund's principal. Anders National Bank was appointed by Lee as trustee of this fund. What journal entry is required on Waller's books?

	Debit	Credit
a) Memorandum entry only		
b) Nonexpendable endowment fund	50,000	
Endowment fund balance		50,000
c) Cash	50,000	
Endowment fund balance		50,000
d) Cash	50,000	
Nonexpendable endowment fund		50,000

3. An unrestricted pledge from an annual contributor to a voluntary not-for-profit hospital made in December 19X1 and paid in cash in March 19X2 would generally be credited to

a) Nonoperating revenue in 19X1

b) Nonoperating revenue in 19X2

c) Operating revenue in 19X1

d) Operating revenue in 19X2

Items (4) through (6) are based on the following data:

Under Abbey Hospital's established rate structure, the hospital would have earned patient service revenue of $6,000,000 for the year ended December 31, 19X3. However, Abbey did not expect to collect this amount because of charity allowances of $1,000,000 and discounts of $500,000 to third-party payers. In May 19X3, Abbey purchased bandages from Lee Supply Co. at a cost of $1,000. However, Lee notified Abbey that the invoice was being canceled and that the bandages were being donated to Abbey. At December 31, 19X3, Abbey had board-designated assets consisting of cash, $40,000, and investments, $700,000.

4. For the year ended December 31, 19X3, how much should Abbey record as patient service revenue?

a) $6,000,000

b) $5,500,000

c) $5,000,000

d) $4,500,000

5. For the year ended December 31, 19X3, Abbey should record the donation of bandages as

a) A $1,000 reduction in operating expenses

b) Nonoperating revenue of $1,000

c) Other operating revenue of $1,000

d) A memorandum entry only

6. How much of Abbey's board-designated assets should be included in the unrestricted fund grouping?

a) $–0–

b) $ 40,000

c) $700,000

d) $740,000

7. Revenue from the gift shop of a hospital would normally be included in

    a) Other nonoperating revenue

    b) Other operating revenue

    c) Patient service revenue

    d) Professional services revenue

8. Cliff Hospital, a voluntary institution, has a permanent endowment fund, the income from which is required to be used for library acquisitions. State law and the donor are silent on the accounting treatment for investment gains and losses. In 19X9, Cliff sold 1,000 shares of stock from the endowment fund's investment portfolio. The carrying amount of these securities was $50,000. Net proceeds from the sale amounted to $120,000. This transaction should be recorded in the endowment fund as a debit to cash for $120,000 and as credits to

    a) Endowment fund principal, $50,000, and endowment fund revenue, $70,000

    b) Endowment fund principal, $50,000, and due to general fund, $70,000

    c) Investments, $50,000, and endowment fund balance, $70,000

    d) Investments, $50,000, and endowment fund revenue, $70,000

(AICPA adapted)

E19-7 **Hospital Accounting: Journal Entries**   Get Well Hospital engaged in the following transactions during the year ending December 31, 19X8.

1. Billings for patient service revenue totaled $210,000, of which $170,000 was for daily patient services and $40,000 was for other professional services.

2. Revenues from cafeteria sales and parking lot permits were $8,000 and $5,000, respectively.

3. Gifts and bequests totaling $16,000 cash were received for research on the sleeping habits of individuals.

4. The plant replacement and expansion fund transferred $60,000 to the unrestricted funds to finance equipment acquisitions.

5. Operating expenses paid relating to nursing services and administrative services were $63,000 and $27,000, respectively.

6. The unrestricted funds incurred research expenses of $10,000 in relation to sleeping habits of individuals [see item (3) above]; the unrestricted funds is reimbursed by the specific purpose fund.

7. The hospital received a donation of $45,000 of bonds as an endowment. Interest on the bonds is to be used to cover the general operating cost of the hospital.

8. Interest income of $2,500 is received on the bonds held in the endowment in item (7).

REQUIRED

Prepare journal entries to record each of the preceding transactions in the appropriate fund or funds of Get Well Hospital. Use the following funds:

- Unrestricted funds
- Specific purpose funds
- Plant replacement and expansion fund
- Endowment funds

Each transaction should be numbered to correspond with the transactions described earlier, and your answers should be organized as follows:

Transaction Number	Fund	Account Title and Explanation	Accounts	
			Debit	Credit

E19-8 **Multiple Choice Questions on Voluntary Health and Welfare Organizations**

1. A reason for a voluntary health and welfare organization to adopt fund accounting is that

   a) Restrictions have been placed on certain of its assets by donors

   b) It provides more than one type of program service

   c) Fixed assets are significant

   d) Donated services are significant

2. Environs, a community foundation, incurred $10,000 in management and general expenses during 19X1. In Environs' statement of revenue, expenses, and changes in fund balances for the year ended December 31, 19X1, the $10,000 should be reported as

   a) A direct reduction of fund balance

   b) Part of supporting services

   c) Part of program services

   d) A contra account to offset revenue and support

3. Why do voluntary health and welfare organizations, unlike some not-for-profit organizations, record and recognize depreciation of fixed assets?

   a) Fixed assets are more likely to be material in amount in a voluntary health and welfare organization than in other not-for-profit organizations.

   b) Voluntary health and welfare organizations purchase their fixed assets and, therefore, have a historical cost basis from which to determine amounts to be depreciated.

   c) A fixed asset used by a voluntary health and welfare organization has alternative uses in private industry, and this opportunity cost should be reflected in the organization's financial statements.

   d) Contributors look for the most efficient use of funds, and since depreciation represents a cost of employing fixed assets, it is appropriate that a voluntary health and welfare organization reflect depreciation as a cost of providing services.

4. Which of the following funds of a voluntary health and welfare organization does *not* have a counterpart *fund* in governmental accounting?

   a) Current unrestricted

   b) Land, building, and equipment

   c) Custodian

   d) Endowment

5. A voluntary health and welfare organization received a pledge in 19X7 from a donor specifying that the amount pledged should be used in 19X9. The donor paid the pledge in cash in 19X8. The pledge should be reported as:

   a) Revenue in 19X7 and a temporarily restricted asset at the end of 19X7 and 19X8.

   b) A deferred credit in the balance sheet at the end of 19X7 and 19X8, and as revenue in 19X9

   c) Revenue in 19X8 and a temporarily restricted asset at the end of 19X8.

   d) Revenue in 19X7 and an unrestricted asset at the end of 19X7 and 19X8.

6. Community Service Center is a voluntary welfare organization that is funded by contributions from the general public. During 19X3 unrestricted pledges of $900,000 were received, half of which were payable in 19X3, with the other half payable in 19X4 for use in 19X4. It was estimated that 10% of all pledges would be uncollectible. How much should Community report as the net contribution revenue for 19X3 with respect to the pledges?

   a) –0–   **c)** $810,000

   b) $405,000   **d)** $900,000

7. Cura Foundation, a voluntary health and welfare organization that is supported by contributions from the general public, included the following costs in its statement of functional expenses for the year ended December 31, 19X3:

Fund-raising	$500,000
Administrative (including data processing)	300,000
Research	100,000

Cura's functional expenses for 19X3 program services included

a) $900,000   **c)** $300,000

b) $500,000   **d)** $100,000

(AICPA adapted)

E19-9   Voluntary Health and Welfare Accounting   Listed here are four independent transactions or events that relate to a voluntary health and welfare organization:

1. $25,000 was disbursed from the current unrestricted fund for the cash purchase of new equipment.

2. An unrestricted cash gift of $100,000 was received from a donor.

3. Listed common stocks with a total carrying value of $50,000, exclusive of any allowance, were sold by an endowment fund for $55,000 before any dividends were earned on these stocks. There are no restrictions on the gain.

4. $1,000,000 face amount of general obligation bonds payable was sold at par, with the proceeds required to be used solely for the construction of a new building. This building was completed at a total cost of $1,000,000, and the total amount of bond issue proceeds was disbursed in connection therewith. Disregard interest capitalization.

REQUIRED
For each of the preceding transactions or events, prepare journal entries, specifying the affected funds and showing how these transactions or events should be recorded by a voluntary health and welfare organization that maintains a separate plant fund.

(AICPA adapted)

E19-10   Analysis of Comments on Accounting Principles and Procedures of "78-10 Organizations"   Indicate whether you agree or disagree with each of the following statements. If you disagree with a statement, provide an explanation as to why.

1. Fund accounting is required for all "78-10 organizations" even in the case where the organization has only unrestricted resources.

2. "78-10 organizations" often have a third source of resources called *capital additions*—contributions and gifts, grants, and bequests that are restricted by the donor to endowment, plant, and loan funds.

3. *Capital additions* received by "78-10 organizations" that are restricted to asset acquisitions are reported under the caption "capital additions" in the statement of activity when the resources are received regardless of when the resources are used for the specified purpose.

4. "78-10 organizations" that have insignificant amounts of restricted resources do not usually use funds. The financial statements of such organizations are similar to those of business enterprises, except that the net worth of "78-10 organizations" is referred to as net assets or equity.

5. Plant assets of "78-10 organizations" are classified as exhaustible or inexhaustible and are depreciated in essentially the same manner as in business enterprises.

6. The basic financial statements generally required of "78-10 organizations" are the balance sheet and the statement of activity.

PROBLEMS

P19-1   **College and University Accounting: Journal Entries**   Selected transactions of Garfield University during the year ending June 30, 19X7, are as follows:

1. Tuition and fees charged to students for the fall and spring semesters totaled $900,000, of which $600,000 was collected in cash. It is estimated that $40,000 of the remaining amount will be uncollectible.

2. A bequest of $30,000 was received in securities, of which the principal and income and gains on the investments are to be used to make loans to students.

3. Federal grants of $200,000 cash were received, of which $150,000 was unrestricted and $50,000 was restricted for accounting history research.

4. An alumnus donated land and buildings that were appraised at $60,000 and $120,000, respectively.

5. Of the restricted grants in item (3), $20,000 was expended for research in accounting history.

6. Accounting computer equipment was purchased for $12,000 from the unrestricted current fund.

7. Cash gifts of $100,000 were received from the faculty to establish an endowment for faculty excellence.

8. Loans totaling $23,000 were made to students.

9. The university chapter of Beta Gamma Sigma deposited $3,000 with the university for safekeeping; the funds can be withdrawn by the organization when necessary.

10. Investments totaling $100,000 were purchased by the endowment fund.

REQUIRED
Prepare journal entries to record each of the preceding transactions in the appropriate fund or funds of Garfield University. Use the following funds:

• Unrestricted current fund
• Restricted current fund
• Loan fund
• Endowment fund
• Annuity fund
• Unexpended plant fund
• Investment in plant fund

Each transaction should be numbered to correspond with the transactions described previously, and your answers should be organized as follows:

| | | | Accounts | |
Transaction Number	Fund	Account Title and Explanation	Debit	Credit

P19-2   **Journal Entries in Plant Fund of Colleges and Universities**   The following transactions relate to the plant funds of Urban University:

1. Bonds payable in the amount of $2,000,000 were issued at par for the purpose of constructing a school of accountancy building. The funds were immediately invested in marketable securities.

2. The university received a $100,000 cash gift for the purchase of equipment for the accounting laboratory.

3. Microcomputers with a fair market value of $30,000 were given to the school of accountancy by a computer manufacturer.

4. The governing board transferred (nonmandatory) $70,000 cash to the renewal and replacement plant fund to replace equipment in the accounting classrooms.

5. Income of $20,000 on the investments in item (1) was received in cash.

6. The equipment for the accounting laboratory noted in item (2) was purchased for $100,000.

7. The investments in item (1) were sold for $2,100,000.

8. The school of accountancy building was completed at a cost of $2,050,000.

9. The equipment was replaced in the accounting classrooms for $65,000.

10. The equipment that was replaced in item (9) was carried on the books at $40,000 and was sold for $15,000. The sale proceeds are accounted for in the unexpended plant fund.

11. The governing board transferred (mandatory) $120,000 to the retirement of indebtedness plant fund for payment of interest on the outstanding debt. The interest payment was made.

REQUIRED
For each transaction, prepare the necessary journal entries for all the plant funds involved. Do not record entries in other funds affected. Use the following headings:

Entry No.	Accounts	Debit	Credit	Plant Fund

In the far-right column, indicate in which plant fund each entry is to be made, using the following coding:

Unexpected plant fund	U
Renewal and replacement plant fund	RR
Retirement of indebtedness plant fund	RI
Investment in plant fund	I

P19-3 **University Accounting: Journal Entries, Financial Statement**   A partial balance sheet of Rapapo State University as of the end of its fiscal year ended July 31, 19X2, is presented as follows:

Rapapo State University
CURRENT FUNDS BALANCE SHEET
AT JULY 31, 19X2

Assets		Liabilities and Fund Balances	
Unrestricted:		**Unrestricted:**	
Cash	$200,000	Accounts payable	$100,000
Accounts receivable—		Due to other funds	40,000
tuition and fees,		Deferred revenue—	
less allowance for		tuition and fees	25,000
uncollectible accounts		Fund balance	435,000
of $15,000	360,000		
Prepaid expenses	40,000		
Total unrestricted . .	$600,000	Total unrestricted . .	$600,000
Restricted:		**Restricted:**	
Cash	$ 10,000	Accounts payable	$ 5,000
Investments	210,000	Fund balance	215,000
Total restricted	$220,000	Total restricted	$220,000
Total current funds	$820,000	Total current funds	$820,000

The following information pertains to the year ended July 31, 19X3:

1. Cash collected from students' tuition totaled $3,000,000. Of this $3,000,000, $362,000 represented accounts receivable outstanding at July 31, 19X2; $2,500,000 was for current year tuition; and $138,000 was for tuition that was applicable to the semester beginning in August 19X3.

2. Deferred revenue at July 31, 19X2, was earned during the year ended July 31, 19X3.

3. Accounts receivable at July 31, 19X2, which were not collected during the year ended July 31, 19X3, were determined to be uncollectible and were written off against the allowance account. At July 31, 19X3, the allowance account was estimated at $10,000.

4. During the year, an unrestricted appropriation of $60,000 was made by the state. This state appropriation was to be paid to Rapapo sometime in August 19X3.

5. During the year unrestricted cash gifts of $80,000 were received from the alumni. Rapapo's board of trustees allocated and transferred $30,000 of these gifts to the student loan fund.

6. During the year restricted fund investments costing $25,000 were sold for $31,000. Restricted fund investments were purchased at a cost of $40,000. Investment income of $18,000 was earned and collected during the year.

7. Unrestricted general expenditures of $2,500,000 were recorded. At July 31, 19X3, the unrestricted accounts payable balance was $75,000.

8. The restricted accounts payable balance at July 31, 19X2, was paid.

9. The $40,000 due to other funds at July 31, 19X2, was paid to the plant funds as required.

10. One quarter of the prepaid expenses at July 31, 19X2, expired during the current year and pertained to general education expenditures. There was no addition to prepaid expenses during the year.

REQUIRED

a) Prepare journal entries to record the foregoing transactions in the university's current funds for the year ended July 31, 19X3. Number each entry to correspond with the number indicated in the description of its respective transaction. Your answer sheet should be organized as follows:

		Current Funds			
		Unrestricted		Restricted	
Entry no.	Accounts	Debit	Credit	Debit	Credit

b) Prepare a statement of changes in fund balances for the year ended July 31, 19X3.

(AICPA adapted)

P19-4 **Hospital Accounting: Unrestricted Funds Journal and Closing Entries, Financial Statement**
Metropolitan Hospital had the following transactions during 19X7:

1. Gross billings to patients, all charged to accounts receivable, for the year were as follows:

Daily patient services	$700,000
Other professional services	140,000

2. Estimated deductions from gross patient service revenues were as follows:

Contractual adjustments with third-party payers	$ 50,000
Provision for bad debts	25,000

3. Accounts receivable of $500,000 were collected. Accounts written off totaled $30,000.

4. During the year Metropolitan received $80,000 of unrestricted gifts, $20,000 of unrestricted income from endowments and a $75,000 cash bequest in the form of a permanent endowment.

5. Operating expenses incurred during the year were as follows. All expenses have been paid except for $10,000.

Nursing services	$475,000
Other professional services	190,000
General services	55,000
Fiscal services	25,000
Administrative services	15,000

6. Depreciation of buildings and equipment was $60,000 and $40,000, respectively.

7. Other operating revenues, all received in cash, for the year were television rentals, $17,000, and cafeteria sales, $13,000.

8. The unrestricted funds received $60,000 cash from the plant replacement and expansion fund to finance equipment acquisitions.

9. The unrestricted funds expended $62,000 for major movable equipment. This included the $60,000 received from the plant replacement and expansion fund, along with $2,000 of unrestricted funds.

REQUIRED

a) Prepare journal entries to record the preceding nine transactions for 19X7. List the transaction numbers (1 through 9) and give the necessary entry in the unrestricted funds only.

b) Prepare closing entries for the unrestricted funds at December 31, 19X7.

c) Prepare journal entries required in funds other than the unrestricted funds for any of the preceding nine transactions.

d) Prepare a statement of activities for the year ending December 31, 19X7, as required by the FASB. Assume beginning-of-the-year balances as follows: $471,000 for unrestricted net assets, $89,000 for temporarily restricted net assets (including restricted current funds, specific purpose funds, and plant replacement and expansion fund), and $220,000 for permanently restricted net assets.

P19-5   **Voluntary Health and Welfare Accounting: Journal Entries in Current; Land, Building, and Equipment; and Endowment Funds**   The Health and Welfare Society of Cityville was formed in 19X1. The following transactions occurred during its fiscal year ending June 30, 19X3:

1. The annual fund drive resulted in cash contributions of $75,000 for unrestricted purposes and $25,000 restricted for the purchase of new equipment.

2. Unrestricted contributions in the form of pledges were received in the amount of $50,000, of which $5,000 is expected to be uncollectible.

3. Revenues from membership dues are received in the amount of $15,000.

4. Since formation of the Health and Welfare Society several years ago, it has been given free use of office space by a local organization; this office space would normally rent for $500 per month.

5. Equipment was purchased, for $12,000 cash, from the land, building, and equipment fund.

6. Program services expenses paid from unrestricted funds for public health education and community services were $20,000 and $18,000, respectively.

7. Cash contributions of $40,000 to the endowment fund are received.

8. Current unrestricted funds of $2,000 are used to acquire equipment.

9. Cash contributions in the amount of $26,000 were received to support research activities.

10. Part-time clerical help during the year totaled $16,000. Based on an agreement with the part-time employees, $10,000 of this amount would be paid in cash and the remaining $6,000 would be considered donated services.

11. Program services expenses paid from restricted funds for research were $8,000.

12. Endowment fund investments that cost $25,000 are sold for $35,000. The gain is available for expenditure in future years only.

REQUIRED

a) Prepare journal entries to record each of the preceding transactions in the appropriate fund or funds of the Health and Welfare Society of Cityville. Use the following funds:

- Current unrestricted fund
- Current restricted fund
- Land, building, and equipment fund
- Endowment fund

Each transaction should be numbered to correspond with the transaction described previously, and your answers should be organized as follows:

			Accounts	
Transaction Number	**Fund**	**Account Title and Explanation**	**Debit**	**Credit**

b) Prepare a statement of activities for the year ended June 30, 19X3, as required by the FASB. Assume beginning-of-the-year balances as follows: $297,000 for unrestricted net assets, $123,000 for temporarily restricted net assets (including the current restricted fund and appropriate parts of the land, building, and equipment fund), and $310,000 for permanently restricted net assets (the endowment fund).

P19-6 **Voluntary Health and Welfare Accounting: Financial Statements** Following are the adjusted current funds trial balances of Community Association for Handicapped Children, a voluntary health and welfare organization, at June 30, 19X4:

Community Association for Handicapped Children
ADJUSTED CURRENT FUNDS TRIAL BALANCES
AT JUNE 30, 19X4

	Unrestricted		Restricted	
	Debit	Credit	Debit	Credit
Cash	$ 40,000		$ 9,000	
Bequest receivable			5,000	
Pledges receivable	12,000			
Accrued interest receivable	1,000			
Investments (at cost, which approximates market)	100,000			
Accounts payable		$ 52,000		$ 1,000
Allowance for uncollectible pledges		3,000		
Fund balances, July 1, 19X3:				
Unrestricted		38,000		
Restricted				3,000
Transfers of endowment fund income		20,000		
Contributions		300,000		15,000
Membership dues		25,000		
Program service fees		30,000		
Investment income		10,000		
Deaf children's program	120,000			
Blind children's program	150,000			
Management and general services	45,000		4,000	
Fund-raising services	8,000		1,000	
Provision for uncollectible pledges	2,000			
	$478,000	$478,000	$19,000	$19,000

REQUIRED
a) Prepare a statement of activities for the year ended June 30, 19X4. Follow FASB rules. The endowment fund had a beginning-of-the-year balance of $212,000 (including term endowments of $78,000), income for the year of $27,000 ($20,000 unrestricted and $7,000 permanently restricted), new permanent endowments contributed during the year of $40,000, and an end-of-the-year balance of $259,000 (including term endowments of $78,000). The endowment fund has no liabilities and all its assets are invested in securities. The organization owns no land, buildings, or equipment.
b) Prepare a balance sheet as of June 30, 19X4, following FASB rules.

(AICPA adapted)

P19-7 **University Accounting: Journal Entries, Financial Statement** Presented here is the current funds balance sheet of Burnsville University, which is under GASB jurisdiction, as of the end of its fiscal year ended June 30, 19X7:

Assets

Current funds:
  Unrestricted:

Cash	$210,000	
Accounts receivable—tuition and fees, less allowance for uncollectible accounts of $9,000	341,000	
State appropriations receivable	75,000	$626,000

  Restricted:

Cash	$ 7,000	
Investments	60,000	67,000
Total current funds		$693,000

Liabilities and Fund Balances

Current funds:
  Unrestricted:

Accounts payable	$ 45,000	
Deferred revenues	66,000	
Fund balance	515,000	$626,000

  Restricted:

Fund balance		67,000
Total current funds		$693,000

The following transactions presented here occurred during the fiscal year ended June 30, 19X8:

  1. On July 7, 19X7, a gift of $100,000 was received from an alumnus. The alumnus requested that one-half of the gift be used for the purchase of books for the university library and the remainder be used for the establishment of a scholarship fund. The alumnus further requested that the income generated by the scholarship fund should be used annually to award a scholarship to a qualified disadvantaged student. On July 20, 19X7, the board of trustees resolved that the funds of the newly established scholarship fund would be invested in savings certificates. On July 21, 19X7, the savings certificates were purchased.

  2. Revenue from student tuition and fees that was applicable to the year ended June 30, 19X8, amounted to $1,900,000. Of this amount, $66,000 was collected in the prior year and $1,686,000 was collected during the year ended June 30, 19X8. In addition, at June 30, 19X8, the university had received cash of $158,000 representing fees for the session beginning July 1, 19X8.

  3. During the year ended June 30, 19X8, the university had collected $349,000 of the outstanding accounts receivable at the beginning of the year. The balance was determined to be uncollectible and was written off against the allowance account. At June 30, 19X8, the allowance account was increased by $3,000.

  4. During the year interest charges of $6,000 were earned and collected on late student fee payments.

  5. During the year the state appropriation was received. An additional unrestricted appropriation of $50,000 was made by the state but had not been paid to the university as of June 30, 19X8.

6. An unrestricted gift of $25,000 cash was received from the alumni of the university.

7. During the year restricted fund investments of $21,000 were sold for $26,000. Investment income amounting to $1,900 was received.

8. During the year unrestricted operating expenses of $1,777,000 were recorded. At June 30, 19X8, $59,000 of these expenses remained unpaid.

9. Restricted current funds of $13,000 were spent for authorized purposes during the year.

10. The accounts payable at June 30, 19X7, were paid during the year.

11. During the year $7,000 interest was earned and received on the savings certificates that were purchased in accordance with the board of trustees' resolution, as discussed in item (1).

REQUIRED

a) Prepare journal entries to record the preceding transactions for the year ended June 30, 19X8. Each journal entry should be numbered to correspond with the transaction described. Your answer sheet should be organized as follows:

Entry No.	Accounts	Current Funds				Endowment Fund	
		Unrestricted		Restricted			
		Debit	Credit	Debit	Credit	Debit	Credit

b) Prepare a statement of changes in fund balances for the year ended June 30, 19X8.

(AICPA adapted)

P19-8 **Hospital Accounting: Journal Entries in Unrestricted, Plant Replacement and Expansion, and Endowment Funds** Presented here is the combined balance sheet of Dexter City Hospital as of December 31, 19X5. Dexter City Hospital is under GASB jurisdiction.

Dexter City Hospital
BALANCE SHEET
AS OF DECEMBER 31, 19X5

Assets			Liabilities and Fund Balances		
UNRESTRICTED FUNDS					
Current:			Current:		
Cash		$ 20,000	Accounts payable		$ 16,000
Accounts receivable	$37,000		Accrued expenses		6,000
Less: Allowance for uncollectible accounts	7,000	30,000	Total current liabilities		$ 22,000
Inventory of supplies		14,000	Long-term debt:		
Total current assets		$ 64,000	Mortgage bonds payable		150,000
Property, plant, and equipment:			Total liabilities		$ 172,000
Land		400,000	Fund balance		2,158,000
Buildings	$1,750,000				
Less: Accumulated depreciation	430,000	1,320,000			
Equipment:	$ 680,000				
Less: Accumulated depreciation	134,000	546,000			
			Total liabilities and fund balances		
Total assets		$2,330,000			$2,330,000

RESTRICTED FUNDS
Plant Replacement and Expansion Fund

Cash		$ 53,800	Fund balance		$ 125,000
Investments		71,200			
Total		$ 125,000	Total		$ 125,000

Endowment Fund

Cash		$ 6,000	Fund balance		$ 266,000
Investments		260,000			
Total		$ 266,000	Total		$ 266,000

During 19X6 the following transactions occurred:

1. Gross charges for hospital services, all charged to accounts receivable, were as follows:

Room and board charges	$780,000
Charges for other professional services	321,000

2. Deductions from gross earnings were as follows:

Provision for uncollectible receivables	$ 30,000
Charity service	15,000

3. The unrestricted funds paid $18,000 to retire mortgage bonds payable with an equivalent fair value. The unrestricted funds will not be repaid.

4. During the year the unrestricted funds received general contributions of $50,000 and an income from endowment fund investments of $6,500. The unrestricted funds has been designated to receive income earned on endowment fund investments.

5. New equipment costing $26,000 was acquired. An x-ray machine, which originally cost $24,000 and which had an undepreciated cost of $2,400, was sold for $500.

6. Vouchers totaling $1,191,000 were issued for the following items:

Administrative service expense	$120,000
Fiscal service expense	95,000
General service expense	225,000
Nursing service expense	520,000
Other professional service expense	165,000
Supplies	60,000
Expenses accrued at December 31, 19X5	6,000

7. Collections on accounts receivable totaled $985,000. Accounts written off as uncollectible amounted to $11,000.

8. Cash payments on accounts payable during the year were $825,000.

9. Supplies of $37,000 were issued to nursing services.

10. On December 31, 19X6, accrued interest income on plant replacement and expansion fund investments was $800.

11. Depreciation of buildings and equipment was as follows:

Buildings	$44,000
Equipment	73,000

12. On December 31, 19X6, an accrual of $6,100 was made for fiscal service expense.

REQUIRED

For the period January 1, 19X6, through December 31, 19X6, prepare journal entries to record the transactions described previously for the following funds of Dexter Hospital:

- Unrestricted funds
- Plant replacement and expansion fund
- Endowment fund

Each journal entry should be numbered to correspond with the transactions described earlier. Your answer sheet should be organized as follows:

			Amounts	
Transaction Number	**Fund**	**Account Title and Explanation**	**Debit**	**Credit**

(AICPA Adapted)

P19-9 **"78-10 Organization" Accounting (Nonprofit Civic Organization): Journal and Adjusting Entries, Financial Statement** In 19X1, a group of civic-minded merchants in Albury City organized the "Committee of 100" for the purpose of establishing the Community Sports Club, a nonprofit sports organization for local youth. Each of the committee's 100 members contributed $1,000 toward the Club's capital and, in turn, received a participation certificate. In addition, each participant agreed to pay dues of $200 a year for the club's operations. All dues have been collected in full by the end of each fiscal year ending March 31. Members who have discontinued their participation have been replaced by an equal number of new members through the transfer of the participation certificates from the former members to the new ones. Following is the Club's trial balance at April 1, 19X3:

	Debit	Credit
Cash	$ 9,000	$
Investments (at market, equal to cost)	58,000	
Inventories	5,000	
Land	10,000	
Building	164,000	
Accumulated depreciation—building		130,000
Furniture and equipment	54,000	
Accumulated depreciation—furniture and equipment		46,000
Accounts payable		12,000
Participation certificates (100 at $1,000 each)		100,000
Cumulative excess of revenue over expenses		12,000
	$300,000	$300,000

Transactions for the year ended March 31, 19X4, were as follows:

1. Collections from participants for dues — $20,000
2. Snack bar and soda fountain sales — 28,000
3. Interest and dividends received — 6,000
4. Additions to voucher register:
   - House expenses — 17,000
   - Snack bar and soda fountain — 26,000
   - General and administrative — 11,000
5. Vouchers paid — 55,000
6. Assessments for capital improvements not yet incurred (assessed on March 20, 19X4; none collected by March 31, 19X4; deemed 100% collectible during year ending March 31, 19X5) — 10,000
7. Unrestricted bequest received — 5,000

Adjustment data:

1. Investments are valued at market, which amounted to $65,000 at March 31, 19X4. There were no investment transactions during the year.

2. Depreciation for the year:

Building	$4,000
Furniture and equipment	8,000

3. Allocation of depreciation:

House expenses	$9,000
Snack bar and soda fountain	2,000
General and administrative	1,000

4. Actual physical inventory at March 31, 19X4, was $1,000 and pertains to the snack bar and soda fountain.

REQUIRED

a) Record the transactions and adjustments in journal entry form (on a functional basis) for the year ended March 31, 19X4. Omit explanations.

b) Prepare the statement of activities for the year ended March 31, 19X4.

(AICPA adapted)

P19-10 **Hospital Accounting: Statement of Revenues and Expenses and Notes** The following selected information was taken from the books and records of Glendora Hospital (a voluntary hospital) as of and for the year ended June 30, 19X2:

• Patient service revenue totaled $16,000,000 ($11,000,000 for daily patient services and $5,000,000 for other professional services) with deductions from patient service revenue for allowances and uncollectible accounts amounting to $3,400,000 ($2,100,000 for charity allowances and $1,300,000 for uncollectible accounts). Other operating revenue aggregated $346,000. Revenue of $6,000,000 recognized under cost reimbursement agreements is subject to audit and retroactive adjustment by third-party payers. Estimated retroactive adjustments under these agreements have been included in allowances.

• Unrestricted gifts and bequests of $410,000 were received.

• Unrestricted income from endowment funds totaled $160,000.

• Income from board-designated funds aggregated $82,000.

• Operating expenses totaled $13,370,000 and included $500,000 for depreciation that was computed on the straight-line basis. However, accelerated depreciation is used to determine reimbursable costs under certain third-party reimbursement agreements. Net cost reimbursement revenue amounting to $220,000, resulting from the difference in depreciation methods, was deferred to future years.

• Also included in operating expenses are pension costs of $100,000, in connection with a noncontributory pension plan covering substantially all of Glendora's employees. Accrued pension costs are funded currently. Prior service cost is being amortized over a period of 20 years. The actuarially computed value of vested and nonvested benefits at year-end amounted to $3,000,000 and $350,000, respectively. The assumed rate of return used in determining the actuarial present value of accumulated plan benefits was 8%. The plan's net assets that were available for benefits at year-end were $3,050,000.

• Gifts and bequests are recorded at fair market values when received.

• Patient service revenue is accounted for at established rates on the accrual basis.

• Specific purpose funds of $125,000 were expended.

• Beginning-of-the-year net asset balances are as follows: $8,957,000 for unrestricted net assets, $623,000 for temporarily restricted net assets (including restricted current funds and specific purpose funds), and $1,670,000 for endowment funds all of which are permanent. The hospital does not have a plant replacement and expansion fund.

REQUIRED

a) Prepare a schedule of patient service revenues and deductions for Glendora Hospital for the year ended June 30, 19X2. (See Exhibit 19-18.)

b) Prepare a statement of activities for Glendora Hospital for the year ended June 30, 19X2.

c) Draft the appropriate disclosures in separate notes accompanying the statement of revenues and expenses, referencing each note to its respective item in the statement.

(AICPA adapted)

ISSUES IN ACCOUNTING JUDGMENT

I19-1 **Joint Cost of Fund-Raising**   Porterfield Art Institute is a nonprofit organization that is subject to FASB rules. Porterfield's executive director, Anne Vanderhoff, is newly appointed to her position and has just completed a major fund-raising effort in conjunction with the annual membership and program registration campaign. She knows that FASB rules require financial statements to include separate amounts for the costs of program services, management and general services, and fund-raising efforts. An expensive consulting firm was employed to redesign Porterfield's campaign approach and materials. As a result, the cost of the campaign was three times the annual cost of past years. In past years, the cost of the campaign has been divided equally between fund-raising and program services. Although the program services have been increasingly successful, charging them half of the cost of the recent campaign would "put them in the red."

REQUIRED
Write a brief essay that addresses the following questions: Why are readers of the Institute's financial statements concerned about this cost allocation problem? Why are the Institute's administrators interested in the problem? How should Anne Vanderhoff resolve the problem? [Hint: Read the AICPA's *Statement of Auditing Procedure 87-2.*]

I19-2 **A Hospital's Community Responsibility**   City Hospital is located in the inner city of a large metropolitan area and is subject to FASB rules. City Hospital receives a total exemption from property taxes while other hospitals located further from the city's center receive only partial exemptions. Recently, City Hospital has been acquired by a consortium of several hospitals most of which are located in the city's suburbs. The consortium's uniform accounting system, which City Hospital is now required to use, does not treat indigent care as a separate program as City Hospital's old system had done. Rather, it is treated as line items in a number of hospital programs.

REQUIRED
Write a brief essay commenting on the effect on City Hospital's financial statements of the consortium's accounting system and the appropriateness of the system for City Hospital.

Index

Account groups, governmental accounting and, 833

Accountability, financial, 830–831

Accountants International Study Group, 154n, 414n

Accounting changes, interim reporting of, 496–498

Accounting Principles Board (APB):
business combinations and, 7–8, 12
Opinions
Opinion No. 9, results of operations, 373, 698
Opinion No. 16, business combinations, 10n, 13–16, 21, 26, 28–32, 33–35, 84, 88, 104, 521, 562
Opinion No. 18, equity method, 135, 140, 145, 215n, 358–359, 363, 365, 414n, 418n, 431, 484–485
Opinion No. 20, accounting changes, 496–497, 555n, 698, 968n
Opinion No. 21, present value reporting, 309n, 528, 564
Opinion No. 22, disclosure of accounting policies, 73, 561
Opinion No. 28, interim financial reporting, 491–496
Opinion No. 30, special income items, 145–146, 369, 484n, 526n
(*See also* Financial Accounting Standards Board)

Accounting Research Bulletin (ARB), 224n
Bulletin No. 51, consolidated statements, 72n, 73, 76, 88, 160n, 168, 224n
Bulletin No. 43, restatement, 493, 527, 646–647

Accounting rule-making agencies, 7–8, 554–556, 557, 968–969

Accounting systems:
branch accounting (*see* Branch accounting)
fund accounting (*see* Fund accounting)
governmental accounting (*see* Governmental accounting)
nonprofit organization accounting (*see* Nonprofit organization accounting)
(*See also specific topics*)

Accounts payable, foreign currency transactions and, 652

Accounts receivable, branch accounting and, 781

Accrual accounting, 834
nonprofit organization accounting and, 972–973
proprietary funds and, 911
(*See also* Generally accepted accounting principles)

Accumulated depreciation, foreign financial statement restatements and, 596–598

Acquired companies, business combination viewpoints of, 5–7

Acquired equity, 150

Acquiring companies, business combination viewpoints of, 4–5

Acquisition(s), 4–7
date-of-acquisition consolidations (*see* Date-of-acquisition consolidations)
interim, 164–170
consolidated income statement forms and, 168–170
equity method and, 167–168
valuation differential and, 170
of outstanding debt, 307–321
gains and losses, 307–309
parent's debt acquired by subsidiary, 309–313
subsidiary's debt acquired by parent, 314–321

Acquisition(s) *(Cont.):*
postacquisition consolidations (*see* Postacquisition consolidations)
of subsidiary common stock
multiple-step, 357–361
new shares, 369–376
ownership changes and intercompany gross margin, 378–382
of subsidiary preferred stock, 422–430
book value of preferred stockholders' equity, 423–424
date-of-acquisition consolidation, 424–426
equity method, 426–427
postacquisition consolidation, 427–430
tender offers and, 6–7
(*See also* Acquisition cost; Consolidations; Mergers; *and specific topics*)

Acquisition cost:
bargain purchase, 84n
contingent considerations and, 35
based on earnings, 34
based on security prices, 34–35
preacquisition contingencies, 35
fair value over cost and, 84–86, 142–144
purchase combinations and, 12–17
allocation, 15–17
measurement, 13–14

Acquisition year, net income and, 26–28

Activity (operating) statements, of 78-10 organizations, 1025

Adjustments:
bankruptcy and, 531–535
branch accounting and, 790–794
merchandise transfers billed in excess of cost, 798–804
omitted entries and errors, 793–794
to consolidation worksheets, 67–68,

Adjustments *(Cont.):*
    79–81, 83, 86–88, 90–91, 148
    interim acquisitions, 168–170
    postacquisition, 158–159, 162–164
    postacquisition, cost method, 173–175
    postacquisition, pooling combinations, 103, 171
    cumulative translation, 606, 606*n*, 608, 664
    deferred income taxes and, 444
    elimination *(see* Elimination adjustments)
    foreign currency forward contracts and, 657
    foreign financial statement restatements and consolidation procedures, 610–616
      equity method, 603–610
      foreign currency restatements, 577–582, 646
      remeasurements, 582, 592
      translation, 583, 584–590, 616, 617
    indirect ownership and, 408–409
    intercompany debt transactions and face-value method, 324–327
      new intercompany debt, 304–307
      outstanding debt acquisition, 312–314, 318–321
    intercompany merchandise transfers and, 223–235
      comprehensive illustration, 228–235
      deferral methods, fractional method illustrated, 236–237
      deferral methods, total vs., fractional, 223–224
      upstream merchandise transfers, 269
    intercompany plant asset transfers and, 262–263
      upstream depreciable asset transfers, 265–266
      upstream land transfers, 258–259
      variations, 269
    intercompany stock transfers and common stock sales, 366–367
      gross margin, 380–381
      multiple-step stock acquisitions, 360–361
    joint ventures and, 432–434
    mutual holdings between parent and subsidiary and, 413–422

Adjustments *(Cont.):*
    preferred stock of subsidiary and date-of-acquisition, 424–426
      postacquisition consolidation, 427–430
    reclassification *(see* Reclassification adjustments)
    (See also Worksheets)
Admission of new partner *(see* Partnerships and partnership accounting)
Affiliated group, 435
Affiliation structures:
    direct ownership and, 70, 403
    discounting and, 328–329
    indirect ownership and, 70, 404–409
      consolidated net income, 406
      consolidation procedures, 406–409
      control, 405
      equity method, 405–406
      minority interest, 406
      ownership percentages, 405
    mutual holdings and, 409–422
      between parent and subsidiary, 413–422
      between subsidiaries, 409–413
    (See also Ownership)
Agency funds, 920–921, 935, 937, 985, 1024
AICPA *(see* American Institute of Certified Public Accountants)
Allocation method, for mutual holdings between parent and subsidiary, 418–422
    date-of-acquisition consolidation, 418–419
    postacquisition consolidation, 418–422
    treasury stock method compared, 414
Allowance(s):
    for depreciation accounts, 985
    for uncollectable current taxes, 852
    for uncollectable delinquent taxes, 849–852
    for unrealized gross margin in branch inventory, 794–796
American Accounting Association, 414*n*
American Institute of Certified Public Accountants (AICPA), 222*n*, 224*n*, 370, 554, 828
    Accounting Standards Executive Committee (AcSEC), 375*n*, 431*n*, 555

AICPA *(Cont.):*
    Auditing Standards Board, 554, 968*n*
    ethics rules of, 554, 554*n*, 555
    nonprofit organization accounting and, 968*n*, 968–969, 971, 972*n*, 992, 999*n*, 1017, 1025
    Statement of Auditing Standards (SAS) No. 69, 554–555, 562
    Statement of Position (SOP) 82-1, 754*n*
    Statement of Position (SOP) 90-7, financial reporting for bankruptcy, 528
    Statement of Quality Control Standards (SQCS) No. 1, 562
Amortization:
    foreign currency transactions and forward contracts, 657–658
      identifiable foreign currency commitments, 661–664
    of goodwill
      common stock sales, 365, 367
      mutual holdings, 420–421
    intercompany debt transactions and outstanding debt acquisition, 307, 310*n*, 315–316
    of valuation differential, 140–141, 144
      cost method, 175
      foreign financial statement restatements and, 605–606
      mutual holdings, 417, 418
      new stock and, 371–373
      postacquisition, 148–149, 159, 164, 170
      stock transfers, 357–359, 367
      unamortized valuation, 152, 164, 170
Annual budgets, governmental accounting and, 840–841
Annual report of governmental unit *(see* Comprehensive annual financial report)
Annuity funds, 980–982, 983
Antitrust Division, Justice Department, 7
Apostolon, Nicholas G., 829*n*
Arm's length transactions, 215–217, 221–222, 222*n*
Arrearage, 369, 429
Arthur Andersen & Co., 22
Articles of partnership, 685
Assessments, special, 917–919

Assets:
  acquisition of, subject to liabilities, 10
  co-ownership of, in partnerships, 686
  depreciable, intercompany plant asset
    transfers and, 263–269
  disposition of, pooling-of-interests
    criteria, 33
  fixed (see Fixed assets)
  foreign currency transactions and
    hedges, 655–658
  foreign financial statement restatements
    and remeasurements, 593–598
    translation adjustments, 616, 617
  governmental accounting and, 833, 853
    capital projects funds, 891–898
  identifiable purchase combinations and,
    15–17
  inexhaustible, 1024
  "infrastructure," 905n
  net (see Net assets)
  noncurrent, 84
    fair value over cost and, 144
  of partnerships, 702–703
  pooling combinations and, 22n
  restricted, 913, 915
  unrecorded, 15
Autonomy, as pooling-of-interests
  criteria, 29
Average capital balances, partnerships
  and, 692–694
Average exchange rates, 580
  remeasurements and, 592

Balance sheets:
  branch accounting and, 791–793
    merchandise transfers billed in
      excess of cost, 799
  consolidations and, 98, 102–103
    date-of-acquisition (see Date-of-
      acquisition consolidations)
    interim acquisitions, 166
    postacquisition (see Postacquisition
      consolidations)
  deferred income taxes and, 441, 445
  foreign financial statement restatements
    and, 584–585, 590, 590n
    remeasurements, 590–602
  governmental accounting and, 857–
    858, 860
    annual financial reporting, 926, 928

Balance sheets (Cont.):
  capital projects funds, 897
  funds, 899, 903
  proprietary funds, 915, 917
  trust funds and, 924, 925
  indirect ownership and, 407–408
  intercompany debt transactions and
    face-value method, 325–327
    new intercompany debt, 305
    outstanding debt acquisition, 313–
      315, 316, 319–321
  joint ventures and, 434
  for leveraged buyout, 522, 524
  mutual holdings between parent and
    subsidiary, 418, 419
  mutual holdings between subsidiaries,
    411
  nonhomogeneous subsidiaries, 472
  nonprofit organization accounting and
    colleges and universities, 985–992
    hospitals, 1006, 1008
    78-10 organizations, 1024, 1025–
      1026
    VHWOs, 1013, 1019
  of partnerships, 698–699, 700
    liquidations, 759–763
  pooling combinations and, 22–24, 102–
    103
  purchase combinations and, 15–20
  push-down, 487
  (See also Financial statements)
Banking industry, 7n, 556–558
Banking regulators, 556–558
Bankruptcy, 519, 527–536
  accounting during, 531–536
  Chapter 7, 527, 528
  Chapter 11, 527, 528–536
  defined, 527
  emerging from, 533–536
  petition, 527, 528, 529–532
  plan of reorganization, 528
  postpetition transactions, 527–528
  prepetition transactions, 527
  reorganization proceedings, 519, 528–
    536
  worksheets for, 531–535
Basis (see New basis accounting)
Baxter, George C., 94n
Beams, Floyd A., 418n
Beginning-of-year balance of minority
  interest, 313

Beginning-of-year balance sheets, 590n
Beginning-of-year capital balances,
  partnerships and, 691–692
Beginning-of-year retained earnings, 259–
  260, 267
Bierman, Harold, Jr., 657n
Bilateral holdings (see Mutual holdings)
Billing, branch merchandise transfers
  and, 798–804
  billed at selling price, 798
  combination worksheet, in excess of
    cost, 798–804
  home to branch, in excess of cost, 796–
    798
Board-designated funds:
  colleges and universities, 972
  hospitals, 993
Bonds:
  debt service funds and (see Debt
    service funds)
  discounts, 892
  general long-term debt account group
    and, 907–911, 912
  governmental accounting and, 892
  interest coupon payments, 900–903
  premiums, 892
  revenue, 914
  serial, 904
  term, 899, 900, 903
  trust funds and, 923
  (See also Long-term debt)
Bonds-payable account, intercompany
  debt transactions and, 309–310, 315–
  316
Bonus method, partnerships and:
  admission by investment, 709–711
  admission by purchased interest, 714–
    716
Bonuses, in partnerships, 694, 718
Book value:
  intercompany stock transfers and new
    stock issues, 371–373
    treasury stock, 377
  investment account, 150–152
  of net assets acquired, 15–17, 77–79
  of partnership equity, 717–719
  pooling-of-interests combinations and,
    12–13, 22–26
  of preferred stockholders' equity, 423–
    424
  purchase combinations and, 15–17

Book value *(Cont.)*:
of subsidiary equity, interim
acquisitions and, 167–168
Borrowing:
by partners, 690
(See also Loans)
Branch accounting, 780–805
combined financial statements and,
790–794, 795, 801
interbranch transfers and, 804–805
merchandise transfers billed in excess
of cost and, 794–804
combination worksheets, 798–804
recording home to branch transfers,
796–798
multiple branches and, 804
transaction records and, 782–790
branch operating transactions and
transfers to home office, 787
end-of-the-period reports and closing
procedures, 787–790
home office accounts, 782–783
investment in branch accounts, 782–
783, 792, 800–801
transfers from home office to
branch, 783–787
Branch investment account *(see*
Investment in branch accounts)
Budgets, governmental accounting and,
839–842, 892
general fund budget, 846–848
Business combinations:
accounting for, 11–28
acquisitions of assets subject to
liabilities, 10
combined net income for acquisition
year, 26–28
consolidations and, 65–68
contingent consideration and, 35
based on earnings, 34
based on security prices, 34–35
preacquisition contingencies, 35
corporate structures of, 11
deferred income taxes and, 12–13,
146, 443–448
defined, 2–3
internal development compared to, 4–5
pooling-of-interests accounting for *(see*
Pooling-of-interests accounting)
purchase accounting for *(see* Purchase
combinations)

Business combinations *(Cont.)*:
tax incentive for, 12–13, 146, 443–
448
types of, 8–10
viewpoints of groups affected by, 3–8
accounting rule-making agencies, 7–
8
acquired company, 5–7
acquiring company, 4–5
regulatory agencies, 7, 11
Business organizations, nonbusiness
organizations compared to, 827
Buying rates, 645*n*

CAFR *(see* Comprehensive annual
financial report)
Capital, contributed versus earned, 686
Capital accounts, of partnerships, 686–
690, 698–699, 700
admission by investments and, 702–
711
admission by purchased interest and,
702–705, 711–717
drawing accounts and, 688–689
financial reporting and, 698–699, 700
income taxes and, 699–701
initial capital balances and, 687–688
interest in partnership capital, 688, 695–
697, 701–705, 711–717
investment bases and, 691–694
liquidation and, 748–763
insolvency, 755–756
installment distributions, 756–763
single-step distributions, 752–756
statement of liquidation, 749–752
withdrawal or death of partner, 717–
719
Capital additions, 1022
78-10 organizations and, 1022
Capital grants, 863, 913
Capital improvements, governmental
accounting and, 918–919
Capital investment bases, 691–694
Capital projects funds, 891–898
bond premium and discounts, 892
budgets and, 892
characteristics of, 934, 936
financial statements and, 897–898
transaction recording, 892–897
Capital-transactions method, 373–374
Carrying amount of acquired debt, 307

Cash:
collection of, partnership liquidation
and, 754
foreign currency restatement of,
current rate and, 579–580
net assets acquired for, 8–9
stock acquired for, 9, 65–66
transfers of, branch accounting and,
783, 793–794
Cash with fiscal agent, 903
Catlett, George R., 21
Chandler, Alfred D., Jr., 3*n*
Changes, interim reporting of accounting,
496–498
Classification:
hospital accounting and, 993–998, 999
of revenues and expenditures, 933–934
Clayton Act of 1914, 7
Closely held corporations, business
combinations and, 6
Closing entries:
branch accounting and, 787–790
governmental accounting and, 841–
842, 856–857
capital projects funds, 896–897
debt service funds, 903
nonprofit organization accounting and,
974, 985
partnership drawing accounts, 689
Co-ownership of assets, 686
College and university accounting, 971–
992
agency funds and, 985
annual financial statements for, 985–
992
annuity and life income funds, 980–
982, 983
closing entries for funds other than
current and, 985
current funds and, 971–978
endowment and similar funds, 978–
980, 981, 992
fund structure and, 970, 971–972
loan funds and, 978, 979
methods and systems, 972–974
plant funds and, 982–989
Combinations *(see* Business
combinations)
Combined financial statements, 782
branch accounting and, 790–794, 795,
801

Combining statements by fund type, 930
Common stock:
    foreign financial statement restatements
        and remeasurement of, 593
    long-term investment accounting for,
        135–146
        cost method, 135n, 135–138
        equity method, 135n, 135–136, 138–
            146
    mutual holdings between parent and
        subsidiary and, 413–422
        allocation method, 418–422
        treasury stock method, 414–418
    parent's calculation of income from,
        426
    preferred stock of subsidiary and, 426
    of subsidiaries (see Subsidiaries,
        common stock of)
    treasury stock, 31–32, 86–88, 376–
        378
Comprehensive annual financial report
    (CAFR), 924–934
    combining statements by fund type,
        930
    general purpose financial statements,
        926–932
    individual fund and account group
        statements, 931–933
Conglomerates, 3, 469
Congress, U.S., governmental accounting
    and, 828–829n
Consolidated financial statements:
    conceptual basis for, 91–102
    date-of-acquisition (see Date-of-
        acquisition consolidations)
    defined, 65
    foreign currency transaction and, 665
    income statement (see Consolidated
        income statements)
    intercompany merchandise transfers
        and, 216
    intercompany plant asset transfers and
        depreciable assets, 263–269
    interim acquisitions, 166
    postacquisition (see Postacquisition
        consolidations)
    purchase combinations and, 82–88
        excess of initial fair value over cost,
            84–86, 142–144
        intercompany loans, 83
        minority interest, 82–83

Consolidated financial statements (Cont.):
    treasury stock of subsidiaries, 86–88
    unpaid subsidiary cash dividends
        and, 83–84
    purposes and limitations of, 74–76
    statement of consolidation policy and,
        73–74
    worksheet completion of,
        postacquisition, 160–161
Consolidated income statements:
    intercompany merchandise transfers
        and, 225
    intercompany plant asset transfers and
        land, 258–259, 262–263
    interim acquisitions and, 166, 168–170
    postacquisition, 154–155, 172
Consolidated net income, 152–154
    defined, 152–153
    indirect ownership and, 406
    intercompany debt transactions and,
        306
Consolidated subsidiaries, 138n
Consolidated tax returns, 435, 445
    intercompany merchandise transfers
        and, 436–438
Consolidations, 65–104
    alternative concepts of, 91–102
        entity concept, 98–101
        parent-company concept, 77, 92–93,
            95, 98, 99–102
        proportionate, 93, 97–99, 100, 431–
            434
        proprietary concept, 91–94, 97–99
        subsidiary net assets, 100–101
        valuation differential analysis, 94–
            97
    business combinations and, 65–68
    consolidated financial statements and
        (see Consolidated financial
        statements)
    criteria related to, 68–74
        controlling interest, 68–72
        foreign consolidation standards, 71–
            72, 610–616
        statement of consolidation policy,
            73–74
        unconsolidated subsidiaries, 72–73,
            138n
    date-of-acquisition (see Date-of-
        acquisition consolidations)
    defined, 11

Consolidations (Cont.):
    full, 431–432
    intercompany debt transactions and,
        304–307, 312–317, 318–321
    intercompany merchandise transfers
        and, 223–235
        comprehensive illustration, 228–235
        deferral methods, fractional method
            illustrated, 236–237
        deferral methods, total vs. fractional,
            223–224
        upstream merchandise transfers, 225–
            228
    minority interest and (see Minority
        interest(s))
    postacquisition (see Postacquisition
        consolidations)
    push-down accounting and, 140n, 486–
        491, 519, 520
    statutory, 11
Constructive retirement of debt, 307
Consumption method of accounting, 837–
    838
Contingent considerations:
    acquisition cost and, 35
        based on earnings, 34
        based on security prices, 34–35
        preacquisition contingencies, 35
    as pooling-of-interests criteria, 32
    purchase combinations and, 35
Contributed capital, 686
Contributed capital accounts, 913, 916–
    917
Contributed goodwill, 705
Contributions, nonprofit organization
    accounting and, 1011
    78-10 organizations, 1023
Control:
    common stock and, 422
    indirect ownership and, 405
    joint, 431n
    leveraged buyouts and, 525–526
    new basis accounting and, 519n, 529n
Control and subsidiary accounts, 842–
    845
Controlling interest, 68–72
Conventional method (see Allocation
    method, for mutual holdings between
    parent and subsidiary)
Conversions, of foreign currency, 577,
    643n, 649

Corporate structures, business combinations and, 11
Cost method of accounting, 135–138
    consolidation procedures and, 173–176
    date-of-acquisition consolidations and treasury stock, 87
    intercompany stock transfers and conversion to equity method, 357–359
    long-term investments in common stock, 135n, 135–138
    subsidiaries and, 72–73
Cost of goods sold:
    foreign currency transactions and, 647
    foreign financial statement restatements and, 596
    intercompany merchandise transfers and, 226–227, 263
        worksheet adjustments, 231
Costs:
    acquisition (*see* Acquisition cost)
    period, 263–264, 492, 494–495
    product, 263, 492
    purchase combinations and direct and indirect costs compared, 14–15
Creditors:
    business combinations and, 3
    partnership liquidation and, 750–751, 754–756
Crumbley, D. Larry, 829n
Cumulative, fully participating stock, 423
Cumulative dividends, 136–137
Cumulative translation adjustments, 606, 606n, 608, 664
Currency, foreign (*see* Foreign currency)
Currency exchange rates (*see* Exchange rates)
Current funds, nonprofit organization accounting and:
    colleges and universities, 971–978
    VHWOs, 1011–1012
Current rate restatements, 579–580, 584, 590–592, 616
Custodian funds, 1013, 1024
Customer deposits, 913
Customers:
    business combinations and, 3
    major, segment information on, 480–484

Date-of-acquisition consolidations, 77–91
    financial statements, 82–91, 102–104, 146–148
    mutual holdings between parent and subsidiary and
        allocation method, 418–419
        treasury stock method, 415
    pooling combinations and, 102–104
    postacquisition consolidations compared to, 146–148
    preferred stock of subsidiary and, 424–426
    purchase combinations and, 77–91
        comprehensive illustration, 88–91
        financial statements, 82–88
        valuation differential analysis, 77–79
        worksheet procedures, 79–81, 86–88, 90–91
Date-of-acquisition translation, 584–585, 603–605, 609
Davis, Michael L., 375n
Death of partner, 717–719
Debt:
    governmental accounting and, 833, 896, 898–905
    intercompany transactions and, 300–329
        discounting of notes, 328–329
        equity method, 302–304, 311, 317–318
        face-value method, 308–309, 323–328
        new debt creation, 301–307
        outstanding debt acquisition, 307–321
    nonprofit organization accounting and, 984
    retirement of, 307, 984
    (*See also* Bonds; Loans; Long-term debt; Notes)
Debt service funds, 896
    characteristics of, 934, 936
    financial statements and, 903–904
    serial bonds and, 904
    special assessments and, 918–919
    transaction recording and, 898–905
    (*See also* General long-term debt)
Decentralization, branch accounting and, 781–782

Deferred gains or losses:
    intercompany plant asset transfers and
        depreciable assets, 268–269
        land, 258–259, 262–263
        production assets, 269
    omissions, effect upon income, 263
Deferred gross margins, 221–222, 222n, 224
    deferred income taxes and, 217n, 438–439
    fractional method and, 224, 236–237
    to future period, 226–227
    intercompany stock transfers and, 378
    from prior period, 227–228
    total vs. fractional, for upstream transfers, 223–224
    worksheet adjustments, 226–227, 229–231
Deferred income taxes, 435–448
    on business combinations, 12–13, 146, 443–448
    comprehensive example, 439–443
    consolidated and separate tax returns, 435, 439–443, 445
    equity method and
        deferred gross margin, 438–439
        downstream merchandise transfers, 220–222, 438–439
        upstream merchandise transfers, 218–220, 439
    intercompany merchandise transactions, 436–439
    separate tax returns and, comprehensive example, 439–443
    undistributed investee income, 435–436
    (*See also* Income taxes)
Deferred revenues, 852–853
Deficiencies, in partnership income, 695–697
Delinquent property taxes, 849–852
DeMoville, Wig, 84n
Deposits, customer, 913
Depreciable assets, intercompany plant asset transfers and, 263–269
    downstream transfers, 268–269
    upstream transfers, 264–266, 267
Depreciation:
    accumulated, foreign financial statement restatements and, 596–598

Depreciation *(Cont.):*
  intercompany merchandise transfers and, 269
  nonprofit organization accounting and, 972n, 972–973
    colleges and universities, 985
  (See also Depreciable assets, intercompany plant asset transfers and)
Direct costs of acquisition, purchase combinations and, 14–15
Direct exchange rates, 578, 644–645
Direct ownership, 70, 403
Disaggregated financial information, 468–498
  defined, 468
  interim financial reporting, 491–498
  need for, historical perspective on, 469
  parent-company-only financial information, 485–486
  reporting nonhomogeneous subsidiaries, 469–470
  segment reporting, 470–484
  separately issued financial statements for subsidiaries and push-down accounting, 486–491
  significant investees and joint ventures, 484–485
Disclosure:
  consolidation policy statement and, 73–74
  defined, 553
  of foreign currency transaction gains and losses, 665
  researching pronouncements on, 554
Disclosure statement, in bankruptcy, 533
Discounts (discounting):
  bond, 892
  forward contracts and, 653n, 653–654
  identifiable foreign currency commitments and, 659
  intercompany debt transactions and, 301–302, 306n, 328–329
  preferred stock of subsidiary and, 426
Disposal date, 484
Disposal of segment of business, 369, 484
Distribution(s):
  on partnership liquidations, 749–763
    installment distributions, 756–763

Distribution(s) *(Cont.):*
    single-step distributions, 752–756
  of proceeds, on new partner admission, 716–717
Dividends:
  consolidations and, 83–84
  earned equity and, 150
  foreign financial statement restatements and, 590
  long-term investments in common stock cost method, 136–137, 138
  preferred stock, 136–137, 145, 426–427, 429
    of subsidiaries, 83–84
      interim acquisition, 169
      postacquisition, 158–159, 164, 171, 174, 175
    subsidiary stock, 145
Dominant segment, 477
Donations, nonprofit organization accounting and, 1011
  78-10 organizations, 1023
Downstream transfers:
  deferred income taxes and, 438–439
  intercompany merchandise and
    defined, 215, 220
    equity method and, 220–222, 438–439
    gross margin, 216
    gross margin deferrals, 221–222, 222n, 228
    worksheet adjustments, 228–231
  intercompany plant asset and
    depreciable assets, 268–269
    land, 261–263
  intercompany stock and, 378
Drawing accounts, partnerships and, 688–689
Due process, 554n

Early extinguishment of debt, 307
Earned capital, 686
Earned equity, 150
Earnings:
  contingent considerations and, 34
  earned equity and, 150
  retained *(see* Retained earnings)
Economic-unit concept of consolidation, 93, 98, 99, 100, 155n
Eisenhart, Larry, 829n

Elimination adjustments, 79
  (See also Adjustments)
Emerging Issues Task Force (EITF), 523, 525, 526, 555, 564, 602n, 652n
Encumbrance accounting (encumbrances), 842–845
  capital projects funds and, 892–896
  general fund and, 853–859
Encumbrances control account, 842–845, 853
End-of-the-year retained earnings, 260, 267
Endowment funds, nonprofit organization accounting and:
  colleges and universities, 978–980, 981, 992
  hospitals, 1005–1006, 1007
  78-10 organizations, 1024
  VHWOs, 1012–1013
Enterprise funds, 911–916, 934, 936
Entitlements, governmental accounting and, 863
Entity-concept consolidation, 98–101
  valuation differential and, 95–97
Entity theory of financial reporting, 91–94
Equipment:
  branch accounting and, 785–786
  foreign financial statement restatements and, 581n
  (See also Fixed assets)
Equity:
  acquired, 150
  changes in, as pooling-of-interests criteria, 30–31
  earned, 150
  marketable, 137n
  in partnerships, 686–690, 702–719
    liquidations, 760–761
    (See also Partnerships and partnership accounting)
  stockholders' *(see* Stockholders' equity)
Equity method of accounting:
  deferred income taxes and, 447
    deferred gross margin, 438–439
    downstream merchandise transfers, 220–222, 438–439
    upstream merchandise transfers, 218–220, 439

Equity method of accounting *(Cont.)*:
  foreign financial statement restatements
    and, 603–608
    remeasured statements, 608–610
    translated statements, 603–608
  indirect ownership and, 405–406
  intercompany debt transactions and,
    302–304, 311, 317–318
    face-value method, 308–309, 323–
      328
    new intercompany debt, 302–304
    parent's debt acquired by subsidiary,
      311
    subsidiary's debt acquired by parent,
      317–318
  intercompany merchandise transfers
    and, 218–223
    comprehensive illustration, 222–223
    downstream transfers, 220–222, 438–
      439
    upstream transfers, 218–220, 439
  intercompany plant asset transfers and
    depreciable assets, 264–265
    land, 257–258, 261–262
  intercompany stock transfers and
    common stock, 357–360
    gross margin, 378–380
  for interim acquisitions, 167–168
  joint ventures and, 432–433
  long-term investments in common
    stock and, 135n, 135–136, 138–146
    fair value in excess of acquisition
      cost, 142–144
    journal entries, 136, 139–141
    special problems, 142–146
  preferred stock of subsidiary and, 426–
    427
  subsidiaries and, 72–73
Errors, branch accounting and, 793–794
Estimates, changes in, 496
Excess of cost *(see* In excess of cost
  billing, branch merchandise transfers
  and)
Excessive withdrawals, from partnership
  accounts, 689
Exchange rates, 577–582, 644–645
  current rate and, 579–580
  forward contracts and, 652–658
  historical rates and, 580–581
  indirect, 578, 644–645
  remeasurements and, 592, 593–596

Exchange rates *(Cont.)*:
  spot, 578, 644, 653, 653n
  transaction periods and, 645–646
Executory contracts, 657n
Exhaustible plant assets, 1024
Expansion, internal development and
  business combination compared, 4–5
Expendable trusts, 920–926, 935, 937
Expenditures:
  governmental accounting and, 836–842
    capital projects funds, 892–896
    classification, 933–934
    debt service funds, 900–903
    encumbrances, 842–845
    general fund, 853–856
Expenditures control, 900
Expenses:
  in branch accounting, transfers and,
    786–787, 787n
  interest, intercompany debt and, 302–
    304
  nonprofit organization accounting and
    hospitals, 998, 999
    78-10 organizations, 1022
    VHWOs, 1011
  of partnership liquidations, 750
Export sales, segment information
  reported by, 480
Extraordinary items, 145–146

Face-value method:
  intercompany debt gains or losses and,
    323–328
    defined, 308–309
Fair value:
  in excess of acquisition cost, 84–86,
    142–144
  goodwill and, 84, 141, 144
  of identifiable net assets acquired, 16–
    17, 21
  of individual identified assets in
    bankruptcy, 534–535
  in leveraged buyouts, 525
  of liabilities, 10n
    in restructuring-reorganization, 526
  partnerships and, 704, 705
  of subsidiary, 95
Fair value over cost, 84–86, 144
FASB *(see* Financial Accounting
  Standards Board)

Federal government *(see* Governmental
  accounting)
Federal Trade Commission (FTC), 7
Fiduciary funds, 832, 833, 919–924
  agency funds and, 920–921, 935, 937,
    985, 1024
  characteristics of, 935, 937
  trust funds and, 920, 921–924
    financial statements, 924–926
FIFO assumptions, intercompany stock
  transfers and, 361, 364
Financial Accounting Foundation, 829
Financial Accounting Standards Board
  (FASB), 554, 555, 827, 829
  business combinations and, 8
  Codification of Accounting Standards,
    555
  Concepts
    Statement No. 1, 553
    Statement No. 4, 967
    Statement No. 6, 82–83, 99n
  Discussion Memorandum, new basis
    accounting, 519
  Financial Accounting Standards
    Statement No. 8, foreign currency,
      646–647
    Statement No. 12, lower-of-cost-or-
      market method, 137n
    Statement No. 14, reporting sales,
      480–481
    Statement No. 15, accounting for
      troubled restructurings, 535
    Statement No. 16, prior-period
      adjustments, 10n, 698
    Statement No. 18, segment
      reporting, 471
    Statement No. 21, public sale of
      securities, 471n, 481
    Statement No. 24, separate financial
      statements, 471n, 473, 477, 480,
      480n
    Statement No. 32, specialized
      accounting and reporting
      principles, 968n
    Statement No. 38, allocation period
      in business combinations, 35
    Statement No. 52, foreign currency,
      578, 581–582, 590, 601n, 602,
      602n, 608n, 643n, 645n, 646,
      653, 655, 658, 659n, 664, 664n
    Statement No. 57, related party

Financial Accounting Standards Board
(Cont.):
    transactions, 490–491
    Statement No. 87, pension plan
        accounting, 16*n*, 562
    Statement No. 93, recognition of
        depreciation by nonprofit
        organizations, 968*n*, 969*n*, 972,
        972*n*, 1024*n*
    Statement No. 94, consolidation, 72,
        73, 469, 485
    Statement No. 106, pension plan
        accounting, 16*n*
    Statement No. 109, disclosure of
        separate-company information,
        142*n*, 435*n*, 490*n*
    Statement No. 116, contributions to
        nonprofits, 969–970, 998*n*
    Statement No. 117, financial
        reporting by nonprofits, 970, 985,
        998, 1007
    Interpretation No. 3, accounting
        changes, 496, 497
    Interpretation No. 4, 16*n*
    Interpretation No. 18, change in
        accounting principles, 496
    Interpretation No. 35, equity method,
        135*n*
    Interpretation No. 40, insurance
        company accounting, 561*n*
    nonprofit organization accounting and,
        968–969
Financial reporting entity, for state or
    local governments, 830–831, 924
Financial reporting pyramid, 925–927
Financial statements:
    combined, 782, 790–794, 795, 801
    consolidated (*see* Consolidated
        financial statements)
    consolidated and separate compared,
        74–76
    foreign (*see* Foreign financial
        statements, restatement of)
    governmental accounting and, 827–
        828, 857–858, 860
        capital projects funds, 897–898
        debt service funds, 903–904
        encumbrance, 842–845
        general fixed assets, 905–909, 911,
            912
        trust funds, 924–926

Financial statements *(Cont.):*
    (See also Comprehensive annual
        financing report)
    interim, 491–498
    for leveraged buyouts, 522, 524, 525
    nonfinancial information in, 553, 558–
        559
    nonprofit organization accounting and
        colleges and universities, 985–992
        hospitals, 1006–1010
        78-10 organizations, 1024–1026
        VHWOs, 1013, 1019–1021
    separate (*see* Separate financial
        statements)
Financial subsidiaries, 73
Fiscal agents, bond interest coupon
    payments on, 900–903
Fiscal periods, consolidations and, 88
Fixed assets:
    branch accounting and, 782, 785–786
    general, 833, 853, 905–909, 911–912,
        935, 937
    governmental accounting and, 833, 853
    inexhaustible, 1024
    (See also Capital projects funds;
        Depreciation; Intercompany plant
        asset transfers)
Fixed rates, 645
Floating rates, 645
Foreign currency, 643–667
    commitment periods, 658
    conversions of, 577, 643*n*, 649
    defined, 643*n*
    functional currency concept, 582–584,
        643*n*
    hedges and, 652–665
        disclosure rules for gains and losses,
            665
        exposure to foreign currency assets
            and liabilities, 655–658
        forward contracts, 652–658
        identifiable foreign currency
            commitments, 658–664
        net investment positions, 664
        qualified, 659
        transactions vs. commitments, 658
    historical perspective on, 646–647
    recording sales and purchases and, 645–
        652
    restatement of, 577–582, 646
        historical, 580–581

Foreign currency *(Cont.):*
    speculative forward exchange contracts
        and, 665–667
    (See also Exchange rates; Forward
        exchange contracts; Foreign
        financial statements, restatement of)
Foreign financial statements, restatement
    of, 577–590
    consolidation procedures and, 71–72,
        610–616
        remeasured subsidiaries, 614–616
    equity method and, 603–610
        remeasured statements, 608–610
        translated statements, 603–608
    foreign currency restatement and, 577–
        582, 646
    functional currency concept and, 582–
        584, 643*n*
    hyperinflation and, 602
    measurement issues and, 578–582
        current rate restatements, 579–580
        generally accepted accounting
            principles of U.S., 578
        historical rate restatements, 580–581
    remeasurement and, 582, 590–602,
        608–610, 614–616
        inventories and lower-of-cost-or-
            market rule, 601–602
        procedures, 593–598
        remeasured financial statements, 598–
            599, 600
        translation of remeasured trial
            balances, 599–601
    translation and, 584–590
        adjustments, 616, 617
        at date of acquisition, 584–585, 603–
            605, 609
        equity method, 603–608
        one year after acquisition, 585–587
        two years after acquisition, 587–590
Foreign subsidiaries, 72–73
Forward exchange contracts, 652–658
    alternatives to, 664
    defined, 653
    exposure to foreign currency assets
        and liabilities and, 655–658
    gains and losses on, 654–655, 661
    identifiable foreign currency
        commitment and, 658–664
    premiums and discounts on, 653*n*, 653–
        654

Forward exchange contracts *(Cont.):*
  speculative, 665–667
  summary of accounting for, 668
Forward rates, 644, 653, 653*n*
Fractional deferral method, 224, 236–237
  total method compared to, 223–224
Fractional revaluation, 719
Free rates, 645
Freight, on transferred merchandise, 785, 785*n*
Freight-in account, 785, 785*n*
Fresh-start accounting, 518
Full consolidation, proportionate consolidation compared to, 431–432
Fully participating preferred stock, 423
Functional currency of the entity, 582–584, 643*n*
Fund accounting:
  governmental accounting and, 831–833
    characteristics of individual funds, 934–937
    combining statements by fund type and, 931–933
    ''reporting pyramid'' and, 925–927
  nonprofit organization accounting and, 969–971
    colleges and universities, 971–972, 974–992
    hospitals, 992–993, 998–1006
    78-10 organizations, 1023–1024
    VHWOs, 1011–1013
  (See also specific types of funds)
Fund balance reserved for encumbrances, 842–845, 853
Fund balance reserved for petty cash fund, 856
Fund fixed assets, 833
Fund long-term debt, 833

GAAP *(see* Generally accepted accounting principles)
Gain-or-loss method, 374–376
Gains:
  on acquisition of long-term debt, 307–309
  foreign currency transactions and, 646–647
    disclosure rules, 665
    forward contracts, 654–655, 661
    identifiable foreign currency commitments, 661, 662–663

Gains *(Cont.):*
  purchases, 651
  sales, 647–648
  speculation, 665–667
  intercompany debt transactions and
    face-value method, 308–309, 323–328
    outstanding debt acquisition, 307–309
    parent's debt acquired by subsidiary, 311
    subsidiary debt acquired by parent, 317–318
  intercompany plant asset transfers and
    comprehensive illustration, 269–274
    depreciable assets, 263–269
    land, 257–263
  intercompany stock transfers and, 363, 365
  interim, 495
  of partnerships, 700, 750
  remeasurements and, 592, 593*n*, 598
  (See also Loss(es))
GASB *(see* Governmental Accounting Standards Board)
General Accounting Office (GAO), 828–829*n*
General determination of forgiveness of debt, 535
General fixed assets account group, 833, 853, 905–909, 935, 937
General fund (general fund accounting), 845–858
  budget recording and, 848
  characteristics of, 934, 936
  defined, 845
  encumbrances and expenditure recording, 853–857
  financial statements and, 857–858, 860
  interfund loans and, 861–863
  ledger accounts and closing entries, 856–857
  revenue recording and, 848–853
General long-term debt, 833, 907–911, 912, 935, 937
  debt service fund and, 904
  interest and principal payments, 838–839
General partnerships, 686
General purpose financial statements for governments, 926–932

Generally accepted accounting principles (GAAP):
  foreign financial statement restatements and, 578
  governmental accounting and, 557, 829–830
  hierarchy of, 554–556, 557, 968–969
  regulatory agencies and, 556–561
  reorganization and, 519, 526–536
Geographic area, segment information reported by, 478–480, 481
Goodwill:
  amortization of
    common stock sales, 365, 367
    mutual holdings, 420–421
  consolidations and, 15, 17, 66–68
    date-of-acquisition, 17, 77–79, 88, 89, 147
    with minority interest, 77–79
  contributed, 705
  fair value and, 84, 141, 144
  foreign financial statement restatements and, 605–607
  implied, 718–719
  investment accounts and, 151
  long-term investments in, common stock, 139–141
  negative, 84, 144
  purchase combinations and, 15–18
Goodwill method, partnerships and:
  admission by investment, 705–709
  admission by purchased interest, 702–705, 711–714
Governance of nonprofit organizations, 967
Government Finance Officers Association, 829
Governmental accounting, 827–864, 891–934
  annual financial reporting and, 924–934
    closing entries, 841–842, 856–857, 896–897, 903
    combining statements by fund type, 931–933
    general purpose financial statements, 926–932
    individual fund and account group statements, 931–933
    schedules, 933
  capital projects funds and, 891–898
    bond premium and discounts, 892

Governmental accounting *(Cont.)*:
  budgets and encumbrances, 892
    characteristics of, 934, 936
    financial statements, 897–898
    transaction recording, 892–897
  debt service funds and, 896
    characteristics of, 934, 936
    financial statements, 903–904
    serial bonds and interest, 904
    special assessments, 918–919
    transaction recording, 898–905
  fiduciary funds and, 919–924
    agency funds, 920–921, 935, 937,
      985, 1024
    trust funds, 920–926
  fundamentals of, 827–864
    budgets and expenditure control,
      839–842, 846–848, 892
    encumbrance accounting, 842–845
    fund accounting systems, 831–833
    generally accepted accounting
      principles, 557, 829–830
    modified accrual method, 833–839
    state and local account standards,
      829–830
  general fixed assets group and, 905–
    909, 911, 912
  general fund and, 845–858
    budget, 846–848
    encumbrances and expenditures, 853–
      859
    financial statements, 857–858, 860
    ledger accounts and closing entries,
      856–857
    revenues and other financial sources,
      848–853
  general long-term debt group and, 833,
    838, 839, 904, 907–911, 912, 935,
    937
  grants, entitlements, and shared
    revenues, 863, 892, 896, 913
  interfund transactions and, 858–863
  nonprofit organization accounting
    compared to, 968–969
  proprietary funds and, 911–917
    enterprise funds, 911–916
    internal service funds, 911, 913, 916–
      917
  reporting entity, 830–831, 924
  special assessments and, 917–919
  special revenue funds, 891

Governmental Accounting Standards
  Board (GASB), 554, 827
  background of, 829
  *Codification of Governmental
    Accounting and Financial Reporting
    Standards*, 555
  Concepts
    Statement No. 1, 828, 829
  depreciation and, 972–973
  nonprofit organization accounting and,
    968–969
  Standards
    Statement No. 8, depreciation by
      nonprofit organizations, 969n
    Statement No. 9, financial reporting
      by proprietary funds, 915, 917
    Statement No. 11, measurement and
      recognition issues, 834–839
    Statement No. 14, financial
      reporting entity, 830–831
    Statement No. 15, nonprofit
      organization accounting, 971,
      971n
    (See also National Council on
      Governmental Accounting)
Governmental funds, 832–833
  characteristics of, 934, 936
Grants, governmental accounting and,
  863, 892, 896, 913
Griffin, Charles H., 418n
Gross margin deferrals and merchandise
  transfers, 221–222, 222n, 224–228
  deferred income taxes and, 217n, 438–
    439
  fractional deferral method, 224, 236–
    237
  intercompany stock transfers and, 378
  total deferral method, 224
  worksheet adjustments, 226–227, 230,
    231
Gross margin rate on sales, 216–223
Gross margins:
  branch accounting and, 794–798
  defined, 217
  intercompany merchandise transfers
    and, 216–235
    comprehensive illustration, 228–235
    consolidation adjustments and, 223–
      235
    deferral methods, fractional method
      illustrated, 236–237

Gross margins *(Cont.)*:
    deferral methods, total vs. fractional,
      223–224
    equity method, 218–223
    upstream merchandise transfers, 224–
      228

Health organizations *(see* Voluntary
  health and welfare organizations)
Hedges, foreign currency and, 652–665
  disclosure rules for gains and losses,
    665
  exposure to foreign currency and
    liabilities, 655–658
  forward contracts, 652–658
  identifiable foreign currency
    commitments, 658–664
  net investment positions, 664
  qualified, 659
  transactions vs. commitments, 658
Hendriksen, Eldon S., 94n
Historical rate restatements, 580–581,
  590–592, 616
Holdings:
  mutual, 409–422
    between parent and subsidiary, 413–
      422
    between subsidiaries, 409–413
  of subsidiary preferred stock, 422–430
    book value of preferred
      stockholders' equity, 423–424
    date-of-acquisition consolidation,
      424–426
    equity method, 426–427
    postacquisition consolidation, 427–
      430
  (See also Ownership)
Home office, branch accounting and, 780–
  805
  accounting systems, 780–781
  branch operating transactions and
    transfers to home office, 787
  combined financial statements, 790–
    794
  elimination adjustments and, 792, 800–
    801
  end-of-the-period reports and closing
    procedures, 787–790
  home office accounts, 782–783
  interbranch transfers, 804–805
  investment in branch accounts, 782

Home office *(Cont.):*
    merchandise transfers billed in excess cost, 794–804
    multiple branches, 804
    transfers from home office to branch, 783–787
Horizontal integration, 2–3, 469
Hospital accounting, 992–1010
    annual financial statements for, 1006–1010
    fund structure and, 970, 992–993
    operating expenses classification and, 998, 999
    restricted funds, 998–1004
    revenue classification and recognition, 993–998
    unrestricted funds, 998, 1000–1003
Hostile takeovers, 6–7
Hylton, Delmer P., 76
Hyperinflation, 582*n*, 590*n*
    foreign financial statement restatements and, 602

Identifiable assets, purchase combinations and, 15–17
Identifiable foreign currency commitments, hedges of:
    accounting for, 658–664
    defined, 658–659
Implied goodwill, 718–719
Improvements, capital, 918–919
In excess of cost billing, branch merchandise transfers and, 794–804
    combination worksheets, 798–804
    recording home to branch transfers, 796–798
Income:
    branch accounting and, 788–790
        elimination adjustments, 792, 800–801
    consolidated financial statements and interim acquisitions, 166, 168–170
        postacquisition, 152–154, 159–160, 166–167, 174, 175
    from investment, 141*n*
        undistributed, 435–436
    from partnerships, 685*n*, 690–698
        allocation bases, 690–691
        capital investment bases, 691–694
        prior period's net income correction, 698

Income *(Cont.):*
        salaries and interest, deficiencies, 695–697
        salaries and interest, in income statement, 697–698
        service contribution bases, 694–695
        specified numerical ratio, 691
    of subsidiaries
        interim acquisitions, 167–168
        postacquisition, 158–159, 164, 171
        taxes, 439, 441
    (See also Net income)
Income-and-loss-sharing ratio, 691, 695–696, 698, 702, 704
Income statements:
    branch accounting and
        merchandise transfers billed in excess of cost, 799
    consolidated *(see* Consolidated income statements)
    intercompany debt transactions and, 303–304
    nonhomogeneous subsidiaries, 471
    in partnerships, 697–699
    (See also Financial statements)
Income taxes:
    basis *(see* New basis accounting)
    on business combinations, 12–13, 146, 443–448
    corporate structure of business combinations, 11
    deferred *(see* Deferred income taxes)
    governmental accounting for receipt of, 835
    interim period, 495–496
    partnerships and, 699–701
Independence, as pooling-of-interests criterion, 29
Indirect costs of acquisition, purchase combinations and, 14–15
Indirect exchange rates, 578, 644–645
Indirect ownership, 70, 404–409
    consolidated net income and, 406
    consolidation procedures for, 406–409
    control, 405
    equity method, 405–406
    minority interest and, 406
    ownership percentage and, 405
Individual fund and account group statements, 931–933
Industry segment, 473–478, 479

Inexhaustible assets, 1024
Inflation:
    foreign financial statement restatements and, 602
    (See also Hyperinflation)
Infrastructure assets, 905*n*
Initial capital balances, in partnerships, 687–688
Insolvency, of partnerships, 755–756
Installment distributions, on partnership liquidations, 751–752, 756–763
    safe-payment calculation, 756–759
    schedules, 759–763
    two-installment, 756
Insurance regulators, 561
Insurance subsidiaries, 73
Interbranch transfers, 804–805
Intercompany debt transactions, 300–329
    consolidation and, 304–307, 312–317, 318–321
    discounting of notes and, 328–329
    equity method and, 302–304, 311, 317–318
    face-value method and, 308–309, 323–328
    issuing-company method and, 308–309
    new intercompany debt creation and, 301–307
    outstanding debt acquisition and, 307–321
        gains and losses, 307–309
        parent's debt acquired by subsidiary, 309–313
        subsidiary's debt acquired by parent, 314–321
    parent-company method, 308–309
Intercompany loans, consolidated financial statements and, 83
Intercompany merchandise transfers, 214–237
    branch accounting and, 783–785, 794–804
        billed at selling price, 798
        billed in excess of cost, 794–804
        omitted entries and errors, 793–794
    consolidation and, 223–235
    deferred income taxes on, 436–439
    depreciable asset adjustments and, 269
    depreciable asset transfers compared to, 263–264
    equity method and, 218–223

Intercompany merchandise transfers
(Cont.):
    comprehensive illustration, 222–223
    downstream transfers, 220–222, 438–439
    upstream transfers, 218–220, 439
    revenue recognition and, 215–218
    gross margins, 216–223
    worksheet adjustments for, 229–231
Intercompany notes, 328–329
Intercompany plant asset transfers, 256–275
    comprehensive illustration, 269–274
    depreciable assets, 263–269
      downstream transfers, 268–269
      upstream transfers, 264–266, 267
    land, 257–263
    preferred stock of subsidiaries, 422–430
Intercompany stock transfers:
    common stock of subsidiaries, 357–376
      new issues, 369–376
      ownership changes and
        intercompany gross margin, 378–382
      parent's transactions, 357–369
      treasury stock, 376–378
Intercompany transactions:
    debt *(see* Intercompany debt
      transactions)
    defined, 214
    dividends paid to parent company by
      subsidiary, 83–84, 136–137, 138
    loans, 83
    merchandise transfers *(see*
      Intercompany merchandise transfers)
    plant asset transfers *(see* Intercompany
      plant asset transfers)
    stock transfers *(see* Intercompany stock
      transfers)
Interest:
    coupon payments, 900–903
    intercompany debt transactions and
      (see Intercompany debt transactions)
    serial bonds, 904
Interest differentials, foreign rates and,
    654
Interest in partnership capital, 688, 695–697
    new partner purchases, 702–705, 711–717

Interest in partnership capital *(Cont.):*
    taxes, 701
Interest income:
    governmental accounting and, 838–839
      delinquent property taxes, 852
    intercompany debt transactions and,
      302–304
Interfund transactions, 858–863
    interfund loans, 856, 861–863
    quasi-external transactions and
      reimbursements, 858–859
    transfers and, 860–861
Interim acquisitions, 164–170
    consolidated income statement forms
      and, 166, 168–169
    equity method and, 167–168
    valuation differential and, 170
Interim expense, 494–495
Interim financial reporting, 491–498
    classes of cost and expense, 492–495
    defined, 491
    financial accounting standards for, 491–496
Internal development, business
    combination compared to, 4–5
Internal service funds, 911, 913, 916–917, 934, 936
International harmonization, in foreign
    consolidations, 72
International Monetary Fund, 602*n*
Intersegment sales, 478
Inventories:
    branch accounting and, 781, 783, 785*n*
      beginning branch inventory, 801–804
      unrealized gross margin, 797–798
    foreign financial statement restatements
      and
      remeasurements, 590, 593, 601, 602
      translation adjustment, 587*n*
    governmental accounting and, 837–838, 856
    intercompany merchandise transfers
      and, 218*n*, 219*n*
      gross margin deferrals, 226–228
    LIFO base, 493
    losses, 493
    periodic, 587*n*, 783, 785*n*
    perpetual, 783
Investees:
    financial statements of, 469, 469*n*

Investees *(Cont.):*
    losses of, 145
    significant, reporting by, 484–485
    undistributed income of, 435–436
Investment accounts:
    consolidations and, 65
      elimination and reclassification, 67–68
      postacquisition, 150–152, 162, 163
    indirect ownership and, 407
    intercompany merchandise transfers
      and, 228–229
    intercompany stock transfers and
      common stock acquisitions, 357–361
      common stock sales, 361–363, 366, 367
      gross margin, 379
Investment-in-bonds accounts,
    intercompany debt transactions and,
    310, 315
Investment in branch accounts, 782–783
    elimination adjustments and, 792, 800–801
Investment in plant funds, 982, 984–985
Investment-in-stock accounts, 65–68
Investments:
    in foreign entities, hedging and, 664
    long-term
      admission, 702–711
      capital balances, 691–694
      new partner admission, 702–711
      (See also Long-term investments, in
        common stock)
    in subsidiary preferred stock, 422–430
      book value of preferred
        stockholders' equity, 423–424
      date-of-acquisition consolidation,
        424–426
      equity method, 426–427
      postacquisition consolidation, 427–430
Issuing-company method, 308–309

Johnson, L. Todd, 657*n*
Joint ventures, 69*n*, 430–434
    alternative accounting methods, 431–432
    joint control, 431*n*
    new basis accounting for, 519

Joint ventures *(Cont.)*:
  proportionate consolidation and, 431–434
  reporting requirements, 484–485
Journal entries:
  in bankruptcy accounting, 535
  branch accounting and, 797, 800–805
    equipment transfers, 785–786
  consolidations and
    acquisition of stock for cash, 65–66
    date-of-acquisition, 83–84, 102–103
  deferred income taxes and, 438–439, 443
  foreign currency transactions and, 644, 646
    collection and conversion, 649
    forward contracts, 655–658, 665–666
    identifiable foreign currency commitments, 659–661
    purchases, 650, 652
    sales, 648
  foreign financial statement restatements and, 605, 607–608
  governmental accounting
    and actual sources and uses of funds, 841
    agency fund transactions, 920–921
    annual budget, 840
    capital projects funds transactions, 892–897
    closing entries, 841–842, 856–857, 896–897, 903
    debt service fund, 899–903
    encumbrances, 842–845
    general fixed assets account group, 908
    general long-term debt account group, 910–911
    inventories, 837
    prepayments, 836–837
    revenues, 836–837
    special assessments, 919
    trust fund transactions, 922–923
  intercompany merchandise transfers and
    downstream, 221
    upstream, 218–219
  intercompany plant asset transfers and land, 257, 261
  intercompany stock transfers and

Journal entries *(Cont.)*:
    common stock acquisition, 359
    common stock sale, 364–365
  for leveraged buyout, 522, 524
  long-term investments in common stock and, 136, 139–141
    cost method, 136
    equity method, 139–141
  mutual holdings between parent and subsidiary and, 417–418, 418n, 421–422
  for partnerships, 687–688, 691–692, 700
    admission by investment, 702–704, 706–708
    admission by purchased interest, 712–716
    withdrawal of partner, 717–719
  pooling combinations and, 22–23, 25
  purchase combinations and, 18–19

King, Thomas E., 224n
Knight, Lee G., 13n
Knight, Ray A., 13n

Land, intercompany plant asset transfers and, 257–263
  downstream transfers, 261–263
  upstream transfers, 257–261
Largay, James A., III, 375n
Laws, governmental accounting and, 829–830
Ledger accounts (*see* T-accounts)
Lembke, Valdean C., 224n
Leveraged buyouts (LBOs), 519, 520–526
  analyzing, 525–526
  defined, 520
  Emerging Issues Task Force and, 523, 525, 526
  financial statements for, 522, 524, 525
  with new basis accounting, 519, 521, 523–526
  stockholders' equity in, 525
  without new basis accounting, 520, 522
Leveraged purchase business combination, 520n
Leveraging, 520
Liabilities:
  acquisition of assets subject to, 10

Liabilities *(Cont.)*:
  fair value of, 10n, 526
  foreign currency hedges and, 655–658
  foreign financial statement restatements and
    remeasurements, 594–595
    translation adjustments, 616, 617
  governmental accounting and, 914, 915
  minority interest in subsidiary and, 154n
  of partnerships, 703–704, 750–756
  unlimited, 686, 752
Liens, tax, 852
Life income funds, 980–982
LIFO base, 493
Limited liabilities, 752
Limited liability corporations (LLC), 685n
Limited life, 686
Limited partnerships, 686
Liquidating gain or loss, 750
Liquidation officer, liability of, 751
Liquidation value, of preferred stock of subsidiary, 423
Liquidations:
  corporate, 11
  defined, 526
  of LIFO inventory base, 493
  of partnerships, 702, 702n, 748–763
    insolvency, 755–756
    installment distributions, 756–763
    single-step distributions, 752–756
    statement of liquidation, 749–752
Loan funds, 978, 979
Loans:
  college and university funds for, 978, 979
  intercompany, 83
  interfund, governmental accounting and, 856, 861–863
  by partnerships, 690
Local government (*see* Governmental accounting)
Long-term debt:
  general, 833, 838–839, 904, 907–911, 912, 935, 937
  governmental accounting and, 833
  intercompany transactions and, 300–329
  nonprofit organization accounting and, 984
  (*See also* Bonds)

Long-term investments, in common stock, 135–146
  cost-method accounting, 135n, 135–138
  equity method accounting, 135n, 135–136, 138–146
Loss(es):
  on acquisition of long-term debt, 307–309
  foreign currency transactions and, 646–647
    disclosure rules, 665
    forward contracts, 654–655
    identifiable foreign currency commitments, 661, 662–663
    speculation, 665–667
  intercompany debt transactions and face-value method, 323–328
    outstanding debt acquisition, 307–309
    parent's debt acquired by subsidiary, 312–313
    subsidiary's debt acquired by parent, 317–318
  intercompany plant asset transfers and comprehensive illustration, 314–321
    depreciable assets, 263–269
    land, 257–263
  intercompany stock transfers and, 365
  interim, 495
  inventory, 493
  investee, 145
  maximum absorbable, 759–760
  maximum unrealized, 756–757
  net unrealized, on marketable equity securities, 137n
  from partnerships, 685n, 690–698, 700
    allocation bases, 690–691
    capital investment bases, 691–694
    liquidations, 750, 754, 756–759
    prior periods net income correction, 698
    salaries and interest, deficiencies, 695–697
    salaries and interest, in income statement, 697–698
    service contribution bases, 694–695
    specified numerical ratio, 691
  remeasurements and, 592, 593n
Lower-of-cost-or-market method, 137n, 493

Lower-of-cost-or-market method (Cont.):
  foreign financial statement restatements and, 601–602

Majority-owned subsidiaries, 72–73
Management, business combination viewpoints of, 4–5, 6
Mandatory transfers, 973
Market value, foreign financial statement restatements and, 601–602
Marketable equity securities, 137n
Markup percentage on cost, 217
Matured interest payable, 903
Matured term bonds payable, 900
Maximum absorbable losses, 759–760
Maximum unrealized losses, 756–757
Measurement date, 484
Measurement issues:
  foreign financial statement restatements and, 578–582
    current rate restatements, 579–580
    generally accepted accounting principles of U.S., 578
    historical rate restatements, 580–581
    remeasurement adjustments, 582
  governmental accounting and, 833–839
  measurement, defined, 552–553
  researching pronouncements on, 553
Merchandise, defined, 215
Merchandise transfers (see Intercompany merchandise transfers)
Mergers:
  defined, 11
  statutory, 11
  (See also Acquisition; Consolidations)
Minch, Roland A., 414n
Minority interest(s), 68n, 68–74
  consolidations and, 68–69
    date-of-acquisition, 80–83, 90, 102–104, 148
    entity concept, 98–101
    parent-company concept, 98, 99–102
    postacquisition, 152–155, 159–160, 175–176
    valuation differential, 95–97
  indirect ownership and, 406
  intercompany debt transactions and new intercompany debt, 307
    outstanding debt acquisition, 308–309
  intercompany merchandise transfers and, 232, 233–235

Minority interest(s) (Cont.):
  deferrals, 224, 224n
  fractional deferral method, 236–237
  intercompany plant asset transfers and depreciable asset transfers, 267
    upstream land transfers, 259–261
  intercompany stock transfers and common stock sales, 367–368
    gross margin, 381–382
    new stock issues, 370–371, 373–376
  mutual holdings between parent and subsidiary and, 418
  mutual holdings between subsidiaries and, 413, 413n
  preferred stock of subsidiary and, 424, 428–429
  ratably subscribed new issues and, 370n, 376
Minority stockholders, 68, 68n, 68–74
  new stock issues and, 373–376
  treasury stock purchased from, 377–378
Modified accrual method of accounting, 833–839
Moonitz, Maurice, 94n, 99n
Multinational companies (see Exchange rates; Foreign currency; Foreign financial statements, restatement of; Subsidiaries)
Multiple-step stock acquisitions, 357–361
Multiple subsidiaries, 403–404
Mutual agency, 686
Mutual holdings, 409–422
  between parent and subsidiary, 413–422
    allocation method, 418–422
    treasury stock method, 414–418
  between subsidiaries, 409–413

National Council on Governmental Accounting (NCGA), 829
  Standards
    Statement No. 1, general, 829n, 831–832, 905, 905n, 933–934, 971
    Statement No. 2, grants, entitlements, and shared revenues, 863
  (See also Governmental Accounting Standards Board)

Negative goodwill, 84, 144

Net assets:
  book value of acquired, 15–17, 77–79
  cash acquisition, 8–9
  fair value over cost and, 84–86, 142–144
  purchase and pooling combinations compared, 11–13, 27–28
  purchase combinations and, 15–17
  stock acquisition, 9
  of subsidiaries, 100–101

Net income:
  for acquisition year, 26–28
  branch accounting and, 791–792
  consolidated, 152–154
    indirect ownership and, 406
    intercompany debt transactions and, 306
  defined, 152–153
  foreign currency transactions and, 649
  intercompany debt transactions and new intercompany debt, 303–304
  interim acquisitions and, 166, 168–170
  of partnerships, corrections to, 698
  postacquisition, consolidations and, 152–154
  of subsidiaries
    intercompany plant asset transfers, 258–261, 264–265, 267
    interim acquisitions, 167–168
    minority interest, 160
  (See also Income; Income statements)

Net investment in plant accounts, 985

Net investment positions, hedges of, 664

Net unrealized loss on marketable equity securities, 137n

Neuhausen, Benjamin S., 72

New basis accounting, 432n, 518–537
  defined, 518
  for joint ventures, 519
  for leveraged buyouts, 519, 521, 523–526
  for partnerships, 703
  for purchase business combinations, 519, 520
  rationales for using, 519
  for reorganizations, 519, 534–535
  types of, 518

New intercompany debt transactions, 301–307
  consolidation procedures for, 304–307

New intercompany debt transactions (Cont.):
  equity method and, 302–304
  parent loans to subsidiary and, 301–302

New issues:
  of subsidiary common stock, 369–376
    decrease in parent's ownership percentage, 373–376
    increase in parent's ownership percentage, 371–373
    minority stockholders, 373–376
    ratably subscribed, 370n, 376

New partner admissions (see Partnerships and partnership accounting)

Non-arm's length transactions, 215–217

Nonbusiness organizations, business organizations compared to, 827

Noncash assets, purchase combinations and, 13–14

Noncurrent assets, 84
  fair value over cost and, 144

Nonexpendable trusts, 919–924, 925, 935, 937

Nonmandatory transfers, 973

Nonoperating revenues, hospital accounting and, 997–998

Nonprofit organization accounting, 967–1027
  colleges and universities, 971–992
    accounting methods, 972–974
    agency funds, 985
    annual financial statements, 985–992
    annuity and life income funds, 980–982, 983
    closing entries for funds other than current, 985
    current funds, 971–978
    endowment and similar funds, 978–980, 981, 992
    fund structures, 971–972
    loan funds, 978, 979
    plant funds, universities, 982–989
  defined nonprofit organizations, 827, 967
  governmental accounting compared to, 968–969
  hospitals and, 992–1010
    annual financial statements, 1006–1010
    fund structure, 970, 992–993

Nonprofit organization accounting (Cont.):
  operating expenses classification, 998, 999
  restricted funds, 998–1004
  revenue classification and recognition, 993–998
  unrestricted funds, 998, 1000–1003
  78-10 organizations and, 970, 1017–1026
    accounting methods, 1022–1023
    annual financial statements, 1024–1026
    fund structure, 1023–1024
  standards for, 968–969
  systems and practices of, 969–971
  voluntary health and welfare organizations (VHWOs), 1010–1017, 1018–1021
    accounting methods, 1011
    financial statements, 1013, 1019–1021
    fund structure, 1011–1013
    transaction recording, 1013–1017

Nontemporary decline in value, 137n, 141n

Notes:
  discounting of, 328–329
  intercompany debt transactions and, 301–302, 306n, 328–329
  tax anticipation, 849

Notes to consolidated financial statements, 469

Notes to financial statements:
  disclosure of consolidation policy in, 73–74
  nonhomogeneous subsidiaries, 474–476, 484
  required, 498

Nurnberg, Hugo, 22n

"Off-balance-sheet financing," 431

Office of Management and Budget, 828–829n

Official rates, 645

Olson, Norman O., 21

Omissions (omitted entries), branch accounting and, 793–794

Omitted deferrals, 263

One line consolidation, 141–142

Operating expenses, nonprofit organization accounting and, 998, 999

Operating funds, nonprofit organization accounting and, 1023–1024

Operating grants, 863, 913

Operating revenues, hospital accounting and, 993, 997

Operating transactions, branch accounting and, 787

Operating transfers, 863

Ordinary income, 495

Other contributed capital account, 365*n*

Other operating revenues, hospital accounting and, 993–997

Outstanding debt transaction, 307–321
gains and losses and, 307–309
parent's debt acquired by subsidiary and, 309–313
subsidiary's debt acquired by parent and, 314–321
consolidation procedures, 318–319
equity method, 317–318

Outstanding shares, 414, 704–705
of subsidiaries, 357–369

Owners, business combinations and, 3, 5–7

Ownership:
consolidated tax returns and, 445
direct, 70, 403
indirect, 70, 404–409
consolidated net income, 406
consolidation procedures, 406–409
control, 405
equity method, 405–406
minority interest, 406
ownership percentages, 405
joint ventures and, 430–434
alternative accounting methods, 431–432
proportionate consolidation, 431–434
mutual holdings and, 409–422
between parent and subsidiary, 413–422
between subsidiaries, 409–413
in partnerships, 686–690
significant influence and, 135–136, 414*n*
subsidiary stock dividends and, 145

Ownership equity accounts, for partnership, 686–690, 702–719, 760–761

Ownership equity accounts *(Cont.):*
(See also Capital accounts, of partnerships)

Ownership percentage:
indirect ownership and, 405
subsidiary common stock transactions and
intercompany gross margin, 378–382
multiple-step acquisitions, 357–361
new issues, decreasing percentage, 369–373
new issues, increasing percentage, 371–373
ratably subscribed, 370*n*, 376
sale of entire investment, 369
sale of shares, 361–369

Pacter, Paul, 71, 71*n*, 94*n*, 154*n*, 236

Par value, pooling combinations and, 24–26

Par-value method in consolidations, treasury stock and, 87

Parent company:
common stock of subsidiaries and, 357–376, 378–382
calculation of income from common stock, 426
ownership changes and intercompany gross margin, 378–382
transactions in new issues, 369–376
transactions in outstanding shares, 357–369
controlling interest and, 68–72
defined, 68–69
extraordinary items and, 145–146
mutual holdings of subsidiary and, 413–422
preferred dividends, 145
ratably subscribed new issues and, 370*n*, 376
treasury stock purchased from, 377–378
(See also Disaggregated financial information; Intercompany transactions *and specific topics)*

Parent-company concept of consolidation, 77, 92–93, 95, 98, 99–102

Parent-company method, 308–309

Parent-company-only financial information, 485–486

Partial liquidation statement, 749

Partnerships and partnership accounting, 431, 684–719
admission by investment and, 702–711
bonus method, 709–711
goodwill method, 705–709
admission by purchased interest and, 702–705, 711–717
bonus method, 714–716
goodwill method, 702–705, 711–714
proceed distribution among partners, 716–717
agreements related to, 685
bonuses, 694, 718
capital accounts of *(see* Capital accounts, of partnerships)
characteristics of, 686
corporate accounting compared to, 686–687, 704–705, 752
deficiencies, 695–697
defined, 684
dissolution of, 702, 702*n*
federal income tax law and, 699–701
financial reporting for, 698–699, 700
general, 686
income or loss allocation and, 685*n*, 690–698
allocation bases, 690–691
capital investment bases, 691–694
liquidations, 750, 754, 756–759
prior period's net income correction, 698
salaries and interest, deficiencies, 695–697
salaries and interest, in income statement, 697–698
service contribution bases, 694–695
specified numerical ratio, 691
income taxes and, 699–701
insolvency of, 754–756
limited, 686
liquidation of, 702, 702*n*, 748–763
insolvent partnerships, 755–756
installment distributions, 756–763
single-step distributions, 752–756
statement of liquidation, 749–752
ownership equity accounts for, 686–690, 702–719, 760–761

Partnerships *(Cont.)*:
withdrawal or death of partner, 717–719
Patient service revenues, 993
Peller, Philip R., 22
Penalties for delinquent property taxes, governmental accounting and, 852
Pension trust funds, 920, 935, 937
Period costs, 263–264, 492, 494–495
Periodic inventory system, 587n, 783, 785n
Permanent differences, deferred income taxes and, 435
Perpetual inventory system, 783
Personal liabilities, 751, 754–755
Peterson, D. Scott, 657n
Petition, bankruptcy, 527, 528, 529–532
Petri, Enrico, 414n
Petrie, A. George, 84n
Petty cash funds, governmental accounting and, 856
Plant and equipment accounts in foreign financial statement restatements, 584–585
remeasurements and, 593, 596–598
(See also Fixed assets)
Plant asset transfers, intercompany, 256–275
comprehensive illustration, 269–274
depreciable asset transfers, 263–269
land transfers, 257–263
(See also Fixed assets)
Plant funds, nonprofit organization accounting and:
colleges and universities, 982–989
hospitals, 1004–1005
78-10 organizations, 1024
VHWOs, 1012
(See also Fixed assets)
Pooling-of-interests accounting, 21–26, 28–33
conditions to qualify as, 28–33
consolidations and
date-of-acquisition, 102–104
postacquisition, 171–173
defined, 21
foreign financial statement restatements and, 585n, 595n
intercompany merchandise transfers, 235
net income and, 26–28

Pooling-of-interests accounting *(Cont.)*:
parent company value considerations and, 24–26
partnership, 704n
purchase combinations compared to, 11–13
recording, 22–23
transactions between companies under common control, 104
Postacquisition consolidations, 146–178
consolidated financial statements, one year after acquisition, 148–161
consolidated net income, 152–154
investment account, 150–152
minority interest in subsidiary net income, 152–155, 154n, 160
subsidiary stockholders' equity, 150
worksheet procedures, 156–161
consolidated financial statements, two years after acquisition, 161–164
adjustments, 162–164
investment account, 162, 163
cost-method accounting and, 173–176
consolidation worksheet, 175–176
worksheet adjustments, 173–175
date-of-acquisition consolidations compared to, 146–148
defined, 135, 146
intercompany merchandise transfers and, 232, 233–235
interim acquisitions and, 164–170
consolidated income statements forms, 166, 168–169
equity method, 167–168
valuation differential, 170
mutual holdings between parent and subsidiary and
allocation method, 418–422
treasury stock method, 416–418
pooling combinations and, 171–173
preferred stock of subsidiary and, 427–430
trial balance format and, 176–178
Postacquisition translations, 585–590, 605–613
one year after acquisition, 585–587, 605–607
two years after acquisition, 587–590, 607–608
Postpetition transactions, bankruptcy, 527–528

Preacquisition contingencies, 35
Preferred dividends, 145
Preferred equity, 423
Preferred stock of subsidiary, 422–430
common stock and, 426
parent's investment in, 422–430
book value of preferred stockholders' equity, 423–424
date-of-acquisition consolidation, 424–426
equity method, 426–427
postacquisition consolidation, 427–430
Preferred stockholders' equity, 423–424
Premiums:
bond, 892
forward contracts and, 653n, 653–654
identifiable foreign currency commitments and, 659, 660–664
preferred stock of subsidiary and, 426
Prepayments, governmental accounting and, 836–837
Prepetition transactions, bankruptcy, 527
Presentation, accounting:
defined, 553
researching pronouncements on, 554
Price Waterhouse, 71
Primary government, 830–831
Principal:
governmental accounting and, 838–839
of trust funds, 922–924
(See also Bonds)
Principle, changes in, 496–497
Prior-period information, 27n
Proceeds of partnerships, 716–717
Product costs, 263, 492
Property taxes, 920–921
delinquent, 852
general fund and, 848–853
governmental accounting for receipt of, 835
Proportionate consolidation, 93, 97–99, 100
full consolidation compared to, 431–432
joint ventures and, 431–434
(See also Proprietary concept of consolidation)
Proportionate treatment, as pooling-of-interests criteria, 32

Proprietary concept of consolidation, 91–94, 97–99
Proprietary funds, 832, 833, 911–917
    characteristics of, 934, 936
    enterprise funds and, 911–916
    internal service funds and, 911, 913, 916–917
Proxy fight, 71
Public support, nonprofit organization accounting and:
    78-10 organizations, 1022
    VHWOs, 1011
Publicly traded securities, 558
    (*See also* Securities and Exchange Commission)
Purchase combinations, 12–21, 82–88, 142–144, 837–838, 856
    acquisition costs and, 12–17
        allocation, 15–17
        measurements, 13–14
    contingent considerations and, 35
    intercompany merchandise transfers, 215–235
    net income and, 26–28
    new basis accounting, 519, 520
        comprehensive illustration, 88–91
        valuation differentials and, 77–79
        worksheet procedures, 79–81, 86–88, 90–91
    pooling-of-interests combinations compared to, 11–13
    recording, 17–21
Purchased interest, new partner admission by, 702–705, 711–717
Purchases:
    foreign currency transactions and, 643*n*, 649–652
        forward contracts, 655–657, 657*n*
    foreign financial statement restatements and, 594
Push-down accounting:
    consolidations and, 140*n*, 486–491, 519, 520
    foreign financial statement restatements and, 606*n*
    for leveraged buyouts (LBOs), 524, 525

Qualified hedges, 658–664
Quarterly reports, 497, 498
Quasi-endowment funds, 978–980

Quasi-external transactions, 858–859
Quasi reorganization, 526–527, 527*n*

Ratably subscribed new issues, 370*n*, 376
Reacquisition of stock, as pooling-of-interests criterion, 33
Realizations, on partnership liquidations, 749–752
Reciprocal accounts, 782
Reclassification adjustments, 67–68, 79–80, 148
    foreign financial statement restatements and, 614
    indirect ownership and, 408–409
    intercompany debt transactions and face-value method, 325–326
        new intercompany debt, 304–307
        outstanding debt acquisition, 312–313, 319–321
    intercompany stock transfers and common stock sales, 366–367
        gross margin, 380–381
        multiple-step stock acquisitions, 360–361
    mutual holdings between parent and subsidiary and, 417
    postacquisition consolidations and, 159, 164
        cost method, 175
Registering securities, 14
Regulatory accounting principles (RAP), 556
Regulatory agencies, 554
    banking, 556–558
    business combinations and, 7, 11
    generally accepted accounting principles and, 556–561
    insurance and utility, 561
    (*See also* Securities and Exchange Commission)
Reimbursements, governmental accounting and, 858–859
Remeasurement of foreign financial statements, 582, 590–602, 608–610, 614–616
    consolidation procedures and, 614–616
    defined, 582–584
    equity method and, 608–610
    gains or losses, 592, 598
    hyperinflation and, 602
    inventories and, 601–602

Remeasurement (*Cont.*):
    objective of, 583
    procedures for, 593–598
        cost of goods sold, 596
        plant and equipment and accumulated depreciation, 593, 596–598
        remeasurement gain, 598
        retained earnings, 594, 598
    remeasured financial statements and, 598–599, 600
    trial balance translation and, 585, 599–601
Renewal and replacement plant funds, 982–984
Reorganization accounting, 519, 526–536
    bankruptcy, 527–536
    generally accepted accounting principles and, 519, 526–536
    liquidation, 526
    new basis accounting in, 519, 534–535
    quasi reorganization, 526–527, 527*n*
    reorganization, defined, 526
    restructuring-recapitalization, 526
Reorganization value, in bankruptcy, 533–534
Reporting entity, changes in, 497
"Reporting pyramid," 925–927
Research, accounting, 552–565
    disclosure, 553, 554
    hierarchy of GAAP and, 554–556, 557, 968–969
    measurement, 552–554
    presentation, 553, 554
    process, 561–565
    regulatory agencies, 556–561
    sample, 562–565
Restated information, 27*n*
Restatement of foreign currency, 577*n*, 577–582, 579–582, 644–647
Restatement of foreign financial statements (*see* Foreign financial statements, restatement of)
Restricted assets, 913, 915
Restricted funds, nonprofit organization accounting and:
    colleges and universities, 972, 973–978
    hospitals, 993, 998–1004
    VHWOs, 1012
Restricted operating funds, 1023

Restructuring-recapitalization, accounting
for, 526
Retained earnings:
branch accounting and, 791, 793
merchandise transfers billed in
excess of cost, 799
consolidated financial statements and
interim acquisitions, 166, 169–170
postacquisition, 161, 166
postacquisition, cost method, 174,
175
postacquisition, pooling
combinations, 172
deferred income taxes and, 441, 445
foreign financial statement restatements
and
remeasurements, 594, 598
translation, 590
governmental accounting and, 913
indirect ownership and, 407–408
intercompany debt transactions and,
319–321
new intercompany debt, 305
outstanding debt acquisition, 314,
319–321
intercompany plant asset transfers and
depreciable asset transfers, 267, 268
upstream land transfers, 259–261
intercompany stock transfers and, 379–
380
joint ventures and, 434
mutual holdings and
between parent and subsidiary, 418,
419
between subsidiaries, 411
preferred stock of subsidiary and, 423,
425–426
reserved, 914–916
Retirement of debt, 307, 984
Retirement of indebtedness plant funds,
984
Revaluation accounting, 518
Revaluation decisions, partnerships and,
703–705, 717–719
Revaluation increments, 151
purchase combinations and, 17
Revenue bond construction account, 914
Revenue bond contingency (renewal and
replacement) account, 914
Revenue bond current debt service
account, 914

Revenue bond future debt service
account, 914
Revenue recognition, intercompany
merchandise transfers and, 215–218
Revenues:
deferred, 852–853
governmental accounting and, 834–
836, 839–842
classification, 933
general fund, 848–853
shared, 863
special revenue funds and, 891
interest
governmental accounting, 838–839,
852
intercompany debt, 302–304
nonprofit organization accounting and,
967
contributions, 969–971
hospitals, 993–998
78-10 organizations, 1022
VHWOs, 1011
during partnership liquidation, 750
shared, 863
Reversal of parent's recording, 158–159,
164, 169, 171
Rita, William, 829n
Rule 203 exception, 555

Safe-payment calculations, 756–759
Salaries, in partnerships, 694–698
Sales:
arm's-length transactions and, 215–
217, 221–222, 222n
branch accounting and, 780–781
estimated interim cost of, 492–493
foreign currency transactions and,
643n, 647–649
in foreign financial statement
restatements, remeasurements and,
594, 596
gross margin rate on, 216–223
intercompany merchandise transfers
and, 214–237
consolidation adjustments, 223–235
equity method, 218–223
revenue recognition, 215–218
major customer, segment information
on, 480–484
of subsidiary common stock, 361–369
disposal of segment of business, 369

Sales (Cont.):
ownership percentage impact, 363
portion of investment sale, 363–368
recognition of gains and losses, 363
Sales agencies, 782
Sales taxes, governmental accounting for
receipt of, 835
Schedule of general fixed assets, 907, 909
Schedules:
governmental annual financial
reporting and, 933
partnerships and, installment
distribution liquidations, 759–763
Scholarship trust funds, 921–924
Scholes, Myron S., 13n
Schwitter, Frank J., 22
SEC (see Securities and Exchange
Commission)
Securities:
marketable equity, 137n
prices of, contingent considerations
and, 34–35
purchase combinations and, 13–14
registration and issuance of, 14
(See also Bonds; Common stock;
Preferred stock, of subsidiary)
Securities Act of 1933, 558, 559, 560–561
Securities and Exchange Commission
(SEC), 7n, 11, 554, 558–561
Accounting Series Release No. 4, 558
Accounting Series Release No. 302, 485
Financial Reporting Codification
(FRC), 485
Financial Reporting Releases (FRRs),
558
Form 8-K, 497, 558, 560
Form 10-K, 485, 497–498, 558, 559–560
Form 10-Q, 497–498, 558, 560
parent-company-only financial
information and, 485–486
quarterly reports, 497, 498
Regulation S-K, 491n, 498, 558, 559
Regulation S-X, 71n, 72n, 146, 470n,
485, 485n, 497n, 558, 560
reporting by significant investees and
joint ventures, 484–485
Staff Accounting Bulletin No. 6,
quarterly disclosures, 498
Staff Accounting Bulletin No. 54, push-
down accounting, 486, 490n
Securities Exchange Act of 1934, 558, 559

Segment reporting, 470–484
  disposal and, 369, 484
  by export sales, 480
  by geographic area, 478–480, 481
  by industry, 473–478, 479
  by sales to major customer, 480–484
  tests for reportability, 477
Selling rates, 645*n*
Separate-company income statements:
  for industry segments, 477–478
  intercompany debt transactions and,
    303–304, 311
    face-value method, 325–327
    outstanding debt acquisition, 311,
      313, 314, 317–318, 320–321
Separate financial statements, 74–76, 146
  branch accounting and, 782–790, 789,
    801, 802
  consolidation worksheet procedures
    and, postacquisition, 156–158
  defined, 469, 470*n*
  income statement (*see* Separate-
    company income statements)
  intercompany merchandise transfers
    and, 216
Separate tax returns, 435
  comprehensive examples, 439–443
  deferred income taxes and, 439–443
  intercompany merchandise transfers
    and, 438–439
Separately issued financial statements,
  469, 469*n*, 486–491
Serial bonds, 904
Service contributions, in partnerships,
  694–695
Settlement dates, 645–646
78-10 (other nonprofit) organization
  accounting, 970, 1017–1026
  annual financial statements and, 1024–
    1026
  fund structure and, 970, 1023–1024
  methods and systems, 1022–1023
Shared revenues, governmental
  accounting and, 863
Sharp, Andrew D., 76
Sherman Act of 1890, 7
Shipments, branch accounting and, 783–
  785
Significant influence, 135–136, 414*n*
Single-step distributions, on partnership
  liquidations, 752–756

Single-subsidiary consolidations, 403
Special assessments, 917–919
Special revenue funds, 891, 934, 936
Specific purpose funds (special purpose
  funds):
  governmental accounting and, 891
  nonprofit organization accounting and,
    999, 1004
Specified numerical ratio, partnerships
  and, 691, 695–696
Speculative foreign exchange contracts,
  665–667
Spinney, James C., 94*n*
Spot rates, 644, 653, 653*n*
  defined, 578
Standard cost variances, 493
Standards, accounting (*see* American
  Institute of Certified Public
  Accountants; Financial Accounting
  Standards Board; Generally accepted
  accounting principles; Governmental
  Accounting Standards Board; National
  Council on Governmental Accounting)
State government (*see* Governmental
  accounting)
Statement of activities, of 78-10
  organizations, 1025
Statement of cash flows,
  nonhomogeneous subsidiaries, 473
Statement of changes in financial
  position:
  governmental accounting and, 930
  nonprofit organization accounting and
    colleges and universities, 985–992
    hospitals, 1006
    78-10 organizations, 1024–1025
Statement of changes in fund balances,
  nonprofit organization accounting and:
  colleges and universities, 985–992,
    994–995
  hospitals, 1007, 1010
  VHWOs, 1013, 1020
Statement of consolidation policy, 73–74
Statement of current funds revenues,
  expenditures, and other changes, 996
Statement of partial liquidation, 749
Statement of partners' capital, 699–700
Statement of partnership liquidation, 749–
  752
Statement of realization and liquidation,
  749–752

Statement of revenues, expenditures, and
  changes in fund balances:
  annual financial reporting and, 926–
    930
  capital projects funds and, 897, 898
  debt service funds and, 903–904
  general fund and, 857–858
  trust funds and, 924–926
Statement of revenues, expenses, and
  changes in retained earnings,
  proprietary funds and, 916, 918
Statement of revenues and expenses,
  1007, 1009, 1011
Statement of support, revenue, expenses,
  and changes in fund balance, 1013,
  1020, 1025
Statutory consolidations, 11
Statutory mergers, 11
Stock(s):
  cash acquisition of, 9
  common (*see* Common stock)
  consolidations and, 65–68
  exchange of, in acquisitions, 10, 30–
    31
  intercompany transfer of (*see*
    Intercompany stock transfers)
  investment in stock account and, 65–
    68
  multiple-step acquisitions, 357–361
  mutual holdings between parent and
    subsidiary and, 413–422
    allocation method, 418–422
    treasury stock method, 414–418
  net assets acquired for, 9
  outstanding, 357–369, 414, 704–705
  pooling combinations and, 22–26
  as pooling-of-interests criteria, 30–31
    exchange of stock, 30–31
    reacquisition of stock, 33
    treasury stock, 31–32
  preferred (*see* Preferred stock of
    subsidiary)
  purchase combinations and, 13–14
    contingent considerations, 34–35
  reacquisition of, 33
  treasury (*see* Treasury stock; Treasury
    stock method, for mutual holdings
    between parent and subsidiary)
  (*See also specific topics*)
Stockholders:
  business combinations and, 3, 5–7

Stockholders *(Cont.)*:
  minority, 68, 68*n*, 68–74
    (See also Minority interest(s))
  purchase and pooling combinations
    compared, 11–13, 27–28
Stockholders' equity:
  consolidations and
    date-of-acquisition minority interest,
      82–83
    date-of-acquisition worksheets, 81
  intercompany stock transfers and
    multiple-step acquisition, 357–359
  in leveraged buyouts, 525
  pooling combinations and, 22–26
  preferred stock of subsidiary and, 423–
    424
  of subsidiaries
    interim acquisitions, 167–168
    postacquisition consolidations, 150,
      164
  treasury stock and, 86–88
Straight-line method, intercompany debt
  transactions and, 310*n*
Subsidiaries:
  acquisition of, 357–361, 369–376, 378–
    382
  common stock of, 357–376
    new issues, 369–376
    outstanding shares, parent's
      transactions, 357–369
    ownership changes and
      intercompany gross margin, 378–
      382
  control of, 68–72, 422
  defined, 69
  dividends of, 83–84, 158–159, 164,
    169, 171, 174, 175
  fair value of, 95
  financial, 73
  financial statements of, 486–491
  foreign, 72–73
    equity-method consolidation
      procedures, 603–616
    foreign currency restatement, 577–
      590
    hyperinflation, 602
    remeasurement of financial
      statements, 590–602
  income taxes and, 439, 441
  insurance, 73
  intercompany plant asset transfers, 258–

Subsidiaries *(Cont.)*:
    261, 264–265, 267
    interim acquisitions, 167–168
    minority interest, 160
  intercompany transactions and, 361–
    376
  majority-owned, 72–73
  multiple, 403–404
  mutual holdings and
    between parent and subsidiary, 413–
      422
    between subsidiaries, 409–413
  nonhomogeneous, reporting, 469–470,
    471, 474–476, 484
  preferred stock of, 422–430
  push-down accounting and, 486–491
  stock dividends, 145
  treasury stock of, 86–88
    transactions, 376–378
  unconsolidated, 72–73, 138*n*
  unpaid cash dividends of, 83–84
  valuation differential and, 95–97
    (See also Disaggregated financial
      information; Intercompany
      transactions *and specific topics)*
Subsidiary stock dividend, 145
Summer terms, 973
Sweeney, Jan, 22*n*

T-accounts:
  foreign currency restatements and, 579,
    581*n*
  foreign financial statement restatements
    and, 606
  governmental accounting and, 840–842
    general fund, 857–859
  intercompany debt transactions and,
    301–302
    outstanding debt acquisition, 309–
      310, 315–316, 319
  long-term investments in common
    stock and equity method, 141
  for partnerships, 689
Takeovers, hostile, 6–7
Tax anticipation notes payable, 849
Tax liens, 852
Taxes:
  consolidated returns, 435, 436–438, 445
  debt service funds and, 898
  governmental accounting and, 834–
    836, 848–853

Taxes *(Cont.)*:
  intercompany merchandise transfers
    and, 217*n*
  intercompany plant asset transfers and,
    256*n*
  partnerships and, 699–701
  property, 835, 850–853, 920–921
  sales, 835
    (See also Income taxes)
Temporary decline in value, 137*n*
Temporary differences, deferred income
  taxes and, 435
Tender offers:
  business combination viewpoints and,
    6–7
  defined, 6
Term bonds, 899, 900, 903
Term endowment funds, 978–980
Thompson, James H., 76
Three-section statement format, 176–178
Time limit, as pooling-of-interests
  criterion, 30
Timing differences, deferred income
  taxes and, 435–448
Total deferral method:
  fractional method compared to, 223–
    224
  intercompany plant asset transfers and
    upstream land transfers, 257–259
Total income, mutual holdings and, 410–
  412
Total revaluation, 719
Total valuation differential, 95–97
Transaction dates, 645–646
Transaction gains, foreign currency
  transactions and forward contracts,
    661, 665–666
Transaction periods, 646
Transfer prices:
  elimination of, 226, 231
  gross margin and, 217
Transfers:
  branch accounting and, 780–805
    accounting systems, 781–782
    branch operating transactions and
      transfers to home office, 787
    combined financial statements, 790–
      794
    end-of-the-period reports and closing
      procedures, 787–790
    home office accounts, 783–787

Transfers *(Cont.):*
    interbranch transfers, 804–805
    investment in branch accounts, 783–787
    multiple branches, 804
    omitted entries and errors, 793–794
    transfers from home office to branch, 783–787
    downstream *(see* Downstream transfers)
    governmental accounting and, 860–861
    mandatory and nonmandatory, nonprofit organization accounting and, 973
    of merchandise, intercompany *(see* Intercompany merchandise transfers)
    of plant assets, intercompany *(see* Intercompany plant asset transfers)
    of stock, intercompany *(see* Intercompany stock transfers)
    upstream *(see* Upstream transfers)
Translation adjustments, 584–587, 616, 617
    cumulative, 606, 608
Translation of foreign financial statements, 584–590, 603–608
    adjustments and, 583, 584–590, 616, 617
    date-of-acquisition translation and, 584–585
    defined, 582–584
    equity method and, 603–608
    hyperinflation and, 602
    objective of, 583
    postacquisition consolidations and translation and, 585–590
        one year after acquisition, 585–587, 605–607
        two years after acquisition, 587–590, 607–608
    remeasurements and, 599–601
Treasury stock:
    consolidations and, 86–88
    as pooling-of-interests criteria, 31–32
    subsidiary transactions in, 376–378
        purchase from minority shareholders, 377–378
        purchase from parent, 377–378
Treasury stock method, for mutual holdings between parent and subsidiary, 414–418

Treasury stock method *(Cont.):*
    allocation method compared, 414
    date-of-acquisition consolidation, 415
    postacquisition consolidation, 416–418
Trial balances:
    foreign financial statement restatement and, 585, 593–595, 599–601
    format of consolidation worksheet, 176–178
    home office and branch, adjusted, 787, 788
Trucking industry, 7n
Trust funds, 920–924
    financial statements and, 924–926
    transaction recording, 920–921
20-percent rule, 135–136

Unaffiliated notes, 328–329
Unaffiliated parties, discounting and, 328–329
Unamortized valuation differential, 152, 164, 170
Uncollectable taxes, 849–852
Unconsolidated subsidiaries, 72–73, 138n
Undivided interests, 431
Unexpended plant funds, 982–985
Uniform Partnership Act, 684, 690, 702n, 703, 750–751, 751n
Unlimited liabilities, 686, 752
Unpaid subsidiary cash dividends, 83–84
Unrealized gross margin in branch inventory, 797–798, 800, 801
Unrecorded assets, purchase combinations and, 15
Unregistered securities, purchase combinations and, 14
Unrestricted funds, nonprofit organization accounting and:
    colleges and universities, 971
    hospitals, 993, 998, 1000–1003
    VHWOs, 1011–1012
Unrestricted operating funds, 1023
Upstream transfers:
    deferred income taxes and, 439
    intercompany merchandise transfers and
        consolidation adjustments, 224–228
        defined, 215, 218
        equity method, 218–220, 439
        fractional method, 236–237
        gross margin, 216–220, 221

Upstream transfers *(Cont.):*
        gross margin deferrals, 221, 222n, 226–227
        total and fractional deferred methods compared, 223–224
        worksheet adjustments, 228–231
    intercompany plant asset transfers and depreciable assets, 264–266, 267
        land, 257–261
    intercompany stock transfers and gross margins, 378, 380–382
Utility regulators, 561

Valuation differentials:
    amortization of, 140–141, 144
        cost method, 175
        foreign financial statement restatements and, 605–606
        mutual holdings, 417, 418
        new stock issues and, 371–373
        postacquisition, 148–149, 159, 164, 170
        stock transfers, 357–359, 367
        unamortized valuation, 152, 164, 170
    consolidations and, 66–67
        date fair value over cost, 84–86
        date-of-acquisition, 77–79, 88, 89, 146–148
        expanded analysis, 94–97
        interim acquisitions, 170
        parent-company concept, 98, 99–102
    fair value over cost and, 144
    foreign financial statement restatements and, 609
    intercompany stock transfers and deferral of upstream gross margin, 379–380
    long-term investments in common stock and, 139–141
    mutual holdings between parent and subsidiary and, 417
    preferred stock of subsidiary and, 425–426
    purchase combinations and, 15–18
    unamortized, 152, 164, 170
Valuation practices, of partnerships, 703–705, 717–719
Value of reorganized entity, 533–534
van Breda, Michael F., 94n
Vatter, William J., 94n

Vertical integration, 3, 469

Voluntary health and welfare
   organizations (VHWOs), 1010–1017,
   1018–1021
   annual financial statements for, 1013,
      1019–1021
   fund structure and, 970, 1011–1013
   methods and systems, 1011
   transaction recording and, 1013–1017

Voting rights, as pooling-of-interests
   criterion, 32

Vouchers, governmental accounting and,
   853

Weighted average assumptions, 361

Weighted average capital balance, 692–
   693

Weil, Roman L., 412n

Welfare organizations (*see* Voluntary
   health and welfare organizations)

Withdrawals:
   of partner, 717–719
   from partnership drawing accounts,
      688–690

Wolfson, Mark A., 13n

Worksheets:
   bankruptcy and, 531–535
   branch accounting and, 790–794
      merchandise transfers billed in
         excess of cost, 798–804
      omitted entries and errors, 793–794
   consolidations and, 79–81, 86–88, 90–
      91, 146–148, 156–161, 162–164,

Worksheets (*Cont.*):
   168–170
      adjustments, 67–68, 79–81, 83, 86–
         88, 90–91, 102–104, 148, 171
      date-of-acquisition, 80–81, 86–88,
         90–91, 102–104, 148
      eliminate and reclassify investment
         accounts, 67–68
      interim acquisitions, 168–170
      postacquisition, 156–161, 162–164,
         171, 173–176
   currency translation, 584–590
   deferred income taxes and, 438–439,
      444, 447–448
   foreign financial statement restatements
      consolidation procedures, 603–616
      equity method, 605–610
      remeasurements, 593–598
      translation, 585–587
   indirect ownership and, 407–408
   intercompany debt transactions and
      face-value method, 324–327
      new intercompany debt, 304–307
      outstanding debt acquisition, 312–
         314, 318–321
   intercompany merchandise transfers
      and, 224–235, 794–804
      first-year consolidation worksheet,
         232, 233
      fractional method, 224, 236–237
      second-year consolidation worksheet,
         233, 234
      upstream transfers, 224–228

Worksheets (*Cont.*):
   intercompany plant asset transfers and
      downstream land transfers, 262–263
      upstream depreciable assets, 265–
         266
      upstream land transfers, 258–259
   intercompany stock transfers and
      common stock sales, 366–367
      gross margin, 380–381
      multiple-step stock acquisitions, 360–
         361
   joint ventures and, 432–434
   mutual holdings, between parent and
      subsidiary and, 417–422
   preferred stock of subsidiary and
      date-of-acquisition, 424–426
      postacquisition consolidation, 427–
         430
   remeasurement of financial statements,
      593–598
   three-section and trial balance formats
      compared, 176–178
   (*See also* Adjustments)

Write-downs, of foreign inventories, 601–
   602

Write-offs, of delinquent property taxes,
   849–852

Wyatt, Arthur R., 21

Year-end note balances, 306n